Twentieth-Century Literary Criticism

Guide to Gale Literary Criticism Series

For criticism on	Consult these Gale series
Authors now living or who died after December 31, 1959	*CONTEMPORARY LITERARY CRITICISM (CLC)*
Authors who died between 1900 and 1959	*TWENTIETH-CENTURY LITERARY CRITICISM (TCLC)*
Authors who died between 1800 and 1899	*NINETEENTH-CENTURY LITERATURE CRITICISM (NCLC)*
Authors who died between 1400 and 1799	*LITERATURE CRITICISM FROM 1400 TO 1800 (LC)* *SHAKESPEAREAN CRITICISM (SC)*
Authors who died before 1400	*CLASSICAL AND MEDIEVAL LITERATURE CRITICISM (CMLC)*
Authors of books for children and young adults	*CHILDREN'S LITERATURE REVIEW (CLR)*
Dramatists	*DRAMA CRITICISM (DC)*
Poets	*POETRY CRITICISM (PC)*
Short story writers	*SHORT STORY CRITICISM (SSC)*
Black writers of the past two hundred years	*BLACK LITERATURE CRITICISM (BLC)*
Hispanic writers of the late nineteenth and twentieth centuries	*HISPANIC LITERATURE CRITICISM (HLC)*
Native North American writers and orators of the eighteenth, nineteenth, and twentieth centuries	*NATIVE NORTH AMERICAN LITERATURE (NNAL)*
Major authors from the Renaissance to the present	*WORLD LITERATURE CRITICISM, 1500 TO THE PRESENT (WLC)*

ISSN 0276-8178

Volume 95

Twentieth-Century Literary Criticism

**Criticism of the
Works of Novelists, Poets, Playwrights,
Short Story Writers, and Other Creative Writers
Who Lived between 1900 and 1999,
from the First Published Critical
Appraisals to Current Evaluations**

Jennifer Baise
Editor

Thomas Ligotti
Associate Editor

GALE GROUP

Detroit
New York
San Francisco
London
Boston
Woodbridge, CT

Library of Congress Catalog Card Number 76-46132
ISBN 0-7876-3208-2
ISSN 0276-8178

Printed in the United States of America
10 9 8 7 6 5 4 3 2 1

Contents

Preface   vii

Acknowledgments   xi

Preface

Since its inception more than fifteen years ago, *Twentieth-Century Literary Criticism* has been purchased and used by nearly 10,000 school, public, and college or university libraries. *TCLC* has covered more than 500 authors, representing 58 nationalities, and over 25,000 titles. No other reference source has surveyed the critical response to twentieth-century authors and literature as thoroughly as *TCLC*. In the words of one reviewer, "there is nothing comparable available." *TCLC* "is a gold mine of information—dates, pseudonyms, biographical information, and criticism from books and periodicals—which many libraries would have difficulty assembling on their own."

Scope of the Series

TCLC is designed to serve as an introduction to authors who died between 1900 and 1960 and to the most significant interpretations of these author's works. The great poets, novelists, short story writers, playwrights, and philosophers of this period are frequently studied in high school and college literature courses. In organizing and reprinting the vast amount of critical material written on these authors, *TCLC* helps students develop valuable insight into literary history, promotes a better understanding of the texts, and sparks ideas for papers and assignments. Each entry in *TCLC* presents a comprehensive survey of an author's career or an individual work of literature and provides the user with a multiplicity of interpretations and assessments. Such variety allows students to pursue their own interests; furthermore, it fosters an awareness that literature is dynamic and responsive to many different opinions.

Every fourth volume of *TCLC* is devoted to literary topics. These topic entries widen the focus of the series from individual authors to such broader subjects as literary movements, prominent themes in twentieth-century literature, literary reaction to political and historical events, significant eras in literary history, prominent literary anniversaries, and the literatures of cultures that are often overlooked by English-speaking readers.

TCLC is designed as a companion series to Gale's *Contemporary Literary Criticism,* which reprints commentary on authors now living or who have died since 1960. Because of the different periods under consideration, there is no duplication of material between *CLC* and *TCLC*. For additional information about *CLC* and Gale's other criticism titles, users should consult the Guide to Gale Literary Criticism Series preceding the title page in this volume.

Coverage

Each volume of *TCLC* is carefully compiled to present:

- criticism of authors, or literary topics, representing a variety of genres and nationalities

- both major and lesser-known writers and literary works of the period

- 6-12 authors or 3-6 topics per volume

- individual entries that survey critical response to each author's work or each topic in
  literary history, including early criticism to reflect initial reactions; later criticism to
  represent any rise or decline in reputation; and current retrospective analyses.

Organization of This Book

An author entry consists of the following elements: author heading, biographical and critical introduction, list of principal works, reprints of criticism (each preceded by an annotation and a bibliographic citation), and a bibliography of further reading.

- The **Author Heading** consists of the name under which the author most commonly wrote,
  followed by birth and death dates. If an author wrote consistently under a pseudonym,
  the pseudonym will be listed in the author heading and the real name given in parentheses
  on the first line of the biographical and critical introduction. Also located at the begin-

ning of the introduction to the author entry are any name variations under which an author wrote, including transliterated forms for authors whose languages use nonroman alphabets.

- The **Biographical and Critical Introduction** outlines the author's life and career, as well as the critical issues surrounding his or her work. References to past volumes of *TCLC* are provided at the beginning of the introduction. Additional sources of information in other biographical and critical reference series published by Gale, including *Short Story Criticism, Children's Literature Review, Contemporary Authors, Dictionary of Literary Biography,* and *Something about the Author,* are listed in a box at the end of the entry.

- Some *TCLC* entries include **Portraits** of the author. Entries also may contain reproductions of materials pertinent to an author's career, including manuscript pages, title pages, dust jackets, letters, and drawings, as well as photographs of important people, places, and events in an author's life.

- The **List of Principal Works** is chronological by date of first book publication and identifies the genre of each work. In the case of foreign authors with both foreign-language publications and English translations, the title and date of the first English-language edition are given in brackets. Unless otherwise indicated, dramas are dated by first performance, not first publication.

- Critical essays are prefaced by **Annotations** providing the reader with information about both the critic and the criticism that follows. Included are the critic's reputation, individual approach to literary criticism, and particular expertise in an author's works. Also noted are the relative importance of a work of criticism, the scope of the essay, and the growth of critical controversy or changes in critical trends regarding an author. In some cases, these annotations cross-reference essays by critics who discuss each other's commentary.

- A complete **Bibliographic Citation** designed to facilitate location of the original essay or book precedes each piece of criticism.

- Criticism is arranged chronologically in each author entry to provide a perspective on changes in critical evaluation over the years. All titles of works by the author featured in the entry are printed in boldface type to enable the user to easily locate discussion of particular works. Also for purposes of easier identification, the critic's name and the publication date of the essay are given at the beginning of each piece of criticism. Unsigned criticism is preceded by the title of the journal in which it appeared. Some of the essays in *TCLC* also contain translated material. Unless otherwise noted, translations in brackets are by the editors; translations in parentheses or continuous with the text are by the critic. Publication information (such as footnotes or page and line references to specific editions of works) have been deleted at the editor's discretion to provide smoother reading of the text.

- An annotated list of **Further Reading** appearing at the end of each author entry suggests secondary sources on the author. In some cases it includes essays for which the editors could not obtain reprint rights.

Cumulative Indexes

- Each volume of *TCLC* contains a cumulative **Author Index** listing all authors who have appeared in Gale's Literary Criticism Series, along with cross references to such biographical series as *Contemporary Authors* and *Dictionary of Literary Biography*. For readers' convenience, a complete list of Gale titles included appears on the first page of the author index. Useful for locating authors within the various series, this index is particularly valuable for those authors who are identified by a certain period but who, because of their death dates, are placed in another, or for those authors whose careers span two periods. For example, F. Scott Fitzgerald is found in *TCLC*, yet a writer often associated with him, Ernest Hemingway, is found in *CLC*.

- Each *TCLC* volume includes a cumulative **Nationality Index** which lists all authors who have appeared in *TCLC* volumes, arranged alphabetically under their respective nationalities, as well as Topics volume entries devoted to particular national literatures.

- Each new volume in Gale's Literary Criticism Series includes a cumulative **Topic Index,** which lists all literary topics treated in *NCLC, TCLC, LC 1400-1800,* and the *CLC* yearbook.

- Each new volume of *TCLC*, with the exception of the Topics volumes, includes a **Title Index** listing the titles of all literary works discussed in the volume. In response to numerous suggestions from librarians, Gale has also produced a **Special Paperbound Edition** of the *TCLC* title index. This annual cumulation lists all titles discussed in the series since its inception and is issued with the first volume of *TCLC* published each year. Additional copies of the index are available on request. Librarians and patrons will welcome this separate index; it saves shelf space, is easy to use, and is recyclable upon receipt of the following year's cumulation. Titles discussed in the Topics volume entries are not included *TCLC* cumulative index.

Citing Twentieth-Century Literary Criticism

When writing papers, students who quote directly from any volume in Gale's literary Criticism Series may use the following general forms to footnote reprinted criticism. The first example pertains to materials drawn from periodicals, the second to material reprinted from books.

[1]William H. Slavick, "Going to School to DuBose Heyward," *The Harlem Renaissance Re-examined,* (AMS Press, 1987); reprinted in *Twentieth-Century Literary Criticism,* Vol. 59, ed. Jennifer Gariepy (Detroit: Gale Research, 1995), pp. 94-105.

[2]George Orwell, "Reflections on Gandhi," *Partisan Review,* 6 (Winter 1949), pp. 85-92; reprinted in *Twentieth-Century Literary Criticism,* Vol. 59, ed. Jennifer Gariepy (Detroit: Gale Research, 1995), pp. 40-3.

Suggestions Are Welcome

In response to suggestions, several features have been added to *TCLC* since the series began, including annotations to critical essays, a cumulative index to authors in all Gale literary criticism series, entries devoted to criticism on a single work by a major author, more extensive illustrations, and a title index listing all literary works discussed in the series since its inception.

Readers who wish to suggest authors or topics to appear in future volumes, or who have other suggestions, are cordially invited to write the editors.

Acknowledgments

The editors wish to thank the copyright holders of the criticism included in this volume and the permissions managers of many book and magazine publishing companies for assisting us in securing reproduction rights. We are also grateful to the staffs of the Detroit Public Library, the Library of Congress, the University of Detroit Mercy Library, Wayne State University Purdy/Kresge Library Complex, and the University of Michigan Libraries for making their resources available to us. Following is a list of the copyright holders who have granted us permission to reproduce material in this volume of *TCLC*. Every effort has been made to trace copyright, but if omissions have been made, please let us know.

COPYRIGHTED ESSAYS IN *TCLC*, VOLUME 95, WERE REPRODUCED FROM THE FOLLOWING PERIODICALS:

Agricultural History, v. 3, Spring, 1989 for "Images of Nineteenth Century Maine Farming in the Prose and Poetry of R.P.T. Coffin and C.A. Stephens" by Mark W. Anderson. © 1989 by Agricultural History Society. Reproduced by permission of the publisher and the author.—*American Literary Realism*, 1870-1910, v. 21, Spring, 1989. © 1989. Reproduced by permission of McFarland & Company, Inc., Publishers, Jefferson NC 28640.—*American Literature*, v. 60, December, 1988. Copyright © 1988 Duke University Press, Durham, NC. Reproduced by permission.—*American Quarterly*, v. 9, Fall, 1957; v. 41, March, 1989. Copyright 1957, 1989, American Studies Association. Both reproduced by permission of The Johns Hopkins University Press.—*Artforum*, v. X, November, 1971 for "The Early Work of Kurt Schwitters" by John Elderfield; v. XII, September, 1973 for "Private Objects: The Sculpture of Kurt Schwitters" by John Elderfield. Both reproduced by permission of the author.—*The Centennial Review*, v. 25, Summer, 1981 for "Broadacre City: Frank Lloyd Wright's Utopia" by James Dougherty. © 1981 by The Centennial Review. Reproduced by permission of the publisher and the author.—*Colby Library Quarterly*, v. VII, December, 1965. Reproduced by permission.—*Columbia Library Columns*, v. XIII, February, 1964; v. XLI, November, 1991. Both reproduced by permission.—*Cross Currents*, Dobbs Ferry, v. XXXIX, Fall, 1989. Copyright 1989 by Cross Currents Inc. Reproduced by permission.—*DAC News*, v. 80, October, 1995. Reproduced by permission.—*Dada/Surrealism*, no. 13, 1984. 1984 © Association for the Study of Dada and Surrealism. Reprinted by permission of the publisher.—*Forum For Modern Language Studies*, v. IX, January, 1973. Reproduced by permission of the publisher.—*The German Quarterly*, v. XLV, January, 1972. Copyright © 1972 by the American Association of Teachers of German. Reproduced by permission.—*Journal of The History of Ideas*, v. XLV, July-September, 1984. © 1984. Reproduced by permission of The Johns Hopkins University Press.—*The Journal of Philosophy*, v. XCIII, May, 1996 for "Desire and Desirability: A Rejoinder to a Posthumous Reply by John Dewey" by Morton White. © copyright 1996 by The Journal of Philosophy, Inc. Reproduced by permission of the publisher and the author.—*The Journal of Religion*, v. 75, July, 1995 for "Emerson and Dewey on Natural Piety" by P. Eddy Wilson. © 1995 by The University of Chicago. All rights reserved. Reproduced by permission of The University of Chicago Press and the author.—*Kenyon Review*, v. 4, Winter, 1942. Copyright © 1942 by Kenyon College. All rights reserved. Reproduced by permission.—*The New York Review of Books*, v. XXXIX, June, 1992. Copyright © 1992 Nyrev, Inc. Reproduced with permission from *The New York Review of Books*.—*Philosophy and Rhetoric*, v. 16, 1983. Copyright 1983 by The Pennsylvania State University. Reproduced by permission of The Pennsylvania State University Press.—*Philosophy Today*, v. 38, Spring, 1994; v. 39, Spring, 1995; v. 41, Summer, 1997. All reproduced by permission.—*Saturday Review of Literature*, V. XI, No. 40, April 20, 1935. © 1935 Saturday Review magazine. Reproduced by permission of Saturday Review Publications, Ltd.—*Soundings*, v. LXXV, Spring, 1992. Reproduced by permission.—*Sulfur*, v. XIV, Spring, 1994. Reproduced by permission.—*The Times Literary Supplement*, October 5, 1973; February 28, 1975; January 20, 1995. © The Times Supplements Limited 1973, 1975, 1995. All reproduced from *The Times Literary Supplement* by permission.—*Walt Whitman Quarterly Review*, v. 6, Summer, 1988 for "Democratic Space: The Ecstatic Geography of Walt Whitman and Frank Lloyd Wright" by John Roche. © Copyright 1988 by The University of Iowa. Reproduced by permission of the publisher and the author.—*Word and Image*, v. 6, January, 1990. Reproduced by permission.

COPYRIGHTED ESSAYS IN *TCLC*, VOLUME 95, WERE REPRODUCED FROM THE FOLLOWING BOOKS:

Brickman, William W. From "Dewey's Social and Political Commentary" in *Guide to The Works of John Dewey*. Edited by Jo Ann Boydston. Southern Illinois University Press, 1970. Copyright © 1970 by Southern Illinois University Press. All rights reserved. Reproduced by permission.—Couser, G. Thomas. From *American Autobiography*. Amherst: The University of Massachusetts Press, 1979. © 1979 by The University of Massachusetts Press. All rights reserved. Reproduced by permission of the author.—Hendley, Brian Patrick. From *Dewey, Russell, Whitehead:*

Robert P. Tristram Coffin

1892-1955

(Full name Robert Peter Tristram Coffin) American poet, novelist, and essayist.

INTRODUCTION

From the 1930s through the 1950s, Coffin was regarded as one of America's foremost regionalists. In poetry, novels, and essays, he wrote about the shaping influence of his birthplace, Maine, on the life and character of its inhabitants, and advocated such values as simplicity and self sufficiency that he believed sprang from its culture. He enjoyed popularity and honor in his lifetime–winning the Pulitzer Prize for poetry in 1936. While some critics praised him for revealing poetic mystery in the commonplace, others found his work sentimental, loquacious, and limited. After his death in 1955, his books were all but forgotten.

Biographical Information

Coffin's life, like his poetry, is marked by robust optimism and unflagging energy. Inspired by his father's love of song and story, he began writing when a boy. His work often celebrated his father, the state of Maine, the primitive currents in human nature, and the resourcefulness and resilience, whether heroic or tragic, of the solitary, self-reliant individual confronting Nature, which he depicted as both holy and brutally unrelenting. He entered Bowdoin College in 1911, where he was twice winner of the Hawthorne prize for short story writing. He graduated *summa cum laude,* and went on to Princeton as a Longfellow scholar. In 1916, he graduated from Princeton and went to Oxford as a Rhodes scholar to study poetry. After serving as a second lieutenant in the artillery during the First World War, he returned to Oxford to complete his studies. Back in the United States in 1921, he began teaching at Wells College in New York State until, in 1934, he was invited to teach in Maine at Bowdoin, where he stayed until his death in 1955. During these years, he won many awards for poetry, published voluminously, developed a hand for pen and ink and water color sketches, participated in the founding of poetry societies, and traveled to numerous universities to read his poems and to speak.

Major Works

Coffin's most characteristic works were poems and stories that endowed common events in the lives of ordinary people with epic proportion and mythic dimension. He drew on his own experience, as in his account of his father in *Portrait of an American,* and in the memoir, *Lost Paradise, A Boyhood on a Maine Coast Farm.* Among his novels, the first, *Red Sky in the Morning,*

concerning a son's sacrificial struggle to gain his father's recognition, is considered his best. Like all his work, it reflects his belief in the lasting influence of the intergenerational male bond, the primacy of men, and the instrumentality of women. Celebration of a male-focused engagement with Nature is central to his major collections of poetry, too, from *Ballads of Square-Toed Americans* in 1933, through the Pulitzer prize-winning *Strange Holiness* in 1935, *Poems for a Son with Wings* in 1945, and *One-Horse Farm: Down-East Georgics* in 1949.

Critical Reception

Rejected by some critics as intellectually uninventive, emotionally pat, out of touch with contemporary realities, and devoid of poetic skill, his work nevertheless enjoyed such widespread recognition and regard at the time of his death that the New York Times printed a page one obituary and declared in an editorial tribute, "His verse was sometimes rough-hewn, unplaned or homespun, but . . . there will always be those who . . . will turn to his work for a glimpse of a life that is simpler, unfettered, and . . . more beautiful."

PRINCIPAL WORKS

Christchurch (poetry) 1924
Book of Crowns and Cottages (essays) 1925
Dew and Bronze (poetry) 1927
Laud, Storm Center of Stuart England (biography) 1930
Portrait of an American (memoir) 1931
The Yoke of Thunder (poetry) 1932
Ballads of Square-Toed Americans (poetry) 1933
Lost Paradise, A Boyhood on a Maine Coast Farm
  (memoir) 1934
Red Sky in the Morning (novel) 1935
Strange Holiness (poetry) 1935
John Dawn (novel) 1936
Kennebec, Cradle of Americans (stories) 1937
Saltwater Farm (poetry) 1937
Maine Ballads (poetry) 1938
Collected Poems of Robert P. Tristram Coffin (poetry) 1939
Thomas-Thomas-Ancil-Thomas (novel) 1941
Christmas in Maine (poetry) 1941
The Substance That Is Poetry (essays) 1942
There Will Be Bread and Love (poetry) 1942
Primer for America (essays) 1943
Mainstays of Maine (essays) 1944
Poems for a Son with Wings (poetry) 1945
People Behave like Ballads (poetry) 1946
Yankee Coast (essays) 1947
Collected Poems of Robert P. Tristram Coffin (poetry) 1948
Coast Calendar (poetry) 1949
One-Horse Farm: Down-East Georgics (poetry) 1949
The Third Hunger & The Poem Aloud (essays) 1949
Apples by Ocean (poetry) 1950
Maine Doings (essays) 1950
Life in America: New England (essays) 1951
On the Green Carpet (lectures) 1951
Hellas Revisited (poetry) 1954
Selected Poems (poetry) 1955

CRITICISM

William Rose Benét (essay date 1933)

SOURCE: A review of *Ballads of Square-Toed Americans,* in *Saturday Review of Literature,* Vol. X, No. 10, September 23, 1933, p. 135.

[*In the following excerpt, Benét reviews* Ballads of Square-Toed Americans *and praises the pictorialism and gusto he finds.*]

This week I have three books on my table for particular comment. All of them are American. Of the three, one is by Robert P. Tristram Coffin, who has now won a place for himself among the best American poets of his time. This is his fifth book of poems—and his prose work includes two books of essays and three biographies. His present volume, ***Ballads of Square-Toed Americans,*** is endemic and chiefly narrative. *The Saturday Review of Literature* first presented one of the longer narratives, **"The Schooling of Richard Orr,"** to Mr. Coffin's public. I am glad to remember that this journal gave so much space to that poem, because, as I reread it, the imaginative reliving on the author's part of an Indian raid strikes me again, in its forthright vividness, as a remarkable feat. And there are other poems in this book no less noteworthy for originality of treatment. **"The Truce of the Mohawks,"** though not one of the poems designed to carry out Mr. Coffin's more patriotic notion of his book, is an account of an early clambake that appeals to me greatly by virtue of its deft pictorial quality:

> Laughing, shrieking with delight
> The squaws turned fat clams to the light,
>   Greeting each big clam with cries.
>   Papooses with their blackberry eyes
>   Grave as owls in their surprise
> On every sloping back would stare
> Down the part in mother's hair.

Mr. Coffin hymns all sorts of upstanding Americans, New Englanders, Chesapeake Planters, even the Mormons. His prologue is a long poem read as the Phi Beta Kappa poem last Commencement at Cambridge. It is "Tristram Winship's" vision of America, an heroic and a poetic vision. It is the idealistic side of the American dream which we forget when we regard some of the more recent results of unbridled American independence. This poem is followed by a Yankee chantey to ancestors whose

>   hands were like square sails,
> They ran the lengths of longitudes,
>   Harpooning spouting whales.

Then there are **"The Men Who Pushed the Forest Down,"** the Mormons, The Tall Axe Men, and so on. There is a swaggering and amusing **"Ballad of a Grandfather,"** there is an eerie legend of **"The Foot of Tucksport,"** with its reflection cast upon the days of witch-burning. There is a sometimes remarkably impressionistic ballad account of **"The Means Massacre,"** and, lastly, **"A Man for a Father"** reveals to us the inspiration behind this volume in praise of early Americans:

> He loved to sing *Belle Brandon* to
>   A mellow old guitar,
> He loved to see his chimney smoke
>   Against the evening star . . .

> Stories he loved, and he kept men
>   With beards upon the chin
> Hanging on such lively tales
>   As Chaucer's at an inn.

His son has inherited something of that gusto. Indeed Mr. Coffin's range is notable. This new book is rather different from anything he has given us before. And in all his books he is apt to ambush you with sudden leaping phrase like a burning arrow. One's fear for him resides in his facility. But he is one of the most pictorial of our poets, and the present book, published by the Macmillan Company, should appeal to those who like a picturesque presentation of certain moments of their country's past—an account flavored with the "tall talking" of true Yankees.

William Rose Benét (essay date 1935)

SOURCE: A review of *Strange Holiness,* in *Saturday Review of Literature,* Vol. XI, No. 40, April 20, 1935, p. 639.

[In the following excerpt, Benét reviews Coffin's Strange Holiness, *praising the poems for the quality of their workmanship and subject matter but regretting that, in them, the poet has not surpassed his previous work.]*

Robert P. Tristram Coffin is a fecund poet. His latest book, **Strange Holiness,** is in contrast to his latest one before that, **Ballads of Square-Toed Americans,** in that this is subjective as that was objective. I am only afraid that Mr. Coffin may have a fatal facility. He shapes and turns his poems well, and he usually has something not only interesting to write about but also seen and felt. Also, his phrase is often extremely good. Moreover, the devotional element in these poems has nothing mawkish about it. One feels that the poet pleasured himself in writing all of them. And yet one also feels that he might have conserved the energy expended in writing a good many of them and poured it all into one poem that would have greatly surpassed them all. Where a man has proved his powers, as Mr. Coffin has already done, I think it is allowable to expect him to surpass himself. This book does not surpass others by the same writer. Were it a first book it would not make nearly the impression upon the reader that certain other books of his have made. That he is a good workman is beyond question. But he is also, at rare intervals, a good deal more than that. In this particular volume those intervals are rare indeed.

Times Literary Supplement (essay date 1935)

SOURCE: A review of *Strange Holiness,* in *Times Literary Supplement,* No. 1750, August 15, 1935, p. 516.

[In the following excerpt, a reviewer commends the theme of Strange Holiness.]

For Mr. Coffin whatever lives is holy and in the longest poem in this collection, entitled **"First Flight,"** he records how he felt "something solemn, something like holiness" in the airplane in which he first took his seat. But while he does full justice in this poem to the cosmic reaches of the air, it is typical of him to turn away soon from these and let his vision pass lovingly over the land unrolled beneath the plane with its small towns and woods and fields and houses that "did not hurry." Far from forgetting his old fidelities in the intoxication of speed and space,

> From his high station Tristram saw that things
> Which meant most to a man were very old,
> A tree before a door, earth turned in furrows,
> A pathway by a brook, a flower-bed,
> The sounds of bees and cowbells, clean, new grass,
> An acre he had planted, sunlit panes . . .
> Doves above a dovecot, a deep sense
> That his two hands had had their fingers in
> Something vast and holy as the growth
> Of seeds to plants, of boughs across a window,
> The patterns of the sunshine and the rain.

This in fact is the theme of almost all his lyrics which run and rhyme easily, like a limpid stream in which the experiences of a farmer who has a keen relish and deep devotion for his work are reflected. Whether he is describing the day's labour of Potato Diggers, a Bull in his stall, milking or the hayfield, or **"The Barn"** in winter or summer, he communicates the sensations of simple elementary things with a fragrant intimacy. His style is at times rather too easily explicit, but his verse is suffused with the grateful tenderness of the devotee who not only lives close to Nature but works with her in watchful harmony.

C. A. Millspaugh (essay date 1938)

SOURCE: A review of *Saltwater Farm,* in *Poetry,* Vol. LI, No. V, February, 1938, pp. 267-70.

[In the following excerpt, Millspaugh reviews Saltwater Farm *and finds nothing to recommend it.]*

That rare person, the serious reader of poetry, may legitimately expect of experienced writers at least a minimum of care in craft, a fairly well-developed point of view from which to inspect society and the men who compose it, a character sufficiently mature to be free of such vulgarities as smugness, self-complacency, and sentimentality, and an imagination disciplined by tradition, compelled by the predicaments of contemporary life, projected by good will and wonder into the astonishing future. Measured against these none too austere standards, the present books of Robert Hillyer and Robert P. Tristram Coffin fail.

Though Mr. Hillyer is of the two the more cultivated and the more accomplished craftsman, neither of these poets achieves a level much higher than that on which the beginner strives. . . .

For the unrestrainedly pat, for machine-like regularity in uninspired loquacity, Mr. Robert P. Tristram Coffin has no competitors. Search as he will, the reader cannot find on any page of **Saltwater Farm** a completed poem. Fragments of pretty scenery, conventionalized characterizations, sentimentalized metaphor, a drouth of passion, a scarcity of insight, are alone discoverable. All the mistakes a beginner is warned against are here—lines padded to fill out the meter and to meet the rhyme; the afflatus, the expanded image traveling on a line of vague feeling to a gaseous end; ignorance of the limits which the physical universe imposes on the fanciful; poetic posing, ingenuity mistaken for imagination, mere words substituted for ideas. As does Mr. Hillyer, Mr. Coffin exhibits a self-complacency that renders him valueless as a commentator on human joy and suffering. A man so thoroughly satisfied with the *status quo* can give the hurt, the poor, the insatiable, and the honestly curious little more than sickly pity and platitudinous Pollyannaism.

To demonstrate Mr. Coffin's aptitude as a versifier, one need only quote the two following excerpts—the first as an example of imprecision of fancy; the second as an example of the inferior quality of Mr. Coffin's ear even when he deals with the New England speech he is supposed to know so well:

> Cows in a pasture faded into bells.

and

> You use your body, not your head,
> When you have a boat's keel spread
> Out before you to put right.
> It is a kind of a delight
> That needs no words to make it go, *etc.*

Both Mr. Hillyer and Mr. Coffin have been awarded the Pulitzer Prize for poetry. Of the first, one must say that he has proceeded with care and a certain dignity; but of the second we can only paraphrase Francis Jeffrey and affirm that Mr. Coffin has dashed his Hippocrene with too large an infusion of saltwater.

Marshall Schacht (essay date 1938)

SOURCE: A review of *Maine Ballads,* in *Poetry,* Vol. LIII, No. II, November, 1938, pp. 92-96.

[*In the following excerpt, Schacht reviews* Maine Ballads *and deplores the poems, which he sees as smug and narrow.*]

In an introduction to his eighth book of poems Mr. Coffin says, in part: "Folk living and folk speaking still go on, in spite of all our modern improvements—the stories are there for the ballads, and the words to them, for anybody who has eyes to see the shape of them and ears to hear the right rhythms and the fall of the words." He ends: "These verses—the more ambitious of them—are not to be judged by the usual poetic standards. Some of them, judged by such, are little more than doggerel. They are to be judged, both in style and in plot, by the principles of folk design."

A foreword of this kind is plainly a defense as well as an explanation of *Maine Ballads* and of Mr. Coffin's poetic work as a whole. It says, in fact: this is my chosen range, my special region, marked off deliberately in a world of modern chaos, my way of speech "in spite of modern improvements." And because Mr. Coffin is obviously a mature poet, he is not to be lightly dismissed by those of

us who feel he has hitched his wagon to a fallen star, one that has already set with the more genuine regionalism of Robert Frost. It can also be argued that a poet's purpose and range are not to be seriously questioned. "It's not what you say, but the way you say it, that counts." If so, it is only fair to take Mr. Coffin as he wishes to be taken—as a listener to, and lover of, what may seem to us disappearing New England folk-ways.

Although Mr. Coffin's poetry is on the surface very different from that of Robert Frost's, one is led to note comparison (and influence) because the purposes of the two poets are so similar. But where Frost is realistic and always uniquely personal, Mr. Coffin is sentimental and general. Where Frost is hard, Coffin is soft. Frost's genuine interest in New England speech-ways is a more intellectual one than Coffin's, which catches the obvious tones and phrases of salty Maine talk, and even the pattern beneath, but with, one tends to feel, a summer artist's bemusement with the quaint, strange, simple natives and their "doin's." Not that Mr. Coffin is an outsider; he comes from Maine. But from his published history of poetic conditioning—from *Christchurch* on—he can be observed gradually to have chosen his poetic range, and to have closed down to home at last, with Robert Frost. Not that one would wish to imply that regionalism is a conscious trick with Coffin, or that regionalism is now a blasphemous ideal in the face of our world of modern improvements. A poet must find his limitations somewhere, so let us grant Mr. Coffin his lovely, salty corner of earth and his worship of vanishing balladry, and see how he manages what he sets out to say.

As in his previous books, at least from *A Yoke of Thunder* on, Mr. Coffin continues with his chosen tricks of speech. In *Maine Ballads* he has curbed somewhat the distressing repetition (poverty) of image and symbol which crusted his earlier books—the incessant mention of "thighs" and "furrows," the habit of dressing holiness in a leather harness and worshipping its masculinity in bulls and farmhands from the otherworld of a lamplighted barn, or from a dainty universe of jewelled snow. He has turned this time further outward, streetward, to folklore and speech-ways of the homely, Frost-incurred short stories of New England humor and tragedy—with the frank foot-beat of an Edgar Guest, and at times with the ubiquitous thread of Housman strangely evident—as in **"Serenity,"** or **"A Hymn at Night."** He still leans on rhyme, often so carelessly that it creaks; sometimes with the desired effect of the inevitable, simple phrase. And through all the poems Mr. Coffin's strong, paternal and loving character reaches out to caress with a warmth few modern poets can express (or wish to), and this is perhaps reason enough for his chosen bulwark against "modern improvements" and the more representative living scenes, for which he has no "eyes to see the shape of them and ears to hear."

In contrast to *Maine Ballads,* Boris Todrin's *7 Men* speaks another man, time and place. This is the newer poet, the unregional modern, with eyes on the world-scene, social injustice, the new city. . . .

The group of poems for which the book is named is its point of contact with *Maine Ballads*. This is a group of portraits and ballads, of "Hughie McPadden—Bantam," of "Olsen," of "John Poor," much in the same groove as Mr. Coffin's portraits and ballads of Jethro Alexander and Tom Bailey of Maine. And, to make the comparison which invites itself, Mr. Todrin's painting is thin portraiture compared to Mr. Coffin's, though set against a more ambitious, cosmopolitan background and concerned with more representative contemporary action. Where Mr. Coffin's portraits smile out from an easy, regional frame, Mr. Todrin attempts the more difficult canvas of the days most of us have to live and know. He includes in his observation modern thinking and social empathy, and if he fails beside Mr. Coffin's smug, popularized miniatures, it is failure which leaves open the possibility of greater success.

Colin E. MacKay (essay date 1965)

SOURCE: "The Novels of Robert P. Tristram Coffin," in *Colby Library Quarterly*, Vol. VII, No. 4, December 1965, pp. 151-61.

[*In the following essay, MacKay examines the theme of permanence running through each of Coffin's three novels and judges it is most effectively expressed in his first.*]

Robert P. Tristram Coffin was a poet who turned frequently to prose; indeed, there was almost no area of prose he did not attempt—biographies, an autobiography, collected lectures, essays, history, criticism, short stories, and novels. This report shall confine itself to the last-mentioned, for (poetry naturally excluded) the novels offered Coffin his greatest challenge.

Coffin's three novels were all written within the seven-year period from 1935 to 1941, when some of his best work as a poet was being done. The first novel, *Red Sky in the Morning,* was published just a year before the author won the 1936 Pulitzer Prize for poetry; the second, *John Dawn,* in that year of national recognition; and the third, *Thomas-Thomas-Ancil Thomas,* five years later. Only brief synopses of the last two books will be necessary; however, as I intend to discuss *Red Sky in the Morning* at some length, a more detailed summary of the plot should prove helpful.

This first novel tells the story of Will Prince, the youngest member of an old Maine sea-faring family whose men used to sail around the Horn, but whose descendants now sell clams and lobsters to the summer people. Will's Uncle Frank still maintains, marginally, the old family home; but, as the story begins, Will's father has already taken Will, an older son, David, and Mrs. Prince, to a shack on a barren coastal island named Whaleboat.

Will's is an unhappy, uneasy childhood. He can neither relate as he feels he should to his devoted mother, nor can he fill the place in his dour father's life that seems the special property of David. But for the affection between Mr. Prince and David, there is no joy in the household. The two men regard Will as a weak sister; and Mr. Prince has spells of jealousy, during which he says things to his wife which suggest to Will "the slime an eel left in your hands when you tried to hold him fast." Will senses his mother's need for love in an intolerable situation, but when she attempts to be affectionate, he feels only a vague affront to his manhood and cannot respond.

After David dies of diphtheria, Mrs. Prince refuses to return to the way of life that killed him, and Will, hoping to take David's place, is rejected too. Thus begins a second stage in Will's life—a life to be lived in Uncle Frank's home, among people, and in an old house full of memories of better days. Will is pleased to be with his uncle; pleased to roam the house, take up school again, work with his nets and lobster-traps, and save money for a future education. But Whaleboat and his father's animal existence there are never out of his mind.

Eventually, a cousin, Rupert Prince—adventurer, world traveler, and successful novelist—visits the family home. Though Will is instinctively repelled by the man's egotism and grossness, he notes that his mother is charmed and excited by the newcomer. For a while, Will swallows his revulsion and enjoys seeing his mother vital and happy, but as the relationship grows he remembers his father's old accusations. Will visits Whaleboat to beg his father to come home, only to be rejected again and to have David thrown in his face as the "manly" son.

Will is now convinced he must act for his father. Almost unconsciously, he weaves a huge net. With this under his coat, he goads Rupert into proving he is no fair-weather sailor by taking his sloop out in a storm. On the open sea, Will tries to sink the craft. When an enraged Rupert attacks him, Will twists the net around his cousin's legs, and they both slip into the water to drown. Their bodies are discovered weeks later, and the net still around Rupert is enough to convince Mr. Prince that his son made the ultimate sacrifice for him. Will is buried beside David, and this time his father turns from the dory that should take him back to Whaleboat and slowly walks into the family home.

Although this first novel is not without flaws, it is, to my taste, the most successful of the three. And paradoxically, its weaknesses and its strengths often overlap.

For example, in *Red Sky* (and to a lesser extent this could be said of the other novels) Coffin tends to make paragraphs primarily out of a series of short, staccato sentences:

> It was a long way to the boiling spring his father wanted the water from for David. The island was full of springs. But just that one would do for David, and no other. One of the white hen's

chickens, David was. That was the way Will's mother often spoke of her older son. Anything he wanted was all right. She often said the sun rose and set by that boy, to hear his father tell. Will knew his father thought more of David than he did of him. David took after his father more in looks. That may have been part of the reason why.

Such passages as the above are presumably designed to suggest the fragmentary thought processes of a young boy. But the entire story is, so to speak, filtered through the mind of this boy; thus scenic and personal descriptions appear in the same style, as do revelations about characters and reactions to events. The "primer-style" can become obtrusive.

Taken individually, many paragraphs are crisp and suggestive:

> The September day was bright as polished silver. High white clouds were flying. But they never got in the way of the sun. The sun poured down on everything and lit the whole of Menhaden up. Houses stood out and glistened like squares of rock candy. Everything was like metal in the clear afternoon light. A puddle in the road was burning like a sheet of melted gold. The seagulls were going over like great snowflakes. Whiter than snowflakes. Whiter than snow.

Here the observant poet is clearly in command of the novelist, and one would not want it otherwise. The staccato effect is still apparent, but what New Englander has not seen just such an Autumn day and wished for the words to describe it?

It must be admitted, too, that Coffin's essentially poetic techniques applied to the novelist's purposes did not always produce happy results such as the lines quoted above. Here, for example, is Coffin's description of a mounting storm:

> The cold day was leaning up hard on Will's left side. As Will came up a mound of frozen spindrift, the whole dark ocean lifted up along the black ledges. A crack of white ran all the way along the island and burst into a row of blossoms like giant lilies. They hung in the air and caught the whole dim shine of coming day. Then they subsided very slowly, all at once, and Will heard thunder across the sky, and the whole granite island trembled under him. He was in a hurry. But he set the jug down carefully and stood there as still as a stone. He waited for the next swell to break. It was a long time coming. It was very quiet. The whole sky was growing unspeakably bright right along the rim of the ocean.

I was tempted to use italics to stress the point here, but even without their help, the reader will notice the repetition of the word "whole": "the whole dark ocean . . . the whole dim shine . . . the whole granite island . . . the whole sky." This could hardly be accidental; if a skilled poet did not deliberately put it there, he would

unquestionably have noticed the repetition in his proofreading. Coffin must have wanted to stress the intensity of his young hero's awareness of physical nature, and he did so. However, he also, thereby, stressed the technique of the description more than the emotional experience of the storm.

There are overlapping weaknesses and strengths, too, in Coffin's creation of characters. The five major characters—David need not be considered; he is an issue more than a person—do not always have the depth of flesh-and-blood creatures. They come close to being stock characters. Mr. Prince is a hard-bitten lobsterman who can love only the son made in his own image. Will is the sensitive, hence rejected, son. Mrs. Prince is the frustrated woman who has been used to better things; Uncle Frank, the always understanding, somewhat ineffectual nice guy; and cousin Rupert, the boastful adventurer and womanizer.

We know who and what all these people are, but they remain, to a degree, peripheral—like the figures in an epic who exist essentially to act upon and react to the hero. And though Will's character is often sharply delineated, even here—again as with the epic characterization—we are not permitted to know everything. Will's feelings about David and his father are obvious and understandable, but his attitude towards his mother is properly a corollary of his attitude towards his father—and we should know about it if Will is to be more than "the rejected son." However, we must settle for Will's own confusion about his mother, or draw our own commonplace psychological implications.

But this cannot be the last word on Coffin's art of characterization. His strength lies, again, in the individual scenes. No reader of *Red Sky in the Morning* will easily forget Will watching his father hold the dying David up to the sun, and almost envying his brother's ability to inspire a God-like look in his father; or could fail to be moved by the scene of an unloved son afraid to touch a pair of his father's trousers because that would seem almost as personal as touching the man himself.

Regrettably, however, such scenes are not enough. Though the analogy may be forced, we do not accept a series of "dramatic monologues" as a cohesive drama; and, similarly, individual scenes in a novel, no matter what their separate force, have got to yield totality of meaning. Flashes of intuition, or feeling, or understanding will not really affect us if we do not, ultimately, identify fully with the people involved in the story. And there's the rub. One is aware that a given page has presented, say, a sensitive and accurate portrait of a "frustrated woman," but she is not often enough a *particular* frustrated woman, Mrs. Prince.

A 1935 reviewer—also reaching for an analogy—put it well, I feel, when he suggested that *Red Sky* "presents single emotions keenly, but with no more analysis than in a lyric." Another reference to the poet!

Coffin's second novel is his least effective, primarily, I would insist, because he tried to make it a novel of action and of generations of characters, and to do so in the too limited space of 300-plus pages, not nearly room enough for a "saga."

John Dawn, the titular hero of the tale, is born on New Year's Day of 1800. He is the son of Captain James Dawn of Merrymeeting, Maine, who, as he toasts both the new century and his new son, promises his comrades the story of a battered pewter cup inscribed "J. Dawn." Suddenly—and one must be alert to catch the shift in time—we find ourselves back in 1751 at the birth of Captain James, the son of Jacob Dawn. The Dawn chronicles have begun. Jacob is killed by marauding Indians, and his wife and children, young James excepted, are burned in their home; James, after fathering John Dawn, is killed in a sea-battle with a British man-o'-war; and John himself, though he lives to a good age, dies after an accident sustained as he watches the launching of his last ship—a sailing ship built despite the new age of steam. Before his story is told, however, John Dawn must bury two sons; the elder, Joel, murdered by cutthroats in a California gold town, and the younger, Robert, killed on a Civil War battleground. When old John dies, therefore, it is the end of the family line, and the end of an era.

John Dawn is the kind of story Kenneth Roberts or C. S. Forester might have chosen to write. The former would have attempted to breathe life into the pages of American history; the latter would have given his attention to the ships and men on the high seas. Both would have specialized in scenes of action. Coffin does not; indeed he seems ill at ease with historical novel heroics and violence. In *John Dawn* the scenes of action and violence are especially creaky:

> The iron missiles had made kindling of the port rail and ploughed up the deck into tall splinters. A man was lying in the midst of them, flat on his face on the deck. His bowels showed below his jacket and glittered evilly in the light of the high moon. Another man had been hit hard, and he was crawling along the deck with his hands alone, for his legs were no use to him. All five of the *Margaretta's* guns were barking now. The men worked them as fast as they could.

There are literally dozens of similar passages. Guns belch smoke; limbs are torn off; wood splinters tear at eyes and faces; and guts are spilled. But there is no smell of sweat and powder, no stink of death, no sense of fear and agony—just statements that they are there.

From time to time, too, the characters are larger than life:

> Fearing Upjohn was sitting on a water bucket with the white bones of his right leg sticking out through his trouser leg, where his knee should have been. He was holding a man up in his arms. John saw that it was Davy Snow. Davy's face was all chalk. His coat was dabbled with blood. He was hurt all over. John bent down to him.

> "Wonderful," Davy was saying as he mopped the blood out of his gray hair and eyebrows, "wonderful fight Johndy! Wouldn't have missed this for Timbuktu! Miriam'll be glad to—to hear what a—a—nice fight we had. Your Daddy will tell—will tell—her what—"

> He slumped forward in Fearing's arms.

> "Davy's gone," Fearing Upjohn whispered fiercely, "gone dead on us. What your father'll ever do without Davy I don't know."

> "You are hurt, too, Fearing," said John.

> "Oh, a scratch—a scratch or two."

One is impelled to ask why Coffin, in his second novel, attempted an uncongenial genre. I think the answer must be that he considered the historical background and the battles on land and sea not vital to his main purpose, which was to assert the value of the continuity of the family—of fathers and sons—and the equal value of the standards of strong and fearless men.

These values are, indeed, implicit in **Red Sky in the Morning** in the relationship of Mr. Prince and David, in the yearnings of Will, and in his foolish but selfless sacrifice of his life for his father's honor. In **John Dawn** the assertions are explicit. Each Dawn male is aware—almost unnaturally aware of his past and of his destiny. The pewter cup is passed from Jacob to James to John to Joel, and it goes into the grave with Robert only when the line of Dawn is ended. Each Dawn male knows he must sire sons, the first always to be given a name beginning with the letter "J" so that he may properly inherit the cup. And captains James and John—the father and son who dominate the novel—are warned of the coming or the presence of death by a vision of a phantom ship, the *Harpswell*, a ship which finally sails off, after John dies, "like a flake of fire . . . burning hot like a candle flame set on the edge of the sea."

There is implicit, also, in **John Dawn** a theme which will become all-important in the last novel and one which is so basic in the poetry: that relationships of men are the ones that matter in the scheme of things, and that fathers live in sons in a special way that transcends the facts of genetics. Whether writing of men of the sea or of the soil, Coffin makes his characters aware of their heritage and convinced that they contain more in their wills and bodies than just themselves. As Captain John Dawn dies in the arms of his beloved natural brother, his whole life runs before his eyes, but just before he dies:

> Someone opened a door on a room full of babies. A door. A door. And it swayed back and forth. The wind outside whistled through a thousand ropes on a mast. The royal yard swayed back and forth across the sky, like a cradle rocking. And babies in it. A single albatross flying lonely across the sea in the sun. And it swayed, like a cradle. Like a cradle rocking babies. Babies that were sons. Babies that were men. Babies. Rocking. Sons. Sons.

In *Thomas-Thomas-Ancil-Thomas,* Coffin seems so pre-occupied with the theme of ancestral influence that it appears not only in the story but in the very dedication: "To my son, Robert, and to my sons in him."

Objection has been raised to the stress on ancestral influence because it seems to suggest that the man who acts as one controlled by three generations of males before him is not sufficiently responsible for his own deeds and valor. This, as far as I am concerned constitutes a moral not an aesthetic criticism. Believe in the idea or not—like it or not—we must ask if the author successfully brings it off. I cannot, for one, accept this "premise," but I can applaud the attempt—often successful—to work with a very complex four-dimensional approach.

It would be inaccurate to say, though it is literally true, that the hero of this last novel is the final Thomas of the title, for that Thomas Coombs is as much his father Ancil, his grandfather Thomas, and his great-grandfather Thomas, as he is himself. The Dawn men were, as has been pointed out, well aware of the stock they came from—but Thomas Coombs *is* the stock he came from, from the age of seven until his death.

In the opening chapter we are introduced to what I have called the four-dimensional approach, and it operates throughout the book. It is a daring and dangerous approach. Certainly Coffin must have known, as he employed it, that he was running two major risks: that the continual stress on four-characters-in-one might keep his readers from identifying with any of the four; and that the leaps from generation to generation might seem merely a series of arbitrary mechanical shifts—might give a kind of "meanwhile, thirty years ago" effect. Coffin was not always successful in minimizing the first risk, but I think he did avoid the second.

Often, he leaps generations by letting the last Thomas dream a special dream—a dream of "timelessness," and of children tumbling along in a great wind. Thomas dreams throughout the novel, but he comprehends the mystery of the dream only when, in the final pages, the dream wind becomes a literal wind that tears him from the top of his barn and tosses him to his death as his sons watch:

> The strong man floated away into the midst of a dream he had always dreamt. And in the fine head the dream was all there was left of life, and that for the time it takes a mayfly to die. The man saw clearly. The man knew. But as in a dream and darkly. He knew how it was with him. For the little time it takes an airy spark to burn out. He knew he was going away from his barn and his farm and his wife forever. He was going away from all wives and all taking in marriage. He was going away. He was going away from his sons. For his sons at last were in a safe place and would not come after him this time rolling on the wind nor fly higher and higher with him as he flew over a dwindling world and into a place where there was no father love, no love of hunger, nor any

eating. No love, no bodies, no hands, no head, no eyes, nor any warm secrets of a man few eyes see and the few trusted ones feel and know.

The dream sequence is an obvious device—like the pewter cup and the phantom ship of *John Dawn*—but it is a much more sophisticated and integral one.

Occasionally, Coffin insists upon the timelessness of his story by duplicating plot action: the father and the friend who are rivals in love and buddies in war play their parts again in their sons, who are rivals in love and buddies in war. Here the author is least convincing, not so much because the parallels are so apparent, but because there is simply not enough difference in fist-fights over girls, generations apart, or between rescues on the battlefield, Civil War and World War I versions, to maintain interest.

Usually, however, Coffin shows us the influence of—really the oneness of—the generations by leading us so gently from the past to the present, or the reverse, that we make the time shifts before we know we have done so.

This ability could only be demonstrated by extensive quotation, which considerations of space forbid, so discussion of one example will have to serve. In the opening pages of *Thomas-Thomas-Ancil-Thomas,* the last Thomas, age seven, is awakened at sunset by his mother and told that he has napped the afternoon away and missed his dinner. She has, however, saved him a generous portion of his favorite dish. As the boy eats hungrily, he looks out of the window and thinks lovingly of his father who explains that world to him and tells him "the best things to know, and they were always right."

The next paragraph briefly describes a freckle-faced, yellow-haired boy; the paragraph after that tells of the wonderful day he had making a trip with his father. Both paragraphs seem to refer to Thomas—but, no, we are already back a generation. If we read carefully, we realize that the boy who slept the afternoon away cannot be the boy who made a day-long trip. Yet, there is no one sentence we can point to and say that the time shift occurred there.

As we read on, the clues pile up. The boy, we learn, likes his father's name, Thomas, and he hopes so to name his own son one day—and the sequence of names in the title reminds us that the father of the first seven-year-old boy we met should be Ancil. Shortly, the boy is actually called Ancil. A bare description of this time shift cannot suggest the smoothness of the transition from present to past, but perusal of just the few pages involved would, I am sure, convince most readers that a very difficult narrative trick has not only been performed, but has been made to appear effortless—the ultimate goal of professionalism.

To sum up, then, the novels of Robert P. Tristram Coffin are—usually for both good and ill—novels whose technical aspects strongly suggest the hand of a man who was a poet before he was anything else. They were written by one who was at his best when he could bring his essentially poetic observation to typical Maine scenes—to a dory being rowed through the sleet of a storm, to the map-covered walls of an old sea captain's harbor home, to mayflowers on a farmer's untilled field, to the delights of an open-air celebration following the successful launching of a new sailing ship. They were written by one who did not sustain characterization, but who captured heightened emotions briefly, and often with great perception and understanding.

The novels were written, too, by a man who seemed sure of his message, though he must have realized many would not share his views. It seems safe enough to suggest that most women would not look with unqualified approval on a scheme of things wherein they exist largely to produce strong sons for strong men who will then regard the sons as their special property. And certainly many men—even men who share Coffin's conviction of the importance of sons—will not accept his insistence on the forces of tradition and genetics as forgers of character.

But I think that very few readers will quarrel with the repeated attempts in the novels to suggest a permanence in the relationship of men and nature that is fundamentally comforting, that is something to draw on. Coffin worked hardest to suggest this permanence in *John Dawn* and *Thomas-Thomas-Ancil-Thomas,* but he was most effective in doing so where he seemed to try the least. *Red Sky in the Morning* has no elaborate machinery; it does not go beyond the lives of the two generations who live together in it; it certainly depends on no involved use of time sequence. We are never told directly the date of the story, and so we begin it assuming it takes place in our own time: then we gradually note that only a sailboat seems available where an emergency situation would seem to call for the speed of a power launch; or we note that a character plans to arrive in town on "the stage." In brief, the first novel, *Red Sky in the Morning,* suggests—pervasively yet unobtrusively—the timelessness, sameness, and the cyclic quality of life which the author tried to recapture in his later novels.

F. Celand Witham (essay date 1965)

SOURCE: "The Essays of Robert Peter Tristram Coffin," in *Colby Library Quarterly,* Vol. VII, No. 4, December, 1965, pp. 161-69.

[*In the following essay, Witham argues that Coffin's skill as an essayist derives from his visionary aptitude as a poet and from his joviality as a person.*]

> *A thrush singing in the woods. . . .* It was the first bird I had ever really heard sing. It was the last marvel in a long chain of marvels. The first violets, like pieces of the sky, the first anemones, like drops of snow left over into April. I had had my first trip out past all houses, out of sight of all windows and doors. I was too tired to take in anything more.

> Then, when the shadow of the earth was climbing up the eastern sky, the bird sang among the distant trees. Three broken little songs rising higher and higher until they faltered and failed. All at once I knew what it was to be alone and among things so lovely that they made your heart ache. For you could never tell how beautiful they were even though you were to live a thousand years and have all the best words on the end of your tongue. My father thought it was weariness that made me burst suddenly into tears. But it was the thrush I have to thank for that.[1]

From the more than 130 collected essays of Robert Peter Tristram Coffin, it would be possible to select literally scores of examples that would illustrate his sharpness of observation and his facility with description. But any number of such examples would show only that Tristram Coffin possesses the essential tools required of any creative writer. What differentiates the work of Coffin from that of many others who have written engagingly and perceptively of the Maine scene is the sensitivity, the intenseness, of the response to his immediate surroundings. Unlike Louise Dickinson Rich, for example, who "took to the woods" and wrote impressively about that temporary experience, Coffin "emerges from" the geographical elements of the Harpswell-Casco Bay area. This is not to say that such a difference makes one writer "better" than another; it is to say that such "goings" and "comings" can have a profound effect upon the writer's attitude toward his subject and, hence, upon the tone of the finished product.

To the extent that "Naturalism" in writing functions on a premise that man is the product of his heredity and environment, Coffin can be said to be a naturalistic writer.[2] His frequently repeated phrase that "Maine is a state of mind" becomes more deeply understood when one encounters such statements as:

> There is a religion to island weather. It has its holy iconography. It comes out in the lines of reachboats and dories, the economies of roof and gables on island fish-houses. It is an awareness to the intangibles of infinity. It is the life-and-death matter of changes of wind and tide which makes up the laws of this religion. An island man is a worshipful man. He goes like a small boy with his hand in the hand of a father too tall to see eye-to-eye with. He trusts and believes, because he knows how to read his salvation in a cud of fog, in the sound of a changed wind, the rote of distant surf on an unseen reef in the night.[3]

or again, when Coffin discusses the day-to-day existence of people in terms of their immediate environment:

> I come of island people. I like to think island people have a special toehold on life. For like mountain people—and Maine people are very much like mountain people, and the sea has washed out all the softness in them—they have come naturally by independence, loneliness, resourcefulness, toughness of body, and sadness . . .[4]

In a lighter vein that is perhaps more commonly associated with Coffin, a similar viewpoint is expressed in these terms:

> . . . when people live in a place a long time, they grow to be like it. The dishes they cook up grow to be like it too. Maine is bayberry and sweetfern and fern-brake and balsams, and I like to think its people and their foods are pungent and sharp-flavored also. A Maine blue-berry cannot help smelling like pitch-pines on a scorching day, for it ripened on just such a day and among those pines. A Maine boy acts the way State of Maine huckleberries taste. He cannot help it, for on any day late in August about half his weight is huckleberries.[5]

Thus it is that the majority of Coffin's essays deal with life as he once knew it off-shore from Harpswell, and hence it follows that many of his pieces are concerned with the close family relationship[6] that such an isolated existence would necessitate. The theme of father idolatry, which occurs frequently in Coffins essays, is better understood, therefore, when seen in terms of the writer's unusually specialized surroundings. Because he has experienced at first hand the family's total dependence upon the wits, resourcefulness, and sheer strength of the father, Coffin can write sensitively of his appreciation of that remarkable man without descending to a level of sentimentality:

> . . . I learned more from my father's stories than I learned from books. I spent half of my time, up till I was seven or eight, on his knee, whenever he was resting, learning to draw pictures or learning what had made my father the man he was. I learned American history and the American philosophy of each tub's standing on its own bottom, I learned about Hannibal and John Paul Jones and what goes into the making of a strong man. I learned about ghosts and Indians also, for my father was up on them, too. He was the best story-teller I have ever heard. His stories stay with me still.[7]

Lest the impression be given that Coffin's essays are mere prose reflections of early childhood, it should be stated now that such is not the case. The self-reliance, hard work, frugality, and isolation of the early life become materials for his definition of individualism and independence as he conceives such terms in his mature years. Coffin's conservative viewpoint regarding contemporary problems emerges as a natural consequence of his background.

> People are being won away from islands and the perilous and hard and narrow life there, won to the mainland, the mainland ways, to the towns. Summer cottages have taken over many islands. Bridges have tied many of them to progress. But more of the islands have fallen vacant in the harder and brighter three-quarters of the year. It seems that the automobile and the movies, manufactured things, the chainstore idea and the herd psychology are winning.

> Yet there are some tough and unherded islanders left. Maybe we can breed from these! They refuse to move over to the mainland and the mass formations of progress.[8]

When he attempts to apply such an island-philosophy to larger issues on the contemporary scene, however, Coffin tends to encounter a problem of over-simplification. In a defense of Wendell Willkie's idea of "one world"—to which Coffin claims to subscribe—one reads the following:

> . . . we Yankees started building ships hand-over-fist all up and down the Atlantic shoreline; and we went off to Havana and took the sugar right out of Britain's mouth. We smelled the rum of Jamaica and down we went for it. We took our potatoes and brought back cotton. We went farther and farther. To Nippon for silks, to Java for coffee, to Sumatra for pepper. We tied the continents together with our shuttles of wood and sail. We became the common carrier of common mankind. We had always been good at horse-trading and shopkeeping. Now we branched out and kept shop and traded for the whole earth.

> And none handsomer than these, the coast men of Maine. Small farmers, but we became big merchants and dressed our ladies in silks that whistled of China . . . We made friends, we made money.[9]

Here Coffin appears to interpret Willkie's concept of "one world" simply as an expansion of the 19th-century American viewpoint. Thus he seems to miss Willkie's argument that traditional concepts of such words as "friends" and "trade" require serious re-thinking in the world of the 1940s. The contrast in viewpoints can easily be seen.

> All the leaks in this priceless reservoir [of goodwill] are of our own making. For the very existence of this reservoir is built on confidence, in our integrity of purpose, our honesty in dealing, our ability in performance . . .

> There are other holes that we are punching in our reservoir of goodwill which can be more easily repaired. One of them is the half-ignorant, half-patronizing way in which we have grown accustomed to treating many of the peoples of Eastern Europe and Asia.[10]

Coffin's limitation as a debater of contemporary affairs becomes evident on the local scene when he attempts to apply his island-philosophy to the issue of conservation of Maine's natural resources. His outrage as presented in his bill of particulars is forceful indeed:

> We have allowed our "white coal"—Maine has limitless waterpower—to get into the hands of monopolists at times. Worse still, we have let the mills at our waterfalls poison our rivers with chemicals and kill out all our famous salmon and shad. That pollution still goes on and makes a desert of some of the best rivers of America. We

have slaughtered our forests, left the slash, and let forest fires burn up our soil and the substance of children to come. Here is our blackest sin. Unintelligence and greed are as common in Maine as elsewhere. I think what the lumber interests have done to the forest which was Maine deserves to rank as a capital crime.[11]

But Coffin's indictment appears to come into conflict with his island-philosophy of individual independence, and his argument consequently founders on a reef of wishful thinking.

We could have made Maine another Norway if we had farmed our forests intelligently. We may do it even yet. For in spite of our greed and shortsightedness, new balsams and pines keep coming up. Maine evergreens are hard to kill. We have always been able to raise a new crop.[12]

In any case, it is for qualities more characteristic of Coffin's sensitive and jovial personality—qualities more closely allied to Coffin, the poet—that readers will turn to his essays. Here, when he is at his best, one can share experiences, either of the distant or recent past, in which Coffin is intimately involved. If he is describing a Christmas homecoming of some forty years past, his reader will be made to feel the cold and sense the swerve of the pung as it glides over the "diamond" ice of Casco Bay. When he provides his reader with a recipe for his father's codfish chowder or lobster stew, he garnishes it with a mouth-watering description of the finished product.[13] To be at his best, Coffin must be dealing with a subject to which he has an intensely personal relationship. There are exceptions, to be sure, such as **"The Harvest of Diamonds"**[14] in which the commercial harvesting of ice is vividly described; but such exceptions are rare.

At the risk of mutilating one of his best pieces, some examples from **"Angel's-Eye View"**[15] will be selected to illustrate the devices by which the characteristic "Coffin tone" is established.

There are lots of ways of viewing the coast of Maine. But the angels have the best one. From high above . . . But you can't have everything. So I am content to see Maine shores in the apocalyptic new way, only a handful of years old.

The best view is from an airplane. Fly over the coast if you want to see it at its *Book of Revelation* best.

One sees here the way in which Coffin juxtaposes typical Maine idiom ("lots of" for "many" and "handful" for an exact number) with Biblical, and less typical, references ("apocalyptic new way" and "Book of Revelation best") which reinforce the angel image. Such juxtapositions occur frequently in Coffin's essays, with varying degrees of success. Many times he will select a phrase of Chaucer's that serves well; at other times his erudition will lead him to introduce Vergil or Donne quite unexpectedly—sometimes, so it seems,

between the fried pork and the onions of a chowder. But such solecisims are infrequent, and they do not seriously affect the over-all enjoyment of any particular essay. It is the easy-going, conversational style, together with the wry humor, that has the long-lasting effect on the reader. Examples of these qualities are abundant in the essay at hand, but one must suffice here:

I wasn't too sure of my friend [Stephen Etnier] as a rival of the angels. He had got his flight training more or less on the correspondence-school level. It was sketchy. It was full of gaps. He did not know too much about the insides of internal combustion engines.

The penchant for understatement, a distinguishing characteristic of the Maine idiom, is discernible in such phrases as "I wasn't too sure" and "more or less on the correspondence-school level." The implication is, of course, that the pilot is either highly incompetent or dangerously irresponsible and that Coffin is extremely apprehensive for his own safety. The humor lies in his refusal to admit openly his fright.

An inclination sometimes to over-write emerges also in this example. Coffin's lack of confidence in the pilot is humorously established by the phrase "correspondence-school level." His addition of such statements as "full of gaps," "sketchy," *et cetera* tend to dull the effectiveness of the original point. Another example occurs three paragraphs later when Coffin describes what appears to him to be an imminent crash into a lighthouse. "But Seguin is an old lighthouse, built in President Washington's time, 1795, and I didn't want anything to happen to it." But the wry understatement here becomes somewhat blunted when Coffin adds: "A good friend of mine tends it, and I shouldn't want anything to happen to him or to his fine family." Lacking the incongruity of concerns that the earlier statement contains, the second tends to call attention merely to itself. The piquant humor of the incident is thereby marred.

Although Coffin does not at all times edit his essays as objectively as one might wish, it must nevertheless be admitted that the flaws become comparatively obscure when his humor, sensitivity, and imagination are all operating at full sail. Evidence again is provided by **"Angel's-Eye View."**

I got excited and reached over to lay hands on whatever controlled our height. It was then my life-belt broke. After that, I had to depend on gravity and native common sense, and the lust to live, to stay put in my seat.

The door on my side, secured with a loop of picture wire, kept coming open every time we leaned my side down . . . I had to hold the door to with my right hand all the time.[16]

By use of careful organization, Coffin achieves a nice balance between farcical and serious elements in a single essay. In contrast to the incident described above, for example, one encounters numerous instances where Coffin the serious man and sensitive observer takes command.

> Down below was my bay—all of it at once—from Cape Small Point to Portland Head Light and the cape named for Gloriana, the glittering queen of the *Faerie Queene*. It was so wide, being all there, that it curved down at each side with the curvature of the earth. There was the marriage of land and sea, islands and hills and forests, that means the center of the universe to me.

Thus **"Angel's-Eye View"** becomes a "Coffin woodcut" by literary means. By either bold strokes of contrast or by subtle lines of transition, Coffin creates here a complete picture of the Casco Bay topography and a self-portrait of the humorous and sensitive artist.

There remains another characteristic of this essayist which leads perhaps most directly to the question of the extent to which Coffin's work is "typically Maine." Almost never in these pieces does he employ dialogue as a means of establishing the native Maine type. When he does, as in the case of **"Hens and Hounds and Hants and Wars,"**[17] the language tends toward a flatness that is wanting in the richness of Coffin, and lacking in the terseness of Maine understatement. One suspects, for two reasons, that Coffin himself is aware of such problems with dialogue: first, he frequently avoids its use; and second, he tends to over-inflate the incidents when dialogue is attempted. In **"Hens and Hounds,"** for example, the incidents become exaggerated to a point that defies credulity.[18]

Most significant, perhaps, is Coffin's reluctance to employ dialogue in the character delineation of his father. Words and phrases that distinguished the father's vocabulary are listed, but the man is never presented as a character speaking in the first person. Similarly, Coffin offers isolated examples of words and phrases that are generally indigenous to the Casco Bay region, but again the "give and take" of dialogue is absent. It has been noted earlier that Coffin adapts some elements of the Casco Bay idiom to achieve his own easy-going style, but such elements are judiciously selected and used in conjunction with the vocabulary of Coffin the poet and well educated man. It is to Owen Davis—another Maine recipient of a Pulitzer Prize—rather than to Coffin, that one should turn for examples of the terse understatement and the rhythm that distinguishes the Maine speech pattern.[19]

What emerges finally from the reading of Coffin's essays is an autobiographical account of an unusual man. To the extent that the essays concern the Maine coast[20] and to the extent that they frequently espouse the virtues of personal independence, hard work, frugality, and conservative thought it can be said that they reflect much that is Maine's natural beauty and its "state of mind."

But what emerges far more poignantly in these pieces is the individuality of Robert Peter Tristram Coffin, the poet, the educated man who views his world in a distinctly uncommon way. It could not be otherwise: Coffin grew up in a geographical environment that is unique; he was raised in the midst of an unusual family by a father who was far from being a common man. All this, together with a sensitive literary talent and a unique educational background, accounts for these essays that reflect, more than anything else, a man's life "as he has found it jovial and beautiful."

NOTES

[1] "First Things", *An Attic Room* (New York, 1929), 6.

[2] Coffin differs from the Zola school of naturalism in that immediate social and economic problems are a secondary concern. Moreover, his outlook is characterized by joviality rather than morbidity.

[3] "Island Living," *Yankee Coast* (New York, 1947), 43.

[4] *Ibid.*, 22.

[5] *Mainstays of Maine* (New York, 1945), ix-x.

[6] Nearly all the members of Coffin's family become subject material for his essays at various times, but everywhere the father is the dominant figure.

[7] "An American for a Father," *Maine Doings* (Indianapolis, 1950), 105-106.

[8] "Island Living," *Yankee Coast*, 45-46.

[9] "Citizens in the Round," *Yankee Coast*, 109.

[10] Wendell L. Willkie, "Our Reservoir of World Respect and Hope," *Vital Speeches of the Day* (Nov. 1, 1942), 36-37.

[11] "Maine: State of Being Oneself," *Maine Doings*, 258-259.

[12] *Ibid.*, Coffin's point is made as part of a more comprehensive discussion in which Arnold Toynbee's statement of "Maine, the 'Museum Piece'" is challenged. (*A Study of History*, abr. I-VI by D. C. Somervell (New York, 1947), 146-147.) The dubious success of Coffin's challenge is similar to that of Kenneth Roberts' as examined by Paul Fullam, *Colby Library Quarterly*, III (May 1951), 21-22.

[13] Coffin's recipes are *not* recommended to either the sick or the squeamish. If it is a beast or a fish, it *all* goes into the pot; if it is a fowl, then everything goes in except the feathers: those go into a pillow!

[14] *Maine Doings*, 38-44.

[15] *Yankee Coast*, 1-14.

[16] Stephen Etnier, an artist who resides in Harpswell, assures the present writer that the plane was "perfectly

air-worthy." Coffin's description of its dilapidated condition is entirely the product of his own creation.

[17] *Yankee Coast,* 69-85.

[18] It may be significant that Coffin is re-telling stories of his brother here. The exaggeration may result from Coffin's personal non-involvement in the incidents.

[19] See *Icebound,* especially Act I.

[20] *Book of Crowns and Cottages* (New Haven, 1925), Coffin's first volume of collected essays, has been purposely omitted from the present discussion because it concerns Coffin's experiences in England as a Rhodes Scholar. "The Dean's Croquet," in that volume, however, is highly recommended.

William C. Wees (essay date 1965)

SOURCE: "Puritanism Versus the Old Green Gods: New England in the Poetry of Robert P. Tristram Coffin," in *Colby Library Quarterly,* Vol. VII, No. 4, December, 1965, pp. 136-50.

[*In the following essay, Wees argues that in its celebration of the male connection to a primal, natural power both destructive and sexual, Coffin's poetry reveals the poet's revolt against New England Puritanism.*]

New England—Maine, in fact—dominates the poetry of Robert P. Tristram Coffin. Like Emily Dickinson, Coffin tried to "see New Englandly." For a poet to so limit his subject matter and point of view, to be so provincial, does not necessarily limit the richness of his work: witness the poetry of Dickinson, herself, and Coffin's contemporary, Robert Frost. Although Dickinson and Frost preferred to make their poems complex, ambiguous and symbolic, and experimented with sound and rhythm patterns, while Coffin tended toward a more open and direct statement of themes and an uncomplicated use or rime and meter, all three poets achieved universality by dealing with New England people and the world they live in.

This world, where man and nature remain close (as farmer to land or fisherman to sea) was the only world that interested Coffin. His decision to ignore industrialized and urbanized America—a decision his thoroughly happy boyhood on a Maine salt water farm apparently made inevitable—allowed him to turn his full attention to creating a poetic response to the world he knew best: the New England world of fishermen, farmers and dwellers in small coastal towns, the sea, the fields and pastures, the rivers, the trees and flowers, the wildlife and, most important of all, the earth itself, which affected Coffin like a deep, strange, primitive power that elicits man's fear and reverence.

It is Coffin's development of an atavistic awe before the power of nature, a nature that destroys man's domesticated world, but at the same time revitalizes man sexually, that I find most interesting in his poetry—interesting, especially, because it led Coffin to repudiate New England's Puritan heritage in favor of a radically anti-Puritan, even pagan, primitivism. To see how Coffin arrived at this commitment to primitivism, we will examine, first, the New Englanders who inhabit Coffin's world and, second, the natural environment in which they live. Then, finally, we will see how the two—people and environment, man and nature—come together in a sexually charged, animistic universe.

I

Some of Coffin's people too much resemble the old lobsterman in the *New Yorker* cartoon, who tells two summer people that he's sorry, but he has already been someone's "Most Unforgettable Character"; others remind one of Sherwood Anderson's "grotesques" in *Winesburg, Ohio,* that is, people who have turned in upon themselves so that they seem "queer" to the outside world, but inside have a touching, bittersweet humanity that makes them sadder and more sensible to the harshness of the world. Most of Coffin's people are neither local characters nor "grotesques," however, but simply ordinary people whose lives most clearly illustrate man's condition and his place in nature.

Typical local characters are Jim Bibber who every Sunday stood on his hill above the town and swore great, booming oaths as the people went to church, and Grandfather Noah Staples who always insisted that only chance had prevented the Confederate Army from capturing Washington "by way of Washington County."[1] Coffin's poems about people such as these do not touch upon basic human problems, but when he writes about "grotesques" like Thief Jones, Lomey Catlin and Roxiney Boody, Coffin reveals universal problems of loneliness and deep unhappiness. Thief Jones steals from everyone in town, but since he always lets the rightful owner have his goods when he comes for them, Thief has become an accepted part of the town's everyday life. But Thief's plight becomes pathetic when we read that although people "liked to hear him lie, . . . Thief ate his victuals by himself." (CP, 223) Pathetic, too is Lomey Catlin who believed that

> The sins of all the world were hers,
> They stuck to her like burdock burrs.
>
> (CP, 331)

She felt responsible when "Sade Carter had a woods-colt child . . . Sim Sinnett did not give up drink . . . a gale blew off the Baptist steeple," and she prayed constantly, "Dear God, I wish I'd never been got!"

The loneliness of Thief Jones and the sense of sin in Lomey Catlin unite in the lamentations of Roxiney Boody, who had danced with all the boys and made love under the spars and nets until "the sun came up, and youth had gone." (CP, 330) Then, old and repentant, she put her misery into a kind of seacoast spiritual:

"If I had the flippers of a seal,
I'd fly to Jesus, and he would heal."

. . . . .

"If I had the wings of a coot or a loon,
I'd fly to my Jesus in Malagoon!"

. . . . .

"If I was a shad with a silver side,
I'd swim to Jesus and be his bride!"

(CP, 328-330)

But Jesus, like Malagoon, was too far away, and Roxiney Boody "spent her groans/ Along Sabino's icy stones." (CP, 329)

Roxiney Boody's isolation also characterizes many ordinary people who must learn to face life, in all its ordinariness, alone. A universal condition, certainly, but given particularity in lonely New England settings along the Maine coast. Thus, the isolation is physical as well as psychological, and the individual's loneliness appears in stark relief against the vast background of sea, sky and rocky, forested shore line.

Coffin captures exactly this sense of physical and psychological isolation when he describes the loneliness of a young wife on a coastal island:

There was the sea, the wall of winds between
The life she knew before and this life here,
Her loneliness was a very steady thing. . . .

(ABO, 48)

This steady loneliness can totally dominate men's lives. In **"Being,"** Coffin presents a clam digger who

had no garden and no friend,
He did not borrow things or lend,
Never in all his silent life
Had he found room for any wife
Of his own or other men's;
He'd never kept as much as hens.

(CP, 224)

Equally lonely is John Popham, a lobsterman who "kept away from other men," and "found his lonely way about/ Shoals and blows and low-ebb hours." (CP, 226) But John loved "being lonely," as he loved "bold water at his door."

Isolation, then, is not necessarily a bad thing, as Coffin shows in **"The Island."** On a treeless, deserted island an old cellar hole gives proof that men lived there once and might return,

When men grow tired
Of being what their neighbors are and find
That things to have are not the things to own.
Men may need frontiers again, and turn
Back to cabins and a loneliness
Which puts them close to stars and tapping rain,
To waters moving, rainbows, and the wind.

(CP, 157)

Men, in other words, may desire loneliness as a way of escaping conformity, finding new frontiers, and returning to a close relationship with nature. Here Coffin touches upon an archetypal image in the American consciousness: man alone in nature.

Coffin's use of this image undoubtedly stems from several impulses: a rejection of today's suburban barracks and urban renewal parking lots; a desire to play the role of the sturdy, self-reliant Yankee; an expansion of his own childhood into a metaphor of general happiness; an innate sympathy with the many American writers who have been drawn to the man-in-nature image. That image stems partly from the Romantic, Rousseauist faith in the beneficence of nature and partly from the direct American experience of being alone in nature, as frontiersman, homesteader and, indeed, even today as fisherman and farmer in Maine. In America the actual experience of being alone in nature was intensified by the peculiarly strong sense of isolation fostered by American Puritanism, with its painful soul-searching and its emphasis on the inevitably lonely confrontation between the individual soul and God. The New England loneliness in Coffin's poetry reflects some of this Puritan-based isolation, but Coffin generally evades its more terrifying and tragic consequences in order to emphasize the positive value of being alone in nature.

Puritanism affects Coffin's ordinary people in another way, by shaping their ethics according to what we might call the old way of doing things, a way that is better because it is harder, simpler and more independent than newer ways of doing things. On this scale of values, labor rates above leisure, farms above cities, thrift above generosity, even sons above daughters. Yet, the hard old way is passing, as Coffin tacitly admits in two poems that ironically undercut the old way of life. **"The Mark"** describes a shining white country church without fallen shingles, loose nails or crooked blinds. Yet, the poet says, "People do not go there any more,/ The church is full of sermons of the dust." (CP, 205) Its only purpose is to satisfy the people's compulsion to have clean, orderly structures, and "to have a good mark when they plow/ To run their furrows by." The church has become an ossified, hollow image of the old way of life. In **"Last Ear,"** Coffin personifies the old way in "one very old New England man" who continues to hunt for the last ear of corn after all the younger men "who have sons in their bodies/ Have called it a day, unhitched, and gone." (PSW, 47) So it is, "'This man with not a seed in him/ Searches for seeds still, searches on." Like the coming winter, like death itself, "he comes ahead of dark . . . holding the last ear like a vise." In the last stanza Coffin specifically applies his metaphor of impotence-winter-death to New England:

This would not be the true New England
Without this old man on weak feet
Bringing the final ear of the year's
Corn he will not live to eat.

The obsession for finding the last misshapen ear of corn is like the obsession for keeping an old, unused church in perfect condition: though the good old way of life is virtually dead, it must not be abandoned.

More directly, Coffin describes the decay of the old standards in four poems that tell a similar story. In **"Thomas King"** we find a man who

> liked straight furrows and clean panes
> And lofty talk at night,
> Weedless corn and pride that keeps
> The shoulders square and right.
>
> (CP, 107)

But Thomas King's son "Let the plowing go/ Took the easy way," and married a woman who left everything "orderless and slack," and finally Thomas King could stand it no longer and killed himself. In **"He Hoes"** another father has a son "mated with a wife/ Coarse and common as the weeds." (CP, 38) The result is again the decay of the old standards:

> Sharp words and dirt are everywhere
> In his house that once was clean.
> His grand-daughters run with the men
> And have a wormy fruit to glean.

And all the father can do is weed the corn until after dark, and remain "clean and shining as his hoe" until death finds him still hoeing and "not a weed in any row." (CP, 39) In **"Head Up Like a Deer's,"** a father has a "weak" son who had an "old streak/ Of his mother's taking the easy way,/ Living for the fun and for the day." (ABO, 45) This boy, too, marries a girl who is "dirty" and for whom "Fun came too easy, she found it everywhere." Rather than see his son "wallow [in]/ All the dirty years he knew would follow," the father kills him with a twelve-gauge shotgun. Finally, in **"The Monument"** Coffin describes a house that is half white and half weathered gray. Old Dan Lord had been busily painting his house when death took him, and

> Thereafter people looking up there knew
> A man had worked the last breath that he drew
> And had a lazy son to be his heir
> Who went on living with his house half bare.
>
> (PSW, 27)

This degeneracy of sons can spread through a whole community, as Coffin shows in **"Run-Out Harbor,"** where the old way has surrendered to the new: the roofs tumble and the gables lean; yards are littered with clam shells and wash hangs on front porches; the people are up to no good long after midnight, and they "loll about and sing/ As they run their shad nets clear." (CP, 208-209)

The degeneracy theme, like the loneliness theme, has direct connections with New England Puritanism. What is degenerating in these poems is the harsh moral standard imposed by the harsh view of man and the world, which was central to Puritan culture. Thus, we find

Coffin revealing the Puritan compulsion for order and cleanliness (dirt equals sinfulness, hence Cleanliness is next to Godliness), its deep suspicion of "having fun," "lolling," and taking the "easy way," of generosity and expansiveness, of the gentler, "weaker" sex, indeed, of sex itself, since it produces degenerate sons and even granddaughters who "have a wormy fruit to glean."

Certainly not all the ordinary people in Coffin's poems live in run-out harbors, marry dirty women, or shoot their sons or themselves; just as not all his people are lonely. But both themes, the decay of the old way and man's isolation from his fellow man, do recur in Coffin's poetry, and they help to explain why nature comes to play such a significant, indeed, dominant, role throughout his work. When man is alone, he is alone in nature; when the world around him is decaying, he can turn to nature to find perpetual vitality. Nature offers an alternative to a world that divides man between a compulsion for weedless fields, clean windows and white-washed empty churches on the one hand, and a degeneration to clamshell littered yards, crooked gables and dirty, loose living on the other. Nature shows man the way to a different and better kind of existence.

II

Although the majority of Coffin's nature poems are simply observations and appreciations of curious and beautiful objects in nature, some take up the more interesting problem of how nature affects man. They show how the seasons, especially winter ("My country has the Winter for its year," [PSW, 831]), affect men's lives. Fog, rain, ice, frost, snow, wind and sun determine when a man can fish, cross bays, plant and harvest crops, and even visit his neighbors. But this sort of man nature relationship is fairly obvious and fairly superficial still. Subtler and more far-reaching are the relationships I would place under two headings: 1, the return (and revenge) of nature; and 2, the sexual potency of nature. In both cases, nature becomes a creative and destructive agent in a deep, primitive relationship with man.

In Coffin's poetry nature constantly threatens to take back man's domesticated world of houses, barns, cultivated fields, orchards and pasture land. This return of nature can be a pleasant thing, or it can take on the more violent complexion of revenge, but in either case it is clear that nature will eventually have its way, whether gradually or rapidly, openly or subversively.

The amicable return of nature appears in the opening stanza of **"The Woodland Orchard"**:

> These apple trees were lost for good
> When the little house which stood
> Nearby to keep them safe and sound
> Sank moldering into the ground
> And the children went away.
> The waiting forest won the day,

And came and took the orphaned trees
Upon its dark and kindly knees.

                                        (CP, 173)

Here is a place, Coffin suggests, "Where tame and wild
for once forgot/ Their old hate," (CP, 174) and yet, he
concludes, "these are trees that have been lost;/ Here one
draws a careful breath,/ This loneliness is so like death."
Death is, after all, an unconditional surrender to nature,
as is implied in **"Foxes and Graves,"** a poem about the
invasion of an abandoned graveyard by foxes, an invasion Coffin accepts as perfectly just: "There is nothing
wrong about wild creatures coming/ Back home again, if
people move away." (CP, 310) But the graveyard conquered by foxes, like the orchard conquered by the forest,
serves to remind man of his own frailty before the impla-
cable return of nature.

In fact, man's death is nature's gain, as Coffin explains in
"Man Sometimes Helps":

> Birds and beasts are glad when farmers grow
> Like Winter on their hair and stiff of knee,
> The rabbits move in through the broken fence,
> The woodchucks take the cellar in staid glee,
> Foxes take over the plots with slanting stones
> Where the farmer hopes to lay his bones.

                                        (ABO, 39)

If people "dread" decay and death, says Coffin, the animals "rejoice." Man's dread of nature's advance becomes
inextricably linked with his sense of his own dissolution,
and it is no wonder that nature's return seems like a reviving of "old hates," to be, in fact, nature's revenge.

Two poems, in particular, capture the sense of dread man
feels before nature's threatened revenge. **"One in a
Darkness"** describes one man's losing struggle against a
malevolent nature that has choked his doorway with
Queen Anne's lace, surrounded his house with hooting
owls, and sent "a thousand subtle roots/ Creeping where
his seeds were sown." (CP, 110) In **"The Haters"** Coffin
explains that, "It is by the cellar they come first,/ The
dispossessed of earth your house stands on." (CP, 203)
The "pale and pindling arms/ Of raspberry plants" begin
to work through the foundations, he says, and a hump, as
if from a rising giant, appears in the cellar floor. The
"dispossessed" make even the "tamed and friendly" potatoes and onions allies in their "secret war" against man:
"They mean death./ You and your house are what these
haters hate." (CP, 204)

With the death of man and the destruction of his house,
nature's revenge is complete. But that is not the end, as
Coffin shows in concluding "The Haters." Now a new
(or, in fact, an older) force takes over—the primitive,
vegetation spirits, the earliest and strongest gods:

> You cannot trust the old green gods men left
> Back in the glooms of time with altars bare.
> They will have vengeance. Their weak, myriad hands
> Will work about your walls until they fall
> And mighty trees inherit your place.

Coffin is not, I think, simply being fanciful by recalling
primitive vegetation rites, for they still echo in the deepest part of man's consciousness and shape many of his
fairy tales, myths and folkways.[2] These rites spring
from what Bronislaw Malinowski calls "the idea of a
certain mystic, impersonal power" in nature, what the
Melanesians call *mana*.[3] Because nature exercises or represents this power, man holds it in dread, but also in awe;
he fears it and worships it. And so it is in Coffin's poetry.

The extent to which Coffin involves his poetry in primitive responses to nature can only be appreciated after we
have examined another man-nature relationship: the sexually revitalizing power of nature. But at this point we
should at least note that Coffin's reference to "the old
green gods" in **"The Haters"** is not the only time suggestions of ancient magic and ritual appear in his poetry. In
"Holy Well" Coffin describes an old well that has become "holy" by having "mystic power" and protecting
taboos. The boy in the poem will not disturb the well
because, "It was not right to do it;/ He did not know the
reason, yet he knew it." (ABO, 8) In **"Totem"** Coffin
describes the carving of jack-'o-lanterns. Every boy, says
the poet, "cuts a face that comes from dim/ Forgotten
ages where men could/ Help the sun and rain and good/
Powers challenge death and win." (PSW, 26) The magical powers of "the old green gods," which guide the
boy's hand, though he may not realize it, also control the
act of a boy who carves his and a girl's initials in a tree.
"Somehow he knew," Coffin says in **"Names in a Tree,"**
"That he was doing a deeper thing than carve/ His name
and a girl's name in a tree." (ABO, 98)[4] He knew that
their relationship was strengthened by the tree's *mana*:

> It was for keeps. She never could escape,
> The long roots of the beech would bring up powers;
> He had planted himself like seeds in her,
> Their sons would come as surely as the flowers.

The "powers" that the boy evokes not only promise to
make the relationship last, but find their expression in
sexual imagery; for, by this magical gesture the boy
has aligned himself with the eternally regenerative
power of nature.

Coffin's most mythical treatment of the sexual force in
nature appears in **"The Red Drummer,"** a poem about
the town girls who are drawn into the fields by a mysterious drumming that Coffin ascribes to an Indian god. In
fact, the god is Dionysus. Coffin uses New England corn-
fields instead of Attic mountain sides, and the ear of corn
instead of the pine-cone tipped wand for the central
sexual symbol, but there can be little doubt that one of
"the old green gods" has brought Dionysian frenzy to
New England:

> No house can hold the girls, no mothers;
> Laws or lamplight, books or brothers;
> Girls dance with strange boys in the gloom,
> And tall corn stands erect in plume.
> The girls come homeward, red and wise,
> And walk the year with averted eyes;

They talk no more of drums or noise,
But carry in Spring their red new boys.

(PBLB, 31)

Dionysus, god of sensuality and rebirth, reveals to these New England corn maidens his regenerative, sexual, power.

Such poems as **"Holy Well," "Totem,"** and **"The Red Drummer"** depend in varying degrees on superstition and myth, in other words, on uncommon circumstances that show nature exerting supernatural power over men. There are other poems that do not call upon the uncommon or obviously magical to present much the same argument: that the return and revenge of nature brings into man's world primitive powers, "the old green gods" who still control men's lives. In these poems, too, Coffin pursues his analysis of nature's sexual potency.

In **"Potato Diggers"** and **"The Catch"** men reach into the living stuff of nature—potatoes in the first poem, fish in the second—to touch a deep, subhuman level of existence and find nature's sexual energy. **"Potato Diggers"** describes men "with levelled backs and hands like forward feet," plunging their hands into the soil:

They have run the dark soil through their hands
And seen it whiten and resign its mysteries.
They have run their fingers through the earth
And felt out fruits which have the feel of flesh
And warmth of flesh, and left them heaped behind.

(CP, 199)

Because Coffin likens these men to pre-human beasts— "They have been creepers/ On the ancient nursery floor"—one would perhaps miss the sexual implications were it not for the close parallels between this poem and **"The Catch,"** which makes the sexual significance more explicit.

In **"The Catch"** men bend over, their hands "dipped in the astounding white/ Of smelts and herring," their "things spread like the thighs of God/ Above the fish," (CP, 192) while around them "the fecund tide/ Swells her bosom to her lover,/ The high moon, leaning cold above her." The fishermen then draw upon this love affair for their own human love-making. The tide is to the moon as the fisherman's wives are to their husbands:

. . . fishermen's wives
Wait to mingle their warm lives
With strange beings cold as death,
With night and starlight in their breath,
Who have had their fingers curled
Around old secrets of the world.

The potato diggers, too, have handled the world's ancient "mysteries," and presumably they too will draw upon the fecundity of the white and flesh-like fruit when they return to their wives.

In both poems sexual implications are indirectly presented through analogy and metaphor, but in **"The Inner Temple"** Coffin is more (though not completely) explicit.

Here we see man making contact with the earth and gaining sexual potency from that contact:

A man can get down there [on the earth] and savor
As all men need to do, the flavor
Of being of the ancient race
Of animals and know his place
Is properly on pungent clay.
And something holy in its way
Will rise out of the earth beneath him
And in a fresh, new garment sheathe him.
So when he will go indoors,
His wife will look up from her chores
And wonder at his seeming new
As when their courtship was not through.

(CP, 152)

Thus the farmer gains renewed sexual potency, the ardor of the young lover before courtship is over, and we notice too, that his new vigor comes from kneeling on the earth itself and merging with the sub-human, animal level of nature. The fishermen, the potato diggers, and the farmer-husband experience a kind of magical union with nature at a sub- or prehuman level in order to learn the "mysteries," the "old secrets of the world," and participate in "something holy."

Two other poems present this magical union more briefly. **"Six Boys in the Sun"** describes "six small boys with legs spread wide," (ABO, 41), lying on a river bank fishing. Coffin first says that they are "tight to earth," then shifting the image, puts them "back on their older mother's knees," and finally, returning to the earlier image, says, "Earth was a globe of hot green joy/ Curved to the right curves of a boy." **"She Was the Spring"** presents a girl sitting on the ground, where she becomes "filled with earth's mysterious heat." (PSW, 24) When she rises, Coffin says, "It was as though she was, herself, the Spring!" This earth maiden clearly experiences the same sexual power, the "heat" of the burgeoning springtime earth, which appears as the boy's maternal and amorous earth, the fishermen's "fecund tide," the potato diggers' warm soil with its fleshy fruit, and the farmer-husband's "pungent clay."

What these poems argue, then, is that man returns—*must* return—to nature for his vital energy, and in so doing he partakes of a sub-human power shared by all nature's creatures. The argument becomes unequivocally clear in **"The Ox-Pull at the Fair,"** in which Coffin depicts man and oxen in the united effort of pulling a stone-boat at the local fair. Urging his animals on, the man "leans like a man bent to caress," and, "He speaks an ancient language, half the brutes',/ Gutturals and words down at the roots/ Of life and of desire." (CP, 264) At the end of the poem Coffin links man and animal and defines the sexual nature of their common "desire":

This thing the farmers stand here to admire
Goes down deep years by thousands to desire
Old as the time when life and strength were one,
Deep as a man's begetting of a son.

(CP, 265)

The mindless, non-individualized, primal origins of all life lie behind a man's "begetting of a son," and it is from the same source that man and animal draw their potency.

In two other poems Coffin rings significant changes on the nature-potency theme. In **"The Stranger"** a boy watches his father plowing, and sees him turn into a hard, "fierce" man who, with his "thighs apart . . . ripped up the sod." (ABO, 93) The violence of his plowing suggests a virtual rape of the earth, and lest we miss the sexual implications, Coffin makes an analogy between the father's plowing and his relationship with his wife:

> It was all strange and far away,
> Yet the boy recalled a day
> He saw his father bend and kiss
> His mother and be a man like this.

Since the scene is presented through the son's eyes, we can easily ascribe the sense of violence in the relationship between father and mother (and father and mother-earth) to the Oedipus Complex, of which this poem gives a perfect example.

The violent plowman-father is counterbalanced by a **"Plowman Without a Plow."** In this poem, an old man, after thirty years of marriage, buys a farm, but he is too old to farm it, and now he "leave[s] the bed" at dawn and goes out into the field. The wife sees him

> On the hill with something in his hand.
> He let it fall, she saw it was plain dirt,
> Yet something in the way he did it hurt.
> He let it crumble through his fingers slow,
> He watched it with his head bent over low.
> When the last of all he held was gone,
> He turned and walked uphill against the dawn,
> And as the walker went, he seemed somehow
> A plowman old and gray without a plow.
>
> (CP, 313)

Thus man must finally admit his human limitations, his defeat in the face of unlimited, undefeated nature. When nature deserts him, he must leave the marriage bed; he is impotent and alone. So man, in Coffin's New England, ends his days.

To conclude a discussion of Tristram Coffin's poetry with an image of man impotent and alone may seem a gross distortion of the poet's work to those who believe Coffin to be an essentially affirmative poet, "a believer in life," as he once called himself.[5] Certainly it is true that many—I suppose, most—of Coffin's poems are written by one who finds life easy to affirm. Yet it is also true that Coffin wrote about loneliness, impotence, and man's degeneration. It is also true that he showed how nature wreaks its vengeance on man by destroying his civilization, reducing him to primitive worship of, and sexual thralldom to, nature. Still, I would argue that Coffin *is* "a believer in life," but in a deeper and more dynamic sense than that phrase, by itself, might

suggest. To see how this is so, let us return to the general terms around which our analysis has grown.

What, finally, is the relationship between man and nature in New England, and how does Coffin view it? Clearly man is subservient to nature. Nature defines the limits and degree of his isolation; nature inevitably obliterates man's attempts to conquer and control it; nature takes on magical powers as man worships "the old green gods"; nature contains at its primal core the power of reproduction, the sexual energy man must have to survive. Nature shatters the rigid Puritan morality as surely as its slender tendrils undermine the foundations of a house. Its hot, pungent, earthiness obliterates cool, clean orderliness and straight-furrowed, weeded decency. Nature tempts the girls to orgies in the corn fields; it draws the young boys down tight against the hot curves of the earth; it offers its fleshy fruit to the potato diggers and plays second wife to the plowing farmer; finally, it deserts old men and leaves them plowless and alone fingering dry, seedless dirt.

Perhaps New England's—Maine's—rocky soil, harsh climate, and harsher Puritan-pioneer tradition finally drive men to throw it all over, to go back to "the old green gods," to embrace a primal life, a sexual, amoral existence man holds in common with the animals. In this sense, Coffin would seem to be carrying out his own rebellion against the Puritan old way of life in order to establish a pagan *older* way, the way of ritual and magic and the union of man and nature in a New England our Puritan forefathers would have condemned to the hottest fires of hell. This would make Coffin "a believer in life," indeed.

NOTES

[1] *Collected Poems* (New York, 1939), 334. The *Collected Poems* hereafter are abbreviated CP; other abbreviations as follows: *Poems for a Son With Wings* (New York, 1945), PSW; *People Behave Like Ballads* (New York, 1946), PBLB; *Apples by Ocean* (New York, 1950), ABO. All references appear parenthetically in the text.

[2] Coffin believed that ancient practices and beliefs reverberate through the ages, as the following passage from one of his lectures indicates: "I am more and more coming to be persuaded to believe in what I call Folk Memory. I believe a man remembers and experiences in timeless and unfading colors the outlines not only what happened to him in his remote bright childhood, but a man goes back into the cumulative memory of those who begot him, and he remembers through the brains of his ancestors. . . . A man lives a hundred ancient lives in living his own." (*The Third Hunger and The Poem Aloud*) [Denton, Texas, 1949], 40.

[3] *Magic, Science and Religion and Other Essays* (Garden City and New York, Doubleday Anchor Books, 1955), 19-20. Malinowski's treatment of this concept is far subtler than my brief quotation indicates, and, of course, his treatment is only one of many with varying points of view.

[4] In *The Third Hunger, op. cit.*, 50, Coffin says that when a boy cuts his and a girl's name on a tree, "that boy is dipping his hands in the warmest fire of folk lore. He is putting his hand into his remote ancestors' hands."

[5] *The Substance That Is Poetry* (New York, 1942), 1.

Mark W. Anderson (essay date 1989)

SOURCE: "Images of Nineteenth Century Maine Farming in the Prose and Poetry of R.P.T. Coffin and C.A. Stephens," in *Agricultural History*, Vol. 3, No. 2, Spring, 1989, pp. 120-29.

[In the following essay, Anderson explores Coffin's writings and those of another Maine author, C.A. Stephens, with regard to their "utility to historians."]

Long before historians turned to matters of daily life as objects of inquiry, poets and novelists dealt with the essentials of the human condition. Authors often have searched for universal elements in the lives of our ancestors. The better poets and novelists offered their readers images that captured the essence of common people's lives. This literature, then, is an often untapped source for the historian trying to understand the experiences in earlier generations.

Life on a nineteenth-century Maine farm is a theme explored by a number of authors of both that century and ours. Two of the most entertaining and insightful writers on farm life were Robert P. Tristram Coffin and C. A. Stephens, both of whom have deep roots in Maine. The writings of Coffin and Stephens illuminate, sometimes in startling ways, farming in nineteenth-century Maine.

R. P. T. Coffin is best known as a poet, in part because he won the Pulitzer Prize in 1937 for his volume of poetry *Strange Holiness.* However, poet is too thin a handle for a man who, in his nearly 50 books, also wrote biographies, novels, criticism, essays, and history. He served for 20 years on the Bowdoin College faculty. However we label him, Coffin wrote intimately of both the farm and the sea. He grew up on a saltwater farm outside of Brunswick, Maine, and both worlds fill his works. He did not merely write about farming and seafaring, he wrote as an insider would view these settings. Even though he wrote in the twentieth century, Coffin's images of nineteenth-century life are profoundly knowledgeable.

C. A. Stephens, on the other hand, was a nineteenth century writer. Born in 1844 in Norway, Maine, Stephens, like Coffin, grew up on a farm. He drew upon this experience in his work as a writer and editor for *The Youth's Companion*, a popular family magazine published in Boston. While Coffin was somewhat more readily accepted in literary circles, Stephens has usually been viewed as "just" a writer of juvenile stories, much like his early mentor, Elijah Kellogg. However, both writers wrote for popular audiences rather than for

the critics. Both used a realistic style embellished with a touch of romanticism for rural life.

Whatever the literary merits of the works of either Coffin or Stephens, the utility of their work to historians need not be overlooked. They both provide us with another window on the past, and thus they serve as models for hundreds of regional authors whose nineteenth-century works are rich sources of historical material, sources that can be a delight to explore.

There are three themes of the farm existence in Maine that this paper explores. It is clear that Coffin and Stephens both knew of the same life, because each explored these three themes. Such complementary images from literary sources provide one way of assessing the historical validity of the ideas.

The first image of the nineteenth-century farm that is inescapable is that of diversity. While the specialization of twentieth-century agriculture leads us to acknowledge rather narrow agricultural occupations such as potato farmers or dairy farmers, their nineteenth-century counterparts were clearly farmers in a broader sense of the word. In a series of books based upon stories that first appeared in *The Youth's Companion*, C. A. Stephens related the details of farm life in Norway, Maine just after the Civil War.[1] In the series, the protagonist's grandfather, affectionately known as the Old Squire, is a progressive farmer of some considerable success. The Old Squire's output included sheep, dairy, apples, vegetables, beans, honey, potatoes, corn, geese, hay, grain, ice (for the dairy), and wood products. Some of these were subsistence items and others were cash crops, but they all had a place in the yearly routine of the farm.

Such diversity was required for several reasons. Most obviously, markets were limited by transport costs, so farmers could not sell their produce if they relied on only one crop produced on a grand scale. Farmers could not reach markets sufficiently large to support specialization. More important, such diversity spread the risk of farming over several enterprises and spread labor more evenly over the year. Diversity was the word of the day, not only among enterprises, but within any enterprise itself. When Stephens' protagonist first arrives at his grandfather's farm as a young boy, his cousin Theodora shows him the apple orchard, among other parts of the farm:

> "I am going to show you the good apple trees," she continued, and led the way through the orchard. "These three great ones, here below the garden wall, are Orange Speck trees; they are real nice apples for winter; and there is the Gillflower tree. Over here is the Early Sweet Bough; and that big one is the August Sweeting; and out there are the three August Pippins. All those down there toward the road are Baldwins and Greenings. Those two by the lane are None Such trees. These by the corn fields are four Sweet Harvey trees; and next below them are two Georgianas. I learned

all their names last year. But this one here by the currant bushes is a Sops-in-wine. Oh, they are so good! And they get ripe early, too, and so do the August Pippins and the Harveys and the August Sweetlings; they are all nice. Those small trees just below the barnyard fence are pears, Bartlett pears, luscious ones! and those vines on the trellises are the Isabella and Concord grapes; some years grapes don't get ripe here in Maine; but they did last year, pretty ripe, in October. (Stephens, *When Life Was Young,* 16-17)

A similar degree of diversity was maintained in the farm's grain production, which was not limited to corn.

After haying came grain harvest. There were three acres of wheat, four of oats, an acre of barley, an acre of buckwheat and three-fourths of rye to get in. The rye, however, had been harvested during the last week of haying. It ripened early, for it was the Old Squire's custom to sow his rye very early in the spring. . . . With the rye we always sowed clover and herdsgrass seed for a hay crop the following year. This we termed "seeding down." (Stephens, *When Life Was Young,* 247)

Since much of farming was for subsistence rather than for market, such diversity in feed grains provided the household a more diverse diet. Grains were held in storage on the farm and then milled as needed, with payment to the miller made in grain itself.

The diversity of the farm in Maine was opportunistic. The Old Squire cut birch logs for sale to a New York dowel manufacturer—Norway is in Maine's hardwood region, not the spruce-fir forest commonly associated with the state. In the farms that Coffin wrote about, the opportunities more often came from the sea than from the forest. In the book *Portrait of an American* Coffin created a fictionalized account of his father's life.[2] A peripatetic man, Coffin's father could never quite settle on a homestead for the family after he had conquered a site. He was always looking for a new home site to challenge him. For several years the family tackled a farm on one of the more remote islands of Casco Bay which presented its own set of opportunities:

William [Coffin's father] was not contented with his island alone. The corks of shad nets were soon bobbing in the path of the June sun, miles out at sea. He seined the smelts in October and dipped them by lantern light as they leaped up along the rock stairway of Spinney's Creek in April nights. William's lobster buoys were soon thick around the island. He would pull fifty traps before breakfast. . . . He loved the smell of tar just as he loved the glow of phosphorescence turned up by his oars on a November night. Rain or shine, no matter what he did, his day was a symphony from the time he rose till he lay asleep on his bed. (Coffin, *Portrait of An American,* 59-60)

With this kind of diversity, life on the Maine farm was never dull.

Another opportunity for diversification that both Coffin and Stephens documented was bee keeping. Coffin's father, according to his son, became an expert at everything to which he put his hand or his mind. Bees were no exception.

William went in for bees. He made the hives and all himself, changing the models as years made him wiser. The whole field back of the kitchen orchard filled up with these tenement houses of workers he loved to have about him, perhaps because they were a kin to himself. He became an expert at handling the new swarms. The children were awed to see him take down a runaway swarm in a dip-net from a tall tree. He encouraged his wife to newer and larger flower-beds for their honey's sake. He came to grief only once; and that was because of one of those unforeseen panics that visit bees on occasion. That day remained marked in his children's memory for the sound of pans and kettles beaten for hours. It was high May, and two swarms departed to set up new housekeeping at the same time. The net went wrong with one of them. The bees separated from their mass and turned into burning bullets. Mrs. William saw her husband streak past the house and over the bank and throw himself into the bay. The dog Snoozer followed his master in. Later, Mrs. William took a dozen drowned bees from her husband's shirt. (Coffin, *Portrait of An American,* 118-19)

In order to keep bees, one had to hive a swarm in this manner, and the earlier in the year the better. Stephens tells a similar story of hiving a swarm early in the year.[2] What he remembered most was the proverb on whether capturing this particular swarm was worth the effort.[3]

This was an early swarm, hence valuable. Gram repeated to us a proverb in rhyme which set forth the relative value of swarms.

A swarm in May is worth a load of hay
A swarm in June is worth a silver spoon
But a swarm in July is not worth a fly

July swarms would not have the time to lay up a store of honey during the season of flowers. (Stephens, *When Life Was Young,* 83)

Enterprising diversity obviously was a necessity, but one that contributed to a richness of life that changed with the seasons. Whether haying in July or cutting wood in March, putting up fruit preserves in summer or slaughtering a pig once the temperature was cold enough in November to keep fresh meat on the hook in the barn, each season of the year had its routine. It was a routine that could be scheduled by the calendar. The custom of the Old Squire was to begin haying the Monday after the Fourth of July, for example.

However, on the Maine farm, in particular, nearly all farm work revolved around the second image of nineteenth-century life—winter.

In both physical and psychological terms, winter was (and to some lesser extent remains) the dominant season in Maine, the one around which all other seasons revolved. Coffin referred to this dominance of winter in his deeply personal poem, **"This is My Country,"**

> These are my people, saving of emotion,
> With their eyes dipped in the Winter ocean
> The lonely, patient ones, whose speech comes slow,
> Whose bodies always lean toward the blow,
> The enduring and the clean, the tough and the clear,
> Who live where Winter is the word for year.[4]

R.P.T. Coffin has a whole book dedicated to chronicling the passage of seasons on the saltwater farm, a beautifully illustrated (by Coffin himself) folio called ***Coast Calendar.*** It is a no coincidence that he begin this work with the month January. It reflects the centrality of winter in Maine life.[5]

Winter was not an idle time on the Maine farm, but it was more relaxed than the short, frantic growing season during which chores never seemed to end. Stephens talked of the need to cut and yard 50 to 60 cords of hard wood for the following year's fires, certainly not an idle undertaking. Yet even the wood harvest and preparation usually came in March, after the back of winter had been broken. Both Stephens and Coffin provided graphic descriptions of ice cutting, doubly hard work for the cold. Stephens' story is one of the family cutting ice on the nearby lake for their farm creamery, supported by their growing herd of Jersey cows. Coffin's is a description of the commercial ice industry on the Kennebec River, an industry that provided winter employment, and thus much needed cash, for many a Maine farmer in the nineteenth century.[6]

But more important than the work, winter was a time through which to survive, to take stock, and to rest. The work of summer had, by contrast, only one purpose, to provide enough to get the household and the farm animals through another year. Coffin described the January world as an interior one:

> The thermometer falls below zero, the high moon blazes like noon, and the lonesome white bays crack for pain of the cold. Honey bees crawl to new combs and warm themselves in the hive at the heat of last summer's sun. The stars snap like sapphires, you hear the hiss of their burning, and the teapot hisses continuously on the back of the stove. The barrel of quahogs in the cellar is halfway down . . .
>
> An old book is a good dish for a long night. Grandfather thumbs the *Old Farmer's Almanac* as he sits on the wood box back of the stove. There will be plenty more snow. The little boy lies under the cookstove and bakes himself through like a biscuit.
>
> The young boy smells the newsprint of the *Boston Transcript* around the hot brick that warms his toes in bed. It snows two feet. The farmer knits a lobster head as he sits with his stocking feet in the oven, which still smells of mince pie. . . .
>
> It is a long month, a hard month, the fish and furrows take a good rest. . . . The January world is as much inside as out, and a good one.

As much as winter was the heart of the year, summer was in some ways to be dreaded in Maine, not only for its hard work, but also for its weather. Those who chose to stay on the Maine farm often found even the brief summer appearance objectionable. Stephens related the Old Squire's wisdom about "dog days" in Maine, days that probably seemed rather temperate to his southern kin.

> I had never heard of "dog days" before and was curious to know what sort of days they were. "They set in," the Old Squire informed me, "on the twenty-fifth of July and last till the fifth of September. Then is when the Dog-star rages, and it is apt to be 'catching' weather. Dogs are more liable to run mad at this time of the year, and snakes are most venomous then." Such is the olden lore, and I gained an impression that those forty-two days were after a manner unhealthy for man and beast. (Stephens, *When Life Was Young,* 249)

Summer weather was perhaps more bearable on the saltwater farm, for Coffin's family had the luxury of picnics spread among the summer chores. He tells of one such picnic on a far island of Casco Bay, perhaps the abandoned island homestead described above.[7] Coffin believed that picnic weather like this could only be found in Maine; it was weather that took the sting out of summer—certainly these were no dog days.

> Then you must have an island with fir trees packed so closely together that you might walk along their tops, if you were spry, and you must have the myrrh of the balsams in your nose along with the smell of the sea all a Summer's day. It must be a day in August and one of the kind that you will find nowhere else on this round earth save Maine; northwest wind blowing the sky as clean and clear as a bell, a blue sky that you can fairly hear ring, and white galleons of clouds with flat keels which sail over by thousands and yet never get in the way of the sun. The sunshine turns everything to amber and crystal and pours over the world like a tide. You can hear it lapping the granite coasts. The whole world is very hot yet airy; you can smell the tar in the caulking of the boats. Your face turns into a russet banner. Your brain turns into sunlight. The ocean grows darker and deeper blue between the whitecrests that are coming in from far Spain. The sea and the sun get in under your soul.
>
> You add spray all over everybody, especially the children; for my picnic would lack spice if all of us were not well drenched down with brine and salted down till our eyes were a fast blue. To have the best spray you need a flooding tide to kick up a chop against the wind.

But these were rare moments, and perhaps all the more beautiful for their rarity. They were simply interludes between one winter survived and one which to prepare.

It is in this survival and preparation that is the final image of nineteenth century Maine farming. This image is that of the simple physical demands placed on the farm family. The hard physical labor of agriculture before mechanization is difficult for many of us to appreciate. Although Coffin was often accused of overly romanticizing rural life in his writings, he never shirked from discussing the hard work of the farm. Nowhere is that clearer than in ***Lost Paradise,*** an autobiographical account of his youth on a saltwater farm.

The story is told by Peter (Coffin's middle name which he never used personally), who at one point was sent away from the farm to a nearby town to live with his older sister so he could attend a proper school. He missed his paradise farm dearly and was trying to cope with the loss. "The game Peter was playing now was trying to think of the hardest work he had to do on the farm. He was doing his best to wean himself of thinking of it as a place that was all apple pie and huckle-berry jam."[8]

Coffin's Peter ran through a list of arduous jobs on the farm to make his confinement to town more palatable. They were sawing wood, cleaning tieups, pounding crabs for hen feed, digging clams, haying, turning the grindstone for his father and brothers to sharpen their scythes, bringing in the salt hay and tending the water fences. Unfortunately for him, Peter found redeeming value in each chore, so was unable to convince himself of the relative benefit of staying where he was.

Even so, bringing in the salt hay from the farm's salt marsh entailed particularly nasty burdens.

> The Marsh was too soft to cut with a horse. Every inch of it had to be mowed by hand. Half of it, the parts up back of the beaver dams, was a poor cross between sweet hay and salt, called black grass. The rest beyond the beaver dams on both sides of the creek was salt thatch. The thatch had not only to be cut, but it had to be carried out of the tide's way green. A middle-sized armful of it weighed more than a man. It had to be carried on handlebars with cross-pieces. Edward did the cutting of it, that was his share, he said. So Peter and Ansel had to do the lugging.

And Ben Sudbury. Peter and his brother stumbled blind with their burden high between them. Their legs sank half to their knees at each step in the blue mud. The black flies stung them in their faces till their faces were big as balloons and they couldn't see out of their eyes. Ben Sudbury swore like a house afire. He didn't care what he said when he was on one end of the handle-bars. The mosquitoes worked on their hands and arms. The hay had to be spread out to dry on the beaver dams and between the brackish pools where they had harvested the black grass. The thatch cut like so much barbed wire.

Stephens was not reluctant to explain the physical demands of the farm either. When his storyteller first came to the Old Squire's farm, he was unprepared for the day's work he would face.

> By the time I reached the farmyard, where the Old Squire had hung up a large iron kettle and had water boiling in it, I was very tired indeed. What with splitting wood in the very early morning, catching seventy sheep and digging and carrying poke, I had put forth a good deal of muscular strength that day . . . (Stephens, *When Life Was Young,* 79)

The best work story, for me, however, is when Coffin describes the work it took to maintain water fences. Since the farm described in ***Lost Paradise*** was a point of land jutting into Casco Bay, the ocean was used as one side of the fence for the pastures. To do this, Coffin's father had constructed a water fence. That is, two barbed wire side fences had to be anchored in the ocean below the low tide line so that the cows could not get around them.

> It was dirty heavy work. You and Ansel had to carry the heavy flat stones to weigh down the three-cornered fence posts your father had run up, to keep your fence from coming up the bay to meet you when next you rowed home. . . . The mud was deep and black and got all over you and finally into your eyes, if there were black flies around. The job was a low-tide job, and low tide was their refreshment hour. . . . Just when you sat back and thought it was done for good till Winter's ice would take it out, you looked up, and there were all twenty cows in the sweet-apple orchard, or knee deep in the beans. (Coffin, ***Lost Paradise,*** 45-46)

As was true of many of Coffin's themes, he came back to this again and in poetic form, a poem called **"Water-Fence"** which appears in another book of poems called ***One Horse Farm.***[9] Construction of the water fence was an annual endeavor; like so much on the salt water farm, one driven by the seasons. While the seasonal change was a source of continuity in the farm life, it was a source for frustration as well, for much work was never really done. A final image of frustration is embodied in the water fence:

> All the wires festooned with green and gray
> Until some sagging barbed-wire strand gives way
> And the cows can step over the top.
> And, of course, some breach cow hip-hop
> Will swim around the fence looking for love
> And bulls, and when the frisking cow will shove
> Off into the ocean, all will follow
> And leave the fence a mockery, plain hollow.
>
> Though the fence is taut enough to bear
> All the tons of rockweed hung like hair
> Upon its strands and no tide can so shift
> The stones that hold it and set it adrift,
> The winter ice will lift it neat's can be
> And take the fence and carry it out to sea.
> Like calf-love and the grasshopper's green song
> A water-fence is but one Summer long.
> The hired man feels his bare backsides itch.
> He sighs to himself, "That elegant son-of-a-bitch!"

NOTES

[1] See, for example, *When Life Was Young at the Old Squire's* (Boston: The Youth's Companion, 1912); *A Great Year of Our Lives* (Boston: The Youth's Companion, 1912); and *A Busy Year at the Old Squire's* (Boston: A Youth's Companion, 1922). The books were collections of stories that first appeared in *The Youth's Companion* beginning in the 1870s.

[2] R. P. T. Coffin, *Portrait of An American* (N.Y.: MacMillan, 1931).

[3] Interestingly, Coffin, in his book *Coast Calendar* (N.Y.: MacMillan, 1912), relates part of the proverb in almost exactly the same language in the chapter on the month of May. His version is:

> A swarm of bees in May
> Is worth a load of hay

[4] This poem first appeared in *Harpers* in 1935 and then in book form in *Saltwater Farm* (New York: Macmillan, 1937), a volume of images of the coastal farm experience.

[5] Similarly in Henry Beston's *Northern Farm* (New York: Rinehard, 1948), a twentieth-century analog to the works of Coffin and Stephens, the chronicle began in January. This is not because January begins the calendar year, it is because that month is the very heart of the year in the Maine farm experience.

[6] Stephens' story is "Cutting Ice at 14 Degrees Below Zero" in *A Busy Year at the Old Squire's;* Coffin's is "Kennebec Crystals" in *Kennebec: Cradle of Americans* (Boston: The Youth's Companion, 1912).

[7] The story is "Codfish Chowder and Sun" contained in his second book of essays, *An Attic Room* (New York: Doubleday, Duran, 1929). Coffin tells another picnic story, this one on the last picnic opportunity in fall, in Chapter 19 of *Lost Paradise* (New York: MacMillan and Co., 1934).

[8] Coffin, *Lost Paradise,* 38-39.

[9] R. P. T. Coffin, *One Horse Farm: Downeast Georgics* (N.Y.: MacMillan, 1949).

FURTHER READING

Bibliography

Cary, Richard. "A Bibliography of Robert P. Tristram Coffin: Part I." *Colby Library Quarterly* VII, No. 4 (December 1965): 170-91.
> Annotated bibliography of books, brochures and pamphlets by Coffin, work included in anthologies, selected biographical and critical articles about him, and several excerpts from Coffin's works on poetry and Maine.

———. "A Bibliography of Robert P. Tristram Coffin: Part II." *Colby Library Quarterly* VII, No. 6 (June 1966): 270-99.
> Lists poems printed in periodicals and newspapers from 1920 to 1945.

Biography

Sanborn, Annie Coffin. *The Life of Robert Peter Tristram Coffin and Family.* New Hampshire: Privately printed, 1963, 111 p.
> A history of the Coffin family written "from memory" by Coffin's sister.

Swain, Charles Raymond. *A Breath of Maine: Portrait of Robert P. Tristram Coffin.* Boston: Branden Press, 1967, 194 p.
> Letters, speeches, poems, accounts of conversations, recollections, and other Coffiniana collected by a friend of long standing.

The following source published by the Gale Group contains additional information on Coffin's life and work: *Dictionary of Literary Biography*, Vol. 45.

John Dewey

1859-1952

American philosopher, psychologist, and educator.

INTRODUCTION

Dewey is recognized as one of the twentieth century's leading proponents of pragmatism, education reform, and pacifism. His work in these three areas derives from his belief that humanity is essentially good, and that social deviancy can be curtailed by specific educational methods.

Biographical Information

Dewey was born in Burlington, Vermont, the son of a grocer. He graduated from the University of Vermont in 1875 and went on to teach high school in Oil City, Pennsylvania, from 1879 to 1881. He returned to Burlington and cultivated his interest in philosophy with the assistance of his former teacher, H. A. P. Torrey. Shortly thereafter, Dewey published two articles in the *Journal of Speculative Philosophy,* and enrolled as a graduate philosophy student at the newly formed Johns Hopkins University, where he studied briefly with American logician and founder of pragmatism Charles S. Peirce, psychologist G. S. Hall, and G. S. Morris, who introduced Dewey to the philosophy of Hegel. He completed his doctoral dissertation on Immanuel Kant in 1884, and began a productive ten-year tenure at the University of Michigan. He strived to make philosophy applicable to all humans by becoming increasingly involved in public education and published several works on psychology. In 1894, Dewey accepted a post as chairman of philosophy, psychology, and education at the University of Chicago. During this period, Dewey worked closely with social reformer Jane Addams, published his *Studies in Logical Theory,* formed the laboratory school commonly known as the Dewey School, and published several works on pedagogy. In 1904, Dewey left Chicago to join the faculty of Columbia University, where he taught until his retirement in 1930, after which he continued to write, travel, and lecture extensively. In 1921, Dewey joined the American Committee for the Outlawry of War, and published the pamphlet *Outlawry of War: What It Is and Is Not,* in which he castigated the League of Nations as the "League of governments pure and simple." Advocating the concept of a World Court, Dewey believed that such an institution could be effective in the moral education of humanity. He also joined the Committee on Militarism in Education to protest ROTC programs and to promote pacifism. He also opposed America's military draft as involuntary servitude and as an example of "totalitarianism." In 1937, Dewey was selected to head the international tribunal in Mexico City formed to investigate charges against Leon Trotsky in the Moscow Trials, resulting in the report *Not Guilty.* Dewey died in 1952 in New York City.

Major Works

Although Dewey's philosophy evolved throughout his life, it is thought by many philosophers and critics to be governed by his concept of experience, which he perceived as a unified albeit constantly changing force, rather than a collection of remembered facts. Differences for Dewey are but variables within a singular, consistent source, a philosophical approach that, along with his rejection of subjectivism and empiricism caused much of his earlier work to be labeled as Hegelian idealism. Dewey, however, eventually rejected the predisposition of idealists to relegate all human experience to knowledge, which he perceived as distorting the initial experience. Humanity, argued Dewey, spends much of its time acting, suffering, and enjoying, not in reflection. Dewey's later work abandoned idealist concepts, instead embracing a theory that life is a sequence of lapidary and concurrent experiences. Borrowing from twentieth-century advancements in the biological and anthropological sciences, Dewey developed a complex and naturalistic theory that an individual's experience is the organic premise of all life. From this concept, Dewey elaborated that there are three levels or plateaus of human interaction with the environment: physiochemical, psychophysical, and human experience. By observing and interacting with the world, humanity's experience grows in knowledge and understanding. This approach directly refutes the scientific theories of Aristotle, which promulgated that science relies on a passive witnessing and contemplation rather than Dewey's view that knowledge relies on active testing and consideration. This theory is consistent with Dewey's writings on logic and education. The objective of inquiry, according to Dewey, is knowledge, but inquiry is a process that continuously alters its original questions and desired conclusions. As for education, Dewey rejected both poles of educational philosophy prevalent during the first half of the twentieth-century. Children were neither passive receptacles of knowledge nor were they mature enough to determine what education they required. Dewey advocated "learning by doing" as a method of active educational inquiry that cultivated a child's inherent curiosity.

PRINCIPAL WORKS

Psychology (nonfiction) 1887
Applied Psychology [with J. A. McLellan] (nonfiction) 1889
Outlines in Ethics [with James Tufts] (philosophy) 1891
School and Society (nonfiction) 1899
Studies in Logical Theory (philosophy) 1903
Child and Curriculum (nonfiction) 1906
Ethics (philosophy) 1908
How We Think (philosophy) 1910
Interest and Effort (philosophy) 1913
Democracy and Education (nonfiction) 1916
Essays in Experimental Logic (philosophy) 1916·
Creative Intelligence (nonfiction) 1917
Reconstruction in Philosophy (philosophy) 1920
Human Nature and Conduct (philosophy) 1922
Experience and Nature (philosophy) 1925
The Public and Its Problems (nonfiction) 1927
The Quest for Certainty (philosophy) 1929
Characters and Events (nonfiction) 1929
Philosophy and Civilization (nonfiction) 1931
Art as Experience (philosophy) 1934
Liberalism and Social Action (nonfiction) 1935
Logic: The Theory of Inquiry (philosophy) 1938
Freedom and Culture (nonfiction) 1939
Problems of Man (nonfiction) 1946
Knowing and the Known [with Arthur Bently] (philosophy) 1949

CRITICISM

Irving King (essay date 1917)

SOURCE: A review of *Democracy and Education,* in *The American Journal of Sociology,* Vol. XXII, No. 5, March, 1917, pp. 674-76.

[*In the following review of Dewey's* Democracy and Education, *King attempts to elucidate Dewey's theories in order to support his thesis that the work is a worthwhile study of sociology, education, and philosophy.*]

All students of philosophy and sociology, as well as of education, welcome this comprehensive and fundamental statement of Professor Dewey's educational philosophy. [*Democracy and Education: An Introduction to the Philosophy of Education*]. It will undoubtedly take its place among the world's enduring classics in these three fields of thought. The educator, to whom it is primarily written, will find here a clarifying account of the principles and the practice which must of necessity characterize all sound educational development that is really an expression of democratic ideals. Such a conception of education cannot be stated in any narrow, isolated fashion, and not the least valuable aspect of its exposition, therefore, lies in the accompanying searching and critical examination of the evolution of philosophical thought and the correlated evolution of the ideals of social democracy.

The method of the work is to be found in a series of statements and expositions of various dualisms of thought and practice which have been at various times more or less dominant in both philosophy and education since the time of the Greeks. The historical analysis which accompanies each discussion presents a viewpoint that is absolutely essential to the adequate understanding of the problems of current educational theory and practice, and on the basis of which alone we can arrive at solutions consistent with our democratic ideals.

The first dualism is the general one between education and life. While a social necessity, education has tended in all times to become more or less isolated from the social order which evolved it, through an inadequate conception of the social function of instruction. This imperfect view of the nature of education has found expression at various times in the conceptions of education as *external direction,* as mere *inner growth,* as *preparation for a remote future,* as *unfolding,* or as *discipline.* These conceptions are criticized as being, in varying degrees, external, retrospective, conservative, and hence inadequate to interpret the educational process that should belong to a progressive democratic society. The worth of such a society depends upon the extent to which "the interests of the group are shared by all its members and the fulness and freedom with which it interacts with other groups." "Such a society must have a type of education which gives individuals a personal interest in social relationships and control, and the habits of mind which secure social changes without introducing social disorder." Professor Dewey's conception of the end of education is developed directly from this viewpoint. It is a statement of the *process of education* at its best rather than external goal which, just because it is external, cannot be put into definite and helpful relation to the process of education with its various resources and difficulties. A real end of education must, if it is to have any practical value, interpret and guide its various expressions rather than be a remote and final goal. One of the most brilliant and stimulating discussions in this book is that in which the ideal as a working hypothesis is developed. Other conceptions of end are discussed and shown to have reality in so far as they admit of statement as interpretative principles rather than as goals.

It is impossible in a review to give even a synopsis of the discussions which follow. The dualisms, which have appeared in the thinking of the Western world and expressed in such contrasts as interest and discipline, play and work, labor and leisure, intellectual and practical studies, naturalism and humanism, individual and world, aesthetic and practical, represent genuine aspects of experience which, in a democracy, education must seek to bring together in an organic relationship. In fact, the realization of a democratic society is seen to be conditioned upon the incorporation of the values of these extremes in everyday social experience. For instance, the separation of the aesthetic and the practical should have a place only in aristocratic conceptions of society. Individual variation is not good in itself. Its highest significance is to be found in relation to a progressive society to which it furnishes the means of progress. In such a society vocational education should represent a union of bodily action and thought, of making a livelihood and the worthy enjoyment of leisure. Certain tendencies in present-day vocational education, if followed up, would tend to perpetuate the old aristocratic distinction between culture and life. Industrial life of today is so dependent upon science and thought that there is no justification for such a distinction. Now, as never before, is it possible for the vocational life to minister to the development of mind and character.

True philosophy is regarded as essentially a theory of education, since the stimulus to its development is to be found in essentially social problems, the solution of which is to be found in a proper type of education.

The problem of moral education is to secure the organic relation and interaction of knowledge and conduct. These scattered points suggest very inadequately the method and conclusions of *Democracy and Education*. The unique and distinctive quality of the thought is lost when one attempts to summarize it.

M. C. Otto (essay date 1920)

SOURCE: A review of *Democracy and Education,* in *The Mississippi Valley Historical Review,* Vol. VII, No. 1, June, 1920, pp. 64-5.

[*In the following review of Dewey's* Democracy and Education, *Otto focuses on the sociological aspects of the work, which Otto expresses as the need for education to reflect common experiences.*]

The present educational situation presents an interesting paradox. We were never so convinced of the social

necessity for public education and never more uncertain what public education should be. We insist that our children must have it even though we do not know what it is they must have. Which is very natural, of course, under the circumstances. With strong vigorous groups threatening the radical reconstruction of the fundamental concepts of life, we are tempted to feel ourselves in a whirl of random movements, a whirl too complicated for analysis and movements too powerful to be resisted. Confused and uncertain, we turn for solace and hope to a compensatory society to be realized through the education of youth. In this we are right—provided we can substitute an intelligent program of education for blind faith in the process itself. In other words, the outstanding need of the contemporary world is an adequate philosophy of education.

Fortunately, a noteworthy statement of such a philosophy is at hand in John Dewey's *Democracy and Education*. The book deserves the widest possible reading and the most careful study. For, in the first place, whatever may be the fate of the philosophy called pragmatism, it is perfectly safe to predict that this expression of it is destined to be one of the world's educational classics; and in the second place, the author's educational theory is being translated into educational facts not only in the United States, but in Europe and in the Orient.

Roughly speaking (if we may murder to be brief) the central doctrine of the twenty-six chapters may be put as follows: as physiological life renews itself through nutrition and reproduction, social life renews itself through education. Education is the sharing of experience to make it become a common possession. In a simple state of society this is secured through direct participation in the common activities, but as life becomes more complex a special environment is set aside for the training of the young. The tendency then is to separate between education and life. This has now taken place to a degree so harmful to the individual and to society that the present problem is to institute a type of education which will reunite the life-customs of the group and the impulses of the young. This is by no means a simple matter, but it will be accomplished to the extent that we make possible education through growth. "The criterion of the value of school education is the extent in which it creates a desire for continued growth and supplies means for making the desire effective in fact." Thus education, technically defined, becomes "that reconstruction or reorganization of experience which adds to the meaning of experience, and which increases ability to direct the course of subsequent experience."

The volume is filled with material illustrating the application of the theory to concrete subjects—history, geography, science, and the like; it is a storehouse of succinct statements of notable theories of education and should succeed in setting right the critics who have misunderstood or misinterpreted the author's position on such controversial subjects as the value of past cultures and vocational training. John Dewey is the enemy of only a certain kind of loyalty to the past and the friend of only a certain kind of vocational training. He is concerned for this one thing: to break down the barriers between people and to add to the meaning and joy of life by transforming education into an adventure for making human life better worth living.

W. H. Werkmeister (essay date 1939)

SOURCE: A review of *Logic: The Theory of Inquiry,* in *Ethics,* Vol. L, No. 1, October, 1939, pp. 98-102.

[*In the following review of Dewey's* Logic: The Theory of Inquiry, *Werkmeister declares Dewey's work as a philosophical landmark.*]

The publication of [*Logic: The Theory of Inquiry*] is most welcome and for at least two reasons. In the first place, it represents the final formulation of basic ideas which Dewey first stated some forty years ago in his *Studies in Logical Theory* and which he subsequently developed and modified somewhat in his *Essays in Experimental Logic* and the more recent little book on *How We Think*. In other words, the new book is important as a landmark in the development of the philosophical system of one of America's most influential thinkers; and it will be interesting to the future historians of philosophy who are concerned with the unfolding and the growth of a philosophical idea. But, beyond this systematic importance, Dewey's *Logic* has a significance also for philosophical discussions at large, notably at a time when the "new" logic is in danger of losing itself in an abstract and intrinsically "irrational" formalism.

Numerous difficulties and confusions of contemporary logic, Dewey believes, are due to "the attempt to retain Aristotelian logical forms after their existential foundations have been repudiated" (p. 94). For, after all, Aristotelian logic was but a more or less adequate expression of "the conditions of science and culture which provided its background and substantial material" (p. 82). The need, therefore, is "for logic to do for present science and culture what Aristotle did for the science and culture of his time" (p. 95). This theme as such, of course, is not a new one. It inspired Bacon no less than Bosanquet and Mill. But Dewey's solution of the problem deserves special attention, for he deals with the specific problems of logic that have only recently (and largely since the development of symbolic logic) been recognized as problems; and he deals with them from a unique point of view.

Dewey's theory, "in summary form," is that "all logical forms (with their characteristic properties) arise within the operation of inquiry and are concerned with control of inquiry so that it may yield warranted assertions" (pp. 3-4). Now, inquiry begins with the "institution of a problem" ("To see that a situation requires inquiry is the initial step in inquiry" [p. 107]) and ends with a "warranted assertion" or judgment ("Judgment may be identified as the settled outcome of inquiry" [p. 120]). The operational process leading from the former to the latter constitutes the "whole of the inquiry," and this "whole" determines all logical forms and conditions all logically relevant matters.

Thus, "to be a datum is to have a special function in control of the subject-matter of inquiry" (p. 124). The "essential" is now readily distinguishable from the "accidental," for "anything is 'essential' which is indispensable in a given inquiry and anything is 'accidental' which is superfluous" (p. 138). "Propositions are the instruments by which provisional conclusions of preparatory inquiries are summed up, recorded and retained for subsequent use. In this way they function as effective means, material and procedural, in the conduct of inquiry, till the latter institutes subject-matter so unified in significance as to be warrantably assertible" (p. 311). And it is interesting to see how Dewey interprets the Aristotelian "square of opposites" from the "functional" point of view (pp. 190ff.). Especially his conceptions of "contrariety" and of "contradictories" deserve attention. The upshot of it all is that "only if propositions are related to each other as phases in the divisions of labor in the conduct of inquiry, can they be members of a coherent logical system" (p. 310).

From Dewey's "functional" point of view the "syllogism" is not in itself the procedural basis of an inquiry but "a generalized formula for logical conditions that must be satisfied if final judgment is to be grounded" (p. 323). It "means that a conclusion is logically warranted, and is only so warranted, when the operations involved in discourse and in experimental observation of existences, converge to yield a completely resolved determinate situation" (p. 324). "Major premise" (as "procedural propositions") and "minor premise" (as "existential propositions") are both indispensable if there is to be grounded judgment.

Of still greater importance is Dewey's reinterpretation of the traditional "laws of thought": identity, contradiction, and the excluded middle. "The Aristotelian interpretation of them as ontological," Dewey maintains, "and any interpretation which regards them as inherent relational properties of given propositions, must certainly be abandoned. But as formulations of formal conditions (conjunctive-disjunctive) to be satisfied, they are valid as directive principles, as regulative limiting ideals of inquiry" (p. 346). They are "*operationally a priori*" with respect to further inquiry" (p. 14). This, of course, raises the whole question of "rationality," and, concerning it, Dewey says: "Rationality is an affair of the relation of *means and consequences,* not of fixed first principles as ultimate premises" (p. 9). And "it is reasonable to search for and select the means that will, with the maximum probability, yield the consequences which are intended" (p. 10). Finally, "the principles state habits operative in every inference that tend to yield conclusions that are stable and productive in further inquiries. . . . The validity of the principles is determined by the coherency of the consequences produced by the habits they articulate" (p. 13).

It seems to me that right here we have before us the weakest point in Dewey's "theory of inquiry"—and it is also a fundamental issue; for does not the relation of "means and consequences" necessarily "transcend" all inquiry in the sense of being ontological rather than purely procedural? And do not the "principles" even as "habits" presuppose a "reasonableness" and interdependence of realities, if you please, which is logically as well as existentially prior to all inquiry? Is it not "reasonable to search for . . . the means that will . . . yield the consequences" only because the "relation of means and consequences" is ontological rather than logical?

These questions are not satisfactorily answered by Dewey's contention that "logical forms accrue to subject-matter in virtue of subjection of the latter in inquiry to the conditions determined by its end" (p. 372), for the possibility of such "subjection" may itself become an issue. But there is at least a suggestion of the required ontology in Dewey's statement that "the purpose for which inquiry is carried on cannot be fulfilled on a wide scale or in an ordered way except as its materials are subject to conditions which impose formal properties on the materials. When these conditions are abstracted they form the subject-matter of logic. But they do not thereby cease to be, in their own reference and function, forms-of-subject-matter" (p. 374). I heartily agree with these statements; but I wonder if they do not contradict the previous contention that principles are but "habits operative in every inference."

In his polemic against Aristotle, Dewey makes much of the fact that "the development of modern science destroyed the conceptions of fixed species, defined by fixed essences, upon which the Aristotelian logic rested." This destruction affected . . . the classic conceptions of universal and particular, whole and part, and the scheme of their relationships with one another. Modern logic, however, attempted to retain the scheme but with the understanding that it is purely formal, devoid of ontological import" (p. 182). And it is Dewey's contention that this very fact is the chief source of trouble in contemporary logical theory. I think Dewey is right in his interpretation of the trend of modern science. Everywhere "thing-concepts" have been, or are being, replaced by "functional" concepts; and present-day logic must adjust itself accordingly. Dewey suggests a reinterpretation that may be required in particular with respect to the notions of "substance" ("'Substance' represents . . . a logical, not an ontological, determination" [p. 128]), and of "causality" ("the category causation is logical; . . . it is a functional means of regulating existential inquiry, not ontological" [p. 462]). And one wonders if such an interpretation does not raise anew—and in a somewhat new form—some of the epistemological problems confronting the neo-Kantians (cf. Cassirer's *Substance and Function*)—and this despite Dewey's belief that the "problems" of epistemology "disappear when the characteristic features of scientific subject-matter are interpreted from the standpoint of satisfaction of *logical* conditions set by the requirements of controlled inquiry" (p. 465).

All philosophers who can see in logic only the formal aspects of intra- and interpropositional relations will be greatly disappointed by Dewey's book; and one must not expect to find in it detailed discussions of "symbolic" logic or the more recent development of this logical line.

But for all who are interested in the broader and genuinely philosophical aspects of logic Dewey's book will be stimulating and valuable.

Joseph Ratner (essay date 1939)

SOURCE: "Dewey's Conception of Philosophy," in *The Philosophy of John Dewey,* Northwestern University, 1939, pp. 49-73.

[*In the following essay, Ratner examines Dewey's personal definition and objectives for his philosophy, concluding that Dewey believed philosophy to be an integral element of all human life.*]

In his opening contribution to *Studies in Logical Theory*, Dewey outlined a conception of philosophy which, from the vantage point of the present time, we can see he has been working on and working out ever since. It has not, however, been a development proceeding on a smooth and unbroken line. It has not been an unperturbed and undeviating unfoldment of an ideally preformed idea, nourished and sustained by an environment ideally preformed for it. Rather has the development been of a more natural, even of a more human sort. Its historic career is marked by crises, by phases of change—and some of them of major importance. Hence in our discussion we shall, to some extent, follow the historic route.

I

Philosophy, as described in the essay referred to (**"The Relationship of Thought and Its Subject-Matter"**) has three areas of inquiry. For the sake of convenience, these may be provisionally represented in the form of three concentric circles. The first area, bounded by the innermost circle, is occupied by reflective thought, by logic, or what Dewey now calls inquiry. In the second area are the typical modes of human experience, such as the practical or utilitarian, the esthetic, religious, socio-ethical, scientific. Philosophic inquiry here concerns itself with analyzing what these modes of experience are and, particularly, with discovering their interrelations, how one leads into and emerges out of the other, how the practical or utilitarian develops, perhaps, into the scientific, the scientific into the esthetic or vice versa or whatever the case may be discovered to be. The third area is that of the socio-cultural world, society in its organized and institutional form, the world which generates what we commonly and quite accurately call "social questions." Of the myriad possible questions that can be found here for philosophy to study and answer, Dewey singled out the following as representative samples: "the value of research for social progress; the bearing of psychology upon educational procedure; the mutual relations of fine and industrial art; the question of the extent and nature of specialization in science in comparison with the claims of applied science; the adjustment of religious aspirations to scientific statements; the justification of a refined culture for a few in face of economic insufficiency for the mass, the relation of organization to individuality."[1]

Today, at any rate, there is nothing new in this conception of the subject-matter of philosophy, taken distributively. To what extent Dewey's own work has contributed to making our contemporary range of philosophic interest and work legitimate, familiar and accepted we need not stop to inquire. But the significance of Dewey's conception is not to be found in the mere extension of the range, significant as that undoubtedly was and is. It is to be found in the idea of the interrelation of the three areas: that they are functional distinctions, discriminable divisions within one inclusive field of experience, the boundary lines being neither fixed nor impermeable, marking off, but not insulating any one from any of the rest.

The fundamental idea then is that the primary subject-matter of philosophic inquiry is a continuously interconnected field of experience. But philosophy, especially in the modern epoch and as an academic pursuit, does not receive its subject-matter in its primary form. It receives it, instead, in derivative forms of various orders of remoteness and complication. It gets bundles of highly intellectualized and generalized problems. Each bundle is outfitted with its own tag: epistemology, ethics, logic, esthetics, social philosophy and whatnot. Philosophy is an enterprise of reflective thought and not only should but can only deal with problems in a reflective or intellectual way. But when each bundle of intellectualized problems is treated as if it constituted a separate and distinct substantive realm, as being the original and primary subject-matter of inquiry, philosophy, instead of prospering as a reflective enterprise, degenerates into a mere dialectical process of untying each bundle in some way and tying it up again in another.

To recur to our three concentric circles for a moment. The contents of those circles, as described above, were all intellectualized contents, that is, problems already given an intellectual form. This is as true of the "social questions" which are the contents of the outer circle as it is of the contents located in the others. "The relation of organization to individuality, the justification of a refined culture for a few in face of economic insufficiency for the mass, the value of research for social progress" and so on, are, with respect to their intellectual form, on a par with any other intellectual problems conceived or conceivable. However, no one of ordinary commonsense would confuse these "social questions," or intellectualized problems, with the actual social conditions that raise those questions or that *are* those problems. And certainly no one of commonsense would substitute the former for the latter, treating the social questions as self-sufficient in themselves, as being the primary and original subject-matter and pushing the social conditions completely to one side as irrelevant, if not even non-existent.

Whether any philosopher ever succeeded in making a complete substitution of the sort indicated, in any field whatsoever, is more than doubtful. Indeed, it is certain that none ever did. Such a feat is beyond the powers even of a philosopher, no matter how "idealistically" or "intellectualistically" he may be constitutioned or conditioned.

However, the temptation to make the substitution is omnipresent in the intellectual class, and the one to which philosophers most frequently and recurrently fall. In the degree that the substitution is made, to that degree does philosophy become a vain dispute and an arid verbal jugglery. The stress falls on *substitution* and in the sense indicated. Reflective inquiry, philosophic or otherwise, can handle an actual condition that *is* a problem only by transforming it into an intellectual form. But such a transformation, when understood and handled as such, is what Dewey calls a surrogate for the actual problem, not a substitute for it. An architect engaged on the problem of remodelling a house uses a blueprint. The blueprint is an intellectualized form of the actual house, a surrogate for it. An architect does not *substitute* his blueprint for the house; he does not consider the blueprint as constituting the original and primary subject-matter of his inquiry; and he does not think that he changes the house when he changes the blueprint—although changing the blueprint may be all that he professionally contributes towards the consummation of that final end.

Let us suppose there is an architect's office, full of blueprints of various orders and descriptions, rolled up in different sets. Now put a philosopher in that office, bolt the door and shutter the windows and what can he do? It all depends upon what the philosopher experienced before he was imprisoned. If he can read the blueprints and has an active and fertile mind, there is no telling what he will be able to do with them, what strange new blueprint or system of blueprints he will be able to fashion out of the blueprints before him. But suppose the philosopher who was sealed in the office was grabbed out of the transcendental blue and was transported and imprisoned so quickly he had no time to have any earthly experience on the way? What could he do with the blueprints? Barring miracles, whatever he did would be a purely transcendental doing, having no relation whatever to the earthly blueprints, what they stand for and where they came from, what they are surrogates of and what they are used for. Our transcendental philosopher would be bottled up in the architect's office much as the mind is still supposed by some to be bottled up in the brain or some part of the brain.

Pictorial analogies or illustrations when taken too literally or when pressed too far are bound to be misleading. However, if in the foregoing illustration the appropriate substitutions are made, the result is a fair picture of the kind of situation in philosophy against which Dewey fundamentally protested in *Studies in Logical Theory* and which his own conception of the nature of philosophic inquiry was designed to correct.

II

The problem of unbolting the door and unshuttering the windows of the philosopher's study is the problem of establishing continuous, functional connection between philosophic inquiry and all other activities of human beings, including among the latter of course other activities of inquiry, such as the scientific.

How can this be done? Poised as an abstract problem at large and this problem itself becomes a dialectical one of the insoluble variety, on the order of the problem of determining whether an "inside" mind can know an "outside" world. If we start off with the mind at large as being "inside" and the world at large as being "outside," the dialectical operation can be pursued indefinitely without ever effecting any connection, let alone a functional connection, between the two. In the course of the dialectic, the mind and the world may exchange positions, recurrently yielding what superficially may seem to be the amazing result of getting the world "inside" and the mind "outside." But such consequence, should it prove unduly unpleasant to contemplate, can always be reversed by carrying the dialectic one round further. Similarly, if we start off with philosophy at large and seek by dialectic .to connect it with the common world of human experience and affairs at large. In fact, the two problems are variants of the same.

The only way in which the connection can be shown to be—for it *is* and does not have to be made—is by giving up the futile task of abstractedly considering "problems in general" and approaching all problems empirically, as a series of specific, concrete problems. Does this beg the question? Dewey has formulated his answer in a great variety of ways, sometimes more clearly and sometimes less. The fundamental idea recurring in all his answers is that this does not beg the question: the only thing it begs is the empirical method and this only at the outset. Thenceforward, the method proves itself by its works.

Of course, the contemporary philosopher in "begging" the adoption of the empirical method for use in philosophy is not asking philosophers to start out on a completely blind hunch. The scientists have been empirical in their procedure for quite some time now, and it is agreed on all hands that it is a good procedure, that, to put it in the vernacular, it produces the goods. The "appeal to example" is as significant in the intellectual as in the moral life. It has at least a quasi-logical force. One scientist does something in a certain way, getting certain results, and that way becomes an "example" for other scientists to follow; not slavishly and blindly, of course, but nevertheless something to follow. There is a logical presumption in its favor—in so far forth. Likewise when it is a case of adopting a method used in one field for use in another field. Of course, the *justification* of a method comes through the fruits of its use where it is used. It is not and cannot be justified by pointing to its fruitfulness elsewhere or whence it was taken. Arguments for adopting empirical method in philosophy because the scientists use that method are, therefore, at the outset, always of the nature of "begging"; they are, in the good sense of the term, hortatory. This of course applies equally to any method *to be* adopted for use in *any* field, or any part of any field.

That a method justifies itself by the goods it produces where it is used is a principle that cuts both ways. It operates to cut a method out as well as to cut a method in. Cutting a method out that is deeply entrenched is no simple, automatic or instantaneous affair. It is accomplished only progressively, only in the course of actually reconstructing the field by the operative use of the new method.

The adoption of the empirical method for use in philosophy may be considered to be in the nature of an initial attitude or standpoint taken towards the work, that is, the assumption of the empirical attitude is of the nature of an overt act whereby the philosopher identifies himself as one human being among other human beings, as one worker among other workers, or what amounts to the same, whereby he identifies his field of work as one field among others and functionally interrelated with them. Since the contemporary philosopher certainly is not in the position of one who stands just in front of the threshold of Creation, what this act means concretely is that all the achievements of the human race, all the methods of work, all the products and results that have already been developed by those methods in all other fields are *legitimately* opened for his use. The whole world of human achievement, the world of goods, becomes a community store to which the empirical philosopher has rightful access and from which he may rightfully take what he needs and as he needs it. (And to which, it may immediately be added, he is under obligation to give something in return.) As a matter of fact, even the most non-empirical philosophers have not hesitated to take what they wanted, no matter how empirical the place where they found it. This fact, which Dewey has very amply documented, is not, to be sure, a reflection on their morals, but it is an indictment of their philosophical position.

III

With the assumption of the empirical attitude, the problems *in* philosophy cease to be unique, parthenogenetic creations. They become formulations in philosophy of common problems arising out of common experience. They all have empirical fathers who can be empirically traced, located and identified. And this precisely becomes the task of empirical philosophy, as Dewey conceives it, with respect to the class of problems in philosophy that have by virtue of their formulation acquired the character of being inherently insoluble. From Dewey's empirical standpoint an insoluble problem is of the nature of an intellectual disease; it is what we may call a "diseased formulation" and the empirical remedy (and the only remedy) consists in tracing the "problem" as it appears in philosophy back to its origins in the primary subject-matter of experience and finding out how, in the course of its intellectual genetic-history, it got that way. How complicated and extensive a process this becomes when carried out in some detail can be seen, for example, in *Experience and Nature* and *The Quest for Certainty*.

The fundamental principle of the remedial process is, however, rather simple. Dewey briefly indicated its nature in *Studies in Logical Theory*, and though brief, it is in some ways the best explanation he has given of his own *modus operandi*. It can be most expeditiously described by referring again to the three concentric circles. They comprise the inclusive area within which philosophic inquiry is going on. Examination of the contents will reveal that at least some of the contents in one area appear in other areas in other forms and on different contextual scales. The method Dewey prescribed and has so extensively and effectively used is that "of working back and forth between the larger and the narrower fields, transforming every increment upon one side into a method of work upon the other, and thereby testing it."[2] Uppermost in Dewey's mind, at the time of writing, was the function this "double movement" performs in testing every increment gained. But it also functions to uncover new clews and leads both for solutions and problems and thus is accumulative as well as corrective. Furthermore, this accumulative and corrective process is the natural matrix out of which develop new varieties of empirical method. For empirical method does not consist of a single, linear rule. It is multi-dimensional and many-potentialed, acquiring different specific forms through use in different specific situations, and displaying new powers with every new way in which it is used. When empirical method is deliberately adopted for philosophic use, it has also to be adapted. Since Dewey's "double movement" is a method of working within the field of philosophy which exhibits the two fundamental features of empirical method as that operates in scientific inquiry it may fairly be considered as being a natural adaptation of that method.

The concentric circles give, of course, a cross-sectional view, or the *area* of philosophic inquiry (as Dewey conceived it in 1903). But the actual field of philosophic inquiry has depth and temporal length as well. It is the socio-cultural world in its full-dimensional, historical character. The method of working back and forth between the narrower and larger fields means, therefore, working back and forth between the technical study of the intellectualized problems in philosophy and the common world of experience, the socio-cultural conditions and activities, including the scientific, which generate or *are* those problems.

IV

In *Studies in Logical Theory*, the distinction between what we may call "problems in general" and "general problems" is clearly recognized and made. All "problems in general" or "problems *überhaupt*" are diseased formulations of general problems. Thus the problem of "knowledge in general" (**"Is Knowledge Possible?"**) is a diseased formulation of the problem of developing a general theory of knowledge or a general logic. From the scientific empirical standpoint Dewey took in those early essays and which he has maintained ever since, it is just as intelligent for a philosopher to ask **"Is Knowledge Possible?"** as it would be for a scientist to ask "Is Motion Possible?" There are specific cases of motion and scientific inquiry begins by observing (and experimenting with) these specific cases. Although there is no "motion in general" (and hence no "problem in general") the scientist none the less has a general problem; namely, the problem of developing a general theory of motion or, what is the same thing for him, formulating general laws of motion. The general laws, furthermore, are not proved valid, are not tested and established by their ability to evaporate out of scientific existence the specific cases of motion going on and observed but, on the contrary, their validity is established by their ability to explain or account for the specific cases.

Similarly with the general problem of knowledge which is the concern of the philosopher in his restricted capacity as logician. Any general theory of knowledge, any general formulation he reaches, must be competent to explain or account for the specific cases of knowing going on. However attractive and admirable his general formulation may be in all other respects, if it does not meet this fundamental requirement it is invalid or incompetent. A great deal of rightful enthusiasm has been poured over Newton's general laws of motion. But suppose the characteristic of those laws was that they accounted for "all motion" only by making every actual motion unaccountable. Would we then be as enthusiastic? To ask the question is to answer it. Why then any enthusiasm over general philosophic formulations which display their competence to account for a total field of inquiry by the method of rendering inexplicable and unaccountable everything that actually occurs within that field? Should we not enforce on philosophic generalizations the same demand we enforce on scientific generalizations? For the philosopher who, like Dewey, has taken the empirical attitude only an unequivocal affirmative answer is possible. For by taking the attitude, by identifying his field of work as one among others, he has given up all special privileges, all claims to exclusive, prerogative treatment and consideration. Hence when he concerns himself with the general problem of knowledge he proceeds with the firm and basic understanding that his solution of that problem, the general formulations he reaches must be such that they will include, not exclude, will account for, not render unaccountable, the actual ways of knowing which occur. The common man and the scientist experience no "metaphysical" problem, they suffer from no "metaphysical" fright, when engaged in the enterprise of knowing. For them, knowing and knowledge do not rend their experience into two inexplicably unjoinable parts. For the common man and scientist, knowledge does not divide off and then hermetically seal the divisions. It does just the opposite: it functions to break through divisions that have for other, non-knowledge causes, occurred. Knowledge, as actually exemplified in experience, does not create breaches but heals them; it does not function to disrupt and disintegrate experience but, on the contrary, operatively functions to deepen and to expand, to re-integrate and integrate experience in adequate and more comprehensive and more fruitful ways. The general formulation of the philosopher must therefore meet these specific conditions. If it does not, there is only one conclusion that can be drawn: the philosopher has, in the course of his work, severed all connection between his field of inquiry and all other fields. He has set himself up as an emperor in a self-created and insulated empire of his own.

The philosophic task, then, is to reach generalizations that meet specific conditions. This is Dewey's position. How is this done? Let us quote:

> Generalization of the nature of the reflective process certainly involves elimination of much of the specific material and contents of the thought-situations of daily life and of critical science. Quite compatible with this, however, is the notion that it seizes upon *certain* specific conditions and factors, and aims to bring them to clear consciousness—not to abolish them. While eliminating the particular material of particular practical and scientific pursuits, (1) it may strive to hit upon the common denominator in the various situations which are antecedent or primary to thought and which evoke it; (2) it may attempt to show how typical features in the specific antecedents of thought call out diverse typical modes of thought-reaction; (3) it may attempt to state the nature of the specific consequences in which thought fulfills its career.[3]

There is, then, according to Dewey, no opposition or conflict between philosophic concern with the general or generic and interest in the specific. In fact, the etiology of all diseased formulations, for example of the diseased formulation of the general problem of knowledge as the problem of "knowledge in general" is, as Dewey then diagnosed the case, chiefly if not exclusively to be found in the fact that logicians apparently believed that there is an irreconcilable opposition between the two and hence in constructing their general theories always worked to eliminate the specific entirely. Wherefore their theories were doomed to end up as one or other of the extant varieties of diseased formulations, that is, were doomed to end up by presenting in an insoluble intellectualized form the original problem they started out to solve.

Dewey's theory of knowledge or general logic of reflective thought is here introduced for illustration not discussion. It is a specific example of an essential, indeed basic element in his general doctrine in *Studies in Logical Theory* regarding philosophy. There the concern of philosophy with general problems is not only admitted as a legitimate concern but the competence of philosophy to arrive at solutions of general problems, its competence to reach general theories or formulations is insisted upon as the foundation of philosophy's ultimate effectiveness as Dewey then envisioned it.

As there described, philosophy, from an initiating and restricted interest in the logic of reflection develops into a "general logic of experience." When thus developed it "gets the significance of a method." Its business ceases to be that of defending any vested interest or traditional order in society or any entrenched conception of Reality. Its business becomes that of freely and unprejudicially (or scientifically) examining the various typical modes of experience and discovering their relationships to each other and their respective claims. When fully realized as a method, Dewey envisioned philosophy as doing "for social qualities and aims what the natural sciences after

centuries of struggle are doing for activity in the physical realm." Philosophy would answer the "social questions" of which some examples were cited earlier. Philosophy alone would answer these questions because only philosophy, in the course of realizing itself, would have acquired the requisite foundation of general method.

The three stages of philosophy's development are diagrammatically represented by our three concentric circles—to refer to this device for the last time. In view of what has already been said, it is clear that Dewey did not conceive of these stages as separate and distinct, as following upon one another in discrete succession. He conceived of the stages in just the opposite way: as indissolubly and interactively interconnected, as discriminable phases of a temporal or natural-historical development. The solution of problems in philosophy can be reached only by working back and forth between the technical or private domain of philosophy and the final or public domain of sociocultural experience. For philosophy to solve its own intellectualized problems it must move into the common field of problematic situations. And just as truly, if philosophy is ever to become able to handle social situations successfully or constructively, it must begin to handle them—its ability progressing in the "double" process: the periodic return of philosophy into its technical domain being an essential phase of the way philosophy perfects its general methods. In sum, for philosophy to develop either way, within its own technical confines or within the inclusive social world, the "double movement" must be continuously maintained. Undoubtedly there is a great temptation to say that answering "social questions" would be "applied philosophy" but such temptation must be resolutely denied. For such a distinction involves the idea that methods and application can be separated, that methods can somehow be developed in some sequestered location and then "applied" to the situations. Which is fundamentally contradictory to Dewey's doctrine. And at any rate in the sphere of "social questions" almost every one admits the inherent absurdity of the idea that methods and application can be separated. This idea is popularly known as sentimentalism or utopianism.

Dewey did not of course see philosophy as maturing to its full powers as a "method" immediately or even soon. But it was in the direction of attaining this maturity that philosophy's destiny lay, the ultimate end in view of which the reconstruction of philosophy was to be undertaken.

v

In the period between 1903 and 1920, the publication dates respectively of *Studies in Logical Theory* and *Reconstruction in Philosophy*, many things happened in the world. For one thing, the brood of social sciences was growing larger and even growing up. And they were obviously increasing their business by taking away the business of philosophy as Dewey had conceived it ultimately to be. By all evidences of the times, philosophy was, in this respect, to repeat its history: its maturation as the science of society was to be achieved through the maturation of the social sciences.

The second thing we need notice here as having happened during this period is the World War. It was largely, though not exclusively, in connection with the social problems created by the War—while it was in progress and for some years after—that Dewey developed his publicist activity, directly participating in current, almost day to day, public affairs. By far the major part of his publicist writings belong to the years 1917-1923. *Reconstruction in Philosophy*, one of the more widely read and known of Dewey's volumes, belongs very definitely to this period. Since it is the only volume of this period that covers the whole field of philosophy, we may fairly take it as representative of one of the major changes in Dewey's conception of philosophy referred to at the outset. If the change were exclusively restricted to this period, or were to be found only in this book, it would deserve some notice, but only of a passing sort. But recurrent echoes of the strain here developed are observable, if not in all Dewey's subsequent writings, at any rate, in a goodly portion of them.

In *Reconstruction in Philosophy* two different, though not unrelated, conceptions of philosophy and its function are advanced. One is the conception that philosophy "is vision" and "that its chief function is to free men's minds from bias and prejudice and to enlarge their perceptions of the world about them."[4] Although this conception of philosophy is not new with Dewey, it is not unreasonable to suppose that the prominence it acquires, not only in this book, but throughout this period and subsequently, is not unconnected with the rise and development of the social sciences.

The other conception of philosophy is a revised version of philosophy as social method, as an "organ for dealing with . . . the social and moral strifes of [our] day."[5] There is, of course, no contradiction or opposition between these two conceptions, they do lead into and out of each other, but there is at least a difference in emphasis between them, which difference sometimes becomes very important, if not crucial. "To say frankly that philosophy can proffer nothing but hypotheses, and that these hypotheses are of value *only* as they render men's minds more sensitive to life about them"[6] is qualitatively different from saying with equal frankness: "the task of future philosophy is to clarify men's ideas as to the social and moral strifes of their own day. Its aim is to become so far as is humanly possible an organ for dealing with these conflicts."[7]

But it is not the relation between these two conceptions of philosophy that we want to discuss just now. It is the second conception only that is of immediate concern. In this book, there is a fundamental conflict in doctrine with respect to this second conception. It occurs throughout, sometimes becoming acute, sometimes practically disappearing entirely. In terms of the foregoing discussion, this conflict may be said to turn on the fact that Dewey recurrently forgets the fundamental distinction he made in *Studies in Logical Theory* and confuses what we

called "problems in general" with "general problems" and because of this mistaken identification repeatedly is led from the argument that the former are intellectual chimeras (which they are) to the conclusion that the latter are of the same character (which they are not).

Thus, for example, in considering various theories of society Dewey

> plunge[s] into the heart of the matter, by asserting that these various theories suffer from a common defect. They are all committed to the logic of general notions under which specific situations are to be brought. What we want light upon is this or that group of individuals, this or that concrete human being, this or that special institution or social arrangement. For such a logic of inquiry, the traditionally accepted logic substitutes discussion of the meaning of concepts and their dialectical relationship to one another. The discussion goes on in terms of *the* state, *the* individual; the nature of institutions as such, society in general.[8]

Now from this thoroughly sound criticism of "notions in general"—"society in general," "the state in general," "the individual in general"—Dewey passes to a conclusion which is tantamount to a denial of the need for any general theory of society, of the state, of the individual, etc. "The social philosopher, dwelling in the region of his concepts, 'solves' problems by showing the relationship of ideas, instead of helping men solve problems in the concrete by supplying them hypotheses to be used and tested in projects of reform."[9] And on the next page he is even more specific: "In the question of methods concerned with reconstruction of special situations rather than in any refinements in the general concepts of institution, individuality, state, freedom, law, order, progress, etc., lies the true impact of philosophical reconstruction."[10]

A great deal of course can be made of the terms "refinement" and "impact" but a dialectical exegesis is uncalled for. On an earlier page, Dewey writes as follows:

> Knowing, for the experimental sciences, means a certain kind of intelligently conducted doing; it ceases to be contemplative and becomes in a true sense practical. Now this implies that philosophy, unless it is to undergo a complete break with the authorized spirit of science, must also alter its nature. It must assume a practical nature; it must become operative and experimental.[11]

Now there can be no doubt that the theory of knowing as contemplative was also "operative" in the very important sense that it operated to influence men's minds and thus to some extent guide their conduct, misguidance being also a form of guidance. In fact, to render this theory innocuous or inoperative was the chief purpose of the book under discussion. In a very real sense, it may truly be said that Dewey has dedicated his life's work to the accomplishment of this myriad-formed, if not hydra-headed task. For the accomplishment of this task requires the reconstruction of all philosophic ideas that were formed under the influence of the conception of knowing as inherently and exclusively contemplative, which means, in effect, reconstructing all of them since none escaped this influence. The implication for philosophy of the operative and experimental character of scientific knowing is not that philosophy must change its nature and itself become operative and experimental in the same direct sense in which laboratory science is experimental: the implication is that philosophy must change its ideas, its conceptions. Above all it must reconstruct its conception of knowing so that the operative and experimental character of knowing is made an *integral* part of its general theory of knowledge. This is not accomplished—unfortunately not, needless to say—when philosophers "insert" the characters of operation and experimentation somewhere in their treatises (take "notice" of them so to speak) and then go on with their business as usual. It is also not accomplished when the element of "contemplation" is shoved back so completely that the process of reconstruction becomes one of substituting the operative for the contemplative. And the trend of Dewey's thought, in the period under consideration, was in the direction of making some sort of a substitution. Wherefore the two conceptions of philosophy which are, in reality, two general conceptions of knowledge.

The title of the book—*Reconstruction in Philosophy*—tells the tale without argument. It is philosophy that Dewey is reconstructing. The impact of this reconstruction is to change the world or some portion of it through changing men's minds or ideas. But whatever the ultimate change philosophy brings about in the world, it is a change that it brings about precisely through changing ideas, through reformulating them, reconstructing them. It is in this way that philosophy "gets the significance of a method." Thus, on the heels of the passage cited where it is asserted that the true impact of philosophical reconstruction does not lie in any refinements in the general concepts, Dewey proceeds exactly to the task of reconstructing the general concept of individuality, etc. Speaking generally, and I hope without any confusing results, it may be said that Dewey's most important line of reconstruction, along which lie his greatest contributions, is his painstaking reconstruction of a considerable number of "concepts in general" into "general concepts." When thus reconstructed, the specific and special are not eliminated or abolished but brought out and embraced. Hence the general concepts can also function as general methods guiding and controlling action to a prospering and not impoverishing issue.

As Dewey very clearly puts it in **"The Need for a Recovery of Philosophy"**:

> There are human difficulties of an urgent, deep-seated kind which may be clarified by trained reflection, and whose solution may be forwarded by the careful development of hypotheses. When it is understood that philosophic thinking is caught up in the actual course of events, having the office of guiding them towards a prosperous issue, problems will abundantly present themselves. Philosophy will

not solve these problems; philosophy is vision, imagination, reflection—and these functions apart from action, modify nothing and hence resolve nothing. But in a complicated and perverse world, action which is not informed with vision, imagination and reflection, is more likely to increase confusion and conflict than to straighten things out.[12]

For good or bad, whether he likes it or not, the philosopher, in his professional capacity, is stuck in the realm of ideas.[13]

VI

In **"The Need for a Recovery of Philosophy"** Dewey writes as follows:

> It is often said that pragmatism, unless it is content to be a contribution to mere methodology, must develop a theory of Reality. But the chief characteristic trait of the pragmatic notion of reality is precisely that no theory of Reality in general, *überhaupt*, is possible or needed. It finds that "reality" is a *denotative* term, a word used to designate indifferently everything that happens. Lies, dreams, insanities, deceptions, myths, theories are all of them just the events they specifically are. Pragmatism is content to take its stand with science; for science finds all such events to be subject-matter of description and inquiry—just like stars and fossils, mosquitos and malaria, circulation and vision. It also takes its stand with daily life, which finds that such things really have to be reckoned with as they occur interwoven in the texture of events.[14]

Here more explicitly than in our earlier examples, we find Dewey going from the proposition that there is no "Reality in general" (which is true) to the conclusion that no general theory of reality is possible (which is false). The passage cited may rightfully be claimed as itself a nuclear or germinal statement of a general theory of reality. But it is quite unnecessary to argue the point. Just as Dewey in *The Public and Its Problems* thoroughly corrected the idea that a general theory of the state and society is not necessary by developing one, so in *Experience and Nature*, which appeared some eight years after the citation above was written,[15] he explicitly developed a general "theory of nature, of the world, of the universe."

Experience and Nature thus marks another major change in Dewey's conception of philosophy, what its task is, what it may and should undertake to do. The only way of getting rid of bad metaphysics is to develop good metaphysics; the only way of getting rid of "Reality in general" is to develop a "general theory of reality." The development of a general theory of reality is not of course to be undertaken as a mere task of riddance. It is a proper and legitimate and needed enterprise on its own. Up to *Experience and Nature* Dewey was preoccupied with the general problem, or the constellation of general problems concerned with locating knowing within experience; and then he took on the still more general problem of locating experience within nature. The more general problem does not abolish or eliminate the less general: it seizes upon the characteristic traits of the latter and includes them in a wider network of meanings. The determination of the place of man within nature is not achieved by eliminating man from the scheme of things. Nor can the scheme of things, or the nature of Nature be determined—as Dewey has comprehensively pointed out—unless we include man as an integral part within that determination. It is a process, again, of working back and forth, only now on an all-inclusive scale, or within an all-inclusive field.

VII

The changes in Dewey's specific doctrines, his changes within the discriminable departments of philosophy, do not concern us here. We may therefore consider *Experience and Nature* as being representative of the final major change in Dewey's conception of the field of philosophy.

In the closing chapter of this book, Dewey redefines his general conception of philosophy as a "criticism of criticisms." In this definitional formula, the two conceptions we distinguished before—philosophy as "vision, imagination, reflection" and philosophy as "social method"—are merged. They are merged but not fused.

Philosophy as a criticism of criticisms differs from other criticisms both by virtue of its generality and of its objective or orientation. Within each specialized occupation, within the boundaries of each profession, technical criticism, competent and restricted to that field, goes on. Specialization, professionalism, even departmentalization are unavoidable and necessary for the successful maintenance and progress of a condition of human society above that of a primordial horde, and of course for such a complex culture as our own. But these necessary conditions, if allowed to develop their particularisms and segregations unchecked would bring about the destruction of culture. The socio-cultural condition—the existential state of affairs, and not some transcendental vision—creates the need for an integrative medium.

> Over-specialization and division of interests, occupations and goods create the need for a generalized medium of intercommunication, of mutual criticism through all-around translation from one separated region of experience into another. Thus philosophy as a critical organ becomes in effect a messenger, a liaison officer, making reciprocally intelligible voices speaking provincial tongues, and thereby enlarging as well as rectifying the meanings with which they are charged.[16]

Although terminologically this differs greatly from the conception of philosophy as a "general logic of experience," it is in its final intent not so very far removed from it. For, clearly, by "liaison officer" Dewey does not mean a Western Union boy. And, equally clearly, by a generalized medium of intercommunication he does not mean a "language" into which all statements of the particular voices can be translated so that by learning this language every one can learn what every one else has said (in so far as their sayings have been translated of course). Dewey's generalized medium is one in which the meanings are enlarged and rectified. Sheer translation does not do this—or if it does then it is bad translation. But to enlarge and rectify is precisely what philosophy is to do—the good of it. Philosophy, as a critical organ, is not critically diaphanous.

From the passage cited one might be tempted to conclude that the process of bringing meanings together from different fields is the whole of philosophic activity. Undoubtedly, the *origination* of the "generalized medium" must be conceived in some such way. However, because philosophy, from its inception, has not been a stranger to the ways of men—something from on high, separate and alone—it has, in the course of its history, been able to acquire a mind of its own. This mind—the complex of ideas and meanings we call philosophic—is, I think, the "generalized medium" whereof Dewey speaks. For to function as such a medium, or perhaps better said, to *be* such a medium, has been and is, according to Dewey, the rôle of philosophy in the history of civilization.

But to *be* a medium, and consciously and systematically to function as a *critical* medium of *intercommunication* are not quite the same thing. The difference is all-important. Philosophy has at various times been set up as a separate and peculiar science, *sui generis*—the holder of the keys to the universe. This, for Dewey, philosophy is not and has not ever been. The keys to the universe are not exclusively retained in any one pair of hands. They are everywhere about. What philosophy does hold is a key position within the development of socio-cultural experience. It is an intermediate between the technical sciences (natural and social) on the one hand, and on the other, the arts and technologies, including among the latter the technologies of associated living, the institutions of society, political and otherwise. An intermediate is not a go-between. An intermediate is a functional activity between two qualitatively differentiated functional activities. Philosophy, as an intermediate between the sciences and the arts, participates in both their functions, being exclusively identifiable with neither. In some phases of its work, philosophy nears the sciences: what Dewey calls the rectification of meanings: this is philosophy as "method." In other phases, it approaches the arts: the enlargement of meanings: this is philosophy as "vision." Neither can be separated from the other. It is a "double movement." And also, it is a "double movement" that does not leave philosophy unchanged. The enlargement and rectification can be effected in the socio-cultural world only as it occurs *in* as well as *through* philosophy. Just as philosophy is not a stranger to the ways of men, so non-philosophic men are not strangers to philosophy. Because of its intermediary function philosophic formulations and ideas have gone out into and penetrated all other fields. A thoroughgoing reconstruction *in* philosophy thus involves reconstruction of ideas in technically non-philosophic domains. And reconstruction of ideas in the latter often brings about and compels reconstruction in philosophy. In the historic spread, the double movement is continuously going on.

The other distinguishing characteristic of philosophy as criticism is its objective. The ultimate orientation of philosophic criticism is towards value. "Criticism is discriminating judgment, careful appraisal, and judgment is appropriately termed criticism wherever the subject-matter of discrimination concerns goods or values."[17] In fulfilling this objective, philosophy accepts "the best available knowledge of its own time and place" and uses this knowledge for the criticism of "beliefs, institutions, customs, policies."[18] If this criticism is not to be a particularistic series of unrelated objections to thises and thats—piecemeal, disconnected, directionless, uncontrolled and uncontrollable—some general concepts, which in their functional sum constitute a "general method" must be developed. In other words, a general logic of experience is necessary. Philosophy, in *Experience and Nature*, just as in *Studies in Logical Theory*, is to be this general logic. And when fully realized, philosophy will do "for social qualities and aims what the natural sciences after centuries of struggle are doing for activity in the physical realm"—*if* by "what the natural sciences are doing" we understand that functional division within the natural sciences which constitutes its theoretical part. When thus understood the comparison is exact: the theoretical division of the natural sciences is the *general logic* of activity in the physical realm and philosophy is (to become) the *general logic* of activity in the socio-cultural realm.

To understand the matter this way, does not involve destroying Dewey's fundamental doctrine concerning the inseparability of theory and practice, for the general logic of experience can be developed only through and in the course of the actual practices of experience as they concretely manifest themselves in the socio-cultural realm. However, in *Experience and Nature* there is a more explicit recognition on Dewey's part of the functional division between theory and practice as this division effects the content and conduct of philosophy itself.

What a general logic of experience looks like, and what is its interwoven relation with practice, can be seen by glancing over the range of Dewey's work. For he has not just been *arguing* that philosophy should become a general logic of experience. He has been *producing* one. This is what his works functionally sum up to, what, in their total integration, they are.

When we take Dewey's works severally, they very naturally group themselves into special (or specific) logics of the typical (or distinctive) modes of experience. Thus to mention only some of his representative works: *Human Nature and Conduct* is the special logic of the socio-ethical mode of experience; *Art as Experience* is the special logic of the esthetic mode; *A Common Faith*—of the religious; the early logical works, *The Quest for Certainty* and *Logic: The Theory of Inquiry*—comprise the special logic of the scientific mode of experience; *The Public and Its Problems, Individualism Old and New,*

Liberalism and Social Action—comprise the socio-practical or utilitarian; and here belong all the publicist writings which in their dealings with concrete socio-practical problems are tryings out, experimental testings and elaborations of the special logic of the utilitarian mode; *Democracy and Education* and the great body of work of which this is only a representative, cut across and include in various ways all the other special logics for within the school, as Dewey conceives it, all typical modes of experience and all forms of socio-practical problems are involved; the school is not a factory which has an outfit of standardized machines and dies for stamping out standardized parts and a conveyor-belt along which the standardized parts are assembled into standardized models ready for sale. The school, or the total educational institution is, for him, both the germinal and cellular structure of society: the means by which society not only reproduces itself as a socio-cultural world but also the means by which it grows. And finally, *Experience and Nature*. All modes of experience are naturally interconnected, being socio-cultural differentiations of common experience. None, therefore, of the special logics enumerated is separated and isolated from the rest. Common strands weave through them all. The interweaving of these common strands, the integration of the special logics into a comprehensive logic of experience, is the special task of this book. *Experience and Nature* is the logic of common experience considered in terms of widest and most inclusive generality. The inclusive general logic of experience is the inclusive integration of the continuities that are disclosed through man in Nature and through Nature in man.

VIII

To sum up. Fundamental to Dewey's conception is that philosophy is not outside of and above all other human pursuits, cultivating in secrecy and silence a remote, staked-off preserve of its own; philosophy is and works within the open and public domain of all human activities, one among others, differentiated by its scope and function, but in no way set apart.

The keys to the universe are not in any one pair of hands. They are everywhere about. In the history of philosophy, one bunch of keys after another has been selected and set up as *the* keys to the universe, philosophy being the sole true keeper, when not also the one and only discoverer of the keys. And then the unappeasable problem has always arisen: How on earth to get rid of the other keys. Dewey's basic conception of the philosophic task—a conception which has persisted through all his changes and deviations—is just the opposite. Here are all these bunches of keys. We cannot do without any of them. The history of thought and ever-present experience prove this. Besides, even if we could dispose of any, it would be a distinct loss: we would impoverish life by just so much. However, just as it is futile and morally unwise to try to get rid of any, so is it morally unwise and theoretically unintelligent merely to collect them and string them along on a series of "ands."

The philosophic task—in which the moral and intellectual, the "vision" and the "method," fuse—is to bring them all into functional relationship with each other.[19] This does not mean, of course, taking all the keys, melting them down and then constructing one great big key that will be the whole works—the idea that seems to prevail in most quarters. It means to reconstruct the keys so that instead of each one allegedly opening a different lock, they will naturally function to assist each other in the common enterprise. For Nature, after all, is not a set of separate locks and human beings the keysmiths. Indeed, in a very important and fundamental sense it may be said that the keys *are* the locks for they *are* Nature in so far as she constructs herself through our reconstructions.

The construction of one great big key is, in more philosophic language, the construction of a formal set or system of principles. In this sense Dewey has no system and, as far as I know, has never aimed to have one. But when we take the outline of the field of philosophic activity presented in **Studies in Logical Theory** as being of the nature of a rough sketch of a philosophic project, we can see that all of Dewey's work is the systematic fulfilling, expanding, revising, deepening, realizing of that project. All his works together comprehend a "system" but it is a system in a new sense, created in a new way. It was created by working back and forth between one field of experience and another, interweaving the threads of continuity as the creative process of reconstruction proceeded.

Dewey has not "solved" the comprehensive problem of the relation of mind to matter which is just the old terminology for his own comprehensive problem of the relation of theory to practice. But if ever this problem is "solved" the solution I venture to say will be reached only by the method so fundamentally characteristic of Dewey's life-long philosophic procedure. For his method of working—the "double movement"—seems to be the way Nature herself works. Every increment Nature gains on one side she converts into a method of work upon the other, thus accumulating as well as testing her increasingly complicated gains.

NOTES

[1] Reprinted in *Essays in Experimental Logic,* 99.

[2] Reprinted in *Essays in Experimental Logic,* 103-104.

[3] *Essays in Experimental Logic,* 83-84; *italics* in original.

[4] *Reconstruction in Philosophy,* 21.

[5] *Ibid.,* 26.

[6] *Ibid.,* 22; *italics* mine.

[7] *Ibid.,* 26.

[8] *Ibid.,* 188; Dewey's *italics.*

[9] *Ibid.,* 192.

[10] *Ibid.,* 193.

[11] *Loc. cit.,* 121.

[12] *Creative Intelligence,* 65.

[13] Perhaps it should be explicitly stated that the intellectual and socio-cultural changes mentioned in this section were only the *conditions* that occasioned the emergence of the conflict in doctrine in *Reconstruction in Philosophy.* (A full list of the *conditions* would include, of course, as supplementary conditions, the philosophical controversies between 1903 and 1920.) The *cause* of the split in doctrine is to be found in a fundamental fault (geologically speaking) which lies deep in the original formulation of instrumentalism in *Studies in Logical Theory.* The limits of this essay make it impossible to go into this matter any further.

[14] *Ibid.,* 55; *italics* in original.

[15] In 1925, to be exact.

[16] *Experience and Nature,* 2nd ed., 410.

[17] *Experience and Nature,* 398.

[18] *Ibid.,* 408.

[19] In the conception of philosophy as a "criticism of criticisms" Dewey's two general theories of knowledge (or of philosophy) are merged but not fused. The actual fusion is attained in his concept of intelligence. Unfortunately, the fusion is implicitly achieved in his writings rather than explicitly recognized and formulated. An adequate discussion of this matter would carry us far beyond the boundaries of this essay. We must content ourselves with saying that "intelligence" for Dewey is a quality of human behavior which is completely actualized when the experience of living has become an intelligently cultivated art. It is not unnatural therefore that one finds Dewey's best and profoundest exposition of his integral conception of philosophy, or the nature of intelligence, in his *Art as Experience.*

Arthur E. Murphy (essay date 1939)

SOURCE: "Dewey's Epistemology and Metaphysics," in *The Philosophy of John Dewey,* Northwestern University, 1939, pp. 195-225.

[*In the following essay, Murphy declares that Dewey's philosophical methods are unsound because they do not adopt scientific or practical methodology.*]

In harmony with Spinoza's observation that Peter's idea of Paul is likely to give us a better notion of Peter than of Paul, it will doubtless be observed that the essays in this volume reflect the preconceptions and interpretative limitations of their authors at least as much as the actual content and implications of Mr. Dewey's philosophy. The danger in such cases is that what is presented as a critical analysis will in fact amount to little more than a translation of what, from the standpoint of an opposing philosophy of questionable validity, Mr. Dewey really must have meant and ought to have said. This risk is not altogether avoidable, for one can only criticize what he takes to be confused and inadequate by reference to clarity and adequacy as he sees them. It can, however, be minimized if the critic states at the outset the standpoint from which his analysis is to be made and the interest that directs it. The reader should then be in a position to consider the interpretation offered explicitly as an hypothesis, to be tested by its success in clarifying a theory which he has, on his own account, been trying to understand.

In the account here presented of Mr. Dewey's theory of knowledge and of nature, primary importance is attached to his insistence on the interpretation and criticism of statements made in terms of their use and testable validity in the contexts in which, prior to either epistemological or metaphysical analysis, they have a discoverable use and meaning. I shall term this reference of ideas to and their testing in specific situations "contextual analysis." The name does not particularly matter, but the procedure it calls attention to does, and the name suggested will serve, I think, as well as any other. It appears to me that a contextual analysis and testing of the ideas used in philosophical discussion is the indispensable basis for any adequate theory of either knowledge or nature and that Mr. Dewey in insisting on this fact and sometimes in carrying out the analysis or criticism required, has contributed very substantially to the progress of inquiry in these fields. I propose, therefore, in the first place, to indicate what this method is and what, by its consistent use, we could reasonably expect to find out about knowledge and its place and function in the natural world.

It will be apparent, however, on further investigation, that the results he has actually reached are in many respects not consistent with the theory thus suggested. The non-philosophical inquirer who studies Dewey's theory of "inquiry" in the *Logic* or of "experience" in *Experience and Nature* will not find what, on the basis of the prospectus offered, he may well feel he had a right to expect. Instead he will discover that the context in terms of which Mr. Dewey interprets knowledge is one not appropriate to the actual procedures and claims of scientific or practical inquiry, and that his theory of nature is compromised and confused by this fact. It becomes necessary, therefore, to discriminate between those elements in the total theory which can be justified by the method recommended and those which tend to impede its satisfactory use. I believe that this discrimination can be made, that the complications and inconsistencies can then be accounted for by reference to the conditions under which Mr. Dewey's theory developed and the controversies in which it was involved, and that, finally, it can be shown that their

elimination leaves the method originally outlined more clearly and reliably usable than it has so far been.

The interpretation thus presented is not offered as an account of what Mr. Dewey really meant, or as a rival theory which might increase its prestige by disposing argumentatively of so formidable a contender for epistemological or metaphysical supremacy. I have not been able to understand Mr. Dewey's philosophy as having any single clear or unequivocal meaning, and I do not suggest that the elements I have selected for favorable attention are any more "really" or "ultimately" what the author had in mind than much else that seems inconsistent with them. And it is certainly not my purpose to "refute" Mr. Dewey. On the contrary, I have learned so much from him that any criticism made will be based, in large part at least, on what, from his own writings, I have come to believe that philosophy ought to be and can be if philosophers take pains to know what they are talking about and to test their theories by reference to situations in which they have a testable meaning. It is in the interest of that sort of philosophy that I have here tried to discriminate those factors in Mr. Dewey's own theories which are permanently useful from those which, as it seems to me, have tended to impede its development.

I

I shall first discuss Mr. Dewey's theory of knowledge since, as will be shown later, it is only in terms of it that the more puzzling features of his empirical metaphysics are to be understood. And here some examination of the use of the term "epistemology" is at once required. In a common philosophical usage "epistemology" simply means "theory of knowledge" or "philosophical analysis of the nature of knowing and the meaning and criteria of truth." In this sense, Mr. Dewey not only has an "epistemology" but gives it a quite fundamental place in his philosophy. He himself, however, has habitually reserved the word "epistemology" as the designation for a particular sort of theory of knowledge of which he disapproves. This has led to some confusion, and has in particular left him open to the specious objection that he has not been able to avoid "epistemology," since he, too, has a theory about knowledge.

The difficulty is easily resolved. There are, on Dewey's view, two main sorts of philosophical accounts of knowledge, the epistemological and the contextual. And he has said quite plainly what the essential difference between these is. For him, as he explains in the first chapter of the *Logic,* "knowledge" has no meaning independent of inquiry so that "that which satisfactorily terminates inquiry, is by definition, knowledge," while for theories of the type to which he objects "knowledge is supposed to have a meaning of its own apart from connection with and reference to inquiry. The theory of inquiry is then necessarily subordinated to this meaning as a fixed, external end. The opposition between the two views is basic."[1]

This distinction seems to me quite fundamental. Any student of the theory of knowledge is acquainted with the interminable and inconclusive controversies which arise when the disputants start with incompatible, but presumably quite evident, notions of what knowing must really be and then proceed to test the validity of all knowledge-claims by reference to or derivation from what is thus really known. If the datum in knowledge must always be other than the "real" object which is the true objective of knowing, since all knowing involves transcendence, then of course all knowing is indirect and we are "epistemological dualists." If, on the other hand, it is quite evident to us that real knowing must be a grasp of being itself as this is directly "present to the mind," then epistemological monism, according to which the real object is itself the given, is the doctrine to be accepted. Such theories are admirably suited to dialectical elaboration and defense against opponents, since the partisan of either view has only to assume the validity of his own definition of knowing in his criticism of his opponent in order to show that the theory criticized either denies the possibility of "knowledge," so defined, and thus reduces to scepticism or else, when its "real" meaning is seen, reduces to his own theory and thus reluctantly and against its will testifies to the essential truth. Since this procedure is open to each of the contestants, if he is sufficiently tenacious in his insistence on his original stipulation, the controversy is in principle endless. Its defect is that it has, as experience has shown, very little connection with what reliable knowing shows itself to be outside the limits and stipulations of the debate, and in terms of the methods by means of which, in the sciences and in practical life, grounded knowledge is distinguished from unsubstantial and unsubstantiated opinion. Hence if we are to get any light on the nature of knowing as it operates in these cases, and to provide the sort of philosophical clarification that is urgently needed of some of the notions that are involved in it, we shall have to turn our attention away from the debate and find out in the first place what such knowing is, what the claims made for it mean in use, and how they are tested in the context of their primary and reliable application. And since it is by inquiry and investigation that most reliable knowledge is acquired, it is to inquiry that we must go to find out what it is.

"Epistemology," in Dewey's usage, is a designation for theories of knowledge that neglect this essential reference.

> Theories of knowledge that constitute what are now called epistemologies have arisen because knowledge and obtaining knowledge have not been conceived in terms of the operations by which, in the continuum of experiential inquiry, stable beliefs are progressively obtained and utilized. Because they are not constructed upon the ground of operations and conceived in terms of their actual procedures and consequences, they are necessarily formed in terms of preconceptions derived from various sources, mainly cosmological in ancient and mainly psychological (directly or indirectly) in modern theory.[2]

The alternative proposed is simply, in the first instance, a reference back to the specific situations in which a difference between true and false beliefs can reliably be made out, and a careful account of what, in these situations, the meaning and validity of various truth claims is found to be. We shall only then be in a position to indulge in philosophical criticism or synthesis.

I shall follow Dewey, in this paper, in describing theories of the first type as "epistemological" and shall designate as "contextual" those that belong in the second group. I do not want to suggest, as Dewey seems at times to do, that all accounts of knowledge prior to his own have been primarily of the epistemological type. There is much careful observation and substantial wisdom in Locke's theory of knowledge, in Spinoza's, and in those of Aristotle and Aquinas, and much that the most up to date devotee of "contextualism" might with much profit learn from them. There is, however, a persistent tendency in theories of knowledge to lose touch with the situations in which knowledge-getting occurs and to substitute a dialectical elaboration of the "real" nature of knowledge for a contextual examination of the specific manner of functioning and meaning in use of the processes and claims of inquiry. In the period during which Mr. Dewey's own philosophy was developed this tendency reached an unhappy maximum in idealistic theories of "thought" and its relation to "reality" and in the great debate among the realists about the real or true object of knowledge and the essential nature of the mind's relation to it. To have insisted on the essential sterility of these theories and the need for philosophy to get into touch once more with the facts of knowledge-getting and testing was a needed contribution to the subject and one that Mr. Dewey has made in quite decisive fashion.

Stated summarily, the standpoint for a philosophical analysis of knowledge by reference to the contexts in which various knowledge-claims have meaning and testable validity in use is substantially this: (1) The philosopher has no special access to the nature of knowledge or of reality, or to the circumstances of their relation to each other. The knowledge-claims that it is his business to examine, understand, and unify so far as possible into a comprehensible whole, occur in the first instance in non-philosophical activities and are to be understood by reference to their rôle in such activities. (2) These activities are various and are concerned not with reality as such or as a whole, but with those aspects or features of the world which are relevant to the particular requirements of the activity in question. (3) A reference to the circumstances under which, in the course of such activities, truth-claims are made and tested, is essential for an understanding of their meaning. To suppose that the statements in which the results of inquiry are summed up can retain their meaning when they are used for other purposes and in other contexts than those of their primary application is quite unwarranted, and leads to confusing results, as when, for instance, the validity of common sense statements is philosophically "criticized" as though they were claims to a sort of knowledge with which, in their ordinary and reliable use, they are not at all concerned, or scientific knowledge is treated as a highly inadequate attempt to characterize reality as a whole and is thus, in its own nature, essentially defective. (4) It is, none the less, philosophically legitimate and important to discover how far what can be found out by any one method of inquiry is relevant to what, on other grounds, we have reason to believe, and especially to our beliefs about what, in the sort of world we live in, is humanly possible and desirable. If "metaphysics" were simply an inclusive and necessarily provisional estimate of the place and prospects of human experience and aspirations within the natural world, then an empirical metaphysics would be a meaningful and useful investigation.

In some aspects of his philosophy, celebrated elsewhere in this volume, Mr. Dewey has given us this sort of theory. In the theory of knowledge, however, his position is much less clear. To see its significance we had best turn directly to his latest and most comprehensive account of the nature of knowledge, in the *Logic*.

Knowledge, as already noted, is to be understood as the appropriate outcome of inquiry. What, then, is inquiry? The answer to this question does not take us, as it should, to such specific sorts of inquiry as serve in practice as our means of finding out about the "antecedent" environment or the consequences of human behavior in it. It refers us instead to a theory about the rôle of ideas as instruments to be used in so altering a present indeterminate situation that an enjoyed future experience, itself non-cognitive but worth while on its own account, will reliably ensue, through the use of procedures which have proved their instrumental value in this capacity. The ultimate objective of knowing is held in all cases to be such an existential transformation of the subject-matter of knowledge, and the only object to which ideas ultimately refer is the experienced outcome of this transformation, as this is later to be "had" or immediately experienced. This does not seem, *prima facie,* to correspond to the intent of knowing or the manner of its use and validation in many sorts of inquiry, and a closer examination will tend to confirm the suspicion that the discrepancy is a radical one. I propose to examine this discrepancy as it first enters into and complicates Dewey's theory of "inquiry," and to show how the confusions it engenders are explained by the antecedent epistemological entanglements in which his notion of the relation of ideas to experience and of cognitive inquiry to practice is involved.

"Inquiry," Mr. Dewey tell us, "is the controlled or directed transformation of an indeterminate situation into one that is so determinate in its constituent distinctions and relations as to convert the elements of the original situation into a unified whole."[3] The appropriate outcome of inquiry is a judgment "warrantably assertible" as following validly from the correct use of appropriate methods, but the objective of this judgment is simply the reconstitution of the situation in which thinking arose as response to the indeterminate or doubtful, in such wise that a final state of determinate resolution and unification is achieved.[4] Propositions about matters of fact or possible courses of action are used in the process of reaching the final judgment and resolution. But these

are neither self-determined nor self-sufficient. They are determined with reference to an intended future issue and hence are instrumental and intermediate. They are not valid in and of themselves, for their validity depends upon the consequences which ensue from acting upon them—as far as these consequences actually ensue from the operations the propositions dictate and are not accidental accretions.[5]

All thought contains a practical factor, "an activity of doing and making which reshapes antecedent existential material which sets the problem of inquiry,"[6] and since the ultimate reference of the ideas involved in this reshaping is to the reconstruction to be achieved, "The ultimate ground of every valid proposition and warranted judgment consists in some existential reconstruction ultimately effected."[7]

Mr. Dewey's development of this theory is accompanied by many illustrations of the way in which inquiry and investigation do alter antecedent situations by bringing to light facts and suggesting hypotheses relevant to the problem being investigated and are thus instrumental to finding out whatever it was that the investigator was previously in doubt about. Equally important in his exposition is the manner in which knowledge once attained is instrumental to further and non-cognitive interests, not least among them the interest in enjoying the outcome of knowing in a cleared-up situation as something worth having on its own account. Of the antecedents in preliminary analysis, hypothesis and the like, and of the consequences of knowing for many other humanly desirable ends Mr. Dewey has a great deal that is enlightening to say. But at the center of the theory there remains an ambiguity that is likely to puzzle even those most anxious to profit by its teachings. One s natural tendency is to suppose that what the ideas used and the analyses performed in the course of inquiry are instrumental to is finding out whatever it is that the particular inquirer was investigating, which might be immediate experience, or unperceived antecedent existence, or the structure of some purely hypothetical logical system, or anything else, existent or non-existent, which can in any way be investigated. And similarly we are inclined to suppose that the worth of knowledge for improving man's estate, or ushering in immediate experiences non-cognitively enjoyed, though enjoyed as the fruit of previous cognition, is essentially distinct from its worth as knowledge, as true belief about its own intended object in the sense that what it asserts to be so is so and is based on adequate evidence or arrived at by a method which leads reliably to true conclusions. Something of this sort seems to be presupposed in inquiry as ordinarily pursued. If we look for its equivalent, however, in Mr. Dewey's description of inquiry, we shall be at a loss to find it.

The most puzzling feature of this instrumental theory of knowledge is that, in the picture of inquiry it offers, knowing, in the sense in which it was understood in the preceding paragraph, seems not to occur at all. There are steps that would ordinarily be thought of as leading up to it—the "jam tomorrow" stage in which experienced events are not simply known on their own account but are used as signs, or instruments, or evidence for something else that is *to be known.* And there are steps leading away from it, the "jam yesterday" stage, at which the use of what is *already* known as a means for the attainment of some further satisfaction is stressed. But what, on the ordinary view, ought to occupy the central place between these two processes and to lend its significance to both, is just not there. It was Mr. Lovejoy, I believe, who observed that "I am about to have known" is the appropriate pragmatic equivalent for "I know." The comment, as applied to Mr. Dewey's theory, is enlightening.

It must not, of course, be supposed that this result is due to any inadvertence on Mr. Dewey's part. It means simply that if he is right, what I referred to as the "ordinary" view of knowing is in need of further analysis, and that when this is supplied the apparent reference to antecedent existence, to a cognitive validity of truth-claims essentially distinct from their efficacy in reconstructing experience, is replaced by a reference of ideas to future experience and to the means for so altering a present situation that a desired and anticipated future will reliably ensue. I am not at present concerned to deny that this is what knowledge "really" is, or that the ultimate objective of knowing may be what he takes it to be. Any decision on these points depends so largely on antecedent epistemological commitments that it is not, on the whole, a matter for fruitful discussion. It is important, however, to observe that this is not what knowing is "known as" when we take it for what it shows itself to be in physical, historical or sociological research and that the attempt to understand these activities in terms of the theory that Mr. Dewey has offered is more fruitful of epistemological controversy, in the disparaging sense in which he uses that term, than of philosophical enlightenment.

The particular issues that will serve best to illustrate the contrast between the theory of knowledge which a contextual analysis would appear to require and that to which Mr. Dewey, as a result of previous epistemological commitments, has been led, are those which concern the true or ultimate object of cognition and the relation of cognition to other and·non-cognitive modes or access to reality. It will appear, I believe, that his discussion of these issues is not intelligible until we refer it back to the idealistic and realistic philosophies in relation and opposition to which it was developed, and that while it can be controversially justified as an alternative to them, its fruits in contextual application are of questionable value.

In *The Quest for Certainty*, Mr. Dewey has insisted at length that the assumption that "the true and valid object of knowledge is that which has being prior to and independent of the operations of knowing" is unwarranted and that on the contrary, "the true object of knowledge resides in the consequences of directed action."[8] This is held to be particularly true and important in the case of the sciences, where it must be seen that "scientific conceptions are not a revelation of prior and independent reality,"[9] but that, on the contrary, "scientific men accepted the *consequences* of their experimental operations as constituting the known object,"[10] and cared nothing for an antecedent archetypal reality.

What precisely do these statements mean? In the procedure of inquiry, whether into the structure of the atom, the cause of infantile paralysis, or, if anyone is interested to investigate, the batting averages of all members of the New York Yankees baseball team in 1921, the true object of knowledge is surely just whatever it is that the inquirer wants to find out about. That antecedent being, as it existed prior to the operations of inquiry, can in this sense be a true and legitimate object of knowledge and even an archetype in so far as knowledge of it must conform to what it was, if it is to be the truth about it, seems not really doubtful. It is of course true that antecedent existence is not *the* true and valid object of knowledge, the only or exclusive one. On this point we should be inclined to say, if we came at the matter directly, that the question as to *the* true object of knowledge is a puerile one, since anything whatever can be *an* object of knowledge if there is any humanly possible way of finding out about it and if anyone is interested in finding out, and that the attempt to set up any such object as preeminently the true or genuine article is inspired by such extraneous moral or epistemological considerations as, e.g., that it is something important or desirable to know about or that it is what we must *really* be knowing if somebody's theory of knowledge is the true one. The objects of science are any objects about which the sciences can give us reliable information; and that some scientific conceptions *are* revelations of a prior and independent reality in that, by the use of them, true and warranted statements can be made about events and objects that existed before cognitive situations ever occurred and independent of such situations, is, I should think, as sure as anything can be in this uncertain world.

The inquirer interested in understanding what scientists are talking about, how their various theories and conceptions are instrumental to finding out, in an approximate but on the whole reliable way what is going on, has gone on and is likely to go on in the world, and what sort of evidence is available for testing statements made on these matters, will get no light from a discussion of the "true" object of knowledge. And when he discovers that Mr. Dewey, in order to emphasize the experimental and operational nature of scientific concepts, is forced to assert that these conceptions do not "ultimately" refer to past events, or indeed to anything but the empirically observable consequences of acting upon them, he is likely to be more confused than enlightened.

Why should Mr. Dewey have introduced such claims into his theory of knowledge? The answer is to be found not in the nature of scientific procedure but in that of Mr. Dewey's antecedent quarrel with a "spectator theory of knowledge." He defined the issue quite clearly in his *Essays in Experimental Logic*.

> The new realism finds that it [thinking] is instrumental simply to knowledge of objects. From this it infers

(with perfect correctness and inevitableness) that thinking (including all the operations of discovery and testing as they might be set forth in an inductive logic) is a mere psychological preliminary, utterly irrelevant to any conclusions regarding the nature of objects known. The thesis of the essays is that thinking is instrumental to a control of the environment, a control effected through acts which would not be undertaken without the prior resolution of a complex situation into assured elements and an accompanying projection of possibilities—without, that is to say, thinking.[11]

Whether or not this characterization of the new realist's position is adequate is not here important. The essential fact is that when thinking is held to be instrumental to a knowledge of "reality" this "reality" is thought of by Dewey as something that is supposed to be known antecedently to and independently of the processes by means of which scientific investigation takes place. The "spectator" theory of knowledge thus stands in his mind for the view that we can know things by passively contemplating them or accepting preconceived ideas about them as adequate bases for conclusions as to their essential natures. It follows of course that scientific method, with its experimental manipulation of given data and constant modification of antecedently accepted ideas, is out of harmony with any such theory of knowledge. If this be knowledge of antecedent being, then neither scientific method nor experimental logic gives such knowledge.

It is clear, I think, that if we want to understand Mr. Dewey's puzzling denial of what seems, on the face of it, the obvious import of some reliably tested knowledge-claims, we must think of him as referring to theories of this sort. His statements are simply not comprehensible apart from such reference. That is why, after burying the spectator theory of knowledge in one volume after another, he has been obliged to dig it up again in subsequent works to justify by contrast his own insistence that *the* true object of knowledge is not only got at by experimental methods but simply *is* the observable outcome of such experimental procedures. But while this is intelligible, in terms of the controversy in question, it is not at all helpful as a characterization of the actual aims of experimental science, where it is not simply what will happen when an experiment is performed that is in question, but also what evidence this supplies about the nature and behavior of other objects which may themselves be beyond the range of observation but can be known about by means of experimental evidence. Mr. Dewey evidently does not mean to deny that in some sense we have such knowledge, but he does insist on stating the nature and aims of knowing in such fashion as to make any clear analysis of it impossible. And this is done because a straightforward statement suggests to him, though it does not by any means imply, an epistemological theory which he is extremely anxious to avoid. The epistemological controversy has thus impeded and confused the contextual analysis that was wanted.

A related matter on which Mr. Dewey finds it very important to insist is the falsity of the assumption "that knowledge has a uniquely privileged position as a mode of access to reality in comparison with other modes of experience."[12] Actually, things can be "had" in immediate experience, as well as known, and in such "having" "we experience things as they really are apart from knowing" while knowing is that *special* mode of experiencing things "which facilitates control of objects for purposes of non-cognitive experiences."[13] Cognition thus is not, as philosophers have in the past assumed, "the measure of the reality found in other modes of experience," and an insistence on this fact is held to be of great significance.

The difficulty one finds in understanding these passages, and many others like them in Dewey, is that knowledge or cognition appears to be used in them in two different but not adequately distinguished senses. Referred to ordinary operations of investigation, knowledge consists of true statements or beliefs arrived at by a reliable method. The cognitive interest is that in the acquisition and adequate testing of such beliefs; and nothing can be directly relevant to the cognitive goodness of a belief or the satisfaction of the interest in knowing except that which tends to confirm or confute the belief in question by serving as evidence of the nature of its object.

It is only because some connection with this meaning for knowledge and the tests of its validity is carried over into Mr. Dewey's discussion that it retains its appearance of pertinence to inquiry in the sciences and practical affairs. But at the same time this is not what Mr. Dewey himself, in his specific epistemological analyses, takes knowing to be. Instead, as we have already seen, he regards it as a use of ideas as signs of possible future experiences and means for effecting the transition to such experiences in a satisfactory manner. These future experiences, in so far as they terminate inquiry, will not be cases of "knowing," i.e., of the use of given experiences as signs of something else. Hence what justifies cognition is not anything in the same sense "known" at all, but the occurrence of a non-cognitive satisfaction, and the goodness of cognition in its own primary aim or intent, is determined by its use in bringing about such experiences.

Each of these accounts is intelligible enough in itself, but when we try to apply to non-philosophical inquiry the results reached on the epistemological level, confusions arise which have always surrounded the "instrumental" theory of knowledge. Are we actually to suppose that the validity of ordinary truth-claims as true is to be determined by something else than what we can find out as to the nature of their objects, or that we are to regard as evidence of their truth the fact they are instrumental to non-cognitive satisfactions? And does the claim that we have non-cognitive access to "reality" mean that we have any way of finding out what really exists or is the case, that is not, just in so far as it *is* a way of finding out, a way of knowing or of cognition? Of course we are related to our environment in many other ways than framing and testing beliefs about it. We "grasp reality" in seeing and handling perceptual objects, in enjoying good health and in doing all manner of things that are not knowing, and may be more satisfactory than knowing. But if the question arises as to what, in any of these ways of experiencing or behaving we *find out* about "reality," the only possible answer is a "cognitive" one, namely, in the first place a statement of what these experiences are, what, other than themselves they are evidence for and how they are relevant to the rest of what, in our various relations with it, we find the world to be. If "practice" reveals the nature of "reality" in any significant sense, it is surely because we find out something through our practical relations with things that we should not otherwise have known. And similarly, if, as Dewey maintains, we experience things as they really are apart from knowing, this is itself something that can be known, where "knowing" is not a reference to some future experience later to be noncognitively enjoyed as a result of present intellectual operations, but a true belief, tested by inspection of the very experiences in question, as to what these experiences are. Mr. Dewey himself makes many statements about immediate experience that he evidently regards as verifiably true in this sense.

In all this, however, we are putting "cognition" in a context other than that to which his own analysis refers. If cognizing is only what, for epistemological purposes, he takes it to be, then there *are* ways of finding out about objects, e.g., observing our own immediate experiences and making a true report of them, which are not "cognitive," since they are not ways of using the experiences in question as signs of future experiences. We then have "access to reality" which is not "cognitive" but nevertheless is a source of information about its intended object. And we have a goodness of ideas in the instrumental sense which bears no clear relation to their goodness as evidence for or information about the objects of which they purport to supply knowledge, but which nevertheless is somehow intended as an equivalent for truth in the more usual sense.

The controversy about pragmatism or instrumentalism has always been a particularly unrewarding one, in which neither party seemed at all able to understand what the other was saying, and any criticism offered from a nonpragmatic standpoint was rejected by the pragmatists as a misrepresentation. It is not my purpose to revive that controversy. What I want to point out is that its inconclusiveness and the misunderstandings on both sides were due to the fact that what Mr. Dewey says about cognition is true of it as he defines it, and false of it as more ordinarily understood, and that the attempt to interpret what he has to say in terms of the ordinary use of the term "truth" leads only to ambiguity. The truth-relation on his view is that of an idea to a future experience, when the idea is intended to suggest a way of behaving that will lead the thinker, if he acts upon it, to enjoy that future experience, and the goodness of an idea in that connection *is* its capacity to serve reliably for the purpose intended. The question of its truth in any other sense does not arise, and it is the essence of this extremely ingenious theory to see to it that it shall not arise. Once admitted into Mr. Dewey's epistemological universe of

discourse, the critic will find himself quite unable to make the objection he had intended. It will be quite impossible to "know" immediate experience as it is in its own qualitative being, since to know anything is not to attend to it on its own account, but to use it as a sign of something else. Yet immediate experience will provide "access to reality," indeed, our only first-hand approach to it. Hence the claims of non-cognitive experience to epistemological primacy. And when ideas are used cognitively their intent as cognitive, as instruments for the resolution of an indeterminate situation, will be to eventuate and find their justification in something not in the same sense known at all. The subtlety with which this theory has been developed is of the highest order.

The crucial question is, however, for what was it devised, and for what is it useful? As an analysis of the interest and criteria of knowing in non-philosophical research it is not really helpful, for the terms in which it is stated and the assumptions on which it is based are not comprehensible except in relation to epistemological controversies on a quite different level, and when applied directly to the ordinary business of truth-seeking, result in endless misunderstanding. But if one recalls the idealism out of which Dewey's theory developed, the situation is altered. The limitation that Mr. Dewey puts on "cognition" and his insistence that it is to be justified by its furtherance of interests and satisfactions not in the same sense cognitive are the direct result of his rejection of his idealistic antecedents, and find their explanation in their relation to it.

In objective idealism "thought" had long since been divorced from the ordinary business of acquiring information. For reasons with which every student of epistemology will be familiar, thought had come to be regarded as a kind of construction, having its point of departure in immediate experience but transcending such experience in its search for an object that would fully satisfy thought's own demand for completeness and consistency. The cognitive interest was just this interest in systematic completeness and coherence, and proofs were not lacking that "Reality" must correspond to our ideas, satisfy the demands of thought, and the like.

The pragmatic revolt against this idealism was a thoroughly salutary one. Thinking, we were told, was to have its test not simply in meeting its own demands for consistency, but in meeting the demands of the situations in which it arose. This reference to "actual situations," which the ***Studies in Logical Theory*** brought to the center of philosophical discussion, was intended to correct the arbitrariness and isolation of a "thought" "absolute and self-inclosed" and to place the tests of thinking in its capacity to serve other ends than its own. That "cognition," in the sense *in which the idealists had understood it,* is "mediate" essentially and finds its justification in its relation to specific situations, is surely true. But that what justifies cognition is its relation to the objects, or facts, or events or whatever else, by its means, we can find out about was not, for Dewey, a live alternative. He was still too much of an idealist to refer directly from thought to its object. The reference was instead to immediate experience, to "practice" and, in general, to the satisfaction of other interests than knowing. The result was that, in denying the right of "thought" to lay down its own laws as to what "reality" must be and insisting on its essential responsibility to something beyond mere thinking, he was impelled to maintain the essential dependence of "cognition" for its validity on its capacity to satisfy "non-cognitive" demands. Such is the primary basis of "instrumentalism."

A position arrived at as a modification of idealism proved further useful in eliminating all reference to "antecedent," "trans-empirical," and otherwise undesirable objects on which the realists were by this time insisting. In the reflective situation as Dewey defines it no such reference occurs, for the only object an idea can be about is that empirically attainable future to which it serves as a guide. As a means of avoiding questions which, given this definition of knowledge, it would be difficult to answer, it is a model of its kind. But that kind is precisely the kind called by Mr. Dewey "epistemology," the kind that stipulates on grounds (mainly psychological in modern philosophy) what knowing is to be, and acknowledges only those operations which can be fitted into its pattern: the preliminary operation in which data are manipulated for use as evidence and the consequent operation in which the results of knowledge are used for the benefit of man's estate, but not the central and primary operation which is the finding out, on the basis of evidence, of those reliably ascertainable conclusions which can be used in a subsequent practical reconstruction because, on their own account, they constitute knowledge of the "situation" to which they refer.

We have now to assess the consequences of this view for an understanding of "knowledge," and an adequate theory of its nature. These will have to be judged on two levels. So far as the epistemological controversy is concerned, the theory is a formidable one. Once inside the "reflective situation" as Dewey describes it, there is no escape from his conclusions, and there are persuasive considerations that recommend such an analysis as opposed to those of its rivals. It is "empirical," "practical," even "operational" and these are all terms of praise in the marketplace of current discussion. The view can be "refuted," of course, as it has been many times, but the refutations proceed from assumptions about knowledge which have their own difficulties and whose results are in many respects out of harmony with facts to which Mr. Dewey and his followers can legitimately refer for support.

When the test is made, however, by reference to the measure in which the theory enables us to understand better and test more justly the knowledge-claims that are made in the course of non-epistemological inquiries, the result is a less favorable one. This does not mean that Mr. Dewey has not made valuable contributions to the subject. No one, certainly, has been at more pains to draw from the procedures of experimental science material illustrative of the thesis he is defending, or to insist that the test of any such theory must be found in its application

to the actual subject. This interest in application, and in experimental procedures gives Mr. Dewey's *Logic* a solid content which more orthodox treatises on the subject rarely possess. He has shown us the environment, physical, biological, and social, in which such inquiry has to operate, and thus provided useful and philosophically relevant information about it. There are very few epistemological theories in the current crop of which as much can be said.

The difficulties that persist in any consistent attempt to apply his theory in contextual analysis or criticism of knowledge, however, are two. The first is an inescapable vagueness, a tendency to see all around the specific object, but never to focus clearly on the object itself. The suggestion that this is the effect of Mr. Dewey's manner of expressing himself is quite misguided. On the contrary, he has said just what, in terms of his epistemology, he *ought* to say, with great skill. The point rather is that his theory focuses attention exclusively on the antecedents and consequences of knowing. Hence when we try to fix our gaze on the object, logical, scientific, or qualitative, as itself an object of knowledge, what at a distance seemed substantial enough becomes diffused and spreads out over its immediate neighborhood. And when we insist on locating it more exactly, we are met by statements not about *it* at all, or our means of finding out about it, but rather about the inaccessibility of an "antecedent" or archetypal reality, the futility of "self-enclosed" thought, and the value of thinking as a means of enriching the life of men. It then becomes apparent that the theory is afflicted with epistemological strabismus, that one eye has been fixed all the time on the defects of opposing theories, and that the specific nature of cognitive inquiry has, in consequence, been blurred.

The second difficulty in application arises not in understanding the various knowledge-claims made but in estimating their validity. Since all thinking is "practical," according to Dewey, and all is justified by the reconstitution of experience it is instrumental in achieving, we should expect to judge of the "worth" of thinking by its results. But here it is important to distinguish between the goodness of knowing for its own primary objective *as knowing* and its goodness as a means to other ends. It is, again, of the essence of Dewey's theory that it prevents us from making this distinction in any clear way. Intellectual inquiry is practical in that it involves making choices, manipulating materials, testing hypotheses, and so far as the inquiry is successful, changing the situation in which the investigator is doubtful into one in which his mind is at rest on the point at issue. Hence "the conduct of scientific inquiry, whether physical or mathematical, is a mode of *practice*; the working scientist is a practitioner above all else, and is constantly engaged in making practical judgments: decisions as to what to do and what means to employ in doing it."[14]

Yet it is quite evident that the outcome of all this "practice" may be a well grounded theory which is not "practical" in the sense that it has the least use in or relevance for any further ends, and, in particular, for those that are socially significant or regarded by wise and good men as of primary importance. Whether all knowledge that a man with a social conscience ought to permit himself to pursue must be in this *further* sense "practical" is a genuine moral question, but it is not the same at all as the question whether the "practice" involved in his inquiry itself has justified, i.e., verified or given grounds for believing in the truth of, the hypothesis with which he was working. There is, then, a practice intrinsic to knowledge-getting, and a "practice" to which it may or may not be relevant, and which is of much moment for its moral or social worth but need be of none at all—unless the hypothesis happened to be about social uses and worth—in testing its truth.

This distinction is, in our own time, of some importance. For earnest men in a hurry are likely to be impatient of inquiries whose relevance to their own socially reconstructive aims is not apparent. If they are encouraged to confuse the practical value of such inquiries for the ends which they take to be of primary importance, with their cognitive validity, they will inevitably judge them unfairly and make utility for the furtherance of their preferred interests the final measure of what is actually true about the world.

That Mr. Dewey himself intends to subordinate scientific method to more immediate social interests is not even plausible enough as a suggestion to make its denial important. No one in this generation has done more than he to celebrate the value of scientific thinking or to discredit attempts to subordinate the pursuit of truth by its means to ulterior interests. But that is precisely because he believes that scientific method is "practical" in the social and moral sense as well. When he comes to deal with intellectual inquiries of whose relevance to the interests he regards as important he is less convinced, his position is a more dubious one. In a recent contribution to the *International Encyclopedia of Unified Science,* he has drawn a sharp line between those types of inquiry that manifest a scientific attitude and are therefore, in his view, to be approved, and those that do not. And one of the bases for distinguishing a scientific from an unscientific attitude is stated as follows:

> Above all, it [the scientific attitude] is the attitude which is rooted in the problems that are set and questions that are raised by the conditions of actuality. The unscientific attitude is that which shuns such problems, which runs away from them, or covers them up instead of facing them. And experience shows that this evasion is the counterpart of concern with artificial problems and alleged ready-made solutions. For all problems are artificial which do not grow, even if indirectly, out of the conditions under which life, including associated living, is carried on.[15]

Now, even artificial problems have presumably grown somehow, since some people are concerned with them, and if the conditions of living are not accountable for

them, this must be because "living" is here used in a eulogistic sense, to refer to such conditions as Mr. Dewey thinks are important. Either all problems whatever arise in conditions of life and actuality since they do actually arise in the life history of human beings, or else "life" and "actuality" stand for the conditions in which *important* problems arise, or those we *ought* to take account of. And when we recall that it was the cognitive goodness of scientific method that was in question here, as opposed e.g. to that of the sort of metaphysics and compensatory religious belief of which Mr. Dewey disapproves, we can see how fatally easy it is to make relevance to conditions felt to be important a primary criterion of the goodness of knowledge as knowledge.

With Mr. Dewey's valuations on this subject I have no quarrel. But with his tendency to make such valuation the test of what is valid as knowledge, I have. The essential fact is that where the distinction between the value of an idea as a means for discovering the truth has been confused with its value as a means for subserving interests felt on other grounds to be important, there is simply no basis left for an independent estimate of truth as such. Mr. Dewey's theory, however liberal its intentions, does involve this confusion and does therefore in practice leave all claims to knowledge at the mercy of ulterior preconceptions about what is "actual," "living," or "socially significant." The theory would be sounder and more useful with this epistemological confusion eliminated.

II

The term "metaphysics," like "epistemology," has often in recent years been used in a derogatory sense. But on this point Dewey does not as a rule adopt the current fashion. In *Experience and Nature*, he takes metaphysics as "a statement of the generic traits manifested by existences of all kinds without regard to their differentiation into physical and mental,"[16] and maintains that an adequate metaphysic can supply a ground-map of the province of criticism. To note, for example, that contingency is a pervasive trait of natural events, and to bring this fact into connection with concrete situations of life, is to provide a metaphysical basis for value judgments. And, in general,

> the more sure one is that the world which encompasses human life is of such and such a character (no matter what his definition), the more one is committed to try to direct the conduct of life, that of others as well as of himself, upon the basis of the character assigned to the world.[17]

The understanding of man with his wants and hopes and limited capacities as a factor in the natural world out of which the human organism has developed and with which, in even its loftiest flights, the human spirit remains essentially continuous, is then the primary task for this metaphysics, and one which, as Mr. Dewey rightly observed. would provide a sound basis for that criticism of values and meanings with which philosophy in his view is primarily concerned.

In one sense this is a very modest project. "This is the extent and method of my metaphysics: the large and constant features of human sufferings, enjoyments, trials, failures and successes together with the institutions of art, science, technology, politics and religion which mark them, communicate genuine features of the world within which man lives."[18] No more "transcendent" reality than the world of natural events is referred to, and the situation of human experience within nature provides the limited but reliable basis on which this "empirical naturalism" is to be built.

In another sense, however, the task that Mr. Dewey has set himself is more arduous than that of traditional metaphysics. For he proposes to use an empirical method throughout, and this has by no means usually been the procedure in these matters. In concrete experience

> things present themselves in characteristic contexts, with different savors, colors, weights, tempos and directions. Experience as method warns us to give impartial attention to all of these diversifications. Non-empirical method sets out with the assumption that some one of these groupings of things is privileged, that it is supreme of its own right, that it furnishes a standard by which to measure the significance and real quality of everything else.[19]

This seems to me a remarkably sound and important point. The word "empirical" is perhaps not happy in this connection, but there is no need to argue over terminology. The fact, which badly needed emphasis, and which in the passage quoted admirably receives it, is that we do come at things in a variety of contexts and that while each of these reveals the "real" nature of things as thus discovered, there is no good reason to believe that any one among them provides a unique approach to "reality" as such, or a preferentially ultimate basis for metaphysics. The attempt to discover a reality thus ultimate and inclusive, to which all that in any fashion we find out about the world must be referred if we are to understand its kind and degree of "reality," whether this be "matter" or "mind," God or Nature, the Absolute or the inevitable dialectical development of history, has not proved, on the whole, an enlightening one. The "reality" discovered is always at best an aspect of the world for which it is supposed to provide the final explanation, and to attempt to unify all experience by reference to or derivation from this metaphysical ultimate will finally confuse our notion of the world and leave us vainly trying to connect this "reality" with what, on other and more substantial grounds we know to be the case. It is no wonder that "metaphysics," thus understood, has fallen into disrepute. Mr. Dewey's attempt to provide a basis for philosophical criticism by reference to the pervasive features of existence which are found alike in human experience and striving and in the world of events with which that striving is inevitably bound up, and to do this without recourse to metaphysical simplification of the sort he condemns as "non-empirical," is an uncommonly hopeful and promising one.

The title of his principal work on metaphysics, ***Experience and Nature***, indicates the point of departure for his theory. Its center is the human situation, as this is disclosed in the whole course of our experience of or commerce with the world. The essential fact is that "this human situation falls wholly within nature. It reflects the traits of nature, it gives indisputable evidence that in nature itself qualities and relations, individualities and uniformities, finalities and efficacies, contingencies and necessities are inextricably bound together."[20] Experience is continuous with the rest of nature in that it is both a consequence of purely natural (physical, biological and social) interactions and also a fair sample of what natural events really are. The pervasive traits of human experience are traits of nature itself and can be used in metaphysics as a guide to its character. "Man fears because he exists in a fearful, an awful world. The *world* is precarious and perilous."[21] And so, as Dewey has so frequently insisted, the indeterminate situation which elicits thought and requires reflection for its adequate resolution is as objective as any other natural situation. A change in it is brought about in a satisfactory and reliable way only when we have altered factors in the environment, not merely our feelings or beliefs about it. Thought in its dealing with the doubtful or precarious is itself a development within the natural world, and the changes it initiates are as "real" as a thunderstorm or an earthquake and as genuinely, though not as a rule as catastrophically, effective in altering the world of nature.

In academic discussion, this view has sometimes been described as "objective relativism," in order to stress the fact that the experienced world is *at once* in some of its major features dependent on and conditioned by the special relations in which sentient (and more particularly human) organisms stand to their environment *and also* a direct presentation of that environment itself, or the order of natural events, as it is under such conditions. Nature is not something essentially beyond the range of perceptual inspection, having its exclusive being in characters independent of all relation to human responses to it. Far more in the natural world than we can ever experience there certainly is and must be. But unless what we experience *also* belongs to and is, under the special but entirely natural conditions of organic interaction, a sample of the nature to which we claim to refer, then our relation to this ulterior nature becomes problematic, and the conditions of interaction which are in fact our means of getting in touch with it are treated as barriers to knowledge of what it is. It is evident, I think, that if metaphysics is to unify our knowledge by stressing the connections between what we experience the world as being and what, more indirectly, we find out about its nature and behavior under conditions in which we cannot ourselves observe it, some such principle is essential. The alternative appears to be, as in fact it has proved to be, an essentially unplausible attempt to predicate of the natural world, as it exists independently of any sentient organism's response to it, the characters which it takes on, sofar as we know, only under these special conditions, or, failing this, to insist that the world as experienced and in its empirically discoverable connections is not the "real" world at all, but only an inadequate subjective counterpart of it. From that point on, the relation between experience and nature will be whatever the metaphysician chooses to take it to be; for his only real ground for supposing that there is a connection will be some remnant of those empirically discoverable interactions which his theory actually has rendered dubious but which for epistemological reasons or as a result of "animal faith" he insists on retaining. In asking philosophers to turn their attention rather to that relation between experience and nature which consists in the fact that what we experience is the outcome of natural and scientifically describable processes and that it is itself an instance and, within its contextual limits, a fair sample, of what nature is and thus a sound basis for a further exploration of it, Dewey has served his subject well and has brought the whole discussion back to a point from which a comprehensive estimate of man's place in nature might profitably proceed.

The "naturalism" of such a theory is founded partly on fact, in so far as it stresses the dependence of the "higher" or more spiritual aspects of human behavior on the physical, biological and social environment in which they are manifested, and partly on a decision that the whole of experience is to be interpreted as falling within the situation which this environment determines. No conclusive proof for such a comprehensive naturalism is possible, since demonstrations of the traditional type that "nature," whether identified with matter, or space-time, or the evolutionary process, is all that can be real, have been ruled out by the method of this empirical metaphysics. It does, however, provide a standpoint for the organization of experience as a whole in which everything on other grounds reliably verifiable finds a credible place, and in which "value" and "meanings" are freed from dubious speculative and supernatural entanglements without being robbed of any of their human validity in the process. As such many reasonable men will prefer it to any speculative alternative and will find it justified to the extent in which it gives order, proportion, and a basic and essential sanity to their total view of things. While it cannot be said that Mr. Dewey has worked out a fully satisfactory theory along these lines, he has made very notable contributions to it.

There is, nevertheless, a skeleton in the closet of this admirably planned metaphysics, which has seriously compromised its good repute and thus given aid and comfort to its speculative rivals. It consists in an unhappy discrepancy between experience as it ought to be if its place in the natural world is to be made intelligible, and experience as it must be if Dewey's epistemology is correct. In the former capacity, "experience" is the essential link between man and a world which long antedates his appearance in it. In the latter, "experience" is the terminus of all knowing, in the sense that all our cognitive claims refer ultimately to what experience will show itself to be in a "resolved" situation and to nothing else. If this latter account is true, all statements about a natural environment outside of these immediate experiences

become on analysis simply means of facilitating cognitive transitions to such enjoyed immediacies and the world which should have provided the background for our experience, and the measure of its metaphysical significance, "collapses into immediacy," and Mr. Dewey's naturalism reduces, as Mr. Santayana has said, to a "philosophy of the foreground."[22]

The difficulty does not arise from Mr. Dewey's laudable attempt to treat experience as continuous with the rest of nature. It is the result of a misinterpretation of the way in which experience functions in knowing, and its consequence is that the reference to "experience" cuts us off from, instead of connecting us with, the circumambient environment, in which experience must be placed if it is to retain its status as a natural event.

The precise nature of this difficulty can be specified by reference to the relation described in **Experience and Nature**, of scientific objects to qualited events as these are immediately experienced. The latter are held to be "ends" both for knowledge and in nature, the former are relational and "instrumental," the conceptual means we use for establishing connections between qualited events. These qualited events are taken as the type of what a natural event, in its concrete individuality, is, and it follows from this that the objects with which the physical sciences deal, representing the statistical outcome of complex processes of measurement and comparison, are not "individual existential objects" in this primary sense at all. "The procedure of physics itself, not any metaphysical or epistemological theory, discloses that physical objects cannot be individual, existential objects. In consequence, it is absurd to put them in opposition to the qualitatively individual objects of concrete experience."[23] The difference between the "world of physics" and the "world of sense" is to be explained as that between objects of thought, when thought is essentially instrumental to the satisfactory reconstruction of experienced and "qualited" situations, and objects of immediate enjoyment—the ends or termini of thinking, in their directly apprehended being.

Thus "the proper objects of science are nature in its instrumental characters"[24] and hence science "is not a final thing. The final thing is appreciation and use of things of direct experience."[25]

This seems to me to violate the primary principle of Dewey's "empirical method" as previously laid down. The objects about which the physical sciences provide abstract and schematic but nonetheless reliable information are not in their own nature "instrumental" at all. Our knowledge of them is instrumental in so far as we can use it to make life in other respects more satisfactory and in this instrumental use science is, of course, not a final thing. But to suppose that the whole meaning of what science tells us about the physical environment is reducible to this instrumental function is to treat one context in which things come to us as ultimate for metaphysics, and this is an irreparable mistake.

For we actually need scientific information *not* merely in this instrumental capacity, but as information about the causes and conditions of human experience, if our naturalism is not to lapse into a hopelessly anthropocentric view of things. Of course the things we directly experience are more "concrete" than the objects of science, since they are the only things we can get at in terms of sensuous content and emotional associations and practical uses. They owe this special status, however, precisely to the fact that we stand in special relations to them. Whatever the "individuality" of an object beyond the range of direct experience may be it will always for *us* remain abstract and relational, since all we can know about it is what can be inferred from its relations to other things. To take "concreteness" in this sense as the measure of individual reality, and abstractness as evidence of a merely "relational" or instrumental character *in nature* is to make the special conditions under which a sentient organism gets into connection with things the measure of their reality. It is the basis for every sort of panpsychism and animism, but hardly for an empirical naturalism.

Since Mr. Dewey has no leanings toward animism or other such attempts to reduce the world to the human scale, it is in a different direction that we must look if this unhappy situation is to be explained. We have not far to look. If conceptual knowing as it functions in physics is a way of finding out by such means as we can what the physical environment is, then experience is not its exclusive object. Objects that cannot be come at directly must of course be known about through such report as other things give of their nature. Experience in such investigation is not the terminus of knowing but a means to knowing about something else. And it is what is thus indirectly known that gives "experience" the meaning that Dewey wants to place on it as a natural event. It would be quite illegitimate to suppose that the reference to such objects renders what we experience "unreal," or "bifurcates" nature. Neither scientific investigation nor empirical observation and enjoyment can be the measure of any other reality than that of its own appropriate object. But it is essential to acknowledge that we know both what the world is like under the conditions of observation and enjoyment and also what, in a much more general and approximate way, the unexperienced environment is by which experience is conditioned. If we could not know this there would be no sense in calling this environment "nature" and regarding experience as our means of finding out about it. On any contextual analysis of knowing this is a feasible and straightforward interpretation.

If, however, the meaning of conceptual inquiry is defined simply as its capacity to refer to and satisfactorily initiate future experiences, experience loses this "vehicular" significance altogether and the limits of what we can enjoy or immediately "have" become the limits of the world to which we can significantly refer. And since these limits are relatively narrow ones, we are left with a reality far too limited for what, outside metaphysics and epistemology, we find the world to be. Mr. Dewey himself warned us of where such a non-contextual metaphysics would lead and the result is an impressive verification of his warning.

The attempt to establish this has necessitated a somewhat ungrateful emphasis on the defects of a theory which, as compared with its rivals, has very much to recommend it and which stands today as the most significant contribution America has made to philosophic enlightenment. It would have been possible, of course, to stress this aspect of the matter more, and to write an essay, as many have been and will be written, in praise of this philosophy. But this outcome, though more laudatory, would have been less appropriate, I think, to the actual merits of its subject. For Mr. Dewey did not compose a philosophy to be appreciated, along with other speculative and literary monuments, as an impressive specimen of man's answer to the riddle of existence. He developed rather a method for clarifying ideas and testing theories in such fashion that men, less interested in even ultimate riddles than in knowing what their statements mean and what, in relation to their own more inclusive purposes, their various activities are worth, could see more clearly and judge more sanely in these matters. In this he has placed us all greatly in his debt. This is a continuing work, and one in which there is still very much to do. We need to know how best to do it, and to decide, more definitely than was possible when Dewey's own work began, what elements in the theory presented are reliable for the purpose in hand. It is because I believe this work is profoundly worth continuing that I have tried here to suggest the line along which work can now most profitably proceed.

The conclusion "warrantably assertible" as the outcome of the preceding analysis is, I believe, the following: Mr. Dewey's epistemology is not, either in its method or results, in harmony with the philosophical procedures he has recommended or the empirical metaphysics he proposes to develop. The procedure would be more directly applicable in non-epistemological contexts and far less open to misconstruction, the metaphysics freed from a serious and quite gratuitous difficulty, if this epistemology were abandoned. In so far as Mr. Dewey's philosophy is one of the rival "positions," developed in the last generation as competing accounts of the "true" object of knowledge and the "final" meaning of truth, this conclusion amounts to the claim that that position is in a fundamental respect untenable. In so far, however, as this philosophy has been, more than any other of the period, a project for the use of philosophic analysis and criticism for the clarification of basic ideas and the coördination of the various aspects of the world as experienced and known, the conclusion offered amounts to a suggestion for its wider and more consistent application. It is the enduring worth of Mr. Dewey's philosophy in this latter aspect that lends whatever significance it may have to this discussion.

NOTES

[1] *Logic*, 8.

[2] *Ibid.*, 534-5.

[3] *Logic*, 104-5.

[4] *Ibid.,* 134.

[5] *Ibid.,* 164.

[6] *Ibid.,* 160.

[7] *Ibid.,* 489.

[8] *The Quest for Certainty,* 196.

[9] *Ibid.,* 165.

[10] *Ibid.,* 185.

[11] *Essays in Experimental Logic,* 30.

[12] *The Quest for Certainty,* 106.

[13] *Ibid.,* 98.

[14] *Logic,* 161.

[15] *International Encyclopedia of Unified Science,* Vol. I, No. I, 31.

[16] *Experience and Nature,* 412.

[17] *Ibid.,* 413-4.

[18] *Journal of Philosophy,* Vol. XXIV, 59.

[19] *Experience and Nature,* 15.

[20] *Ibid.,* 421.

[21] *Ibid.,* 42.

[22] See Santayana's review of *Experience and Nature* in the *Journal of Philosophy,* Vol. XXII, 680ff., and Dewey's reply in Vol. XXIV, 57ff.

[23] *The Quest for Certainty,* 241.

[24] *Experience and Nature,* 137.

[25] *The Quest for Certainty,* 221-2.

Stephen C. Pepper (essay date 1939)

SOURCE: "Some Questions on Dewey's Esthetics," in *The Philosophy of John Dewey,* Northwestern University, 1939, pp. 371-89.

[*In the following excerpt, Pepper examines Dewey's writings on esthetics, which he finds are often contrary to Dewey's purported allegiance to Pragmatist tenets.*]

A personal item may more quickly reveal the grounds of certain issues I sense in Dewey's esthetic writings than anything else I could offer to the same end, and will also perhaps furnish him with a more direct focus for reply than the customary impersonal and more distant modes of statement. About 1932 I came to the point in a manuscript, which I was preparing on types of esthetic theory, where I wished to give an exposition of the pragmatic esthetics. I was not aware of any well considered work on the subject, and accordingly dug the matter out for myself, taking most of the details from scattered remarks on art and esthetic experience to be found in Dewey's writings up to that time, and for the rest following what I believed to be the implications of the general pragmatic attitude in the face of relevant facts. The section I tentatively prepared, therefore, amounted to a prediction of what I thought a pragmatist of importance would write if he undertook to make a carefully considered and extended statement. Accordingly, when Dewey's **Art as Experience** came out in 1934, I turned to it with avidity to see how nearly correct my predictions had been.

I was excited to discover that all of the features I had thought important were emphasized by Dewey, together with others along the same line revealing further insights that I had not previously noticed. But I was also amazed to find Dewey saying many things which I had deliberately excluded from my tentative pragmatic account, believing them to be contrary to the spirit of pragmatism— things which an organic idealist would have said, and which I should have thought Dewey would rather have bitten his tongue than to have said, implying as they did a view he has often vigorously repudiated. In fact, Dewey said so much about the organic character of art that, when I had finished reading his book, this side of his work stood out for me more than the pragmatic. Was Dewey reverting to Hegelianism in his later years? Or had I so widely missed the character of pragmatism that I had seen only half of it, and that perhaps the lesser half?

The more I thought about the issue, the more convinced I became that I had been right in my predictions of the nature of pragmatic esthetics and that it was Dewey who had here gone astray. Accordingly, I set about myself to write what I thought a pragmatic esthetics should be. My *Aesthetic Quality,* of course, amply verifies my own predictions. But there is very little stated in *Aesthetic Quality* that is not also better stated in **Art as Experience**. The point is merely that many things are *not* stated in *Aesthetic Quality* which are said in **Art as Experience**, and which I believe should not be said by a pragmatist.

The criticisms to follow are now obvious. I shall try to show, first, that an organistic esthetics cannot be harmonized with a pragmatic esthetics. If one of these theories is unequivocally accepted, the other must be rejected. For even though the insights of the one can often be adjusted to the framework of the other, this can only be accomplished with considerable alterations or with loss of prestige to the insights in question.

I shall next try to show the presence of an almost fully developed organistic esthetics in **Art as Experience**. The presence of the pragmatic view I shall take for granted, assuming that it will be obvious enough to any reader.

I shall then point out certain unfortunate results that seem to me to arise from the mixture of the two views. Since my own solution of such a difficulty is to present the views separately (to use an old phrase, clearly and distinctly), I am virtually asking Dewey what objections he has to this solution, or why he prefers the mixture. This is a question of method which I believe reaches down into questions of fact, truth, and probability.

Finally, I shall hint that much of Dewey's polemic against Platonic and materialistic theories loses its force, unless he comes to terms with the criticisms that have preceded.

The characteristics of an organistic esthetics have, to my mind, been ably and summarily presented by Bosanquet in his *Three Lectures on Aesthetics.* The basic traits seem to be the following: First, the general organistic principle that experience is intrinsically coherent or internally related, from which it follows, that the process of elucidating or of comprehending or of adequately seeing into experience consists in making explicit out of the fragments of experience as we originally find them the implicit coherence that lies there.

Second, the value of any sort of finite or relatively fragmentary experience is proportional to the degree of coherence that has been achieved in it.

Third, the differences among values are based solely on the materials organized. So truth is an organization of judgments in experience, ethical goodness an organization of acts in experience, beauty an organization of feelings in experience. It follows that the differences among values become less and less apparent the more organized the experience. Clear-cut classifications are accordingly signs of inadequate organization, comprehension, evaluation. All of our human experience, however, is, we note empirically, fragmentary in various degrees and incomplete. No *man* is the absolute, though men in different degrees according to their achievements approach the absolute or the real structure and coherence of the world. And relatively few men achieve coherent organizations of considerable stability.

Fourth, applying these principles to the field of art and esthetic appreciation, we find that this field is defined by the feelings (primitively mere pleasures) in materials which have trends, *nisuses,* demands for other feelings to enlarge and complete them. The man of taste or the artist of genuine creative capacity follows these trends, and in so doing constructs organizations of feelings having cumulative satisfaction. The process of constructing such esthetic organization has, after Coleridge, come to be called creative imagination. The greatness of a work of art is judged by the degree of imaginative construction it contains. A good appreciative critic is accordingly of the same nature as a good artist. The only difference between the two is that the latter actually draws the materials together out of experience and exhibits their coherence, whereas the former follows the coherence achieved by the latter. Both activities are active, and in a sense creative,

because the organization achieved even by the appreciative critic is not precisely that achieved by the artist since every man or center of experience is different from every other and in the intimate organization of *his* feelings the appreciator draws upon *his* experience which is not precisely that of the artist. However, the firmer the organization, the greater the degree of communion or esthetic communication between artist and appreciator, since the two have come nearer to certain intrinsic structures of the world.

Fifth, just as differences among values in general are determined by differences of experience in general, so the specific practical criteria of esthetic judgments are determined by the materials of the arts. Every art in its selection of certain materials to work with determines its own detailed critical criteria. These criteria are intrinsic to the art, namely the potentialities and directions of coherent esthetic construction in those materials. The critical criteria are themselves discovered in the process of the development of the art. Hence painting cannot be judged by the criteria of literature, nor the painting of the impressionists by the criteria of the painting of the post-impressionists, though it may be fitting to say that the esthetic materials of the impressionists have less constructive potentiality than those of the post-impressionists.

The traits of an organistic esthetics, then, are: (1) coherence, (2) value as degrees of coherence, (3) differences of value as differences of cohering materials, the esthetic field being that of feelings rendered coherent, (4) creative imagination or the process of rendering feelings coherent, (5) potentialities for coherence in specific esthetic materials as the intimate criteria of value in the arts.

Now, turn to the traits of a pragmatic esthetics: First, experience is an enduring historical process with a past sloughing off, a central present, and a future coming in. For any man, his experience is embedded in an environment, which enters into his experience, and with which he is constantly interacting.

Second, there is a relational phase of experience with a web or texture-like nature, so that whatever experience one has is felt as interconnected with other experiences. The threads of these webs can be followed and their terminations to considerable degree predicted, or by means of instruments attained. But there are also frustrations, blockings, and downright novelties intrinsic to experience.

Third, there is a qualitative phase of experience, which may often be regarded as a 'fusing' or a 'funding' of certain of its relational phases resulting in an immediacy of perception of various degrees of vividness. The 'having' of a very vivid quality may be called a 'seizure.' In a broad sense (and perhaps in a final sense) the esthetic field can be identified with that of the qualitative phase of experience.

Fourth, it follows that the criteria of esthetic value are the extensity, depth, and degree of vividness of quality in experience.

Fifth, as secondary esthetic criteria, may be added those factors instrumental to the production of extensity, depth, and vividness of quality. Roughly speaking, organization is the chief instrument for increasing the extent and depth of an esthetic experience, and conflict the chief instrument for increasing vividness.

Sixth, a *physical* work of art is a continuant in the environment constructed so as to control esthetic values by acting as a stimulus to an organism whence an *esthetic* work of art is generated. This last is a qualitative experience partly contributed out of the organism and partly out of the environmental physical work of art (cf. 108-9).[1] It follows that the esthetic work of art is discontinuous, and that its quality will vary with the organism, with the amount of 'funded' experience available, and consequently with the culture or epoch. One cannot, therefore, legitimately speak of *the* value of a work of art in pragmatism as one can in organicism. A physical work of art has no absolute potentiality but only a potentiality relative to an epoch, for no man can develop beyond the limitations of his epoch. The esthetic value of a work of art, accordingly, changes with its epoch, and incidentally every epoch demands an art and a criticism of its own. The judgment of the value of a work of art should, accordingly, be distinguished from that of the esthetic value of an experience had. The latter is the genuine esthetic judgment; the former is an estimate of the potentiality of a certain continuant or set of continuants to produce the genuine esthetic judgment.

The traits of a pragmatic esthetic then are: (1) experience as historical duration, (2) relational texture of experience, (3) quality as the esthetic differentia of experience often unifying a texture of relations through 'fusing' and 'funding,' (4) extensity, depth, and vividness of quality as the basic criteria of esthetic judgment, (5) organization and conflict as secondary criteria, and (6) the work of art as an instrument for the control of esthetic values with its own (though related) criteria of evaluation.

That there are incompatibilities between these two theories must be evident from these summaries. For the moment, the question is not which is the more adequate theory (to me personally, they appear about equally adequate), but whether they are not definitely incompatible.

There is first a fundamental difference of emphasis on the defining feature of the esthetic field. For organicism the coherence of feelings is central, while for pragmatism it is secondary and instrumental. And for pragmatism quality is central, while for organicism, though quality is not actually neglected, it is only a sort of corollary, being the very concreteness of experience which is automatically attained with greater organization. But by this very fact, the quality envisaged by the organicist is not the same as that of the pragmatist, for the organicist disparages fusion as a limitation of finiteness and a species of confusion. The organicist recognizes 'funding' as part of the synthetic process of coherence, but in so far as 'funding' exhibits itself as a fused unity of quality it is incomplete

and lacking in value. In other words, fusion, and therefore quality as the fused sense of the character of an experience, is appearance and not reality. Pragmatic quality is noticed by the organicist in finite experience and is preferable to singular and more abstract stages of experience; it is not, however, valuable in itself, but on the contrary a sign of disvalue. And for an organicist 'seizure' is little better than emotionalism. The organicist conceives *the* work of art as a complete clear whole in which every part or aspect implies every other and is implicit in it without blur or compromise or focus or fringe. That completely integrated whole is the individual thing, the character. Finite perceptions approximate it in various degrees, but in reality there is no fused quality of it. For the pragmatist, however, such a fused quality is as ultimate a reality as there is. The basis for this difference, of course, is that the organicist embeds his work of art in the absolute structure of the world, whereas the pragmatist finds the esthetic experience in historical processes as they come, and considers nothing more real or ultimate than an actually had experience.

A second major incompatibility is closely allied to the first. For the organicist there is really only one work of art, that integrated whole of feelings which has been achieved. Various finite centers enter into the work of art to the best of their abilities. If the work of art is really highly coherent, the variations of perceptions among the different perceivers only indicate men's own various limitations and failures to achieve the organization that is really there to be found. The value of the work is objectively there, the variations and incapacities to appreciate merely indicate a "weakness of the spectator" and his own lack of integration and reality.

For the pragmatist, there is no ground for belief in such a single real integrated whole, for he rejects the hypothesis of an absolute coherent structure of nature. He must therefore distinguish between immediate experiences had (the esthetic work of art), and the environmental instrument for the control of these experiences (the physical work of art). The pragmatist cannot adequately account for the facts of art without dividing the common sense 'work of art' into at least two factors. The result is a relativity of judgment about the value of a work of art. This relativity does not dissolve all objectivity of judgment, but it justifies differences of judgment in terms of inadequacy of experience and epochal changes in whole environments. For a pragmatist there is no absolute judgment of the value of a work of art, though the judgments about some works of art have a high degree of stability.

Thirdly, the organicist sees nothing in conflicts and frustrations but appearance and illusion and disvalue. For a pragmatist there is nothing more real or ultimate than a conflict had, and under certain conditions a conflict is valuable in its own right. The pragmatist notes that conflicts are actually sought after and valued in games, in comedy, in tragedy, and, if he looks carefully, even throughout all art subtly in the minutest details. He does not explain these away by suggesting that they are transcended and thereby converted into harmonious integrations in the organic wholes in which they appear. He stresses and savors them and suggests that the organization sought in works of art is mainly an organization of conflicts. For he finds conflict a principal source of the vividness of quality, and thereby esthetically valuable in its own right, and to be sought after up to that point where it cannot be endured and debouches into practical action.

These three incompatibilities are sufficient, I think, to demonstrate that one cannot consistently have organicism and pragmatism present at once in the same theory. If coherence is fundamental, then fused, had quality is not, and *vice versa.* If a work of art is a single absolute entity, then it is not a multiple relative entity, and *vice versa.* If conflict is always disvalue, then it is not sometimes a positive value, and *vice versa.* I have personally obtained esthetic insights from both of these theories, and believe for the present we ought to keep them both separately and consistently in mind; but I think a mixture of the two only blurs and damages both and adds nothing to general esthetic understanding. My criticism of Dewey's *Art as Experience* is that it contains a mixture of these two theories, and consequently results not only in many implicit contradictions and vacillations but also in mutual inhibitions such that some of the important insights of both theories are concealed.

I wish now to show by some references that a fairly complete organistic esthetics is present in *Art as Experience.* As for the pragmatic esthetics, that, as I said, can be assumed to be there, and is obvious in any ten pages of the book. The disturbing thing is that the organistic theory is equally obvious to one who is aware of what is going on, and that in large degree and at critical points, notably in Chapter XIII, the chapter specially devoted to esthetic criticism, it submerges the pragmatic view. Let us now consider Dewey's exposition of an organistic esthetics.

Let us follow *seriatim* the evidences for the five traits previously mentioned of an organistic esthetics.

(1) *Coherence.* That there is great emphasis on this principle will appear in the evidences for the other traits. It would be too much to expect of a deeply imbued pragmatist that he would ever slip into identifying reality with coherence. Had Dewey been aware that the evidences for the other traits went far towards committing him to this fundamental organistic principle, he would, I suspect, have drawn back and cleared his book of these implications.

(2) *Value as degrees of coherence.* This also is a general organistic principle which will exhibit itself so far as esthetics is concerned in the three remaining traits.

(3) *The esthetic field is that of the coherent organization of feelings.* Let us compare this with Dewey's definition of esthetic beauty.

> In case the term [beauty] is used in theory to designate the total esthetic quality of an experience,

it is surely better to deal with the experience itself and show whence and how the quality proceeds. In that case, beauty is the response to that which to reflection is the consummated movement of matter integrated through its inner relations into a single qualitative whole. (130)

Now, if Dewey had written, "Beauty is the consummated movement of feelings and their qualities integrated through their inner relations into a single individual whole," he would have given an orthodox organistic definition. What he did write is obviously far from a pragmatic definition as outlined recently. The emphasis is on integration, singleness, and wholeness, and quality comes out as the differentiating guide of the integrative process. There may be other kinds of integration, but the sort of integration that is esthetic is the sort that integrates quality. The question is how far Dewey conceived this quality in the organistic rather than the pragmatic sense. The two senses easily slip into one another but at extremes, as I have shown, they are very different. The quality of organicism (the individual, or the characteristic) is the coherent whole developed from the internal relations of the affective materials. The 'had' quality of pragmatism is the awareness of experience itself, and is not necessarily coherent, may even be indefeasibly incoherent. In Dewey's definition of beauty, which seems to me from its context to have been rather carefully considered, the meaning of 'quality' appears ambiguous. I am suggesting that it was so felt by Dewey—not, of course, with any intention to confuse, but possibly with an underlying (though I believe mistaken) intention to enrich. This same ambiguity runs through most of the book. I would even go so far as to say that the weight of significance for this and many other passages is predominantly organistic.

The definition quoted comes near the end of a chapter on "Substance and Form." Near the beginning of the chapter Dewey writes,

> The *material* out of which a work of art is composed belongs to the common world rather than to the self, and yet there is self-expression in art because the self assimilates that material in a distinctive way to reissue it into the public world in a form that builds a new object. This new object may have as its consequence similar reconstructions, re-creations, of old and common material on the part of those who perceive it, and thus in time come to be established as part of the acknowledged world—as "universal." The material expressed cannot be private; that is the state of the mad-house. But the *manner* of saying it is individual, and, if the product is to be a work of art, induplicable. Identity of mode of production defines the work of a machine, the esthetic counterpart of which is the academic. The quality of a work of *art* is *sui generis* because the manner in which general material is rendered transforms it into a substance that is fresh and vital. (107-8)

And immediately thereafter comes an approving reference to A. C. Bradley, the most consistent and illuminating organistic critic since Coleridge. The foregoing passage might very well have been written by A. C. Bradley, or F. H. Bradley, or B. Bosanquet, or any other imbued organicist. Coherence is the evaluating principle which assimilates, objectifies, universalizes material. Incoherence and privacy are "the state of the madhouse." The result of coherence embodying material is a concrete universal, to use the technical term, to be strictly contrasted with the repetitive abstract universal which develops academism, and is but another mode of incoherence. "The quality [value?] of a work of *art* is *sui generis*," a concrete universal, which is individual and common to every aspect, since every aspect is internally related with every other though a unique center in its own right.

Hence A. C. Bradley can be aptly quoted as saying: "Poetry being poems, we are to think of a poem as it actually exists; and an actual poem is a succession of experiences—sounds, images, thought—through which we pass when we read a poem. . . . A poem exists in unnumerable degrees." (108) That is, different finite individuals approximate the potential integration of the poem according to their capacities of integration in reference to the material at hand. It is true that immediately after this passage is another into which Dewey slips by imperceptible transitions and which stresses the absoluteness of pragmatic relativity as emphatically as anywhere in the whole book. But that, of course, is just my point. A passage like the preceding can grow only out of organistic modes of thought leading to the conception of *the* work of art as a "public" object of the 'common world,' as 'universal,' 'individual' and 'induplicable' because it exhibits the necessary logic of the affective materials out of which it is made. And there is no justification in such a passage for an inalienable diversity of interpretations or for the idea that "it is absurd to ask what an artist 'really' meant by his product" (108), and that "if he could be articulate, he would say 'I meant just *that* and *that* means whatever you or any one can honestly, that is in virtue of your own vital experience, get out of it" (109)—unless by "honestly, that is in virtue of your own vital experience" is meant precisely the inevitable logic of the affective materials themselves, "the inevitable self-movement of a poem" (70) which eventuates in "material completely and coherently formed" (116), *the* work of art *"sui generis."* Just what weight and direction is given to "honestly" here? Is it the pragmatic relativistic honesty of "whatever anyone can get out of it?" Or is it the absolutistic organistic honesty of "vital experience" following "the inevitable self-movement of a poem?" Throughout ***Art as Experience***, phrases are indecisive on this matter, as here in the midst of a typically pragmatic statement. But evidences for the interpretation of "honestly" in the organistic terms of "the inevitable self-movement of a poem" multiply in the passages dealing with the creative imagination.

(4) *Creative imagination.* This term owes its currency to Coleridge, who got the idea it contains from the purest early organistic sources and projected it into the literary world where, though generally half understood, it has still proved very effective. As Dewey says, "it is a *way* of seeing and feeling things as they compose an integral whole." (267) In the next paragraph,

Coleridge used the term 'esemplastic' to characterize the work of imagination in art. . . . But one may pass over his verbal mode, and find in what he says an intimation not that imagination is the power that does certain things, but that an imaginative experience is what happens when varied materials of sense quality, emotion, and meaning come together in a union that marks a new birth in the world. . . . Possibilities are embodied in works of art that are not elsewhere actualized; this *embodiment* is the best evidence that can be found of the true nature of imagination. (267-8)

The next paragraph is a quite orthodox organistic description of the processes of the creative artist:

There is a conflict artists themselves undergo that is instructive as to the nature of imaginative experience. . . . It concerns the opposition between inner and outer vision. There is a stage in which the inner vision seems much richer and finer than any outer manifestation. It has a vast, an enticing aura of implications that are lacking in the object of external vision. It seems to grasp much more than the latter conveys. Then there comes a reaction; the matter of the inner vision seems wraith-like compared with the solidity and energy of the presented scene. The object is felt to say something succinctly and forcibly that the inner vision reports vaguely, in diffuse feeling rather than organically. The artist is driven to submit himself in humility to the discipline of the objective vision. But the inner vision is not cast out. It remains as the organ by which outer vision is controlled, and it takes on structure as the latter is absorbed within it. The interaction of the two modes of vision is imagination; as imagination takes form the work of art is born. (268)

From the vague appearance to the clear reality; from the abstract and conflicting to the concrete and coherent; thesis, antithesis, synthesis; "enticing implications" becoming explicit in organic form and full "embodiment"; the internally constructive logic of the relations through which "the artist is given to submit himself in humility to the discipline of the objective vision." Is not this the very chorus voiced by Schelling, Hegel, Bradley, and Bosanquet? An "instructive" chorus, indeed, and to be well heeded, but where does it fit in or harmonize with the pragmatism of ***Experience and Nature***, of ***The Quest for Certainty***, and of the dominant message of Dewey?

Passages of this sort are not sporadic and unrepresentative. They constitute a theme that recurs with and without variations, and that is possibly (as I have suggested) the main theme of the book. It comes out most clearly and frequently in the form of the typical organistic principle that a work of art is the coherent embodiment of the esthetic implications of its materials.

(5) *Coherence of a work of art as the implications of its media.* This theme is the basis of Dewey's exposition of form, of the differences (or classification) of the arts, and of the critical esthetic judgment itself.

"Form," he says, *"may be defined as the operation of forces that carry the experience of an event, object, scene, and situation to its own integral fulfillment.* The connection of form with substance is thus inherent, not imposed from without. It marks the matter of an experience that is carried to consummation." (137) It follows that "each medium has its own efficacy and value" (227), and that "we may safely start any discussion of the varied matter of the arts with this fact of the decisive importance of the medium: with the fact that different media have different potencies and are adapted to different ends." (226) The examination of the different arts (229-244) is carried through on this principle and he concludes,

> I have been concerned with the various arts in but one respect. I have wished to indicate that, as we build bridges of stone, steel, or cement, so every medium has its own power, active and passive, outgoing and receptive, and that the basis for distinguishing the different traits of the arts is their exploitation of the energy that is characteristic of the material used as a medium. (243-4)

Moreover, "when the effect appropriate to one medium becomes too marked in the use of another medium, there is esthetic defect." (229)

The transition from this insight to the typical organistic theory of criticism is natural. Practically the whole of Chapter XIII on "Criticism and Perception" is occupied with this theory either in positive exposition or in polemic against rival theories. And this chapter as next to the last in the book comes to the reader as a sort of summary of the esthetic doctrine of the book, the last chapter being reserved for reaffirmation of the social implications. It is largely because of the location of this chapter and its strongly organistic trend, that one comes out of reading *Art as Experience* wondering if Dewey has not turned Hegelian.

After some pages of probing into the superficialities of what he calls "judicial criticism," what the orthodox organicist calls "abstract" criticism, in which "criticism is thought of as if its business were not explication of the content of an object as to substance and form, but a process of acquittal or condemnation on the basis of merits and demerits" (299), Dewey presents his constructive view of the critical judgment.

> If there are no standards for works of art and hence none for criticism (in the sense in which there are standards of measurement), there are nevertheless criteria in judgment, so that criticism does not fall in the field of mere impressionism. The discussion of form in relation to matter, of the meaning of medium in art, of the nature of the expressive object, has been an attempt on the part of the writer to discover some of these criteria. But such criteria are not rules or prescriptions. They are the result of an endeavor to find out what a work of art is as an experience. . . . Criticism is judgment. The material out of which judgment grows is the work, the object, but it is this object as it enters into the experience of the critic by interaction with his own sensitivity and his knowledge and funded store from past experiences. As to their content, therefore, judgments will vary with the concrete material that evokes them and that must sustain them if criticism is pertinent and valid. Nevertheless, judgments have a common form because they all have certain functions to perform. These functions are discrimination and unification. Judgment has to evoke a clearer consciousness of constituent parts and to discover how consistently these parts are related to form a whole. (309-10)

The last sentences of the chapter are,

> We lay hold of the full import of a work of art only as we go through in our own vital processes the processes the artist went through in producing the work. It is the critic's privilege to share in the promotion of this active process. His condemnation is that he so often arrests it. (325)

All of this with certain alterations of style might have been written by Bosanquet.

Well, what of it? If it is good doctrine, why shouldn't a pragmatist write it? What's in a label? A good deal, I think, if it is a significant label. 'Pragmatism' and 'organicism' I think are significant labels. Dewey's eclecticism in *Art as Experience* has damaged his pragmatism without adding anything we could not gather elsewhere concerning organicism. This damage is of two sorts: the pressure of organicism inhibited the full growth of a pragmatic esthetics in Dewey's hands, and the simultaneous presence of both theories produced a confused book. I will say nothing about the confusions, but let me show some of the effects of the inhibitions.

First, we have been deprived of a pragmatic theory of criticism. The germs of it are repeatedly stated—quality, fusion, seizure, realization, vivid perception, novelty, uniqueness, conflict—but they are toned down or suppressed to make way for the organistic theory. We get occasionally a few sentences that summarize the view:

> I have had occasion to speak more than once of a quality of an intense esthetic experience that is so immediate as to be ineffable and mystical. . . . All direct experience is qualitative, and qualities are what make life-experience itself directly precious. . . . A work of art may certainly convey the essence of a multitude of experiences, and sometimes in a remarkably condensed and striking way. (293)

But such "directly precious" realization or "seizure" is elsewhere derogated to the vague confusion that precedes organistic integration: "Artist and perceiver alike begin with what may be called a total seizure, an inclusive qualitative whole not yet articulated, not distinguished into members." (191) This precious vital kernel of a new esthetic and a new criticism struggles to grow in three eloquent pages (192-4), but is finally mulched under a rich layer of organicism:

The undefined pervasive quality of an experience is that which binds together all the defined elements, the objects of which we are focally aware, making them a whole. The best evidence that such is the case is our constant sense of things as belonging or not belonging, of relevancy, a sense which is immediate. (194)

Second, we are deprived of a theory, or let us say a solution, of tragedy in art. Organicism is a theory of harmony culminating in the great cosmic harmony of the absolute. Pragmatism is a theory of conflict, celebrating struggle and vigorous life in which every solution is the beginning of a new problem, in which every social ideal is an hypothesis of action, in which values thrive on conflicts. The inference almost comes of itself that vital quality will thrive on tragedy, so that artists will seek out great conflicts for the esthetic values that directly sprout from them. Conflict is not something to be overbalanced or transcended in art, but something to be brought prominently forward and emphasized. What organization is required in art (and much is, of course, required) is instrumental to realization of the very quality of experience, of its conflicts. Yet Dewey gives us the conciliatory organistic theory of tragedy: "This sense of the including whole implicit in ordinary experiences is rendered intense within the frame of a painting or poem. It, rather than any special purgation, is that which reconciles us to the events of tragedy." (194) And again,

The peculiar power of tragedy to leave us at the end with a sense of reconciliation rather than with one of horror forms the theme of one of the oldest discussions of literary art. . . . The positive fact is that a particular subject matter in being removed from its practical context has entered into a new whole as an integral part of it. In its new relationships, it acquires a new expression. (96)

There is just a hint now and then of the pragmatic view, as in the reference to

Shakespeare's employing the comic in the midst of tragedy. . . . It does more than relieve strain on the part of the spectator. It has a more intrinsic office in that it punctuates tragic quality. Any product whose quality is not of the very 'easy' sort exhibits dislocations and dissociations of what is usually connected. The distortion found in paintings serves the need of some particular rhythm. But it does more. It brings to definite perception values that are concealed in ordinary experience because of habituation. Ordinary prepossession must be broken through if the degree of energy required for an esthetic experience is to be evoked. (173)

But this point of view is never developed further.

Third, we are deprived of a pragmatic theory of ugliness (or rather of its absence) and meet instead with statements that might have come out of Schasler, Hartmann, or Rosencrantz—for instance: "The explanation of the fact that things ugly in themselves may contribute to the esthetic effect of a whole is doubtless often due to the fact that they are so used as to contribute to individualization of parts within a whole." (204) The context indicates that Dewey is identifying dullness and conflict with ugliness. Why the problem obsesses orthodox organicists is easily understood. But though Dewey avoids the obsession, he does not escape the inhibition to look into the status of the concept in pragmatic terms. Unless I am mistaken, ugliness is a pseudo-concept in pragmatic terms, and some interesting consequences follow from this discovery.

Lastly, we are deprived of an intensive investigation into the nature of quality. Here is for pragmatists a fact correlative in importance with the fact of relations. The mutuality of the two was ably exhibited in *Experience and Nature*. In the *Quest for Certainty* the nature of relations in scientific procedures was intensively studied. In *Art as Experience*, we might have expected the corresponding intensive investigation into the nature of quality. We are not, to be sure, altogether disappointed. But there is so much to be said on this topic, and so much to be found out, that the spaces given up to the processes of integration in the book are a frustration to our hopes. Who more competent to tell us about the shades and discriminations and the scope and depth of quality, its fusions and its fundings, than Dewey? We are on the point of learning some new detail, our ears are pricked up, our heads turned to attend, and instead we are given another fragment of Hegelianism.

It is not that we should regret anything that Dewey writes, for his writing always has the glow of truth in it. These Hegelian insights are as valid, I think, as any. And Dewey presents them with his own personal flavor. But these insights are not new, and Dewey has insights that are. And those of us who feel what he might have given us, if he had not been drawn aside by the fascinations of the integrated whole, wish a little that he had not noticed these fascinations. Would he perhaps yet turn his eyes aside for a while, and give us what we are waiting for? There is no one else who can do it with his authority.

The comments I have made here on Dewey's esthetics come, it is clear, under two heads: comments on what I suggest to be shortcomings in the material and comments on shortcomings in the method. I believe the shortcomings in the material arise out of those in the method. Let me therefore summarize the preceding paragraphs in the following questions:

1. Is it not true that the method is eclectic—*i.e.*, employs two incompatible theories in the presentation of the relevant facts?

2. If so, would it not have been better to have given separate expositions of the two theories?

3. And if so, does not much of the polemic against certain other theories in terms of the pragmatic and organistic theories lose its force? By what criteria does Dewey justifiably distinguish between acceptable and unacceptable theories? Why, for instance, is a coherent whole to be accepted but a recurrent form of the Platonic type to be rejected?

4. But if not so, and if it is held that esthetic facts are obvious, indubitable, certified as such, and need no theories to assist their discrimination, how account for the inconsistencies suggested?

Of the social message in *Art as Experience*, its plea to break down the separation between art and life, to realize that there is beauty in the commonest and meanest things, and on Tuesdays and Wednesdays as well as on Sundays, I have said nothing. Possibly this message is the chief intention of the book. Dewey is ever a reformer. And here as elsewhere he has shown the contemporary evil and the direction to take for eliminating it. I have commented on the book only as on something that intends to be sound and true, and have only asked how far that intention has been realized.

Nor have I tried to bring out the reasons for the greatness of the book. I am personally convinced that *Art as Experience* is one of the four or five great books on esthetics, and is a classic though but five years old. I am assuming that any one who reads the book with understanding will see that. But even the greatest books are not flawless. The most elementary student in philosophy now sees the inconsistencies of Spinoza, and, if a reply could be expected, would like to write him about them. This is such a letter to Dewey.

NOTES

[1] All references are to *Art as Experience*.

Charles E. Merriam (essay date 1940)

SOURCE: A review of *Freedom and Culture*, in *The American Political Science Review*, Vol. XXXIV, No. 2, April, 1940, pp. 339-42.

[*In the following review of Dewey's* Freedom and Culture, *Merriam concludes that Dewey has a firm grasp on the theories of political science.*]

[*Freedom and Culture*] by the Nestor of American philosophy, writing at the age of eighty, is one of the most penetrating and stimulating contributions yet made to modern political science. The theory of government is already deeply indebted to Dr. Dewey's previous contributions—*Democracy and Education* (1916), *Human Nature and Conduct* (1922), *The Public and Its Problems* (1927), *Individualism Old and New* (1930), and *Liberalism and Social Action* (1935), not to speak of many other articles and reviews and volumes covering his observations on politics for a generation. This distillation of these works is presented in brief form in the present volume on *Freedom and Culture*. Space does not permit an analysis of the important philosophical background of Dewey, or of his earlier political writings. In a later discussion, I shall deal more fully with the basic philosophy underlying Dr. Dewey's politics and estimate the trends and meaning of his very important work in political science.

The writer discusses and analyzes at the outset the confusion of the modern day regarding the nature and implications of democratic society. Many of the older forms, he points out, have been upset by unexpected economic developments which have brought confusion and uncertainty into the works of popular government and have subjected the whole plan to a basic strain. The government has found it necessary to take on broader functions and to organize these new governmental powers more effectively than before. This combination has brought about a state of affairs in which what he calls "wholesale theories" arise in opposition to one another, such as "individualism" or "socialism"—an antithesis, he maintains, not warranted by experience or analysis.

The facts that justify economic emphasis are not, in Dewey's judgment, to be taken as indicating that the economic interpretation of social relations is a complete explanation either of the present or the future. The idea of a "pre-established harmony between the existing so-called capitalistic régime and democracy is as absurd a piece of metaphysical speculation as human history has ever evolved." Marxism eliminates psychological as well as moral considerations, yet unconsciously assumes the existence and operation of factors in the constitution of human nature which must coöperate with "external" economic or "material" conditions in producing what actually happens. I do not know what Professor Sidney Hook may say after his generous attempt to prove the near Marxian quality of the distinguished Dr. Dewey. "It is ironical," Dewey continues, "that the theory which has made the most display and the greatest pretense of having a scientific foundation should be the one which has violated most systematically every principle of scientific method"; for science not merely tolerates but welcomes diversity of opinion.

Of Mr. John Strachey's assertion that Communists, in "refusal to tolerate the existence of incompatible opinions . . . are simply asserting the claim that Socialism is scientific," Dr. Dewey says: "It would be difficult, probably impossible, to find a more direct and elegantly finished denial of all the qualities that make ideas and theories either scientific or democratic than is contained in this statement. It helps to explain why literary persons have been chiefly the ones in this country who have fallen for Marxist theory, since they are the ones who, having the least amount of scientific attitude, swallow most readily the notion that 'science' is a new kind of infallibility."

Democracy needs fundamentally a new psychology of human nature, for trust in the "common man" has no significance save as an expression of belief in the intimate and vital connection of democracy and human nature. But the picture of human nature drawn by some of its nineteenth-century democratic defenders was only a sketch of existing institutions generalized as basic laws of human nature. A special type of economic organizations was made the essential condition of free and democratic institutions, he declares, and interference with its profits, a violation of the laws of human nature. Democracy, however, implies faith in the potentialities of human nature in a far broader sense than this. It involves faith in the values of tolerance and in the method of persuasion and discussion. The democratic road is a hard one to take, and backsets will continue to occur, but what is its weakness at a particular time is precisely its strength in the long course of human history.

The question of what is involved in self-governing methods is far more complex in our times than in earlier days, and for this reason the task of those who retain belief in democracy is to revive and maintain in full vigor the original conviction of the intrinsic moral nature of democracy. "We have advanced far enough to realize that democracy is a way of life. We have yet to realize that it is a way of personal life and one which provides a moral standard for personal conduct."

But if democracy is a moral problem, what then is the relation of science to democracy? It is no longer possible, Dr. Dewey maintains, to hold the simple faith of the Enlightenment that the advance of science will automatically produce free institutions by dispelling ignorance and superstition. Already the progress of natural science has been even more rapid and extensive than was imagined, but it has also produced unexpected results: in industry, creating corporations and the concentration of capital; giving to dictators new means of controlling opinion and sentiment and reducing through organized propaganda all previous agencies of despotic rulers to a mere shadow.

This leads to the old question whether science has any part to play in the formation of human ends and purposes. Liberal and progressive movements based themselves on the principle that action is determined chiefly by ideas, and neglected the importance of emotions and habits in the determination of conduct. In more recent times, the opposite has been true, and the older doctrine has been stood upside down by emphasis on the emotional and non-rational. Science is not, however, in Mr. Dewey's view, merely a body of technical conclusions. It is an attitude embodied in habitual will to employ certain methods of observation, reflection, and test rather than others. Scientific men themselves have often created confusion by disclaiming any social responsibility for scientific results or by advocacy of personal conclusions in scientific terminology and with scientific prestige. The real question is whether science has "intrinsic moral potentialities."

Historically, the position that science is devoid of moral quality has been held by theologians and their metaphysical allies. But if control of conduct amounts to conflict of desires scientifically implemented, with no possibility of the determination of desire and purpose by scientifically warranted beliefs, then the practical alternative is only competition and conflict between unintelligent forces for control of desire. To say that there are no such things as moral facts because human desires control formation and valuation of ends is in truth but to point to desires and interests as themselves moral facts requiring control by

intelligence equipped with knowledge. If, says Dr. Dewey solemnly, science is "incapable of developing moral techniques which will also determine these relations, the split in modern culture goes so deep that not only democracy but all civilized values are doomed. . . . A culture which permits science to destroy traditional values but which distrusts its power to create new ones is a culture which is destroying itself. War is a symptom as well as a cause of the inner division."

Liberty and democracy must in the end be set in a framework of culture and of human nature without which it has no enduring meaning, without which it has no power of adaptation and adjustment. The most serious threat to our democracy is not the existence of totalitarian states; it is the existence within our own personal attitude, and within our own institutions, of disordered and unintegrated conditions similar to those which have given a victory to external authority, discipline, uniformity, and dependence upon the Leader in some foreign countries. The battlefield is also accordingly here within ourselves and within our institutions. This battle Dewey asserts can be won only by extending the application of democratic methods, methods of consultation, persuasion, negotiation, communication, coöperative intelligence, all in the effort to make our politics, industry, education, and culture an evolving manifestation of democratic ideas. "An American democracy can serve the world only as it demonstrates in the conduct of its own life the efficacy of plural, partial, and experimental methods in securing and maintaining an ever-increasing release of the powers of human nature, in service of a freedom which is coöperative and a coöperation which is voluntary."

This is not an easy volume to read or to review fairly. In arrangement, it is somewhat disorganized, and the discourse is at times repetitive. Some of the paragraphs are condensed to a point where they require many readings to interpret. But it must be said that if one must search, there is much to be found. Dr. Dewey's *Freedom and Culture* is a gold mine which students of political science cannot afford to pass by. I do not know of any study which examines more sharply and intelligently the basic problem of human relations that threatens the whole civilization of the Western world. If Dr. Dewey had known more of economics, of politics, of administration, and of law, he might have written with greater sophistication and sureness in these fields, but he might have lost the broad sweep and perspective of his present view. The design of lifting the problem of democracy above economic determination, above emotional violence, above outdated psychology, tribal or industrial, and of elevating the discussion to a scientific-moral, cultural basis, is a noble and challenging one, even if not fully achieved.

Herbert W. Schneider (essay date 1970)

SOURCE: "Dewey's Psychology," in *Guide to the Works of John Dewey,* edited by Jo Ann Boydston, Southern Illinois University Press, 1970, pp. 1-14.

[In the following essay, Schneider presents an overview of Dewey's writings on the various aspects of human psychology.]

During his years as a student under George Sylvester Morris, from 1882 to 1886, John Dewey thought of psychology not as a science but as a philosophical method and "standpoint." In part, his studies in Vermont, the influence of Coleridge and the writings of the romantic idealists, and in part, the systematic version of this standpoint as it took shape in the mind of Morris led Dewey to believe that for a "critical" understanding of life-mind-nature as an organic whole, it was necessary to show the identity of psychological, logical, and ontological procedure. Morris had conceived such a "dynamic idealism" as a more adequate "experimental" method than the methods of British Empiricism, which had reduced the idealizing functions of mind to a "hard concretion in the sphere of actual particular fact."[1] The "psychological standpoint" would liberate philosophy and philosophical imagination so that it could "freely work . . . to reach certain intellectual ends."[2]

Morris, under whom Dewey did his Ph.D. research at Johns Hopkins, had worked out this standpoint during his studies in Germany under Adolf Trendelenburg and Hermann Ulrici. Trendelenburg had worked out a biological and Aristotelian reformulation of Hegel's theory of the objectification of mind. He conceived mind as constructive movement (*konstruktive Bewegung*) in the context of natural activity (*Aktivität*) conceived as the process of living, and had applied this philosophy to knowing, willing, and feeling by making the category of purpose (*Zweck*) basic for both organic and logical analysis. Ulrici had applied this general method to the interpretation of religious experience and to problems of pedagogy. Morris's version of this philosophical psychology and psychological philosophy reads as follows:

> [The method in which the British Empiricists] put all their trust, and which they style "experimental" is . . . abstract, partial, incomplete, and not commensurate with the whole nature and content of experience; requiring, therefore, to be supplemented by a larger and more liberal, but not less strictly scientific, method, which is not unknown to philosophy and which, not being arbitrarily conceived and forcibly imposed on experience but simply founded in and dictated by the recognition of experience in its whole nature, is alone entitled to be termed fully and without qualification "experimental."

> The science of knowledge has nothing to do with unknowable objects. It has no ground on which to posit their existence. It has positive ground for absolutely denying their existence, for *knowing* that they do not exist. . . . The phenomenal object is not a veil or screen effectually to shut out from us the sight of the noumenal object. Nor is the former separated from the latter by an impassable interval. On the contrary, to thought it instrumentally reveals the true object.

> In other words, that *is* which is *known*. Knowledge and being are correlative terms. When we know

therefore what is the true *object of knowledge,* we know what is the final and absolute significance of the terms *being* and *reality.*[3]

Dewey's researches as a student, culminating in his doctor's dissertation in 1884 on **"The Psychology of Kant"** and in his paper on **"Knowledge and the Relativity of Feeling"**[4] were preoccupied with a criticism of British Empiricism and of Kant's contrast between feeling and knowing. But when he went in 1884 to the University of Michigan as Instructor under Morris[5] he cooperated with his teacher in developing the more positive and philosophical aspects of this psychology, which came to be known as "dynamic idealism."

In his articles in *Mind* in 1886[6] Dewey referred to "known objects" as "objective consciousness." This use of "consciousness" was attacked at once by Shadworth Hodgson, to whom Dewey replied as best he could, but he was evidently finding it difficult to justify such language and method as empirical and experimental.

Meanwhile, in 1883, Dewey at Johns Hopkins had become acquainted with the more recent trends in experimental psychology as represented by G. Stanley Hall, and had read a paper at a meeting of the Metaphysical Club (presumably in the presence of G. Stanley Hall) on **"The New Psychology,"** later published in the *Andover Review.*[7] On this occasion he discussed "the bearings of the theory of evolution on psychology" and in general showed that he was trying to adapt his ideas and expressions to a more naturalistic biology and to shift his conception of psychology as the philosophical standpoint of "objective consciousness" to that of an experimental science.

Arrived at Michigan in 1884, Dewey devoted himself to developing the "newer" psychology in the framework of an *ethics* of dynamic idealism. A few references to the *Psychology* and to its 1891 revisions will indicate some of the attempts to bring his science up to date. His first revisions in content, for the 1889 printing, centered in an improved analysis of sensation. The more philosophical changes in his revisions for the 1891 printing reveal that the author's thinking was already moving beyond the idealistic theory of self-realization to which his ethical theory was devoted. The reader should consult the context out of which these references are taken if he wishes to get the evidence for the emergence, even in these old-fashioned pages, of doctrines which transformed his theory of mind from "idealization" to "reconstruction," and from "objectification" to "adjustment."[8]

> *Retention:* Retention is the process by which external, actually-existing material is wrought over into the activities of self, and thus rendered internal or ideal. (1887)

> *Conception:* The conception, like every other mental content, is particular in its existence. . . . It is only its meaning that is universal. . . . What is experienced is only the symbolic quality of the image. (1887)

Compare the revision in 1891:

> . . . *as to its existence,* every idea must be particular and have more or less sensuous detail. But it is not the existence that we mean by concept. The concept is the power, capacity, or function of the image or train of images to stand for some mode of mental action, and it is the mode of action which is general (p. 179).

> *Judgment:* A judgment expressed in language takes the form of a proposition. . . . [It] may either idealize a real thing, by stating its meaning, or it may, so to say, realize an idea by asserting that it is one of the universe of objects. As matter of fact, it always does both. (1887)

> *Truth:* Truth is but another name for intelligence. . . . [It is] not only harmony with all intelligences, but harmony with the universal working of one's own intelligence. (1887)

Compare the revision in 1889:

> The mind always tests the truth of any supposed fact by comparing it to the acquired system of truth . . . if there is irreconcilable conflict, one or the other must be false. . . . The worth of the criterion will evidently depend upon the degree in which the intelligence has been realized and knowledge acquired (p. 190).

> *Reasoning:* There is no such thing as purely *immediate* knowledge. Any cognition is dependent; that is, it is *because of* some other cognition (p. 192).

> *Process of Mind in Knowledge:* Fact and law cannot be regarded as anything except two ways of looking at the same content. . . . Each of these functions is an abstraction; in actual knowledge we always identify and distinguish. . . . All actual knowledge proceeds from the individual to the individual (p. 199).

> *Will:* What gives the conflict of desires its whole meaning is that it represents the man at strife with himself. He is the opposing contestants as well as the battle-field. . . . The process of choice is that process by which some one of the conflicting desires is first isolated and then identified with the self to the exclusion of others. . . . Choice is the identification with self of a certain desire (p. 314). We realize the self only by satisfying it in the infinite variety of concrete ways. . . . The self is the end, because it is the organic unity of these various aspects of self-realization (p. 319). The whole process is will (p. 328). The process of our actual life is simply that by which will gives itself definite manifestation, bodies itself forth in objective form. Just what will is, we can tell only so far as it has thus realized itself (p. 330). A man's will is himself (p. 345). Character is the will changed from a capacity into an actuality (p. 352).

The need for reconstructing his psychology more radically did not become critical until 1893 when he began to see that a new ethics as well as a new psychology was forming. In 1893 when Dewey was preparing to get out a revised edition of his 1891 *Outlines of a Critical Theory of Ethics*, in which the language of the *Psychology* had been retained, the old bottles burst, and in 1894 when he published the small *Study of Ethics: A Syllabus*, he explained that the new work was "in no sense a second edition of the previous book." It laid the foundation for his own philosophy and his own terminology.

Dewey's interest and competence in psychology continued to develop throughout his life, and all his works reflect this development. But he abandoned the writing and amending of a textbook on psychology after 1891. Several years after the American Book Company took over the printing of the book, its Editor-in-Chief wrote to Harry Ambrose, then president of the company, "Dewey's *Psychology*: A revision of this book means entirely re-writing it, and when I last wrote to Dr. Dewey on the subject he was not ready to undertake the job."[9] Once, during Dewey's years in Chicago, a friend asked him for information about a certain small college in Michigan. Dewey replied that he knew little about it except that "it is benighted enough still to be using my *Psychology* as a text."

Two radical developments in his thinking during the years 1893 to 1896 gave to Dewey's psychology a new significance and direction. One found expression in his paper presented to the Herbart Society in 1895 at Jacksonville, Illinois, on **"Interest as Related to Training of the Will"** (published in the Society's *Year Book* for 1895). The other was published as an article in *The Psychological Review* in July 1896, under the title **"The Reflex Arc Concept in Psychology."** Both essays have been reprinted several times and remain basic expositions of Dewey's contributions to psychology.

The idealistic theory of self-realization through the mediation of desires by the will, with which Dewey had struggled, was now transformed by the theory that the self is the organization of interests. The substitution of "interests" for "desires" enabled Dewey to revise his theory of motivation and emotion in terms of Darwinian biology and social psychology. Interests are not "subjective" feelings or desires, but patterns of overt activity that are objectively directed and socially interrelated. Dewey emphasized these points in his 1894 *Syllabus:* "Interest is active, projective . . . implies an object—the end, or thought, which claims attention, . . . dominates activity, . . . implies the relation . . . to *character*, . . . expresses the *identification* of the object with the subject" (p. 54).[10] The educational implications of this psychological insight for the theories of effort and discipline became obvious at once to Dewey and led directly to his own dominant interest in experimental schools and socialized schoolrooms.

His revision of the reflex-arc concept led directly to his "experimental logic." Developing the psychology which he discovered in William James's treatment of "conception," he pointed out that a response to a stimulus leads not merely to a decision that re-directs activity but also to a re-construction of the environment or the stimulating situation, which reconstruction makes a difference in future stimuli. The human art of adapting the environment to the organism as well as the organism to the environment gave Dewey the psychological analysis that he needed for a general theory of the reconstructive power of intelligence. This reconstruction takes place both in the reformation of the habits and character of an individual and also in the reform of institutions. He now had a psychology that implied a philosophy of science, of education, and of democracy. The volumes that followed rapidly—*School and Society*, *How We Think*, *Democracy and Education*—gave systematic expression to his revision of the traditional reflex-arc concept and to his revision of motivation on the basis of interests.

Dewey had worked out this new psychology with the cooperation of George H. Mead and James H. Tufts. As a result, Dewey, during his years at Michigan and Chicago, relied on his two colleagues to develop the social aspects of the psychology while he concentrated on the psychology of intelligence in the individual organism, emphasizing its implications for the theory of knowledge and the self. He continued to use the term "experience" largely in relation to personal conduct and organic action, pointing out that he did not limit the concept to *conscious* experience nor to the process of *experiencing* to the exclusion of objects-experienced. His method was to insist on "activity" or "experience" as an operation that implied the co-operation of organism and environment. The separation of the subjective and the objective factors in this activity, as if only the organism were an agent, is useful and valid only for certain technical and subsidiary operations (logical), and is false or arbitrary if interpreted as a presupposition of psychological science. For this reason Dewey became a leader in advocating "behavioral" methods in the human sciences.

The only attempt Dewey made to formulate such a behavioral psychology systematically in both its individual and social aspects was in his *Human Nature and Conduct* (1922). In the Preface he stated the theme of this volume concisely:

> The book does not purport to be a treatment of social psychology. But it seriously sets forth a belief that an understanding of habit and of different types of habit is the key to social psychology, while the operation of impulse and intelligence gives the key to individualized mental activity. But they are secondary to habit so that mind can be understood in the concrete only as a system of beliefs, desires, and purposes which are formed in the interaction of biological aptitudes with a social environment.[11]

The three parts of the work ("Habit," "Impulse," "Intelligence") were designed to shift the emphasis from the then popular preoccupation in social psychology and ethics with human nature, instincts, moral sentiments and values. Dewey regarded custom and habit as more significant environmental factors than "herd instincts" and universal "drives." Human nature, he thought, is an unorganized mass of reflexes and impulses, which are shaped by custom, habit, institutions, rather than by an order of nature. The changes in the cultural environment necessitate continual re-constructions of habits and impulses through intelligent "deliberation." In the course of such deliberation, ends, values, and ideals are also reformed.

Dewey was thus prepared to accept the growing emphasis in psychology on unconscious factors in motivation. He was especially interested in the discoveries of the physiologists concerning the important functions of the autonomic nervous system, and he discussed critically Sherrington's thesis that the central nervous system is at the service of the autonomic system. He regarded this thesis as an exaggeration, on the ground that no part of man's natural endowment determines fixed ends or values beyond conscious control. For the same reasons he was ready to accept the findings of clinical psychiatry, but rejected the "metaphysical" concepts and construction of the Freudian theory of the subconscious, which he regarded as an inheritance from Schopenhauer's romantic theory of the will. Dewey continued to believe that conflicts tended to generate conscious emotions and that intelligent analysis of the tensions could "sublimate" the emotions into effective interests.

The problem for social psychology that emerged in *Human Nature and Conduct* was that the analysis of the so-called "interaction" between human nature and cultural habits and customs made it increasingly difficult to give a precise content to the natural or inherited endowment of the organism. It became fashionable among social psychologists to read into human nature a variety of instincts ("herd," "moral," "religious," "imitative," etc.) that were clearly in part cultural acquisitions. It was necessary to make a more careful and physiological examination of the distinction between biological and cultural "inheritance." In Dewey's own interests and method, attention shifted from the analysis of will or of impulses as elements of human nature to an analysis of social behavior. From the beginning of his emphasis on "psychological method in philosophy" it was evident that for Dewey psychology was the handmaiden of ethics and logic; and the problem of "self-realization" was something he had "inherited" from the idealists. He now consciously subordinated psychology to more general methods and problems of human existence as it was exhibited in politics, art, labor, and in human relations generally; his philosophy became intimately associated with the social sciences and cultural anthropology. Accordingly, the problems of self-realization became also problems of cultural reconstruction. He summed up this situation by saying that "what passed as psychology was a branch of political doctrine,"[12] and in more detail:

> Any movement purporting to discover the psychological causes and sources of social phenomena is in fact a reverse movement, in which current social tendencies are read back into the structure of human nature; and are then used to explain the very things from which they are deduced. . . . Love of power is put forward to play the role taken

a century ago by self-interest. . . . What are called motives turn out upon critical examination to be complex attitudes patterned under cultural conditions, rather than simple elements in human nature.[13]

For this reason the further developments in Dewey's psychology will appear best where they should appear in this Guide, as aspects of broader problems and other sciences. But it may be well to extract from the other chapters a summary statement of the general features of Dewey's later psychology.

In *Experience and Nature* he presented a general historical outline to emphasize the importance of the shift from the classical to the modern concept of mind. He pointed out that in the classical tradition mind and will were regarded as objective, cosmic entities, and that even in modern times this classic tradition was kept alive by the Cartesian doctrine of "thinking substance," by Spinoza's "conatus," and by the universalization of thought and will in the romantic philosophies of Schopenhauer and Nietzsche and in the Hegelian philosophy of history and *Phänomenologie des Geistes*. In reaction to such speculation, modern scientific psychology drifted into the opposite extreme of subjectivism, taking consciousness in individuals as the essence of mind. The social scientists were tempted to adopt one or the other of these extremes: thus, the Durkheim School interpreted the mind as a collective construct, while Bergson regarded the individual *élan* as a source of creative energy. Dewey conceived his own theory of mind as taking an intermediate position between these extremes: mind, self, and personality are active centers of reconstruction and find themselves realized in intelligent reform.

In his *Logic* he made continual reference to the *process* of inquiry and to the continuity not only between stimulus and responsive inquiry (which he had been emphasizing) but also between natural relationships or "connections" (to use his technical name for them) and the *relations* as they are logically formulated by language and conceptual thought.

His political writings and especially his *Art as Experience* led Dewey to explore the less cognitive dimensions of experience. In addition to the arts of intelligence and inquiry, he analyzed the arts of expression and of "impulsion." He realized that there is an important difference between the scattered raw material of innate impulses and reflexes and urges in human nature and the "impulsion" or propulsion and adventure in the world of objects that is exhibited by sustained imagination and self-expression. These psychical processes are also social and institutional, involving the mind not only in inquiry but also in enjoyments as they are found in the arts and crafts, in politics and sports. The relation of motivation to expression, and of both to culture became an increasing psychological problem to him, especially during the years of war, depression, and revolt. In such a context, he realized how absurd it is to speak of the environment as "external world." To use his own words (taken over in part from his friend Arthur F. Bentley):

The epidermis is only in the most superficial way an indication of where an organism ends and its environment begins. There are things inside the body that are foreign to it, and there are things outside of it that belong to it *de jure,* if not *de facto.* . . . The need that is manifest in the urgent impulsions that demand completion through what the environment—and it alone—can supply, is a dynamic acknowledgment of this dependence of the self for wholeness upon its surroundings. . . . But the impulsion also meets many things on its outbound course that deflect and oppose it. In the process of converting these obstacles and neutral conditions into favoring agencies, the live creature becomes aware of the intent implicit in its impulsion. . . . The attitudes of the self are informed with meaning.[14]

Dewey developed in many new ways his central idea that the self is not to be conceived as a metaphysical agent but as an agency of responsibility. The problems of self-control over the imagination and other adventures of the mind in view of the demands made upon them by a particular "human situation" or crisis led Dewey to involve psychology and philosophy continually in "the problems of men" as these become urgent. His responsiveness to such problems and his conception of democratic self-government and responsibility induced him to make continual applications of his psychology to a great variety of cultural problems and interests. He became irritated and worried when he witnessed the fashion among philosophers of dismissing such problems as not a philosopher's business. His activities during the last decades of his life gave eloquent testimony to his own character, for to him the critical concern about such problems was a most "consummatory experience."

These interests and insights led him to co-operate gladly with his friends, especially Albert C. Barnes and Arthur Bentley, and the editors of the *New Republic,* in the critical study of international relations, of the fine arts, and of the behavioral sciences.

During the final decade of his career Dewey was preoccupied with the theory of "transactional" activity which he and Arthur Bentley expounded in joint works. Bentley tried to push Dewey into an extreme behaviorist theory of knowledge. Dewey agreed that the usual conception of the "interaction" of organism and environment failed to do justice to his theory that "activity" is a single process of which organism and environment are merely factors; and he welcomed the term "transaction" as recognizing the "partnership." But he resisted Bentley's suggestion that the concept of "experience" is too ambiguous to be useful. Dewey concluded, on the contrary, that "human experience" in the broad, popular sense that implies nobody's private experience but rather a general process of learning, is still needed in both psychology and philosophy. In this sense, Dewey was quite content to abandon the traditional emphasis on "the subject" and "subjectivity" and to encourage Bentley's pan-objectivism. But he was less willing to agree to the Neo-Positivist doctrine that things are as they are said to be. He continued to the end to think of language as communication and of communication as a kind of manipulation of things for social purposes. This way of thinking about knowledge as endless "inquiry," without ever assuming that any discovery is final, was circumstantial evidence that for John Dewey the most "consummatory experience" or enjoyment was to let things be reconstructing themselves, including his own psychology.

NOTES

[1] *Psychology* (The Early Works of John Dewey, 1882-1898, Vol. II [Carbondale: Southern Illinois University Press, 1967]), p. 175.

[2] *Early Works,* II, 175.

[3] George S. Morris, *Philosophy and Christianity* (New York: Robert Carter and Bros., 1883), pp. 28, 44-45, 70.

[4] "Knowledge and the Relativity of Feeling," in *Early Works,* I, 19-33.

[5] For an excellent account of this Michigan period in Dewey's life and development, see George Dykhuizen, "John Dewey and the University of Michigan," *Journal of the History of Ideas,* XXIII (1962), 512-44.

[6] "The Psychological Standpoint," *Early Works,* I, 122-43; "Psychology as Philosophic Method," *ibid.,* 144-67.

[7] "The New Psychology," *Early Works,* I, 48-60.

[s] See *Psychology* (Early Works, II). All revisions are tabulated in the List of Emendations in the Copy-Text, pp. lix-lxxxvi. Page references are to the *Early Works,* II.

[9] H. H. Vail, handwritten annual report (1906?), quoted by Mauck Brammer, letter of 21 May 1965.

[10] *The Study of Ethics: A Syllabus* (Ann Arbor: Register Publishing Co., 1894), p. 54.

[11] *Human Nature and Conduct* (New York: Henry Holt and Co., 1922), p. iii.

[12] *Freedom and Culture* (New York: G. P. Putnam's Sons, 1939), p. 29.

[13] *Freedom and Culture,* p. 108.

[14] *Art as Experience* (New York: Minton, Balch and Co., 1934), pp. 58-59. Dewey and Bentley had been discussing "the human epidermis" in connection with the "problem of the external world" before the publication of *Art as Experience,* but Bentley made the point emphatically in an amusing article, "The Human Skin: Philosophy's Last Line of Defense," *Philosophy of Science,* VIII (1941), 1-19.

CHECKLIST

"Knowledge and the Relativity of Feeling," in *The Early Works of John Dewey, 1882-1898,* Vol. I, pp. 19-33. Carbondale: Southern Illinois University Press, 1969.

"The New Psychology," in *Early Works,* I, 48-60.

"The Psychological Standpoint," in *Early Works,* I, 122-43.

"Psychology as Philosophic Method," in *Early Works,* I, 144-67.

Response by Shadworth Holloway Hodgson, "Illusory Psychology," in *Early Works,* I, xli-lvii.

Reply by Dewey, "Illusory Psychology," in *Early Works,* I, 168-75.

Psychology (The Early Works of John Dewey, 1882-1898, Vol. II). Carbondale: Southern Illinois University Press, 1967. cix, 366 pp.

"Speculative Psychology," [Prof. John Dewey, Feb. 23, 1887]. Class lecture notes, handwritten by C. E. Goddard, University of Michigan. 180 pp. [Michigan Historical Collections.]

"Professor [George T.] Ladd's *Elements of Physiological Psychology,*" in *Early Works,* I, 194-204. [Review.]

"Knowledge as Idealization," in *Early Works,* I, 176-93.

"Galton's Statistical Methods," in *The Early Works of John Dewey, 1882-1898,* Vol. III, pp. 43-47. Carbondale: Southern Illinois University Press, 1969. [Review of *Natural Inheritance* by Francis Galton.]

"On Some Current Conceptions of the Term 'Self'," in *Early Works,* III, 56-74.

The Study of Ethics: A Syllabus. Ann Arbor: Register Publishing Co., 1894. iv, 151 pp. [2d ed., Ann Arbor: George Wahr, 1897. 144 pp.]

"The Psychology of Infant Language," *Psychological Review,* I (Jan. 1894), 63-66.

Review of *The Psychic Factors of Civilization* by Lester Frank Ward, *Social Evolution* by Benjamin Kidd, *Civilization During the Middle Ages* by George Burton Adams, and *History of the Philosophy of History* by Robert Flint, *Psychological Review,* I (July 1894), 400-411.

"The Theory of Emotion," I. Emotional Attitudes, *Psychological Review,* I (Nov. 1894), 553-69; II. The Significance of Emotions, *ibid.,* II (Jan. 1895), 13-32.

The Psychology of Number and Its Applications to Methods of Teaching Arithmetic, with James Alexander McLellan (International Education Series, Vol. XXXIII, ed. William Torrey Harris). New York: D. Appleton and Co., 1895. xv, 309 pp.

Review by Henry Burchard Fine, *Science,* n.s. III (Jan. 1896), 134-36.

Reply by Dewey, "Psychology of Number," *Science,* n.s. III (Feb. 1896), 286-89.

Review of *Johnson's Universal Cyclopædia,* I-V, *Psychological Review,* II (Mar. 1895), 186-88.

"Interest as Related to [Training of the] Will," in *Second Supplement to the Herbart Year Book for 1895,* pp. 209-46. Bloomington, Ill.: National Herbart Society, 1896. [Rev. ed., Chicago: The Society, 1899; reprinted in C-16, pp. 260-85, with the title "Interest in Relation to Training of the Will."]

"The Reflex Arc Concept in Psychology," *Psychological Review,* III (July 1896), 357-70. [Reprinted in C-7, pp. 233-48, with the title "The Unit of Behavior."]

Review of *Studies in the Evolutionary Psychology of Feeling* by Hiram Miner Stanley, *Philosophical Review,* V (May 1896), 292-99.

Educational Psychology: Syllabus of a Course of Twelve Lecture-Studies. Chicago: University of Chicago Press, 1896. 24 pp.

"The Psychology of Effort," *Philosophical Review,* VI (Jan. 1897), 43-56.

"Some Remarks on the Psychology of Number," *Pedagogical Seminary,* V (Jan. 1898), 426-34. (Reply to: Daniel Edward Phillips, "Number and Its Application Psychologically Considered," *Pedagogical Seminary,* V [Oct. 1897], 221-81.)

"Psychology and Philosophic Method," *University [of California] Chronicle,* II (Aug. 1899), 159-79. [Reprinted separately, Berkeley: University of California Press, 1899, 23 pp.; also reprinted in C-2, pp. 242-70, with the title "'Consciousness' and Experience."]

Mental Development. [Chicago], 1900. 21 pp., mimeographed.

"Psychology and Social Practice," *Psychological Review,* VII (Mar. 1900), 105-24; *Science,* n.s. XI (Mar. 1900), 321-33. [Reprinted separately as University of Chicago Contributions to Education, No. 2. Chicago: University of Chicago Press, 1901. 42 pp.]

"Interpretation of Savage Mind," *Psychological Review,* IX (May 1902), 217-30. [Reprinted in C-7, pp. 173-87.]

Review of *Analytical Psychology* by Lightner Witmer, *School Review,* X (May 1902), 412.

"Report on the Fairhope [Alabama] Experiment in Organic Education," *Survey,* XXXII (May 1914), 199.

Human Nature and Conduct. New York: Henry Holt and Co., 1922. [Enl. ed. with Foreword, New York: Modern Library, 1930. ix, vii, 336 pp. Also, Armed Forces ed. (from original plates), 1944.]

Experience and Nature (Lectures upon the Paul Carus Foundation, First Series). Chicago, London: Open Court Publishing Co., 1925. xi, 443 pp. [2d ed., with a Preface, New York: W. W. Norton, 1929. ix, 1a-4a, 1-443 pp. 3d ed., LaSalle, Ill.: Open Court Publishing Co., 1958. xviii, 360 pp.]

"Foreword," in *Human Nature and Conduct,* pp. v-ix. New York: Modern Library, 1930.

"Marx Inverted," *New Republic,* LXX (Feb. 1932), 52. [Review of *The Emergence of Man* by Gerald Heard.]

Art as Experience. New York: Minton, Balch and Co., 1934. viii, 355 pp.

Freedom and Culture. New York: G. P. Putnam's Sons, 1939. 176 pp.

John Dewey and Arthur F. Bentley: A Philosophical Correspondence, 1932-1951, eds. Sidney Ratner and Jules Altman. New Brunswick, N.J.: Rutgers University Press, 1964. ["Means and Consequences—*How, What, and What For,*" pp. 647-54, and "Importance, Significance and Meaning," pp. 655-68, are previously unpublished articles by Dewey.]

William W. Brickman (essay date 1970)

SOURCE: "Dewey's Social and Political Commentary," in *Guide to the Works of John Dewey,* edited by Jo Ann Boydston, Southern Illinois University Press, 1970, pp. 218-56.

[*In the following essay, Brickman—a professor of Educational History and Comparative Education—defends his conclusion that Dewey's commentaries on politics and society form a cohesive and consistent whole.*]

A milestone in Dewey's intellectual development was his lecture, **"The Ethics of Democracy,"** delivered in 1888 to the Philosophical Union of the University of Michigan. To Merle Curti, this paper was evidence that Dewey possessed "a thoroughly democratic and even radical social point of view as early as 1888."[1] The philosopher argued that democracy was a broad concept which necessarily embraced not merely politics, but also the economy and industry. He combined "a criticism of quantitative individualistic theory of political democracy with a definitely moral interpretation in terms of 'liberty, equality, fraternity.'"[2] His insistence that no political democracy is possible without economic and industrial democracy was evidently derived from the thought of Henry Carter Adams, a colleague in the field of political economy, who urged "a development in economic life parallel to that which had taken place in politics, from absolutism and oligarchy to popular representation."[3] As interpreted by his daughter, Dewey's political philosophy at this stage in his career was probably not as radical as it sounded. In any event, it was alarming enough to his parents, who came to live with him during the closing years of his tenure at the University of Michigan. "While his father was hurt at his sons' recreance to the Republican party, associated in his mind with the preservation of the union, and his mother at their defection from the religious teachings of their boyhood, both were sufficiently liberal in their views and had sufficient confidence in their children to keep the family relation a close one."[4]

Externally, to be sure, Dewey maintained a posture of conformity throughout the Michigan period. He "remained the devout Congregationalist, participating in Bible institutes, teaching Bible classes, giving courses on the life of Christ, Paul's Epistles, and Church history, and attending Congregationalist conventions."[5] Yet, either his parents were highly perceptive or else the socialist ideas were penetrating his outward conformist attitude to a degree at the end of his Michigan sojourn. At any rate, Dewey absorbed the spirit of social service, which was manifesting itself in the form of a back-to-the-people movement in literature, sociology, economics, and adult education, both in the United States and abroad. Faculty and students at Michigan became involved in dreaming about and working toward a better society. Dewey, James H. Tufts, George H. Mead, and Alfred Lloyd, philosophers all, and Robert E. Park, a sociologist, "constituted the core of a 'leftist' group," rejecting New England orthodoxy and seeking "liberation in social movements and the new psychology."[6]

Particularly of significance was Dewey's association with the brothers Corydon and Franklin Ford, social reformers of the type of Henry George, Edward Bellamy, and socialists of every description. One outcome was the planning in 1892 of a monthly, "Thought News," under Dewey's editorship, with the objective of discussing political, educational, religious, and scientific issues "as parts of one moving life of man."[7] What Dewey intended to do in this publication was to demonstrate that philosophy was not simply "a matter of lunar politics," but that it had "some use." He disclaimed any notion of a social revolution but stressed instead the role of philosophic ideas "as tools to point out the meaning of phases of social life," thereby having "some life value."[8] Even though this publication was stillborn, the idea underlying it came to life years later in Dewey's political writings in the *New Republic*.

The upshot of Dewey's association with the Ford brothers was the acceleration of his assimilation of socialist thought and action. One example of this was his analysis, in an article published in January 1891, in the *International Journal of Ethics*, on the moral justification of strikes. In a basic work on ethics, *Outlines of a Critical Theory of Ethics*, published in the same year, Dewey again referred, by way of illustration, to the labor problems and summed up his definition of a moral law as "the principle of action, which, acted upon, will meet the needs of the existing situation as respects the wants, powers, and circumstances of the individuals concerned. It is no far-away abstraction, but expresses the *movement* of the ethical world."[9] He ended this discussion by stating that "the consideration of specific institutions, as the family, industrial society, civil society, the nation, etc., with their respective rights and laws, belongs rather to political philosophy than to the general theory of ethics."[10] With these words, Dewey made it clear that moral questions were not to be treated as abstruse philosophic speculation, but rather as issues to be resolved by thought processes leading to action.

It is noteworthy that, in the *Outlines*, his second work on philosophy, Dewey mentioned appreciatively Thomas Hill Green, Francis H. Bradley, Edward Caird, Samuel Alexander—Britons all—as sources of his ideas on ethics. He even was generous enough to pay tribute to Herbert Spencer and Leslie Stephen, with whom he expressed disagreement. To his inspirers Dewey gave credit for the core of his theory: "the conception of the will as the expression of ideas, and of social ideas; the notion of an objective ethical world realized in institutions which afford moral ideals, theatre and impetus to the individual; the notion of the moral life as growth in freedom, as the individual finds and conforms to the law of his social placing."[11] In addition, Dewey acknowledged his indebtedness "to my friend, Mr. Franklin Ford," for the point concerning "the treatment of the social bearings of science and art."[12] Interestingly, while he cited the works of the British thinkers, he made no reference to any of the writings by his friend.

Dewey's effort to make philosophy practical in Michigan, in the manner of the Ford brothers, did not turn out to be successful, apparently because their procedures did not suit precisely his character and temperament.[13] However, his talents and ambitions along these lines were furthered to a better degree during the decade, 1894-1904, when he served as chairman of the Department of Philosophy, Psychology, and Pedagogy at the University of Chicago. Here he taught, among others, courses on the History of Political Ethics and Contemporary Theories Regarding Ethical Relations of the Individual and Society.[14] In the field of education, one of his courses was the Evolution of the Curriculum in the Fifteenth to the Seventeenth Centuries "with reference to general social and intellectual conditions."[15] It will be seen that Dewey was stressing the socio-political content in his academic work. Moreover, his initiative in the establishment of a Laboratory School at the University of Chicago involved constant attention to social values and problems.

But Dewey, as might have been expected, was not satisfied to operate within the confines of the campus. America at the turn of the century was seething with political and social unrest related to unemployment, the Populist movement, capital-labor tensions and violence, and revolutionary ideology. Chicago, by the time Dewey arrived, had become "the center of radical thought in the United States," and Jane Addams's Hull House, founded in 1889 to help the impoverished, immigrant laborers, was "its moral spokesman."[16] At Hull House, the philosopher found a fertile field and kindred spirits to encourage him to undertake fresh ventures in the application of his discipline to the problems of man and society. The persons associated with Hull House, "though filled with idealism, were intensely practical, and had a sense of how to achieve social legislation, and how to make democracy meaningful to persons who had never experienced its workings. They were not single-ideaed, quasi-crack-pots such as the brothers Ford but people who combined vision with resourcefulness."[17] Here Dewey met and exchanged ideas with such individuals as Florence Kelley, translator of Friedrich Engels' *The Condition of the Working Class in England in 1884*; and Henry Demarest Lloyd, the muckraker whose *Wealth against Commonwealth* attacked monopolies, especially the Standard Oil Company. "The Hull House circle was the American analogue of the English Fabians, with an admixture of the self-sacrifice of the residents of Toynbee Hall."[18]

During his association with Hull House, John Dewey was able to meet foreign radical and revolutionary thinkers who were guests of the house. Probably the most noted of these was the Russian Prince Peter A. Kropotkin, the theoretical architect of revolutionary anarchism who advocated the substitution of mutual-aid communities for state authority and private property. Among the other socially conscious foreigners met by Dewey was Alexander Zelenko, a Russian engineer who resided during 1903-4 at Hull House and who carried back with him the settlement idea of Jane Addams and most likely Dewey's educational principles as well.[19] Through Zelenko, other Russian educators were influenced to experiment in education along the lines exemplified by Dewey in his Laboratory School. Thus, the celebrated Stanislav T. Shatskii acknowledged his debt to the careful analysis by John Dewey, "especially his 'philosophy of pragmatism' which persistently demanded careful examination of theoretical ideas in their practical application."20 On another occasion, Shatskii stated: "In 1904 new educational principles coming from American settlements penetrated into Moscow. These principles were based upon the idea of social reform through education."[21] This phrase expressed fully what Dewey was trying to accomplish not only through the Laboratory School, but also through his lectures on social psychology and on the socio-economic philosophy of Henry George at Hull House.[22] This is what he derived from his association with Jane Addams and others in the settlement house.[23]

Since Russia has been mentioned and since it was to occupy at a later date a significant place in Dewey's socio-political thought, it would be appropriate to mention at this point a possible source of his interest in that country. While he must have read about Russia in his undergraduate and graduate periods, he very likely learned even more from his future wife, Alice Chipman, who "was active at the University of Michigan in the Samovar Club which spent its senior year discussing Turgenev, the great novelist of the Russian back-to-the-people movement."[24] No doubt Jane Addams shared with Dewey her impressions of her visit in 1896 with Count Leo Tolstoi at Yasnaya Polyana.[25] Likewise, he may have heard about Tolstoi and his work from President William Rainey Harper of the University of Chicago. These vicarious contacts, plus the awareness of the growing acceptance of his educational doctrines in Russia, must have made Dewey more sensitive to the situation of that country and to the growing momentum toward political and social change.

During his stay in Chicago, there were other important developments in Dewey's thinking. For one thing, he began his gradual divorce from the logic and metaphysics of Hegel.[26] For another, he became more active in psychological circles, to some extent in connection with his educational interests. During 1899-1900, he served as president of the American Psychological Association and emphasized the relation of psychology to education and social practice in his presidential address in 1899. He indicated that "education is primarily a social affair" and that "educational science is first of all a social science,"[27] as is psychology. He deplored "the gap between psychological theory and the existing school practice,"[28] as well as the ethically defective teaching method, which, "while giving the child a glibness in the mechanical facility of reading, leaves him at the mercy of suggestion and chance environment to decide whether he reads the 'yellow journal,' the trashy novel, or the literature which inspires and makes more valid his whole life."[29] To him, precept and performance were no less significant in pedagogy than in society.

The teacher "lives in a social sphere—he is a member and an organ of a social life. His aims are social aims; the development of individuals taking ever more responsible positions in a circle of social activities continually increasing in radius and in complexity."[30] Even his methods have to be social and ethical. In short, Dewey was convinced of "the social and teleological nature of the work of the teacher."[31] It is the teacher who must bring about the interrelatedness of pupil, the school, and social life.

The application of psychology to the school constitutes a clear example of the necessity of similar application to other social institutions. Psychology will afford "insight into the conditions which control the formation and execution of aims, and thus enable human effort to expend itself sanely, rationally and with assurance."[32] And the psychologist, even if concerned with technical problems, is a contributor "to that ordered knowledge which alone enables mankind to secure a larger and to direct a more equal flow of values in life."[33] The same, of course, might be said, from Dewey's standpoint, of all the other areas of knowledge.

It would be helpful at this point in the review of the historical high spots in the development of John Dewey's sociopolitical involvement to take stock of his published works through 1904. Virtually all of his writings embraced the categories of philosophy, psychology, and education. The social element appears from time to time, but the political is seldom to be seen, except as intertwined with considerations of society. By way of early example, in his address in 1892 to the Students' Christian Association of the University of Michigan, the theme of the relation of Christianity to democracy, Dewey substituted democracy for religion as the road to truth and freedom. "Democracy, as freedom, means the loosening of bonds; the wearing away of restrictions, the breaking down of barriers. . . . Democracy is, as freedom, the freeing of truth."[34] Furthermore, "It is in the community of truth . . . that the brotherhood which is democracy, has its being."[35] Through the medium of democracy the truth based on the social equality of human beings will prevail.

In 1894, Dewey published reviews of works in social psychology and a penetrating review of James Bonar's book on the historical relations of philosophy and political economy.[36] This was perhaps his formal, inchoate initiation into the turbulent world of writing in the arena of applied social sciences.

The social emphasis appeared in such writings on education as **"Ethical Principles Underlying Education"** and **"My Pedagogic Creed,"** both published in 1897. In the former, he proclaimed that, "apart from the thought of participation in social life the school has no end nor aim,"[37] and that "the only way to prepare for social life is to engage in social life."[38]

Before leaving Chicago, Dewey wrote again on sociopolitical topics of interest to him. The views expressed in his classic, *The School and Society*, found expression once more in an address, **"The School as Social Center,"** which he delivered in 1902 to the National Educational Association. In addition, he published the first of his numerous statements on the nature and significance of academic freedom, a subject which was to occupy his mind and energies for many years.

The period from 1904 to 1930, when Dewey served as professor of philosophy at Columbia University in New York City, was undoubtedly the most fruitful one in his life, especially from the standpoint of socio-political thought and activity. New York, even more than Chicago, was a cosmopolitan center of liberal politics, social welfare, and labor organization. During this quarter-century, the philosopher published more than a score of books and a large number of articles and book reviews. In 1915, he helped to found and served as the first president of the American Association of University Professors, an organization devoted to the preservation of academic freedom. The following year he became a charter member of the Teachers Union in New York City and was one of the few educational leaders to write and work for this type of organization.[39]

Some students of the life and work of Dewey have called attention to the fact that, during the decade of 1904-14,

he was chiefly absorbed by technical philosophical problems. His writings were not concentrated on socio-political questions as such. However, "It was the war that precipitated his production for political publics *per se*. And his political public was possibly already recruited to some extent by his educational work."[40] Along with other liberals, Dewey found himself catapulted into the socio-political struggle of ideas and public policy.

In *Ethics*, of which he was coauthor with his former colleague, Professor James H. Tufts, Dewey inveighs against corruption in politics, especially as practiced by the large public utility companies. As he saw it, the proposals for reform involve, at bottom, "questions of the right and wrong use of political power and authority."[41] In other words, Dewey was applying the principles of ethics to the controversies and conflicts engulfing industry, labor, commerce, and government. He summed up his moral criterion to judge social institutions and political acts in the following formula: "The test is whether a given custom or law sets free individual capacities in such a way as to make them available for the development of the general happiness or the common good."[42] Stated from the standpoint of society, "The test is whether the general, the public, organization and order are promoted in such a way as to equalize opportunity for all."[43] Dewey did not merely play around with words; his actions correlated highly with his statements.

The philosopher rejected both the subordination of the individual to the group and that of the majority to the minority. "A true public or social good will . . . not subordinate individual variations, but will encourage individual experimentation in new ideas and new projects, endeavoring only to see that they are put into execution under conditions which make for securing responsibility for their consequences."[44] A "just social order," in his view, was one in which there existed a balance of the individual and the group. This balance was constituted by the promotion of criticism and the reorganization toward the better distribution of goods. "Not order, but orderly progress, represents the social ideal."[45]

One thought in the *Ethics* deserves special attention. Dewey noted with appreciation the development of national states during recent decades but was also aware of the dangers of unrestrained nationalism. He criticized the notion of *si vis pacem para bellum* and urged instead the consideration of "an international State of federated humanity, with its own laws and its own courts and its own rules for adjudicating disputes."[46] He warned against the dangers of the armament race on the ground that "the possession of irresponsible power is always a direct temptation to its irresponsible use."[47] It was "unmitigated nonsense" to argue for the necessity of war as a preventive measure against "moral degeneration." Dewey thus aligned himself with the historic and contemporary ideas and programs which strove for peace and international political co-operation. What he said did not represent anything novel; long before Kant's essay on "Perpetual Peace" of more than a century prior to Dewey's book, there were projects by thinkers of various countries to bring about lasting peace and harmony among nations. No doubt, Dewey's voice helped in the formulation of intellectual opinion in behalf of a League of Nations.

The advent of World War I provided John Dewey with much upon which to reflect. His major contribution toward the understanding of some of the issues at stake was *German Philosophy and Politics* (1915). This volume contained the text of three lectures delivered in February 1915 at the University of North Carolina. The air in the United States had not been charged as yet with suspicion against Germany. Dewey acknowledged that Germans had "philosophy in their blood" and that Germany was "the modern state which provides the greatest facilities for general ideas to take effect through social inculcation."[48] While he appreciated that there was "freedom of academic instruction" in Germany, he was also keenly aware that the state played a crucial role in the selection of professors and teachers, especially in fields closely related to political policy. Dewey's sensitivity to academic freedom was evident in his writings[49] and in the fact that in January 1915 he had become one of the founders and the first president of the American Association of University Professors. Moreover, in his capacity as president of this organization, he wrote a letter protesting an editorial in the New York *Times* supporting the dismissal of Scott Nearing, assistant professor of economics, from the University of Pennsylvania.[50]

The "educational and administrative agencies of Germany provide ready-made channels through which philosophic ideas may flow on their way to practical affairs."[51] Such ideas may be those of Kant, Schleiermacher, and Hegel. Yet, Germany lacked, in Dewey's view, a political public opinion such as found in France, Britain, or the United States. It was the university, rather than the newspaper, that gave public opinion its "articulate expression." And this, to Dewey, was a mixed blessing. In point of fact, he saw serious dangers in the indoctrination of the public in *a priori* truth by German philosophers, either directly or through the intermediacy of war planners and generals.

Apart from the justification of war by German philosophers, Dewey was also aware of their contribution to the development of a racial ideology in Germany. "A purely artificial cult of race has so flourished in Germany that many social movements—like anti-Semitism—and some of Germany's political ambitions cannot be understood apart from the mystic identification of Race, Culture and the State."[52] To an extent, such ideas were seen by him as stemming from the teachings of Fichte and Hegel.

When the United States entered the war in April 1917, the entire nation was mobilized. The government, in cooperation with the schools and colleges, made an organized attempt to channel the energies of all children, teachers, and administrators to aid the war effort. In 1917, Columbia University, where Dewey was professor of philosophy, issued a series of Columbia War Papers.

The first of these pamphlets was Dewey's "Enlistment for the Farm." Here the philosopher, rejecting the idea of military drill for adolescent boys, proposed "training drills with the spade and the hoe,"[53] so that the pupils and teachers might help in increasing the nation's food supply. He urged "educators and teachers to develop Constructive Patriotism . . . to help evolve in the growing generation the idea of universal service in the great battle of man against nature, which is something American, something great; and which is not a military idea transplanted from Europe."[54] In this way, the educators will not only contribute toward the conclusion of the war, but they will also have "a chance to link the school with life. It is a chance to develop for the first time in the history of the world in time of war a constructive and industrial instead of a destructive and militaristic patriotism. All can join without distinction of race and creed, or even of previous sympathy. It is service not only for our own country and for the countries on whose side we are fighting, but a service to the whole world when peace shall again dawn."[55]

Dewey spoke like a true patriot. He recognized the reality of the war and wished to do what he could to terminate it. His contribution lay in participation on as educational a level as possible, with an eye toward the realization of democratic values and of the values of the peace to come.

In World War I, Dewey proved that he was not a professional pacifist. He did not advocate or practice opposition to or sabotage of the war effort. While not giving up his devotion to peace, he was convinced that peaceful activity, such as agriculture, would in time help bring a more lasting peace than that achieved by force of arms. In any event, this seems to have been the rationale by which he was able to remain at peace with himself.

All through the war, Dewey focused his attention on the peace ahead. In June 1918, for example, he commented on President Wilson's doctrine of a world safe for democracy and insisted that democracy could be safely anchored in the world only if there would be a development toward "a federated world government and a variety of freely coöperating self-governing local, cultural and industrial groups."[56] Autocracy involves uniformity and the straining of human nature to the breaking point. Democracy, the great hope of the future, signifies diversification. It releases and relieves the stresses and strains of human nature—and this, to Dewey, "is the ultimate sanction of democracy, for which we are fighting."[57]

When the possibility of the League of Nations came under increasing discussion and debate in the closing months of the war, Dewey offered his views. His position in November 1918 was in favor of a League, but one which was more than a legal and political organization. As he saw it, the dominant idea of a League which would be engaged in arbitration, conciliation, and military enforcement of its decisions "is negative not constructive, and doomed to fail at some critical moment. . . . The real problem is one of organization for more effective human association and intercourse."[58] This was the lesson drawn by Dewey from the war and he may have had a premoniton of the debacle that the League of Nations was to suffer from about 1935 to the beginning of World War II. He made this point repeatedly in speeches and articles, but again he had to suffer neglect and opposition. When the pressure for the United States' joining the League was stepped up in liberal circles with the passing 1920s, Dewey felt it necessary to take a definitive stand. In March 1923, he addressed himself in the *New Republic* to the question, **"Shall We Join the League?"**[59] Dewey stressed that, among other reasons, the League was weak and "its international character is a farce" so long as Germany and Russia were not permitted to join. Moreover, "Europe does not want and will not tolerate our coöperation except on its own terms, and it is divided against itself as to those terms."[60] The people of the United States, in Dewey's view, were also "ignorant, inexperienced, governed by emotion rather than by information and insight" and, accordingly, "the notion that we have only to offer ourselves as universal arbiter—and paymaster—and all will be well is childish in the extreme."[61] The very fact, he concluded, that "only appeal to emotion can possibly be successful in engaging us to enter the League of Nations is the most conclusive reason possible for our staying out of it."[62] Dewey continued to uphold this position even after criticism in the periodicals. In his reply to a critic, he added another point: "The League is *not* honestly named. It is a League of governments pure and simple."[63]

Dewey was no isolationist. He was in favor of genuine international co-operation on *all* fronts and in relation to *all* peoples. The League of Nations was weighed in his scale of values and was found wanting. Hence, his opposition.

Before leaving the war period, it will be appropriate to refer to an unpublicized inquiry conducted under the direction of Dewey, at the request of Albert C. Barnes, in the spring and summer of 1918, among the Polish immigrants in Philadelphia. The aim of the inquiry, as stated by Mr. Barnes, was to discover the barriers to democratic living among the Poles, so that a practical plan might be devised "to eliminate forces alien to democratic internationalism and to promote American ideals in accordance with the principles announced by President Wilson in his various public communications."[64] Dewey's team, which included two young philosophers, Brand Blanshard and Irwin Edman, gathered the data on the life of the Polish immigrants, especially with reference to the conflict between the conservatives and radicals and to its relation to events in Europe. That this information had bearing on the war was evident from the fact that Dewey presented his confidential report in August 1918 to the Military Intelligence Bureau of the Army in Washington. It is possible that recommendations of this eighty-page report may have had some impact on the development of postwar United States policy with regard to the reconstitution of Poland. Probably few philosophers have had the opportunity that Dewey had to participate directly in the process leading to the formation of international policy.

The postwar period was a time of international intellectual exposure for Dewey. During February and March 1919, he lectured at the Imperial University in Tokyo and these lectures resulted the following year in the publication of *Reconstruction in Philosophy*. From 1919 to 1921, he lectured at the National Universities of Peking and Nanking in China. In 1924, he studied the education in Turkey; in 1926, in Mexico; and in 1928, in Soviet Russia.

His *Letters from China and Japan*, written informally in collaboration with his wife, showed considerable insight into the international dynamics of politics, economics, education, and culture.[65] In a more formal way, he presented in *China, Japan and the U.S.A.* (1921) a series of seven articles published originally in the *New Republic*. Here Dewey discussed international political problems and tried to draw some inferences for United States foreign policy in the Far East. His conclusion, typically enough, was that there was a need for China and the Orient to have "freer and fuller communications with the rest of the world"—not merely an open door to commerce, but even more "to light, to knowledge and understanding."[66] He called upon liberals to "work for the opened door of open diplomacy, of continuous and intelligent inquiry, of discussion free from propaganda."[67] Dewey thus extrapolated his doctrine of interaction in a democratic society on an international scale.

John Dewey's experiences with thinking on international problems during the war and his sojourn abroad after World War I no doubt sensitized him more than ever before to political and social issues involving various nations in different parts of the globe. His writings, whether in book or article form, touched on these problems to a greater or lesser extent. His firsthand exposures to the social and educational systems of Turkey (1924), Mexico (1926), and Soviet Russia (1928) were too brief to permit him to attain any degree of depth. Furthermore, Dewey had no more knowledge of Russian, Spanish, and Turkish than he had of Chinese and Japanese. Since he did quote from original writings, he evidently had to depend upon interpreters, foreigners who were well acquainted with the English language, and any available translations. Consequently, even though he was able to gain insight into social, educational, and political problems in these countries, it is likely that he would have had a clearer understanding had he had the necessary linguistic skills and had his residence there been of longer duration. In any event, this period in Dewey's life, which culminated in his retirement in 1930 from his professorship at Columbia University, was characterized by frequent participation in international cultural and educational activities.

This is not to imply that Dewey did not give due attention to domestic problems in American society. In 1929 alone, he became president of the People's Lobby and national chairman of the League for Independent Political Action. All through the 1920s he was critical of the materialistic values underlying the era of prosperity. Not that he failed to appreciate the importance of economic advances in a democratic society, but he insisted that genuine cultural values be kept free from exploitation by the wealthy. Although Dewey was aware of the existence of a struggle among classes in the United States, he rejected the doctrine of utilizing the class struggle in the achievement of social change. Unlike other educators, he possessed a "more realistic economic interpretation of institutions and culture";[68] yet, with many of them, he maintained that education was the major means by which to bring about the improvement of society and of man.

The year 1929 saw the publication of numerous articles and four books: *Characters and Events* (2 vols.), *Impressions of Soviet Russia*, *The Quest for Certainty*, and *The Sources of a Science of Education*. The first of these, subtitled **"Popular Essays in Social and Political Philosophy,"** was a timely collection of articles on recent and current issues at home and abroad originally published in the *New Republic* and in a multitude of other magazines. The first volume includes the material published separately as *Impressions of Soviet Russia*. In the words of the editor, Joseph Ratner, who was Dewey's disciple, this compilation reveals the application of the philosophy of instrumentalism to the criticism of current issues. Instrumentalism states that the home of intelligence is in this world, where it acts "as critic and regulator of the forces operative within it. This doctrine, which is the philosophic *raison d'être* of these essays, is also one of their fundamental unifying principles."[69] A reading of the chapters of both volumes will disclose the correctness of this observation. Dewey was consistent in relating his abstract principles of socio-economic thought to the specific problems of everyday life.

In *Impressions of Soviet Russia*, Dewey brought together fifteen articles which had appeared from 1920 to 1928 in the *New Republic*. Here is a record of his observations and analyses of education, society, culture, and other aspects of life in the USSR, Mexico, China, and Turkey, countries which he had visited. He endeavored to be as objective as possible, and he made certain to express his appreciation, wherever he thought it advisable, of ways of life other than his own. On the other hand, his effort at being fair did not blind him to the dangers of dictatorship. Thus, he referred to the existence of "secret police, inquisitions, arrests and deportations," but went on to balance this by observing that "life for the masses goes on with regularity, safety and decorum."[70] It is debatable as to what extent Dewey attained depth during his visits to Soviet Russia and the other countries. Nevertheless, it is well, especially in the light of later controversies involving Dewey and the Soviet Union, to take note of the fact that the American philosopher did not see Soviet Russia as all black or all white or even all red.

Another work made up of articles reprinted from the *New Republic* is *Individualism, Old and New* (1930). In this little book, Dewey discussed critically various problems of the day and upheld the role and status of the individual in a world where he seemed to be submerged. He urged once more that due attention be paid to the values of the scientific method of thought. "The general adoption of the scientific attitude in human affairs would mean nothing less than a revolutionary change in morals, religion, politics and industry."[71] Possibly one instance of Dewey's use of this type of thinking may be the following statement: "I cannot obtain intellectual, moral or esthetic satisfaction from the professed philosophy which animates Bolshevik Russia. But I am sure that the future historian of our times will combine admiration of those who had the imagination first to see that the resources of technology might be directed by organized planning to serve chosen ends with astonishment at the intellectual and moral hebetude of other peoples who were technically so much further advanced."[72] Let it be noted that these were written three to four years before the coming of the New Deal.

John Dewey, aged seventy when he retired from his professorship at Columbia University, was named professor emeritus of philosophy in residence and he continued in this capacity until 1939. During this decade, he lived through the worldwide economic depression; the New Deal; the emergence and consolidation of dictatorships in Germany, Italy, the USSR, Japan, and Spain; the crises of the Spanish Civil War, the Italo-Ethiopian War, and the Munich Pact; and the onset of World War II. From 1939 to 1952, the year of his death, he experienced the devastating World War II and the early stages of the Cold War.

In the socio-political realm, he published *Liberalism and Social Action* (1935), *Freedom and Culture* (1939), and the revision of *German Philosophy and Politics* (1942). Of special interest were the reports issued under his direction: *The Case of Leon Trotsky* (1937) and *Not Guilty* (1938), containing data on the allegations by Stalin against Trotsky; and *The Bertrand Russell Case* (1941), a critique of the ban upon the appointment of the British philosopher at the City College of New York. In addition, he wrote countless articles and reviews in the *New Republic*, the *Social Frontier*, the *Journal of Philosophy*, and other journals, as well as numerous small publications. His productivity went on, seemingly undiminished by advancing age. He was intensely interested, as always, in everything pertaining to man and he gave expression to this interest in his multifarious writings. He followed closely the course of educational development in the United States, participated assiduously in the debate over Progressive Education, and contributed a vigorous volume, *Experience and Education* (1938), in defense of his concept of education and in opposition to the distortions of his doctrine.

One example of Dewey's doctrine of freedom is his advocacy of the objective appraisal of social planning as a method of stabilizing society in a period of turmoil. He stated his conviction that all forms of knowledge and skill should be applied to a social problem without regard necessarily to the fact that a particular procedure is in operation in an antidemocratic milieu. Society should be free to experiment with the technique of organized planning even if it is associated with the Soviet Union. "To hold that such organized planning is possible only in a communistic society is to surrender the case to communism."[73]

Instead, the Soviet Russian effort should spur those of a diverse political faith to expend their effort to use all possible knowledge to improve their own social organization and institutions. As Dewey saw it, the situation did not call for a choice between capitalism and communism, but rather "between chaos and order, chance and control: the haphazard use and the planned use of scientific techniques."[74] It will be seen that Dewey anticipated the thought and activity of those who undertook to set society and its economy aright after the dislocation of the Depression.

The socio-economic crisis of the Depression in the early 1930s led Dewey and other educators to interrelate the situation of society and the school even more closely than ever before. One product of such an effort was a collaborative volume, *The Educational Frontier* (1933), edited by William H. Kilpatrick. Two chapters, "a joint product" of the thought of Dewey and John L. Childs, were "written out" by the former. Here was expressed the conviction that an educational philosophy which is to be meaningful for the United States "must be the expression of a social philosophy and . . . the social and educational theories and conceptions must be developed with definite reference to the needs and issues which mark and divide our domestic, economic, and political life in the generation of which we are a part."[75] The "moral and human import" of the democratic tradition is at the foundation of the social organization. Planning is necessary for a sound society, but not in the way already in practice in Russia and Italy. What is needed is not a planned society, but rather a *planning* society, and herein lies the crucial difference "between autocracy and democracy, between dogma and intelligence in operation, between suppression of individuality and that release and utilization of individuality which will bring it to full maturity."[76]

As a conclusion to the entire volume, Dewey stresses that "life based on experimental intelligence provides the only possible opportunity for *all* to develop rich and diversified experience, while also securing continuous coöperative give and take and intercommunication."[77] The experimental method, as "the only one compatible with the democratic way of life," makes possible an enlarged area of human understanding and consensus. This is not to say that there must be full agreement. The experimental method extends "intelligence as the method of action," so that, in cases of differences, "it will conduce to agreement to differ, to mutual tolerance and sympathy, pending the time when more adequate knowledge and better methods of judging are at hand."[78] The processes of desirable social change and of education are "correlative and interactive. No social modification, slight or revolutionary, can endure except as it enters into the action of a people through their desires and purposes. This introduction and perpetuation are effected by education. But every improvement in the social structure and its operations releases the educative resources of mankind and gives them a better opportunity to enter into normal social processes so that the latter become themselves more truly educative."[79]

The growth of interest in communism and in the USSR in various circles in the early 1930s was a great factor in increasing Dewey's writings, speeches, and activities along socio-political lines. As Communists became more outspoken and activistic in American life, Dewey felt called upon to restate the principles of democracy. In a symposium of philosophers on Marxism, he made clear five reasons why he was not a Communist: The United States is "profoundly different [from the USSR] in its economic, political, and cultural history"; communism uses a "monistic and one-way philosophy of history"; the class war is not *the* means by which such [class] conflicts can be eliminated and genuine social advance made"; "the emotional tone and methods of discussion and dispute . . . are extremely repugnant"; and "a revolution effected solely or chiefly by violence can in a modernized society like our own result only in chaos."[80] Dewey did not beat around the rhetorical bush; he called a hammer and sickle a hammer and sickle: "official Communism has made the practical traits of the dictatorship *of* the proletariat and *over* the proletariat, the suppression of the civil liberties of all non-proletarian elements as well as of dissenting proletarian minorities, integral parts of the standard Communist faith and dogma."[81] He accused the Communists of responsibility for the growth of fascism. "As an unalterable opponent of Fascism in every form, I cannot be a Communist."[82]

The danger of the Communist and Fascist dictatorships for a democratic society also occupied Dewey's mind in *Liberalism and Social Action* (1935). On the very first page he called attention to the attacks upon liberalism by "those who want drastic social changes effected in a twinkling of an eye, and who believe that violent overthrow of existing institutions is the right method of effecting the required changes."[83] He pointed out that in "three of the great nations of Europe" liberalism ceased to flourish with the suppression of civil liberties. Classical liberalism, in his view, was characterized by the three values of "liberty; the development of the inherent capacities of individuals made possible through liberty, and the central role of free intelligence in inquiry, discussion and expression."[84] One should "look with considerable suspicion upon those who assert that suppression of democracy is the road to the adequate establishment of genuine democracy."[85] Dewey recognized that an apparent exception "to dependence upon organized intelligence as the method for directing social change is found when society through an authorized majority has entered upon the path of social experimentation leading to great social change, and a minority refuses by force to permit the method of intelligent action to go into effect. Then force may be intelligently employed to subdue and disarm the recalcitrant minority."[86] The trouble with the historical liberals was they did not apply organized effort to attain their social objectives. "Earlier liberalism regarded the separate and competing economic action of individuals as the means to social well-being as the end. We must reverse the perspective and see that socialized economy is the means of free individual development as the end."[87]

In *Liberalism and Social Action*, Dewey threw out a direct challenge to his fellow liberals and to the antiliberals. It is not at all surprising that Sidney Hook predicted that this little work "may well be to the twentieth century what Marx and Engels' *Communist Manifesto* was to the nineteenth."[88] Dewey later characterized the views he expressed in *Liberalism and Social Action* and in *Individualism, Old and New* as those of a "democratic socialist." Such a position, it might well be understood, would invite criticism and censure from both right and left.

Dewey's activities in relation to communism and Soviet Russia were stepped up in the following years. An investigation of the charges made against Leon Trotsky in the Moscow Trials of 1936 was made by a commission under the chairmanship of John Dewey. After hearings in Mexico, Dewey and his colleagues published two volumes in which Trotsky was exonerated from Stalin's charges.[89] In various writings,[90] as well as in these two reports, Dewey reaffirmed his opposition to dictatorship of any kind and his commitment to democracy. The second report, *Not Guilty,* was described by James T. Farrell as "an example of democratic thinking, reasoning, procedure and of Dewey's own conceptions of free inquiry."[91]

Dewey returned to criticize specifically the Marxist theory in his *Freedom and Culture* (1939). While he contrasted democracy with all forms of totalitarian ideologies throughout the book, he devoted an entire chapter to a critique of Marxism, especially as practiced in Soviet Russia. To begin with, Dewey deplored the neglect by many democrats of the relation of culture to democracy. He stated his conviction that "works of art once brought into existence are the most compelling of the means of communication by which emotions are stirred and opinions formed" and that "emotions and imagination are more potent in shaping public sentiment and opinion than information and reason."[92] Totalitarian countries have recognized this principle and have taken full advantage of it in controlling their people. Democracy cannot be taken for granted, insisted Dewey, and democratic conditions cannot be expected to maintain themselves automatically. Constant caution, eternal vigilance, and the maximum use of culture and education will enable a society to retain its democratic integrity in the face of the totalitarian threat.

The critique of Marxism and of the Soviet Union appears as Chapter 4, "Totalitarian Economics and Democracy," in *Freedom and Culture*. Marxism, states Dewey, isolates a single factor, economics, which cannot be isolated from the other forces of society. The view of the Marxist, as summed up by Dewey, is that "the state of the forces of economic productivity at a given time ultimately determines all forms of social activities and relations, political, legal, scientific, artistic, religious, moral."[93] Economic determinism did not appeal to Dewey, who was convinced that causation is derived from a broader base. He insisted that effects could be traced to causes by concrete investigation only. The adoption of this method of study would result in the abandonment of the single

economic cause. "It would put us in the relativistic and pluralistic position of considering a number of interacting factors—of which a very important one is undoubtedly the economic."[94]

Dewey was not simply a critic of Marxism and totalitarianism; he was a devotee of democracy, not just in name but in fact. His standards for society were his own. His faith in man did not permit him to give weight to some of the forces of tradition, the biblical for instance, which taught the equality of man in a context other than the natural. Such a force also proved a potent weapon in the struggle against totalitarianism. Be that as it may, Dewey's *Freedom and Culture* was apparently as severe an indictment of the totalitarian nature of Stalinist communism and of its parent theory, Marxism, as had been written up to his time and, to a very large extent, for some time afterward. At the same time, it should also be regarded as a blueprint for democratic thought and action.[95]

During the World War II years, he continued to uphold the cause of democracy and to denounce dictatorship, whether of the right or the left. He refused to go along with other intellectuals in climbing the bandwagon of conformity at any particular time. Nor did he bow to the pressures which sought to impose views upon the public at large. When he was convinced that a fellow philosopher, Bertrand Russell, with whom he was often in intellectual disagreement, was deprived of his academic freedom, he did not hesitate to speak up orally and in writing. In *The Bertrand Russell Case* (1941), coedited by Dewey and Horace M. Kallen, he assembled statements and documents to illustrate the inequity of the judicial decision preventing the British philosopher from assuming his post at the City College of New York. To this symposium, Dewey contributed an introduction and a chapter, **"Social Realities *versus* Police Court Fictions."** In his Introduction, Dewey stressed the consensus by the authors of the book with regard to the "belief in the social importance of public discussion of moral problems, when it is conducted upon the plane of scientific method and with a sense of public responsibility."[96] The alternative to a serious discussion by competent individuals disciplined by the scientific method is the adoption of totalitarian methods. Dewey expressed the hope that the book may contribute to "the freedom of the human spirit and the democratic way of life."[97]

In his chapter, Dewey deplored the hypocrisy whereby public opinion delighted in "the mass of cheap sexuality presented on the stage and in public prints," but "is easily rallied to oppose serious intellectual discussion of sex and to revile those who act upon a belief that such discussion is a precondition of a better social ethic."[98] This is a situation of darkness where it becomes "easier for evil customs to endure and to flourish."[99] However, there is hope for the dispelling of such darkness through the co-operation of learned men, educators, and public-minded citizens to defend the academic and scientific freedom of men like Bertrand Russell.

During World War II, Dewey found himself in a relatively lonely position among America's intellectual circles. It had become fashionable, inasmuch as the United States and the USSR were now allies in a common struggle against Nazi totalitarianism, to regard the Soviet Communist society as an equal to the free society in a democracy. Dewey was firmly convinced of the falsity and danger of this doctrine. As one who had realized the nature of communism as far back as 1932, when members of the party tried to take over the New York Teachers Union, he lost little time in emphasizing that Soviet Russia had not changed its stripes.

During World War II, Dewey did not permit himself to be blinded by the great pressure in behalf of Soviet-American amity to the extent that he was able to minimize the realities of Stalin and the Communist dictatorship. He called public attention to the need for evaluating Stalin's actions in historical perspective. In addition, he warned against "the fatuous one-sided love feast now going on in this country," whereby Communist sympathizers demanded full consideration for the Soviet Union while giving little or nothing in return.[100] This attitude did not endear Dewey to the Communists, whether in the USSR, the United States, or any other country. The cold war between Dewey and the Communists continued to the year of his death—and beyond.

On the other hand, Dewey contributed to the war effort by writing, in behalf of the United States government, an open letter to the Chinese people. He identified the common goal of the Chinese and the Americans—"to preserve our independence and freedom. We both want to see a world in which nations can devote themselves to the constructive tasks of industry, education, science and art without fear of molestation by nations that think they can build themselves up by destroying the lives and the work of the men, women and children of other peoples."[101] Together with the Chinese, Dewey looked forward to a new and better postwar world, in which good will, kindness, and humaneness would prevail.

At the end of World War II, the philosopher, now beyond the age of eighty-five, continued his interest in the problems of men. In 1946, he joined nineteen Americans, including John Haynes Holmes, Sidney Hook, Robert MacIver, and Norman Thomas, in protesting the deportation of Sudeten Germans and Hungarians from Czechoslovakia.[102] His writings embraced philosophy and education for the most part. His socio-political statements appeared at rather rare intervals, in part possibly due to the fact that age made his active participation in human affairs less likely.

On the occasion of his ninetieth birthday, Dewey summed up his socio-political viewpoint in a type of swan song. Again, as on countless earlier occasions, he restated his firm conviction that democracy was the way of life, the basis of education, and the foundation of human society. He was thankful for the widespread recognition given him on his ninetieth milestone and interpreted it "as a

sign that faith in the will to realize the American dream through continued faith in democracy as a moral and human ideal remains firm and true even in a time when some people in their despair are tending to put their faith in force instead of in the cooperation that is the fruit of reciprocal good will and shared understanding:—and of nothing else."[103]

John Dewey passed away on 1 June 1952 after a long life of putting these principles into practice to the utmost of his power. He made use of the word—spoken and written—but he also resorted to action in relating his socio-political theory to life. He was a thinker and a doer.[104] If he was repetitive, it was because of many demands upon his time and talent, as well as of his recognition that his basic points required restatement in order to attain effectiveness: respect for human nature and dignity, faith in democracy and social intelligence, and progress through co-operation—toward the attainment of the ideal society.

It would be appropriate to conclude with a statement by Paul Arthur Schilpp: "[Dewey] lived what he taught and preached, without regard to the applause of either his professional colleagues or of the masses. Dewey thus showed by action as well as by doctrine his faith in man's intelligent capacities to cope with any situation, with any problem—*provided* man be willing to pay the price in patient, vigorous, continued cooperative inquiry."[105]

NOTES

[1] Merle Curti, *The Social Ideas of American Educators* (New York: Charles Scribner's Sons, 1935), pp. 502-3.

[2] Jane M. Dewey, ed., "Biography of John Dewey," in *The Philosophy of John Dewey* (The Library of Living Philosophers, Vol. I, ed. Paul Arthur Schilpp [Evanston, Chicago: Northwestern University, 1939]), pp. 12-13.

[3] Jane Dewey, "Biography of John Dewey," pp. 12-13.

[4] Jane Dewey, "Biography of John Dewey," pp. 12-13.

[5] Lewis S. Feuer, "John Dewey and the Back-to-the-People Movement in American Thought," *Journal of the History of Ideas,* XX (1959), 553.

[6] Feuer, "John Dewey and the Back-to-the-People Movement," p. 548.

[7] Prospectus, quoted in Feuer, "John Dewey and the Back-to-the-People Movement," p. 552.

[8] Interview in Detroit *Tribune,* 13 Apr. 1892.

[9] *Outlines of a Critical Theory of Ethics,* in *The Early Works of John Dewey, 1882-1898,* Vol. III (Carbondale: Southern Illinois University Press, 1969), p. 351.

[10] *Outlines,* p. 352.

[11] *Outlines,* p. 239.

[12] *Outlines,* p. 239.

[13] Feuer, "John Dewey and the Back-to-the-People Movement," p. 555.

[14] George Dykhuizen, "John Dewey: The Chicago Years," *Journal of the History of Philosophy,* II (1964), 233.

[15] Quoted in Dykhuizen, "John Dewey: The Chicago Years," p. 240.

[16] Feuer, "John Dewey and the Back-to-the-People Movement," p. 556.

[17] Feuer, "John Dewey and the Back-to-the-People Movement," p. 556.

[18] Feuer, "John Dewey and the Back-to-the-People Movement," p. 557.

[19] William W. Brickman, "Soviet Attitudes Toward John Dewey as an Educator," in *John Dewey and the World View,* eds. Douglas E. Lawson and Arthur E. Lean (Carbondale: Southern Illinois University Press, 1964), pp. 68-69.

[20] As quoted in Thomas Woody, *New Minds: New Men?* (New York: Macmillan Co., 1932), pp. 47-48.

[21] S. Shatzky [*sic*], "The First Experimental Station of Public Education of the People's Commissariat of Education, U.S.S.R.," *New Era,* IX (1928), 13.

[22] Jane Addams, *Twenty Years at Hull House* (New York: Macmillan Co., 1920), p. 435; Robert L. McCaul, "Dewey's Chicago," *School Review,* LXVII (1959), 275.

[23] Jane Dewey, "Biography of John Dewey," p. 30.

[24] Feuer, "John Dewey and the Back-to-the-People Movement," p. 548.

[25] Addams, *Twenty Years at Hull House,* pp. 267-73.

[26] Dykhuizen, "John Dewey: The Chicago Years," p. 235.

[27] "Psychology and Social Practice," *Science,* n.s. XI (1900), 321.

[28] "Psychology and Social Practice," p. 323.

[29] "Psychology and Social Practice," p. 328.

[30] "Psychology and Social Practice," p. 328.

[31] "Psychology and Social Practice," p. 329.

[32] "Psychology and Social Practice," p. 333.

[33] "Psychology and Social Practice," p. 333.

[34] "Christianity and Democracy," in *Religious Thought at the University of Michigan* (Ann Arbor: Inland Press, 1893), p. 66.

[35] "Christianity and Democracy," p. 67.

[36] *The Psychic Factors of Civilization* by Lester Frank Ward, *Social Evolution* by Benjamin Kidd, *Civilization During the Middle Ages* by George Burton Adams, *History of the Philosophy of History* by Robert Flint, and *Philosophy and Political Economy in Some of Their Historical Relations* by James Bonar.

[37] "Ethical Principles Underlying Education," in *Third Yearbook* (Chicago: National Herbart Society, 1897), p. 12.

[38] "Ethical Principles Underlying Education," p. 14.

[39] "Professional Organization of Teachers," *American Teacher,* V (1916), 99-101.

[40] C. Wright Mills, *Sociology and Pragmatism: The Higher Learning in America,* ed. Irving Louis Horowitz (New York: Paine-Whitman, 1964), p. 316.

[41] *Ethics,* with James H. Tufts (New York: Henry Holt and Co., 1908), p. 481.

[42] *Ethics,* pp. 482-83.

[43] *Ethics,* p. 483.

[44] *Ethics,* p. 485.

[45] *Ethics,* p. 485.

[46] *Ethics,* p. 482.

[47] *Ethics,* p. 482.

[48] *German Philosophy and Politics* (New York: Henry Holt and Co., 1915), p. 14.

[49] "Academic Freedom," *Educational Review,* XXIII (1902), 1-14; and "Freedom, Academic," in *A Cyclopedia of Education,* II, ed. Paul Monroe (New York: Macmillan Co., 1911), 700-701.

[50] New York *Times,* 22 Oct. 1915.

[51] *German Philosophy and Politics,* p. 16.

[52] *German Philosophy and Politics,* p. 100.

[53] *Enlistment for the Farm* (Columbia War Papers, Series I, No. 1 [New York: Division of Intelligence and Publicity of Columbia University, 1917]), p. 5.

[54] *Enlistment for the Farm,* p. 5.

[55] *Enlistment for the Farm*, p. 10.

[56] "What Are We Fighting For?" *Independent*, XCIV (1918), 483.

[57] "What Are We Fighting For?" p. 483.

[58] "The Approach to a League of Nations," *Dial*, XVII (1918), 341.

[59] "Shall We Join the League?" *New Republic*, XXXIV (1923), 36-37.

[60] "Shall We Join the League?" p. 37.

[61] "Shall We Join the League?" p. 37.

[62] "Shall We Join the League?" p. 37.

[63] *New Republic*, XXXIV (1923), 139-40, in answer to Arthur Oncken Lovejoy's letter, *ibid.*, XXXIV (1923), 138-39.

[64] *Confidential Report: Conditions Among the Poles in the United States* ([Washington?], 1918), p. 2.

[65] See, for example, *Letters from China and Japan*, with Alice C. Dewey, ed. Evelyn Dewey (New York: E. P. Dutton and Co., 1920), pp. 74-76, 179-80, 190, 209, 243-47, and 305-11.

[66] "A Parting of the Ways for America," II., *New Republic*, XXVIII (1921), 317.

[67] "A Parting of the Ways for America," II., p. 317.

[68] Curti, *Social Ideas of American Educators*, p. 514.

[69] Joseph Ratner, "Preface," in *Characters and Events*, I (New York: Henry Holt and Co., 1929), vi.

[70] "Impressions of Soviet Russia," II. A Country in a State of Flux, *New Republic*, LVII (1928), 12.

[71] *Individualism, Old and New* (New York: Minton, Balch and Co., 1930), p. 155. [Published originally as "Individualism, Old and New," VI. Individuality in Our Day, *New Republic*, LXII (1930).]

[72] *Individualism, Old and New*, p. 95.

[73] *Philosophy and Civilization* (New York: Minton, Balch and Co., 1931), p. 328.

[74] *Philosophy and Civilization*, p. 328.

[75] "The Social-Economic Situation and Education," in *The Educational Frontier*, ed. William Heard Kilpatrick (New York, London: Century Co., 1933), pp. 35-36.

[76] "The Social-Economic Situation in Education," p. 72.

[77] "The Underlying Philosophy of Education," in *The Educational Frontier*, p. 317.

[78] "Underlying Philosophy of Education," p. 317.

[79] "Underlying Philosophy of Education," p. 318.

[80] "Why I Am Not a Communist," *Modern Monthly*, VII (1934), 135-37.

[81] "Why I Am Not a Communist," p. 135.

[82] "Why I Am Not a Communist," p. 137.

[83] *Liberalism and Social Action* (New York: G. P. Putnam's Sons, 1935), p. 1.

[84] *Liberalism and Social Action*, p. 32.

[85] *Liberalism and Social Action*, p. 87.

[86] *Liberalism and Social Action*, p. 87.

[87] *Liberalism and Social Action*, p. 90.

[88] Sidney Hook, *John Dewey: An Intellectual Portrait* (New York: John Day, 1939), p. 165.

[89] *The Case of Leon Trotsky* (New York: Harper and Bros., 1937); *Not Guilty* (New York: Harper and Bros., 1938).

[90] E.g., *"Truth Is on the March,"* Report on the Trotsky Hearings in Mexico (New York: American Committee for the Defense of Leon Trotsky, 1937).

[91] James T. Farrell, "Dewey in Mexico," in *John Dewey: Philosopher of Science and Freedom*, ed. Sidney Hook (New York: Dial Press, 1950), p. 375.

[92] *Freedom and Culture* (New York: G. P. Putnam's Sons, 1939), p. 10.

[93] *Freedom and Culture*, p. 77.

[94] *Freedom and Culture*, p. 77.

[95] For other contemporary reaffirmations of democracy, see "Experience, Knowledge and Value: A Rejoinder," in *The Philosophy of John Dewey*, pp. 607-8; ["I Believe"] in *I Believe*, ed. Clifton Fadiman (New York: Simon and Schuster, 1939), pp. 347-54; and "Creative Democracy—The Task Before Us," in *The Philosopher of the Common Man: Essays in Honor of John Dewey to Celebrate His Eightieth Birthday*, ed. Sidney Ratner (New York: G. P. Putnam's Sons, 1940), pp. 220-28. For an interesting interpretation of Dewey as a political philosopher, see Hu Shih, "The Political Philosophy of Instrumentalism," pp. 205-19, in the 80th anniversary *Festschrift*.

96 "Introduction," in *The Bertrand Russell Case,* eds. John Dewey and Horace M. Kallen (New York: Viking Press, 1941), p. 9.

97 "Introduction," in *Bertrand Russell Case,* p. 9.

98 "Social Realities *versus* Police Court Fictions," in *Bertrand Russell Case,* p. 73.

99 "Social Realities *versus* Police Court Fictions," p. 73.

100 Letter to the New York *Times,* 11 Jan. 1942.

101 "Message to the Chinese People," in National Archives, Washington, D.C., 2 pp.

102 *Tragedy of a People: Racialism in Czecho-Slovakia* (New York: American Friends of Democratic Sudetens, 1946), pp. 3-6.

103 "John Dewey Responds," in *John Dewey at Ninety,* ed. Harry W. Laidler (New York: League for Industrial Democracy, 1950), p. 35.

104 George R. Geiger, "Dewey's Social and Political Philosophy," in *The Philosophy of John Dewey.*

105 Paul A. Schilpp, "The Faith of John Dewey," in *Horizons of a Philosopher: Essays in Honor of David Baumgardt,* eds. Joseph Frank et al. (Leiden: Brill, 1963), p. 373.

CHECKLIST

Outlines of a Critical Theory of Ethics, in *The Early Works of John Dewey, 1882-1898,* Vol. III, pp. 239-388. Carbondale: Southern Illinois University Press, 1969.

"Thought News," Detroit *Tribune,* 10 Apr. 1892.

"News for Thought," Detroit *Tribune,* 11 Apr. 1892.

"He's Planned No Revolution," Detroit *Tribune,* 13 Apr. 1892. [Interview.]

"Christianity and Democracy," in *Religious Thought at the University of Michigan,* pp. 60-69. Ann Arbor: Inland Press, 1893.

Review of *The Psychic Factors of Civilization* by Lester Frank Ward, *Social Evolution* by Benjamin Kidd, *Civilization During the Middle Ages* by George Burton Adams, and *History of the Philosophy of History* by Robert Flint, *Psychological Review,* I (July 1894), 400-411.

Review of *Philosophy and Political Economy in Some of Their Historical Relations* by James Bonar, *Political Science Quarterly,* IX (Dec. 1894), 741-44.

"Ethics and Politics," *University Record,* III (Feb. 1894), 101-2. [Report of an address to the Philosophical Society in Dec. 1893.]

"Ethical Principles Underlying Education," in *Third Yearbook,* pp. 7-33. Chicago: National Herbart Society, 1897. [Reprinted separately by University of Chicago Press, 1908, 34 pp.; also reprinted in C-16, pp. 108-38.]

"Psychology and Social Practice," *Psychological Review,* VII (Mar. 1900), 105-24; *Science,* n.s. XI (Mar. 1900), 321-33. [Reprinted separately as University of Chicago Contributions to Education, No. 2. Chicago: University of Chicago Press, 1901. 42 pp.]

"Academic Freedom " *Educational Review,* XXIII (Jan. 1902), 1-14.

Ethics, with James Hayden Tufts (American Science Series). New York: Henry Holt and Co., 1908. xiii, 618 pp.

[Statement] in "Symposium on Woman's Suffrage," *The International,* III (May 1911), 93-94.

"Freedom, Academic," in *A Cyclopedia of Education,* II, ed. Paul Monroe, 700-701. New York: Macmillan Co., 1911.

German Philosophy and Politics. New York: Henry Holt and Co., 1915. 134 pp. [Reset and reprinted with "verbal corrections," a Foreword and new Introduction, New York: G. P. Putnam's Sons, 1942.]

> Comments by William Ernest Hocking, "Political Philosophy in Germany," *New Republic,* IV (Oct. 1915), 234-36.

> Dewey's "In Reply," letter in *New Republic,* IV (Oct. 1915), 236.

"Professorial Freedom," letter in New York *Times,* 22 Oct. 1915. [Reprinted as "The Control of Universities," *School and Society,* II (Nov. 1915), 673.]

"Universal Service as Education," I, *New Republic,* VI (Apr. 1916), 309-10; II, *ibid.,* VI (Apr. 1916), 334-35. [Reprinted in C-10, pp. 465-73; C-12, pp. 92-100.]

"The Schools and Social Preparedness," *New Republic,* VII (May 1916), 15-16. [Reprinted in C-10, pp. 474-78; C-12, pp. 101-5.]

"Professional Organization of Teachers," *American Teacher,* V (Sept. 1916), 99-101.

"The Hughes Campaign," *New Republic,* VIII (Oct. 1916), 319-21.

"Ill Advised," letter in *American Teacher,* VI (Feb. 1917), 31.

Enlistment for the Farm (Columbia War Papers, Series I, No. 1). New York: Division of Intelligence and Publicity of Columbia University, 1917. 10 pp.

"In a Time of National Hesitation," *Seven Arts*, II (May 1917), 3-7. [Reprinted in C-10, pp. 443-46, with the title "The Emergence of a New World."]

"Professor Dewey of Columbia on War's Social Results," New York *World*, 29 July 1917. [Interview with Charles W. Wood.]

"What America Will Fight For," *New Republic*, XII (Aug. 1917), 68-69. [Reprinted in C-10, pp. 561-65, with the title "America and War."]

"Conscription of Thought," *New Republic*, XII (Sept. 1917), 128-30. [Reprinted in C-10, pp. 566-70.]

"War Activities for Civilians," *New Republic*, XII (Sept. 1917), 139-40. [Review of *National Service Handbook*.]

[Statement], New York *Times*, 9 Oct. 1917.

"In Explanation of Our Lapse," *New Republic*, XIII (Nov. 1917), 17-18. [Reprinted in C-10, pp. 571-75.]

"The Case of the Professor and the Public Interest," *Dial*, LXII (Nov. 1917), 435-37.

"Democracy and Loyalty in the Schools," New York *Evening Post*, 19 Dec. 1917; *American Teacher*, VII (Jan. 1918), 8-10.

"Public Education on Trial," *New Republic*, XIII (Dec. 1917), 245-47. [Reprinted in C-12, pp. 133-38.]

Confidential Report: Conditions Among the Poles in the United States. [Washington?], 1918. 80 pp.

"Vocational Education in the Light of the World War," Vocational Education Association of the Middle West, *Bulletin No. 4*, Jan. 1918. [Chicago, 1918]. 9 pp.

"America in the World," *Nation*, CVI (Mar. 1918), 287. [Reprinted in C-10, pp. 642-44, with the title "America and the World."]

"Internal Social Reorganization After the War," *Journal of Race Development*, VIII (Apr. 1918), 385-400. [Reprinted in C-10, pp. 745-59, with the title "Elements of Social Reorganization."]

"What Are We Fighting For?" *Independent*, XCIV (June 1918), 474, 480-83. [Reprinted in C-10, pp. 551-60, with the title "The Social Possibilities of War."]

"Autocracy Under Cover," *New Republic*, XVI (Aug. 1918), 103-6.

"The Approach to a League of Nations," *Dial*, LXV (Nov. 1918), 341-42. [Reprinted in C-10, pp. 602-5.]

"The Cult of Irrationality," *New Republic*, XVII (Nov. 1918), 34-35. [Reprinted in C-10, pp. 587-91.]

"The League of Nations and the New Diplomacy," *Dial*, LXV (Nov. 1918), 401-3. [Reprinted in C-10, pp. 606-9.]

"The Fourteen Points and the League of Nations," *Dial*, LXV (Nov. 1918), 463-64.

"The Post-War Mind," *New Republic*, XVII (Dec. 1918), 157-59. [Reprinted in C-10, pp. 596-601.]

"A League of Nations and Economic Freedom," *Dial*, LXV (Dec. 1918), 537-39. [Reprinted in C-10, pp. 610-14.]

"The New Paternalism," *New Republic*, XVII (Dec. 1918), 216-17. [Reprinted in C-10, pp. 517-21, with the title "Propaganda."]

"Japan and America," *Dial*, LXVI (May 1919), 501-3.

"The Student Revolt in China," *New Republic*, XX (Aug. 1919), 16-18.

"The International Duel in China," *New Republic*, XX (Aug. 1919), 110-12.

"Militarism in China," *New Republic*, XX (Sept. 1919), 167-69.

"Liberalism in Japan," I. The Intellectual Preparation, *Dial*, LXVII (Oct. 1919), 283-85; II. The Economic Factor, *ibid.*, LXVII (Oct. 1919), 333-37; III. The Chief Foe, *ibid.*, LXVII (Nov. 1919), 369-71. [Reprinted in C-10, pp. 149-69.]

"Transforming the Mind of China," *Asia*, XIX (Nov. 1919), 1103-8. [Reprinted in C-10, pp. 285-95.]

"Chinese National Sentiment," *Asia*, XIX (Dec. 1919), 1237-42. [Reprinted in C-10, pp. 222-36, with the title "The Growth of Chinese National Sentiment."]

"The American Opportunity in China," *New Republic*, XXI (Dec. 1919), 14-17. [Reprinted in C-10, pp. 296-303, with the title "America and China."]

"Our Share in Drugging China," *New Republic*, XXI (Dec. 1919), 114-17.

Letters from China and Japan, with Alice Chipman Dewey. Ed. Evelyn Dewey. New York: E. P. Dutton and Co., 1920. vi, 311 pp.

"The Sequel of the Student Revolt," *New Republic*, XXI (Feb. 1920), 380-82.

"Shantung, as Seen from Within," *New Republic*, XXII (Mar. 1920), 12-17. [Reprinted in C-4, pp. 9-21.]

"Our National Dilemma," *New Republic*, XXII (Mar. 1920), 117-18. [Reprinted in C-10, pp. 615-19.]

"The New Leaven in Chinese Politics," *Asia*, XX (Apr. 1920), 267-72. [Reprinted in C-10, pp. 244-54, with the title "Justice and Law in China."]

"What Holds China Back," *Asia*, XX (May 1920), 373-77. [Reprinted in C-10, pp. 211-21, with the title "Chinese Social Habits."]

"Americanism and Localism," *Dial*, LXVIII (June 1920), 684-88. [Reprinted in C-10, pp. 537-41.]

"China's Nightmare," *New Republic*, XXIII (June 1920), 145-47. [Reprinted in C-10, pp. 193-98.]

"How Reaction Helps," *New Republic*, XXIV (Sept. 1920), 21-22. [Reprinted in C-10, pp. 815-19.]

"A Political Upheaval in China," *New Republic*, XXIV (Oct. 1920), 142-44. [Reprinted in C-4, pp. 27-32.]

"Industrial China," *New Republic*, XXV (Dec. 1920), 39-41. [Reprinted in C-5, pp. 237-51.]

"Is China a Nation?" *New Republic*, XXV (Jan. 1921), 187-90. [Reprinted in C-10, pp. 237-43, with the title "Conditions for China's Nationhood"; C-5, pp. 252-70. (Reply to: J. W. Helburn, letter in *New Republic*, XXV [Jan. 1921], 187.)

"The Siberian Republic," *New Republic*, XXV (Jan. 1921), 220-23. [Reprinted in C-10, pp. 185-92.]

"The Far Eastern Deadlock," *New Republic*, XXVI (Mar. 1921), 71-74.

"The Consortium in China," *New Republic*, XXVI (Apr. 1921), 178-80.

"Old China and New," *Asia*, XXI (May 1921), 445-50, 454, 456. [Reprinted in C-10, pp. 255-69, with the title "Young China and Old."]

"New Culture in China," *Asia*, XXI (July 1921), 581-86, 642. [Reprinted in C-10, pp. 270-84.]

"Hinterlands in China," *New Republic*, XXVII (July 1921), 162-65. [Reprinted in C-4, pp. 21-27.]

   Response by Dora Winifred Black, "American Policy in China," *New Republic*, XXVIII (Nov. 1921), 297.

   Rejoinder by Dewey, *New Republic*, XXVIII (Nov. 1921), 297.

"Divided China," I., *New Republic*, XXVII (July 1921), 212-15; II., *ibid*., XXVII (July 1921), 235-37. [Reprinted in C-4, pp. 33-44.]

"Shantung Again," *New Republic*, XXVIII (Sept. 1921), 123-26.

"Tenth Anniversary of the Republic of China: A Message," *China Review*, I (Oct. 1921), 171.

"Federalism in China," *New Republic*, XXVIII (Oct. 1921), 176-78. [Reprinted in C-4, pp. 44-50.]

"China and Disarmament," *Chinese Students' Monthly*, XVII (Nov. 1921), 16-17.

"A Parting of the Ways for America," I., *New Republic*, XXVIII (Nov. 1921), 283-86; II., *ibid*., XXVIII (Nov. 1921), 315-17. [Reprinted in C-4, pp. 51-64.]

"The Issues at Washington," I. Causes of International Friction, Baltimore *Sun*, 14 Nov. 1921; II. The Anglo-Japanese Alliance and the United States, *ibid*., 15 Nov. 1921; III. China's Interest, *ibid*., 16 Nov. 1921; IV. Suggested Measures, *ibid*., 17 Nov. 1921.

"Public Opinion in Japan," *New Republic*, XXVIII (Nov. 1921), Sup. to No. 363, 15-18. [Reprinted in C-10, pp. 177-84, with the title "Japan Revisited: Two Years Later."]

"Shrewd Tactics Are Shown in Chinese Plea," Baltimore *Sun*, 18 Nov. 1921.

"Four Principals [*sic*] for China Regarded as but Framework," Baltimore *Sun*, 23 Nov. 1921.

"Underground Burrows Must Be Dug Open," Baltimore *Sun*, 29 Nov. 1921.

"Angles of Shantung Question," Baltimore *Sun*, 5 Dec. 1921.

"The Conference and a Happy Ending," *New Republic*, XXIX (Dec. 1921), 37-39.

"Chinese Resignations," Baltimore *Sun*, 9 Dec. 1921.

"Three Results of Treaty," Baltimore *Sun*, 11 Dec. 1921.

"A Few Second Thoughts on Four-Power Pact," Baltimore *Sun*, 17 Dec. 1921.

"Education by Henry Adams," *New Republic*, XXIX (Dec. 1921), 102-3.

"As the Chinese Think," *Asia*, XXII (Jan. 1922), 7-10, 78-79. [Reprinted in C-10, pp. 199-210, with the title "The Chinese Philosophy of Life."]

"America and Chinese Education," *New Republic*, XXX (Mar. 1922), 15-17. [Reprinted in C-10, pp. 303-9, with the title "America and China."]

"The American Intellectual Frontier," *New Republic*, XXX (May 1922), 303-5. [Reprinted in C-10, pp. 447-52.]

"Mind in the Making," letter in *New Republic*, XXXI (June 1922), 48. (Reply to: "Liberalism and Irrationalism," editorial on *The Mind in the Making* by James Harvey Robinson, *New Republic*, XXX [May 1922], 333-34.)

"Future Trends in the Development of Social Programs Through the Schools," in *Proceedings of the National Conference of Social Work, Washington, May 16-23, 1923*, pp. 449-53. Chicago, 1923. Also in *Journal of Social Forces*, I (Sept. 1923), 513-17.

"A Sick World," *New Republic*, XXXIII (Jan. 1923), 217-18. [Reprinted in C-10, pp. 760-64.]

"China and the West," *Dial*, LXXIV (Feb. 1923), 193-96. [Review of *The Problem of China* by Bertrand Russell.]

"Shall We Join the League?" *New Republic*, XXXIV (Mar. 1923), 36-37. [Reprinted in C-10, pp. 620-24; C-11, pp. 499-502, with the title "On International Coöperation."]

> Response by Arthur Oncken Lovejoy, "Shall We Join the League of Nations?" letter in *New Republic*, XXXIV (Mar. 1923), 138-39.

> Reply by Dewey, *New Republic*, XXXIV (Mar. 1923), 139-40. [Reprinted in C-10, pp. 625-28; C-11, pp. 502-3, with the title "On International Coöperation."]

"If War Were Outlawed," *New Republic*, XXXIV (Apr. 1923), 234-35. [Reprinted in C-10, pp. 672-76.]

"What Outlawry of War Is Not," *New Republic*, XXXVI (Oct. 1923), 149-52.

"War and a Code of Law," *New Republic*, XXXVI (Oct. 1923), 224-26. [Reprinted with "What Outlawry of War Is Not," as *Outlawry of War: What It Is and Is Not*, Chicago: American Committee for the Outlawry of War, 1923, 16 pp.; also reprinted in C-10, pp. 677-84, 685-90.] (The two articles are in answer to: Walter Lippmann, "The Outlawry of War," *Atlantic Monthly*, CXXXII [Aug. 1923], 245-53.)

"Shall the United States Join the World Court?" Pt. II, *Christian Century*, XL (Oct. 1923), 1329-34. [Reprinted in C-10, pp. 650-65, with the title "Which World Court Shall We Join?" C-11, pp. 511-25, with the title "International Law and the War-System."] (See: Manley Ottmer Hudson, "Shall the United States Join the World Court?" Pt. I, *Christian Century*, XL [Oct. 1923], 1292-97; and "Shall the United States Join the World Court?" Pt. III, *Christian Century*, XL [Oct. 1923], 1367-70. [This installment includes statements by Dewey and Hudson and exchanges between them.])

"Science, Belief and the Public," *New Republic*, XXXVIII (Apr. 1924), 143-45. [Reprinted in C-10, pp. 459-64.]

"Secularizing a Theocracy: Young Turkey and the Caliphate," *New Republic*, XL (Sept. 1924), 69-71. [Reprinted in C-10, pp. 324-29, with the title "Young Turkey and the Caliphate"; C-5, pp. 220-34.]

"Angora, the New," *New Republic*, XL (Oct. 1924), 169-70. [Reprinted in C-10, pp. 330-34; C-5, pp. 208-19.]

"Dewey Aids La Follette," New York *Times*, 23 Oct. 1924.

"The Turkish Tragedy," *New Republic*, XL (Nov. 1924), 268-69. [Reprinted in C-10, pp. 335-39; C-5, pp. 197-207.]

"The Problem of Turkey," *New Republic*, XLI (Jan. 1925), 162-63. [Reprinted in C-10, pp. 340-45.]

"Highly-Colored White Lies," *New Republic*, XLII (Apr. 1925), 229-30. [Reprinted in C-10, pp. 312-16, with the title "The White Peril."]

"Is China a Nation or a Market?" *New Republic*, XLIV (Nov. 1925), 298-99. [Reprinted in C-10, pp. 316-21, with the title "The White Peril."]

"We Should Deal with China as Nation to Nation," *Chinese Students' Monthly*, XXI (May 1926), 52-54.

"America and the Far East," *Survey*, LVI (May 1926), 188. [Reprinted in C-10, pp. 309-11, with the title "America and China."]

"A Key to the New World," *New Republic*, XLVI (May 1926), 410-11. [Review of *Education and the Good Life* by Bertrand Russell.]

"Church and State in Mexico," *New Republic*, XLVIII (Aug. 1926), 9-10. [Reprinted in C-10, pp. 352-57; C-5, pp. 137-49.]

"From a Mexican Notebook," *New Republic*, XLVIII (Oct. 1926), 239-41. [Reprinted in C-10, pp. 358-63, with the title "The New and Old in Mexico"; C-5, pp. 168-80.]

"Bishop Brown: A Fundamental Modernist," *New Republic*, XLVIII (Nov. 1926), 371-72. [Comments on *My Heresy* by William Montgomery Brown.] [Reprinted in C-10, pp. 83-86, with the title "William Montgomery Brown."]

"America's Responsibility," *Christian Century*, XLIII (Dec. 1926), 1583-84. [Reprinted in C-10, pp. 691-96; C-11, pp. 503-8.]

"Introduction," in *Militarizing Our Youth: The Significance of the Reserve Officers' Training Corps in Our Schools and Colleges* by Roswell P. Barnes, pp. 3-4. New York: Committee on Militarism in Education, 1927.

"Imperialism Is Easy," *New Republic*, L (Mar. 1927), 133-34. [Reprinted in C-10, pp. 372-77, with the title "Mexico and the Monroe Doctrine"; C-5, pp. 181-94.]

"The Real Chinese Crisis," *New Republic*, L (Apr. 1927), 269-70.

"Psychology and Justice," *New Republic,* LIII (Nov. 1927), 9-12. [Reprinted in C-10, pp. 526-36.]

"A Critique of American Civilization," *World Tomorrow,* XI (Oct. 1928), 391-95.

"To the Chinese Friends in the United States," *Chinese Students' Bulletin,* I (Mar. 1928), 4.

"As an Example to Other Nations," *New Republic,* LIV (Mar. 1928), 88-89. [Reprinted in C-10, pp. 697-702.]

Response by James Thomson Shotwell, "Divergent Paths to Peace," *New Republic,* LIV (Mar. 1928), 194.

Rejoinder by Dewey, *New Republic,* LIV (Mar. 1928), 194-96.

"China and the Powers: II. Intervention a Challenge to Nationalism," *Current History,* XXVIII (May 1928), 212-13. [Reprinted in C-10, pp. 321-23, with the title "The White Peril."] (Reply to: Major General William Crozier, U.S.A. [Ret.], "China and the Powers: I. What Hope for China?" *Current History,* XXVIII [May 1928], 205-12.)

"Outlawing Peace by Discussing War," *New Republic,* LIV (May 1928), 370-71. [Reprinted in C-10, pp. 703-6.]

"Why I Am for Smith," *New Republic,* LVI (Nov. 1928), 320-21.

"Impressions of Soviet Russia," I. Leningrad Gives the Clue, *New Republic,* LVI (Nov. 1928), 343-44; II. A Country in a State of Flux, *ibid.,* LVII (Nov. 1928), 11-14; III. A New World in the Making, *ibid.,* LVII (Nov. 1928), 38-42; IV. What Are the Russian Schools Doing? *ibid.,* LVII (Dec. 1928), 64-67; V. New Schools for a New Era, *ibid.,* LVII (Dec. 1928), 91-94; VI. The Great Experiment and the Future, *ibid.,* LVII (Dec. 1928), 134-37. [Reprinted in C-10, pp. 378-431; C-5, pp. 3-133.]

"Introduction," in *Humanity Uprooted* by Maurice Hindus, pp. xv-xix. New York: Jonathan Cape and Harrison Smith, 1929.

"Labor Politics and Labor Education," *New Republic,* LVII (Jan. 1929), 211-14.

Response by Matthew Woll, *New Republic,* LVIII (Feb. 1929), 19-20.

Reply by Dewey, *New Republic,* LVIII (Feb. 1929), 20.

Further reply by Dewey, "Mr. Woll as a Communist Catcher," *New Republic,* LVIII (Mar. 1929), 99.

"What Do Liberals Want?" editorial in *Outlook and Independent,* CLIII (Oct. 1929), 261.

[Statement on Censorship], *Laughing Horse,* No. 17 (Feb. 1930), p. [5].

"What I Believe," *Forum,* LXXXIII (Mar. 1930), 176-82. [Revised statement in *I Believe,* ed. Clifton Fadiman, pp. 347-54. New York: Simon and Schuster, 1939.]

"In Response," in *John Dewey, the Man and His Philosophy: Addresses Delivered in New York in Celebration of His Seventieth Birthday,* pp. 173-81. Cambridge: Harvard University Press, 1930.

"Religion in the Soviet Union: An Interpretation of the Conflict," *Current History,* XXXII (Apr. 1930), 31-36.

"Individualism, Old and New," I. The United States, Incorporated, *New Republic,* LXI (Jan. 1930), 239-41; II. The Lost Individual, *ibid.,* LXI (Feb. 1930), 294-96; III. Toward a New Individualism, *ibid.,* LXII (Feb. 1930), 13-16; IV. Capitalistic or Public Socialism? *ibid.,* LXII (Mar. 1930), 64-67; V. The Crisis in Culture, *ibid.,* LXII (Mar. 1930), 123-26; and VI. Individuality in Our Day, *ibid.,* LXII (Apr. 1930), 184-88. [Reprinted in C-6, pp. 35-171.]

Individualism, Old and New. New York: Minton, Balch and Co., 1930. 171 pp. [" . . . material that originally appeared in the columns of (the *New Republic*) . . . now incorporated in connection with considerable new matter, in this volume." Prefatory Note.]

"Our Illiteracy Problem," *Pictorial Review,* XXXI (Aug. 1930), 28, 65, 73.

[Letter to Senator George William Norris], *New York Times,* 26 Dec. 1930.

Philosophy and Civilization. New York: Minton, Balch and Co., 1931. vii, 334 pp. [Reprints, with revisions, of previously published articles.]

"The Need for a New Party," I. The Present Crisis, *New Republic,* LXVI (Mar. 1931), 115-17; II. The Breakdown of the Old Order, *ibid.,* LXVI (Mar. 1931), 150-52; III. Who Might Make a New Party? *ibid.,* LXVI (Apr. 1931), 177-79; IV. Policies for a New Party, ibid., LXVI (Apr. 1931), 202-5.

"Surpassing America," *New Republic,* LXVI (Apr. 1931), 241-43. [Review of *The Challenge of Russia* by Sherwood Eddy, *The Soviet Challenge to America* by George Sylvester Counts, and *These Russians* by William Chapman White.]

"Is There Hope for Politics?" *Scribner's Magazine,* LXXXIX (May 1931), 483-87.

"Full Warehouses and Empty Stomachs," *People's Lobby Bulletin,* I (May 1931), 1-3.

"The President and the Special Session," *People's Lobby Bulletin,* I (June 1931), 1.

"Secretary Klein Asked Basis of Optimism," *People's Lobby Bulletin,* I (June 1931), 3-4.

Response by Klein, *People's Lobby Bulletin,* I (Aug. 1931), 3-4.

Reply by Dewey, *People's Lobby Bulletin,* I (Aug. 1931), 4-5.

"Challenge to Progressive Senators to Act for Relief," *People's Lobby Bulletin,* I (June 1931), 5.

"The Key to Hoover's Keynote Speech," *People's Lobby Bulletin,* I (July 1931), 3-6.

"Lobby Challenges Senator Borah's Opposition to Reconsideration of Interallied Debts," *People's Lobby Bulletin,* I (July 1931), 7-8; "Contradicts Borah on Debt Revisions," New York *Times,* 15 July 1931.

"Should America Adopt a System of Compulsory Unemployment Insurance?" *Congressional Digest,* X (Aug. 1931), 212.

"The People's Lobby," *New Republic,* LXVIII (Aug. 1931), 48.

"President Dewey Opposes Blanket Freight Increase," *People's Lobby Bulletin,* I (Aug. 1931), 6-8.

"President Dewey Calls on Hoover to Recognize Government Responsibility for Unemployment," *People's Lobby Bulletin,* I (Sept. 1931), 1.

"President Dewey Opposes Community Chest Drives for Unemployed," *People's Lobby Bulletin,* I (Sept. 1931), 1-2.

"Setting New Goals at Seventy," New York *World-Telegram,* 4 Nov. 1931. [Interview with William Engle.]

"The Federal Government and Unemployment," *People's Lobby Bulletin,* I (Dec. 1931), 5.

Ethics, with James Hayden Tufts. New York: Henry Holt and Co., 1932. xiii, 528 pp. [Rev. ed., with Preface to the 1932 Edition. The 1908 edition has been completely revised, with "about two-thirds of the present edition . . . newly written, and frequent changes in detail . . . in the remainder."]

The Place of Minor Parties in the American Scene (Government Series Lecture No. 13). [Chicago]: University of Chicago Press, 1932. ii, 9 pp.

"Foreword," in *The Coming of a New Party* by Paul Howard Douglas, pp. vii-viii. New York: Whittlesey House, 1932.

"Education and Birth Control," *Nation,* CXXXIV (Jan. 1932), 112.

"A Third Party Program," *New Republic,* LXX (Feb. 1932), 48-49.

"The Only Way to Stop Hoarding," *People's Lobby Bulletin,* I (Mar. 1932), 1.

"To Replace Judge Cardozo," *New Republic,* LXX (Mar. 1932), 102.

"Instrument or Frankenstein?" *Saturday Review of Literature,* VIII (Mar. 1932), 581-82. [Review of *Man and Technics* by Oswald Spengler.]

"Peace—by Pact or Covenant?" *New Republic,* LXX (Mar. 1932), 145-47.

"Church Leaders Ask Church to Act on Unemployment," John Dewey et al., *People's Lobby Bulletin,* I (Mar. 1932), 2.

"Prosperity Dependent on Building From Bottom Up," *People's Lobby Bulletin,* I (Apr. 1932), 1.

"You Must Act to Get Congress to Act," *People's Lobby Bulletin,* II (May 1932), 1.

"The Senate Birth Control Bill," *People's Lobby Bulletin,* II (May 1932), 1-2.

"Joint Committee on Unemployment Demands Congress Act; Speeches at Morning Session," *People's Lobby Bulletin,* II (May 1932), 3-4.

Are Sanctions Necessary to International Organization? Yes [by] Raymond Leslie Buell; No [by] John Dewey. (Foreign Policy Association Pamphlet No. 82-83, Series 1931-32, June 1932.) New York: Foreign Policy Association, 1932. 39 pp. [Reprinted in C-11, pp. 566-602, with the title "Sanctions and the Security of Nations."]

"Voters Must Demand Congress Tax Wealth Instead of Want," *People's Lobby Bulletin,* II (June 1932), 1.

"Making Soviet Citizens," *New Republic,* LXXI (June 1932), 104. [Review of *New Minds: New Men?* by Thomas Woody and *History of Russian Educational Policy* by Nicholas Hans.]

"President Dewey Asks Senators to Stay on Guard," *People's Lobby Bulletin,* II (June 1932), 2-3.

Democracy Joins the Unemployed. New York: League for Independent Political Action, 1932. 4 pp.

"Prospects for a Third Party," *New Republic,* LXXI (July 1932), 278-80.

"John Dewey Surveys the Nation's Ills," New York *Times,* 10 July 1932. [Interview with S. J. Woolf.]

"Get Mayor and Governor to Demand Relief," *People's Lobby Bulletin,* II (Nov. 1932), 1.

"The Social-Economic Situation and Education" and "The Underlying Philosophy of Education," with John Lawrence Childs, in *The Educational Frontier*, ed. William Heard Kilpatrick, pp. 32-72, 287-319. New York, London: Century Co., 1933.

"Outlawry of War," in *Encyclopaedia of the Social Sciences*, XI, 508-10. New York: Macmillan Co., 1933.

"Preface" [to the English edition], *Terror in Cuba* (Paris: Courbevoie, la Cootypographie, 1933), pp. 9-10, trans. Jo Ann Boydston, in "Terror in Cuba in 1933," *School and Society*, XCVI (Nov. 1968), 444-46.

Steps to Economic Recovery (Pamphlets on the Economic Crisis of 1929, Vol. IX, No. 9). New York: Robert Schalkenbach Foundation, [1933?]. 15 pp.

"Unemployed and Underpaid Consumers Should Not Pay Billion Dollar Subsidy to Speculators," *People's Lobby Bulletin*, II (Jan. 1933), 1-2.

"The Future of Radical Political Action," *Nation*, CXXXVI (Jan. 1933), 8-9.

Review of *Mr. Justice Brandeis*, ed. Felix Frankfurter, *Columbia Law Review*, XXXIII (Jan. 1933), 175-76.

"Relief Is Vital," *People's Lobby Bulletin*, II (Feb. 1933), 1-2.

"The Banking Crisis," *People's Lobby Bulletin*, II (Mar. 1933), 1-2.

"The Drive against Hunger," *New Republic*, LXXIV (Mar. 1933), 190.

"Social Stresses and Strains," *International Journal of Ethics*, XLIII (Apr. 1933), 339-45. [Review of *Recent Social Trends in the United States;* Report of the President's Research Committee on Social Trends.]

"Congress Faces Its Test on Taxation," *People's Lobby Bulletin*, II (Apr. 1933), 1-2.

"The Real Test of the 'New Deal'," *People's Lobby Bulletin*, III (May 1933), 1.

"Superficial Treatment Must Fail," *People's Lobby Bulletin*, III (June 1933), 1-3.

"Inflationary Measures Injure the Masses," *People's Lobby Bulletin*, III (July 1933), 1-2.

"Plenty *vs.* Scarcity," *Commerce and Finance*, XXII (Aug. 1933), 751-52.

"The Imperative Need for A New Radical Party," *Common Sense*, II (Sept. 1933), 6-7.

"Wild Inflation Would Paralyze Nation," *People's Lobby Bulletin*, III (Sept. 1933), 1-2.

"Lobby Asks Special Session on Debts," *People's Lobby Bulletin*, III (Oct. 1933), 1.

"Unemployment Committee Asks Adequate Relief," *People's Lobby Bulletin*, III (Oct. 1933), 5-6.

"Farm Processing and Other Consumption Taxes Must Be Repealed," *People's Lobby Bulletin*, III (Nov. 1933), 1.

"The Next Session [of Congress] and the People's Lobby," *People's Lobby Bulletin*, III (Dec. 1933), 1.

"Introduction," in *Challenge to the New Deal*, eds. Alfred Mitchell Bingham and Selden Rodman, pp. v-vii. New York: Falcon Press, 1934.

"President's Policies Help Property Owners Chiefly," *People's Lobby Bulletin*, III (Jan. 1934), 1-2.

"New Deal Program Must Be Appraised," *People's Lobby Bulletin*, III (Jan. 1934), 5.

"A Real Test of the Administration," *People's Lobby Bulletin*, III (Feb. 1934), 1-2.

"America's Public Ownership Program," *People's Lobby Bulletin*, III (Mar. 1934), 1.

"Facing the Era of Realities," *People's Lobby Bulletin*, III (Apr. 1934), 1-2.

"Why I Am Not a Communist," *Modern Monthly*, VII (Apr. 1934), 135-37.

"What Keeps Funds Away from Purchasers?" *People's Lobby Bulletin*, IV (May 1934), 1-2.

"Acquiescence and Activity in Communism," *New Humanist*, VII (May-June 1934), 22. [Review of *A Philosophic Approach to Communism* by Theodore B. Brameld.]

"No Half Way House for America," *People's Lobby Bulletin*, IV (Nov. 1934), 1.

Liberalism and Social Action. New York: G. P. Putnam's Sons, 1935. viii, 93 pp.

"Needed—A New Politics," in *World Fellowship* by Charles Frederick Weller, pp. 119-25. New York: Liveright Publishing Corp., 1935.

"Socialization of Ground Rent," *People's Lobby Bulletin*, IV (Jan. 1935), 1.

"International Cooperation or International Chaos," *People's Lobby Bulletin*, IV (Feb. 1935), 6-7.

"Toward Administrative Statesmanship," *Social Frontier,* I (Mar. 1935), 9-10. [Reprinted in C-8, pp. 66-69, with the title "Democracy and Educational Administration."]

"Taxation as a Step to Socialization," *People's Lobby Bulletin,* IV (Mar. 1935),1-2.

"United, We Shall Stand," *Social Frontier,* I (Apr. 1935), 11-12; *School and Community,* XXI (Apr. 1935), 143-45. [Reprinted in C-8, pp. 72-76, with the title "The Teacher and His World."]

"When America Goes to War," *Modern Monthly,* IX (June 1935), 200.

"Our Un-Free Press," *Common Sense,* IV (Nov. 1935), 6-7.

[Letter to the editor], *New Republic,* LXXXVIII (Oct. 1936), 249.

The Case of Leon Trotsky. New York, London: Harper and Bros., 1937. xix, 617 pp. [Stenographic report of hearings in Mexico City.]

"Truth Is On the March." Reports and Remarks on the Trotsky Hearings in Mexico. New York: American Committee for the Defense of Leon Trotsky, 1937. 15 pp.

Report of radio broadcast by Dewey and rejoinder by Corliss Lamont, New York *Times,* 14 Dec. 1937.

    Response by Sidney Hook, "Corliss Lamont: 'Friend of the G.P.U.','" *Modern Monthly,* X (Mar. 1938), 5-8, including telegram from Dewey, p. 8.

"Pravda on Trotsky," *New Republic,* LXXXX (Mar. 1937), 212-13.

"Righting an Academic Wrong," *New Republic,* LXXXX (Mar. 1937), 242.

"The Future of Democracy," *New Republic,* LXXXX (Apr. 1937), 351.

"John Dewey, Great American Liberal, Denounces Russian Dictatorship," Washington *Post,* 17 Dec. 1937. [Interview with Agnes Ernst Meyer (Mrs. Eugene Meyer).]

"In Defense of the Mexican Hearings," in "Violence, For and Against: A Symposium on Marx, Stalin and Trotsky," *Common Sense,* VII (Jan. 1938), 20-21.

"Introduction," in *Looking Forward: Discussion Outlines,* p. 3. New York: League for Industrial Democracy, 1938.

Freedom and Culture. New York: G. P. Putnam's Sons, 1939. 176 pp.

"Experience, Knowledge and Value: A Rejoinder," in *The Philosophy of John Dewey* (The Library of Living Philosophers, Vol. I, ed. Paul Arthur Schilpp), pp. 517-608. Evanston, Chicago: Northwestern University, 1939.

"No Matter What Happens—Stay Out," *Common Sense,* VIII (Mar. 1939), 11.

"The Basis for Hope," *Common Sense,* VIII (Dec. 1939), 9-10.

"The Case for Bertrand Russell," *Nation,* CL (June 1940), 732-33.

"Introduction" and "Social Realities *versus* Police Court Fictions," in *The Bertrand Russell Case,* eds. John Dewey and Horace M. Kallen, pp. 7-10, 55-74. New York: Viking Press, 1941.

"Creative Democracy—The Task Before Us," in *The Philosopher of the Common Man: Essays in Honor of John Dewey to Celebrate His Eightieth Birthday,* ed. Sidney Ratner, pp. 220-28. New York: G. P. Putnam's Sons, 1940.

"Address of Welcome," in *Thirty-five Years of Educational Pioneering* (L.I.D. Pamphlet Series), pp. 3-6. New York: League for Industrial Democracy, 1941.

"Foreword to Revised Edition" and "The One-World of Hitler's National Socialism," in *German Philosophy and Politics,* 2d ed., pp. 5-7, 13-49. New York: G. P. Putnam's Sons, 1942. [New Foreword and Introduction to 1915 edition, which was "reprinted without change, save for a few verbal corrections."]

"Foreword," in *S. O. Levinson and the Pact of Paris: A Study in the Techniques of Influence* by John E. Stoner, pp. vii-viii. Chicago: University of Chicago Press, 1942.

"Message to the Chinese People," 2 pp., typewritten. [Original English version in National Archives, Washington, D.C.]

"Russia's Position: Mr. [Joseph Edward] Davies's Book [*Mission to Moscow*] Regarded as Incorrect Picture," letter to New York *Times,* 11 Jan. 1942; reprinted as "Can We Work with Russia?" *Frontiers of Democracy,* VIII (Mar. 1942), 179-80.

    Comments by John Lawrence Childs, *Frontiers of Democracy,* VIII (Mar. 1942), 181-82.

    Reply by Dewey, "Dr. Dewey on Our Relations with Russia," *Frontiers of Democracy,* VIII (Apr. 1942), 194.

["Several Faults Are Found in 'Mission to Moscow' Film"], letter of John Dewey and Suzanne La Follette to the editor, New York *Times,* 9 May 1943.

    Response by Arthur Upham Pope, New York *Times,* 16 May 1943.

Reply by Dewey and Miss La Follette, New York *Times,* 24 May 1943.

Reply by Pope, New York *Times,* 12 June 1943.

Reply by Dewey and Miss La Follette, New York *Times,* 19 June 1943.

"Hitler's Spirit Still Lives: Introduction," John Dewey et al., in *Tragedy of a People: Racialism in Czecho-Slovakia,* pp. 3-6. New York: American Friends of Democratic Sudetens, June 1946.

"Behind the Iron Bars," *New Leader Literary Section,* 13 Sept. 1947. [Review of *Forced Labor in Soviet Russia* by David J. Dallin and Boris I. Nicolaevsky.]

"American Youth, Beware of Wallace Bearing Gifts," *Liberal* (Organ of the New York State Liberal Party), II (Oct. 1948), 3-4; *New Leader,* XXXI (Oct. 1948), xliv, 1, 14, with the title "Wallace vs. a New Party."

"How to Anchor Liberalism," *Labor and Nation,* IV (Nov.-Dec. 1948), 14-15.

"Communists as Teachers," New York *Times,* 21 June 1949.

"John Dewey at 90, Finds Tension of World May Result in Good," New York *Herald Tribune,* 15 Oct. 1949. [Interview with Lester Grant.]

"John Dewey, at 90, Reiterates His Belief that Good Schools Are Essential in a Democracy," New York *Times,* 16 Oct. 1949. [Interview with Benjamin Fine.]

"John Dewey Responds," in *John Dewey at Ninety,* ed. Harry Wellington Laidler, pp. 32-35. New York: League for Industrial Democracy, 1950.

"Mr. Acheson's Critics: Their Attacks Feared Damaging to Our World Prestige," letter to the New York *Times,* 19 Nov. 1950.

"Modern Labor Leader" and "Master Craftsman of Labor," in *David Dubinsky: A Pictorial Biography,* pp. 13-19, 21-28. New York: Inter-Allied Publications, 1951.

[Contribution to a Symposium], in *Democracy in a World of Tensions: A Symposium Prepared by UNESCO,* eds. Richard McKeon and Stein Rokkan, pp. 62-68. Chicago: University of Chicago Press, 1951.

Christopher Lyle Johnstone (essay date 1983)

SOURCE: "Dewey, Ethics, and Rhetoric: Toward a Contemporary Conception of Practical Wisdom," in *Philosophy and Rhetoric,* Vol. 16, No. 3, 1983, pp. 185-207.

[In the following essay, Johnstone finds similarities between the interrelation of ethics and rhetoric in the writings of Aristotle and Dewey.]

Rhetoric and wisdom are often linked in discussions of the practical functions of speech. For Plato, a genuine art of rhetoric is rooted in wisdom—in knowledge of the true Forms of things—and serves to communicate this knowledge to others.[1] Aristotle views rhetoric both as an exercise of practical intelligence and as generative of practical wisdom.[2] In the Ciceronian scheme, wisdom without the aid of eloquence is essentially useless, while eloquence without wisdom is deemed harmful.[3] Recent inquiries have sought to illuminate further the relationship between these two ideas. Lloyd Bitzer writes that "rhetoric at its best sustains wisdom in the life of the public."[4] Kneupper and Anderson argue that "wisdom would not exist without eloquence," and suggest that the unification of the two is the proper concern of rhetorical invention.[5]

The connections between wisdom and rhetoric, nonetheless, remain unclear, as does the nature of wisdom itself. Indeed, whereas for Plato, Aristotle, and the ancients the idea had roots in language and culture, and served as a significant social ideal, we have no contemporary vision of wisdom or of the means of its attainment. I will address this deficiency by examining both the components of a modern conception of *practical* wisdom, and the role of rhetoric in its creation.

If we are fully to understand the wisdom-generating powers of rhetoric, we must consider the role of the subject, the person, in the activities of knowing and acting. For knowing is rooted in and is shaped by the character of the knower.[6] One thinker whose work provides rich insight into the connections among self, speech, and the growth of wisdom is John Dewey. "Perhaps no philosopher since Aristotle," Don Burks writes, "has more to offer the rhetorician than does John Dewey."[7] Still, Dewey's work remains largely unexamined by contemporary theorists and philosophers of rhetoric.[8] Particularly in his work on aesthetics, ethics, and the philosophy of knowledge, Dewey explores and clarifies the relationships among character, communication, and "practical intelligence."

My principal aim is to examine how an art of rhetoric can be employed to create wisdom. Dewey's writings illuminate three ideas in this. He examines the nature and functions of art, and concludes that all art serves finally to enhance the growth of the human personality: "it is the office of art in the individual person to compose differences, to do away with isolations and conflicts among the elements of our being, to utilize oppositions among them to build a richer personality."[9] Rhetoric, if it is to function genuinely as an art, must fulfill this office. Of rhetoric itself Dewey has little to say; but of the instrumental uses of communication—which I shall take to be rhetorical—he says much. Indeed, he observes that "all communication is like art,"[10] and thus maintains that human communication serves to stimulate and guide the development of individual mind and character, that is, of the self. Again, about "wisdom" per se Dewey writes little; but his elaboration of "creative intelligence" and "moral selfhood" yields significant insight into the nature of what Aristotle terms "practical wisdom" or *phronesis*. In what follows I shall summarize Dewey's discussions of these ideas and examine the implications of his discussions for the use of the rhetorical art, and for the direction of contemporary rhetorical theorizing.

I

"Practical wisdom," Aristotle tells us, "must be a reasoned and true state of capacity to act with regard to human goods."[11] It is, moreover, a capacity resting upon the exercise of *logos,* upon the soul's capability for intelligent direction of conduct. Aristotle grounds his conception of moral virtue, indeed, his entire ethical theory, upon the development and use of practical wisdom. The life lived according to the dictates of practical wisdom, after all, for Aristotle most fully reflects and realizes human nature.

Dewey's ethical theory is quite at home with Aristotle's emphasis on the practical, and with his concentration upon the formation of character in the pursuit of wisdom. One of Dewey's principal aims was to help individuals meet the problems of life, and his entire philosophy is at bottom an argument for the method of intelligence as the most promising tool in the quest for significant and satisfying experience. His ethical philosophy in particular identifies both the foundations and the features of this method, and in doing so illuminates a useful and distinctly post-Aristotelian conception of practical wisdom. Dewey's "method of intelligence" is essentially a complex of mental habits and attitudes that compose the individual self; and his moral theory recommends a conception of selfhood that will serve best as a ground for choosing good conduct. A brief review of his views will clarify the idea of wisdom to which Dewey's thought leads.

Dewey's moral theory is rooted finally in the life-process itself, and he derives from the facts of this process a view of value that centers upon the satisfaction of legitimate desire and upon the expansion and enrichment of the content of experience. Dewey emphasizes the significance of intelligent methods of deliberation and choice in determining conduct, and finds the foundation of moral value in the growth of the *self,* the author of judgment.

Goods and values, on Dewey's view, inhere in the very processes of life. Any attempt to understand human behavior, therefore, including the activities of valuing and choosing, must begin with an awareness of the human being as a living, experiencing creature that functions in and through relations with its environment. In its persistent ebb and flow of energies, the environment presents both the obstacles that impede the life-process and the materials and conditions that are used to restore harmony. Discord in the environment-organism relation is experienced as need, lack, or privation; and the restoration of harmony creates enjoyment or satisfaction.[12]

Such satisfactions are the foundation of values; for an object has worth to an individual when it satisfies need or desire. But not all enjoyments are to be *pursued* as values. In order for an experienced good to be considered valu*able,* it must be approved as such after critical inquiry into the conditions and consequences of its occurrence. Without the intervention of thought, Dewey observes, "enjoyments are not values but problematic goods, becoming values when they reissue in a changed form from intelligent behavior. . . . [We should] regard our direct and original experience of things liked and enjoyed as only *possibilities* of values to be achieved; . . . enjoyment becomes a value when we discover the relations upon which its presence depends."[13]

Since not all goods are of equal value, the "moral situation" requires that one judge the relative worth of competing possibilities. Dewey's theory concentrates on the methods by which and the grounds upon which such judgments are made. His aim is to provide insight into the ways of judging and choosing that promise most in generating truly valuable conduct. These methods are described by the idea of intelligence, which I identify with the idea of practical wisdom.[14]

Dewey's "method of intelligence" involves, first, a set of factors that are to guide practical deliberation; and second, a conception of the habits and attitudes to be cultivated in the individual in order to extend the capacity for intelligent judgment and conduct. It is in response to some problematic situation that one envisions as ends-in-view possible reconstructions of affairs that will satisfy existing lacks, and that one chooses from among competing alternatives a course of action intended to bring about the desired reconstruction. Prospective conduct is appraised first, accordingly, in terms of its efficacy as means to desired ends—and this idea, of course, is the one most often linked with the pragmatic method. Practical judgments are predictions or anticipations of consequences, based upon insight into the tendencies of actions to bring about certain results. Judgments are tested and confirmed, then, only by acting and comparing actual outcomes with those anticipated.

A second factor in valuation grows out of Dewey's recognition that actions have multiple consequences. In responding to the idea that "the end justifies the means," Dewey emphasizes the multiplicity of effects and the need to consider them impartially when deliberating about conduct. "Certainly," he says, "nothing can justify or condemn means except ends, results. But we have to include consequences impartially. . . . Not *the* end—in the singular—justifies the means; for there is no such thing as the single all-important end. . . . [We must] note the plural effects that flow from any act. . . . "[15] Among the most important of these effects, we shall see, is the development of the selves touched by the act.

One of Dewey's most significant contributions to value-theory is the idea that there is no final distinction between ends and means. For all ends-in-view are also means to further ends; they are transitional points between two phases of experience. Just as one's proposed conduct is subject to appraisal as means, therefore, so are one's aims. We must evaluate the states of affairs to be brought into existence through our actions because these are themselves conditions of further accomplishment, and thus will affect subsequent valuations, conduct, and enjoyments. The ends toward which proposed conduct is aimed must be appraised in terms of how they will serve the "continuum of action."

This notion of "endless ends" has led some critics to wonder what, if anything, finally warrants value judgments.[16] If no end is ultimately and intrinsically good, what is the foundation of the specific values in terms of which particular choices are made? In his answer to this question lies what may be most provocative and compelling in Dewey's moral theory. The intelligent person chooses aims and conduct with a view both toward the satisfaction of immediate wants and toward the maintenance of conditions that will make future satisfactions the more likely and extensive. Why? asks the critic. What is the value of deeper, more significant satisfactions? It is in life itself—in how people actually do seek to live—that Dewey finds the final authority for value-judgments.[17] We must seek a life that is "fruitful and inherently significant" because "the only ultimate value which can be set up is just the process of living itself."[18] Since "life is its own excuse for being," means and ends can be justified finally "only because they increase the experienced content of life itself."[19] The ultimate ground of valuation, therefore, is a *fact:* as a matter of *fact* people who are committed to life seek to live in ways that reward them with experiences that are enjoyed, that satisfy, that are good. What makes a life significant and worthwhile is just that it brings one to more enduring, more deeply satisfying, more inclusive enjoyments.[20] And the capacity for living in such a way as this, I suggest, is precisely what practical wisdom consists in.

If the individual is to maintain conditions that will make valuations and choices meaningful and productive, then particular attention must be paid to the factors that most directly affect inquiry, judgment, and conduct; and these are the habits and tendencies comprising the self. Accordingly, while it is true for Dewey that "consequences fix the moral quality of an act," he stresses that "consequences include effects upon character, upon confirming and weakening habits, as well as tangibly obvious results."[21]

Conduct is a manifestation of the self; for the self is the "interpenetration of habits" through which impulses are filtered as they instigate activity. One must seek in one's responses to the problematic, therefore, to cultivate habits that make for broader, more sensitive, more inclusive, i.e., wiser, choices. The central factor in moral judgment, then, is the growth of the self: the cultivation of habits and dispositions that will sustain the capacity for intelligent choice. "The real moral question," writes Dewey, "is what *kind of* a self is being furthered and formed. And this question arises with respect to both one's own self and the selves of others."[22] The quest for growth becomes the moral imperative that should guide all practical deliberation and choice: "We set up this and that end to be reached, but *the* end is growth itself."[23]

The self is formed, Dewey argues, by the choices it makes and by the experiences that flow from them. The very act of choosing forms character because, as a mode of conduct, it reinforces certain habits of mind at the expense of others. In deciding how to respond to the difficulties encountered in living, we reinforce in ourselves as habits and dispositions certain ways of inquiring, of reasoning, of choosing and acting. Choice also forms the self by determining the nature of the experience to which it will be led by its own acts. On this view, *any* choice can give formative impulse to the developing self, and thus can have moral import.[24] When we attempt to remake the world in ways that will institute our values, we remake ourselves.[25] Because growth is the "only moral end," the obligation attending any attempt to respond to the problematic in life is to look for methods of doing so that will respect the demand for growth.

Dewey's ethical theory culminates in the development of characteristics he identifies with the "moral self." And in his conception of moral selfhood we find the key elements of a contemporary vision of practical wisdom. For the moral self is defined by its capacity for sagacious judgment and by its attentiveness to opportunities for the continued growth of all who are affected by one's conduct. The dimensions of moral selfhood can be summarized by the ideas of *creative intelligence, responsibility, freedom,* and the *expansion of mind.*

While the wisdom of particular practical decisions is confirmed ultimately by the consequences that accrue to them, it is certified at the moment of choosing by the quality of the decision-making process itself. What makes a choice intelligent is that it is guided by openminded and impartial inquiry and deliberation, and that it is regarded as tentative, flexible, and capable of modification as experienced outcomes dictate.[26] We should note particularly that this conception emphasizes imagination and sensitivity. As a power to plan and to anticipate the outcomes of action, intelligence is also a power to conceive the unseen; to perceive and manipulate in the mind the potentialities that dwell in actual experience.[27] Moreover, underlying this power is a habit of sensitivity or heightened awareness, a habit of "being wide-awake, alert, attentive to the significance of events." As this habit is intensified, more intelligent direction of action is made possible, and so prudence is cultivated in the person.

Responsibility, responsiveness to the well-being and growth of others, is a second characteristic of the prudent person. Dewey's is not a hedonistic nor anegoistic perspective. Because the individual is deeply rooted in and dependent upon the community of which he or she is a functioning member, one has a fundamental stake in the welfare of those with whom one associates. "Selfhood is not something which exists apart from association and intercourse."[28] Moreover, "the *kind* of self which is formed through action which is faithful to relations with others will be a fuller and broader self than one which is cultivated in isolation from or opposition to the purposes and needs of others."[29] The moral self, then, is responsive to others' interests because they are bound up with one's own. The habit of responsibility—attentiveness in one's practical deliberations and choices to the implications of one's conduct for the growth of others—is to be cultivated because of the fundamental connections between individual and community.

A chief requirement of sound valuation is that judgments and choices be made and conduct performed with a view toward maintaining the widest possible range of opportunities for further action and enjoyment. One thing demanded by this requirement is that the individual aim at maintaining a maximum of personal freedom, an openness to the possibilities presented by experience for continued activity and development. What is essential is that choices reinforce the "habit of growth": the disposition to open oneself to what is new in experience, the attitude of exploration and the willingness to look for new avenues of development. Thus conceived, personal freedom, "A mental attitude rather than external unconstraint of movements", is fundamental to moral selfhood, and to the vision of wisdom suggested by Dewey's philosophy. As he concludes, "in the degree in which we become aware of the possibilities of development and actively concerned to keep the avenues of growth open, in the degree in which we fight against induration and fixity, and thereby realize the possibilities of recreation of our selves, we are actually free."[30]

Finally, intelligent or sagacious judgment requires an understanding of the relations of events to one another, a grasping of the patterns or regularities in experience. It requires, that is, that actions and events be perceived in terms of their meanings. The cultivation of practical wisdom rests in part upon the enrichment and extension of the meanings given to experience. It is in part a growth in one's recognition or awareness of the recurring events in human experience and of the implications held by these events. Thus we find Dewey remarking that "morals means growth of conduct in meaning; at least it means that kind of expansion of meaning which is consequent upon observations of the conditions and outcome of conduct. It is all one with growing."[31]

Conduct and ends-in-view, consequently, must be appraised in terms of the degree to which they will clarify and extend the meanings given to events. Moral growth, in sum, must include the expansion of *mind*.[32] This indicates not merely the addition of bits of information to memory, but a diversification, expansion, and integration of meanings, of "the sense things make," wherein actions and other events are understood not as isolated and simple occurrences, but in terms of their connections with one another. Growth of mind is growth in the integrity of experience so that what is apprehended constitutes a genuine universe, a unified system of events that "fit in" with one another. It is growth in awareness of the wholeness of experience.

What emerges from John Dewey's moral theory is a provocative, yet satisfying view of value and intelligence. We might summarize his thinking as follows: *In attempting to respond to the problematic in experience, do in any situation that which, after careful inquiry, reflection, and deliberation, seems to hold the greatest promise for satisfying existing lacks, maintaining opportunities for fuller, more significant experience, and facilitating the growth of those affected by the act.* On this view, practical wisdom is a disposition to choose conduct based upon an awareness of an attentiveness to its implications for the quality of subsequent experience and for the continued enhancement of this very disposition, in oneself and in others.

II

If a contemporary art of rhetoric is to contribute to the quest for wisdom, theorists must formulate artistic principles that will aid in the generation of discourse capable of fostering the growth of moral selves. These principles derive from an understanding of how communication in its pragmatic functions contributes to the growth of persons, and particular to the development of those features of selfhood that constitute practical intelligence. Dewey's discussion of communication and its moral functions provides for just such an understanding. Indeed, we are led by his views to conceive rhetoric as the primary agency of moral growth, and consequently as the principal means to the development of wisdom.

The implications for rhetoric of Dewey's ethical philosophy emerge from the role of communication in the growth of personality. Growth, he tells us, is a social process; it occurs in the context of one's associations with others. "Morality is social," he writes, because "the formation of habits of belief, desire, and judgment is going on at every instant under the influence of the conditions set by men's contact, intercourse, and associations with one another."[33] Communication is for Dewey the highest form of human activity; for it makes possible shared experience, "the greatest of human goods."[34]

Several features of communication are particularly pertinent here. First, it is the basis of all personal development. Human beings, in Dewey's view, are not born as such: they emerge through participation in the thinking, purposes, and knowledge of other humans.[35] When he holds that the self "comes to itself" only through interaction with others, Dewey observes that such characteristically human activities and capacities as thinking, inquiring, deliberating, and planning are stimulated and formed by sharing in the mental activities of others.

Beyond this, as the agency through which meanings are generated and refined, communication serves as the essential tool for creating and testing knowledge. In the first place, the act of self-expression completes the activity of thinking: "Ideas which are not communicated, shared, and reborn in expression are but soliloquy, and soliloquy is but broken and imperfect thought."[36] Second, in sharing the thoughts and conclusions to which one is led by one's own experience lies the path to genuine knowing; for knowledge is generated when individual perceptions and beliefs are examined and tested in dialogue and debate. "Record and communication are indispensible to knowledge," Dewey contends. "Knowledge cooped up in a private consciousness is a myth, and knowledge of social phenomena is peculiarly dependent upon dissemination, for only by distribution can such knowledge be either obtained or tested."[37]

We must recognize also that communication has reflexive as well as objective force. Just as the experience encountering another's message affects one's ideas, outlooks, and habits, so does the experience of creating messages. "Communication," we are told, "is a process of sharing experience till it becomes a common possession. It modifies the disposition of *both* the parties who partake in it."[38] The reflexive potency of communication is particularly important, for it suggests that as we communicate with others we give impetus to our own self-modification. We act not only upon others when we speak; we act upon ourselves.

Finally, we note that Dewey's perspective on communication and growth applies most especially to the pragmatic functions of language, to the uses of speech to deal with the problematic, that is, to the rhetorical. "In a world like ours," writes Dewey, "where people are associated together, and where what one person does has important consequences for other persons, attempt to influence the action of other persons so that they will do certain things and not do other things is a constant function of life. On all sorts of grounds, we are constantly engaged in trying to influence the conduct of others."[39] Such attempts occur because, in our efforts to respond satisfactorily to the difficulties that experience brings us to, our interests and purposes are entwined with others'. Now the use of communication to affect the decision-making and conduct of people as one seeks to address problematic situations is the function to which we customarily apply the term "rhetorical."[40] Dewey's thought thus has significance for our conceptions of the functions and uses of rhetoric.

Dewey tells us two things about communication that illuminate the wisdom-generating functions of rhetoric. Communication is *educative* and it is *artistic*. To say that communication is educative is to say that it encourages growth; for "education is . . . a fostering, a nurturing, a cultivating process . . . [it] implies attention to the conditions of growth."[42] This is to say that communication forms character, that it selects and integrates native tendencies and acquired habits so that they may better be employed in the direction of conduct and in the quest for more meaningful experience. At least, communication at its best does these things.

Dewey's discussion of art helps explain the way in which communicating can effect these results. Art is an activity through which one clarifies, intensifies, and vivifies experience for another and for oneself by "selecting those potencies in things by which an experience—any experience—has significance and value."[43] Art expresses a subjective perception of some subject matter in a form that serves to enhance another's experience of it. This heightened perception of the matter being expressed, culminating in what Dewey calls an "esthetic perception," occurs because the expression itself brings to a completion the recipient's experience of the subject matter. In doing so, the expression shapes one's consciousness of the matter, and thus modifies the perceptual field (i.e., the mind) of the beholder.

Expression gives form to subject matter.[44] The matter of communication, consequently, exists only as a potentiality unless and until it is given concrete, intelligible shape by being expressed as linguistic forms: as particular metaphors, names, lines of reasoning, narrative structures, etc. Form brings matter into being as a perceivable, graspable, knowable thing.

How does an auditor experience the matter thus formed? When one encounters discourse, one is led by the structured complex of forms to *form*ulate in one's own mind a system of ideas or images that, for the moment, constitute one's awareness of the matter being expressed. Whatever antecedent ideas the auditor might have about the subject, interpreting a message compels one to construct meanings for the particular configurations one is experiencing. It is the form itself to which the auditor attaches meaning; and the meaning attached is constructed from previous experiences with the same or similar forms. The effect of assimilating discursive forms, then, is to guide the mind in remaking its meanings so as to account for the configurations appearing in a novel combination and context.[45]

When the experienced forms are routine, the mind assimilates them routinely, unconsciously. But this is not communication-as-art. In order for one to experience a discourse consciously, there must be in the forms employed an element of the unfamiliar. When one encounters a discursive formulation that is not to be accounted for routinely, owing to originality of expression, to novelty of application, or to limited experience with the forms employed, the system of meanings in terms of which interpretation occurs is thrown into disorder. One struggles to make sense of the configuration, to determine how it fits in with what one already knows about things. One is puzzled, momentarily confused. This disorder occasions redirection of meanings in an effort to account for the event; and this is the essence of consciously experiencing a message. For "consciousness. . . is that phase of a system of meanings which at a given time is undergoing re-direction, transitive transformation. . . . Consciousness *is* the meaning of events in the course of remaking. . . . "[46]

We experience another's ideas *as* the linguistic forms he or she uses to express them; and these forms direct and intensify our awareness of particular elements in each idea and of relationships among ideas. Through this heightened awareness of the subject matter, the system of meanings itself is reconstructed, and a new, more inclusive structure emerges from it. When the new structure serves to unify previously disparate elements of the self, when one's experience of the world is made more meaningful, communication has been artistic and growth-inducing, and so has contributed to the creation of wisdom in the participants.

Note again the reflexive effect of communicating. Not only is the *auditor's* consciousness shaped by the sharing of experience through language. Expression molds the speaker's awareness of the very matter to be communicated. In order to be shared, one's idea must be formed as a particular symbolic configuration; and in the process of forming, one's own awareness of the idea is given a particular set. Prior to its first utterance, an idea is an internal, unstable complex of feelings, impulses, and images, capable of any of a number of concrete embodiments. Once articulated, it exists as a particular form. Of the possible configurations it might have taken, one alone is realized; and in articulating the idea for another one realizes for oneself what the idea is. In the act of saying, one brings into being an objective formulation of thought or intelligence, of one's self. This form is created in the act. It is original, born in the moment of expression. Thus is one's mind re-created in the act of expression.

Communicating also directs and initiates the formation of habit, and thus influences the emergence of the self in yet another way. When we encounter discourse and are led by it to form ideas about its subject matter, we do more than have an idea. Because interpretation is an activity, we are led by a message through a process of coming to an idea or conclusion. We are guided in the activity of thinking. A message thus predisposes us to employ similar methods of thought on other occasions. It gives impetus to habits of attention, deliberation, inquiry, sensitivity, outlook, definition, formulation, and interpretation. The formal characteristics of discourse, then, shape the configuration of intellectual habits, predispositions, and tendencies that will henceforth guide us in understanding and responding to our experience.[47]

Dewey's views imply finally that communication is the essential means to acquiring practical wisdom. More acutely than any other mode of conduct, the conscientious generation and interpretation of discourse function to promote the formation of those habits and meanings in which moral selfhood consists; and wisdom is identified with this form of selfhood. What is true of communication in general is especially true of the rhetorical mode; for this function of discourse is distinguished by its interest in influencing perceptions, beliefs, judgments, and choices. When one seeks to affect others' conduct, the ways one chooses to use language, to reason, explain, argue, describe, or exhort both form one's own character and recommend a way of being to another. It is the direction of development that is at stake in the rhetorical transaction.

The use of the rhetorical art, more than any other form of conduct, has a fundamental and inherent connection with the coming of wisdom. Those who employ and participate in it, accordingly, are subject to a significant obligation, both to themselves and to one another. Rhetoric must serve as the principal tool in the liberation and development of those who participate in it. This art is the energizing agency of our shared undertakings. As such, it ultimately creates the most promising opportunities for growth in wisdom. Primarily through our efforts to share our minds while trying to agree upon goals and methods in living together, we can enlighten and enrich one another and ourselves.

III

Dewey's views have implications for our conceptions of the nature of rhetoric, its aims, and the responsibilities attending its use. Viewed as an art, rhetoric involves the application of artistic principles to the generation of pragmatic discourse. The medium of the art is language, and the artifact it produces, at least immediately, is a message. This immediate product of the art, however, is productive of additional artifacts: a particular mode of experiencing some aspect of the world, and through this a mode of consciousness and a self. At its best, rhetoric functions to create forms of awareness that will resolve themselves through such a transformation and reintegration of meanings and activities of the self as will result in a fuller, richer, more liberated personality. As art, moreover, rhetoric serves to emphasize the aesthetic dimensions of the activities it stimulates, and thus to generate experience that will carry participants to fuller, more significant modes of awareness, thought, and action.

Art finds its excellence in what Dewey calls "eloquence."[48] Eloquence occurs when the act of expression creates for communicators an experience in which unresolved elements of previous efforts are unified and completed. This, for Dewey, is the essence of the aesthetic experience. The expression calls forth meanings from earlier undertakings, and it completes these in the present "undergoing," thus fulfilling a particular course of experience.[49]

Eloquence is marked by the feeling of harmony, by the sense that the expressed matter is "in agreement with the ideal nature of the self."[50] The aesthetic completes, unifies, and harmonizes the self in one or more of its aspects by integrating impulses and perceptions that were previously inchoate or discordant. In doing so, it illuminates a vision of selfhood toward which development should be directed.

When viewed as art, rhetorical activity finds its excellence in precisely this idea of eloquence. Dewey writes of the activity of thinking, of having an idea, as being art when "it marks the conclusion of long continued endeavor; of patient and indefatigable search and test."[51] Communicating creates *an* experience when it brings to fruition a previously embarked-upon endeavor. Encountering and assimilating a message, when it is wisdom-generating, is a bringing-to-consciousness of ideas that unify previously fragmented and incomplete feelings, images, and yearnings. It "satisfies" and completes the course of experience into which it injects itself because it integrates the disparate ideas about the subject matter it calls forth.

One important implication of Dewey's view is that, in order for rhetorical eloquence to occur, an auditor must be in a condition of uncertainty or unsettledness about the subject matter. The matter must be problematic, the mind fragmented in its apprehension. A message that doesn't deal with a matter about which an "unfinishedness" is felt cannot really speak to a person. It cannot create the sort of experience that unifies disparate elements, because no disparity exists. When a message functions to evoke the ambiguities and uncertainties that can be felt about a subject, and then to integrate these, it is eloquent in Dewey's sense.

Such integration occurs, I believe, when the message brings together ideas in a way that provides insight into an attitude to be taken toward the subject matter, into a way of seeing it. This attitude is an orientation taken toward the matter that allows one to perceive unifying connections among its disparate elements. It grows out of an act of imagination, combining these elements in a novel way, thus creating a more inclusive apprehension of the matter in terms of its connections with other ideas. Rhetorical discourse, to be eloquent, must cultivate such a sense of discovery that conclusions are experienced as fulfillments of a quest, not merely as repetitions of clichés or catch phrases. To do so, it must present the subject meaningfully, in terms of its antecedents and implications; and thus it must bring the auditor to a fuller perception of the unity of experience.

As it brings the mind to a new attitude toward the subject, discourse brings the self to new and richer patterns of action, both mental and overt. It liberates thought from habitual channels; it extends the power of imagination to unify disjointed ideas and thus to generate new meanings; it focuses attention on new lines of inquiry; it cultivates tendencies and dispositions that allow one to be open to such satisfactions and enjoyments as subsequent experience may bring. Indeed, it helps create the habits that make such enjoyments more likely. Dewey's is not primarily a rhetoric of persuasion, then, but one of growth; and the measure of quality is not practical effect only, but also eloquence.[52]

Communicating involves a partnership between speaker and listener. Responsibility for the quality of the transaction, consequently, is shared. Eloquence is not an accomplishment of the speaker acting alone; it is an achievement of speaker and listener acting in concert. In order to contribute to eloquence, a speaker must approach the subject matter and the situation intelligently, sensitively, imaginatively, responsibly, freely. But if one would fulfill one's obligations as a rhetor, a person must also approach communication artistically, lovingly: "Craftsmanship to be artistic in the final sense," Dewey writes, "must be 'loving'; it must care deeply for the subject matter upon which skill is exercised." Moreover, "the artist embodies in himself the attitude of the perceiver while he works."[53] These are particularly important ideas; for they bring us to the heart of the creative act. In order to contribute to eloquence, a speaker's expression must grow out of a deep caring for and excitement about the subject, and from a sensitive understanding of the auditor.

And what of the listener's duties? Certainly, again, we must seek as listeners to be intelligent and sensitive in our interpretation of and response to another's expression. But most especially, we must be receptive to it. This does not mean that we must dispose ourselves to agree with what another proposes; rather, that we should allow the other to speak to us, to touch us, to affect us. To be intelligent in our interpretation, we must always be self-possessed, autonomous. But to experience communication fully, to perceive and exploit in it whatever potential it has for creating wisdom in us, we must be willing for a moment to surrender ourselves to it. The aesthetic experience requires a "yielding [of] the self."[54] To assist in the attainment of eloquence, a listener must truly *listen*. In interpreting another's message, one must seek genuinely to experience it, not merely to assimilate and translate it in a routinized, comfortable, customary way, but to ponder it, to delve into it, to examine one's own mind through it, to come to a new awareness of the matter formed by it, to become more conscious because of it. One must seek to be brought by it to a new level of understanding through communion with another human mind.

These are our obligations as communicators, the duties to which we implicitly commit ourselves when we agree to share with one another the insights, the conclusions, the inquiries, the uncertainties to which we have been led by our own experience. These, at any rate, are the conclusions concerning the nature and uses of rhetoric to which we are led by Dewey's thought. Indeed, Dewey's contributions to our thinking about rhetoric are multiple. His views serve to integrate the practical and the aesthetic dimensions of discourse, and to emphasize the artistic functions of rhetoric. They imply that the rhetorical is a dimension of all communication, and that the poetic functions of language can have rhetorical dimensions. More particularly, Dewey forces us to concentrate upon the *participants* in communication, upon their attitudes and mental activities as they prepare for and engage in pragmatic dialogue, rather than upon messages only. We are led to examine the conditions and resources out of which discourse emerges, hence to the preliminary phases of communication. The implications of this shift in emphasis for the teaching of rhetoric are worth exploring further.

Two and one-half millennia ago, Aristotle described practical wisdom as a capacity for prudent choice and conduct in the quest for a good life. He characterized this capacity, moreover, in terms of *logos,* the ability to perceive the grounds of legitimate choice. And this ability itself, we might conclude, rests upon the power of the mind to perceive the *Logos,* the patterns or order among things, the logic of experience. Dewey's view is a contemporary counterpart of this ancient and profound idea. It is grounded, not in a teleological and hierarchical conception of the universe, but in one that is scientific, phenomenological, and evolutionary. The vision of practical wisdom that emerges from his writings, nonetheless, shares with Aristotle's the recognition of *logos* or intellect as a capacity for recognizing the *Logos,* the patterns in the flow; and the commitment to the idea that this capacity, when applied to practical pursuits, is the best guide available to humans in seeking a life that is significant and satisfying. Dewey refines the idea of practical wisdom by elaborating the particular features of character that are most closely associated with the capacity for sagacious choice, and thus that are to be cultivated if one is to grow in wisdom. Dewey's parallels Aristotle's view further in the respect that both observe the centrality of the *word,* of human intercourse, especially in its pragmatic dimensions, in the creation and exercise of wisdom. Again, Dewey illuminates more fully than Aristotle the ways in which language can be used to generate wisdom, and thus provides more elaborate grounds for a theoretical link between rhetoric and wisdom.

If we embrace growth in wisdom as the highest aim of a humane life,[55] then the greatest task facing our discipline is to illuminate and clarify the ways in which the rhetorical art can fulfill its philosophical office. Dewey's thought provides a starting point in this undertaking.[56]

NOTES

[1] See both the *Gorgias* and the *Phaedrus* for elaboration of Plato's views. See also such recent studies as Peter J. Schakel, "Plato's *Phaedrus* and Rhetoric," *Southern Speech Journal,* 32 (1966), 124-33; K. E. Wilkerson, "Interpreting Plato's *Phaedrus,*" *Quarterly Journal of Speech,* 56 (1970), 310-13; and Steven Rendall, "Dialogue, Philosophy, and Rhetoric: The Example of Plato's *Gorgias,*" *Philosophy and Rhetoric,* 10 (1977), 164-79.

[2] See Aristotle, *Nicomachean Ethics,* Bk. X, Chs. 7-8. See also Christopher Lyle Johnstone, "An Aristotelian Trilogy: Ethics, Rhetoric, Politics, and the Search for Moral Truth," *Philosophy and Rhetoric,* 13 (1980), 1-24.

[3] See *De inventione,* 1.1.

[4] Lloyd F. Bitzer, "Rhetoric and Public Knowledge," in Don M. Burks, ed., *Rhetoric, Philosophy, and Literature:*

An Exploration (West Lafayette: Purdue University Press, 1978), p. 68.

[5] Charles W. Kneupper and Floyd D. Anderson, "Uniting Wisdom and Eloquence: The Need for Rhetorical Invention," *Quarterly Journal of Speech,* 66 (1980), 321.

[6] Michael Polanyi observes that "all knowledge is ultimately personal," *Personal Knowledge: Towards a Post-Critical Philosophy* (New York and Evanston: Harper and Row, 1964), p. xi. Later (p. 71) he notes that "to affirm anything implies . . . an appraisal of our own art of knowing, and the establishment of truth becomes decisively dependent on a set of personal criteria of our own which cannot be formally defined."

Henry W. Johnstone, Jr. is another who has addressed this issue at length and insightfully. His views are developed and presented in several places, but are summarized cogently in his *The Problem of the Self* (University Park: The Pennsylvania State University Press, 1970).

[7] Don M. Burks, "John Dewey and Rhetorical Theory," *Western Speech,* 32 (1968), 126.

[8] Dewey's views about communication in general and about rhetoric in particular have been examined on occasion, but there has been no systematic effort to integrate those views and to apply them to the issues outlined here. For a sampling of recent scholarship on Dewey, see Gerald L. Steibel, "John Dewey and the Belief in Communication," *Antioch Review,* 15 (1955), 286-99; James Carey, "A Cultural Approach to Communication," *Communication,* 11 (1975), 1-22; and Jerome Nathanson, *John Dewey: The Reconstruction of the Democratic Life* (New York: Scribner, 1951).

[9] John Dewey, *Art as Experience* (New York: Capricorn Books, 1934), p. 248.

[10] John Dewey, *Democracy and Education* (New York: The Free Press, 1944), p. 6.

[11] Aristotle, *Nicomachean Ethics,* trans. W. D. Ross, 1140b 20-21.

[12] In *Experience and Nature* (New York: Dover, 1958), p. 253, Dewey clarifies the character of the "harmony" as it is experienced by the living organism: "By satisfaction is meant [the] recovery of equilibrium pattern, consequent upon the changes of environment due to interactions with the active demands of the organism."

[13] John Dewey, *The Quest for Certainty* (New York: Capricorn Books, 1960), p. 259.

[14] "A moral situation," Dewey writes, "is one in which judgment and choice are required antecedently to overt action. The practical meaning of the situation—that is to say the action needed to satisfy it—is not self-evident. It has to be searched for. There are conflicting desires and

alternative apparent goods. What is needed is to find the right course of action, the right good. Hence, inquiry is exacted; observation of the detailed makeup of the situation; analysis into its diverse factors; clarification of what is obscure; discounting the more insistent and vivid traits; tracing the consequences of the various modes of action that suggest themselves; regarding the decision reached as hypothetical and tentative until the anticipated or supposed consequences which led to its adoption have been squared with actual consequences. This inquiry *is* intelligence." John Dewey, *Reconstruction in Philosophy* (Boston: Beacon Press, 1957), pp. 163-64.

[15] John Dewey, *Human Nature and Conduct* (New York: The Modern Library, 1930), p. 212.

[16] Henry Aiken, for one, has taken to task the instrumentalist approach to ethics. "To be sure," he writes, "consequentialists have sometimes claimed to justify particular moral rules in terms of their effects. But this merely transfers the burden of obligation to something else which is taken to be intrinsically desirable on its own account. When this point is reached, the consequentialist, whether he knows it or not, is at the end of *his* rope. His principle provides a justification of secondary moral rules or prima facie duties, and through them particular moral imperatives; but the rule itself has and can have no such justification. If the consequentialist supposes to the contrary, he is simply confused and fails to understand the logic of his own consequentialist arguments. All that he or anyone can do in the end is to reiterate the intrinsic desirability of the end which he believes to be the proper goal of moral action. And if someone should stubbornly ask, 'Why should I accept that as intrinsically desirable?' he has and can have no answer. For him the question must be simply tantamount to the question 'Why should I accept as intrinsically desireable what is really so?' which is tantamount to the tautology, 'Why should I do what I really ought to do?'" Henry David Aiken, *Reason and Conduct* (New York: Alfred A. Knopf, 1962), p. 83.

[17] "Still," Dewey writes, "the question recurs: What authority have standards and ideas which have originated in this way? What claim have they upon us? In one sense the question is unanswerable. In the same sense, however, the question is unanswerable whatever origin and sanction is ascribed to moral obligations and loyalties. Why attend to metaphysical and transcendental ideal realities even if we concede they are the authors of moral standards? Why do this act if I feel like doing something else? Any moral question may reduce itself to this question if we so choose. But in an empirical sense the answer is simple. *The authority is that of life.* Why employ language, cultivate literature, acquire and develop science, sustain industry, and submit to the refinements of art? To ask these questions is equivalent to asking: Why live? And the only answer is that if one is going to live one must live a life of which these things form the substance. The only question having sense which can be asked is *how* we are going to use and be used by these things, not whether we are going to use them. . . . [One] cannot

escape the problem of *how* to engage in life, since in any case he must engage in it in some way or other—or else quit and get out." *Human Nature and Conduct,* p. 75.

[18] *Democracy and Education,* p. 240.

[19] *Ibid.,* p. 243.

[20] "The aim and end," he writes (*The Quest for Certainty,* p. 37), "is the securer, freer, and more widely shared embodiment of values in experience by means of that active control of objects which knowledge alone makes possible." What saves Dewey's theory from ethical egocentrism, as we shall see shortly, is that the quest for significant and satisfying experience is fundamentally social—a shared undertaking.

[21] *Human Nature and Conduct,* pp. 43 and 45. Elsewhere Dewey tells us that "whenever anything is undergone in consequence of a doing, the self is modified. The modification extends beyond acquisition of greater facility and skill. Attitudes and interests are built up which embody in themselves some deposit of the meaning of things done and undergone. These funded and retained meanings become a part of the self. They constitute the capital with which the self notes, cares for, attends, purposes. In this substantial sense, mind forms the background upon which every new contact with surroundings is projected. . . . Mind as background is formed out of modifications of the self that have occurred in the process of prior interactions with the environment." *Art as Experience,* p. 264.

[22] John Dewey, *Theory of the Moral Life* (New York; Holt, Rinehart, & Winston, 1960), p. 159.

[23] *Ibid.,* p. 172. Again, "growth itself is the only moral 'end.'" *Reconstruction in Philosophy,* p. 177.

[24] "Every choice," Dewey writes (*Theory of the Moral Life,* p. 149), "is at a forking of the roads, and the path chosen shuts off certain opportunities and opens others. In committing oneself to a particular course, a person gives a lasting set to his own being. Consequently, it is proper to say that in choosing this object rather than that, one is in reality choosing what kind of person or self one is going to be. Superficially, deliberation which terminates in choice is concerned with weighing the values of particular ends. Below the surface, it is a process of discovering what sort of being a person most wants to become." He writes in another place that "each act as it is performed has . . . its effect on personality. It organizes it in a certain direction. It gives it a specific set or bent." John Dewey, *Psychology,* in *The Early Works of John Dewey, 1882-1898* (Carbondale: Southern Illinois University Press, 1969), II, 352.

[25] "All voluntary action is a remaking of the self, since it creates new desires, instigates to new modes of endeavor, brings to light new conditions which institute new ends. . . . In the strictest sense, it is impossible for the self to stand still; it is becoming, and becoming for

the better or the worse. It is in the *quality* of becoming that virtue resides." *Theory of the Moral Life*, p. 172.

[26] "The moral," Dewey concludes (*Human Nature and Conduct*, p. 194), "is to develop conscientiousness, ability to judge the significance of what we are doing and to use the judgment in directing what we do, not by means of direct cultivation of something called conscience, or reason, or a faculty of moral knowledge, but by fostering those impulses and habits which experience has shown to make us sensitive, generous, imaginative, impartial in perceiving the tendency of our inchoate dawning activities. . . . Therefore, the important thing is the fostering of those habits and impulses which lead to a broad, just, sympathetic survey of situations."

[27] "The highest form of imagination," Dewey tells us, " . . . is precisely an organ of penetration into the hidden meanings of things—meanings not visible to perception or memory, nor reflectively attained by the processes of thinking. It may be defined as the direct perception of meanings. . . . " *Psychology*, p. 171.

[28] *Theory of the Moral Life*, p. 163. Elsewhere he writes that "the individual comes to himself and to his own only in association with others." John Dewey, "Intelligence and Morals," in *The Influence of Darwin on Philosophy* (Bloomington: Indiana University Press, 1965), p. 55.

[29] *Theory of the Moral Life*, p. 167. In another work he writes that "we wish the fullest life possible to ourselves and to others. And the fullest life means largely a complete and free development of capacities in knowledge and production—production of beauty and use. Our interest in others is not satisfied as long as their intelligence is cramped, their appreciation of truth feeble, their emotions hard and uncomprehensive, their powers of production compressed. To will their true good is to will the freeing of all such gifts to the highest degree." John Dewey, *Outlines of a Critical Theory of Ethics*, in *The Early Works*, III, 318.

[30] *Theory of the Moral Life*, pp. 171-72. Elsewhere (*Democracy and Education*, p. 175), he says that "open-mindedness means retention of the child-like attitude. . . . " In another refinement of this idea, Dewey adds (*Experience and Nature*, pp. 245-46) that "surrender of what is possessed, disowning of what supports one in secure ease, is involved in all inquiry and discovery; the latter implicate an individual still to make, with all the risks implied therein. For to arrive at new truth and vision is to alter. The old self is put off and the new self is only forming, and the form it finally takes will depend upon the unforeseeable result of an adventure."

[31] *Human Nature and Conduct*, p. 259.

[32] Mind, for Dewey, consists in the organized system of meanings in terms of which one interprets experience; for "meanings are rules for using and interpreting things; interpretation being always an imputation of potentiality for some consequence." *Experience and Nature*, p. 188.

[33] *Human Nature and Conduct*, p. 295.

[34] *Experience and Nature*, p. 202.

[35] "To learn to be human is to develop through the give-and-take of communication an effective sense of being an individually distinctive member of a community; one who understands and appreciates its beliefs, desires and methods, and who contributes to a further conversion of organic powers into human resources and values." John Dewey, *The Public and Its Problem* (Chicago: The Swallow Press, 1927), p. 154.

[36] *The Quest for Certainty*, p. 151.

[37] *The Public and Its Problems*, pp. 176-77. The sort of dialogue Dewey envisions is best carried on in direct conversation: "the winged words of conversation in immediate intercourse have a vital import lacking in the fixed and frozen words of written speech. Systematic and continuous inquiry into all the conditions which affect association and their dissemination in print is a precondition to the creation of a true public. But it and its results are but tools after all. Their final actuality is accomplished in face-to-face relationships by means of direct give and take. Logic in its fulfillment recurs to the primitive sense of the word: dialogue" (p. 218). An important implication of this view is that the wisdom-generating functions of communication are realized most fully in dialogue. When this dialogical orientation is applied to rhetoric, it emphasizes the transactional nature of rhetorical activity. Such an emphasis is consistent with recent work on the epistemic dimensions of rhetoric. See, for example, Richard Cherwitz, "Rhetoric as a 'Way of Knowing': An Attenuation of the Epistemological Claims of the 'New Rhetoric,'" *Southern Speech Communication Journal*, 42 (1977), esp. p. 217.

[38] *Democracy and Education*, p. 9. Italics added.

[39] *Theory of the Moral Life*, p. 155.

[40] See Lloyd F. Bitzer, "The Rhetorical Situation," *Philosophy and Rhetoric*, 1 (1968), 6.

[41] "All communication," we are told (*Democracy and Education*, pp. 5-6), "is educative. To be a recipient of a communication is to have an enlarged and changed experience. One shares in what another has thought and felt and in so far, meagerly or amply, has his own attitude modified. Nor is the one who communicated left unaffected. . . . All communication [furthermore] is like art. . . . It enlarges and enlightens experience; it stimulates and enriches imagination: it creates responsibility for accuracy and vividness of statement and thought."

[42] *Ibid.*, p. 10.

[43] *Art as Experience,* p. 11. See also Bertram Morris, "Dewey's Theory of Art," in Jo Ann Boydston, ed., *Guide to the Works of John Dewey* (Carbondale: Southern Illinois University Press, 1970, pp. 156-80.

[44] "This is what it is to have form," Dewey writes (*Art as Experience,* p. 109). "It marks a way of envisaging, of feeling, and of presenting experienced matter so that it most readily and effectively becomes material for the construction of adequate experience on the part of those less gifted than the original creator. Hence, there can be no distinction drawn, save in reflection, between form and substance. The work itself *is* matter formed into esthetic substance." Moreover, as he points at later (p. 137), "form is a character of every experience that is an experience. *Form may thus be defined as the operation of forces that carry the experience of an event, object, sense, and situation to its own integral fulfillment.* The connection of form with substance is thus inherent, not imposed from without."

[45] Polanyi notes that "every use of language to describe experience in a changing world applies language to a somewhat unprecedented instance of its subject matter, and thus somewhat modifies both the meaning of language and the structure of our conceptual framework." *Personal Knowledge,* pp. 104-05.

[46] *Experience and Nature,* p. 308. Later (p. 312) he adds "the apex of consciousness . . . is the point of *re*-direction, of *re*-adaptation, of *re*-organization."

[47] Nor again is the one who creates a message left unaffected. Communicating, especially when one communicates with a view to influencing another's practical judgments, is a voluntary, deliberate form of activity. It is conduct, and as such it is chosen. Just as with other forms of conduct, the choices we make in communicating with others reinforce certain habits in ourselves. If we choose our words carelessly, semi-consciously, insensitively, ignorantly, or selfishly, we set ourselves on one developmental path. If we communicate conscientiously, responsibly, knowledgeably, imaginatively, caringly, we nurture the same habits or inquiry, judgment, and action that any morally sound conduct would cultivate. Indeed, because of the intimate connection between communication and habits of intelligent action, the nurturing effects of our discursive activities are even more pronounced than most other forms of conduct.

[48] "Whenever any material finds a medium that expresses its value in experience . . . it becomes the substance of a work of art. The abiding struggle of art is thus to convert materials that are stammering or dumb in ordinary experience into eloquent media." *Art as Experience,* p. 229. Kenneth Burke maintains a similar view, and applies it more explicitly to discourse, when he writes that "eloquence is formal excellence," and that it "is simply the end of art, and is thus its essence." *Counter-Statement* (New York, 1931), pp. 49ff.

[49] Dewey describes *an* experience as involving two phases: a *doing* or undertaking in which a movement is begun, and a *suffering* or undergoing in which the outcomes of the movement are perceived, and thus in which the movement itself is brought to a fulfillment. See *Art as Experience,* esp. Ch. 3.

[50] *Psychology,* p. 273.

[51] *Experience and Nature,* p. 371. See also *Art as Experience,* pp. 38 and 172.

[52] It should be emphasized that eloquence is not indifferent to effectiveness of expression. As a quality of *pragmatic* discourse, eloquence includes the objective of responding appropriately and adequately to the defects or exigencies of the situation to which discourse is addressed. Eloquence is the moral standard by which practically efficacious discourse is to be judged. See Don M. Burks, "John Dewey and Rhetorical Theory," p. 126.

[53] *Art as Experience,* pp. 47-48. He also writes (p. 65) that "when excitement about subject matter goes deep, it stirs up a store of attitudes and meanings derived from prior experience."

[54] *Art as Experience,* p. 53.

[55] For an elaboration of this idea, see my essay entitled "Ethics, Wisdom, and the Mission of Contemporary Rhetoric: The Realization of Human Being," *Central States Speech Journal,* 32 (1981), 177-88.

[56] I wish to express appreciation to the Center for Dewey Studies and the John Dewey Foundation at the Southern Illinois University, and to the Institute for the Arts and Humanistic Studies at the Pennsylvania State University for support provided during work on this project.

Michael Buxton (essay date 1984)

SOURCE: "The Influence of William James on John Dewey's Early Work," in *Journal of the History of Ideas,* Vol. XLV, No. 3, July-September, 1984, pp. 451-463.

[*In the following excerpt, Buxton examines the movement of Dewey's thought from idealism to pragmatism, and identifies William James as a singular influence on the evolution of Dewey's beliefs.*]

William James has generally been regarded as the source of John Dewey's rejection of neo-Hegelian absolute idealism in favor of a naturalist position. The intellectual relationship between the two men during the late nineteenth and early twentieth centuries is an important aspect of the history of American philosophy and psychology. Their early association occurred when Dewey was developing his philosophy of education. Yet until recently, Dewey's early work between the years 1882-1899 has been relatively ignored. This has led to the general acceptance of the myth of James's central influence over Dewey particularly between the years 1890-96. Recent textual examination of Dewey's early work has been made under the influence of, and has perpetuated, this myth.

The conventional view of James's influence has been accepted for over fifty years. Wayne Leys writing in 1970 effectively illustrates it. He claims that James "obviously" forced Dewey to reconsider the German theories of the self; that the James-Lange theory of emotion changed Dewey's conception of activity; that even in ***The Study of Ethics*** (1894) he was still an idealist, resisting relativity; and that in 1893 he was still under the influence of an idealist logic. It is safe to say, Leys argued, that Dewey put ethics and all other specialized studies into a larger picture as a result of his reflections upon James's *Principles of Psychology* (1890). Finally Leys also claims that Dewey failed to proceed "in one jump" to an ethical naturalism and that in 1894 "Dewey was in the process of rejecting the Idealist doctrine of an absolute self as the end of 'the tortuous path', but he was not abandoning the idea of the tortuous path."[1] The evidence supports none of these claims.

Before 1890, Dewey's views were clearly dominated by absolute idealist philosophy; after this date his familiar functionalist ideas became more clearly recognizable. The central difficulty is how to account for this change and adequately describe his views during the transition years 1890-94. The most attractive explanation has been the appeal to a single extraneous source. This argument relies on the similarity between James's and Dewey's beliefs, the possibility of influence, and Dewey's autobiographical comments as evidence of a causal connection. Dewey's biography states that "William James's *Principles of Psychology* was much the greatest single influence in changing the direction of Dewey's philosophical thinking." In referring to the *Principles* Dewey specifically excludes James's *The Will to Believe,* his *Pluralistic Universe* or his *Pragmatism.* Similarly, Dewey states in his autobiography that James's influence was the "one specifiable philosophic factor which entered into my thinking so as to give it a new direction and quality."[3]

A second approach to these years analyzes Dewey's idealist and instrumentalist thought as a continuum demonstrating an intrinsic relationship between each phase. Morton White has most noticeably argued this position but does not mention James.[4] I shall reassess the intellectual relationship between James and Dewey and argue that Dewey's movement from an absolute idealist to a functionalist orientation occurred when he independently reinterpreted his previous work by applying an early interest in the concept of biological function to his idealist concerns of the late 1880s. James and others later reinforced part of this process. Dewey's own reassessment was affected by the interaction of many people and events including James's writings in the late 1880s and in his *Principles.* The change in Dewey's thought was sudden and took place without the extent of difficulty

usually suggested. It was well under way by the time Dewey appointed George Herbert Mead to Michigan University in 1891 and began to assess James's work critically. By then Dewey had abandoned absolute idealism and had begun to formulate the basis of his functionalism. The argument will be supported by an examination of Dewey's early writings and of James's comments on Dewey's importance, and by assessing the reliability of Dewey's comments on the question of influence.

Early Influences on Dewey.—Dewey said that the chapters in James's *Principles* which influenced him most were those dealing with conception, discrimination and comparison, and reasoning.[5] For both James and Dewey, an analysis of the process of conception was basic to their view of mind as functionally active, to their attack on the insufficiency of disparate isolated sensations, and to their attempts to derive interactionist theories of knowledge. Dewey's views on the relationship between concepts and percepts provide the key to understanding the process of his change from absolute idealism to functionalism. His idealist writings during the 1880s show that he developed his views on this issue from experimental, psychological, and Kantian idealist and absolute idealist sources. His early functionalist work between 1890 and 1894 arose through his reexamination of the relationship he drew between conception and perception as an absolute idealist, particularly in 1887-88. The interactionist theory of mind Dewey adopted after 1890 differed markedly from that of James.

Dewey's views on conception and related subjects were published three years before the publication of James's book, in his ***Psychology,*** **"Knowledge as Idealization,"** and in **"Illusory Psychology"** (1887). In **"Knowledge as Idealization"** for example, Dewey anticipates James's comments in the *Principles* not only on the importance of the mind's interpretive activity in the process of conception but also on the abilities to discriminate, identify, relate, associate, attend and compare, and on the presentation of mind as a teleological and mediating factor. The mind constructs its own reality, Dewey argued; meaning is mediate and our view of reality is a function of our ideas. There is no perceptual world apart from conceptual order: a perception is a judgment based on an inference and sensations are meaningful only by being discriminated and mediated through concepts.[6]

Dewey's 1887 views on conception had three sources. First, he was influenced by idealists as diverse as Berkeley, Kant, and Bradley. Kant's account of mind actively interpreting sensations through the categories of self-consciousness particularly impressed Dewey. Secondly, Dewey agreed with Herbert Spencer's argument that sensations are nothing until discriminated, and with Lewes' emphasis on the importance of mental activity in organizing phenomena. Earlier, Dewey had strongly criticized the evolutionary theory of Spencer and "other materialists" in such articles as **"Soul and Body"**[7] (1886). Thirdly he was influenced by psychological experimentation, particularly Wundt's experimental school at Leipzig. Although Dewey rejected Wundt's empiricist philosophical assumptions, he attempted to combine the results of the Leipzig experiments (on mental content and the introspective experimental method) with the absolute idealists' concentration on mental phenomena. The result he hoped would be a psychology of interpreted or mediated experience in place of an "externally given. . . fixed conception of reality."[8] Dewey also refers to early experiments on reaction time in relation to astronomical measurement and, like James three years later, to Hermann von Helmholtz's famous work on tone, to illustrate the phenomenon of selective attention and the use of a conceptual structure to interpret sensations.[9]

Like Dewey, James argued that perception does not take place independently of the processes of interpretation and selection. "No one ever had a simple sensation by itself," James argued in his *Principles*; consciousness "from our natal day, is of a teeming multiplicity of objects and relations, and what we call simple sensations are results of discriminative attention." The Law, he argued, "is that all things fuse that *can* fuse, and nothing separates but what must"; a baby "feels it all as one great blooming, buzzing confusion." The notion that psychology should begin with sensations as the simplest mental facts is an assumption which wreaks havoc.[10]

As early as 1878, James argued that Spencer's theory made mind too mechanical and reduced it to a passive faculty which must adjust to a fixed environment. In contrast an organism is active in its reactions with an environment, striving for the ends presented by its interest, for the knower has an active mind that makes truth in transforming the world. It has a vote in the game and is not a mere looker-on.[11] James repeated this view in his *Principles of Psychology* where he argued that purposive action distinguished an intelligent from a mechanical performance.[12] In 1879 and 1882, in essays later reprinted as "The Sentiment of Rationality" in *The Will to Believe* (1897), James also discussed concepts in terms of the subjective interests of the interpreter. "No abstract concept can be a valid substitute for a concrete reality except with reference to a particular interest in the conceiver."[13] James consistently maintained this position. "Nothing," he said again in 1912, "shall be admitted as fact . . . except what can be experienced at some definite time by some experiment. . . . Everything real must be experienced somewhere and every kind of thing experienced must be something real."[14] James's 1878, 1879, and 1882 statements were published respectively in the *Journal of Speculative Philosophy, Mind,* and the *Princeton Review.* These journals were read by Dewey and James's comments would have been known to him.[15] Yet recollecting over forty-five years after the publication of James's *Principles,* Dewey specifically rejects them as influences.

Dewey and James were influenced by similar psychological and to a lesser extent philosophical sources. They quote the same physiological and psychological experiments and other sources independently of each other.

This was not unusual. The rapid growth of an American interest in German physiological and psychological experimentation and German philosophy affected thousands of young Americans in the 1880s. Both men rejected the then standard British empiricist view of consciousness, *viz.,* that the basic elements of mind are atomic sensations produced either by external objects or impressions of internal mental events, and that our ideas are formed by a combination of these discrete perceptions. James's and Dewey's rejection of elementarism and atomism led them away from structuralist and associationist psychologies. They rejected specifically the elementarism and psychological parallelism of Wilhelm Wundt's physiological psychology then dominant in Europe. Wundt's separation of body and mind had no appeal for Dewey.[16]

As an idealist between 1884 and 1890, Dewey emphasized the same teleological, active, mediating, and antimechanistic features in his account of mind as James had in 1890. James's work provided a reconciliation between teleology and materialism, two concepts which Dewey as an idealist had regarded as irreconcilable. However, by 1890 Dewey had already begun to reinterpret his own idealist views on conception and perception in a functionalist manner.

Dewey's Writings 1890-94—Three aspects of Dewey's thought between 1890 and 1894 show the quite sudden development of his functionalist views and their derivation from his early idealist account of conception. These are his views on logic, ethics, and psychology.

(1) *Logic.* Four articles[17] written between January 1890 and October 1891 take up the criticism of formal logic made in **"The New Psychology"** (1894) in **"Psychology as Philosophic Method"** (1886) and in **"Leibniz's New Essays Concerning the Human Understanding"** (1888). He argues for a "transcendental logic" and still shows the absolute idealist influence of George S. Morris who initiated him into a study of Hegel's logic.

Yet Dewey's continued interest in the question of how perception and observation are logically related to thinking, led him to enlarge on the analysis found in his ***Psychology*** and **"Knowledge as Idealization."** In his articles published in January and April 1890 and written before James's *Principles* was published, he argues that the mind isolates relations from facts, forms a hypothesis and compares it with other facts. Both idea and "facts" are flexible, and verification is the process of mutual adjustment, of organic interaction. This reciprocal action is exemplified by the theory of evolution. Theory and data are not fixed or unchangeable either in amount or quality: theory may be pliable so that it "fits the facts"; data may also be transformed, "elastic to the touch of the theory." His conclusion is that "there is no other test of a theory than this, its ability to *work,* to organize "facts" into itself as specifications of its own nature . . . on the other side, the particulars attacked by the universal do not remain indifferent; through it they are placed in a new light, and as facts gain a new quality."[18]

Dewey here conveys much that is characteristic of his later instrumentalism. The interactionist relationship between "theory" and "fact" and his emphasis on future results i.e., on a theory which "works" was an early statement of his later view that concepts and theories are instrumental towards the production of future facts, and that a hypothesis is a step towards solving a felt problem by means of concepts translated into action. His explanation of the role of concepts is an important step in showing the mediating role of intelligence, for his logical theory of concepts and inferences which formed the bases of his instrumentalism. His attack on fixed and final logical categories became an essential part of his later thought. The examples he gives also show the changing tendency in his thought: he not only now refers to Darwin's evolutionary theory approvingly, but later in October 1891, in the context of justifying Hegel's dialectic, Dewey uses a functional analysis; just as a human organism sustains any one organ, so the organ "in turn, contributes to and thus helps constitute the organism."[19]

Dewey accepted transcendental logic at that time, because he believed it made knowledge of reality depend upon forms and categories which the mind imposed rigorously on all interpretation; but he showed that the emphasis in idealist logic upon the reciprocal dependence of mind and matter could be restated in an essentially functionalist view of the relationship between theory and fact.

(2) *Ethics.* Between 1891 and 1893, Dewey in his writings on ethics decisively and rapidly rejected absolute idealism and its associated metaphysical positions such as those developed by T. H. Green and F. H. Bradley. His rapid acceptance of a functionalist position was illustrated at first not by reference to James but by his reassessment of the work of the British absolute idealist philosopher, T. H. Green. In April 1889 and January 1890, Dewey had continued the unqualified praise of Green which had characterized his thought from 1884,[20] but in March 1890, he criticized Green for the first time[21] and continued this reassessment in three further articles published between 1891 and November 1893.[22]

Dewey there developed his idealist views on the concept-percept, or general-particular relation by stressing the concrete and the particular in preference to what he calls the remote and abstract ethical categories of metaphysicians such as Green. Thus he continued his rejection of fixed and abstract categories of thought which he had first adopted as an idealist in his **"Knowledge as Idealization"** (1887).

He now talks of practice in discussing the relation between fact and theory. A theory, he says, is a generalization of facts. The active process and practice of enquiry inevitably leads to theory formulation; practice therefore is theory in action. Metaphysical moral theories are abstract and remote from engagement with action, for their ideas cannot be used. Moral conduct results from an individual's perception of practical, concrete relationships; "it is what and where and how to the last inch." Moral rules are therefore working tools of analysis. They are no different in kind from those we use to measure goods, sell wheat or invent the telephone.[23]

Dewey also reexamined and rejected the absolute idealists' concepts of self-realization and activity and again used Green as his main target. In **"On Some Current Conceptions of the Term 'Self'"** (1886) and **"Psychology as Philosophic Method"**[24] (1886), Dewey accepted the absolute idealist belief that an individual self must be actively realized in absolute self-consciousness. In **"Self Realization as the Moral Ideal"** (1893) he argued that this metaphysical definition makes moral experience a process of gradually attaining a fixed, remote, and empty ideal. In its place, we should substitute a working definition of the self, the notion of a working or practical self. To realize our capacity we must act concretely and see knowledge only in relation to action.[25] Similarly, to concentrate on activity only in terms of the active union of the individual in the absolute, as Green did, is to ignore the fact that all action is concrete and individualized. Ethical theory then should also be concrete and particular in its rules of "action stated in its more general terms."[26]

As early as January 1891, in **"Moral Theory and Practice"** Dewey understood that these sentiments meant he had moved from a metaphysical to a naturalistic ethics, by attacking the distinction between "ought" and "is" statements. In determining what we ought to do, we consider only the existing practical situation, and our concrete relations to others. The "'ought' always rises from and falls back into the 'is' and . . . the 'ought' is itself an 'is'—the 'is' of action."[27]

(3) *Psychology.* Dewey's functionalist analysis of the concept-percept relationship also redirected his psychological thought. During the 1880s Dewey had attempted a psychological analysis of experience from an absolute idealist perspective, but in **"How Do Concepts Arise From Percepts?"**[28] (November 1891), his new functionalist beliefs are as clearly applied to psychology as to logic and ethics at that time.

He rejected the early structuralist model of independent, isolated conceptual elements and adopted a functionalist view of parts which operate as members of an interconnected unity and which "go together and work together" and actively serve a general purpose. A functionalist approach emphasizes "the *work* done by that thing and its value for the organism." This model leads him to his functionalist explanation of the meaning of a concept according to which a whole is viewed in relation to its working parts. A concept does not denote a passive mental state or isolated existence but has an intellectual function or active role. The notion of activity is inseparably related to its function just as that of function is inseparable from the characteristic meaning of a concept to "be grasped only in and through the activity which constitutes it."[29]

In **"The Superstition of Necessity"**[30] (April 1893) Dewey again showed that his re-examination of the concept-percept relationship redirected his thought from idealism to instrumentalism. Those who accept the relativity of knowledge agree that "objects, *as known,* are not independent of the process of knowing, but are the content of our judgments . . . that the 'object' (anyway as known) is a form of judgment. . . . " If so, then objects as they are known change with the development of our judgments. Dewey then made two claims from this argument which became central to his later instrumentalist position. First, if such change occurs then truth "must attach to late rather than to early judgments."[31] This suggests something of the pragmatic conception of truth as developed later by Dewey and James whereby truth is not static but grows, and an idea "becomes true" if it "successfully leads" from one part of our experience to another.[32] For James in his *Pragmatism* (1907) the test of ethical truth is in grasping the consequences of an idea in action. The basis of this important pragmatist principle is evident in Dewey's writings years before James systematized and more broadly publicized his own views on the matter late in the 1890s and restated them in more extended form in 1907.

Second, in speaking of the importance of judgment in conception Dewey states that the distinction between two interpretations apparently of the same object, is "not simply a superimposition of new qualities upon an old object, that old object remaining the same; it is not getting new objects; it is a continual qualitative reconstruction of the object itself . . . the first judgments do not make the object once for all, but . . . the continued process of judging is a continued process of 'producing' the object."[33]

This statement further elaborates the argument on truth, and introduces the notion of reconstruction which was to be such a central aspect of his later philosophy. To illustrate this argument Dewey used Venn's *Empirical Logic,* rather than the work of William James.

Dewey's work on ethics at this time was derived from the same psychological account of experience which characterized his early idealist and functionalist writings.[34] This psychological account was derived from German idealism and stressed the active interactionist role of mind in concept formation. It opposed the passive atomic and dualist account identified with British empiricism and its derivative structuralist and associationist psychologies. Dewey's two books on ethics during this transition period, *Outlines of a Critical Theory of Ethics* (1891) and *The Study of Ethics: A Syllabus* (1894), show a process of change similar to what appeared in his articles.

His *Outlines* contains details of his undergraduate ethics course at Michigan University; Dewey's description of that course shows how he applied his "critical theory."[35] This book is usually taken to be the work of an idealist, and the functionalist sentiments of *The Study of Ethics* as evidence of James's influence; however, the *Outlines* is far from the work of an uncompromising idealist. The book speaks initially of an absolute which was not rigid but could be applied as a method of action to concrete cases.[36] It also uses the word "ideal" in a functionalist manner. By 1892-93 Dewey had rejected all theories of an absolute ideal whether these were concerned with a fixed absolute or one which could adjust and change. In 1894, in his *Study of Ethics*, he enlarged on this rejection. There in the section on "Theories of Abstract Ideals" he wrote that the absolute as "ideal" was a fixed, remote, unattainable, idealistic metaphysical concept. Absolute ideas cannot be translated "into items of a concrete, individual act—and every *act* is concrete and individual." They do not and cannot become a working principle for what has to be done. We need working hypotheses of action.[37]

Dewey himself called attention to the *Outlines'* "analysis of individuality into function including capacity and environment."[38] In particular, the *Outlines* emphasized the two functionalist uses of "mind" as the means of adapting an individual to and reconstructing the environment. "Even a plant must do something more than adjust itself *to* a fixed environment; it must assert itself *against* its surroundings, subordinating them and transforming them into material and nutriment." Thus, the transformation of existing circumstances rather than the mere reproduction of them describes moral action. The *Outlines'* application of this argument to learning anticipated one of the central stances of *Democracy and Education* (1916): in learning we may not only appropriate the general intellectual environment already in existence, but may also actively increase or even reconstruct the prior environment.[39] Individuality means not separation from, but a defined position in, a whole.

Part II of the *Outlines*, in particular, shows clearly the beginning of the change the Dewey's philosophy through its emphasis on function, the practical, the inseparability of "ought" and "is," and the definition of a rule as a tool of analysis. The similarity between the functionalist ideas and language used in Dewey's article **"Moral Theory and Practice"** (Jan. 1891) and part of the final section of his *Outlines* in striking. The *Outlines* shows Dewey reexamining his own idealist position and rapidly incorporating new functionalist ideas into the argument of the book. Similarly, much of *The Study of Ethics* was the result of Dewey's incorporation of articles on ethics published after the *Outlines*, into a revision of the 1891 book.

Dewey's and James's Comments—Dewey later claimed that he was influenced by two "unreconciled strains" in James's *Principles of Psychology*.[40] First, the book restated the traditional view of psychology as a theory of consciousness; however I have shown above that Dewey had adopted this tradition as an idealist, as his concentration on the role of concepts in the mental construction of reality shows. From 1890, he then reinterpreted and stated this view in a functionalist form, while retaining its emphasis on mental activity, teleology, and interactionism.

The second and most important influence of James's *Principles* on his thought, Dewey stated, was "the objective psychology theory . . . founded on biology" which he discovered in James's book. James's application of the idea of biological function, arising from physiological experimentation, to a theory of mind was what Dewey believed "worked its way more and more into all my ideas and acted as a ferment to transform old beliefs."[41] Is this assessment accurate?

Dewey was thoroughly familiar with the concept of function in physiology, biology, and psychology from his college years before 1882. By 1894, in **"The New Psychology,"** he showed he was impressed by the implications of the biological concepts of organism and function for a theory of mind. He knew of James's early instrumentalist work, the details of Huxley's and Tyndall's writings, and the work of philosophers such as Herbert Spencer who attempted to explain mind in terms of his Lamarckian evolutionary theory. He then ignored their work for the rest of the decade and became a committed idealist influenced by Hegel, the American Hegelian George S. Morris, and British absolute idealists particularly T. H. Green and Edward Caird. Nevertheless these early evolutionist and functionalist writings became a key element in his reinterpretation of his views after 1890 when he applied his early interest in function to his idealist account of conception. Dewey's self-assessment thus ignores his extensive knowledge of evolutionary biology and function applied to a theory of mind prior to 1890 and James's earlier work on this subject between 1878 and 1882. It also neglects the contribution to his own thinking by others such as George Herbert Mead and Alfred Henry Lloyd at the University of Michigan after 1891, and Mead and the functional psychologist James R. Angell at the University of Chicago after 1894. Most of all it ignores the process of change well under way by 1890. Dewey's recollections forty-five years after the event did not benefit from hindsight.

Dewey played the central role in the formulation of an account of instrumental intelligence during the 1890s and early twentieth century. His educational views arose and were inseparable from this philosophical and psychological account. He was an originator influenced by a wide variety of people and ideas. This central role was recognized by James. On March 11, 1903 James wrote to Dewey that having just read A. W. Moore's *Existence, Meaning and Reality* he saw "an entirely new 'school of thought' forming, and, I believe, a true one." Soon after, James added: "It humiliates me that I had to wait till I read Moore's article before finding how much on my own lines you were working. Of course I had welcomed you as one coming nearer and nearer, but I had missed the central root of the whole business, and shall now re-read you. . . . I fancy that much depends on that place one starts from. You have all come from Hegel and your terminology *s'en ressent,* I from empiricism, and though we reach much the same goal it superficially looks different from the opposite sides."[42]

James's repeated references in letters between March and November 1903 to Dewey's new Chicago school of functionalist thought were an indication of his enthusiasm for his discovery. He first publicized the name "Chicago School" in January 1904 in his review of Dewey's *Studies in Logical Theory* announcing: "Professor John Dewey, and at least ten of his disciples, have collectively put into the world a statement, homogeneous in spite of so many co-operating minds, of a view of the world, both theoretical and practical, which is so simple, massive, and positive that, in spite of the fact that many parts of it yet need to be worked out, it deserves the title of a new system of philosophy."[43] By 1907 he was referring to the central importance of "the instrumental view of truth taught so successfully at Chicago" adding that "our contemporary pragmatists especially Messrs. Schiller and Dewey, have given the only tenable account of this subject."[44]

James's own assessment of Dewey's importance in the context of a school of thought and the times is the correct analysis. To it can be added Edwin Boring's view that James was only a symptom of what was about to happen: " . . . all this excitement getting the new psychology under way in America in the 1880s and 1900s is not to be accounted for by any personal act of James." America was ready for what the times had for it and created something unique from the "efforts of many men."[45] Dewey's own recollections are therefore not quite supported by his own writings or by a review of others; relevant evidence.

EXPERIMENTAL IDEALISM

Finally, Dewey is commonly supposed to have attempted to combine his idealism and a developing biologically based functionalism during these years of transition. Morton White, for example, in an influential argument, could not accept the alleged simultaneous adherence by such an anti-dualist as Dewey during these transition years, to the seemingly contradictory positions of instrumentalism and idealism. He therefore argues that during this period Dewey attempted to combine the two positions and became an "instrumental Hegelian." The organicism of each position is alleged to have provided a means by which they were reconciled.[46] This argument is now universally accepted. The evidence usually cited in its support is twofold. Firstly, there is Dewey's own description of his philosophy in *The Study of Ethics: A Syllabus* (1894) as "experimental idealism."[47] Secondly, Dewey also spoke in retrospect of his alleged attempt to combine both positions, saying: "There was a period extending into my earlier years at Chicago, when in connection with a seminar in Hegel's Logic, I tried reinterpreting his categories in terms of "readjustment" and "reconstruction." Gradually I came to realize that what the principles actually stood for could be better understood and stated when completely emancipated from Hegelian garb."[48]

Recent studies have also interpreted Dewey's early work from this position. George Dykhuizen, for example, accepts the "undeniably pragmatic slant" of Dewey's work after 1890 and produces no satisfactory examples to show that Dewey tried to combine both positions. But against all the evidence of Dewey's writings, and contemporary accounts such as James's, he then interprets these writings by the criteria White identified. Dykhuizen states that Dewey throughout the 1890s believed that an active dynamic individual adjusting to an environment can be best explained in relation to an absolute mind manifesting itself as a rationally structured universe. The first published indication of Dewey's break with "experimental idealism" and Hegelian logic and metaphysics was in 1900, Dykhuizen claims.[49] This ignores the direction of a decade of work, and places the change in Dewey's thought ten years too late.

There is no evidence of any attempt to reconcile both positions. Where both positions are included in the same work, as in his **Outlines,** Dewey expressed later functionalist thoughts in a work begun as an idealist. I have argued here that Dewey ceased to be an idealist in any meaningful sense in 1891 and from then on, rapidly adopted the basis of his later functionalism which he gradually systematized during the remaining years of the decade. He always saw philosophical absolute idealism and evolutionary biology as contradictory. During the early 1880s, he was impressed with biological holism, but after his 1884 article **"The New Psychology"** decisively rejected it along with all forms of materialism. After 1890-91, Dewey continued to see both positions as incompatible, but then rejected absolute idealism. The writings of his transition years of 1890-94 clearly show the absence of any attempted reconciliation.

NOTES

[1] Jo Ann Boyston *et al.,* (eds.), *John Dewey: The Early Works 1887-1898* (Carbondale, 1969-1972), 4. Introduction by Wayne Leys, *passim.*

[2] "Biography of John Dewey," in Paul Arthur Schilpp (ed.), *The Philosophy of John Dewey* (Chicago, 1939), 23.

[3] John Dewey, "From Absolutism to Experimentalism," in Richard Bernstein (ed.), *John Dewey, On Experience, Nature and Freedom* (Indianapolis, 1960), 15-16.

[4] Morton White, *The Origins of Dewey's Instrumentalism* (Cambridge, Mass., 1943)

[5] Schilpp, *op. cit.;* Dewey, *op. cit.*

[6] *Early Works,* I, 179-187. First published in *Mind,* 12 (July 1887), 382-96.

[7] *Early Works,* I, 93-115. First published in *Bibliotheca Sacra,* 43 (April 1886), 239-63.

[8] "Knowledge as Idealization," *Early Works,* I, 192-93.

[9] *Ibid.,* 180-81. James refers to Helmholtz in *The Principles of Psychology* (New York, 1890), I, 284-89, and *The Will to Believe and Other Essays in Popular Philosophy* (New York, 1897), 85. Dewey and James were

referring to Helmholtz's *On the Sensations of Tone as a Physiological Basis for the Theory of Music,* translated by Alexander J. Ellis (London, 1875).

[10] *The Principles of Psychology,* I, 224, 448.

[11] "Remarks on Spencer's Definition of Mind as Correspondence," *Journal of Speculative Philosophy,* 12 (1878), 18.

[12] *The Principles of Psychology,* I, 8.

[13] *The Will to Believe and Other Essays in Popular Philosophy* (New York and London, 1897), 70. Parts of the Chapter "The Sentiment of Rationality" were first published in *Mind,* 4 (1879), 317-46, and the *Princeton Review,* 2 (1882), 58-96.

[14] *Essays in Radical Empiricism* (New York and London, 1912), 160.

[15] See Lewis S. Feuer, "John Dewey's Reading at College," *Journal of the History of Ideas,* 19 (1958), 415-21.

[16] Dewey showed an extensive knowledge of nineteenth-century experimental psychology and its origins in "Knowledge as Idealization," "The New Psychology," *Andover Review,* 2 (Sept. 1884), 278-89, *Psychology* (New York, 1887), and his review of George T. Ladd's *Elements of Physiological Psychology* in *New Englander and Yale Review,* 46 (June 1887), 528-37. Among the hundreds of authors cited in these works (236 in *Psychology* alone) he shows a familiarity with the work of Weber, Muller, Lange, Fechner, Helmholtz, Lotze, Wundt, Ebbinghaus, Ward, Ladd, Hall, and James McKeen Cattell. He studied sources such as Wundt's Journal *Philosophische Studien* since at the time there was no good history of psychology in English or French (*Psychology, Early Works,* 2, 17). James possessed a similarly thorough knowledge and in 1875 offered a graduate course on "The Relations between Physiology and Psychology" and began the first psychological laboratory in the United States of America at Harvard.

[17] "On Some Current Conceptions of the term 'Self'," *Mind,* 15 (Jan. 1890), 58-74. "Is Logic a Dualistic Science?," *Open Court,* 3 (Jan. 1890), 2040-43, "The Logic of Verification," *Open Court,* 4 (April, 1890), 2225-28. "The Present Position of Logical Theory," *Monist,* 2 (October 1891), 1-17.

[18] *Early Works,* 3, 87-88.

[19] *Ibid.,* 138.

[20] "The Philosophy of Thomas Hill Green," *Andover Review,* 11 (April 1889), 337-55. "On Some Current Conceptions of the term 'Self'."

[21] Review of Edward Caird, *The Critical Philosophy of Immanuel Kant, Andover Review,* 13 (March 1890), 325-27.

[22] "Moral Theory and Practice," *International Journal of Ethics,* 1 (Jan. 1891), 186-203. "Green's Theory of the Moral Motive," *Philosophical Review,* 1 (Nov. 1892), 593-612. "Self Realization as the Moral Ideal," *Philosophical Review,* 2 (Nov. 1893), 652-64.

[23] *Early Works,* 3, 95, 98.

[24] "Psychology as Philosophic Method," *Mind,* 11 (April 1886), 153-73.

[25] *Ibid.,* 4, 53-54; *ibid.,* 43, 50, 53.

[26] "Green's Theory of the Moral Motive," *ibid.,* III, 156-59, 163.

[27] *Ibid.,* 105-09.

[28] *Public School Journal,* 11 (Nov. 1891) 128-30.

[29] *Early Works,* III, 142.

[30] *Monist,* 3 (April 1893), 362-79.

[31] *Early Works,* IV, 21-23.

[32] William James, *Pragmatism: A New Name for Some Old Ways of Thinking* (New York, 1907), 201.

[33] *Early Works,* IV, 23.

[34] See *The Study of Ethics,* Prefatory note; and Schilpp (ed.), *op. cit.,* 23.

[35] "The Ethical Record," 2 (Oct. 1889), 145-48.

[36] *Early Works,* III, 325.

[37] *Ibid.,* 4, 286-62.

[38] *Ibid.,* 3, 239; see also Schilpp (ed.), *op. cit.,* 22.

[39] *Early Works,* III, 325, 304, 376, 313-14.

[40] Schilpp (ed.), *op. cit.,* 23.

[41] "From Absolutism to Experimentalism," 16.

[42] R. B. Perry, *The Thought and Character of William James.* Briefer edition. (New York, 1954), 306-07.

[43] William James, "The Chicago School," *The Psychological Bulletin,* 1 (Jan., 1904) 1. See also Perry *op. cit.,* 308; and *The Letters of William James,* 2 vols (Boston, 1920), II, 201-02.

[44] *Pragmatism . . .* 49, 197.

[45] Edwin G. Boring, "The Influence of Evolutionary Theory Upon American Psychological Thought," in Stow Persons (ed.), *Evolutionary Thought in America* (New York, 1956), 272-73; see also Perry *op. cit.,* 304.

[46] *Op. cit.,* 79-113.

[47] *Early Works,* IV, 264.

[48] Schilpp (ed.), *op. cit.,* 8.

[49] George Dykhuizen, *The Life and Mind of John Dewey* (Carbondale, Ill., 1973), 68-70, 82-83.

Brian Patrick Hendley (essay date 1986)

SOURCE: "John Dewey and the Laboratory School," in *Dewey, Russell, Whitehead: Philosophers as Educators,* Southern Illinois University Press, 1986, pp. 14-42.

[*In the following essay, Hendley presents a history of Dewey's Laboratory School, and focuses on Dewey's philosophical and educational goals for the school.*]

> I went to the Dewey School one day,
> And saw the children all at play.
> But when the tardy bell had rung,
> All the classes had begun.
> Some to Science, some to French,
> Some to shop to work at the bench.
>
> L.o.t.D.o.E., Dewey, Dewey, Dew-ee-ee.
>
> When Thursday afternoon is here
> There are excursions if it's clear
> To Stony Island in Highland Park,
> And they often stay till nearly dark.
> Mister Gillett points here and there,
> Showing things both strange and fair.
>
> L.o.t.D.o.E., Dewey, Dewey, Dew-ee-ee.[1]

Thus the students immortalized in song the experimental school run by the Department of Pedagogy of the University of Chicago and headed from 1896 to 1904 by John Dewey. The refrain of the song is shorthand for "Laboratory of the Department of Education." Although the school was officially called the University Elementary School, it became popularly known as the "Dewey School" or, on the suggestion of Ella Flagg Young, the "Laboratory School."[2] Dewey himself often compared the function of this school in his department to that of laboratories in biology, physics, or chemistry. "Like any such laboratory," he said, "it has two main purposes: (1) to exhibit, test, verify, and criticize theoretical statements and principles; (2) to add to the sum of facts and principles in its special line."[3]

Having a school to test educational theories and ideas suited Dewey's pragmatic temper nicely. He thought that "the mere profession of principles without their practical exhibition and testing will not engage the respect of the educational profession" and that without such exhibition and testing, "the theoretical work partakes of the nature of a farce and imposture—it is like professing to give "thorough training in a science and then neglecting to provide a laboratory for faculty and students to work in."[4] Rather than separate the theory from the practice, we should bring the two together. This will result in a more viable, realistic set of ideas and principles of education as well as give direction and guidance to our day-to-day educational activities.

Dewey felt strongly that in education as in other areas of thought and action a well-ordered experiment requires that "There must be a continual union of theory and practice; of reaction of one into the other. The leading idea must direct and clarify the work; the work must serve to criticize, to modify, to build up the theory."[5] In pedagogy especially, Dewey felt that we must escape the dualism between general principles and empirical routine or rule of thumb and instead promote a "vital interaction of theoretical principle and practical detail."[6] How he saw this taking place he spelled out in greater detail in an essay entitled **"The Relations of Theory to Practice in Education."**[7]

Dewey distinguishes two ways to approach practice in education: from the point of view of the apprentice and that of the laboratory. The apprentice approach would have us seek to give teachers a working command of the tools of their trade, a skill and proficiency in teaching methods, a control of the techniques of class instruction and management. With the laboratory approach, we "use practice work as an instrument in making real and vital theoretical instructions; the knowledge of subject-matter and of principles of education."[8] Here the immediate aim is not to produce efficient workmen but to supply the intellectual methods and materials of good workmanship, just as in other professional schools (architecture, engineering, medicine, law, etc.) where the aim is "*control of the intellectual methods* required for personal and independent mastery of practical skill, rather than at turning out at once masters of the craft."[9]

Dewey always insisted that teaching is a profession, and the training of teachers should follow scientific lines. Too often it had been thought that "anybody—almost everybody—could teach. Everybody was innocent at least until proved guilty."[10] The time had come to pay greater heed to the theory and practice of teaching. Although he favored the establishment of practice schools for teachers, he recognized that most practice schools only approximate ordinary conditions of teaching and learning, usually safeguarding the children's interest and supervising their activities to such an extent that "the situation approaches learning to swim without going too near the water."[11] He criticized normal practice work in education for depriving the practice teacher of responsibility for discipline in the classroom, and for its unrealistic aspects such as the continued presence of an expert teacher, the reduction of class size, and the use of predetermined lesson plans. The very context of such training for teachers militates against an immediate practical application because it fails to connect the theory with experience, even

with the very practical experience of life that the apprentice-teacher has had before coming to learn how to teach in the first place.

Another factor often missing in such schemes is a lack of instruction in subject matter. Since there are obviously good teachers who have never had any training in practical pedagogy but show only a mastery of and enthusiasm for their subject matter (one wonders if Dewey had himself in mind here since he reputedly followed very few of the accepted methods for effective teaching[12]), "scholarship per se may itself be a most effective tool for training and turning out good teachers."[13] There is, Dewey points out, method in subject matter, scientific method, the method of the mind itself. True scholars are "so full of the spirit of inquiry, so sensitive to every sign of its presence and absence, that no matter what they do, nor how they do it, they succeed in awakening and inspiring like alert and intense mental activity in those with whom they come in contact."[14]

For Dewey, this applies to teachers at an elementary level of education as well as to those engaged in higher education. What is needed in the training of teachers is more of a continuity of classroom experience with actual conditions of teaching and learning as well as with real life experiences, more emphasis on the subject matter to be taught, more freedom and responsibility for the practice teacher. In a later formulation, Dewey said that the method of teaching is the method of an art. It involves the study of past operations and results that have been successful, thorough acquaintance with current materials and tools, and careful scrutinizing of one's own attempts to see what succeeds and fails.[15] This is what Dewey sought to provide in his Laboratory School.

The school was not meant to be a practice school in the ordinary sense; nor did Dewey see the training of teachers to be the main goal of the Department of Pedagogy. Rather, he saw the school as taking "teachers who have already considerable experience, and who now wish to acquaint themselves more thoroughly with the rational principles of their subject, and with the more recent of educational movements."[16] What he had in mind were former superintendents and normal school teachers. The Laboratory School would serve as a focus to keep the theoretical work in touch with the demands of practice and experimentally to test and develop methods of teaching. Dewey believed there was nothing the primary schools needed more than "the presentation of methods which are the offspring of a sound psychology, and have also been worked out in detail under the crucial tests of experience."[17]

He did not intend his school to "turn out methods and materials which can be slavishly copied elsewhere."[18] It sought to demonstrate certain principles as fundamental in education. It could be seen as having an indirect influence on public education by serving as an example of new experimental lines of thought and thereby preparing the public for the acceptance of similar changes in the system, by training specialists in theory and practice who could begin to make such changes, and by publishing the results of the experiment to make them available to teachers elsewhere.

Dewey undoubtedly saw this as an opportunity to break down the isolation he so often decried in education. Here at Chicago the beginning phases of the educational system (kindergarten and the elementary grades) were to be in vital contact with the highest (university and graduate school), and the more concrete and practical problems were to interact with the more abstract, theoretical speculations to the benefit of both. The traditional dualism between thought and action was thus to be overcome, and working hypotheses in education were to be exhibited and tested to prove their worth. In all this we could say that Dewey himself was attempting to practice what he preached about knowledge in general and about teaching and learning in particular. Students in the Department of Pedagogy were to be instructed in the history and theory of school systems, "the theory of the best attainable organization and administration in our own country under existing conditions," the historical development of ideas concerning education, and the bearings of psychology and sociology upon the curriculum and on teaching methods.[19] "The nerve of the whole scheme," said Dewey in an early statement to President William Rainey Harper of the University of Chicago, is "the conduct of a school of demonstration, observation, and experiment in connection with the theoretical instruction."[20]

Harper evidently agreed that such a school would be a valuable component in the training of teachers, and Dewey's proposals were approved by the Board of Trustees and an appropriation of $1,000 made to help get the school started. The rest of its income was expected to come from tuition and gifts from parents and friends.[21] The tale of this initial appropriation sheds some light on Dewey's subsequent falling out with Harper over the school. According to his wife, Alice Dewey, "The trustees of the University had felt the need of a laboratory of Psychology, but they were suspicious of a laboratory of Education. It so happened that in October of 1895 a sum of one thousand dollars had been appropriated for a Psychological laboratory. As no room or other facility for utilizing that fund could be provided, it was likely to revert. Influence upon the president at that moment brought him to consent to its use for Education, thus officially sanctioning the Educational phase of the new department."[22] Although it is certainly not unusual for a University administrator to reallocate funds already provided for in his budget, this does not seem to me to indicate the kind of enthusiastic support of the school that some have attributed to Harper.[23]

Even the thousand dollars had strings attached to it, for it was "not in cash, but in tuitions of graduate students who were to teach in the school."[24] As his daughter, Jane Dewey, put it, "The University allowed one thousand dollars in free tuition to teachers in the school, but gave no further financial aid. For the seven and a half years of its existence friends and patrons contributed more to the support of this school than did the University."[25] On top of this, Dewey was required to submit an annual budget to Harper for consideration and approval by the university trustees. Small wonder that Dewey reportedly found the financial relationship between his school and the university "trying and, at times, even vexing."[26] Some of the financial difficulties faced by the school can be gleaned from Dewey's Report to the President for the year July 1898-July 1899. Total expenses were listed as $12,870.26, of which tuition covered $4,916.00. "The University gave seven free scholarship tuitions, aggregating $840.00 in return for service in the school," according to the report, and the rest of the money had to be made up by personal gifts. About $350.00 was realized from a series of lectures given by Dewey to parents, students, and friends of the school and subsequently published as the book *The School and Society*.[27]

The school opened in January 1896, with sixteen pupils, aged six to nine, and with Miss Clara I. Mitchell, formerly of the Cook County Normal School, in charge and Mr. F. W. Smedley, a graduate student of pedagogy, directing the manual training work.[28] In October 1896, the school changed locations and added Miss Katherine Camp, formerly of the Pratt Institute, to teach science and the domestic arts. She later became Mrs. Katherine Camp Mayhew and with her sister, Anna Camp Edwards, a history teacher and special tutor for older children, wrote a thorough and detailed history of the school. After several changes of location and the addition of more staff, the school's enrollment eventually grew to 140 students of from four to fifteen years of age with a teaching staff of twenty-three and ten part-time assistants.[29] Dewey served as director, Mrs. Dewey as principal, and Ella Flagg Young, who was later to become Chicago's first superintendent of schools, as supervisor of instruction.[30]

Each of these women exerted a strong influence on Dewey. Jane Dewey claimed that her father "regards Mrs. Young as the wisest person in school matters with whom he has come in contact in any way. . . . Contact with her supplemented Dewey's educational ideas where his own experience was lacking in matters of practical administration, crystallizing his ideas of democracy in the school and, by extension, in life."[31] His wife was said to be a moving force behind the school. According to Max Eastman, Dewey would never have started a Dewey school had it not been for his wife Alice. "Dewey never did anything, except think . . . unless he got kicked into it . . . Mrs. Dewey would grab Dewey's ideas—and grab him—and insist that something be done. . . . Dewey's view of his wife's influence is that she put 'guts and stuffing' into what had been with him mere intellectual conclusions."[32]

The Deweys had more than an academic interest in the school since by 1902 four of their own children were enrolled.[33] Even before they came to Chicago, Alice was said to be keen on trying out some of John's theories on their children at home. While Dewey was at the University of Michigan, this was said to have led to "many unconventional and unexpected situations which, when created in the presence of outsiders, caused considerable merriment and comment, 'Old Ann Arborites,' according to one report, 'still regale themselves with tales of how the Dewey methods worked.'"[34] However amusing these early attempts might have been to some outside observers, the experimental approach of the Laboratory School was no laughing matter among professional educators. In 1900, A. B. Hinsdale, professor of the Science and the Art of Teaching and a colleague of Dewey's at the University of Michigan, claimed, "More eyes are now fixed upon The University Elementary School at Chicago than upon any other elementary school in the country and probably in the world—eyes watching to see the outcome of the interesting experiment."[35]

Mayhew and Edwards state that the students in the Laboratory School came mainly from professional families.[36] McCaul estimates that most were faculty children from middle- or upper-class backgrounds.[37] The vast majority of parents were strong supporters of the school. At the beginning of the second year a Parents' Association was formed "to assure financial support for the school and to provide information about its radical departures in method and content." For three years "a parents' class was formed, open to all members, in which Mr. Dewey set forth his theories, discussed them, and answered questions regarding the activities of the school.[38] Although Dewey counted on the parents for moral and financial support for his endeavors, not all of them were totally enamoured with what was going on in the school. One father made this caustic comment about his son's experiences there: "One year at the University Preparatory Laboratory, otherwise known as the D—School (supply the proper word, not on Sunday, please!) nearly ruined him. We have to teach him how to study. He learned to 'observe' last year."[39]

Ella Flagg Young maintained that people who came to the school with preconceived notions on how teaching and learning were to be carried out often went home disappointed with what they had seen. Traditional ideas of order and discipline, of the role of the teacher and the place of the student, of how it should be manifest that something had been learned, even of the posture of the child in his or her seat, all these tended to obscure what was actually being accomplished.[40] Laura Runyon has described her first visit to the school as a curious parent who found that her initial scepticism gave way to an enthusiastic endorsement of what was happening.[41] She liked what she saw so much that she became a teacher of history at the school and wrote an M.A. thesis at the University of Chicago on *The Teaching of Elementary History in the Dewey School* (1906, unpublished).

Unfortunately, most of our information about the school and its achievements is of just that sort of personal and impressionistic writing. Harold Rugg bemoans the fact that no systematic and critical appraisal of Dewey's educational experiment was ever made. He points out, "Mayhew and Edwards assembled scattered comments on the success of the School made by visiting educators, parents, and former pupils—'thirty years after.' But these are all pro-Dewey and so far as I can see contribute nothing to the needed critical appraisal of the educational product. Students of educational reconstruction will regret . . . that the Dewey group did not conduct a *systematic and objective inquiry* into the traceable effects of the school's work in the later lives of its graduates."[42]

It is not entirely fair of Rugg to chide the Dewey group for failing to employ methods of social scientific investigation and evaluation which it happened were themselves in a very embryonic stage at the turn of the century. The teachers did manage to write a number of accounts of the ongoing activities of the school and the rationale behind them which were published in the *University* [of Chicago] *Record* from 1896 to 1899. During 1900, Dewey edited nine issues of *The Elementary School Record,* "which dealt exclusively with the practices, content, and rationale of the University School."[43] Typed reports and summaries of 1901 and 1902 were collected and edited by Laura L. Runyon. Alice Dewey had collected a great deal of material pertinent to the school, intending to write its history; but she died in 1927, and the task fell to Katherine Mayhew and her sister Anna Edwards. Dewey collaborated with them and contributed parts of the book, some from previous writings and some new. The most important of the latter eventually became "The Theory of the Chicago Experiment," an appendix to their book. In addition, some of Dewey's writings and talks at the time (for example, those collected in the book, *The School and Society*) make specific reference to the school and its operations.

I would like to consider this material in order to explain the operations of the Laboratory School and, so far as can be gathered, why things were done as they were. My aim is not to pass judgment on the educational products of the school, nor is it primarily to make comparisons with what Dewey tried to do and what is being done in elementary education today. What I hope to find is some link between the practice and the theory, some indication of whether the theoretical principles and the practical details did indeed interact, some indication of the way the leading ideas affected the day-to-day practice and whether or not the ensuing practical results had any impact on the theory. It should be especially interesting to see if a case could be made for Dewey's having changed any of his important educational theories because of what happened when he tried to put them into practice in the Laboratory School. The remainder of this chapter is a summary of the educational practices of the Laboratory School together with an evaluation of how these relate to its underlying theories. A final section considers some recent criticisms of Dewey's educational views in light of what we have seen of their practical exhibition and testing.

DEWEY'S SCHOOL: THE THEORY BEHIND IT

The social and intellectual milieu in which Dewey set up his school was a vibrant one. Chicago was growing rapidly, with a large influx of immigrants and with diametrically opposed levels of great wealth and abject poverty. Dewey was to become directly acquainted with people on both levels. The mood of the city fathers was for progress, which many thought could be purchased, given the right amount of cash. Marshall Field, Cyrus McCormick, Philip Armour, Gustavus Swift, and George Pullman typified the powerful businessmen of the day who amassed great fortunes and began to think of leaving behind a legacy, something that would carry on their names after they had fought their last financial battle. Many turned to educational projects for this purpose. Thus, Philip Armour founded the Armour Institute of Technology of 1892, giving it a million dollars a year for five years. George Pullman willed a million dollars in 1897 to found a manual-training school for boys. Not to be outdone, Mrs. Emmons Blaine, daughter of Cyrus McCormick, donated a million dollars to support the educational endeavors of Colonel Francis Parker.[44]

Parker was the principal of the Cook County Normal School (later the Chicago Normal School) from 1883 to 1899. He was forced to contend with the educational authorities on behalf of his extremely child-centered approach to elementary education. In 1899, Mrs. Blaine decided to free him from such harassment and offered him a million dollars so he could train teachers and instruct children in full accordance with his theories and ideals.[45] President Harper at the University of Chicago became quite interested in this bequest and persuaded Mrs. Blaine to turn the money over to the university board of trustees for the purpose of erecting a new building on campus and assimilating Parker and his staff into the university's faculty.[46] As we shall see, this would eventually have bad effects upon the status of Dewey's school.

This renewed interest in education in Chicago came at an opportune moment. J. M. Rice had spent five months in 1892 visiting schools across America. Having personally observed more than 1,200 teachers at their work in the schools of thirty-six cities and some twenty institutions for the training of teachers, he deplored the lack of public interest in the education of the young, saying that it smacked of "criminal negligence."[47] Rice was highly critical of the meager training required of public school teachers. Only a small percentage were normal school graduates. Some had attended a normal school or high school for one or more terms, while a very large number were licensed to teach based on their having been educated at a grammar school and perhaps having received a "little extra coaching."[48] Obviously, this did not make for much of a grasp of the subject matter to be taught or for much formal training in the methods of teaching or the principles of pedagogy—the very things Dewey deemed necessary for a properly trained teacher.

Rice was especially critical of the public schools of Chicago, which, he charged, used unscientific, antiquated, and often absurd methods of teaching. They concentrated on "busy work," the students mechanically copying words from the book or on the board. One class had been

supplied with only one reading book, which was dutifully read and reread until the end of the term. Some schools ran for only a half day, but with no break for recess. In a typical geography lesson, students read a question from their books and then searched for the answer on the map. Heavy emphasis was placed on learning by rote, usually to no apparent purpose. The only exception he saw was the school run by Parker which stressed the freedom and growth of the child and attempted to "bring the child into close contact with nature in the beautiful park of twenty acres in which the school is situated."[49]

Dewey was familiar with such shortcomings in the schools and frequently argued against resorting to heavy-handed discipline, memorization, or even sugar-coating the material in order to arouse the child's interest. He explained that interest (from *inter-esse*: to be between) involves breaking down the distance between the pupil and the subjects to be studied in order to develop their organic union. Genuine interest implies that one is whole-heartedly involved with what one is doing.[50] Dewey thought that the curriculum was too often thought of as fixed and final, something to be handed down in a ready-made fashion to the student. But the subject matter, which represents the accomplished results of adult experience, cannot be made a substitute for the child's own experience, nor can it be simply imposed or grafted upon it. We must recognize the connection between the reflectively formulated, logical, and more objective human experience of the curriculum and the relatively disjointed, emotional, subjective experiences of the child. A key point of Dewey's is that there is no difference in kind between the child's experience and the forms of study that make up the curriculum.[51] The child and the curriculum are two limits defining a single process. Education is a process of continuous reconstruction of the child's present experience by means of the adult experience represented by "the organized bodies of truth that we call studies."[52] We show proper concern for the child by using the subject matter as the means to develop his or her individual abilities. The subject matter is the working capital which enables the teacher to determine the environment of the child so that he or she may grow to full potential. "It says to the teacher: Such and such are the capacities, the fulfillments in truth and beauty and behavior, open to these children. Now see to it that day by day the conditions are such that *their own activities* move inevitably in this direction, toward such culmination of themselves."[53]

Dewey is not, as is often charged, advocating a strictly child-centered approach to education. He does not downplay the importance of the materials to be studied. They represent our intellectual and cultural heritage, the best that man has accomplished thus far. What he objects to is forgetting that this subject matter stems from human experience of the same kind as that of the child in the classroom. Instead of trying to impose it upon the child or clothe it "with factitious attraction, so that the mind may swallow the repulsive dose unaware,"[54] we should treat it as a means to reconstruct the child's experience and promote his or her growth. Dewey would have us appreciate that the curriculum has a logical and a psychological side to it. It is a more reflective, abstract, logical rendering of experience. It needs to be psychologized, reinstated or restored to the experience from which it has been abstracted, "turned over, translated into the immediate and individual experiencing within which it has its origin and significance."[55] The function of this subject matter for Dewey is "strictly interpretative or mediatory"—it enables the child to reconstruct his or her experience and grow.[56] Education, for Dewey, is growth in and of experience.

In addition, Dewey believes that "all education proceeds by the participation of the individual in the social consciousness of the race."[57] This involves not only coming to understand the reflectively formulated experience conveyed by the subjects of study in school, it also entails living and working and thinking with other human beings at all stages of the individual's development. He wanted his school to be neither child-centered, nor curriculum-centered; it was to be "community centered."[58] This meant that the school should be a living community in which the child was an active participant. As he put it, "Education being a social process, the school is simply that form of community life in which all those agencies are concentrated that will be most effective in bringing the child to share in the inherited resources of the race, and to use his own powers for social ends."[59]

Since the child lives and grows in communities such as the family, the neighborhood, the school, and the state, Dewey stressed continuity of community activity as much as possible. School activities were to connect with home activities so that the child would be interested in pursuing them. They were then to lead, by means of the curriculum, toward habits of doing, thinking, and feeling that would be part of the productive social life of an adult. Our social inheritance was the means to personal growth and to the progress of society for Dewey. One way to pursue such individual and social growth was by introducing the child to the kind of occupations that he or she would be familiar with (and, it is hoped, interested in) from the home. In Dewey's school, therefore, students engaged in cooking, sewing, manual training, pottery making, weaving, and so on. Dewey thought that these activities "represent, as types, fundamental forms of social activities; and that it is possible and desirable that the child's introduction into the more formal subjects of the curriculum be through the medium of these activities."[60] He saw activities such as cooking, carpentry, and sewing as being constructive in themselves "while socially they represent the fundamental activities of the race."[61]

Thus, the visitor to the Laboratory School would not see children sitting in neat rows, quietly reading or reciting according to some set format. Instead, he would find them engaged in activities Dewey felt recapitulated man's past and provided a good introduction to the more formal studies of the traditional curriculum. In weaving, for example, the child can learn of the different types of material and where they came from and how important this was for early mankind geographically as well as economically. Some elementary mathematics and science might also be included while putting the finishing touches on the end product. In describing how this occurred at his school, Dewey somewhat rhapsodically proclaimed that "you can concentrate the history of all mankind into the evolution of the flax, cotton, and wool fibres into clothing."[62] Ordinary household occupations served both a retrospective and a prospective purpose for Dewey. They showed students where man had come from and how he had reached his present level of knowledge skills, while preparing for their own future thinking and activity as adults, which was to be achieved by the more formalized studies of mathematics, history, geography, and science.

At no time did Dewey have in mind a kind of primitive job training for the students. As he himself pointed out, "Coming as the children did mainly from professional families, there was little prospect of any utility of this sort."[63] Nor did he have in mind the kind of "culture-epoch" theory popular at the time. This was a notion, derived from Herbart, that there was a direct parallelism between the development of the child and the historical development of the human race. This parallelism was supposed to guide our selection and arrangement of the materials to be studied in the curriculum so that "the appropriate basis of the content of study at each period of child growth is the culture products (literature especially) of the corresponding period of race development." Dewey said the theory could best be summed up by a line from Goethe: "The youth must always begin anew in the beginning, and as an individual traverse the epochs of the world's culture."[64] Although he admitted that one could trace a general correspondence between the cultural products of each epoch and the stages of development of the child, Dewey himself denied that there was an exact parallel and argued that we should focus our primary attention on the personal growth of the child. He also objected to the emphasis placed by the theory on the products of a given age without much consideration of the "physical conditions which originated those products."[65]

The main thing, in Dewey's eyes, was to have children in school engage in social occupations providing a link with their home lives, have an active participation in the social life of the school, and enjoy a good introduction to the more formal, disciplined, abstract modes of adult thought and activity that would prepare them to be productive workers and responsible citizens when they left school. The underlying factor was experience: the experience the child had before coming to school, the experience in school itself, and the development of dispositions and habits which make up a large part of adult experience. In this way Dewey saw no major problem of creating interest in the subjects to be studied because they were not foreign to the experience of the students. Nor would it be difficult to relate one subject to another or show their relevance to life. As he put it, "Experience has its geographical aspect, its artistic and its literary, its scientific and its historical sides. All studies arise from aspects of the one earth and the one life upon it. . . . Relate the school to life, and all studies are of necessity correlated."[66]

Dewey was insistent that it was the process of learning, rather than the products that were learned, that was most important. He thought that the scientific attitude of mind was particularly worth promoting. This did not come about by offering more science courses or nature-study projects but by encouraging students to follow a certain method of thinking.[67] This was to be more than a merely mechanical skill or an empty formal listing of rules for correct thinking. Teachers were to establish conditions in school that were conducive to critical, problem-solving thinking. Such thinking, according to Dewey, passed through five logically distinct steps: "(i) a felt difficulty; (ii) its location and definition; (iii) suggestion of possible solution; (iv) development by reasoning of the bearings of the suggestion; and (v) further observation and experiment leading to its acceptance or rejection."[68] This was the kind of experimentalist or instrumentalist approach to thinking that Dewey was to elaborate on in his later works, and in regard to education most notably in *Democracy and Education* published in 1916.[69] He saw these steps as characterizing reflective experience in general and scientific thinking in particular, and he never ceased to urge that the learning environment be such that genuine problems could arise in the course of the student's own activity and that the student would be expected to come to grips with them and to formulate at least tentative answers.

Dewey's concern for the process of education, for the continuity of experience between home and school, child and adult, for the social dimension of education and the connection of living and learning, and for the importance of scientific problem solving can all be seen as part of his underlying faith in democracy and education. The best environment for the type of participatory activity and problem-solving thinking that he envisaged was one of free discussion and shared possibility. On the other hand, the surest guarantee for such freedom was the very sort of open exchange of ideas and respect for evidence that characterized what he called the scientific attitude. Rather than simply equating democracy with freedom of action, Dewey would have us see its link with freedom of thought. Thus, it is not surprising that he sees a close relationship between democracy and education.

This he extended to the need to preserve democracy *in* education. If we are indeed to recognize and protect the "spiritual basis of democracy, the efficacy and responsibility of freed intelligence,"[70] we must see to it that teachers are given their proper say in the selection of materials for the curriculum, the methods of teaching used, questions of discipline, and so on. It will not do to farm these tasks out to pedagogical experts. How can we justify our belief in the democratic principle if we refuse to put it into practice in our schools? This applies to the role of the students as well. We cannot claim to respect their freedom of intelligence when we seek to impose ready-made subject matter upon them from without. All too often, says Dewey, we let acquiring take the place of inquiring in school; that is to say, we encourage passive and obedient reception of cut-and-dried materials. What

we need to do is to allow for the actual problem-solving thinking of the child, to provide materials and situations that will bring about such thinking. We need to make the school "a place for getting and testing experience, as real and adequate to the child upon his existing level as all the resources of laboratory and library afford to the scientific man upon his level."[71]

This is not easily accomplished in a traditional classroom setting. As he was to put it later in *Democracy and Education*: "The physical equipment and arrangements of the average schoolroom are hostile to the existence of real situations of experience. . . . Almost everything testifies to the great premium put upon listening, reading, and the reproduction of what is told and read. . . . There must be more actual material, more *stuff*, more appliances, and more opportunities for doing things, before the gap can be overcome."[72] Dewey describes the difficulty he had in buying the right kinds of desks and chairs for his school. Finally, he says, one dealer, more perceptive than the rest, told him, "I am afraid we have not what you want. You want something at which the children may work: these are all for listening."[73] He also sought to make the school a community in which teachers and students, not ignoring the very real differences in their training, abilities, and temperament, are mutually engaged in inquiring rather than acquiring, in directly experiencing rather than docilely memorizing bits and pieces of second-hand experience and are conscious of and dedicated to the ethical principle upon which democracy rests: "the responsibility and freedom of mind in discovery and proof."[74] This commitment to democracy animated all of Dewey's views on education. Many years later he was to restate it as follows: "Democracy is faith that the process of experience is more important than any special result attained. . . . Since the process of experience is capable of being educative, faith in democracy is all one with faith in experience and education."[75] Let us now turn to the actual operation of his Laboratory School to see whether or not this faith was justified.

DEWEY'S SCHOOL: THE ACTUAL PRACTICE

The children in the school were divided into eleven groups according to age. From the very start, the social aspects of learning were emphasized. The youngest children (ages four and five) were encouraged to talk about their own home life and the various persons helping in the occupations of the household. They discussed the family's dependence upon the daily visit of the milkman, grocer, iceman, postman, and the occasional visits of the coalman and others. They helped to prepare, serve, and clean up after their midmorning luncheon, an activity which was said to afford many opportunities for self-management and initiative.[76]

The six-year-olds spent the first fifteen minutes of the day in group conversation. They took excursions, played floor games, built a farm house and barn out of blocks, and then cleared a small plot of land outdoors to plant their winter wheat. They planted cotton seeds in pots, ginned and baled the cotton, built a train of cars to transport it to market, and then put on a play summarizing the whole process.[77] The seven-year-olds began to study primitive life and did experimental work with the materials that primitive people would use. They tried to work out cave life, with its weapons, utensils, and clothing, in a tangible form, while also reading Stanley Waterloo's *Story of Ab.* They came to some understanding of the use of textiles and the discovery of metals. Museums and books were used as sources. According to Mayhew and Edwards, "This natural setting of man and his occupations, the basis of their future, was clothed with human significance to these little actors of primitive life as they imaginatively wandered in the sandbox hills and valleys of their tribal habitation. In the process, many scientific facts of geology, of chemistry, of physics, or of biology, found their way into the sinews of their intellectual wings."[78]

The eight-year-olds centered their occupational work around the trading and maritime activities of the Phoenicians. This made them directly aware of the need for a system of weights and measurements, as well as the necessity for a more accurate method of written record. One year they made a large map and another year a rough version of a boat. Science was taken up "as involved in the study of cooking, or of history, and not as a subject by itself."[79] They studied the travels of Marco Polo, Prince Henry, and Magellan and kept their own "Journal" of these trips. They studied the life and voyages of Columbus and began to read *Robinson Crusoe.* All of this was in accord with Dewey's desire to avoid what he called "The Primary Education Fetich," which consisted of starting too soon with the teaching of reading and writing. Dewey, not unlike Rousseau before him, would have us hold off until the child has the interest and experience to want to learn to read and write. We must avoid the premature use of the child's analytic and abstract powers. We must start first with activities that engage the child's positive and creative impulses "and direct them in such ways as to discipline them into the habits of thought and action required for effective participation in community life."[80] Language study is needed to provide discipline, organization, and the effective means of communication. It can best be taught when the child has an awareness of this need and seeks for itself such discipline. The child will make the effort to learn to read and write when he or she sees some point in doing so.

The nine-year-olds were divided into two sections and "In order to secure more time for practice in reading and writing, the school day was lengthened an hour in the afternoon."[81] They studied local history and geography, with many visits to local museums and historic spots. They learned about early French exploration and one year built a model of Fort Dearborn. Field trips were frequent, says Ida DePencier in her history of the Laboratory School, "to the quarry on Stony Island where glacial markings were observed, to the cotton mills in Aurora to see the spinning of cotton, and others to Ravinia to see the clay bluffs, to Miller Station to see the sand

dunes and desert, and to Sixty-third Street and the city limits to see a typical prairie area."[82]

The children were said to be anxious to attain greater facility in writing and number work in order to carry on their projects to a desired conclusion.[83] Some German and French were introduced. The children were even more involved in the general social activities of the school, helping out with the printing of school materials, the running of assemblies, and indoor and outdoor games. The ten-year-olds studied colonial history and built a colonial room. Here the teachers observed one of the first instances where the children themselves decided on a division of labor by gender: The boys built the furniture for the room and the girls made the fabrics. Heretofore boys and girls had participated in the same activities together.[84] There was much collateral reading on the American colonies, and a relief map was made of the campaigns of the American Revolution. The origin of flax was studied, and its spinning and dyeing were demonstrated to the class by a German woman.[85] Whenever possible the school made use of immigrant workers in Chicago for firsthand information on such occupations.[86] The physiology of digestion was discussed, with some experimental work being done with foods in the cooking laboratory. Many excursions were made to Jackson Park to gather specimens of plant and animal life. Mayhew and Edwards make the claim, "With proper laboratory facilities and proper organization of subject-matter into topics, a group of ten-year-olds, that are shielded from distraction and waste of energy, can make much progress in many directions."[87]

The eleven-year-olds looked at the European background of the colonists. The students were divided into two sections on the basis of previous school experience. One section studied the lives of great men of the period, the other English village life. There was more drill in writing and spelling. Electricity was studied and the working of simple machines. "An account of Faraday's experiment with an iron core and a coil was the starting-point for their construction of a dynamomotor." As preparation for a visit to the technological displays of the Armour Institute, they reviewed the things they would want to see; there were, in their preferred order: "a motor, a dynamo, a galvanometer (which they called a tester), a storage battery, and an apparatus for telegraphy."[88] The students made a pair of scales. They dissected the heart and lungs of a sheep and examined the circulatory, respiratory, and digestive system of a frog. They worked out the school tax bill and studied taxes in general. More teamwork was stressed in physical education, and with help from the university coach considerable proficiency was developed in basketball.

The twelve-year-olds' activities took on the nature of occupations. They saw more and more clearly their need for certain skills to achieve desired results. Since the child himself saw this need, "his need for skill thus became sufficient to engage himself in its acquisition; he had an impelling motive from within for analysis and mastering rules."[89] They were led to appreciate the importance of a scientific attitude of mind. Throughout their study of changing civilization, it had been brought continually to their attention that "it was always science and scientific method that had broken down physical barriers, conquered disease, and eliminated evils once thought insurmountable."[90] Science was seen as a means to the control of nature and to the perpetuation of social progress. Some of the boys in this and the older groups "were irked by the historical approach to their school subjects and seemed to require a shift in method." In one of their rare admissions of failure, Mayhew and Edwards state, "These boys were finally taken out of the class and allowed to follow their own diverse and individual lines until the general trend of their interest could be determined." Most of them eventually ended up working in the shop.[91]

The thirteen-year-olds, most of whom had been in the school since its beginnings, reviewed U.S. history. "A large number of books were listed and each child was urged to seek out his own sources and to get the help of parents and friends in writing up his topics."[92] They studied photography (the use of the camera, its parts) and made visits to university laboratories to see perfected instruments. This led to the formation of a Camera Club and the subsequent need for darkroom facilities; another club, the so-called Dewey Club for discussion and debating, was also looking for a meeting place. So it was decided that the students would build their own club house. Although Mayhew and Edwards bemoan the fact that "Lack of a library, lack of quiet, lack of beauty, lack of adequate space for club meetings all made it impossible to carry out many individual and group plans,"[93] they do admit that the project of building the club house drew the whole school into an exciting cooperative effort which turned out to be one of its most memorable accomplishments.

The final group of students were of ages fourteen and fifteen. The oldest were given special tutoring and review courses in preparation for their college board examinations. One visitor to the school says he was initially quite disturbed "when I learned that three or four of the older pupils, whom I saw over in one corner, were being drilled up for college examinations in the old way, the regular work of the school having failed to prepare them to pass such tests. As I considered the matter on my way home, I satisfied myself that the fault lay with the type of examination, rather than with the kind of training which these children had received."[94] Wherever the fault lay, this group of students seemed more difficult for the school to deal with. They were allowed to choose their own shop work, and "the results were unsatisfactory." Their writing style was clear and fluent but loose and inaccurate in sentence structure. It was thought that their skill in artistic expression should keep pace with their intellectual concepts, but "this was an ideal difficult to attain and more often than not failed of achievement."[95] The pressure of college preparatory examinations made it necessary to drop from the program for the older children a planned course in the techniques of cooking. Despite these shortcomings, Ella Flagg Young noted that they all did well in their later schooling. She said, "It may be well

for those who incline to the opinion that philosophy is attractive in theory, but not possible in practice, to know that the valuation put by the high school on the preparation of this class was high."[96]

Throughout the school year, the teachers held weekly meetings to review, discuss, and improve upon the past week's work. They also had almost daily contact at lunch or after school. The teachers came from different backgrounds, but they usually had a college education or training in a technical school such as Pratt, the Drexel Institute, or the Armour Institute of Technology. Most of the teachers were said to be strongly supportive of the school and of what it was trying to accomplish. Over the course of time, the weekly meetings became more structured and more formal, with Dewey himself and later Mrs. Young and Mrs. Dewey present.[97]

Dewey maintained an active interest and involvement in the activities of the school, which he visited almost daily.[98] When it became apparent that a new building would be made available through the generosity of Mrs. Blaine, he sent her a detailed, two-page handwritten letter setting forth his view on the location of rooms, kitchen facilities, work equipment, space for reading and writing in the library, the need for an assembly room, and so on.[99] As mentioned previously, Dewey often gave lectures to parents and friends of the school.

A close relationship was maintained with the University of Chicago. The children made use of many of its facilities, and Dewey enlisted the help of a number of faculty members from outside his department. Robert McCaul notes that there was a substantial core of professors at the university sympathetic to what Dewey was trying to accomplish. "Excluding Dewey and members of the Department of Pedagogy, there were thirty-seven full professors in the arts, literature, and science departments in 1896-7. Of these sixteen had had previous experience as teachers or administrators in subcollegiate schools."[100] Dewey could count on men such as Chamberlin (geology) and Starr (anthropology) for support. Others, for example Small and Vincent in sociology, Coulter in botany, and Hale in Latin, gave occasional lectures to the children, offered teacher education courses in their departments, and showed an active interest in pedagogical theory.[101] Their cooperation and creative help seemed to justify Dewey's criticism of the amount of waste in our educational system owing to the isolation of its component parts. For all his battles over finances, Dewey would have heartily endorsed the view of Mayhew and Edwards that the close relationship of the school to the university "was of incalculable help and importance in maintaining the stability and reality of the experiment."[102]

Despite some notable successes and achievements,[103] outside events began to overtake the noble experiment. Harper succeeded in winning Mrs. Blaine's million-dollar donation to the University of Chicago, and with it came Colonel Parker, his school, and its staff. Dewey and his supporters resisted the amalgamation of the two schools, so Chicago for a time had two University Elementary schools, one heavily endowed and the other struggling to pay its bills. This caused inevitable confusion and not a little bickering, much of it between Dewey and Wilbur Jackman, Parker's aide. Parker died in 1902, and Dewey was made director of the School of Education and the two elementary schools were consolidated under his direction. The administrative task facing Dewey seemed awesome. "His previous administrative experience had been confined to a department of philosophy with seven faculty members, a department of education with four, and a Laboratory School staffed by a coterie of fifteen devoted females and one devoted male. Now he was in command of some one hundred persons and a budget of several hundred thousand dollars a year.[104] Small wonder that he wrote to Mrs. Blaine in August 1902 that although his relations with the staff of the School of Education had thus far been amicable and he sincerely hoped they would continue to be so, "the administrative work is not just in my line."[105]

Things came to a head when Mrs. Dewey was made principal of the newly formed University Elementary School for the year 1903-4. This did not set well with the Parker staff who feared they would lose their identity, if not their jobs, in such a family affair as the Dewey School was becoming. Harper as usual tried to please all parties concerned by interpreting Mrs. Dewey's appointment as being for a one-year period only. She evidently did not think of it this way; when he informed her of this in an interview of March 1904, she was furious and resigned: "Because your attitude toward my position on the Faculty of the School of Education places my work on a personal rather than on an educational basis."[106]

Dewey's reaction was equally swift. He wrote in a letter of resignation to Harper on 6 April that "since the administrative side of the work which I undertook in assuming the Directorship of the School of Education has now been accomplished, and since the conditions as you outline them are not favorable to development upon the educational side," he could no longer continue as director of the School of Education. On 11 April, he also resigned as professor and head of the Department of Philosophy, though he politely thanked Harper for his past support. Such politeness went by the board when Dewey heard that Harper was telling people he had resigned because his wife was not to be allowed to stay on as principal. This was not so, he protested, perhaps a bit too strongly. In a letter of 10 May to Harper he asked that it be made clear to the board that "the question of the alleged failure to reappoint Mrs. Dewey as Principal of the Elementary School is in no sense the cause of my resignation, and that this question had never been discussed between us till after our resignations were in your hands. Your willingness to embarrass and hamper my work as Director by making use of the fact that Mrs. Dewey was Principal is but one incident in the history of years."[107]

"With the resignation of Mr. Dewey and the subsequent dispersal of all save three or four of the faculty of the Laboratory School," says Mayhew and Edwards, "this experiment in education ended."[108] Not, we might add, with a whimper but with a bang. Some say Dewey left with a sense of failure and never again tried to engage in this kind of practical experimentation in the schools.[109] His defenders, such as Mayhew and Edwards, maintain that the experiment worked and that Dewey's basic approach to education was vindicated. In the remaining part of this chapter, I evaluate the experiment and in particular try to trace out the interaction between the theory and the practice. I consider what Dewey thought of it after the fact as well as some recent criticisms that have been made of both the practice and the theory behind it, and conclude with some remarks on what I see as the proper relationship between theory and practice.

DEWEY'S REACTIONS TO THE SCHOOL

From his comments written for the Mayhew and Edwards book, we can see that Dewey was aware of certain problems with the school and the approach it took. Since the principles upon which the school was founded were taken to be "working hypotheses," he had felt that their application, development, and modification should be left largely in the hands of the teachers. After the fact, Dewey speculated that perhaps too much responsibility was imposed upon the teachers. "In avoiding hard and fast plans to be executed and dictation of methods to be followed, individual teachers were, if anything, not given enough assistance either in advice or by way of critical supervision. There might well have been conditions fairer to teachers and more favorable to the success of the experiment."[110]

This is a surprising comment for him to make, given the frequency of teachers' meetings, discussions, and written reports and the active involvement of Dewey himself with the teachers. What happened, says Dewey, was that the discussions tended to revolve around the peculiarities and difficulties of individual children, and the underlying principles "were too much taken for granted as being already understood by all teachers; in the later years an increasing number of meetings were allotted to the specific discussion of underlying principles and aims."[111] Even then one wonders how open and wide-ranging such discussions could be for a young teacher facing the impressive triumvirate of John and Alice Dewey and Ella Flagg Young.[112] One problem with having a coterie of devoted followers is that there is less likelihood of frank assessment of pet theories.

Because they were working comparatively unbroken ground, Dewey realized that much trial-and-error experimentation was required in order to bring the needs and interests of the child into view as well as to determine the desirable components of the curriculum. He admitted that "the school was overweighted, especially in its earlier years, on the 'individualistic' side in consequence of the fact that in order to get data upon which we could act, it was necessary to give too much liberty of action rather than to impose too much restriction."[113] The ideas and policy of the school were modified in light of such experimentation in regard to two points:

(1) The children were originally intended to be mixed together, older and younger, so "the younger children might learn unconsciously from the older." The increase in enrollment made this unfeasible, and the children were grouped, as we have seen, primarily according to age.

(2) The original assumption was that "an all-round teacher would be the best, and perhaps it would be advisable to have one teacher teach the children in several branches." This was abandoned in favor of having different teachers specialize in different subjects.[114]

No grades were assigned, although there was indication that "some of the children desired external marks as proof of their own development." The ever-present need to prepare the older children for their college entrance examinations often intruded into other school activities for that group. Yet even with them, "Written or oral review on completion of the work to be done took the place of examination."[115]

Without a doubt the biggest problem the school faced, from Dewey's point of view, was the financial one. In one of his reports on the school in *The Elementary School Record,* Dewey reviews the work of the past five years and states that "practically it has not as yet been possible, in many cases, to act adequately upon the best ideas obtained, because of administrative difficulties, due to lack of funds—difficulties centering in the lack of a proper building and appliances, and in inability to pay the amounts necessary to secure the complete times of teachers in some important lines."[116] While we can sympathize with him about meager finances, we should not forget that when the Blaine money became available and Dewey was put in charge of the newly consolidated University Elementary School, things got worse instead of better. While generally praising Dewey's handling of the staff in his school, Arthur Wirth acknowledges that "Dewey was not the perfect administrator. He was far from blameless in the wrangles with Colonel Parker's staff, particularly with Wilbur Jackman."[117]

Even sharper criticisms have been made of Alice Dewey. She was said to be extremely critical of some of the staff of the Parker school and quick to dismiss teachers from her own faculty.[118] Max Eastman, a friend of the family, said that as an administrator she had "the faults of her virtues. She was not a good mixer. She had an uncanny gift of seeing through people who were faking, and made such witty game of them that she alarmed even those who were not faking. . . . And she had a kind of inside-out timidity, a fear of being presumptuous, that because of her obvious superiority looked sometimes like snooty coldness."[119] Here too Dewey may well have erred as an administrator by putting his wife in such an influential position in his own school. It certainly would make it more difficult to bring about radical changes in policy or guiding principles.

A more fundamental criticism that has been made is that the school itself was too much of a special situation to be much of a test of Dewey's ideas. The students were mainly from middle- and upper-class families. Their parents were highly interested in and supportive of the school. The teachers were better trained and more committed to the enterprise than one would normally find. Classes were small,[120] and the vast resources of the University of Chicago were close at hand. No doubt, as McCaul suggests, with a more heterogeneous school population Dewey would have been forced to adapt his theory and approach more to the capacities, interests, and goals of the average child, and as a result he might have achieved "some sort of educational synthesis of theory and practice, of scientific inquiry and direct experience, and of the ideal as prevailing in his school and the actual as existing in the typical schools in which his students would later teach."[121]

Henry Perkinson makes an even more pointed comment about the idealistic nature of the Dewey experiment: "Dewey's educational philosophy depicts a school or school enterprise that never existed and probably never could exist. To carry it out would require superteachers and superstudents." The teachers in his ideal school are expected to have "a thorough understanding of his philosophy plus a knowledge of the subject matter, including its history, its logical structure, and its connection with other subject matters, plus a sociological-psychological understanding of the child and his development." The students, for their part, were learning to be dedicated scientists, "indefatigable in the pursuit of inquiry into the problems of men. . . . "[122] Perkinson doubted whether the entire nation could produce enough such teachers and students to fill a single classroom.

As we have seen, Dewey had not claimed to be setting up a model school of practice turning out materials and methods to be slavishly copied elsewhere. Even Professor Hinsdale, who is often quoted as saying the eyes of the country were on Dewey's experimental school, went on to say that, of course, "No man of sense expects to see the children of the people generally taught in schools like the one that Professor Dewey has set up, but there are many who are hoping that this school may contribute something of value to the progress of elementary education."[123] Dewey realized that in many respects, though hardly in its financial setup, his school operated in nearly optimal conditions. He even admitted, "Like every human enterprise the Laboratory School came far short of achieving its ideal and putting its controlling ideas into practice."[124] Some years after he had severed his connections with Chicago, he dealt with the question of why educational ideals so often fail to be put into practice, speculating that perhaps it is because "the research persons connected with school systems may be too close to the practical problems and the university professor too far away from them, to secure the best results."[125] In his own case he might have added more candidly that the theoretician is not necessarily the best person to enact practical policies. As Plato says, few of us are capable of being philosopher-kings.

Another thing Dewey might have said in his own defense was that the ideals he set for the school were high ones and therefore were going to be difficult to attain under any circumstances. For example, when Mayhew and Edwards claimed that one of the school's goals was to see to it that "the music, the literary and dramatic efforts of the children, and their artistic expression . . . all should represent the culmination, the idealization, the highest point of refinement of all the work carried on," Dewey replied that "the school can justly be said to have failed more often at this point than at any other. This failure, however may be taken as evidence that the difficulty of achievement in this direction is proportionate to its importance."[126] Taking this line of thought, Dewey could defend his "working hypotheses" that the child's experience can be made continuous with that represented by the studies in the curriculum, that the child should be an active member of a democratic, social community in the school, and that the model for all thinking is the scientific, problem-solving method of science; all these he might say are worthwhile objectives, no matter how difficult—or expensive—they may be to reach. Some recent critics of Dewey would challenge these very hypotheses and claim the theory was wrong even before he tried to put it into practice. Let us turn to them now.

SOME RECENT CRITICISMS OF DEWEY'S EDUCATIONAL THEORY

Many contemporary philosophers of education, particularly in Great Britain, have moved away from Dewey's key notion of the unity of knowledge and experience, and from his primary concern with the interests and growth of the child toward an analysis of the component parts of an ideal curriculum and the logical characteristics of the subjects to be studied. Paul Hirst, for example, argues for a return to the Greek ideal of a liberal education based on the nature of knowledge itself.[127] For Hirst, this entails initiating the young into the forms of knowledge. These are "the complex ways of understanding experience which man has achieved, which are publicly specifiable and which are gained through learning."[128] They include mathematics, physical sciences, human sciences, history, religion, literature and fine arts, and philosophy. Each form has its own distinct set of concepts, logical structure, statements and expressions, and ways of testing these against experience. It is by means of the forms of knowledge that experience has become intelligible to man. As educators we want our students to be able to deal with experience in terms of these forms (i.e., to think mathematically or scientifically) and to recognize that they are mutually irreducible (e.g., to do mathematics is not the same kind of activity as doing science), though interdependent (e.g., to do physics requires a knowledge of mathematics). The proper way to learn a form of knowledge is to study its paradigms from someone who has already mastered it.

John White uses Hirst's analysis of the forms of knowledge to construct an argument for a compulsory curriculum.[129] For White, our aim in education is to equip our students to make autonomous choices. This requires that they be made aware of all the possible activities they might choose to engage in for their own sake. But some

activities, most notably those of mathematics, science, and philosophy, cannot be understood unless one has engaged in them. That is to say, nothing in a child's prior experience is a sufficient basis for understanding curricular activities of this sort, so we are justified in compelling students to study such subjects in order to be properly equipped to make those autonomous choices. Some external imposition is unavoidable in school because of the very nature of the subject matter, such interference in the child's liberty being justifiable as being in his or her own best interests.

Because of their views of the nature of knowledge, White and Hirst would doubtless agree with Frederick Olafson in his criticism of Dewey's notion of learning as reconstruction of experience. Olafson asserts that education has to do with a process of "internalizing the distinctive procedures of a preexistent discipline . . . , rather than in terms of discovery and reconstruction."[130] There is a sudden and precipitate jump from the familiar world of common sense to the domain of abstract thought. For Olafson, "the process of mastering, of internalizing a preexistent idiom of thought is very different in respect of the kind of communication and sociality it entails from the form of experience that precedes such a process."[131]

He also charges Dewey with having misconstrued science as a kind of cooperative consensual activity on a par with democratic decision making. This view of science fails to take account of the fact that there are accepted canons of scientific procedure and a special symbolic code and that the processes of scientific inquiry involve a movement to conceptual levels other than those of common sense.[132] Kathryn Morgan echoes this sentiment by charging it is absurd to claim that children have a natural bent for scientific investigation, since they lack most of the features necessary for scientific orientation toward the world, features such as the "detachment of the object from the self . . . ; a capacity for engaging in sustained disinterested speculation; and the systematic naturalization of and deanthropomorphizing of object predicates."[133]

Has Dewey overstated the continuity of experience? Does he illegitimately resolve the dualism between the child and the curriculum by romantically idealizing the capacities of the former while defining away the distinguishing characteristics of the latter? Richard Peters warns us not to forget that the children who come to us to be educated start off as barbarians outside the gates. "The problem is to get them inside the citadel of civilisation so that they will understand and love what they see when they get there."[134] It will not do to ignore, as Dewey does, whole dimensions of the human condition: man's irrationality, his emotional sensitivities and susceptibilities, his life and death predicaments as well as his problems.[135]

Richard Hofstadter calls Dewey's approach to education "anti-intellectual." He claims that Dewey adopts a romantic, primitivist conception of the child, that his notion of growth is nothing but a mischievous metaphor designed to gloss over the need for an externally imposed, adult vision of the good society, that his method of overcoming dualisms is utopian, and his idea that all learning has to be overtly shared in social action is highly questionable. Dewey has placed the child so firmly at the center of things that questions about the content of what is to be taught and the structure of the curriculum are subsumed under those of method and motivation. But, according to Hofstadter, "the moment one admits that it is not all of life which is presented to children in school, one also admits that a selective process has been set up which is determined by some external end; and then one has once again embraced the traditional view that education is after all not a comprehensive attempt to mirror or reproduce life but a segment of life that is specialized for a distinct function."[136]

Dewey would not deny that the school is a special environment. He called it a simplified, purified, broadening kind of environment.[137] Simpler than our complex civilization and our numerous social relationships, in school we select features of life and thought that are "fairly fundamental and capable of being responded to by the young" and proceed toward those that are more complicated. This occurs in what Dewey calls a "purified medium of action" in which we have weeded out what is antisocial, immoral, or downright perverse. School seeks to reinforce the power of the best. Finally, by bringing children into contact with a larger, more diverse social group, school aims to create a new and broader environment in which to grow.

This was not meant simply to mirror or reproduce life; Dewey's term is "reconstruction." We help the child develop from relatively crude and narrow experience into the more critically refined, socially responsible experience of the adult. The way to accomplish this is not to center all our attention on the child[138] any more than it is to be so enamored of the logical features of the curriculum that we fail to appreciate the need to "psychologize" the material so it can be learned by the child. Dewey sought to strike a balance between both factors in the educative process. He set up a school in which the attempt was made for the child to interact with the curriculum in a new and creative way. To those who chide him for neglecting what was to be learned, I would throw back his own challenge of how *they* proposed to teach it. In real life one seldom has the luxury of settling all philosophical differences before commencing to educate. Dewey at least attempted to practice what he preached.

But did the practice have any lasting effect upon his theory of education? We have seen how the leading ideas were meant to direct and clarify the work; but in what important ways did the actual work serve to "criticize, modify, and build up the theory"? In a recent review of Dewey's writings from 1899 to 1909, J. O. C. Phillips remarks that for all Dewey's talk about the value of the scientific method, he himself was never really an exponent of it. He did not dirty his own hands with experiments in psychology laboratories, and his school "functioned far more as a public demonstration of his views than as a genuinely experimental laboratory." Even his writing does not appear to us now as very scientific. "The research seems thin, the factual evidence impressionistic. Statistics are rare; most of the conclusions are based on deduction."[139]

A similar appraisal was given by Lawrence Cremin in the course of a generally favorable review of Dewey and his school: "Actually, there were few dramatic changes in Dewey's pedagogical theory as a result of the Laboratory School. Rather, he was able to state his initial hypotheses with ever greater confidence and specificity."[140] According to Joe R. Burnett, the lack of direct influence of Dewey's educational practices upon his theory is not so surprising in light of the fact that by 1900 he was already moving away from a direct concern with practical pedagogy and becoming a philosopher of culture. "Within four years," says Burnett, "he stopped discussing matters of practical pedagogy at any length. Even *Democracy and Education* . . . is a work of social, political, and educational philosophy rather than of practical pedagogy."[141]

This is not to say that none of Dewey's ideas were vindicated by the school. His belief that teaching should be a profession and teachers trained in their subject matter, the latest teaching methods, child psychology, and the history of education, as well as be given the opportunity to practice in a real school situation, seems to be almost taken for granted today. We should not forget how radical some of these ideas appeared to be at the turn of the century. I think his experience with the school also supports his point about the amount of waste in our educational system caused by the isolation of its parts. He showed how much the elementary level of education could gain by interacting with the university level. It might be added that universities would likewise benefit from this exposure to the practical problems of educating children.

Finally, whatever the shortcomings of his notion of the role of social occupations in the curriculum, Dewey did establish the point that children will learn more readily if we can overcome the distance between them and the subject matter. This should involve making them aware of the origins of much curricular material in the lives and experiences of human beings. The approach to the school as a kind of community in which teachers and students are active participants is another way to overcome an unproductive conflict between the child and the curriculum. Democracy itself he saw as a working hypothesis to be tested in our educational activities. He wanted it not simply to be studied but to be lived.

SOME CONCLUDING REMARKS ON THEORY AND PRACTICE IN EDUCATION

Some conceptual problems remain with theory and practice in education. Do they refer to distinct domains of thought and action? Is there a dualism here that cannot be overcome? Or is the problem that they do not normally interact in the same person? Perhaps we all suffer from a kind of split between what we say and what we do. Is this because of some ingrown tendency in ourselves or is it part of the very nature of things?

Perhaps there is something about education that promotes a division between theory and practice. We tend to espouse very high educational ideals. Education is an act of faith and hope, as well as love: faith in the future of the human race, hope that the young will carry on what we have accomplished and go beyond us, love in the sense of an active concern for their growth and a willingness to sacrifice for their welfare. It has been said that what we want in education is what all good parents want for their own children. If so, then it is not altogether surprising that our aspirations often exceed our accomplishments. Failure to achieve our educational ideals in practice usually serves to prod us to try harder rather than to modify or abandon the ideals altogether.

Another problem has to do with the evaluation of practice. How is it to be evaluated, by whom, and when? There are long-term as well as short-term results in education. Which are we to judge and in what fashion? Not even the great advances by the social sciences since the days of Dewey's school have completely resolved the old issues of the relative importance of nature and nurture in the upbringing of a child, what methods are most effective for teaching various individuals or a class full of them, what content is most worthwhile from the point of view of society and from the individual student's own point of view. Is it obvious that massive increases in equipment and personnel will improve the quality of education? Do we seek to produce happy individuals or good citizens? What things do the young need to learn and how can they best be taught?

Clearly, Dewey's experiment in education has not answered such questions. If anything it has added to our perplexities. This can be seen in a positive light as a stimulus to the kind of thinking about the problems involved in educating the young that Dewey felt was so crucial. In Dewey's eyes this is an ongoing inquiry where the answers are tentative at best. Whatever theoretical conclusions we might reach, we must also take account of their practical consequences. The most lasting lesson from his experiment may well be that if we are to make progress in education, the duality between theory and practice is one that must be overcome.

NOTES

[1] This is from a copy of the Dewey School song found in the Katherine Camp Mayhew papers in the library of Teachers College, Columbia University.

[2] George Dykhuizen, "John Dewey: The Chicago Years," *Journal of the History of Philosophy*, 2, (October 1964):240 n. 60. "Laboratory School" was shortened even further to the "Lab School."

[3] John Dewey, "The University School," in *The Early Works of John Dewey*, ed. Jo Ann Boydston (Carbondale,

Illinois: Southern Illinois University Press, 1972), 5:437. All subsequent references to either the Early Works or the Middle Works of Dewey will be made in the standard format, i.e., EW or MW.

[4] "The Need for a Laboratory School," EW 5:434. As a graduate student at Johns Hopkins, Dewey had personal experience of the use of the laboratory for observation and experiment in his psychology course taught by G. Stanley Hall. See Dorothy Ross, *G. Stanley Hall* (Chicago: University of Chicago Press, 1972), 154. According to Ross, Hall opposed the renewal of Dewey's fellowship at Hopkins and later rejected a suggestion that Dewey be engaged to handle undergraduate instruction in philosophy (p. 146). Hall wrote a mildly critical review of Dewey's book, *Psychology* (New York: Harper and Bros., 1887), in the *American Journal of Psychology,* vol. I, no. 1. (November 1887):146-59; and Hall referred to Dewey's work in "paidology" as having nothing new to offer in his autobiography, *Life and Confessions of a Psychologist* (New York: D. Appleton & Co., 1924), 500.

[5] "Pedagogy as a University Discipline," EW 5:288.

[6] "Report of the Committee on a Detailed Plan for a Report on Elementary Education," EW 5:454.

[7] "The Relation of Theory to Practice in Education," MW 3:249-72.

[8] *Ibid.*, 249.

[9] *Ibid.*, 251 (italics are Dewey's).

[10] This is from remarks of John Dewey recorded in a shorthand report of a departmental conference on "The Training of Teachers" held at the University of Chicago on 13 May 1904 and found in the Anita McCormick Blaine Papers, The McCormick Collection, State Historical Society of Wisconsin in Madison.

[11] "The Relation of Theory to Practice in Education," MW 3:252.

[12] For some firsthand accounts on Dewey as a teacher, see George Dykhuizen, "John Dewey and the University of Michigan," *Journal of the History of Ideas,* 23 (1962):528; Sidney Hook, "Some Memories of John Dewey," in *Pragmatism and the Tragic Sense of Life* (New York: Basic Books, 1974), 101-14; Corliss Lamont, ed., *Dialogue on John Dewey* (New York: Horizon Press, 1959); Harold Larrabee, "John Dewey as Teacher," in *John Dewey: Master Educator,* ed. William W. Brickman and Stanley Lehrer (New York: Society for the Advancement of Education, 1959), 50-57; Una Bernard Sait, "Studying Under John Dewey," *Claremont Quarterly,* vol. 11, no. 2 (Winter, 1964), pp. 15-22; and Herbert W. Schneider, "Recollections of John Dewey," *Claremont Quarterly,* vol. II, no. 2 (Winter 1964):23-35.

[13] "The Relation of Theory to Practice in Education," MW 3:263.

[14] "The Relation of Theory to Practice in Education," MW 3:265.

[15] *Democracy and Education* (New York: Macmillan, 1916); MW 9:177.

[16] "A Pedagogical Experiment," EW 5:244.

[17] *Ibid.*

[18] "The University Elementary School," MW 1:319.

[19] "Pedagogy as a University Discipline," EW 5:285-87.

[20] "The Need for a Laboratory School," EW 5:434.

[21] Robert L. McCaul, "Dewey and the University of Chicago," part I: July 1894-March 1902, *School and Society* (25 March, 1961):153.

[22] Alice Dewey in an unpublished sketch of the school, quoted by Lawrence A. Cremin, *The Transformation of the School* (New York: Knopf, 1961), 136 n. 8.

[23] Cf. Robert L. McCaul, "Dewey's Chicago," *The School Review* (Summer 1959):266-67; Arthur Wirth, *John Dewey As Educator* (New York: John Wiley & Sons, 1966), 35; and Dykhuizen, "John Dewey: The Chicago Years," 231.

[24] Katherine Camp Mayhew and Anna Camp Edwards, *The Dewey School* (New York: D. Appleton-Century Co., 1936; reprint, Atherton Press, 1966), 12.

[25] Jane Dewey, ed. "Biography of John Dewey," in *The Philosophy of John Dewey*, ed. Paul Arthur Schlipp (New York: Tudor Publishing Co., 2d ed., 1951), 28. It should be noted that this biography was "written by the daughters of its subject from material which he furnished" (p. 3).

[26] McCaul, "Dewey and the University of Chicago," Part 1, 153; this point was made by McCaul despite his own views on how supportive Harper was of the school.

[27] "The University Elementary School," MW 1:317.

[28] "The University Elementary School," MW 1:325. Smedley eventually became director of the Child Study Department of the Chicago Public Schools; cf. Wirth, *Dewey As Educator*, 195.

[29] Mayhew and Edwards, *Dewey School*, 8.

[30] Cremin, *Transformation*, 135.

[31] Jane Dewey, "Biography of Dewey," 29. For a good recent biography of Mrs. Young, see Joan K. Smith, *Ella Flagg Young* (Ames: Iowa State University Press, 1979).

[32] Max Eastman, *Great Companions* (New York: Farrar, Straus and Cudahy, 1959), 273.

[33] McCaul, "Dewey and the University of Chicago," Part 1, 157.

[34] Dykhuizen, "John Dewey and the University of Michigan," 534. He in turn is quoting from De Witt Parker and C. B. Vibbert, "The Department of Philosophy," in *The University of Michigan: An Encyclopaedic Survey*, vol. 2, ed. Wilfred B. Shaw (Ann Arbor: University of Michigan Press, 1951), 674.

[35] B. A. Hinsdale, *Journal of Proceedings and Addresses of the Thirty-ninth Annual Meeting of the National Educational Association* (Chicago: University of Chicago Press, 1900), 326-27. For Dewey's relationship to Hinsdale as a colleague at the University of Michigan, see McCaul, "Dewey's Chicago," 260-61. There is also a reference to a debate between Dewey and Hinsdale at Michigan in John A. Axelson, "John Dewey 1884-1894: Decade of Ferment for Young Michigan Teacher," *Michigan Education Journal* (1 May, 1966), 14. The Hinsdale quote is incompletely given and incorrectly attributed to a meeting of the National Council of Education by Wirth, *Dewey As Educator*, 215-16. Wirth is quoting Hinsdale as presented in Ida B. DePencier, *The History of the Laboratory Schools: The University of Chicago, 1896-1957* (Chicago: University of Chicago, 1960; 2d printing, Quadrangle Books, 1967), 16. The latter is a chatty but not very scholarly account of the Laboratory School.

[36] Mayhew and Edwards, *Dewey School*, 57.

[37] McCaul, "Dewey's Chicago," 275.

[38] DePencier, *Laboratory Schools*, 23-24.

[39] Richard J. Storr, *Harper's University, The Beginnings* (University of Chicago Press, 1966), 298.

[40] Ella Flagg Young, "Democracy and Education," *Journal of Education*, vol. 84, no. 1 (6 July, 1916):5-6. This review of Dewey's *Democracy and Education* by his trusted follower and confidant is surprisingly missing from the list of reviews of the book listed in MW 9:379 n. 10.

[41] Laura L. Runyon, "A Day with the New Education," *Chautauquan*, vol. 30, no. 6 (March 1900):589-92.

[42] Harold Rugg, *Foundations for American Education* (New York: World Book, 1947), 555-56 (italics are Rugg's).

[43] George Eastman, "John Dewey on Education: The Formative Years," D.Ed. diss., Harvard University, 1963, 495; for a list of Dewey's Contributions to *The Elementary School Record*, see p. 646. Lawrence Cremin states that "The published records of the school are more voluminous and detailed than for any similar venture of the time," Cremin, *Transformation*, 139 n. 3.

[44] Two excellent introductions to the Chicago of Dewey's times are: Ray Ginger, *Altgeld's America* (Chicago: Quadrangle, 1965), and Wayne Andrews, *Battle for Chicago* (New York: Harcourt, Brace, 1946). Also of interest is Bessie Louise Pierce, *A History of Chicago,* vol. 3, 1871-1893 (Chicago: University of Chicago Press, 1957). Good studies of the University of Chicago at the turn of the century are those of Storr, *Harper's University,* and McCaul "Dewey's Chicago." A lively portrait of the life of the immigrant in Chicago at that time is Jane Addams, *Twenty Years at Hull-House* (New York: Macmillan, 1910; reprint, New American Library, 1961).

[45] McCaul, "Dewey and the University of Chicago," Part 1. A short summary of Parker's views and practices can be found in Cremin, *Transformation,* 128-35. Angela Fraley claims that Dewey simply adopted Parker's theories and used his methods. "At best," she says, "he can be said to have replicated Parker's less formally recorded experimental work"; *Schooling and Innovation* (New York: Tyler Gibson Publishers, 1981), 45. No one else, to my knowledge, sees the two men in this light. See, for example, Jack K. Campbell, *Colonel Francis W. Parker, The Children's Crusader* (New York: Teachers College Press, 1967). For Parker's own words, see his *Talks on Teaching* (New York: A. S. Barnes, 1883) and *Talks on Pedagogics* (New York: E. L. Kellogg & Co., 1984).

[46] McCaul, "Dewey and the University of Chicago," Part 1.

[47] J. M. Rice, *The Public-School System of the United States* (New York: The Century Co., 1893), 19. For more background on Rice and his study see Wirth, *Dewey As Educator,* 31-33. Lawrence Cremin dates the beginning of the progressive movement in American education to the publication of Rice's study; Cremin, *Transformation,* 22.

[48] Rice, *Public-School System,* 15.

[49] *Ibid.,* 210-11; McCaul, "Dewey and the University of Chicago," Part 1, 155.

[50] *Interest and Effort in Education* (Boston: Houghton Mifflin, 1913).

[51] "The Child and the Curriculum," MW 2:277-78.

[52] *Ibid.,* 278.

[53] *Ibid.,* p. 291 (italics are Dewey's).

[54] "The Psychological Aspect of the School Curriculum," EW 5:166.

[55] "The Child and the Curriculum," MW 2:285.

[56] "The Psychological Aspect of the School Curriculum," EW 5:174.

[57] "My Pedagogic Creed," EW 5:84.

[58] "The Theory of the Chicago Experiment," in Mayhew & Edwards, *Dewey School,* 467. Dewey often took pains to dissociate his own view from the more extreme child-centered stance of many progressive educators. See, for example, his article, "How Much Freedom in New Schools," *New Republic* (9 July, 1930), 204-6, and his book, *Experience and Education* (New York, 1938). Despite his efforts, he continues to be described as a child-centered educational theorist. A recent example of this can be found in Christopher J. Lucas, *Foundations of Education* (Englewood Cliffs, N.J.: Prentice-Hall, 1984), 304-9.

[59] "My Pedagogic Creed," EW 5:86-87.

[60] *Ibid.,* 90.

[61] "Plan of Organization of the University Primary School," EW 5:230-31.

[62] *The School and Society,* MW 1:15. Dewey showed such enthusiasm for the possibilities for learning to be derived from such simple social occupations that he might be criticized for the very thing that he found fault with in the Montessori method—i.e., being so eager to introduce children to the intellectual distinctions that adults have made that he ignores or reduces the amount of time devoted to the immediate crude handling of the familiar material of experience (*Democracy and Education,* MW 9:153-54). Margaret Naumberg makes this point when she claims that in the Dewey School "the making and doing of things was always subordinated to a social plan, not related to the individual capacities and tastes of the children," and that "neither individual nor group entities initiated much in the way of original planning, however much they may have expanded and adapted the social projects suggested by the teacher"; *The Child and the World* (New York: Harcourt, Brace, 1928), 111.

[63] Dewey in Mayhew & Edwards, *Dewey School,* 47 n. 5. Walter Feinberg charges that Dewey's proposals for curriculum development differed significantly, depending upon the socioeconomic class of the children he was dealing with. After looking at *Schools of Tomorrow* (New York: E. P. Dutton, 1915), Feinberg asserts that we can see different assumptions in Dewey's treatment of all-black or working-class schools from middle- or upper-class schools, especially in Dewey's acceptance of the relative neglect of academic subjects in the former; Walter Feinberg, *Understanding Education* (New York: Cambridge University Press, 1983), 263 n. 17. A far-ranging rebuttal to this charge could be constructed from Dewey's writings and actual practices; suffice it to say that the book in question was written by Dewey in collaboration with his daughter Evelyn and that *she* was responsible for the chapters that described specific schools of the type mentioned by Feinberg (see the preface to *Schools of Tomorrow*).

[64] "Culture Epoch Theory," MW 6:408.

[65] "Interpretation of the Culture-Epoch Theory," EW 5:250. A recent article claims that Dewey was closer to

the Herbartian viewpoint than he cared to admit; Herbert M. Kliebard, "Dewey and the Herbartians: The Genesis of a Theory of Curriculum," *Journal of Curriculum Theorizing,* vol. 3, no. 1 (Winter 1981):154-61. For more on Herbart and the Herbartians see: Johann Friedrich Herbart, *Outlines of Educational Doctrine* (New York: Macmillan, 1901); Gabriel Compayre, *Herbert and Education by Instruction* (New York: Thomas Y. Crowell, 1907); Charles De Garmo, *Herbart and the Herbartians* (New York: Scribner, 1895); and Harold B. Dunkel, *Herbart and Herbartianism* (Chicago: University of Chicago Press, 1970). A good summary of Dewey's reactions to the Herbartians and to the other educational movements of his time can be found in Melvin C. Baker, *Foundations of John Dewey's Educational Theory* (New York: Atherton Press, 1966), 86-108.

[66] *The School and Society,* MW 1:54-55.

[67] "Science as Subject-Matter and as Method," MW 6:69-79.

[68] *How We Think,* MW 6:236-37. Although this book was originally published in 1910, some years after he had left the school, Dewey acknowledged in the preface his indebtedness to his wife for inspiring the ideas of the book and "through whose work in connection with the Laboratory School . . . the ideas attained such concreteness as come from embodiment and testing in practice" (MW 6:179). Indeed, reviewers of the book praised its clear and simple style (MW 6:517-18).

[69] *Democracy and Education,* MW 9.

[70] "Democracy in Education," MW 3:239.

[71] "Democracy in Education," MW 3:237.

[72] MW 9:162.

[73] *The School and Society,* MW L:21.

[74] "Democracy in Education," MW 3:230.

[75] "Creative Democracy," in *The Philosopher of the Common Man,* ed. Sidney Ratner (New York: Greenwood Press, 1968), 227.

[76] Mayhew & Edwards, *Dewey School,* 64-66.

[77] *Ibid.,* chapter 5.

[78] *Ibid.,* 113.

[79] *Ibid.,* 126.

[80] "The Primary Education Fetish," EW 5:268.

[81] Mayhew & Edwards, *Dewey School,* 144.

[82] Depencier, *Laboratory Schools,* 33-34.

[83] Mayhew & Edwards, *Dewey School,* 155.

[84] *Ibid.,* 166.

[85] *Ibid.,* 175.

[86] Baker, *Foundations,* 144.

[87] Mayhew & Edwards, *Dewey School,* 183.

[88] *Ibid.,* 208.

[89] *Ibid.,* 200.

[90] *Ibid.,* 203.

[91] *Ibid.,* 213-14.

[92] *Ibid.,* 221.

[93] *Ibid.,* 248.

[94] *Ibid.,* 396.

[95] *Ibid.,* 240-48.

[96] Young, "Democracy and Education," 6.

[97] Mayhew & Edwards, *Dewey School,* 370-75.

[98] *Ibid.,* 382.

[99] Letter from Dewey to Mrs. Emmons Blaine, 2 August, 1900, Anita McCormick Blaine Papers, The McCormick Collection, State Historical Society of Wisconsin in Madison.

[100] McCaul, "Dewey's Chicago," 264.

[101] Ibid.

[102] Mayhew & Edwards, *Dewey School,* 438.

[103] A recent appraisal credits Dewey with applying many innovations at his schools, such as "new methods of instruction, reduction in student conformity, students' evaluations of their own work, and the elimination of grading"; *Conflict and Continuity,* ed. John R. Snarey, Terrie Epstein, Carol Sienkiewicz, and Philip Zodhiates, *Harvard Educational Review,* Reprint Series No. 15, 1981, ix.

[104] Robert McCaul, "Dewey and the University of Chicago," Part 2: April 1902-May 1903, *School and Society* (8 April, 1961):180.

[105] Letter from Dewey to Mrs. Emmons Blaine, (4 August, 1902, Anita McCormick Blaine Papers, The McCormick Collection, State Historical Society of Wisconsin in Madison.

[106] Letter from Alice Dewey to William Rainey Harper, 5 April 1904, President's Papers 1889-1925, Department of Special Collections, University of Chicago Library.

[107] Letters from Dewey to Harper, *ibid*. McCaul attributes Dewey's peevishness in the matter to the tremendous strain caused by the intellectual and social stimuli of Chicago; McCaul, "Dewey's Chicago," 278-79. I think a simpler and more reasonable explanation is that Dewey became angered when his wife was told she was no longer wanted as principal.

[108] Mayhew & Edwards, *Dewey School,* 18.

[109] See, for example, Rugg, *Foundations,* 554-55.

[110] Mayhew & Edwards, *Dewey School,* 366.

[111] *Ibid.*, 370.

[112] An example of this approach is the experience of Miss Emily Rice (a staunch follower of Parker), whom Dewey consulted about the merger of the two schools and the question of his wife's assuming the principalship. She did not oppose the plan to Dewey's face but expressed reservations privately in a letter to Mrs. Blaine, claiming that she felt unable to speak frankly to him or to Mrs. Young on such a delicate, personal matter; McCaul, "Dewey and the University of 'Chicago," Part 2, 182 and George Dykhuizen, "John Dewey in Chicago: Some Biographical Notes," *Journal of the History of Philosophy,* 3 (April 1965):228 n. 67. Presumably, Mrs. Blaine communicated Miss Rice's reservations to Dewey: he strongly criticized Miss Rice for this in his own letter to Mrs. Blaine and sarcastically remarked that "Miss Rice has so completely and repeatedly misrepresented both Mrs. Young and my own statements that I attach no further importance to any statement she makes about other people, so far as that reflect upon them"; Dewey to Mrs. Blaine, 30 April 1903, Anita McCormick Blaine Papers, The McCormick Collection State Historical Society of Wisconsin in Madison.

[113] Mayhew & Edwards, *Dewey School,* 467-68.

[114] *Ibid.*, 35.

[115] *Ibid.*, 376.

[116] "The Psychology of Elementary Education," MW 1:73. This statement is also quoted with a slight change of wording in Mayhew & Edwards, *Dewey School,* 248.

[117] Wirth, *Dewey As Educator,* 71.

[118] See McCaul, "Dewey and the University of Chicago," Part 2, 182, and Dykhuizen, "John Dewey in Chicago," 228.

[119] Eastman, *Great Companions,* 277. Joan K. Smith reports that Wilbur Jackman had been advised by the Board of Trustees to document any difficulties occurring between Mrs. Dewey and the faculty of the school. He found the basic problem lay in her nature: "so critical that it becomes destructive . . . making it impossible for her to direct others . . . without continual combat"; Smith, *Ella Flagg Young,* 98.

[120] R. S. Peters, among others, has noted the extremely favorable teacher-pupil ratio in the Dewey School and suggests that this be kept in mind when we evaluate its apparent success; "John Dewey's Philosophy of Education," in *John Dewey Reconsidered,* ed. R. S. Peters (London: Routledge & Kegan Paul, 1977), 108.

[121] Robert McCaul, "Dewey and the University of Chicago," Part 3: September 1903-June 1904," *School and Society* (22 April 1961):205.

[122] Henry J. Perkinson, *Two Hundred Years of American Educational Thought* (New York: McKay, 1976), 215.

[123] Hinsdale, *Thirty-ninth Annual Meeting,* 237. Hinsdale's cautious sentiment was echoed in a review of Dewey's *School and Society* that appeared in *Dial,* 29 (16 August 1900):98, coauthored by Hinsdale and A. S. Whitney: "While no one can tell what the future of the University Elementary School may be, it does not require much foresight to see that it can never become the type of the public elementary school; its cost and the delicacy of the organization make this impossible." A more extreme reaction is that of Maxine Greene, who claims that "a look at the *Addresses and Proceedings* of the NEA in the years immediately following Dewey's Chicago experiments shows us that his work impressed public-school teachers little, if at all"; "Dewey and American Education, 1894-1920," in Brickman and Lehrer, *John Dewey,* 40. I am not sure that such a conclusion is warranted. From the evidence she cites, the most one could say is that those who gave addresses to the NEA during that period did not seem to be talking much about Dewey. A similar observation has been made on the apparent lack of influence of Dewey on educational reformers in England who were at work in the period of 1914-24; "Furthermore the textbooks of the period while respectful, show no signs that Dewey's ideas had penetrated the minds of their writers." R. W. Selleck, *English Primary Education and the Progressives,* 1914-1939 (London: Routledge and Kegan Paul, 1972), 113.

David Hawkins goes even further and asserts, "Dewey has so far had almost no influence at all on the practical level except, for a time, in a few private schools for children most of whom would have succeeded academically in any case." "Liberal Education: A Modest Polemic," in *Content and Context,* ed. Carl Kaysen (New York: McGraw-Hill, 1973), 156. Unfortunately, Hawkins provides no evidence whatsoever to back up this assertion; William Boyd and Wyatt Rawson in their book, *The Story of the New Education* (London: Heinemann, 1965), make the same point: "The schools of Parker and Dewey at Chicago were day schools for city children; but they had their most interesting outcome in the later establishment of private-venture Country Day Schools, in which children could grow up in free conditions which afforded greater scope for individual initiative and effort than the ordinary public schools of America" (p. 3).

[124] Mayhew & Edwards, *Dewey School,* 7.

[125] *The Sources of a Science of Education* (New York: Liveright, 1929), 43.

[126] Mayhew & Edwards, *Dewey School,* 361-62.

[127] Paul Hirst, "Liberal Education and the Nature of Knowledge," in *The Philosophy of Education,* ed. R. S. Peters (New York: Oxford University Press, 1973), 87-111. Many of Hirst's writings on this topic have been collected in his book, *Knowledge and the Curriculum* (London: Routledge & Kegan Paul, 1974). A response to Hirst, somewhat in the spirit of Dewey, is that of Richard Pring, *Knowledge and Schooling* (London: Open Books, 1976).

[128] Hirst, "Liberal Education," 96.

[129] John White, *Towards a Compulsory Curriculum* (London: Routledge & Kegan Paul, 1973). Also of interest are Keith Thompson and John White, *Curriculum Development: A Dialogue* (London: Pitman Publishing Company, 1975), and Robin Barrow, *Common Sense and the Curriculum* (London: George Allen & Unwin Ltd., 1976).

[130] Frederick Olafson, "The School and Society: Reflections on John Dewey's Philosophy of Education," in *New Studies in the Philosophy of John Dewey,* ed. Steven M. Cahn (Hanover, N.H.: University Press of New England, 1977), 195.

[131] *Ibid.,* 201.

[132] This criticism is also made by Charles Frankel, who argues that a scientific community is a community of specialized competence whose opinions are checked against the evidence; whereas democracy is a procedure for melding and balancing human interests. "John Dewey's Social Philosophy," in Cahn, *New Studies,* 20.

[133] Kathryn Morgan, "Children, Bonsai Trees, and Open Education," in *Philosophy of Education: Canadian Perspectives,* ed. Donald B. Cochrane and Martin Schiralli (Don Mills, Ontario: Collier Macmillan Canada, 1982), 314.

[134] R. S. Peters, "Education as Initiation," in *Philosophical Analysis and Education,* ed. R. D. Archambault (London: Routledge & Kegan Paul, 1965), 107.

[135] Peters, *Dewey Reconsidered,* 121. Some early critics saw Dewey's pragmatism as an inadequate philosophy of life in the face of the irrationality of war. Thus, Randolph Bourne wrote in 1917 that Dewey's philosophy assumes the existence of a society that is peaceful, prosperous, and has a strong desire for progress; *War and the Intellectuals, Essays by Randolph S. Bourne, 1915-1919,* ed.

Carl Resek (New York: Harper & Row, 1964). John C. Farrell believes that the outcome of the World War I did not shake Dewey's faith in reason, progress, and the scientific method, because this was really in the nature of an a priori assumption on Dewey's part; "John Dewey and World War I: Armageddon Tests a Liberal's Faith," *Perspectives in American History,* 9 (1975):337. A good counter to such objections to pragmatism can be found in Hook, *Pragmatism and the Tragic Sense of Life.*

[136] Richard Hofstadter, *Anti-intellectualism in American Life* (New York: Knopf, 1970), 385. Anthony Quinton (in Peters, *Dewey Reconsidered* has also characterized Dewey's approach as anti-intellectual but only in the sense that his theory of knowledge disagrees with the Cartesian tradition. Quinton looks favorably upon Dewey's anti-Cartesian contentions that all our beliefs are fallible and corrigible, that the knower is an active experimenter, and that the pursuit of rational belief is an essentially social undertaking. Part of my objection to analytic philosophy of education may well be a response to its Cartesian elements— i.e., the view that we can have beliefs that are certain and definitions for which we can find necessary and sufficient conditions, and the assumption that the knower is some kind of contemplative theorist pursuing truth in isolation from his or her fellow investigators.

[137] See, for example, *Democracy and Education* MW 9:24-26.

[138] Thus, in a review of Dewey's Lectures in the *Philosophy of Education: 1899,* John Childs remarks that these lectures show that Dewey recognizes that "adult guidance is written into the very constitution of the school," and the regard for the individuality of the child and his interests "is no substitute for adult interpretation, evaluation and selection from among genuine social alternatives, each with its own pattern for the molding of the immature." *Studies in Philosophy and Education,* 5 (Winter 1966-67):69.

[139] J. O. C. Phillips, "Dewey in Mid-Passage," *History of Education Quarterly,* vol. 20, no. 1 (Spring 1980):123. This view also finds support in a recent article on Dewey that concludes that he seems to have been "more of a social engineer than a pure scientist"; Merle Borrowman, "The School and Society: Vermont in 1860, Chicago in 1890, Idaho in 1950, California in 1980," *Educational Studies,* 11 (Winter 1981):381.

[140] Cremin, *Transformation,* 140.

[141] Joe R. Burnett, introduction to *The School and Society,* MW I:xix-xx. Burnett's judgment is overly harsh. Dewey continued to write on practical pedagogy throughout the rest of his life. In 1924, for example, he went to Turkey to prepare a "Report and Recommendation upon Turkish Education." The report has been described as speaking directly "to the problems of school systems in all developing countries, today and for many coming decades"; MW 15:xx and 275-97. Even near the end of his life, Dewey was writing about practical pedagogical

matters such as the "project method" developed by Professor Kilpatrick at Teachers College; Dewey's introduction to Samuel Tenebaum, *William Heard Kilpatrick* (New York: Harper & Brothers, 1951).

Steven C. Rockefeller (essay date 1989)

SOURCE: "John Dewey, Spiritual Democracy, and the Human Future," in *Cross Currents*, Vol. XXXIX, No. 3, Fall, 1989, pp. 300-21.

[*In the following essay, Rockefeller—writing from the perspective of the collapse of communism in Eastern Europe and the Soviet Union, as well as the student revolts in China—enumerates several concepts from Dewey's social agenda as a desirable antidote to spiritual and social oppression.*]

The human race faces the urgent challenge of creating a global community marked by economic opportunity, equal justice, freedom and respect for nature, or its survival as a species is in doubt. The obstacles to achieving community locally as well as internationally are great, for almost everywhere peoples suffer from moral confusion, bitter social conflicts, fragmentation of experience and knowledge, and the deterioration of the environment. In the poet's words, the center no longer holds. There is, then, an urgent need for ideas with integrating spiritual power, for a unifying moral and social faith that is able to affirm the value of cultural pluralism in the process of liberating and harmonizing the self and society on a national, regional and global basis. Such a faith must be comprehensive enough to integrate the technological, economic, social, environmental, moral, and religious dimensions of experience; it cannot otherwise bring the wholeness and harmony that we need.

This essay focuses on an idea that has roots in the moral vision of the Hebrew prophets and in the social ideals of ancient Athens. It concerns an idea that has steadily grown in influence over the centuries and has had extraordinary transformative power throughout the world for over two hundred years. In short, it is the purpose of this essay to explore the global moral, social, environmental, and religious significance of democracy. As symbolized by the construction of the Statue of Liberty in Tiananmen Square last spring and the appearance of glasnost in the Soviet Union, it is probably already the most widely shared moral value in the world today. Reflecting on the widespread disillusionment with communism in the Soviet bloc and China, Francis Fukuyama has even gone so far as to argue in a widely debated essay that Western liberal democracy, which is based on the ideas of freedom, equality, and the consent of the governed, has already won "an unabashed victory" over Marxist-Leninism and all other ideological rivals. Democracy as a mode of political and economic organization has decisively established itself, declares Fukuyama, as "the ideal that will govern the material world in the long run."[1] These developments are cited,

not to enter the debate over the correctness of Fukuyama's thesis about current history, but as a way of calling attention to the worldwide potential that lies in the democratic ideal. Also, it is not being implied that the word democracy always possesses a consistent meaning in international discourse, and it may well be that the full significance of democracy as a social ideal is yet to be revealed as different peoples throughout the world explore experimentally its possibilities and meaning in their own social and spiritual contexts.

The question at issue can be stated briefly: Is there a distinctively democratic way of liberation and community, and does it involve an ideal possibility for the future development of the social, economic, moral and religious life of the human species worthy of humanity's shared faith and devotion? This essay argues that the democratic ideal may be understood in such a way as to justify the claim that it does possess this broad significance. Sustaining this argument involves demonstrating that the idea of democracy has, at least in some quarters, historically involved a depth and fullness of meaning that is not commonly appreciated and that it has a potential for acquiring even greater meaning as democratic societies adjust to the challenge of the environmental crisis.

In reflecting on the significance of the democratic ideal, it is helpful to turn back to earlier American intellectual traditions, and especially the thought of John Dewey. Dewey's philosophy of "creative democracy" took form in the late nineteenth century under the influence of Hegel, the St. Louis Hegelians, T. H. Green, and Walt Whitman. Hegel had taught that universal freedom is the goal of the world historical process. Developing Hegel's prophecy that America is "the land of the future," Whitman called for realization in America of "a sublime and serious Religious Democracy."[2] For Whitman the democratic ideal is a "fervid and tremendous idea" of "vast, and indefinite, spiritual and emotional power" that gives to American life its moral purpose and underlying unity. He called for the emergence of "a cluster of poets, artists, teachers fit for us, national expressers, comprehending and effusing for men and women" the meaning and values associated with this great idea.[3]

Having learned to respect democratic values as a youth in Vermont, John Dewey was deeply moved early in his philosophical career by Whitman's vision, and he aspired to be one of those "poets, artists, teachers" interpreting for the people the profound spiritual meaning of the democratic ideal. Starting with Protestant Christian social values and the Neo-Hegelian philosophy of the organic unity of the spiritual and the material, the ideal and the real, he set out to construct his own philosophy of individual liberation, social transformation, and harmony with the divine. As he reconstructed his early Neo-Hegelian ethical idealism and developed a new brand of humanistic naturalism, which charts a middle way between a tough-minded and tender-minded world view, the idea of democracy remained of central importance.[4]

As has been suggested, thinkers like Whitman and Dewey understand the idea of democracy to involve much more than a theory of political organization and economic opportunity, important as this is. It is more fundamentally a great moral and social ideal that comprehends all human relations and has important implications also for humanity's relations with nature and the divine. Understood in this more comprehensive sense, the democratic ideal embraces for Dewey both a philosophy of ongoing social reconstruction and a philosophy of "a personal way of individual life." It was his conviction that democracy as a mode of social, political and economic life could be sustained and perfected only if democracy also became a personal philosophy and faith, a unifying way of ethical life and spiritual growth.

Democracy as an individual way "signifies the possession and continued use of certain attitudes, forming personal character and determining desire and purpose in all the relations of life."[5] As a comprehensive moral ideal, Dewey argues that it should govern human relations in family life, the school, the church, business and industry as well as in government. Moreover, the democratic way becomes an individual path of moral and spiritual growth, a personal way of liberation and transformation. It involves, in other words, a form of spiritual practice in the sense of a way to grow and realize the enduring meaning of life and to find peace, wholeness, and harmony with the world and the divine. In his mid-thirties, Dewey broke with the Congregational church, in which he had been an active member since boyhood, and thereafter had little interest in institutional religion. He never ceased to believe, however, that his work was consistent with the Christian spirit, and was convinced that if the Christian tradition with its gospel of freedom and hope had ongoing relevance and meaning in the contemporary world, it was to be found in the thorough-going democratic reconstruction of experience and all social institutions and interactions.

In what follows, I will explore Dewey's vision of the democratic ideal. In conclusion, the essay will briefly consider the possibilities of a further environmental reconstruction of the idea of democracy and discuss the democratic reconstruction of the religions.

1

In Dewey's view, the American democratic ideal has roots in Christian ideals, and he arrived at his own philosophy of "creative democracy" by undertaking a radical reconstruction of the Protestant Christian tradition in the eighteen eighties and nineties. It is important, however, to make clear in this regard that as mature thinker, Dewey did not believe that faith in democracy necessarily requires any particular metaphysical or theological foundation for its validation. As one of the founders of American pragmatism, he looked for confirmation of the meaning and value of the democratic life in the consequences that flowed from it as revealed by human experience. It is nevertheless illuminating to consider Dewey's understanding of the interconnection between Christian and democratic values.

In 1894, in his last major religious statement before leaving the institutional church, Dewey summarized what he viewed as the three most fundamental Christian ideals or values. First he mentions the idea of "the absolute, immeasurable value of the self" or human personality. Second, he cites the notion of a kingdom of God, that is, the idea of a community of free persons bound together in all their relations by mutual love and support and by shared values, that is, devotion to the common good. Third, he cites the idea of the revelation of liberating truth to humanity, and he has in mind primarily practical truth sufficient for the guidance of life.[6] Even after Dewey abandoned traditional theism and Neo-Hegelian idealism, he continued to associate God or the divine with practical wisdom, especially unifying social ideals, and all those cosmic processes that support realization of the ideal. The reality of the divine is found for Dewey chiefly in the animating spirit of authentic community and is experienced as a living reality in and through all relations informed by sympathy, moral wisdom, and affection.[7]

Dewey goes on to point out that at the time Christianity emerged, these three basic ideas found little opportunity for realization in the everyday world, because politically and industrially society to a large extent treated the mass of people not as persons but as things, means to ends external to themselves. The church justifiably existed as an institution where these ideals could be nurtured separate from society. Given the social situation, the faithful understandably hoped for realization of these values by supernatural means in some future eschatological event. A spirit of world denial and other-worldliness was pervasive. However, over time the gradual spread of basic Christian values caused a transformation of society, and democracy as a social reality was born. The emergence of democracy was coupled with the industrial revolution and the rise of the middle class, causing a major shift in human orientation and aspiration. These social, political and economic forces generated a new spirit of world affirmation and created unheard of possibilities for earthly liberation and fulfillment. As a result, Dewey argues, it became possible for the first time to appreciate fully "the direct, natural sense" of Christian teaching, which calls for liberation of all persons regardless of race, class or gender, in and through the revelation and incarnation of the truth, or, in other words, realization of a kingdom of God that embraces all and finds expression in all social relations.[8]

Given the vast changes in the social situation caused by science and democracy and in the light of their transformative potential, the objective of Christianity and religious persons everywhere should be, Dewey contends, "a society in which the distinction between the spiritual and the secular has ceased, and as in the Greek theory, as in the Christian theory of the Kingdom of God, the church and the state, the divine and the human organization of society are one."[9] The practice of democracy in the context of a technological age makes this a real ideal possibility, Dewey argues. "Democracy, the crucial expression of modern life, is not so much an addition to the scientific and industrial tendencies [of contemporary culture] as it is the perception of their social or spiritual meaning."[10]

In 1892 Dewey stated clearly the momentous social and spiritual meaning that is for him the promise of democracy.

> The next religious prophet who will have a permanent and real influence on men's lives will be the man who succeeds in pointing out the religious meaning of democracy, the ultimate religious value to be found in the normal flow of life itself. It is the question of doing what Jesus did for his time.[11]

Dewey acquired from the Neo-Hegelians the belief that there is no fundamental dualism of God and the world, the ideal and the real, the spiritual and the material, and he retained the conviction as a naturalist that everyday life is inherently full of positive meaning and value. His later thought as well as his early thought is inspired by a passion for unification, or more specifically, for unification of the ideal and the real. He labored as a philosopher to develop a way of living, working, thinking and interacting with the world so as to realize in experience the ideal meaning in life. Democracy as a mode of social organization and a way of personal life has momentous import according to Dewey, because it provides for the first time in human history an opportunity for all persons regardless of race, class, ethnic origin, or gender to realize "the ultimate religious value to be found in the normal flow of life itself," that is, in nature and in everyday life in the secular world. Democracy so understood is, then, the great spiritual challenge and opportunity of the new age.

These convictions make it clear why Dewey does not view the death of the god of supernaturalism as in the final analysis a spiritual catastrophe. Though undeniably painful for many people, it involves a critical transformation in the evolution of human consciousness that opens the door to a deeper and fuller ideal possibility in the religious and moral life of humanity. In the midst of the secularized world, which the atheist and religious conservative alike view as godless and devoid of ultimate meaning, Dewey finds a situation that has made it possible for religious meaning and value to emerge in new, vital, freer forms. His vision is something much more profound than a liberal dream of ongoing material progress, and he lamented the excessive materialism and externalism in American life. To dramatize the point, one might say, using a Mahayana philosophical vocabulary, that democracy for Dewey promises a way of life that offers all persons the opportunity to awaken to the identity of *nirvana* and *samsara*. Furthermore, he understood as few others have that, if men and women in contemporary civilization are to find the wholeness, inner peace and meaning that are the fruit of a healthy religious life, and, if the terror and suffering of modern history are to be overcome in the social sphere, then religious life and social life must not only be reconstructed, but they must also be fully integrated. Part of the power and ongoing relevance of Dewey's thought is to be found in the way that he seeks to address the social, moral and religious problems of the age by holding them together and thinking them through as interrelated aspects of a single whole.

Dewey argues that the fundamental link between Christianity and democracy is to be found in the emphasis on equality, freedom and shared experience in the ethics of democracy. The social ideal of equality recognizes the absolute worth of human personality and the individual person. It requires that all persons be treated as ends and not as a means only. It implies most fundamentally, according to Dewey, guaranteeing to every man, woman and child the opportunity "to become a person," to realize his or her distinctive capacities.[12] Realization of personality, or ongoing human growth (to use the language of his later thought), becomes in Dewey's philosophy the most fundamental social objective and a supreme moral good.

Dewey considers freedom a basic democratic value because it is necessary to realization of personality and the pursuit of happiness. The self, he argues, is essentially a self-determining will, and if personality is to be perfected "the choice to develop it, must proceed from the individual." Hence, the development of the self is thwarted in authoritarian social structures where power and control are centralized in the hands of the few. Dewey points out that self-realization requires the development of moral will, moral responsibility, the capacity for moral choice. The self becomes and is the self it chooses to be in its concrete activities. In Dewey's view persons are genuinely free only insofar as they have developed a capacity for intelligent judgment and choice. People are not born with this capacity. It must be developed, and the achievement of positive freedom is conditioned by the quality of the social institutions in which an individual lives, learns and works.

Democracy as a social ideal also means a community of free persons in which all are bound together by shared experience and a commitment to the common good. "Since democracies forbid, by their very nature, highly centralized governments working by coercion," Dewey points out, they depend upon shared interests and experiences for their unity . . ."[13] Freedom of inquiry, assembly and speech become essential, for "free and open communication . . . is the heart and strength of the American democratic way of living." Class divisions, religious or racial prejudices, and discrimination on the basis of sex, "imperil democracy because they set up barriers to communication, or deflect and distort its operation." The democratic spirit is antithetical, then, to all social barriers that estrange human beings from one another and limit the potential for shared experience. "Democracy is a name for a life of free and enriching communion."[14]

Free communication and the sharing of experience characterize both the internal and external relations of a democratic institution or society. Any social group imbued with the democratic spirit seeks a free give and take with its neighbors. In this way the sharing of experience, the discovering of common values, and the building of community expand. Such is the democratic strategy for the progressive enlargement of authentic community until it embraces all of humanity. In Dewey's world community, the primary social entities would not be nation states, but those voluntary associations formed by men and women from around the world to pursue their shared interests in education, the arts, the sciences, the humanities, business, athletics. The chief task of government is to protect and facilitate the "life of free and enriching communion" which is the very life of democracy.

"If democracy has a moral and ideal meaning," Dewey writes in ***Democracy and Education***, "it is that a social return be demanded from all and that opportunity for development of distinctive capacities be afforded to all."[15] In other words, as he points out elsewhere, in a democratic community every person is both a "sustaining and sustained" member of the whole.[16] In this regard, the question may be asked: What makes Dewey think that educating people, developing their capacities for freedom of choice, and creating opportunities for free communication will result in commitment to the common good and an attitude of social service?

In the final analysis, Dewey believes that human beings educated in a genuinely liberating environment will act in a socially responsible fashion because it offers them a path to the deepest and richest fulfillment possible. He rejects the idea of a fundamental dualism between the individual and society, self and world, as the product of a false psychology. The individual person is not an atomic entity that can develop itself and find satisfaction as an isolated self. Humans are social beings interconnected with their environment, and the communities in which they choose to live shape their character, habits and beliefs. They have a basic need to feel that they belong to the larger whole and find enduring meaning in life by achieving a deep-seated adjustment with their world. According to Dewey's psychology and theory of education, developing one's distinctive capacities in and through responding to the needs of the community is the soundest approach to self-realization. A person best serves the common good by devotion to the capacities with which he or she is endowed and by loyalty to the needs of the social environment. "There is something absolutely worthwhile, something 'divine' in the demands imposed by one's actual situation and powers."[17] The ideal towards which a democratic society should work, then, is creation of a community in which all individuals are provided with the opportunity to develop and employ their special abilities. The individual in this way finds realization of self and the community is sustained.

In developing these ideas about equal opportunity, freedom and community, Dewey sought a way of humanizing the industrial sphere, of making industrial relations subordinate to human relations. This endeavor led him to embrace the concept of "industrial democracy," which is central to his social philosophy. In brief, Dewey's point is that all social institutions—business, industry and government as well as the family, school and religious bodies—are responsible for providing an environment that makes it possible for the people working in these institutions to grow as persons and to develop their distinctive capacities. Social institutions exist first and foremost, not as means of producing things, but as "means of *creating* individuals," as agencies for developing responsible, self-motivated, resourceful and creative persons.[18] In other words, all social organizations have an educational task to perform:

> . . . the test of all the institutions of adult life is their effect in furthering continued education. Government, business, art, religion, all social institutions have a meaning, a purpose. That purpose is to set free and to develop the capacities of human individuals without respect to race, sex, class or economic status. And this is all one with saying that the test of their value is the extent to which they educate every individual into the full stature of his possibility. Democracy has many meanings, but if it has a moral meaning, it is found in resolving that the supreme test of all political institutions and industrial arrangements shall be the contribution they make to the all-around growth of every member of society.[19]

Dewey further explains what this entails: "Full education comes only when there is a responsible share on the part of each person, in proportion to capacity, in shaping the aims and policies of the social groups to which he belongs."[20] Emancipation from external oppression and social welfare programs cannot set a people free unless their living and working environment develops in them the powers of initiative, inventiveness, deliberation and intelligent choice.

In an effort to facilitate the development of industrial democracy, Dewey as a philosopher labors persistently to break down the long standing Western dualisms between the spiritual and the material, the ideal and the natural, and means and ends. These dualisms, he argues, have the effect of degrading the material or natural by stripping it of inherent moral and spiritual meaning. This in turn has a dehumanizing and dispiriting effect on the life of the mass of people whose lives are largely bound up with material and industrial concerns. Dewey's point is that the material and spiritual, means and ends, are organically connected so that the ideal values that illuminate human life are realized and made manifest only in and through the natural and material. In other words, true ideals are properly understood as possibilities of nature. Ends are constituted by means so that properly understood means have all of the meaning and value attributed to ends. Industrial democracy means realizing the inherent meaning and value of industrial work and reconstructing the industrial sphere so that they are actualized for those involved in it.

Dewey's ideal of industrial democracy has been criticized as impractical and utopian. Its realization does involve overcoming complex educational, social, and economic problems. Nevertheless it remains a valid definition of a genuinely liberated society and an ideal by which a democratic culture should be guided. It is furthermore an ideal that gives concreteness to the idea of integrating the spiritual and the secular and to the notion of "the religious meaning of democracy."

2

To appreciate Dewey's idea of democracy fully, it is necessary to explore further some of the fundamental attitudes that he associates with the democratic spirit. First of all, the democratic way of life is animated by a faith in human nature, a "faith in the potentialities of human nature, as that nature is exhibited in every human being irrespective of race, color, sex, birth and family, of material or cultural wealth."[21] Dewey adds "that this faith may be enacted in statutes, but it is only on paper unless it is put in force in the attitudes which human beings display to one another in all the incidents and relations of daily life." Dewey has often been criticized for maintaining a faith in human nature that is naive and unduly optimistic. In response he explains his position:

> Democracy is a way of personal life controlled not merely by faith in human nature in general but by faith in the capacity of human beings for intelligent judgement and action if proper conditions are furnished. I have been accused more than once and from opposed quarters of an undue, a utopian, faith in the possibilities of intelligence and in education as a correlate of intelligence. At all events, I did not invent this faith. I acquired it from my surroundings as far as those surroundings were animated by the democratic spirit. For what is the faith of democracy in the role of consultation, of conference, of persuasion, of discussion, in formation of public opinion, which in the long run is self-corrective, except faith in the capacity of the intelligence of the common man to respond with common sense to the free play of facts and ideas which are secured by effective guarantees of free inquiry, free assembly, and free communication? I am willing to leave to upholders of totalitarian states of the right and the left the view that faith in the capacities of intelligence is utopian.[22]

Reinhold Niebuhr, who in the 1930s was a harsh critic of Dewey's liberal optimism, conceded in 1944 that a consistent pessimism regarding human nature leads invariably to "tyrannical political strategies." Niebuhr concluded: "Man's capacity for justice makes democracy possible; but man's inclination to injustice makes democracy necessary."[23] Dewey would agree.

Second, Dewey gives special attention to what he calls "intelligent sympathy" as an essential democratic virtue. "Sympathy as a desirable quality is something more than feeling. It is a cultivated imagination for what men have in common and a rebellion at whatever unnecessarily divides them."[24] It involves the will "to join freely and fully in shared or common activities." More specifically, sympathy is sensitive responsiveness to the interests, sufferings, and rights of others. He finds sympathy "the animating mold of moral judgment . . . because it furnishes the most efficacious intellectual standpoint."[25] "Sympathy . . . carries thought out beyond the self," "renders vivid the interests of others," and "humbles . . . our own pretensions," encouraging the development of impartial moral judgments. Sympathy "is the tool, par excellence,

for resolving complex situations." Dewey, however, did not believe that feelings of compassion by themselves are an adequate guide in the moral life. He urged development of what he calls "intelligent sympathy," that is, a union of benevolent impulses and experimental inquiry into conditions and consequences.

Third, Dewey argues that the democratic way of life involves an attitude of cooperation and peace that includes a commitment to non-violent methods of resolving conflicts whenever possible.

> . . . democracy as a way of life is controlled by personal faith in personal day-by-day working together with others. Democracy is the belief that even when needs and ends or consequences are different for each individual, the habit of amicable co-operation—which may include, as in sport, rivalry and competition—is itself a priceless addition to life. To take as far as possible every conflict which arises—and they are bound to arise—out of the atmosphere and medium of force, of violence as a means of settlement, into that of discussion and of intelligence, is to treat those who disagree—even profoundly—with us as those from whom we may learn, and in so far, as friends. A genuinely democratic faith in peace is faith in the possibility of conducting disputes, controversies, and conflicts as co-operative undertakings in which both parties learn by giving the other a chance to express itself, instead of having one party conquer by forceful suppression of the other—a suppression which is none the less one of violence when it takes place by psychological means of ridicule, abuse, intimidation, instead of by overt imprisonment or in concentration camps. To co-operate by giving differences a chance to show themselves because of the belief that the expression of difference is not only a right of the other person but is a means of enriching one's own life-experience, is inherent in the democratic personal way of life.[26]

The depth of good will demanded by Dewey's idea of the democratic spirit is revealed in his counsel "to treat those who disagree—even profoundly—with us as those from whom one may learn, and in so far, as friends." Regarding Dewey's attitude toward non-violence, he was led to support World War I, but the consequences of the war left him deeply disillusioned. During the 1920s and 1930s he worked tirelessly in support of the international movement to outlaw war and consistently attacked the communist advocacy of class war as the means of social progress.

3

The democratic way of life, Dewey teaches, is an ethical way guided by "intelligent sympathy" and concern for the common good. Such a way of life fosters ongoing growth in the individual and transforms and sustains the community. At this juncture it is useful to seek clarification of Dewey's democratic ethics of intelligent sympathy and social reconstruction. Here one finds him working out his interpretation of the "direct, natural sense" of Christian belief in the revelation of liberating practical truth.

As a philosopher of democracy, Dewey seeks in his approach to ethics a middle way between absolutism and subjectivism, just as in his metaphysics he seeks a middle way between supernaturalism and an atheistic scientific materialism. Moral absolutism has the advantage of affirming the objective validity of moral values. However, it also involves ideas of an external authority and a fixed hierarchy of ends and goods that reflect aristocratic social values and feudal class divisions, Dewey asserts. It frequently is an obstacle to progressive social change. It may be used to obstruct the development of independent thought and has all too often in human history fostered fanaticism and the gross abuse of power. Subjectivism respects the freedom of the individual and the authority of direct personal experience, but it leaves society and the individual at the mercy of whim, prejudice, passion, uncriticized habit and narrow self-interest.

Dewey argues that the democratic spirit in ethics charts a course between the extremes of absolutism and subjectivism by looking for guidance to experience and intelligence, or, more specifically, to the experimental method of knowledge. By giving authority in matters of knowledge, including moral values, to experimental intelligence rather than to something external to experience, Dewey seeks to develop a method of moral knowledge consistent with the democratic faith in human nature, education, free inquiry, and public debate. By adapting the experimental method of the sciences to the process of moral valuation, he endeavors to overcome the split between science and moral and religious values and to give moral judgments an empirical foundation and objective validity. Moreover, Dewey's larger theory of the moral life becomes a theory of the unification of the spiritual and the material and pursues the full integration of the moral good with ordinary life. In his democratic reconstruction of Christianity, then, the experimental method becomes the instrument for the ongoing revelation of practical truth, and the authentic moral life becomes the incarnation of liberating truth in everyday existence.

Dewey's pragmatism and democratic experimental ethics reflects the marked influence of Darwinian biology and William James' functional psychology and instrumentalist view of mind. The mind according to James and Dewey is chiefly an organ designed to assist the human being in adapting to its environment. They view ideas and beliefs first and foremost as guides to action. Knowledge may possess for thinkers a certain inherent aesthetic meaning, but it has a fundamentally instrumental function. Ideas are to be evaluated according to their effectiveness as guides to ongoing growth and to well-being in the fullest sense. Ideas, like the tools of a craftsman, are not only to be respected and prized but also to be redefined and reconstructed so as to better meet the demands of the situation. As an evolutionary naturalist, Dewey emphasizes the pervasive presence of change and rejects all ideas of fixed final causes. There are no absolute fixities in nature. Even species come to be and pass away. Moral and religious values, he reasons, may and should change in response to the needs of a changing human situation.

Instead of seeking absolute ideals and offering ready-made solutions to moral problems, pragmatism adopts a genetic and experimental approach that focuses on developing a method for dealing with specific moral difficulties as they arise in concrete situations. It directs a person facing a moral dilemma to carefully clarify the nature of the problem and then to give attention to specific alternative values or ideal possibilities that might guide conduct in the situation, noting especially the conditions necessary to actualize them, that is, the means to their realization. With the aid of this knowledge of conditions or means, it studies the actual consequences that will flow from acting under guidance of the alternative values in question. In the light of knowledge of consequences, it then evaluates these ideals taking into consideration the specific needs of the moral problem at hand. Pragmatism, then, evaluates moral values or ideals with reference to specific problematic situations and in the light of the means involved in their realization and the consequences that necessarily follow.

In Dewey's middle way, true moral values are relative to the situation, but since moral judgments are based on an examination of conditions and consequences, they possess objective validity. Much of the popular discussion of moral values today incorrectly assumes that the only alternative to absolutism is subjectivism, because it is thought that relativism inevitably means subjectivism. Dewey clearly demonstrates that this is not the case. It is also widely assumed that science and empirical methods of knowledge support moral subjectivism. Again, Dewey's ethical experimentalism shows that this is not necessarily true. The experimental method of knowledge cannot prove that the values of beauty and goodness are objectively real, but Dewey asserts that this is hardly necessary and not its function. The reality of values—social, moral, aesthetic, religious—is disclosed in direct, immediate experience.

One does not need philosophy and science—reflective experience—to reveal or demonstrate that values are real unless one adopts an "arbitrary intellectualism" and makes the unempirical assumption that "knowledge has a monopolistic claim to access to reality."[27] However, the experimental method of inquiry may become a way of evaluating and reconstructing the many goods and related purposes that are discovered in and through direct experience, that is, it may serve as an instrument for deepening and refining the human vision of the ideal possibilities of life. It also may help in the process of realizing these ideal possibilities by disclosing the means necessary to chosen ends. In this fashion Dewey seeks to overcome the division between science and human values and to develop a method of moral guidance adequate to the demands of a democratic and technological age.

Regarding the criteria for making moral decisions, Dewey points out that deliberation is called into play when a problematical situation arises, and the criteria for evaluating alternative courses of action are supplied by the situation itself. The end of action is judged good which overcomes the original problems and reestablishes a harmonious situation.[28] He also emphasizes "a plurality of changing, moving, individualized goods and ends."[29] His point is that the good will vary according to individual need and capacity and the situation. Each situation is unique having "its own irreplaceable good." It is the task of intelligence using the method of experimental empiricism to determine just what the good is in any particular situation. The supreme value at any one time varies with the situation, which is a further reason for rejecting the idea of a fixed hierarchy of goods.

> Every case where moral action is required becomes of equal importance and urgency with every other. If the need and deficiencies of a specific situation indicate improvement of health as the end and good, then for that situation health is the ultimate and supreme good.[30]

It is "a final and intrinsic value" and "the whole personality should be concerned with it." Dewey here broadens the idea of what constitutes moral action and again seeks to break down the dualism of spiritual and material. He would liberate people to live wholeheartedly in the present, realizing the inherent meaning and value of even the most ordinary everyday tasks. He seeks to locate the center of gravity and attention in the moral life within the process of living. It is the difference between what Paul calls living under the law and living in the spirit.[31]

As an evolutionary naturalist who views the universe as unfinished and open to novel creative possibilities, Dewey opposes any idea of a fixed supreme good, but he was not without his own general definition of the moral good and a comprehensive end of moral action. He argues in *Experience and Nature* (1925), for example, that to common sense "the better is that which will do more in the way of security, liberation and fecundity for other likings and values," because "the best, the richest and fullest experience possible" is "the common purpose of men."[32] Dewey assumes, then, that there is a common sense, common purpose generated by experience and shared by all, which is growth toward the richest and fullest experience possible. He has, however, abandoned the Hegelian idea of some pre-established notion of the universal self and every other idea of a fixed end. His thought shifts the emphasis from achievement of a pre-established goal to a concern with the process of growing itself, emphasizing the intrinsic value of the process as lived each day and its ongoing open-ended nature: "Not perfection as a final goal, but the ever-enduring process of perfecting, maturing, refining is the aim in living."[33]

In his discussion of moral virtue, Dewey returns to a classical Christian theme, asserting that love may be understood as the comprehensive moral virtue. He then proceeds to give his own democratic experimentalist's definition of love. By love he means wholehearted interest in those objects, ends, and ideals which the process of experimental moral evaluation recognizes as good. In other words, love is the whole self responding with complete interest and intelligent sympathy to the needs of the situation and the perfect union of subject and object, of self and activity—the activity dictated by the ideal possibilities of the situation. The good person "is his whole self in each of his acts," and "his whole self being in the act, the deed is solid and substantial, no matter how trivial the outer occasion."[34] "To find the self in the highest and fullest activity possible at the time and to perform the act in the consciousness of its complete identification with self," that is, its ultimate meaningfulness in this situation, is to live as a liberated and enlightened moral being. So defined, love realizes the full positive value of the present situation. It ensures responsibility. It also involves the classical Greek virtues of courage, self-discipline, justice and wisdom.[35] Love so defined is the way of freedom and growth for the individual and the community. It is the perfection of democracy as a creative way of personal life.

Dewey's experimental reconstruction of the moral life involving the ideas of sympathetic responsiveness, complete identification of self and activity, and wholehearted living in the present, reminds one of the spiritual practice of teachers as diverse as St. Francis of Assisi, Zen Master Dogen, and Martin Buber.[36] They all emphasize that a vital spiritual life involves being able to respond to a situation with the energy and attention of the whole self. In other words, one finds here in Dewey a theory of what might be called a secular democratic form of spiritual practice.

Dewey's democratic strategy for ongoing creative social change emphasizes the development of the social sciences, experimental ethical valuation, education, and communication. In this regard, he has been justly criticized for failing to appreciate fully the depth of the contradictions that divide social groups in the contemporary world and for not recognizing the necessity for "confrontational politics and agitational social struggle."[37] Nevertheless, Dewey's approach remains fundamental, for without experimental inquiry and evaluation confrontation will be without intelligent purpose, and without communication the peace of authentic community will never be more than a dream.

4

In her essay on *Democracy and Social Ethics* (1902), Jane Addams, the founder of Hull House in Chicago, writes that the democratic way brings "a certain life-giving power" and a sense "that we belong to the whole, that a certain basic well-being can never be taken away from us whatever the turn of fortune."[38] Dewey, who worked closely with Addams on many liberal social fronts and learned much from her about the meaning of democracy, shared these sentiments. In short, he found the democratic way of life to be a source of sustaining religious experience.

As a Hegelian idealist Dewey had embraced a certain ethical as well as aesthetic mysticism arguing that the democratic life leads to an experience of union with God, the Universal Self. As a naturalist, he ceased to think of God as in any sense a being. Nevertheless, in *A Common*

Faith (1934), he asserts that, if a person wishes to use the term God, or the divine, it may quite properly be used to refer to all those conditions and processes in human nature, society and the universe at large that have a liberating and unifying effect on human life and contribute to the actualization of the ideal. So defined, the divine includes the creative democratic life.

Furthermore, Dewey argues that the democratic faith and way of life have the power to give to experience a distinctly "religious quality." He identifies the religious quality of experience with a deep enduring sense of unification of self and of self and world.[39] It includes feelings of belonging to the larger whole, cosmic trust, and peace, and it involves a sustaining sense of the meaning and value of life. Reflecting on the religious significance of the democratic life in 1920, he borrows some imagery from Wordsworth and writes: "When the emotional force, the mystic force one might say, of communication, of the miracle of shared life and shared experience is spontaneously felt, the hardness and crudeness of contemporary life will be bathed in the light that never was on land or sea."[40] Even in the midst of failure and tragedy a person committed to the ethics of democracy may be "sustained and expanded . . . by the sense of an enveloping whole."[41] Given the unifying and sustaining effects of a moral faith in democracy, Dewey argues that it may properly be called a form of religious faith.

He also points out that philosophical reflection and aesthetic intuitions of a mystical nature may reinforce and deepen the religious quality of experience generated by a faith in democracy. In short, there is divine grace flowing in the democratic life and natural experience as Dewey understands it. One could even argue that his account of the religious quality of experience implies more about the nature of the divine than is expressed in his philosophy, but that is not a matter which can be explored in this essay.

5

Today the human race faces a major environmental crisis which will make the planet uninhabitable unless there are major changes in humanity's moral values and behavior in relation to nature. Dewey's philosophy lays the foundation for such a development by rejecting all dualisms of spirit and nature and of mind and body and by proposing an ecological world view. As a philosophical naturalist, Dewey identifies nature as the all-encompassing whole of which humanity is a part interrelated with all other parts. Nature is the primal matrix out of which the human spirit has evolved, and humanity's creativity and spiritual life are viewed as expressions of possibilities resident in nature and as dependent on nature as well as human effort for full realization. Having a keen sense of the interrelation of culture and nature, Dewey counselled "piety toward nature," and expressed appreciation of the Taoist spirit of living in harmony with nature.[42] He conceived the democratic community to be intimately interrelated with all those aspects of nature which support and help to make possible the flowering of human civilization,

but he did not explore the idea of extending the ethics of democracy to encompass the rights of nature outside the human sphere. Today this further step is imperative. Some thinkers have already proposed such a development.

In recent decades animal rights activists and environmentalists have been working to extend the liberal tradition of natural rights to embrace plant species, animals and eco-systems as well as human beings. This has resulted in an expansion of the idea of the democratic community. The first to make the connection with democracy explicit was an Englishman and champion of animal rights, a contemporary of John Dewey's named Henry J. Salt. As early as 1894 Salt is found calling for the perfection of democracy by including "all living things within this scope."[43] More recently, the American theologian and medieval historian Lynn White, working in the tradition of St. Francis of Assisi, has advocated a new spiritual democracy that recognizes all living things as possessing intrinsic value and ethical rights.[44] In a Pulitzer prize-winning book of poetry, Gary Snyder, who has been influenced by Zen Buddhism and Native American traditions, calls for a new definition of democracy that conceives it to involve a social order in which plants and animals are given legal rights and represented in the councils of government.[45] There is, of course, already legislation in many nations forbidding certain kinds of animal abuse and protecting endangered species and wilderness areas.

The expansion and deepening of the idea of the democratic community proposed by Salt, White, and Snyder involve constructive proposals for giving the democratic ideal a necessary added dimension of ethical meaning. In an age that is learning how to think ecologically, the ethics of creative democracy must integrate the values of economic well-being and equal rights for humans with respect for the needs and rights of other life forms and ecosystems.[46]

6

Fukuyama in his essay on the triumph of Western liberal democracy sees the future as "a very sad time," because he identifies liberal democracy with consumerism and finds it suffering from "impersonality and spiritual vacuity . . . at the core."[47] Dewey, who arrived at his idea of the democratic ideal by reconstructing Christian ethics, would argue that, even if Fukuyama is correct about the current spiritual condition of liberal democratic societies, his assessment suffers from a failure to appreciate the full ethical meaning of the idea. Democracy as Dewey conceives it offers liberal democratic societies an opportunity to recover their spiritual center and to become profoundly ethical at the core. The democratic way involves a full integration of religious life and secular life. It offers the religious person a meaningful way to be religious in the contemporary world, and it offers society a way to find the meaning and value that consumerism cannot provide.

These observations raise questions about the relation of creative democracy, or what could also be called spiritual democracy, to the great world religions. The democratic faith can be practiced within the framework of a humanistic and naturalistic world view, and it does not necessarily require the support of traditional institutional religion. It is also quite capable of living peacefully in association with different religious faiths, provided they respect the ethics of democracy in living together. Furthermore, it can be actively supported by a variety of religious world views, and the democratic life can be deepened and enriched by this association. The religions in turn are developed in a positive fashion by undergoing a democratic reconstruction that brings their symbols, ideas and practices fully into harmony with democratic values.

Historically, the world religions have been a mixed blessing for humanity. On the one hand, they have been treasure houses of faith, wisdom and compassion providing beneficial methods of spiritual growth and transformation. On the other hand, they have often suffered moral corruption, and they have been a source of superstition, fanaticism, persecution, and war. The greatest single moral failing of the religions has been their inability to instill in the mass of their followers an attitude of respect for the rights and dignity of all human beings including those of different religious faiths. Where the influence of democratic social change has been strong, many religious groups have endeavored to revise official doctrine and teaching in this regard. Wherever the spirit of religious absolutism and fundamentalism is strong, this issue can be a serious problem, and throughout the world social and political conflicts continue to be exacerbated by religious exclusivism and intolerance.

Another particularly pressing moral issue is the discrimination against women within many religious institutions, which has been unmasked by feminist theology in recent decades. The corrective to interfaith hostility, religious bias against women, and other forms of unjust religious discrimination is to be found in the ethics of democracy and the abandonment of those patriarchal, monarchical and imperialistic images of God that foster undemocratic attitudes and behavior. This is fundamental to what is meant by the democratic reconstruction of the religions. In line with a transformation of the democratic ideal into a vision of a community of all life, democratic reconstruction would also support those movements within the religions that are developing an environmental ethics and a supporting ecological world view.

The democratic spirit also works to break down completely the dualism of the sacred and the secular, and it focuses religious concern first and foremost in the life of relationship and intelligent sympathy. Whole-hearted ethical action is the finest flower of the religious life, and the deepest mystical insight and union with the divine comes in and through its radiant energy. As Martin Buber has expressed it, turning inward and concentration by means of prayer and meditation are preparation for going forth, and the Eternal Thou is encountered in everyday life in and through relationship to persons—and also to dogs, trees, and stones—insofar as each is treated as a thou and not only as an it. In all the world religions there are traditions which emphasize some variation on this teaching. A democratic reformation of the religions would make it central and seek to clarify its implications for an understanding of God, the moral life, and spiritual practice in societies being transformed by ongoing technological change, democratic reform, and destruction of the natural environment.

Writing in 1946, Albert Schweitzer, who embraced an ethics of reverence for all life as essential to the survival of civilization, states the general issue within a Christian theological vocabulary:

> Belief in the Kingdom of God now takes a new lease of life. It no longer looks for its coming, self-determined, as an eschatological cosmic event, but regards it as something ethical and spiritual, not bound up with the last things, but to be realized with the cooperation of men.
>
> . . . Mankind to-day must either realize the Kingdom of God or perish. The very tragedy of our present situation compels us to devote ourselves in faith to its realization.[48]

The growing nuclear threat only adds urgency to Schweitzer's words, which in the democratic spirit stress human responsibility and invention rather than divine control and intervention.

Devotion to the community of God in its democratic transformation means commitment to the creation of social institutions that would enable all human beings to develop fully their capacities for spiritual freedom, intelligent judgment, aesthetic enjoyment, creating, sharing, cooperating and loving. At its best, the democratic mind knows that none are truly free until all are free, and that the spiritual meaning of our time is to be found by working to build a world where freedom is universal. This is especially true at the end of the twentieth century, because advancement towards the goal of freedom is a possibility as never before, even if the complexities and difficulties are greater than ever. Also, as Schweitzer understood, the concept of liberation must be extended to the entire biosphere.

Ethical principles with democratic implications have been at work in a variety of traditions within the great world religions for centuries. Various forms of liberation theology have in the last two hundred years worked to overcome the dualism of the religious and the secular. The democratic reformation of the religions under the impact of democratic social change and interfaith dialogue is far advanced today in some quarters. It remains to make men and women fully conscious of the meaning and potential of this process and to extend it. Space does not permit discussion of democratic change within specific traditions, but a few general comments are in order. What is being contemplated would respect the unique identity of each of the religions and of the many traditions within them. Many paths can be followed as ways into the democratic life. The objective is not to impose on the religions some moral ideal external to their traditions; that would be an undemocratic procedure. It is rather to encourage development from within each tradition of those ethical principles and images of the divine which have creative democratic and ecological implications and support freedom, human rights, equal opportunity, collective participation, peace in living together, and respect for nature. The democratic reformation of the religions will be accomplished only when they come to recognize in the democratic way the deeper practical meaning of their own spirituality.

This discussion would be incomplete without considering the contradiction between the democratic faith and authoritarianism and absolutism. Democracy rejects authoritarianism as the fundamental method of education and government, because it is inconsistent with the goal of a free self-governing individual. The defenders of authoritarianism, like Dostoevski's Grand Inquisitor, can at times mount strong arguments. Authoritarianism may have popular appeal: witness the rise of fascism in the 1930s and theocracy in Iran more recently. Respect for duly constituted, responsible authority has its place. Obedience to the moral truth is an important virtue, and a vow of obedience to a superior authority in a monastic situation may be an effective instrument for getting rid of ego.

However, the democratic faith opposes authoritarianism. In the final analysis it believes that the full meaning of human life is realized only in and through the challenge and risk of freedom. There are great risks, as the abuse of freedom in liberal democratic societies reveals again and again. There is much to be learned from a democratic social philosopher with a profound appreciation of the problem of evil in human nature such as Reinhold Niebuhr. Nevertheless, the central concern in a democratic environment is always the creating of free persons—persons with independent minds capable of intelligent responsible choice—not obedient persons whose minds and wills are subordinate to an external authority. Autonomy and direct personal realization of the truth constitute the critical issue.

Commitment to the liberation of the individual is the most fundamental aspect of the great spiritual significance of democracy. When a school system, an economic system, a religious community or a government lose sight of this ultimate objective, democracy begins to die. The democratic objective of a self-governing individual does not necessarily imply moral subjectivism. The democratic faith as outlined in this essay is identified with an ethical experimentalism that affirms the reality of objective moral truth and the critical social significance of an enlightened sense of moral responsibility. Autonomy is not an end in itself, but without it the individual cannot undertake the great social and religious challenges of life.

The problems with absolutism have already been discussed in connection with Dewey's theory of ethics. It remains to make clear that it is quite possible for the democratic spirit to embrace a faith in the Absolute, the Eternal One or God, while standing firmly opposed to absolutism in the sense of a belief that one particular revelation, creed or set of dogmas contains a fixed and final formulation of the absolute truth. The democratic faith may be harmonized with a trust that there is at work in the cosmos an ultimate meaning that transcends the threats of evil, time and death. However, such a faith when consistent with the democratic spirit would insist that by its very nature the Truth cannot be grasped by the discursive intellect alone and formulated in concepts once and for all. Socrates, who firmly believed in the reality of the Absolute Truth and may well have directly experienced it, makes the critical point when he asserts that the wisest human being is one who knows his or her own ignorance. The highest wisdom of the Buddha is expressed in a thunderous silence. One Christian mystic speaks of God as a dazzling obscurity.

A person may find a way to the Absolute in and through the symbols and beliefs, of a particular religious tradition, but symbols and beliefs should not be confused with the Absolute itself. One may rightfully trust a particular religious tradition without adopting the arrogant and dangerous belief that one possesses the absolute truth and that other religious paths are necessarily inferior or wrong. Faith in God or the Absolute is consistent with democracy when it leads an individual to spiritual poverty and the humble effort to help others knowing always that, while the Truth may possess us as its instruments, we do not possess it. Such faith offers the deepest support to creative democracy as a unified way of social, economic, moral and religious life.

The task of criticizing and developing the democratic ideal can give post-analytic philosophy a coherent social purpose, and it offers liberation theology—especially in North America—the possibility of a more comprehensive and integrated vision than it has yet achieved. A thoroughgoing democratic reconstruction of the religions in a world experiencing democratic social transformation will breathe new life into the religions and fresh energy into democracy as a way of liberation. It will enable men and women in the midst of their every day existence to look anew to the great religious traditions for guidance in wrestling with the deeper mysteries of life and death. It will unify social, moral and religious life, bringing a wholeness, peace and joy that many seek and few today are able to find.

NOTES

[1] Francis Fukuyama, "The End of History?" *The National Interest,* 16 (Summer 1989), 4.

[2] G. W. F. Hegel, "America is Therefore the Land of the Future, in *The American Hegelians,* ed. W. H. Goetzmann (New York: Alfred A. Knopf, 1973), p. 20. Walt Whitman, *Democratic Vistas,* in *Walt Whitman,* ed. Mark Van Doren (New York: Viking Press, 1945), p. 365.

[3] *Ibid.,* pp. 323-324.

4 See Steven C. Rockefeller, "John Dewey: The Evolution of a Faith," in *History, Religion, and Spiritual Democracy, Essays in Honor of Joseph L. Blau,* ed. Maurice Wohlgelernter (New York: Columbia University Press, 1980), pp. 5-35.

5 John Dewey, "Creative Democracy—The Task Before Us," in LW 14:226. EW, MW, LW refer to the Early, Middle and Later *Works of John Dewey* edited by JoAnn Boydston and published by Southern Illinois University Press, Carbondale, Ill.

6 John Dewey, "Reconstruction," in EW 4:98-102.

7 John Dewey, *A Common Faith,* in LW 9:29-37.

8 John Dewey, "Christianity and Democracy," in EW 4:7-8.

9 John Dewey, *The Ethics of Democracy,* in EW 1:248-249.

10 John Dewey, "Intelligence and Morals," in MW 4:39.

11 John Dewey, "The Relation of Philosophy to Theology," in EW 4:367.

12 Dewey, *The Ethics of Democracy,* pp. 244-248.

13 John Dewey, "The Need of an Industrial Education in an Industrial Democracy," in MW 10:137-138.

14 John Dewey, *The Public and Its Problems,* in LW 2:350.

15 John Dewey, *Democracy and Education,* in MW 9:129.

16 John Dewey, *Individualism Old and New,* in LW 5:68.

17 John Dewey, *Outlines of a Critical Theory of Ethics,* in EW 3:321.

18 John Dewey, *Reconstruction in Philosophy,* in MW 12:191.

19 *Ibid.,* p. 186.

20 *Ibid.,* p. 199.

21 Dewey, "Creative Democracy," p. 226.

22 *Ibid.,* p. 227.

23 Reinhold Niebuhr, *The Children of Light and the Children of Darkness* (New York: Charles Scribner's Sons, 1944), pp. xii-xv.

24 Dewey, *Democracy and Education,* pp. 127-128, 130.

25 John Dewey, *Ethics,* in LW 7:251-252, 270, 299-300.

26 Dewey, "Creative Democracy," p. 228.

27 John Dewey, *Experience and Nature,* in LW 1:28; John Dewey, *The Quest for Certainty,* LW 4:20.

28 John Dewey, *Theory of Valuation,* in LW 13:231-233.

29 Dewey, *Reconstruction in Philosophy,* p. 173.

30 *Ibid.,* pp. 176, 180.

31 Dewey, *Ethics,* p. 279.

32 Dewey, *Experience and Nature,* pp. 311, 321.

33 Dewey, *Reconstruction in Philosophy,* p. 181.

34 John Dewey, *The Study of Ethics,* in EW 4:245, 293.

35 *Ibid.,* p. 361; Dewey, *Ethics,* p. 259.

36 See for example, John C. Maraldo, "The Hermeneutics of Practice in Dogen and Francis of Assisi: An Exercise in Buddhist-Christian Dialogue," in *Eastern Buddhist,* 14 (1981), 22-46.

37 Cornel West, *The American Evasion of Philosophy: A Genealogy of Pragmatism* (Madison: University of Wisconsin Press, 1989), pp. 101-107.

38 Jane Addams, *Democracy and Social Ethics* (Cambridge, Mass.: Harvard University Press, 1964), p. 276.

39 Dewey, *A Common Faith,* pp. 8-17.

40 Dewey, *Reconstruction in Philosophy,* p. 201.

41 John Dewey, *Human Nature and Conduct,* in MW 14:181.

42 Dewey, *A Common Faith,* pp. 18, 36; John Dewey, "As the Chinese Think," in MW 13:222-224.

43 Henry S. Salt *Animals' Rights Considered in Relation to Social Progress* (New York, 1894) as quoted in Roderick Frazier Nash, *The Rights of Nature* (Madison: The University of Wisconsin Press, 1989), p. 28.

44 Lynn White, Jr., "Continuing the Conversation," in Ian G. Barbour, ed., *Western Man and Environmental Ethics* (Reading, Mass., 1973), p. 61 and Lynn White, Jr., "The Future of Compassion," *Ecumenical Review* 30 (April 1978), 107. See Nash, *The Rights of Nature,* Chapter 4.

45 Gary Snyder, "Energy is Eternal Delight" and "Wilderness" in *Turtle Island* (New York: New Directions Publishing Corporation, 1974), pp. 104, 106-110.

46 I am particularly indebted to conversations with Professor J. Ronald Engel and his work on a world conservation ethic, which will soon be published, for first bringing to my attention the possibilities for integrating the ethics of democracy and environment ethics.

[47] Fukuyama, "The End of History?" pp. 14, 18.

[48] Albert Schweitzer, "The Conception of the Kingdom of God in the Transformation of Eschatology," in *Religion From Tolstoy to Camus,* ed. Walter Kaufmann (New York: Harper Torchbooks, 1961), pp. 420, 424.

Louis Menand (essay date 1992)

SOURCE: "The Real John Dewey," in *The New York Review of Books,* Vol. XXXIX, No. 12, June 25, 1992, pp. 50-55.

[*In the following review of Robert B. Westbrook's* John Dewey and American Democracy, *Menand gives an overview of Dewey's life and work, and touches briefly on the influence Jane Addams and Dewey's wife, Alice Chapman, had on his social consciousness.*]

1

In the minds of most people born after the Second World War, John Dewey is an exceedingly dim presence, a figure apparently left stranded on the far side of the Sixties. He has seemed the spokesman for a world view whose day has passed. His ideas have not been thought worth knowing better, and his books, by and large, have not been read.

Once, of course, it was different. For more than half a century, from the time his experimental school for children, founded in 1896, achieved its worldwide renown until his death, in 1952, at the age of ninety-two, Dewey was one of the most celebrated public intellectuals in America. He published forty books, and lectured before almost every kind of audience. He helped to create some of the most prominent political and educational organizations established in his time: the American Civil Liberties Union, the NAACP, the League for Industrial Democracy, the New York Teachers Union, the American Association of University Professors, the New School for Social Research. His writings on education changed the way children were taught in places as far away as China; and his views were solicited on nearly every subject. "It is scarcely an exaggeration to say," wrote Henry Steele Commager in 1950, "that for a generation no major issue was clarified until Dewey had spoken."[1]

Robert Westbrook, who teaches history at the University of Rochester, thinks that neither of these Deweys—the Dewey lionized as "the national philosopher" in his own time and the Dewey generally dismissed in ours—is the real Dewey. The real Dewey, he believes, was "a deviant among American liberals," "a minority, not a majority, spokesman within the liberal community," "a more radical voice than has been generally assumed." The key to this Dewey, he proposes, is his idea of democracy, and the purpose of his book is to explain what that idea was and why it remains important.

John Dewey and American Democracy is an exceptionally intelligent, rigorous, and thorough book. Although it is offered as an interpretation of one aspect of Dewey's thought, it makes a first-rate guide through the enormous (and, many have complained, often turgid) mass of Dewey's writing.[2] Westbrook's call for a renewed appreciation of Dewey's relevance—his implicit claim that Dewey really belongs to the generation that failed to read him rather than to the generation that actually did—is strengthened by great learning and conviction, and it will find many responsive echoes.

Westbrook does not have much to say about Dewey's personal life, but neither did Dewey. Dewey was born in Burlington, Vermont, in 1859 (which, as few commentators have been able to resist pointing out, also happens to be the year of *On the Origin of Species,* a work whose influence on Dewey was paramount). Both parents were descended from generations of Vermonters. His father was a storekeeper, a witty man who recited Milton and Shakespeare around the shop, but whose greatest ambition for his sons is said to have been the hope that one of them might grow up to become a mechanic. Dewey's mother was a strong-minded and evangelical woman. He attended the local public school, the local Congregationalist church, and, eventually, the local college, which was the University of Vermont. He graduated in 1879; there were eighteen students in his class.

Dewey was, in short, a prime example of what used to be called a New England Yankee, and the standard thing to say about his upbringing is that it bred into him the values of American democracy in their most pristine and aboriginal form. This is an understanding encouraged by Dewey himself, in one of the few places in which he commented on his own life, a curious essay of 1939 called "Biography of John Dewey," said to have been "written by the daughters of the subject from material which he furnished."[3] In Burlington, this authorial committee explains, "life was democratic—not consciously, but in that deeper sense in which equality and absence of class distinctions are taken for granted." (The essay goes on to remark that "the few who attended private schools were regarded as 'sissies' or 'stuck-up' by the majority," which suggests that class distinctions were not as absent as all that from nineteenth-century Burlington.)

Westbrook dismisses this explanation for Dewey's later egalitarianism as a myth, and he's quite justified in doing so. Burlington was not a Yankee village in 1859; it was an industrializing community with a large working-class population of French Canadian and Irish immigrants. In other respects, it was merely provincial: Dewey later described the religious culture, impressed upon him most insistently by his mother, as "a painful oppression," and it is hard not to believe that he struck on what was, at the time, the extremely novel idea of going to graduate school as a means of escaping the entire scene. Dewey was not, despite his famous country-mouse appearance, a small-town boy at heart. He spent ten years, from 1894 to 1904, in Chicago, which he thought "the greatest place in the world"; in 1905, he moved to New York City, where he lived (ultimately on Fifth Avenue) for the rest of his life. He used to say to his colleagues at Columbia that he didn't see why they had summer places in Vermont. "I got out," he told them, "as soon as I could."[4]

Dewey's homespun aura is, in fact, the one truly deceptive thing about him. His lack of affectation and self-regard was perfectly genuine, of course, and it could make him seem not only simple but simple-minded. There is a story, apparently once enjoyed as somehow emblematic of Dewey's sense of himself, about the time he joined a parade down Fifth Avenue on behalf of one of the many liberal causes he supported, women's suffrage. He was handed a placard and dutifully set off, but became increasingly puzzled by the laughter of the spectators he passed along the route. He had not bothered to read the sign he was carrying, which said, "Men Can Vote, Why Can't I?"

But Dewey was not a naif, a Jimmy Stewart character whose native common sense triumphs over the pretensions of the sophisticates. His thought was formed by influences the Jimmy Stewarts of his time would have regarded with horror: Darwin, Hegel, and functional psychology. He admired Jefferson, but he rarely referred to any of the other founders, and his entire social and political philosophy was an assault on the kind of pioneer individualism conventionally associated with the early American spirit. He did not think this country had forgotten its core principles, that it had gone forward too fast. He thought it had not gone forward fast enough, and that devotion to its "core principles" was one of the things holding it back. Compared to Dewey, William James was a nostalgist.

The graduate school Dewey chose was Johns Hopkins, and it is an indication of his eagerness to leave Burlington that after his applications for fellowships had been twice turned down, he borrowed the money from a relative and went anyway. Although the three-man philosophy department at Hopkins in 1882 included G. Stanley Hall, whose work in psychology helped lay the foundations for the progressive movement in education of which Dewey would later become the hero, and Charles Sanders Peirce, whose studies in the logic of science were eventually the model for much of Dewey's own work, Dewey chose to study with the third, now largely forgotten, member of the department, George Sylvester Morris, who was a Hegelian.

Under Morris's tutelage, Dewey became a Hegelian, too, and, says Westbrook, he "never completely shook Hegel out of his system." Dewey did not deny it. Hegel's organicism—his synthesis of spirit and matter, subject and object, human and divine—"operated," he later wrote, as "an immense release, a liberation" from "the sense of divisions and separations that were, I suppose, borne in upon me as a consequence of a heritage of New England culture, divisions by way of isolation of self from the world, of soul from body, of nature from God"; and it left, he said, "a permanent deposit in my thinking."[5]

Hegel glued his system together, of course, with an Absolute—a transcendental Mind whose Idea the ongoing evolution of human history is supposedly working to make manifest—and Dewey began his career as an absolute idealist. He took his degree in 1884, and then (following a shake-up in the Hopkins department) accompanied Morris to the University of Michigan, where, apart from a year spent at the University of Minnesota, he worked for the next ten years.

The sort of idealism Dewey espoused put him in the mainstream of late-nineteenth-century academic philosophy. His effort, in his early work, to integrate the Hegelian system with Darwinian evolutionary theory and other developments in science on the one hand and Christian belief on the other was very much the sort of thing an ambitious young philosophy professor was expected to be doing. Dewey's use of the findings of recent psychological research to support the notion of an Absolute, culminating in his *Psychology* (1887), brought him professional renown; and when, in 1894, the president of the recently established University of Chicago, William Rainey Harper, went searching for a distinguished scholar to head the philosophy department, Dewey's was the name that came up.

It was at Chicago that Dewey transformed himself into a public intellectual. He had married, while at Michigan, Alice Chipman, a woman with an intense interest in social reform, and he began to write (though circumspectly: it was not unheard of in the 1890s for professors to be fired for expressing opinions offensive to trustees) about political and economic issues, such as the Pullman strike of 1894. He involved himself in local social welfare efforts, notably Hull House, with whose founder, Jane Addams, the Deweys became close friends. And he started his school.

Dewey's interest in education had begun while he was at Michigan, where it was one of his duties to visit the public high schools to determine whether their graduates were qualified to enter the state university. He now began to formulate a philosophy of education, spelled out in a series of essays and in a best-selling and much-translated book, *The School and Society* (1899); and in 1896, he opened the Laboratory School, an experimental educational facility run by the department of pedagogy, of which Dewey was chairman, and dedicated to the principle of learning by "directed living."

As his name for it implied, Dewey regarded the school as a testing ground for his philosophical ideas: it gave him the chance, he later explained, "to work out in the concrete, instead of merely in the head or on paper, a theory of the unity of knowledge."[6] The Platonic-sounding phrase "unity of knowledge" is a good example of Dewey's notorious imprecision. He did not mean that everything we know is one; he meant that knowing is inseparably united with doing. For knowledge, Dewey believed, is in the first place a by-product of activity: people do things in the world, and the doing results in learning something that, if deemed useful, gets carried along into the next activity. In the traditional method of education, in which the things considered worth knowing are handed down as disembodied information from teacher to pupil, knowledge is cut off from the activity in which it has its meaning, and it thus becomes a false abstraction. One of the consequences (besides boredom) is that an invidious distinction between knowing and doing—a distinction Dewey thought socially pernicious as well as philosophically erroneous—gets reinforced.

At the Dewey School, therefore, children were involved in workshop-style projects—on primitive life, say, or colonial history—in which learning was accomplished in a manner that simulated the way Dewey thought it was accomplished in real life: through group activity. Since the project is being carried out in the present, and since it is supposed to proceed in accordance with the natural interests of the children, what is learned is precisely what is useful: relevance is built in, so to speak, to the system.

The most common charges against the Dewey approach (Dewey was not, it ought to be said, the first American educator to adopt a progressive system, only the best known) are that it makes the child the classroom authority instead of the teacher, that it emphasizes skills instead of information, and that it means that what doesn't interest the child doesn't get taught. "A pupil's 'genuine concern' to learn Latin was for Dewey sufficient proof of its value," complained Richard Hofstadter in 1963. "If for 'Latin' one substitutes 'driver education' or 'beauty culture,' considering each as justified if it makes 'an immediate appeal,' one senses the game that later educators played with Dewey's principles."[7]

Westbrook makes a strong case for regarding these criticisms as a misrepresentation of Dewey's actual doctrine. "It is difficult to read through descriptions and accounts of the Laboratory School," he says, "and understand how Dewey came to be seen by critics as a proponent of 'aimless' progressive education. . . . He valued mankind's accumulated knowledge as much as the most hidebound traditionalist." Dewey *was* concerned about transmitting the cultural heritage, Westbrook maintains; he just didn't see how, if the goal was the eventual application of that heritage to the pupils' own lives, simply handing over abstracted bits of information was supposed to do this. "The facts and truths that enter into the child's present experience," he wrote, "and those contained in the subject-matter of studies, are the initial and final terms of one reality."[8]

Westbrook thinks that Dewey's respect for content was deep enough to have satisfied even E. D. Hirsch, whose best-selling criticism of American education, *Cultural Literacy* (1987), is largely an attack on Deweyism. Hirsch's program for reform, with its prescriptive list of the information schoolchildren ought to have, is "consistent," Westbrook suggests, "with Dewey's own vision of American democracy," and he calls Hirsch's book "a friendly companion" to the work that is the summa of Dewey's educational philosophy, *Democracy and Education* (1916).

This may be bending over backward a little too far. Hirsch certainly believes with Dewey that the purpose of education is to prepare children to become active participants in a democratic culture. Hirsch is not (despite the rather pronounced monoculturalism, as it were, of his famous list) an educational elitist—on the contrary. But at the center of Dewey's method is the idea that the child's natural movement of mind in ordinary activity mimics the operation of mature intelligence. "The native and unspoiled attitude of childhood, marked by ardent curiosity, fertile imagination, and love of experimental inquiry, is near, very near, to the attitude of the scientific mind," he wrote in *How We Think* (1910).[9] This is what Hofstadter complained about as the pre-Darwinian romanticism embedded in the progressive philosophy; and it is not an attitude found in Hirsch.

Dewey eventually came to feel that his proposals had been taken to extremes. In his last major work on education, *Experience and Education* (1938), he scolded progressive educators for becoming hostage to their own abstract principles (some of which, of course, had once been Dewey's abstract principles), and for making a fetish of the child and its freedom. The school at Chicago, though, was an immense success. It opened in 1896 with sixteen students and two teachers; by 1903, it had 140 students and a staff of twenty-three. It helped persuade many people of the need for educational reform, and it was widely referred to as "the Dewey School."

Then, in 1904, Dewey quit. He had had a run-in with Harper about the role in the school of his wife, who served as the director; he seems to have had some longstanding financial grievances, as well. His resignation brought an end to the school. Dewey let it be known to a friend at Columbia that he was unemployed, and Columbia, then in its great period of expansion under Seth Low and Nicholas Murray Butler, snapped him up.

2

At Chicago, Dewey had shed two elements of his thinking. One was his Christianity (displaced, as Westbrook is probably right to suggest, onto his philosophy of education: "The teacher," he wrote in 1897, "always is the prophet of the true God and the usherer in of the true kingdom of God").[10] The other was his absolutism, and his efforts to produce a philosophy that would preserve the Hegelian (and Darwinian) emphasis on organicism and change, but dispense with the metaphysics, culminated in a volume, written in collaboration with some of his colleagues, called *Studies in Logical Theory* (1903).

The book was rescued from likely obscurity by William James, who praised it as an example of the kind of thinking he had begun to call "pragmatism." Dewey welcomed the association enthusiastically: he had dedicated the book to James, in fact, and he regarded James's *Principles of Psychology* (1890) as his greatest inspiration. And the rest of Dewey's career can be divided into two parts: from his arrival at Columbia until America's entry into the war in 1917, he defended pragmatism against the arguments of other philosophers;[11] from the war until the end of his life, he addressed the issues of his time in a pragmatist spirit.

Put most simply, pragmatism is what follows from the view that there is nothing external to experience—no World of Forms, City of God, independent cogito, a priori category, transcendental Mind, or far-off divine event to which the whole creation moves, but only the mundane business of making our way as best we can in a universe shot through with contingency. "All 'homes' are in finite experience," said James; "finite experience as such is homeless. Nothing outside the flux secures the issue of it."[12]

Distinctions are valid, therefore, only when they make a practical difference, since there is no other authority for them to appeal to. Separate a distinction from its use, or change the context in which it is made, and it becomes an idle abstraction. This was exactly the line Dewey had taken in his educational writings on the distinction between "knowing" and "doing," and he now began to see everywhere the tendency to talk about provisionally useful distinctions—subject and object, stimulus and response, means and end, individual and society, culture and nature—as though they were real and independent entities. The abstraction Dewey attacked most consistently in his academic writing was "mind"; in his public writing, it was "individual."

Philosophers, Dewey thought, have mistakenly insisted on making a problem of the relation between the mind and the world, an obsession that has given rise to what he called "the alleged discipline of epistemology"[13]—the attempt to answer the question, "How do we know?" The pragmatist responds to this question by pointing out that nobody has ever made a problem about the relation between, for example, the *hand* and the world. The function of the hand is to help the organism cope with its environment; in situations in which a hand doesn't work, we simply try something else, such as a foot, or a fishhook, or an editorial. Nobody worries, in these situations, about a lack of some preordained "fit"—about whether the physical world was or was not made to be manipulated by hands. They just use a hand where a hand will do.

But philosophers do worry about whether the world is such that it can be known by the mind, and they have produced all sorts of accounts of how the "fit" is supposed to work—how the mental reflects the real. Dewey's point was that "mind" and "reality" name nonexistent entities: they are abstractions from a single, indivisible process. It therefore makes as little sense to talk about a "split" that needs to be overcome between the mind and the world as it does to talk about a "split" between the hand and the environment. "Things," he wrote in 1905, " . . . are what they are experienced as."[14] Knowledge is not a copy of something that exists independently of its being known, he explained a few years later: *it is an instrument or organ of successful action.*"[15]

Dewey regarded the tendency to ascribe an independent objective existence to the mind as a reflection of class bias. The Greek philosophers belonged to a leisure class, and this made it natural for them to exalt reflection and speculation at the expense of making and doing—to talk about "reasoning" as something that goes on unaffected by the circumstances of the being who reasons. Philosophy since the Greeks, Dewey thought, amounted to a history of efforts to establish, in the interests of similar class preferences, the superiority of one element over the other in a series of false dichotomies: stability over change, certainty over contingency, the fine arts over the useful arts, what minds do over what hands do.

The penalty was anachronism. While philosophy pondered its artificial puzzles, science, taking a purely instrumental and experimental approach, had transformed the world. It was time for philosophy to catch up. "Philosophy recovers itself when it ceases to be a device for dealing with the problems of philosophers," Dewey announced in 1917, "and becomes a method, cultivated by philosophers, for dealing with the problems of men."[16] He repeated the argument many times, most fully in *Reconstruction in Philosophy* (1920) and *The Quest for Certainty* (1929).

How well did Dewey deal with "the problems of men"? Westbrook thinks the crucial episode is Dewey's support of American intervention in the First World War. "I have been a thorough and complete sympathizer with the part played by this country in this war and I have wished to see the resources of this country used for its successful prosecution,"[17] Dewey declared in 1917. He dismissed reservations about the use of force as squeamishness, and he argued that the means were justified by the likely outcome, which was the chance for the United States to take a formative role in the establishment of democracy in Europe.

In other words, Dewey echoed the official position of the American government, and this put him at odds with one of his admirers, the critical prodigy Randolph Bourne. Bourne had been Dewey's student at Columbia and a champion of Deweyan pragmatism—a philosophy which, he wrote in 1915, "has an edge on it that would slash up the habits of thought, the customs and institutions in which our society has been living for centuries."[18] Bourne felt betrayed by Dewey's support for Wilson's policy, though, and in 1917, in an essay called "Twilight of Idols," he attacked pragmatism for being "against concern for the quality of life as above machinery of life."

Bourne's criticism of pragmatism has been repeated many times: it is that, however admirable a pragmatist's own instincts may be, the philosophy itself provides no stable criteria by which values can be judged. Dewey "always meant his philosophy . . . to start with values," Bourne argued. "But there was always that unhappy ambiguity in his doctrine as to just how values were created, and it became easier and easier to assume that just any growth was justified and almost any activity valuable so long as it achieved ends." Thus excitement among the Deweyites about the machinery of war had obscured the simple fact that "war always undermines values."[19]

Westbrook calls Bourne's quarrel with Dewey "very much a family affair." It was, he thinks, not Bourne who had parted company with pragmatism, but Dewey, who had been seduced by Wilsonian rhetoric, and had fallen "prey to the very mistakes his philosophy was designed to prevent." The disastrous treaty of Versailles, in which, despite the American presence, the world was simply carved up to suit the victorious imperial powers, brought him to his senses; and although Dewey never again referred to Bourne (who died during the flu epidemic of 1918, at the age of thirty-two), Westbrook thinks his subsequent treatment of political issues "amounted essentially to a reconsideration of positions he had taken during the war along lines suggested by Bourne's criticisms."

The effort to present Bourne as a true pragmatist is not very persuasive: Bourne's characterization of Dewey's philosophy as an instrument for "slash[ing] up" established customs and institutions belongs to a cultural politics much more radical than anything in Dewey. But Bourne is, in a sense, the hero of Westbrook's book, the voice of conscience that rescued Dewey from the technocratic implications of his philosophy, and from the sort of liberal messianism that destroyed Wilson. And it is after 1919 that Westbrook's "radical" Dewey really emerges.

A summary of Dewey's political positions gives an idea of the extent to which he departed from what is thought of as the standard liberal line. He supported the Progressive Robert La Follette for president in 1924, and the socialist Norman Thomas in 1928 (though he voted for Al Smith on practical grounds). His great cause in the 1920s was the quixotic Outlawry of War movement. He tried, without success, to organize a third political party in 1930. He regarded the New Deal as an unworthy effort to patch up an economic system he thought inherently unjust; and in 1932, 1936, and 1940, he voted for Thomas against Roosevelt. Until the attack on Pearl Harbor, he argued against American intervention in the Second World War—six months before the Nazi invasion of Poland, he was still insisting that "no matter what happens," the United States should "stay out."[20] And he quarreled with two of the leading liberal "realists" of the time: Walter Lippmann, who in *Public Opinion* (1922) and *The Phantom Public* (1925) had questioned the ability of people in a mass society to make informed political decisions (Dewey replied in **The Public and Its Problems** [1927]), and Reinhold Niebuhr, who attacked pragmatism in *Moral Man and Immoral Society* (1932) for taking too sanguine a view of human nature, and for discounting the role played by self-interest in human affairs.

But Dewey's radicalism was unusual, as Westbrook points out, because of its indifference to Marx. Despite the urgings of his disciple Sidney Hook, Dewey read little of Marx's work, and he dismissed the scientific pretensions of the Marxian theory of history out of hand. His anticommunism led, during the era of the Popular Front,

to a split with *The New Republic,* to which he had been a regular contributor. He also resigned from Local 5 of the New York Teachers Union, of which he was a charter member and former vice-president, and from the ACLU, on whose national committee he had served for many years: both organizations, he felt, had been infiltrated by Communists whose methods were undemocratic.

Dewey's most renowned encounter with communism, though, was his leadership of the inquiry into the charges against Leon Trotsky in 1937. The committee Dewey headed, which traveled to Mexico to conduct its investigation (Dewey was seventy-eight), cleared Trotsky of Stalin's accusations; but although Trotsky and Dewey made a celebrated show of mutual respect during the hearings, Dewey emerged from them even more opposed to Marxism than he had been. Trotsky's answers to his questions convinced him that even the most dialectically supple Communist was, at bottom, the prisoner of his own iron law of historical progress. Trotsky, he later remarked, "was tragic. To see such brilliant native intelligence locked up in absolutes."[21]

After the war, Dewey supported the anti-Communist policies of the Truman administration, and this seems to Westbrook to represent another betrayal of pragmatist principles. Like Sidney Hook (with whom he had by then become closely allied), Dewey "played a role," Westbrook says, "in the escalation of rhetoric which prepared the ground emotionally, if not logically, for the reactionary attack against radicalism by Senator Joseph McCarthy and others."

This is one of the few places in his book where Westbrook fails to provide sufficient evidence for an assertion, and the charge seems unfair. Dewey did not subordinate means to ends in the anti-Communist cause: he expressly condemned, for instance, efforts to root Communists out of the public schools and the teaching profession generally. And it is hard to see why an unambivalent opposition to totalitarianism is unpragmatic. The totalitarian is the pragmatist's natural enemy.

What sort of liberal was Dewey, then? He was a liberal who believed that the liberalism of his own day was founded on an error. The liberalism that emerged in the eighteenth century, he argued, was based on the idea of natural rights and the theory of the social contract—the notion that society is an aggregation of autonomous individuals, who are endowed with guarantees of personal liberty against the claims of the group as a whole. These beliefs helped liberate the individual from an oppressive political order; but in the nineteenth century, Dewey thought, liberals like Jeremy Bentham and John Stuart Mill failed to see that this atomistic conception of society—which, through Adam Smith, had become the basis for liberal economic as well as political theory—was interfering with their efforts at social reform. And this division within liberalism, between the desire to protect the freedom of the individual and the desire to compel individuals to act in the best interests of the group, persisted, he felt, into the twentieth century.

The problem, Dewey believed, was the abstraction "individual." Just as it makes no sense to talk about knowing apart from doing, or about the mental apart from the real, it is a mistake to think of the individual as something separable from society. This is not a view Dewey arrived at in the 1930s: it is one of his earliest positions, and predates his association with pragmatism. "The non-social individual is an abstraction arrived at by imagining what man would be if all his human qualities were taken away," he wrote in **"The Ethics of Democracy"** in 1888. "Society, as a real whole, is the normal order, and the mass as an aggregate of isolated units is the fiction. If this be the case, and if democracy be a form of society, it not only does have, but must have, a common will; for it is this unity of will which makes it an organism."[22]

Dewey did believe in individuality; he just thought that genuine individuality is achieved *through* the collective will rather than in opposition to it. He regarded it as the purpose of societies, in fact, to provide the means by which people can achieve "the fullest and freest realization of [their] powers"[23]:

> When an individual has found that place in society for which he is best fitted and is exercising the function proper to that place, he has obtained his completest development, but it is also true (and this is the truth omitted by aristocracy, emphasized by democracy) that he must find this place and assume this work in the main for himself.[24]

Thus, as Westbrook argues, the centrality of the idea of democracy in Dewey's thought: it is by intelligent participation in what Dewey called "associated living" that self-realization—in his view, the only true end of life—is achieved.

This is why, therefore, the school must be, in Dewey's own phrase, "a miniature community"[25] ("The only way to prepare for social life is to engage in social life,"[26] he wrote in 1897); and it is why industrial capitalism is deficient, since it denies the worker full participation in the task at hand. It is why so-called "democratic realists" like Lippmann, who argued for the superior efficiency of a top-down system of governing, and Niebuhr, who stressed the limitations of the popular will, seemed to Dewey to be calling for less democracy in a society in which too little democracy was precisely what ailed it. And it is why, despite his admiration for socialist economies, Dewey denounced all forms of state socialism, and particularly the Marxist form. It was not, in his view, a question of reaching the same goal by other means; for apart from democratic means, there was no independent "goal" to be reached.

It is this all-embracing conception of democracy, Westbrook argues, that distinguishes Dewey from the liberals of his own time (who took, he thinks, a more elitist or "statist" view) and makes him our contemporary. Dewey's ideals "echo . . . resoundingly," he says, "in the 'Port Huron Statement,'" the manifesto drafted by Tom Hayden (a reader of *The Public and Its Problems*) and ratified by the Students for a Democratic Society in

1962. And they are compatible, he believes, with much of the academic political theory that has been produced since the 1960s.

3

Westbrook's sense that the time has arrived for a reconsideration of Dewey is one that has recently begun to be shared by many people. The writer who has done the most to keep Dewey's name alive during the last ten years is the philosopher Richard Rorty, who has argued that the side of Dewey that tried to use philosophy to answer questions like "What are the proper ends of life?" is better left ignored. What really matters to us, Rorty thinks, is Dewey's pragmatism—his debunking of the truth-claims of other philosophical systems, and his insistence on the provisional and practical nature of our beliefs, the way we use ideas not to "know" the world, but to help us get what we want from it.

Westbrook, of course, dissents sharply from this estimation of Dewey's significance, since it is precisely the normative features of Dewey's political philosophy—the importance it attaches to self-realization through collective activity—that he wants to rescue. He's right to insist that the side of Dewey Rorty is eager to dispense with is essential to Deweyism as Dewey, at least, conceived it; and it's worth contemplating some of the implications of this aspect of Dewey's thought before we all begin calling ourselves Deweyites again.

It is misleading, to begin with, to associate Dewey with the radicalism of the 1960s. Whatever the intentions of the Port Huron Statement, New Left "participatory democracy" proved (as Westbrook himself concedes) a wildly atomistic and existentialist affair, an umbrella for radical viewpoints of every stripe—including (and this is where it departed most dramatically from Dewey) undemocratic ones.

Uncoordinated ideological and cultural laissez-faire is, in fact, exactly what Dewey opposed. He complained, in 1915, about the danger of fragmentation implicit in the philosophy of "cultural pluralism" (then being promoted by his admirer Horace Kallen), and insisted on the overriding importance of "general social unity"; and he argued, in *Liberalism and Social Action* (1935), that force is justified in compelling recalcitrant minorities to accept majority choices; he believed that the state was the representative of "the public," in whose interest it could intervene in the affairs of smaller groups. Dewey was interested in greater social control (so long as it was democratically established and genuinely egalitarian); most of the radicals of the 1960s were interested in less.

For if we follow Westbrook's Dewey far enough, we eventually find ourselves in what Isaiah Berlin once called "the Temple of Sarastro"—the domain of the most benign and considerate of despots, someone who knows what is best for us, and who only wants to help us achieve it by disabusing us of the bad ideas we mistakenly think we benefit from having. The hallmark of Sarastroism is the refusal to countenance the separation of realms—public from private, thought from action, work from leisure—since the image of the good life must be reflected fully in every facet of experience. Everything becomes a "site" for whatever process the philosopher thinks leads to the proper ends of life.

Hence there is a kind of blurring in Dewey's thought of the aesthetic experience, the religious experience, the educational experience, the work experience, and the political experience: they all tend to turn into versions of the same thing, which is the activity through which the human organism realizes itself. The requirement that these experiences be accessible to everyone, and that they be conceived of collectively, is what Dewey meant by "democracy."

It may seem ungracious to decline the invitation to join a world in which every activity leads to the same process of fulfillment; yet there are reasons to prefer the incommensurabilities of the world we actually live in. Liberalism's greatest achievement, it seems to me, is its separation of a private realm from public life. It's perfectly true that the separation is pure only in theory—that even in liberal societies, the state gets into the bedroom, and so forth. But Dewey's political philosophy is only a theory, too, and one that moves—particularly as Westbrook conceives it—in the opposite direction.

"Democracy" is the name for a kind of politics. As a method for running affairs in the public realm (which, I think Dewey was right to argue, ought to include the economic life), it is the best we have come up with. But as a requisite feature of education, or religious observance, or any other department of life which does not directly involve the interests of the public at large—which deals, so to speak, with selected or "volunteer" publics—"democracy" means politicization, a continuous arbitration among competing interests. One of the things liberty means is the opportunity *not* to submit to political processes—the opportunity to opt out of the system of values that obtains, quite properly, in public life. Sometimes "self-realization" (an exceedingly flexible concept anyway, it seems to me) is achieved by disagreement. Dewey didn't disparage disagreement: disagreement is part of the process, the event that starts up the engines of social change. But the process is what matters.

It is not hard to see why Westbrook feels encouraged to align this emphasis in Dewey's thought with recent academic theorizing about the priority of the community to the individual—theorizing that turns up in a rather debased form in the thinking called "political correctness." "We know the attitudes and behaviors that will make people feel most fulfilled in their association with others," this way of thinking runs, "and we will therefore compel people to adopt those attitudes and behaviors in their own best interests."

In the larger world, this is the sentiment behind the current impatience—evident, for example, in some of the feminist efforts to censor pornography—with the reluctance of liberals to regulate kinds of behavior and expression they disapprove of. "Culturally," Westbrook says, by way of explaining why a reconsideration of the Deweyan mode of liberalism is so important,

> liberals have left it to conservatives to worry over the absence of a common culture grounded in a widely shared understanding of the good life and adopted a studied neutrality in ethics and art which favors a segmented market of competing "life styles" in which the good life is reduced, both morally and aesthetically, to a set of more or less arbitrary preferences among bundles of signifying commodities.

Those who feel that concern for the common culture is better expressed by tolerating other people's choices than by regulating them will have reservations about the kind of liberalism Westbrook is urging. They may also feel that at this point the argument has moved beyond Dewey.

At a moment when the existence of a public realm—a place in which people participate in common activities, uninsulated by money or privilege—seems dangerously threatened by an official insistence that everything be "privatized," Dewey's vision of the democratic commonweal is deeply appealing. In particular (and regardless of the merits of his theory of pedagogy), his argument that the public school experience should be understood as the foundation of democratic life deserves to be renewed and loudly repeated.

Still, there has to be a way out of the temple, too. "Society," after all, is as much an abstraction as "the individual"—something that becomes strikingly apparent the moment one tries to define it. If "society" does not mean the whole of the species (an entity whose interests are impossible to calculate, and which is irrelevant to most of the practical decisions we have to make), what determines the boundaries of the organism we are to consider ourselves indivisibly connected to? Is it nationality? Ethnicity? The local community? A common culture or religious faith? Each of these categories can seem arbitrary and oppressive to some of the people who find themselves inside the groups they define, and exclusionary and discriminatory to the people left outside. It's also true, of course, that they can all command allegiance to some degree: people are often willing to subordinate their interests as individuals to the interests of the larger entity in which they feel they have their identities—as Americans, or black people, or New Yorkers, or Jews. But surely one of the lessons of this century is that such allegiances are desirable when they are limited allegiances, or checked by competing allegiances, and profoundly undesirable whenever they assert themselves as absolute.

Dewey understood very well the danger inherent in the kinds of appeals that can be made in the name of the group. In 1939, at the end of a decade in which antidemocratic and antipluralist ideologies had shown themselves capable of enormous power, he announced, in an essay written for a collection called *I Believe,* that "I should now wish to emphasize more than I formerly did that individuals are the finally decisive factors of the nature and movement of associated life. . . . I am led to emphasize the idea that only the voluntary initiative and voluntary cooperation of individuals can produce social institutions that will protect the liberties necessary for achieving development of genuine individuality."[27] The statement expresses, I think, the essence of the pragmatism Rorty admires in Dewey's thought: when contexts change, or when results fail to match expectations, beliefs need to be reformulated. Westbrook doesn't cite this essay of Dewey's, but it makes an appropriate coda to his study.

As Rorty complains, Dewey did undertake, in books like **Human Nature and Conduct** (1922) and **Experience and Nature** (1925), to write philosophy for a post-Darwinian age—to draw a conceptual map for experience in a world that seemed to many of his literary and philosophical contemporaries to be (in Max Weber's famous phrase) incurably disenchanted. Perhaps, as Rorty argues, this was an unpragmatic mistake on Dewey's part. But those books hold a certain kind—perhaps it is only a literary kind—of fascination.

For unlike almost every other writer of his time, Dewey did not regard modern life as a deprivation, a sort of cultural wound which the absence of traditional kinds of religious and civic faith made it impossible to heal. He was perfectly, almost serenely, at home in a world without certainty—much more so than his hero William James, who always seems to be fighting his way toward an accommodation with own principles. Dewey saw that life in that world was morally deep and suffused with meaning; and in his books, as in almost no other writing of the time, we can watch the twentieth century come to recognizable life on its own terms, without being defined by comparison to ways of life it is supposed to have supplanted. Stylistically, I suppose, Dewey was one of the least novelistic of writers; but he had a novelist's grasp of experience. Whatever else it may have been, his philosophy was a consolation.

NOTES

[1] *The American Mind: An Interpretation of American Thought and Character Since the 1880s* (Yale University Press, 1950), p. 100.

[2] The reputation for turgidity, which has become the one thing everyone knows about Dewey, is exaggerated. All of Dewey's writing is now available in an extraordinary new edition, which includes excellent introductions and many collateral items, among them some of the notable reviews of Dewey's books by other philosophers. Almost any of the volumes provides a fascinating, well-documented look at the variety of Dewey's work. *John Dewey: The Early Works, 1882-1898*, Vols. 1-5; *John Dewey: The Middle Works, 1899-1924*, Vols. 1-15; and *John Dewey: The Later Works, 1925-1953*, Vols. 1-17, edited by Jo Ann Boydston (Southern Illinois University Press, 1969-1991), index also available.

[3] In Paul Arthur Schilpp, editor, *The Philosophy of John Dewey* (Northwestern University Press, 1939), pp. 3-45.

[4] Quoted in Mary V. Dearborn, *Love in the Promised Land: The Story of Anzia Yezierska and John Dewey* (Free Press, 1988), p. 8.

[5] "From Absolutism to Experimentalism" (1930), *Later Works*, Vol. 5, pp. 153-154.

[6] "The Theory of the Chicago Experiment" (1936), *Later Works*, Vol. 11, p. 204.

[7] *Anti-intellectualism in American Life* (Knopf, 1963), p. 377.

[8] *The Child and the Curriculum* (1902), *Middle Works*, Vol. 2, p. 278.

[9] *Middle Works*, Vol. 6, p. 179.

[10] "My Pedagogic Creed" (1897), *Early Works*, Vol. 5, p. 95.

[11] Many of these debates were conducted in the pages of the *Journal of Philosophy*; these have been helpfully collected by Sidney Morgenbesser and reprinted as *Dewey and His Critics* (The Journal of Philosophy, 1977).

[12] *Pragmatism: A New Name for Some Old Ways of Thinking* (1907), *The Works of William James* (Harvard University Press, 1975), p. 125.

[13] "Brief Studies in Realism" (1922), *Middle Works*, Vol. 6, p. 111.

[14] "The Postulate of Immediate Empiricism" (1905), *Middle Works*, Vol. 3.

[15] "The Bearings of Pragmatism Upon Education" (1908-1909), *Middle Works*, Vol. 4, p. 180 (Dewey's italics).

[16] "The Need for a Recovery of Philosophy," *Middle Works*, Vol. 10, p. 46.

[17] "Democracy and Loyalty in the Schools," *Middle Works*, Vol. 10, p. 158.

[18] "John Dewey's Philosophy" (1915), in Randolph Bourne, *The Radical Will: Selected Writings 1911-1918*, edited by Olaf Hansen (Urizen, 1977), p. 332.

[19] *The Radical Will*, pp. 342, 344.

[20] "No Matter What Happens—Stay Out!" (1939), *Later Works*, Vol. 14, p. 364.

[21] Quoted in James T. Farrell, "Dewey in Mexico," in *John Dewey: Philosopher of Science and Freedom*, edited by Sidney Hook (Dial, 1950), p. 374.

[22] *Early Works,* Vol. 1, p. 232.

[23] *Ethics* (1908), *Middle Works,* Vol. 5, p. 273.

[24] "The Ethics of Democracy," *Early Works,* Vol. 1, p. 243.

[25] *The School and Society* (1899), *Middle Works,* Vol. 1, p. 12.

[26] "Ethical Principles Underlying Education," *Early Works,* Vol. 5, p. 62.

[27] "I Believe," *Later Works,* Vol. 14, pp. 91-92.

Bob Pepperman Taylor (essay date 1992)

SOURCE: "John Dewey in Vermont: A Reconsideration," in *Soundings,* Vol. LXXV, No. 1, Spring, 1992, pp. 175-98.

[*In the following essay, Taylor discusses the contradictory nature of Dewey's attitude toward his birth-state Vermont.*]

John Dewey was always somewhat ambivalent about his Vermont background. At times he praised the "democratic" character of his Vermont heritage and even drew close parallels between the development of his own ideas and the ideas of his teachers at the University of Vermont. At other times, perhaps more frequently, he distanced himself as much as he could from these political and intellectual roots.

For example, in 1929 Dewey delivered an address at the University of Vermont commemorating the one-hundredth anniversary of the publication of James Marsh's "Introduction" to Samuel Taylor Coleridge's *Aids To Reflection*—a book of profound significance to the whole university community in the nineteenth century and one that Dewey, as a member of the class of 1879, had read as an undergraduate.[1] Toward the end of this talk, Dewey reflected on his own Vermont background and education at the university in a now oft-quoted passage:

> If I may be allowed a personal word, I would say that I shall never cease to be grateful that I was born at a time and a place where the earlier ideal of liberty and the self-governing community of citizens still sufficiently prevailed, so that I unconsciously imbibed a sense of its meaning. In Vermont, perhaps more than elsewhere, there was embodied into the spirit of the people the conviction that governments were like the houses we live in, made to contribute to human welfare, and that those who lived in them were as free to change and extend the one as they were the other, when developing needs of the human family called for such alterations and modifications. So deeply bred in Vermonters was this conviction that I still think that one is more loyally patriotic to the ideal of America when one maintains this view than when one conceives of patriotism as rigid attachment to a form of the state alleged to be fixed forever, and recognizes the claims of a common human society as superior to those of any particular political form.[2]

Here Dewey pays tribute to what he understands to be the best of his Vermont inheritance and suggests that the independence, flexibility, and common sense contained in this heritage had greatly influenced the development of his mature political thinking—and continued to do so even fifty years after his graduation.

It is evident from other writings, however, that Dewey was not entirely uncritical of his background. In his only published autobiographical statement, an essay entitled **"From Absolutism To Experimentalism,"** Dewey maintains a superficially respectful attitude toward his college experience. He refers to the importance for him of his "senior year course," taught by President Matthew Buckham, and of a number of books that he read, especially Thomas Huxley's textbook in physiology.[3] He also has kind words for his teacher of philosophy, H. A. P. Torrey: "I owe him a double debt, that of turning my thoughts definitely to the study of philosophy as a life-pursuit, and of a generous gift of time to me during a year devoted privately under his direction to a reading of classics in the history of philosophy and learning to read philosophic German."[4] Nonetheless, despite these comments, there is a strong ambivalence in these reflections. Although Torrey was a fine teacher, Dewey comments that "in a more congenial atmosphere than that of northern New England in those days, [he] would have achieved something significant."[5] The implication is clearly that there was much in this "northern New England" environment that was uncongenial, presumably because it in some way prevented complete intellectual freedom and self-expression.

In fact, Dewey explained that his attraction to Hegel in graduate school and during the early part of his professional career served an almost therapeutic function for him, necessitated by his "uncongenial" Vermont background:

> It [Hegelianism] supplied a demand for unification that was doubtless an intense emotional craving, and yet was a hunger that only an intellectualized subject-matter could satisfy. It is more than difficult, it is impossible to recover that early mood. But the sense of divisions and separations that were, I suppose, borne in upon me as a consequence of a heritage of New England culture, divisions by way of isolation of self from the world, of soul from body, of nature from God, brought a painful oppression—or, rather, they were an inward laceration. . . . Hegel's synthesis of subject and object, matter and spirit, the divine and the human, was, however, no mere intellectual formula; it operated as an immense release, a liberation.[6]

As the very title of his essay suggests, Dewey viewed his own development as a thinker as a movement away from the "absolutism" of his youth. His later instrumentalism represented a break from the philosophical and religious dogmatism of his childhood environment.

Elsewhere Dewey has similarly critical things to say about organized religion, which had played a central role in the communities to which he belonged in Vermont. In

The Quest for Certainty he argues that the exclusivity of religious communities is one of the most divisive of human practices. "Men will never love their enemies until they cease to have enmities. The antagonism between the actual and the ideal, the spiritual and the natural is the source of the deepest and most injurious of all enmities."[7] In *A Common Faith*, Dewey writes in a similar vein: "The opposition between religious values as I conceive them and religions is not to be bridged. Just because the release of these values is so important, their identification with the creeds and cults of religions must be dissolved."[8] Dewey, by 1934, had come a long way from his early Congregationalist piety. He could now view organized religions as no more than cults subscribing to unjustifiable dogmas.

Dewey's biography is very much the story of a man who left his hometown far behind him. After he graduated from college in 1879, Dewey spent a brief period teaching school in Oil City, Pennsylvania. He then returned to Vermont to teach school. During this time he resumed private studies with H. A. P. Torrey, and then decided to attend graduate school in philosophy. He left to study at Johns Hopkins University in 1882, and for all intents and purposes this event signifies his permanent break with Vermont. After graduate school, he would hold faculty positions at the Universities of Michigan and Minnesota, and at Chicago, and Columbia. From 1904, when he first went to Columbia, until his death in 1952, Dewey would become a central figure in the intellectual life of New York City. He enjoyed life in the big city. He could not, he once said, understand why so many of his colleagues vacationed in Vermont: "I don't see why you fellows want to go back to summer places in Vermont. I got out of there as soon as I could." Vermont was, he confided to another friend, "that God-forsaken country."[9]

Dewey's discomfort with his Vermont background is nicely illustrated by his appearance at a celebration held for him at the University of Vermont in honor of his ninetieth birthday in 1949. Arriving in Burlington, he was greeted by marching bands and cheerleaders, much as though he were a returning athletic hero. Dewey took a tour of Burlington and met with a few people he had known during his childhood. But like a man who had been away from the city long enough, he boarded the return train to New York well before the dinners and speeches were held in his honor that evening.

. . . . .

John Dewey, then, had mixed feelings about his Vermont background. This is neither unusual nor surprising—many of us have similar feelings and confusions regarding our origins, upbringing and early life. But this ambivalence is paralleled by a lack of clarity about Dewey's Vermont inheritance in the secondary literature. On the one hand, it is common for commentators to make claims about how Dewey's mature thinking reflects values "imbibed" from the democratic political culture of Burlington and Vermont. On the other hand, some Dewey scholars have emphasized the significant distance between the intellectual background of Burlington and Dewey's mature democratic theory (produced, we must note, in the great cities of Chicago and New York).

Jane Dewey, John's daughter and biographer, most clearly claims that Dewey's thought reflects the political culture of nineteenth-century Vermont: "His boyhood surroundings, although not marked by genuine industrial and financial democracy, created in him an unconscious but vital faith in democracy. . . ."Again, " . . . in spite of the especial prestige of the first few families, life was democratic [in Burlington]—not consciously, but in that deeper sense in which equality and absence of class distinctions are taken for granted."[10] Sidney Hook, too, argues that Dewey's egalitarianism can be explained by the democratic Burlington of his childhood: "It was a community in which no great disparities of wealth or standards of living were to be found, and in which a man was judged as the saying went, not by what he had but by what he did."[11] These are but two well-known examples of interpreters explaining Dewey's democratic sensibilities by reference to his Vermont heritage. Dewey is thus frequently thought of as a representative of small town democratic America, giving the ideals of this environment their highest philosophical expression. More critically, but much in the same vein, Dewey is sometimes thought of as bound by his background in a way that never allowed him to break out of his provincialism.[12] Whether critical or admiring, many authors think of Dewey's philosophy as in some (not necessarily very clear) way reflecting his small town New England origins.

In contrast, other scholars have argued that in order to understand the origins and nature of Dewey's political beliefs and social theory we must concentrate on his experiences after he left Vermont.[13] From this perspective there is a great gulf between Dewey's Republican background and his mature democratic socialism, his Congregationalist background and his mature view of religion, the presumed Protestant dogmatism of his teachers at Vermont and the pragmatism of his mature instrumentalism. For Lewis Feuer, "Dewey resented his Puritan upbringing because of the repressions it imposed."[14] Dewey's mature ideas have to be understood as expressions of his rebellion against and rejection of Vermont.

We find, then, in the secondary Dewey literature both a tendency to make connections, however vague and weak, between the tone and sensibilities of Dewey's philosophy and his Vermont background, and an emphasis upon the substantive distance between Dewey's professional work and the intellectual environment of Burlington and UVM.

Both of these tendencies, whether in Dewey's self-understanding or in the commentaries and autobiographies, are quite misleading. The view that Dewey's work reflects small-town New England culture points in a useful direction, but it does so in a most misleading way. As we will see below, Dewey has much more in common with his teachers and peers in Burlington than is revealed by vague comments about his Vermont sensibilities—comments that are frequently based upon an inaccurate understanding of the social realities in Burlington in the last half of the nineteenth century. On the other hand, the view of Dewey as a rebel against his Vermont origins is in many ways more satisfying—the intellectual distance between Dewey and his Vermont background is generally more carefully drawn than the contrary claims. But, this literature has paid insufficient attention to the ideas of those who influenced Dewey in his youth. When we look more carefully at these ideas, we find that Dewey had much more in common with the folks back home than even he understood or appreciated.

Consider first those who understand Dewey's intellectual development as an extension of his Vermont inheritance.[15] The implication of this literature is that the Burlington of Dewey's childhood was a sleepy, homogeneous New England town with little or no class conflict or political strife found in larger urban settings. Although it is true that Dewey's ideas and values owed much to his experiences in Burlington and his education at the university, it is simply untenable to contend that he was deeply impressed by a small New England town and its "town meeting" political culture. Burlington was much more of a city during Dewey's childhood than this stereotype would allow. The growth of the lumber trade had made it the third largest lumber center in the country in 1850.[16] Town meetings were abolished when Burlington was incorporated as a city in 1865, when Dewey was only six years old (although they survive to this day in surrounding towns). Dewey's childhood actually coincided with the dramatic growth in Burlington that prompted municipal incorporation. This was accompanied by sharpening class, ethnic, and political cleavages. In the five years following the end of the Civil War and the establishment of city government, the population of Burlington doubled, causing serious public health problems, overcrowding, and social and political friction between the old Protestant Yankees and the immigrants who were primarily French-Canadian and Irish-Catholic working people. It was the growth of these working-class and Catholic groups that led old Yankee business leaders to fear that they would lose control of town meetings and thus political power. This, along with concerns over public health and public works in the face of population growth, led to the adoption of the city charter in 1865. In short, the sociology of Burlington during Dewey's childhood and adolescence belies the mythology of Dewey as a product of small town America.

The real lesson Dewey seems to have learned from the political culture of Burlington was less about town meeting democracy than about America's catapult into modern urban industrial society. The world of his childhood was a rapidly changing and expanding one, in which the personal, informal, and small-scale institutions of the earlier American experience were quickly becoming inadequate. This was the lesson that Dewey was sensitive to even as a college student, and it was to inform the central message of his lifelong philosophical project.

Consider, on the other hand, the views of those who have emphasized the great distance between Dewey's mature political thinking and activism and the conservative Republicanism of his Vermont heritage. What is most unsatisfying about his reading of Dewey is that it leaves so little room for any substantive influence from his early life. It is true that Dewey did rebel against his Vermont background; when he left for graduate school in 1882, he left pretty much for good. Nonetheless, even in this break with his childhood and youth, there was much more continuity than is conventionally recognized—even by Dewey himself.

John Dewey's academic career at Vermont was respectable, but in no way outstanding. As Max Eastman wrote, "He slid through his first three college years . . . without throwing off any sparks, or giving grounds to predict anything about his future."[17] The story is often told, however, about his reading during his junior year a physiology text by the Darwinian T. H. Huxley that had a deep impact on him. Dewey himself traces his interest in philosophy to this event.[18] He then went on to perform very well in his senior year, especially in a year-long course in social and political morals offered by President Buckham. In his final year of study Dewey improved his rather average academic standing enough to graduate second in a class of eighteen.[19]

There is evidence, however, primarily in the form of library records of his reading habits, that Dewey was interested in philosophical and political affairs quite early in his college career. During his first year, for example, Dewey read Walter Bagehot's *Physics and Politics,* Alexis de Tocqueville's *Democracy in America,* and a more obscure, but for our purposes very interesting, volume by Richard Josiah Hinton, *English Radical Leaders.*[20] Bagehot's book is a discussion of the importance of Darwinism for political thinking and institutions.[21] Tocqueville's monumental work, of course, is one of the most insightful studies of America's democratic political culture. Hinton's book is a series of profiles of liberal and progressive English politicians. As Hinton writes, the book is about "a class of men who seem destined to lead their nation through the peaceful ways of ameliorative reforms, into the larger liberties and ordered equities of a practically democratic future."[22] These three books indicate that Dewey, even in his first year of college, was interested in and sensitive to major intellectual changes (most notably the development of Darwinist scientific and social theory), social change (the growth of the labor movement, the increasing concentration of capital, the woman's movement), and the importance of these developments for democratic politics and society.

This freshman interest was not short-lived. Dewey's sophomore essay was a discussion of municipal reform, a topic of some significance in Burlington, which had incorporated as a city a little more than a decade earlier.[23] His commencement speech, entitled **"Limits Of Political Economy,"** was also obviously of political interest.[24] Throughout his four years of college Dewey read extensively in the most advanced literary, philosophical, and political periodicals of the day, such as *Edinburgh Review, Westminster Review, North American Review, Atlantic,* and *Journal of Speculative Philosophy.* And in addition to his coursework he read Spencer, J. S. Mill, Bain, and Comte among others.[25] In all of this reading, Dewey was confronting the most advanced English-language philosophical and political discussions of the period.

Dewey comments in **"From Absolutism To Experimentalism"** that at this time what interested him the most in Comte's writings was "his idea of the disorganized character of Western modern culture, due to a disintegrative 'individualism,' and his idea of a synthesis of science that should be a regulative method of an organized social life. . . ."[26] In general, Dewey learned from all these readings about the tremendous flux in traditional ideas and social practices, a sense of openness and change for the future, the importance of new developments in science, and the excitement and apprehension accompanying these profound intellectual and social developments. It is clear that from his earliest years in Burlington Dewey became sensitive to change and development in American society and that this sensitivity led him in college to seek out literature which would help him to explain these developments and project their future. The University of Vermont, at the very least, provided Dewey with the environment and resources necessary to pursue this interest.

But there were more direct influences at the university. Dewey was grateful to H. A .P. Torrey both for his educational attention and for his encouragement in pursuing philosophy as a vocation. Torrey was primarily a teacher, and he never wrote very much. Looking back over the written materials he did leave, however, one is at first struck by the great differences in tone and perspective between Torrey's writing and that of Dewey. For example, after Abraham Lincoln was assassinated, Torrey wrote an essay (unpublished) in remembrance of the dead President. The moral certainty and stern piety of this discussion of the Civil War reminds one that Torrey was only the latest in a long line of Puritan thinkers in New England. The war had been, to Torrey, a conflict between the just and righteous Union and the evil and ungodly Confederacy, and God, working through Lincoln, had assured the Union victory. "For if ever the Hand Of Providence is visible in human history, it is visible in the history of this war, and in the career of him whom God chose to guide the nation through it."[27] Two qualities of this document provide a noticeable contrast with Dewey's later political writings. First is its extreme moral certainty. There is no attempt to understand the moral complexity of the Civil War or the possibility of moral guilt on the part of the North as well as the South. Torrey views the conflict in much simpler terms, as a conflict between good and evil. Dewey would never be guilty, in his mature work, of exhibiting such a contempt for moral complexity. Although he would never lose the capacity for moral indignation, he would spend much of his adult life attacking precisely the "quest for certainty" so clearly illustrated in Torrey's essay.[28]

Second, Torrey's understanding of the political world is still informed by Puritan orthodoxy: the basic reason for political organization is original sin. Because of sin, war is and always will be a necessary institution in human life, for "persuasion comes more of suffering than of conscience."[29] In fact, "the strength of government is still in the sword."[30] Dewey would become very critical of the conception of original sin, which he considered to be indicative of philosophical laziness (for assuming that which needs explaining). Referring to Reinhold Niebuhr's insistence on the importance of original sin, Dewey once commented to Sidney Hook, "A man doesn't have to be an S.O.B. S.O.B.'s are made, not born."[31]

Despite these differences with Dewey, in Torrey's most extensive published writings, a three-article series on "The 'Theodicy of Leibniz,'" we find that Dewey has much more in common with his old teacher than the above comments suggest. Torrey criticizes Leibniz for practicing philosophy on a level too highly abstracted from the realities of life as experienced by everyday men and women. Referring, for example, to Leibniz's definition of suffering as metaphysical evil, Torrey sarcastically observes, "The philosopher may define suffering as metaphysical evil, but the victim is not eased by the definition."[32] His point, of course, is that Leibniz's definition is a pure abstraction, removed from the facts and realities of life and experience. In terms of pure metaphysical knowledge, Torrey suggests, the problem of theodicy may be intractable (at least until the "end of history"). Yet, this is not the only kind of knowledge, nor even the most important knowledge available to Christians. Torrey suggests that "Light comes more from living than from thinking. Moreover, this practical way of dealing with a problem too hard for the intellect is like that which God himself has offered to our consideration and acceptance." It is possible, through Christian faith, to live and feel the solution to theodicy, if not to strictly "understand" it in philosophical terms.[33] There is a hardheaded practicality to Torrey's discussion here. It is this type of appeal to lived reality and the distrust of "philosopher's problems" that suggests a strong similarity with Dewey's later pragmatism. In addition, Torrey writes, "Pessimism is artificial, non-natural. Every man is at heart an optimist."[34] Dewey, too, was an optimist, although by no means an uncritical or complacent one.

What we find in Torrey's work is a surprising mix of characteristics. On the one hand, the content of much of his thought appears almost diametrically opposed to Dewey's mature writings. On the other, there are elements of great similarity. When we look at some of the other individuals in a position to influence Dewey at the University of Vermont and in the Congregational Church during these years, we find the same mix of elements. President Buckham, was "looked upon as the very embodiment of tradition, a kind of fortress of conservatism."[35] And when we read through his essays, there is material that sets him very much apart from what we recognize in Dewey. For instance, when discussing the "college ideal of life," Buckham writes: "It would not have human life dominated by the philosophy of the average man. It says to that philosophy, there are more things in heaven and earth than you have dreamed of."[36] This elitism and idealism is a far cry from the thought of the "philosopher of the common man," as Dewey was not infrequently called.[37] There is also in these essays a sort of Horatio Algerism, a belief that individuals, through hard work and determination, are able to overcome all obstacles and adverse circumstances that is incongruous with Dewey's communitarianism and his analysis of the organizational and structural constraints in complex urban industrial society.[38]

Yet despite these differences with Dewey, some of the other elements in Buckham's writings are quite similar to the sensibilities of the later Dewey. Like Dewey, Buckham was committed to an understanding of the moral life as an activist life: "the life nurtured by Christianity is a life of action."[39] Although he warned his students against the temptations of radicalism, Buckham was sensitive to the changes taking place in American society and the need to rethink many of our moral and political ideals and categories.[40] Most interesting, however, is his attack on what he views as too great an emphasis on individualism and individual rights in contemporary society.

> We in this country . . . have been living too long in the primitive stage of human society. We have built our social fabric too much out of a mere assertion of rights. At times we have been lifted into a glorious forgetfulness of our selfishness, but have soon dropped back again into our old ways. Save as religion modifies the temper of our people, the spirit of American life is too much that of individualism. Every man is for himself. Politically we are democratic: socially we are intensely aristocratic. The strongest are the best.[41]

A society built merely on the assertion of individual rights would, Buckham thought, be a chaotic one. In Buckham's mind America has been saved from this chaos only by its all too infrequently recognized Christian morality and fellowship:

> To found society on the rights of man, his rights only, is simply to incorporate the principle of multiple self-assertion. The experiment has been tried, and its various phases have been hate, cruelty, bloodshed, anarchy, insurrections, massacres, the reign of terror, military despotism. History furnishes no single instance of a community beneficently organized upon a mere assertion of rights. The French anarchists were fond of justifying themselves by appealing to the American Declaration of Independence. But that document represented the spirit of American liberty only when taken in connection with the profound respect for law and the deep sense of religion which informed the substance of the American character.[42]

Dewey's sense of the limitations of liberal individualism are not at all surprising against this intellectual background. Like Dewey, Buckham believed that unbridled individualism was both morally and empirically incorrect.

During his college years and directly afterward, while he still lived in Burlington, Dewey was active in the First Congregational Church; he was elected president of the church's newly founded youth group in 1881.[43] From the church's minister at this time, Lewis Orsmond Brastow (subsequently a professor at the Yale Divinity School), Dewey certainly heard much Congregational orthodoxy. In a discussion of religion and government, for example, Brastow tortuously attempts to prove that ours is a Christian state and can therefore favor Christian activity and morals even if there is a formal separation between these two spheres. He concludes his case by observing, "It is God, not man, who creates government."[44] Nonetheless, there is also much in Brastow's career and writings which is similar to Dewey's convictions. He bravely defends toleration of diverse opinions within the Congregational Church from an attempt by conservatives at the 1887 state convention to impose greater doctrinal standards upon the clergy and laity.[45] After his death, one of his colleagues at Yale eulogized him as a man whose theology "arms one against all movements in the direction of intolerance and dogmatism."[46] Like Dewey, Brastow firmly believed that "doctrines that fear liberty confess weakness."[47] From Brastow Dewey also probably heard criticisms of the individualism of contemporary life.[48] Most striking are comments Brastow made in a special sermon during Dewey's senior year in college, in which he emphasized the importance of personal growth and development: "Every man is a man of whom more might have been made. No one attains his full measure. We all die half-grown. . . . It belittles a man not to grow."[49] Life as a moral opportunity for personal growth would, of course, become an idea of central importance for Dewey's moral and political theory.

Probably the most significant intellectual presence at Vermont when Dewey attended was the ghost of the late president of the university, James Marsh. Marsh had been an important figure in the New England transcendentalist movement, and his introductory essay to Coleridge's *Aids To Reflection,* along with a collection of his writings published after his death and edited by his friend and colleague Joseph Torrey (H. A. P. Torrey's uncle), were perhaps the most important texts of moral philosophy taught and read at Vermont during the middle part of the nineteenth century. Marsh expounded a philosophy highly critical of the Lockeanism that he (like Coleridge) believed dominated contemporary philosophy and moral theory. He felt that Lockean epistemology was subversive of religious orthodoxy because it radically split the worlds of faith and reason.[50] On the contrary, Marsh argued, "Christian faith is the perfection of human reason."[51] The worlds of faith and reason are complementary when properly understood, rather than antagonistic or simply unrelated. Philosophy and religion are mutually compatible and, in reality, interdependent. True religion must be philosophical, just as true philosophy must become religiously informed.[52]

From this perspective, Marsh was critical of philosophical systems that had purely intellectual integrity but seemed far removed from the concerns of Christian life and activity. Joseph Torrey commented that Marsh "felt altogether dissatisfied with the old method of the Scottish and English philosophers, which he thought too formal, cold and barren. They did not, he said, keep alive the heart in the head."[53] Philosophical thinking must grow out of the experiences that individuals have in the course of their daily lives. In turn, for philosophy to be significant, it must influence the living of these lives: "No living and actual knowledge can be arrived at simply by speculation. The man must become what he knows; he must make his knowledge one with his own being; and in his power to do this, joined with the infinite capacity of his spirit, lies the possibility of his endless progress."[54] So Marsh was impatient with philosophical systems of merely academic or speculative interest. Philosophy must be activist, intimately concerned with the moral problems raised by the facts of life.[55]

Marsh believed that this moral perspective was in direct conflict with the currently fashionable Lockeanism, with its emphasis on individualism and self-interest.[56] Philosophy must be intimately associated with, if indeed not subordinated to, the claims of religion and moral duty. Marsh and those who followed him at UVM held that we are obliged to think seriously not because it is fun or interesting or exciting or creative but because without doing so we simply do not know how to live appropriately. Any philosophical system that does not inform such concerns and is not proved in the living is false, vain, or irrelevant.

Even though Dewey would eventually hold few if any of Marsh's religious beliefs, there is a great deal of common ground between Dewey and his Congregationalist forebear. Marsh, Dewey points out in his centennial address, condemned all attempts to separate knowledge from action. "Marsh constantly condemns what he calls speculation and the speculative tendency, by which he means a separation of knowledge and the intellect from action and the will."[57] Dewey also quotes extensively from a speech Marsh gave at the dedication of the University chapel in 1830, in which he discussed the democratic nature of American government:

> We can hardly, indeed, be said to be the subjects of any state, considered in its ordinary sense, as body politic with a fixed constitution and a determinate organization of its several powers. . . . With us there is nothing so fixed by the forms of political and civil organizations as to obstruct our efforts for promoting the full and free development of all our powers, both individual and social. Indeed, where the principle of self-government is admitted to such an extent as it is in this state [i.e., the United States], there is, in fact, nothing fixed or permanent, but as it is made so by that which is permanent and abiding in the intelligence and fixed rational principles of action in the self-governed. The self-preserving principle of our government is to be found only in the continuing determination and unchanging aims of its subjects.[58]

Dewey finds that his own pragmatic perspective and understanding of democratic values is not greatly different from this view.

When we look at these intellectual influences of a few key individuals on Dewey the young man and student, we find many more similarities between Dewey's developed democratic philosophy and the ideas of his teachers and of clergy back home in Burlington than the secondary literature or even Dewey's own personal reflections would lead us to expect. It was common for him in the early years to hear criticisms of philosophical individualism and conventional Lockean theory. It was equally common to hear criticisms of all philosophy and intellectual life that was not intimately involved with human activity and life as it is lived. Individual growth and development were held by others in Burlington and the University to be of ultimate moral concern for personal moral life and social life in general. Democracy, at least as it was understood by Marsh, is less a fixed form of government than an open opportunity for the development and growth of the citizenry. And finally, all of those in a position to have influenced Dewey strongly opposed any radical separation between the world of facts and the world of values, between intelligence and morality, between means and ends. On all of these counts, which are so important to Dewey's mature democratic thought, there are important precedents in the thought of those who taught and influenced him at the University of Vermont.

. . . . .

Dewey's democratic theory is distinctive in a number of ways. He distrusted the individualism of much conventional liberal theory, both in its natural rights (Locke) and utilitarian (Mill) incarnations. His criticisms were twofold: on the one hand, the theory is empirically inaccurate (especially in the twentieth century); on the other, it has become a mere rationalization for institutions and social behavior that are actually contrary to the spirit of the liberalism from which it developed. On the first count, liberal individualism simply fails to understand the objective interdependency of individuals in the modern world. Because of this the theory is not terribly useful in guiding moral action in the world that individuals actually live in. Thus, in *The Public and Its Problems*, Dewey refers to "the enormous ineptitude of the individualistic philosophy to meet the needs and direct the factors of the new age."[59] In an equally characteristic passage in *Liberalism and Social Action*, Dewey argues that the "beliefs and methods of earlier liberalism were ineffective when faced with the problems of social organization and integration."[60]

On the second count, Dewey argues that it is largely because of this theoretical limitation that liberalism has so easily been corrupted and vulgarized as an ideology serving narrow, selfish interests. Thus, for example, liberal individualism has come to be associated with the rights of capitalists to engage in unrestricted economic activity, regardless of the consequences for the community as a whole.[61] The individualism of earlier liberal democratic theory, which had been formulated as a theory of freedom for all members of the political community, has easily been co-opted and put to work for particular class interests.

The political implications of Dewey's democratic theory are strongly participatory: against the thrust of much twentieth-century political theory he warns us to be wary of the power of political experts and elites. As social and political life has become increasingly complex, centralized, and national (or international) in scope, the temptation for democratic theorists is to give up on the possibilities for direct citizen participation and to view democratic politics as primarily a method for the periodic control of elite behavior and policies. In fact, the tendency has frequently been for theorists to attempt to protect and isolate political elites as much as possible from the influences of mass opinion so that they will be able to develop the expertise necessary for political activity and have the power to practice their skills.[62] Dewey, in contrast, argued that the challenge for democratic politics in the twentieth century was to find new ways for citizens to participate meaningfully in political affairs despite the increasing complexity and impersonality of those affairs. To hand over political life to a class of political experts would be a disaster, because their expertise is illusory. "A class of experts is invariably so removed from common interests as to become a class with private interests and private knowledge, which in social matters is not knowledge at all."[63] If politics is concerned with common affairs, then it is the individuals who hold those affairs in common—that is, the citizenry—who must, to the greatest degree possible, participate in the direction and determination of public life.

This characteristic of Dewey's democratic theory is related to a third, and perhaps most important, aspect of his thinking: democracy is viewed not simply as a political form or a set of institutions but as a way of life. From Dewey's perspective the ultimate moral value, as far as we can define such a thing, is found in what he refers to as individual growth: "Growth itself is the only moral 'end.'"[64] Because it is the highest of all social goals, democracy is to be cherished as the greatest of social values because it maximizes the opportunities for personal growth for all individuals in a society. "Democracy has many meanings, but if it has a moral meaning, it is found in resolving that the supreme thrust of all political institutions and industrial arrangements shall be the contribution they make to the all-around growth of every member of society."[65] The way democracy promotes this value is through its insistence on free and open communication, which allows every member of a community the opportunity to contribute to the development of social life and shared interests. Thus, "regarded as an idea, democracy is not an alternative to other principles of associated life. It is the idea of community life itself."[66] To the degree that a genuine community life is achieved, the opportunity for individual growth and communication with others is maximized. Dewey's theory is, obviously, a highly moralized theory of democracy, rather than simply

descriptive or empirical (like much contemporary democratic theory). For Dewey, democracy places a premium on communication, and "Of all affairs, communication is the most wonderful."[67]

Because Dewey thinks of democracy as a way of life, his theory differs markedly from those theories that view democracy only as a set of institutions or political practices. Although elections and constitutional protections of individual liberty are essential ingredients of a democratic society, for Dewey they are not enough to form a community where communication is nurtured, protected, and stimulated. In fact, the institutions necessary for a democratic community change from society to society and from time to time, depending upon the particular needs of each community. In small, local communities, town meeting democracy may be the appropriate vehicle for democratic participation. In a large urban area, different institutional arrangements (for example, neighborhood organizations or the like) become necessary. The final form of a democratic state, therefore, cannot be defined, nor should current or past institutional arrangements be fetishized. "The formation of states must be an experimental process."[68] Institutions must constantly be revised, created, or abolished as required to maximize the democratic communication and participation of the citizenry. Dewey's theory emphasizes democratic process, change, and development, and is hostile to democratic theories which are overly formalistic, static, or ahistorical. There is nothing sacred in political forms in and of themselves. Only to the degree that they cultivate democratic life are they to be valued.

Finally, Dewey's theory is a critique of the tendency in much contemporary political thought and political practice to separate political means from political ends. Dewey believed that such a separation was based upon a misunderstanding of the relationship between means and ends and, more generally, between facts and values. In a 1937 essay, Dewey wrote:

> The fundamental principle of democracy is that the ends of freedom and individuality for all can be attained only by means that accord with those ends. . . . The value of upholding the banner of liberalism in this country . . . is its insistence upon freedom of belief, of inquiry, of discussion, of assembly, of education: upon the method of public intelligence in opposition to even a coercion that claims to be exercised in behalf of the ultimate freedom of all individuals. . . . But democratic means and the attainment of democratic ends are one and inseparable.[69]

The maintenance and protection of democratic society requires not only that we use democratic methods but also that we reject the split between facts and values found in much contemporary philosophy.[70]

What we find, then, in Dewey's mature political thinking is a theory based on strong communitarian and participatory principles, which views democracy as much more important than political institutions alone and, in fact, thinks of democracy as a way of "associated life." His theory is pragmatic and antiformalistic. It sees democracy as an experimental process of development, not something achieved once and for all. Finally, Dewey emphasizes the intimate relationship between means and ends, and he argues that to sacrifice democratic means is to also sacrifice democratic ends.

. . . . .

Given Dewey's personal ambivalence about his background, as well as the emphasis in much of the secondary literature on the gulf between Dewey and his Vermont origins, it is at first a little surprising to find that those with whom he came into contact when he was a young man studying at Vermont prefigured so many of the ideas in his later philosophical work. Perhaps the most striking similarity is in what we might call the pragmatic perspective. Dewey agreed with his teachers that thought divorced from the problems of action is at best vanity and at worst dangerous and irresponsible. There is a deep sense of earthly vocation in the writings of Dewey's teachers, alive and dead, and their strong religious sensibilities served less to separate their thoughts from this world than to moralize the entirety of their worldly activities. Although the theological component of this moralism would disappear from Dewey's thought, the moral perspective of instrumentalism is very much in the tradition of his Puritan forebears. Paul Conklin has been one of the few to recognize this relationship; he writes, "He never repudiated most of the values of his childhood. Instead, he correlated them with a new knowledge of man and his environment, a knowledge never possessed by his less sophisticated forebears."[71] With his pragmatic perspective, Dewey "was the best of the Puritans."[72] He had no tolerance for philosophy apart from the real problems faced by common men and women in everyday life, anymore than his forebears had tolerance for those who professed religious belief but did not allow this belief to guide them in the mundane details of living.

It is this characteristic of Dewey's Vermont inheritance, in fact, which may have led him to overemphasize the practical significance of philosophical activity. It is the Puritan in him that made him believe that wrong thinking necessarily leads to wrong acting, in ways, I think, that simply cannot be sustained empirically. This view, for example, led him to exaggerate the importance of Kantian idealism for the growth of German political absolutism before the World Wars.[73]

On the other hand, it is this same characteristic that made Dewey so important to his generation and potentially to our own. He always had, even in his choice of reading at college, a strong sense of the movement and change in his society. This was not unusual for men and women of his generation—the Progressive movement as a whole, of which he was a central figure, was very much a movement struggling to come to terms with the new American society emerging from the post-Civil War era. What

made Dewey so important and attractive to his peers was not the uniqueness of his concerns so much as the strength of his vision and his supreme sensitivity to the problems of social change. If it is true, he argued, that the world has changed in ways such that our old ideas are no longer reliable guides for everyday life, then it is our moral duty to develop new ways of thinking so as not to be cut adrift in this new world (which, he was afraid, was becoming more and more the case). All the while he insisted, in the tradition of James Marsh, that it was unacceptable to separate moral from intellectual concerns, and that to do so was not only an intellectual error but also a grave danger to moral integrity.

Cushing Strout has rightly observed of Dewey: "He was a man of notable common sense and decency, and if he seems remote now it is partly because we find it difficult to conceive of a philosopher so effective in the world."[74] This effectiveness was at least in part the result of his early moral and intellectual training in Vermont. It was not simply intellectual curiosity that drew the young Dewey to the debates about Darwin and Comte, Spencer and Hegel, in the intellectual journals he found in the University library. It was the same moral concern that would later lead him to attempt a "reconstruction in philosophy" in order to make philosophy a more effective tool for action.

Dewey's objection to the theological perspective of his forebears, then, was not that it was too moralistic but that the moralism it brought to bear on life was dogmatic and pragmatically indefensible—quite simply, it would not do the work required of it. In fact, he argues that if we are to maintain the moral concern and responsibility taught by his Puritan elders, the content of their theology and philosophy must change. This position is nicely illustrated by an article written in 1935 by Dewey's childhood friend, John Wright Buckham (the son of President Buckham), discussing Dewey's *A Common Faith*. A professor at the Pacific School of Religion, Buckham had stayed much closer than Dewey to the Congregationalist orthodoxy of his youth, and he was quite unsympathetic to Dewey's pragmatism (which he understood only imperfectly). He sensed, nonetheless, that he and Dewey had maintained a much closer similarity in moral perspective than he had yet appreciated—in fact, he believed that in *A Common Faith* Dewey had transcended his pragmatism and returned to the fold.[75] Buckham was both right and wrong. Dewey had not renounced pragmatism, nor had he really returned to the fold. Yet he was not as far away from the views of his childhood friend as Buckham had thought.

If the relationship between Dewey and his Vermont inheritance has been overlooked or misunderstood, the result is that we have missed an opportunity to understand a crucial chapter in the development of modern American democratic theory. The relationship between secular democratic theory and the theistic philosophies out of which it grew is a complex and not always happy one. But Dewey's democratic theory grew not only out of a rebellion against Congregationalist society. Nor is it the simple reflection of the values of the supposed political culture of his youth. His preoccupation with the democratization of American life grew quite naturally out of his moral and intellectual education in Vermont. Dewey had more in common with the folks back home than most commentators have realized.

NOTES

[1] Referring to Marsh's edition of Coleridge's book, Dewey said to his friend and colleague, Herbert W. Schneider: "Yes, I remember very well that this was our spiritual emancipation in Vermont. Coleridge's idea of the spirit came to us as a real relief, because we could be both liberal and pious; and this *Aids to Reflection* book, especially Marsh's edition, was my first Bible." Corliss Lamont, ed., *Dialogue on Dewey* (New York: Horizon Press, 1959) 15.

[2] John Dewey, "James Marsh and American Philosophy," *Journal of the History of Ideas* II (April 1941): 147.

[3] John Dewey, "From Absolutism to Experimentalism," in George P. Adams and William Pepperill Montague, eds., *Contemporary American Philosophy,* vol. 2 (NY: Macmillan, 1930) 13.

[4] Dewey, "From Absolutism" 14-15.

[5] Dewey, "From Absolutism" 14.

[6] Dewey, "From Absolutism" 19.

[7] John Dewey, *The Quest for Certainty* (NY: Paragon Books, 1929) 308.

[8] John Dewey, *A Common Faith* (New Haven, CT: Yale 1934) 28.

[9] Lamont 89.

[10] Jane Dewey, "Biography of John Dewey," in Paul Arthur Schlipp, ed., *The Philosophy of John Dewey* (Evanston and Chicago: Northwestern University, 1939) 43, 3.

[11] Sidney Hook, *John Dewey: An Intellectual Portrait* (New York: John Day, 1939) 5.

[12] For example, see Neil Coughlan, *Young John Dewey* (Chicago: U Chicago P, 1973) 112. For a general criticism of pragmatism as a "provincial" philosophy, see Ernest Gellner, "Pragmatism and the Importance of Being Earnest," in Robert Mulvaney and Philip Zeltner, eds., *Pragmatism: Its Sources and Prospects* (Columbia, SC: U South Carolina P, 1981) 41-65.

[13] Coughlan 90-91; Lewis Feuer, "John Dewey and the Back to the People Movement in American Thought," *Journal of the History of Ideas* 20 (1958): 545-68.

[14] Feuer 565.

[15] Lewis Feuer writes, "Dewey's metaphysics indeed was Vermont village democracy projected upon the universe as a whole." "H. A. P. Torrey and John Dewey: Teacher and Pupil," *American Quarterly* 10 (1958): 53.

[16] "Burlington, Vermont 1865-1965" (Burlington, VT: League of Women Voters, n.d.) 7.

[17] Max Eastman, "John Dewey," *Atlantic* 168 (1941): 672.

[18] In a letter to George Dykhuizen, Dewey wrote on October 15, 1949: "I think I've referred in print to the influence of a course with Dr. Perkin's father in physiology in our Junior year—text by T. H. Huxley—I imagine that was the beginning of my interest in philosophy." University of Vermont Archives, Dykhuizen File #16.

[19] George Dykhuizen, *The Life and Mind of John Dewey* (Carbondale: Southern Illinois UP, 1973) 12.

[20] The records of Dewey's library transactions were discovered and published by Lewis Fuer, "John Dewey's Reading at College," *Journal of the History of Ideas* 19 (1958): 415-21.

[21] The following passage also is interesting because it reads very much like Dewey's later political thinking: "Nothing promotes intellect like intellectual discussion, and nothing promotes intellectual discussion so much as government by discussion." *Physics and Politics* (NY:—1873) 199.

[22] R. J. Hinton, *English Radical Leaders* (NY: G. P. Putnam's Sons, 1875) 76.

[23] Julian Ira Lindsay, *Tradition Looks Forward* (Burlington, VT: The University of Vermont, 1954) 234.

[24] Lindsay 252.

[25] There is no reference in Feuer's list to Dewey having checked out writings by Comte from the library, but Dewey mentions having read Comte in the library. See Dewey, "From Absolutism to Experimentalism" 20.

[26] Dewey, "From Absolutism to Experimentalism" 20.

[27] "In Memoriam—Abraham Lincoln," 18. This manuscript is located in the University of Vermont Archives. Page numbers refer to typewritten transcription of the document made by Lewis Feuer (located with original).

[28] The phrase comes from Dewey's book, *The Quest for Certainty.*

[29] Torrey 13.

[30] Torrey 9.

[31] Sidney Hook, *Pragmatism and the Tragic Sense of Life* (New York: Basic Books, 1974) 101.

[32] H. A. P. Torrey, "The 'Theodicy of Leibniz'," *Andover Review* 4 (Oct.-Dec. 1885): 497.

[33] Torrey, "The 'Theodicy of Leibniz'" 511.

[34] Torrey, "The 'Theodicy of Leibniz'" 509.

[35] Levi P. Smith, introductory essay, "A Masterpiece in Living," in Matthew Buckham, *The Very Elect* (Boston: Pilgrim Press, 1912) 5.

[36] Buckham 48.

[37] Sidney Ratner, *The Philosopher of the Common Man* (NY: G. P. Putnam's Sons, 1940).

[38] See Buckham 34.

[39] Buckham 80.

[40] Buckham 329.

[41] Buckham 201.

[42] Buckham 200.

[43] Minutes of the first meeting of Young People's Society of Christian Endeavor of First Congregational Church of Burlington, VT, 21 November 1881; Special Collections, Bailey Howe Library, UVM, First Congregational Church documents, vol. 15.

[44] Lewis O. Brastow, "Religion and Government," *Burlington Free Press* 6 (April 1876): 4.

[45] Minutes of the Eighty-Fourth Annual Meeting of the General Convention of Congregational Ministers and Held at Burlington, June 1879 (Montpelier: Vermont Chronicle, 1879) 19-20.

[46] Frank C. Porter, "Lewis Orsmond Brastow, D.D.," *Yale Divinity Quarterly* (January 1913): 6.

[47] Quoted, Porter 10.

[48] Brastow remarked, for example, that it was the "extreme development of the theories of individualism which have resulted in a loose public sentiment." "Comments about a Divorce Reform Bill," *Burlington Free Press* (16 February 1884):1. Although Brastow made this comment well after Dewey had left Burlington, it is the type of opinion Dewey was likely to have heard from him.

[49] Lewis O. Brastow, "The True Estimate of Life," *Burlington Free Press* (17 February 1879): 2.

[50] James Marsh, introduction to Samuel Taylor Coleridge, *Aids to Reflection* (Burlington, VT: Chauncey Goodrich, 1829) xlv.

[51] Marsh xiv.

[52] Marsh xx.

[53] Joseph Torrey, *The Remains of the Rev. James Marsh, With a Memoir of His Life* (Boston: Crocker and Brewster, 1843) 42.

[54] Torrey, *Remains* 115.

[55] Torrey, *Remains* 114-15.

[56] Torrey, *Remains* 490.

[57] Dewey, "James Marsh and American Philosophy" 142.

[58] Quoted in Dewey, "James Marsh" 145.

[59] John Dewey, *The Public and Its Problems* (Athens, Ohio: Swallow Press, 1927) 96.

[60] John Dewey, *Liberalism and Social Action* (New York: Capricorn Books, 1963) 28.

[61] Dewey, *Liberalism and Solid Action,* see especially chap. 1.

[62] In Dewey's own time, the best expression of this perspective is found in Walter Lippmann's *Public Opinion* (New York: Harcourt, Brace, 1922).

[63] Dewey, *The Public and Its Problems* 207.

[64] Dewey, *The Public and Its Problems* 207.

[65] Dewey, *The Public and Its Problems* 186.

[66] Dewey, *The Public and Its Problems* 148.

[67] John Dewey, *Experience and Nature* (LaSalle, Illinois: Open Court, 1925) 138.

[68] Dewey, *The Public and Its Problems* 33.

[69] John Dewey, "Democracy is Radical," *Common Sense* 6 (January 1937): 11.

[70] See, for example, his attack on Kantianism and his understanding of its political implications in John Dewey, *German Philosophy and Politics,* in Jo Ann Boydston, ed., *John Dewey: The Middle Works,* vol. 8 (Carbondale: Southern Illinois UP, 1979) 135-204.

[71] Paul Conklin, *Puritans and Pragmatists* (New York: Dodd, Mead, 1968) 346.

[72] Conklin 402.

[73] See Dewey, *German Philosophy and Politics.*

[74] Cushing Strout, *Intellectual History in America,* vol. II (Ithaca, NY: Cornell UP, 1968) 77.

[75] John Write Buckham, "God and the Ideal: Professor Dewey Reinterprets Religion," *The Journal of Religion* 15 (January 1935): 1-9, 309-15. The specific reference here is to 311.

Frank X. Ryan (essay date 1994)

SOURCE: "Primary Experience as Settled Meaning: Dewey's Conception of Experience," in *Philosophy Today,* Vol. 38, No. 1, Spring, 1994, pp. 29-42.

[*In the following excerpt, Ryan examines Dewey's views on personal experience, concluding that he never was able to reconcile his seemingly contradictory views.*]

This essay will examine and attempt to clarify Dewey's conception of immediate or primary experience. In particular, my aim is to extricate Dewey's actual view from an interpretation still popular among pragmatists consisting of: 1) the phenomenology of "blooming, buzzing, confusion" and 2) its ontological correlate designating a "brute" encounter with "primal, pulsative" reality. Dewey himself, to the contrary, is ahead of his contemporary supporters in overcoming this paradigm whose roots lie in Locke and traditional empiricism. His is not the ontology of other versus self, in-itself existential event versus subjective object of experience, even given the "pragmatic" codicil that the latter knows the former by "interacting" with it. Instead, these denote phases of inquiry—settled havings versus problematic challenges that produce knowings.[1]

We will begin with Dewey's ontology of "mediate-immediacy," whereby a thing of primary experience *is* just what it is experienced as. But it will be made clear that this sense of immediacy necessarily implicates a mediating network of meanings without which experience shifts from "directly enjoyed" to problematic. From this follows the important consequence that even feelings "make sense"—that so-called qualities, sensations, and tonalities are directly experienced only insofar as they cohere to a background of settled meanings. For without such a coherence they mark the interruption of primary experience, a shift from background to focus requiring cognitive disposition. Finally, we will see how inquiry informs us about what is not inquiry—including those natural processes comprising the causal conditions of inquiry itself. It is here we may speak, if we must, of "pulsations," "anteceptions," or "raw feels," but with the full realization that these are products of highly refined reflection—far removed from the true ontological primitives that comprise the subject-matters of everyday experience.

FROM KNOWING TO HAVING

The movement of inquiry that girds Dewey's philosophy cannot be understood without a grasp of the respective roles of knowing and having. To trivialize knowing is to requicken the old "associationalist" psychology that was at a loss to explain how knowledge arises from a hodgepodge of sensations. To trivialize having is to hide behind idealistic blinders in assuming that all experience must be cognitive experience. Any appreciation of Dewey's philosophy as a bona fide alternative to traditional empiricism, idealism, and realism, must accordingly account for the relationship between having and knowing.[2]

Dewey himself began to work out this relationship in the "pattern of inquiry" first articulated at the turn of the century.[3] In this famous model, a direct "having" or "enjoyment" of primary experience is interrupted by confusion or doubt marking the onset of a problematic situation. The resolution of this uncertainty calls forth the formulation of a hypothesis or "end-in-view," data and instrumentalities for testing this hypothesis, and finally actual experimentation. If this is successful, the hypothesis is confirmed as an "object of knowledge." Yet inasmuch as it is no longer problematic, this newly-ascertained meaning itself becomes something directly had or enjoyed—an enrichment of primary experience and a potential resource to be drawn upon in future problematic situations.

Early on, therefore, Dewey's theory of inquiry circumscribed the relationship between having and knowing as a cyclic pattern from having to knowing to having once again. But his chief concern in this period involved warding off misconceptions about the cognitive element within this pattern—to demonstrate that an object of knowledge is a consequence of inquiry and not a self-sufficient antecedent "reality," to develop a supporting logical account of knowledge, truth, belief, and judgment, and to distance himself from contemporary forms of idealism and realism.[4]

The need to extinguish kitchen fires ignited by the debate over cognition and knowledge in these formative years amply justifies Dewey's relegation of noncognitive experience to a back burner. The chief exception to this is his "postulate of immediate empiricism," introduced in 1905 to characterize having or nonreflective experience. According to this intriguing and important ontological credo, immediate empiricism postulates that things—anything, everything—are what they are experienced as. Hence if one wishes to describe anything truly, his task is to tell what it is experienced as being (MW 3:158).[5]

Dewey's point is not that "we" have "direct access" to things "as they are outside of experience,"[6] but that nonreflective experience is ultimate and ontologically primitive: the direct experience of typewriter-in-use undercuts both the object-subject dichotomy of the "typewriter-presented-to-me" and the epistemological quicksand of a supposed correspondence to an ultimately real "typewriter-in-itself."[7]

Yet in its original formulation, the postulate of immediate empiricism seems to obviate analysis of primary experience itself. After all, what more need, or indeed can we say about the typewriter of everyday experience beyond the "common sense" observation that it is what it is experienced as in a determinate context?

From the 1916 *Essays in Experimental Logic* onward, however,[8] Dewey increasingly turns his attention to the full elaboration of what he variously terms "gross," "nonreflective," "direct," or "primary" experience. The reasons for this renewed interest are manifest. For one thing, despite a comprehensive analysis of truth and knowledge, the nature of conditions that precede and follow cognition remained undetermined. For another, critics continued to distort his actual view of "having" by interpreting it in terms of sense data popularized by Moore, Russell, and Price. Finally, Dewey's ultimate aim of discovering the integral bond between practice and theory, common sense and science, required a capstone promised by a tenable theory of nonreflective experience. Above all else he wanted to show that encultured values and scientific advance need not conflict—for culture benefits by supplanting blind custom with intelligently directed inquiry, and science enriches itself and humanity by acknowledging an intrinsic involvement with values. But this meant replacing the traditional separation of social values and scientific facts with the realization that each represents a different level of problem-solving activity arising from a common nonreflective source.

Many of Dewey's most influential students see his transition from instrumentalism to naturalism as a delayed attempt to overthrow the idealism of his youth for a hard-headed realism. But I see Dewey as continually and consistently developing a middle way between these traditional alternatives. The notable "shift" in such later classics as *Experience and Nature* and *Art as Experience* marks not a fundamental conversion from idealism to realism but a shift in focus from reflective to primary experience. In Dewey's very late works, primary experience is ultimately elevated to the "alpha and omega"[9] of a transactional "circle" of having-knowing-having sketched at the dawn of this century yet not fully closed until the very end of his life.[10]

IMMEDIATE VERSUS REFLECTIVE EXPERIENCE

In order to understand primary experience we must first grasp the essential yet initially quixotic-sounding concept of "mediate immediacy." In all settled experience, Dewey tells us, is "something obdurate, self-sufficient, [and] wholly immediate" (LW 1:105). It is, in fact, this very finality that distinguishes having from knowing, experience immediately possessed and enjoyed from that cognitively engaged in the determination of hypotheses and data needed to resolve encountered problems. Yet the core of this finality, and the reason why immediacy is mediate, is a sense of relatedness, connectedness, or, as more recently phrased by Hilary Putnam, "fit."[11] The familiar arrangement of furniture in a room, the hypnotic passage of lines on a highway, the egg-salad sandwich grabbed on the run, are what they are in a familiar context. It is the interruption of this integrated whole—the chair discovered mysteriously overturned, the suddenly onrushing barricade, the crack of a tooth on an eggshell—that marks the transition to cognitive focus, the conscious discrimination of "myself" and "other," and the

recognized need for a plan. Both knowings and havings are charged with relations, but whereas cognitive relations are deliberately directed to some external and as yet unattained end, in having this connectedness is directly enjoyed and terminal—its *mediacy* reinforces its *immediacy*.

Keeping in mind this double aspect of primary experience also helps us avoid the empiricist fallacy of equating the "something obdurate" in direct experience either with "incorrigible" sense-data or with "objects" as complex constructs of these. As Dewey frequently points out, such data, let alone their constructs, signify not "simples" but products of refined and discriminating analysis. Indeed, some of us eminently capable of getting around in a world of yellow bananas and yellow caution lights, where yellow is qualitatively what it is within a vast context of things and hues, are pressed to come to grips with the epistemological import of G. E. Moore's alleged experience of "indefinable" yellow.[12]

Primary and reflective experience may be said to differ in other ways as well. Whereas primary experience is frequently transitory and marked by random juxtaposition, reflective experience strives for order, homogeneity, and classification by kinds and species. Reflection further enhances our capacity for problem solving by reformulating common experience into causal explanations and scientific laws (LW 1:114-17).

To say primary experience is mediate immediacy and to note several differences between it and reflective experience merely offers a starting point for its analysis, of course. But before we develop the positive conception of primary experience as settled meaning, it is crucial to distinguish Dewey's general outlook from one popular among pragmatists and often attributed to Dewey himself. This alternative view has two related phases: 1) a phenomenological axiom that primary experience is inherently undifferentiated or "confused," and 2) a metaphysical correlate that this marks a primal or "brute" encounter with "independent reality." Although Dewey clearly regards both as legitimate phases of experience, it is misleading to interpret them in terms of a realist ontology Dewey in fact rejects.

A PHENOMENOLOGICAL PREMISE
PRIMARY EXPERIENCE
AS "BUZZING, BLOOMING, CONFUSION"

In humans and other higher animals, Dewey tells us, feeling arises as a "vague and massive uneasiness," a pervasive sense of need requiring response (LW 1:197). According to James Gouinlock, this suggests that primary experience is aptly characterized as a "welter:" a "jumble of characteristics and events" the metaphysician sorts "into common traits for all situations."[13]

Both Gouinlock and S. Morris Eames agree that James' memorable "blooming, buzzing, confusion" aptly portrays the initial phase of experience from which intellectual operations and products are subsequently derived.[14]

Eames, however, adds the proviso that primary experience must already be "layered with" or contain "germs of critical reflection."[15] And because immediate and critical components are interwoven, for Dewey an object cannot merely consist of a "bundle of sense qualities," as Russell and the logical empiricists held. Instead, it must be a "bundle of sensory qualities functioning as signs."[16]

A METAPHYSICAL COROLLARY
PRIMARY EXPERIENCE AS THE "BRUTE" ENCOUNTER
WITH INDEPENDENT REALITY

In itself, the claim that primary experience is "confused" or a "welter" is merely a phenomenological description.[17] It need carry no metaphysical import regarding the "structure of reality." Dewey himself, however, at times seems quite concerned with articulating just such a structure. To ward off any "chemical trace" of subjective idealism, he repeatedly reminds us that immediate experience is a natural product of the interaction of an organism and its environment (see, e.g., **"Conduct and Experience,"** LW 5:220; *The Quest for Certainty*, LW 4:138).

Nowhere is Dewey's naturalism of organism-environment interaction spelled out more boldly than in *Experience and Nature*. In the rising and setting sun, in the seasons, in the pulse of life itself, nature reveals a "characteristic rhythmic order" (LW 1:65).

Dewey identifies this naturally occurring rhythmic order with "events," to be distinguished from "objects of experience" that denote interpretations of events:

> The nearest approach that occurs in ordinary life to making the distinction is when there occurs some brute dumb shock, which we are constrained to interpret, to assign meaning to, to convert into an "object." (LW 1:245)

Reflection, therefore, takes "events which brutely occur and brutely affect us, [and] convert[s] them into objects by means of inference to their probable consequences" (LW 1:245).

Such passages have convinced some of Dewey's most able followers that primary experience is the point of connection between "independent reality" and "objects of experience," i.e., between "events" that causally produce yet are devoid of human experience and distinctively human interpretations.[18] In short, although all *knowing* involves interpretation and the overlay of meaning, at some primal level *having* confronts or at least approaches reality "itself."

For Raymond Boisvert, this implies that "object" is no longer a suitable term for existential entities. For the experienced object must be distinguished from the existing thing and "should no way be confused with it."[19] Nevertheless, if knowing is about something, an adequate ontology must provide "a theory of beings which would provide the generic characteristics of these 'somethings.'"[20]

According to Boisvert, such a theory is to be founded upon 1) "data," described in oddly Lockean phrasing as "the immediate givens received by the individual"; and 2) Brentano's intentionality, whereby an idea is the "mental inexistence of an object" that nonetheless "includes something as object within itself."[21]

In Sandra Rosenthal's "speculative" pragmatism, the "brute" interface of independent reality with experience is captured by the important notion of "anteception," borrowed from Peirce.[22] Rosenthal acknowledges that objects of experience, of what she terms the world of human involvements, are infused with meaning structures established by habit and are not merely "constructed" from brute data. She also admits that a "bare reaction event" is only a component in the ultimate reality she terms "processive concreteness." Nevertheless, she insists that a "blind reacting thing" is a substantive "slab" of this whole, and as such expresses the "brute presence" of reality wholly independent of human involvements.[23]

According to Rosenthal, what we would normally consider objects of everyday experience are in fact "abstractions" from this far richer "primordial" or "anteceptive" experience.[24] Rooted in fundamental organism-environment interaction, anteception is brute sensation that "thickens" awareness to "the ontological presence of an independently there otherness."[25] Whereas Dewey's perceptual "focus," "fringe," and "background" are all possessive of meaning to some degree, Rosenthal's anteceptive experience overflows these "meaning containers."[26]

BRUTE ENCOUNTER AS "INTENTIONAL TRIPPING"

As suggested earlier, characterizations such as "brute sensation" and "independent otherness" are unfortunate not so much because they are wrong but because they fail to articulate the degree to which Dewey's conception of primary experience undercuts the traditional paradigm of internal versus external, self versus other. Primary experience is, to be sure, 1) inevitably interrupted by shock or confusion, without which inquiry would be unnecessary and in fact impossible. There is also 2) a legitimate, *reflective* sense where we may quite properly conclude that experience is produced as an organism encounters the external world. The distortion occurs only when either 1) the confusion that terminates or marks a transition from primary experience is identified with such experience itself; or, 2) as we will spell out shortly in the distinction between process and function, organism-environment interaction is taken as a processive causal condition of experience in neglect of the crucial functional corollary that such conditions themselves, like all facts about the world, cannot be posited without appeal to reflective inquiry.

Inasmuch as it tends to reduce Dewey's radical innovation to an "interactive" version of realism,[27] the metaphysics of "brute encounter" will be taken up first. To begin with Boisvert's analysis, any hint of an affinity between Dewey and Brentano on intentionality also insinuates the company of Frege, Meinong, Russell, and the logical empiricism of which Brentano was an influential progenitor.[28] Whereas Dewey, as even Boisvert allows, was attempting to "avoid realistic and idealistic theories" altogether,[29] Brentano's conception of intentionality virtually self-destructs in an effort to remain faithful to realism. Stung by allegations of subjectivism arising from his appeal to "mental inexistence," Brentano insists that the ground of any intention is always some physical existence and never a mental attitude or disposition. This, of course, precludes all intentionality toward counterfactuals, whether 1) by design, e.g., "the golden mountain does not exist," or 2) by mistake, as in assuming "my uncle is at the station," when in fact he's delayed in traffic. For Brentano, such statements can only be improper uses of language requiring "translation" into something with bona fide existential reference.[30]

By this criterion, any allegorical or fictional reference is technically nonsense. But must my idea about Vanya's nihilism, for example, really intend ink on a page or electro-chemical traces in the brain of Dostoyevsky? Certainly Dewey didn't think so. For him, as for William James before him, dreams, hallucinations, fictions, even errors, are as "real" as spatio-temporal sticks and stones.[31] The issue is not between reality and non-reality, but between success and failure when different sorts of beliefs are acted upon. Checks written on the belief there is money in the account will have adverse consequences if in fact you are overdrawn.

But the ultimate defect in Brentano's translation scheme, as illustrated by the example of erroneous reference, is that it ultimately destroys the very principle it attempts to specify. For on his interpretation I cannot rightfully claim to "intend" an external object unless I already possess an incorrigible guarantee of its existence. Nor can I be sure I "intend" a property or quality of an object without a similar guarantee of that property's existence. But if I can only intend what I already incorrigibly possess, what is the purpose of intentionality?

Dewey would undoubtedly regard Brentano's intentional realism, including his translation scheme amounting to physical reductionism, as but another instance of the "intellectualist" fallacy where both the intentional "state of mind" and its physical referent must be known a priori by some allegedly "superior" act of cognition or "God's-eye view." His alternative, not sketched until 1950,[32] suggests that intentionality signifies neither a subjective "mental inexistence" nor secured terminal objects alone. Instead, intentionality incorporates elements of both in the context of a hypothetical meaning linked to specific behavior. Here the so-called "mental" or "ideational" component takes the form of the hypothesis "if *x then y*," where *y*— an "end in view"—is what would be achieved if *x*—existential entities employed as data and instruments in coordinated activity—successfully procures *y*.

Intentionality as hypothesis avoids the intellectualist fallacy because neither the end-in-view nor the data utilized are authentically "known." The end-in-view is not known because it is not yet achieved. The data are not known because they possess settled meanings merely had in this inquiry.[33] This avoids subjectivism because the so-called "mental" component has nothing to do with some mere attitude or state of mind; it literally means or intends something beyond itself. What it intends is not, to be sure, some antecedent thing-in-itself, but a concrete consequence or consummation.

Once Dewey's intentionality is distinguished from Brentano's, a related misconception about the nature of "data" may be avoided. From a traditional perspective, Boisvert's description of data as the "immediate givens received by an individual" suggests a manifold of primitive sense-data somehow "synthesized" into objects by inquiry. But as we saw earlier, the postulate of immediate empiricism explicitly reverses the notion that objects are constructs of data. To the contrary, common sense things and affairs, and not their isolated characteristics, are our true primitives. Given that they are what they are experienced as, they carry their own ontological credentials. To repeat, this in no way disbars us from seeking their causal conditions, components, or qualities; nor does it discourage the conclusion that such determinations unavoidably alter the character of future havings. But it does forcefully remind us that such conditions and components are, to repeat, products of prolonged and often sophisticated reflection. The more we wish to know about the world beyond our feeble flailings the harder we must push the horizons of inquiry. There is no getting "behind" experience, no pretense of primitive data or undifferentiated feeling as a threshold to "independently there otherness."

Recalling that Boisvert initially appealed to Brentano's intentionality and to immediate data to try to determine the general character of "events" beyond the purview of "objects of experience," it should now be clear why neither device offers much promise. Intentionality certainly fails once we replace the notion that the intended "thing" is not some extra-experiential event constitutive of reality "itself," but the coordination of a meaning-hypothesis and an activity designed to confirm or disconfirm it.[34] Data certainly fail once we realize these mark not the primitive encounter with "reality" but instrumentalities chosen to procure ends-in-view.[35]

An appraisal of Rosenthal's more fully developed system also follows along the same lines. To begin with, Dewey would have no difficulty accepting what Rosenthal at times calls the "analytic categorical" sense in which "blind reacting things" may be identified in nature.[36] In certain contexts, this sort of specification may serve inquiry well, just as Newton's laws work better than Einstein's in certain contexts, and Euclid's geometry fits better than Reimann's. Dewey would caution us, however, never to forget that specifications such as "blind reacting thing" and "processive concreteness" are products of highly refined reflection. And claims about "reality itself," if permissible at all, call forth even more rarified levels of inquiry.[37]

This seems just what is neglected in the attempt to force the arcane notion of "anteception" onto primary experience per se. Whatever its value to physics, physiology, or psychology, "pulsating anteception" seems a peculiar and expressly nonempirical way to characterize having. Dewey's phenomenological assessment, that such experience is populated with everyday things and affairs, has far more prima facia plausibility. In my own experience a sense of immediacy-in-connectedness does indeed seem to pervade everyday doings and involvements. But Rosenthal's "ontological presence of an independently there otherness" utterly eludes me on all but those mercifully rare occasions when I've been pressed into reading Heidegger late into the night.

These difficulties merely illustrate what appears to be the underlying problem with Rosenthal's conception of anteceptive experience—that it seems an unwarranted inversion of what Dewey calls focus and fringe. In Dewey's terms, blind reacting things—stubbing a toe, being hit in the face by a softball, suffering a bee sting—present themselves as immediately focal, not as vague presences that overflow our fringe. They require immediate attention, the preparation and execution of some directed course of action.[38] Nor is the experience of a bare reaction event "thick" or "rich," as Rosenthal avows. To the contrary, richness is a product of the systematic replacement of such events with objects of knowledge in inquiry. Objects become richer, unfolding what Dewey at times calls their nature or essence, as directed intelligence uncovers new levels of utility and relatedness to other objects. A background is rich, therefore, not because it bumps up against primordial reality, but because it contains a wealth of meanings developed in previous inquiries that are at least provisionally secure in this inquiry.

THE "BLOOMING, BUZZING, CONFUSION" CONFUSION

Once it is evident we primarily encounter a world of things and affairs and not shocks or crude sensations, the phenomenology of perceptual "confusion" requiring cognitive processing or "layering" also may be rectified. Certain physio-psychological states, such as infant perception, might well be regarded as "confused."[39] But it is apocryphal to suppose some such primordial state as underlying normal adult perception. Indeed, even James intends his famous "stream of consciousness" metaphor to demonstrate that confusion marks the *interruption* of a "substantive resting place." Consciousness as a "stream" thus designates not vagueness or confusion but "perchings and flights" whose beginnings and ends are always coherent settled states.[40]

Even from his earliest writings on the topic, Dewey, too, takes great pains to show that primary experience is neither vague nor confused. For him, to suggest that having is a kind of "unconscious" experience would amount to "suicide" for empiricism. Quite to the contrary, primary experience is characterized by "assurance or control," or even "the peace which passes understanding." Primary experience, then, is saturated with content and value and

"unconscious," only in the sense that it is not concerned with *reflective* reference (**"The Knowledge Experience Again,"** MW 3:179).

This conclusion is also confirmed by the postulate of immediate empiricism itself: since immediate presences are "just what they are, it is illegitimate to introduce such notions as obscurity or confusion into them." Confusion and doubt mark the transition from having to diagnosis of the problem. They also can arise when proposed data or instrumentalities are found inadequate or inappropriate (**"Logic of Judgments of Practice,"** MW 8:57).

PRIMARY EXPERIENCE AS SETTLED MEANING

The lesson here is that it is folly to portray primary experience either in terms of a brute encounter with independent reality or as a bundle of sensory qualities "synthesized" into a cognitive object. To be sure, there is something obdurate about everyday experience, but this is better characterized as a *settled* state of affairs than as an intrusion. The actual perception of disturbance usually marks a transition from primary experience to the inquiry situation resolved in the procurement of a new cognitive object.

It is in this context alone that the distinction between event and object makes sense. Dewey overthrows the whole mind-set of a bare existential event as a thing-in-itself set over against an object of experience as a mental appearance or phenomenon. For him, the important distinction is not between event and object at all, but "between events which are challenges to thought and events which have met the challenge and hence possess meaning." (LW 1:246) In other words, events assert themselves as "brute existences" when connections have been severed and thus require reconstruction into reflective objects—objects returned to primary experiences as existential, to be sure, yet certainly not as "brute."

Hence although is clear that an event is spatio-temporally antecedent to an object, the fact that inquiry is a circle reminds us of a legitimate sense in which it is a consequent as well:

> What is signified [by primary experience] is that there is a direct possession and enjoyment of meanings to be had in that experience of objects which issues *from* reflective knowledge. (*The Quest for Certainty*, LW 3:177)

Here Dewey is making two crucial points:

1) The pattern of inquiry is a circle exhibiting closure, for in addition to the movement from having to knowing, each thing directly had "issues *from*" something previously known. Stated otherwise, the immediacy of primary experience is mediated by its relation to an established pattern of doubt-resolution activity.

2) Our "direct possession and enjoyment" is of things-with-meanings, not of brute shocks or "raw feels," though

these meanings are clearly noncognitive or "settled" and, as such, no longer part of the foreground of cognitive objects of reflective inquiry. For once a problem is resolved, and knowing returns to having, a cognitive solution becomes a settled meaning—a habituated set of relations no longer requiring conscious attention. We no longer have to think about riding the bike, stopping for the red light, booting up the computer. These, in a simple and straightforward sense, are natural existences, things, or events.[41]

Once we understand that Dewey's true ontological primitives are such directly possessed havings it becomes possible to grasp the boldness and originality of his reaction against both traditional philosophy and the "problem of knowledge" it generates. Dewey rejects not only the ontological priority of a passive "correspondence" between spectator and object of knowledge, but that of an interactive naturalism of organism and environment as well.[42]

Yet the total repudiation of metaphysical realism conveyed in the redescription of objects as cognitive meanings and events as settled meanings has frequently provoked the opposite charge of idealism: Isn't Dewey, after all, "making everything meaning?"[43]

To reply to this, we must again revisit the postulate of immediate empiricism. Dewey never tires of reminding us that having is not an experience of *experience,* but an experience of *things.* Nor is experience of meaning, but of *things* with meaning. What holds for "independent reality" holds for the conception of meaning as well—both are products of reflective inquiry. Although we speak of, e.g., hypothetical meanings and settled meanings, in its "purest" sense, meaning is synonymous with the movement of inquiry itself: the means-consequence activity denoting the successful consummation of an end-in-view.[44] Hence the subject matters addressed by the conception of meaning are logical, epistemic, and semiotic, and not to be confused with physical processes or causal explanations.

Here an important distinction must be made between Dewey and Peirce, who gratuitously cast perfectly serviceable logical categories across the firmament of the physical cosmos.[45] The same holds true for James, who even lured an unwitting Russell into flirting with the notion of a "neutral stuff."[46] To the contrary, Dewey consistently avoids such pitfalls Whitehead pegged as "category mistakes."

FUNCTION AND PROCESS

Despite his acuity in identifying the shortcomings of his predecessors, it was not until late in his career that Dewey himself began to develop the distinction between function and process that distinguishes an ontology of existence and meaning from causal or physical accounts of their development and employment.[47] Function discriminates the general patterns of existences as they are encountered in inquiry—the circle of primary and reflective experience encompassing having-knowing-having. Process is a core conception of a pragmatic theory of

nature, especially crucial in establishing the continuity between comparatively rare and highly specialized human problem-solvings and more primitive "pushes and pulls" generic to all existences. It is here that an analysis of organism-environment interaction is warranted as a causal account of the origination and development from "significant gestures" to a sophisticated system of symbols. Circles abound here as well: an organism doesn't merely "react" to an environmental stimulus. Instead, what *counts* as a stimulus, and thus helps initiate an appropriate response, depends upon patterns habituated in previous organism-environment interactions.[48] Nor is it possible to develop a conception of a "self" without an empathetic understanding of an "other."[49]

Yet Dewey's ultimate "circle," approached only in his final "transactional" phase, is that of process *and* function. As the idea of a circle suggests, each half presupposes yet reinforces the other. From a transactional perspective we readily affirm, on the one hand, that inquiry is the causal and historic outcome of natural processes; on the other hand, however, we insist that process is always delineated within a functional context of inquiry, without which no claim to "independence" or "existence" can be coherent. Dewey's naturalistic legacy has spawned an able and enthusiastic defense of his philosophy of process. At this time, however, both the task of developing his correlative conception of function and that of employing it to close the transactional circle remains tantalizingly incomplete.

NOTES

[1] Unless otherwise noted, all citations of Dewey's writings are from John Dewey, *The Early Works, 1884-1898* (EW); *The Middle Works, 1899-1924* (MW); and *The Later Works, 1925-1953* (LW), ed. Jo Ann Boydston (Carbondale and Edwardsville: Southern Illinois University Press, 1969-1990). Hereafter references to EW, MW, and LW will appear in the text.

[2] Even in his early writings on pragmatism, Dewey identifies the "intellectualist" fallacy underlying traditional empiricism, idealism, and realism. 1) Empiricism (and presentative realism, see note 7 below) attempts a correspondence between ideas and things, yet renders any sense of "agreement with reality" unintelligible by insisting that things are exclusively known through ideas. 2) Idealism absurdly assumes that the world itself has the characteristics of ideas (or hypotheses) that are in fact instrumentalities for change in the world. 3) Direct realism, in making truth a property of things or events apart from the context of their discovery, unwittingly joins intellectual rationalism in conceiving of the natural universe as a truth system. Dewey thus boldly throws his philosophical rivals into reductio ad absurdum by declaring that "the non-pragmatist, if logical, thus appears as either a pure subjectivist or an objective absolutist" ("The Dilemma of the Intellectualist Theory of Truth," MW 4:76-77).

[3] The well known articulation of the pattern of inquiry in *Logic: The Theory of Inquiry,* LW 12:109-22, is clearly

foreshadowed as early as the *Studies in Logical Theory* (1902), where Dewey develops the notion of "the movement of experience in its reconstructive transition" (MW 2:360).

4 "The Dilemma of the Intellectualist Theory of Truth," noted above (n. 2), is representative of Dewey's overriding concern for correcting misconceptions about the nature and scope of knowledge in the period prior to 1916. Despite their surface disagreements, realism and idealism alike regard mere perception as knowledge and thus falsely conclude that knowledge is a "ubiquitous" relation ("Brief Studies in Realism II," MW 6:111-12). Hence realists such as F. J. E. Woodbridge, who held that knowledge is a "privileged" kind of experience ("The Knowledge Experience and its Relations," MW 3:73), and James Evander McGilvary, who equated knowledge with consciousness ("A Reply to Professor McGilvary's Questions," MW 4:74), were equal to any idealist in their intellectualism.

5 The postulate of immediate empiricism supports Dewey's specific denial of the charge, leveled by critics such as Arthur Kenyon Rogers, William Ernest Hocking, and Morris Cohen, that he is concerned only with the "actual advance of knowledge" rather than with a "faithful report of reality" ("Realism Without Monism and Dualism," MW 13:59). Dewey is in fact building upon Kant's famous thesis that objects must conform to mind—a reversal of traditional empiricism's claim that mind consists of impressions and associations acquired from external reality. Yet Dewey conceives of "mind" and "experience" in a wholly nonsubjectivistic sense: "mind" does not primarily reside within "someone's head." Instead, it encompasses 1) a conscious foreground of things, data, and instrumentalities needed to resolve problematic situations; 2) a rich background of things and events with settled meaning ultimately constitutive of culture, and 3) problem-solving activities by which the former may be reconciled with the latter. My essay, "The Kantian Ground of Dewey's Functional Self," *Transactions of the C. S. Peirce Society* 28 (1992): 127-44, explores the affinity between the young Dewey and an ontology he ascribed to a "liberated" Kant. For Dewey's mature conception of mind, experience, and culture, see *Experience and Nature* (LW 1:365-92; 230-36).

6 To the contrary, this expresses the epistemological monism of direct realism. Ralph Barton Perry, for example, held that "physical nature" can be "directly present in consciousness" ("The Program and Platform of Six Realists," MW 6:477), a claim not illuminated by the assertion that "one knows truly because one's knowledge merges into its object." See "A Review of Pragmatism as a Theory of Knowledge," reprinted in S. Morgenbesser, ed., *Dewey and His Critics* (New York: Journal of Philosophy, 1977), p. 221.

7 "Presentative" or "critical" realists rejected the epistemological monism of direct realism for an epistemological dualism positing a "correspondence" between percept and object perceived. Beyond this, however, they shared no common "program and platform" about either the nature of this correspondence or the underlying reality represented. George Santayana embraced metaphysical materialism; Bertrand Russell, Durant Drake, and Roy Wood Sellars promoted "scientific" objects and relations; Arthur O. Lovejoy and James Bisset Pratt remained metaphysical as well as epistemological dualists in positing an ineradicable psychic element without which knowledge of the physical world is impossible.

8 In the introduction to the *Essays in Experimental Logic* (MW 10:322-23), Dewey first develops the conception of primary experience in terms of 1) internal relatedness and organization and 2) focus and context, important themes later developed in *Experience and Nature*.

9 See Kenneth Chandler, "Dewey's Phenomenology of Knowledge," *Philosophy Today* 21 (1977): 43-55. In this exceptional essay, Chandler both recognizes primary experience as the "alpha and omega of all theorizing" (p. 51) and suggestively links it to Husserl's life-world, Heidegger's *Verhandensein*, and Dewey's own Hegelian roots.

10 In recent years Dewey scholarship has begun to emerge from an almost exclusive focus upon the naturalism of *Experience and Nature* promoted by influential successors such as John Herman Randall, Jr., Sidney Hook, and Ernest Nagel. Ralph Sleeper, who for years accepted Randall's dismissal of *Logic: The Theory of Inquiry* (1938) as a "geriatric whim," has recently praised this as the best statement of Dewey's "first philosophy" ("Commentary on 'Epistemology as Hypothesis,'" *Transactions of the C. S. Peirce Society* 26 (1990): 437-38. See also *The Necessity of Pragmatism* [New Haven and London: Yale University Press, 1986], pp. 5-10; 66-71; 90-92; 134-67). I hope future scholarship will come to acknowledge the Logic as merely the headwaters of a remarkable project, undertaken with Arthur F. Bentley, to integrate logical method, metaphysical function, and naturalistic process within an overarching principle of transaction.

11 Not unlike Dewey, Putnam also replaces the "external" affirmation of things-in-themselves with the "internal" assertion that objects "fit" within conceptual schemes, with practices and discovered utilities that eliminate the paradoxes of standard correspondence theories. See, e.g., *Reason, Truth, and History* (Cambridge, Cambridge University Press, 1981), pp. 49-54.

12 The point here is not to challenge conceptions such as, e.g., the "indefinability of yellow," but to bring attention to the fact that such characterizations are not "building blocks" of everyday experience, but products of sophisticated reflection. For recent empirical documentation of Dewey's claim that so-called "simple" sensations of color in fact require discrimination within a context, see C. L. Hardin, *Color for Philosophers: Unweaving the Rainbow* (Indianapolis: Hackett, 1988), pp. 41-43; see also Putnam, pp. 70-71.

13 James Gouinlock, *John Dewey's Philosophy of Value* (New York: Humanities Press, 1972), p. 29.

[14] Gouinlock, p. 25; S. Morris Eames, "Primary Experience in the Philosophy of John Dewey," *Monist* 48 (1964): 409. In fairness, Gouinlock also provides a very apt characterization of primary experience in the example of a swimmer moving effortlessly through the water (p. 28). My intent is merely to note that such experiences are neither "confused" nor a "jumble."

[15] Eames, pp. 408, 416.

[16] *Ibid.*, p. 410.

[17] "Phenemological" in the sense of what "appears" or "shows itself."

[18] For a recent example, see Barry E. Duff, "'Event' in Dewey's Philosophy," *Educational Theory* 40 (1990). Duff finds it necessary to distinguish nonconscious "bare" events from events that express "ordinary happenings" in human experience (p. 466).

[19] Raymond D. Boisvert, *Dewey's Metaphysics* (New York: Fordham University Press, 1988), p. 86.

[20] *Ibid.*, p. 85.

[21] *Ibid.*, pp. 86 n. 14, 96.

[22] Sandra B. Rosenthal, *Speculative Pragmatism* (Amherst: University of Massachusetts Press, 1986), p. 45.

[23] Rosenthal offers the caveat that a "bare reaction event" is an "analytic distinction" (p. 126). This initially suggests that Rosenthal is echoing Dewey's insistence that "bare reaction event," like the "indefinability of yellow," is a product of reflection rather than an ontological primitive. But she is clearly intending a different, physicalistic account of such events in characterizing them as "slabs" of the "processive concreteness" that "comprises the natural universe."

At this point a profound gulf appears to open between Dewey's postulate of immediate experience and Rosenthal's speculative pragmatism. For Dewey, the objects and affairs of ordinary experience are the true "ontological primitives:" all "underlying" processes or reaction-events, though equally real, are products of sophisticated reflection. Rosenthal, to the contrary, restricts ordinary experience to the "world" of human involvements that must be set apart from the truly ontological processes of the independent "universe." In this scheme,

> the general categorical features of the natural universe independent of man's activities will provide the categorical features for understanding man and the emergent features of [a human-determined] world" (p. 110; also see pp. 156-60, 170).

Dewey would likely regard this as but another attempted "correspondence" ultimately resulting in a dualism between "human world" and "in-itself universe." The ontological primacy of primary experience, to the contrary, explains how scientific experience (including causal accounts of the emergence of intelligence and culture within nature) grows out of the common ground of primary experience without recourse to a futile "correspondence."

[24] Rosenthal, p. 61.

[25] *Ibid.*, p. 68.

[26] *Ibid.*, p. 42.

[27] It is universally known that Dewey opposed the "Spectator Theory of Knowledge" whereby the external world is held as passively conveyed to or impressed upon the mind. But we must equally guard against the complacent view that the problem is overcome by replacing the passive model with an "interactive" one that still clings to the notion of distinct organisms and environments that "interact." For Dewey and Bentley's usurpation of external interaction by internal transaction ("external" and "internal" in Putnam's sense, see n. 11), see *Knowing and the Known,* LW 16:67-68.

[28] There is room for doubt about the degree of the affinity Boisvert perceives between Dewey and Brentano. In one place (p. 85) Boisvert says Dewey's "intentionality" is a term borrowed from another tradition, suggesting that the affinity may be slight. Elsewhere, however, he concludes a detailed statement of Brentano's position by citing Victor Kestenbaum's monograph "comparing Dewey to the phenomenological tradition" (p. 96 n. 14). Unfortunately Boisvert fails to mention that Kestenbaum's comparison (*The Phenomenological Sense of John Dewey: Habit and Meaning* [Atlantic Highlands, N.J.: Humanities Press, 1977], p. 1) is to Merleau Ponty's "internal" intentionality, and not to Brentano's "external" version.

[29] Boisvert, p. 86.

[30] For an elaboration of this exchange between Brentano and Meinong, see Dagfinn Follesdal's comments in Hubert L. Dreyfuss, ed., *Husserl, Intentionality, and Cognitive Science* (Cambridge: MIT Press, 1982), pp. 32-34.

[31] In *The Principles of Psychology,* Vol. 2 (Cambridge: Harvard University Press, 1981), p. 925, James recounts Kant's teaching that the mere affirmation of something's reality of existence adds no qualitative or quantitative content to it: one hundred real dollars is not a greater sum than one hundred imagined dollars. What we regard as unreal, therefore, are those things perceived to be irrelevant to a given context (p. 920). Within the context of my dream, for example, the winged horse is real: it has no reality, however, in my waking world of physical objects (p. 919). In "Beliefs and Existences" Dewey affirms the point that "the radical empiricist, the humanist, the pragmatist . . . believes not in fewer but in more 'realities' than the orthodox philosophers allow" (MW 3:94-96). But he avoids James' subjectivistic tone by insisting that objectively achieved consequences, and not

merely personal perceptions of relevance or interest, are the ultimate determinants of operative realities.

[32] In fact, Dewey's last two letters to Bentley, written as his health began to fail in late 1951, are about intentionality, see S. Ratner and J. Altman, eds., *John Dewey and Arthur F. Bentley: A Philosophical Correspondence* (New Brunswick: Rutgers University Press, 1964), pp. 644-46.

[33] This is not to deny, of course, that data possess settled meanings on this occasion inasmuch as they themselves have been objects of knowledge on prior occasions, nor that the selection of appropriate data may involve their cognitive evaluation.

[34] This strongly suggests that Dewey's conception of intentionality is much closer to Husserl's than Brentano's. Husserl, aware of the difficulties of an intentional stance toward in-itself reality, reconstrued intentionality as directed to a noema. According to this thesis, the directedness of intentionality is accounted for not by the external object alone but by the very structure of experience. This structure, or noema, is a hypothetical orientation that coordinates our activities "as if" there were an external object. Dewey's late description of intentionality as the ideational hypothetical seems quite similar to the "as if" of Husserl's noema. Nevertheless, whereas the status of the external object "itself" remains problematic for Husserl and invites the possibility of subjectivism, for Dewey both the ideational plan or hypothesis and its object or consummation are "open and above board" at all times.

[35] For Dewey's insistence that a datum is a product of reflective experience, see "Realism Without Monism or Dualism II," (MW 13:57); also see "In Reply to Some Criticisms," (LW 5:211).

[36] In *Knowing and the Known* (LW 16:68) Dewey and Bentley call this "specialized interactional treatment within the wider transactional presentation." For Rosenthal's characterization, see note 23.

[37] Dewey, though well known for eschewing reality *überhaupt* for specific encountered reals, nevertheless reserved a philosophical niche for what he called "infinity" words such as being, reality, and universe—words that are "transcendental, noumenal, a priori . . . [with] emotional, esthetic, or mystical impact but no definite meaning." Any immediacy, had or known, is what it is because of a mediating network of relations that "shades off" into an indefinite background. Similar to Kant's regulative ideas, infinity words provide direction toward achievable ends while preserving the wonder and open-endedness of the procurement of future consummations. For a development of this little-known dimension of Dewey's thought, and the obscure yet colorful character who helped inspire it, see Dewey's "First Introduction to *Universe*, by Scudder Klyce" (MW 13:412-19).

[38] In *Experience and Nature*, Dewey specifies focus as the perception of immanent need or urgency, fringe as

that recently requiring or soon to be in need of attention, and background as the remote field of stable meanings that "may be dependably counted upon in dealing with immanent need" (LW 1:235-36).

[39] But even here a cautionary word is in order. In the past two decades the trend in infant and child psychology has reversed the model of, as Susan Caey phrases it, Piaget's "confused child." ("Cognitive Development in Childhood," in Steven Schiffer and Susan Steele, eds., *Cognition and Representation* [Boulder: Westview Press, 1988], p. 131.) Lila Ghent Braine, "Early Stages in the Perception of Orientation," in *Cognitive Growth and Development: Essays in Memory of Herbert G. Buch* (New York: Brunner Mazel, 1979), pp. 105-06, 131, observes that the "orientation errors" once thought to accompany the development of motor skills are in fact remarkably advanced "orientation judgments" limited, however, by insufficient experience and habituation. Note also Hardin (p. 41), who documents the surprising finding that infant color discrimination is remarkably similar to that of adults.

[40] James, *Principles,* vol. 1, p. 290. See also p. 268, where he specifically repudiates the notion of a "manifold of sense" requiring synthesis.

[41] In *Experience and Nature* Dewey expressly captures the reciprocal relation between objects and events in his assertion that a "bare existence event" is not something that precedes inquiry, but something so settled or habituated that its connection to a problem-solving activity has been "lost":

> A solution ceases to be a solution and becomes a bare incident of existence when its antecedent generating conditions of doubt, ambiguity, and search are lost from its context. (LW 1:58)

Here "lost" clearly conveys the sense of being "resolved" or "rendered innocuous" rather than "forfeited." In early childhood, for example, we habituate the ability to walk to the degree that it soon becomes a bare existential event requiring little or no reflection. Should this habituation become truly "lost," say through accident or stroke, we would have to reestablish walking as an objective of inquiry.

[42] For a representative example of the latter, see Arthur O. Lovejoy's "Time, Meaning, and Transcendence," MW 15:360. Lovejoy eschews the passive Spectator Theory of Knowledge for a vigorous interaction where

> all our knowledge (beyond bare sensory content) is a kind of foreign commerce, a trafficking with lands in which the traffickers do not live, but from which they may continually bring home good store of merchandise to enrich the here-and-now.

Such "trafficking" organisms need only 1) the ability to represent things in the external environment as "present as absent" and 2) the belief "that the characters which as present they bear are the same characters which they bear as absent" ("Pragmatism Versus the Pragmatist," MW 13:474).

Dewey's rejoinder attacks the notion that some "psychological percept" grasps or points to "some entity immediate or complete in itself" ("Realism Without Monism or Dualism II," MW 13:52). For this psychical experience of "present-as-absent" constitutes the knowing experience that somehow—magically or mysteriously, but in any case transcendent of experience itself—"hooks up" or "converses" with "ready-made" existences. In fact, however, what is delivered is not a real existence but only its psychic surrogate ("Some Comments on Philosophical Discussion," MW 15:40).

[43] See Boisvert (p. 56) for an impressive documentation of accusations of idealism against Dewey raised, among others, by Charles Bakewell, George Santayana, Benedetto Croce, Bertrand Russell, Stephen Pepper, and Evander Bradley McGilvary.

[44] Despite the charge that Dewey's use of "meaning" is ambiguous or equivocal (see, e.g., Everett W. Hall, "Some Meanings of Meaning in Dewey's *Experience and Nature*," LW 3:401-14), he is in fact both clear and consistent regarding its "primary sense." From as early as "The Control of Ideas by Facts II" (1907), this sense denotes the active doing that brings an end-in-view "into" a hypothesis in literally "fulfilling its own meaning" (see Morgenbesser, p. 199). This is reiterated in *Experience and Nature*, where meaning "is primarily a property of behavior, and secondarily a property of objects" (LW 1:141).

[45] Dewey's admiration for Peirce expanded with his own renewed interest in logic and semiotics in the period following *Experience and Nature*. For Dewey, Peirce was a master of the phenological/logical analysis of experience: "the matter of experience as experienced" ("Peirce's Theory of Quality," LW 11: 86), and pioneered a realism where

> it is only the outcome of persistent and joint inquiry which enables us to give intelligible meaning in the concrete to the expression "characters independent of what anybody may think them to be. ("The Pragmatism of Peirce," MW 10:77)

Nevertheless, by hyperinflating qualities encountered in the phenomenological analysis of inquiry—feeling, doubt, freedom, striving—into physical properties of the cosmos itself, Peirce succumbed to an unfortunate "pan-psychic metaphysics" (LW 11:86). In terms to be introduced shortly, we might say Peirce confused function with process, and one wonders whether a similar inference could not be drawn to Rosenthal's "processive concreteness."

[46] Dewey's foreshadowing of his later distinction between function and process is even more pronounced in the 1917 essay "The Concept of the Neutral in Recent Epistemology." Here he carefully distinguishes a beneficial logical sense, where certain distinctions such as subjective/objective, physical/mental, are suspended for certain phases of inquiry, from a harmful metaphysical sense suggesting some "neutral stuff" in nature that is the object of "pure experience." James, says Dewey, unfortunately fails to separate these two senses of "neutrality" (MW 10:49-51).

[47] Although a prototype of the function/process distinction occurs in *Experience and Nature* (LW 1:139) with an acknowledged difference between a logical sense of relation and one constituted by physical "pushes and pulls," the first clear statement occurs in *The Quest for Certainty* (LW 4:130), where Dewey uses the example of a machine to distinguish the constant function of its operation from the particular spatio-temporal variations that comprise its processes.

[48] Dewey's first and masterfully prescient articulation of this theme, enveloped consistently for more than five decades, is the "reflex circuit" of "The Reflex Arc Concept in Psychology" (1896), EW 5:96-109.

[49] Dewey's conception of "self" is indebted to his colleague and former student George Herbert Mead. See Patrick L. Bougeois and Sandra B. Rosenthal, "Role Taking, Corporeal Intersubjectivity, and Self: Mead and Merleau Ponty," *Philosophy Today* 34 (1990): 117-28, for an enlightening discussion of Mead's theory of empathetic role-taking in the development of a sense of self compared to Merleau-Ponty's "primordial generality" of self and other.

Randolph Feezell (essay date 1995)

SOURCE: "Sport, the Aesthetic, and Narrative," in *Philosophy Today*, Vol. 39, No. 1, Spring, 1995, pp. 93-104.

[*In the following essay, Feezell humorously examines competitive collegiate sports in light of Dewey's* Art as Experience.]

From Paul Weiss's relatively early and legitimating reflections in *Sport: A Philosophic Inquiry*, to more recent ruminations in books and scholarly publications, numerous philosophers have been fascinated by the fascination of sport. For example, in his recent book, *Philosophy of Sport*, Drew Hyland again wonders about the "significant and apparently transcultural appeal" of play and sport.[1] I won't attempt to catalogue the various attempts to understand why so many of us are attracted to sport, especially those sports that involve the playing of games. Like many people, I've wasted a good part of my life playing and watching these games, and I've given up being ashamed or apologetic about it. But I still want to understand the attraction, as any reflective human being should. I suppose one could read the writings of Hyland (a former college basketball player), George Will, or Bart Giamatti as wholesale rationalizations in defense of triviality. But there must be something "deeper" going on here. Or so we think. What could be deeper?

According to my students (and, of course, many others), the deeper attractive realities of sports relate to competition, victory, and the pursuit of excellence. Each semester, at the beginning of my classes, I ask my students to write a paragraph telling me something about themselves.

Invariably the most common response expresses a strong interest in sports. These responses cross the boundaries of race, sex, class, religion, and region. (After all, ESPN is as committed to equality and democratic viewing as is MTV.) Whenever I have the occasion to ask my students to explain their attraction, the responses are as predictable as they are obvious and facile. Perhaps I shouldn't be so harsh. Surely part of the nature and attractiveness of sport does involve the intense and often satisfying experiences involved in competing, striving for victory, and becoming better. But such a view of sport is partial; it leaves out too much of the joy. It makes sport sound too much like winning a war or closing a big business deal. It robs the thing of its magic and its imaginative appeal, and it impoverishes the rich vocabulary that can be used to reveal sport's possibilities. Previously I've tried to make the case for the view that sport is a form of human play. A play theory of sport is more phenomenologically adequate in showing the attractive possibilities of sport and in showing what sort of attitudes and comportment are appropriate when engaging in playful activity.[2] The play theory of sport seems to me to be a more powerful explanation of the attraction experienced by the player. However, it is not obvious that the people who view sport, the fans (in the broadest sense), are attracted in the same way as the player.

In this essay I want to suggest another fruitful response to the question concerning the appeal of sports. I begin with an intuition and I hope to develop the intuition and its implications more fully in what follows. Consider the notion that one of the significant elements in the fan's love of watching games like baseball, football, and basketball has something to do with the way in which sport structures experience and represents it to us. We can see here a close relationship between the kinds of experiences associated with art and the experiences of watching games. Perhaps the aesthetic element plays an important role in the fan's love of the game. Furthermore, in certain kinds of aesthetic experiences we are captivated by our involvement with another temporally articulated world. In the world of the aesthetic object we are taken up by an alternative context of meaning and significance, so much so that these very involvements seem not only to give us a momentary reprieve from the ordinary world; they also help give sense to our lives. If such a response concerning the appeal of sports is enlightening with regard to the fan's experience, I believe it will also disclose something important about the participant's experience. Thus two central notions will emerge from these reflections. (My method will be, roughly speaking, phenomenological.) First, sport provides the occasion for intrinsically interesting experiences and insofar as it does, it is aesthetically valuable. Second, sport also provides contexts of meaning for people, narratives that become existentially valuable for selves seeking a sense of meaning in life.

To work toward these conclusions let us begin with an alternative account of human experience. Against the backdrop of the view of experience described by Sartre in his early novel, *Nausea,* the aesthetic and narrative possibilities of experience will emerge more sharply.

. . . . .

Nausea is the purported diary of a young man, Antoine Roquentin, whose life is undergoing fundamental changes.[3] Antoine is writing a biography of a minor nineteenth century historical figure while he attempts to understand the recurring revelatory experience named by the title of Sartre's great existentialist novel. Antoine's nausea supposedly reveals the brute facticity of being, the utter contingency of himself and all other things, a contingency concealed by various philosophical, religious, and practical strategies. To exist is simply to be there, superfluous (*de trop*). One shows up on the scene and must realize that any attempt to understand human nature in terms of some kind of rational necessity is to falsify what it means to be. Sartre's novel is a sustained reflection on the theme of contingency. For our purposes, however, it is Antoine's related remarks on adventure that are most significant, for the feeling of adventure, he insists, relies on the imposition of narrative structures that falsify the basic contingency of experience.

Prior to returning to Bouville to use the library for his historical researches, Antoine had traveled widely. The pathetic little "humanist," the Self-Taught Man, systematically reading all of the books in the library in alphabetical order, envies Antoine's adventurous past. The "autodidacte" wants to pursue adventures after he has finished his own instruction. As they talk, the Self-Taught Man's adoring interrogations occasion Antoine's reflective denial of the possibility of adventure, because he realizes he has lost the sense that adventurous events can make moments of life special or particularly meaningful. He attempts to understand and explain this loss of meaningfulness.

Antoine says that he "had imagined that at certain times that my life could take on a rare and precious quality. There was no need for extraordinary circumstances: All I asked for was a little precision" (N, p. 37). The "precision" would be constituted by a series of events with a "beginning." "The beginnings would have to be real beginnings. Alas! Now I see so clearly what I wanted. Real beginnings are like a fanfare of trumpets, like the first notes of a jazz tune, cutting short tedium" (N, p. 37). Antoine believes that when one experiences an adventure, the experience of time is altered. "Each instant appears only as part of a sequence," unlike the daily routine of life. The felt sense of a "real beginning" is dragged forward by a sense of immanent direction in the experience, like the notes of a melody. A sense of fitness shapes each developing moment. Antoine summarizes his analysis of adventure:

> This is what I thought: for the most banal event to become an adventure, you must (and this is enough) begin to recount it. This is what fools people: a

man is always a teller of tales, he lives surrounded by his stories and the stories of others, he sees everything that happens to him through them; and he tries to live his own life as if he were telling a story. (N, p. 39)

Antoine expresses here the familiar contemporary theme that our stories attempt to give some narrative shape to our otherwise fragmentary and amorphous experience. But he now denies that our stories capture the true nature of our experience. Storytellers are condemned to falsify experience which has no such narrative form. Storytelling is just another mode of self-deception; it is the attempt to hide from contingency. "But you have to choose: live or tell" (N, p. 39). Live or tell! Truth or storytelling—you can't have it both ways. "Nothing happens while you live. The scenery changes, people come in and go out, that's all. There are no beginnings. Days are tacked on to days without rhyme or reason, an interminable, monotonous addition" (N, p. 39). Antoine realizes that life is just one damn thing after another, with no internal coherence, no direction, no unity.

One can attempt to transform the past by telling about it, but the structure is imposed, a projection in which the end artificially transforms the nature of the events. "As if there could possibly be true stories" (N, p. 39). This model of projection, the imposition of structures on the events of experience, is clearly explained in Antoine's following comments. (Note, here, as in other parts of the book, the Humean character of his reflections.)

> This feeling of adventure definitely does not come from events: I have proved it. It's rather the way in which the moments are linked together. I think this is what happens: you suddenly feel that time is passing, that each instant leads to another, this one to another one, and so on; that each instant is annihilated, and that it isn't worth while to hold it back, etc., etc. And then you attribute this property to events which appear to you in the instants; what belongs to the form you carry over to the content. You talk about the amazing flow of time but you hardly see it. (N, pp. 56-57)

Such reflections should be disturbing to a biographer, and it is easy to understand why Antoine gives up his writing project. But where does he go after he realizes that stories falsify? Direction is puzzling, contingency is inescapable. He no longer has the luxury of seeking adventures. "I wanted the moments of my life to follow and order themselves like those of a life remembered. You might as well try and catch time by the tail" (N, p. 40). Antoine's future is only hinted at in the book, but his salvation will have something to do with the necessity he perceives in the unfolding character of songs. Of course, he's not a musician, but he embraces an ontology of art that allows for the salvific qualities of the experiences of composer, performer, and perceiver. Works of art don't "exist" like the brute facticity of contingent beings in the world. In the artwork, there is a felt necessity that transcends the contingency of ordinary life. Perhaps he would write a book:

> Another type of book. I don't quite know which kind—but you would have to guess, behind the printed words, behind the pages, at something which would not exist, which would be above existence. A story, for example, something that could never happen, an adventure. It would be beautiful and hard as steel and make people ashamed of their existence. (N, p. 178)

Sartre's narrator leaves us with a challenging but somewhat dreary view of life. On the one hand, life would make sense if all or parts of it had an immanent, story-like character. If life is just one damn thing after another, it's going nowhere; it's not even a tale told by an idiot, since it is not a tale at all. No wonder Antoine wanted the moments of his life to have the order of a story. We do often experience parts of our life as essentially storyless. On the other hand, must we agree that such structures are added only in retrospect, reflectively modifying, transforming, and thus falsifying a mere dissociated sequence of events as the sequence is represented or reflectively reenacted? Antoine hints that one might find salvation in the experience of aesthetic necessity, "above existence," but he leaves no doubt that ordinary life is without such order. Is there an unbridgeable gap between ordinary experience and the narrative reconstruction of it associated with our stories and our other aesthetic transactions? I don't think so, and to show this we should look at another account of experience.

. . . . .

One of the main problems with Antoine's view of experience is that his own diary belies the general account his diary expresses. Obviously, the "form" of a diary might be an appropriate way to express the fragmentation that he describes. His diary was found, supposedly, among his papers. Does it begin? Only in the sense that there is a first entry, but there is no "real beginning." The reader merely shows up at a point at which the diary is in progress, not that this date is of any particular significance. Neither is there some specific "end" to transform the sequence of events. In the final entry we find that Antoine will drift into indeterminacy, his future hinted at yet shrouded in uncertainty. But the life described in the diary is no undifferentiated flow. Antoine recounts a series of situations and events: lunch with the Self-Taught Man; the meeting with his former lover, Anny; the final tragic scene when the Self-Taught Man is caught flirting with a young boy and chastely caressing the boy's hand. It is this last scene, especially, that is expressed with tautness and suspense. The situation unfolds with dramatic necessity. When the Corsican smashes the Self-Taught Man's face and the little humanist retreats in humiliation, his abstract love of humanity suffocated by the realities of real human hatred and disgust, it's not that Antoine's telling has transformed the experience. The narrative has disclosed the immanent development of the situation.

Life is simply not necessarily like Antoine's description of it: "No beginnings. Days are tacked on to days without rhyme or reason, an interminable, monotonous addition." I think of my own life. I'm a teacher. For many years at least part of my life has been structured by the rhythms of an academic calendar (an academic "season" in the language of baseball). My life, in part, consists of semesters, courses, and classes. Parts of my life stand out from the general flow of experience. For example, most teachers can recall an especially excellent and pleasurable course, and within such a course certain days in which the class discussion developed in an exciting and wonderful way: perhaps a new line of inquiry, novel comments, an interesting new argument, effective Socratic direction, the material coming together in an unsuspected way leading to a satisfying conclusion. Such an experience is integrated and fulfilling. Contrast that with courses and classes in which there is no smooth development; there are starts and stops, gaps and edges, and there is no sense of completion or satisfactory windup. Contrast the alluring and satisfying character of the good class with the unappealing quality of the bad class. Our lives are not simply "one damn thing after another," in one undifferentiated flow of experience. (Later we will see the way in which experience can be interpreted in terms of the concept of narrative. For now, we will be most interested in the aesthetic possibilities of experience.)

John Dewey has described this with acuteness in *Art as Experience*.[4] "For life is no uniform uninterrupted march or flow. It is a thing of histories, each with its own plot, its own inception and movement toward its close, each having its own particular movement; each with its own unrepeated quality pervading it throughout" (AE, pp. 35-36). Dewey speaks of the difference between experience in general and having an experience, when "the material runs its course to fulfillment. Then and only then is it integrated within and demarcated in the general stream of experience from other experiences" (AE, p. 35). I have given as an example of an experience my own experience as a teacher, but such possibilities are pervasive in life. Dewey mentions such possibilities in relation to finishing a piece of work, solving a problem, eating a meal, writing a book, having a conversation, and (obviously important for the purposes of this paper) playing a game. He offers an extended description of an experience of thinking to show when it is possible that an experience is "so rounded out that its close is a consummation and not a cessation. Such an experience is a whole and carries with it its own individualizing quality and self-sufficiency" (AE, p. 35).

Dewey stresses two important features of an experience. First, there is a temporal structure of connection within the experience. There is a structure of organization and growth: "inception, development, fulfillment" (AE, p. 55). "In such experiences, every successive part flows freely, without seam and without unfilled blanks, into what ensues" (AE, p. 36). Such experiences are temporally integrated. The second feature is somewhat more difficult to get at phenomenologically. There is a felt unity within an experience, "constituted by a single quality that pervades the entire experience in spite of the variation of its constituent parts. This unity is neither emotional, practical, nor intellectual, for these terms name distinctions that reflection can make within it" (AE, p. 37). In some experience one of these elements may dominate, and reflection can apprehend such dominance. If I recall an experience of philosophical reflection, the intellectual elements would predominate, but Dewey insists that the experience as lived would be emotional as well. "No thinker can ply his occupation save as he is lured and rewarded by total integral experiences that are intrinsically worthwhile" (AE, p. 37).

We are now ready to connect Dewey's account of experience to the aesthetic and ultimately to sport. Dewey insists that every experience so constituted as an experience has "esthetic quality." Aesthetic experience proper, for example, the creation and experience of works of fine art, differ from predominantly intellectual and practical activities in the dominating interest, intent, and materials. But here as elsewhere, Dewey wants to deny what he sees as a pernicious dualism. He denies the radical separation of the aesthetic and the non-aesthetic. In practical activity ("overt doings") and in intellectual activity ("thinking") there are latent aesthetic possibilities. Even in an experience of thinking, "the experience itself has a satisfying emotional quality because it possesses internal integration and fulfillment reached through ordered and organized movement. The artistic structure may be immediately felt. Insofar, it is esthetic" (AE, p. 38). I believe Dewey calls such a quality of an experience "esthetic" for two related reasons: because the quality is felt or perceived in an immediate acquaintance and because such a structure is intrinsically satisfying or valued. In fact, Dewey believes that art involves the intention to make objects whose sensuous qualities are immediately enjoyable to perception because of the aesthetic structure he describes.

It is clear that the upshot of Dewey's analysis of the aesthetic is to alter the normal view that aesthetic experience is different in kind from acting and thinking. He attempts to show that "the esthetic is no intruder in experience from without, whether by way of idle luxury or transcendent ideality, but that it is the clarified and intensified development of traits that belong to every normally complete experience" (AE, p. 46). It is striking to read Dewey's account of "an experience" with sport in mind, since the description captures so sharply the experiences of viewing (and playing) sports. Consider a baseball game. The game is initiated by a real beginning, not merely an accidental first occurrence associated with clock time. The first inning is internally related to all future occurrences in the game; events that occur later will invest early moments with novel significance and earlier moments will be meaningful in relation to later moments (a kind of hermeneutic circle). The pitcher attempts to establish his fastball, probes the weaknesses of certain hitters, and attempts to gain a sense of the umpire's strike zone. Fielders position themselves according to their judgment of the swing and strength of the hitters, and they must remember previous at bats. Coaches learn and respond as the game proceeds. The pitcher has a poor move to first; the catcher's arm is strong but his release is slow and his feet are plodding. The pitcher never throws breaking balls when he's behind in the count. A decision is made to steal second base. And so on. The game involves "overt doings," but these practical activities are invested with strategic meanings. Each moment is pregnant with future possibilities as the game develops. If the game is a good one, the action is tense and occasions excitement and suspense. From the fan's perspective, attention is intensely focused on the actions, decisions, and meanings inside the world of the game. If one knows baseball well, the complexity of a particular game is quite amazing. An entire book might be written describing one game![5] The teleology within the development of the game finally leads to a consummating moment when victory or defeat makes the experience complete. In Dewey's language, the game has constituted an experience, an integral experience with aesthetic quality.

Dewey describes a mundane practical activity: a stone rolling down a hill, towards a resting place. But he imaginatively adds an interesting possibility. Suppose the stone is self-conscious:

> Let us add, by imagination . . . the idea that it looks forward with desire to the final outcome; that it is interested in the things it meets on the way, conditions that accelerate and retard its movement with respect to their bearing on the end; that it acts and feels toward them according to the hindering or helping function it attributes to them; and that the final coming to rest is related to all that went before as the culmination of a continuous movement. Then the stone would have an experience, and one with esthetic quality. (AE, p. 39)

Let's change Dewey's example slightly. Suppose that the stone is a self-conscious leather ball filled with air, but it allows others to act in order to achieve its final resting place, and those others are interested in its movement. Together, the ball and other self-conscious beings (persons) make some arbitrary decisions in order to make possible intrinsically enjoyable actions (playful activities) and experiences. They decide to construct a goal, allow the ball to be advanced only by kicking, place boundaries on the space within which the ball can be advanced, the time it takes to have opportunities to kick the ball into the goal, and the number of players who will either attempt to make a goal or keep others from kicking the ball into the goal. The players, interested in such activities, would have an experience. Likewise, if we let others watch and these self-conscious beings were knowledgeable about the rules of the activity and interested in the outcome, they would also have an experience with aesthetic quality.

Why would people be captivated or fascinated by watching such activities? One reason, I believe, is the contrast they would find between the satisfying structures of an experience and the typical experiences of ordinary life. Recall Antoine's interpretation of human experience: life is merely a series of events leading nowhere. Things happened to him, but with no apparent meaning that related these events to one another. Life can be like that, as we have said. Again, to use Dewey's language, it is to see life as an aimless succession of events. We drift, towards nothing or nowhere in particular. The drift of aimlessness leads to boredom. At the other extreme, parts of our life may be so ruled by a kind of order or structure that each moment seems to succeed the previous one in mechanical determination. Here the paradigm example would be factory work, in which some task is repeated over and over, activities strictly determined by time, tightly governed rules, and technical expertise. Aesthetic interest, constituted by acute attentiveness, anticipation, tension, and teleologically directed captivation, is contrasted with the boredom of aesthetic looseness and the oppressiveness of aesthetic constriction. Moments of experience are aesthetically interesting when integration is mediated by novelty; unity in development is colored by uncertainty; initiations are fulfilled by consummating moments, not mere endings. Dewey is right to insist that it is incorrect to distinguish sharply between aesthetic experience associated with art proper and supposedly ordinary "non-aesthetic" experience, simply because so much of our experience consists of one of these two poles: loose succession with no internal development and consummation or mechanical succession:

> There exists so much of one and the other of these two kinds of experience that unconsciously they come to be taken as norms of all experience. Then, when the esthetic appears, it so sharply contrasts with the picture that has been formed of experience, that it is impossible to combine its special qualities with the features of the picture and the esthetic is given an outside place and status. The account that has been given of experience as dominantly intellectual and practical is intended to show that there is no such contrast involved in having an experience; that, on the contrary, no experience of whatever sort is a unity unless it has aesthetic quality. (AE, p. 40)

If Dewey is correct, experiences of sport and in sport, like the experiences associated with reading books, listening to music, going to movies, etc., can be seen as attempts to replace aesthetically impoverished ordinary experiences with experiences that have aesthetic quality. Of course there are differences, but it is the Deweyan similarities that I want to stress. These similarities, it seems to me, offer a plausible explanation of at least part of the attraction of sport.

Let me end this section with some brief related remarks that confirm the association I have suggested. Monroe Beardsley's well known notion of aesthetic value depends heavily on Dewey's description of aesthetic experience.[6] Beardsley says that, among other things, aesthetic experiences are intense, unified (they "hang together"), and internally complete, in the sense that they are differentiated from the "general stream of experience." All of this is quite familiar to us after having looked carefully at Dewey's account. Beardsley adds that the characteristics of aesthetic experience are found in other experiences but that they are combined differently. He even mentions playing games in which we enjoy activities having "no practical purpose." But, according to Beardsley,"it seems not necessarily to be an experience of a high degree of unity. Watching a baseball or football game is also generally lacking in a dominant pattern and consummation, though sometimes it has these characteristics to a high degree and is an aesthetic experience."[7] Beardsley's comments confirm the notion that sport offers aesthetic possibilities. However, these possibilities may be more available to those whose interests in and knowledge of the sport are keen, just as the aesthetic possibilities of a work of art are more available to the sensitive and knowledgeable consumer of art.[8]

. . . . .

As we have seen, one way to respond to Antoine's phenomenology is to think about the concept of the aesthetic in Deweyan terms. But recall that Antoine specifically uses the language of narrative and story. As storytellers we are condemned to falsify our experience. Sartre's narrator wanted the moments of his life to be ordered, like a story, but that would merely be a life remembered, not lived. However, the aesthetic structure of an experience is not merely imposed. There are "real beginnings," in sport and elsewhere in life. What Dewey calls the aesthetic structure of a developed and integrated experience, rounded out and differentiated in the general stream of experience, could also be described as a narrative. As Dewey has said, life consists of histories, with different plots, rhythms of development, distinctive "emotional" qualities, and consummating moments. Life consists of stories we live, not simply artificially reconstruct in reflection.

Alasdair MacIntyre has stressed the role of narrative in life, in the context of a criticism of the modern conception of a self who is unable to be the bearer of the traditional virtues.[9] For our purposes, a narrative conception of selfhood will be another significant ground for the attractiveness of sport. Briefly, MacIntyre criticizes modernist conceptions of life that either attempt to explain human action atomistically or radically separate the individual from the social roles he inhabits. He shows that action can be adequately explained only by referring to an agent's intentions, and that these intentions are themselves embedded in "settings" that have histories. (Settings may be practices, institutions, or other situations.) To explain what a person is doing is to refer to narratives within which individuals live and act. An act of gardening may be a way of sustaining the family, helping a marriage, or attaining a more healthful personal life. "Narrative history of a certain kind turns out to be the basic and essential

genre for the characterization of human actions."[10] Narrative interpretation makes action intelligible by placing it in a historical context.

MacIntyre insists that even such a common and familiar type of situation as a conversation must be understood in terms of narrative. Conversations "have beginnings, middles, and endings just as do literary works. They embody reversals and recognitions; they move towards and away from climaxes."[11] Likewise, human transactions in general have a narrative structure: "battles, chess games, courtships, philosophy seminars, families at a dinner table, businessmen negotiating contracts."[12] He concludes that "both conversations in particular then and human actions in general are enacted narratives."[13] He is quite clear that Antoine's view of life is simply a false picture typical of modernity:

> It is now becoming clear that we render the actions of others intelligible in this way because action itself has a basically historical character. It is because we all live out narratives in our lives and because we understand our own lives in terms of narratives that we live out that the form of narrative is appropriate for understanding the actions of others. Stories are lived before they are told—except in the case of fiction.[14]

What do we make of MacIntyre's narrative conception of selfhood in relation to the possibilities associated with sport? Perhaps MacIntyre is right that narrative is the essential way we make sense of life. Of course, there is a complex relationship among the various narratives we live as individuals. MacIntyre speaks of narratives being "embedded" in one another. A person may be a mother, wife, friend, teacher, scholar, poet, and amateur chef, all embedded in one life. But whether it's merely an aberration of modernity or an inevitable part of any human life, individuals often appear to lose the sense that important parts of their life or life in general have any narrative structure. Marriages fail and important friendships fade. Flowering careers are displaced by unemployment, and health is replaced by disease and suffering. Families disintegrate and communities or small groups are wrecked by dissension. It is often quite difficult to see where all of this, or even discrete parts of it, could be going. MacIntyre's account of the narrative structure of human life is tainted by nostalgia, as if fragmentation is merely an accidental historical condition.

Richard Lischer has expressed a halting pessimism in the face of attempts to make story pervasive in life. In his useful article, "The Limits of Story,"[15] he expresses a middle way between MacIntyre's optimism and Antoine's deep and abiding pessimism that narratives falsify our life. Arguing against theologians and preachers who have embraced the primacy of story, Lischer believes that parts of our life are indeed shapeless and storyless, that "story falsifies those vast and deep non-narrative domains of human life."[16] Narratives impose a structure on a disordered life, and "may provide the sense of order so desperately needed or they may appear transparently palliative to those whose experience has resisted the broom that sweeps in one direction."[17]

We may experience our life or parts of our lives as essentially storyless. And when we do, it is natural to seek out new stories, or return to areas of experience which offer the meaningful possibilities of story. I can think of no area in modern life that offers more possibilities for story-like experiences than sports. Certainly, viewing sports and being a "real fan" may appear to be more "transparently palliative" than reading our scriptures or praying to our gods. Nonetheless, it seems to me that the ways in which people identify with the narratives associated with sports are important strategies for finding a sense of meaning and concern in an otherwise anarchical life. I don't want to appear to be saying that the only role that sports play in the life of individuals is therapeutic, keeping the wolf of despair at bay. For the psychologically fit as well as the despairing, sport is there. But if our gods are dead, our politics shallow, our cultural life thin, our work alienated, and our relation to the world overly technological, we may need the atmosphere of play and narrative more than ever. (The overcommercialization of sport may be cause for despair as well.)

Lischer offers apt comments on the storyless places in our lives:

> They exist wherever episodic complications have stagnated and cease to develop with any organic connection toward new episodes and new complications. Life continues as a series of unrelated episodes, as in a collection of short stories by many authors, or it proceeds by a series of "slices" or scenes, as in a cabaret show or picture gallery. An objective thread of identity may persist, but to those caught in this kind of life, the "I" known long ago in Act One has become a stranger. Indeed, if one is to make sense of such a life, it will not be by casting it into acts and rationalizing its plot but by rediscovering the continuity of identity throughout the confusion of broken plots, botched lines, and embarrassing non-sequiturs.[18]

Think about these comments in relation to the games we played in childhood and the games we still care about as adults. One might consider the deep love so many have for baseball. (I use baseball only as an apt example. There may be nothing particularly "special" about our national pastime as a source of certain kinds of story-like experiences.) For many who played baseball as children, it meant really caring about something, about hopes and dreams, special moments, enduring relationships, magical situations, and joy. It also meant having heroes, collecting baseball cards, listening to and watching games, sometimes heated conversations, and yes—fathers playing catch with their sons. So one grows up and gets on with life. Winter comes to a close, days get longer, and spring rolls around. It's baseball season again! At least there may seem to be one thing in life that makes sense in its captivating and

alluring qualities. The unity of a life may reappear as spring training begins. If "episodic complications have stagnated" in one's life, and have ceased "to develop with any organic connection toward new episodes and new complications," there are still available the narrative experiences of sport. To watch a baseball game is to move from ordinary life to a realm of experience in which episodic complications are alive with possibilities, organically developing in a teleologically directed movement. But a game may be "embedded" (MacIntyre's term) in a series, and a series may be embedded in an entire season. If we think about major league baseball, the narrative possibilities that we may identify with and vicariously experience are practically endless. For each game, each inning, even every pitch and at bat, are embedded in a complex historical setting. Players, coaches, teams, and leagues have careers, statistical relationships abound, and strategic maneuvers are omni-present. To love baseball is to immerse oneself in a world of transparent meanings, efficacious actions, and admirable excellences. It is to identify with the story of a game, a team, a career, and even one's own life. If there is a need for story in our lives, as there was for Antoine, one may momentarily keep the wolf at bay by being a fan. And the distance between the transparently palliative experiences of the fan and "real life" may be closed by sustaining an internal relationship to sport by playing or coaching.[19]

Recall that Antoine's diary ends on a somewhat hopeful note. He says he may write a book, create a story "which would not exist, which would be above existence." His ontology of art is the basis for an act of transcendence, beyond the contingency of the ordinary, as if participation in the structure of a story would give some hope of salvation. Although I've insisted that ordinary experience has aesthetic and narrative possibilities, the experience of sport is not quite ordinary. If Antoine can be saved by or through art, "above existence," the story-like experiences of sport are also insulated, in some sense, from real life, and that is why sport is such a fecund arena for these possibilities. This is the point at which sport as aesthetic and sport as narrative naturally reconnect with sport as play. Recall Huizinga's famous account of play.[20] Play is not ordinary or real life; it is a free activity standing outside of ordinary life, in which a distinctive order reigns. Kenneth Schmitz has also emphasized the notion of play as "suspension of the ordinary," the world of play as a "distinctive order," and sport as a rule-governed activity grounded in the spirit of play.[21] We are now in a position to see the peculiar order of the world of play in aesthetic and narrative terms. Since persons find aesthetic quality intrinsically satisfying and since persons need stories in order to experience life as having some shape, pattern, or end, it is natural that so many people would be drawn to sport—not merely because of a thirst for victory, a desire to make the other submit, or a need to be excellent. Lovers of sport need not be apologetic about their appreciation of the aesthetic nor their need for story in life.

NOTES

[1] Drew Hyland, *Philosophy of Sport* (New York: Paragon House, 1990), p. 125.

[2] See the following articles by Randolph Feezell: "Sport: Pursuit of Bodily Excellence or Play? An Examination of Paul Weiss's Account of Sport," *The Modern Schoolman* 58 (May, 1981): 257-70; "Play, Freedom, and Sport," *Philosophy Today* 25 (Summer, 1981): p. 166-75; "Play and the Absurd," *Philosophy Today* 28 (Winter, 1984): 319-28; "Sportsmanship," *Journal of the Philosophy of Sport* 13 (1986): 1-13; "On the Wrongness of Cheating and Why Cheaters Can't Play the Game," *Journal of the Philosophy of Sport* 15 (1988): 57-68; "Sport, Character, and Virtue," *Philosophy Today* 33 (Fall, 1989): 204-20.

[3] Jean-Paul Sartre, *Nausea,* trans. Lloyd Alexander (New York: New Directions, 1964). I will abbreviate the title and refer to it as N. Also, I will cite all specific references to the novel in the body of the paper.

[4] John Dewey, *Art as Experience* (New York: Capricorn Books, 1958). I will abbreviate the title and refer to it as AE. Also, I will cite all specific references to Dewey's text in the body of the paper. All quotations will come from Chapter 3, "Having an Experience."

[5] As a matter of fact, a recent book has been written describing and analyzing only two games. See Keith Hernandez and Mike Bryan, *Pure Baseball: Pitch by Pitch for the Advanced Fan* (New York, Harper Collins, 1994).

[6] Monroe Beardsley, *Aesthetics: Problems in the Philosophy of Criticism* (Indianapolis: Hackett Publishing Co., 1981), pp. 524-56.

[7] *Ibid.*, p. 530.

[8] Also see Joseph Kupfer, *Experience as Art: Aesthetics in Everyday Life* (Albany: State University of New York Press, 1983), for a more lengthy treatment of the aesthetic possibilities in ordinary life. Kupfer has also been influenced by Dewey. Chapter 5, "Sport—The Body Electric," is especially interesting.

[9] Alasdair MacIntyre, *After Virtue* (Notre Dame, Indiana: Notre Dame University Press, 1984).

[10] *Ibid.*, p. 208.

[11] *Ibid.*, p. 211.

[12] *Ibid.*

[13] *Ibid.*

[14] *Ibid.*, p. 212.

[15] Richard Lischer, "The Limits of Story," *Interpretation* 38 (January, 1984): 26-38.

[16] *Ibid.*, p. 30.

[17] *Ibid.*

[18] *Ibid.*, p. 31.

[19] See A. Bartlett Giamatti, *Take Time for Paradise: Americans and Their Games* (New York: Summit Books, 1989), especially Chapter 3, "Baseball as Narrative," for a loving reflection related to these comments.

[20] Johan Huizinga, *Homo Ludens: A Study of the Play Element in Culture* (Boston, Beacon Press, 1955), especially Chapter 1, "Nature and Significance of Play as a Cultural Phenomenon."

[21] Kenneth Schmitz, "Sport and Play: Suspension of the Ordinary," in Morgan and Meier, eds., *Philosophic Inquiry in Sport* (Champaign, Illinois: Human Kinetics, 1988), pp. 29-38.

P. Eddy Wilson (essay date 1995)

SOURCE: "Emerson and Dewey on Natural Piety," in *The Journal of Religion,* Vol. 75, No. 3, July, 1995, pp. 329-46.

[*In the following excerpt, Wilson examines the differences and similarities between the naturalism espoused by Dewey and Ralph Waldo Emerson.*]

Today many find themselves to be alienated from a religion with a strong textual tradition and in rebellion against the idea of a transcendent deity. In the nineteenth century, Friedrich Nietzsche said, "it is in one particular interpretation [of distress], the Christian moral one, that nihilism is rooted."[1] Rather than simply abandoning religion, some, convinced by Nietzsche's analysis, have sought to combat nihilism by turning to other religious resources. Two American philosophers who have attempted to demonstrate that modern man may yet have a significant religious experience in relation to nature are Ralph Waldo Emerson and John Dewey. Both Emerson and Dewey described forms of naturalism wherein humanity might pursue the ideal ends of their lives in a structured, valuable pattern of practical activity as they interact with nature. It was Dewey who made use of the term "natural piety," but both urged mankind to practice a form of natural piety.[2]

In this essay, I want to explore the ways that natural piety would be expressed if one adopted the naturalism of Emerson or Dewey. Of course, Emerson was a transcendentalist, Dewey was an instrumentalist. At first glance it may appear that there is only a verbal dispute between Emerson and Dewey regarding the practice of naturalism. The practical reasoning required by both for the practice of natural piety initially appears to be the same. A closer comparison, however, may reveal that the natural piety described by each is fundamentally different. Such a comparison may also demonstrate a methodology for formulating a meaningful response to nihilism. I shall begin with a brief sketch of the naturalism of each author.

I. EMERSON'S VIEW OF NATURE AND NATURAL PIETY

Emerson's view of natural piety emerges from his view of nature. Emerson, who was influenced by Zoroastrianism and Hindu thought, rejected supernaturalism and abandoned Unitarianism in favor of Transcendentalism. He declared his New England transcendentalism to be a form of idealism. In his address to the Masonic Temple in Boston in 1841, "The Transcendentalist," Emerson said, "What is popularly called Transcendentalism among us, is Idealism; Idealism as it appears in 1842. . . . Mind is the only reality, of which men and all other natures are better or worse reflectors."[3] Emerson also believed in a form of intuitionism whereby man could become aware of his primordial relation to nature. In his seminal work, *Nature,* he wrote,

> The world proceeds from the same spirit as the body of man. It is a remoter and inferior incarnation of God, a projection of God in the unconscious. But it differs from the body in one important respect. It is not like that, now subjected to the human will. Its serene order is inviolable by us. It is therefore, to us, the present expositor of the divine mind. It is a fixed point whereby we may measure our departure. As we degenerate, the contrast between us and our house is more evident. We are as much strangers in nature, as we are aliens from God.[4]

Thus, in Emerson's monistic, idealistic view of nature, individuals find themselves to be in direct communion with nature. In this view, one may consciously abet or suppress one's communion with nature. If one does consciously abet that relationship, one may experience the influx of the divine as a reward for self-reliance. Emerson said, "Revelation is the disclosure of the soul."[5] Such a disclosure is described as "an influx of the Divine mind into our mind."[6]

Emerson's emphasis on self-reliance had a popular appeal among early nineteenth-century North American culture because of the value it attached to independence and its reliance upon natural resources. Yet, Emersonian self-reliance would not produce ungrateful, self-made individuals. Humanity's indebtedness to nature was reaffirmed in Emerson's description of self-reliance, since one's self-reliance was the occasion for the conscious influx of the Divine mind. In his essay "Experience," Emerson said, "Into every intelligence there is a door which is never closed, through which the creator passes."[7]

I have used the term "natural piety" in connection with Emerson to designate an individual's devotion to nature, that is, one's religious response to nature. For Emerson, this religious response to nature is an outgrowth of one's intuitive grasp of his or her relation to nature. It is not a forced or falsified relationship to nature. In addition, it refers to a state of being in which an individual might become reflectively aware of his or her relation to nature. Let us explore this idea at greater length.

Individuals, who experience themselves as conscious beings, may find themselves alienated from nature. This was a form of insanity, according to Emerson, who said, "The tradesman, the attorney comes out of the din and craft of the street, and sees the sky and the woods, and is a man again."[8] The renewal that comes to one who regains a sense of his or her primordial relation to nature in this instance is not the result of some metaphysical transformation. Through a change of one's own conscious perspective one becomes aware of one's metaphysical dependence upon nature. Nature, to which humanity is indebted, stands ever ready to be appreciated. Emerson said, "The simplest person who in his integrity worships God, becomes God; yet for ever and ever the influx of this better and universal self is new and unsearchable."[9]

The worshiper becomes aware of his or her relation to nature in a state of heightened consciousness. So, does the worshiper arrive at this state of heightened consciousness by artificial inducements? Emerson stressed that this heightened consciousness is not something that the worshiper can force upon himself or herself. Emerson said, "never can any advantage be taken of nature by a trick. The spirit of the world, the great calm presence of the Creator, comes not forth to the sorceries of opium or of wine. The sublime vision comes to the pure and simple soul in a clean and chaste body."[10]

Only by quietly attuning oneself to nature can an individual enhance his or her relation to nature. One must become insensitive to the hurly-burly lifestyle of the masses so that the voice of nature can be heard. Proximity to natural surroundings may become the occasion for this enhanced awareness of nature, but it is not the cause of that enhanced awareness. Through such simple, natural efforts, one may become aware of a shift of perspective regarding the world. One moves out of a strictly egoistic view to a transcendental view. In a much-cited passage, Emerson said: "In the woods I return to reason and faith. . . . Standing on the bare ground,—my head bathed by the blithe air, and uplifted into infinite space,—all mean egotism vanishes. I become a transparent eye-ball. I am nothing. I see all. The currents of the Universal Being circulate through me; I am part or particle of God."[11]

In Emerson's view, if individuals were to change their perspective regarding their metaphysical relationship to nature, then a change of perspective would manifest itself in their practical expressions of natural piety. For that reason, intuitionism plays a key role in Emerson's view of humanity's relation to nature. As one turns away from the crowd and the world toward nature, the Oversoul may reveal itself to the listener.

What happens as a result of this experience of worship? First, the worshiper becomes aware of a qualitatively superior relation to nature. Emerson said, "The soul gives itself, alone, original and pure, to the Lonely, Original and Pure, who, on that condition, gladly inhabits, leads and speaks through it."[12] So the individual whose life was once plagued by a multitude of competing ends and motivations finds a new sense of integrated purpose and existence. "He will weave no longer a spotted life of shreds and patches, but he will live with a divine unity. He will cease from what is base and frivolous in life and be content with all places and with any service he can render."[13]

Many of the competing and mutually exclusive finite ends that would otherwise distract an individual would come to be abandoned or reintegrated in a positive way in the life of one who displayed natural piety. Certainly there would be a greater sense of self-confidence in the person displaying natural piety, since the person would learn not to belittle his or her own inner glimmer of truth. Furthermore, a person displaying natural piety might be identifiable as a nonconformist on the strength of his or her self-reliance. As Emerson wrote, "Whoso would be a man, must be a nonconformist. Nothing is at last sacred but the integrity of your own mind. Absolve you to yourself. And you shall have the suffrage of the world."[14]

Second, adherents to natural piety might also display a different relation to society. On the one hand, they would not enter society as mere conformists. On the other hand, as they entered into social relations, there would be a greater respect for an other because of the recognition of the divine element in the other. Emerson said, "Jove nods to Jove from behind each of us."[15] Encountering an other as an embodiment of the divine spirit was certain to influence the social relation that those individuals shared. If the other was not in touch with the divine element in his or her own life, that would limit the possible exchange between the individuals. As Emerson put it, "Everywhere I am hindered of meeting god in my brother, because he has shut his own temple doors and recites fables merely of his brother, or his brother's brother's God."[16] Emerson's penetrating insight into human relations led him to condemn slavery openly. He realized that it was a petty-spirited individual who would campaign for world relief for some ethnic group while tolerating the enslavement and victimization of a fellow human within that individual's own community.

Third, if a person were to display natural piety, this would be evident in his or her relation to the surrounding world. That individual would discover that he or she was working in harmony with nature. Likewise, that individual would find that nature was meant to be used for his or her purposes, providing that those were the purposes of nature itself. Emerson realized that much of what passed for prayer within orthodox religious circles was cheap begging. His own view of prayer offers an alternative to that type of practice, while demonstrating how someone displaying natural piety works in cooperation with the world spirit for good:

Prayer that craves a particular commodity, anything less than all good, is vicious. Prayer is the contemplation of the facts of life from the highest point of view. It is the soliloquy of a beholding and jubilant soul. It is the spirit of God pronouncing his works good. But prayer as a means to effect a private end is meanness and theft. It supposes dualism and not unity in nature and consciousness. As soon as the man is at one with God, he will not beg. He will then see prayer in all action. The prayer of the farmer kneeling in his field to weed it, the prayer of the rower kneeling with the stroke of his oar, are true prayers heard throughout nature, though for cheap ends.[17]

Emerson might be identified as a pantheist.[18] The Oversoul or the divine mind is identifiable in all the world. In the case of humanity, the Oversoul is present to inspire the individual, if he or she consciously attended to its prompting. "Idealism sees the world in God. It beholds the whole circle of persons and things, of actions and events, of country and religion, not as painfully accumulated, atom after atom, act after act, in an aged creeping Past, but as one vast picture which God paints on the instant eternity, for the contemplation of the soul. Therefore the soul holds itself off from a too trivial and microscopic study of the universal tablet."[19] Natural piety is not only a state of mind but also a state of being that might manifest itself in action as an individual behaved in organic harmony with the leading of nature. The person who is moved to act upon the basis of natural piety is an individualist rather than a conformist.[20]

II. DEWEY'S VIEW OF NATURE AND NATURAL PIETY

Having examined Emerson's view of nature and natural piety, we are in a better position to understand Dewey's views. Dewey, an instrumentalist, was a firm critic of traditional religion and was committed to an instrumentally valuable form of religiousness that he called natural piety. Most of the observations that I shall make here about Dewey's view of nature and natural piety are drawn from a work he offered in his mature years, *A Common Faith*.

Throughout the writings of Dewey, one may find an opposition to dualisms, especially the dualisms of classical supernaturalism. Dewey's work *A Common Faith* is an attempt to show that what is genuinely religious can be emancipated when it is freed of the encumbrances of supernaturalism.[21] As we shall see, for Dewey this also meant that the emancipation of the genuinely religious lay in its being freed of metaphysical commitments.

Consider Dewey's comments about mystical experience. Dewey believed that an individual who was committed to supernaturalism had a hermeneutical mind-set that would exploit religious experience for self-validation. Dewey did not deny that one could have a mystical experience, but his criticism was directed against the circular reasoning used to analyze the experience. He wrote, "This dualism as it operates in contemporary interpretation of mystic experience in order to validate certain beliefs is but a reinstatement of the old dualism between the natural and the supernatural, in terms better adapted to the cultural conditions of the present time."[22] Dewey thought that a belief in supernaturalism biased our understanding of experience and interfered with our pursuit of ideal ends. "In the degree in which we cease to depend upon belief in the supernatural, selection is enlightened and choice can be made in behalf of ideals whose inherent relations to conditions and consequences are understood. Were the naturalistic foundations and bearings of religion grasped, the religious element in life would emerge from the throes of the crisis of religion."[23]

Dewey's reactionary comments against supernaturalism are insufficient to determine whether Dewey's naturalism was either pantheistic or atheistic. However, Dewey did not want to have his view of religious experience identified as an atheistic view, because of the pragmatic consequences of that view. Dewey thought that, if the universe were regarded atheistically, it would foster the impression that man's environment is indifferent or hostile to his presence.[24] Dewey said, "A religious attitude, however, needs the sense of a connection of man, in the way of both dependence and support, with the enveloping world that the imagination feels is a universe."[25] So, Dewey wanted humanity to view the universe as being pragmatically cooperative with humanistic projects, but he did not want to suggest that there was some personal or metaphysical basis for nature's congeniality toward or cooperativeness with humanistic projects.

We may use the term "theistic naturalism" to describe Dewey's viewpoint only if we give a proper account of his use of the term "God." Dewey said, "It is the *active* relation between ideal and actual to which I would give the name 'God.'"[26] He uses the term in a pragmatic sense rather than a strictly metaphysical sense. For instance, "The idea [of God] is, as I have said, one of ideal possibilities unified through imaginative realization and projection. But this idea of God, or of the divine, is also connected with all the natural forces and conditions—including man and human association—that promote the growth of the ideal and that further its realization."[27]

This usage is consistent with Dewey's instrumentalism, but has generated considerable confusion. Part of the confusion seems to have arisen when Dewey's readers used metaphysical categories to analyze his instrumentalism. Corliss Lamont attempted to alleviate some of this confusion regarding Dewey's metaphysical commitments by corresponding with Dewey. The letters exchanged by Dewey and Lamont for several weeks led Lamont to the following conclusion: "John Dewey was not, then, in any sense a theist, but an uncompromising naturalist or humanist thinker who saw the value of a shared religious faith free from outworn supernaturalism and institutional fanaticism."[28]

If one is to determine, on the basis of Dewey's usage, the meaning that he attaches to the term "nature," then one needs to appreciate two distinct ways that the term may be used. On the one hand, one may make an undifferentiated use of the term, in which case one does not set nature apart as a conglomerate per se but refers to it as an aggregate. The parts are not taken to be distinguishable from the whole. In a similar vein, one may speak of beings while refraining from speech about Being per se. On the other hand, the term "nature" may also be used to pick out the whole, as such, as opposed to the parts. Something like this happens when ontologists speak of Being per se and juxtapose this term with beings in particular. What usage of the term "nature" do we find in Dewey's writings?

In light of Dewey's special instrumental use of the term "God," I think we are better able to understand his view of nature. Dewey is found to have used the term "nature" in two different senses. Above, Emerson makes use of the term "Nature" in a differentiated sense, so that it is synonymous with God, the Divine mind, and the Oversoul. Dewey is found to have used the term in both a differentiated and a nondifferentiated sense. John Smith observed, "By 'nature' [Dewey] did *not* mean a cosmic system or order of that sort envisioned by those who adhered to the classical conception of a 'Chain of Being' wherein nature stands as something distinct from man and God . . . at the same time he actually used the classical differential sense when opposing idealists, theists and others bent on denying that the cosmic system exhausts what there is."[29]

Dewey used the term "nature" in a strictly differentiated sense in his replies to supernaturalists, but these replies were meant to be understood only dialectically. It was suggested above that Dewey's usage of the term "God" was best understood in light of his instrumentalism. It would seem inappropriate to label Dewey a naturalist in the same sense that the label is used for Emerson. Dewey's instrumentalism was opposed not only to dualisms but also to noninstrumentally valuable metaphysical dogmas such as pantheism. A nondifferentiated view of nature is consistent with Dewey's instrumentalism. One might be able to substitute the term "nature" for the term "God" in Dewey's later works, providing that one did not misunderstand the term to be used in some metaphysical or ultimate sense.

For Dewey, natural piety was a way to ennoble individuals and to ally them with the resources of the world so that they might better pursue the ideal ends of a good life, that is, a humanistically good life. Compare the views of Emerson and Dewey regarding the effects of natural piety upon individuals' relations to one another and to society. First, Dewey observed that the particular problems of humanity that the churches of his generation addressed were merely symptoms of a more fundamental problem—the disintegration of the self; and Dewey attempted to show that a holistic solution was needed for this fundamental problem facing humanity. Through the practice of natural piety, one's life became reintegrated with an ideal self, society, and nature: "The self is always directed toward something beyond itself and so its own unification depends upon the idea of the integration of the shifting scenes of the world into that imaginative totality we call the Universe."[30] Dewey's point is that, when faced with humanitarian problems, traditional religious practitioners are often standoffish. They refrain from intervening in situations where human welfare is at risk and where their input could contribute to the resolution of the situation. Dewey claimed that "dependence upon an external power is the counterpart of surrender of human endeavor."[31] Under the pretense of waiting for divine intervention, followers of traditional religions have too often deliberately refrained from intervening in dire situations.

Emerson held a similar view. He condemned the religious practice of making gratuitous prayers. Emerson held that one's best prayers were the prayers of action, acts done in pursuit of some end. Recall the following quote from Emerson: "The prayer of the farmer kneeling in his field to weed it, the prayer of the rower kneeling with the stroke of his oar, are true prayers heard throughout nature, though for cheap ends."[32] Emerson thought that one could interactively communicate with nature through one's behavior rather than by verbal communication. In so doing, one could act for the betterment of one's self.

Second, Dewey's natural piety promoted social intervention rather than supernatural intervention. He wrote, "The old-fashioned ideas of doing something to make the will of God prevail in the world, and of assuming the responsibility of doing the job ourselves, have more to be said for them, logically and practically."[33] Dewey did not simply disparage the laxness of traditional religion in resolving social problems, but he emphasized the value of religiousness for effecting the welfare of mankind. In Dewey's view, not in religion but in religiousness there is "the conviction that, if human desire and endeavor were enlisted in behalf of natural ends, conditions would be bettered."[34] In his view, the betterment of the human condition, such as the social relations of humanity, is dependent upon human rather than supernatural intervention.

Third, Emerson and Dewey held very different views on the effect of natural piety upon one's relations to the world. Earlier I discussed how, in Emerson's view, a change of perspectives would follow from reestablishing one's primordial relation with nature. In Emerson's view, that could effectively alienate those quietly attuned to nature from others who were not so attuned. In Dewey's view, no special metaphysical attunement was required, and it is likely that Dewey would have identified that element of Emerson's naturalism as "a romantic idealization of the world." Dewey summarized his view of natural piety as follows: "Natural piety is not of necessity either a fatalistic acquiescence in natural happenings or a romantic idealization of the world. It may rest upon a just sense of nature as the whole of which we are parts, while it also recognizes that we are parts that are marked by

intelligence and purpose, having the capacity to strive by their aid to bring conditions into greater consonance with what is humanly desirable."[35]

III. PRACTICAL ACTIVITY AND PRACTICAL REASONING

Above, I have attempted to compare the descriptions of natural piety by Emerson and Dewey. The way that practitioners of natural piety would express their faith may be a more pressing consideration. If one were convinced of the value of natural piety how would one implement a program of natural piety? To understand that, we must examine how one moves from faith to practice. Here I give a brief account of how one's faith may be implemented by means of one's practical reason.[36] Practical reasoning is goal-directed reasoning that has a performative dimension.

Aristotle understood practical reasoning to be a type of reasoning that issued in practical activity, that is, it was a type of reasoning that had a performative dimension. "Practical wisdom," he claimed, "must be a reasoned and true state of capacity to act with regard to human goods."[37] In addition, "understanding and practical wisdom are not the same. For practical wisdom issues commands, since its end is what ought to be done or not to be done; but understanding only judges."[38] Understanding is important for making judgments, but one does not necessarily act upon the judgments of one's understanding. In the passage just cited, Aristotle said that understanding "is about the same objects as practical wisdom." Yet, my practical reasoning gives rise to judgments about my personal behavior in a way that my understanding does not. Aristotle said, "'understanding' is applicable to the exercise of the faculty of opinion for the purpose of judging of what some one else says about matters with which practical wisdom is concerned—and judging soundly."[39] An individual acts upon the judgments of her own practical reasoning.

Consider a strikingly modern example of practical reasoning found in Aristotle: "If a man knew that light meats are digestible and wholesome, but did not know which sorts of meat are light, he would not produce health, but the man who knows that chicken is wholesome is more likely to produce health."[40] In the example, light meats are a healthy type of meat. Yet, much more must be known, if that knowledge is to benefit the conscientious consumer. The consumer must also know what meat tokens are included in this meat type. Poultry and fish could be two meat tokens that would be included in this meat type. Finally, if this knowledge is to be valuable for the individual's health, then the reference to light meat must be extensionally meaningful. To consume a healthy meat, as the example suggests, the individual must be able to identify and procure an available chicken product from the meat market.

Perhaps the best way to examine practical reasoning is to analyze further some of Aristotle's examples. On the one hand, practical reasoning was thought to issue in action.

On the other hand, practical reasoning, as Aristotle describes it, was formally similar to classical, syllogistic reasoning. It offers us a logical cross section of action that describes both the origin and end of action. If one acts intentionally, then practical reasoning can demonstrate the origin of that action. Aristotle said, "The origin of action—its efficient, not its final cause—is choice, and that of choice is desire and reasoning with a view to an end." Of course the end of action is the primitive bodily movement intended to precipitate some desirable end. Consider two examples offered by Aristotle:

PS I: I should make something good.

A house is something good.

At once I make a house.

PS II: "I have to drink," says appetite.

"Here's a drink," says sense perception.

At once he drinks.[41]

These examples demonstrate not only the logical progression in practical reasoning, but also the problems associated with it. First, consider how they exemplify practical reasoning. The conclusion of the syllogism is a performative statement reached by a process of reasoning along two lines. One premise is a prescriptive statement of what is desirable.[42] The other premise states the means for attaining that desirable end. Of course, the conclusion brings the means and the end together in the form of a plan of action. Douglas Walton said, "Aristotle postulates practical reasoning as a linkage between appetite and sense perception."[43]

Second, these examples demonstrate some of the problems associated with practical reasoning. Aristotle wrote, "No one deliberates about things that are invariable, nor about things that it is impossible for him to do."[44] It seems clear that the efficient cause of choice is both desire and reasoning with a view to an end. G. E. M. Anscombe said, "Aristotle would seem to have held that every action done by a rational agent was capable of having its grounds set forth up to a premise containing a desirability characterisation."[45] Such declarative statements of what is desirable, though, prove to be notoriously suspicious. Stating the means for practical reasoning within the intentional plan is doubly problematic. R. M. Hare has argued that we must carefully distinguish between necessary and sufficient conditions for the satisfaction of a practical syllogism.[46] For instance, a house may be a good thing, but it can be only a sufficient condition for the satisfaction of the premise that a man must do something good. Furthermore, if the practical syllogism does link sense perception to appetite, then there is an implicit assumption that the judgments of sense perception are warranted. If one were to take action on the basis of a statement of sense perception like "this is water," whether the statement was warranted or unwarranted would be of utmost importance.

So, the background beliefs of an actor would play a major role in determining whether that actor was warranted in employing the available means to execute his or her intentional plan.

Practical reasoning is not inevitably doomed to failure. We do routinely engage in practical reasoning, and we do experience a high success rate. The fact that almost all of my audience are not now thirsty is ostensible proof that we are successful at practical reasoning. Nevertheless, I suspect that the practical reasoning required for an agent to perform an act of natural piety is often beset with these problems.

The examples drawn from Aristotle have been used to demonstrate the structure and logical progression employed in practical reasoning. That may now be applied to the naturalism of Emerson and Dewey. I would like to suggest that an actor who displays natural piety has engaged in some form of practical reasoning. I would suggest that the actor has reasoned along the following lines:

PS III: I ought to display natural piety, i.e., to display reverence toward nature.

This is nature.

Therefore, I should display reverence toward this.

Here one should not be misled to believe that this syllogism standardizes expressions of natural piety. Not everyone who displays natural piety will perform the same act tokens, just as not everyone who sets out to do a good thing will construct a house. Suppose that someone said, "I should engage a contract with Sawz Lumber Company to erect a number 34 Williamsburg house." This is a token of a type of behavior, house building behavior. To build a house, one does not merely perform a basic act but engages in an elaborate, intentional plan.[47] Likewise, a practitioner of natural piety may adopt an elaborate intentional plan that will make use of act tokens different from those used by another practitioner of natural piety.

IV. COMPARING SOME ENTAILMENTS OF APPLIED NATURAL PIETY

It may appear as if the practical reasoning of a person inspired by Emerson to practice natural piety is indistinguishable from that of a person inspired by Dewey. However, there is a deep-seated difference between the natural piety inspired by Emerson and that inspired by Dewey. To explore this point I shall consider again the three areas where the practice of natural piety manifests itself—in one's self-awareness, in one's social relations, and in one's relations to the environment.

For Emerson and Dewey, the practice of natural piety entails the reintegration of the self. Emerson suggested that we abandon frivolous and mean pursuits when we practice natural piety. Dewey suggested that the otherwise competitive, finite goals that we would pursue are subordinated to a primary, integrating goal—an ideal, imaginary self. Both authors suggest that the person who does not practice some form of natural piety may experience the disintegration of the self. In other words, apart from an expression of natural piety, man may experience himself as someone going in all directions at the same time. Intentional plans formulated for the sake of expressing one's natural piety may counteract the disintegration of the self. From this, one might conclude the following: a necessary condition for all types of natural piety would be the adoption of a self-integrating intentional plan.

The ideal self envisioned by Dewey as an entailment of natural piety could not serve as a substitute for the ideal self envisioned by Emerson. For Dewey, an ideal self is an ideal possibility unified through the imagination. Thus, "God" could influence the formulation of an ideal self, but that would be only an imaginative influence devoid of metaphysical implications. Dewey said, "Suppose for the moment that the word 'God' means the ideal ends that at a given time and place one acknowledges as having authority over his volition and emotion, the values to which one is supremely devoted, as far as these ends, through imagination, take on unity."[48] In contrast, Emerson suggested that one obtained a vision of the ideal self under divine inspiration. The metaphysical indebtedness is clear. Emerson said, "within man is the soul of the whole; the wise silence; the universal beauty, to which every part and particle is equally related; the eternal One."[49] Given the metaphysical indebtedness of humanity to the Oversoul it is not surprising that such pursuits must be subordinated to the ultimate will of nature. Emerson said, "nature has a higher end, in the production of new individuals, than security, namely ascension, or the passage of the soul into higher forms."[50] While Emerson and Dewey both envisioned the reintegration of the self as an entailment of natural piety, their understanding of the nature and emergence of an ideal self differed vastly.

For both Emerson and Dewey, another entailment of natural piety is that one's social relations are enhanced by a sense of dignity, although natural piety does not necessarily drive humanity toward social existence with fellow humans. For Emerson there was a heightened sense of dignity because the practitioner of natural piety recognized the same divine spirit to be in all creatures. Emerson said, "Jove nods to Jove from behind each of us."[51] Yet, Emerson attached a negative value to some forms of social existence with fellow humans. Often social existence amounted to nothing more than conformity and herd existence. Emerson stressed that individuals should be related to nature even at the expense of social company. For Dewey individuals carried a heightened sense of dignity to social existence because of their natural piety. Their natural piety liberated individuals from a dependence on otherworldly resources. Thus, individuals developed a newfound sense of dependence upon one another for the achievement of their ideal ends. Rather than driving an individual away from social existence, the natural piety of Dewey turned individuals back to social existence with a newfound zeal for cooperation.

By comparison, Emerson's naturalism might appear to be antisocial, but that would be a misreading of Emerson. According to Emerson the social company that was expendable was infected with insanity, that is, it was mere herd existence that had forsaken its natural heritage. Emerson was quite willing to encourage social relations, provided that the individuals who entered into these relations could reciprocate the spirit of naturalism that he was promoting. While he might have been willing to tolerate other social relations, he found them less than edifying in those instances where the other individual had forsaken or left uncultivated his or her primordial relation to nature.

Perhaps the most evident difference between the natural piety of Emerson and that of Dewey arises in connection with the relation of the individual to the environment. To act reverentially toward nature, one must successfully make the judgment "this is nature." One of two different background beliefs about nature could be held by the practitioner of natural piety. In Emerson's account, nature was described in a differentiated, pantheistic sense; but Dewey's used a nondifferentiated sense of nature. Both recognized the instrumental value of nature, and both urged individuals to make full use of the potential of nature rather than appealing to some otherworldly force. Emerson said, "Nature is thoroughly mediate. It is made to serve. It receives the dominion of man as meekly as the ass on which the Savior rode."[52] Yet, we should not overlook the fact that, in Emerson's naturalism, Nature itself had ultimate ends that man was meant to serve. Emerson said that "prayer as a means to effect a private end is meanness and theft. It supposes dualism and not unity in nature and consciousness. As soon as the man is at one with God, he will not beg."[53] Dewey could offer his approval of the turn toward nature and away from supernaturalism, but Dewey regarded nature as something instrumentally valuable only. Since the instrumental value of nature was grounded on whatever proved to be instrumentally valuable to humanity, this type of natural piety could justify the displacement of not only ultimate purposes like those envisioned by Emerson but also the purposes of coexistent species. So, the natural piety of Dewey might lead to the exploitation of nature.

It may be enlightening to consider how individuals persuaded by either Emerson or Dewey would react to a current situation, where man's action could place nature at risk. In its July 1994 report to stockholders, one California-based oil and gas company, Unocal, explained its projected expansion program in Southeast Asia.[54] Roger Beach, the CEO of the company, emphasized that the company would endeavor both to have a positive impact on local people and to take environmental responsibilities seriously. The expansion program outlined in the report proposes that a natural gas pipeline running through Myanmar to Thailand be installed. The pipeline would cross some rain forest areas. To find out how to minimize environmental damage, the company consulted both a research scientist specializing in rain forests and a tropical botanist. The current plan is to make a minimal clearing for the pipeline and to provide reforestation wherever it is needed. The same research scientist who reviewed the plan said, "there appears to be a way of designing and routing the line to maintain the integrity of the forests."[55] While the expansion program will benefit humankind in terms of providing jobs and available energy resources, the proposed plan is also environmentally sensitive in that it promises to minimize the pipeline's environmental impact. The CEO's report was written in response to shareholders who had expressed a concern about humanity's moral obligation to be environmentally sensitive.

One who was persuaded by Emerson to practice natural piety could easily understand the obligation to develop an environmentally sensitive expansion program in this situation. One who was persuaded by Dewey to practice natural piety would not experience the same sense of obligation to act in an environmentally sensitive way. The latter person might reason that, if a plan of action were not more instrumentally valuable for humanitarian ends, it would not be obligatory. In other words, in Dewey's view there is no justification for an obligation *ab extra* to be environmentally conscientious, whereas in Emerson's view there is. In Dewey's view, environmental conscientiousness would be justified only if it proved to be more instrumentally valuable for humanitarian ends.

V. CONCLUSION

Both Ralph Waldo Emerson and John Dewey included within their naturalism descriptions of natural piety. The person who reflectively reveres nature and who manifests that reverence for nature in practical activity is a practitioner of natural piety. Yet, Emerson and Dewey demonstrated that there may be two vastly different forms of natural piety. Practitioners of both types of natural piety engage in a similar process of practical reasoning, but the practical activity that results differs widely; therefore, through this comparison one finds an apparently verbal dispute that is a genuine dispute. At the heart of the genuine dispute are the different attitudes of Emerson and Dewey toward religion. Emerson's description of natural piety is religious, and the reverence for nature it inspires is metaphysically grounded. Dewey's description of natural piety makes use of an instrumental view of religiousness, and the reverence for nature it inspires is subject to instrumental criteria.

In light of the fact that man resorts to natural piety to combat nihilism, the significance of the latter observation should not be underestimated. Emerson's naturalism would combat nihilism by a return to a metaphysical commitment, whereas Dewey's naturalism would combat nihilism through a plan of action that is fundamentally self-affirmative. Within Emerson's naturalism, individuals travel a path to meaningful existence as they reaffirm their primordial relation to the Oversoul. As they cultivate that relation and allow it to influence all other personal relations, those individuals reclaim for themselves meaningful existence.

Within Dewey's naturalism, to travel a path to meaningful existence one must be disengaged from an otherworldly religious orientation. Then, by focusing upon the potentiality available within nature, one may turn nature toward the service of a humanistically good life. Nature is to be respected for its potentiality and happily engaged in light of its convivial instrumentality, but nature does not become a substitute for some otherworldly deity such that one's efforts are turned toward its service per se. Within Dewey's natural piety, one does not find any justification for Nature worship.

This essay examines two naturalistic solutions to nihilism.[56] Nevertheless, there is an important methodological point to be observed here, for anyone attempting to formulate a solution to nihilism. Emerson's description of naturalism is metaphysically grounded, whereas Dewey's description of naturalism is not. Dewey's naturalistic solution to nihilism, without metaphysical grounding, demonstrates how we may resort to self-authenticating tactics to combat meaninglessness. To the extent that these self-authenticating tactics for combating nihilism are environmentally insensitive, they may upon reflection prove to be ultimately self-effacing.

NOTES

[1] Friedrich Nietzsche, "The Will to Power," in *Existentialism from Dostoevsky to Sartre,* ed. Walter Kaufmann (New York: New American Library, 1975), p. 131.

[2] John Dewey, *A Common Faith* (New Haven, Conn.: Yale University Press, 1934), p. 25.

[3] Ralph Waldo Emerson, "The Transcendentalist," in *The Complete Essays and Other Writings of Ralph Waldo Emerson* (New York: Modern Library, 1940), p. 87.

[4] *Emerson's* Nature: *Origin, Growth, Meaning,* 2d ed., ed. Merton M. Sealts, Jr., and Alfred R. Ferguson (Carbondale: Southern Illinois University Press, 1979), p. 31. Hereafter, this work shall be cited as *Nature*. Other references drawn from Emerson's essays shall be cited simply by the name of the essay and the page. References to his essays come from *Ralph Waldo Emerson: "Essays and Journals,"* selected by Lewis Mumford (Garden City, N.Y.: International Collectors Library, 1968).

[5] "Oversoul," p. 204.

[6] *Ibid.*, p. 203.

[7] "Experience," p. 273.

[8] *Nature,* p. 11.

[9] "Oversoul," p. 208.

[10] "The Poet," p. 260.

[11] *Nature,* p. 8.

[12] *Ibid.*, p. 210.

[13] *Ibid.*, p. 212.

[14] "Self-Reliance," p. 92.

[15] "Oversoul," p. 202.

[16] "Self-Reliance," p. 106.

[17] *Ibid.*, p. 105.

[18] There is some debate whether Emerson should be labeled simply a pantheist or a panentheist. I shall not take up that discussion here. However, I find the possibility that he was a panentheist unlikely, since he took a monistic, idealistic position regarding nature.

[19] *Nature*, p. 28.

[20] Emerson's description of natural piety is roughly comparable to William James's description of nature mysticism. In *Varieties of Religious Experience* (New York: New American Library, 1958), James described several incidents where nature awakened within some individual "mystical moods." In a footnote (p. 302) James commented on an incident involving nature mysticism. He said, "The larger God may then swallow up the smaller one." Thus, in James's view, when one encounters the divine element in nature, one may experientially transcend the muffling effect of religious tradition on an encounter with the divine. Recall that Emerson himself found his own religious tradition to be stifling by comparison with his encounter with the Oversoul through nature. James might easily include Emerson within his corps of nature mystics.

[21] Dewey, p. 2.

[22] *Ibid.*, p. 38.

[23] *Ibid.*, p. 57.

[24] *Ibid.*, p. 53.

[25] *Ibid.*

[26] *Ibid.*, p. 51.

[27] *Ibid.*, p. 50.

[28] Corliss Lamont, "New Light on Dewey's Common Faith," *Journal of Philosophy* 58, no. 1 (1961): 27.

[29] John E. Smith, *Purpose and Thought: The Meaning of Pragmatism* (New Haven, Conn.: Yale University Press, 1978), pp. 224-25, n. 86.

[30] Dewey, p. 19.

[31] *Ibid.*, p. 46.

[32] "Self-Reliance," p. 105.

[33] Dewey, p. 79.

[34] *Ibid.*, p. 46.

[35] *Ibid.*, p. 25.

[36] Above, I explore the way in which one moves from a faith in natural piety to a practice of natural piety. For devotees of natural piety, some of the problems associated with this move from faith to practice may arise as a result of the absence of a firm dogma or revelation in naturalism. More traditional religions rely heavily upon a written or spoken voice of authority to facilitate the move from faith to practice. Nevertheless, I suspect that practitioners of more traditional forms of religion are not exempt from some of the same difficulties associated with the move from faith to practice through practical reasoning, and I hope to explore that idea in an upcoming project.

[37] *The Works of Aristotle,* ed. J. A. Smith and W. D. Ross, vol. 5 (Oxford: Clarendon Press, 1912), *Nicomachean Ethics,* 1140b20; hereafter cited as Aristotle, *NE.*

[38] *Ibid., NE* 1143a8.

[39] *Ibid., NE* 1143a13-15.

[40] *Ibid., NE* 1141b18.

[41] Here I give Walton's modernized rendition of Aristotle's syllogisms. See Douglas Walton, *Practical Reasoning: Goal-Driven, Knowledge Based, Action-Guiding Argumentation* (Totowa, N.J.: Rowman & Littlefield, 1990), p. 11. Aristotle said, "For the actualization of desire is a substitute for inquiry or reflection. I want to drink, says appetite; this is drink, says sense or imagination or mind: straightaway I drink. In this way living creatures are impelled to move and to act, and desire is the last or immediate cause of movement, and desire arises after perception or after imagination and conception" (see Aristotle, *NE* 701a30-40; PS = Practical Syllogism).

[42] Some further work has been done on the analysis of practical reasoning by Michael Bratman. In his book, *Intention, Plans, and Practical Reason* (Cambridge, Mass.: Harvard University Press, 1987), Bratman suggested that practical reasoning occurred on two levels. He said, "Prior intentions and plans pose problems and provide a filter on options that are potential solutions to those problems; desire-belief reasons enter as considerations to be weighted in deliberating between relevant and admissible options" (p. 35). The prescriptive statement of what is desirable could be correlated with Bratman's first level of practical reasoning. One develops an intentional plan that designates some desirable end as its goal.

[43] Walton, p. 11.

[44] Aristotle, *NE* 1140a33.

[45] G. E. M. Anscombe, *Intention* (New York: Cornell University Press, 1963), p. 72.

[46] R. M. Hare, *Practical Inferences* (Berkeley: University of California Press, 1972), p. 60.

[47] See n. 34 above. If we were to make use of Bratman's analysis of practical reasoning here, we could say that the decision to build a particular house took place on the second level of practical reasoning. At that level, one could develop a subplan that included all the specific details of the contract with Sawz Lumber Company. Thus, the performance of basic acts would be understood to take place within an elaborately structured plan that would also include specific subplans such as the one described in the text.

[48] Dewey, p. 42.

[49] "Oversoul," p. 197.

[50] "The Poet," p. 258.

[51] "Oversoul," p. 202.

[52] *Nature*, p. 20.

[53] "Self-Reliance," p. 105.

[54] "Unocal in Myanmar: Report to the Stockholders" (Los Angeles, Calif., Corporate Communications Department, Unocal Corp., 1994).

[55] *Ibid.*, p. 7.

[56] I myself am inclined to believe that an effective way to combat nihilism lies along a path similar to the one taken by Emerson though significantly different. To me it seems that the panentheistic solution to the problem that has been described by Charles Hartshorne and has been developed within process theism by thinkers like Schubert Ogden and John B. Cobb may be an effective way to combat nihilism. I leave the discussion of that line of thought to be developed elsewhere.

Morton White (essay date 1996)

SOURCE: "Desire and Desirability: A Rejoinder to a Posthumous Reply by John Dewey," in *The Journal of Philosophy,* Vol. XCIII, No. 5, May, 1996, pp. 229-42.

[In the following article, White recounts Dewey's response to White's book Social Thought in America, *and White's answer to Dewey's charges.]*

Shortly after his ninetieth birthday, John Dewey[1] acknowledged receiving from me two publications in which I had criticized some of his views in ethics: my *Social*

Thought in America, and my "Value and Obligation in Dewey and Lewis," both published in 1949.[2] Since I never heard anything more from Dewey about them, I surmised that he had probably not read them or that, if he had, he did not think it worth bothering to discuss my criticisms. I was therefore very surprised when I read in the final volume of his *Collected Works* that he *had* paid attention to them in a piece entitled **"Comment on Recent Criticisms of Some Points in Moral and Logical Theory,"**[3] published in 1990, along with other posthumous writings of his which testify to his remarkable intellectual vigor in old age. His editors indicate that Dewey's reply was probably written as late as 1950, and this is confirmed by his reference in it to another criticism of my views by Sidney Hook in his article, "The Desirable and Emotive in Dewey's Ethics,"[4] published in that year.

Despite the fact that all of this discussion took place more than forty years ago, I think that an examination of Dewey's reply is warranted today, partly because Dewey said there that the subject of the discussion occupied "a central position in the theory of *method* underlying [his] views on all philosophical topics" (*op. cit.,* p. 480); and partly because Alan Ryan, in his recent widely praised study, *John Dewey and the High Tide of Liberalism,*[5] has referred to my differences with Dewey on the relation between the desirable and the desired in a way that needs correction. By publishing a rejoinder to Dewey at this late date, I may make my exchange with him one of the longest-running ones in the history of philosophy as well as one in which he unfortunately cannot have the last word; but I think the current revival of interest in his thought fully justifies the attention I give here to ideas that Dewey regarded as fundamental in his philosophy. I am bound to say, however, that his reply does not convince me that my criticism of his view was unjustified.

1. TWO DIFFERENT CRITICISMS OF DEWEY'S ANALYSIS OF DESIRABILITY

At one point, Dewey writes: "The specific criticisms made by Dr. White already have been so amply and so adequately dealt with by Dr. Sidney Hook on the base [sic] of an extensive and critically accurate knowledge of my writings that I have only as concerns the particular views criticized to refer interested persons to Dr. Hook's discussion and express my deep and grateful appreciation" (*op. cit.,* pp. 480-81). Dewey then goes on to comment on what he, following Hook, calls "one variant" of my criticism of his views on the relation between '*X* is desir*ed*' and '*X* is desir*able*'. The variants of which Hook and Dewey speak are two different criticisms by me of what I regarded as two different versions of Dewey's view of the relationship between what is desired and what is desirable, when the latter is understood as what we ought to desire or have a moral duty to desire. I dealt only with the first of these versions in the article mentioned earlier, but in the book, which appeared a little later in 1949, I dealt with it along with the second version.

It seemed to me that, in the first version, Dewey regarded moral statements of the form '*X* ought to be desired' as synonymous with 'If *X* is considered by a normal person under normal conditions, *X* will be desired by that person', following the pattern used by some philosophers—notably C. S. Peirce—when analyzing the nonmoral statement 'This is objectively red' as synonymous with 'If this is looked at by a normal person under normal conditions, it will appear red to that person'. In so analyzing 'desirable', I said Dewey had tried unsuccessfully to generate a moral de jure proposition by performing a logical operation on two merely de facto propositions. I said that Dewey had linked a de facto proposition such as 'Adam considers this apple under normal conditions' and the de facto proposition 'Adam desires this apple' as antecedent and consequent, respectively, of the conditional proposition 'If Adam considers this apple under normal conditions, then Adam desires this apple', and then asserted that this conditional proposition was synonymous with the moral proposition 'This apple ought to be desired by Adam'. I thought that joining these two de facto propositions in a conditional proposition did not yield the equivalent of a moral proposition any more than joining them in a conjunction would, and said that, if it did, it would also generate a related embarrassment for Dewey's view. I pointed out that, if the moral proposition 'This apple ought to be desired by Adam' were synonymous with the conditional 'If Adam considers this apple under normal conditions, Adam desires this apple', then by parity of reasoning the conditional 'If Adam looks at this apple under normal conditions, then this apple appears red to Adam' should be synonymous with 'This apple ought to appear red to Adam'. This, I said, would make 'This apple is objectively red' synonymous with a statement that is false or nonsensical, since 'ought to appear red' contains the moral 'ought' of 'ought to be desired' and not the predictive 'ought' of a sentence such as 'The sun ought to set in a minute'.[6]

I added in *Social Thought in America* that Dewey seemed to defend a second version of the relationship between 'desirable' and 'desired' in which a thing is said to be desirable just in case we know the causal antecedents and consequences of desiring it (*op. cit.*, pp. 216-17). In commenting on this reference to causal antecedents, I repeated what I had said about the first version, that knowing the causal antecedent of a desire not to smoke opium would not establish the moral desirability of not smoking it, for knowing that my desire not to smoke opium came about after I had considered not smoking it while in a normal state and under normal conditions would not make that desire morally obligatory. And merely knowing in addition the causal *consequences* of my desire if acted upon, such as preservation of my health, would not contribute to showing that my desire was obligatory. Therefore, I wondered whether Dewey might say in reply that I ought to desire not to smoke the opium just in case I knew the causal antecedents of my desire not to smoke it and also knew that the consequences of this desire would be . . . , where the dots were to be filled in by Dewey himself. First I asked whether Dewey could complete the

task by putting the word 'desirable' in place of the dots. No, I said, because that would produce a circular definition or analysis of 'desirable'. And when I asked whether Dewey should put 'desired' in place of the dots, I made some observations that I now expand in order to facilitate later discussion of my exchange with Dewey and Ryan's account of it.

If Dewey were to put 'desired' in place of the dots, then saying 'Not smoking opium is desirable' would be false if one did not desire the consequences of desiring not to smoke. If I said that not smoking opium was desirable and learned that my desire not to smoke it had consequences that I did *not* desire, I would have to recant my statement. To my mind, this raised a question about putting 'desired' in place of the dots in the definiens of 'desirable', because doing so required that *the consequences* of a desire for *X* be *desired* and not that they be desired by a normal person under normal conditions or be desirable. I wondered, therefore, whether Dewey would be willing to say that knowledge of this *raw* desire, so to speak, for the *consequences* of the original desire could play this role in his analysis of the desirable. On the other hand, as we have seen, if Dewey were to say that the consequences had to be *desirable,* he would be involved in the circle I mentioned earlier.

II. DEWEY'S VIEW AND MILL'S COMPARED AND CONTRASTED

In order to discuss Ryan's views about my differences with Dewey in an intelligible way, I must also repeat what I said in my paper[7] concerning the relations between J. S. Mill's views and those of Dewey. I said that although these views were more alike than is usually supposed, Mill held that we can prove that something is desirable by showing it is desired, whereas Dewey avoided this view in the first version of his definition of the desirable since it is obvious that a thing may be desired without being desirable, according to that version of his definition, if the desire were not that of a normal person under normal conditions. After pointing this out, I made some remarks on a difference between the so-called dispositional terms 'soluble' and 'objectively red' which I thought would illuminate the relationship between Dewey's first version of desirability and Mill's view. I said that we can infer '*a* is soluble' from '*a* is dissolving now' whereas we cannot infer '*a* is objectively red' from '*a* appears red now', because '*a* is soluble' means the same as the statement that *there are conditions* under which *a* dissolves whereas '*a* is objectively red' does not mean the same as the statement that *there are conditions* under which *a* appears red, but rather is synonymous with the statement that *a* appears red under specific conditions, namely, to a normal observer who looks at *a* in white light. That is why Dewey's view that the analysis of 'desirable' resembles that of 'objectively red' does not license the inference of '*a* is desirable' from '*a* is desired now'. Mill, I held, thought that 'desirable' resembled 'soluble', whereas Dewey avoided Mill's error by saying that 'desirable' resembled 'objectively red'. Nevertheless, I said,

Dewey's first version was defective for the reasons I have given earlier, even though Dewey had not been misled by the 'ble' at the end of 'desirable' into thinking that it was a dispositional predicate like 'soluble', but instead had made the more subtle error of thinking that 'desirable' was like 'objectively red'.

All of this makes it comparatively easy to see a misunderstanding in what Ryan says about my exchange with Dewey. Ryan writes: "Dewey, said White, had committed the same mistake as Mill and had confused the *desired* with the *desirable*. Dewey thought the 'data' of ethics were our likings and wishings and longings and seemed to be reducing ethical argument to the discussion of what we desired rather than what we *ought* to desire" (*op. cit.*, p. 337). This, I submit, is a very inadequate summary of my view. In my discussion of the *first* version of Dewey's view, I objected to Dewey's effort to assimilate 'desirable' to 'objectively red', while stating explicitly that Dewey did *not* make Mill's error of inferring '*a* is desirable' from '*a* is desired' or that of confusing them. Nor in my examination of the *second* version did I accuse Dewey of doing this, for there I merely asked whether Dewey wished his definition or analysis of *desirable* to require that the *consequences* of desiring a thing be (1) *desirable* or (2) *desired*, and I pointed to difficulties in both answers. I must therefore protest against Ryan's defense of Dewey's view as "infinitely far from collapsing the desirable into the desired" (*op. cit.*, p. 337), as if to imply that I had accused Dewey of *confusing* the desirable with the desired or of *collapsing* one into the other.

III. TWO INEFFECTUAL CRITICISMS OF MY VIEW BY DEWEY

Now I turn to Dewey's own effort to answer my criticisms. He begins by referring to what he calls a fundamental methodological difference between my view and his, but in stating that difference he unfortunately relies too much on what Hook claims I say. This leads Dewey to misunderstand my statement that the second version of his definition of 'desirable' might be circular. Because he accepted Hook's misleading summary of my view, Dewey wrongly took me to hold that "knowledge of the causes and consequences of our desire and of what is desired does not make the desired desirable unless . . . we can get back to some rock-bottom *desirable in itself*" (*op. cit.*, p. 481). In other words, Dewey mistakenly thought I held that the expression 'desirable in itself' must appear in the *definiens* of 'desirable'. Having got this wrong impression, Dewey then associated me with what he probably regarded as two of the most objectionable ideas in the history of philosophy, saying that my alleged "dependence upon that which is 'desirable in itself', that is, in complete independence of and isolation from investigation of the existential context of 'conditions and consequences', involves the assumption of what has been known in ethics as the method of *Intuition* and in epistemology as the necessity of the *a priori* to warrant the validity of statements made on empirical grounds" (*op. cit.*, p. 481). In my book and

article, however, I never appealed to the notion of *desirable in itself*. Indeed, if the phrase means something different from 'desirable'—as it seems to for Dewey—I would not have complained that its introduction into the *definiens* of 'desirable' created a circle. Furthermore, I did not defend ethical intuitionism and was probably less of an advocate of the necessity of the a priori than Dewey himself was.[8] So much, then, for one of Dewey's ineffectual criticisms of my views.

I turn now to another such criticism that emerges in Dewey's response to my claim that he had generated a normative or de jure proposition by performing a suitable operation on merely de facto propositions. He admits that such generation would constitute "a variety of intellectual magic" (*op. cit.*, p. 482) but does not admit that his view is open to this criticism. Instead, he uses my remark about performing an operation on propositions as an occasion for complaining that in using the word 'operation' in this way I completely neglect a view of his according to which an operation is performed not *on* propositions but *with* them (*op. cit.*, p. 482). I knew, of course, that Dewey had used the word 'operation' differently from the way in which I used it, but this hardly affected the point I made while using 'operation' as I used it. Therefore, Dewey's remark about his operating *with* propositions rather than *on* them fails to rebut anything I said in criticism of his views.

IV. DEWEY'S MORE SERIOUS ARGUMENTS

After Dewey ironically says that I have the "personal right to take" a position which is a "heritage from times when scientific method as now practiced did not exist and when the rational as distinct from the observational had to be invoked to guarantee the validity of beliefs and statements," he adds that the method *he* "employed in making the distinction between the *de facto* desired and the *de jure* desirable is simply the method pursued in all sciences which conduct inquiries intended to find out what is fact—'objective' fact to indulge in a pleonasm—and in distinction from what is taken to be fact apart from inquiry into 'conditions and consequences'" (*op. cit.*, p. 482).

Dewey also says: "Dr. White's reduction of the desirable to that which is desired 'under normal conditions' is wholly satisfactory to me provided the literally terrible ambivalence in normal is cleared away—which I do not find he even tries to do" (*op. cit.*, p. 483). I shall postpone dealing with Dewey's view of the word 'normal', but I wish to emphasize here that he accepts the wording of the reduction or analysis of 'desirable' which I attribute to him as well as the similarly worded analysis of 'objectively red' or 'really red' which I attribute to him. But since I maintained that his analysis of 'This apple is desirable'—where 'desirable' is synonymous with 'ought to be desired'—is *not* acceptable whereas the parallel analysis of 'This apple is really red' *is* acceptable, Dewey tries to show that they are both acceptable because both reflect the method used in science "to find out what is *fact* . . . in distinction from what is taken to be fact apart from inquiry into 'conditions and consequences'" (*op. cit.,* p. 482). Unlike Dewey, however, I think that the distinction between what is *taken to be* fact and what *is* fact is involved when we distinguish between the statements 'This appears to be red' and 'This is really red', but that it is *not* involved when we distinguish between the statements 'This is desired' and 'This is desirable, that is, ought to be desired'. Indeed, I think Dewey's main error is to identify the distinction between the de facto 'This is desired' and the de jure 'This is desirable, that is, ought to be desired' with the distinction between what is taken to be fact and what *is* fact. Therefore, one way of stating my criticism of Dewey in traditional philosophical language might be to say that the distinction between the de facto and the de jure is not the same as that between the apparent and the real. I elected to say in less traditional philosophical language, however, that though the statement 'This apple is really red' may be analyzed (following Peirce) as synonymous with the statement 'If this apple is put before a normal eye in daylight (normal light), it looks red', the statement 'This apple is desirable, that is, ought to be desired' is *not* synonymous with the statement 'If this apple is considered by a normal person under normal circumstances, it is desired'.

In arguing that the de facto/de jure distinction is not the same as the apparent/real distinction, I might have said that the expression 'de facto' does not mean the same as 'apparent' and that the expression 'de jure' does not mean the same as 'real'. But I chose another way of arguing the point because I did not wish to use terms that some readers might find very obscure, and so I argued instead that, if the correct analysis of the moral statement

> (a) This apple ought to be desired (is desirable).

is given by

> (b) If this apple is considered by a normal person under normal circumstances, it is desired.

then the statement

> (c) If this apple is put before a normal eye in normal light, it looks red.

should be the analysis of .

> (d) This apple ought to be seen as red (ought to look red).

But since (c) by hypothesis gives the analysis of

> (e) This apple is really (objectively) red.

then (e) should also be synonymous with (d). In that case, a statement of the real color of an object would become synonymous with an ethical statement, which (d) is because its 'ought' is, as I have said, the 'ought' of (a). This would be absurd, however, and would lead us to say that all attributions to objects of their real or objective colors

are made in statements synonymous with ethical statements and therefore to the unacceptable conclusion that many obviously nonethical descriptive scientific truths are ethical. Here, I was not arguing against ethical naturalism construed as asserting that all ethical statements are synonymous with scientific statements of behavioral science; I was protesting against a view that had as a logical consequence the view that 'This apple is really red' is an ethical statement.

Parenthetically, I suggest that the statement 'If this apple is considered by a normal person under normal circumstances, it is desired' might be regarded as the analysis of the statement 'This apple is *really* desired' by those who seek an analogue involving desire for Peirce's analysis of 'This apple is really red'. One of these analogous analyses would say that the real color of an apple is the color it appears to have in the eye, so to speak, of a normal beholder under normal circumstances; the other would say that the real attitude toward the apple is the attitude the normal reactor to it has under normal circumstances. I merely *suggest* this, as I say; I do not advocate it. But I do continue to maintain that although the Peirceian approach connects the real color of an object with the way in which the object looks or appears, it does not connect the attitude we *ought* to have toward an object with the attitude we *do* have toward it.

I turn now to the difficult and crucial concept of normativeness that figures in Dewey's reduction of the desirable to what is desired under normal conditions, for his reflections on it contain the heart of his argument against my view. In my opinion, only the *outlines* of that argument may be made out with confidence. Dewey thinks that the word 'normal' is used normatively when it appears in the conditional statements (b) and (c) above, and from this he concludes that (a) and (e) are also normative in a sense that allegedly undermines my contention that (b) *does not* give the correct analysis of moral statement (a). Dewey never answers my complaint that his view leads to the absurd conclusion that statements about real colors are ethical, but since he insists that (a), (b), (c), and (e) are all scientific and *therefore* all normative, I shall try now to penetrate the outlines of his view in order to look more closely at his idea of the normal as normative and to see whether it can sustain the great philosophical load he puts on it.

Dewey tells us that 'normal' in the sense of what happens usually or on the average is "certainly de facto" and therefore not normative. But then, as I have already pointed out, he says that a statement like (e) of the form '*X* is objectively (really) red' *is* normative and that the expression 'normal' in (c) has what he calls *normative force*. He also says in a crucial passage that the normal conditions referred to in statements like (c) are "not those of a majority or even the total number of cases in which *X* appears red. They are conditions instituted by continued experimental inquiries conducted for a definite end-in-view" (*op. cit.,* p. 483). Dewey seems to imply here that Peirce's condition of being before a normal eye in normal light applies neither to *the majority* of cases in which *X* appears red nor to *the total number* of such cases. I doubt whether he is correct in saying that the number of cases in which *X* is before a normal eye in daylight does not constitute the majority of cases in which *X* appears red, but I shall not quarrel about that since I do not know how to settle the issue. Dewey needs to say, however, that *some* cases in which *X* looks red are cases in which *X* is *not* before a normal eye in daylight, since that will allow him to say that an experimenter must *put X* before a normal eye in normal light in order to discover whether a statement such as (c) is warranted. Dewey seems to think that the condition 'is before a normal eye in normal light' has normative force because it expresses a norm or standard to be met which is not always met, and therefore the scientist must institute such a condition in order to test (c) and its synonym (e). Dewey's point seems to be that because objects that appear red are not always before a normal eye in normal light, the scientist puts them there to see whether (c) and therefore (e) are true.

Once it is recognized that normal conditions are normative in his sense, Dewey says he welcomes "the formal or methodological identification of the statement '*X* is desirable' with '*X* is objectively red', for if 'objective' has any distinctive *relevant* sense in the latter proposition, that sense, like that of 'normal' as having any relevance to the point at issue in the phrase 'normal conditions', is itself intrinsically normative or *de jure*" (*op. cit.,* p. 483). Furthermore, Dewey says he welcomes the "identification when its direction is completely reversed," which means, I think, that Dewey assimilates the analysis of '*X* is objectively red' to that of '*X* is desirable' just as he does in the reverse direction. In short, he seems to hold that (a) and (e) are both normative because they are respectively synonymous with (b) and (c). These two singular statements seem to be normative for him because the generalizations that support them, respectively, are the following allegedly normative scientific statements:

> (b′) Whenever this apple is considered by a normal person under normal circumstances, it is desired.

and

> (c′) Whenever this apple is put before a normal eye in normal light, it looks red.

And these generalizations seem to be normative because their antecedent statement forms are said to express conditions that require institution by an experimenter, for a reason that Dewey conveys at the end of his "Comment": "Unfortunately, or perhaps fortunately, 'normal' conditions for and of an experiment that yields a warranted conclusion do not lie around nor force themselves upon us. They are obtained by undertaking the kind of activities which the best available knowledge at the time informs us *should be* tried in order to find out their specific consequences in and for further knowing" (*op. cit.,* p. 484). Dewey's use of the phrase '*should be* tried' conveys his idea that the activity of putting an apple before

a normal eye in daylight is dictated by a normative judgment. But surely it is not a moral judgment, one is tempted to add.

Having said as much as I can in elucidation of Dewey's view as to why (a), (b), (c), and (e) are normative, I now ask: Does all of this show what he thinks it shows? In other words, does he succeed in showing that all scientific propositions are normative in a way that undermines my claim that his analysis or reduction of 'ought to be desired' cannot be modeled on the Peircean analysis of 'really red' or 'objectively red'? I am afraid not. Even if one accepts what Dewey says, it is hard to see how it makes statement (a) a statement of moral duty. Moreover, according to a strict application of Dewey's own criterion for being normative, statement forms of the antecedents in statements such as (b′) and (c′) are normative in his terminology, since his word 'normative' strictly applies only to antecedent conditions or statement forms like '*X* is considered by a normal person under normal circumstances' and '*X* is put before a normal eye in normal light'. But how does it follow from the fact that these antecedent conditions or statement forms *are* normative in Dewey's sense and that the tester of (b′) and (c′) must institute those conditions so that he can perform an experiment to discover the truth of (b′) and (c′), that statement (b′) expresses a moral duty? And if it does follow, why should it not follow for the very same reason that (c) expresses a moral duty and is synonymous with (e)—a consequence I have said is absurd? So far as I can see, Dewey has no answer to these crucial questions.

Furthermore, I am not convinced that Dewey's characterization of *all* scientific generalizations is adequate. I am not sure that he is right when he says that all statements of the form 'For every *X*, if *X* is *A*, then *X* is *B*' are scientific if and only if the experimenter must *put* things in normative condition *A* in order to see whether they are also in condition *B*. 'All bodies attract each other' is a scientific generalization even though there is no verb like 'put' in its antecedent when it is transformed into 'For every *X* and *Y*, if *X* and *Y* are bodies, *X* and *Y* attract each other'. This is a scientific generalization which contains no experimental directions, and I cannot imagine an experimenter saying 'Let us put *X* and *Y* into the condition of being bodies to see whether they attract each other'. This is not to say that the law of universal attraction is not tested empirically by the use of scientific method, but it is to say that not every scientific generalization contains antecedents that contain experimental directions like those which Dewey regards as essential components of the antecedents of scientific generalizations. I want to emphasize, however, that, even if he had characterized all scientific generalizations correctly, his view of science as normative would not support his answer to my criticism of his view of moral duty. Even if all scientific generalizations were to contain antecedent conditions that are normative in Dewey's sense, that would not show that they support statements saying that we have a moral duty to desire certain things—that they are desirable. And if they did show that, they would also support statements that say absurdly that we have a moral duty to see certain things as red.

V. ETHICAL NATURALISM: REDUCTIVE AND HOLISTIC

Throughout my discussion of Dewey's ideas in my earlier writings, I assumed that his views on what is objectively red and what ought to be desired were analytic or reductive. I based this on Dewey's[9] favorable quotation of a passage in which Peirce asks: "of the myriads of the forms into which a proposition may be translated, which is that one which is to be called its very meaning"; to which he replies: "It is, according to the pragmaticist, that form in which the proposition becomes applicable to human conduct" (*ibid.*, p. 303). And I also had in mind passages like the following one in Peirce[10]: "to say that a Jacqueminot rose really is red means, and can mean, nothing but that if such a rose is put before a normal eye, in the daylight, it will look red" (*ibid.*, p. 194). Therefore, I feel vindicated in my interpretation of Dewey when he says in his reply: "Dr. White's reduction of the desirable to that which is desired 'under normal conditions' is wholly satisfactory to me," even though Dewey goes on to say things about 'normal' that I do not fully accept or even understand. But I am sure that readers of my later work might see some irony in my saying this because in *What Is and What Ought To Be Done* and *The Question of Free Will: A Holistic View*[11]—especially in the first—I urge that we abandon the reductive search for the *meanings* of ethical terms partly because of my increasing doubts about analyticity and analysis as expressed in my *Toward Reunion in Philosophy*.[12] I therefore came to focus instead on the epistemology rather than the semantics of ethics, which I later approached holistically under the influence of Pierre Duhem, W. V. Quine, and Alfred Tarski.[13]

When I approached ethics in this non-Mooreian way, I came to believe that the purpose of ethical thinking was to organize a heterogeneous flux that contained not only sensory experiences but also moral feelings, and that some heterogeneous systems or bodies of statements that are used to organize such a flux contain not only logical statements and those of descriptive science but also moral statements. Just as Quine's holism and Tarski's are used by them to argue against a sharp epistemological distinction between the method of testing logical statements and that of testing statements of natural science, I use my holism—which I label *corporatism* merely because I include moral feelings among experiences and moral statements in some of the systems we test—to argue against a sharp epistemological distinction between the methods of testing statements such as 'This is desirable' and 'This is objectively red'. Descriptive and ethical statements, I argue in my later work, appear in conjunctions of statements that organize heterogeneous experiences in a way that permits no sharp distinction between the methods used in testing such statements. By regarding ethical argument in this way, I have come to a view *like that* of Dewey insofar as the aim of his analysis of 'This is desirable' was to erase a

sharp epistemological distinction between the method of testing it and the method of testing 'This is objectively red'. Because my corporatism requires Duhemian testing of conjunctions of statements by experience, I call myself an *ethical naturalist* but not a *naturalistic reductionist* like Dewey, who seems to seek synonyms for statements asserting moral duties and for statements attributing objective colors while engaging in what he calls reduction in his reply to me. And because I think scientists test extended hypothetico-deductive systems rather than isolated statements, Dewey's view that all "scientifically grounded propositions" contain or need experimental directions for testing them individually strikes me as excessively isolationist, so to speak. I say this because he regards *each* scientific generalization or law as experimental in a way that I criticized earlier, and because I do not think that such a criticism may be justly made when a scientific theory is viewed as a conjunction of statements that is confirmed as a whole by experience and not by separate experimental testings of each generalization contained in that whole. I believe that there is an important affinity between my present rejection of a sharp distinction between testing moral statements and testing descriptive statements, and what I took to be the antidualistic, naturalistic motive behind Dewey's effort in *The Quest for Certainty*[14] and elsewhere. Like him, I do not think that the moral judge has any data except sensory and emotional experiences against which to test his theories, but I do think that Dewey's ethical naturalism was reductive and therefore subject to criticism of the kind I have made earlier.

In concluding, I want to say something about Dewey that Bertrand Russell[15] once said so felicitously about William James after criticizing his views. I wish "to express, what in the course of controversial writings does not adequately appear, the profound respect and personal esteem which I felt for him, as did all who knew him. . . . For readers trained in philosophy, no such assurance was required; but for those unaccustomed to the tone of a subject in which agreement is necessarily rarer than esteem, it seemed desirable to record what to others would be a matter of course" (*ibid.*, p. v). I say this about Dewey on the chance that even readers trained in philosophy might need such assurance while reading the present article, and I wish to add that I owe him a great intellectual debt as well. He was a towering figure in philosophy, one from whom I learned an enormous amount even when I disagreed with him.

NOTES

[1] Dewey wrote me on November 6, 1949: "Many thanks for a copy of your *Social Thought in America* which I've just received and [am] looking forward to reading soon. I want also to thank you for your reprint from the *Philosophical Review*. I had been waiting till I have had a chance to read it carefully, as I have been swamped and am only now beginning to get my head above water. I haven't even yet been able to study it but shall soon." This was the last letter I had from Dewey, the end of a cordial

correspondence that began in 1941, when I was writing *The Origin of Dewey's Instrumentalism* (New York: Columbia, 1943). It saddens me to think that he might not have written me again because he did not wish to say in a letter what he says in the piece to which I reply here.

[2] *Social Thought in America* (New York: Viking, 1949); same pagination in paperback editions: (Boston: Beacon, 1957) and (New York: Oxford, 1976). "Value and Obligation in Dewey and Lewis," *The Philosophical Review,* LVIII (July 1949): 321-29; this article is reprinted with some alterations in my *Pragmatism and the American Mind* (New York: Oxford, 1973), pp. 155-67; the altered version also appears in J. E. Tiles, ed., *John Dewey: Critical Assessments, Volume III* (New York: Routledge, 1992), pp. 28-36.

[3] In Jo Ann Boydston, ed., *The Later Works: 1925-1953, Volume XVII* (Carbondale: Southern Illinois UP, 1990), pp. 480-84.

[4] In Hook, ed., *John Dewey: Philosopher of Science and Freedom* (New York: Dial, 1950), pp. 194-216.

[5] New York: Norton, 1995.

[6] "Value and Obligation in Dewey and Lewis," p. 326.

[7] "Value and Obligation in Dewey and Lewis," pp. 324-25. For a more extended discussion of the relation between Dewey's views and Mill's, see the altered version in *Pragmatism and the American Mind* and the reprint thereof in Tiles.

[8] This reference to the a priori should be read with the following in mind. I had contributed my essay, "The Analytic and the Synthetic: An Untenable Dualism," to *John Dewey: Philosopher of Science and Freedom,* the same volume to which Hook had contributed his essay, "The Desirable and Emotive in Dewey's Ethics" (*op. cit.,* pp. 194-216). Had Dewey read mine, he would have known that I was sympathetic to his views on the dualism I was considering. Indeed, Hook wrote me upon receiving my manuscript on November 5, 1949, that it was "squarely in the context of [Dewey's] thinking." When I say that I was probably less of an advocate of the necessity of the a priori than Dewey, I have in mind some views I set forth in "Experiment and Necessity in Dewey's Philosophy," *Antioch Review,* XIX (Fall 1959): 329-44; reprinted, as "The Analytic and the Synthetic," in my *Pragmatism and the American Mind.*

[9] "The Pragmatism of Peirce," in Peirce, *Chance, Love, and Logic,* M. R. Cohen, ed. (New York: Harcourt, Brace, 1923).

[10] *Collected Papers,* A. W. Burks, ed. (Cambridge: Harvard, 1958).

[11] (New York: Oxford, 1981) and (Princeton: University Press, 1993).

[12] Cambridge: Harvard, 1956.

[13] Duhem, *La Théorie physique: son objet, sa structure* (Paris: 1914, 2nd ed.), pp. 278-89; Quine, "Two Dogmas of Empiricism," *Philosophical Review,* LX (1951): 20-43; and my "A Philosophical Letter of Alfred Tarski," this JOURNAL, LXXXIV, 1 (January 1987): 28-32.

[14] New York: Putnam, 1960.

[15] *Philosophical Essays* (London: Longmans, 1910).

Alan B. Spitzer (essay date 1996)

SOURCE: "John Dewey, the 'Trial' of Leon Trotsky, and the Search for Historical Truth," in *Historical Truth and Lies about the Past,* The University of North Carolina Press, 1996, pp. 13-34.

[*In the following essay, Spitzer examines Dewey's role as commissioner of the committee to defend Leon Trotsky, its eventual finding that Trotsky was not guilty of the Moscow purges or of corroborating with Nazi Germany, Dewey's rejection of historical objectivity, and Dewey's conclusion that Trotsky was right although Dewey abhorred his political views.*]

> For truth, instead of being a bourgeois virtue, is the mainspring of all human progress.—John Dewey

Consider the following historical text:

> In 1937, new facts came to light regarding the fiendish crimes of the Bukharin-Trotsky gang. The trial of Pyatakov, Radek and others, the trial of Tukhachevsky, Yakir and others, and, lastly, the trial of Bukharin, Rykov, Rosengoltz and others, all showed that the Bukharinites and Trotskyites had long ago joined to form a common band of enemies of the people, operating as the "Bloc of Rights and Trotskyites."

> The trials showed that these dregs of humanity, in conjunction with the enemies of the people, Trotsky, Zinoviev and Kamenev, had been in conspiracy against Lenin, the Party and the Soviet state ever since the early days of the October Socialist Revolution. The insidious attempts to thwart the Peace of Brest-Litovsk at the beginning of 1918, the plot against Lenin and the conspiracy with the "Left" Socialist-Revolutionaries for the arrest and murder of Lenin, Stalin and Sverdlov in the spring of 1918, the villainous shot that wounded Lenin in the summer of 1918, the revolt of the "Left" Socialist-Revolutionaries in the summer of 1918, the deliberate aggravation of differences in the Party in 1921 with the object of undermining and overthrowing Lenin's leadership from within, the attempts to overthrow the Party leadership during Lenin's illness and after his death, the betrayal of state secrets and the supply of information of an espionage character to foreign

espionage services, the vile assassination of Kirov, the acts of wrecking, diversion and explosions, the dastardly murder of Menzhinsky, Kuibyshev and Gorky—all these and similar villainies over a period of twenty years were committed, it transpired, with the participation or under the direction of Trotsky, Zinoviev, Kamenev, Bukharin, Rykov and their henchmen, at the behest of espionage services of bourgeois states.

The trials brought to light the fact that the Trotsky-Bukharin fiends, in obedience to the wishes of their masters—the espionage services of foreign states—had set out to destroy the Party and the Soviet state, to undermine the defensive power of the country, to assist foreign military intervention, to prepare the way for the defeat of the Red Army, to bring about the dismemberment of the U.S.S.R., to hand over the Soviet Maritime Region to the Japanese, Soviet Byelorussia to the Poles, and the Soviet Ukraine to the Germans, to destroy the gains of the workers and collective farmers, and to restore capitalist slavery in the U.S.S.R.

These Whiteguard pygmies, whose strength was no more than that of a gnat, apparently flattered themselves that they were the masters of the country, and imagined that it was really in their power to sell or give away the Ukraine, Byelorussia and the Maritime Region.

These Whiteguard insects forgot that the real masters of the Soviet country were the Soviet people, and that the Rykovs, Bukharins, Zinovievs and Kamenevs were only temporary employees of the state, which could at any moment sweep them out from its offices as so much useless rubbish.

These contemptible lackeys of the fascists forgot that the Soviet people had only to move a finger, and not a trace of them would be left. The Soviet court sentenced the Bukharin-Trotsky fiends to be shot.

The People's Commissariat of Internal Affairs carried out the sentence.

The Soviet people approved the annihilation of the Bukharin-Trotsky gang and passed on to next business.[1]

What should we make of this passage? Today, many readers would simply say with Pierre Vidal-Naquet that "the history of the communist party of the Soviet Union that appeared under Stalin is a lasting monument of the most murderous historical lies." But as historians we might not wish to leave it at that. What seems self-evident now was the object of bitter debate and agonizing uncertainty then. The Stalinist version of the great purges of the 1930s was not only affirmed as revealed truth but glossed, as Vidal-Naquet observes, by "liberal, apparently scholarly versions of Stalinist history" ornamented by numerous references and bibliographical notes.[2] The trials were authenticated for world opinion by appeals to the "facts" established by inference from the evidence provided in great part by the confessions of the accused.

This chapter will examine one of the most influential challenges to the authenticity of the trials, presented in public hearings before a Preliminary Commission of Inquiry headed by John Dewey (henceforth referred to as the commission or the Dewey Commission). The commission was the subcommittee of a body organized to allow Leon Trotsky—condemned in absentia as the soul of the conspiracy to overthrow the Soviet state—to present his side of the case. In effect, the Dewey Commission presided over something like a mock trial of Trotsky that simultaneously placed the entire system of Soviet political justice in the dock.[3]

The debate over the validity of the trials was a debate over the nature of the Soviet experiment, and one, as James T. Farrell and many others saw it, that posed stark, categorical alternatives. "At the time," Farrell wrote, "I, as well as others, posed this question: if the official version of the trials were true, then the co-workers of Lenin and the leaders of the Bolshevik Revolution must be considered as one of the worst gang of scoundrels in history; if the trials were a frameup then the leaders of Soviet Russia were perpetuating one of the most monstrous frameups in all history."[4] This either/or had special poignancy for those thousands throughout the world, located on the political Left, whose attitude toward the Soviet regime was crucial to their political and moral self-definition.

Poignancy of a different sort might inform our own reading of those Stalinist texts in the light of the historical skepticism that leaves us and Vidal-Naquet with the question, On what grounds might we refute "murderous historical lies?" The question of how to distinguish historical truth from falsehood was starkly posed in the irreconcilable interpretations of the purge trials, which tore apart the political Left in the 1930s. In the Soviet version, the "facts" of the case were authenticated by the deadly authority of Stalinist discourse. No one who fell within the orbit of the Soviet regime in those years needed a Foucault to remind them of the integral relationship between "knowledge" and power.

The language of Marxo-Stalinism had its peculiar structure and its linguistic figures—its tropes, modes, and emplotments, or, in Hayden White's words, its own "strategies of explanation . . . with an ideological implication that is unique to it." We might then simply stand on White's "moral and aesthetic" grounds for preferring alternative versions of the past and choose to reject this one. We suspect, however, that White would not wish to insert such a text under his rubric of "mutually exclusive, though *equally legitimate,* interpretations of the same set of historical events or the same segment of the historical process" (my emphasis).[5] That was scarcely how contemporaries in any camp would have disposed of it then.

There were some who did simply reject the Stalinist version on what Richard Rorty might now identify as ethnocentric grounds. Their intellectual solidarity—to use another Rortyan term—entailed the conviction that Stalinist discourse was integrally false.[6] Few, however, would have argued, like Rorty, that "people think that intellectuals have to give a reason why these dictators [Hitler and Stalin] were wrong. This seems to me to be a ludicrous hope."[7] It seemed very important then, especially to those aligned in the socialist and democratic camps, to know whether and wherein Stalin was right or wrong, and this was important not only in the abstract but also with reference to specific issues of great political and moral significance. One could not simply assume that Stalinists lied about or were wrong about everything and that their liberal and social-democratic antagonists were correct. I am one of those who believe that representatives of liberal and democratic regimes such as Anthony Eden and Léon Blum, who defended the noninterventionist policy in the Spanish Civil War, were wrong and that the Soviet apparatchiks, apologists, and international fellow travelers who called that policy a farce were right.

While there were a great many people whose minds were made up about the validity of the Moscow Purge Trials prior to the examination of evidence, there were many who were convinced in the light of what they perceived as evidence, and others who waited to be convinced. Ambassador Davies, whose duty was to report to Washington the truth about the trials, became convinced of their authenticity; John Dewey, who agreed to head a commission of inquiry into the case of Leon Trotsky, would conclude that the trials were a cynical travesty.

I do not intend to retell the fascinating story of the mock trial of Leon Trotsky convened in Mexico City in April 1937 by the commission chaired by John Dewey, or to beat Stalinism with an old stick, but to examine the arguments through which contemporaries justified their conclusions about the truth of contradictory histories of a recent past. The Dewey Commission was not convened to write history, and the recent past it examined was remembered as well as recorded, but issues raised with regard to the grounds for the justification of historical propositions are as applicable to the commission's conclusions as to any historical text.

In March 1936 an American section of an international committee for the defense of Leon Trotsky was organized to allow Trotsky to answer the accusations leveled against him at the Moscow trials. The question of Trotsky's guilt or innocence was practically and symbolically central not only to an evaluation of the purge trials but also to the reading of the history of Russia since 1917—practically because if the charges brought against Trotsky were false, the entire structure based on the confessions of the accused, which assigned Trotsky a central role, would disintegrate; symbolically because Leon Trotsky had become the great protagonist of a modern political Paradise Lost, expelled from the workers' paradise but still "going to and fro on the earth and walking up and down on it."

As the Preliminary Commission of Inquiry had been organized by the Committee for the Defense of Leon Trotsky, it was predictably dismissed as a tool of the "Trotskyites." This view did not plausibly dispose of John Dewey, who was certainly not a Trotskyist, who refuted Trotsky on various occasions, and who, in his seventy-eighth year, was venerated as an icon of liberal rectitude. He could, of course, be dismissed as deluded or, even better, senile; but it would be difficult to argue the latter, given the publication in 1938 of *Logic, The Theory of Inquiry*, Dewey's magnum opus in technical philosophy.

The organization and procedures of the hearings in Mexico City would be vulnerable to the criticism of those who opposed the commission's conclusions. The commission disclaimed any pretense at conducting a trial; it was to function "solely as an investigating body" to decide whether "Mr. Trotsky had a case warranting further investigations."[8] As its critics would emphasize, however, the commissioners functioned as something like magistrates and jurors, setting the ground rules, posing questions, and drawing conclusions.

The commission had four members in addition to Dewey: Benjamin Stolberg, a journalist with labor connections and a qualified admirer of Trotsky; Susan La Follette, niece of Senator Robert La Follette, writer for *The Nation,* and art critic; Otto Ruehle, a German Marxist emigré with distinguished socialist credentials; and Carleton Beals, a left-wing journalist and widely read author of books on Latin America.[9] His abrupt resignation from the commission, and condemnation of its procedures, would supply powerful ammunition to its detractors.

Trotsky was "represented" by a labor lawyer, Albert Goldman, as if in a conventional adversarial procedure, but the commission's attorney, John Finerty, did not play the role of a prosecuting attorney so much as that of a European examining magistrate orchestrating a search for the truth. This too would be a target. The arguments over procedure certainly did bear on evaluations of the commission's conclusions, but ultimately the burden of conviction would be borne by the arguments over the substance of the hearings.

There were three sorts of arguments brought to bear on the results of the investigation in Mexico City which I shall label, at some risk of parody, pragmatic, hermeneutic, and epistemological. By pragmatic arguments I intend those that spoke to the possible consequences of the trial, and therefore "what was good in the way of belief" to those somewhere on the political Left; by hermeneutic I refer to interpretations of the meaning of the trials and the commission's hearings in the larger historical context, and with reference to the values and perspective of the interpreter; and by epistemological I mean the treatment of the evidence regarding what allegedly occurred.

A prologue to the pragmatic argument over the findings of the Dewey Commission appeared two months before the inquiry in Mexico City in an "open letter to American liberals" published in the *Daily Worker* and printed a month later in *Soviet Russia Today.* This manifesto, signed by many distinguished figures on the American Left, was intended to warn American liberals against the machinations of the American Committee for the Defense of Leon Trotsky, notably its organization of an investigation of the Moscow trials. It pointed out "the real nature" of the committee as a Trotskyist front and therefore an ally of fascist and reactionary enemies of the Soviet Union, which "should be left to protect itself against treasonable plots as it saw fit." The open letter concluded:

> We ask you [The American liberals] to clarify these points, not merely because we believe that the Soviet Union needs the support of liberals at this moment when the forces of fascism, led by Hitler, threaten to engulf Europe. We believe that it is important for the progressive forces in this country that you make your position clear. The reactionary sections of the press and public are precisely the ones to seize most eagerly on the anti-Soviet attacks of Trotsky and his followers to further their own aims. We feel sure that you do not wish to be counted an ally of these forces.[10]

The argument about consequences was, of course, a principal line of the communist and fellow-traveling press, but it also weighed heavily in the balance of all those whose primary concern was the inexorable advance of fascist power. Even for those who knew the trials were wrong, Alfred Kazin recalls, "the issue was not so simple. . . . The danger was Hitler, Mussolini, Franco. . . . Although I had been revolted and disgusted by still more Moscow trials[,] . . . Fascism was still the major threat to peace."[11]

According to the editors of the *New Republic,* to open the question in the manner of the Dewey Commission would simply add to the confusion over the trials. "Meanwhile, there are more important questions than Trotsky's guilt"—among them, "the question of whether American liberals and progressives are going to work toward the end they have in common, or whether they are going to dissipate their influence by quarrels among themselves over questions that concern them at second hand."[12]

When Malcolm Cowley, influential editor and literary critic of the *New Republic,* set down his reminiscences—"without apologies or recriminations," as he puts it—of the political line he followed in the 1930s, he drew a distinction between two "factions" on the Left. One group was essentially anti-Stalinist and the other anti-Hitlerite. The latter, Cowley recalls, was primarily concerned with promoting the anti-Nazi alliance which included the Communists. Whatever one thought of Stalin's brutality, vindictiveness, and so forth, "the only sound policy was to check Hitler by any possible means and with the greatest number of allies, including Beelzebub." That wasn't precisely how Cowley had characterized Stalin at the time. In comparing the great Bolshevik antagonists in the April 7, 1937, issue of the *New Republic,* Cowley wrote, "it is now a question of war and peace and the world our children are going to live in. Stalin with all his faults and virtues represents

the Communist revolution. Trotsky has come to represent the 'second revolution' that is trying to weaken it in the face of attacks from the fascist powers."[13]

Like many other liberals whose primary loyalty was to a viable Popular Front, Cowley was concerned not only with the practical political consequences of one's reading of the purge trials and therefore of the Soviet system but also with its meaning—its implications for the intelligibility of the political universe and one's relation to it. A judgment on the trials was an interpretation, a making sense of patterns of political behavior in light of each individual's moral and political location. This was an issue raised at the Mexico City hearings and elsewhere by Trotsky and his partisans, who argued that a reading of Trotsky's career and, indeed, the history of the Bolshevik revolution that granted the allegations of counterrevolutionary conspiracy and betrayal was simply unintelligible.

The Dewey Commission did give some credence to this argument, although it was also available to those antagonists who were happy to quote Trotsky against himself. In various published documents Trotsky had asserted that the Soviet bureaucracy would not relinquish power without a fight and could only be removed by "a revolutionary force." Considering this issue from a broader, "more objective," liberal perspective, some would argue that as completely consequential political actors, Trotsky and his followers had no choice but to take up any method, even alliance with fascist enemies of the Soviet Union, that might bring down the regime, which incarnated the betrayal of the workers' cause. Indeed, the regime had given them no choice, and Stalinist despotism was in effect a self-fulfilling prophecy of the treasonable activity of its proponents, who were afforded no other outlet.[14] Thus, one could both accept the essential authenticity of the trials and criticize an authoritarian regime that equated opposition to conspiracy. This was still to accept the official Soviet version of what had actually occurred.

The interpretation of the Soviet apologists was the reverse of the Trotskyists' version. The entire history of the revolution and the Soviet regime was unintelligible if the trials had been a brutal farce. For Corliss Lamont, "the Soviet regime and its achievements are indivisible; and we cannot believe that its system of justice is completely out of step with its splendid accomplishments in practically all other fields."[15] The Dewey Commission was to find this version of historical intelligibility less convincing than that of Trotsky but would ultimately base its conclusions on its understanding of what it would call "historic truth." Both the defenders of Trotsky and the Communist Party's polemicists insisted that their positions were founded on factual bedrock. And it was there that the commission intended to build its case. Evidence about past events was at the center of the hearings in Mexico City.

Since the confessions at the Moscow Trials constituted the substance of the prosecution's case against Trotsky, the Dewey Commission's investigation was to a considerable extent an evaluation of their validity. As the commission remarked, despite Vyshinsky's talk of documenting the immense conspiracy, that conspiracy had left no paper trail: none of the letters or messages, not a scrap of incriminating paper, had been preserved by the horde of inept conspirators—nothing but their word, in tailored response to the prosecutor's questions.

However, the confessions did refer to alleged events that had occurred outside the Soviet Union, and these references could be checked against publicly accessible information. This was Vyshinsky's great blunder, fully exploited by Trotsky in Mexico City, and the decisive contribution to the conclusions of the commission.

The entire case against Trotsky at the second purge trial was predicated on the confessions of Radek and Pyatakov that they had followed Trotsky's orders in orchestrating the campaign of sabotage and political terror in the Soviet Union. These orders had to have been received abroad from Trotsky or his agents—specifically, on three major occasions that were crucial for the prosecution's scenario and became the targets of Trotsky's defense. According to the confessions, (1) several defendants met Trotsky and his son L. L. Sedov in Copenhagen in 1932 to receive seditious instructions; (2) Vladimir Romm, a former correspondent for *Izvestia,* had met Trotsky and received instructions from him in the Bois de Boulogne in July 1933; and (3) G. L. Pyatakov, a former supporter of Trotsky and a key figure in the industrialization of the Soviet Union, the self-confessed linchpin of the entire conspiratorial machine in the Soviet Union, had flown to Oslo in December 1935 and met Trotsky outside the city.

The first of these allegations had to do with testimony at the first great purge trial by one Holtzman, a self-identified courier for the conspiracy. Holtzman described a trip to Copenhagen where he had put up at a Hotel Bristol and met Trotsky's son, who took him to see his father. Holtzman's confession was implausible on various counts—notably the considerable (if not absolutely conclusive) evidence that Trotsky's son Sedov could not have been in Copenhagen on that date. But the really embarrassing gaffe lay in the fact that the only Hotel Bristol in Copenhagen had been destroyed by a fire in 1917. The answer to this would be a photograph—published, among other places, in *Soviet Russia Today*[16]—which showed that there was an establishment described as the Café Bristol near a hotel, purporting to demonstrate that the witness had simply confused the café with the hotel. This line was shredded by Trotsky in his peroration in Mexico City: the shop was not a café but a candy store; it was not next to the hotel but two doors away, and it faced on another street. Holtzman had testified that he had put up at the hotel and met Sedov in the lobby. A glance at the photograph, which blacked out an area between the candy store and the hotel, carries considerable negative authority.

Vladimir Romm, who described himself as the link between Trotsky and the old Bolshevik leader Radek, testified to a meeting in the Bois de Boulogne during Trotsky's sojourn in France in 1933. The Trotsky defense presented many witnesses to the chronology of Trotsky's journey from the Mediterranean village of Cassis, where he entered France, to his French residence at Royan, where he arrived on July 25, and to the state of his health, which made it impossible for him to travel for the rest of the summer. The answer to this, of course, would be to claim that every relevant witness had lied.

The most important and contestable matter of fact would be contained in Pyatakov's testimony, which was the keystone of the entire structure erected by Vyshinsky at the second purge trial and was really indispensable for the plausibility of all three of the great trials. Pyatakov had confessed that he had been in Berlin in December 1935 on Soviet business, had flown with a forged passport to an aerodrome in Oslo and driven to Trotsky's residence, where he received instructions and learned that Trotsky was working with the Nazis. Before the trial had even concluded, Norwegian newspapers uncovered the fact that no foreign aircraft had landed at Oslo's airport during the month of December 1935 and that no foreign plane at all had used the field between September 1935 and May 1936. This rather remarkable discrepancy was assigned decisive weight in the Dewey Commission's conclusions because the entire edifice of "contradictions and deliberate falsifications" that had been erected by the prosecution depended on Pyatakov's testimony.[17]

The evidence about matters of fact constituted the basis for the commission's findings in its report *Not Guilty,* published at the end of the year. The commission assayed the credibility of the trials in the larger context of the shoddy legal procedures, the absence of relevant documentation, the perspective of Trotsky's life and writings, and the implausibility of the entire conspiratorial scenario; but the basis of its conclusions rested on the evidence that the key confessions involved factual fabrications.

In effect, the commission applied canons of evidence appropriate to both historical and legal investigations. Especially relevant were those characterized in Nicholas Rescher and Carey B. Joynt's article "Evidence in History and in the Law"[18] as the Argument from Silence and the Best Evidence Rule, and the Critical Use of Witness Testimony. The first rule proceeds from the assumption that when the best evidence relevant to the case is not produced by the party that controls it, "the law draws the inference that it would be unfavorable" to that party. Vyshinsky's crew sedulously avoided the pursuit of evidence that would have undermined the credibility of the confessions, such as the official records of the flight to Norway. As to the evaluation of witness testimony, the decisive criterion would be "the physical improbability of the facts related," and that criterion was, and remains, central to any judgment of historical truth in the case of Leon Trotsky.

It is, of course, much easier to assay the weight of the evidence now than it was then. The mutually corroborating confessions carried considerable authority. This sort of evidence is given due weight by juries and historians. But the evidence about "physical improbability" takes priority. A "cast-iron alibi" such as the absence of the accused from the scene of the crime carries an authority rarely outweighed by other evidence.

The contemporary responses to the commission's report, to Dewey's speeches setting out its conclusions, and to the entire procedure in Mexico City were more or less predictable in the light of political *partis pris.* From the beginning the hearings had seemed a dubious enterprise, not only to hard-line Stalinists and consistent fellow travelers but also to many "open-minded" liberals and independent radicals.[19] Once underway they were denigrated by ad hominem slander and coarse vituperation but also by clever argument. Consider, for example, the masterful application of selective skepticism by the journalists sent down to Mexico City by the *New Masses* to observe the hearings.[20]

Their obvious task was to disparage the entire procedure—to present it as a travesty of a trial, in which the Trotskyite "court" had stacked all of the cards in favor of the defendant. They were provided with powerful ammunition by the resignation of a member of the commission. Carleton Beals, who had been the only hostile interrogator of Trotsky, quarreled with the other members, resigned before the end of the hearings, and issued a widely published statement that described them as a whitewash: "The hushed adoration of the other members of the Commission for Mr. Trotsky throughout the hearings has defeated all spirit of honest investigation."[21]

Beals's motives are still subject to debate. He has been described as a Stalinist plant. His indignant denials of bias, publicly and in private correspondence, have been accepted by his biographer. In my view they are not convincing.[22]

The two reporters for the *New Masses* addressed not just the form of the hearings but also their substance, outlining an analysis of Trotsky's defense under two rubrics: "argument from personality, devoted to showing that it was morally and psychologically impossible for him to have engaged in treasonable counterrevolutionary activities," and "argument from 'actual facts' designed to show by circumstance and 'documentation' that Trotsky had not met or conspired with Moscow trial defendants."[23] The *New Masses* handled the first category by referring to those writings by Trotsky which asserted that the Soviet bureaucracy could be overthrown only by a new political revolution and that opposition to the will of the Soviet masses would be answered with violence.

What is more interesting for our purposes is the deft disposal of the key factual allegations. The treatment of the visit to Copenhagen emphasized the reliance on the unsupported word of Trotsky, his son, and his friends;

cited Beals's questions designed to raise the possibility that Sedov could have entered Denmark with a false passport; and played on the location of a Café Bristol as featured in the photo published in *Soviet Russia Today.* The writers disposed of the issue of the meeting in the Bois de Boulogne by remarking that all of the supporting testimony came from Trotsky's friends and disciples, that the French government had made public no documentation of Trotsky's movements, and that therefore "the inquiry commission would simply have to take his own word for it." This was also the way they handled the Pyatakov trip to Norway. As the statement regarding the absence of foreign flights to the Oslo airport between September 1935 and May 1936 was never confirmed by the Norwegian government, "again you had to take Trotsky's word for it."[24]

Readers of the *New Masses* might have believed in its writers' objectivity; they scarcely expected impartiality. But there were plenty of ostensibly impartial observers who arrived at the same conclusions as the *New Masses* or *Soviet Russia Today.* Walter Duranty in the *New York Times* and Joseph Barnes of the *Herald-Tribune* underwrote the validity of the purge trials. The *New Republic* published Duranty's "Riddle of Russia," where he simply summarized the Soviet line on the crimes of the Trotsky center, qualified by the familiar observation that opponents in the Soviet state had no choice but to work underground, therefore to conspire, therefore to commit treason.[25]

For many liberals and social democrats who stood somewhere between consistent fellow travelers and the anticommunist Left, the polemical cacophony over the trials induced something like logical anomie. At various times in 1937 and even after the third purge trial, in 1938, the editors of the *New Republic* and the *Nation* assumed a position of "Agnosticism on the Moscow Trials"—the title of a *New Republic* editorial. Perhaps the confessions were not completely convincing, they argued, but as it was impossible for foreigners fully to explore the evidence on either side, the fairest position was to suspend judgment.[26] As Frank Warren observed in his book *Liberals and Communism,*[27] the agnostic position and the argument that American intellectuals should suspend judgment to preserve unity in the Left effectively supported the Soviet status quo.

I don't intend to examine the various motives of the liberal intellectuals who more or less swallowed the party line (a subject thoughtfully treated in Warren's book), except with regard to the way that evidence about Trotsky's guilt or innocence was assimilated, refuted, or explained away. Nor do I wish to score points off my deluded predecessors with the complacency of facile hindsight, or to suggest that a qualified defense of historical objectivity is an affirmation of political conservatism.

By April 1937, the agnostic position had been superseded, to the satisfaction of Malcolm Cowley and many others, by the conviction that "the major part of the indictment was proved without much possibility of doubting it." Cowley did grant that some points depending on the testimony on Pyatakov's flight to Oslo seemed less firmly established. "On these points," he wrote, "we might suspend our judgment until more conclusive evidence is produced by one side or the other. The main question to be decided here is the scrupulousness and good faith of the Soviet authorities. It does not seem to me that Trotsky's moral guilt or innocence is really at stake."[28]

This remarkable approach was restated by the editors of the journal in response to the publication of the Dewey Commission report (which they hadn't "fully read"). The fact of Leon Trotsky's guilt or innocence did not answer the question of whether there was a conspiracy or speak to its obvious repercussions on international politics and the peace of the world. "Americans were more concerned with that than with allegations that Trotsky was its master mind."[29]

That chord was struck again by F. L. Schuman in a full-scale treatment of the case in the *Southern Review,* which reads something like "The Fellow Traveler's Guide to the Trials."[30] Having described himself as a political scientist and a liberal who "abjures both Stalinism and Trotskyism and abhors dictatorship and terrorism in all their forms," Schuman summarized the contradictory interpretations of the Trials, stated that there was insufficient evidence for an outside observer, such as the Dewey Commission, to arrive at a definitive judgment, and then did arrive, concluding that "the available testimony points unmistakably to the guilt of the accused and to the sincerity and substantial accuracy of the confessions."[31]

Schuman managed to ring changes in the various pragmatic, hermeneutic, and epistemological arguments that affirmed the truth of the trials. Thus along with reflections on the political meaning of Trotsky's role as the fallen angel of the revolution, and the worldwide consequences of opposition to the practical, consequential, anti-fascist leadership of the Soviet regime, Schuman confronted the evidence about actual events produced by the Trotsky defense before the Dewey Commission. In considering the three crucial allegations of the Trotsky defense—no meeting in Copenhagen, no rendezvous at the Bois de Boulogne, no Pyatakov journey to the empty airfield in Oslo—Schuman pleaded the absence of any verifiable testimony. As for Copenhagen, there were only the denials of Trotsky and his son and the testimony of their friends (Schuman did grant in passing that Moscow's photographic evidence on the Café Bristol is not quite convincing); as for the Paris rendezvous, "it is Trotsky's word against Romm's with no conclusive evidence from the French authorities available"; as for Pyatakov's flight, he "travelled incognito and his plane may have landed in some obscure spot without being officially noticed." Trotsky had been caught in politically expedient falsehoods in the past, Schuman continued, so there was no reason to suppose

that his unsupported testimony outweighed the mutually supporting confessions at the trials.

On top of all of this Schuman took out a little polemical insurance: "Even should all the allegations be disproved, Trotsky must remain under suspicion of complicity until he has demonstrated convincingly that he proposed to remove Stalin and to organize revolution against 'the bureaucracy' by methods other than those he was said to have employed."[32]

In subsequent issues, the *Southern Review* featured correspondence for and against Schuman's essay that followed the factional fault line on the American Left.[33] In a characteristic, ferociously cogent article, Sidney Hook concentrated his fire on Schuman's attempt to explain away the evidence regarding matters of fact presented before the commission in Mexico City.[34] Here, as throughout the debate on the trials, Hook hammered away at the factual question. "Guilt on all the matters charged," he wrote, "is a matter of evidence."[35]

This was Dewey's emphasis, too, as he presented and defended the conclusions of the Preliminary Commission of Inquiry. In a speech that he delivered after the deliberations of the commission but before publication of its final report, Dewey remarked that many honest liberals seemed to assume Trotsky's guilt because they believed that his theories and policies were mistaken. Here they suffered from the "intellectual and moral confusion that is the great weakness of professed liberals, for Trotsky was not convicted upon charges of theoretical and political opposition to the regime which exists in the Soviet Union. He was convicted upon certain definite charges whose truth or falsity is a matter of objective fact." The Dewey Commission was "trying to get at the truth as to the specific charges upon which he was convicted. This work is one of evidence and objective fact, not of weighing theories against each other."[36]

In his refutations of the commission's critics, Dewey seems to grant a hard autonomy to the "objective facts." Whether this approach is compatible with his instrumentalist version of inquiry and his conviction that "truth-falsity is not a property of propositions,"[37] or can be reconciled with Richard Rorty's celebration of "Dewey's suspicion of attempts to contrast an objective 'given' (e.g., 'the evidence,' 'the facts') with human 'takings,'"[38] I leave to those who are better equipped than I to say.

In the brief section on historical inquiry in Dewey's *Logic* there are passages that seem to promise small comfort to the historical objectivist. Dewey argues that the notion that historical inquiry simply reinstates the events that once happened "as they actually happened" is incurably naive, that "all historical construction is necessarily selective [and] necessarily written from the standpoint of the present [and] of that which is contemporaneously judged to be important in the present," and that "the writing of history is itself an historical event—it has existential consequences. . . . [T]here is no history except in terms of movement toward some outcome[;] . . . history cannot escape its own process. It will, therefore, always be rewritten."[39]

On the other hand, in the same section of the book Dewey refers to the control that must be exercised "with respect to the authenticity of evidential data" and grants that "it is certainly legitimate to say that a certain thing happened in a certain way at a certain time in the past, in case adequate data have been procured and critically handled." Dewey then qualifies this concession to an objectively discernible past: "But the statement, 'it actually happened in this way' has its status and significance *within* the scope and perspective of historical writing. It does not determine the logical conditions of historical propositions, much less the identity of these propositions with events in their original occurrence."[40]

Even with this qualifier, it is the assumption that statements about the past can be categorically true or false that allows the Dewey Commission to state "in the most categorical fashion that on the basis of all the evidence we find them [the accused at the purge trials] not guilty of having conspired with Leon Trotsky and Leon Sedov for any purpose whatsoever."[41]

Presumably, the commission and Dewey himself had answered to their satisfaction Dewey's question, which in my view is the question to put to all claims of historical truth: "What conditions must be satisfied in order that there may be grounded propositions regarding a sequential course of past events? The question is not even whether judgments about remote events can be made with *complete* warrant much less is it whether 'History can be a science.' It is: upon what grounds are some judgments about a course of past events more entitled to credence than certain other ones?"[42]

Dewey's "upon what grounds" is not equivalent to "according to what facts." Past events are not immediate; they are inferred. The authentication of Pyatakov's testimony depended not on immediately perceptible events but on inference from evidence. The point at which conflicting histories become incommensurable is not in contradictory versions of what actually happened but in fundamentally different criteria for establishing the truth.

The criteria for establishing the truth—the norms of valid inference—affirmed by the Dewey Commission and by the Soviet court were ostensibly identical but actually incommensurable. This was because the grounds for Stalinist belief were located in the party line. The Leninist argument that conceptions of truth were relative to social class, but that the class truths of the proletariat were congruent with reality, had been streamlined into a sort of Stalinist Thomism where the faithful had only to reaffirm by Reason the articles of faith bestowed by Revelation. Or, to borrow David Joravsky's characterization, Soviet ideology did not distinguish "between service of group interests and objective verification as essentially different bases for belief."[43]

What I wish to emphasize with regard to the international debate over the purge trials is that this essential criterion could not be acknowledged by the apologists for the Soviet line. That is, however sincerely they believed in the inerrancy of the Soviet leadership, or however cynically they lied in the light of that assumption, they could not simply assert it as their sole claim to authority. Their polemics did not afford the clarity about conflicting criteria for truth that one can see, for example, in those fundamentalists who assert the inerrancy of Scripture irrespective of any sort of evidence bearing the authority of science or common sense. In principle, this is where the argument ends. In fact, even creationists whose ultimate authority is a certain reading of biblical text are glad to cite "scientific" refutations of carbon dating. When it is polemically convenient, they too claim the cognitive authority of science and common sense. So did Stalin.[44]

For communist polemicists circa 1937 there could be no question about the objective validity of the findings of Soviet courts. The confessions alone were sufficient to establish the truth beyond any reasonable doubt. However, like a tongue to a sore tooth, party-line apologists kept returning to the manifest discrepancies between the confessions and the evidence regarding relevant time and place outside Russia. Even before the end of the Pyatakov trial Vyshinsky was impelled by the reports of the absence of flights to the Oslo airport to put "in the records" the following communication: "The consular department of the People's Commissariat of Foreign Affairs hereby informs the Procurator of the U.S.S.R. that according to information received by the embassy of the U.S.S.R. in Norway the Kjellere Aerodrome near Oslo receives all the year round, in accordance with international regulations, airplanes of other countries, and that the arrival and departure of airplanes is possible also in the winter months."[45] This feeble attempt to shore up the system of interdependent fabrications at its weakest point was followed some months later by the circulation of the "Café" Bristol photograph intended to validate the testimony on the Copenhagen connection.

William Z. Foster's *Questions and Answers on the Piatakov-Radek Trial* is a fair example of the many made-to-order polemics against the critics of the trials.[46] Foster did a rather good job of steering away from the evidential issues. He dismissed the absence of supporting documentation as the obvious result of the practical imperatives of conspiring, and he persuasively argued the implausibility of scripting and staging the complex scenario required by the trials, applying Ockham's razor, as it were, to Trotsky's throat. This argument seemed plausible to many reasonably open-minded liberals, as it appealed to the sense of how things worked in general without requiring the consideration of the credibility of specific claims. However, Foster felt obliged to dispose of the hard factual issues in passing: he straightened out the question of the location of the Café Bristol and dismissed "other Trotsky attacks upon the Oslo airplane incident, the Russian visit to Trotsky, etc." as based on "similar quibbles."

A more subtle response to the embarrassing factual discrepancies in the confessions was suggested by Joshua Kunitz in the *New Masses*. Kunitz surmised that some of the accused had made absurd confessions describing events that could not have occurred in order to discredit Soviet justice.[47] This line worked to defuse the critique of the obvious flaws in the confessions by vaguely granting their existence without drawing the specific consequences for the credibility of the entire indictment.

These examples of party-line polemic illustrate the fact that the Stalinists and the Dewey Commission ostensibly spoke the same language—that is, appealed to the same criteria of historical judgment in the case of Leon Trotsky. According to Soviet spokesmen it was perfectly clear that the facts of the case imposed the conclusion of the courts. For Dewey, Hook, and other critics of the Trials, as the confessions were demonstrably false, the entire case collapsed.

For the worldwide agglomeration of dedicated anti-fascists, fellow travelers, left-leaning liberals, and independent socialists who did not, or believed they did not, receive the party line as if from Sinai, things were not so simple. They too accepted the rules of rational discourse and "objective" investigation yet wished to evade their unwelcome conclusions. That is why some of them arrived at the phenomenally incoherent thesis of the irrelevance of the issue of Trotsky's guilt or innocence—a formulation as unacceptable to hard-line party liners as to anti-Stalinist logicians.

The thesis of the irrelevance of Trotsky's guilt or innocence was raised to a higher level of abstraction in arguments that attempted to substitute the authority of ultimate meaning for that of plausible inference. In this version the highest court of appeal was a hypostatized History whose judgment was validated not by an understanding of the past but by a reading of the future. If argued with excessive clarity, this approach simply reads as vulgar pragmatism—"The winners write the history"; but given the appropriate transcendental twist, it lifts the conversation above the question of mere fact into a higher realm. This sort of argument was only brought to full continental flower after the war, by Maurice Merleau-Ponty.[48]

A rather inchoate contemporary historicist interpretation of the trials was advanced in the *Workers' Age,* organ of the Lovestoneites, the American partisans of Bukharin. The issue of February 13, 1937, drew an analogy between the purge trials and the political trials of the French Revolution, remarking that it was pointless to pass judgment on the validity of the condemnations of the Girondists and the other victims of Jacobin justice. "In effect, we practically ignore the charges, refutations and counter-charges, and ask ourselves: which tendency was carrying forward the interests of the revolution, and which was obstructing it?" Projecting this criterion into the twentieth century, an "objective judgment" on the Moscow Trials proceeded from the view that "the course of events has generally confirmed the viewpoint of Stalin as against that of Trotsky on the vital questions of socialist construction in the Soviet Union, on the tempo of industrialization and on the collectivization of agriculture." This interpretation coincided with the conviction that there was indeed a "substantial bedrock of fact" supporting the accusations against the followers, or former followers, of Trotsky and Zinoviev.[49]

As the "course of events" came to include more trials and other victims, the Lovestoneites began to reexamine the grounds for judging Soviet justice. By the time the handwriting on the wall spelled Bukharin, Will Herberg and Bertram Wolfe had been convinced by the Dewey Commission report that the crucial admissions of Holtzman, Romm, and Pyatakov were a tissue of falsehoods constituting a "brazen . . . political frame up." The trials were still best understood from a "historico-political rather than a juridical point of view," but from that viewpoint it was apparent that the trials were actually a phenomenon of Stalin's desperate attempt to preserve an oppressive, reactionary regime.

A more sophisticated attempt to transform a vulgar argument from consequences into an interpretation of the trials' essential meaning (without completely avoiding the question of consequences) was Merleau-Ponty's critique of Koestler's *Darkness at Noon*. In a series of articles in *Les Temps Modernes* in 1946 and 1947, collected in his book *Humanism and Terror*, Merleau-Ponty staked out grounds for judgment that were, I would argue, incommensurable with those asserted by Dewey *or* his procommunist antagonists in the 1930s.

Merleau-Ponty located the authority for interpreting past events in a possible reading of the future, such that a record of what Dewey had called the objective facts was not the decisive consideration for the evaluation of the trials. While he recognized the extreme implausibility of Vyshinsky's scenario—he remarked that "it would truly be strange if Lenin had surrounded himself with supporters all of whom except one were capable of crossing over into the service of capitalist governments"[50]—he dismissed such criticisms as inessential.

To some extent Merleau-Ponty did accept the argument from consequences. He interpreted Bukharin's testimony in the third trial as an admission by Bukharin himself of the treasonable implications of what might have been a perfectly honest and rational critique of the regime: "The Moscow Trials might be seen as the drama of subjective honesty and objective treason."[51] Under certain circumstances an interpretation based on an "enlargement and falsification of the facts . . . remains historically permissible because political man is defined not by what he himself does but by the forces on which he counts." Thus, in a political universe in which to make any choice is to do violence to others, "to tell the truth and act out of conscience are nothing but alibis of a false morality; true morality is not concerned with what we think or what we want but obliges us to take a historical view of ourselves."[52]

Yet according to Merleau-Ponty, such a historical view is always problematic, because of the radical contingency of human destinies. The question of whether the Soviet system would be the political expression of a proletariat that was to fulfill its assigned role as the universal class remained open. Therefore, the ultimate judgment of the trials rested with the tribunal of the future—a position that, as Raymond Aron observed, would logically postpone history's judgment on the trials until the Last Judgment.[53]

Although John Dewey's philosophy seems light-years away from the Marxism-existentialism of Merleau-Ponty circa 1947, Dewey too argued that the question of whether a proposition about the past is true depends on present and future events. Valid propositions about events that occurred in the past can only be based on what is presently observable, and furthermore, the history under determination extends into the future. Only when past, present, and future events are brought into "temporal continuity with each other" are propositions about past events fully warranted.[54] This is Dewey's way of approaching the historical evidence. The definition of something presently experienced as historical evidence depends on the questions posed to the past—in Dewey's terms, "the inquiry." Thus the report on the absence of flights to the Oslo airport is evidence in the context of the investigation of Pyatakov's testimony about what actually happened in the past, which itself is significant because it relates to the ongoing inquiry regarding the alleged anti-Soviet conspiracy. This process suggests further investigation, thus projecting our assessment of judgments about the past into the future. Dewey's emphasis on the temporal continuum of validation is far different from Merleau-Ponty's location of judgment in some undefined future. In Merleau-Ponty's language it does not essentially matter whether Pyatakov made that trip to Oslo; to Dewey, that is precisely what matters.

For John Dewey, the obligation to tell the truth as a necessary constituent of a democratic polity took priority over the immediate, or distant, political consequences of any particular inquiry. Such a commitment entails one of the senses in which objectivity is ordinarily defined. Dewey's objectivity in this sense is recalled in James T. Farrell's description of his response to the evidence presented to the commission: "He [Dewey] went to Mexico more or less thinking that Stalin rather than Trotsky was right. On the basis of the evidence that Trotsky presented plus what Dewey read on the Moscow Trials, he came to the conclusion that Trotsky and the other defenders were right. However, he did not agree with Trotsky's political views."[55]

If Farrell's recollections were correct, Dewey was objective in the ordinary sense of what people mean when they say that someone is disinterested. "Disinterested," however, is not the equivalent of "neutral"; it is possible to be passionately dispassionate. Or to put it in currently fashionable language, Dewey's commitment to objectivity in this sense did not transcend the "historicity" of such a commitment. The decision to tell the truth according to his lights, irrespective of the consequences, was a socially, historically, morally mediated choice—just as one might have chosen to ignore the facts and grind an axe.

Objectivity in another sense was involved in Dewey's choice of the criteria for judging the truth of propositions about the past, in his choice of "the grounds on which some judgments about a course of past events [are] more entitled to credence than certain other ones." These are the grounds that impelled Dewey to identify some arguments about Trotsky's guilt or innocence as good—for example, those which spoke to the "physical improbability of the facts related"—and others as bad—for example, those emphasizing Trotsky's personality, or the virtues of the Soviet system, or the consequences for the Popular Front.

To put it another way, the correct assertions that past events are mediated through present preconceptions, that conflicting interpretations of complex events are rarely settled by definitive demonstrations, that historical interpretations are dependent on the language in which they are cast, or that it is impossible to evaluate discrete bits of evidence outside of temporal and ideological contexts, do not justify the stance of agnosticism toward the Moscow trials that was affected by many of the 1930s liberals. It is understandable that men and women of good will took that stance; they were mistaken. The sound arguments on Pyatakov's flight now seem virtually self-evident, independent of Khrushchev's revelations or anything else we have learned since 1956. No one now accepts the bad arguments.

We now find the commission's conclusions more persuasive than those of William Z. Foster, Malcolm Cowley, or F. L. Schuman, not because of their superior tropological strategies, or because of a skillful parade of rhetorical figures, or the hermeneutic fusing of historical horizons, or a dialogic interaction between this reader and those texts, but because they satisfy familiar criteria of empirical inference and rational discourse. This is not to deny that all arguments, including Dewey's and mine, are rhetorical in some sense, but to argue that rhetorical preferences do not exempt historical discourse from evidential norms.

Perhaps one might say that all of this amounts to kicking an open door, that no sane person denies that some statements about past events are true and some are false. But that brings us back to Dewey's question: on what grounds do we prefer one historical account to another; on what grounds do we identify errors and refute lies?

According to Sidney Hook's memoirs, his answer to that question was crucially affected by the experience of the trials:

> The upshot of the Moscow trials affected my epistemology, too. I had been prepared to recognize that understanding the past was in part a function of our need to cope with the present and future, that rewriting history was in a sense a method of making it. But the realization that such a view easily led to the denial of objective historical truth, to the cynical view that not only is history written

by the survivors but that historical truth is created by the survivors—which made untenable any distinction between historical fiction and truth—led me to rethink some aspects of my objective relativism. Because nothing was absolutely true and no one could know the whole truth about anything, it did not follow that it was impossible to establish any historical truth beyond a reasonable doubt. Were this to be denied, the foundations of law and society would ultimately collapse. Indeed, any statement about anything may have to be modified or withdrawn in the light of additional evidence, but only on the assumption that the additional evidence has not been manufactured. At any point in time, the upshot of converging lines of evidence must guide judgment.[56]

I am sure that there are those who would ask Hook to justify the universal standards that distinguish historical fiction from truth—to specify the location of some historical Archimedes' point. But he would not have to answer them if they justified their arguments, explicitly or implicitly, in his language. And if they spoke a completely different language there would be no dialogue. If Hook's political opponents had simply located the criterion of truth-value in Stalin's bosom there would have been no way for Hook to refute them, but they would have lost all credibility even with those who were desperate to be credulous.

Hook's decision too was a moral choice, but without that choice there are no grounds on which to refute murderous historical lies.

NOTES

[1] Commission of the Central Committee of the C.P.S.U.(B.), ed., *History of the Communist Party of the Soviet Union (Bolsheviks)* (New York, 1939), 346-48.

[2] Pierre Vidal-Naquet, "A Paper Eichmann?," *Democracy* (April 1981): 91. The work to which Vidal-Naquet refers is Michael Sayers and Albert E. Kahn, *The Great Conspiracy: The Secret War against Soviet Russia* (Boston, 1946), which now reads as a crude party-line product.

[3] For the published transcript of the hearings and the commission's conclusions, see the Preliminary Commission of Inquiry's *The Case of Leon Trotsky: Report of Hearings on the Charges Made against Him in the Moscow Trials* (New York, 1937); and *Not Guilty: Report of the Commission of Inquiry into the Charges Made against Leon Trotsky in the Moscow Trials* (New York, 1937). For useful descriptions of the hearings and the attendant controversy, see James T. Farrell, "Dewey in Mexico," in *John Dewey: Philosopher of Science and Freedom,* ed. Sidney Hook (New York, 1950), 351-77; Sidney Hook, *Out of Step: An Unquiet Life in the Twentieth Century* (New York, 1987), 218-47; Isaac Deutscher, *The Prophet Outcast: Trotsky, 1929-1940* (London, 1963), 371-82; Gary Bullert, *The Politics of John Dewey* (Buffalo, 1983), 134-41; Alan Wald, "Memories of the John Dewey Commission: Forty Years Later," *Antioch Review* 35 (1977):

438-51, and *The New York Intellectuals: The Rise and Decline of the Anti-Stalinist Left from the 1930s to the 1980s* (Chapel Hill, 1987), 128-39; and Robert B. Westbrook, *John Dewey and American Democracy* (Ithaca, 1991), 480-87.

[4] Farrell, "Dewey in Mexico," 358n.

[5] Hayden White, *Metahistory: The Historical Imagination in Nineteenth-Century Europe* (Baltimore, 1980), 428, 433.

[6] Richard Rorty, "Solidarity or Objectivity?" in *Post-Analytic Philosophy,* ed. John Rajchman and Cornel West (New York, 1985), 3-19.

[7] Joel Foreman and Richard Rorty, "The Humanities: Asking Better Questions, Doing More Things: An Interview with Richard Rorty," *Federation Review* 7 (March/April 1985): 17. Rorty's point is, "The fact that the Nazis were bad is so clear and evident that I cannot imagine getting more conviction on the subject from one's study in literature, history, or philosophy."

[8] Preliminary Commission of Inquiry, *Case of Leon Trotsky,* xv.

[9] The Preliminary Commission was actually a subcommittee of the Commission of Inquiry, which also included John R. Chamberlain, Alfred Rosmer, E. A. Ross, Wendelin Thomas, Carlo Tresca, and F. Zamora.

[10] "An Open Letter to American Liberals," *Soviet Russia Today,* March 1937, 14-15.

[11] Alfred Kazin, *Starting Out in the Thirties* (New York, 1965), 85, 137.

[12] *New Republic,* March 17, 1937.

[13] Malcolm Cowley, *And I Worked at the Writer's Trade: Chapters of Literary History, 1918-1978* (New York, 1978), 148-52. In 1984 Cowley granted that he "grossly deceived" himself about the trials (Cowley, "Echoes from Moscow: 1937-1938," *Southern Review* 20 [January 1984]: 3).

[14] For example, "Behind the Soviet Trials," *Nation,* February 6, 1937.

[15] Corliss Lamont, "The Moscow Trials," *Soviet Russia Today,* January 1938, 26.

[16] *Soviet Russia Today,* March 1937, 7.

[17] Preliminary Commission of Inquiry, *Not Guilty,* 361.

[18] Nicholas Rescher and Carey B. Joynt, "Evidence in History and in the Law," *Journal of Philosophy* 66 (June 1959): 561-78.

[19] For example, "The Trotsky Commission," *Nation,* May 1, 1937; *New Republic,* March 17, 1937; Selden Redman, "Trotsky in the Kremlin," *Common Sense,* December 1937.

[20] Marion Hammett and William Smith, "Inside the Trotsky Trial: A Report by Two Eye-Witnesses," *New Masses,* April 27, 1937, 6-11.

[21] See, for example, "Mr. Beals Resigns from Trotsky Commission," *Soviet Russia Today,* May 1937, 38.

[22] John A. Britton, *Carleton Beals: A Radical Journalist in Latin America* (Albuquerque, 1987), 166-86. Beals's break with the commission was precipitated by his question as to whether Trotsky had instructed the Soviet agent Borodin to foment revolution in Mexico in the 1920s. This seemed to threaten the security of Trotsky's asylum in Mexico.

[23] *New Masses,* April 27, 1937, 6.

[24] *Ibid.,* 9.

[25] Walter Duranty, "The Riddle of Russia," *New Republic,* July 14, 1937. On Duranty's dubious journalistic career see E. J. Taylor, *Stalin's Apologist: Walter Duranty, The* New York Times*'s Man in Moscow* (New York, 1990); and Malcolm Muggeridge, *Chronicles of Wasted Time: The Green Stick* (New York, 1973), 254-56.

[26] The paradigmatic assertion of agnosticism was the analysis of the trial materials by the Yale law professor Fred Rodell, in "Agnosticism in the Moscow Trials," *New Republic,* May 19, 1937.

[27] Frank Warren, *Liberals and Communism* (Bloomington, 1966), 185-92.

[28] *New Republic,* April 7, 1973, and December 22, 1937.

[29] *Ibid.,* December 22, 1937.

[30] Frederick L. Schuman, "Leon Trotsky: Martyr or Renegade?" *Southern Review* 3 (1937-38): 51-74.

[31] *Ibid.,* 64.

[32] *Ibid.,* 68.

[33] *Ibid.,* 199-208, published responses by Malcolm Cowley, Max Eastman, John Dewey, Carleton Beals, and James T. Farrell.

[34] Sidney Hook, "Liberalism and the Case of Leon Trotsky," *Southern Review* 3 (1937-38): 267-82. This was followed by further correspondence between Hook, Beals, Schuman, and Farrell (pp. 406-16). For a similar debate on the English Left, see Peter Deli, "The Image of the Russian Purges in the *Daily Herald* and the *New Statesman,*" *Journal of Contemporary History* 20 (April 1985): 261-82; "How They Saw the Moscow Trials," *Survey* 41 (April 1962): 87-95; *New Statesman,* January 30, April 10, and November 6 and 13, 1937; and *Nation,* March 5, 12, and April 23, 1938.

[35] *New Republic,* June 2, 1937.

[36] "Dewey Rebukes Those 'Liberals' Who Will Not Look into Facts," *New Leader,* May 15, 1937. In his answer to Selden Rodman's piece on Trotsky in *Common Sense,* Dewey wrote, "The question is one of fact, based on one side on the testimony of the Moscow Trials, and on the other side upon the evidence, oral, written and documentary, which the Commission itself gathered" (*Common Sense,* January 1938). In a subsequent critique of Leon Trotsky's "Their Morals and Ours" (*New International,* June 1938, 163-73), Dewey remarks that the means presumably directed to the liberation of mankind "have to be viewed and judged on the ground of their actual objective results" (Dewey, "Means and Ends: Their Interdependence and Leon Trotsky's Essay on 'Their Morals and Ours,'" *The Later Works, 1925-1953* [Urbandale, 1988], 13:351).

[37] John Dewey, *Logic, The Theory of Inquiry* (New York, 1938), 287.

[38] Richard Rorty, *Objectivity, Relativism, and Truth* (Cambridge, 1994), 65. For an introduction to the controversy over Rorty's Dewey, see Westbrook, *John Dewey and American Democracy,* 539-42.

[39] Dewey, *Logic,* 234-39.

[40] *Ibid.,* 236-37.

[41] Preliminary Commission of Inquiry, *Not Guilty,* 361.

[42] Dewey, *Logic,* 231. Ernest Gellner, *Legitimation of Belief* (London, 1974), 31, puts it this way: "For modern philosophy, and its epistemological stress, gain enormously in plausibility when they are read, not as a descriptive or explanatory account of what knowledge 'is really like,' but as a formulation of norms which are to govern and limit our cognitive behavior."

[43] David Joravsky, "Soviet Ideology," *Soviet Studies* 18 (1966): 6.

[44] In the 1920s Bertrand Russell remarked on the "practical pragmatism" of frameups in Russian political trials which the Russian police made every effort to conceal: "This effort after concealment shows that even policemen believe in objective truth in the case of a criminal trial" (*The Will to Doubt* [New York, 1958], 11).

[45] People's Commissariat of Justice of the U.S.S.R., *Report of Court Proceedings in the Case of the Anti-Soviet Trotskyite Centre* (Moscow, 1937), 443.

[46] William Z. Foster, *Questions and Answers on the Piatakov-Radek Trial* (New York, 1937).

[47] Joshua Kunitz, "The Moscow Trial," *New Masses,* March 15, 1938.

[48] Maurice Merleau-Ponty, *Humanism and Terror: An Essay on the Communist Problem,* trans. John O'Neill (Boston, 1969).

[49] *Workers' Age,* February 20, 1937. See also the issues of February 13, April 24, and December 18, 1937; and Bertram Wolfe, *New Republic,* June 16 and November 24, 1937.

[50] Merleau-Ponty, *Humanism and Terror,* 73.

[51] *Ibid.,* 44.

[52] *Ibid.,* 53, 103.

[53] Raymond Aron, *The Opium of the Intellectuals,* trans. Terence Kilmartin (New York, 1967), 133.

[54] Dewey, *Logic,* 237-39.

[55] Farrell quoted in Corliss Lamont, ed., *Dialogue on John Dewey* (New York, 1959), 69.

[56] Hook, *Out of Step,* 218-19.

Shannon Sullivan (essay date 1997)

SOURCE: "Democracy and the Individual: To What Extent is Dewey's Reconstruction Nietzsche's Self-Overcoming?" in *Philosophy Today,* Vol. 41, No. 2, Summer, 1997, pp. 299-312.

[*In the following essay, Sullivan finds similarities between Dewey's esthetics and the writings of Friedrich Nietzsche.*]

The mere combination of the names of John Dewey and Friedrich Nietzsche in the title of an essay might offend some readers. Many of the scholars of American pragmatism I have met view Nietzsche as just one more of those Continental, postmodern philosophers whose work, while perhaps stylish and currently *en vogue,* contributes little of value to philosophy because the issues with which they concern themselves in no way connect with the lives of the most people. The reaction of many scholars of Continental philosophy I know to American pragmatism has been to dismiss it as concerned only with "utility" narrowly conceived, e.g., with the usefulness of an idea for making money, ensuring that parking places are available at work, securing good health care, etc.[1] I do not want to suggest that members of the two philosophical camps are always or necessarily antagonistic toward one another—certainly there are some who find the intersection of Continental philosophy and American pragmatism to be fruitful.[2] Nonetheless, the relationship between scholars of American pragmatism and Continental philosophy is often cool, if not, at times, openly hostile.

Thus to claim, as I will here, that Dewey and Nietzsche have much in common and, furthermore, that the work of Dewey continues and perhaps even improves upon that of Nietzsche probably seems at best provocative, at worst ridiculous.[3] After all, the principal aim of Dewey's work seems to be to support and promote everything Nietzsche abhorred: a humanistic, liberal democracy that has the goal of helping humans find ways to eliminate suffering in their lives. As an acquaintance at a recent meeting of the APA remarked, connecting Nietzsche and American pragmatist William James might be plausible, but not Nietzsche and Dewey. A friend and Nietzsche scholar even went so far as to claim that Dewey's pragmatist is Nietzsche's "last man."

Indeed, with only a glance, Dewey's program of pragmatic democracy does appear much like that of the "levelers" described by Nietzsche in *Beyond Good And Evil* and the "last," or "ultimate," man described by Zarathustra:

> These falsely so-called "free spirits"—being eloquent and prolifically scribbling slaves of the democratic taste and its "modern ideas"; they are all human beings without solitude. . . . What they would like to strive for with all their powers is the universal green-pasture happiness of the herd, with security, lack of danger, comfort, and an easier life for everyone. . . .[4]

> The earth has become small, and upon it hops the Ultimate Man, who makes everything small. . . . "We have discovered happiness," say the Ultimate Men and blink. They have left the places where living was hard: for one needs warmth. . . . They still quarrel, but they soon make up—otherwise indigestion would result.[5]

The levelers and last men are primarily characterized by their inability to overcome themselves. They shun the danger, pain and turmoil of the sacrifice of themselves that is necessary for the birth of the *Übermensch.* They are not strong enough to produce greatness out of themselves, and so they make virtues out of their weakness and call rest, peace, and security humanity's ultimate happiness.[6]

If it is true that Dewey's pragmatism excludes self-transformation and extols the "virtues" of uninterrupted calmness and security, then Dewey indeed offers the democratic ideals of the last man. However, as we will see, Dewey's pragmatist is much closer to Nietzsche's free spirit than to the last man, and Dewey's promotion of democracy need not obscure this connection. The democracy that Nietzsche rejects is *not* the same democracy that Dewey endorses.[7] Dewey's democratic pragmatism is characterized by what Dewey calls reconstruction, and reconstruction, particularly as applied to the self, is a type of self-transformation remarkably similar to the self-overcoming described by Nietzsche.[8]

My exploration of the connections between Nietzsche and Dewey will be composed of the following four parts. First, I will briefly review Nietzsche's self-overcoming, followed by a more detailed examination of Dewey's reconstruction.[9] Then I will explore the similarities of Dewey's reconstruction and conception of the self as organism and Nietzsche's self-overcoming and conception of the self as body. Finally, I will return to the topic of democracy and find that the question of the irreconcilability of Nietzsche and Dewey's differences regarding democracy turns on the issue of Nietzsche's individualism. If a philosopher who is a "cultural physician" conceives the individual as atomistic (as Nietzsche appears to do), then it is possible for him or her to "cure" the culture by aristocratically caring for just a few individuals. However, if one conceives the individual as having fluid boundaries between it and others in its society (as Dewey does), then the cultural physician must democratically try to cure all individuals in the culture. If Nietzsche's individual is not atomistic (and, I will argue, we should hesitate to conclude that it is), then Nietzsche must abandon his aristocratic approach for a (Deweyan-style) democratic one so that his goal of great cultural health in the West might be reached. Dewey's democracy is not necessarily opposed to, but instead can be seen as complementing and even improving upon Nietzsche's philosophy of self-overcoming.[10]

NIETZSCHE AND SELF-OVERCOMING

To understand self-overcoming best, we must remember that for Nietzsche, the self is bodily and multiple—or, rather, because the self is bodily, it is multiple. To claim that the self is the body is not to say that "spirit" and "consciousness" do not exist, but rather that they are (merely) out-growths and instruments of the many drives and affects of the body and thus are secondary to the body.[11] Through these instruments, the body organizes and simplifies its plurality to produce conscious thought. Or, we might say, conscious thought is precisely the organization and simplification of plurality, one particular perspective of the body and its multiplicity.[12] The multiplicity of the body is unified, but this unity is not the elimination of multiplicity.[13] Rather, the body produces a functional unity, a temporary organization of itself in the form of an alignment of its drives that will be renegotiated again and again. We may continue to talk of the "soul," but only if we acknowledge that it is no mysterious immortal essence but instead the changing "social structure of the drives and the affects,"[14] that is, the behaviors of and relations between the various bodily instincts.[15]

The shifting plurality of the "unified" self helps explain how self-overcoming is indeed *self*-overcoming. Self-overcoming is the "law of life:" "all great things bring about their *own* destruction through an act of self-overcoming."[16] To bring about one's own destruction means that self-overcoming is not done to one by something other but is something done to oneself. One destroys what one is now to make possible the creation of the new. That which must self-overcome will be the power that fuels its self-overcoming. Because the self is a plurality and not merely the one drive or affect that dominates and gives the self its "character," the self contains within itself

the possibility of a reorganization of drives, producing a new configuration of the "soul."[17] For example, our old values are the very means by which the new will be produced.[18] It is our herd-like virtues, such as chastity, poverty and humility, that can provide the energy and discipline that make possible their own self-overcoming.[19]

The possibilities for reconfiguration of the "unity" of the self are infinite, and thus self-overcoming is never complete. In Zarathustra's words, "life itself told me this secret: 'Behold,' it said, 'I am that *which must overcome itself again and again.*"[20] While self-overcoming is a goal that Nietzsche holds out for those who are strong enough for it, it is not a goal in the sense that it can ever be finally and completely achieved. It is not something to be done once only, but rather again and again. This is why life tells Zarathustra that it is both a goal and "conflict of goals."[21] Self-overcoming conflicts with the idea of goals because it interrupts all goals by requiring that they eventually self-overcome, i.e., sacrifice themselves for other, new "goals."

DEWEY AND RECONSTRUCTION

While Dewey never uses the term "self-overcoming," he sounds remarkably similar to Zarathustra in *Art as Experience* when Zarathustra speaks of the role of *untergang* in self-overcoming.[22] Dewey writes:

> There is . . . an element of undergoing, of suffering in its large sense, in every experience. Otherwise there would be no taking in of what preceded. For "taking in" in any vital experience is something more than placing something on top of consciousness over what was previously known. It involves reconstruction which may be painful.[23]

According to Dewey, reconstruction is a transaction between self and world in which there is a "yielding of the self"[24] to that which is "taken in." In and through experience, the self remakes itself and, in the process, its environment is remade as well.

To further our understanding of Dewey's notion of reconstruction, we must first realize that for Dewey, the self is an organism made up of habits and impulses. Impulses are "blind dispersive burst[s] of . . . energy,"[25] "something primitive, yet loose, undirected, initial,"[26] which push us in various and often conflicting directions. They are much like what Nietzsche refers to as the body's plurality of drives and affects and are that which we and Nietzsche often call "instincts." Dewey prefers "impulse" to "instinct" because he believes the latter is too heavily laden with the connotation of necessary and definite organization, which impulses do not have. Impulses can be organized and unified, but in and of themselves, they are chaotic and purposeless.

Habits are that which provide impulses with direction; habits are the acquired patterns of activity that organize the energy of impulses. Already we can see that, for Dewey, just as "impulse" means something different from our usual use of the word, so does "habit." Habits are much different from "bad habits," and they are not, as we often think, restricted to repetition and routine. Habits are dispositions to ways that an organism responds to its world.[27] For example, when I sit down in a chair, my body responds to the chair with a particular posture, say, slumping. This posture is a readiness to act in a certain fashion whenever I am presented with a situation that calls forth a response from me and thus is one of my habits.

We should note two important points in conjunction with this example: first, my bodily posture is not a conscious response to my world. Habits are more the style that an organism has than specific acts it chooses. Second, while many habits, such as slumping, are physiological, habits are mental as well. People have particular methods or styles of thinking about life, approaching and solving problems, and so on. But this second point must not be construed as affirming a firm distinction between body and mind, the physical and the mental. Like posture, thinking is a particular way an organism organizes impulses and replies to its world. Human rationality is not something located in a realm apart from habit and the body. It is "embedded" in the organism in that it is the organism's attainment of a harmonious organization of its many impulses and habits.[28] It is our failure to realize rationality's relation to habit that has produced our tradition's division of mind and body. To claim that thought is a habit not only eliminates a sharp mind-body distinction, it also insists that much of our thought is not conscious. Certainly conscious thought exists, but it is only a small fraction of the thinking that humans do. Habits, both of the body and thought, are that which fund our conscious thoughts and ideas. This means that a way of thinking that is not ingrained in habit is ineffective and will be betrayed by thinking methods that are so ingrained.[29]

We can see this point most clearly in the above example of body posture and, in particular, how I might change my posture. We tend to assume that my failure to sit up straight is a failure of reason or "will power." But Socrates was wrong when he said that to do the good, all one needed was knowledge of the good. Conscious knowledge of what good posture is, is not sufficient for the attainment of good posture. By itself, it will help me sit differently for a while, but differently as "only a different kind of badly."[30] After a brief spell of my different kind of poor posture, such as awkwardly over-arching my back in order to (over)compensate for my tendency to slump, I will likely revert to my usual bad way of sitting (i.e., slumping). The key to achieving good posture is not to consciously think my way to good posture but to find an act that keeps me from falling into my usual bad posture and that initiates the development of a new, improved posture.[31] That is, I must find a way to change my habits to change my bad posture. To understand just how habits might be changed and thus how the self might reconstruct itself, we need to look more closely at the relationship of habit to impulse in the human organism.

I have said that impulses are the raw energies that are organized by our habits. As these raw energies, impulses are also that which makes the change of habits possible. "Impulses are the pivots upon which the re-organization of activities turn, they are agencies of deviation, for giving new directions to old habits and changing their quality."[32] The impulse of fear, for example, may become either cowardice, bravery, skepticism, respect for authority, or something else, depending on the way that fear is woven together with other impulses and existing habits.[33] But how exactly is impulse the impetus for change if habit is always organizing impulses in its own image?[34] That is, if my habits have developed such that I always become cowardly when scared, how can my impulse of fear help give that habit "new direction?"

We seem to have stumbled into a vicious circle in which impulses, once habituated, work only to further reinforce one's habits. How can habits change if "habits once formed perpetuate themselves, by acting unremittingly upon the native stock of abilities?"[35] To see our way out of this circle, we must understand that the self is not an atomistic, but a culturally constructed self. When Dewey defines habit as a readiness to act in response to the world, he is in effect claiming that there is no self separate from the world in which it exists. Dewey compares habits to physiological functions like breathing and digesting not only to emphasize the importance of the body in his account, but also to argue that habits emerge as a product of the interaction between organism and environment. For example, bodies take things from their environment (food), which are integrated into and transform the body (nourishment), and the body in turn releases things back into the environment (excrement), which are used to transform the environment (fertilizing the soil, which produces more food). Likewise, "breathing is an affair of the air as truly as of the lungs," which means that "habits are ways of using and incorporating the environment in which the latter has its say as surely as the former."[36]

By "environment," Dewey not only means things like food and air. Because society and culture are human environments no less than nature is, a human organism's interaction with its physical environment is always social and cultural. An individual's habits affect social customs, and social customs, which are "widespread uniformities of habit,"[37] in turn shape the personal customs and habits of individuals. Thus, because the self interacts with its environment, new material is always "entering" the self, disrupting and challenging the established self. When the organism is in a fairly stable, unchanging environment, habits can indeed become ruts in which change is nearly impossible. But when the organism finds itself in a new or unusual situation, the old habits no longer function smoothly as they did in the old situation, and the organism's peaceful coordination of impulses and habits is thrown into disarray. It is at this point, in the midst of tension, conflict and confusion, that growth and change can occur. The organism must create new patterns by which to organize its impulses, new ways of responding to its environment, which disrupt old habits and lay the groundwork for new ones. These new habits, in turn, contribute to the shaping and reshaping of larger patterns, or customs, that exist in the organism's cultural environment.

We should not confuse the interdependency of self and environment with a determinism of the self. While voluntarists might charge that the Deweyan self is determined by its environment's construction of it and thus unfree, in fact, "the self acts as well as undergoes, and its undergoings are not impressions stamped upon an inert wax but depend upon the way the organism reacts and responds."[38] The relationship between self and environment is that of a creative cycle. Change in the environment motivates change in the organism, which (because the organism is part of and not set apart from its environment) changes the environment in return, which stimulates yet more change in the organism, and so on. This cycle is best represented by the figure of a spiral since the organism never returns to exactly the same "place" it was before a cycle of change began.[39] The interaction between organism and environment produces a new organism and a new environment. While we have been emphasizing one half of the cycle—the reconstruction of the organism—we cannot fully or adequately understand self-reconstruction unless we include the other half—the reconstruction of the environment. For Dewey, reconstruction is at once the reconstruction of the self and the reconstruction of society.

SELF-TRANSFORMATION IN NIETZSCHE AND DEWEY

For Dewey, the self is a plurality of impulses, organized and unified by its conscious and unconscious habits and constructed by means of interaction with others. The self becomes artist, sculpting herself through her transactions with her environment: "it is the office of art in the individual person, to compose differences, to do away with isolations and conflicts among the elements of our being, to utilize oppositions among them to build a richer personality."[40] Yet, as is the case for Nietzsche, the created unity of the self does not eliminate the self's multiplicity. According to Dewey, selfhood is always in the making because of "the relative fluidity and diversity of the constituents of selfhood."[41] "There is no one ready-made self behind activities," and in fact, "any self is capable of including within itself a number of inconsistent selves, of unharmonized dispositions."[42] The embodiment of the Deweyan organism ensures that the organism is always a plurality, and the unity of the Deweyan organism occurs as a temporary harmony of impulses and desires that will be interrupted and reconfigured.[43] Like a good artist, the "good" self is one who blends plurality and unity such that her "work" has the capacity "to hold together within itself the greatest variety and scope of opposed elements."[44]

As the earlier image of the spiral suggests, self-reconstruction includes a continuity between the old self and the new self, just as self-overcoming does. It is out of an organism's old habits that new ones are created.[45] As we have seen, to create new habits is to reconfigure the plurality of impulses of the self, allowing for new expressions of impulses through new organizations of them. An organism does not "magically" create new habits that have no connection to the old. That we often think change occurs in this way is evidence of our stubborn insistence upon the "free will."[46] Habits, not free will, effect change. Without a corresponding change in habits, any decision made by the "will" is ineffectual. In that sense, habits are our will.[47]

Nor should we think that because impulses are fresh while habits are sometimes stale, impulse by itself effects change. A particular combination of habit and impulse must be in place for change to occur because habits without impulses are too rigid and impulses without habit are too chaotic to effect self-reconstruction. "Impulse is a source, an indispensable source, of liberation; but only as it is employed in giving habits pertinence and freshness does it liberate power."[48] By themselves, impulses are unintelligent, merely "a surging, explosive discharge."[49] They may instigate change, but it is habit that must carry out the hard work of making the change.[50] It is only when channeled, directed, "sublimated" that impulses can become creative and intelligent forces that furnish the dynamic to carry out an organism's projects.[51] The image of the spiral is also helpful for our understanding of self-reconstruction because it indicates a process without end. Reconstruction, like self-overcoming, is not a one-time procedure. It has no final goal of completion because to be alive is, to use imagery common to both Dewey and Nietzsche, to be continually growing, putting out new "leaves" and dropping the old.[52] To what end is this growth? For Dewey, as for Nietzsche, the "end" of growth is growth itself; there are no final, fixed ends, no point at which the organism is finished changing and reconstructing itself.[53] "If it is better to travel than arrive, it is because traveling is a constant arriving, while arrival that precludes further traveling is most easily attained by going to sleep or dying."[54]

Dewey insists that such "traveling" is important for human organisms and, furthermore, that welcoming such adventures is the sign of a particularly healthy and vibrant organism. Our account of reconstruction has been incomplete up to this point because it has implied that "traveling" occurs only because an unstable environment throws a reluctant organism onto the highway of reconstruction. Unfortunately, it is true that many people undergo self-reconstruction only because their environment forces them into it. And because so much of many people's lives is dull, uninterrupted routine, many people grow very little. Because they are still physically alive, we must acknowledge that a minimal amount of reconstruction does occur in their lives.[55] But since "the process of life *is* variation,"[56] it is not too much of an exaggeration to say that on the continuum of life, they are very near the end that is (literal and figurative) death.

It is these reluctant "travelers" that are very similar to Nietzsche's last man. They want sleep, peace, and rest.

Conflict, turmoil and upheaval are viewed by them as only extremely painful disruptions and never also as opportunities for new growth. Strife is something to be avoided at all costs, not something to be welcomed for the change that is made possible by it. But not all avoid self-reconstruction. The main difference between those who shun and those who welcome reconstruction is in the type of habits that each has. Habits can be either unintelligent and routine or intelligent and artful.[57] The former are enslaved, stuck in old ruts. They are mechanical, inflexible and stubbornly resist any sort of change. The latter, on the other hand, are flexible and plastic. Much like Nietzsche's free spirits, those with artful habits see resistance, obstacles, and the resulting tension within themselves as enriching elements and moments.

As is the case for Nietzsche, the artist and the scientist are models for and often instances of Dewey's free-spirited pragmatist.[58] Their creativity and experimentalism are styles of living and thinking—habits—that ideally all organisms would have in all aspects of their lives.[59] In learning habits, these organisms have learned the habit of on-going learning and growth.[60] Dewey, like Nietzsche, refers to the child when describing what he hopes humanity might become: "for certain moral and intellectual purposes adults must become as little children."[61] While Dewey's uses of the figure of the child may be more literal than Nietzsche's, Dewey also finds in the child a type of life in which originality and playfulness have not been tamed or transformed into seriousness.[62] According to Dewey, childhood "remains a standing proof of a life wherein growth is normal not an anomaly, activity a delight not a task, and where habit-forming is an expansion of power not its shrinkage."[63]

However, Dewey's use of the imagery of childhood does not signal a brand-new beginning for the organism in which the organism is free to adopt any belief or habit at will.[64] The organism is never a "clean slate" on which a new picture is painted. Recalling that old habits are the material for the creation of new habits, to insist upon change is not to abandon the past for the future but to insist upon the alteration of the past in order to make possible the future.[65] Dewey's pragmatist is a questioning experimenter who lives knowing that when "we once start thinking no one can guarantee where we shall come out,"[66] but she also realizes that habits are the medium through which change occurs. At any one time, some habits must be taken for granted in order for the organism's project of self-questioning to be possible.[67] Total plasticity of the self does not turn the pragmatist into a more free, more spontaneous adventurer but instead into chaotic, ineffectual pulp.[68]

Zarathustra, on the other hand, tells us that the child is "a new beginning" and "a first motion,"[69] suggesting that for Nietzsche, the self overcomes herself entirely all at once. Many of Nietzsche's other descriptions of the free spirit make it easy to think that his experimentalism calls everything into question at the same time. In *The Gay Science,* the free spirit is one who, having not just left behind but destroyed the secure land she once stood on, is now afloat on the ocean, amazed and excited (as well as somewhat scared) at the vast openness of her new seas.[70] In that work, Nietzsche also tells us that the degree that one needs something firm to believe in is an indication of one's weakness.[71] Even more striking is the description of the habitual as a net of spider webs in *Human, All Too Human.* These webs, which we have spun around ourselves, turn into cords that choke and bind, so much so that we are dying because of them. For that reason, the free spirit "hates all habituation and rules" and thus rips apart the net that surrounds him.[72] And Nietzsche's admonition against getting trapped by some belief or conviction is repeated later in his passage on "stuckness" in section 41 of *Beyond Good and Evil,* as well as in several passages in *The Anti-Christ.*[73]

These various passages suggest another, related difference between Nietzsche and Dewey. Nietzsche's free spirit not only welcomes the turmoil that accompanies self-overcoming, she seems deliberately to disrupt any tranquillity in her life in an effort to ensure that she never becomes stuck. Any need for security appears to mark one as a member of the herd and thus is something to be overcome. Unlike Nietzsche's free spirit, however, Dewey's pragmatist does not seem to seek out turmoil. This is explained by Dewey's claim that life is very difficult for organisms if there is no structure or stability in their world. Because the world is precarious, unstable and thus provides little stability apart from human control of it, humans seek out the stable, organized and unified.[74] In the midst of the turmoil of self-reconstruction, what is sought after is not ongoing fluctuation but the restoration of the stability of self and environment, habit and impulse. And in the midst of such stability, in which activity and belief are confident and undisturbed, the human organism tends merely to "march on," enjoying his uninterrupted life.[75]

The pragmatist's restriction of experimentation and her appreciation for security may make her seem more like a member of the herd than a free spirit, but only until we remember the positive role that Nietzsche tells us habit plays in his life, and thus, presumably, in the life of a free spirit. After explaining that he loves brief habits but hates enduring ones, Nietzsche says that "most intolerable, to be sure, and the terrible par excellence would be for me a life entirely devoid of habits, a life that would demand perpetual improvisation."[76] Walter Kaufmann is correct when he says that this passage indicates that Nietzsche holds that "some stability and temporary equilibrium are needed to permit the concentration of all mental and emotional resources on the most important problems."[77] Questioning everything all at once would not produce a playful irreverence but instead a chaotic anarchy. To have perpetually to improvise means that one never has the luxury of a directed focus, which is what makes all projects and creations possible.

While we often think of the artist as one who creates in a frenzied, uncontrolled moment of inspiration, Nietzsche tells us that her creation is made possible by strict and subtle obedience to a "thousandfold laws," which order and give form to the creation.[78] Those "laws" are the artist's habits. They are the order and pattern that the artist gives to her creation, not as a result of conscious decision (hence our use of the term "inspiration") but because they have become the way by which the artist handles her brush, her paints, her values, and her virtues. In the midst of creating, she does not, indeed must not question those particular laws for they are that by which her creation is possible. Without those laws, vulgarity, not artistry is the result. "This is the *first* preliminary schooling in spirituality: *not* to react immediately to a stimulus, but to have the restraining, stock-taking instincts in one's control. . . . All unspirituality, all vulgarity, is due to the incapacity to resist a stimulus."[79] To recognize the need for laws or habits is not to say that they are never to be questioned. Nietzsche, like Dewey, grants nothing permanent immunity to questioning. But, like Dewey, Nietzsche does qualify the experimentalism of free-spiritedness: we cannot question everything at once.

There is no Archimedean point for either philosopher. The creative free spirit as much as the creative pragmatist must have a place of stability within her fluid and shifting self from which she can "move" herself. But this place of stability is no more permanent for Dewey than it is for Nietzsche. While restoration of the stability of the self is a "goal" for the pragmatist, it is not a final goal because it is soon surpassed by the next unsettling of the self. Stability and security are important to the pragmatist, but only as part of the whole of rhythm of life, which is a movement from disruption to recovery, to disruption again, and so on.[80] By itself, "love for security, translated into a desire not to be disturbed and unsettled, leads to dogmatism,"[81] not pragmatism.

Does this then mean that Dewey's pragmatist, like Nietzsche's free spirit, has "a desire to be disturbed and unsettled" and thus seeks out turmoil? Dewey is ambiguous on this point. We have seen why it seems that the pragmatist does not have such a desire. Significantly, Dewey characterizes "scrupulous" thinking (as distinct from "ordinary" thinking) as thinking which "takes delight" and "enjoys" disruption,[82] which implies that pragmatism welcomes but not necessarily pursues strife. However, he also claims that the artist "cultivates" "moments of tension and resistance" and that the scientific person "does not rest in [resolution]" but "passes on to another problem using an attained solution only as a stepping stone from which to set on foot further inquiries,"[83] which suggests that the pragmatist does deliberately bring upheaval into her life.

I will not be able to resolve this ambiguity here. While Nietzsche and Dewey may differ in their views on strife, because they both value and promote an openness and questioning attitude toward even that which is most precious to us, the difference is perhaps one of degree only. Both appreciate the important role that both upheaval and stability play in life. Without periods of turmoil and

chaos, the self would never remake itself and thus would stagnate and die. And without periods of harmony, the self would never be able to concentrate its energies into its projects, making creation impossible. Albeit, perhaps with different emphases upon self-destruction, both Nietzsche and Dewey establish a balance in the self and in the process of self-transformation between strife and calm, chaos and harmony, plurality and unity.

NIETZSCHE, DEWEY, AND DEMOCRACY

In exploring the connections between Dewey's reconstruction and Nietzsche's self-overcoming, I have suggested that there are great similarities between the two philosophers' visions of what humanity could become. Like Nietzsche, Dewey presents continuous self-transformation as a "goal" for human beings. Dewey's pragmatism is about growth and the creation of meaning and value in life, not about mere practicality, efficiency or commonsensical business practices, as it is often misunderstood to mean.[84] Dewey, as much as Nietzsche, holds out hope for the regeneration and transfiguration of Western culture through the greatness of individuals.[85]

However, in Nietzsche's case, we must add that self-overcoming can be a "goal" only for certain individuals because, according to Nietzsche, the masses are too weak to self-overcome. In fact, most people are so sickly that Nietzsche has already declared them virtually dead: too weary to die and thus living on in sepulchers.[86] Because a *pathos of distance* which grows out of the ingrained difference between strata" is crucial for those who would self-overcome,[87] the sick should care for the sick, leaving the healthy ones free to pursue their "great health." To associate with the rotting corpses of the herd is for the free spirit to risk becoming fatally ill herself.

The sickliness of most people explains why Nietzsche's books are written only for the very few, that is, for fellow free spirits.[88] Nietzsche explains that "all the nobler spirits and tastes select their audience when they wish to communicate; and choosing that, one at the same time erects barriers against 'the others.'"[89] In contrast to the exclusivity of Nietzsche's audience, the audience for Dewey's books is everyone. This is not to say that Dewey's books were not written for academic philosophers—many of them were—but rather that they are addressed to everyone in that all people have the potential for self-transformation. While Dewey admits that much of us avoid self-transformation and thus might even grant that some of us are closer to dead than alive,[90] every person is at least minimally capable of self-reconstruction. The difference between Dewey's and Nietzsche's intended audiences is an important one. "Books for all the world are always foul-smelling books,"[91] according to Nietzsche, and thus from his perspective, the fact that Dewey does not limit his audience only seems to prove that Dewey's philosophy of self-reconstruction is tainted by the uncleanliness of the last man. Dewey's appeal to everyone is irreconcilable with Nietzsche's aristocratic disdain for the herd, making reconstruction and self-overcoming, for all their similarities, crucially different.

To be fair to Dewey, it must be acknowledged that reconstruction is not meant to reduce all to the level of the lowest but to lift even the lowest to the level of the experimental and daring pragmatist. In that sense, Dewey's democracy is a democracy of aristocrats. But this means that Dewey has transformed aristocracy into a club to which all can belong. Thus, Deweyan aristocracy eliminates the hierarchical distance between types of people, something that Nietzsche insisted was necessary to generate the tension needed to propel humanity upward into the greatness of the *Übermensch*. There seems to be no way to avoid a fundamental clash between the catholicism of Dewey's reconstruction and the elitism of Nietzsche's self-overcoming.

The issue of Dewey and Nietzsche's different views of human nature is at heart a conflict between the social philosophy of the former and the individualism of the latter. While Dewey wanted to change social institutions so that individuals could transform themselves, Nietzsche thought free spirits had a future only if they separated themselves from society. When the issue is recast in this way, however, it becomes clear that the fundamental difference between Dewey and Nietzsche's ideas about self-transformation is in their differing conceptions of individuality. As we have seen, for Dewey, the individual is transactional, not atomistic. Instead of the "old" individualism that strictly divides the individual from society, Dewey's "new" individualism holds that the boundaries between the individual and society are always fluid.[92] If Nietzsche's concept of individuality is fundamentally atomistic, then the differences between self-overcoming and reconstruction are indeed irreconcilable.

Nietzsche's endorsements of an "old"-style, radical individualism are too numerous and well known to repeat here. There is little in Nietzsche's corpus that explicitly encourages us to label his individualism "new."[93] However, perhaps implicit in Nietzsche's demand that we go beyond dualisms such as good and evil is an acknowledgment of lack of fundamental opposition between the dualism of individual and society. Also, Nietzsche's claim that a self is primarily a body implies at least a minimal commitment to a transactional self on his part if it is true that the body is only able to live and grow by means of its interactions with its environment. Furthermore, as Nietzsche's comments about the artist demonstrate, Nietzsche's call for a return to the body is not a demand that we "return to nature" in the sense of a "return" to an unbridled, "raw" world of instincts.[94] This suggests that Nietzsche does not subscribe to a sharp nature-culture division, which means he would agree with Dewey that the body never interacts with a purely "natural" environment. Thus Nietzsche's emphasis upon the body might ultimately translate into an implicit claim that the human body must and does interact with its social, as well as physical environment in order to live. If so, the

boundaries between the individual and society cannot be rigid, impermeable ones for Nietzsche. This is not to claim that Nietzsche himself held that the boundaries are not rigid. Rather, it is to say that, given Nietzsche's emphasis upon the body, the boundaries should not be considered rigid. Whether Nietzsche fully thought through the implications of his "return to the body" will not be established here. However, if we think through his emphasis upon the body, we must abandon "old"-style, atomistic individualism.

While much more needs to be said in support of these suggestions and, in particular, the last claim, I will not be able to pursue the question of the nature of Nietzsche's individuality further.[95] However, we have reason to wonder if Nietzsche's individualism is closer to the "new" variety than his explicit remarks on the individual suggest. If Nietzsche's individual is transactional rather than atomistic, then Nietzsche must broaden the audience for his work if self-overcoming is to have a chance at success. Poor soil will only produce unhealthy plants. If one's social and cultural, as well as physical environments are important components in an individual's self-transformation, then they need to be as rich, vibrant, and diverse as possible. The environment becomes richest only if all the individuals in it are growing, enriching and transforming themselves. The more thriving individuals there are in society, the more rich the social environment for each individual. A rich environment offers individuals, in the form of other individuals, the greatest "diversity of stimuli" to which they must respond, thus promoting the greatest amount of disruption and subsequent growth on their part.[96] If the boundaries between Nietzsche's individual and society are fluid, then Nietzsche's refusal to include all people as candidates for self-transformation only depletes the soil in which his free spirit grows.

Dewey's philosophy is a social one not because he does not value the individual and not because he is too weak to maintain a height for his pragmatist to look down upon the masses, but because the pragmatist can only reach such heights if those around him attain them too. Democracy, for Dewey, is just such a community in which social structures are such that they encourage and even enable all to attain such heights. Dewey's democracy is like the spiral described above, in which growth of individuals leads to growth of the culture which produces even greater growth of individuals, and so on. And the spiral includes all individuals, even the weak "herd." Of course, if the individual is atomistic and thus must begin the process of self-transformation purely on her own, the weak individual will not have enough strength to do so and thus must be written off as a hopeless case. But if one holds that the self is transactional, no person necessarily need be considered incapable of reconstruction. Granted, changing habits such that growth itself is a habit will be difficult and take time, but changing social structures so that they encourage rather than discourage critical inquiry will begin the process of the spiral of change.[97]

Whether Nietzsche can embrace Dewey's democracy ultimately becomes a question of the construction of the self for Nietzsche.[98] However, even if Nietzsche's individuality is atomistic, we have reason to believe that the democracy that Dewey promotes is not the "foul-smelling" democracy that Nietzsche scorns. As Dewey scholar Thomas Alexander puts it, Dewey's "democratic community takes itself experimentally and therefore artistically and intelligently."[99] Because of its experimentalism, Dewey's democracy perpetually disrupts and ideally eliminates the comfortable, unchallenging happiness of the last man. As Dewey puts it, "to 'make others happy' except through liberating their powers and engaging them in activities that enlarge the meaning of life is to harm them."[100] Dewey's democracy is so radical in its emphasis upon the continual growth and self-reconstruction of the individual that we can embrace it as a continuation of Nietzsche's own ideas about what a vibrant and flourishing culture should be. And if we reject atomistic individuality, Dewey's philosophy can even be considered an improvement of that of Nietzsche. Because Dewey explicitly acknowledges the interaction between individual and society, he is able to address both halves of the cycle of reconstruction. Rather than focus solely on changing the individual so that humanity might have a transformed future, Dewey gives us a double-barreled approach to transformation by demonstrating that change can and should start at once on the part of the individual and society.

No doubt Nietzsche and Dewey differ in many ways not addressed here and in which Deweyans might well profit from Nietzsche.[101] However, the striking similarities between self-overcoming and reconstruction have shown us that exploration of the intersections of their work can be fruitful. Dewey once wrote that "ultimately there are but two philosophies. One of them accepts life and experience in all its uncertainty, mystery, doubt, and half-knowledge and turns that experience upon itself to deepen and intensify its own qualities."[102] Reconstruction, as well as self-overcoming are examples of the philosophy Dewey describes. We could say that Dewey's pragmatist has recovered from the death of God because she welcomes the free-spirited experimentalism with life that comes from a rejection of our tradition's quest for certainty. For that reason, Nietzscheans should recognize a kindred spirit in Dewey's pragmatist.[103]

NOTES

[1] Ted Honderich, ed., *The Oxford Companion to Philosophy* (New York: Oxford University Press, 1995) notes a similar reaction to pragmatism on the part of Continental philosophers in the dictionary's entry on "pragmatism" (p. 712).

[2] See, for example, Vincent M. Colapietro, "The Vanishing Subject of Contemporary Discourse: A Pragmatic Response," *The Journal of Philosophy* 87 (1990): 644-55; Victor Kestenbaum, *The Phenomenological Sense of John Dewey: Habit and Meaning* (Atlantic Highlands,

NJ: Humanities Press, 1977); Mark Okrent, *Heidegger's Pragmatism: Understanding, Being, and the Critique, of Metaphysics* (Ithaca: Cornell University Press, 1988); Richard Rorty, "Overcoming the Tradition: Heidegger and Dewey," *The Review of Metaphysics* 30 (December 1976): 280-305; Sandra B. Rosenthal and Patrick L. Bourgeois, *Mead and Merleau-Ponty: Toward a Common Vision* (Albany: State University of New York Press, 1991); R. W. Sleeper, "The Pragmatics of Deconstruction and the End of Metaphysics," in John J. Stuhr, ed., *Philosophy and the Reconstruction of Culture* (Albany: State University of New York Press, 1993), pp. 241-56; John J. Stuhr, "Can Pragmatism Appropriate the Resources of Postmodernism? A Response to Nielsen," *Transactions of the Charles S. Pierce Society* 29 (Fall 1993): 561-72; Michael A. Weinstein, *The Wilderness and the City: American Classical Philosophy as a Moral Quest* (Amherst: The University of Massachusetts Press, 1982), especially chapter 7; Cornel West, "Nietzsche's Prefiguration of Postmodern American Philosophy," *boundary 2* 9 (Spring/Fall 1981): 241-69; Michael Zimmerman, "Dewey, Heidegger, and the Quest for Certainty," *Southwestern Journal of Philosophy* 9 (Spring 1978): 87-95.

For discussions of the particular question of whether Nietzsche's epistemology and conception of truth are pragmatic, which I will not address in this essay, see Alfred L. Castle, "Dewey and Nietzsche: Their Alethiology Compared," *Southwest Philosophical Studies* 3 (April 1978): 25-29; Ken Gemes, "Nietzsche's Critique of Truth," *Philosophy and Phenomenological Research* 52 (March 1992): 47-65; Max O. Hallman, "Nietzsche and Pragmatism," *Kinesis* 14 (Spring 1985): 63-78; Friedrich Nietzsche, *Philosophy and Truth: Selections from Nietzsche's Notebooks of the early 1870's,* ed. and trans. Daniel Breazeale (Atlantic Highlands, NJ: Humanities Press, 1979), pp. xxxi-xxxviii, and footnote 38 on page 17; George J. Stack, "Nietzsche's Influence on Pragmatic Humanism," *Journal of the History of Philosophy* 20 (October 1982): 369-406; John T. Wilcox, "A Note on Correspondence and Pragmatism in Nietzsche," *International Studies in Philosophy* 12 (Spring 1980): 77-80; John T. Wilcox, "Nietzsche's Epistemology: Recent American Discussions," *International Studies in Philosophy* 15 (Summer 1983): 67-77.

[3] I have found only one instance of such a suggestion. See David Michael Levin, *The Body's Recollection of Being: Phenomenological Psychology and the Deconstruction of Nihilism* (Boston: Routledge & Kegan Paul, 1985), p. 230. Levin discusses Dewey's progress beyond Nietzsche (only) in the area of education.

[4] Friedrich Nietzsche, *Beyond Good and Evil in Basic Writings of Nietzsche,* ed. and trans. Walter Kaufmann (New York: Random House, 1968), p. 44, emphasis in original. Hereafter cited as BGE. I will cite section numbers for all of Nietzsche's works except *Thus Spoke Zarathustra,* for which I will give section and page numbers.

[5] Friedrich Nietzsche, *Thus Spoke Zarathustra,* trans. R. J. Hollingdale (New York: Viking Penguin, Inc., 1969) I:46. Hereafter cited as TSZ.

[6] Friedrich Nietzsche, *Genealogy of Morals* I, *passim* (in *Basic Writings of Nietzsche*). Hereafter cited as GM.

[7] Stuhr, "Can Pragmatism Appropriate the Resources of Postmodernism?" p. 569.

[8] My focus on the reconstruction of the self and self-overcoming of the self is not meant to imply that these concepts apply only to the self. Both concepts relate to much more in the work of Dewey and Nietzsche (e.g., society, morality and values); however, in this essay I will focus on their application to the self.

[9] The reason for my unequal treatment of Nietzsche and Dewey in these first two sections is that I assume a contemporary audience more familiar with Nietzsche than Dewey.

[10] At least, upon Nietzsche's philosophy prior to 1888, Nietzsche apparently rejected the notion of self-overcoming in the preface of his 1888 work *The Case of Wagner* (in *Basic Writings of Nietzsche,* p. 611). Nietzsche writes there, "If I were a moralist, who knows what I might call it [his fight against "Wagnerizing"]? Perhaps self-overcoming.—But the philosopher has no love for moralists. Neither does he love pretty words." However, whether this indeed means that he rejected self-overcoming is not clear since he goes on to describe his fight as a demand "to overcome his time in himself" and a requirement to "take sides against everything sick in [himself]" (*ibid.*)—descriptions which sound like a warring, destructive and creative multiplicity overcoming itself. In any case, Dewey's self-reconstruction can be profitably connected to Nietzsche's self-overcoming as described prior to 1888 in his main works.

[11] TSZ I:61-62; Friedrich Nietzsche, *The Gay Science,* trans. Walter Kaufmann (New York: Random House, 1974), §333. Hereafter cited as GS.

[12] Friedrich Nietzsche, *The Will To Power,* ed. Walter Kaufmann, trans. Walter Kaufmann and R. J. Hollingdale (New York: Random House, 1967), §518. Hereafter cited as WP.

[13] Eric Blondel, *Nietzsche: The Body and Culture,* trans. Sean Hand (Stanford: Stanford University Press, 1991), pp. 206-08.

[14] BGE §12. See also WP §§490, 492.

[15] For more on Nietzsche's self as embodied and multiplicitous, see Walter A. Brogan, "The Decentered Self: Nietzsche's Transgression of Metaphysical Subjectivity," *The Southern Journal of Philosophy* 29 (1991): 419-30; Daniel W. Conway, "Disembodied Perspectives: Nietzsche contra Rorty," in *Nietzsche Studien,* vol. 21 (Berlin: Walter de Gruyter, 1992), pp. 281-89; Michel Haar, "Heidegger and the Nietzschean 'Physiology of Art'" in David Farrell Krell and David Wood, eds. *Exceedingly Nietzsche: Aspects of Contemporary Nietzsche-Interpretation* (New York: Routledge, 1988), pp. 13-30; David Michael Levin, *The Body's Recollection of Being* (New York: Routledge and Kegan Paul, 1985), pp. 34-35; David Owen, "Nietzsche's Squandered Seductions: Feminism, the Body, and the Politics of Genealogy," in Keith Ansell-Pearson and Howard Caygill, eds., *The Fate of the New Nietzsche* (Brookfield, VT: Ashgate Publishing Company, 1993), pp. 189-209.

[16] GM III:27, emphasis added.

[17] This also means that the self contains within itself the possibility of disorganization, chaos and decadence.

[18] *TSZ* II:139.

[19] GM III:8. This is not to say that Nietzsche simply rejects these qualities when encouraging their self-overcoming. Rather, through their overcoming as ascetic virtues, they can become conditions for the strength and fruitfulness of the *Übermensch.*

[20] *TSZ* II:138.

[21] *Ibid.*

[22] See *ibid.,* I:44: "What is great in man is that he is a bridge and not a goal; what can be loved in man is that he is a *going-across* [*übergang*] and a *down-going* [*untergang*]. . . . I love those who do not first seek beyond the stars for reasons to go down [*untergehen*] and to be sacrifices: but who sacrifice themselves to the earth, that the earth may one day belong to the Superman [*Übermensch*]."

[23] John Dewey, *Art as Experience* in *John Dewey: The Later Works, 1925-1953,* vol. 10, ed. Jo Ann Boydston (Carbondale and Edwardsville, IL: Southern Illinois University Press, 1989), pp. 47-48. Hereafter cited as AE. While one of Dewey's main goals in this passage is to demonstrate that viewing artwork is just as creative and active a process as the production of a piece of art, his comments, and indeed the entire book, do not apply to the experience of viewing artwork only. They apply to all of experience because all of experience is a reconstructive interaction between self and world.

[24] *Ibid.,* p. 59.

[25] John Dewey, *Human Nature and Conduct,* in *John Dewey: The Middle Works, 1899-1924,* vol. 14, ed. Jo Ann Boydston (Carbondale and Edwardsville, IL: Southern Illinois University Press, 1988), p. 65. Hereafter cited as HNC.

[26] *Ibid.,* p. 75, note 1.

[27] *Ibid.,* p. 32.

[28] *Ibid.,* p. 136; John Dewey, *Experience and Nature* in *John Dewey: The Later Works, 1925-1953,* vol. 1, ed. Jo Ann Boydston (Carbondale and Edwardsville, IL: Southern Illinois University Press, 1988), p. 61. Hereafter cited as EN.

[29] HNC, p. 49.

[30] *Ibid.,* p. 24.

[31] *Ibid.,* p. 28. For more on the relation of body and consciousness in Dewey's thought, see Bruce Wilshire, "Body-Mind and Subconsciousness: Tragedy in Dewey's Life and Work," in *Philosophy and the Reconstruction of Culture: Pragmatic Essays after Dewey,* pp. 257-72.

[32] HNC, p. 67.

[33] *Ibid.,* p. 69.

[34] *Ibid.,* p. 88.

[35] *Ibid.,* p. 88.

[36] *Ibid.,* p. 15.

[37] *Ibid.,* p. 43.

[38] AE, p. 251.

[39] *Ibid.,* p. 19. Dewey uses the image of a spiral in HNC, p. 225.

[40] AE, p. 253.

[41] HNC, p. 96. Dewey talks at length of the (re)creation of the self in the chapter "The Moral Self," in *Ethics* in *John Dewey: The Later Works, 1925-1953,* vol. 7, ed. Jo Ann Boydston (Carbondale and Edwardsville, IL: Southern Illinois University Press, 1989), pp. 285-310. Hereafter cited as *Ethics.* See also John Dewey, "Experience, Knowledge and Value: A Rejoinder," in *John Dewey: The Later Works, 1925-1953,* vol. 14, ed. Jo Ann Boydston (Carbondale and Edwardsville, IL: Southern Illinois University Press, 1991), pp. 70-71.

[42] HNC, p. 96. See John Dewey, *The Study of Ethics: A Syllabus* in *John Dewey: The Early Works, 1882-1898,* vol. 4, ed. Jo Ann Boydston (Carbondale and Edwardsville, IL: Southern Illinois University Press, 1971), pp. 311-12 for a discussion of identity issues relate to a plural self in which internal struggle occurs. Hereafter cited as *Early Ethics.*

[43] For the role that imagination and faith play in effecting the unity of the self, see John Dewey, *A Common Faith,* in *John Dewey: The Later Works, 1925-1953,* vol. 9, ed. Jo Ann Boydston (Carbondale and Edwardsville, IL: Southern Illinois University Press, 1989), pp. 14, 23.

[44] AE, p. 184.

[45] *Early Ethics,* pp. 312-13.

[46] Nietzsche is also critical of the "free will"; see, e.g., BGE §§17-21. As is the case for Dewey, Nietzsche's emphasis upon the plurality of the drives and affects of the body and his account of the intellect as (merely) an instrument of the body works to disrupt our tradition's notions of agency by eliminating the "free will." Of course, this is not to say that Nietzsche (or Dewey) is a determinist or that agency of all kinds has been eliminated. Rather, for both Nietzsche and Dewey, agency becomes bodily, instead of disembodied.

[47] HNC, p. 32.

[48] *Ibid.,* p. 75.

[49] *Ibid.,* p. 108.

[50] *Ibid.,* p. 176.

[51] *Ibid.,* p. 108. Much like Nietzsche, Dewey talks of undirected, sublimated and suppressed impulses on ibid., pp. 108-09. And Nietzsche would agree with Dewey that transforming oneself into an *Übermensch* is not about an undirected release of animal drives and instincts, which would be a sensualism far removed from the ordered form-giving of the artist (see BGE §188; TSZ I:71).

[52] HNC, p. 204; BGE, §44.

[53] HNC, p. 159; Robert L. Holmes, "John Dewey's Social Ethics," *The Journal of Value Inquiry* 7 (Winter 1973): 274-80.

[54] HNC, p. 195. *Cf.* TSZ I:56-58, I:71-73.

[55] Since Nietzsche would not be willing to grant that members of the herd undergo even a minimal amount of self-overcoming, this point differentiates his self-overcoming from Dewey's self-reconstruction. I will return to this difference in the final section of this paper when I examine the two philosophers' conceptions of the individual.

[56] AE, p. 173. See also John Dewey, *Democracy and Education,* in *John Dewey: The Middle Works, 1899-1924,* vol. 9, ed. Jo Ann Boydston (Carbondale and Edwardsville, IL: Southern Illinois University Press, 1980), pp. 54, 56. Hereafter cited as DE.

[57] HNC 48, 51, 55. See also DE 57.

[58] For Nietzsche, the scientist can be just another version of the ascetic ideal (*GM* III, *passim; GS,* 344). I refer here to Nietzsche's "gay scientist," who has called his remaining piety—the will to truth—into question.

[59] AE, pp. 21, 148.

[60] HNC, p. 75, note 1; DE, p. 50.

[61] *Ibid.*, p. 47.

[62] HNC, pp. 70-72; AE, p. 294; *cf.* TSZ I:55.

[63] HNC, p. 71.

[64] EN, pp. 169-170.

[65] HNC, p. 168.

[66] EN, p. 172. See also *ibid.*, pp. 188-89.

[67] HNC, pp. 30-31.

[68] HNC, pp. 72, 125; *Early Ethics*, p. 312.

[69] TSZ I:55.

[70] GS, §§124, 343.

[71] *Ibid.*, §347.

[72] Friedrich Nietzsche, *Human, All Too Human*, trans. R. J. Hollingdale (New York: Cambridge University Press, 1986), §427. Hereafter cited as HATH. See also *ibid.*, §§483, 629-38.

[73] See, for example, Friedrich Nietzsche, *Twilight of the Idols/The AntiChrist*, trans. R. J. Hollingdale (New York: Viking Penguin, 1968), §§54-55. Hereafter cited individually as TI and AC.

[74] See AE, pp. 19-20; EN, chapter two; John Dewey, *The Quest for Certainty*, in *John Dewey: The Later Works, 1925-1953*, vol. 4, ed. Jo Ann Boydston (Carbondale and Edwardsville, IL: Southern Illinois University Press, 1988), p. x and chapter one (hereafter cited as QC).

[75] HNC, p. 127.

[76] GS, §295.

[77] *Ibid.*, note 18.

[78] BGE, §188.

[79] TI, p. 65.

[80] HNC, p. 125; AE, pp. 19-20.

[81] QC, pp. 181-82.

[82] *Ibid.*, p. 182.

[83] AE, p. 21.

[84] Mary L. Coolidge, "The Experimental Temper in Contemporary European Philosophy," *Journal of Philosophy* 52 (1955): 493; Sidney Hook, "Pragmatism and Existentialism," *The Antioch Review* 19 (1959): 155.

[85] Wilshire, "Body-Mind and Subconsciousness," p. 261. *Cf.* Richard Rorty, "Nietzsche, Socrates and Pragmatism," *South African Journal of Philosophy* 10:3 (1991): 63.

[86] TSZ II:156. See also GM I:12.

[87] BGE, §257.

[88] Nietzsche is explicit on this point in HATH, which is subtitled "A Book For Free Spirits."

[89] GS, §381.

[90] See John Dewey, *Individualism, Old and New*, in *John Dewey: The Later Works, 1925-1953*, vol. 5, ed. Jo Ann Boydston (Carbondale and Edwardsville, IL: Southern Illinois University Press, 1984), pp. 52-53. Hereafter cited as ION.

[91] BGE, §30.

[92] While it is true the category of the individual is given very little role to play in Dewey's early work, by the time of his middle and late works, the asymmetry between the social and the individual had been balanced out (see Abraham Edel and Elizabeth Flower's Introduction to *Ethics,* pp. xviii-xix). The individual plays an important role in Dewey's mature philosophy for it is the locus of change for our culture (HNC, p. 62; *Ethics*, p. xix).

[93] He does comment cryptically in *The Will to Power* about the "false dogmatism regarding the 'ego': it is taken in an atomistic sense, in a false antithesis to the 'non-ego'" and "the false autonomy of the 'individual,' as atom" (WP, 786).

[94] *Cf.* Laurence Lampert, *Nietzsche and Modern Times: A Study of Bacon, Descartes, and Nietzsche* (New Haven: Yale University Press, 1993), p. 342.

[95] See Haar, "Heidegger and the Nietzschean 'Physiology of Art,'" and Mary Elizabeth Windham, "Nietzsche's Philosopher of the Future as an Ethicist: Experimentalism in Ethics," *International Studies in Philosophy* 24 (1992): 115-24, for arguments that Nietzsche's individual is not isolated from the world in which she lives. For an example of the view that Nietzsche's body-self does remain separate from the world, see Arifuku Kogaku, "The Problem of the Body in Nietzsche and Dogen," trans. Graham Parkes, in Graham Parkes, ed., *Nietzsche and Asian Thought* (Chicago: The University of Chicago Press, 1991), p. 224.

[96] DE, p. 93.

[97] ION, p. 74.

[98] For an argument for the compatibility of Nietzsche's self-overcoming and (a non-Deweyan) democracy that is

very different from the one that I have presented, see Aharon Aviram, "Nietzsche as Educator?" *Journal of Philosophy of Education* 25 (1991): 226-31. Aviram claims that it is precisely Nietzsche's individualism that allows his philosophy to complement the goals of democracy.

[99] Thomas M. Alexander, *John Dewey's Theory of Art, Experience & Nature: The Horizons of Feeling* (Albany: State University of New York Press, 1987), p. 273.

[100] HNC, p. 202.

[101] The difference of "tempo" is the most obvious one and one which Nietzsche would find very important. Dewey's writing has been described as "swimming through oatmeal" (Alexander, p. xii)—hardly the brisk and playful *allegrissimo* of Nietzsche's work. The different tempos of their work are probably related to the different audiences intended for it, a suggestion that I will not be able to pursue here. See BGE, §§27-28 for instances of Nietzsche's views on tempo and style.

[102] AE, p. 41.

[103] I wish to thank Phillip McReynolds and Brian Domino for their helpful suggestions and comments and Miami University for its support of this project through the award of a Summer Research Grant.

FURTHER READING

Bibliography

Levine, Barbara, ed. *Works about John Dewey: 1886-1995*. Carbondale and Edwardsville: Southern Illinois University Press, 1996, 526 p.
Combines the *Checklist of Writings about John Dewey* (1974; revised 1978) in addition to works published about Dewey since 1977, including books and articles about Dewey, reviews of Dewey's works, an author index, and a title key-work index.

Thomas, Milton Halsey. *John Dewey: A Centennial Bibliography*. Chicago: The University of Chicago Press, 1962, 370 p.
Divided into listings of works by and about Dewey.

Biography

Dykhuizen, George. *The Life and Mind of John Dewey*. Carbondale and Edwardsville: Southern Illinois University Press, 1973, 429 p.
Dedicates equal space to each phase of Dewey's life, beginning with his Vermont boyhood, and ending with Dewey's retirement years from 1939 to 1952.

Criticism

Alexander, Thomas M. *John Dewey's Theory of Art, Experience, and Nature: The Horizons of Feeling*. Albany: State University of New York Press, 1987, 325 p.
Traces Dewey's philosophy from his early embracement of Hegelian Idealism to his later writings, concluding that Dewey's philosophy contained several contradictions.

Gouinlock, James. *John Dewey's Philosophy of Value*. New York: Humanities Press, 1972, 377 p.
Examines Dewey's moral philosophy as but one element of what he believes is a consistent, multifaceted body of work.

Hickman, Larry A. *John Dewey's Pragmatic Technology*. Bloomfield and Indianapolis: Indiana University Press, 1990, 234 p.
Asserts that Dewey is the first postmodern philosopher, and the firstphilosopher to examine questions regarding modern science and technology.

Hook, Sidney. *John Dewey: An Intellectual Portrait*. New York: The John Day Company, 1939, 242 p.
Attempts to convey Dewey's complex philosophical views for readers new to philosophy.

Kuklick, Bruce. *Churchmen and Philosophers: From Jonathon Edwards to John Dewey*. New Haven and London: Yale University Press, 1985, 253 p.
Concludes with two essays on Dewey: the first on Absolutism and Idealism; and the second on Instrumentalism.

Peters, R. S., ed. *John Dewey Reconsidered*. London, Henley and Boston: Routledge & Kegan Paul, 1977, 128 p.
Collection of essays by Anthony Quinton, Alan White, Martin Hollis, Anthony Flew, Jerome Brunner, Eileen Caudill, and others.

Ratner, Sidney. "John Dewey, Empiricism, and Experimentalism in the Recent Philosophy of Mathematics" in *Journal of the History of Ideas* (July-September 1992): 467-79.
Examines Dewey's concepts of logic, placing him in direct contrast with Bertrand Russell and Alfred North Whitehead.

Ryan, Alan. *John Dewey and the High Tide of Liberalism*. New York: W. W. Norton and Company, 1995, 414 p.
Finds many similarities between Dewey and the nineteenth-century British philosopher Thomas Hill Green, declaring that the two men shared many liberal humanist traits.

Westbrook, Robert B. *John Dewey and American Democracy*. Ithaca, N.Y.: Cornell University Press, 1991, 570 p.
Focuses on Dewey's social theories and his concepts of democratic ideals.

Wirth, Arthur G. *John Dewey as Educator: His Design for Work in Education (1894-1904)*. New York: John Wiley & Sons, 1966, 322 p.

> Details Dewey's theories on education, believing much of his philosophy to be centered on supporting his concepts for school reform.

Additional coverage of Dewey's life and career is contained in the following source published by The Gale Group: *Contemporary Authors*, **Vol. 114.**

Edgar A. Guest

1881-1959

(Full name Edgar Albert Guest) American journalist, and poet.

INTRODUCTION

Throughout the first half of the twentieth century, Guest was the foremost American writer of mass-circulation newspaper and magazine verse. Sentimental, homiletic, and inspirational, his work was not esteemed by serious readers of poetry, but enjoyed enormous success with the general public. Guest's poems proclaim and celebrate the domestic, industrious, patriotic, and religious virtues, and are characterized by common phrases, a folksy idiom, regular meters, word inversion, humor, nostalgia, and regular rhyme schemes.

Biographical Information

Born in England, Guest was brought to the United States when he was ten, and begin his writing career in 1895 at the age of fourteen when he was hired as a copy boy at the Detroit Free Press. He rose to cub reporter and began contributing verse soon after. He began a weekly column of verse and observation in 1904, which soon appeared daily, and at its height was syndicated in over three hundred papers. With his brother he published privately the first of the many collections of his verse. Soon, however, the Detroit Rotarians and then a commercial house began publishing them. He enjoyed commercial success throughout his life, appeared on radio in the 1930s and on television in the early 1950s, and was honored by the Boy Scouts of America in 1951 with the Silver Buffalo award. When he died in 1959, the flags of Detroit , by order of the mayor, were flown at half staff.

Major Works

Throughout his career, Guest's work was uniform and predictable. No piece stood far above any other. The most significant work in Guest's canon, however, is the 1916 volume which propelled him to fame, *A Heap o' Livin'*. It touches on Guest's principle theme: celebrating domestic family life. His World War I volume of patriotic verses *Over Here* was distinguished by being bound in khaki and distributed by the army to the troops in Europe.

Critical Reception

Guest's verse reflects the sensibility of his era, and is hardly read today. Those who enjoyed Guest's verses admired them for their sentiment and skill. Those who were dismayed by his success and found his verses banal

were generally at a loss for comment, and in place of critiquing, resorted to parodying the verses and their values. Guest himself made no pretensions to poetry or sophistication but said he was "a newspaperman who wrote verse for folks."

PRINCIPAL WORKS

Just Glad Things (poetry) 1911
A Heap 0' Livin' (poetry) 1916
Just Folks (poetry) 1917
Over Here (poetry) 1918
The Path to Home (poetry) 1919
When Day Is Done (poetry) 1921
All That Matters (poetry) 1922
My Job as a Father, and What My Father Did for Me (essays) 1923
The Passing Throng (poetry) 1942

CRITICISM

The Dial (essay date 1916)

SOURCE: A review of *A Heap o' Livin'*, in *The Dial*, Vol. 61, November 2, 1916, p. 355.

[*In the following excerpt, a reviewer warmly praises Guest's verse.*]

There is one glory of the new poetry, and another of the old-fashioned sort, and another (it may be) of the kind that is neither poetry nor prose; for one form of verse differeth from another in glory. Without instituting invidious comparisons, one 'may heartily commend the style of verse that flows so readily from the pen of Mr. Edgar A. Guest, and one may at the same time rejoice that he has found leisure to provide rhymes for all his lines. He chooses the old familiar themes of domestic joys and sorrows, the ups and downs of life, the high hopes and the grievous disappointments common to our lot. Those who like Will Carleton and James Whitcomb Riley will not dislike Mr. Guest. His book, *A Heap o' Livin'* is by no means his first appearance in print, and to his old friends he needs no introduction. Let those who still have before them the pleasure of making his acquaintance try his quality in such poems of the present collection as **"My Creed," "Spring in the Trenches," "The Other Fellow," "Father,"** and **"Mother."** The verses entitled **"Canning Time"** are savory of the autumn's fruitage. **"Opportunity"** surpasses the well-known older poem of the same name in that the knock at one's door is, with truth, represented as not a single and never-to-be-repeated summons. **"At Sugar Camp"** disappoints the New England reader in giving no hint of the sweet delights of maple-sugar making, though the glad freedom of the return to nature and the simple life is well depicted. Here and there the book shows a limping line, perhaps not oftener than in many a greater poet, but in some instances the limp could easily have been cured. In a writer so much to one's liking even slight blemishes cause regret.

Leonard Cline (essay date 1925)

SOURCE: "Eddie Guest: Just Glad," in *The American Mercury*, Vol. VI, No. 23, November 1925, pp. 322-27.

[*In the following parody of an idealized biography of Guest, Cline alludes to Guest's verse in order to create his own rendition of Guest's life.*]

Doty's drug-store has spawned prolifically in the last thirty years. Fecundated by Henry Ford, it has become a chain of stores from end to end of Detroit. The old place at Sibley and Clifford streets, where Mr. Doty himself used to compound prescriptions for our mothers, is probably gone now. Mr. Doty travels in Europe and vicarious hands paste the labels on the bottles. There is one-way traffic in Clifford street, and the brick residences that once bordered the adjacent avenues, each sedately aloof in its iron-fence enclosure, have given way to garages and motor salesrooms and rearing efficiency apartments.

It was in Cass avenue, five blocks north of Sibley, that I spent my childhood, and it was on Doty's marble that I spilled my first ice-cream soda. Summer and Winter, green and white, the years passed. When it was July Cass avenue would be the sleepiest street in Detroit. Once a morning John Blessed's grocery wagon would jog somnolently up the street under the maples. Blessed's delivery boy would let me ride with him now and then, and from his seat I learned how to drive a horse. At Doty's I would get off and have a soda. When it was January the sporting folk of Detroit, the horsemen, the *noblesse,* would have cutter races down Cass avenue from the Central High-school to Sibley. How merrily the snow flew! We children of the neighborhood would gather at the finish line and watch there until our paws got stiff with cold in our mittens and the hot baked potatoes that Ma put in our pockets had become quite frigid. Then we would go into Doty's and have a soda.

Who were we all, in those halcyon days? Philip Worcester and his sister Mabel; God knows where they may be now. And Hudson Pirie. Dear old friend! He and my sister and I were the whole membership of the White Swan Club, named for the laundry: Hudson was president, and Elizabeth was vice-president, and I was ex-president. And Hallie Burton and . . . and who besides? They are all grown, those brave fine children; they have carried their burdens with a grin; America is the richer and the world the wiser for them. As I muse with a tear in my heart the music of Eddie Guest comes singing:

Youth is the golden time of life, and this battered
   old heart of mine
Beats fast to the march of its old-time joys, when
   the sun begins to shine.

Eddie Guest! And he, in those sweet far years that are
now but tenuous memories, tinted and fragrant—years
when Ma and Pa and Granpa and my seven sisters and
brothers did a heap o' livin' in that little gray brick cottage that shall always be home to me—he, in those years,
worked at the soda fountain in Doty's.

II

From soda fountain to Parnassus, from potwasher to Poet
of the Plain People, Poet of America indeed, whose
books—I have the authority of his publishers, Reilly
and Lee, for it—have sold more than a million copies!
Never has Providence wrought its wonders in stranger
and more romantic fashion. John Masefield, to be sure,
swept out Luke O'Connor's barroom at one time; and
Knut Hamsun, as we all know, was conductor on a Chicago street-car in the days before his triumph. But where
is there another record of a soda fountain clerk becoming
immortal! It is a story of indomitable will, the story of
Eddie Guest. It never could have been written had there
not burned in the soul of the man the challenging conviction that, as he phrases it, "No one is beat till he quits":

Fate can slam him and bang him around,
   And batter his frame till he's sore,
But she never can say that he's downed
   While he bobs up serenely for more.

We ignorant children, of course, discerned no least glare
of celestial fire in the dark-haired, dreamful lad who
mixed our chocolate and soda water and took our nick-
els. It remained for a humble book-keeper employed
by the Detroit *Free Press* to be the first to recognize
in Eddie those qualities of mind and spirit which have
made him, as he is, the outstanding figure in our national
literature—qualities

That all men picture when they see
The glorious banner of the free.

This was a book-keeper who, even in that Golden Age of
Rum, preferred his ice-cream soda to his growler of bock,
and regularly dropped in at Doty's on his way home,
weary after a hard day of white collar toil.

One can imagine the scene. The book-keeper, honest fellow, sucking at his straw, twirling idly on his stool, gazing curiously at the industrious little shaver who polished
the glasses on the other side of the counter. He was a
self-made man, a Christian no doubt—one who had made
his way dauntlessly against all adversity; self-educated,
leaning on no one for support. He had himself all the
high qualities that he admired in the dark-haired, serious
boy who worked so earnestly while other lads his age
frittered away their time in frivolities. He was a master of
the science of book-keeping.

"Eddie," he said, putting his glass down and meditatively
wiping a drop of cream from his beard; "Eddie, son, what
do you expect to make of yourself in life?"

And Eddie, without ceasing his toil, replied, "God grant
me the strength to do some needed Service. I pray for
wisdom to be Brave and True, and for the gift of Clear
Vision, so that I may see the Deeper Purposes and the
Finer Significances of the tasks that are set me. To be
content to keep on in the station where God has put me,
to do always a little more than I am paid for, to get early
to the job and never leave until the rest are gone. I may
never be famous, but I'll not leave any sign of wrong
behind me when I pass out."

Up from his stool jumped the book-keeper, and he
stretched a white hand across the marble to the laddie,
and he vowed then and there that the first opening for an
office boy in the business department of the Detroit *Free
Press* should go to Edgar Albert Guest. Who was there to
witness the scene? I myself cannot remember having
been there. Mr. Doty was probably dozing in the back
room. They were alone, Eddie and the book-keeper, in
that solemn and historic moment.

The words that Eddie said were from the bottom of his
great heart. In almost all his poems the echo of them
sounds; particularly in the noble **"Plea"** that dignifies the
pages of ***Poems of Patriotism.*** And the book-keeper's
promise was fulfilled when, in 1895, Eddie went on the
pay-roll of the Detroit *Free Press.* He has been there ever
since, not now indeed as office boy, but as staff poet.

III

There are apple-trees and sand-lot baseball games and
country roads and swimmin' holes in Eddie Guest's
memory of his boyhood, but the bustle of the down-
town streets is his principal heritage of dream from
those days. He was born on August 20, 1881, in Birmingham, England, and his parents brought him to the
land of the free when he was ten. Through the public
schools he made his studious way. The family, it appears, was not opulent, and Eddie began to work after
school hours as soon as he was able. In 1895, as we have
seen, he mixed his last soda, polished his last glass, and
went to the *Free Press.*

His duties at first were arduous. One of them was marking the baseball scores on the bulletin-board in front of
the *Free Press* Building. Attentively the serious little
fellow studied the jostling morons who waited through
the innings, and no doubt he wondered now and then how
it would feel to be himself the hero they applauded. "Promotion," he told himself, "will come to me if I work
unselfishly in my employer's interests. If I think less of
what is in my envelope and more of my opportunity to
serve, I will get there!" And sure enough, after two years
of diligent and unwearying effort as office boy in the
business department, Eddie was given his reward—promotion to the post of office boy in the editorial rooms!

Eddie's thoughts on this occasion were to become, later, that ode to **"Promotion"** which has inspired so many American youths to ever more assiduous toil:

> Promotion comes to him who tries
> Not solely for a selfish prize,
> But day by day and year by year
> Holds his employer's interests dear. . . .
> The man who would the top attain
> Must demonstrate he has a brain.

But not yet was that epiphany of beauty in Eddie's heroic spirit. He still had no idea of poetry. He confronted instead the problem of demonstrating that he was a useful lad, of winning still another promotion in another two years. Indeed, he told himself, I may even sometime be made a reporter! And so he buckled into his new job.

Craps he eschewed, it would appear; the cigarettes and the profanities and the viciousness of the other newspaper office boys never seem to have smirched him. He kept the paste pots full, he purveyed caramels for the switchboard gal, he saw that there was always an abundance of copy-paper on the desks. Early and late he worked; he did the tasks of two, of six, of a dozen ordinary office boys. And his joy can be easily imagined when one afternoon the editor summoned him and gripped his hand and said, "Eddie, I've been watching your career. Your intelligence and your devotion demand greater opportunities. Here's your chance, boy! You are promoted!"

And so, just as the Nineteenth Century which had cradled him was yielding place to the Twentieth which was destined to immortalize him, Eddie found himself exchange editor of the *Free Press.*

"The exchange desk! A meaningless phrase to those who have never helped in the building of the daily paper!" exclaims Mr. R. Marshall, his official biographer, in *A Little Book About the Poet of the Plain People.* "Every daily newspaper has an exchange desk. In fact many of them haven't much else! But on the big dailies, the man who sits all day in a four-by-six room, completely surrounded by wave upon wave of printed sheets, from the Boston *Transcript* to the Wahoo *Bugle*—he is the man who looks at the world through wideangle lenses. Across the desk of the exchange editor sweeps the flood of the world's opinion, the sum total of the world's woe, the tinkling brooks of the world's joys. To him come the banker and the burglar, the women of high and low degree. To him," Mr. Marshall continues with jolly alliteration, "come the poet and the plunderer, musicians and murderers, jokesmiths and junkers, prophets and perjurers. It is he who sees history in the making—to him is shown the panorama of the world's fight in the midst of the fighting."

It is the ordinary practice, on the half-dozen metropolitan newspapers to which I have yielded Service, to assign to the exchange desk men who can be spared with least detriment from the work of writing news. But the *Free Press,* no doubt, was an unusual institution; and so we find Eddie clipping and pasting and studying through those wide-angle lenses the panorama of the world's fight.

It was here, on the exchange desk, that he first burst into song. The golden bell sounded, the finger of eternity anointed his temples, he leaned his ear to the clarion call, he discerned for the first time the throb of the heart of the great American people: that audience which he was to make so completely and so significantly his own, "the plain folk who sit in front of base-burners, who wear overalls, and pay their grocery bills on Saturday nights, and say grace at meals, and stick up for the under-dog, and fish for trout in brooks."

Mr. Marshall in his careful way records the moment. "A poetry microbe wriggled out from between one of Marse Henry Watterson's virile editorials and bit Eddie Guest good and proper. Eddie started to write verse and more verse, and those verses that got into print were read and were then cut out and preserved in family albums."

But who first saw the flare of the levin, who bated his breath, who set eyes on that first epochal poem, while the shy lad, its creator, kicked his heels in embarrassment? Mr. Marshall does not say. But it is not difficult to picture the scene.

Back to Eddie the gray-haired, scholarly copy-reader hands the poem, with a faint smile. "Well . . . it *does* rhyme, in places, doesn't it?" he comments; reluctant but stern in the integrity of his own understanding. "Eddie, whatever made you think you could write poetry? Stick to your shears and paste-pot, old man. You'll get to be a good newspaper man yet."

So into Eddie's pocket went the firstling of his genius, rejected. With eyes downcast he lingered a moment, the everlasting poet on the drear threshold of derision, until he could control his emotions enough to mutter an abashed "Thanks!" Then into the corridor he groped his way; and there, ah! there at last the tears came, storming down his cheeks. Was this the end? Was this denial all he had struggled to achieve? Could he never write those poems that were already beginning to flower in his heart, poems that would leave the simple hearts of men gladder when he had gone: poems that would memorialize the goodness of Ma and Pa, the joys of the plain and wholesome grub that the missus prepares for one, the nobleness of toil, the nearness of God and the transcending glory of Yankee Doodledom? Even as he wept he felt the songs in his spirit too wildly sweet to be hushed, a pæan of hope and courage renewed that swelled in a tumultuous diapason.

"I will!" he cried, his eyes shining, his fist clenching. "They may say that it can't be done, but I for one am not convinced until I try it! They scoff at me, they jeer! But I shall buckle in with a grin and win!"

And he did. It is in Eddie's own words that we have the inner, spiritual story of what Mr. Marshall has but hinted at, and of what I have tried in my lame way to revivify: the poem **"It Couldn't Be Done"** from *The Path to Home,* whose periods are graven deep on the hearts of many a proudly aspiring, never faltering warrior of these splendid days:

> There are thousands to tell you it cannot be done,
>   There are thousands to prophesy failure;
> There are thousands to point out to you one by one,
>   The dangers that wait to assail you.
> But just buckle in with a bit of a grin,
>   Just take off your coat and go to it;
> Just start in to sing as you tackle the thing
>   That "cannot be done," and you'll do it.

He did it, and it was not long before dawn spread her rosy wings over the burgeoning gardens of his life.

IV

There has been little development since then in Eddie Guest's literary style. From book to book, as the years pass, it runs along the same high plane of brave delicacy. From the crest of the wave his genius sprang full-formed to life. One reads the lyrics of *A Heap o' Livin',* the first book of his poetry brought out by Reilly and Lee, in 1916, and one finds them exactly as sweet and juicy as the pieces in *All That Matters,* published in 1922. They are the same in style and in theme; his particular genius was mature in its first manifestation; it lisped never, it chanted full-throated. Yet for a little while after his beginnings in beauty Eddie continued a humble private in the cohorts of the *Free Press.*

From the exchange desk he graduated to the position of police reporter. Mr. Marshall lets us see him as he was in those remote days. "The crime reporter is the young man who knows all the policemen in town, who can point out the dope-fiends as they pass on the street, who wears a badge that lets him inside the lines at the big fires, who sits with the lawyers at the murder trials and who plays dominoes with the night chief when they're both doing 'the dog watch' in the small hours of the morning. The crime reporter knows the side of life where the seams are. And that, too, is a good experience for one who would school himself in the humanities."

I remember myself the reporters' room in the old Detroit Police Headquarters. We did not in my time play dominoes; we played poker, and the drawers of the rickety desks were filled with packs of greasy cards and chips. I remember the walls pasted thick with lickerish pictures from the *Police Gazette;* I remember the spittoons, the dirt, the jovial obscenities of the cops. And as I muse I find it incredible almost that Eddie, after this compulsory proximity to nastiness and crookedness and vice, could have preserved so chaste and unsullied the gentle ideals of his childhood: I am more and more amazed by the fact that he has yet to write "a line that father had to skip when he read to the family."

But he did not have to languish many years in that grotesquely uncongenial atmosphere. Presently the *Free Press* began to publish a short column of his poetry once a week, under the caption of "Chaff." And not long after that, as Mr. Marshall says, "they took Eddie off the crime beat and ordered him to be funny for a column every day." Again . . . he did it.

A poem a day! Perhaps his average was not, at first, so high as that. Yet in the decade up to 1910, so great was his facility, so indomitable his persistence, that he turned out some 3,650 poems. And so the time came when he determined to get out a book. Like Whitman, he was his own publisher. He produced a volume called *Home Rhymes,* for which his brother Harry set type in the attic of their house. The edition ran to 800 copies.

Two years later 730 new poems had accumulated and the Guest boys made another book—*Just Glad Things*—of which they printed 1,500 copies, In 1914 still another batch of 730 songs was on hand, and a third book was projected. But here the Rotary Club of Detroit intervened. Was not this a poet indeed, this slender, serious youth with the frank smile, who could dash off a poem a day? And poetry, too, that a red-blooded, high-powered Rotarian could understand: a poet who hymned in his swinging way "the peaceful warriors of trade," a poet who extolled the deliciousness of raisin pie in strophes one could sing to the tune of "The Battle Hymn of the Republic":

> There are pies that start the water circulatin' in
>   the mouth;
> There are pies that wear the flavor of the warm
>   an' sunny South;
> But for downright solid goodness that comes
>   drippin' from the sky
> There is nothing quite the equal of a chunk o'
>   raisin pie.

So the alert minds of the Rotary Club intervened. Boy still, Eddie was summoned by those men of Vision. "We want Guest!" they shouted. They instructed him to make this new book in an edition big enough to go around. It must be of 3,500 copies! And the Rotarians themselves printed it so.

Noon, bright noon! Winds of popular acclaim swept away the mists, and Eddie, looking at his feet, saw them set firmly on the pinnacle! The sun hung above him. The world of his admirers bade it stand still, and it stood. It hangs above him to this day.

Came *A Heap o' Livin',* reaching eight editions in twenty months and a total circulation of 50,000. Since then seven more books have been published, and a first edition of 50,000 is considered conservative.

North, South, East and West the word winged its flaming way: Look to the heights! And the world looked, and there was Eddie: and the list of his poems in a quarter of a century numbered 9,125, and the number of his books in the homes of America was more than a million! The man who did it when they said it couldn't be done!

It remained for a prose-minded nomothete, a politician flaunting his efficiency-methods, a governor more interested in problems of reforestation, public schools and police protection than in the very essential spiritual thing without which all these mean nothing, to rob Eddie Guest of his final reward. In the Michigan legislature early in 1925 Representative Howell introduced Act No. 74, providing for the post of poet-laureate of the State, to be filled by the governor. Through both houses the act went without a murmur of dissent. For once, at the beckon of the Hon. Mr. Howell, both bodies of lawgivers turned from the crass needs of industrial and economic life to gaze a moment on Parnassus. There was never any doubt who would be honored as the first laureate of Michigan. The Kiwanis Club, eager to match the snobbish Rotarians, had already dubbed him such. It was admitted in press dispatches that Eddie was to have the job. And then the governor vetoed the act.

Why? Ah, why indeed! He explained idiotically that "such an office has no place in a republican form of government!"

V

But Eddie goes on. "Mr. Guest, as every one knows, writes a poem each day," marvels the reporter for the *Telegram Mail* who interviewed him last February. "Mr. Guest admits that some days it's a hard pull, but he often finds that the poem that has been the hardest to write and which he has thought his poorest has turned out to be the most popular of all."

He works without crutches. I well remember the consternation of a literary friend of mine, who, being in need of a rhyming dictionary, and being informed that Eddie had one in his office, knocked on his door and asked for it. I am afraid that Eddie spoke rather curtly to my friend. But it is not hard to understand what an affront the request may have seemed to him. He makes up all his own rhymes.

For some time, at least up to a year ago, he conducted once a week "The Edgar A. Guest's Young Verse Writers' Corner." Children were invited to submit their poems. Eddie undertook to correct them, and gave instructions in the art whose confines he himself has so largely expanded. He printed every day a number of the pieces sent to him, with comment. A prize, an autographed copy of one of his own books, was awarded weekly.

One week he printed a stanza by a nine-year old child in Bay City:

> If I were a singer
>   I would sing a bonny song,
> And all those who stopped to listen
>   Would be happy all day long.

His own emended version—infinitely more precise, more measured; the thumbprint of the master!—he printed at the same time:

> If I were a singer
>   I'd sing a bonny song,
> And all who stopped to hear
>   Would happy be, day-long!

Eddie went on to comment upon the form. He cited the iambic structure with alternating tetra—and trimeter verses: Ta dum ta dum ta dum ta dum, Ta dum ta dum ta dum. This, he said, "is a very good form, and we recommend it to all readers who aspire to write good verse."

Good verse, indeed! It is to far more than that that Eddie himself aspires. In the *American Magazine* he once published an intimate, sympathetic, encouraging little essay called **"My Job as a Father."** In it he revealed the real aspiration which, beneath and beyond his quest for beauty, dominates his life. It is not to be an artist at all! "To be the father of a great son is what I should call Success," he declares. There stands the man in a gesture.

John Bakeless (essay date 1930)

SOURCE: "Laureate of the Obvious: Portrait of Edgar A. Guest," in *Outlook and Independent*, Vol. 155, No. 14, August 6, 1930, pp. 527-9, 556.

[*In the following excerpt, Bakeless uses humor to criticize Guest's verse and its admirers.*]

> *And, Mr. Sneering Critic, you certainly cannot disturb my peace of mind with your gibes and taunts unless you have my co-operation.*

—From the prose writings of EDGAR A. GUEST

This article really ought to be entitled *Profits from Poems, Reaching Results with Rhymes, Living on Lyrical Literature,* or something like that, for Edgar A. Guest, the sweet singer of Detroit, inventor of the mass-production lyric, is the first man in the long and lively history of English literature who has succeeded in Putting Over Poetry in a really big way.

Not for nothing does Mr. Guest live in Detroit. It is even rumored that the Guestian lyrics are built on a moving belt which carries them from the Scansion and Structure Department to the Rhyme Production Department, thence to the Sunshine Department for the insertion of the "just folks" and "everyday" qualities—and finally to the Religious Department, where faith, hope and charity are mortised in, a little toning up is done with sunsets, and the whole product is inspected to make sure it is perfectly moral. After that the new lyric can be run out of the factory on its own wheels and is ready for shipment, f.o.b. Detroit, terms net cash.

Only two modern poets make a living out of poetry. The other one is Alfred Noyes, who also resembles Mr. Guest in being of English birth. Otherwise they are very different. Mr. Guest came to our shores at an early age, went straight west to Detroit, and grew up with the country and Henry Ford. Alfred Noyes came later in life, lingered in the academic shades of the effete East, returned to the tyrannous monarchy of Great Britain, Ireland, and the British Dominions beyond the Seas—and now look at him!

In the ecstatic language of Messrs. Reilly and Lee, who seem to admire the Guestian works with that glad, free sincerity which is so characteristic of publishers when they are speaking of the genius that they nurture and pay royalties:

> Mr. Guest speaks to everyday people on everyday themes in everyday language in the columns of more than two hundred American newspapers, morning or evening. His Books of Verse [don't blame me for the capitals] are read in a million American homes. His voice is heard from the speaker's platform, over the radio or on the phonograph every day in the year.

Indeed, one indignant lover of poetry (not the Guestian variety) once protested in the columns of Miss Harriet Monroe's little magazine of verse, that the only way to escape him was to smash the radio. Escape, alas, is not so easy. One would also have to stop the morning paper, censor the sermon before going to church, and sedulously avoid Rotarian luncheons and Chamber of Commerce banquets. You cannot say that about Alfred Noyes—indeed, you cannot say it about far greater poets. But you can say it about Edgar A. Guest, the unlaureled laureate of the illiterate, the beloved, the admired, the applauded, the highly paid, and the generally agreed with—in short, Mr. Edgar A. Guest, of 17471 Hamilton Drive, Detroit.

THE story of Edgar A. Guest is the story of a poor boy who felt the call to Service, the urge to Higher Things. He said to himself:

> Brave youth must rise! Each Age demands
> Clear brains, strong hearts and willing hands.
> There is no limit placed on fame;
> Tis something any boy can claim.
> Hold fast! Work hard, be strong, be true—
> The future keeps a place for you! . . .
>
> Poor boys with glory shall be crowned,
> And men shall pass their stories round.
> This great success which thrills you through
> Tomorrow may belong to you.

It was even so. Within a few years he had taken the Kingdom of Rotararia by storm.

Edgar A. Guest was born on August 20, 1881, the son of Edwin and Julia Wayne Guest. His parents brought him to the land that he was subsequently to celebrate in song, at the age of nine. They settled in Detroit, and within six months knew everybody on the block—not exactly an English way of doing things.

In fact it leads one to suspect that perhaps the emphasis on the personal element in much of Guest's later work may be just the result of English reserve trying hard to be American—and overdoing it.

He was educated in the grammar schools and high school of Detroit. He never went to college—like Shakespeare. His learning, rather, was in the busy marts of men, at the communing places of the active, directing brains, the stamping ground of strong, silent men, the meeting place folks, plain, everyday people—in short he was the soda-jerker at Doty's drugstore, Sibley and Clifford Streets, Detroit. But not for long. And so—

> He risked for much, and risking, knew
>   What failure meant.
> His all into the game he threw,
>   And as it went,
> He stood prepared to pay the cost
> And not to whimper when he lost.

But the harsher trials were spared him. He soon had the job of office boy in the business department of the Detroit *Free Press;* again like Shakespeare, you see, who, legend avers, once held horses outside the theatre. The budding bard can't hold horses in Detroit. The next best thing is to be office boy in the busy marts of trade. It leads to poetic heights just the same.

It is recorded that Edgar A. Guest was an earnest office boy. He said to himself:

> Two ways there are for youth to go, and
>   one is gay with song;
> The other calls for earnest men and
>   rugged hearts and strong.
>   Bewitching sirens lure the feet
>   Of those who sigh for pleasures sweet,
> But when the purse is empty, boy, in
>   scorn they pass you by;
>   'Tis time enough to dance and sing
>   When you have done some useful thing,
> And youth must strike for goals afar
>   which old men dare not try.

Young Edgar struck for goals afar, and within two years he had advanced upstairs to be office boy in the editorial department.

It is not known that he washed the windows or that he swept the floor or that he polished up the handle on the big front door. It is not even known whether the big front door of the Detroit *Free Press,* at that early date, had a handle that required polishing. But young Edgar A. Guest did the next best thing. He said to himself:

> For the many, more's the pity,
>   Seem to like to drift along.
> But the steeps that call for courage
> And the task that's hard to do,
> In the end result in glory
> For the never-wavering few.

In practically no time he was exchange editor of the Detroit *Free Press!*

Mr. R. Marshall, author of *A Little Book About the Poet of the Plain People,* has hymned the event in poetic prose: "Across the desk of the exchange editor sweeps the flood of the world's opinion, the sum total of the world's woe, the tinkling brooks of the world's joys. To him come the banker and the burglar, the women of high and low degree. To him come the poet and the plunderer, musicians and murderers, jokesmiths and junkers, prophets and perjurers. It is he who sees history in the making—to him is shown the panorama of the world's fight in the midst of the fighting."

Mr. Guest became a naturalized American citizen in 1902, he married a Detroit girl in 1906, his son was born in 1912, and his daughter in 1922. Such was the genesis of America's most famous home, whose inmost privacies have since been publicized in thousands of newspaper and magazine columns. *The New Baby in Our Home* was written and published about the time the new baby was a year old. Mr. Guest has even told in a magazine article, just **"What I Shall Teach Bud and Janet about Marriage."** He has explained for a woman's magazine why **"My Youngsters Don't Worry Me,"** besides providing detailed descriptions of the Guest backyard and the Guest neighbors, all mentioned by name.

Before long, Mr. Guest became police reporter for the *Free Press.* His official biographer has written another exquisite prose romance about what the inside of a Detroit police station was really like in those days, a place where the reporter "plays dominoes with the night chief when they're both doing 'the dog watch' in the small hours of the morning." Apparently a nice place for mother to do her knitting.

Then came the transformation. Out of the earnest office boy, the exchange editor afire with the lust for Service, and out of the pure-minded police reporter, emerged the gifted columnist and poet. Eddie Guest took charge of a daily column, which was appropriately named "Chaff." But the wind did not blow it away. Ever since there has been something or other of Eddie Guest's on the editorial page of the *Free Press;* though the "Chaff," following excellent precedent, has long since been made into breakfast food and is now called "Edgar A. Guest's Breakfast Table Chat."

But, long ere this, had dawned the light of a new day. By 1910, Edgar A. Guest had written 3,650 poems. Most versifiers become impatient for the dignity of cloth bindings long before that, but they have not the Guestian spirit of Service to sustain them. When at length even he aspired to book publication, his brother Harry set the type for **Home Rhymes** in the attic. An edition of 800 was printed. A single copy of this home-made first edition would be a notable addition to any collection of Americana, but copies are almost undiscoverable today.

One volume, however, is no Aristotelian eatharsis for a man who can write more than three thousand poems before thirty. Within two years there were more than 730 new poems, and another volume had to be printed, appropriately titled **Just Glad Things.** Passed another two years and there was born another book, **Breakfast Table Chat.** It, too, was about to be privately printed when the Rotary Club of Detroit decided that the poetry of Edgar A. Guest was simply swell, besides being literary and high class and bursting with the spirit of Service. They published the new book for him, in an edition of 3,500 copies.

His first commercial publication was *A Heap o' Livin',* named from one of his most famous poems, **"It Takes a Heap o' Livin' t' Make a House a Home."** This book was published in 1916. Its far from subtle rhythms and even less subtle thought made an instantaneous hit. Service, home, mother, and the little ones, dogs, lilies, and the ol' swimmin' hole, embalmed in iron-clad iambics were precisely what the great throbbing heart of the plain folksy people yearned for. In ten years they bought a quarter of a million copies. In the meantime, the mills of Guest ground on, and they ground exceeding thin. The result was eight more books of verse—a total of nine in a decade, all of which sold and sold and sold. A first edition of 50,000 copies for a Guest book of verses is now regarded as ridiculously conservative. A good many of these are given away as gift books, for which purpose they are brought out in seven different bindings, four with an "art box."

When the World War came, Mr. Guest sprang to the defense of the Detroit front with *Over Here,* since republished as *Poems of Patriotism.* He swallowed, and helped others to swallow, a vast dose of war-time propaganda:

> Old women pierced by bayonets grim
> And babies slaughtered for a whim,
> Cathedrals made the sport of shells,
>   No mercy, even for a child,
> As though the imps of all the hells
>   Were crazed with drink and running wild.

A kind of versified Bryce report.

The book was full of the clichés of battle poetry, as the earlier books had been full of clichés about home and mother. It is curious to reflect that those years which tried the souls of all the world—which called forth the best work of Housman, Brooke, Seeger, Kilmer, and Sassoon—meant to the bard of Detroit merely lines about "bloodstained tyrants," "worn warriors," "mountain peaks . . . freedom shrieks," "battling for the right . . . cruel might," "lead of shame . . . cannons flame," "war's alarms . . . call to arms."

The book reached its depth of unreality in the sage asseveration that "no soldier will complain." The man who wrote that doesn't know soldiers. From Caesar's legionaries to Napoleon's "Grognards," and on down to the last scuffle in North Africa, every good soldier has at all times in all armies "groused" to high heaven in all moods and tenses, with expletives thrown in.

The chorus of praise which Mr. Guest's mass of versified platitudes has elicited—particularly from the clergy—is beyond belief. It is rather the fashion to compare Guest with Burns, neglecting the fact that Burns wrote as graceful and delicately varied lyric verse as has ever been written in English, while the prosody of Edgar A. Guest is a wooden succession of monotonous iambics.

Yet, "he is the Burns of America," observes that distinguished critic, the Grand Prelate of the Knights Templar of Indiana. Says another clerical enthusiast: "If Robert Burns sang at times with more rhythmic beauty and smoother cadence, there shines through the crystalline character of Edgar A. Guest an unsullied sincerity born of purity of heart such as is pathetically lacking in the poet from Scotia's hills. . . . He sees God everywhere, with an eye which gleams with 'the light of faith.' He sees God in friendship and he sees Him in the trees; he sees Him in the hollyhocks 'swaying in the breeze;' he sees Him in the 'rippling brooks' and in 'blue skies overhead;' he sees Him in the robins and in 'roses white and red.' His faith is founded on the years and all that he has seen; something of God's he's looked upon no matter where he's been."

Which simply means that a Bishop of the Methodist Episcopal Church is so mixed up in a Guestian lyric enthusiasm that he has mistaken the simplest pantheism for orthodox Christianity. Other parsons are quite as ludicrous in their praises of Guest's verse.

"He is trying with all his heart and soul to be a good picture of Jesus Christ and get us all better acquainted with the Sweet Father," murmurs the rector of an Episcopal Church in Detroit. "Guest's poems are singing a needed challenge 'round the family fireside," declares a shepherd of souls in Indianapolis. Heaven knows what that means.

"Our night with him was one of happiness and uplift," murmurs a Pittsburgh parson, without the ghost of a smile. Guest's, says no less a personage than a Methodist District Superintendent, is "a blessed ministry of laughter, love, and song."

One gasps as one reads the astounding array of bad taste that has been published as *Edgar A. Guest: Some Appreciations of the Man and his Work, by his Friends of the Pulpit.* One wonders how any men who must daily read the austere magnificence of the English Bible can honestly applaud the jingle-jangle of Guest's verse. It is appalling to think that men presumably familiar with the eternal human truths can confuse them with the ephemeral truisms of the Detroit seer.

It was the Rev. Phillips Endecott Osgood, rector of St. Marks, Minneapolis, who once and for all explained the

hold that Guest's verse has on the man in the street and his children in the fifth grade. Guest expresses, he said, "an average man's conclusions crystallized from life as it is." Or, as the president of a denominational university puts it: "He does not wear long hair; he dresses after the approved style of civilization [i.e., Detroit, Michigan]; he has none of the picturesque vices of the old-fashioned writing man [a roué, for example, like Tennyson]; and he does not entertain eccentric views about any of the big questions of life."

Mr. Guest's verse is without beauty, distinction, or honest intellectual content. He apparently has no idea of metrical substitutions or the use of the run-over line—what the French prosodists call *enjambement.* As a result, the monotonous humdrum of his verse is enough to madden a trained ear. His only variation is an occasional inversion of word order of the simplest kind, which usually makes the "poem" worse. A few years ago, when he was running a Sunday department called *Edgar A. Guest's Young Verse Writers' Corner*—with his own autographed works as prizes—a nine-year-old in Bay City, Michigan, sent in these simple little lines:

> If I were a singer
> I would sing a bonny song,
> And all those who stopped to listen
> Would be happy all day long.

Now that, for a nine-year-old, isn't bad. At least it has freshness and simplicity, and the naïve charm of childhood, even if it does not bear comparison with the juvenile lyrics of Chatterton.

But Edgar A. Guest revamped it relentlessly into his own tom-tom beat. He advised the child to write:

> If I were a singer
> I'd sing a bonny song,
> And all who stopped to hear
> Would happy be, day-long!

A jingle as monotonous and mechanical as the rattle of a Ford car.

But Mr. Guest is popular, not in spite of the machine-made quality of his verse but because of it. He is also popular because he re-enforces the prejudices and "beliefs" of the average man. His subjects are the conventional sentimentalities—he must have written at least a dozen "poems" on mother love—and the wish-fulfilments, defense-mechanisms, baseless optimisms, and success motifs which constitute nine-tenths of the after-dinner oratory of North America.

The "mother" poems are the worst. One of this year's crop concludes:

> Though broken promises destroyed
> The faith of others all,
> With help she ran unto the man
> Whene'er she heard him call.

Friends oft divide and pride forgets
   The ones it climbs above,
But there's no sin man wallows in
   Can change a mother's love.

Bad as this is, Mr. Guest reached the ultimate in one called, **"Weaning the Baby,"** which reaches its climax thus:

No more upon her gentle breast
   That little face may lie,
No more that little nose be pressed
   Against her food supply.

When one considers the nature of the subject, the banality of the verse seems debasing as only shoddy art can be. Yet the offense to good taste in much of Mr. Guest's writing is not the head and front of his offending. For twenty years he has unconsciously been drumming into the average heads of average American voters the most dangerous belief that a great nation can entertain: Its own flawlessness. Smug self-satisfaction is more fatal to democracy than any number of amateur Machiavellis in Moscow.

It is comforting to add that not all criticism has been so sugary as that of the clerics whom I have quoted. Occasionally, Mr. Guest gets precisely what is coming to him. Benjamin de Cassères, writing in the *American Mercury,* once summed him up as "the Cerberus that guards us against the great Blond Beast, against the sex-prickings of jazz, against the Seven Deadly Pleasures, . . . the upsprung backbone of middle-class morality."

But such are the views of the literati, and as every honest yokel knows, the literati are no better than they should be. They did not prevent the Michigan Legislature, in 1925, from passing a bill providing for a poet laureate—who, as every one knew, was destined to be Edgar A. Guest. That inconsiderable fellow, Robert Frost, was Fellow in Letters at the University of Michigan at the time, but as his poems don't even rhyme, the Legislature did not consider him.

On the second day of March, in that memorable year, the Hon. Chester M. Howell, of Saginaw, introduced "a bill to provide for the appointment of a poet laureate of the State of Michigan." It was considered in Committee of the Whole—along with a bill "to fix the weight per bushel of certain vegetables," and another enactment "to provide that the term 'live stock' shall include poultry."

After one failure, the bill passed the House by 82 to 5, and the Michigan legislators turned in relief to the question of "spearing red horse, suckers, and mullet in the Clinton and Belle Rivers." By April it looked as if Michigan were destined to be the only state in the Union with an official laureate all its own; for the Senate also passed the bill and returned it to the House—together with another "to permit the taking of speckled bass and crappies from certain waters of Muskegon County."

But at this interesting juncture, up in gubernatorial wrath rose the Honorable Alex J. Groesbeck, Governor of Michigan. He vetoed the bill on the ground that "no compensation seems to have been provided for the Poet Laureate in the event of his appointment, and I can scarcely conceive of one such, serving without a salary. At least this is my understanding of this monarchial [sic] job." Considering the fact that the official payment of the British poet laureate has for centuries been a generous measure of wine, this was indeed a difficulty. Besides, argued Governor Groesbeck: "Speaking more seriously, as the saying goes, such an office has no place in a Republican form of government and for this reason I withhold my approval."

J. P. McEvoy (essay date 1938)

SOURCE: "Sunny Boy," in *Post Biographies of Famous Journalists,* edited by John E. Drewry, The University of Georgia Press, 1942, pp. 128-45.

[*In the following biographical sketch, McEvoy humorously and affectionately draws a portrait of Guest from glances at his life and verse.*]

It takes a heap o' livin' in a house t' make it home, . . .

Who wrote that? Does he believe it? And how does he get that way?

The answer to all these questions is Eddie (Edgar A.) Guest. He wrote it because he is Eddie. He wrote it about home because he hardly ever stirs out of it. He wrote it because he believes it; he believes it because he wrote it.

You'd believe it, too, if it had supported you for years, put your son through college, bought you a $50,000 home, sold 1,000,000 copies and made you that rarest thing in history—a prophet with honor in your own country.

I've known Eddie Guest for more than twenty years. In all that time I've never heard so many things that aren't so about anybody. And that is very odd, because an oyster on the half shell is a closed book compared to Eddie Guest. Every day, including Sundays, for thirty-two years he has written a "pome," and practically every one of them is about himself or his family or his friends. More than 300 newspapers told their readers when Bud cut a tooth, or Nellie cooked a pie, or how the installment collector came and took away the furniture, and yet people still ask, "Who is Eddie Guest?"

Who indeed! Why, so revealing were his daily songs of poverty and personal inefficiency that his mother, her traditional English reticence outraged, would weep and say, "Eddie, have you no shame?" What is he like indeed? My friends, he is just like that. Simple as a child, common as an old shoe, friendly as a puppy, foolish like a fox.

A heap o' sun an' shadder, and ye sometimes have
    t' roam
Afore ye really 'preciate the things ye lef'
    behind, . . .

That's Eddie too. Countless thousands have nodded acquiescence as Eddie, in a voice that would coax a robin out of its nest, painted a picture of far wanderings and glad returnings. To them, Eddie was a world-weary traveler—Eddie, who in his own words "ain't never been nowheres and ain't never seen nothin'." At the age of nine he came straight from England to Detroit. That was forty-seven years ago, and he's been in Detroit ever since. Some lecture trips, to be sure; and last year a session in Hollywood, where he went to be an actor; and one trip to Yucatan on Charles F. Kettering's yacht, during which he wirelessed home every hour on the hour until he landed, and then telephoned Nellie so often that she made him come home to save expenses.

"Without going out-of-doors, one may know the whole world" says Lao-tse, the Old Rogue of China; "without looking out of the window one may see the way of heaven. The further one travels, the less one may know. Thus it is without moving ye shall know; without looking ye shall see; without doing ye shall achieve." There's a lot of the Old Rogue in Eddie. Sitting in Detroit, he has let the world come to him. Without stretching forth his hand, fame, success, riches have tracked him down and forced their vulgar attentions on him. Living in this modern fairyland where the most fabulous dreams have come true, where one played golf with Midas in the morning and poker with Croesus at night, Eddie closed his ears to the siren song. He was a pal of Henry Ford's when Henry was tinkering with his first car, and they used to meet late at night in a little beanery and match pennies to see who would pay for the sandwiches. Eddie's grocer put $1200—all of his savings—into Ford's hands, and Ford bought back the stock for $12,000,000. But Eddie was unmoved. He has never put a dime in any kind of speculation. He knows all the big shots in Detroit and during the boom played golf with many of them. Every day they would greet him with "Well, I made a hundred and fifty thousand dollars this morning," or some such catty remark, but Eddie only smiled and said,

"It don't make any differunce how rich ye get t' be,
How much yer chairs an' tables cost, how great
    yer luxury;
It ain't home t' ye, though it be the palace of a king,
Until somehow yer soul is sort o' wrapped round
    everything."

Apparently their souls weren't wrapped very tightly around what they had, because they lost it, but when the smoke cleared away and the dust settled, Eddie still had his home and Nellie and Bud and Janet, and a lot of friends. And today his soul is still sort o' wrapped round all of 'em in a double bow knot.

Twenty years is a long time to know anybody, and to find them unchanged in all that time is rare indeed. When they

ain't spoiled by success, they're apt to be soured by failure. (He's got me talkin' that way now.) We met first in Chicago at a convention of American Press Humorists—if you can imagine anything so grim. Professional humorists, column conductors, cartoonists, toastmasters—we got together three, four, five times a day, luncheons, breakfasts, teas, dinners. Women's clubs entertained us, and men's clubs, and even the little children didn't escape. All day and far into the night and every day for a week, we went around together and listened to one another's jokes and stories. We started out suspicious of one another, but long before the week was over, our worst suspicions were confirmed. We began hating one another's jokes and stories, and wound up hating one another's collars and hats, hopes and fears, wives and children. But when I tell you that Eddie Guest is the only one who has survived this horror, you will get some idea of his indestructible quality. None of the other visitors could ever come back to Chicago. And we who lived there had to move away, but Eddie has come back many times by special request and has told the same audiences the same stories and recited the same "poems" to them. And they laugh and cry in the same places, and the only difference is that every year they have to pay him more.

Home ain't a place that gold can buy or get up in
    a minute; . . .

For a fellow who goes around knocking gold all the time, an amazing amount has managed to cling to Eddie. More than 3,000,000 of his books have been sold at an average of $1.50 apiece, and if you figure 10 per cent of that as Eddie's annual insult—known in the vulgar mart as royalty—it amounts to what better poets have called a "pretty penny." But then they would know more about pennies than Eddie. Since 1916 his daily "pome" has been syndicated in anywhere from 200 to 300 papers seven times a week. For the last six years he has been on a half-hour radio program, Coast to Coast, every week. His take for that is a thousand bucks on the nose every Tuesday.

When Hollywood started on a hunt for another Will Rogers, it was logical that they would turn to Eddie, the Poet of the People. He told the scouts and lawyers and the producers and everybody that he couldn't go to Hollywood, he couldn't be happy there.

"Afore it's home there's got t' be a heap o' livin'
    in it; . . ."

Eddie reminded them mechanically, and they told him he could do a heap o' livin' on $2500 a week, even in Hollywood. But Eddie went right on:

"Within the walls there's got t' be some babies
    born, and then
Right there ye've got t' bring 'em up t' women
    good, an' men; . . ."

and then he walked out into the yard and started playing with his robins. Well, it takes a heap o' givin' in a place to make it Hollywood, so they followed him right out into the yard and explained that babies are born out West, too, and you could do an awful lot about bringin' "'em up t' women good, an' men" on $3000 a week. So Eddie compromised on $3500, because as he put it himself:

> " . . . gradjerly, as time goes on, ye find ye
>   wouldn't part
> With anything they ever used—they've grown into
>   yer heart:
> The old high chairs, the playthings, too, the little
>   shoes they wore
> Ye hoard; an' if you could, ye'd keep the thumb
>   marks on the door."

There were a lot of thumb marks on Eddie, too, before he got out of Hollywood—but that's another story.

It would seem that Eddie's public is not so indifferent to money as Eddie tells you he is. People either want to know where Eddie gets all his wonderful ideas, or how much of that wonderful dough does he get? Where he gets his ideas is simple enough. He gets them from Eddie. Where he gets the dough is even simpler. He gets it from Eddie's public. But trying to find out how much of it he gets is like trying to learn how many planes in the Soviet air force. You pass out of the realm of reporting into the stratosphere of spy work. However, putting this and that and those together, it is pretty safe to say that Eddie has an annual income of more than $100,000, and has enjoyed this and more for many years, for not only does he collect from radio, the newspapers, movies and books, but he has a tremendous income from greeting cards, calendars, novelties and what the Authors' League painfully refers to as "small rights." Well, they may be small for you and me, but they ain't for Eddie.

Yes, Eddie has an enormous public, and it is not surprising that he has an enormous mail. Eddie's customers love to read and like to write, but occasionally he gets a surprise. Eddie was on the air one night, reciting one of his "pomes" about Nellie, his wife. "When my ship comes in," sighed Eddie in effect, "I will buy Nellie a comb for her hair and a new gingham dress. When my ships comes in," he went on, and his voice trembled with love and tenderness, "I will buy fine gloves for her toilworn hands and new shoes for her weary feet." All over the country, Eddie's audiences wept with emotion, but one of them wrote in and said, "Dear Eddie, I see the Government reports your income last year as $128,000. Don't you think you could spare enough to buy Nellie a comb for her hair? Or, if that is rank extravagance, surely you could manage a pair of new shoes."

Eddie chuckled when he read that one. He knew what the writer didn't know—that this was an old, old "pome," written many years ago, when he and Nellie were living on twenty-five dollars a week in a flat they rented from the cop on the corner. He was writing poetry then on the Detroit *Free Press,* but his early training was that of a bookkeeper, and every night he used to sit down with Nellie and figure out how far they were running behind.

No matter how they figured, it always came out the same—every week they had a nine-dollar deficit. So Eddie wrote a letter to the publisher, E. D. Stair—he is still the publisher and Eddie is still working on the Detroit *Free Press*—in which he pointed out that he was steadily losing nine dollars a week, and eventually, at this rate, he would go under. Mr. Stair, in the immemorial manner of newspaper publishers, solved Eddie's problem by raising him three dollars a week. This masterpiece of high financing so dazzled Eddie that he could never break away from Mr. Stair, always went to him for advice, and refers to him today as the smartest businessman he knows.

One is inclined to agree with Eddie when one learns that only after many years did Eddie succeed in getting his salary up to fifty dollars a week, and he was never able to get it any higher. Today, after forty-two years of continuous service, it is lower even, for he was cut during the depression to $37.50, and he has never been put back. However, Eddie never sees the check, although it is collected and faithfully cashed every week. Nellie gets it. Incidentally, Eddie's son, Bud, now a reporter and radio commentator on the Detroit *Free Press,* got his father's check by mistake one week and was so insulted he almost quit.

Eddie's formal education stopped with one year of high school, but his informal education has been going on ever since. He graduated *magna cum laude* as a soda jerker and then won a scholarship as an office boy for the Detroit *Free Press.* Here he mastered in posting baseball scores, providing his own board and tuition out of the weekly grant of $1.50 from the Stair foundation. A fellowship was then offered him in the accounting department, where he occupied the chair of ledger entries, with an honorarium of six dollars weekly. This led to an exchange professorship on the editorial faculty, where his work consisted principally of research in the police stations, supplemented by intensive case studies in abnormal psychology provided by the continuous poker games going on among his associates in the field.

A chair awaited him at the exchange desk—a chair and an eyeshade, a pair of shears and a pot of paste. He read papers from all over the country—big-city dailies, country weeklies—and mined countless little nuggets of wit and wisdom. As Eddie snipped out pieces of poetry to be reprinted, he began to write rhymes of his own and sneak them into the paper as exchange items. Finally he was caught at this, and for one breathless moment, the fate of America's Poet of the People teetered on the brink of oblivion. This was the turning point. After this, Eddie became more daring. He expanded from four-line verses to eight lines, to sixteen. His poetic feet left tracks all over the Detroit *Free Press*—flat tracks, a lot of them, to be sure, but Eddie was feeling his way.

"Groping blindly" describes it better, perhaps—blindly and desperately—for Eddie knew by this time that he didn't want to grow old and die in the newspaper harness.

"I can't say I planned my life this way," Eddie tells me. "A lot of things have happened to me that I didn't foresee and a lot of things have come my way that I don't deserve, but as I look back, one of the turning points of my life was a funeral. It was a simple enough funeral—just the body and the undertaker and I and a bugler. The bugler was there to blow taps over the grave. It was raining, too, I remember, and the man we were burying had been a newspaperman for forty-five years, and nobody came to the funeral but the undertaker and I, and we buried him in the rain, and then the bugler blew taps, and he was in a hurry because it was raining so hard, and we gave him the five dollars we promised him, and he beat it without even looking back. I said to myself, right there and then, 'This won't happen to me, if there is any way I can help it.'"

And then I asked him that old bewhiskered question, "To what do you attribute your success?" and he replied, "When I was a child in England, a terrible panic hit everybody, but it knocked us out. I can still see the furniture disappearing, melting away as we sold it for food. Then my father came to this country, looking for work. And he landed in the middle of another panic. Poverty is no fun, and I suppose more than ambition or anything else, the dread of it has kept me trying. That's the secret, I guess. I've always kept trying."

"Don't you believe in luck?"

"The wind usually blows one way or the other," said Eddie, "and if it happens to be blowing your way, that's luck. If it's blowin' against you, you tack. If it stops blowin', you wait until it starts again. But if you aren't out there trying, it won't make any difference which way it blows."

Eddie has been trying for more than forty years, and friends of Eddie who knew him when—Detroit is full of them—say success hasn't changed him a bit. He's still simple and kindly—a small, wiry man who talks with the same drawl and makes the same half-helpless gestures with his hands. Twenty years later, when I met him first, he was still small and slight and dark, and he gave you the impression of being embarrassed to death, unless you looked into his eyes, and then you saw they were keen and twinkling with laughter. I've heard him talk to any number of audiences and he always gives them the impression that they are scaring him stiff.

In his shrewd knowledge of human nature, Eddie is as smart as Will Rogers ever was. To watch him handle an audience is an education in crowd psychology. He tells them a little story that does a lap dissolve into a little "pome" right under their eyes, and before they have finished laughing at the story, they are crying at the verse. They never hear anything that they haven't known since childhood, but it all sounds new when Eddie tells it. At first they feel terribly sorry for him as he shuffles nervously and explains that he really doesn't know why he's there, and he hopes they don't mind if he tells them a

little story, because this happened to him that morning—he's been using that same story for thirty years and it's good for thirty more. They feel sorry for him, and then they laugh at him because now they feel so much superior to him—and then they're hooked.

Eddie doesn't lecture very much any more. The women's clubs finally beat him down. Women like Eddie because he makes them cry. Other lecturers would come and try to make them think, but succeeded only in making them feel uncomfortable. But Eddie would stand up there, a pale poetic figure, with his shock of black hair falling into his eyes, his hands making timid, helpless gestures, and in a sobbing cello voice tell them:

> "Ye've got t' weep t' make it home, ye've got t'
> sit an' sigh . . ."

Years of fighting his way home through crowds of adoring women finally convinced Eddie that he'd rather stay at home. But he still does quite a bit of talking in and around Detroit, and if Nellie didn't protect him, he would be out every night and every afternoon and every morning. Churches—any church—boy scouts, girl scouts, hospitals—Eddie will talk to any of them at any time of the day or night and never charge them a cent. Just the week before I visited him he agreed to go over and talk to the colored Y. W. C. A. one night. It wasn't until he got there that he realized a dreadful mistake had been made. The meeting had been scheduled on the same night as the Joe Louis-Nathan Mann fight, and, horror on horror, his talk was scheduled to start at ten o'clock, when the fight started in New York.

"I watched them getting more nervous," said Eddie, "and finally, sure enough, their worst fears were realized. Just two minutes to ten I was called on, and at ten the radio broadcast was supposed to start from Madison Square Garden. So I got up and said, 'Folks, with the best will in the world, I can't make a fifteen-round talk. Besides, I'm just as anxious to hear about the fight as you are. Suppose we delegate one of our members here to sit by the radio and bring in the results round by round. I'll just go on talking, and you don't have to listen if you want to.' So I rambled along and a girl ran in and shouted, 'End of the first round, Joe Louis!' and then I recited the little poem about old-fashioned flowers, 'I love them all, the morning-glories on the wall, the pansies in their patch of shade, the violets stolen from their glade. The bleeding hearts and columbine have long been garden friends of mine, but memory every summer flocks about a clump of hollyhocks,' and the girl runs in and hollers, 'End of the second round, Joe Louis!' So I acknowledged the applause and continued to tell them that 'the bright spots in my life are when the servant quits the place, although that grim disturbance brings a frown to Nellie's face. The week between the old girl's reign and the entry of the new is one that's filled with happiness and comfort through and through. The charm of living's back again, a charm that servants rob—I like the home, I like the meals, when Nellie's on the job,' and just then the girl ran in screaming, 'Joe Louis wins by a knockout!' so I didn't have to talk any more that night."

Millions have read Eddie Guest's verses in books and newspapers, more millions have heard his voice on the radio, and hundreds of thousands have seen him on lecture platforms, but only his intimates have seen Eddie at work and Eddie at play—in short, have seen Eddie at home. For home isn't just something Eddie writes about. He lives in it all day every day, and hardly stirs out of it except to play golf, and then he doesn't need to stir far, because his house is right on the edge of the golf course, thirty minutes from the heart of the city. In fact, he and his neighbors live on lots that were cut out of the original tract. The lots were laid out first and then the course, and Eddie can tee off his back porch and play the twelfth hole. Incidentally, he goes around in the low eighties and has shot a seventy-five. Not bad for a poet.

It is a comfortable gracious house with a white column portico and a garden in the back, full of flowers and birdhouses. For the information of housewives who may read this for homely details, there are nine rooms and four baths on the second floor, and on the first floor there are kitchen, dining room, breakfast room, living room, library. The furniture is simple, comfortable and so unobtrusive that if it belongs to any period, style, school or era, it rings no bells in my memory. After two days of lounging, sleeping, eating and sprawling all over the house, I have only a general impression of color and comfort and a lot of outdoors looking in.

In addition to this, I hear a typewriter upstairs. It clicks along for a few minutes and then there is a shuffle of feet on the stair and Eddie comes into the library, looking for Nellie. If she isn't sitting in the corner knitting, he goes around the house looking for her. As soon as he has located her, he seems satisfied, because he goes back upstairs and pecks out two or three more lines of poetry on his battered typewriter. Should Nellie leave the house to shop or visit or go to the hairdresser, Eddie is finished writing for that day. After thirty years, Nellie is still trying to get his hair to lie down, and would like to have him do something about that old velvet jacket he works in. She straightens his little bow tie and takes off his glasses for him when he isn't using them, and tucks them in his pocket, but it's all done so automatically that you know she has done it ten thousand times, and that, though he doesn't notice that she does it, he would miss it if she didn't.

The old velvet house jacket is more than just a working uniform. There's just a slight suspicion of genteel elegance about it which warms Eddie's secret soul—a suggestion of formality which Eddie sternly suppresses in all his other attire. He really likes to wear his tuxedo, but he feels that his public wouldn't understand, so, whenever photographers surprise him in this outfit, he rushes to get an overcoat and puts it on with the collar turned up as though he had just come in from feeding the stock. It is quite possible that Eddie didn't identify himself as a Poet

of the People in the beginning, but willy-nilly he was cast in the role, and now the role and the man are so inextricably commingled that it is impossible even for Eddie to know where one begins and the other ends. He reminds you of Frank Bacon in his last years, when he had played Lightnin' Bill Jones so long that Bacon was Jones and Jones was Bacon.

"Does he do all his work at home?" I asked Nellie, because Eddie doesn't want to talk about his work. Nellie says, "Yes, and he's always running up and down the stairs, and some days it takes him all day to write one poem and other days he can write two, but he never gets very far ahead, and after thirty years he is still fighting the dead line. He started to retire at fifty," says Nellie, who has white hair, but a young face, "and he went right to bed to enjoy ill health. The house was full of doctors and none of them could find anything wrong with him, which made Eddie very angry, because he was sure he was falling all to pieces. Well, this went on for at least a year, and then one day I said, 'Eddie, get up. We can't afford to have you retire.' This seemed like good news to Eddie. He got up out of bed, and he hasn't talked about retiring since. I don't think now he'll ever retire."

> *Ye've got t' sing an' dance fer years, ye've got t'*
> *romp an' play, . . .*

Eddie can't carry a tune and, stranger than that for a rhymester, Eddie "aint got rhythm." When I sat with him in the broadcasting station in Chicago while Frankie Masters and his band swung "Mama, That Moon is Here Again," every foot in the studio tapped in time—every foot but Eddie's.

Perhaps he is willing to let his young daughter, Janet, take care of that department. She is just sixteen and she fills the Guest house with all the rhythm it could take without falling apart. Rhythm and boys who come for breakfast and stay for dinner and are finally shooed home. When the boys aren't there, Janet isn't either, for this is a typical American household. She's either at a girl friend's or going to the movies. When Benny Goodman came to Detroit, Janet and her friends took their lunch to the theater, got there for the first show and stayed until the theater closed. They did this every day, until finally they knew all the dialogue of the picture, and the whole theater of youngsters would recite it out loud with the actors. Then Benny Goodman and his band came on, and the kids would truck up and down the aisles and shriek for all the world like a Holy Roller meeting.

I was a guest of the Guests for two days, and I caught one glimpse of Janet. She was having dinner with her gang, after which she was scheduled to leave and spend the night with a girl friend. "Come back for breakfast, dear," said Nellie, but she wasn't back for breakfast, nor luncheon either. When Eddie came down from upstairs, where he had been writing all morning on a poem about home and children, he looked around the table for Janet. "Doesn't she live here any more?" said Eddie plaintively.

The boy, Bud, doesn't live there any more either, but that's only because Eddie built him and his new wife a brand-new house. It's the kind of a house that fathers who didn't have anything when they were young build for their sons. Every day Eddie was over there suggesting new gadgets and getting in the architect's hair. Now that it's finished, Eddie goes over and gloats at least once each day. It has a paneled library nook and a game room with bar downstairs. The garage doors open with an electric eye. The guest room is much too good for any guest—even Eddie. A sweeter, gayer, more complete little chromium-trimmed love-nest you couldn't imagine. But it is all of a piece with the Detroit of today, just as the three-room flat on the second floor of the crossing cop's house where Eddie and Nellie started out was all of a piece with the Detroit of yesterday. The village that was Detroit is a dynamic city now, and Bud is a grown man, making good on the same paper his father started on, and Janet is a young lady who trucks where Nellie, her mother, waltzed—everything and every place and everybody have changed—except Eddie.

It takes a heap o' something to be a hero to your own children. If Eddie is proud of his son, Bud is twice as proud of his father. Not that he has any illusions about his father's poetry. He calls it verse—Eddie thinks most of it isn't even that. "Rhymes, doggerel, anything you like to call it," says Eddie. "I just take simple everyday things that happen to me and figure that they probably happen to a lot of other people, and I make simple rhymes out of 'em, and people seem to like 'em."

"But my father reads everything," Bud tells me proudly, "and his favorite poets are Walt Whitman and Browning," and he adds, "Can you imagine anything more different than Browning and the stuff my father writes? He reads all the modern poets, too, even though he suspects that they don't read him, except to poke fun at him."

"Does he mind?" I inquire, and Bud says "No. Would you? Of course, I think away back there somewhere, it worried him a little bit, but a lot of those who criticized him then are forgotten now, and those who criticize him now aren't read very much, except by each other—and even they seem to mellow as they grow older and have the same kind of troubles that everybody has and find that they can't wisecrack their way out of them."

"I suppose you know your father pretty well?"

"I play golf with him every day when the weather's good and I play poker with him one night a week. You get to know a man that way. In fact, he won't play golf with any other partner but me. I suspect he's afraid I might beat him some day if I played against him. But there's no doubt about the poker. We have a game here at the house every week—mother and dad, Betty—that's my wife—and I, and Betty's father and mother. The blue chips are three cents, the red chips two, and the white chips, one cent, and dad always cleans us out

regularly. He does pretty well down at the club, too—that's the Detroit Club. Some of the fellows there play a pretty stiff game and occasionally they coax dad into sitting in. He always tells them he doesn't want to, that he doesn't understand what they're doing, and he has such an honest face that they always believe him. They still think he doesn't know what he's doing, that he's just lucky, but he always takes 'em just the same."

"When I was in college," Bud continues, "I didn't have as much fun as I might have had, because I realized if I got into a jam, it wouldn't be me, but 'Eddie Guest's son.' You have no idea the way a lot of people think of dad, as though he was hardly of this world."

I assured him I could believe it, for only that day Charlie Hughes, secretary of the Detroit Athletic Club, who has known Eddie for thirty-six years, told me the story of a member who came in one morning, all excited, and asked, "Is it true that Eddie Guest is getting a divorce?"

Charlie said, "I hadn't heard of it and I can't imagine it."

"I've got to find out right away," said the member, "because my wife heard it on the train yesterday coming from Chicago, and she cried all night."

Charlie Hughes has a lot of stories about Eddie, but I like especially the one he tells about the motor trip Eddie took with Henry Ford and Harvey Firestone. It seems they were riding in a flivver and stopped at a farmhouse upstate for a glass of buttermilk. In the yard the farmer was fighting an old Model T which was tired of it all and wouldn't fight back.

Finally Henry couldn't stand it any longer. He took off his coat and said, "Let me look at it. Maybe I can do something with it."

The farmer didn't think the stranger could, but was willing to let him try. Ford rolled up his sleeves and reached down into the decrepit innards, twisting a muscle here, tying off an artery there. And finally it started to rasp and wheeze, kick off the bedclothes and sit up.

"It'll go now," said Henry, "but when you take it down to the garage, tell them to do such-and-such with it."

The farmer was grateful and wanted to pay. Ford laughed it off and he and his party climbed into their car. The farmer insisted. It would have cost him several dollars to get the car fixed, he argued, and there was no reason why he shouldn't give that money to the stranger.

Finally, to get rid of him, Eddie said, "He doesn't need the money. He has all the money he can possibly use."

"I don't believe it," snorted the farmer cynically. "If that's true, what the hell are you all riding around in that thing for?"

The people who cry when they think of Eddie and Nellie being divorced are the same ones who write indignant letters every week to their local radio stations and protest against the singing of popular songs and the playing of swing music on the same program with their poet-philosopher. If they had their way, it would be all chimes and organ music. How many of them are there?

Last Christmas week an announcement was made to the effect that 100,000 calendars with the picture of Eddie Guest and a facsimile of his signature would be sent to the first 100,000 applicants. Requests poured in by telegraph, special delivery, practically everything but carrier pigeons and dog sleds. When the calendars were exhausted, there were still 250,000 applications, and more were coming by every mail.

How many of them are there?

The Reilly & Lee Co., who publish the Eddie Guest books in stiff board and limp leather, in library editions, pocket editions, and boxed for gifts, tell me that a first printing of an Eddie Guest book of verse is anything from 150,000 down to 100,000. There are twelve titles, and one of them, ***A Heap o' Livin'***, has sold more than 1,000,000 copies, and is still selling as strong as ever. I have been able to find only two books that consistently outsell Eddie Guest year after year. One is the *Bible*, the other is *Fannie Farmer's Cook Book*. Even the most devout of Eddie's readers would tell you that he combines the best features of each.

How many of them are there? So many who talk so rapturously about him that you grow positively weary trying to add them up.

Here are two real stories out of hundreds that have been told to me. It seems that for years now Eddie has taken the same train out of Detroit every Monday night, occupies the same stateroom, has the same porters, is met at the Twelfth Street station in Chicago by the same redcaps, driven by the same taxi drivers, and his progress from train to hotel, to broadcasting station and back to the train again, is like a triumphal procession. One night there was a new porter on Eddie's car, and Eddie learned that his old porter was ill in a South Side hospital. Now, most men would say, "Isn't that too bad?" and let it go at that. A few might send a note, practically none would send flowers, but Eddie dropped everything and drove out to visit him in the hospital.

The second story has to do with Henry Klein, the hard-boiled radio executive who produces Eddie's weekly program. The Kleins built a little house, and they were so proud of it they insisted that Eddie come out and see it. Which he did.

"Where's your garden?" inquired Eddie, and Klein said, "We've done pretty well to get a house. A garden can jolly well wait."

Eddie said he didn't think a house without a garden could possibly amount to much, and went away talking to himself.

"The next day my wife called up," said Klein, telling me the story. "She was having hysterics. 'The WPA is out here,' she said. 'There are trucks full of trees all over the place and they're tearing up the whole yard.'

"I calmed her down by telling her I'd look into it, and then I promptly forgot it. But that night when I got home I passed right by the house without recognizing it. The yard was full of tall trees and flowering shrubs and flower beds in bloom. There was an old turf lawn and roses round the door. It wasn't the WPA; it was just Eddie Guest."

Now, most of Eddie's readers know nothing of rhyme and less of meter, they wouldn't know a pentameter from a speedometer, but Eddie's verse suits them right down to the ground and deep into their very roots. And it is true that many of Eddie's poetic feet have flat arches, and his muse sings less like a heavenly being than the girl next door, and it is true that you could fill Soldier Field tomorrow with contemporary poets and rhymesters and versifiers of all kinds, any and all of whom can write rings around Eddie Guest, but the public, the dear, queer, busy, dizzy, sad, glad public, wouldn't swap one Eddie Guest "pome" for the whole kaboodle.

Why?

Perhaps it is because the bright lads and lassies are so proud of being bright that they can't believe that other people on the road wish they would learn to dim their lights. You can be mighty bright and still not know that you can't put your heart in your work and your tongue in your cheek at the same time. Eddie's heart is in his songs. Small wonder then that his songs go straight to the heart.

> Even the roses 'round the porch must blossom
>   year by year
> Afore they 'come a part o' ye, suggestin'
>   someone dear
> Who used t' love 'em long ago, an' trained 'em
>   jes' t' run
> The way they do, so's they would get the early
>   mornin's sun;
> Ye've got t' love each brick an' stone from cellar
>   up t' dome:
> It takes a heap o' livin' in a house t' make it home.

Bruce Walker (essay date 1995)

SOURCE: "Edgar A. Guest," in *DAC News*, Vol. 80, No. 7, October, 1995, pp. 49-51.

[In the following excerpt, Walker relies on biographical information provided by Guest's grandson, Edgar A. Guest III, and from contemporaneous newspaper accounts to assess Guest's poetic legacy.]

"To his generation he was, through the lilt of his words, a bestower of pleasure, a kindler of hopes and an assuager of sorrow."—The Detroit Free Press *on Edgar A. Guest*

A regular contributor to the DAC NEWS and Detroit Athletic Club mainstay, Edgar A. "Eddie" Guest endeared himself to thousands with his insightful and witty, yet down-to-earth verses during his more-than-50-year career as a *Detroit Free Press* syndicated poet.

To show how much members appreciated Guest, the DAC held annual Edgar A. Guest Nights in the 1940s. Edgar A. Guest III, Guest's grandson, says because he never read his verses aloud at home, the first time he heard his grandfather recite his verses was at a DAC Edgar A. Guest Night. He recalls the dining room was packed. "It was the first time I saw him and it astounded me that he could do so well," he says.

Literary critics, however, did not share DAC members' views of Guest's work; they deplored his simple verses aimed at the general public. Dorothy Parker was among the literaries who berated his verses. A *Detroit Times* article after his death stated the literaries were not who Guest was trying to impress: "First let us admit that people who read Harriet Monroe or Carl Sandburg were not among the buyers of the Guest books. Most of these buyers never read poetry at all, but they wanted *A Heap O' Livin'*." Similarly, a *Detroit News* article stated, "he was deeply admired by the mass of men and women who lead quiet lives, pay their debts, bring up their children properly and seldom get their names in the papers except in connection with a golden wedding anniversary." Although he was dubbed a "poet for the masses," Guest refused the title of poet. His son, Edgar "Bud" Guest II, wrote in a 1966 *Free Press* article that because his father didn't accept that title, critics' opinions never made him lose any sleep. Guest called himself a "newspaperman."

While running errands, polishing glasses, and tending the soda fountain for Robbins' Drug Store at the age of 14, Guest caught the attention of one of the regulars, a *Detroit Free Press* accountant named Charles Hoyt, who got him a summer job at the paper as a bookkeeper's office boy in 1895. From that day until his death in 1959, Guest was on the *Free Press* payroll. Guest's father, who had brought the Guest family to Detroit in 1891 from Birmingham, England after his business collapsed the year before, died when Guest was 16. Because of this, he thought it'd be best to quit school and get a job as a "cub reporter." Among his first jobs in the editorial department was clipping bits of poetry and prose for a column. Along with the clips, Guest would throw in bits and pieces of his own rhymes. It wasn't long before he had his own "Blue Monday Column."

Eventually Guest was put on the police beat, during which he entertained policemen and colleagues with his verses. One of his companions on the beat was a former night engineer at Edison who had decided to build

horseless carriages—Henry Ford. Guest would meet Ford for a late-night chat at a lunch wagon in front of City Hall. Eventually, he was taken off the police beat altogether to concentrate on his verses, which the paper began to demand daily. However, not everybody thought Guest should be a "versifier." A copy editor once told him: "It rhymes here and there, Eddie, my boy, but if you cut out that poetry, you'll probably make a fair reporter."

Guest found universal subjects for his verses in everyday life and conversations. He said in a 1956 *Detroit Times* article, "If an idea appeals to me, I figure it might appeal to someone else. I've just tried to express people's hopes and pleasures. They are pretty much the same for all of us." His most famous poem, **"Home,"** came from an exchange with a construction worker who was building a house next door to his. The man said, according to Bud, "We're building a home for Dr. J. W. Smith." Eddie told the man he couldn't possibly build a home; the worker could build a house, but only a family could build a home.

Guest once wrote a poem based on a conversation he had overheard between two young men on a Detroit streetcar. One of them was said he didn't think he was going to go home for Christmas. Guest didn't say anything directly to the man, but it bothered him because he thought the man was making a mistake. Instead, he wrote a verse which appeared in the *Free Press*. The next day, he received letters from 30 young men saying they hadn't planned on going home for Christmas, but because of Guest's verse they had changed their minds.

Though Guest was established at the *Free Press*, no publishers were willing to take a risk on putting his work in book form. In 1909, his brother, Henry, set Guest's first collection of poems in type. Henry could print eight pages at a time, but only if there weren't too many "E's." If there were too many of the English language's most common vowel, those poems would be held until the next eight-page batch. Seven years later, only 3,500 copies of Guest's most famous book, **A Heap O' Livin',** were published. Eventually 500,000 copies were run.

Guest wrote everyday, says his grandson. He says his grandfather had a set time when he would work for about three hours and he stuck to it. Even when the family went to their cottage near Port Austin, the younger Guest remembers his grandmother telling him and the other children to be quiet because his grandfather was going to write. "We would just sit there and hear the tippity-tap of the typewriter," he says.

By 1945, Guest had published 14 verse collections and had attracted millions of readers from the 200 newspapers which picked up his syndicated verses. Upon his death, those readers from as close as Fenton, Mich., to as far away as Long Beach, Calif., and Boston, Mass., sent letters to the *Free Press* bereaving his death and writing of the joy and comfort he brought them. People also got to know Guest over the airwaves on an eight-year national radio show he hosted from Chicago, although people said he sounded more like a preacher than a radio personality. He also appeared in a weekly television program, but did not protest cancellation of the show because he thought commuting to New York City was too difficult. Hollywood also wanted him; Universal Studios offered Guest $3,500 a week to become "Will Rogers' successor." Guest stayed one week, didn't like the scripts and went home. Though he broke his contract, Universal Studios did not pursue it.

Guest, a fairly short man with heavy eyebrows and dark hair in his younger years, was known for his kind-heartedness. A *Detroit News* article once stated he "never wrote an unkind word about anyone, never was unkind to anyone—and, insofar as such things may be known, never harbored an unkind thought about anyone." Guest said in a *Detroit Times* article that he had no reason to distrust people. He said, "I think people are essentially decent. Even a man in jail didn't start out deliberately on that path." Guest did as he said, also; though he played golf with Cardinal Edward Mooney, he also corresponded with prison inmates.

Possessor of a soft spot for children, Guest was deeply involved with the Boys' Club of Detroit. Once a president of the group, he asked friends to send contributions to the Boys' Club as their Christmas gift to him. Likewise, at his death, memorial contributions were to be sent to the club. Because of his devotion to the club, one of the organization's facilities was named after him. Another building, a high school in Roseville, also bears the Guest name. Bestowed in the 1950s, it was one of the few times a school was named for a person while he was still alive.

Though Guest never got more than a sixth-grade education, says his grandson, he was well-read. The younger Edgar's early memories of his grandfather are times when his grandfather read children's books, including Dr. Seuss, to his grandchildren. Later, though, the grandson says he remembers discussing William Shakespeare's *Julius Caesar* with his grandfather. He says he was telling his grandfather how wonderful the play was when Guest began to quote from the play.

"I remember being very impressed that he memorized Shakespeare," says the younger Guest. "He said, 'I like it, I read it, I memorized it.'"

Guest was given many honors, including one of his favorites, the Elks' Outstanding Newspaperman of 1906. A state-wide Edgar A. Guest Day was proclaimed by Michigan Gov. Frank D. Fitzgerald in the mid 1930s. In honoring Guest, the governor said, "It is appropriate that Michigan join in this honor to one who had done so much to spread the spirit of cheer and kindness among millions of people." DAC members, along with members from other clubs to which Guest belonged, were among the 3,000 invited guests at the Hotel Statler on February 14, 1936. Mayor Albert Cobo of Detroit also declared a Detroit Edgar A. Guest Day in 1951, complete with honorary speeches and the music of the Belle Isle Concert Band. Even after his death in 1975, Michigan Gov. William Milliken pronounced August 20 (Guest's birthday) Edgar Albert Guest Day.

In the early 1950s, Guest's health started to slip. He had major surgeries in 1953 and 1954. The next year a heart attack incapacitated him for months. Toward the end of his life, Guest had a large-type typewriter and floodlights installed in his bedroom because of his failing vision. But throughout his career, even in times of poor health, his verses appeared every day in the paper. He would write several verses while he was feeling up to it, in case he didn't have the strength later. He kept his writing up so well that on the day of his death, his column appeared.

Guest died in his sleep August 5, 1959, 15 days short of his 78th birthday, of a cerebral hemorrhage. The next day the *Detroit Free Press* announced his death with a yellow banner across the top of the front page reading, "The Eddie Guest Story." Much of the front section was devoted to honoring him. Detroit Mayor Louis Miriani called for flags to be at half-mast; State Rep. Edward H. Jeffries proposed Guest be named "Detroit's poet laureate." In the days following, the Legislature also passed a resolution calling him "America's most popular and beloved verse writer." It stated he had won "an enduring place in the hearts of his countrymen as their unofficial poet laureate."

FURTHER READING

Criticism

De Casseres, Benjamin. "The Complete American." In *The American Mercury* X, No. 38 (February 1927): 146.
    Included in a series of iconoclastic parodies of renowned Americans, a short sketch of Guest humorously challenges the values and themes he wrote about.

Brander Matthews

1852-1929

(Full name James Brander Matthews; also wrote under the pseudonyms Arthur Penn and Hallitt Robinson) American critic, essayist, short story writer, and novelist

INTRODUCTION

Matthews is best known as one of the most popular and influential American literary critics of the late nineteenth and early twentieth centuries. Despite a continuing bestowal of honors by established colleagues on both sides of the Atlantic, however, his formidable reputation as a man of letters and widespread influence in determining a writer's place in the literary canon began to decline during the first decades of the twentieth century. Although in the past he had championed contemporary authors, he became reluctant to grant the new writers canonical credentials and was alarmed by their modernism; they, in turn, along with their influential advocates, dismissed him as an academic and reactionary remnant of a genteel, moribund Victorianism.

Biographical Information

When Matthews was seven, his family moved from New Orleans, his birthplace, to New York City, where he lived for the rest of his life. His early years were shaped by his family's immense wealth: Matthews was raised to pursue the career of a millionaire, to be a gentleman able to supervise the family fortune. The year he graduated from Columbia Law School, 1873, his father lost most of his fortune in a stock market panic. (The young man, however, still received an inheritance from his mother.) Matthews later asserted that this reversal provided him the opportunity to pursue his real ambition, to be a writer. He published prolifically in English and American magazines, and his plays were successfully staged in both countries. He wrote criticism, fiction, pamphlets on such topics as simplifying English spelling and securing transatlantic copyrights for American and European authors, and an autobiography. He edited anthologies, joined established literary clubs and participated in starting new ones. He took the side of realism in the "war" between the realists and the romanticists. He gave heartfelt support to the foreign and domestic policies of Theodore Roosevelt, with whom he shared a long friendship, and revised Roosevelt's writings before their publication. He counted numerous celebrated literary figures of Europe and the United States among his friends. Foremost was the American Realist novelist William Dean Howells. For Matthews, Howells and Roosevelt were a pair of ideologically conflicting mentors between whom he moved gracefully, maintaining loyalty to both. For

years he wrote a weekly column in *The New York Times Book Review*. At Columbia University, he established the study of American Literature as a national literature. In 1900, he was made professor of drama at Columbia. He was awarded the French Legion of Honor in 1907, served as president of the Modern Language Association in 1910, was a founder of the National Institute of Arts and Letters, and served as its president from 1912 to 1914. He was chancellor of the American Academy of Letters from 1920 to 1924. Matthews died in 1929.

Major Works

Matthews's most significant works were those in which he discussed genre, structure, plot, and character. Starting with *The Theaters of Paris* in 1880, followed the next year by *French Dramatists of the Nineteenth Century*, he established himself as an acknowledged critical intelligence and a renowned scholar of the theater. His 1896 *Introduction to the Study of American Literature* sold over a quarter of a million copies. Over the years, up until his death, he published many volumes dealing with diverse aspects of literature and drama, work respected even by those who otherwise objected to his opinions and assertions. His books on Molière and Shakespeare represent his practice of examining drama as a theatrical rather than a literary medium. He also published five collections of essays and several volumes of short stories, including *Vignettes of Manhattan* and *Outlines in Local Color*. In these he tried to render representative images of New York City streets, haunts, characters, and situations. His three novels, *His Father's Son, A Confident Tomorrow,* and *The Action and the Word* all are set in the Manhattan he knew well: Wall Street and its environs. Studies in realism tempered with faith in the ability of people to redeem themselves, they confronted the social, psychological, and economic issues and attitudes of the day.

Critical Reception

Matthews's novels and short stories were never a popular success, and he abandoned fiction writing at the turn of the twentieth century after completing his third novel. Nevertheless, such divergent commentators as Roosevelt and Howells often praised his fiction and encouraged him to continue writing. Matthews's critical work met with greater success than his fiction and made him both an academic authority and a popular oracle on literary matters. Both his appointments at Columbia were less the result of academic credentials than they were recognition of his achievements as a playwright, practicing critic, and theorist. Mark Twain, who had recommended that Matthews's high appraisal of James Fenimore Cooper's books be taken with "a few tons of salt," expressed his age's admiration for the professor when he wrote, "Brander knows literature and loves it; . . . he has a right to be a critic."

PRINCIPAL WORKS

The Theaters of Paris (criticism) 1880
French Dramatists of ,the Nineteenth Century (criticism) 1881
Cheap Books and Good Books (nonfiction) 1888
Pen and Ink: Papers on Subjects of More or Less Importance (essays) 1888
American Authors and British Pirates (nonfiction) 1889
Americanisms and Briticisms, with Other Essays on Other Isms (essays) 1892
The Story of a Story, and Other Stories (short stories) 1893
Studies of the Stage (criticism) 1894
Vignettes of Manhattan (short stories) 1894
His Father's Son (novel) 1895
Aspects of Fiction, and Other Ventures in Criticism (criticism) 1896
An Introduction to the Study of American Literature (criticism) 1896
Outlines in Local Color (short stories) 1898
The Action and the Word (novel) 1900
A Confident Tomorrow (novel) 1900
The Historical Novel, and Other Essays (essays) 1901
The Philosophy of the Short Story (criticism) 1901
The Development of the Drama (criticism) 1903
Inquiries and Opinions (essays) 1907
Moliere, His Life and His Works (criticism) 1910
A Study of the Drama (criticism) 1910
Shakespeare As a Playwright (criticism) 1913
On Acting (criticism) 1914
These Many Years: Recollections of a New Yorker (autobiography) 1917
The Principles of Playmaking and Other Discussions of the Drama (criticism) 1919
The Tocsin of Revolt, and Other Essays (essays) 1922
The Clown in History, Romance and Drama (essays) 1924
Suggestions for Teachers of American Literature (essays) 1925
Rip Van Winkle Goes to the Play, and Other Essays on Plays and Players (criticism) 1926

CRITICISM

Augustine Birrell (essay date, 1894)

SOURCE: "Americanisms and Briticisms," in *The Collected Essays & Addresses of the Rt. Hon. Augustine Birrell 1880-1920*, Vol. Three, Charles Scribner's Sons, 1923, pp. 168-73.

[*In the following review of* Americanisms and Briticisms, *Birrell lambastes what he sees as Matthews's project to erect a barrier of nationalism between national literatures.*]

Messrs. Harper Bros., of New York, have lately printed and published, and Mr. Brander Matthews has written, the prettiest possible little book, called *Americanisms and Briticisms, with other Essays on other Isms.* To slip it into your pocket when first you see it is an almost irresistible impulse, and yet—would you believe it?—this pretty little book is in reality a bomb, intended to go off and damage British authors by preventing them from being so much as quoted in the States. Mr. Brander Matthews, however, is so obviously a good-natured man, and his little fit of the spleen is so evidently of a passing character, that it is really not otherwise than agreeable to handle his bombshell gently and to inquire how it could possibly come about that the children of one family should ever be invited to fall out and strive and fight over their little books and papers.

It is easy to accede something to Mr. Matthews. Englishmen are often provoking, and not infrequently insolent. The airs they give themselves are ridiculous, but nobody really minds them in these moods; and, *per contra,* Americans are not easily laughed out of a good conceit of themselves, and have been known to be as disagreeable as they could.

To try to make "an international affair" over the "u" in honour and the second "l" in traveller is surely a task beneath the dignity of anyone who does not live by penning paragraphs for the evening papers, yet this is very much what Mr. Matthews attempts to do in this pleasingly-bound little volume. It is rank McKinleyism from one end to the other. "Every nation," says he, "ought to be able to supply its own second-rate books, and to borrow from abroad only the best the foreigner has to offer it." What invidious distinctions! Who is to prepare the classification? I don't understand this Tariff at all. If anything of the kind were true, which it is not, I should have said it was just the other way, and that a nation, if it really were one, would best foster its traditions and maintain its vitality by consuming its own first-rate books—its Shakespeares and Bacons, its Taylors and Miltons, its Drydens and Gibbons, its Wordsworths and Tennysons—whilst it might very well be glad to vary the scene a little by borrowing from abroad less vitalising but none the less agreeable wares.

But the whole notion is preposterous. In Fish and Potatoes a ring is possible, but hardly in Ideas. What is the good of being educated and laboriously acquiring foreign tongues and lingoes—getting to know, for instance, what a "freight" train is and what a bobolink—if I am to be prevented by a diseased patriotism from reading whatever I choose in any language I can? Mr. Matthews' wrath, or his seeming wrath—for it is impossible to suppose that he is really angry—grows redder as he proceeds. "It cannot," he exclaims, "be said too often or too emphatically that the British are foreigners, and their ideals in life, in literature, in politics, in taste, in art" (why not add "in victuals and drink"?) "are not our ideals."

What rant this is! Mr. Matthews, however frequently and loudly he repeats himself, cannot unchain the canons of taste and compel them to be domiciled exclusively in America; nor can he hope to persuade the more intelligent of his countrymen to sail to the devil in an ark of their own sole construction. Artists all the world over are subject to the same laws. Nations, however big, are not the arbiters of good taste, though they may be excellent exemplars of bad. As for Mr. Matthews' determination to call Britons foreigners, that is his matter, but feelings of this kind, to do any harm, must be both reciprocal and general. The majority of reasonable Englishmen and Americans will, except when angry, feel it as hard to call one another foreigners, as John Bright once declared he would find it hard to shout "bastard" after the issue of a marriage between a man and his deceased wife's sister.

There is a portrait of Mr. Matthews at the beginning of this book or bomb of his, and he does not look in the least like a foreigner. I am sorry to disappoint him, but truth will out. The fact is that Mr. Matthews has no mind for reciprocity; he advises Cousin Sam to have nothing to do with John Bull's second-rate performances, but he feels a very pardonable pride in the fact that John Bull more and more reads his cousin's short stories and other things of the kind.

He gives a countrywoman of his, Miss Agnes Repplier, quite a scolding for quoting in a little book of hers no less than fifteen British authors of very varying degrees of merit. Why, in the name of common-sense, should she not if they serve her turn? Was a more ludicrous passage than the following ever penned? It follows immediately after the enumeration of the fifteen authors just referred to:

> But there is nothing from Lowell, than whom a more quotable writer never lived. In like manner, we find Miss Repplier discussing the novels and characters of Miss Austen and of Scott, of Dickens, of Thackeray, and of George Eliot, but never once referring to the novels or characters of Hawthorne. Just how it was possible for any clever American woman to write nine essays in criticism, rich in references and quotations, without once happening on Lowell or on Hawthorne, is to me inexplicable.

O Patriotism! what follies are committed in thy name!

The fact is, it is a weak point in certain American writers of "the patriotic school" to be for ever dragging in and puffing the native article, just because it is native and for no other reason whatever; as if it mattered an atom whether an author whom, whilst you are discussing literature, you find it convenient to quote was born in Boston, Lincoln, or Boston, Massachusetts. One wearies of it indescribably. It is always Professor This or Colonel That. If you want to quote, quote and let your reader judge your samples; but do not worry him into rudeness by clawing and scraping.

Here we all are, Heaven knows how many million of us, speaking, writing and spelling the English language more or less ungrammatically in a world as full as it can hold of sorrows and cares, and fustian and folly. Literature is a solace and a charm. I will not stop for a moment in my headlong course to compare it with tobacco; though if it ever came to the vote, mine would be cast for letters. Men and women have been born in America, as in Great Britain and Ireland, who have written books, poems, and songs which have lightened sorrow, eased pain, made childhood fascinating, middle-age endurable, and old age comfortable. They will go on being born and doing this in both places. What reader cares a snap of his finger where the man was cradled who makes him for awhile forget himself? Nationality indeed! It is not a question of Puffendorf or Grotius or Wheaton, even in the American edition with Mr. Dana's notes, but of enjoyment, of happiness, out of which we do not intend to be fleeced. Let us throw all our books into hotch-pot. Who cares about spelling? Milton spelt "dog" with two g's. The American Milton, when he comes, may spell it with three, while all the world wonders, if he is so minded.

But we are already in hotch-pot. Cooper and Irving, Longfellow, Bryant and Poe, Hawthorne, Lowell, and Whitman, and living writers by the score from the other side of the sea, are indistinguishably mixed with our own books and authors. The boundaries are hopelessly confused, and it is far too late for Mr. Brander Matthews to come upon the scene with chalk and tape, and try to mark us off into rival camps.

There is some girding and gibing, of course. Authors and critics cannot help nagging at one another. Some affect the grand air, "assume the god," and attempt to distinguish, as Mr. Matthews himself does in this little book of his, "between the authors who are not to be taken seriously, between the man of letters who is somebody and the scribbler who is merely, in the French phrase, *quelconque*, nobody in particular." Others, again, though leading quiet, decent lives, pass themselves off in literature as swaggering Bohemians, cut-and-thrust men. When these meet there must be blows—pen-and-ink blows, as bloodless as a French duel. All the time the stream of events flows gigantically along. But to the end of all things Man will require to be interested, to be taken out of himself, to be amused; and that interest, that zest, that amusement, he will find where he can—at home or abroad, with alien friends or alien enemies: what cares he?

W. P. Trent (essay date 1895)

SOURCE: "Mr. Brander Matthews as a Critic," in *The Sewanee Review,* 1895, pp. 373-84.

[*In the following appreciation, Trent argues that Matthews's other impressive achievements ought not be permitted to eclipse his reputation as a major critic.*]

While there are few living American writers better known or more heartily admired than Mr. Brander Matthews, it has long seemed to me that the public does not sufficiently appreciate a special phase of his versatility. What that phase is, will be learned from the title I have given this paper. Mr. Matthews is a playwright, a story-teller, a composer of *vers de société*, a genial humorist, a bibliophile, a professor in Columbia College, and all, or most of these facts are known to the public. The variety, the wit, the charm of his writings are familiar to the people that read the magazines as well as to the people that read books; the wit and charm and sincerity of the man are familiar to his friends; but I doubt if his friends or the reading public, although they may be acquainted with his essays, whether in their detached or collected form, are fully cognizant of the fact that their favorite writer is entitled to high rank among our living critics. Now we have too few genuine critics, living or dead, to be able to afford the extravagance of sinking one of them in a novelist, a playwright, a humorist, or even in a professor, and I purpose, if possible, in this brief appreciation, to try to keep Mr. Matthews posing as a critic long enough for a satisfactory sketch to be made of him in that attitude. But this is not putting the matter fairly, perhaps, for Mr. Matthews has already collected his critical work into four easily obtainable volumes, and so has done all that can justly be expected of him. If, therefore, my sketch of him in the rôle of critic be unsatisfactory, the blame must be laid on my own defective eye and unsteady hand.

The four volumes that sum up Mr. Matthews' work as a critic are entitled, respectively, *French Dramatists of the Nineteenth Century* (1881 and 1891), *Pen and Ink* (1888), *Americanisms and Briticisms* (1892), and *Studies of the Stage (1894).* A small book on American Literature, made up from articles contributed to *St. Nicholas,* is announced for publication next fall, but neither this nor his scattered essays will be considered here. The four volumes named represent our critic fully and well, for each stands for a distinct phase of his critical endowment and of his accomplished work. In his *French Dramatists* he appears as a scholarly specialist, the product of whose serious and sustained labors is a treatise of permanent value as well as of present interest. In *Pen and Ink* the subtle critic appears combined with the kindly humorist, and the result is a book that charms while it enlightens. In *Americanisms and Briticisms* the critic and humorist displays in fuller measure that sturdy, but never overbearing love of country that has made him one of the most distinctively national of all our writers, and the result is a volume that incites to patriotism and stimulates to the pursuit of high ideals in life as well as in literature. In *Studies of the Stage* the critic returns to the field of his earliest labors, but lays aside to some extent his rôle of scholarly specialist and allows us to perceive that like a true humorist he

loves Charles Lamb, that like an old theatre-goer and playwright he loves Paris, and that like a good patriot he loves America and New York.

I wish I were a competent critic of the drama from the point of view of dramatic construction, and that I were more familiar with the dramatic achievements of France, in particular, in order that I might feel qualified to speak with some authority about Mr. Matthews' most elaborate work of criticism. I do not possess the proper qualifications, however, and I cannot speak with authority. Yet it is possible for a worker in one field of literature or art to pass more or less valuable general judgments upon the work of another in a different field. It is possible, I think, for one specialist to recognize the thoroughness and soundness of the methods of research followed by another specialist; and it may happen that his recognition may be more stimulating and valuable, because less biased and prejudiced, than that vouchsafed by rivals in the same field. It is only on some such grounds as these that I can at all justify my attempt to appraise the merits of the *French Dramatists of the Nineteenth Century.*

I am not sure but that what most pleases me in the book is the evidence it gives of the courage possessed by its author. It requires considerable courage for a young writer (*The French Dramatists* appeared in 1881) to devote an enormous amount of conscientious labor to a phase of contemporary literature, and to a little-understood phase of a foreign literature at that. With a student preparing his thesis for a doctor's degree, the case is, of course, different, and after all such a student usually chooses as the subject of his lucubrations a classical theme fully weighted down with real or sham dignity. Criticism of contemporary work in the nature of the case lacks finality, and while many men are willing to devote a hasty sketch to it, we find few willing to devote a careful treatise. Yet with all due regard to the past, we are assuredly still more vitally concerned with the present, and I am by no means certain that the preponderating study devoted by us to the work of our ancestors over that of our contemporaries is not due to our better understanding of the principles of historical research than of those of philosophical criticism. Be that as it may, I heartily admire the courage evidenced by this serious attempt to trace the development of a contemporary phase of foreign literature.

That it is a serious and successful attempt is apparent to any careful reader. The easy style, the general absence of foot-notes, the brevity of the book might, indeed, tempt the casual reader to believe that it is a mere sketch and not what I have already termed. it, a serious and worthy treatise. But a labored style, a superfluity of foot-notes, and portentous length are by no means essential to a serious and worthy treatise. Full knowledge of the subject in hand, general knowledge of literature and life, sympathy, enthusiasm, and a love of truth that shrinks at no self-sacrifice are essential to such a treatise, and I find them all in Mr. Matthews' book.[1] Of the hundreds of plays produced by Frenchmen during this century, he has read a large proportion, and has seen many of them acted. He has studied the development of the drama in every country and period, and has looked at each play of importance as something to be acted, not as something to be read. His point of view is therefore that of the scientific specialist, and he has produced a book that is a model of its kind. But he is something more than a dramatic critic who knows his business. He is a man who, having read and travelled widely, has thereby enlarged his knowledge of life and his human sympathies. He possesses, too, an abundant humor, that makes his judgment as kindly as it is keen. This is but to say that Mr. Matthews' critical work is informed and thorough as befits a scholar, and sane, sympathetic, and sincere as befits a man.

To prove the truth of these assertions to the satisfaction of even the most exacting reader would be difficult anywhere, and is clearly impossible in a piece of impressionist criticism. I may, however, be able to give a few grounds for the judgments I have just ventured to pass. The second chapter of the book under discussion is devoted to M. Victor Hugo, who is, perhaps, the writer of all moderns that most severely tries the sanity of a critic. He has tried Mr. Swinburne's sanity to such an extent that the result long ago ceased to be doubtful. That Mr. Matthews, however, has stood the ordeal unscathed must be apparent to anyone who will study his treatment of "Hernani." There is in it nothing hysterical, nothing subservient or extravagant. Its dominant note is sanity, but not the pseudo-sanity of the eighteenth century, which was often but another name for inappreciation. Our latter-day critic possesses too sound a judgment not to perceive clearly that "Victor Hugo is not a great dramatic poet of the race and lineage of Shakespeare," but he has too keen an appreciation of what is true and beautiful in art not to perceive with equal clearness that "Victor Hugo is a great poet, although not a great dramatic poet." These two balanced judgments are fused by a genuine enthusiasm into certain fine concluding paragraphs, too long to be given here, but to which the reader may be referred with confidence.

Almost as good as the chapter on Hugo are those devoted to Dumas *Père* and Eugéne Scribe: fully as good is that on Emile Augier, with whose masculine genius Mr. Matthews is in entire sympathy. But even in dealing with the author of that excellent comedy, *Le Gendre de M. Poirier,*[2] Mr. Matthews' admiration is kept within just bounds, a feat which it is needless to say grows easier when he has to deal with M. Alexandre Dumas *fils* and M. Victorien Sardou. The cleverness of the latter dramatist, as illustrated, for example, in the well-known use of the scrap of paper in the *Pattes de Mouche,* receives some neat left-handed compliments that serve well to prepare the reader for the rapier thrusts at M. Octave Feuillet in the chapter that follows. It is a broadsword, however, with which Mr. Matthews thrusts at M. Feuillet, when in his resumé of the dramatic work of the decade, 1881-1891, he says of the latter's *Parisian Romance:*

The sudden death of a dissipated atheist at the supper table just when he is proposing a toast to Matter strikes me as tricky, cheap, childish; as Dr. Klesmer, in "Daniel Deronda," said of an aria of Bellini's, it indicates "a puerile state of culture—no sense of the universal."

Here is a home thrust, indeed, yet with a broadsword, as I have said, not with a rapier; but, if another metaphor may be allowed, we have here a piece of criticism that clears the air with the efficacy of a stroke of lightning. Fortunately, however, our genial critic is not compelled to make much use of his heavier weapon. MM. Labiche, Meilhac, and Halvéy are more to his liking than M. Feuillet, and although he has to say some sharp words about M. Emile Zola, he is too fully alive to the latter's great epic and lyric powers to be wanting in a courtly, if somewhat distant admiration. In short, the main note of this volume as of all good criticism, is hearty admiration for what is true and worthy.

In *Pen and Ink* Mr. Matthews has given us what is to me not only his most charming book, but one of the most delightful books of our generation. I forget that it is made up mostly of previously published essays and think of it as a book *per se*—a book that can be read through at a sitting, and then taken up again and again. There is not a dull page in it, which is equivalent to saying there are many wise ones. Certainly there is a deal of common sense, a most rare and acceptable form of wisdom in the essay on **"The Ethics of Plagiarism"** which I should be tempted to recommend to the plagiarist-hunter were I not sure that his small brain would never let him know what hit him, if indeed it let him know that he had been hit at all. There is also a deal of common sense hid snugly away in the banter of **"The True Theory of the Preface"**—a bit of clever humor which I shall not spoil by attempting its condensation here. The essay that follows on **"The Philosophy of the Short Story"** is more serious in tone and is, perhaps, Mr. Matthews' most important contribution to formal criticism. It belongs to the very limited class of authoritative essays—essays whose value is the same in kind, if not in degree, with that of a definitive treatise. In other words it may be fairly termed an achievement in criticism just as the two sketches that follow it may be called a feat of criticism. These sketches are brief appreciations of Mr. Frederick Locker (now Mr. Locker-Lampson) and Mr. Austin Dobson who are appropriately designated as **"Two Latter-Day Lyrists."** Good contemporary criticism always partakes more or less of the nature of a feat, and this is especially true when the critic has to pass judgment upon a personal friend. The least straining of the praise bestowed will offend the reader who knows or suspects the relationship, as well as the friend himself, if his nature be at all sensitive. If the critic be transparently sincere, he can, perhaps, avoid the Charybdis of flattery, not to speak of the rapids into which our modern log-rollers have pushed their logs, yet his very sincerity is not unlikely to cast him upon the Scylla of depreciation. But depreciation, however slight, is an infallible solvent of friendship, and friendship, the Greeks have taught us, is the best part of life; the man, then, that criticizes his friend takes his life in his own hands. From the ease and spontaneity, however, apparent in Mr. Matthews' tributes to his two English friends, I should infer that he was hardly aware of the danger he was incurring. This means that he was not self-conscious, and perhaps we find just here the reason why his two sketches are models of their kind—as delightful to the general public as they must have been to Mr. Locker and Mr. Dobson.

Of the three remaining essays, I confess that I could easily spare one, although I should not mind seeing it transferred to *Americanisms and Briticisms,* if its author is desirous of preserving it on account of the original data it contains. This is the paper entitled **"The Songs of the Civil War,"** which, while in excellent taste, appears to me to be but a slight performance and out of place in a volume of such distinction and charm as *Pen and Ink.* But I should not willingly part with the disquisition **"On the French spoken by those who do not speak French;"** and I should pull a revolver as well as a royal flush on any individual so lost to all sense of propriety as to suggest that a self-respecting American citizen could do without **"Poker-talk"** after having once read it. Mr. Matthews is an authority on the short story and the French drama, but he is more than an authority on poker; he is the tried and true knight-champion of that high-born and winsome, but often calumniated damsel. I cannot conceive of any more delightful treat for a native American with a sense of humor and a knowledge of our national game—and what true American is without these?—than a first perusal of this essay, unless, indeed, it be a game of poker with the author of **"Poker-talk."**

The buoyant patriotism of this unique closing essay of *Pen and Ink* makes the transition from that volume to *Americanisms and Briticisms* natural and easy. At least this is true for an American reader, although I should hardly say that it is true for the average British reader if Mr. Augustine Birrell's review[3] of the book is to be taken as typical of the way a Briton often fails to understand the spirit of an American writer, especially if the latter chance to be of a humorous turn. "It is rank McKinleyism from one end to the other," is Mr. Birrell's judgment upon what he calls "a pleasingly-bound little volume." Mr. Birrell is nothing if not epigrammatic, but he seems to forget the dangers that beset this style of writing. The sentence I have just quoted illustrates these dangers strikingly, for it shows that Mr. Birrell is as far from understanding the true nature of the McKinleyism, of which he writes so glibly, as he is from appreciating the real spirit in which Mr. Matthews wrote his book. For he immediately proceeds to quote a sentence from the American essayist to the effect that "every nation ought to be able to supply its own second-rate books, and to borrow from abroad only the best the foreigner has to offer it." As if a true McKinleyite would not dread the pernicious influences of "the best the foreigner has to offer," far more than the influences of that foreigner's second best—always supposing, of course, that a true McKinleyite could stop to think of distinctions between best and second best

(except, perhaps, in the matter of giving sops to the rich) in the presence of the horrible spectre evoked by the mere mention of the Unspeakable Foreigner! McKinley and Matthews! This is indeed a brilliantly logical combination, almost fit for a presidential ticket!

No, in spite of Mr. Birrell, Mr. Matthews is not a McKinleyite, nor is he an anarchist, as the unwary British reader might infer from his countryman's reference to the bomb contained in the American book. Neither is any "wrath" to be discovered in our amiable critic or in his pages. I grant that there was some force in Mr. Birrell's point as to the invidiousness implicit in the distinction between best and second-rate, but it would seem that he pushed his point too far. I grant, too, that Dr. Fitzedward Hall, writing in the *Academy,* made good certain philological points against the volume we are considering, such points having, when made against a piece of pure literature, as complete a lack of tangibility as their geometrical congeners. But I am sure that neither Mr. Birrell nor Dr. Hall has ever thoroughly comprehended the purpose of the book they criticized.

Mr. Matthews did not set out to defend the American use of "elevator" for "lift," or to laugh at the English lady who wrote her brother in America to hold himself in readiness to cross the Atlantic, as he might "have to come over on a *wire,*" or to gird at the Saturday Reviewer's cock-sure and invincible ignorance, or even to take up arms for American spelling. He was hunting down other game, although his keen wit did occasionally lead him off on a side scent. And the game he was hunting down was a legitimate object of sport, and at the same time a noxious beast most fit to kill—a beast which we dignify too much when we call it the colonial *spirit.*

That Americans have in the past shown too great subservience to British literary judgment and taste, and that many of our countrymen continue in this state of bondage is a fact too patent to be denied. That such subservience should be exterminated, whether by ridicule or by serious argument, is a fact equally patent. Exactly how the ridicule and the argument are to be applied are questions on which I should not like to have to pronounce a decided opinion. It does, perhaps, seem a little hard on Miss Repplier to have Mr. Matthews proffering friendly advice as to the authors she should do her quoting from; and yet it is impossible to deny one's self the wish that so clever a woman would develop an independent spirit, and by critisising, at least at times, writers of her own country render more positive and valuable services to a literature she is well fitted to adorn. This, I suspect, is mainly what Mr. Matthews wished to say in those pages devoted to Miss Repplier that gave Mr. Birrell such unnecessary concern. Mr. Matthews himself appreciates Charles Lamb just as fully as Miss Repplier does, and has written charmingly about him. He has even written, as we have seen, an entire book on a phase of foreign literature; certainly a most illogical thing for a rank McKinleyite to do. But he has not neglected to praise his own countrymen when they have done worthy work, and he has therein displayed, in my judgment, sound sense, good taste, and wholesome patriotism. I know at least one American scribe who is deeply grateful to him for a piece of kindly criticism which, whether deserved or not, came at a time when encouragement was greatly needed. It is in praise not in blame that Mr. Matthews does his best and main critical work, which is fitting in the author of the sound essay on **"The True Duty of Critics"** that finds itself in this volume. It is hearty praise that is the dominant note of the much-needed appreciation of Cooper republished here, as well as of the discerning tribute to Mark Twain's best story. It is hearty praise, finally, coupled with discriminating patriotism that underlies the dedication of *Americanisms and Briticisms* to that countryman of ours who has written the best biography of an American man of letters and the most notable recent treatise on a great English poet, Professor Thomas R. Lounsbury, of Yale. If this be McKinleyism, I am anxious to abjure my free-trade principles.

Studies of the Stage offers less occasion for comment than the volumes that preceded it. The "Prefatory Note" shows plainly the point of view of the writer, who argues "that dramatic literature must approve itself as drama first, before it need be discussed as literature." If this seem to the casual reader a self-evident proposition, he may be requested to attend a class in English literature in one of our colleges, or else to read through a few textbooks on the subject. When he has finished such a course of training, he will be pretty sure to welcome this small book as a much-needed contribution to the study of what must be regarded by every unbiased critic as the highest achievement of the human mind in art. Of the essays that make up the volume, the most valuable is that on **"The Dramatization of Novels"** which, while not equal to the masterly essay on the **"Short Story,"** is nevertheless clear-cut in its analysis and lucid in its expression. The second paper describing the **"Dramatic Outlook in America"** is optimistic with the optimism of a man who is, above all things, sane. The essay that follows is an accurate and therefore delightful description of **"The Players,"** the club founded in New York by Edwin Booth, and then we have a characteristic paper on **"Charles Lamb and the Theatre."** After Lamb we are introduced to **"Two French Theatrical Critics"**—M. Francisque Sarcey and M. Jules Lemaitre, who are sketched with the light, sure touch that we recognized in the essays on Mr. Locker-Lampson and Mr. Dobson. In conclusion, we have three brief papers on themes that always take our critic at his best, on **"Shakspere, Molière, and Modern English Comedy,"** on **"The Old Comedies,"** and on the timely propriety of making **"A Plea for Farce."** It is hardly necessary to add that with this list of subjects Mr. Matthews could not help putting together a book that should instruct as well as charm.

But this article has already exceeded the limits usually allotted to impressionist criticism, and it is time to cry halt, although there are many things still that I should like to say. I have not commented sufficiently on the graceful ease and effectiveness of Mr. Matthews' style

when it is at its best; nor have I, perhaps, laid enough stress on the fact that his style is not always at its best, owing, doubtless, to the hurry incident to periodical publication. Such comment is not needed, however, by so trained and experienced a writer, and the reader can without difficulty judge in this matter for himself. Yet, I cannot part from Mr. Matthews, the critic, without expressing a hope which I shall not be sorry to have him take as an exhortation. It seems to me that, judging from what he has already given us, we have the right to expect from his pen in the future critical work of even better quality and higher aims. Indeed, I am going to be bold enough to tell him definitely what he ought to do for us. He ought to write that exhaustive biography and study of Molière which is so needed in our literature, which is perhaps the most needed treatise on any foreign author at the present time. For this noble task Mr. Matthews possesses every qualification. No man living knows and loves Molière better than he does. No one has a more exact and technical knowledge of the acted drama. No one can bring to the work more genial humor, more sound tact, more serious purpose. In fine, I must protest that I do not exaggerate when I maintain that Mr. Matthews *owes* us a *Life and Works of Molière*.

NOTES

[1] A comparison of *The French Dramatists* with Dr. Joseph Sarrazin's scholarly monograph *Das Moderne Drama der Franzosen in seinen Hauptvertretern* (a later book) is by no means to the disadvantage of the American work.

[2] I cannot help feeling that perhaps, *Le Gendre de M. Poirier* is not as great a work of art as Mr. Matthews holds it to be, but I am hardly entitled to an opinion on the subject. Antoinette seems to me to be too much of a heroine and too little of a flesh and blood woman. I should be almost tempted to say that Francine of *Maitre Guérin* (a less successful play) is a better character but for the fact that she is plainly indebted for her existence, as Mr. Matthews has observed, to the noble figure of Marguerite Claes in Balzac's great novel, *La Recherche de l'Absolu*.

[3] Included in his *Men, Women, and Books*.

Brander Matthews (essay date 1885)

SOURCE: "The Philosophy of the Short-Story," in *The New Short Story Theories*, Edited by Charles E. May, Ohio University Press, 1885, pp. 73-80.

[*In the following essay, Matthews spells out the difference between the novel and the short story and defines the short story as a specific genre.*]

The difference between a Novel and a Novelet is one of length only: a Novelet is a brief Novel. But the difference between a Novel and a Short-story is a difference of kind. A true Short-story is something other and something more than a mere story which is short. A true Short-story differs from the Novel chiefly in its essential unity of impression. In a far more exact and precise use of the word, a Short-story has unity as a Novel cannot have it.[1] Often, it may be noted by the way, the Short-story fulfils the three false unities of the French classic drama: it shows one action, in one place, on one day. A Short-story deals with a single character, a single event, a single emotion, or the series of emotions called forth by a single situation. Poe's paradox[2] that a poem cannot greatly exceed a hundred lines in length under penalty of ceasing to be one poem and breaking into a string of poems, may serve to suggest the precise difference between the Short-story and the Novel. The Short-story is the single effect, complete and self-contained, while the Novel is of necessity broken into a series of episodes. Thus the Short-story has, what the Novel cannot have, the effect of "totality," as Poe called it, the unity of impression.

Of a truth the Short-story is not only a chapter out of a Novel, or an incident or an episode extracted from a longer tale, but at its best it impresses the reader with the belief that it would be spoiled if it were made larger, or if it were incorporated into a more elaborate work. The difference in spirit and in form between the Lyric and the Epic is scarcely greater than the difference between the Short-story and the Novel; and the "Raven" and "How we brought the good news from Ghent to Aix" are not more unlike the "Lady of the Lake" and *Paradise Lost*, in form and in spirit, than the "Luck of Roaring Camp," and the "Man without a Country," two typical Short-stories, are unlike *Vanity Fair* and the *Heart of Midlothian*, two typical Novels.

Another great difference between the Short-story and the Novel lies in the fact that the Novel, nowadays at least, must be a love-tale, while the Short-story need not deal with love at all. Although there are to be found by diligent search a few Novels which are not love-tales—and of course *Robinson Crusoe* is the example that swims at once into recollection—yet the immense majority of Novels have the tender passion either as the motive power of their machinery or as the pivot on which their plots turn. Although *Vanity Fair* was a Novel without a hero, nearly every other Novel has a hero and a heroine; and the novelist, however unwillingly, must concern himself in their love-affairs. . . .

While the Novel cannot get on easily without love, the Short-story can. Since love seems to be almost the only thing which will give interest to a long story, the writer of Novels has to get love into his tales as best he may, even when the subject rebels and when he himself is too old to take any delight in the mating of John and Joan. But the Short-story, being brief, does not need a love-interest to hold its parts together, and the writer of Short-stories has thus a greater freedom; he may do as he pleases; from him a love-tale is not expected.[3]

But other things are required of a writer of Short-stories which are not required of a writer of Novels. The novelist may take his time; he has abundant room to turn about. The writer of Short-stories must be concise, and compression, a vigorous compression, is essential. For him, more than for any one else, the half is more than the whole. Again, the novelist may be commonplace, he may bend his best energies to the photographic reproduction of the actual; if he show us a cross-section of real life we are content; but the writer of Short-stories must have originality and ingenuity. If to compression, originality, and ingenuity he add also a touch of fantasy, so much the better.

In fact, it may be said that no one has ever succeeded as a writer of Short-stories who had not ingenuity, originality, and compression; and that most of those who have succeeded in this line had also the touch of fantasy. But there are not a few successful novelists lacking, not only in fantasy and compression, but also in ingenuity and originality; they had other qualities, no doubt, but these they had not. If an example must be given, the name of Anthony Trollope will occur to all. Fantasy was a thing he abhorred; compression he knew not; and originality and ingenuity can be conceded to him only by a strong stretch of the ordinary meaning of the words. Other qualities he had in plenty, but not these. And, not having them, he was not a writer of Short-stories. Judging from his essay on Hawthorne, one may even go so far as to say that Trollope did not know a good Short-story when he saw it.

I have written "Short-stories" with a capital S and a hyphen because I wished to emphasize the distinction between the Short-story and the story which is merely short. The Short-story is a high and difficult department of fiction. The story which is short can be written by anybody who can write at all; and it may be good, bad, or indifferent; but at its best it is wholly unlike the Short-story. In "An Editor's Tales" Trollope has given us excellent specimens of the story which is short; and the narratives which make up this book are amusing enough and clever enough, but they are wanting in the individuality and in the completeness of the genuine Short-story. Like the brief tales to be seen in the British monthly magazines and in the Sunday editions of American newspapers into which they are copied, they are, for the most part, either merely amplified anecdotes or else incidents which might have been used in a Novel just as well as not.

Now, it cannot be said too emphatically that the genuine Short-story abhors the idea of the Novel. It neither can be conceived as part of a Novel, nor can it be elaborated and expanded so as to form a Novel. A good Short-story is no more the synopsis of a Novel than it is an episode from a Novel. A slight Novel, or a Novel cut down, is a Novelet: it is not a Short-story. Mr. Howells's *Their Wedding Journey* and Miss Howard's *One Summer* are Novelets,—little Novels, Mr. Anstey's "Vice Versa," Mr. Besant's "Case of Mr. Lucraft," Hugh Conway's "Called Back," Mr. Julian Hawthorne's

"Archibald Malmaison," and Mr. Stevenson's "Strange Case of Dr. Jekyll and Mr. Hyde" are Short-stories in conception although they are without the compression which the Short-story requires. . . .

It is to be noted as a curious coincidence that there is no exact word in English to designate either *vers de société* or the Short-story, and yet in no language are there better *vers de société* or Short-stories than in English. It may be remarked also that there is a certain likeness between *vers de société* and Short-stories: for one thing, both seem easy to write and are hard. And the typical qualifications of each may apply with almost equal force to the other: *vers de société* should reveal compression, ingenuity, and originality, and Short-stories should have brevity and brilliancy. In no class of writing are neatness of construction and polish of execution more needed than in the writing of *vers de société* and of Short-stories. The writer of Short-stories must have the sense of form, which has well been called "the highest and last attribute of a creative writer." The construction must always be logical, adequate, harmonious.

Here is a weak spot in Mr. W. H. Bishop's "One of the Thirty Pieces," the fundamental idea of which—that fatality awaits every successive possessor of every one of the coins paid to Judas for his betrayal of Jesus—has genuine strength, not fully developed in the story. But other of Mr. Bishop's stories—the "Battle of Bunkerloo," for instance—are admirable in all ways, conception and execution having an even excellence. Again, Hugh Conway's, "Daughter of the Stars" is a Short-story which fails from sheer deficiency of style: here is one of the very finest Short-story ideas—the startling and fascinating fantasy that by sheer force of will a man might have been able to draw down from the depths of the sky a lovely astral maid to share his finite human life—ever given to any mortal, but the handling is at best barely sufficient. To do justice to the conception would tax the execution of a poet. We could merely wonder what the tale would have been had it occurred to Hawthorne, to Poe, or to Theophile Gautier. An idea logically developed by one possessing the sense of form and the gift of style is what we look for in the Short-story.

But, although the sense of form and the gift of style are essential to the writing of a good Short-story, they are secondary to the idea, to the conception, to the subject. Those who hold, with a certain American novelist, that it is no matter what you have to say, but only how you say it, need not attempt the Short-story; for the Short-story, far more than the Novel even, demands a subject. The Short-story is nothing if there is no story to tell;—one might almost say that a Short-story is nothing if it has no plot,—except that "plot" may suggest to some readers a complication and elaboration which are not really needful. But a plan—if this word is less liable to misconception than "plot"—a plan a Short-story must have, while it would be easy to cite Novels of eminence which are wholly amorphous—for example, *Tristram Shandy.*

Whatever its length, the Novel, so Mr. Henry James told us not long ago, "is, in its broadest definition, a personal impression of life." The most powerful force in French fiction today is M. Emile Zola, chiefly known in America and England, I fear me greatly, by the dirt which masks and degrades the real beauty and firm strength not seldom concealed in his novels; and M. Emile Zola declares that the novelist of the future will not concern himself with the artistic evolution of a plot: he will take *une histoire quelconque,* any kind of a story, and make it serve his purpose,—which is to give elaborate pictures of life in all its most minute details.

It is needless to say that the acceptance of these stories is a negation of the Short-story. Important as are form and style, the subject of the Short-story is of more importance yet. What you have to tell is of greater interest than how you tell it. . . . As a Short-story need not be a love-story, it is of no consequence at all whether they marry or die; but a Short-story in which nothing happens at all is an absolute impossibility.

Perhaps the difference between a Short-story and a Sketch can best be indicated by saying that, while a Sketch may be still-life, in a Short-story something always happens. A Sketch may be an outline of character, or even a picture of a mood of mind, but in a Short-story there must be something done, there must be an action.[4] Yet the distinction, like that between the Novel and the Romance, is no longer of vital importance. In the preface to the *House of the Seven Gables,* Hawthorne sets forth the difference between the Novel and the Romance, and claims for himself the privileges of the romancer. Mr. Henry James[5] fails to see this difference. The fact is, that the Short-story and the Sketch, the Novel and the Romance, melt and merge one into the other, and no man may mete the boundaries of each, though their extremes lie far apart. With the more complete understanding of the principle of development and evolution in literary art, as in physical nature, we see the futility of a strict and rigid classification into precisely defined genera and species. All that is needful for us to remark now is that the Short-story has limitless possibilities: it may be as realistic as the most prosaic novel, or as fantastic as the most ethereal romance.

The Short-story should not be void or without form, but its form may be whatever the author please. He has an absolute liberty of choice. It may be a personal narrative, like Poe's "Descent into the Maelstrom" or Mr. Hale's "My Double, and how he Undid me"; it may be impersonal, like Mr. Frederick B. Perkins's "Devil-Puzzlers" or Colonel J. W. De Forest's "Brigade Commander"; it may be a conundrum, like Mr. Stockton's insoluble query, the "Lady or the Tiger?" it may be "A Bundle of Letters," like Mr. Henry James's story, or "A Letter and a Paragraph," like Mr. Bunner's; it may be a medley of letters and telegrams and narrative, like Mr. Aldrich's "Margery Daw"; it may be cast in any one of these forms, or in a combination of all of them, or in a wholly new form, if haply such may yet be found by diligent search.

Whatever its form, it should have symmetry of design. If it have also wit or humour, pathos or poetry, and especially a distinct and unmistakable flavour of individuality, so much the better.[6] But the chief requisites are compression, originality, ingenuity, and now and again a touch of fantasy. Sometimes we may detect in a writer of Short-stories a tendency toward the over-elaboration of ingenuity, toward the exhibition of ingenuity for its own sake, as in a Chinese puzzle. But mere cleverness is incompatible with greatness, and to commend a writer as "very clever" is not to give him high praise. From this fault of super-subtlety, women are free for the most part. They are more likely than men to rely on broad human emotion, and their tendency in error is toward the morbid analysis of a high-strung moral situation.

The more carefully we study the history of fiction the more clearly we perceive that the Novel and the Short-story are essentially different—that the difference between them is not one of mere length only, but fundamental. The Short-story seeks one set of effects in its own way, and the Novel seeks a wholly distinct set of effects in a wholly distinct way. We are led also to the conclusion that the Short-story—in spite of the fact that in our language it has no name of its own—is one of the few sharply defined literary forms. It is a *genre,* as M. Brunetière terms it, a species, as a naturalist might call it, as individual as the Lyric itself and as various. It is as distinct an entity as the Epic, as Tragedy, as Comedy. Now the Novel is not a form of the same sharply defined individuality; it is—or at least it may be—anything. It is the child of the Epic and the heir of the Drama; but it is a hybrid. And one of the foremost of living American novelists, who happens also to be one of the most acute and sympathetic of American critics, has told me that he has often distracted by the knowledge of this fact even while he was engaged in writing a novel.

In the history of literature the Short-story was developed long before the Novel, which indeed is but a creature of yesterday, and which was not really established in popular esteem as a worthy rival of the drama until after the widespread success of the Waverley Novels in the early years of the nineteenth century. The Short-story also seems much easier of accomplishment than the Novel, if only because it is briefer. And yet the list of the masters of the Short-story is far less crowded than the list of the masters of the longer form. There are a score or more very great novelists recorded in the history of fiction; but there are scarcely more than half a score Short-story writers of an equal eminence.

From Chaucer and Boccaccio we must spring across the centuries until we come to Hawthorne and Poe almost without finding another name that insists upon enrolment. In these five hundred years there were great novelists not a few, but there was no great writer of Short-stories. A little later than Hawthorne and Poe, and indeed almost contemporaneous with them, are Mérimée and Turgenef, whose title to be recorded there is none to dispute. Now at the end of the nineteenth century we find two more that no competent critic would dare to omit,—Guy de Maupassant and Rudyard Kipling.

NOTES

[1] In a letter to a friend, Stevenson lays down the law with his usual directness: "Make another end to it? Ah, yes, but that's not the way I write; the whole tale is implied; I never use an effect when I can help it, unless it prepares the effects that are to follow; that's what a story consists in. To make another end, that is to make the beginning all wrong. the denouement of a long story is nothing, it is just 'a full close,' which you may approach and accompany as you please—it is a coda, not an essential member in the rhythm; but the body and end of a short-story is bone of the bone and blood of the blood of the beginning." *Vailima Letters,* Vol. I, p. 147.

[2] See his essay on "The Philosophy of Composition," to be found in the sixth volume of the collected edition of his works, prepared by Messrs. Stedman and Woodberry.

[3] In an essay on "The Local Short-story" contributed to the *Independent* for March 11, 1892, Colonel T. W. Higginson points out the disadvantages the novelist labours under when he knows that his work is to be published in instalments; and he declares that this possible serial publication "affords the justification of the short-story. For here, at least, we have the conditions of perfect art; there is no sub-division of interest; the author can strike directly in, without preface, can move with determined step toward a conclusion, and can—O highest privilege!—stop when he is done. For the most perfect examples of the short-story—those of De Maupassant, for instance—the reader feels, if he can pause to think, that they must have been done at a sitting, so complete is the grasp, the single grasp, upon the mind. This completeness secures the end; they need not be sensational, because there is no necessity of keeping up a series of exciting minor incidents; the main incident is enough. Around the very centre of motion, as in a whirlwind, there may be a perfect quiet, a quiet which is formidable in its very response. In De Maupassant's terrific story of Corsican vengeance, *"Une Vendetta,"* in which the sole actor is a lonely old woman who trains a fierce dog so that he ultimately kills her enemy, the author simply tells us, at the end, that this quiet fiend of destruction went peacefully home and went to sleep. *Elle dormit bien, cette nuit-là.* The cyclone has spent itself, and the silence it has left behind it is more formidable than the cyclone."

[4] This difference is considered briefly by Mr. F. B. Perkins in the characteristically clever preface to the volume of his ingenious Short-stories, which takes its title from the first and best—"Devil-Puzzlers" (New York: G. P. Putnam's Sons).

[5] In the narrow but suggestive biography of Hawthorne contributed to Mr. John Morley's "English Men of Letters."

[6] In a chatty and somewhat uncritical paper on the "Rise of the Short-story" contributed by Mr. Bret Harte to the "International Library of Famous Literature" and published also in the *Cornhill Magazine* for July, 1899, we find the assertion that the secret of the American Short-story is "the treatment of characteristic American life, with absolute knowledge of its peculiarities and sympathy with its methods, with no fastidious ignoring of its national expression, or the inchoate poetry that may be found hidden even in its slang; with no moral determination except that which may be the legitimate outcome of the story itself; with no more elimination than may be necessary for the artistic conception, and never from the fear of the fetish of conventionalism." This is cleverly phrased; but it is open to the obvious objection that it is not so much an adequate definition of the Short-story as a form as it is a defence of the special kind of Short-story Mr. Bret Harte himself had chosen to write.

W. P. Trent (essay date 1901)

SOURCE: "Brander Matthews as a Dramatic Critic," in *The International Monthly,* Vol. IV, July-December 1901, pp. 289-293.

[*In the following essay, Trent rejoices that Matthews's dramatic criticism is being collected for publication in book form and extols his merits as a critic.*]

For some years, not a few of Mr. Brander Matthews' many readers and friends have wished that he would devote more and more attention to critical work, and that the public would recognize him as a writer whose attractive versatility set off rather than detracted from his serious qualities. Mr. Matthews' critical essays were, however, scattered through magazines and several books issued by different publishers; they thus failed to produce their due effect, failed perhaps to produce as much effect as the more uniform series of his novels and short stories. Now they are to be gathered by the Scribners into five uniform volumes, of which the two named below have already appeared.[1] These books will sufficiently indicate the range of his powers, the attractive qualities of his style, his humor, his buoyant and aggressive, but not chauvinistic, patriotism, the keenness of his perceptions, and the essential soundness of his judgment.

I say "essential soundness" advisedly, because I believe that in his grasp upon life and upon the most important principles of art Mr. Matthews is not excelled by any of his contemporaries, although I am quite free to confess that I do not entirely sympathize with some of the critical opinions that are evidently dear to him. I find less inevitability than he does in certain forms of modern fiction, and I am still able to laugh over *The Pickwick Papers.* The critical canons of Mark Twain and Mr. Howells,—if they have any such incumbrances—are apparently of more importance to Mr. Matthews than they are to me. But these matters are trifles, and trifling too is the question whether Mr. Matthews gets the better of Mr. Lang, or Mr. Lang of Mr. Matthews in their perennial philological tilts. What is important to American letters is the fact that we have in Mr. Matthews a critic who is wholly fearless, remarkably suggestive, always clean-minded and sound-hearted, possessed of wide sympathies, and democratic in the best sense of the term. It is a pleasure to have the critical work of such a man winnowed and collected in a permanent form, even though it shows us plainly that the author's first book is also his best. For it proves just as plainly that dramatic criticism is Mr. Matthews' *forte,* and that he can, if he will, give us in the future a great and elaborate treatise in his chosen line of study,—a line of study hitherto practically ignored by Anglo-Saxon critics, with the honorable exceptions of the late George Henry Lewes and of Mr. William Archer.

"A critic of the acted drama" is what Mr. Matthews, in one of his essays, terms Mr. William Archer, but the phrase is also accurately descriptive of Mr. Matthews himself. He has abundant literary appreciation, but he never forgets, or allows his readers to forget, that after all "the play's the thing." As he has written plays, his criticism of the drama has the technical merits that characterize good art criticism, and alas! so little literary criticism. No one can put down an essay or a book of his relating to the drama without perceiving why the plays he has been discussing are good or bad. In other words, Mr. Matthews is not an impressionist, describing in culled phrases the fortuitous impressions produced upon him, in a fortuitous mood, by a fortuitous combination of words arranged in acts and scenes.

French Dramatists of the Nineteenth Century appeared in 1881, and was Mr. Matthews' first important book. As I have just said, it seems to be also his best. It is practically the only thing we have in English on a subject of great interest, and its soundness and usefulness have been tested by time. Its preparation involved an enormous amount of labor, yet it does not read like a ponderous treatise. Perhaps this absence of ponderosity accounts for the fact that the book is not more frequently referred to as a scholarly performance of very high merit. Perhaps, however, the title itself is partly responsible for this. The nineteenth century had twenty years to run when Mr. Matthews began his criticisms of the modern French drama, and it appeared that little finality could attach to his judgments of plays and playwrights that were but little older than their critic. When his book was reissued, in 1891, with a supplementary chapter, it seemed to carry distinctly more weight; and since that time, competent writers upon French literature have borne ungrudging witness to its worth. Now that it has almost literally reached its majority, we may fairly claim that it deserves to rank high among the critical studies of decided value produced in America during the last two decades.

Minute criticism of such a well-known book will not be expected now. I must express, however, my appreciation of Mr. Matthews' success in dealing with that very perplexing writer,—all the more perplexing on account of his indubitably great genius,—Victor Hugo. His treatment of *Hernani,* for example, is sane in the best sense. He perceives clearly that Hugo is not "a great dramatic poet of the race and lineage of Shakespeare," but he perceives with equal clearness that, if Goethe be credited to the eighteenth century, Hugo is the greatest poet of the nineteenth. Quite as good as the chapter on Hugo is the one devoted to that virile genius, Émile Augier, whose masterpiece *Le Gendre de M. Poirier* is a most notable play. As for the criticism of Feuillet, especially of his *Parisian Romance,* it seems to me to be as deserved as it is severe, and to make, as all Mr. Matthews' criticism does, for intellectual and moral soundness.

Whether or not many readers will agree with him in his treatment of M. Rostand's *Cyrano,* in the supplementary chapter,—which, it will be remembered, first appeared in the pages of this journal,—is somewhat doubtful. Allowing M. Rostand considerable, though not perhaps sufficient, credit as a poet,—for he has a narrative and idylic faculty as well as a lyrical,—Mr. Matthews credits him with little originality as a playwright, and asserts that his most famous play, while "clean externally," should be characterized as "essentially immoral,—in so far as it erects a false standard and parades a self-sacrifice which, to use Mr. Howells' apt phrase, is 'a secret shape of egotism.'"

Personally, I recognize the truth involved in Mr. Matthews' strictures, yet I think something may be said on the other side. *Cyrano* does lie open to the charge of being romantically sentimental in parts, and of thus being both inartistic and essentially immoral. But it is this only to critics and philosophers. The public cares more for effectiveness than for artistic felicity, and with the instinct of self-preservation, it tracks, if I may so express it, the dominant moral motive of the play—Cyrano's self-abnegation—upwards not downwards. It does not perceive the misery that might have been wrought if the facile Christian had lived as Roxane's husband, but it does perceive that Cyrano was ready to cut out his heart-strings for the woman he loved. All the world loves a lover, nor does the average man inquire too curiously into every cause and effect of a passion without the higher phases of which this life would be brutal and unendurable. Yet, after all, I agree so thoroughly with Mr. Matthews in regretting the *opera bouffe* and other discordant elements to be found in *Cyrano,* that I fear many of M. Rostand's admirers would consider me as complete a heretic as my colleague who occupies the chair of Dramatic Literature. I confess to a malicious wish that in his closing chapter, which is written with such a firm hand, Mr. Matthews could have paid his respects to M. Rostand's attempt to resuscitate the chronicle play in his more or less melodramatic *L'Aiglon.* But if he had, he might have suffered the fate, reserved for a Harvard Professor, of falling a victim to the patriotic fury of the great French actress,—which might have made him a less militant patriot himself. But I did not intend to be drawn so near the perilous ring in which critical encounters come off. I intended only to emphasize the merits of Mr. Matthews' dramatic criticism and to call attention to the reissue of an admirable book, which, experts tell us, is the best single volume on its subject, and, apparently, not in English alone.

NOTES

[1] *French Dramatists of the Nineteenth Century.* By Brander Matthews, D. C. L., Professor of Dramatic Literature in Columbia University. Third edition brought down to the end of the century. New York: Chas. Scribner's Sons, 1901. 12mo., pp. ix, 321. Price, $1.25.

The Historical Novel and other Essays. By Brander Matthews, same publishers. 12mo., pp. iii, 321. Price, $1.25.

William Lyon Phelps (essay date 1908)

SOURCE: "A Cosmopolitan Critic," in *The Forum,* Vol. XXXIX, No. 3, January, 1908, pp. 377-381.

[*In the following review of* Inquiries and Opinions, *Phelps offers some minor reservations about Matthews's literary judgments, but, on the whole, enthusiastically endorses them.*]

Among American teachers of English, Professor Brander Matthews is notable for the breadth of his culture and the openness of his mind. He is a quite different person from the modern Ph.D. product, "made in Germany." The latter is no doubt useful in his way, but his way is not always human, or humanizing. The attitude of Professor Matthews toward literature has always been characterized by two distinguishing features: first his treatment of literature as a whole, without regard to the language in which it happens to have been written; second, his willingness to treat contemporary authors as definitive subjects of study. In discussing the history of the drama—which happens to be his specialty—he has never insulated any particular nation, but has studied every great dramatist in the light of the world's intellectual life of that particular time. Nor has he ever had a vestige of the familiar academic contempt toward the literary output of our own day. These two qualities have made him a true cosmopolitan in scholarship; for the real scholar should be the broadest, not the narrowest, man in the world. And as literature is primarily written not as text-book but as an interpretations of life, it is impossible to write a penetrating criticism of it unless the critic have a keen sympathy with life as he has with books. Owen Wister's cowboy was not a bad critic of Browning.

Professor Matthews' latest volume, ***Inquiries and Opinions*** is well named, for of the twelve essays it contains, nine are on themes too modern to admit of anything like a final word. We do not yet know for certain whether Ibsen is an immortal writer, or merely a person who has had a tremendous effect on nineteenth and twentieth century drama. All we do know is that in the year 1908 he is a vital force that cannot be ignored, and that his effect on the technique of the modern stage is as good as his effect on the moral nature of certain individuals has been bad. A moral anarchist, who believed in only one law—the law of copyright—he showed his age how a play could be made highly interesting without scenic display. Professor Matthews treats him, therefore, not as a philosopher but as a playwright—for we who go to hear Ibsen on the stage have the same reason that the lovers of the Belasco melodrama have—we go not because we are "highbrows" but because we find him interesting, and we would not go if he were dull. Intelligent men and women hate to be bored fully as much as those who are incapable of thought, only both are not always bored by the same things.

The chapter on **"The Literary Merit of Our Latter-Day Drama"** is in a way a defense of Henry Arthur Jones, to whom the volume is affectionately dedicated. This essay is written with shrewd sense, insisting that literary merit should be something integral and inherent, not something foisted on from the outside. The dramas of Jones and Pinero do not have the same kind of literary merit as the dramas of Tennyson; but they would have far less literary merit if (let us say) *Mrs. Dane's Defense* had been written in the style of Tennyson's *Harold*. Professor Matthews is also right in insisting that what Tennyson desired was exactly the same kind of success as that enjoyed by Pinero and Jones; and that he failed where they succeeded, because their plays had actually more literary merit than his if we admit that style should be adapted to subject.

The least successful essay in the volume is the one called **"The Supreme Leaders."** I do not know where it originally appeared, but it sounds as if it were intended for a distinctly lower grade of readers than the rest of the book appeals to, and therefore it seems perhaps out of place here. It is, of course, both useful and entertaining; but it would be better as an address at some high school graduation exercises, or as an article in some cheap and popular magazine. The tone of the essay is by no means cheap; quite the contrary, for it insists on what we are all prone to forget, that the masters are few; and it could have a chastening effect on the use of superlatives. Possibly Professor Matthews included it to serve as a counterweight to the essay on Mark Twain, whom he ranks tentatively with Moliere and Cervantes. Little fault can be found with his roll-call of geniuses, except that one may query whether Frederick really ranks in military history with Hannibal, Alexander, Caesar and Napoleon. And is it not a slip, however trivial, to say that "those who speak French . . . fare no better when we turn . . . to the art of war"? On the next page, the Italian descent of Napoleon is insisted upon, but surely, "those who speak French" may claim him. At all events, they seem to have done so,

In his anxiety to prove the contrary of the prevailing opinion, which declares that a man of genius is usually not appreciated by his contemporaries, and that he is "discovered" only by future generations, Professor Matthews is possibly a little too positive and a little too

sweeping. It is, of course, true that Shakespeare was a popular playwright; that Dickens and Thackery were immensely admired by their contemporaries, that Goethe was adored one hundred years ago. But can we unreservedly assent to such a statement as this; "Those books that survive are always chosen from out the books that have been popular, and never from those that failed to catch the ear of their contemporaries"? What shall we say to Herrick's *Hesperides?* The first edition of Herrick's poems appeared in 1648, the second in 1823! No real poet of his time was more neglected. Suppose Browning had died in 1860. In that year he received a copyright statement for the preceding six months. This proved that not one single copy of *Men and Women,* published in 1855 had been sold during the six months ending in 1860. How about Keats? Still, while it is certain that many exceptions can be found to Professor Matthews remark, it is no doubt true that he is largely right, and that most of us need his emphasis.

The first paper in the book, **"Literature in the New Century,"** was read in 1904, at the International Congress of the Arts and Sciences, held at St. Louis. This essay is fully worthy of the great occasion that produced it. It shows the breadth of view that always characterizes its author's utterances; it also shows a philosophical grasp, command of material, delicacy of insight, and accuracy of phrase, which makes us proud that it is the fruit of American scholarship. Professor Matthews discusses the "four legacies from the nineteenth century to the twentieth: first, the scientific spirit; second, the spread of democracy; third, the assertion of nationality; and fourth, that stepping across the confines of language and race for which we have no more accurate name than 'cosmopolitanism.'" There is not space here to set forth or to analyze these separate portions of the essay; suffice it to say that the book is worth purchasing for this chapter alone. Two other chapters, one on an abstract, the other on a concrete subject, may be briefly noted. The discussion of **"Invention and Imagination"** is exceedingly valuable and stimulating, and will be comforting to good writers who lack originality in conceiving situations. Our essayist is wholly right in insisting upon the superior quality of true imagination, as shown supremely by Shakespeare in comparison with more original dramatists, and as shown by Poe in contrast with Conan Doyle. But I am not so sure of the felicity of the choice of Rudyard Kipling to prove the writer's point. Not all readers will agree that Mr. Kipling can be correctly described as a writer "not seething for originality." It is the strenuous search for originality that has marred so much of the later work of this extraordinarily gifted man. And can we heartily assent to the statement concerning the tales of the *Jungle Book,* even cheerfully admitting their undeniable power and charm? We are told "They seem as assured of survival as anything which the nineteenth century has transmitted to the twentieth." Is the *Jungle Book* really as good as *David Copperfield, Esmond, The Mill on the Floss, Pride and Prejudice, Ivanhoe,* not to mention the poetry of Byron, Wordsworth, Keats, Shelley, Tennyson, Browning?

The essay on the concrete subject deals with the work of Guy de Maupassant. Just before writing this, Professor Matthews would have found it profitable to reread Tolstoy's remarkable and powerful discussion of the same author. It is not quite true that Maupassant "began by caring little or nothing for the heart or the soul or the mind, and by concentrating all his skill upon a record of the deeds of the human body. . . . But in time the mind came to interest Maupassant as much as the body." The thing is unfortunately more the other way around. The real tragedy of Maupassant's career is the steady moral deterioration in his novels, which Tolstoy has so grimly pointed out. His early work, as shown in the incomparable *Une Vie,* is full of amazing mental analysis, and is in a way profoundly spiritual; whereas his last novels, *Notre Coeur* and *Fort Comme La Mort,* are given up to sensations rather than thoughts, and are excellent examples of that wholly vicious school of literature, which, in the words of Turgenev, shows us not how people think, but how they feel. Of course, Professor Matthews has in mind chiefly the short stories, whereas Tolstoy is talking about the novels; but the direction of Maupassant's mind was the opposite from that pointed out by our essayist.

I have no hesitation expressing divergent views from those set forth in this volume, not only because the book is in the main so fine, but because its author enjoys honest dissent fully as much as praise. For the benefit of the next edition, one or two minute slips may be mentioned. Simplified spelling, like "the wos of Romeo," seem to the present unbeliever not wholly agreeable; but if its object is economy, why say "benefitted?" And surely, "Hannible" is a typographical error. Stevenson's novel, written in collaboration with Osbourne, was called *The Wrercker,* not "Wreckers." It is curious to see the old error concerning the origin of the name "Mark Twain" repeated, especially by one who knew him so intimately, and writes so admirably of his work. *Tom Sawyer* was first published in 1876, not 1875. Nor is it necessary to go back four hundred years to find a parallel to Maupassant's terror of death. If any one reads my review as far as the closing sentence, he will not need to be reminded of Dr. Johnson.

The Literary Spotlight (essay date 1924)

SOURCE: "I: Brander Matthews," in *The Literary Spotlight,* George H. Doran Co., 1924, pp. 15-23.

[*In the following essay, the critic depicts Matthews as a literary dilettante mired in the past and of little contemporary importance.*]

The year 1922 was an *annus mirabilis* in many ways. One of the most unexpected occurrences was the inexplicable departure of Professor James Brander Matthews from the weekly book review of our largest daily newspaper. Professor Matthews had been like death and taxes in one respect. He was always with us. Fifty-two times a year his name was to be discerned appended to printed matter in the *New York Times Book Review.* This matter took various forms. Sometimes it seemed to be a review of a current publication. At other times it wasn't. Professor Matthews's article could often be identified by certain phrases. One of them was "Forty years ago, etc." Another was the quotation of Jules Lemaître's fallacious but epigrammatic, "Criticism of our contemporaries is not criticism, it is only conversation." No epigram, of course, can be more than partially true; its very neatness defeats its own logic. But for Professor Matthews this statement by a distinguished Frenchman was the text of his life. He made his literary existence a long sermon in defence of it.

When Professor Matthews was not writing a review (he insists, quite rightly, that he does not write criticism) he was enlarging upon M. Lemaître's epigram. When he was not doing this he was rewriting himself. He made quaint admissions. He affirmed that he did not have time to read the younger men, but nevertheless he could not sleep for the horrendous tocsin of revolt that re-echoed in the streets adjacent to his mossy tower. Because of his attitude toward the younger men Professor Matthews is an important figure in current letters. His humanity is charming. He is so much what one would expect a representative of the older order to be that most of the younger generation experience a warming of the cockles of the heart when they think of him. It is true that they do not think of him very often, not so often, for instance, as they think of Stuart P. Sherman, but this is mainly because of Professor Matthews's repetitiousness. He scrapes away on the same old fiddle at the same old tune, and the younger generation (not barbarians really but rather nice young men who are mostly guilty of the attempt to think for themselves) know it by heart.

Professor Matthews was the Jeremiah of *The New York Times Book Review.* He did not criticize; he judged. His weekly articles were the dumplings in the stew. About them gathered the beefy chunks of Dr. Maurice Francis Egan, the carrots of Professor William Lyon Phelps, the parsnips of Austin Hay, the Irish potatoes of Herbert S. Gorman, and the thin gravy of Richard Le Gallienne. Now and again the concoction was enlivened by a dash of paprika from Benjamin De Casseres, who ate the mystics and was mad. The dish was quaint and one can but note with some consternation that it exists no longer.

Professor Matthews as the dumpling in the stew was naturally in a position of some importance. It is to be suspected that he had merely to nod his head toward a certain book and that book leaped toward him on the wings of the parcel post. His range of enthusiasms extended from Gelett Burgess's idea of *Æsop's Fables* to Gilbert Murray's Greek theories. Poetry of the lighter sort (*vers de société*) titillated him. Now this was but natural, for is not Professor Matthews himself the author of that deathless panegyric to the young Yankee maiden? Lest any of the younger generation have failed to memorize this effort it is drawn from its obscurity and set down here.

AN AMERICAN GIRL

She's had a Vassar education,
  And points with pride to her degrees;
She's studied household decoration;
  She knows a dado from a frieze,
  And tells Corots from Boldonis;
A Jacquemart etching, or a Haden,
  A Whistler, too, perchance might please
A free and frank young Yankee maiden.

She does not care for meditation;
  Within her bonnet are no bees;
She has a gentle animation,
  She joins in singing simple glees.
  She tries no trills, no rivalries
With Lucca (now Baronin Raden),
  With Nilsson or with Gerster; she's
A frank and free young Yankee maiden.

I'm blessed above the whole creation,
  Far, far above all other he's;
I ask you for congratulation
  On this the best of jubilees:
  I go with her across the seas
Unto what Poe would call an Aiden,—
  I hope no serpent's there to tease
A frank and free young Yankee maiden.

Envoy

Princes, to you the western breeze
  Bears many a ship and heavy laden.
What is the best we send in these?
  A free and frank young Yankee maiden.

Can one read this without affection for Professor Matthews? One wonders if he was not the F. Scott Fitzgerald of his day, and yet there is a certain naïveté that precludes any such opinion. Professor Matthews was and is as naïve as Jackie Coogan. Yet behind his unsophisticated humanity is a sound and important intellect. He has written admirably about Molière and Shakespeare. His scholarship in certain lines must remain unchallenged. His naïveté rests in his inability to understand when it is time to stop and where he should pause. He protests, without much reason, when the younger generation fails to adapt its pace to his. He belongs to the Bunner school of letters (a school that played delightfully and superficially with life) but he does not quite accept the fact that that movement is a thing of the past. They were gentle scholars, sound and sunny and sometimes close to saccharinity. One can but note with regret that the sweetness once implicit in Professor Matthews's work has grown a bit acidulous. This is mainly because he insists upon concerning himself with a modern movement of mind and spirit with which he has nothing in common. His blood does not tingle to that tocsin which he hears so loudly ringing in the streets of his Little Old New York. A new race has sprung up about him with other dreams. They are not interested in the things about which Professor Matthews's mind revolves. They don't care about Jules Lemaître's epigrams. They can roll their own.

Professor Matthews has written more than one article (or rather he has rewritten the same article several times)

striving doggedly to prove that book reviewing and criticism are two separate things. Very well. They are. Very well. They aren't. It is simple enough to grant that a book review is not necessarily criticism and it is equally simple to grant that criticism is not necessarily a book review. But when Professor Matthews asserts, as he does, that a book review may not be a criticism if it is concerned with a book by a contemporary author, he is merely expressing a personal opinion that other readers are not bound to accept. The idea that one may not criticize one's contemporaries because, presumably, of the nearness of the subject and the consequent lack of proper perspective, is a controversial subject with as much evidence on one side as on the other. Certainly Ben Jonson's opinion of Shakespeare (*his* contemporary, Professor Matthews will grant) has not been seriously destroyed as a piece of criticism by subsequent Shakespearian scholars. This is a subject assuredly in which one example will serve to destroy Professor Matthews's argument. If it has been done once it may be done again, and one does not need to search the archives of literature for an abundance of examples. So much has been written about this attitude of Professor Matthews that the foregoing statements are designed, not to destroy his attitude—for that would take an article in itself—but to illustrate one facet of his mind which is revelatory of his character. Professor Matthews is dogmatic, settled in his convictions, and not open to argument. He knows what he thinks; his opinions crystallized years ago; and the shiftings and fluctuations of the intellectual world have not moved him from his sturdy stand. He is in himself an epitome of that older order that grudgingly observes the younger generation and slams a ponderous fist upon it almost as soon as it opens its infant mouth.

It is futile for the older order to summon up a smile and assert that it does not deprecate the younger generation, that it likes youth and the thoughts that go with youth, and that it views with disapproval only the aberrations of the younger generation, the false experimentations and elaborate extravagances, etc. For the older order the younger generation itself is an aberration. The older order likes its own scheme of things and measures all movements accordingly. It is not qualified to judge either the merits or demerits of the experimentations of the younger generation, for it cannot enter into the spirit of them. It stands outside and observes objectively. The turmoil of the spirit, the urge to discovery and self-expression that lead the younger generation into such queer paths are meaningless gestures to the older order whose traveling days are done, whose roads have been made smooth in the days when its members were too young to realize that they themselves moved through the disadvantages and obstacles of a still older order. Castle after castle crashes down and the progress of art continues. No one generation can affirm that it has reached the appointed goal. The secret of great art is that the goal is never reached.

These are the things that Professor Matthews does not understand, and so clearly defined is his position that he is a welcome signpost for the younger generation. That much maligned group is glad to have him there, for he stands for the outworn things that have hardened, that have perished from a spiritual arteriosclerosis. It is futile for Professor Matthews or any representative of the older order to assert that the younger men are contemptuously flinging aside Shakespeare, Goethe, Dante, Shelley, and such divine constellations as squeezed oranges, for this has never been the case. The younger generation is as reverend as any where genius is concerned and past achievements are still past achievements. The difference between the older order and the younger generation is that the youthful group is not content to retravel roads that long ago were exhausted, to bask itself in an old tradition which indubitably has its place in the whole perspective of world literature but which is nothing more than a starting point for younger feet. The younger generation cannot think Professor Matthews's thoughts and exist; it would automatically destroy itself in the attempt.

Various tales (which may not be true) have arisen from Professor Matthews's attitude toward life and letters. There is the one about the young student taking his father's notebooks to a class conducted by Professor Matthews and discovering that he need take no new notes. Even the jokes fell in the same places. There is also the tale regarding Professor Matthews's explanation that he could not lecture on Emerson to his class as he had neglected to bring his notes along. These stories are possibly mere apocrypha, jaunty dramatizations of an atmosphere by impertinent youths, but they serve to show what Professor Matthews and all that he stands for suggest to the younger men.

He is the essentially personal prophet of the older order. Anything that he considers derogatory to the fetishes of his youth (which have remained fetishes all his life) he takes as a personal matter. An insult to Emerson is an insult to him. One can but observe this militant oldster (born in 1852) with admiration as he sallies into the vexed arena of modern letters bearing his frayed gonfalon. He will die fighting and he will die with the respect of the younger generation, for his sincerity is undoubted and in spite of criticism the younger men revere sincerity. But he will not be taken seriously, since he never possessed any value as a constructive thinker. His literary animosities rather reveal this deficiency. The tocsin of revolt peals in his streets of the mind and he rushes forth; but he is neither trampled upon nor thrust aside by the impatient youngsters who follow the alarum of that bell. They merely dart past him and far up the street. Farther than Professor Matthews's eyesight carries, he may hear the shouting of the young warriors.

Stuart P. Sherman (essay date 1924)

SOURCE: "Brander Matthews and the Mohawks," in *Points of View,* Charles Scribner's Sons, 1924, pp. 251-60.

[In the following essay, Sherman contrasts what he sees as the mean-spiritedness of the attacks upon Matthews by the new generation of writers and the sweetness of his response.]

Criticise the book before you, and don't write a parallel essay, for which the volume you have in hand serves only as a peg. This is No. VII of Twelve Rules For Good Reviewers, formulated by Brander Matthews in an essay on **"The Whole Duty of Critics,"** 1892.

I should try to follow this rule if its maker himself had not led me astray by sub-announcing in ***"The Tocsin of Revolt"*** a theme which he does not develop. Here is the theme which lurks in the first short essay:

> When a man finds himself at last slowly climbing the slopes which lead to the lonely peak of three-score-and-ten he is likely to discover that his views and his aspirations are not in accord with those held by men still living in the foothills of youth. He sees that things are no longer what they were half a century earlier and that they are not now tending in the direction to which they then pointed. If he is wise, he warns himself against the danger of becoming a mere praiser of past times; and if he is very wise he makes every effort to understand and to appreciate the present and not to dread the future. He may even wonder whether he is not suffering from a premature hardening of the arteries of sympathy. He finds himself denounced as a reactionary; and he doubts whether he has the courage of his reactions.

Whenever I turn away from this paragraph to comment on the other essays in this volume, I seem to see Brander Matthews peering into a dusky street, and to hear the sound of the tocsin bell.

"The younger generation is knocking at the door." That is the pretty phrase which used to be employed to describe the coming of age of a numerous group of new talents. It evokes the image of eager but modest youngsters, rather timorously offering their maiden speeches, their first poems, and their unsunned paintings to the critical scrutiny of their elders and their masters. And as a matter of fact one can call up out of literary history actual instances of such behavior on the part of the younger men—even in America, and even among critics and poets. With such deference the youthful William Dean Howells approached James Russell Lowell. With such reverence, Whitman offered his *Leaves of Grass* to his master Emerson. For the moment I am unable to think of other American cases. But then consider the respect of Johnson for Pope, of Pope and Congreve for Dryden, of Dryden for Honest Ben, or the religious tribute of the young Milton to his immediate predecessor, Shakespeare. The graceful antique mode of "knocking at the door" is now so completely forgotten that I must be allowed to present one exquisite illustration of it by a Son of Ben:

> When I a verse shall make,
>   Know I have pray'd thee,

> For old religion's sake,
>   Saint Ben, to aid me.
>
> Make the way smooth for me,
>   When I, thy Herrick,
> Honouring thee on my knee
>   Offer my lyric.
>
> Candles I'll give to thee,
>   And a new altar
> And thou, Saint Ben, shalt be
>   Writ in my psalter.

The beauty of this antique relation between the elder and the younger writers is lost because the younger generation no longer knocks at the door. It thunders at the door, it batters, it hammers, it bangs, it thumps, it kicks, it whacks, it wrenches, it lunges, it storms—it would require a Rabelaisian vocabulary to express all the indignities which the younger generation substitutes for knocking at the door. This somewhat barbaric performance, Brander Matthews, with his unfailing courtesy of phrase, calls sounding a "tocsin" at the door.

The ringleaders of this innovation in manners, the most impatient of our young people, are hardened journalists of forty, with a following of youths upon whose caustic lips the maternal milk is hardly dry. They are determined to have a better time than their fathers had. I sympathize with the object. But I am not always sure that they are going about "the great task of happiness" in the best way. From Samuel Butler of saintly memory, for example, they have adopted the theory that the chief obstacle to happiness in the path of children is their parents. At first thought the idea perhaps commends itself as offering to youthful impatience—generally so vague and objectless—something definite to work upon. But then I pick up the morning paper and read that one of our young people has confessed to having placed poison in her father-in-law's coffee because "he was old and such a care." That obstacle to her happiness is removed, but now another has arisen in its place. To put the matter in the happiest light, there is a certain want of amenity in the act, which one suspects, will rather poison the pleasure which the act was intended to procure. There is an inauspicious rowdiness about the present picnic on Parnassus. Laurel wreaths snatched from the heads of others seem somehow to lack the significance of laurel wreaths bestowed—the leaves are scattered, the garland is bare.

It may be due to a Chinese prejudice, but I have never been able to join with any great alacrity of spirit in the nearly universal contemporary sport of deriding the classics, or indeed any perpetuated mold in which the human spirit of a bygone age or generation expressed all that it knew of grace or charm or power. In cruel old myths, in grotesque images of primitive art, in the hard brilliance of early eighteenth century verse, in the perhaps excessive saccharinity of early Victorian representations of women, even in fashion-plates five years old, there is the pathos of things that Time, the "eternal philanderer,"

once loved and caressed and swore eternal fidelity to, and then left behind him in the vacant banquet halls and the grey solitudes of history. One of our newspapers has the custom of displaying every Sunday, side by side with the latest idols of stage and society, the idols of 1900, in all the borrowed glories that twenty years have filched. If we think a guffaw the right reaction to the best effect that 1900 could produce, we had better laugh quickly and have it over with, before our laughter is drowned by an outburst from the chucklers at our heels. But in the contemplation of these contrasts, the finer sense will shiver, knowing how soon *le dernier cri* becomes the farewell of warm life frozen into the past.

The literary Mohawks, however, are somewhat deficient in the finer sense. As the fighting organization of the younger generation, they fear the past as an enemy at their rear, and they hold that military considerations demand the devastation of the territory immediately behind their lines, and the destruction of all able-bodied men who will not actively enlist in their band. For some time, as everyone knows, they have been trying to blow up the National Academy of Arts and Letters as the stronghold, precisely, of the preceding generation. At frequent intervals their chieftains have advanced whooping to the portals of that serene citadel, and, uttering every taunt known to them, have challenged the Academicians collectively and severally to come forth and do battle. In the interior of a national academy there broods the quiet of a club organized by old field marshals. Its membership is made up for the most part of men who are remembering, not fighting, their campaigns. In the judgment of their peers, they have reached the head of their professions. They have passed through the cold spring of experimentation and the dusty summer of struggle and unrecognized achievement to that clear autumnal season in which one writes one's memoirs, and composes tributes to one's departing comrades, and turns an eye of curiosity and unenvious welcome upon the promising work of younger men.

If you are a member of the Academy, as Brander Matthews is, and if you hear ringing through the streets and alleys of the Republic of Letters the shouts of the Mohawks and the detonation of their bombs against your door, you will probably feel some astonishment at the alteration in literary manners during the last decade, and some irritation at the disturbance of your peace. You do not understand what grievance the Mohawks have against you.

You have, to be sure, reached the age when the transitory fashions of the hour no longer impress you as overpoweringly interesting, nor the fashions of twenty years ago as overwhelmingly funny. You are interested now rather in those permanent human passions and virtues and powers, in that play of wit and imagination, in that instinct of craftsmanship, in that study of perfection, in all those fluid elements of the intellectual and artistic life which are present in every great age, and which make the artists and scholars of all ages, in the higher sense, contemporary. You can appreciate the talent of Charlie Chaplin, and yet remember without humiliation your admiration for Coquelin and Edwin Booth. Your relish for the work of contemporary playwrights does not, to you, seem to require the "scrapping" even of so old a workman as Molière. You have given many younger men their "start," and have been the first to salute their maiden efforts; and yet you have not denounced your own masters, Arnold and Lowell, nor renounced your own coevals. You have dared to honor the memory of many men, friends of yours, who were born in your own time or a few years earlier or later—Aldrich, Bunner, Lounsbury, Stevenson, Austin Dobson, Andrew Lang, Howells, Stedman, McDowell, Mark Twain, Saint-Gaudens, and innumerable others.

With that eagerness to understand the world you are living in, which has always characterized you, you lean from your window to catch the hostile shouting of the Mohawks in the street, so that you may learn the head and front of your offending. From the cries that come up, you find that they hate all things that begin with P. They are carrying on a propaganda against the following: Propagandists, Prohibitionists, Prudes, Purists, Puritans, and Professors. You scrutinize your conscience. You find that in strictness you are none of these.

You were ever a "clubbable" man. You stepped without struggle into a congenial and intelligent society which you had no desire to "reform." You have regarded literature and the arts not as instruments of social salvation but rather as part of the accomplished expression of society. You have sought to give distinction to the American short story by perfecting its technique. You have been a zealous friend to the living drama and to all the arts of the theatre. You followed Lowell in your graceful defense of the independence of American writers and of the free creative American use of the English tongue.

They may charge you on technical grounds with being a professor; but in your own conscience you know that you have never been that. You were formed before pedagogy had a chance to deform you. You were forty before you ever told anecdotes in a professorial chair or brought the intoxicating airs of Bohemia and the great world of letters within the drab walls of a classroom. No Mohawk hates the pedantries of scholarship more sincerely than you do. You have successfully resisted the laws of gravitation. You are a lover of artistic form, you are a craftsman, and in whatever you have touched, criticism, the informal essay, the story, the drama, even *The New York Times,* you have shown your delight in literary workmanship. Your immense acquaintance with the interesting people of your time at home and abroad, your French clarity and ease of expression, and your sense that the highest use of learning is to increase the vivacity and the charm of human intercourse during a man's own lifetime—these things have made you what the Mohawks are howling for, a man of letters who is also a man of the world.

What, then, is the young people's grievance against you? Your unpardonable sin is that you are seventy. Therefore they batter at your door. It is the new manners.

In these circumstances a wise man, after due reflection, will probably be inclined to treat the disturbance like the bombardment of Halloween revellers. But there are three methods of dealing with Halloween revellers. One is to close shutters and say nothing. That is what is called "giving the absent treatment." One is to discharge a shotgun among the crowd. This is bucolic incivility. Brander Matthews is incapable of incivility. It is an incapacity which he shares with most of the distinguished writers of his generation. He adopts the third method. He steps out on his verandah, makes a charming speech to the Mohawks on youth and age and their common need of the traditions of their art, and then he distributes cider and apples—he blandly discusses American aphorisms, American architecture, repartee, conversation, cosmopolitan cookery, the length of Cleopatra's Nose, the modernity of Molière, Roosevelt, and memories of Mark Twain.

A. A. Milne (essay date 1929)

SOURCE: "Dramatic Art and Craft," in *By Way of Introduction,* E. P. Dutton and Company, Inc., 1929, pp. 62-8.

[*In the following review Milne addresses the criticism of George Jean Nathan and Matthews, dismissing the ideas of the former.*]

Mr. George Jean Nathan comes from the "Mother, look at George!" school of criticism, and is now enjoying a post-graduate course of "Oh, Mr. Nathan, you *do* say things!" As a professional dramatic critic he has been saying things for years, and this book is a collection of his best bits. Evidently he is a person of some consequence in America just now. "Much is made of the fact that I often leave the theatre in the middle of the second act of a play," he tells us. Under this stimulus he writes (and who would not?) with a buoyant swagger which is delightful, but which may lose some of its buoyancy when the fact that he has left the theatre in the middle of the second act is made much of no longer. Meanwhile, he is sufficiently exciting. When he says: "The lesser British playwrights . . . such playwrights as A. A. Milne, for example. . . . The net impression that one takes away from their exhibits is of having been present at a dinner-party whereat all the exceptionally dull guests have endeavoured to be assiduously amusing"—when he says this, he may give more pleasure to my friends than to me; but I do not leave the theatre. I stay to the end, and am rewarded a hundred pages later by the most charming piece of ingenuousness imaginable. He is telling us that, during the last year, he has met personally eleven men whose work he had criticized: four sound artists whom he had praised, seven incompetents whom he had damned. "When I met the seven incompetents I found them agreeable and amiable men, interesting to talk with and extremely companionable." But as for the four sound artists, "I could scarcely bear them. They were devoid of social grace; they were stupid; they were as heavy as lead; they were bores." It is a fascinating picture. Mr. Nathan and the seven amiable second-raters getting on charmingly together. . . . Mr. Nathan, the smile from his last good thing still on his lips, moving confidently across to the four first-raters. . . . I must not spoil it by a word of comment. Let us leave it there, with all its delightful implications.

Professor Brander Matthews' book takes us into a different atmosphere. *Playwrights on Playmaking* is a collection of essays which should be read by every critic of the theatre who is also interested in the theatre. With Professor Matthews the play is the thing, even if Mr. Nathan is feeling for his hat. With Mr. Nathan, Mr. Nathan is the thing, even if the play is so good that nobody but Mr. Nathan goes to it. "If I were appointed official dramatic censor," says Mr. Nathan, "I should, with negligible exception, promptly shut down every play that was doing more than 3,000 dollars a week." Molière, whom Professor Matthews quotes, thought differently: "I am willing to trust the decision of the multitude; and I hold it as difficult to combat a work which the public approves as to defend one which it condemns." The Professor agrees. "The eternally dominating element in the theatre is the audience," he says. If the dramatist cannot win the approval of the playhouse crowd, he should write, not plays, but novels. The printed play is nothing. "To judge a play by reading it is like judging a picture by a photograph." The dramatist must please, not the play-readers, but the playgoers, "and if they render a verdict against him he has no appeal to posterity. It is a matter of record that a play which failed to please the public in its author's lifetime never succeeded later in establishing itself on the stage."

Professor Matthews, you see, is quite definite about it, and he has Molière and others behind him. We cannot just say "Rubbish!" in the Nathan manner. We cannot content ourselves with a comparison of *Strife* with *Tons of Money,* or *Heartbreak House* with *Chu Chin Chow.* We shall have to examine the matter. Now, the first thing to be noted is that play-writing is not an art alone, but also a craft. I suppose that the difference between an art and a craft is this: that an art is something personal to the artist, whereas a craft is inevitably a collaboration. A sonnet is complete in itself; that Wordsworth wrote it is all that matters. But a chair wants not only Chippendale to make it, but a collaborator to sit in it. If, in his lifetime, humanity had suddenly become two sizes broader in the beam, and three sizes shorter in the leg, Chippendale's chairs would have taken on a different beauty; but Keats would not have changed by a word his "Ode to a Nightingale." Indeed, we may almost say that a chair would not be a beautiful thing at all if mankind had been so constructed that we could never sit down; in other words, that it is only beautiful because it is useful. As another writer has suggested, the reason why a castle is beautiful, and a castellated mansion an abomination, is

that the ancient castle was built for use and the modern castellation was only built for ornament. Left to himself a craftsman is without inspiration.

A dramatist is both artist and craftsman. He is a stage-craftsman by reason of the fact that he collaborates with the public. To put it vulgarly, every play is a bluff. Things didn't happen so, and couldn't happen so, but the dramatist is going to bluff the audience into believing (for three hours anyway) that things did happen so. The manner of his bluff depends upon the attitude to the stage of the contemporary audience; the intelligence of the people; the conventions of the period; and so forth. That is to say, it is dictated to him by his collaborators, the playgoers. Suppose that a dramatist wishes the audience to know what his hero's thoughts are in a certain crisis. If the conventions of his time allow of soliloquy, he makes his hero soliloquize. A soliloquy is neither good art nor bad art in itself; it is merely good craftsmanship or bad craftsmanship according to whether the audience is prepared or unwilling to accept it. But it is bad art if the speech, as *thought,* is untrue to character. On the modern stage soliloquy is unacceptable by the audience. A modern dramatist, then, has to find some other way in which to get his hero's thoughts across the footlights. Perhaps he makes him, under the stress of great emotion, burst out with them in the presence of other of the characters. It does not follow that the dramatist conceives his hero capable of exposing himself thus in public. All that the dramatist says is, "My hero would *think* like this (or I am no artist). His thoughts will eventually become known to the other characters, privately, one by one. To show you these scenes, one by one, would take up too much of your time. So I am trying to bluff you into believing, just while the scene lasts, that he might actually reveal himself to all of them together. And if I can't make you believe it, then I shall try to make the speech so good that you won't stop to ask yourself whether he could or couldn't have spoken it in public; you will let yourself be carried away by it."

It is obvious, of course, that in this matter the author is very much in the hands of his players. I emphasize again that, in detail, no play can be in the least like life; the essentials are true, but the details only masquerade truth. The author puts up a bluff, and the players carry it out. But the author is also very much in the hands of his audience. If they won't be carried away, they won't be carried away. If a scene, written to be judged by their hearts in a moment of emotion, is referred coldly to the judgment of their heads, so much the worse for him. Professor Matthews, on this point, speaks with great understanding of *Agamemnon.* The beacons announce that Troy is taken; within an hour Agamemnon (absurdly enough) is home again! Modern criticism labours to explain that what Æschylus really meant was this, that, and the other. The simple explanation is that Æschylus knew that his audience, seeing the beacons through the eyes of the watchman, would now want to see Agamemnon, and would want to see him at once. Whether Agamemnon could do a three weeks' journey in an hour had nothing to do with the play, and still less to do with their enjoyment of the play. You may call them unsophisticated, or you may call them uncommonly wise; but, whatever they were, Æschylus knew them and wrote for them. For a more sophisticated (or less wise) public he would have written very different plays. But, since he was an artist, they also would have been the plays of Æschylus.

And now we might ask ourselves (and Professor Matthews): What do we mean by "the plays" of Æschylus, or Shakespeare, or Sheridan? What do we mean by *Hamlet?* Do we mean Irving's *Hamlet,* or Tree's, or Forbes-Robertson's? We mean none of these. We mean Shakespeare's *Hamlet.* And Shakespeare's play of *Hamlet* can only be found in the printed book. The Professor himself tells us how certain characters in *The School for Scandal* should be played. How does he know? Because he has read the play. When a critic damns Barker's production of *A Midsummer Night's Dream* (as does Mr. Nathan), he means that, from his *reading* of the play, he feels certain that Shakespeare meant something different. To the dramatist as artist the printed play is everything; it is his appeal to posterity. To the dramatist as craftsman the acted play is something less than everything; for, until he shares with the Almighty the privilege of creating flesh-and-blood people, it can never be played as he saw it. It is useless to say that Shakespeare wrote *Hamlet* for Burbage. He may have seen Burbage as he began to write, but after a dozen lines he saw only Hamlet. But if to the dramatist as craftsman the acted play is never all that he meant, the play acted three hundred years later, under a different convention, would be a nightmare. Many critics write of a Shakespearean production as if the ideal *Macbeth* (or whatever it may be) were waiting round the corner for the ideal producer and the ideal cast. The ideal *Macbeth* is an impossibility; just as an ideal production of *Man and Superman* would have been an impossibility in Shakespeare's day. We may read and enjoy Shakespeare's plays, because he was a great artist; but we can never see them performed. He was much too great a craftsman for that.

Nicholas Murray Butler (essay date 1929)

SOURCE: "Brander Matthews," in *Commemorative Tributes of the American Academy of Arts and Letters,* American Academy of Arts and Letters, 1942, pp. 234-38.

[*In the following tribute, Butler, president of Columbia University from 1902 to 1945, commemorates his departed friend and colleague with deep and affectionate praise.*]

There are men who do important and interesting work in the world, whose personalities loom larger through the years than do any of their performances. Brander Matthews was one of these. No matter what he wrote or how excellent it may have been, no matter what he taught or how abundant an inspiration it was, the personality of the man puts it all into the shade. His manner, his merriment, and his charm were all his own, and were never failing. By good fortune he wrote for us an autobiographical sketch which he called *These Many Years.* He gave to it, as subtitle, the words "Recollections of a New Yorker." And a New Yorker he certainly was, in some respects the last of his kind.

Those mingled Scottish and English strains which gave to America its possibilities as well as its ideals and so much of its competence, united to produce this charming man and to guide his feet toward the metropolitan city which he truly loved and mightily adorned. One does not easily think of Brander Matthews as finding the home of his father's origin on Cape Cod, but there it was. From a parentage in which New England and Virginia were mingled, our dear friend and associate of so many years was born in New Orleans when the Nineteenth Century had just passed its middle point. But neither Cape Cod nor Virginia nor New Orleans was the suitable setting for this amazing personality. He was a cosmopolitan by his very nature and through his every taste, and it was only one of the world's capitals which could lure and hold him.

He probably was the first youth, and doubtless one of the very few youths, to be consciously educated and trained for the highly exclusive profession of millionaire. His father, who was a man of immense wealth as fortunes were counted in those days, and who would be deemed a very rich man even now, told his son repeatedly that he need never work for a living, but must fit himself to care for the great properties which his father possessed. All through his undergraduate days in Columbia College, and during his subsequent study of the law, Brander Matthews was fitting himself to pass through life as an educated gentleman possessed of a vast fortune which he should be competent to manage. Hardly had he entered upon this attractive task, however, when the fates decided that his life was to be something wholly different. They swept away his father's fortune, reduced the family possessions to practically nothing, and invited the young man to turn his attention to making a living by his own efforts. Most men confronted by such a situation would almost certainly lapse into a state of despair and helplessness, or become bitter cynics with no interested concern for life or for their fellow men. Not so Brander Matthews. He paid little more attention to this astonishing happening than if he had merely stumbled and fallen while walking through his father's garden. He picked himself up, metaphorically tightened his belt, took pen in hand, and started to make a living by the practice of the art of letters. His early travels in England and in France, the delightful acquaintance with men of letters and of the arts which he had been enabled to make, all now stood him in good stead. His dominant interest was the literature of the drama, whether creative or critical. With the French drama, both classical and contemporary, he became quickly familiar. With the playwrights of the day, whether to be found in Paris, in London, or in New York, he was speedily intimate companion and friend. His name as author became known, his reputation grew, and the livelihood of which he had gone in search came into his happy possession.

No one ever heard Brander Matthews refer to the dashing of the cup of gold from his lips, save with philosophical detachment or in amused contemplation. Even had the Golden Calf been in his possession, he was not the sort of man ever to fall down and worship it.

Forty years ago, when Columbia University was in the building, it was my fortune to propose to the governing authorities that provision should be made to have English literature taught and interpreted not simply by academically trained scholars, but also by men who were themselves of established and growing reputation in the world of letters, whether critical or creative. Once this proposal was accepted, it was yet my official duty to seek for the individuals who might best satisfy the requirement which had been set. The two who were selected, George Edward Woodberry and Brander Matthews, both became members of the Academy, both became distinguished in high degree, and both wrote their names high on the roll of honor of the University which was so fortunate as to secure their glad and notable service.

Brander Matthews hugely enjoyed his academic life and associations. He formed every sort and kind of intellectual contact. He attracted to his lectures and intimate discussions the most ambitious and eager students from all parts of this country and from many other countries as well. He never permitted himself to be cast in the traditional academic mold. He did not know how to be solemn or aloof or distant or coldly disinterested. That rich and delightful personality of his poured itself over everything which he said and did. At one moment those who were following his words were convulsed with laughter; at another their eyes were fixed upon him with rapt attention.

Brander Matthews knew and had known every man of letters of importance in this country, in Great Britain, and in France, for full forty years. He could relate personal anecdotes concerning them, each and all. He described incidents of their lives and work which made them live again, really live, in the hearts and minds of the younger generation which crowded about him. His friends were legion, and on their roll are many names celebrated in more lands than one. This delightful man moved through the years on intimate terms with Mark Twain and Howells, with Lowell and Henry Cabot Lodge, with George William Curtis and John Hay, with Richard Watson Gilder and Thomas Bailey Aldrich, with Edward L. Godkin and Edmund Clarence Stedman, with Edwin Booth, Coquelin and Henry Irving, with Henry James and Austin Dobson, with Andrew Lang, Thomas Hardy and Laurence Hutton, with Sir Martin Conway and Edmund Gosse, with H. C. Bunner and George Du Maurier, with Florence and Sothern and Crane and Gilbert, with Theodore Roosevelt and Rudyard Kipling. What other life than his was set in such a firmament of

brightly shining stars? He instructed, inspired and stimulated, not tens or hundreds, but actually thousands, of the ambitious youth of this land who had a wish to gain some true insight into the significance of letters, and to be led up to the high places from which they could look out upon the undying achievements of the spoken and the written word.

Brander Matthews took the keenest interest in his fellow workers in letters. He was an unfailing ornament of the old and famous Saturday night gatherings at the Century, and never missed a stated dinner of the Round Table. He was a familiar figure at the Saville Club in London and later at the Athenaeum. Literally he rocked the cradle of the Authors' Club, of the Players, and of this Academy. His place was never vacant when the members of the Academy assembled, and no mind among all its membership was more alert than his, to seek out ways and means of new and broader and higher usefulness.

Brander Matthews was truly a New Yorker. He loved the metropolitan city, its good cheer, its joyousness, its liberality, its open-mindedness, its varied companionships, and its enjoyments. Isolation had no charms for him. The country was merely a delightful place from which to come back to town. He wished to be where men were, where power was generated, and where great deeds were planned and done.

There are men of letters, fortunately, of every sort and of every kind. It would not be easy to trace relationship between an Emerson and a Whitman, or between a Browning and a Kipling. Yet they are each and all men of letters of the highest order of excellence, and each and all have carved their names on the undying roll of literature's immortals. Brander Matthews eludes classification or comparison. He was unique—unique in the circumstances of his education and early training, unique in what the world thought was the calamity which overtook him, unique in the fashion in which he turned himself with persistent cheerfulness to his new and unexpected task, unique in the quality and character of his academic service, unique in his odd and inviting intermingling of creative and critical writing with many-sided and keenest human interest, unique in his good humored faith in mankind, unique in the strong affections which his friends had for him and he for them, unique in the place which he holds in the hearts of all of us and on the rolls of this Academy.

Jack E. Bender (essay date 1960)

SOURCE: "Brander Matthews: Critic of the Theatre," in *Educational Theatre Journal*, Vol. XII, No. 3, October, 1960, pp. 169-76.

[*In the following essay, Bender provides an appreciative overview of Matthews's involvement with the theater as playwright, theoretician, critic and teacher.*]

The recent publication of ***Papers on Playmaking***[1] and ***Papers on Acting***[2] has brought back into print the name of an American theatrical figure who has almost been forgotten except on the campus of Columbia University where it is perpetuated in the name of the Brander Matthews Dramatic Museum and the Brander Matthews Chair of Dramatic Literature. Yet for almost half a century the opinions and theories of Brander Matthews loomed most importantly over the American dramatic scene. And even today, although the name is known to few, the theories evolved by Matthews remain important in much of our thinking regarding the theatre and the criticism of drama.

There is a special interest in the name of Brander Matthews for those working in the educational theatre, for he was the first in the United States to bring drama into education. When Matthews died in 1929, an anonymous writer in *Commonweal* noted: "Today the colleges are redolent of drama, experimental and otherwise. Not a few of the initiates forget that what they are attempting would probably never have become possible but for the witty, somewhat old-fashioned sage who really talked to the United States from his pulpit on Morningside Heights."[3] In the *Review of Reviews,* Montrose Moses wrote: "One might call him the Father of Our Interest in Drama in this country. . . . "[4] And a few years previously, Clayton Hamilton commented that it was "not excessive to state that there was no dramatic criticism—in the theoretic, philosophic sense—until Brander Matthews formulated his code in the last decade of the century. In the worldwide history of dramatic criticism, the contribution of America is, almost entirely, the contribution of Brander Matthews. . . . "[5] Extravagant perhaps, but in essence it is the truth. Certainly, in 1908, it was the bitter complaint of Oliver Sayler that "Brander Matthews monopolized the shelves of books about the theatre."[6]

Matthews really talked to the United States. Yet he exerted his influence upon the theatre, not as a practicing theatrical critic, but as a theorist who spoke from numerous essays in magazine and book form and from the classroom at Columbia University.[7] Born in New Orleans on February 21, 1852, Matthews was educated in private schools. Columbia College, and Columbia Law School for a career as a millionaire. Not only was his maternal grandfather a wealthy southern merchant, but his father was one of the wealthiest men in the United States. In the panic of 1873, however, the career for which Matthews had been educated came to an end, for his father was able to rescue only the remnants of a fortune.

At an early age he was introduced to the theatre and to Europe, and as he matured he was a frequent visitor to both. It was from Europe and from the theatre that Matthews chose his wife, Ada S. Smith, who was a member of Lydia Thompson's chorus. And it was the combination of the theatre and the many family trips to France that made him a student of the French theatre. "From my youth up," Matthews declared in his autobiography,[8] he was determined to be a playwright. Over a period of

thirty years, he wrote twelve plays, six of which were adaptations from the French. With the exception of the ***Silent System,*** which was adapted in 1889 for Coquelin on his first visit to the United States, all these adaptations were made in the seventies. Of the original plays, ***A Gold Mine,*** written in collaboration with George H. Jessop in 1887, was one of Matthews' most popular works and was played for a number of years by such actors as John Raymond and Nat C. Goodwin. His last attempt at playwriting was ***Peter Stuyvesant,*** written in collaboration with Bronson Howard. This was produced by William H. Crane in 1899, but it was a failure.

In the same decade that Matthews made his initial attempts toward what he hoped would be a career as a playwright, he also made his initial attempts at other aspects of literature. Although most of his work was written under his own name, a few of the early essays and poems were written under the *nom-de-plume* of Arthur Penn. In 1870 he "made a beginning toward the acquisition of the difficult craft of composition" by contributing to the London *Figaro* reviews of·American plays and books. It was not long, however, before he was writing for most of the important magazines in the United States, pouring forth a stream of book reviews, play reviews, essays of various types, literary criticism, dramatic criticism, poetry, novels, and short stories as well as plays.

By the nineties Matthews had become a figure of stature; he was known not only in New York, but in London and Paris as well. Laurence Hutton, in 1894, asserted that "no man in America is more thoroughly familiar with the history and the literature of the drama than is Mr. Brander Matthews."[9] Three years earlier, Matthews began his career at Columbia, teaching courses in American literature, modern fiction and English versification. The following spring a new professorship of literature was created for him, and to his other courses, Matthews added a fourth, concerned with the dramatists of the nineteenth century. Such a subject was unprecedented in contemporary colleges and universities. As these courses might indicate, Matthews was the champion of American art and of contemporary literature in an age described by Lewis Mumford as one in which, "for the dominant generation of the seventies, the new personalities that had begun to humanize America did not exist: art and culture meant the past; it meant Europe; it meant over the seas and far away."[10] ·

The education of the American playwright and the American public early became Matthews' objective. But at the same time, it became the search of a man attempting to evolve an aesthetic of the theatre which should satisfy both his "sacred and profane love of the theatre,"[11] as John Mason Brown would term it. The theatres of Paris were exciting, but the theatres of New York were frequently dull. The difference was not in the acting, Matthews believed, for the theatre of the United States offered as fine acting as the theatre of France. On the other hand, the French were not "cursed with the· 'star' system."[12] Got, Coquelin, and Delaunay might frequently play together; this certainly was not true of American star actors. Yet American acting could be exciting.

Dullness in the American theatre frequently was in the plays themselves; they were thin and uninspired, or they were simply dull and unplayable. Matthews was ever fond of citing a cartoon which depicted a "dramatic critic ordering a second cup of coffee, and saying, 'Make it strong, for I'm going to see an American comedy tonight, and I must keep awake somehow.'"[13] That until about 1890 American drama was dull, Matthews readily admitted. The importation of European plays to the exclusion of American plays, and even more so the adaptation of European plays, he condemned. The American drama was poor, but he was optimistic about its future. Only two things were necessary for the United States to have a superior drama of its own: the American playwright must learn the "grammar of the dramatic art"[14] and the public must be educated.[15]

In 1877, in a consideration of Bret Harte and Dean Howells as dramatists he wrote: "The misfortune hitherto of American dramatic literature has been that those who made plays did not make literature, and that those who made literature did not make plays."[16] A play must first prove itself in the theatre before it could be considered as literature. This dichotomy of the drama, appearing early in his writing about the theatre, persisted throughout his life time. What made for success in the theatre? What was literature? How could the two be brought together? This was the search of Brander Matthews.

The first twenty-five years of his critical career, i.e., the last quarter of the nineteenth century, were devoted to a questioning of the state of the theatre and the drama and to a campaign to raise the standards of American drama. As George Jean Nathan was the early critic of the doctrine advanced by Matthews, so was Matthews in his own fashion the critic of the doctrine preached by William Winter.[17] In the theatre of the latter, the actor was the focal point, and beauty was the single objective. Amusement had no place herein, for the theatre of Winter was a temple to be approached with reverence; it was a theatre of manners and morals in which the actor delightfully instructed the audience. As such, the critic was its priest. He was the judge of standards of acting, the leader of public taste, and the protector of public morals.

It was in this theatre that both Matthews and Bronson Howard made their appearance in the seventies, each as a theatrical critic and as a playwright. Although they travelled divergent paths, the former as a critic and the latter as a playwright, they met on common ground in their collaboration on *Peter Stuyvesant,* and they shared the objective of the elevation and promotion of American drama. Howard accepted the theatre of his day, borrowed his formula from Scribe, and attempted to portray the American character in a realistic fashion. What he established was taken up by other playwrights of lesser and greater ability. The form persevered, although seriousness of purpose varied, and the well-made play went

virtually unchallenged until the war years, meeting with organized resistance only in the twenties.

That which Howard, his contemporaries, and his successors practiced, Matthews championed in his criticism. Yet, the ideal for which he struggled was never realized by these practitioners. It was not simply for the well-made play that he battled, but for a drama which should truly entertain in the theatre. The theatre, he argued, was a separate art in its own right, as valid and as important as the other arts. Functioning as non-practical activity, in their most perfect forms the arts engaged the attention of the complete individual. Thus, aesthetic experience involved sensuous, emotional, and intellectual activity. An absolute, however, was based on Darwinian evolution, and intellectual activity was the superior activity. The theatre was a means to an end: a "criticism of life" and the communication of "the best that is known and thought" by means of mimetic representation.

The relationship of drama to literature was the subject of a long series of discussions carried on by Matthews. Most important to our present consideration were **"The Literary Merit of Our Latter-Day Drama"** and **"Putting Literature into the Drama."** In the earlier essay, appearing in 1907, he wrote:

> It seems absurd that at this late day it should be needful to repeat once more that literature is not a matter of rhetoric; that it is not external and detachable, but internal and essential. It has to do with motive and character, with form and philosophy; it is a criticism of life itself, or else it is mere vanity and vexation.[18]

In this instance literary merit was found in the content as the expression of a view of life. It is to be noted, however, that "form" also was an important aspect of literature. This at least suggests the position taken twelve years later in the second essay:

> True "literary merit" does not reside in the smoothness of the external rhetoric but in the vigorous harmony of the internal elements which enable the play to stand four-square to all the winds that blow. It is by the force of these internal elements that a drama maintains itself in the theatre.[19]

Herein the literary merit of a play was placed within the total achievement of a work as performed in the theatre. It was not a matter of a play first achieving success in the theatre and then achieving permanence in the library, but of maintaining itself in the theatre by the force of the internal elements. Literature was not equated with reading, but with permanence, with truth. As Matthews had previously observed, "Only literature is permanent." The drama might be read, but the reading of a play was an imagined performance. The truth of a play was in its function in the theatre.

Literature and theatre were made one by means of Brunetière's law of drama. In *The Development of the*

Drama, Matthews observed that drama was interesting to people in many ways: in its philosophy, studies of character, simple amusement, or as the loftiest form of poetry.

> And to the scantiest group of all, perhaps, dramatic literature is ever interesting because it is the highest manifestation of the dramatic instinct universal in mankind. . . . To me, I admit, it is always most interesting when it is considered simply as drama—as a work of dramaturgic craftsmanship prepared especially to be performed by actors, in a theater, before an audience. . . . Praise is abundant for the poetry that adorns the great plays, for their sentences of pregnant wisdom, for the subtlety of their author's insight into conflicting human motives; but due consideration is seldom bestowed on the skill with which the action is conducted—the action, which is the heart of the play, and without which it is lifeless and inert.[20]

Action was the essential element of any play, and by action Matthews meant mimetic representation in the telling of a story. Drama was but the evolution of the mimetic from what was "communal" and "spontaneous" into "an accepted way of telling a story in action." By means of Brunetière's law, Matthews identified this action of mimetic representation with action as truth, and thus, he shifted the emphasis within the drama from the theatre to this truth. "The soul of the drama," said Matthews, "is the assertion of the human will which is the cause of the conflict."[21] The "inner stiffening of the human will" was all-important, for "to exert one's own will is the final proof of man's existence; and therefore what the drama necessarily deals with is the most significant action of human life."[22]

Thus, action in terms of the auditory and visual stimuli of the theatre, was but a demonstration of "a will which knows itself," and the action of theatre was identified with the action of truth, a quality of literature. Brunetière's law Matthews accepted not as a definition of drama, but as a measure of its value. He might have agreed with John Mason Brown's assertion that the theatre was whatever it happened to present on any particular night, but at the same time Matthews would undoubtedly have asserted that this was no measure of the drama. He distrusted the simple pleasure of the senses unless this pleasure was associated with higher values. He had "profane love" for the theatre, but he valued this love primarily for the greater appreciation through his "sacred love."

Truth was the determinant of value, but there was a relativity in truth, the larger being the more valuable. This was not to deny, however, the value of the lesser truth. The theatre was a truth in itself, and the visual and auditory stimuli of the theatre were values in themselves. Considered in a larger view, however, they were merely the means toward larger values. The drama, being of the theatre, must be true to itself, and its values were revealed only in the theatre or as imagined in the theatre. The theatre was an art in its own right and was to be considered only in terms of this art; but the ultimate value of drama was in its "literary" aspects, the truth of free will. The representation of such will was, if not a definition of drama, at least the essence of drama.

Art was a matter of giving form to eternal truth, and the aesthetic experience was the realization of this truth in an organized fashion. The art of the dramatist was the fashioning of a single episode from life, isolated from other activity, into a symmetrical whole so as to bring into play the sensuous, emotional, and intellectual activity of the individual in a realization of truth. The purely sensuous play, i.e., the work which simply told a story in theatrical terms, was perfectly valid as amusement for this was the first objective of art, but it lacked value for consideration as the highest endeavor of man and as a product in the continuity of culture. The play without this quality, however, likewise lacked value for it failed to satisfy the first objective of the art of the theatre: mimetic story telling.

Apart from politics and religion, there were few themes which Matthews would deny to the dramatist; treatment was the important consideration. He approved of the attempts of Ibsen, the French realists, and the naturalists to utilize the contemporary problems of the day and to examine the various levels of society, but he did not always approve of the plays. In some instances, his failure to approve was based on his concept of dramatic form: in others, it was based on the treatment. Realism, in his view, did not imply the minute examination of a subject, but a broad examination; it was the duty of the dramatist to tell the truth as he saw it, but he did not necessarily have to tell the whole truth. While Matthews could not agree with Winter that the objective of art was sweetness and light, neither could he accept the extreme pessimism of the naturalists. In encouraging the examination of life, Matthews at least loosened the bonds of decorum even though he was linked to Winter as a symbol of gentility.

Thus, Matthews preached to the American public a theory of the theatre which supported the well-made play yet encouraged realism in subject matter and truthfulness in character portrayal. In so doing, he shifted the focus of attention from the actor to the play; the drama was no longer for the display of the emotional intensity of the actor, but the actor existed to interpret the play which was a view of the life about us. There might appear to be agreement between Winter and Matthews when the latter wrote: "What we go to the theatre to see is—in the final analysis—acting. Whatever we may like in the library, in the theatre we prefer the plays which give most scope to the actors."[23] This was not meant to minimize the role of the playwright, however. The expression of the actor was valid expression in the theatre, but it was interpretative in nature, while that of the playwright was creative: "the player is ever overshadowing the playwright, altho the actor is but the interpreter of what the author has created."[24] The two arts of the dramatist and the actor were inseparable. Upon the actors the dramatist "had to depend for the proper presentation of what he has imagined. They and they alone can bring his work before the public."[25] And without the playwright, the actor had nothing to act.

That the drama was an art of the theatre—to be more exact, that the drama was *the true art* of the theatre—was the first principle in Matthews' doctrine: a play was to be performed by actors in a theatre. The second principle was really a corollary of the first. Because the drama is an art of the theatre and because the theatre is dependent upon an assembled audience, the drama must be a democratic art; it must appeal to the collective tastes of an average audience. But Matthews' dictum that a play must appeal to the "average audience" was not as democratic as it might at first seem. In a book review, he once wrote: "'The man in the street,' when he goes into his house and sets himself down before the fire under the evening lamp, has no difficulty in understanding and enjoying Walter Bagehot's 'Physics and Politics,' William James's 'Principles of Psychology' and William G. Sumner's 'Folkways.'"[26] The drama was democratic in the sense that it must make its appeal to an assembled group, but it was aristocratic in the sense that it appealed to a group with similar cultivated tastes. Such an aristocracy of taste, however, was based upon the premise of an absolute good. It allowed for individual differences within the absolute, but it had no place for the individual personality. Matthews could not comprehend an intellectual aristocracy which was based upon the principle of freedom of taste unbound by a cultural absolute. In this respect, Matthews was linked to Winter as a "symbol of gentility." But there was an important difference between these two individuals. Winter remained the provincial in his tastes, while Matthews was the cosmopolitan always returning to the roots of his nationality. Thus, the tastes of the "average audience," in the view of Matthews, were rooted in the absolute good of the traditions of the Anglo-Saxon.

When writing *The French Dramatists of the 19th Century*[27] Matthews was a cosmopolite, and the drama which he then found the most exciting in the world he established as the model for the American playwright who was prone to be dull or unskilled. This work and *Studies of the Stage*[28] were written while he was active in his study of the contemporary stage and while he himself was still attempting to write plays. In his humanistic approach to the theatre, and in his bringing to bear upon a study of the drama the influences of the theatre, Matthews helped make possible our present methods of the study of the theatre. *The French Dramatists of the 19th Century* and *Studies of the Stage* were the early works, but *The Development of the Drama. A Study of the Drama,*[29] *Molière, His Life and His Works,*[30] and *Shakespere As a Playwright*[31] were the fruition of this theory and method. *The Development of the Drama* was the first attempt to consider the history of the drama of the western world as an art of the theatre. It was an attempt at an objective evolutionary treatment of the history of the drama from the point of dramatic form. *A Study of the Drama,* published in 1910, was also a study in form, but approached, first, from the view of the technique of the

playwright, and secondly, from the historical view in the presentation of each aspect of technique. The former work was approached inductively, the latter was approached deductively. And the premises and the conclusions were the same. The two remaining works were also studies in form approached from the same point of view. It might benoted in passing that his briefer study, **"Ibsen the Playwright,"**[32] was in the same category. These works together with the many studies of the drama and the theatre published under Matthews' supervision by Columbia University and the many models of theatres of the past built for the Dramatic Museum provide the American beginnings of our present methods of dramatic criticism and study of the drama.

In the twentieth century, however, Matthews drew further and further away from the contemporary theatre, and the influence of Matthew Arnold and Ferdinand Brunetière became increasingly apparent as he became more concerned with the cultural ideal and the codification of a doctrine of the theatre. Although he constantly attended the theatre in both the United States and Europe, no playwright of the twentieth century received more than a passing comment in his essays. For all practical purposes in the criticism of Matthews the development of the drama ceased with the French realists, Jones, Pinero, and Ibsen. Notable is the following reference to the drama of the 1920s: "Of a truth, a theatrical season is memorable when it sees the production of American dramas as diverse and as outstanding as *What Price Glory?* and *They Knew What They Wanted,* and *Desire Under the Elms.*[33]

Attacks upon the doctrine of Matthews, instigated largely by Nathan, began to appear shortly before the First World War. In the years immediately following the war, the attacks increased, and Matthews became truly a symbol of gentility out of touch with modern thought in the theatre. He might privately admire much in this new theatre, but he never discussed it. That he did not discuss it was not because of his aversion to it, but because of his philosophy of criticism. "Four parts of what is contemporary must be temporary," he often wrote, noting Jules Lemaître's observation that "criticism of our contemporaries is not criticism—it is conversation." Discussion of contemporaries was journalism. Criticism was literature and dealt with what was permanent.

For half a century, however, Matthews really talked to the American public. "Exposition of what the theatre meant, of what it was and had been, restored to the footlights their humanistic appeal." He took up the education of the American playwright and the American public in behalf of a drama which should be both interesting and serious in its intention. And to the dramatic critic he expounded the doctrine that criticism of the drama must be considered in terms of the theatre since the drama was an art of the theatre.

Brander Matthews was both a force in the American theatre and a force in the development of a new method of dramatic criticism. If the theatres represented by William

Winter and George Jean Nathan are radically different theatres, the theatre of Brander Matthews is representative of the transition between the two. His domination of dramatic criticism made possible the theatre of a Nathan. Moreover, if in serious dramatic criticism the drama is treated as an art of the theatre, it is done so largely because of the work of Matthews. Clayton Hamilton did not exaggerate when he declared that American dramatic criticism began with Matthews. Nor would it be an exaggeration to say that Brander Matthews has been a potent force in the development of American thought pertaining to the theatre.

NOTES

[1] (New York: Hill and Wang, Inc., 1957). This series of papers was originally published by the Dramatic Museum of Columbia University in 1926.

[2] (New York: Hill and Wang, Inc., 1958).

[3] IX (April 17, 1929), 669.

[4] LXXIX (June, 1929), 146-147.

[5] "Brander Matthews as a Dramatic Critic," *Literary Digest International Book Review,* I (November, 1923), 90.

[6] *Our American Theatre* (New York, 1923), p. 3.

[7] Contrary to the statements made in many places. Matthews was not a working critic of the theatre. It is true that he wrote a few reviews in the seventies and the eighties, but this was the work of a neophyte.

[8] *These Many Years* (New York, 1917).

[9] "Literary Notes," *Harper's Monthly,* LXXXVIII (April, 1894), 812.

[10] *The Golden Day* (New York, 1926), p. 204.

[11] *Two on the Aisle* (New York, 1938), p. 265.

[12] "Actors and Actresses of New York," *Scribner's Monthly,* XVII (April, 1879), 770.

[13] "The Dramatic Outlook in America," in *Studies of the Stage* (New York, 1894), p. 67.

[14] Ibid., p. 69.

[15] Ibid., p. 76.

[16] "Bret Harte and Mr. Howells as Dramatists," *Library Table,* III (September 13, 1877), 174.

[17] For the most authoritative discussion of the career of Winter, see, Charles McGaw, "An Analysis of the Theatrical Criticism of William Winter" (Unpublished Ph.D. dissertation, University of Michigan, 1940). A part of

this material has been presented by McGaw in *The Quarterly Journal of Speech* for April, 1945, under the title of "William Winter: Critic of the Brown Decades."

[18] *Inquiries and Opinions* (New York, 1907), p. 214.

[19] *The Principles of Playmaking and Other Discussions of the Drama* (New York, 1919), p. 51.

[20] (New York, 1903), pp. 15-17.

[21] *A Study of the Drama,* p. 102.

[22] *The Development of the Drama,* p. 61.

[23] "On Certain Parallelisms between the Ancient Drama and the Modern," in *Aspects of Fiction and Other Ventures in Criticism* (New York, 1896), p. 87.

[24] "The Art of Acting," in *Rip Van Winkle Goes to the Play and Other Essays on Plays and Players* (New York, 1926), pp. 237-38.

[25] "The Playwright and His Players," *Scribner's Monthly,* XLV (1909), 116.

[26] *New York Times Book Review,* April 16, 1922, p. 9.

[27] (New York, 1881; revised 1891 and 1901).

[28] (New York, 1894).

[29] (Boston, 1910).

[30] (New York, 1910).

[31] (New York, 1913).

[32] *Bookman,* XXII (1906), 568-75; XXIII (1906), 18-29.

[33] "American Plays and Home-Made Calicoes," *Literary Digest International Book Review,* IV.

H. L. Kleinfield (essay date 1964)

SOURCE: "The Tutelage of a Young American: Brander Matthews in Europe, 1866," in *Columbia Library Columns,* Vol. XIII, No. 2, February, 1964, pp. 35-42.

[*In the following essay, referring to a travel diary Matthews kept when he was fourteen, Kleinfield examines the boy's impressions of and responses to a European excursion.*]

In five centuries, Europe has played for Americans many roles, the point of departure, the home base, the mother country, the fountain of culture, the raging war god, the artist's haven, the wounded ally, the first line of defense. Through these many contacts with the Protean old world, the fledgling new has grown steadily in strength, size, vigor, and complexity. Always there has remained, however, a desire—sometimes merely a curiosity, often a passion—to visit, explore, and challenge the teeming parent beyond the seas. Today jet planes make Europe a weekend resort, but not until the advent of the steamship in the mid-nineteenth century did Europe lay within ready reach. A half-forgotten manuscript picked from Columbia's library shelves now gives us a candid picture of one such eastward pilgrimage made a hundred years ago when hundreds of affluent American families gained prestige, refinement, and knowledge by following the popular guide-book routes to the geographical and cultural monuments of England, France, Switzerland, Italy, and Germany.

That manuscript, a journal of James Brander Matthews from June through December, 1866, also puts flesh on a name once alive to thousands but now lingering in the shadowy corners of aging memories. Suddenly a new generation of Americans, born of an incredible political and social experiment, with ease could cross the ocean which was itself a symbol of their freedom. Brander Matthews, Professor of Dramatic Literature at Columbia for more than twenty-five years and member of the English faculty for ten earlier, made a literary career for himself, writing fiction, drama, and criticism before he joined the academic community. Class of '71 and law graduate of '73, he remembered Columbia College as a dilettante's club far more than as an educational seminary. He recounted in his autobiography the amazing change he found when he undertook his first teaching duties two decades later, in 1891, to fill the temporary void left by someone on a sabbatical year in Europe. That new serious purpose and intellectual character in the College grew many fold as he himself gained in stature, range, and reputation. One consequently opens the youthful journal of Brander Matthews, aged fourteen, aware that it offers a glimpse into the formative experience of a significant figure on the intellectual scene, as well as a canto of the American Odyssey.

His father, Edward Matthews, who was a merchant at Broad Street and Exchange Place, had made a great deal of money. He lived in an elegant house at 101 Fifth Avenue, and traveled in style with his wife, three children, a tutor, and two servants. Embarked on the Cunard steamer, *Scotia,* 27 June 1866, the Matthews family quickly encountered rough seas which, on the very first day out of port, sent the fourteen-year-old son and heir away from the dinner table. Brander Matthews soon recovered, however, for this was by no means his first trans-Atlantic crossing, and he noted in his journal the weather and the distance traveled each day, a practice on European voyages he continued in later life with his brief notations of day-to-day activities. After three days of fog and rolling seas, the weather appropriately cleared on 4 July for "a grand dinner in the after saloon," where the healths of the Queen and the President were drunk and cheered under American, English, and French flags. When the uneventful crossing on this his third visit abroad drew to its close at Queenstown on the following night, Brander Matthews stood once more on foreign soil after nine years.

His journal pictures a well-behaved youth seeking contact with the familiar landmarks, opening his eyes and mind to this foreign but not altogether unfamiliar world, and moving contentedly and affectionately in the bosom of his family. With Mr. Carroll, his tutor, he walked about a great deal, visiting monuments and observing city or town. Often the family rode together to see the sights and usually dined together at their lodgings or hotel. The "Armoury" in the Tower of London held his eye with a "very beautiful" arrangement of weapons in the shapes of flowers, and Hampton Court was "very beautiful." Madame Tussaud's Wax Works were interesting but the "Indian and Esquimana curiosities" in the British Museum drew special attention because they "called to my mind immediately the accounts I had read of the voyages and explorations of Parry, Kane and Hall." There was always something of interest to see, the Poet's Corner in Westminster Abbey, the Houses of Parliament, the Zoological Gardens in Regent Park, Leotard, "the celebrated gymnast." A week later the Matthews entourage reached Paris. The Vendôme monument gave the young traveler a disappointing view of the city after a long climb up a narrow stairway, and looking at pictures in the Louvre he found "rather dull" although "the building was very fine." But Paris offered the opera, the theatre, stamp collecting, the waterworks at St. Cloud.

At Basle diversion was natural, rather than man-made, and Brander Matthews rowed on the lake with his father and had his first swimming lesson, "being held up by a cord around my waist." The Matthews family spent nearly two months in Switzerland, visiting all cities of interest. In spite of predominantly rainy weather, they persisted in mountain climbing, occasionally being rewarded with "a magnificent view of the Alps, covered with snow," and enjoying a lake or a waterfall. Perhaps they reached the high point on a trip to the Jungfrau "after 3 hours hot and disagreeable ride." Standing before the mountain, we "*heard* four avalanches and saw one of them, which looked like a waterfall." From the grounds of Baron Rothschild's house near Geneva, open by card to visitors on Fridays, Mont Blanc and Lake Leman looked especially beautiful. In Geneva, of course, the Swiss watchmaker beckoned. At Pateks, after a tour of the establishment, "Papa bought two watches just alike, one for himself and one for me, and Mamma bought a very little one for herself. Papa also bought me a chain and a scarf-pin." With the purchases made of a Saturday, the following Monday Brander excitedly ran out after breakfast, bought a guide-book, and "went to the watchmakers to see about the watches." At Baden-Baden he paid his first visit to a gambling casino, only to be bewildered by both Trente-et-un and Roulette. "I could not understand either of them at first but I bought a little book in French which explains them, and after that I found it quite interesting to watch the playing, which appeared to me, in a good many cases, rather wild."

The tour continued through Heidelberg, Frankfort, Hamburg, and Cologne. At Aix-la-Chapelle, the relics at the church drew from the young tourist a remark typical of his friend of later years, Mark Twain, in that eccentric travel book, *Innocents Abroad.* "They also showed us the vase used at Capernaum to hold the water, at the marriage feast, but as it was made of alabaster and the only vases then in use in Judaea were made of earthen ware, it can't be the real one!" At Brussels, there were churches, palaces, picture galleries and, of course, "Mamma went to some lace shops and bought some lace."

The Matthews family returned to Paris early in October and appear to have remained three months. After recounting sight-seeing and other activities for nearly two weeks, Brander Matthews neglected his journal between 16 October and 7 December. The brief glimpse he gives of his stay includes a good deal of walking, often in the company of a cousin who came over from London under the escort of their grandfather. There were rides to the Bois, "as they always call the 'Bois de Boulogne' here," stamp collecting, and Italian lessons. Theatre-going, however, provided the single greatest interest. On their second night in Paris, the family trouped to the "Gaieté," only to be disappointed, for "as we got there only ten or twelve minutes before it commenced we had no chance of getting seats, so we came home in despair." Eventually, however, their dramatic appetites were satisfied, for Brander Matthews recorded attendance at eight different performances, including opera, ballet, and drama, before the party left Paris for Marseille, 7 December, in a private railroad car.

The remainder of Brander Matthews's journal covers two additional weeks of touring the French Riviera, then following the Corniche Road through Italian villages, to Genoa and Florence. Only an occasional beautiful church or a pretty scene from the carriage relieved the fatigue of travel and the discomfort of poor accommodations and bad food. At Florence, however, the party halted to enjoy the riches of both art and nature. Nestling in the Tuscan hills, the ancient city offered "splendid" views of the surrounding countryside and fascinating sights of man's ingenuity like "the old Estruscan walk which is built of immense-sized stones, without any cement or mortar, their own weight keeping them together." Then there were the galleries, the Uffizi and the Pitti Palace, and the frescoes of Andrea del Sarto in the Church of the Annunciata. Dutifully appreciative, young Brander noted one picture of the Madonna and Child in which "the expression of the Virgin's face was very beautiful," and he remarked on the "splendid statuary including the Venus de Medici and the Knife-sharpener, both of which are very beautiful." The journal abruptly ends on 21 December with visits to studios of American sculptors in Florence, including Hiram Powers' where his "Greek Slave" drew notice.

As yet an unformed youth and scarcely able to articulate any serious reactions he may have had to works of art, people, or experiences, Brander Matthews could not flavor his journal with meaningful insights into the benefits he enjoyed as a scion of America's moneyed aristocracy. The account he left of these few months in Europe fits very convincingly, however, the picture one holds of him and his era. Here is the typical American pilgrimage to the Old World, with its sense of cultural inferiority, its energy, its impulse for exploration, its quest for identity, its self-consciousness. At the age of fourteen, to parade the Champs Elysées, climb the highest Alp, ogle the Venus de Medici meant to slip on the robes of cosmopolitan urbanity. The costume fit not only a fortunate youth but also a youthful nation. Still to come of age, America was scarcely a stripling in the family of nations.

In the ensuing decades, as the United States grew to manhood, Brander Matthews also gained his place in the world, a place far different than that expected for and by him in 1866. For Edward Matthews suffered disastrous reverses in the panic of '73. Taking up his pen for livelihood, Brander Matthews worked determinedly to compose a literary career, and he turned first to a youthful interest in the theatre. By 1876 he had had under consideration at least half a dozen plays. At the end of the same year, a number of magazines had printed nearly forty of his articles, mostly on dramatic subjects, and had paid him in the neighborhood of four hundred dollars. In 1880 appeared his first full-length book, *The Theatres of Paris,* clearly the product of an interest already formulated before this youthful grand tour. As Professor of Dramatic Literature, biographer of Molière, disciple of Sarcey, and intimate of Coquelin, Brander Matthews assuredly capitalized later on his youthful advantages.

Interest in Brander Matthews must go beyond the personal or biographical, however, for his career, active and extensive though it was, does not hold any major achievement. It is, rather, the breadth and variety of his work, with its dozens of books, thousands of essays and reviews, hundreds of students, endless correspondence, multiple clubs, amazing energy, and inexhaustible confidence that catch and hold the eye. Actors, playwrights, novelists, artists, critics, bankers, editors, statesmen, clergymen, publishers, all the figures of the cultural scene composed the *dramatis personae* of his life. That life came to have its focus in Columbia University where officers, faculty, students, and alumni alike delighted in his presence. The fruit of his work grew out of a soil nourished by the accidents of fortune as well as by his indefatigable labor and uncommon mind. Without formal academic training, he drew on other sources of knowledge and experience to tutor students, foster young playwrights, and issue critical judgments over half a century. In these roles he became an intellectual figure of representative, if not dominating, importance. The knowledge of the formulating elements of his personality, as reflected in this slight journal, helps to strengthen likewise an understanding of the American character.

Lawrence J. Oliver (essay date 1988)

SOURCE: "Brander Matthew's Re-visioning of Crane's *Maggie,*" in *American Literature,* Vol. 60, No. 4, December, 1988, pp. 654-8.

[*In this essay, Oliver contrasts Matthews' version of Realism with Stephen Crane's by comparing Matthews' short story "Before the Break of Day" with Crane's short novel,* Maggie: A Girl of the Streets.]

Reviewing Stephen Crane's *Maggie,* Hamlin Garland praised the novella as the most truthful and unhackneyed tale of the slums he had ever read, but he qualified his praise of Crane's compelling study in naturalism by contending that it "is only a fragment. It is typical only of the worst elements of the alley. The author should delineate the families living on the next street, who live lives of heroic purity and hopeless hardship."[1] Garland's critique of *Maggie* will be familiar to most Crane scholars; less known, however, is the fact that two months before his review appeared, Garland, apparently intending to promote *Maggie,* had urged Crane to send a copy of the book to Brander Matthews. An influential literary critic and professor of drama at Columbia University, Matthews was an intimate friend of and was highly regarded by not only Garland but William Dean Howells and Mark Twain as well. During the "war" being waged in the United States at the time between the literary romanticists and realists, Matthews was a staunch ally of the latter; and he especially encouraged accurate fictional portraits of New York City life. Matthews himself published a number of what he termed "snapshot" sketches of New York in the early 1890s, reprinting twelve of them in a volume titled ***Vignettes of Manhattan*** in 1894. Thus Garland had good reason for suggesting that Crane send his novella to the professor.

Crane took Garland's advice. In a letter dated 21 March 1893, he wrote to Matthews that he was, at Garland's suggestion, sending him a "very small book." Crane closed his brief note with a request: "If you write me what you think of [the book], you would confer a great favor."[2]

Whether Matthews conferred the favor and expressed his opinion of *Maggie* to Crane is not known; but there is no doubt that the tale of Rum Alley evoked a written response from the professor—not in expository but in fictional form. In his short story **"Before the Break of Day,"** first published in the July 1894 issue of *Harper's Monthly* and reprinted in ***Vignettes of Manhattan,*** he revisioned Crane's work, transforming it from a tale of tragic defeat into one of heroic triumph. In doing so, he produced, ironically, the very kind of romanticized fiction that Crane parodied in *Maggie,* and that Matthews himself repeatedly seemed to disparage in his polemical defenses of literary realism.[3]

"Before the Break of Day" opens with one Maggie O'Donnel asleep in her dingy, rat-infested apartment above a saloon she and her husband Terry own, Terry having left the tenement before dawn to lend a hand in preparations being made for the Fourth of July celebration to occur later that day. The date is significant, for this tale, in sharp contrast to Crane's novella, is an endorsement of the American Dream. Maggie's life, we learn from the omniscient narrator, has been hard. She

spent her childhood in the squalor of Hell's Kitchen; like Crane's Mag Johnson, she was often beaten by her alcoholic stepmother (her natural mother died when Maggie was five years old) and her late father (who, inebriated, fell down the stairs to his death after missing a blow at his daughter). At age fourteen, she was forced to work in a sweat shop. But where Crane's Maggie found the factory a "dreary place of endless grinding" (p. 20), Matthews' heroine reflects that her first days of work were the happiest of her girlhood: "She remembered the joy which she felt at her ability to earn money; it gave her a sense of being her own mistress, of being able to hold her own in the world."[4]

Maggie's happy world began to disintegrate, however, when she became infatuated with a Bowery tough named Jim McDermott, who is as insensitive and brutish as the Jimmie and Pete of Crane's *Maggie.* Refusing to break off her relationship with him, she was, like her counterpart in Crane's novella, locked out of her apartment by her stepmother. Under the pernicious influence of Jim, Maggie quit her factory job and began spending her evenings at a Bowery dance hall. When Jim was convicted of a crime and sentenced to jail, Matthews' Maggie found herself as lonely and vulnerable as Crane's after Pete jilted her: "the thing plainest before [Mag O'Donnel] was the Morgue; she was on the way there, and she was going fast, and she knew it" (p. 92).

But this forlorn Maggie did not continue her downward trajectory; her slide toward the abyss was halted by the arrival of Terry, a bartender who is the very "beau ideal of a man" (*Maggie,* p. 19) that Crane's Maggie idealized Pete to be. Terry, the narrator informs us, took pity on Maggie and thrashed Jim when that villain emerged from prison and harassed her; falling in love with the poor girl, he took her to the Tombs and married her as soon as he was able. With a lot of hard work and a bit of luck (good luck, of course, is not to be found in Mag Johnson's indifferent universe), Terry and Maggie were able to buy the saloon that employed Terry.[5]

Thus, like the protagonist of the romantic play that Crane's Maggie attended with Pete, Maggie O'Donnel has marched from poverty to, if not wealth exactly, at least economic security: "Terry was doing well. . . . He was sure to make money; and perhaps in two or three years they might be able to pay off the mortgage on the fixtures. Then they would be rich" (p. 94). As she lies awake in bed in the narrative's present tense, Maggie does indeed have reason to celebrate the Fourth of July.

Melodramatic as is the narrator's account of Maggie's rise from the Hell's Kitchen gutter toward a modest version of the American Dream, this section of the tale is bland in comparison to what follows. When she hears a noise in the room below, Maggie suspects that someone is attempting to rob the saloon safe, which contains her and Terry's life savings; though alone and unarmed, "she was not in the least afraid" (p. 94). Her only course of action, she determines, is to proceed downstairs and call the police on the saloon telephone. When she reaches the phone, however, she finds herself staring into the shifty eyes of her nemesis, Jim: "You try to squeal and I'll shoot—see?" he warns. Undaunted, Maggie picks up the phone, tells the operator that Jim McDermott is in the act of burglarizing her saloon, then faces Jim and cries: "Now shoot, and be damned!" (pp. 96-97). He does, but misses; for some inexplicable reason, she laughs "tauntingly," and he fires again, wounding her in the arm. When the police arrive, she is bloodied and unconscious but not seriously injured, and Jim has fled, without the money he sought to steal. Maggie's American Dream remains intact.

"Plainer than ever before is the duty of the novelist now to set up no false ideals, to erect no impossible standards of strength or courage or virtue, to tell the truth about life as he sees it with his own eyes."[6] So wrote Matthews the literary critic in his essay **"The Study of Fiction"** (1898). Yet in **"Before the Break of Day"** he re-visioned one of American literature's most powerful examples of realistic fiction as a tale of romantic ideals and improbable if not impossible standards of courage; moreover, we find idealized characters and improbable incidents in many other of Matthews' vignettes of the metropolis. Why, one wonders, would Matthews the fiction writer so blatantly violate his own critical standards? The answer, I would suggest, is that Matthews perceived no discrepancy between his critical views and his fictional productions; put simply, he considered **"Before the Break of Day"** to be a more truthful vision of slum life than Crane had constructed in *Maggie.*

Like so many other literary critics of his generation, Matthews was greatly influenced by Hippolyte Taine's theory that the best literature is that which is rooted in and reflects "racial identity." In **"The Study of Fiction,"** Matthews insists that "serious" fiction reveals "race-traits"; and since, he further argues, the Anglo-Saxon "race" is essentially energetic, courageous, and cheerful, truly "Realistic" portraits of American (i.e., Anglo-American) life will emphasize those traits. He even goes so far as to suggest that anyone steeped in American and Spanish literature could have predicted the United States victory in the Spanish-American War![7]

Thus, like Garland—who once stated that Realism and Americanism were virtually synonymous—Matthews believed that Crane's *Maggie* was a "fragment," typical only of the worst elements of the slums.[8] In the dedication to Theodore Roosevelt (one of the professor's closest friends and most ardent supporters) that prefaces *Vignettes of Manhattan,* Matthews expressed his disdain for those New Yorkers who "maligned" the city that he and Roosevelt so loved. Perhaps the professor had Crane in mind when he wrote that dedication. In any case, it is clear that in **"Before the Break of Day"** Matthews set out to correct what he perceived to be Crane's distorted and "unrealistic" vision of the slums and of American "race-traits" in general. Heeding the advice Garland offered Crane in the review of *Maggie,*

Matthews delineated the family on the next street from Rum Alley, living the more typically American life of "heroic purity."

In Matthews' rewriting of *Maggie,* then, we have a vivid illustration of how ideology can govern a writer's perceptions of what is or is not truthful fiction.

NOTES

[1] "An Ambitious French Novel and a Modest American Story," *Arena,* 8 (June 1893), xi-xii; rpt. in Stephen Crane, *Maggie: A Girl of the Streets,* ed. Thomas A. Gullason (New York: Norton, 1979), pp. 144-45. All page references to *Maggie* refer to this edition (a reprint of the 1893 edition of the novella) and will appear in parentheses within the text.

[2] *Stephen Crane: Letters,* ed. R. W. Stallman and Lillian Gilkes (New York: New York Univ. Press, 1960), p. 15. Stallman and Gilkes identify the "very small book" as *Maggie.*

[3] For a sample of Matthews' arguments for a truthful realism and against an invidious romanticism in fiction, see his review of Howells' *Criticism and Fiction* in *Cosmopolitan,* 12 (Nov. 1891), 124-26; and the essays "Romance against Romanticism" and "The Study of Fiction" in his *The Historical Novel and Other Essays* (1901; rpt. Freeport, N.Y.: Books for Libraries Press, 1968).

[4] "Before the Break of Day," in Matthews, *Vignettes of Manhattan* (New York: Harper, 1894), p. 92. Subsequent page references to "Before the Break of Day" refer to this edition of *Vignettes* and will appear parenthetically in the text.

[5] Matthews' description of the saloon's bar reveals that he borrowed details as well as major plot and character elements from Crane's work. Compare Matthews' "The bar curved across the saloon, and behind it the sideboard with its bevelled-edge mirrors lined the two inner walls. The sideboard glittered with glasses built up in tiers, and a lemon lay yellow at the top of every pyramid" (p. 87), to Crane's sketch of the bar in which Pete works: "Upon its shelves rested pyramids of shimmering glasses that were never disturbed. Mirrors set in the face of the sideboard multiplied them. Lemons, oranges and paper napkins . . . sat among the glasses" (p. 34).

[6] "The Study of Fiction," p. 83.

[7] "The Study of Fiction," pp. 98-100. Taine's influence on Matthews' criticism is especially evident in this essay as well as in "The Historical Novel," where Taine is cited (*The Historical Novel,* p. 13).

[8] See Jane Johnson, Introduction, *Crumbling Idols,* by Hamlin Garland (Cambridge; Harvard Univ. Press, 1960), p. xxiii.

Lawrence J. Oliver (essay date 1989)

SOURCE: "Theodore Roosevelt, Brander Matthews, and the Campaign for Literary Americanism," in *American Quarterly,* Vol. 41, No. 1, March, 1989, pp. 93-111.

[In the following essay, Oliver explores Matthews's long friendship with Theodore Roosevelt and the influence of the relationship on his fiction and nonfiction.]

> Yet the fact remains that the greatest work must bear the stamp of originality. In exactly the same way the greatest work must bear the stamp of nationalism. American work must smack of our own soil, mental and moral, no less than physical, or it will have little of permanent value.
>
> —Theodore Roosevelt, "Nationalism in Literature and Art"

No president of the United States was better acquainted with and took a greater interest in the literary canon than Theodore Roosevelt. Though the Harvard-educated Rough Rider strove to project a "cowboy" image to the public, he was at heart a "literary feller," as he confided to his friend Brander Matthews.[1] In Roosevelt's mind, the literary and the political were inextricably linked, as is vividly revealed in a letter he wrote to Matthews in June, 1894.

The letter is worth a close reading. Roosevelt, then Civil Service Commissioner, begins by expressing support for a check on immigration because "we are getting some very undesirable elements now." He then states that he is looking forward to visiting his Dakota ranch in September. That comment leads to a paragraph on Hamlin Garland's *Crumbling Idols* (1894), which Matthews had sent him. Roosevelt admired Garland's depictions of the strenuous life out West, but was displeased by Garland's insistence in *Crumbling Idols* that the literary classics have little to say to the present; in a bit of "rough writing," Roosevelt complains that Garland's "ignorance, crudity, and utter lack of cultivation make him entirely unfit to understand the effect of the great masters of thought [such as Shakespeare, Homer, and Milton] upon the language and upon literature." But if Garland is wrong in arguing that the idols are crumbling, he is absolutely correct, Roosevelt maintains, in trumpeting American literary independence. "We must," exclaims Roosevelt, in words echoing Emerson's "American Scholar," "strike out for ourselves; we must work according to our own ideas, and must free ourselves from the shackles of conventionality." In the next paragraph, Roosevelt denounces the *Yellow Book,* which represents the "last stage of degradation," as well as Henry James, whose "polished, pointless, uninteresting stories about the upper social classes in England make one blush to think that he was once an American." As an antidote to such "diseased" literature, Roosevelt recommends Rudyard Kipling's works, which offer a "fresh, healthy, out-of-doors" vision of life, and the western fiction of Owen Wister (who would later dedicate *The Virginian* to Roosevelt).[2]

Roosevelt's letter counterpoints undesirable aliens to the strenuous life of the western frontier, and "decadent" foreign and expatriate writers to such "wholesome" ones as Wister and the imperialist Kipling; at its center, a strong endorsement of American literary nationalism. Here is the essence of Roosevelt's political-literary ideology, which he would fully articulate in such essays as "The Strenuous Life" (1900), "Race Decadence" (1911), and "Nationalism in Literature and Art" (1916). Richard H. Collin's recent assertion that the formulator of the "big stick" foreign policy was not a territorial expansionist is debatable, but he is undeniably correct in arguing that Roosevelt waged throughout his life a vigorous campaign for American *cultural* imperialism.[3] That campaign, however, had to be won at home before it could be exported abroad. Though the quest for cultural independence had been underway since the American Revolution and had culminated in the 1830s and 1840s, many of Roosevelt's contemporaries shared his perception that the Emersonian tradition of literary Americanism was being threatened by a resurgence (most notable among cultivated "Easterners") of the "colonial" attitude that worshipped European and denigrated American culture, as well as by the influx of those "undesirable" Southern and Eastern European immigrants who, even if they could read English, would view the classic American texts through alien eyes.[4] Roosevelt found many allies in his campaign for literary nationalism (including Wister and Garland), but he valued none more than the man who was for over three decades his literary advisor as well as trusted friend, Brander Matthews.

By the time Roosevelt wrote the 1894 letter to Matthews, New York City had dethroned Boston as the nation's literary capital, and Matthews was one of its most influential men of letters. Professor of literature and drama at Columbia University from 1892 to 1924, Matthews played a significant role in the expansion of American literature in the academy and in the formation of the American literary canon during the 1890s and first decade of the twentieth century. In 1892, for example, he developed one of the first college courses in American literature, and his *An Introduction to the Study of American Literature* (1896) was among the earliest texts in the field. Intimate friends with Mark Twain and William Dean Howells, Matthews published numerous essays and reviews defending them and other realist writers during the "Realism War" of the 1880s and 1890s. His role as Roosevelt's literary mentor began as early as 1888, when, as an advisory editor for Longmans, Green & Company's American branch, he persuaded Roosevelt to write a history of New York City for that publisher's "Historic Towns" series.[5] Matthews was active in many literary organizations, serving as president of the Modern Language Association in 1910 and of the National Institute of Arts and Letters during 1913-14. His voluminous scholarly writings include a chapter in the *Cambridge History of American Literature* (1917-21). The senior editor of that landmark in the history of the canon was William P. Trent, whose appointment to Columbia's faculty in 1900 was sponsored by Matthews and by the governor of New York then, Theodore Roosevelt.[6] Trent's appointment was one of numerous instances in which the politician and the professor collaborated to ensure that American literature and literary criticism would promote the ideology of "true Americanism," a "manly" ideology that the Rough Rider repeatedly set in contrast to the "over-civilized, over-sensitive, over-refined" culture of the Eastern establishment.[7] The behind-the-scenes maneuvering of Matthews and Roosevelt provides an instructive glimpse into the politics of canon formation.

. . . . .

Ironically, Matthews's life almost perfectly conforms to that of the caricatured "Easterner" in Roosevelt's writings. The only child of a wealthy cotton speculator (related on his mother's side to the Pilgrim governor William Brewster) and a New Orleans belle, Matthews was, as he candidly admits in his autobiography, raised to be a professional millionaire.[8] Seven years old when the family moved from New Orleans, the place of his birth, to Manhattan's Fifth Avenue, Matthews spent his youth among the genteel class; he attended private academies and enjoyed extended visits to London and Paris. Though the senior Matthews lost his fortune in the Panic of 1873, just as his twenty-one-year old, Columbia-educated son was about to help administer it, the latter never fell from the upper ranks of New York society. The small inheritance he received from his mother and his substantial earnings from magazine journalism allowed him to maintain his aristocratic lifestyle. He lived in fashionable New York neighborhoods, spent summers in Europe or Narragansett, and helped found several clubs that formed the center of New York's social and literary life during the Gilded Age.

Matthews's only "Western" experience occurred the summer of his seventeenth year. With a friend and a teacher who acted as escort, he toured the Great Lakes and upper Mississippi River region. Matthews was neither a soldier nor a hunter (in one letter, Roosevelt remarks that he would enjoy Matthews's company on a hunting trip but knows that he is "not sufficiently a devotee of 'le sport' to go to it"). He and his wife were the parents of one child, a daughter. The eminent professor, in short, was hardly the "good fighter and good breeder" the Rough Rider believed essential to English-speaking white men if they were to avoid the "race suicide" he so dreaded: "If all our nice friends in Beacon Street, and Newport, and Fifth Avenue, and Philadelphia have one child, or no child at all," Roosevelt once remarked to Wister, "while all the Finnegans, Hooligans, Antonios, Mandelbaums and Rabinskis have eight, or nine, or ten—it's simply a question of the multiplication table."[9]

While Roosevelt was charging San Juan (actually Kettle) Hill, Matthews remained stationed in Manhattan, sending the Colonel reading material. But if he was not on board the ship that transported Roosevelt to Cuba and national prominence, he was, as Roosevelt put it, "on deck" when it came to "Americanism." The campaign to save the country from the pernicious influences emanating from Wall Street, labor union halls, and "decadent" writers such as Oscar Wilde, Emile Zola, and Lyof Tolstoy required not the sword but the pen. Though Roosevelt himself did not shrink from action on the verbal firing line, he considered Matthews to be his better in this sphere: "I decidedly envy you your reputation as being the champion of American methods and ways in literature, in spelling [Matthews spearheaded the vain attempt to simplify the English spelling system], and in all other directions," he once wrote his friend.[10]

Indeed, Matthews's literary efforts ran in many directions. Though primarily a scholar and critic of drama, his writings covered matters literary, social, and political. He authored three novels, several plays, and numerous short stories, one volume of which (*Vignettes of Manhattan* [1894]) was dedicated to Roosevelt. Most of Matthews's fictions were situated in New York, and explored manners and mores of the genteel class. In style and tone they exemplified the "polish and daintiness" that Roosevelt set in disparaging contrast to the art of Wister, Kipling, and other writers whose tales of "strong men" bore no traces of a "cloistered intellect."[11] But if Matthews's fictions were "genteel" rather than rugged on the surface, they were Rooseveltian at the core, their subtexts promoting Roosevelt's belief that plutocrats, anarchists, and "liberated" women were leading the country to ruin. Matthews's first novel, *His Father's Son* (1895), for example, indicted the materialist values and corrupt practices of wealthy Wall Street investors. His second, *A Confident To-morrow* (1899), suggested that radical Socialists were as pernicious to the national health as the despised plutocrats. *The Action and the Word* (1900), his final novel, caricatured the New Woman and implicitly endorsed Roosevelt's conviction that "the question of woman's voting is a thousandth or a millionth part as important as the question of keeping, and where necessary reviving, among the women of this country, the realization that their great work must be done in the home."[12] Certainly Roosevelt—who denounced Howells for projecting a "jaundiced view of life" in his fictions—would have agreed wholeheartedly with the progressive-minded hero of *A Confident To-morrow* when he asserts that "it has always seemed to me that the way to make the world better is to tell people it is getting better, and to prove it to them; to encourage them and not to discourage them; to inspire hope and confidence and energy to fight a good fight, with a certain victory in the distance."[13]

Only once did the professor depart from an urban East Coast setting and attempt to portray the strenuous life of the American West. Titled **"Memories,"** the story (published in 1889) is situated in the Northwest at a fort named, not insignificantly, "Roosevelt." Here U.S. troopers must battle not only the red men but fierce winter weather. As he sits by the fireside during a blizzard, the protagonist Robert Douglas reflects on his days at an Eastern military academy, where the older boys made life painful for him—but not nearly as painful as his unrequited love for a beautiful young woman who shattered his soul by marrying an Italian nobleman. She has recently died, he has learned, of an illness caught at a costume ball in Rome at which she represented "America." Douglas's reveries are broken, however, when news arrives that two children have been lost in the storm. In the howling wilderness he and nine volunteers (connected by a rope that symbolizes group solidarity) search for the children. "There was no use in repining; a strong man does not die of a broken heart. Work there is in plenty in the world for a man to do, if he be but willing," declares the narrator.[14]

Upon reading the story, Roosevelt wrote Matthews: "As soon as I saw your article, I knew that you had written the piece about which you spoke to me two years ago. . . . I was electrified when I struck the name of the fort. It may be prejudice on my part, but I really think it is one of the best of your stories, and I am very glad to have my name connected with it in no matter how small a way." Roosevelt would have admired the piece even if the fort bore another name, for the tale dramatizes the heroic ideal of the "strenuous life" and fulfills the literary prescription he once gave Wister, "Leave your reader with the feeling that life, after all, does-go-on." Moreover, **"Memories"** would have struck a deeply personal chord in Roosevelt, for there are obvious parallels between Matthews's fictional hero and his real-life friend. Five years before the story was published, Roosevelt had lost his beloved wife (and, almost simultaneously, his mother); deeply grieved, he headed to the Dakota territory, where he attempted to lose his sorrows in physical labors of ranch life. Like Douglas, he did not wallow in pity. After "finding himself" out West, Roosevelt returned East and resumed his patriotic duty running for mayor of New York City in 1886 (the year before Matthews discussed the outline of the story with him). **"Memories"** is thus a thinly veiled tribute to Roosevelt's personal triumph over the morbid self-depression or neurasthenia that, in the eyes of many late nineteenth-century Americans, seemed to be a national contagion.[15]

But as much as Roosevelt admired Matthews's fictions, he valued his essays and reviews even more. He was particularly impressed by Matthews's performance in *Americanisms and Briticisms* (1892). Though the eleven articles collected in the volume cover a wide range of topics, together they form a polemic against the "colonial" mind as it manifested itself not only in English condescension toward Brother Jonathan but in certain American writers' excessive deference to British opinion. Kermit Vanderbilt has recently observed that Matthews believed British literature was superior to his own country's. But he was hardly the staunch anglophile that Vanderbilt suggests, as *Americanisms and Briticisms* makes clear.[16]

"Americanisms and Briticisms," the collection's title essay, is a spirited refutation of the view, widely proclaimed by English critics and journalists of the day, that the Americans—their professional humorists, in particular—were "mongrelizing" the English language. Arguing that, since language is always evolving, a fixed and "pure" English language never has existed, and demonstrating that many of the degrading "Americanisms" cited by English critics are actually "Briticisms" (that is, of British origin), Matthews proclaims: "The English language is not bankrupt that it needs to have a receiver appointed; it is quite capable of minding its own business without the care of a committee of Englishmen." The attacks from across the Atlantic, he charges, result not from linguistic inquiry but from England's supercilious attitude toward Americans, the same attitude, he adds, against which Fenimore Cooper had struggled earlier in the century.[17]

Essentially a defense of American speech and literature, **"Americanisms and Briticisms"** is not politically innocent. Like Roosevelt, Matthews was an imperialist at heart. In his essay **"American Character,"** for example, he speaks proudly of the "warlike temper, the aggressiveness, the imperialistic sentiment" that is "in our blood." What might be called the "manifest destiny" subtext of **"Americanisms and Briticisms"** surfaces when Matthews announces that "we may be sure that branch of our Anglo-Saxon stock will use the best English, and will perhaps see its standards of speech accepted by the other branches, which is most vigorous physically, mentally, and morally, which has the most intelligence, and which knows its duty best and does it most-fearlessly." It is easy to see why the author of "The Strenuous Life" would recommend the essay to Henry Cabot Lodge and would declare (in a review of another of Matthews's works) that **"Americanisms and Briticisms"** is "by far the most noteworthy critical or literary essay which has been published by any American writer for a score of years."[18]

Nor is it surprising that Roosevelt would admire the professor's essay on Fenimore Cooper in *Americanisms and Briticisms*. Roosevelt loved Cooper's fiction, and the Leatherstocking novels were, as Richard Slotkin emphasizes, a shaping influence on Roosevelt's myth-ideological system. Roosevelt's ideology, in turn, seems to have shaped Matthews's perceptions of Cooper: ignoring Cooper's aristocratic temperament, his bitter quarrel with his countrymen, and the pessimistic vision of such later novels as *The Crater*, Matthews recreates Cooper in Roosevelt's image when he states that Cooper's two defining traits are a "hearty, robust, out-of-doors and open-air wholesomeness" and an "intense Americanism—ingrained, abiding, and dominant."[19]

In contrast to Cooper's "stalwart Americanism," the outspoken essayist Agnes Repplier (1855-1950) represents the "colonial" attitude that is targeted throughout *Americanisms and Briticisms*. Philadelphia's most prominent woman of letters, Repplier was as erudite and articulate as any critic of her day, but her essays during the late 1880s and early 1890s virtually ignore native writers. As anglophilic as her good friend Andrew Lang, the British essayist whose denigrating remarks on American culture always enraged Roosevelt, Repplier chose not to participate in the campaign for literary Americanism. Matthews makes disparaging references to Lang and Repplier in an essay lauding Henry Cabot Lodge's *Studies in History* and Thomas Wentworth Higginson's *The New World and the New Book,* both of which deplore American intellectual dependence on Great Britain. He notes with satisfaction, for example, that one of Higginson's verbal "transatlantic darts" struck Lang, drawing a "cry of pain" from him. Though he admits that Higginson's aggressive nationalism might seem excessive to some, Matthews insists that all Americans would profit from reading the book, especially Miss Repplier. While acknowledging that Repplier's essays are often brilliantly expressed, they are marked, Matthews charges, by a grovelling deference to English opinion. "Although a Philadelphian," he gibes at one point, "she has apparently never heard of the Declaration of Independence." Perhaps, he continues, "some of Miss Repplier's Philadelphia friends could take this 'British sparrow' hatched in the United States to Independence Hall the next Fourth of July, and on the way home purchase her copies of Higginson's and Lodge's books." That Matthews's hostility toward Repplier may have been a reaction to her gender as well as to her "colonialism" is suggested by his remark, "In literature as in some other things a woman's opinion is often personal and accidental; it depends on the way the book has happened to strike her."[20] Women, in other words, read capriciously rather than critically.

In his study of Repplier, George Stewart Stokes notes that though Roosevelt and Repplier developed a mutual respect after she was introduced to the former president in 1914, he "may not have approved entirely" of her. That is an understatement, for Roosevelt initially shared Matthews's disdain for Repplier's anglophilism, and his contemptuous remarks about her, like Matthews's, reveal the fear of feminization lurking beneath the "manly Americanism" both men sought to promote. In one letter to Matthews, for example, Roosevelt declares that "Miss Repplier, whose original essays were no good, is beginning to write like Andrew Lang gone crazy"; in another, he refers to her as a "female idiot" and a "sporadic she-fool."[21]

Roosevelt's denunciations of Repplier went beyond private correspondence. After reading a draft of Matthews's essay which sniped at Repplier, Roosevelt wrote to express his admiration for it, adding that the "cringing provincialism and lack of patriotism" of Repplier's recently published "The Praises of War" (*Atlantic Monthly,* December 1891) so irritated him that he was about to launch his own attack against her in an article he intended to submit to Howells, editor of *Cosmopolitan* at the time. His piece, he added, would not be merely a criticism of Repplier, but rather a discourse on Americanism, "using her partly as a peg and partly as an awful object lesson." Several months later, Roosevelt informed Matthews that he had written Howells about "having you see the article—though I am ashamed of myself for doing so," a comment which suggests that Roosevelt sought (and no doubt received) Matthews's help in preparing the essay

for *Cosmopolitan,* where it appeared under the title "A Colonial Survival" in December, 1892.[22]

Roosevelt does not call Repplier a "female idiot" in "Colonial Survival," but that is precisely what he implies. After firing salvos at several of his favorite targets—Kipling, the vulgar rich, effete literary men, "brainless women of fashion," "émigré novelists," and all Americans who were "by education and instinct entirely un-American"—Roosevelt turns his attention to "The Praises of War."[23] Though in accord with Repplier's attempt to analyze literary treatments of war and patriotism, he complains that her critiques seem "unreal" because she delights "only in battles that are won by the expenditure of nothing more violent than rose-water"; her perspective, in other words, is feminine. Only a man who has the capacity to experience the "joy of battle." Roosevelt continues, "knows that he feels [that joy] when the wolf begins to rise in his heart; he does not then shrink from blood and sweat, or deem that they mar the fight; he revels in them, in the toil, the pain and the danger, as but setting off the triumph." Seeking to refute Repplier's argument that battles seldom generate first-rate literature, he points to such "immortal tales of prowess" as the *Nibelungenlied,* Chaucer's "Knight's Tale," Longfellow's "Saga of Olaf," and, of course, the battle fictions of Fenimore Cooper (a writer to be "read and reread again and again"). Repplier's remark that the American Civil War evoked only doggerel poetry is, he exclaims, "colonialism gone crazy."

Roosevelt and Matthews's skirmish with Repplier blazed for some time, but by 1894 Roosevelt felt that their female foe had been vanquished: "Do you know," he wrote Matthews, when calling attention to Repplier's complimentary allusion to one of the professor's short fictions, "I think you have had a decidedly chastening effect on that young lady?"[24] Whether Matthews had, as Roosevelt implies, verbally beaten Repplier into submission to their views is arguable, but Repplier did in fact come to embrace militant Americanism. In fact, when Roosevelt later waged his campaign against Woodrow Wilson and the policy of neutrality before the United States entered World War I, Repplier was firmly on the side of the Warrior against the Priest. In her *Counter-Currents* (1916), a collection of nine essays previously published in the *Atlantic Monthly,* she stridently mocks Woodrow Wilson's isolationism and pacifism; deplores American "loss of nerve"; argues that Christianity and war have "walked together down the centuries"; and, in the essay titled "Americanism," expresses her support for "Americanization Day" programs and warns that unassimilated immigrants threaten national security.[25] The author Roosevelt once disparaged for her lack of patriotism and "rose-water" view of battle was now writing like a Rough Rider.

"Colonial Survival" was not the only Roosevelt writing that Matthews read in draft and helped through the publication process. The Rough Rider often leaned on the professor's genteel arm for editorial assistance. "The only thing that unnerves President Roosevelt," wrote Joseph Gilder after the Colonel assumed the presidency, "is literary composition," and in his correspondence with Matthews, Roosevelt reveals the anxiety that plagued him when he performed as a "literary feller." Expressing, for example, his frustration over his inability to "get the hang" of writing book reviews, he in one letter confides to Matthews: "I struggle and plunge frightfully, and when written my words don't express my thought"; in another letter to the professor, he assumes the posture of admiring pupil, remarking that he has not "sat under your teaching so long entirely in vain."[26]

In the preface to the history of New York City that Matthews solicited from him in 1888, Roosevelt trumpeted the theme that would preoccupy him throughout his literary career—"the necessity for a feeling of broad, radical, and intense Americanism." Of course, it is easier to urge one to practice Americanism that it is to precisely define the term, and when Roosevelt finally did attempt such definition in an 1894 essay titled "True Americanism," he sent an outline of the piece to Matthews, penciling at the top, "How will this do?"[27] Matthews also critiqued a draft of Roosevelt's "Politics in a Democracy," and advised Roosevelt and Lodge on how to make their *Hero Tales from American History* more appealing to teachers.[28] As late as 1915, Roosevelt was writing Matthews asking for his assistance in submitting an essay to *Harper's Monthly.* And when he was not reading Roosevelt's writings on Americanism, the professor was attending his friend's lectures on the topic: in the letter in which he speaks of Matthews as being "on deck," Roosevelt, for example, thanks Matthews for attending an address he gave in Boston, remarking that "the perpetual wonder both to myself and the hard-featured Lodge is that you should come to any of my lectures."[29]

In 1891 the "hard-featured Lodge" was among the eminent politicians and men of letters called upon to speak at a banquet celebrating the American Copyright League's eighth anniversary and, more important, the recent passage of a new copyright act. Lodge may have hyperbolized when he called the bill a "monument and a milestone in the march of American civilization," but by largely eliminating the problem of book piracy, the Copyright Act of 1891 was a crucial victory in the campaign for American literary independence.[30] Neither Lodge nor any of the other speakers at the banquet mentioned Matthews or Roosevelt, but both men were "on deck" throughout the long and often bitter struggle to get the legislation enacted.

The first meeting of the American Copyright League was held at Matthews's home on April 16, 1883. As the League organized its lobbying efforts, Matthews became chair of the subcommittee on publicity. In that capacity, he wrote several essays advocating an international copyright act, including **"American Authors and British Pirates,"** which the League published as a pamphlet in 1889, and **"The Evolution of Copyright,"** which appeared in the December 1890 number of the *Political Science Quarterly.* Matthews sent a copy of the latter

article to Civil Service Commissioner Roosevelt, a fellow League member, who was so impressed by the piece that he immediately gave it to Thomas B. Reed, Speaker of the House. According to Matthews, the essay converted Reed to the League's cause and influenced his decision to grant the bill a vote during the close of the 1891 Congressional session. However, before the bill was passed in 1891, it met stiff opposition from its adversaries. On February 10, 1890, Roosevelt wrote Matthews: "Can't you get down here [Washington] some time this winter? I would like you to see some of our 'men in action' in congress. They are not always polished, but they are strong, and as a whole I think them pretty good fellows. I swear by Tom Reed; and I tell you what, all copyright men ought to stand by him." As the congressional debates continued, Roosevelt became increasingly frustrated, so much so that he urged Matthews to "write a scathing article . . . holding up *by name* the chief congressional foes of copyright to merited ridicule" (emphasis Roosevelt's). Matthews wisely ignored the suggestion of his pugnacious friend and kept his essays on copyright "polished" rather than "strong."[31]

Roosevelt and Matthews's literary politics on behalf of "true Americanism" extended beyond the halls of Congress and into the schoolrooms later in the decade, for both men strongly believed that students be taught American literature and study textbooks which would, as Roosevelt and Lodge's *Hero Tales from American History* aimed to do, promote the "manly" virtues and a strong sense of nationalism. As noted earlier, Matthews's course in American Literature at Columbia was among the first college courses to focus on American writers. Matthews sent copies of the course syllabus and examinations to Roosevelt, who expressed praise for course topics (he was particularly pleased to see Lincoln on the reading list) and test questions. Within a year after Matthews assumed his position at Columbia, Roosevelt urged him to write a "school hand book of American literature," a "series of reviews . . . of our different American authors and schools of literature. If you would only do this . . . you would make a book of the utmost permanent value of interest."[32]

Matthews undertook the project. First published serially in the juvenile magazine *St. Nicholas,* the group of biographical-critical essays—their appeal to students enhanced by sketches or photographs of the authors discussed and reproductions of original manuscript pages—appeared in textbook form as. *An Introduction to the Study of American Literature* in 1896. In eighteen chapters, the book surveys the history of American literature from the Puritans to the late nineteenth-century realists, the treatment afforded individual writers reflecting the literary biases of Matthews and his milieu. Thus the poets Fitz-Greene Halleck and Joseph Rodman Drake and the historian Francis Parkman (whom Roosevelt idolized) enjoy chapters unto themselves; whereas Whitman (whose verse, Matthews states, is "irregular, but often . . . beautifully rhythmic") and Melville are relegated to the section on minor writers.[33]

The year before the textbook appeared, Matthews had published a revised edition of his ***Poems of American Patriotism*** (1882; 1895), an anthology of poems including "Paul Revere's Ride," "Old Ironsides," "O Captain! My Captain!" and "The Star-Spangled Banner." When Roosevelt received the book, he exclaimed that it ought to be distributed, copy for copy, with his and Lodge's *Hero Tales* "as a missionary tract." That ***Introduction to the Study of American Literature*** is likewise a "missionary tract" for "true Americanism" is evident at the outset; the introduction announces that "there is such a thing as Americanism" and that it has left its indelible mark on the writings of the American authors in the book. Matthews informs his intended audience of students that a language can be only as strong and vibrant as its people; then, echoing the cry of literary imperialism with which he closed **"Americanisms and Briticisms,"** he proclaims that since the English-speaking "race" is steadily spreading across the globe, English literature is bound to expand. Moreover, as the people of the United States are as vigorous and aggressive as their British cousins, "it seems likely that hereafter the Americans, rather than the British, will be recognized as the chief of the English-speaking peoples."[34]

Like many critics during his day, Matthews accepted Hippolyte Taine's theory that great works of art project "race traits"; in an essay addressed to teachers of American literature, Matthews declared that it was their duty to "seize and make plain to . . . pupils the [race] characteristics" revealed in literary works.[35] Though the essays composing his introduction to American literature give attention to literary merit, Matthews is preoccupied throughout with illuminating the admirable "race traits" he detects in the lives and works of the authors discussed. As a group, our literary ancestors were, Matthews implies, morally wholesome (with the exception, of course, of Poe, who is portrayed as a genius destroyed by his depravity), good-humored, sturdy, optimistic, idealistic yet practical, egalitarian, and, of course, intensely patriotic. James Russell Lowell, for example, is described as a "true American, not only in his stalwart patriotism in the hour of trial, but in his loving acceptance of the doctrine of human equality." Oliver Wendell Holmes is lauded for his kindliness and "sunny sagacity." Ralph Waldo Emerson's essays ever reveal a "sturdy and wholesome Americanism." Henry David Thoreau's *Walden* is commended for its "wholesome warning against the pursuit of luxury." And Whitman—whom Roosevelt considered a "warped, although a rugged genius of American poetry"—is described as an "intense American" whose "stalwart verse" looked to the future with "splendid confidence."[36] That Matthews and Roosevelt praise the "obscene" author of *Leaves of Grass* testifies that when their Victorian prudery came into conflict with their devotion to literary nationalism, the latter dominated.

Though Matthews's textbook is not the work of "utmost permanent value" Roosevelt hoped it would be, it was clearly a success from the author's standpoint with sales reaching the quarter-million mark within twenty-five years after its release. A significant portion of those sales, no doubt, could be attributed to the sterling review the text received in *The Bookman* shortly after publication. ***Introduction to the Study of American Literature,*** asserts the *Bookman* reviewer, is "a piece of work as good of its kind as any American scholar ever had in his hands." Furthermore, "the principles upon which Mr. Matthews insists with such quiet force and good taste are those which must be adopted, not only by every student of American writings, but by every American writer if he is going to do work that is really worth doing." The reviewer finds the sketch of Cooper to be "capital," and concurs with Matthews's assertion that Parkman is the greatest of American historians. The author of the review is Roosevelt—who wrote the critique at Matthews's request, and received his assistance in getting it published.[37]

This was not the only case of literary back-scratching between the two men. Shortly after Roosevelt's *New York* appeared, Matthews published an unsigned essay titled **"New York as a Historic Town"** in the *Century Magazine.* Though the piece is ostensibly concerned with establishing New York's historical importance, it is actually an advertisement for Roosevelt's book; in a letter to Matthews, Roosevelt expressed his gratitude for the piece, remarking that the *Century* was the best place to promote his book. And Matthews's *Bookman* review of Roosevelt's *Autobiography* and *History as Literature* is as lavishly praiseworthy of those works as Roosevelt's is of Matthews's American literature text. Matthews proclaims that since Roosevelt's memoirs are as interesting and as representatively American as Benjamin Franklin's, they should be read by every American citizen. If Roosevelt's *Autobiography* rivals Franklin's, his *History as Literature,* Matthews declares, places him in the good company of Parkman. Reminding his audience that Roosevelt was an elected president of the American Historical Association and that *The Winning of the West* "may be considered as a necessary continuation of Parkman's great work," Matthews maintains that the essays forming *History as Literature* reveal Roosevelt's "possession of the interpreting imagination which can survey the whole field of history past and present" in order to find the laws of human history.[38]

Matthews's efforts to enhance his friend's political and literary reputation did not cease with Roosevelt's death in 1919. Several months after Roosevelt was laid to rest, Matthews, for example, published an article in *Outlook* magazine that eulogizes the Square-Deal president as being the equal of Jefferson and Lincoln in practical idealism, erudition, devotion to democracy, and moral character. Though certain of his comments inadvertently reveal Roosevelt's bullying self-righteousness (as, for instance, when we are told that he sought to make others obey his moral code, "even if they did not believe it"), Matthews's purpose throughout is to justify Roosevelt's ways to man. The professor also delivered the commemorative tribute to Roosevelt at the American Academy of Arts and Letters, in which he praised the late historian's "plumbing vision," likened his oratorical powers to those of a Roman statesman, and again compared *Winning of the West* to Parkman's history. Roosevelt's writing style, Matthews informed the Academy, was "masculine and vascular"; at his best, Roosevelt achieved the ideal—"the speech of the people in the mouth of the scholar." And when Joseph Bishop's biography of Roosevelt appeared, Matthews reviewed it at length in the *New York Times,* asserting that "Mr. Bishop has given us a work which does for one President of the United States what was done for an earlier President by the publication of Grant's 'Personal Memoirs.' And neither of these great men would object to the comparison."[39]

Matthews's culminating tribute to Roosevelt the "literary feller" is **"Theodore Roosevelt as a Man of Letters,"** which first appeared in *Muncey's* magazine (March, 1919), and was later reprinted as the introduction to the volume of literary essays in Roosevelt's collected *Works.* Drawing together the threads of praise he wove into his earlier adulations of Roosevelt, Matthews here idolizes his deceased friend. Surveying completely Roosevelt's literary accomplishments, Matthews declares that Roosevelt's career was fuller and richer than Franklin's; that his *Great Adventure* equals Lincoln's "Gettysburg Address" in its attainment of the "serener heights of pure literature"; that, like Parkman, he was a "severely trained scientific investigator" as well as a "born story-teller," his *Winning of the West* exemplary in its "absolute impartiality" and "manly" prose; and that the "pure fire of patriotism" burning in his political addresses roused the nation to "do our full duty in the war which saved civilization from the barbarian."[40]

While Matthews was attempting to canonize Roosevelt, the canon and its keepers faced fierce assault by H. L. Mencken, Van Wyck Brooks, Ludwig Lewisohn, and their fellow "Mohawks," as Stuart Sherman (one of the *Cambridge History of American Literature* team of editors) derisively labeled them in an essay defending Matthews. The revolt started as early as 1910 (the year in which Matthews was elected president of the Modern Language Association), but it gained full force following World War I. In 1898 Matthews could write that, though he lamented the reckless jingoism displayed by some of his countrymen, he believed the Spanish-American conflict would produce a "welding effect" on the nation and would strengthen the national fiber. "In a community as wealth-seeking as ours," he contends, "it is well that the warlike virtues have a chance to show themselves now and again." At about the same time, Roosevelt, who once publicly declared that a "just war is in the long run far better for a man's soul than the most prosperous peace," was expressing his hope that England would colonize all Africa—by force where necessary—so as to establish a splendid "race for all time." But the slaughter wreaked by the Great War had a divisive rather than welding effect on the country. Members of the "lost generation" who had witnessed the carnage perceived not a splendid "race for all time" but a civilization that seemed, as Brooks expressed it in "Toward a National Culture" (1917), to be "falling into a void." He no doubt had Roosevelt in mind

when he criticized the intellectually immature "old boys" whose thoughtless sense of nationalism drove the country to war. The United States, Brooks concluded, must in the future offer the world "something better than what is at present called 'Americanism.' For two generations the most sensitive minds in Europe . . . have summed up their mistrust of the future in that one word. . . . The shame of this is a national shame, and one that the war, with all the wealth it has brought us, has infinitely accentuated."[41]

"The accepted canons in letters and . . . the accepted canon lawyers" must be overthrown, declared Brooks's champion, Mencken, in the opening essay of *Prejudices Second Series* (1920), a diatribe against Matthews and his fellow academic "Prussians" who fueled the recent war fever with "bogus history, bogus philosophy, bogus idealism, bogus heroics." The next essay in the volume is a verbal "autopsy" on the politician and military hero who, in Mencken's eyes, personified all that was "bogus" in American culture—Theodore Roosevelt. Between Roosevelt's death in 1919 and Matthews's in 1929, Mencken and his band of "immigrant iconoclasts," as he referred to them, succeeded in placing writers whom Roosevelt would judge "morbid" or "decadent" (for example, Poe, Melville, and Dreiser) at the center of the canon and in banishing or at least marginalizing many of the authors privileged by Matthews's *Introduction to the Study of American Literature* and the *Cambridge History of American Literature.* This re-visioning of the canon, however, was not a repudiation but actually a continuation of the literary nationalism that inspired Roosevelt and Matthews. Thus we find Mencken, for example, invoking the spirit of "The American Scholar" as he launches his attack on the professors and the "genteel" tradition for which they stood.[42] But where Roosevelt and Matthews associated "true Americanism" with such Anglo (or "Western") "race traits" as manly courage, patriotism, moral wholesomeness, and optimism, Mencken and Brooks identified the authentically American with nonconformity, protest, subversiveness, alienation[43]—and also with *aliens,* with the immigrants who were streaming through the gates of Ellis Island at the time. Turning Roosevelt's theory of "race decadence" on its head, Mencken argues that the "Anglo-Saxon strain, second-rate at the start, has started to degenerate steadily to lower levels." Consequently, it was up to the immigrants, whose sensibilities had not been thwarted by a repressive Puritanism, to revitalize the desiccated state of American letters. The canon, Mencken charges, had become feeble precisely because Matthews and other Anglo-American "canon lawyers" worshipped mediocre but patriotic writers like Wister and Garland, while excluding such distinctively American artists as Dreiser and Eugene O'Neill, whose "sturdy animality" and probing of moral decay offend the *bourgeois* mind. Delivering his *coup de grâce,* Mencken contends that the guardians of the canon never really freed themselves from the shackles of Anglophilism, "Despite all the current high-fallutin about melting pots and national destinies the United States remains almost as much an English colonial possession, intellectually and spiritually, as it was on July 3, 1776."[44] After their thirty-years' crusade for American literary independence, Matthews and Roosevelt were indicted as colonial-minded impediments to the development of a vibrant American literature.

That accusation, of course, was not entirely just: the campaign for literary nationalism did result in the growth and influence of American literature, especially of realist fiction. But, as Emerson said, each generation must write (and, one might add, canonize) its own books. To reshape the American literary tradition to fit their ideology, Mencken and the immigrant iconoclasts had to crumble the idols of the Progressive Era. Roosevelt, needless to say, was too monumental a figure to completely crumble (indeed, he continues to be idolized by some historians today, as Richard Collin's book testifies), but Matthews's reputation was so pulverized by the "Mohawk" assault that, despite his prominent stature during his own times, he all but disappeared from American literary history after his death in 1929.

. . . . .

Today, some seventy years after Mencken launched his attack on Matthews, Roosevelt, and the *Cambridge History of American Literature,* new histories of American literature by Cambridge and Columbia University Presses reshape the canon, invigorating it, according to some "canon lawyers," vitiating it, according to others.[45] The debate over the canon, however, has taken a new turn: a growing number of critics, many of them influenced by poststructuralist literary theories, are challenging the very existence of a "distinctively American" literature. Arguing, for example, that in any *literary* history, works of literature must be situated in a linguistic (for example, English language) rather than national (United States) tradition, William C. Spengemann has contended that the "reigning theory of American literature as an independent, autochthonous, unique collection of writings with a history of its own appears to be little more than a political fiction."[46] Should those who embrace Spengemann's position (which is as political as the one it seeks to depose) ultimately prevail, the campaign for literary Americanism will have met its final defeat.

NOTES

[1] Roosevelt to Matthews, 5 Oct. 1888, Brander Matthews Papers, Columbia University, New York. The Brander Matthews Papers at Columbia University include over 250 pieces of correspondence from Roosevelt to Matthews, mostly unpublished; permission to quote from the correspondence granted by Columbia University. The earliest dated letter in this collection was written by Roosevelt on 1 Oct. 1888, but its tone and content suggest that the two men were on familiar terms by this time. It is possible that Matthews and Roosevelt first met when they were children, for Matthews remarks in his autobiography that as a boy he lived for a time on the same New York street as the Roosevelts (*These Many Years: Recollections of a New Yorker* [New York, 1917], 165).

Roosevelt's literary career has been the subject of scholarly attention from his own times to the present. See, for example, Joseph B. Gilder, "A Man of Letters in the White House," *Critic* 29 (1901): 401-09; Henry A. Beers, *Four Americans: Roosevelt, Hawthorne, Emerson, Whitman* (1919; reprint, Freeport, N.Y., 1968); Charles Fenton, "Theodore Roosevelt as an American Man of Letters," *Western Humanities Review* 13 (1959): 369-74; Edmund Morris, *The Rise of Theodore Roosevelt* (New York, 1979); Aloysius A. Norton, *Theodore Roosevelt* (Boston, 1980); and Richard Slotkin, "Nostalgia and Progress: Theodore Roosevelt's Myth of the Frontier," *American Quarterly* 33 (1981): 608-37. Surprisingly, only Norton mentions Matthews's literary relationship with Roosevelt (28).

[2] Roosevelt, *The Letters of Theodore Roosevelt,* ed. Elting E. Morison, 8 vols. (Cambridge, Mass., 1951-54), 1:389-90.

[3] Richard H. Collin, *Theodore Roosevelt, Culture, Diplomacy, and Expansion: A New View of American Imperialism* (Baton Rouge, 1985).

[4] Benjamin T. Spencer, *The Quest for Nationality: An American Literary Campaign* (Syracuse, 1957), 300.

[5] Roosevelt, *The Works of Theodore Roosevelt: National Edition,* ed. Herman Hagedorn, 20 vols. (New York, 1926), 10:359.

[6] Kermit Vanderbilt, *American Literature and the Academy: The Roots, Growth, and Maturity of a Profession* (Philadelphia, 1986), 7. The evolution and significance of the *Cambridge History of American Literature* are the subject of Book One of Vanderbilt's massive study, which makes more than a dozen references to Matthews and includes a photograph of him (238). Matthews's relationship with Howells and his efforts on behalf of the realists during the "Realism War" are examined in Lawrence J. Oliver's "Brander Matthews and the Dean," forthcoming in *American Literary Realism.*

[7] Roosevelt, "True Americanism," *Forum,* Apr. 1894; reprint *Works* 13:19.

[8] Matthews, *These Many Years,* 7.

[9] Roosevelt to Matthews, 31 Dec. 1900, Brander Matthews Papers. Quoted in Owen Wister, *Roosevelt: The Story of a Friendship, 1880-1919* (New York, 1930), 66. Roosevelt's racial views are examined in depth by Thomas G. Dyer, *Theodore Roosevelt and the Idea of Race* (Baton Rouge and London, 1980).

[10] Roosevelt, *Letters* 2:866; Roosevelt to Matthews, 18 Dec. 1893, Brander Matthews Papers; Roosevelt, *Letters* 1:376.

[11] Roosevelt, "A Teller of Tales of Strong Men," *Harper's Weekly* 21 Dec. 1895, 216. The essay is a review of Wister's *Red Men and White.*

[12] Roosevelt, *Works* 13:635. On Roosevelt's fear that the women's movement would lead to "race suicide," see Dyer, 150-53. Matthews's male chauvinism is evident not only in *The Action and the Word* but in his efforts to prevent women from becoming members of the American Academy of Arts and Letters and from enrolling in his Columbia classes (Matthews to Hamlin Garland, 27 Jan. 1919, Brander Matthews Papers; Blanche Colton Williams, "Brander Matthews—A Reminiscence," *MS.*, 1 [July 1929], 1, 9).

[13] Roosevelt, *Letters* 1:410; Matthews, *A Confident Tomorrow: A Novel of New York* (New York and London, 1900), 178.

[14] Matthews, "Memories," *Scribner's Magazine*, 6 Aug. 1889, 174.

[15] Roosevelt, *Letters* 1:177; Wister, 319; Victorian-American society's preoccupation with neurasthenia is discussed by T. J. Jackson Lears, *No Place of Grace: Antimodernism and the Transformation of American Culture 1880-1920* (New York, 1981), 47-58.

[16] Vanderbilt, 206-07.

[17] Matthews, *Americanisms and Briticisms with Other Essays on Other Isms* (New York, 1892), 7, 11.

[18] Matthews, *The American of the Future and Other Essays* (1909; reprint Freeport, N.Y., 1968), 29-30; idem, *Americanisms and Briticisms*, 31; Roosevelt, *Letters* 1:254; *Works* 12:294.

[19] Slotkin, 611, 619; Matthews, *Americanisms and Briticisms*, 93.

[20] Matthews, *Americanisms and Briticisms*, 135-50.

[21] George Stewart Stokes, *Agnes Repplier: Lady of Letters* (Philadelphia, 1949), 168; Roosevelt to Matthews, 2 Jan. 1891, Brander Matthews Papers; *Letters* 1:351. On the Victorian-American male's fear that American culture was being feminized, see Lears, 103 ff.

[22] Though he later condemned Howells as a "feeble apostle of Tolstoi" (*Letters* 3:142), Roosevelt and the novelist were at this time on good terms; Howells shared Roosevelt's high opinion of Matthews as a person and a literary critic; Roosevelt to Matthews, 25 Feb. 1892, Brander Matthews Papers; Roosevelt, *Letters* 1:288.

[23] Roosevelt, *Works* 12:300-06. Roosevelt initially disliked Kipling because of his criticisms of American culture, but Matthews, who was an intimate friend of Kipling, succeeded in reversing Roosevelt's opinion: in 1895 Roosevelt wrote Matthews that he had "come round to your way of looking at Kipling," adding that what he most likes about the Englishman is that "he seems almost as fond of you as I am" (*Letters* 1:439); Roosevelt, *Works* 12:303, 309.

[24] Roosevelt, *Letters* 1:370.

[25] Agnes Repplier, *Counter-Currents* (Boston and New York, 1916).

[26] Gilder, 405; Roosevelt, *Letters* 1:288; Roosevelt to Matthews, 23 May 1893, Brander Matthews Papers.

[27] Roosevelt, *Works* 10:360. The outline held at Columbia University bears no date nor formal title, but in the accompanying note to Matthews, Roosevelt refers to the document as the "Americanism piece." Matthews's response, if extant, has not been located.

[28] Roosevelt to Matthews, 10 Oct. 1892, Brander Matthews Papers; *Selections from the Correspondence of Theodore Roosevelt and Henry Cabot Lodge 1884-1918*, ed. Henry Cabot Lodge (New York, 1925), 1:145.

[29] Roosevelt, *Letters* 8:973; Roosevelt to Matthews, 18 Dec. 1893, Brander Matthews Papers.

[30] "American Copyright League Celebration of the Passage of the Bill," *Publishers' Weekly*, 11 Apr. 1892, 568. The 1891 Copyright Act's importance to the development of American literary independence is emphasized by Spencer (337).

[31] Matthews, *These Many Years*, 225, 228; Roosevelt, *Letters* 1:213-14, 216.

[32] Roosevelt to Matthews, 27 Sept. 1897, Brander Matthews Papers; Roosevelt, *Letters* 1:288, 307.

[33] Matthews, *An Introduction to the Study of American Literature* (New York, 1896), 224.

[34] Roosevelt, *Letters* 1:436; Matthews, *An Introduction to the Study of American Literature*, 11-13.

[35] Matthews, "Suggestions for Teachers of American Literature," *Educational Review*, Jan. 1901, 12. Taine's pervasive influence on late nineteenth-century American literary criticism is traced by John W. Rathbun and Harry H. Clark, *American Literary Criticism, 1860-1905*, vol. 2 (Boston, 1979), 94-102.

[36] Matthews, *An Introduction to the Study of American Literature*, 136, 177, 98, 193, 224; Roosevelt, *Works*, 12:326.

[37] Matthews, *These Many Years*, 404; Roosevelt, *Works* 12:292-95. In a letter to Matthews dated 11 Nov. 1895 (Brander Matthews Papers), Roosevelt remarked that both *The Forum* and *Atlantic* had rejected his proposition to review *Introduction to the Study of American Literature*, adding "I am rather at a loss to know what to do." Matthews, it seems, then made arrangements to have Roosevelt publish the review in *The Bookman*, for on 6 Dec. 1895, Roosevelt wrote him: "Of course I will gladly review your *Introduction of [sic] the Study of American*

Literature in the February number. I suppose they will write me about it. I will have to get them to send me a stenographer" (*Letters* 1:499). Though not mentioned by name in the letter, *The Bookman* did publish the review in its Feb. 1896 number. In light of Kim Townsend's illuminating analysis of sexist, racist, and violent language in Parkman's writings, Matthews's and Roosevelt's admiration for the historian is telling ("Francis Parkman and the Male Tradition," *American Quarterly* 38 [1986]: 97-113).

[38] "New York as a Historic Town," *Century Magazine* 41 (1890-91): 476-77; Roosevelt to Matthews, 1 Jan. 1891, Brander Matthews Papers; Matthews, rev. of Roosevelt's *Theodore Roosevelt: An Autobiography* (1913) and *History as Literature and Other Essays* (1913), *The Bookman* 38 (Dec. 1913): 418-22.

[39] Matthews, "Roosevelt as a Practical Politician," *Outlook,* 16 July 1919, 433-35; Matthews, "Theodore Roosevelt," in *Commemorative Tributes of the American Academy of Arts and Letters 1905-1941* (1942; reprint, Freeport, N.Y., 1968), 110-15; Matthews, rev. of Joseph Bishop's *Theodore Roosevelt and His Time: Shown in His Own Letters* (New York, 1920), *New York Times,* 3 Oct. 1920, sec. 3.

[40] Matthews, "Theodore Roosevelt as a Man of Letters," in Roosevelt, *Works* 12:ix-xx. Roosevelt may have read an early draft of the essay, for in a letter to Matthews dated 4 Sept. 1917, Brander Matthews Papers, he expresses thanks for an unspecified article Matthews wrote about him, adding that he is particularly pleased with the praise of *Winning of the West.*

[41] Stuart P. Sherman, "Brander Matthews and the Mohawks," in Sherman, *Points of View* (New York, 1923), 251-60; Matthews to William P. Trent, 9 May 1898, Brander Matthews Papers; Roosevelt, quoted in Morris, 12; *Letters* 2:1052; Van Wyck Brooks, "Toward a National Culture," *Seven Arts* 1 (Mar. 1917): 535-47.

[42] H. L. Mencken, *Prejudices Second Series* (New York, 1920), 83. Mencken debunks Matthews by name in this essay (11) and in other writings as well; ibid., 102-35, 9. The article is titled "Roosevelt: An Autopsy."

[43] See Sacvan Bercovitch, "The Problem of Ideology in American Literary History," *Critical Inquiry* 12 (1986): 641-42.

[44] Mencken, 47, 91.

[45] *Columbia Literary History of the United States,* ed. Emory Elliott et al. (New York, 1988); the Cambridge history of American literature, under the general editorship of Bercovitch, is forthcoming. For a sample of the controversy generated by these works, see "The Extra" essays in *American Literature* 58 (1986): 99-108; and 59 (1987): 102-14, 268-76.

[46] William C. Spengemann, "American Writers and English Literature," *ELH* 52 (1985): 224. See also Peter Carafiol, "The New Orthodoxy: Ideology and the Institution of American Literary History," *American Literature* 59 (1987): 626-38.

Lawrence J. Oliver (essay date 1989)

SOURCE: "Brander Matthews and the Dean," in *American Literary Realism 1870-1910,* Vol. 21, No. 3, Spring, 1989, pp. 25-40.

[*In the following essay, Oliver examines the forty-year literary relationship between Matthews and William Dean Howells.*]

Recollecting his experiences as a member of the Saturday Club, Bliss Perry, after suggesting that William Dean Howells was never as happy in New York City as in Brahmin Cambridge, reports that the Dean complained to him in the 1890s: "No one ever drops in any more to talk about books, no one except once in a while Brander Matthews."[1] Perry continues his reminiscence without another word about Howells' book-loving visitor. Matthews in fact frequently appears on the scene in biographical and critical studies of Howells (and of other realists as well) only to disappear, as in Perry's essay, almost as soon as he arrives, most scholars apparently considering his literary relationship with Howells too insignificant to merit much attention.[2] Yet that relationship, though obscured by the shadows of Mark Twain, Henry James, Stephen Crane, and other prominent writers who occupied privileged positions in Howells' life, spanned four decades and generated an extensive chain of correspondence. And though Matthews might seem a slight figure today, published and unpublished letters reveal that the Dean considered him one of the realist movement's sturdiest allies as well as a trusted friend.

Professor of literature and drama at Columbia University from 1891 to 1924, founder of several of the social and literary clubs that helped make New York City the nation's literary center during the 1890s, and influential literary critic, Matthews (1852-1929) did more than discuss books with the father of the realists. Trained as a lawyer before he became a man of letters, Matthews assumed the role of Howells' public defender during and after the Realism War, and he offered private encouragement when the Dean most needed it. Howells, in turn, supported Matthews' literary activities by favorably reviewing his books, citing him in essays, and praising him—often in the most enthusiastic terms—in personal correspondence. Yet, the two men held sharply divergent views on certain social and political issues. Indeed, one of the more intriguing aspects of their relationship is that while he was defending Howells against those who questioned both his literary doctrines and his patriotism, Matthews was an ardent supporter of Theodore Roosevelt, the living symbol of the imperialistic ideology that Howells deplored. But if Matthews did not always share Howells' perspective on what the "truth" was, he stood firmly with the Dean in insisting that fiction writers should aim to represent life as they perceived it, free from all "effectism." The friendship between the Dean and the professor thus vividly illustrates how devotion to the ideal of literary realism could transcend ideological barriers.

Though Howells and Matthews did not meet in person until the early 1890s, after the Dean had taken up residence in New York City, their literary relationship began some fifteen years earlier, when Matthews was a fledgling drama critic. Howells, as is well known, had a lifelong passion for the theatre; he was one of the leading drama critics in America during the late nineteenth century and author of some three dozen plays.[3] And though his desire to achieve the same success as a playwright he enjoyed as a novelist brought frustration and disappointment, he nonetheless remained, as he put it to Henry James, irresistibly attracted to the tormenting "blue fire of the theatre."[4]

Matthews' first published comments on Howells fanned that flame. In an unsigned review of *The Parlor Car* in *The Nation* (31 August 1876, p. 136), twenty-four-year-old Brander expressed high praise for Howells' "bright little play," which, like the Dean's novels, struck "just the light-comedy key." (Howells' darker vision, of course, had not yet fully manifested itself in his fiction, but even after it did, Matthews preferred to emphasize the more "smiling aspects" of the Dean's writings.) Matthews continued and heightened his praise of Howells the playwright a year later in a brief review essay titled **"Bret Harte and Mr. Howells as Dramatists"** (*The Library Table*, 13 Sept. 1877, pp. 174-75). Both *The Parlor Car* and *A Counterfeit Presentment* are well-made plays, Matthews asserts; and if *Out of the Question* (the focus of Matthews' review) is perhaps too slight to be a success on stage, the author "has never worked with a lighter hand or a firmer touch than in many passages of this little comedy."

In his autobiography, Matthews remarks that it took him years to have an essay accepted for publication in Howells' *Atlantic;* but Howells' rejection letters apparently did not discourage the young New Yorker from fully committing himself as an ally to Howells and the realists during the late 1880s, after the publication of *The Rise of Silas Lapham*—which impressed Matthews with its "miraculous veracity"—drew the furor of Howells' adversaries.[5] By 1889, Hamlin Garland (who came to respect Matthews as much as he did Howells) was writing Matthews to praise his essay **"The Dramatic Outlook in America"** (*Harper's Magazine,* May 1889, pp. 924-30) and to invite him to speak in Boston, adding that since "there are so few of us . . . we should be able to work together" for literary Americanism and realism.[6] **"The Dramatic Outlook in America"** caught the attention of Howells as well as of Garland, and in fact was the first of Matthews' writings to earn the Dean's public praise. The essay's central thesis is that, although the drama had

been on the decline for a century and a half, it was showing signs of a revival. Put simply, Matthews attributes the decline to the pernicious influence of romanticism, and the revival to the healthy influence of realism. Great playwrights such as Shakespeare and Moliere have, he observes, always attempted to reflect the life of their times.[7] In the early nineteenth century, however, the success of Scott's Waverley Novels and of technically sophisticated but artificial French drama drove realism and therefore the life out of the theatre in England and in the United States. But "the French dramatists of to-day are conscious of the realistic movement which dominates the fiction of France, of Russia, and of America. The younger playwrights especially are aware of the increasing public appreciation of the more exact presentation of the facts of life" (p. 927). The more accurately a French play reflects French life, the less adaptable it will be to the English or American stage; thus, as "Realism, and its younger brother, Naturalism, gain in power in Paris, fewer and fewer French plays will be fit for the American market" (p. 928), and, consequently, the demand for native drama will increase.

Needless to say, Howells, who disdained the French-style "well-made play" and who championed the efforts of Edward Harrigan, James A. Herne, and other playwrights to inject realistic content and technique into American drama of the day, welcomed Matthews' views. "Mr. Matthews," he wrote in his July 1889 "Editor's Study," "is one of the very few people among us authorized by knowledge and experience to treat of a matter so many are willing to handle without either. His wide acquaintance with dramatic literature affords him the right critical perspective, and his ventures as a playwright [Matthews authored several farces] enable him to conceive of the subject from the theatrical point of view, and to represent those claims of the stage which literary men are sometimes disposed to contemn."[8]

Matthews' review of *Criticism and Fiction* two years later left no doubt that he approached literature with what Howells considered to be the "right critical perspective."[9] Here, as in virtually all his defenses of Howells, Matthews' strategy is to disarm the opposition by insisting that the Dean's controversial views evolve from rather than revolt against traditional literary theory. Matthews concedes at the outset that Howells tends to be combative in propounding his ideas, so much so that it at times seems as if he "longed to see all mankind wearing one coat that he might tread on the tail of it." But Matthews then proceeds to argue that though good critics should, as a rule, avoid being polemical, Howells' militant posture in *Criticism and Fiction* is justifiable, for it is a counterattack against the assaults of sneering British critics and "colonial-minded" American ones. What Howells demands, Matthews emphasizes, is nothing more than truth in fiction; and American writers will attain that goal only if they study American, rather than British, life. The professor also takes Howells to task for failing to appreciate the art of Thackeray. But even when Howells is wrong, Matthews contends, his thoughtfully expressed critical opinions are ever stimulating and force his adversaries to analyze more carefully their own views. Howells, Matthews asserts, has thus raised the level of critical discussion and done a great service to literature.

And as Howells recognized, Matthews had done him a great service. His personal letter of appreciation to Matthews reveals the high esteem in which he had come to hold this young ally of the realists. "I have sometime had it in mind and heart to tell you what very fine work I thought you were doing in criticism for the *Cosmopolitan*," he opens, adding that the remark is sincere and not merely an attempt to repay a compliment. He then goes on to say:

> I told Mr. [Henry] Alden, the last time I saw him . . . what I tell you now: that your work is better than that of any other critic of your generation among us. I had to make exception of your elders of course [such as Henry James]. I like your fighting in the open; I like your spirit, and I like your manner.[10]

During the two decades following his review of *Criticism and Fiction,* a period during which realism began to wane under the persistent counterattacks of the neoromanticists, Matthews continued to fight in the open for literature that would accurately reflect the life and character of his contemporary America, and often received Howells' praise and appreciation for doing so. In, for example, **"Text-Books of Fiction,"** an essay that promoted scholarly study of the modern novel at a time when the great majority of Matthews' academic colleagues held that genre in contempt, the professor declares that literary historians ought to trace

> the successive steps of the story-tellers who narrated at the first things quite Impossible; and then things only Improbable—in which stage the romanticists still linger even in this last decade of the nineteenth century, when riper artists have already tried to pass from the description of the merely Probable to a depiction of the absolutely Inevitable.[11]

That "riper artists" refers to Howells and his fellow American realists is suggested earlier in the same essay when Matthews castigates the "colonial-minded" American professor William Edward Simonds for completely ignoring, in his survey of contemporary fiction, "the extraordinary skill with which almost every locality in the United States has been translated into literature. Nowhere does he praise the vigor with which American character has been presented by the best of our later writers of fiction" (p. 227).

"That is a capital paper of yours on fiction text books," wrote Howells a year before the essay was published in Matthews' *Aspects of Fiction* (1896). "Why don't you write a listing of fiction for scholars and collegers? Nobody else could do it so delightfully and so well."[12] Though he did not produce the kind of "great novels" list

that Howells suggested, Matthews in the following year did publish a textbook on American literature, one that would sell over a quarter of a million copies.[13] Titled *An Introduction to the Study of American Literature,* the book surveys the rise of American literature from Colonial times to Matthews' present day. Implicitly rebuking those "colonial-minded" critics of American literature on both sides of the Atlantic, Matthews confidently asserts that American literature, still in a state of infancy, will one day supplant its British elder brother as the dominant branch of English-language literature. In his closing chapter, **"The End of the Nineteenth Century,"** he remarks that while there is no "towering figure" in American letters, the average quality of literary work is perhaps higher than ever before. Though he mentions no authors by name, pictures of Howells, Twain, and Edward Eggleston indicate what literary school he has in mind. Lauding such writers for examining the richly variegated American scene, Matthews strikes a Howellsian note when he argues that the best works of contemporary fiction tell the truth about life.

One of the more interesting things about Matthews' textbook is that it earned a flattering review not only from Howells but from that outspoken advocate of virile neoromanticism and imperialism, Theodore Roosevelt. Howells and Roosevelt did not, of course, always see eye to eye on literary or political principles, but they were united in their opposition to condescending British critics and in their championing of a distinctively American literature.[14] Writing in *The Bookman,* Roosevelt declared that *Introduction to the Study of American Literature* was "a piece of work as good of its kind as any American scholar ever had in his hands," and he urged that not only every student of American literature but every American writer would profit from the professor's sound principles of literary criticism.[15] Perhaps Howells had in mind the fiercely nationalistic Roosevelt, who disdained "émigré" American writers like Henry James, when he penned his critique of Matthews' book, for he announces at once that nationalism in literature becomes a vice rather than a virtue if carried to extremes, and that he does not necessarily find value in a book simply because of its "Americanism." But, after thus distancing himself from those who, like Roosevelt, allowed the ideology of "true Americanism" to govern their taste in art, Howells proceeds to admit that the "Jingo" in him is touched by Matthews' study, which "heartens us with a true sense of the greatness of our native republic of letters."[16]

Attempts to distinguish a healthy from a pernicious sense of patriotism were, of course, legion during the late nineteenth century, especially during the years leading up to the Spanish-American War; and 1897 found both Howells and Matthews publishing essays that attempted to draw the vital distinction. Howells offered his views on "true Americanism" in "The Modern American Mood" (*Harper's Monthly,* 95 [July 1897], 199-204). Stating that the country was finally sobering up from its intoxication with Gilded Age prosperity, Howells argued that Americans facing the new century were as patriotic as their forefathers, but that their patriotism was quieter and more self-assured. Their devotion to the development of a "truly national literature," furthermore, had not been, as some suggested, extinguished by the lust for materialistic wealth. Implicitly criticizing those who (like Roosevelt) practiced a bellicose and imperialistic form of patriotism, Howells declared that true patriots are like people "whose religion has become their life; it is no longer an enthusiasm, and it is certainly not a ceremonial. They do not seek for a sign; the light is in them" (p. 203). The new Americanism, he insisted, was more patient and tolerant than its post-Civil War era predecessor. If ever Howells engaged in wishful thinking, it was here; his misplaced confidence in his compatriots was of course soon shattered by the triumph of the enthusiast Jingoes.

Matthews immediately wrote Howells to express his praise for the essay, and Howells wrote in reply, "Well, I did like your liking my paper, and I do think what I said is true. The thing seems to have prospered somewhat, but your favor is far its greatest fortune. I shall try to see what you say in the Round Table" (*Selected Letters* IV, 153). What Matthews says in his *Harper's Round Table* essay, titled **"Americanism,"** reveals a mind pulled between the conflicting ideologies that his friends Howells and Roosevelt represented.[17] Where Howells indirectly attacks jingoistic fervor, Matthews is explicit: the Jingoes, he asserts, may be patriotic, but "their patriotism is too frothy, too hysteric, too unintelligent, to inspire confidence." America, he declares, is a great country, but it is not perfect; nor are all European countries inferior to the United States in every aspect. Howells would have been pleased thus far. But then Matthews becomes rather "frothy" himself when he declares that true Americanism implies a "confidence in [the country's] destiny, a buoyant hopefulness that the right will surely prevail." That this cheery perspective derives from a Spencerian view of evolution is implicit in his remark that in the struggle for life, weak races will be "crushed" by races of "stronger fibre and of sterner stock"; thus the world, he believes, is "getting better, if not year by year, at least century by century," and the United States is "destined" to do its full share in contributing to this "steady improvement of the condition of mankind." The endorsement of Manifest Destiny and the militant imagery demonstrate that the professor was being "swollen by the . . . race conceit" and "muscular ideals" that Howells would later argue were indirectly responsible for the Spanish-American War and America's deplorable conduct in the Philippines.[18] When the war erupted in 1898, the author of **"Americanism"** did in fact align himself with Roosevelt and the Jingoes; and in the early 1900s he vigorously defended America's actions during the conflict and readily admitted the "warlike temper, the aggressiveness, the imperialistic sentiment" that are "in our blood."[19]

Yet, surprisingly, the political differences separating Howells and Matthews during the closing years of the century did not rupture their friendship. In fact, at the same time he was congratulating the Colonel of the Rough Riders for his San Juan (Kettle Hill) victory, Matthews was offering encouragement to Howells and waging verbal battle on behalf of the realists. Plagued by feelings of depression and a lack of enthusiasm for his own work, Howells needed the support of friends more than ever during these dark years (see *Selected Letters* IV, 193). Thus an 1898 letter thanking Matthews for praising a new novel (*The Story of a Play* apparently) is especially significant: "You make it worth one's while to do one's best," Howells wrote, adding "I would be willing to write a far more popular novel than mine will be for such advice as yours."[20] And in September of 1899, as he prepared to undertake his successful lecture tour of the Midwest, he waxed enthusiastic over an essay by Matthews, exclaiming "The paper on 'Novels' is all you wish one to think, and I am in such entire agreement with it, I felt almost as if I had written it. In fact, it telepathetically occupies nearly the same ground as that in which I have laid the line in my lecture on 'Novel Writing and Novel Reading.'"[21] The paper that so pleased the Dean is presumably **"The Study of Fiction"**; Matthews wrote it at the request of the American Society of the Extension of University Teaching, which offered a series of lectures on "Books and Reading" in 1898-99. Since the lecture on novel-reading and novel-writing that Howells delivered during his tour repeats many arguments expressed in previously published essays, it hardly required mental telepathy for one as steeped in Howells' writings as Matthews was to make such assertions as "Plainer than ever before is the duty of the novelist now to set up no false ideals, to erect no impossible standards of strength or courage or virtue, to tell the truth about life as he sees it with his own eyes," or "The Romanticistic fictions are more exciting than the veritistic; surprise follows surprise, and so-called effects are heaped one on the other. Life as we all know it, with its commonplace duties, seems drear and gray after these excursions into fairy-land with impossible heroes who face impossible perils with impossible fortitude."[22]

But though **"The Study of Fiction"** bears many parallels with Howells' lecture, Matthews goes far beyond Howells—and toward neoromanticism—in applying Hippolyte Taine's literary principles to the study of literature. Taine's influence on Howells and on American realism in general is well known.[23] One must not forget, however, that the Frenchman's theory of "race, moment, and milieu" was also warmly received by neoromantic nationalists like Roosevelt (whose essay "Nationalism in Art and Literature" has a Tainean subtext).[24] Rather schizophrenic in its trumpeting of Howellsian and Rooseveltian ideals, Matthews' essay vividly demonstrates how Taine could be employed in the service of imperialism as well as realism. Insisting that a nation's "serious" fiction—which he defines as "Realistic fiction, the fiction in which the author has tried to tell the truth about life as he sees it" (p. 100)—inevitably reveals its people's "race-traits," Matthews urges teachers of literature to focus classroom discussions on "the accuracy with which race-characteristics are recorded in the fiction of a language—how, for example, the energy and the humor of the

Anglo-Saxon stock dominate the novels of the English language" (p. 84). Those statements in themselves might not have much distressed the man who in 1896 had admitted that the Jingo in him responded to Matthews' *Introduction to the Study of American Literature.* But one can only imagine how the pacifist-minded Dean reacted to the following passage:

> Whoever [Matthews declares] had read and understood the recent serious fiction of the United States, the 'Rise of Silas Lapham' and the 'Hazard of New Fortunes,' the stories of Mr. Hamlin Garland and Mr. Owen Wister, the tales of Miss Wilkins and of "Octave Thanet," might have sized up us Americans, and might have made a pretty good guess at the way [the Spanish-American War], once entered upon, would bring out the energy of the race, the tenacity, the resolution, the ingenuity—and even the good-humored and easy-going toleration which is perhaps our chief defect as a people, and which is responsible in some measure for the preventable sufferings of our sick soldiers. (pp. 99-100)

Howells must have been aghast at such a "compliment"! But if Matthews at times played the role of Job's comforter in his relationship with Howells, he nonetheless was, as I have stated, one of the Dean's most ardent supporters at the turn of the century, as essays like **"Romance against Romanticism"** and **"Mr. Howells as a Critic"** testify.

Anticipating Louis J. Budd's "W. D. Howells' Defense of the Romance" by more than half a century, Matthews' **"Romance against Romanticism"** defends Howells against the unjust charge that he was inimical to any work of literature that failed his test of realism.[25] Though Matthews does not cite Howells' own careful attempt in his September 1889 "Editor's Study" to distinguish between the authentically romantic and its bastard brother, the "romanticistic," Matthews echoes Howells' definitions of the two terms when he proclaims that "Romance is genuine, while Romanticism is pinchbeck. True Romance, whether ancient or medieval or modern, is as sincere and as direct and as honest as the Classic itself. And it needs to be distinguished sharply from Romanticism, which is often insincere, generally indirect, and sometimes artistically dishonest."[26] Those who have accused Howells of being hostile to Romance, Matthews argues, have failed to see that "it is only barren Romanticism [Howells] detests and despises" and that he "has more than once gladly recorded his delight in true Romance" (p. 38), such as that created by Hawthorne and Stevenson. Howells might have cringed somewhat at the professor's more martial remarks, his assertion, for example, that the heroes of the age-honored Romances are "brave boys, all of them, hearty and honest and sturdy" (p. 44); but he must have appreciated the piece overall.

And he had even more reason to be pleased with Matthews' **"Mr. Howells as a Critic,"** an essay that will be familiar to many students of Howells. Gathering together arguments formulated in his earlier praises of Howells,

Matthews constructs his most persuasive case for the Dean and the literary realism for which he stood. After declaring Howells the most multifarious of all American writers at the opening of the twentieth century, Matthews argues, as he had done in his 1891 review of *Criticism and Fiction,* that the controversy aroused by that book and other of Howells' earlier writings stemmed more from the often aggressive and blunt manner in which the Dean presented his views than from the views themselves.[27] Matthews once again admits that Howells has at times been over-strenuous in pointing out the faults of earlier masters (of Thackeray, in particular) and has not always been judicious in his praise of contemporary writers, but he emphatically denies the charge—leveled by certain "stupid" and "malevolent" critics—that Howells elevates such realists as John De Forest or H. B. Fuller to the rank of literary master. From the vantage point of the opening of the twentieth century, Matthews contends, *Criticism and Fiction* hardly seems iconoclastic: "At bottom all that Mr. Howells had done was to voice once again the demand that art, and more especially the art of fiction, should deal with life simply, naturally, and honestly. This has ever been the watch-cry of the younger generation in every century" (p. 69). Indeed, Howells would have aroused little controversy had he not had the courage to question the merits of authors who had become sacred in the eyes of less critical minds: "Those who refuse blindly," Matthews asserts (in the same aggressive tone, ironically, that he faults in Howells), "to see any blemishes in the art of Balzac or of Cervantes, those who persist in upholding Scott and Dickens and Thackeray as impeccable artists, need to be reminded that ancestor-worship is no longer esteemed the highest form of religion" (p. 76). In criticism as in fiction, proclaims the professor in his concluding paragraph, character counts as much as talent; and both in his fiction and his criticism, Howells reveals himself to be "a man large of nature and of a transparent sincerity, liberal in his appreciation, loyal to his convictions, and little hampered by mere academic restrictions" (p. 77).

"Your praise," Howells wrote in response to the review, "seems the more reasonable because your blame is so just. I know I have those faults which you hint, and if I were not nearly sixty-five years old I should, under the inspiration of your censure, set about correcting them. But as it is I shall have work enough cultivating the merits which you recognize so charmingly that I should love them almost as much if they were some one else's. . . . Now it shall never matter to me whatever meaner critics say—Matthews has forever secured me from their harm" (*Selected Letters* IV, 278-79).

Matthews also sought to secure the Dean from the harm of those "meaner critics" who—outraged by his defense of the Haymarket anarchists; his celebration of such "decadent" writers as Zola, Tolstoy, and Ibsen; and his opposition to the Spanish-American War and to imperialistic nationalism—denounced him for being "un-American." Roosevelt even went so far as to charge that Howells and other "feeble apostles of Tolstoy" were indirectly responsible for the assassination of President McKinley.[28] Though he was, as already noted, ideologically closer during the 1890s to the Rough Rider than to the "apostle" of Tolstoy, Matthews never doubted Howells' loyalty to country; indeed, in **"Mr. Howells as a Critic"** and in several other pieces written during the two decades prior to Howells' death, Matthews labored to portray the Dean and his writings as being quintessentially American. In **"Mr. Howells as a Critic,"** for example, Matthews insists that though Howells may take a cosmopolitan perspective in his literary criticism, he is nonetheless "intensely American, irresistibly American; and he is never conceivably anything else" (p. 634). Paying tribute to the Dean on the occasion of his seventy-fifth birthday, Matthews emphasizes that the great writer's sense of patriotism is "all the more truly American in that it is free from every taint of spread-eagleism."[29] In a review essay titled **"American Character in American Fiction"** (1913), Matthews—after taking a retrospective glance at the "dark ages of a score of years ago, when Mr. Howells was engaged in stirring up the critics in their cages"— lauds *New Leaf Mills* for its "restful portrayal of a group of very American characters in very American conditions."[30] As late as 1917 Matthews was still proclaiming that the Dean (now eighty years old) was "the most intensely national and the most truly cosmopolitan [of American writers], with that sound cosmopolitanism which burgeons bounteously because it is deeply rooted in the soil of its nativity."[31]

That final observation, that nationalism is not inimical to but rather requisite for cosmopolitanism, is the central theme of Matthews' **"Literature in the New Century,"** an address he delivered at the International Congress of the Arts and Sciences in St. Louis on 24 September 1904. And though the essay (which reveals at every turn Matthews' debt to Taine and Spencer) never mentions Howells, it implicitly defends him against the "meaner critics" who equated cosmopolitanism with un-Americanism. Matthews begins by identifying the four legacies from the nineteenth century that would shape the literature of the new century: the scientific spirit; the spread of democracy; the assertion of nationality; and, finally, "that stepping across the confines of language and race, for which we have no more accurate name than 'cosmopolitanism.'"[32] Twentieth-century writers, Matthews proceeds to argue, will examine life from the scientific perspective of evolution; they will, in addition, reflect the spirit of democracy, tolerance, and compassion that has spread throughout the globe, a spirit exemplified by such democratic-minded (and Howells-favored) authors as Hawthorne, George Eliot, Turgenev, and Tolstoy. Accompanying the spread of democracy, Matthews observes, has been a surge of nationalism, and since each nation possesses distinct "racial characteristics" inherited from its ancestors, the writers of the twentieth-century will explore and dramatize racial differences—intranational as well as international ones. Arriving at the fourth and final legacy, Matthews declares that "The deeper interest in the expression of national qualities and in the representation of provincial peculiarities

[provided by local colorists] is to-day accompanied by an increasing cosmopolitanism which seems to be casting down the barriers of race and of language" (p. 22). This cosmopolitanism, however, is primarily a borrowing or sharing of literary *forms,* whereas it is the "national spirit" (or "race-traits") that breathes life into the work. Thus—and here is the key point—though literary works of various nations may be similar in their artistic formulae and structures, they must needs be "radically dissimilar in their essence, in the motives that move the characters and in their outlook on life; and this dissimilarity is due not alone to the individuality of the . . . authors,—it is to be credited chiefly to the nationality of each" (p. 23). In short, what accounts for the *international* appeal of such writers as Turgenev, Twain, and D'Annunzio is the *nationalistic* (or racial) core of their writings. "This racial individuality," Matthews concludes, "is the best safeguard against "mere craftsmanship"; it permits a writer "to frequent the past without becoming archaic and to travel abroad without becoming exotic, because it will supply him always with a good reason for remaining a citizen of his own country" (p. 25). Thus Matthews nicely fuses realism, Americanism, and cosmopolitanism. That Howells' writings epitomized this fusion goes without saying.

If some readers may have failed to recognize the implied endorsement of Howells, the Dean himself did not: **"Literature in the New Century,"** he wrote its author, is a "capital paper. . . . I agree with it so perfectly that I do not see why I did not write it, except that I could not. I promise myself the pleasure of reading everything in the volume [Matthews' *Inquiries and Opinions*].—I always read anything of yours I come upon by chance, and enjoy it, tho' my age and my make are against my telling you so."[33]

Howells clearly did not, however, wholly enjoy and agree perfectly with at least one of the essays reprinted in *Inquiries and Opinions,* **"Ibsen the Playwright."** Here again Matthews reveals his divided Victorian mind. Beginning on a note of high praise, he declares that Ibsen is a "poet-philosopher who wishes to make people think, to awaken them from an ethical lethargy, to shock them into asking questions for which the complacent morality of the moment can provide no adequate answer."[34] He goes on to argue that the Norwegian is a playwright of "surpassing technical dexterity" (p. 253) who exhibits a genius for creating fully founded and lifelike characters and for probing the "naked human soul, in its doubts and its perplexities" (p. 254). But the line of argument takes a sudden turn when it focuses on the ideology underlying Ibsen's social dramas. Contending that the "romanticist is forever wrestling with the realist" in Ibsen, Matthews is disturbed by a "romanticistic clamor, a tocsin of anarchy" (p. 274) he detects in the plays. He also complains that Ibsen's later dramas are somewhat mystical and moralistic; and he suggests that the Norwegian was never able to overcome the village mentality of his boyhood (a comment that might have stung a certain novelist who grew up in rural Ohio). If the essay began in the voice of

Howells, it ends in that of Roosevelt, with the professor predicting that the anarchistic ideology and the "hint of abnormal eccentricity or of morbid perversity" in Ibsen's plays will prevent them from gaining broad popularity and from withstanding the critical scrutiny of the twentieth century (p. 279).

Though drafted in 1903, three years before Matthews' essay appeared, the famous tribute to Ibsen that Howells published in the *North American Review* in 1906 is virtually a point-by-point refutation of the professor's denigrating criticisms of the Norwegian (*Selected Letters* V, 181-82). Ibsen, Howells passionately argues, is the greatest of modern dramatists, a supreme realist and a completely honest artist. His quarrel with his countrymen arose from the fact that "Norway was provincial and Ibsen was not," European travel developing in him (as it did in Howells himself) a "cosmopolitan" outlook.[35] Where detractors like Matthews detected "morbid perversity" in the Norwegian's art, Howells perceives a "wholly sanative" integrity (p. 441). As for the anarchistic element in his life and plays, Ibsen, states Howells, "grew strong by standing alone"; he "lived as he has died, 'a very imperial anarch,' for . . . the note of this mighty solitary, hermited in the midst of men, was anarchism. Solidarities of any sort he would not have. The community was nothing to him, and, if not quite despicable as the majority, was still a contemptible substitute for the individuality. That alone was precious" (p. 444). Ibsen may be unpopular with the public, Howells concedes, but popularity, he argues, has nothing to do with literary value nor with a writer's influence; and Ibsen is "one of those masters . . . who are more accepted through those they have influenced than in themselves" (p. 445). Perhaps, Howells admits in closing, Ibsen's reputation and influence will fade in the twentieth century, but "it would not be altogether impossible that some in the future should know him with the passionate joy with which a few in the present have had the courage to know him" (p. 445). Matthews must have felt soundly chastized by the Dean's remarks.

But if the Howells-Matthews friendship could survive the tensions caused earlier by the Spanish-American War and United States imperialism, it could weather a difference of opinion over Ibsen. And when Matthews published his autobiography *These Many Years* (1917) a decade later, eighty-year-old Howells (who the year before had facetiously written Matthews "I am getting uselesser every way. I am old, old! . . . Zest is gone"[36]) found enough energy to be of good service to his friend one last time, expressing publicly the fond sentiments he had spoken privately over the years. Reviewing the autobiography in the *New York Times,* Howells proclaims that "among all our literary folk there are no truer Americans, no more genuine, than Mr. Matthews and Mr. Garland," and that the former is without doubt the country's foremost scholar of the drama.[37] Noting that Matthews (who published three novels, six plays, and dozens of short stores) ceased writing fiction and drama some years earlier because he did not achieve the success he sought,

Howells faults the reading public for failing to recognize the delicate beauty of the professor's novels; and if the theatre could not appreciate Matthews' farces, "all the worse for the theatre" (p. 405).

Of course, the Dean's opinion of Matthews' or any other writer's work had little influence on the American literary scene in 1917, as the iconoclastic new generation of writers and critics sought to gain control of literature in the new century by verbally guillotining their literary elders. And as Howells' fellow traveller, Matthews was often the target of the sometimes vicious denunciations levelled by the "literary Mohawks," as Stuart Sherman labelled them in an essay defending the professor.[38] Thus we find the once buoyant Matthews writing Howells in 1918 that he wished they "could foregather and swap bitter opinions about the upstart young."[39] If they did foregather to commiserate, their conversation likely would not have dwelled on definitions of literary "realism," for by the time he wrote his autobiography, Matthews had in fact abandoned the term. His explanation for doing so sounds as if it were written by one of today's reader-response critics rather than by a Victorian "genteel": The meaning of any word, he observes, is not intrinsic and fixed, but rather is the product of individual interpretation. "If this uncertainty and this variableness" of meaning, he continues, "is obvious in ordinary speech about ordinary things, it is intensified in all discussions of art." Thus, he concludes, terms like "romantic," "realistic," and "naturalistic" are "will-o'-the-wisps and chameleons, changing color while one looks at them."[40]

But if tne word "realism" was will-o'-the-wisp, its chief American promoter remained as solid as ever in the professor's eyes. Reviewing Howells' edition *Great Modern American Stories* (New York: Boni and Liveright, 1920) in April, 1920, just weeks before the Dean died, Matthews praised Howells' introduction to the anthology as being "altogether charming . . . , written with the exquisite perfection of expression which is ever the delight and despair of his fellow-craftsman in the difficult art of writing."[41] Implicitly denouncing what he earlier would have labelled "romanticistic" fiction and yoking local-colorism to Americanism once again, Matthews asserts that the stories in the collection (by Twain, Henry James, Garland, Mary E. Wilkins, and Sarah Orne Jewett, among others) would not suit readers whose "taste has been depraved by sensation," but would appeal to those who desire an "intimate revelation of American life and character." The professor would not change his colors; he continued advocating for Howells and American literary realism even after the "upstart young" had dismissed the case.

NOTES

[1] Bliss Perry, "Recollections of the Saturday Club," *The Saturday Club: A Century Completed 1920-1956,* ed. Edward W. Forbes and John H. Finley, Jr. (Boston: Houghton Mifflin, 1958), p. 5.

[2] Edwin Cady briefly discusses Matthews' support of Howells during the Realism War (*The Realist at War: The Mature Years 1885-1920* [Syracuse: Syracuse Univ. Press, 1958], pp. 51-52, 210-211), but none of Howells' other biographers makes more than passing reference to the professor. Robert Falk, who notes that Matthews was an ally of Henry James and Mark Twain, merely lists Matthews as one of several young critics influenced by the Dean (*The Victorian Mode in American Fiction 1865-1885* [East Lansing: Michigan State Univ. Press, 1964], pp. 55, 165, 194).

[3] In his *An Outline History of American Drama* (Totowa, N.J.: Littlefield, Addams, 1965), p. 313, Walter J. Meserve cites Howells, Henry James, and Matthews as the three most scholarly American drama critics of the late nineteenth century. Brenda Murphy's recent study of Howells' drama criticism and playwriting is a welcome addition to Howells scholarship, but her failure to discuss Matthews' significant role in the development of American drama and drama criticism (she mentions his name only once) is a lamentable oversight (*American Realism and American Drama, 1880-1940* [Cambridge, England: Cambridge Univ. Press, 1987]).

[4] Howells, *Selected Letters of W. D. Howells,* ed. Thomas Wortham et al. (Boston: Twayne, 1981), IV, 181-82. Subsequent references to this volume of Howells' letters will appear parenthetically in the text.

[5] Brander Matthews, *These Many Years: Recollections of a New Yorker* (New York: Scribner's, 1919), pp. 160, 167.

[6] Garland to Matthews, 29 Dec. 1889, Columbia University. Permission to quote from this and subsequent unpublished letters in the Brander Matthews Papers at Columbia granted by the Butler Library. Garland's admiration for Matthews is evident in his many letters to Matthews held at Columbia as well as in his autobiographical works. See, for example, his *Companions on the Trail* (New York: Macmillan, 1931), pp. 252-53, and *My Friendly Contemporaries* (New York: Macmillan, 1932), pp. 272-73.

[7] In a later essay titled "How Shakespeare Learnt His Trade" (*North American Review,* 177 [Sept. 1903], 424-33), Matthews fully developed the argument that Shakespeare's greatness lies in his "realism," his attempts to portray truthfully and completely Elizabethan life. "Bravo!" exclaimed Howells after reading the article (*Selected Letters,* ed. William C. Fischer and Christoph K. Lohmann [Boston: Twayne, 1983], V. 62).

[8] Howells, "The Editor's Study," *Harper's Monthly,* 79 (July 1889), 314-15.

[9] Matthews, "Recent Essays in Criticism," *Cosmopolitan,* 12 (Nov. 1891), 124-26; rpt. *Critical Essays on W. D. Howells, 1866-1920,* ed. Edwin H. and Norma W. Cady (Boston: G. K. Hall, 1983), pp. 114-16.

[10] Howells, *Selected Letters,* ed. Robert C. Leitz III et al. (Boston: Twayne, 1980), III, 323. Subsequent page references to this volume of Howells' letters will appear parenthetically in the text.

[11] Matthews, "Text-Books of Fiction," *Aspects of Fiction and Other Ventures in Criticism* (1896; rpt. Upper Saddle River, N.J.: Literature House/Gregg Press, 1970), pp. 224-234.

[12] Howells to Matthews, 3 May 1895, Columbia Univ. Permission to quote from Howells' unpublished letters granted by William White Howells; the letters quoted in this article may not be republished without Mr. Howells' permission.

[13] Matthews, *These Many Years,* p. 404.

[14] Howells' ambivalent relationship with Roosevelt is detailed in William M. Gibson's *Theodore Roosevelt Among the Humorists* (Knoxville: Univ. of Tennessee Press, 1980), pp. 9-23.

[15] Theodore Roosevelt, "An Introduction to American Literature," *The Bookman,* 2 (Feb. 1896); rpt. *The Works of Theodore Roosevelt* (New York: Scribner's, 1926), XII, 292-95.

[16] Howells, "Life and Letters," *Harper's Weekly,* 40 (28 March 1896), 294.

[17] Matthews, "Americanism," *Harper's Round Table,* 6 July 1897, pp. 873-74.

[18] Howells, "The New Historical Romances," *North American Review,* 171 (Dec. 1900); rpt. *W. D. Howells as Critic,* ed. Edwin H. Cady (London and Boston: Routledge & Kegan Paul, 1973), pp. 301, 309.

[19] Matthews, "American Character," *The American of the Future and Other Essays* (1909; rpt. Freeport, N.Y.: Books for Libraries Press, 1968), pp. 29-30. Matthews read this essay before the Phi Beta Kappa Society at Columbia University in June, 1905.

[20] Howells to Matthews, 23 June 1898, Columbia Univ.

[21] Howells to Matthews, 10 Sept. 1899, Columbia Univ. Howells wrote his lecture on novel writing and reading in the spring of 1899, several months before he began his lecture tour and wrote the letter to Matthews. See Harrison T. Meserole, "The Dean in Person: Howells' Lecture Tour," *Western Humanities Review,* 10 (1956), 337-47; and Thomas Wortham, "W. D. Howells' 1899 Midwest Lecture Tour: What the Letters Tell," *American Literary Realism,* 11 (Autumn 1978), 265-74.

[22] Matthews, "The Study of Fiction," *The Historical Novel and Other Essays (1901;* rpt. Freeport, N.Y.: Books for Libraries Press, 1968), pp. 83, 100. Subsequent page references to this essay will appear parenthetically within the text.

[23] See Everett Carter, *Howells and the Age of Realism* (Philadelphia and New York: J. B. Lippincott, 1954), pp. 94-101.

[24] Roosevelt, "Nationalism in Art and Literature," *Works* XII, 325-336.

[25] Louis J. Budd, "W. D. Howells's Defense of the Romance," *PMLA*, 67 (March 1952), 32-42.

[26] Matthews, "Romance against Romanticism," *The Bookman*, 12 (Jan. 1901); rpt. *The Historical Novel*, p. 37. Subsequent page references to this essay will appear parenthetically within the text. Howells' essay defining "romanticistic" literature is reprinted in *W. D. Howells as Critic,* pp. 157-160.

[27] Matthews, "Mr. Howells as a Critic," *Forum,* 31 (Jan. 1902); rpt. *Howells: A Century of Criticism,* ed. Kenneth E. Eble (Dallas: Southern Methodist Univ. Press, 1962), p. 68. Subsequent page references to this essay will appear parenthetically within the text.

[28] Roosevelt, *The Letters of Theodore Roosevelt,* ed. Elting E. Morison (Cambridge, Mass.: Harvard Univ. Press, 1951), III, 142.

[29] "William Dean Howells at 75," *Boston Evening Transcript,* 24 Feb. 1912, sec. 3, p. 2.

[30] Matthews, "American Character in American Fiction," *Munsey's Magazine,* 49 (Aug. 1913), 796.

[31] "Birthday Tributes to Wm. D. Howells," *New York Times,* 25 March 1917, sec. 1, p. 9.

[32] Matthews, "Literature in the New Century," *North American Review,* 179 (Oct. 1904); rpt. *Inquiries and Opinions* (New York: Scribner's, 1907), p. 5. Subsequent page references are to this volume and will appear parenthetically within the text.

[33] Howells, *Selected Letters,* V, 230.

[34] Matthews, "Ibsen the Playwright," *Bookman,* 22-23 (Feb.-March, 1906); rpt. *Inquiries and Opinions,* p. 229. Subsequent page references are to this volume and will appear parenthetically within the text.

[35] Howells, "Henrik Ibsen," *North American Review,* 183 (July 1906); rpt. *W. D. Howells as Critic,* p. 444. Subsequent page references are to this volume and will appear parenthetically within the text.

[36] Howells, *Selected Letters,* ed. Gibson and Lohmann (Boston: Twayne, 1983), VI, 81.

[37] Howells, "An Appreciation," *New York Times Review of Books,* 21 Oct. 1917, p. 405. Subsequent page references will appear parenthetically within the text.

[38] Stuart P. Sherman, "Brander Matthews and the Mohawks," *Points of View* (New York: Scribner's, 1924), p. 251-60.

[39] Matthews to Howells, 11 March 1918, Harvard Univ. Permission to quote granted by Houghton Library.

[40] Matthews, *These Many Years,* pp. 288-89.

[41] Matthews, "Choosing America's Great Short Stories," *New York Times Review of Books,* 18 April 1920, pp. 179, 182, 189.

Robert A. Colby (essay date, 1991)

SOURCE: "Quill and Olive Branch: Walter Besant Corresponds with Brander Matthews," in *Columbia Library Columns,* Vol. XLI, No. 1, November, 1991, pp. 13-22.

[*In the following essay, Colby documents the collaboration between Matthews and Walter Besant, founder of the British Society of Authors, as they attempted to secure transatlantic copyright protections for British and American writers and to make the work of American writers familiar in England.*]

From December 1894 through December 1895 there appeared in the *Author,* organ of the British Society of Authors, edited by Walter Besant who had founded the Society in 1883, a column entitled **"New York Letter."** These contributions at first were signed Hallett Robinson, shortened subsequently to H. R., a pseudonym adopted by Brander Matthews (by then a professor of literature at Columbia), as revealed in letters from Besant to Matthews in the Rare Book and Manuscript Library.

These twenty-nine letters, spread out in time from 1884, the year of the incorporation of the Society of Authors, to 1900, the year before Besant's death, reflect a remarkable confluence of interests between the two men. Both were versatile writers, as well as actively engaged in the promotion of international copyright. A conviction they shared that American writers were inadequately appreciated by English readers prompted Besant to commission Matthews's pieces for the *Author.*

Matthews was a transatlantic figure, visiting London frequently in connection with his books, in the course of which he met Besant among other British literary figures. The first letter in the Library's collection, dated January 24, 1884, bears the seal of the Savile Club, one of the associations to which the two belonged. This letter is accompanied by a Prospectus of the Society of Authors, which had been brought into being just the previous September. Besant solicited Matthews's opinion, along with a plea: "Perhaps you can see your way to helping on the cause. Could you for instance establish a 'Company of Writers' in New York? The members of your Company could be honorary members of ours and vice versa."

The Company of Writers was the name under which the Society of Authors was first organized. Unknown to Besant, an Authors' Club had been founded in New York City at the home of Richard Watson Gilder, with Matthews a charter member, on October 1, 1882, actually antedating the Society of Authors. An immediate offshoot of the Authors' Club was the formation of the American Copyright League the following year at Matthews's home. Besant obviously had wind of the League by the time of his next letter, dated December 5, 1884, in which he informed Matthews that international copyright was foremost on the agenda of the Society, concluding, "and we cannot but acknowledge with gratitude the efforts made by American Authors to bring about this result." This letter was sent from the office of the Incorporated Society of Authors, which had been granted this formal status by Act of Parliament earlier that year. It was accompanied by a list of Vice Presidents (which included Matthew Arnold, Thomas Henry Huxley, and Wilkie Collins), Fellows, and Associates. Matthews was invited to become a Foreign and Honorary Fellow, an honor he accepted, to be joined by Mark Twain, James Russell Lowell, Henry James, and Bret Harte, among others.

Matthews spoke out and wrote frequently on copyright, most vehemently in two pamphlets brought out under the auspices of the American Copyright League. In *Cheap Books and Good Books* (1888), he complained that, in the absence of international copyright, the American market was flooded by cheap English fiction, "and this at a time . . . when the English novel is distinctly inferior to the novel of America, of Russia, and of France." In *American Authors and British Pirates* (1889), he pointed out conversely that "The Black Flag still flies alongside the Union Jack—as it does alas! by the side of the Stars and Stripes." Besant referred to Matthews and this second pamphlet in his *Autobiography* (1902): "It was absurd to keep calling the Americans thieves and pirates while our people did exactly the same thing on a smaller scale. It exasperated Americans and weakened the efforts of those who were manfully fighting in the cause of international honesty."

Besant's *Autobiography* was published posthumously, but these words had actually been delivered at the annual meeting of the Society of Authors early in 1892, shortly after the passage of the landmark U.S. Copyright Act of 1891, which, after more than a half century of struggle on both sides of the ocean, extended legal protection to British authors. This legislation marked a major victory for the American Copyright League, which had campaigned vigorously for it with the cooperation of the Society of Authors. In fact, prior to its passage Matthews was sent by the League to London to confer with Besant on the technicalities of copyright. "Well— it seems we have got it at last," Besant wrote to congratulate Matthews on July 1, 1891, the day the bill took effect, from the office of the Society. Matthews was apparently in London again at the time, for this letter opens with an invitation to him and Mrs. Matthews to attend the annual dinner of the Society in Holborn.

Besant goes on to extend the invitation to several noteworthy martyrs to the cause:

> I shall write Charles Dickens—Charles Reade— Wilkie Collins and Lord Lytton—not Thackeray because he never seemed to care. I shall pay for their tickets out of the fortune they ought to have made—You may write your Ghosts if you please— We shall be glad to meet Fenimore Cooper & Nathaniel Hawthorne—especially—You have funds— ghostly funds—their fortunes made here—on your side to meet the expense of bringing them over.

Even after the passage of the Copyright Act of 1891, Besant warned his friend not to relax his vigilance. On October 15, 1892, after acknowledging the gift of Matthews's book for young people *Tom Paulding*, which he turned over to his son, Besant asked: "Have you secured copyright here? Pirates still abound you know."

This letter concludes by soliciting Matthews's advice about a forthcoming Congress of Authors in Chicago in which Besant had been invited to participate. The next letter, dated February 14, 1893, indicates that with Matthews's encouragement he was seriously contemplating the voyage, "but I don't know if it will come off. I am so horribly afraid of Asthma." Besant did lead the delegation from the Society of Authors to the Congress held in July 1893 in connection with the Columbian Exposition; in fact, from his side he helped plan the conference with its chairman Francis Browne, editor of the *Dial*, then Chicago's leading literary journal.

On what proved his only visit to the United States, Besant, before taking the railway journey to Chicago, traveled through the East and spent some time in New York prior to returning to England. This experience led to his engaging Matthews the following year as a contributor. "Returning to our talk about the New York Letter to the Author," he wrote on July 22, 1894, from his home in Hampstead to his colleague then on his annual summer visit to England. "I have been thinking of it again and I believe it would be an excellent thing for us. Can we try for a year?" While allowing Matthews a free hand, he exerted some editorial direction:

> We do not want personal details—a few may help the understanding of a book, e.g. that Cable is a Louisiana man (It is also interesting but not for publication to have seen him & to know what an ugly creature he is). Then we want to know what is going on in the literary world—its clubs—papers etc.—I assure you there is great scope. The writer might be the means of introducing to us some most valuable writers.

"Remember that our ignorance of American literature is really colossal," Besant remarked earlier in the letter, recalling that he found his countrymen well represented in bookshops in Boston and New Haven, "but in our shops—where are your books?" On this trip Besant also swooped up "all the living American poets that Messrs Little & Co. could rake together for me" to bring back with him. He thought American poets in general rather shabbily treated in English reviews, with reference specifically to one of Matthews's colleagues on the Columbia faculty, who had participated in the Chicago Authors' Congress: "George Woodberry for instance. I brought him over & gave him to a man to read and not to deride. The result at all events was a short notice of appreciation in the S[aturday] R[eview]."

His own animadversions fueled by Besant's charge, it is not surprising that a note of chauvinism pervades Hallett Robinson's letters to the *Author.* He begins by boasting that with the quadrupling of the population of the United States since the days of the Knickerbockers, literary production has fanned out through the land, and by now "there are many more accomplished writers than there were formerly and the average of merit is undoubtedly higher." A later piece announces the establishment of New York branches by the venerable firms of Longman's and Macmillan's, pointedly adding that they are flourishing on their American authors. In other columns he refutes with facts and figures assertions of superiority in the British press, such as that English novelists still outsell American in the United States, and that no American magazine approaches the *Strand* in circulation.

Concurrently H.R. observed with special pride that the teaching of English literature was more widespread in American schools and universities than in British, Columbia being in the forefront, second only to Harvard. He hails the launching of the Columbia University Press, "which has been founded to do for Columbia what the Clarendon Press does for Oxford." This banner year (1895) gave him opportunity also to announce the establishment of "a public library worthy of the chief city of a great nation," to which Columbia had offered a site eventually rejected.

In one of his letters, Besant requested that Matthews discuss American literary magazines. The last of H.R.'s contributions (December 1, 1895) gave his editor perhaps more than he asked for. He contended, for example, that the columns of the *Nation* and the *Critic* were "absolutely free from the sickening self-puffery of their own contributors which disgrace certain of the London reviews." (His barbs were aimed specifically at the *Spectator* and the *Academy.*) To his praise of New York's *Bookman,* "a brisk and lively review abundant in trenchant and lively criticism" under the editorship of Columbia's classics professor Harry Thurston Peck, he adds that this magazine has "too much sense of proportion and too wide a knowledge of books to give up to the infusoria of contemporary literature the space they are allowed to fill in the Bookman*'s* London namesake."

Obviously in putting America's best foot forward, Matthews did not hesitate to step on English toes, but Besant, far from objecting, was reluctant to lose him: "I am indeed grieved to learn that 'H.R.' will cease after December," he wrote on September 2, 1895, in response to a letter of resignation, "You must find some one, some

how, who will console our readers for the loss." Two months later on November 14 he reiterated:

> Your papers were just what we wanted. If your successor will only bear in mind that people here are very ignorant about almost everything in American literature! I don't think you can walk around us yet in letters as you can in yachts. But I like a good honest American belief in thine own article.

Shortly afterward Norman Hapgood took over the "New York Letter" in the *Author,* apparently on Matthews's recommendation.

Occasionally Besant found Matthews a useful sounding board on his own writing. In his first letter where he informed him of the Society of Authors he also consulted him on the publishability of a contemplated story on the War of Independence from the Loyalist standpoint. Matthews cited Besant's early collaboration with James Rice as an example of a literary "marriage" in the introduction to his collection **With My Friends: Tales Told in Partnership** (1891), and Besant in turn requested permission to draw on this book for his article "Authors Individual and Corporate." He also took interest in Matthews's pioneering courses, which separated the teaching of literature from language and rhetoric: "A thousand thanks for your Exam Paper . . . I have said in the 'Author' that you were the first Professor of Literature who has done this on the novel. Your paper is a stiff one—I should like to know what sort of marks were obtained on it but I suppose I must not ask" (February 23, 1893). From time to time he fed his correspondent club gossip. His letter of April 27, 1895, accompanying a check, carried news of a persecuted fellow author:

> We have all been afflicted with the real horror of the Oscar Wilde business. As I write he is standing his trial in the Old Bailey. I wish he could be acquitted. It seems like a national disgrace—tho' he is not a big enough man of letters to make it so. However, it is sufficiently horrible.

"He is not a member of the Savile," Besant added, "tho' he tried to get in two years ago."

With the tapering off of Matthews's visits to England after 1895, Besant's letters to him record mainly exchanges of books and ideas. A proposal to make the Authors' Club of New York and the Society of Authors "of mutual help" (August 15, 1896) apparently did not materialize. A letter dated January 2, 1898, carries the heading "The Survey of London," the major undertaking of Besant's last years ("I am the successor of Stow and Strype—if you know these great men," he had previously announced). A paper by Matthews entitled **"The Future of the English Language"** (*Munsey's Magazine,* October, 1898), in which he predicted that English and Russian would become the dominant languages of the world, overtaking French, German, Italian, and Spanish, elicited this reaction from Besant:

I think that you overrate the future importance of Germany and France. Neither country could support a much larger population than they have at present unless Science assists. As for the future supremacy of Russian or Anglo-Saxon, I think there should be very little doubt as to the result. The Russian is curiously lacking in the qualities of enterprise and self-reliance that are so conspicuously present in ourselves. It remains to be seen, however, whether we can arrive at a federation of six great countries speaking our language and governed by our institutions. (January 11, 1899)

This letter was accompanied by a present of Besant's *The Rise of The Empire,* "a little book which I wrote some time ago for schools."

"Are you coming over to see the Exhibition and the Savile Club?" inquired Besant in the last letter, dated April 16, 1900. "It is now the third year since you were here. Some of us are not growing any younger." This letter begins with praise for Matthews's latest novel *The Action and the Word,* which "I read in bed when I was a prisoner with certain ailments," and ends with an expression of curiosity about the infant National Institute of Arts and Letters, to which Matthews had recently been elected, among the first to be so honored. Besant died in June of the following year.

"The generation now coming forward knows nought of [William] Black and it cares as little for Walter Besant, whose cheerful stories used to join fellowship with Black's, month after month, week after week," Matthews wrote toward the conclusion of his memoir *These Many Years* (1917). The author of some thirty topical novels and numerous popular histories who thought of himself as no more than a writer for his own day, who indeed rarely retained a copyright, not expecting any of his books to go into a second edition, Besant would probably not have been bothered by these words. However, at the time they were written, a memorial plaque to him had been installed in the crypt of St. Paul's, and the *Author* still bore on its masthead "Founded by Walter Besant." Moreover, the Society of Authors flourishes to this day. A man of letters and a man of causes, Besant's talent went into his writing, his genius into his enterprise.

Lawrence J. Oliver (essay date, 1992)

SOURCE: "Ideological "Snap-Shots" of the New York Metropolis: Matthews's Fiction," in *Theodore Roosevelt, Brander Matthews, and the Politics of American Literature,* University of Tennessee Press, 1992, pp. 145-63.

[*In the following excerpt, Oliver reviews Matthews' three novels and considers the effect of his attitudes about race, class, and gender on his vision and practice of Realism.*]

In addition to his voluminous scholarship and criticism, Matthews produced a sizable and varied corpus of fiction: three full-length novels, several books of short stories, and a juvenile romance. Matthews admitted that many of his early stories, written during the late 1870s and early 1880s, were done purely for fun and were imitative of the "clever" but superficial fictions of Thomas Bailey Aldrich. But, as he crusaded for Howells and literary realism during the eighties, Matthews became increasingly interested in exploiting the "local color" potential of his beloved New York. As he explains in his autobiography:

> The field was here, and it was fertile, and furthermore, it had not been pre-empted. Yet there were very few of us who then [the late 1880s] recognized the richness of the soil or who had confidence in the crop that could be raised. London had been painted on the broad canvases of a host of robust novelists. . . . but New York had not yet attracted either the novelists [with the exception of Henry James, of course] or the tellers of brief tales. Her streets were paved with gold . . . but the men of letters who strayed here and there in her thorofares had not the vision to perceive they were living in a Golconda of opportunity.[1]

With this vision in mind, Matthews set out to "write short stories saturated with local color," verbal "snap-shots" that would capture and fix the "color, unending movement, and incessant vitality" of the great metropolis.[2] In 1894 he collected a dozen of these previously published "snap-shots" into a volume titled *Vignettes of Manhattan,* and followed it in 1897 with a second volume, *Outlines in Local Color.* Realizing that the short-story form could not contain the "movement of the mighty city," he approached his subject with a larger camera, producing three novels: *His Father's Son* (1895), *A Confident Tomorrow* (1899), and *The Action and the Word* (1900). Though none of these works was the best-seller he hoped for, each was, he remarks, well-received by reviewers and by his "fellow-craftsmen in the practice of fiction."[3] Matthews's novels were not as well received as he suggests, but they did win praise from several literary fellows, including the craftsman he most wanted to please—Howells.

In 1893, as he struggled to overcome his penchant for producing "clever" stories and to create enduring "snap-shots," Matthews, reflecting on a recent conversation with Howells, wrote him: "What you said the other night about my stories not being your kind of stories is true, I'm afraid. Not only is my natural gift less, but both my temperament and my training are very different from yours. Yet your kinds of stories are the stories I like best, read oftenest, praise most highly. From no American author have I learned as much as from you of the ways, customs, traditions, thoughts and characters of my fellow citizens." Matthews closed by declaring that, though his own works fell short of the realist mark, he did not "belong in the other [what Howells termed the "romanticistic"] camp."[4]

Why Howells would place Matthews's fiction in the "other camp" is suggested by a story like **"Memories,"** which, is a thinly veiled tribute to Roosevelt and promotes the Rough Rider's code of the "strenuous life" and "manly duty." Roosevelt was very pleased also with *Vignettes of Manhattan,* which Matthews dedicated to him. No doubt the volume includes several of the pieces that prompted Howells to reprimand Matthews for being a romanticistic writer. In **"Before the Break of Day,"** for example, Matthews responded to the copy of *Maggie* that Stephen Crane had sent him by re-visioning it into an improbable tale of heroism that celebrates the American Dream. The tale is set in the Bowery, and its heroine is named Maggie. Like Crane's, this Maggie's life has been hard and gets worse after she is jilted by a young tough. But Matthews's heroine does not slide into the naturalistic abyss; rescued from its edge by an honest bartender, she and her new beau get married, buy a saloon of their own, and feel confident that they will be rich if they keep working hard. In another vignette, a father succeeds in securing a governor's pardon for his son, who had been unjustly imprisoned for manslaughter. The youth, however, is killed in a prison riot the very day the pardon is granted; when the father reads the newspaper account of his son's death, he falls dead on the spot, "still tightly grasping the pardon."[5]

After receiving Howells's frank criticism in 1893, however, Matthews attempted to replace the melodramatic lens through which he had envisioned his vignettes with a realist one. His first success as a Howellsian "realist" was, in the Dean's as well as his own eyes, *His Father's Son,* a novel that was serialized in two parts in *Harper's Weekly* in 1895 before being published in volume form in 1896. As Howells had sarcastically observed in an 1891 "Editor's Study" piece, the millionaire had become the new subject for the romance.[6] The central character of *His Father's Son* is a millionaire, but he is no more romanticized than is Jacob Dryfoos of *A Hazard of New Fortunes.* In his fictions set in Fort Roosevelt or the ghetto, Matthews was swimming in alien waters; but in depicting the Wall Street scene he was in his own element. Before the Panic of 1873 financially ruined his father, young Brander spent a good deal of time at his father's business office on Wall Street, observing first-hand the making and breaking of millionaires. Those observations had convinced him that the majority of Wall Street tycoons were not heroes to be idolized but unprincipled materialists whose lust for profits was a cancer of the national spirit. That view was, of course, shared by Roosevelt and most other progressivists. In the opening chapter of *His Father's Son,* Ezra Pierce (the father) preaches to his son Winslow that, though some may consider investors to be mere gamblers, they are actually the "greatest benefactors of humanity the world has ever seen."[7] Subsequent events in the novel, however, refute that claim: under the well-intentioned but inevitably pernicious tutelage of his father—who refuses to see the immorality of many of his business dealings—Winslow gradually becomes possessed by the gambling demon and is transformed from a moral idealist into a selfish cynic. By the end of the narrative, he has destroyed his marriage and has fled to Europe to escape prosecution for fraud. There he marries a Parisian socialite and pesters his heartbroken father for more money.

Reviewing the first installment of the novel when it appeared in *Harper's,* Howells showered it and the author with praise. Matthews's essays and drama criticism have been consistently brilliant, states the Dean, but the fictions preceding *His Father's Son* are, as he had told Matthews personally in 1893, tainted by elements of the fantastic.[8] "I have had to ask myself," Howells continues, "Hasn't his knowledge of literature got the better of his knowledge of life at this point or at that [in his stories]? Will he be able to go forward in the light of the verity dear to his artistic conscience, or will he advance in the flicker of the trickery fancy that amuses him?" But with *His Father's Son,* Howells declares, Matthews seems to have abandoned the fanciful and sensational and has joined the American school of fiction best represented by the recent work of such accomplished realists as Henry B. Fuller. The first half of Matthews's novel reveals a "firm texture of character, a fidelity of circumstance, a quiet truth of local color"; this is Wall Street as never before depicted in American literature. If the second and final installment of the novel sustains the artistic virtues present in the first, then Matthews, Howells contends, will have established himself as a novelist of true quality.

Matthews, needless to say, was greatly flattered and wrote Howells to say so. Admitting that most of his previous fictions—even those that "pretended to be realistic"—were essentially "fantastic," he declares that *His Father's Son* is his attempt to face life seriously and truthfully, as writers such as Turgenev and, of course, Howells himself have done. "I hope," Matthews states, "you will like the story to the end; however much it may fall off, it does not change its manner at all. The end is too sad, I fear, for the study ever to be popular; and so your praise of it is doubly precious."[9]

Though one particularly uncharitable critic dismissed the completed novel as a "sad dog,"[10] most reviewers praised the book's theme and its detailed depiction of the Wall Street scene. But they also faulted Matthews for creating characters lacking psychological depth, and at least one critic found Winslow's slide from moral idealism to selfish cynicism improbable.[11] Most critics today would, I think, concur with these complaints. Howells's review, however, offers a much more positive perspective: filled with superlatives, it grants the high marks that Matthews had hoped for. Announcing that Matthews "kept faith with me to the last word" of the novel, Howells reports that he has not read a "cleaner, finer, straighter piece of work" in a long time; *His Father's Son* is a "tragedy of principles, of conditions, of moral forces, but so livingly embodied that it is too intensely human, too like us all, to suffer us to be very self-confident in condemning this or that person in it."[12] In seeking to present a truthful vision of Wall Street, argues Howells, Matthews could not help but accuse the "whole economic system," though "that is scarcely what the author meant [to do]." significantly, further on in the same review essay, Howells only lukewarmly recommends Crane's *The Red Badge of Courage,* judging it psychologically realistic but somewhat immature.

Works of art, Theodor Adorno has written, achieve greatness only insofar as they "let speak what ideology conceals. They transcend, whether they want to or not, false consciousness."[13] Adorno's proposition helps explain, I think, why Howells—who at this point in his life was a socialist in his politics, if not in his life-style—would value Matthews's banal novel over Crane's masterpiece of psychological impressionism. As his admiration for and friendship with Andrew Carnegie testifies, Matthews did not share the Dean's view of capitalism as an "infernal" economic system; like Roosevelt, he condemned plutocracy but not the economic system that created plutocrats. Thus, from a Marxist perspective, Matthews was clearly a prisoner of "false consciousness." But, in conceiving *His Father's Son* he had, Howells suggests in the review, transcended his bourgeois ideology and produced a work whose subtext indicts capitalism, though that was "scarcely what [he] meat [to do]." (Howells may have preferred *Maggie* over *The Red Badge of Courage* because the ghetto tale, too, implicitly condemns the "whole economic system.") Yet Howells's interpretation—one might say appropriation—of *His Father's Son* as an attack on socioeconomic principles that Matthews himself embraced did not, apparently, chafe the professor, for he expressed his deep appreciation for the review, remarking, "You were in my mind always as I wrote. I was trying to tell the truth according to your precepts and was hoping that you would like the tale."[14]

When Matthews undertook writing his second novel, *A Confident To-morrow,* four years later in 1899, Howells was again in his mind, so much so that the book contains a thinly disguised portrait of him. But the portrait is not entirely flattering, and the novel overall projects Matthews's growing disenchantment with Howells's praxis, if not theory, of literary realism. In this book Matthews sought not to "keep faith" with his literary father but to rid himself of what Harold Bloom would diagnose as the "anxiety of influence."

Described as a "determined realist," Frank Sartain, the novel's central character, comes from Topeka, where he had spent several years as a journalist, to New York City in hopes of publishing his first novel, titled *Dust and Ashes*.[15] Mirror image of *His Father's Son,* Sartain's fictional study of the metropolis focuses all its attention on the villains of Wall Street and their victims. Having had no firsthand experience with the New York scene, however, Sartain based his depiction of it entirely on other books as well as on his unpleasant boyhood experiences at Narragansett Pier, where as a hack-driver for the rich during summers, he was exposed to the "hollowness of our boasted civilization" and to social snobbery. The shortcomings of American culture and social snobbery are, of course, two prominent themes in Howells's novels, including *A Hazard of New Fortunes,* which was, one suspects, among the urban fictions that shaped Sartain's perceptions of big-city life. Upon arriving in New York, Sartain immediately seeks the acquaintance of Meredith Vivian, a novelist whose "delicate art" Sartain admires with the same "profound reverence" as Matthews did

Howells's. That Howells was the model for Vivian seems beyond question. Like Howells, Vivian, who advises Sartain to write about what he knows best rather than what seems interesting "literary" material, rose from humble beginnings to become the most successful and influential novelist of his era and a sort of father figure to the younger generation of writers. Howells, as his six volumes of *Selected Letters* reveal, wrote numerous letters of encouragement and advice to fledgling writers and critics. Matthews's essays and reviews praising Howells's works earned him many notes of appreciation and support, including the one in which the Dean proclaimed: "your work is better than that of any critic of your generation."[16] The description of Vivian's relationship and correspondence with his literary sons suggests, however, that Matthews may have suspected that ulterior motives lurked beneath the surface of such flattering remarks. Vivian, one character sarcastically observes, has

> a habit of attaching to him by bonds of gratitude for favors received all the rising young men of letters in the country. [He] writes one of his clever little notes to every man who reviews one of his books—and if the fellow who did the notice is young, he takes it as a great compliment to himself and as proof that his critical faculty is singularly acute.

Sartain, who upon reviewing one of Vivian's novels receives a letter from him commending the review for its "justice both in the praise and the blame," wonders if all those "clever little notes" are Vivian's self-seeking attempts to maintain his prominent stature among upcoming writers like himself. In a letter expressing his appreciation for Matthews's **"Mr. Howells as a Critic"** in 1902—three years after *A Confident Tomorrow* was written—Howells, curiously enough, echoed Vivian's urbane note to Sartain: "Your praise," the Dean remarked, "seems the more reasonable because your blame is so just."[17] Emerson Adams, a painter whose character fuses the idealism of an Emerson with the prickly cynicism of a Henry Adams, assures Sartain, however, that the elder writer is by nature kind, sincere, and generous—just as Matthews assured his contemporaries that Howells was a man "large of nature and of a transparent sincerity."[18] These qualities, not any manipulative practices on Vivian's part, have kept him "solid" with the younger writers, declares Adams. Sartain accepts Adams's assessment, but by merely raising the question of Vivian's sincerity, Matthews plants in the reader's mind the seed of doubt about Vivian's character and, by implication, about Howells's as well.

Subsequent events in the narrative deepen the ambivalent image of Vivian and therefore of Howells. *Dust and Ashes,* Sartain admits, was an attempt to follow in Vivian's footsteps; not surprisingly, though he finds its art rather immature, Vivian responds favorably to the Wall Street novel, just as the author of *A Hazard of New Fortunes* had to *His Father's Son.* But the longer he investigates the city for himself, the more Sartain is "seized by a sense of the beauty inherent in modern life."

Influenced by Emerson Adams, who is at his most sarcastic when castigating those who denigrate the modern and idealize the ancient (Matthews, we recall, disparaged Ibsen for desiring to return to the "sun-dial"), Sartain comes to equate the metropolis with vitality and progress rather than with degeneracy. In an epiphanic moment brought on by Adams's passionate outburst celebrating the city, Sartain discovers that his "realism had been rather sordid," that he had "looked down for his facts rather than up." His second novel, he therefore determines, will offer a much more positive perspective on New York than did his tale of Wall Street villains and victims.

An upbeat perspective on New York is precisely what Matthews provides in *A Confident To-morrow,* for this novel, in contrast to *His Father's Son,* is a success story with a happy ending. After Sartain comes to New York and meets Vivian, he falls in love with the charming Esther Dircks, whose father is a socialist radical. Intellectually vacuous, ignorant of political issues, and not interested in gaining the right to vote, Esther is a far cry from the "New Woman." When her father, Raphael, inherits a large sum of money, he launches a reformist newspaper and offers the editorship to Sartain, whose disdain for the plutocrats appeals to the cranky old man. Sartain, however, is as opposed to Dircks's anarchism as he is to laissez-faire capitalism and crass commercialism. Sartain's politics are unmistakably progressivist; he supports abolition of the patronage system, subsidized housing, and other social and political reforms that Roosevelt and the progressivists championed in real life. As one who believed that "public opinion, if only sufficiently enlightened and aroused, is equal to the necessary regenerative tasks and can yet dominate the future," Roosevelt must have been delighted by Sartain's exclamation, in the passage that embodies the novel's central theme, that "It has always seemed to me that the way to make the world better is to tell people it is getting better, and to prove it to them; to encourage them and not to discourage them; to inspire hope and confidence and energy to fight a good fight, with certain victory in the distance." And Roosevelt—who in 1894, the year of the bloody Pullman riots in Chicago, admitted to Matthews that he liked to see a "mob handled by the regulars, or by good State guards, not over-scrupulous about bloodshed"—would without doubt have concurred with Sartain's condemnation of the strikers' violent actions against the police during the New York street-car strike.[19] Though Dircks's sympathies are entirely with labor, Sartain—who has come to believe that the "boyish iconoclasm" he brought with him to New York was "rather foolish"—feels morally compelled to write an editorial in which he argues that "If we attack the robber barons because they set themselves above the law, we must also call the strikers to order when they put themselves outside the law." Outraged, the fanatical Dircks refuses to put another cent into a tabloid that "stood up for law." (Since he has by this point gone bankrupt, he could not provide more money for the enterprise even if he wanted to.) The paper goes under. Sartain is unemployed but not dismayed; he remains confident about tomorrow. His optimism is

borne out when he is hired—at a larger salary—by a New York publishing house, this stroke of good fortune allowing him to marry the fair Esther. And Sartain's faith in the common sense of his fellow New Yorkers is validated by their electing an honest reformer to the mayor's office, as reform-minded New Yorkers had done in 1894 by voting for William L. Strong and against the Tammany machine. In the novel's closing lines, as Sartain and his new bride gaze, arm in arm, at the New York skyline, we are told that, whereas two years earlier the mighty city seemed a "frowning fortress" to the callow young man, it now appears "friendly and inviting."

Noting the obvious parallels between Dircks and the anarchist Lindau of *A Hazard of New Fortunes,* Matthews's Columbia colleague Harry Thurston Peck suggested in his review of *A Confident To-morrow* that "Mr. Matthews's well-known admiration for the work of Mr. Howells has led him unconsciously to assimilate some of Mr. Howells's material."[20] Peck missed the point: Matthews indeed assimilated material from *A Hazard of New Fortunes*—not only Dircks's portrait but major plot elements as well—but he acted intentionally. As he had earlier done with Crane's *Maggie,* Matthews transformed a grim work that seeks to subvert the status quo into a middlebrow celebration of the American Dream. Where Howells's novel portrays the strikers sympathetically and condemns the brutality of the police, Matthews's puts the strikers in a negative light and insists that the police had to meet violence with violence in order to prevent anarchy. Where the plutocrat Jacob Dryfoos is the central target of Howells's scorn, the anarchist-socialist Dircks is the butt of Matthews's. Looking down rather than up for the facts when constructing his first New York novel, Howells produced his darkest fiction; turning his gaze upward—as Sartain physically does in the book's closing—Matthews created a progressivist novel that aims to "inspire hope and confidence and energy to fight a good fight."

Matthews's re-visioning of Howells's *Hazard of New Fortunes* should not, however, be interpreted as a repudiation of the doctrine of literary realism, which, as we have noted, he defined as the attempt to render life honestly and truthfully, for he believed that *A Confident To-morrow* presented a more accurate cross-section of New York life than did Howells's novel. It was Howells, after all, who in that famous quote of 1886 urged the American writer to dramatize the "more smiling aspects of life" since they were the "more American." The Haymarket tragedy of 1886 and the terrible death of his daughter in 1889 darkened Howells's vision, as *A Hazard of New Fortunes* testifies. Matthews, however, never wavered in his conviction that the "smiling aspects" *were* the more American. As previously discussed, Matthews was ideologically much closer to the jingoistic Roosevelt than to the deeply distressed Dean in the late 1890s. When he embarked upon his first novel in 1895, Matthews set out to produce a somber "Howellsian" critique of Gilded Age commercialism, the result, as Howells observed, being an implicit denunciation of capitalism. But the Spanish-American War fanned the flames of Matthews's burning sense of patriotism, and *A Confident To-morrow*—the title itself implying Matthews's "bully" Americanism—projected, as such essays as **"The Study of Fiction"** also did, his belief that the "race traits" most manifest in the "typical" Anglo-American were courage, tenacity, energy, good humor, and so on. Put simply, Matthews's quarrel with Howells was not over the aesthetic of realism, which Matthews, we recall, vigorously defended in **"Mr. Howells as a Critic"** (1902) and in other post-1900 essays, but over the Dean's vision of America and the ideology in which that vision was grounded.

In 1894 Roosevelt, who admired Howells's early works, complained that the Dean's view of life had turned "jaundiced."[21] As he breaks away from Vivian's influence in *A Confident To-morrow,* Matthews's persona employs a synonymous metaphor in describing the "damning defect" of the elder writer's novels: they lack, he says, the "ruddy drop of human blood." By the end of the novel Sartain, though he maintains his friendship with and respect for Vivian, discovers that he "could no longer assign to the elder author so high a place as he had hitherto given him. It came upon him with a certain shock that he had outgrown Vivian, that he had passed beyond the stage in which such writing as Vivian's was to be admired inevitably, and that perhaps, after all, he had been setting too high a value upon Vivian's work." With that comment, Matthews completed the figurative slaying of his literary father.

Surely Howells, who had reviewed Matthews's first novel with such enthusiasm and who commented, either publicly or privately, on virtually every book his friend published, must have read *A Confident To-morrow,* yet he does not mention it in any of his published writings or in any of the numerous letters he wrote to Matthews after 1900. Assuming he did read the book and recognized, as he could hardly avoid doing, its ambivalent portrait of him, he apparently did not allow the experience to sour his relationship with Matthews; the two men remained close friends until Howells's death. Matthews was one of many writers, most notably Garland and Wister, who drifted from Howells's to Roosevelt's camp during the late 1890s, and in such cases the Dean generally proved to be a tolerant literary mentor.[22] In his 1917 review of *These Many Years* Howells was as generous as ever with his praise: not only did he laud Matthews's accomplishments as a scholar and educator, he also expressed admiration for Matthews's "two . . . best novels."[23] Two, not three; since Howells, as explained below, considered Matthews's final novel, *The Action and the Word,* to be an even better work of art than *His Father's Son,* the novel he tactfully excluded must be *A Confident Tomorrow.*

The Action and the Word (1900) concerns itself with one of Howells's favorite themes, the Woman Question; and, as in several of his marriage novels, that question is implicitly answered by affirming the value of marriage as a bulwark against anarchic desires that threaten both self and society.[24] But if Matthews followed Howells in this respect, he sought to go "beyond" the elder writer's "jaundiced" fiction by injecting his narrative with the element of passion he felt was wanting in the Dean's novels. In **"Of Women's Novels"** Matthews, as noted, had observed that women writers were "more willing than men [such as Howells?] to suggest the animal nature that sheathes our immortal souls; they are bolder in the use of the stronger emotions; they are more willing to suggest the possibilities of passion lurking all unsuspected beneath the placidity of modern fine-lady existence."[25] In *The Action and the Word,* Matthews, one might say, sought to write passionately "like a woman"—but the result would hardly have pleased feminists like Charlotte Perkins Gilman.

The novel's central character is Carla, a beautiful, dark-eyed Creole whose "supple" and "undulating" walk never fails to attract an admiring male eye. Daughter of a race-horse breeder, she spent her youth in an environment where "animal nature" could hardly be more apparent—a stud farm. When she marries into the upper stratum of Manhattan society, she becomes bored with her role as a wife and mother. The source of her frustration, Matthews all but explicitly states, is sexual repression. Dr. Brookfield (Carla's father-in-law), who represents the wisdom that comes with maturity, suspects that she is dissatisfied with domestic life because she did not "sow her her wild oats" as a youth, as males have the opportunity to do. She finds an outlet for her suppressed desires in amateur acting. Like her contemporary fictional actress, Carrie Meeber, Carla thrills her audiences with her ability to "exert the potent fascination of sex" on stage.[26] That acting is for Carla, as for Carrie, a sublimation of her sexual urges is vividly suggested when, in an agitated state after a successful performance, she remarks that the experience on stage reminded her of an exciting adventure she had when she was fifteen years old: in an act of intentional disobedience, she had gone bare-back riding on one of the studs, "astride like a man." Describing how her horse broke into a wild gallop, she exclaims: "There we were, flying down the pike, and I couldn't hold him, and my hair got loose, and I didn't know whether he was running away and whether he'd even stop. That was splendid, too! Excitement and success,—just like to-night,—for I conquered him after a while; and I rode him home on the snaffle."

Though Matthews could be bold enough to reveal the passions lurking beneath the placidity of modern fine-lady existence, he nonetheless shared Howells's fear of the "unbridled" libido in women. As the story proceeds, it becomes clear that, if Carla's mild-mannered husband, Evert, does not take the reins, she will ride roughshod over him, thus destroying their marriage and jeopardizing the future happiness of their infant son. When she broaches the idea of going on the road as a professional actress and placing the baby under the care of a governess, Evert seeks counsel from Dr. Brookfield, who informs him that, however passionately they cry for independence, women desire to be *mastered* by their man. Inspired by his father's advice, Evert takes his stand. A bitter quarrel ensues, with Carla crying out: "I was a woman before I was a mother, wasn't I? And I think a woman has some rights, after all. She has a right to live her own life, hasn't she?" She further exclaims that she will be no "slave," no "talking doll, to be wound up and dressed and undressed [!] again." Carla of course speaks—or rather screams—here in the voice of the New Woman, but though her arguments may sound persuasive to feminist ears, they are dismissed as the rantings of a spoiled child by her husband, and, clearly, by the novel's author, who once complained that the ending of *A Doll's House* was improbable because Ibsen denied Nora the "most permanent and most overpowering of woman's characteristics—the maternal instinct."[27] In the end, that instinct does indeed overwhelm Carla: after nursing her child through a serious illness, she decides, as Dr. Brookfield knew she would, that she prefers the nursery to a room of her own. The closing scene finds her disparaging the author of *A Doll's House* as an "old bore" who knows nothing about "American girls," and chirping that "It's a wife's duty to wait on her husband."

The reference to *A Doll's House* suggests that Matthews meant his novel to be a rebuttal of Ibsen's "unrealistic" play. But he may also have been targeting Kate Chopin's *The Awakening,* which had appeared a year before ***The Action and the Word.*** The many parallels between these works suggest that Matthews—who, as a native of New Orleans, had a special interest in fictional portraits of Creole life—had Chopin's novel in mind as he composed his own.[28] Both works dramatize the struggle of a passionate woman to break the constricting bonds imposed by American Victorianism, and both set in opposition the Creole and Anglo (Puritan) attitudes toward sexual desire. Like Carla, Edna came to New Orleans from Kentucky, where her father bred race horses.[29] Finally, the title that Chopin chose for her novel would fit Matthews's perfectly, for the climactic event of ***The Action and the Word*** is Carla's "awakening" to her responsibilities as a wife and mother, responsibilities that Edna escapes through suicide.

The Action and the Word no doubt struck a responsive chord in those "manly" readers who shared Theodore Roosevelt's fear that *fin de siècle* American culture was becoming dangerously feminized. Yet the most lavish praise of the book came not from the Rough Rider but from Howells, who must have somehow discovered in it the "fidelity to experience and probability of motive" that he demanded in the realist novel. In an essay in *Literature and Life,* Howells placed ***The Action and the Word*** in the good company of Crane's *Maggie,* Abraham Cahan's *Yekl,* and James's *Washington Square;* after speaking of the "masterly skill" with which Matthews had sketched New York's genteel society in ***His Father's Son,*** the Dean lauded Matthews's third novel as "one of the best American stories I know."[30] In a letter to Garland he called it "a capital story about a stage-tempted wife— the best thing [Matthews] has done." To Matthews himself, Howells gushed that the work was "one of the most perfect pieces of fiction in the language," adding: "The delicate beauty of such a book as The A[ction] and the W[ord] is obscured in a brute time for a while, but it will

count you 12 in minds of true critics." And when he was asked to be general editor of a series of novels by prominent American and British writers (a project later aborted), Howells solicited a book from Matthews, asking him if he could produce "a novel of 50,000 words as good as 'The A[ction] and the W[ord]?'"[31]

From his own day to the present, Howells's attitude toward women has generated heated debate. To such admirers of Howells as Edwin H. Cady, the Dean's support of the suffrage movement, his well-known statement that women were, in general, morally superior to men, and the many sympathetic portraits in his novels of women trapped in the patriarchal net of Victorian American culture qualify him for the title of "ardent feminist." But Gail Thain Parker and other feminist critics have argued that the subtexts of Howells's works endorse male hegemony and reveal his unconscious fear of the independent woman.[32] Critics on both sides of the fence have been vexed by Howells's silence on *The Awakening.* We know that he admired "Boulet and Boulotte," one of Chopin's vignettes of Creole life, for he sent her a letter telling her so. No other correspondence between the two writers exists, however, and Howells makes no mention of Chopin or *The Awakening* in his writings.[33] But if ***The Action and the Word*** is, as I have suggested, a patriarchal re-visioning of *The Awakening,* then Howells's exuberant praise of Matthews's novel may be read as an implicit comment on Chopin's. In any case, Howells's discovery of "delicate beauty" in Matthews's crude caricature of the New Woman provides telling evidence for those in Parker's camp.

"Don't you be down-hearted; you are all right, and your day is coming," Howells assured Matthews in the letter commending the "delicate beauty" of ***The Action and the Word.***[34] By that time, however, a thoroughly discouraged Matthews had faced the fact that his day as a novelist would never come; in 1900 he abandoned novel-writing, complaining to Trent (before the breach of their friendship occurred): "I don't sell—and I don't get praised."[35] A year earlier (1899), Howells had composed his lecture essay "Novel-Writing and Novel-Reading," perhaps his most thoughtfully expressed proclamation of his realist credo. In it he stated that "truth to life is the supreme office of the novel," and he contended that the novelist "is rarely the victim of such a possession, or obsession, that he does not know when he is representing and when he is misrepresenting life. If he does not know it fully at the time, he cannot fail to be aware of it upon review of his work."[36] The naïveté of that theory is clearly exposed by Matthews's assessment of his work. Though the reception of his novels (outside the flattering reviews provided by Howells, Trent, and other close friends) disheartened him to the point that he ceased writing fiction, Matthews never came to recognize what seems obvious to a contemporary critic: that his supposedly "objective" representations of the great metropolis were mediated by his race, class, gender, and ideology. In his retrospective analysis of why his novels failed to achieve the popularity and critical acclaim he had hoped for, Matthews insisted that the "picture I painted [in the novels] was true to life." The main reason his "snapshots" had not won a wide readership, suggested the creator of such cardboard stereotypes as Ezra Pierce, Raphael Dircks, and Carla Brookfield, was that they were "too quiet in tone, too subdued, too moderate, to thrust themselves into the favor of the general public"; the merits of his novels, he was convinced, could be appreciated only by the "inner circle" who "relish deliberate workmanship."[37] That progressive-minded inner circle, one can be sure, included no Wall Street plutocrats, socialists, or "New Women."

NOTES

[1] Matthews, *These Many Years,* 383.

[2] Ibid., 383-84.

[3] Ibid., 389.

[4] Matthews to Howells, 25 Dec. 1893, William D. Howells Papers, Houghton Library, Harvard Univ. Subsequent references will be to "Howells Papers."

[5] Matthews, *Vignettes of Manhattan* (New York: Harper, 1894), 85-97, 13-21.

[6] Howells, "The Editor's Study," *Harper's Monthly* (Nov. 1891); rpt. in *W. D. Howells as Critic,* 204.

[7] Matthews, *His Father's Son: A Novel of New York* (New York: Harper, 1895, 1896), 17.

[8] Howells, "Life and Letters," *Harper's Weekly* 39 (Aug. 3, 1895): 725-26.

[9] Matthews to Howells, 3 Sept. 1895, Howells Papers.

[10] Anon., "Recent Fiction," *The Nation* 62 (1896): 81.

[11] See, for example, Hamlin Garland's review in *The Bookman* 2 (1895-96): 416-20. Garland commends the novel for avoiding the sensational and sentimental, and he maintains that the portrait of Ezra Pierce is as impressively drawn as that of Silas Lapham; but, remarking that the "theme is greater than the treatment," he finds the book in general to be merely "perfectly adequate" within its limits. William Morton Payne's review of the novel in *The Dial* 19 (1895): 384-85, takes a similar position. In *Companions on the Trail,* written after Matthews's death, Garland offered a more frank assessment of his friend's novels: they tended, he said, to be cold and formal, lacking "juice" (252-53).

[12] Howells, "Life and Letters," *Harper's Weekly* 39 (26 Oct. 1895): 1012-13.

[13] Qtd. in Leo Lowenthal, "Sociology of Literature in Retrospect," trans. Ted R. Weeks, *Critical Inquiry* 14 (Autumn 1987): 5.

[14] Matthews to Howells, 27 Oct. 1895, Howells Papers.

[15] Matthews, *A Confident To-morrow: A Novel of New York* (New York: Harper, 1899), 6-7. Subsequent page references will appear parenthetically within the text.

[16] Howells, *Selected Letters* 3: 323.

[17] Ibid., 4: 278.

[18] Matthews, "Mr. Howells as a Critic," 77.

[19] Roosevelt, *Letters* 5: 795; 1: 412.

[20] Harry Thurston Peck, "A Confident To-morrow," *The Bookman* 10 (1899-1900): 328. Though Matthews would later consider Peck an "abscess" in the Columbia English Department, he was on friendly terms with him at this time, as witnessed by his dedication of *The Philosophy of the Shortstory* (1901) to him. Peck admired French realist fiction, Balzac's in particular, but he considered Howells's novels to be trivial.

[21] Roosevelt, *Letters* 1: 410.

[22] See Cady, *The Realist at War,* 209-10.

[23] Howells, "An Appreciation," 405.

[24] Howells's treatment of marriage in his fiction has been the subject of numerous studies, the most recent and comprehensive of which is Allen F. Stein's *After the Vows Were Spoken: Marriage in American Literary Realism* (Columbus: Ohio State Univ. Press, 1984), 19-53. As Stein argues, for Howells marriage was a vehicle of liberation from the "prison of the self," offering those whose marriage was based on an affectionate partnership rather than passion a "little sphere of civility and order in a world that otherwise is often chaotic and threatening" (20).

[25] Matthews, *Americanisms and Briticisms,* 175-76.

[26] Matthews, *The Action and the Word: A Novel of New York* (New York: Harper, 1900), 171. Subsequent page references will appear parenthetically within the text.

[27] Matthews, *Inquiries and Opinions,* 258.

[28] Matthews was an intimate friend of the day's most prominent Creole writer, George Washington Cable, as well as of *Century* editor Richard Watson Gilder, with whom Chopin had an uneasy relationship. Gilder opened the *Century*'s doors to her; but he considered some of her fiction "immoral," and he twice refused to publish short stories of hers unless she softened their self-assertive women characters (see Per Seyersted, *Kate Chopin: A Critical Biography* [Baton Rouge: Louisiana State Univ. Press, 1980], 68-69). Given Matthews's interest in Creole fiction and Gilder's relationship with Chopin, it seems reasonable to assume that the two men discussed her work.

[29] Kate Chopin, *The Awakening and Selected Stories,* ed. Nina Baym (New York: Modern Library, 1981), 273.

[30] Howells, "American Literary Centres," *Literature and Life* (New York: Harper, 1902), 179.

[31] Howells, *Selected Letters* 4: 204, 233.

[32] Cady, ed., *W. D. Howells as Critic,* 406; Gail Thain Parker, "William Dean Howells: Realism and Feminism," in *Uses of Literature,* ed. Monroe Engel, Harvard English Studies 4 (Cambridge, Mass.: Harvard Univ. Press, 1973), 133-61. Occupying the middle ground between Cady's and Parker's positions is John W. Crowley's "W. D. Howells: The Ever-Womanly," in *American Novelists Revisited: Essays in Feminist Criticism,* ed. Fritz Fleischmann (Boston: G. K. Hall, 1982), 171-88.

[33] Seyersted, *Kate Chopin,* 54.

[34] Howells, *Selected Letters* 4: 233n.

[35] Matthews to Trent, 9 Sept. 1900, Matthews Papers.

[36] Howells, "Novel-Writing and Novel-Reading," in *The Norton Anthology of American Literature,* ed. Nina Baym et al., 2d ed. (New York: Norton, 1985), 284, 300.

[37] Matthews, *These Many Years,* 388-89.

FURTHER READING

Criticism

Lewisohn, Ludwig. "The Critic and the Theater." In *The Drama and the Stage,* pp. 12–18. New York: Harcourt, Brace and Company, 1922.
> Argues that Matthews's dictum that a play's value must be judged by its appeal to its audience falters when one analyzes the quality and composition of contemporary audiences.

Payne, William Morton. "Recent Fiction." *The Dial* XXIX, No. 341 (September, 1900): 125.
> Concludes that *The Action and the Word,* is not a "deep" story but shows "deft workmanship," and is "exceptionally entertaining."

Perry, Thomas S. "Memories of the Golden Age." *The Yale Review* VII, No. 3 (April 1918): 641-45.
> Reviews autobiographies by Hamlin Garland, Henry James and Matthews, offering friendly dissent on Matthews's campaigns for spelling and copyright law reform.

Kurt Schwitters

1887-1948

German artist, poet, essayist, dramatist, novelist, and short-story writer.

INTRODUCTION

Schwitters is recognized for his unique contribution to twentieth-century art and literature. Influenced by Dadaism, Cubism, German Expressionism, and similar avant-garde movements of the early twentieth century, Schwitters offered his idiosyncratic vision of postwar bourgeois culture in the form of collage, sculpture, experimental poetry and prose. Furnishing the neologism *Merz*—a name derived from a discarded scrap of paper bearing the phrase "Kommerz und Privatbank" ("Commerce and Private Bank")—to describe his projects, Schwitters produced a series of visual and literary works collected from the rubbish of the modern industrial landscape. In his *Merz* collages and assemblages Schwitters attached found fragments to one another in an apparently chaotic fashion. Using the concept of *Merz* figuratively in his written works, Schwitters presented an absurdly ironic view of life in modern society in poetry, prose, and performance pieces.

Biographical Information

Schwitters was born in Hanover, Germany in 1887, the only child of prosperous middle-class parents. He was educated at the Kunstgewerbeschule, in Hanover and later studied at the Kunstakademie (Academy of Art), Dresden between 1909 and 1914. Schwitters married Helma Fischer in 1915 after a six year engagement, and served briefly in the German army as a draughtsman in an ironworks at the close of the First World War. In 1918, Schwitters produced his first *Merz* piece, a collage. The following year his works were displayed at the Der Sturm Gallery in Berlin under the direction of Herwarth Walden, editor of the journal *Der Sturm*. In 1919 Schwitters's essays and poetry, including his best-known work "An Anna Blume," were published in the journal. Due to the success of this poem and his visual works during this period, Schwitters quickly established himself as a noted German avant-garde artist. He also became increasingly associated with artists of the Berlin Dadaist movement, although he never became an orthodox member of the group. In 1922 he befriended Dutch artist Theo van Doesburg, an influential member of the De Stijl movement in art and architecture. Schwitters also began to publish his journal *Merz* in 1923, and continued work on his visual art and Dadaist sound poetry. During the Weimar years of the 1920s in Germany, Schwitters created the first of his grand *Merz* assemblages, or *Merzbau*, with the *Kathedrale des erotischen Elends* ("Cathedral of Erotic Misery"), which was later destroyed by Allied

bombing during World War II. By the 1930s, Schwitters was splitting his time between Germany and Norway, where he emigrated in 1937 after the Nazi government confiscated 13 of his works for their *Entartrete Kunst* (Degenerate Art) exhibit in Munich. Schwitters was forced to flee following the 1940 Nazi invasion of Norway; he sought refuge in England. After spending some time in London with his son, he suffered a stroke and retreated to the Lake District in 1944. Meanwhile, Schwitters, who enjoyed notoriety in England the United States, continued his work, attempting to recreate his destroyed assemblages. He died on 8 January 1948 in Kendal, England.

Major Works

One of Schwitters's principal goals was the production of a "Gesamtkunstwerk" or "total work of art" that would encompass all artistic mediums. This he endeavored to do with his *Merzbau*. The first of these assemblages, "The Cathedral of Erotic Mystery," Schwitters began constructing in his Hanover house in 1923. Using various scrap materials and personal effects from friends and strangers—including toe-nail clippings and jars of urine—Schwitters created a strange structure filled with myriad columns and semi-enclosed grottos arranged to symbolize postwar bourgeois culture and materialism. As the accumulation of detritus rapidly progressed, the assemblage gradually expanded to the upper floors of Schwitters's home. As with his other artworks, his *Merz* collages are formed from bits of trash he found on city streets—discarded train tickets, candy wrappers, and the like—arranged in seemingly chaotic fashion on canvas.

As for Schwitters's poetry and prose, his collected writings contained in the five-volume *Das literarische Werk* feature a variety of experimental stories and lyrics that subvert conventional norms. Many of his early poems were written in a compressed, Expressionistic style heavily influenced by the work of August Stramm. A representative poem, Schwitters's famous "An Anna Blume" uses such elements of parody and nonsense verse as exaggeration, unusual metaphors, and bathos to express the speaker's mystical love for Anna Blume. Other examples of Schwitters's *Merz* poetry, most of which originally appeared in *Der Sturm*, include such abstract works as "Gedicht 25", which uses patterns of numbers instead of words, and the song poem "Meine Sonate in Urlauten," which was designed for recitation. Among Schwitters's prose works, the satirical story "Die Zwiebel" ("The Onion") vividly describes the narrator's grotesque slaughter by a butcher followed by the reintegration of his body, which is left with no scars or apparent mental side effects. The Expressionist tone of "Die Zwiebel" is sustained in the first chapter of Schwitters's unfinished novel, *Franz Müllers Drahtfrühling*, in which a group of people gather to condemn a man as he stands, doing nothing, in public. As the man leaves, an absurd hysteria strikes the crowd causing many to be trampled to death. Later, a boy proclaims that Müller's movement has precipitated a great and glorious revolution in the town of Revon (Schwitters's imaginary name for Hanover).

Critical Reception

Because of the intensely personal vision of his work, Schwitters was never fully accepted by his contemporary, Hans Richter, the presiding force within the Berlin Dada group, who disliked what he thought of as Schwitters's bourgeois sensibility. Nonetheless, Schwitters's artistic work is frequently considered Dadaist work. He has since been credited with making Hanover a major center for art in Germany and his work has been compared to the geometrical pieces of the Russian Constructivists and the products of the Dutch De Stijl movement. While his large assemblages no longer exist except in photographic images, Schwitters's collages continue to be highly valued pieces of abstract expressionism. Since his death, many critics have viewed his work as strikingly original and have reaffirmed his contribution to modern visual art and his importance as an early creator of concrete poetry. Most commentators on his work have celebrated his endeavor to liberate humankind "from the chaos and tragedy of life" through art.

PRINCIPAL WORKS

Anna Blume, Dichtungen (poetry) 1919
Franz Müllers Drahtfrühling. ["Revolution: Causes and Outbreak of the Great and Glorious Revolution in Revon"] (unfinished novel) 1922
Elementar. Die Blume Anna. Die neue Anna Blume (poetry) 1922
Memoiren Anna Blumes in Bleie (poetry) 1922
Tran Nr. 30. Auguste Bolte (ein Lebertran) (novella) 1923
Die Scheuche [*The Scarecrow*; with Kate Steinitz and Theo van Doesburg] (children's book) 1925
"Meine Sonate in Urlauten" (poetry) 1927
Zusammenstoß [*Collision*] (drama) 1927
Anna Blume und Ich. Die Gesammelten Anna Blume-Texte (poetry and prose) 1965
Das literarische Werk. 5 vols. (poetry, drama, and prose) 1973-1981
Merzhefte als Faksimile-Nachdruck (facsimile reprints) 1975
Wir spielen, bis uns der Tod abholt: Briefe aus fünf Jahrzehnten (letters) 1975
pppppp: Poems Performance Pieces Proses Plays Poetics [edited and translated by Jerome Rothenberg and Pierre Joris] (poetry, drama, and prose) 1993

CRITICISM

Sidney Tillim (essay date 1963)

SOURCE: "Schwitters: Dada as Fine Art," in *Arts Magazine,* Vol. 38, No. 3, December 1963, pp. 54-59.

[*In the following essay, Tillim explores Schwitters's relationship to orthodox Dada.*]

The artistic substance of Dada has rarely, if ever, been treated to purely aesthetic dissection. The works of visual art that came of the movement conceived in a Zurich cabaret in 1916 are invariably regarded as the extension or expression, or both, of a disturbance that went far beyond the limits of art and which gained its artistic context, since music, literature, drama and architecture were also involved, simply because artists happened to be associated with it. Artists, in fact, never ranked high in the Dada bureaucracy. As George Ribemont-Dessaignes explained in 1931, "What has been called the Dada movement was really a movement of the mind . . . and not merely a new artistic school." Dada was in fact Romanticism at its most self-conscious, ironic and, in a few instances, its most extreme. It was a protest against absolutely everything, including even Cézanne. An authentic Dada did not have to create at all in the conventional sense; he had only to be different, to despise the bourgeoisie, show contempt for its civilization and culture and be passionately interested in freedom, usually his own. Only a few years ago Marcel Janco retrospectively conferred the title of Grand Dada on Chaplin, Machiavelli and Napoleon.

Needless to say Dada contradicted itself, as Dadaists readily admitted it did, but many moons had to pass before a final contradiction asserted itself—the appreciated art of Dada's anti-art. For with the emergence in time of several Dada personalities, especially Kurt Schwitters, as respectable fine artists, Dada's social and political involvements can now be interpreted as largely the measure of the state of despair to which artists had been reduced during and following the First World War, not merely by the condition of society but by the condition of art. Dada artists were faced with a problem not only of style but of iconography. They could not go "back" nor could they advance without courting the abstraction of which they were the sworn enemies. Indeed, the obscenities, like the politics, of Dada reflect largely the repressions Dadaist artists felt at the hands of "modern aesthetic art," a contradiction in terms and a redundancy I am forced to employ because of the nature of my subject. Dada was violent because it could not create without admitting the authority of art which it was committed to destroy. And it died because it could not tolerate even its own authority. Gradually its demonstrations failed to sustain the feeling of a liberating novelty. The movement broke up amidst charges of betrayal from within. Members came to blows, others were merely disgusted. Some quit art altogether. Duchamp, already in America, ceased painting in the twenties. Huelsenbeck, a founder, was to become Charles R. Hulbeck and a New York analyst (Jungian) whose running feud with Tristan Tzara, the impresario of French Dada (Huelsenbeck represented the German and, at the time, Communist camp; eventually the positions were reversed) continues to this day. One Dadaist, Jacques Rigaut, committed suicide as had an early Dada, Jacques Vache, ten years earlier; others experienced religious conversion (Hugo Ball); still others passed into all but complete obscurity. Then Surrealism took over. Emotionally, art is very expensive.

It is interesting then to note that those Dadaists who survived as artists were principally Germans—Ernst, Arp (who as an Alsatian is only superficially an exception) and, of course, Schwitters. There is a good reason for this. Though the historical image of Dadaism is principally French in coloration simply because under Tzara's direction it became identified with the avant-garde, it is Northern sensibility that defines Dada's aesthetic. The appeal of Dadaism to an artist like Duchamp, who along with Picabia was Dada prior to its baptism in Zurich, lay precisely in the conceptual tendencies of Northern art and the hospitality the fantastic has always found there—from Bosch and Brueghel to the Expressionists. These qualities Duchamp identified with—which is to say the affinity existed, in his opposition to French métier and good taste. Doubtlessly Picabia, the Latin, was similarly attracted to the meticulousness and the "lunacy" of the North, just as today geometric art and antiseptically modern architecture are popular in South America. It is

revealing of Dada's aesthetic orientation that Surrealism, replacing Dada in the late twenties, served as a reaction to Northern clarity; Dali's limpid watch perfectly expresses the aesthetic inertia (and "paranoia") induced by a conflict between linear and painterly pride. Surrealism, in short, throws Dada's sense of style into clear relief by amounting, as it were, to a French counter-revolution against the North, reopening the case for painterly painting. This was important in France because French primacy in the arts was based on it.

Dadaism in the North, however, had different motives. For one thing it hoped to profit sensuously from the exchange of ideas with the South, that is, it hoped to mitigate the rigidity of Northern conceptualism, which had already been attacked by the Expressionists. It succeeded as well as it did because first of all it did not violate Northern sensibility altogether. But more important, it enabled artists such as Ernst and Schwitters to link up with mainstream modernism and yet to preserve their conceptual habits to a certain necessary extent. Schwitters courted Cubism as one might cultivate a celebrity, while Dada for Ernst was largely a bridge to Surrealism. Advancing his education as a painter, Surrealist automatism permitted Ernst to break out of the repressive Northern idiom literally with a splash. Schwitters was himself all thumbs as a painter, but even the career of so negligible and perennial a Dadaist as Hans Richter shows a thwarted lust after the plastic, failing in which he became involved with concepts of time and movement and finally film—"plastic" substitutes. And look what happened to George Grosz.

There is more, however, to Dada's aesthetic significance than a conceptual sensibility. Dada's relationship to subject has been ignored, while its position on color has been unheard of. As for subject matter, a cornerstone of the Dada platform was its opposition to abstraction as devoid of the human, that is, social content. Already in Dada's politics and tactics we see demands for social restitution and involvement of, and in, the arts; and on the artistic front itself, the Dadaists closed ranks on the issue of representation by advancing one that was protectively coated with irony, perversion and disjunction of sense. But it was these shock values that enabled the Southern Dadaists to ignore the protest implicit in Duchamp's "ready-mades" in favor of the affront to respectable taste they otherwise constituted. (In France Dadaism was dissipated on bigger and bigger insults which more and more came to publicity and less to protest.) While the subversive content in the form of old prints, typeface, newspaper reproductions and the like in the collages of Ernst, Arp and Schwitters went similarly unremarked. (In Cubist collage realistic fragments did not carry the same ideological force; they merely paved the way for a compromise—Synthetic Cubism.) The upshot of this frustrated impulse to represent was Surrealism. As Dada petered out, Breton became interested in psychoanalysis and the *content* of the unconscious, which, adapted to Surrealist theory, provided the pretext for a new representationalism.

Color, however, is a more complex issue. For one thing the very idea of it runs counter to the representational tendencies of Dada. But this is natural because color was a traditional concern and besides that a *mere detail*. Theoretically, Dadaists had no patience with either. For another, it applies almost entirely (Ernst used color eventually but in a "literary" way) to the work of Kurt Schwitters. Color for Schwitters was the bridge between German Expressionism and Analytical Cubism. Analytical Cubism employed subdued earth colors to emphasize planar form. The ochers of Analytical Cubism were color but not important *as* color except as an oblique recollection of the primitive: they were connotative rather than denotative. Synthetic Cubism permitted the analytical Cubists to employ color in a way structurally comparable to the analytical style but only at the expense of introducing a conflict between the real and the abstract. The real, admitting painterly feeling previously "classicized" or "primitivized" by the analytical phase, eventually divided (as we have known for years) no less an artist than Picasso down the middle. Schwitters, in using castoff matter like stamps, labels, packaging, stubs, transfers, plus papers with printed matter or images on them, made the figurative data seem both incidental and accidental, focusing one's attention instead on abstract elements of form, space and color—but particularly color.

Since color in a way symbolizes all that certain fanatical Dadaists found objectionable in Schwitters, more or less ostracizing him, I prefer to elaborate the issue and sum up Dada's aesthetic position in the context of the inspired Schwitters exhibition at the Galerie Chalette (October, November). It is a compactly comprehensive and (obviously) provocative exhibition that is comprised of a private collection balanced by loans from collectors and museums, plus documents, first drafts and periodicals relating to Schwitters' career. In all there are some sixty works dating from 1918 to 1947, the year before his death. The exhibition is accompanied by another of the handsome catalogues which this gallery produces regularly; it includes four color plates, excerpts from Schwitters' writings and personal reminiscences by Jean Arp and Hans Richter.

The typical Schwitters collage is so well known that it barely requires description. It is a mixture of formality of design and informality of means—castoff bits of paper junk interrupting and lapping the verticals and horizontals of more or less geometric designs. These are pasted onto surfaces that, rarely large, were sometimes no larger than a book of matches. This scale is important because it proves that Schwitters recognized the anti-heroic implications of his medium, which, precluding vast designs, insisted instead on a scale commensurate with its ignoble character. Schwitters' famous grottos, The "MERZ-bauen" (MERZ-structures), including the first one in Hanover (destroyed during the Second World War) and a second one in London, which along with his unique palette of trash and his sound-poems apparently satisfied some Dadaists as to his basic good faith, were large. Built into a room, they were three-dimensional collages one could live in; but they were also private temples in which he celebrated the ritualistic impulse of his art for his own spiritual enrichment and apparently for the fascinated entertainment of his friends. At any rate, between 1918 and roughly 1931 (there is an understandable gap in the exhibition between 1931 and 1937), Schwitters produced the bulk of his best work. The exhibition includes some of the best of these that I have seen—*Red on Red* (1924), *Okolade* (1926), *Einhundert-tausend Mark* (1924), *"R"* (1929). Excepting *Untitled* (1920) and *P (Dada)* (1921), I care less for his more complex compositions—the means seem to me too much stressed—but cannot deny their more sumptuous effect which might have meant more coloristically had not tatters of the former structural sense, which it was the function of color to enlighten, remained to obscure their intention.

Had Schwitters been a better painter, the entire neo-Dada trend, deriving largely from his collage idea, would have been inconceivable. For the least of his works are those in which paint is involved, such as the corrupt Neo-Plastic *Das Gustave-Finzler-Bild,* with wood additions, and the messy *Cherry Picture* from the collection of the Museum of Modern Art which somehow suggests a pinball machine destroyed by Futurist fire. They prove at least why Schwitters opted for collage; he simply froze when handling paint and what is more could not produce color with the subtlety and variety he demonstrated in collage. Nevertheless, his collages show a general decline in quality after 1931 (some have said sooner). Growing obscurity now extends to color and organization, which in some examples is simply chaotic. Structural unity giving way, a spewing forth of wildly overlapping shapes resulted, destroying the base plane with "holes" that were frequently implemented by illusionistic details. In the confusion these details became equal and assertive. In fact the old conflict between the real and the abstract asserted itself. And in an apparent effort to introduce movement, Schwitters had become too "painterly."

Doubtless the increasing social disorder at home and Schwitters' inevitable exile first to Norway and then, following the Nazi invasion, to Great Britain, all played a role in destroying both Schwitters' consistency and concentration. But the passing of Dadaism from the scene earlier contributed greatly to his vulnerability. Schwitters, who derived a great deal of psychological support from Dada despite criticism and rejection from German Dada militants such as Huelsenbeck, tried to keep it alive through his magazine, MERZ. It ran for twenty-four issues between 1923 and 1932, after which he joined the Abstract Creation group in Paris in an effort to relocate himself in the post-Dada era. He never gave up. There is a collage by Schwitters in the Kate Steinmetz Collection of the Pasadena Art Museum, entitled *For Kate* and dated 1947. It was reproduced in an issue of *Art International* (January 25, 1963) which dealt extensively with pop art. Not only does this collage of comic-book images seem to anticipate pop art, but it also recalls two of his collages of 1918, which I shall mention later. I submit the following interpretation. Schwitters' own art had become too rarefied for him, and his old Dadaist fighting spirit emerged, not without nostalgia, a final time, protesting to Schwitters the desperately place-less bourgeois he had become. Nobody seems to have noticed this last bright star falling in the darkness.

In approaching Schwitters' work it helps to bear in mind the intensely factional and political character of the Dada movement, because the very qualities that some Dadas found suspect in his art are precisely the ones we admire today—their ingratiating wit, their intelligibility, their *aesthetic* irony. Schwitters was in short a *serious* artist at a time when it was neither fashionable nor simple to be one, especially if you claimed to be Dada. Outwardly observing the mores of Dadaism, he nonetheless insisted on creating fine art with it. A first step was to establish MERZ, a word derived from one of his collages, as the name of his version of Dada which he felt was true Dada, "Kerneldadaism" as opposed to "Huelsendadaism," and essentially abstract. To both French and German Dadas this was treason. A casual remark by Charles Hugnet in *The Dada Spirit in Painting* sums up the least acrimonious but official disenchantment with the renegade artist. Wrote Hugnet, "Holding steadfastly to the poetic sphere he remained prudently bourgeois in politics." [1932, 1934, reprinted in *The Dada Painters and Poets,* edited by Robert Motherwell. Wittenborn, Schultz, Inc., New York, 1951.]

Yet Schwitters was the only Dadaist, however *manqué*, to do something *concrete* about the crisis of mainstream modernist painting. (Sculpture was only just beginning to assimilate Cubism, and Arp's Dadaism was pre-Surreal-ist.) The orthodox Dadaists avoided the challenge by insisting that the body wasn't worth saving. Surrealism likewise ignored the challenge, and it wasn't until Surrealism encountered Cubism in the United States in the late thirties that it engaged the problem. But Schwitters subjected it to an emergency operation. He grafted his bits of refuse to Cubism and Neo-Plasticism and sent these ideas back into the world, patched like a beggar, but intellectually presentable again. The primary aesthetic fact of Schwitters' medium was that its colors must have obviously been fascinating to a German who had Expressionism in his blood but not its desperation or, perhaps, its courage. For another thing, Schwitters was enough of a Dadaist to feel the inhuman chill held out to art by analytical abstraction. Surprisingly, he got much of his dexterity in manipulating the Cubist format from Neo-Plasticism, which allowed him to move freely over the picture plane. Futurism helped of course, but, as I have said, in the interests of an analogous painterliness. But it was his benign scraps of weather-beaten color that brought the blush of life back into abstract art. Schwitters' popularity today is fitting when once more color is an issue in an abstract art for which Surrealism provided only a placebo, just as his "classicism" strikes a responsive chord wherever the hard-edge idiom seeks relief and expansion of sensibility in chromatic brilliance and clarity.

Nor can one ignore the significance of Schwitters to pop art. Collages like *King Edward and Emperor William II*

and *Die Handlung Spielt in Theben* (both 1918), not to mention details elsewhere, must have seemed in their day, with their montages of newspaper photographs and prints of events, fashions and mores of the day, like pop art to the general. After seeing them, it is impossible to accept the proto-pop artist Robert Rauschenberg, for instance, as a major artist, for Rauschenberg converts Dada irony *à la* Schwitters into the very aestheticism it was designed to subvert—not to mention his grand scale. Perhaps Donald Judd is right in treating him strictly as a formalist.

Dadaism, at least French Dadaism, and now pop art, fell into a similar aesthetic trap. What Schwitters was doing was actually restoring the primitivistic bias of modernism in bourgeois terms. He brought it out of the jungle and relocated it in the gutters of the modern world. But the Dadaists were unwilling to descend to this level with him, a descent which purged him of aesthetic affectation. They had become the aristocrats of anarchy—too abstract! Instead they confused literal anarchy for symbolic anarchy and could only degenerate into spectacle. Correspondingly, contemporary pop art, which is a form of Establishment Dadaism, cannot raise the level of the vitality of a once more depleted modern art because it cannot lower itself wholeheartedly beneath the level of the established aesthetic.

I seem to have shown, on the one hand, that Dadaism unconsciously entertained a new figuration, while on the other I have stressed the fact that Schwitters' strength lay primarily in the abstract. But this of course is only the difference between Schwitters and orthodox, theoretical Dadaism. Otherwise, I have also shown that color for Schwitters possessed an emotional value that was inseparable from its physical sources and implications—that is, it cannot be construed as entirely denotative of itself. The hidden connotations of Schwitters' color take us back to his means, to the fecal litter of bourgeois culture. Schwitters also used color, then, to defy the impoverishment of the particular.

Still, I must say that I am, with all my admiration for his work, uncertain of its durability. Schwitters gave Cubism only a few extra years, not an eternity. No matter how remote a Dadaist Schwitters finally appears, he shared Dadaism's impetus and perhaps its fatality too. For without the socio-aesthetic correlation of Dada in mind it would have been impossible for me to make the observation above, connecting medium and culture, and noting their implications for each other. To a certain extent this interaction still matters. But the possibility is that in time the medium will turn back into itself, into what it is, and seem cheap. This is the real "homeless representation" of Dada. Age is not all that gives Schwitters at his best a certain faded quality. So far, however, no Schwitters has dated nearly so quickly as, say, Duchamp's ready-mades. Because of his acquired sophistication, that is, art, Schwitters escapes the basically provincial character of the Northern mind, though as I have said it was just this almost "stupid" provincialism, hard and ungainly, that acted as a tonic to Southerners who had reacted against refinement in art. What distinguished Schwitters from the rest of Dada was not his policy of aesthetic appeasement, but his ability to grow in spite of it, probably because of it, and his natural death from it and other causes.

John Elderfield (essay date 1971)

SOURCE: "The Early Work of Kurt Schwitters," in *Artforum* Vol. X, No. 3, November, 1971, pp. 54-67.

[*In the following essay, Elderfield examines the structure of Schwitters's collages and assemblages of 1917 to 1923, discussing aesthetic developments in his art during this period.*]

> An object that tells of the loss, destruction, disappearance of objects. Does not speak of itself. Tells of others. Will it include them.
>
> —Jasper Johns

In 1919, Kurt Schwitters chose the word "Merz" to describe what he called his "pasted and nailed pictures" because he could not "define them with the older conceptions like Expressionism, Cubism, Futurism or whatever" and because he wished to make them "like a species."[1] This insistence on a generic title reflects Schwitters' consciousness of having achieved an independent and original status for his art. Schwitters' historical reputation rests largely on the innovations of his early years. These established the framework for all his subsequent work, work which at no time repudiated the initial premise of an assembled art using found elements as tools for forming. Yet this premise was not in itself original: the modern use of collage was at least six years old when Schwitters first adopted it, and the formal character of his early work is in fact not free from a dependence of "older conceptions," as Schwitters would have it. In this sense, Schwitters was not an innovator at all. Like many of the artists associated with Dada he willingly utilized devices and techniques from earlier vanguard art (and only after the German period for which he is best known did he break with established pictorial conventions, and then not completely).[2] Of course, no art can be entirely innovating, but when considering Schwitters' one finds constant reference to contemporary advanced styles—be they Cubo-Expressionist ones in the early years or Elementarist ones in the mid- and later '20s. If Schwitters was an innovator it was despite his derivations, or even because of his finely developed exploitation of derived techniques. This essay considers the structures of Schwitters' art from 1917 to 1923 and seeks to clarify these principal issues: the nature of Schwitters' development from painted to constructed abstraction; the significance to that development of Schwitters' parallel "stealing" from earlier art and lifting of nonart elements into an art context; and the crucial differences, both in procedure and in implication, between a structure founded in paint and a new "object vocabulary."

I

Although Merz was not so named until 1919, Schwitters' first assembled works date from 1918 and his first abstract paintings from the year before that. This hectic and speculative period was, however, preceded by some ten years of painting in different realist styles, from a very early concern for exact mimetic effects to a later more flexible and "expressive" use of the oil painting medium stimulated by an ever increasing awareness of modernist idioms. Schwitters' years as a student at the Dresden Kunstakademie (1909-14) coincided with the dissemination of the major German Expressionist styles; but it was not until he had left the Academy that his work began its move through borrowed modern forms and not until 1917 that its movements through these forms became rapid enough, or its results interesting enough, to deserve serious attention. Since Schwitters' Merz was patently abstract in composition and constructive in approach most of this naturalistic early work seems of little direct significance for what follows; except for the fact that Schwitters never entirely abandoned naturalistic painting but continued to produce landscapes and portraits right up to his death in 1948, and that he often affirmed the importance of all aspects of what he made, without too much hierarchical distinction.

Although Schwitters' introduction of found objects in replacement for more conventional pictorial materials appears in principle a dramatic change of approach, it was in fact a natural extension of preoccupations developed within the more convention-bounded work and coming to a head in 1917. For Schwitters, the importance of naturalistic painting was that "it rests essentially on measurement and adjustment. . . . For me it was essential to learn adjustment, and I gradually learned that the adjustment of the elements in painting is the aim of art."[3] That is, painting is an art which manipulates a variable number of pictorial "elements." This conception forms a bridge between the early naturalistic works, where the manipulation was a means to an end—accuracy of representation—and the later "conscious elaboration of purely artistic components in the Merz object."

In an article written in 1920, when this bridge had been crossed, Schwitters described how his art had changed: "First I succeeded in freeing myself from the literal reproduction of all details. I contented myself with the intensive treatment of light effects through sketchlike painting (impressionism)." His landscapes from about 1914 represent this position. But they are only very superficially Impressionist in style: Schwitters' color sense and touch is heavy and somber and his interpretation of painting as tonal and tactile already well established. Importantly, the objects are fused not in terms of light but of expressive mood. Loosening the means of his representation was for Schwitters the first significant step towards making the forms work for their places in his pictures. That is, by denying himself a predefined spatial context, the painterly translations of objects had to create their own intuitive, self-determined, spatial cohesion.

Moreover, the newly emphatic material density of the pigment stressed the physical "building" nature of the compositions, exploiting the special properties of oil painting to create a unity of separate statements of color on different planes, and subsuming illusionistic space to that created by the surface adjustment of heavy impastos. It was, in fact, an approach more Expressionistic than Impressionistic; it heralded a breakthrough beyond representation to abstraction in 1917—a breakthrough almost equal in significance for Schwitters' development as was the use of extra-artistic elements a year later since the character of his transition to abstract art held implicit this later innovation. Schwitters described it thus: "I emphasized the main lines by exaggeration, the forms by limiting myself to what was most essential and by outlining, and the color tones by breaking them down into complementary colors." He was approaching the idea of a pictorial vocabulary where "every combination of lines, colors, forms has a definite expression." The basis was as ever adjustment; but he "adjusted the elements of the picture to one another . . . not for the purpose of reproducing nature but with a view to expression."

The result of this procedure was not, however, necessarily an abstract art, but often a still referential manner developed "from an impressionist foundation (that) had, as its first aim, not the beautifying of the organic form, but a strong characterization through an omission of incidental details."[4] Kandinsky, whose words these are and to whose own early "abstractions" Schwitters' work of this period frequently referred, called this "stylization." But stylization led the way to an autonomous abstract art by turning away from the copying of perceived effects towards what Kandinsky called "the creation of the various forms which, by standing in different relations to each other, serve the composition of the whole"[5]—hence creating the possibility of going beyond the "external" expression of stylization for an "internal" one. "Natural forms make boundaries which often are impediments to this expression. Thus they must be set aside and the freed space used for the objective side of the form—construction for the purpose of composition."[6] The descriptive titles of some of Schwitters' 1917 paintings were thus preceded by the classification, "Expression," and these usually very awkward works make overt reference to Brücke and Blaue Reiter sources. But more interesting, and the link between the stylized realism of the "Expressions" and Merz itself, was a series of "Abstractions" of 1917-18. While evidencing the same Expressionist sources (substantiated by titles such as *Die Gewalten*—close to Marc—or *Schlafender Kristall*—reminiscent of many German "angularists"), they tighten and simplify the pictorial grammar to a two-part structure of loosely gestural painting and tense linear scaffolding. This is, of course, a structure particular to early Cubism, and (to anticipate a little) it should be noted that for Schwitters (as for all his contemporaries) coming to terms with Cubism was the single most crucial factor for his first mature works. It was Schwitters' misfortune to learn his Cubism through Expressionism and, not yet understanding its premises, to mistake its looks for its logic.[7] But the very

nature of his misunderstanding is itself informative. Schwitters' interpretation of modernism was heavily indebted to Herwarth Walden's *Der Sturm* propaganda, and by 1918 Schwitters identified himself enough with this interpretation to make a point of introducing himself to the Sturm circle in Berlin. (This in itself separates Schwitters from other German Dadaists who repudiated Sturm Expressionism as outmoded.) It is difficult to locate particular Sturm characteristics within painting since in that field Walden was primarily a promoter of already existing Expressionist forms. More easily specified, however, is a Sturm style in poetry. Schwitters, we remember, was not only an Expressionist painter at this time, but also an Expressionist poet (closest, perhaps, to Stramm). And much of his early verse displays typical Sturm concerns with a highly compressed language system of "clenched" forms, often within a "word-chain" arrangement—hence creating a structure of individual word-units, each holding rich "meanings," which serve as sources for "readings." The implications of this structure for Schwitters' assemblages are readily apparent. And an analogous concern for "presented meanings" seems significant even in the earlier "Abstractions."

For all their heaviness of painting, works like *Die Gewalten* (1917) and *Schlafender Kristall* (1918) depend totally on their drawing. Modulation is virtually replaced by infilling and the linear framework of "signs" which (both specifies the implied volumes and holds compressed the last vestiges of realist content) carries the entire formal and iconographical weight. The relation of this framework to the loose painting which surrounds it is as yet unclear. Schwitters vacillates between an integration and distinction of linear and tonal structures, between a positioning of lines and tones so that their relationship is sometimes contiguous and sometimes reciprocal. Just how the two components of the structure interact was to be of crucial importance in the assembled works and came to imply a choice between metaphoric and metonymic order. That is, if lines and tones (later objects and surfaces) are contiguous this affirms their syntactical connections; if they are spatially separated (reciprocal in relationship) the likelihood of lines (later objects) functioning metaphorically is increased. In 1918, however, this contradistinction was not yet fully apparent, and the implied choice at this stage was between the "form" (tone meeting line and hollowing out volume) and "plane" (tone and line in separate spatial zones) interpretations of painting. A more advanced and cohesive "Abstraction," *Entschleierung* of 1918, shows that while tone and line are often spatially adjunctive Schwitters has opted for an essentially flat painting-object. But the separate identities of, and tension and reciprocity between, linear scaffolding and painterly surroundings remain. The tension in this relationship was an integral part of original Cubism; and just as the Cubists' increased concern for the conventional identity of pictorial elements led them to concentrate more and more on the potentiality of a semiotic interpretation of art-making, so Schwitters paralleled their development, and, like them, arrived ultimately at a collage solution—taking from the world a repertory of descriptive forms without simply imitating it.[8]

But Schwitters' early assemblages are so very different from Cubist collages that this analogy is soon exhausted. From 1917, Schwitters' preoccupations came increasingly to center on creating a vocabulary of pictorial expression to which any kind of referential space structure (such as was retained in Cubist collage) was irreconcilable. The precise chronology of his development into assemblage is not easily fixed. The three "Abstractions" discussed show an increasing sophistication from one to the next (and their order is confirmed by Schwitters numbering these works), but, generally speaking, Schwitters' course to Merz was most erratic. A sensitive, totally abstract drawing of 1917 seems, for example, amazingly advanced in its intuitive order when compared to a conventionally Expressionist figurative work of 1918. Already implicit in the earlier drawing was the possibility of an autonomous space created neither from the analysis of perception nor by the synthesizing of conventional deductive signs but (as Schwitters was to put it) from the "relationship of form to form, surface to surface, line to line, regarded in a nonaccumulative sense,"[9] that is by an all-over "continual intersection" of formal devices.

II

A great deal is often made of Schwitters' broadness of endeavor—of the unpredictable nature of his creativity and of the way Merz encompassed many separate disciplines. While not entirely disputing this, it should not, however, obscure the fact that the formal boundaries of his art are narrowly defined. True, a wide range of effects may be observed in the collages and constructions,[10] but they are all generated from relatively few structures. As has been already suggested, Schwitters' art (whatever genres it occupied) was prescribed by his reactions to Cubism; and his formal vocabulary is a Cubist one tempered by other brands of modernism (firstly Expressionism but also Futurism in these early years). The morphology set forth here examines first the early "assemblages" which show most clearly the logic of Schwitters' move from painting into constructionist art, and later the collages which draw on sources unavailable to the larger assemblages which, as we shall see, are at first really "paintings modified" to include new materials where the crucial issue, both formal and psychological, is the nature and effectiveness of their inclusions.

Schwitters' early assemblages from 1919 to 1921 form a distinct group within his oeuvre. Their general characteristics may be specified as follows: in scale, they are relatively large. Most are 30 to 50 inches in height (although a few are in the region of 14 to 26 inches) whereas most collages are around 6 inches, and few more than 12 inches, high. The components of these pictures, as befitting their scale, are similarly large. Some works are technically large collages; but as many combine both low relief pieces of paper and card and more bulky three-dimensional elements (wooden planks, wheels, chicken

wire, etc.). All involve a greater or lesser degree of oil painting. As to their forms, they are linear in emphasis—circles and straight lines predominating—and nearly always contained within a vertical format. The color (as much dependent on the oil painting as on the added materials) is tonal and spatial. And the sources of these works are patently Schwitters' own Expressionist-influenced paintings with strong Futurist overtones.

Weltenkreise of 1919 is remarkably close in format to the "Abstraction," *Entschleierung,* of the previous year, except of course that the linear scaffolding of the purely painted work is now composed of extra-artistic materials. By affixing (or sometimes just anchoring) "lines" and "circles" on top of (or even above) a painterly surface, these relief elements inevitably push themselves forward into the perceiver's space—establishing themselves as belonging as much to the world outside as to the plane to which they are fastened. That is, the implications of a complementary forward/backward structure visible in the painted work is here maximized, while the "life" sources of the forward scaffolding metaphorically confirms its relative displacement. The painting is unavoidably a kind of theater for forms where materials inhabit rather than occupy (quite belong to) the pictorial space, and none of the assemblages quite escape this effect. But what would be unacceptable in a purely painted work is justified in pictures that are in essence "containers." Moreover, a too blatant figure/ground effect is reduced by Schwitters' carrying oil painting over and around the relief elements, and thus camouflaging them back to the plane. And this work is the baldest of the early assemblages. Most contain materials of widely varying degrees of relief—some of which, therefore, have spatially (and hence connotatively) ambiguous functions. In *Konstruktion für edle Frauen* (1919), juxtaposed elements, similar in form but varied in bulk, work to grade (through) the space, except where they cross the darkly painted (and hence deeply hollowed) areas of exposed ground which set them in relief. The effect is partly of a neo-Picabian machine of weights and balances standing on the bottom edge of the frame. Unlike *Weltenkreise,* where the ground "presents" its superimposed forms, here it seems to recede behind the edge-anchored materials, and produces the look of a figure grounded on the "proscenium" plane, parts of which are occasionally drawn back into the central graded space. The nature of edge liaisons was to remain crucial for Schwitters' art. Here, the unevenness of bonding is successfully countered by the insistent rectilinearity of the lower materials forcing themselves forward and the firm frontality of the planks, discs, and wheels. But where there are few planar materials and no significant edge bondings (as in *Weltenkreise),* the perimeter of the work seems too much simply the edge of a sample of transmitted information, and the work itself comes dangerously close to being but a "channel" for the presentation of effects. The problem Schwitters posed for himself was to relate added materials to the surface and edges of a picture in a way close enough to affirm its totality without yet forcing everything else but high relief forms into an illusionistic hollowed space. Or, to put it in another way, to reconcile what he called the "personality poison" of the materials to the demands of picture-making.

One of the smallest of the early assemblages, *Das Undbild* (1919), only 14 inches high, shows that Schwitters' early difficulties had a lot to do with scale. If less imposing than the *Konstruktion für edle Frauen*, the smaller work is certainly more coherent spatially. The reduced size of materials meant that they could more easily be managed in an intuitive manner cognizant of the procedures involved in the collage technique. More than the previous works discussed, this breaks from the linear emphasis of Schwitters' earlier style. Material forms do not simply replace painted ones; rather, their common planarity but individual-unit nature (identified by the differences in printed matter) locks the work as surface. And while as yet tonal in effect the single blue triangle offers the new possibility of intense planar color so crucial to the mature collages. And, like the collages, the far more standardized relief of the materials here goes far to avoid the formal and metaphorical ambiguities which combinations of high and low relief elements involved. But in this respect the work is exceptional. Mostly the early assemblages achieve their special character from the particular nature of these ambiguities, which deserve, therefore, further attention.

In using "life" materials within established esthetic structures Schwitters created a duality of formal design and associative reference. By using high relief elements on top of worked grounds he created the likelihood that these elements belong equally to the outside world and to their formal "containers." That is, they alternate between achieving a self-sufficient denotive status and being sucked back into the greater object which contains them. Neighborhood, therefore, is the factor which dictates metaphorical functioning. Nevertheless, the likelihood of high relief elements being *only* metaphorical because of their forward positions is reduced by their acting as formal replacements for more conventional materials. Reworking originally painted themes with materials which allowed colors, surfaces, and textures impossible to produce by painting alone, was for Schwitters a way of broadening the scope of his art while the "conventional" nature of the compositions these new materials filled was enough to stress their primarily formal intent. Doubtless aware of the inherent associative strength of his material sources (as well as the irony of using them for esthetic purposes) he was always compelled to emphasize in his writings their potentialities for "forming." "In a piece of art," he wrote, "it is only important that all the parts are correlated to the whole. It is irrelevant whether materials had any established value before they were used for producing a piece of art. They receive their evaluation through the creative process."[11] But since the assemblage technique can only with difficulty create structures exclusively dependent on syntactical connections, a tension between inner and outer reference always remains. Moreover, despite the compositional similarities of Schwitters' "Abstractions" and assemblages, the procedural bases of

the two genres are very different; and the earlier planning of "expressive" effects became irreconcilable with the demands that process itself now made. Expression as such seemed to Schwitters "injurious to art": "The work of art comes into being through artistic evaluation of its elements. I know only how I make it, I know only my medium, of which I partake, to what end I know not."[12] In fact, the means were coming to be the end.

The means was not so much the potentiality of the material or medium chosen as the "forming" process it underwent. "The medium," Schwitters wrote, "is as unimportant as I myself. Essential is only the forming." This did not mean, however, that the choice of materials lacked importance; rather that material *consistency* was unimportant. "Because the medium is unimportant, I take any material whatsoever if the picture demands it. When I adjust materials of different kinds to one another, I have taken a step in advance of mere oil painting, for in addition to playing off color against color, line against line, form against form, etc., I play off material against material. . . . " The artist thus creates by "the gathering together" of any kind of material compositional elements, "considering the importance of the individual materials" (their special formal properties), and "by his choice, division of and removal of the form of materials."[13] This insistence on the "removal" of individual identity from materials might suggest an inevitable development towards using materials whose nonformal aspects were already purged, that is, clean papers, without texts, stains, or other markings which might divert from their being integrated into the work of art. This did happen to an important degree in the mid- and later '20s; but works of this kind surely miss out on that special balance of metaphoric and metonymic factors central to Schwitters' art. The inconclusive and irresolved character of spatial and referential reciprocations produces the strangely powerful impact of the early assemblages. The added objects push and pull in space, alternating between being parts of the total object they help to create and individual objects in their own right. The problem, as I mentioned earlier, is how "alien" objects can be introduced into the art object without destroying its autonomy. In analyzing Schwitters' solutions, two issues seem most useful to explore. First: since the style of Schwitters' assemblages derives from that of his earlier paintings, the assemblages inevitably take over morphological features which belong to painting. If the most successful modernist art is that which best expresses the uniqueness of its medium, the specific status of Schwitters' new medium must be basic to an understanding of his art. Second: if Schwitters' early assemblages involved the "affixing" of new morphological features to established ones, this is particularized by the manner in which the surface of a work accommodates its added objects ("Will it include them?"). Investigating the reciprocations of surface and objects in Schwitters' assemblages is, therefore, to evaluate their success as new classes of art objects. This suggests some further questions: if the added objects can never perform simultaneously as metaphoric and metonymic elements, how can the picture best contain (or express) this ambiguity without itself becoming indecisive? Also: since the added objects fulfill the functions previously performed by painted elements, how does a "vocabulary of object conditions"[14] differ from a purely "artistic" one?

III

Some years after the first assemblages had been made, Schwitters made the following statement on what had motivated them:

> When, along with pictures painted entirely with oil paint, I also produced these Merz pictures, I did not . . . intend to demonstrate that from now on pictures could only be made out of junk; in them I merely made exclusive use of materials which other artists, such as Picasso, had employed only in conjunction with other materials. . . . Now, if I have been successful with these compositions . . . I believe I have somewhat enlarged the domain of art, without thereby endangering the standing of great works of art in any age.[15]

He makes it quite obvious that his intentions were not at all didactic (or Dadaist, really) but that he sought new forms to extend (or even to preserve) tradition. And he recognized that to make art exclusively from found materials was for him far more significant than merely to use found materials *in* art. That is, he understood (and herein lies his importance) that collage could achieve a newly separate status within a neo-Cubist style. Besides Schwitters, the only artists of his generation to find significant new possibilities for major art within geometric Cubism were Mondrian and Malevich.[16] Schwitters' contribution was to define so fully the medium of collage as to virtually close it up as a vehicle for Cubist art.

What most characterizes the collage style is that it creates an art of additive surfaces. It affirms planarity and shape, and it declares the procedures by which it is made. Moreover, it can readily hold color as a property of its surfaces and reference as an innate attribute of its contents. To this end, it is most coherent when it is all collage, and Schwitters' pictures confirm this. A reliance on added painting usually weakens the enterprise, as does a reliance on devices culled from painting. The early assemblages subsume the special properties of the medium to features associated with painting; but the presence of nonpainting elements inevitably works to modify the "painting language" because Schwitters insisted on the elements' own "forming" characteristics. This was to become the underlying logic of his art. In the assemblages, however, the "forming" has not yet entirely replaced the earlier "expressive" concerns (although Schwitters theoretically repudiated expression in the passage quoted earlier in this essay). Simply substituting representations of his environment with its representative tokens was not itself the crucial issue in his art. True, the "reality" is now of a different kind, but this simply puts expression to work in a new way. And if the new materials are just left stranded on the surfaces of what are in effect paintings, they tend to form individual

relationships with the beholder, often at the expense of the integrity of the internal structure. And simply pushing the materials into archaic Expressionist arrangements could only be an expedient solution. Similarly, in the material substructure (the forming of the "ground") flatter elements seem often to merely fill in a preconceived compositional framework (like the painterly infillings of the "Abstractions"). These elements seem to speak far less of their own logic than to create a linear patterning from the intersections of their edges. Schwitters' art could only achieve maturity by avoiding such compositional preconceptions, and this was only possible "beyond painting" itself.

I will suggest later that Schwitters was only able to achieve this by sidestepping some of the (particularly spatial) problems large-scale assemblage posed; but even in the assemblages he approached this "constructive" stance since he had moved into assemblage itself as a way of reinforcing existing concerns with relationships. Relationship came to be identified with value. "All values exist only in so far as they are related to one another," he said.[17] The putting-together of objects thus became the primary concern. Although Schwitters challenged the boundaries of existing art by introducing alien objects into an established art context, his preoccupation with forming maximized the distinctly "artistic" potentialities of these objects—their aspects which readily formed an association with the qualities of the context they had invaded—thus extending their identities away from their utilitarian origins. However, the special formal properties of these objects modified their new context by expanding its artistic vocabulary (of colors, lines, and planes) to include the "vocabulary of object conditions." As Schwitters himself put it: "In the relationship of a known and an unknown quality, the unknown varies and modifies the known."[18] To maximize a forming based on "the gathering together" of materials, the inherited formal devices were to give way to the spontaneously additive process which itself became the structure of the new work. Both "compositional" notions and materials (in their semantic roles) were to be subsumed to process itself.

A "material" vocabulary thus differs from a purely "artistic" one in stressing the additive, constructive nature of the art work and the process by which it is made. And yet, the kind of process open to Schwitters was inevitably determined by his sources, both material and stylistic. In this sense, process as such was prevented from achieving its autonomy. The Cubist style restricted Schwitters' intuitive forming to the confines of its established grid, and only a lot later—in some of the more randomly composed post-German works—did Schwitters risk breaking with Cubism. Moreover, although the visibly different identities of individual materials affirms the additive effect of the pictures, this same individuation of materials cannot but arrest the continuity of the additions by affirming reference. And of all the aspects of Schwitters' art, it is reference that has continually provoked most comment. If, however, we follow Schwitters' lead, the metaphoric implications of his work should be passed over. The materials are but so much "stuff" for that "self-related entity," the picture, which "has no longer an outward relationship to the material elements that formed it."[19] But this is not the impression received from the works themselves. The best of Schwitters' pictures evoke complex feelings from the identity of the materials used and the nature of their juxtapositions, without in any way diminishing their formal impact. This psychological side of his art has occasioned interpretation of Schwitters' intentions as ranging from social satire to some mystic infiltration of matter. This concern for intentions has too frequently involved a quarrying for latent content which subsumes the manifest structure of the work, and ignores the fact that the structural and psychological aspects of Schwitters' forming are parallel and complementary. And certainly (as I hope this essay shows) Schwitters' work can do without any of those special dispensations favoring psychological "rightness" over formal quality sometimes demanded for artists in the Dada-Surrealist tradition. Nevertheless, the referential status of the materials in Schwitters' pictures does deserve attention on its own terms. Towards this end we need first to consider the kinds of paper collage work he was making in the early years of Merz since the more limited relief of their materials, when compared to the assemblages, assists an understanding of how Schwitters' use of collage differed from that of other artists. Moreover, in some of his early collages Schwitters allowed himself far more specifically anecdotal references than ever got into the contemporary assemblages. And in this context emerges the significance of his Dadaism to his work as an artist. We shall see that for Schwitters "even if dada created the basis for excellent works of art, that was not the aim of the time—it was, in fact, the means for making art, art which is not dada, but the result of it."[20]

IV

Pictorial complexity was the most characteristic feature of the early Merz assemblages of 1919-21. These works reveal how Schwitters had developed from purely painterly conceptions into assemblage by allowing added materials to hold locum-tenency for pictorial forms; and they express his realization that the new transactions between surface and objects differed from those between surface and paint. The problem of carrying over painterly ideas to high relief formats was the irreconciliation of forward and backward interest: that in works where the substructure is dominated by material "scaffolding," the paper planes functioned less on their own account than for the linear structure their edges created. And even in the foregrounds, Schwitters' choice of often predominantly linear materials reinforced this effect. The *Weltenkreise* of 1919 was a case in point of this line-replacement, except that the lines were positioned on a ground that contained no other materials. This idea of arranging relief forms on a simply stated support was one of the principal directions taken by the later German assemblages since it avoided the spatial difficulties of works with a complicated ground structure. *Das Kegelbild* of 1921 shows this even more. But here the physical bulk of the material elements is greater and the sense of these elements standing as replacements for painted forms is less. This principle of materials simply functioning as themselves first emerges in the very earliest paper collages which are from the first "constructed." It seems significant, however, that the problems of transition between different modes of forming is most apparent in the larger assemblages, closer in size to a normal art context than the often very tiny collages. Indeed, Schwitters first called the collages "Merz-drawings," thus separating them from the painting genre, and only later felt the need to explain that they should also be regarded as pictures. It is also interesting that Schwitters' later stylistic reassessments are likewise more easily recognized in larger high relief works (this is no less true of the Constructivist-biased reliefs of the later '20s than of the "rural" assemblages of the '30s and '40s), while the collages reveal changes of stylistic emphasis more subtly. The smaller size of the collages seems to have allowed a greater and more personalized control by being more separate from a painting context than the works I have described as "paintings modified." What is more, the flat material planes of the collages could more easily perform simultaneously as structural and referential motifs, thus tending to resolve the semantic/syntagmatic ambiguities which give the assemblages of the early "revolutionary" years their special character.

It might seem that the confusion of genres in the early assemblages speaks directly of their period character—of social and political turmoil—and that the more orderly but less dynamic reliefs from around 1924 tell of the new stability of the post-Dawes Plan era. But such easy generalizations are confounded by the structural resolution of many of the earliest collage works. And the fact that Schwitters' assemblage and collage developments are parallel refutes any suggestion that the collages simply consolidate principles of forming first approached in high relief form. Indeed, the opposite viewpoint is more easily supported; for while no relief assemblages have dates previous to 1919, at least two collages are dated 1918.

From its very inception the referential status of collage received as much critical attention as its formal properties. Apollinaire, one of the first to refer to the technique, wrote of its relationship and relevance to the modern city, and (in words more appropriate to Schwitters than to Picasso or Braque) that its materials were "already steeped in humanity."[21] But the iconography of Cubism was well formed before collage, and collage did little to expand it. If there were urbanistic metaphors at work in Cubist collages they referred but to a very small section of the city. The real beginning of collage as a kind of "vernacular realism"[22] lies more truly in Futurism. Schwitters took formal devices from Futurist painting, notably the centrifugal composition, but another important source for his esthetic was the Futurists' positive attitude to using a wide range of materials in discontinuous juxtaposition to express the conditions of contemporary life. Undoubtedly the *Der Sturm* propaganda for Futurist art and theory was strongly influential in Schwitters' formative years. But it is not to raw Futurist tactics that Schwitters' earliest collages refer, rather to the more factual use of life materials, and sometimes life images, that characterize the Dadaists' modification of Futurist devices. In 1918, the same year Schwitters introduced himself to Herwarth Walden and the Sturm group, he met Arp and Hausmann in Berlin. If we are to seek any local sources for Schwitters' first collages, it must be with these two artists. Arp's collages of 1916-17 inform some of Schwitters' very simple first experiments. Hausmann's 1918 photomontages appear to have directly motivated a little-known but very significant group of works in the same medium by Schwitters.

What the Berlin Dadaists called "the new medium" dealt with "the absolutely self-evident that is within reach of our hands . . . it participates in life itself. . . . The new medium is the road from yearning to the reality of little things, and this road is abstract."[23] Although Schwitters never shared the Berliners' political concerns, he could readily identify with philosophies like this, especially since he was himself repudiating expression ("yearning") for abstraction and "reality." His early photomontages are among the most Dadaist of his works—their illustrative bases press them towards subject matter, unlike most of Schwitters' collages. Because his art developed from abstract sources, very few of his works permitted the introduction of narrative relationships and fewer still contained the human figure. Yet the works of this kind made in 1918 formed the prototypes for a small but interested thread in Schwitters' later development. Not the least remarkable aspect of his art was the swiftness with which it moved in the early years, and the way it opened up many different futures. *Die Handlung spielt in Theben* of 1918 shows Schwitters simply presenting the odd mixture of images with an eye to their greatest legibility—as if they were on a notice board. In consequence, the freedom from compositional preconceptions is very apparent. Although it is impossible to know the exact chronology of individual works in this period (and it could be that the purely abstract collages of 1918 precede this work), it does appear that this concern for legibility—directly stating the individual content-holding fragments—itself either suggested or confirmed the possibility of an art whose logic would be entirely that of the materials themselves. Disregarding for a moment the wealth of descriptive incident this work contains, its composition is entirely based on horizontal and vertical forms so different from the tilting ones of the contemporary paintings. Moreover, since Schwitters' materials purvey information, their planarity rather than their edge-patternings is emphasized. But here, anecdote wins over forming. *Die Handlung* is an early pictorial version of Schwitters' "Anna Blume" theme, his mockery of the fashionable bourgeois lady. Annas from photographs and fashion drawings are mixed up with her art-historical counterparts—the smiling angel of Rheims, a madonna by Stefan Lochner—and set among scenes of her own period.

As with Schwitters' collages in general, the iconographies of the photomontages interrelate. If the inclusion of high art fragments in *Die Handlung* seems to be satirizing them, this impression is even greater in a later work, *Wenzel Kind* of 1921, where a racehorse nudges into Schwitters' reworking of the Sistine Madonna; and the madonna herself is defiled by an Anna Blume head (like Duchamp's whiskered Mona Lisa), while the putti (who in Raphael's painting represented the presence of ordinary human nature) are replaced by machine parts. The racehorse here refers back to a 1918 picture, *König Eduard,* which celebrates the prewar meeting of the Kaiser and Edward VII, while the machinist-woman theme is specified in *Frau-Uhr* (1921), close in sentiment to many of Hausmann's photomontages. Again, the irreverent attitude to woman in this last work is echoed in *Das Kotsbild* (1920), which is in effect a verbo-visual pun on the word "bitch." Although "Frauschen" itself does not appear, the meaning is clear enough. Space prohibits a fuller investigation of Schwitters' iconographies, but these few examples should suffice to indicate something of their scope.

The only other works that are so Dadaist in mood are some contemporary watercolors and drawings. But these, like the photomontages, eschew any of that aggressive feeling so much a part of the Berlin Dadaists' makeup. Although Schwitters derived techniques from that quarter, his lighthearted irreverence has little to do with their expression of anger. And only rarely did the rampant fantasy of his literary works affect his visual production. But what is interesting about his Dadaist drawings is that, unlike the first photomontages, they owe a great deal to the Expressionist sources I discussed earlier. Thus, an abstract lithograph of 1919 which Schwitters made for the journal *Der Zweemann* is remarkably close in format to the nonsensical watercolor, *Das Herz geht vom Zucker zum Kaffee,* or to the cover illustration for the first edition of *Anna Blume* (both also 1919). In this latter drawing, a toy train chugs along what are in essence Expressionist *Kraftlinien.* Even the "drawings" made by rubber stamps, like *Der Kritiker* (1921), are composed along Expressionist lines. It was not until the "Merzmappe" lithographs of 1923 that Schwitters' graphic work really reached that equilibrious expression of shape and edge which characterizes the earliest collages, and then only after the new proformalist orientation of that year.[24] Drawing was at first an appropriately private avenue for whimsicality. The assemblages are hardly ever at all bizarre (*Der Irrenarzt* of 1919 is a rare exception), and the collages—though sometimes containing humorous or provocative images or word-fragments—are essentially committed to "forming." Although the use of waste elements was itself at that time a sociorevolutionary gesture, Schwitters had no strong social feelings. And though the amusing titles of some works belie their visible seriousness, with the passing of time it is their art that makes them last.

v

At first sight the collages display a somewhat bewildering diversity, but it very soon becomes apparent how close to each other they are. This is not to say that the effects which Schwitters creates are limited. Clearly this is not so. Emphasis might be placed predominantly on color, on tone, or on texture; the compositions might suggest stability, or rising or falling movements; the materials might be dirty and worn or clean and sharp. But formally they all depend either on a radiating Futuro-Expressionist device or on a Cubist grid.

Hansi of 1918 is one of a small group made that year which represent (with the contemporary photo-montages) Schwitters' first collage works.[25] From the start, therefore, he discards the linearism of the assemblages for an uncomplicated expression of flatness. The paper fragments already work as frontal surfaces and already assert themselves as, first of all, stated areas of color. While he was still struggling with illusionism, tonality, and inherited style in the larger assemblages, this more "advanced" *Zeichnung* was in existence. This apparent contradiction in stylistic development (which has led some to doubt the date of works like this) is only explicable if we remember Schwitters' openness to influences. There is no reason why this collage should not belong to 1918 since its total freedom from Expressionism seems itself to indicate a *first* experiment with abstract collage, directly motivated by Arp's idea of its essentially flat properties. And that Schwitters' collages of the following few years look not less but more Expressionist implies that he then began to try to use Arp-derived collage ideas in a way closer to what his own style was then like. Perhaps distrusting the manifest simplicity he had created, he tried to make collage more his own—although this meant that the work he produced was sometimes less "advanced." And not until around 1922, in works like *blauer Funken,* could Schwitters regularly accept the openness of effect which characterizes the 1918 collage. Instead, he opted by and large for a complicated closely knit design; and some large-scale collages of 1919-21 show how the assemblage and collage modes overlapped. In *Das Grosse Ichbild* (1919), only very rarely are materials left as Schwitters found them. Nearly everything is glazed over with tonal painting which at the same time sublimates the referential function of materials, creates the luminous angularity of the work (the shading of paint towards drawn lines emphasizing this), and imposes an expressive mood. By 1920, in *Merzbild Einunddreissig,* this glaze had gone and relatively more raw materials are visible, but now a heavy dose of thicker oil painting is used to apply the mood. Like the assemblages, these are clearly hybrid works (though possessing the commensurate dramatic properties this status effects) and suffer from compositional preconceptions. Materials are still forced into patterns and the treatment of edges remains uncertain. In contrast, smaller works of this same period more successfully express their medium and its own particular qualities.

Schwitters' collages depend in essence on three procedural devices and two stylistic forms. These are best explained by considering how collages are made, and a group of 1921 works can serve to show this. The pasting of papers in collage has a beginning and an end which the work can reveal to a greater or lesser degree. If all parts of the surface are worked together, the location of beginning and end is disguised; and the effect is an all-over contrapuntal one. If the work is built outwards, the last pastings occupying its perimeters, the edges achieve prominence. If the last-pasted elements are free from the edges (the work built inwards) then this will locate some materials as more or less floating on the surface. The degree to which any of these procedures achieve prominence dictates the effect of the work—although this effect will be modified by the color and relative areas of the materials used, and whether their compositions stress either a Futuro-Expressionist radiating pattern or an all-over Cubist grid. The all-over effect of *Mz 322, bunt,* is thus emphasized by the relative smallness of its materials, the evenness of its textures and the chromatic counterpointing of its hues. And, interestingly here, the last-pasted materials pull loose from the perimeter of the work, except along the bottom edge, therefore giving the effect of space somehow tipping back away from the observer. This again may have something to do with the procedural bases of Schwitters' art. We noticed something similar in the assemblage, *Konstruktion für edle Frauen.* Also, several collages are composed themselves along an implied central vertical axis. *Mz 222* and *Mz 299* (both also 1921) do this; materials converging or splaying in a direct relationship to the body position of the artist. But both these works, especially the former, are outward-built, which itself emphasizes this effect. Works of this kind have also the advantage of seeming to very directly express how the materials themselves create and delimit spaces—until the boundaries arrived at are just large enough to accommodate them—while edge-positioned materials themselves both define literal shape and reflect back into the center. In another collage, *Mz 334, Verbürgt rein,* this works to locate a focus of interest; but uneven edge-positioning can create distinct directional movements across the whole area (as in *875 G,* 1921-24). There are far fewer instances of collages with no edge alignments, and this serves to confirm just how much Schwitters' style was a synthetic Cubist one. *Mz 308, Grau* appears mainly inner-built—its central forms being strongest—but here the Cubist axiality could hardly be more pronounced, being emphasized by the "pureness" of the materials and the sharpness of their cut edges. And even in the rare cases when Schwitters tears all the edges in one work, the axiality of the printed matter used once more reminds us of his Cubist sources.

Another link to Cubism is Schwitters' use of color. Although Cubist collage did not itself make significant use of color, it changed the surface of Cubist painting so that color could be used. The surface was no longer broken to suggest the illusion of interior depths to the degree it was before, but could become instead a flat support for the planes of added materials, each of which could function as an unbroken color-holding surface. Color, being a property of surface, could thus collaborate the flatness of the entire work while creating a tie between individual materials. And in the best of Schwitters' works, color unifies, ties and flattens, and does this although harsh contrasts and strong complementaries are used. These can be accommodated because the colors physically occupy the individual planes of which the work is composed. However, illusion is never—and here can never be—absent: on the one hand, the spatial position of colored areas (materials) is physically determined (by the order in which they were pasted down); on the other, color may either support the "real" space (in some of the inner-built collages, the last-added planes float Hofmannesque forward of the surface) or act as an incitement to deny physicality (early-pasted materials pushing up from below). Moreover, the degree to which in any given work materials either suppress (totally cover) the ground plane or allow themselves to appear to be resting on it must also affect the perception of their colors. Locked objects defy physicality in direct proportion to the complexity of their locking (total cover with relatively small units confounds the search for just where the ground is), and consequently assist in establishing the interrelationships of colors. Similarly, the size of colored areas (materials) and their degree of "problematic" identity is significant. Materials or colors which give the appearance of being unusual (either in hue or in terms of the incident they contain) increase the relational difficulty, while as the size of objects increase they are not so easily managed in an intuitive way. Schwitters' predilection for usually worn materials of an intimate size therefore contributes to the optical tying of their colors. Inevitably, the colors are physically inseparable from the nostalgia of the materials that contain them. Although there are some works of this period (*Mz 308, Grau,* for example) where the colors do operate purely, mostly the stains, crumples, added paint marks, texts, pictures, and varied textures, modify their impact—and these markings also encourage one to react somehow bodily to the work itself. To read the mixture of signs, one's manner of access must keep changing. This response is analogous to the way the collages were made.

VI

Earlier I suggested that the esthetic and psychological aspects of Schwitters' art are complementary. By this I mean that the works are only successful if they announce simultaneously their formal and associative structures. The danger is that they might be only mnemonic devices, and it should not be denied that occasionally a collage comes close to betraying itself artistically by depending overmuch on its role as a trigger for the viewer's (nonpictorial) emotions. Nevertheless, by either signaling responses within established formal structures (in the assemblages) or letting the signals or triggers create their own structures (in the collages), Schwitters was by and large successful in producing an abstract art whose "content" was both esthetic and moral. And the mechanism of moral content becomes rather like Eisenstein's "series of connecting shocks arranged in a certain sequence and directed at the audience."[26] It may be argued that what I have discussed here does not touch enough on this "content," on the emotive or poetic side of Schwitters' art. The point, however, is that the emotion—or, rather, the

sincerity of the emotion—can only exist if the esthetic structure possesses the conviction to hold it. To be other than simply pathetic fallacies, the subjectivities of these works must be included, and the mechanism of Schwitters' "inclusions" has been my theme here. Since it has been noted that the extent to which materials are "included" directly affects their referential functions, we might, in conclusion, speculate a little on what implications this holds for the viewer.

Since any given work is not referential as one image (because its parts assume neither a narrative or spatial relationship paralleling that of the world), reference can exist only in terms of the individual, added objects. This means that in theory there are two opposite possibilities: added objects may or may not depend on each other, that is, may make relationships between themselves or may affirm their individual autonomy. If individual object autonomy exists, the likelihood of outer reference is maximized; if relationship is maximized (and this relationship is itself in no way metaphorical), then reference is limited. The objects can never be perceived to function simultaneously as both form and reference though they may exist as such. (A useful analogy here is the figure/ground illusion.) This we have observed in the assemblages. We have also seen that the capacity of objects to form relationships depends essentially on their capability to associate themselves with the real surface of the work (as well as on the extent of their interlocking). Maximum reference thus exists on the forward plane when an object seems alienated from those surrounding it. And yet, Schwitters' concern with "relationships" meant that an extreme alienation of individual objects rarely occurred. Although the very nature of Schwitters' procedures made absolute pictorial homogeneity an impossibility (the identity of materials being irrepressible), his concern for relationships created a situation wherein the viewer can only momentarily settle on individual objects that can be separately "translated." An individual object is no sooner recognized that one is forced to let it go in favor of the neighboring object to which it is adjusted. In terms of reference, therefore, the "fixation pauses" during which associative reactions can occur are at odds with the "saccades" between them.[27] Since it takes a deliberate effort to keep focusing on individual materials, the viewer is pushed into searching for a common denominator between them (in an emotional as well as structural sense). In an important sense, therefore, a work is only fully experienced by the viewer somehow reconstructing the activity of Schwitters' forming.

Schwitters' special brand of forming ("considering the importance of the individual materials") involved the relationship or interaction of the artist and his material environment in terms not only of its pictorial usefulness but, equally significantly, in terms of its existential status. Since, in this forming, "form" might be understood as meaning "the form his procedures took," materials therefore function in accordance with their behavioral access—become, as "stuff," important in terms of their manipulable physicality—and, when in the work, make reference not only as individual iconographical elements but, in relationships, to the character of his procedures. This allying of form and process—approximating of ends and means—identifies Schwitters' phenomenological approach to art-making.[28] He does, in a very real sense speak "not only *with* things . . . but through the medium of things: giving an account of his personality and life by the choices he makes."[29] Like still life, collage, as Schwitters practiced it, expresses "an empirical standpoint wherein our knowledge of proximate objects . . . is the model or ground of all knowledge. . . . 'The reality of what we see is what we can handle'"[30] And individual collage or assemblage thus refers to its environmental sources in both iconographic and behavioral terms. Though Schwitters softened the disassociation between the material elements he used, this could never entirely "succeed." Discontinuities could never be completely bridged since the presence of objects in new contexts, while regenerating their formal properties, also revalued their metaphorical roles—replacing their worn-out utilitarian functions with ones belonging to an esthetic situation. That is, while objects *do* refer to their original uses, equally they refer to how they have changed from these uses. They act as evidence of their own transformation (in function, though not in looks) through the forming process. The autobiographical iconography of the materials thus acts as a factual reminder of Schwitters' "forms" of behavior—and the relationships of the materials demand some degree of "completion" by the viewer, who is invited to reconstitute the manner of the behavior (while yet aware of individual iconographic references). Schwitters' work—emphasizing its procedures—places an important formative responsibility on the viewer, demanding, as it were, not only to be seen but to be known to be seen. In this way, there is no hard and fast line between the art and its audience. These works are art (the objects are included); but by the precariousness of their inclusions (referring beyond their unique art contexts to earlier stylistic conventions and stealing from life) they function also as systems expediting the perception of art, as perceptual fields within which the viewer is encouraged to perform.

NOTES

[1] *Merz,* no. 20, 1927.

[2] My essay, "The Last Work of Kurt Schwitters" (*Artforum,* VIII, 2, October, 1969. pp. 56-64), first discussed some of the problems presented here, and details Schwitters' later solutions.

[3] "Merz" (1920), *Der Ararat,* 1921. From the translation in Robert Motherwell, ed., *The Dada Painters and Poets,* New York, 1951, pp. 57-65; and for the following quotations.

[4] Wassily Kandinsky, *Concerning the Spiritual in Art,* New York, 1947, p. 48, note 6.

[5] *Ibid.,* p. 49.

[6] *Ibid.,* p. 73.

[7] For the problems of learning Cubism through German modernism see Clement Greenberg's essay on Kandinsky in his *Art and Culture, Boston,* 1961, pp. 111-114.

[8] In terms of Schwitters' opting for a flat painting solution, the comment by Maurice Reynal, the first critic to discuss collage, is interesting. He inferred that collage emerged as a solution for dealing with the representation of flat objects in a picture. While volumes can be painted, he suggested, "plane surfaces cannot . . . since they are not bodies; if one does so, one falls back into imitation. . . . If I think of a bottle and wish to render it as it is, the label on it appears to me simply as an unimportant accessory which I might leave out, for it is only an image. If I feel I must show it, I could copy it exactly, but that is a useless labour; so I place the actual label on the picture." ("L'Exposition de la Section d'Or," *La Section d'Or,* Paris, 1912, p. 5.)

[9] Quoted by Carola Giedion-Welcker, *Contemporary Sculpture,* London, 1941, p. xix.

[10] I do not discuss here Schwitters' few early sculptures, his Hannover Merzbau (begun ca. 1923) nor his creative writing, but it would be no exaggeration to say that my remarks here apply equally to these other aspects of his work.

[11] *Merz,* no. 1, January, 1923.

[12] "Merz" (1920) in Motherwell, p. 59; and for the following quotations.

[13] Quoted by Christof Spengemann, "Kurt Schwitters," *Der Cicerone,* no. 40, 1919, p. 580.

[14] The phrase is Alan Solomon's, of Jasper Johns' work.

[15] Unpublished text of 1926. Quoted by Werner Schmalenbach, *Kurt Schwitters,* New York, 1969, p. 96.

[16] Here I am excepting figures close to the center of original Cubism (like Léger or Delauney) or those of Schwitters' generation who only later developed their personal styles (like Hofmann or Albers). But all found that their first task (taken up also by Synthetic Cubism) was to overcome the way a Cubist grid dissolves at its edges; and all their solutions involved (to a greater or lesser degree) creating some kind of pictorial "container" for the "dramatic" interaction of forms or colors.

[17] Quoted by Hans Bolliger, in *Kurt Schwitters,* Marlborough Fine Art, London, 1963, p. 14.

[18] *Merz,* no. 1, January, 1923.

[19] *Ibid.*

[20] Letter to Raoul Hausmann, March 29, 1947. In Raoul Hausmann and Kurt Schwitters, *Pin,* London, 1962, p. 17.

[21] Cf. Apollinaire's "Die Moderne Malerei," *Der Sturm*, no. 148/149, 1913, p. 272, and *Les Peintres Cubistes*, Paris, 1913, p. 38. But Apollinaire was also aware of the formal changes collage brought, importantly that "the object is the inner frame of the picture and marks the limit of its depth."

[22] William Seitz's phrase in *The Art of Assemblage*, New York, 1961, p. 87.

[23] Richard Hülsenbeck, *En Avant Dada* (Hanover, 1920) in Motherwell, pp. 36-37.

[24] These six lithographs were published as a special issue (no. 3, 1923) of Schwitters' magazine, *Merz*.

[25] *Hansi* is numbered "Zeichnung A2." A stylistically similar "Zeichnung A6," also dated 1918, is the only known survivor of what was presumably a small group of first collage experiments bearing the designation "A." Schmalenbach (p. 120) finds the 1918 dating "curious," although he also locates the Arp influence I discuss below—but without drawing the same conclusions. The unique numbering sequence for these collages separates them from those with the more common designation "Mz" or "Mzz" (for "Merz-Zeichnung"), which Schwitters began using in 1919. But the sequence of Schwitters' titlings is confusing (cf. Schmalenbach, p. 119), and the "A" designation itself doesn't date *Hansi* as 1918. However, one of a "J" series of Zeichnungen remains from 1920 (*Zeichnung 19, Hebel* 2), so presumably the "A" series predates this. Schwitters did sometimes make mistakes in dating works, but there is, I feel, enough evidence here (as well as such other indications of his tactics as the 1918 photomontages) to justify my suggestion that in these early years he moved first and asked questions afterwards.

[26] Quoted by Peter Wollen, *Signs and Meaning in the Cinema*, London, 1969, p. 39 (itself highly relevant to this discussion of Schwitters' "meanings"). For Eisenstein, however, this was a mixture of Pavlov and the Marxist dialectic. He also wrote of montage as *collision:* "A view that from the collision of two given factors arises a concept." Schwitters sometimes talked of collision (it was the title of his comic-opera of 1928), but does this imply the dialectic as it did for Eisenstein? A footnote isn't the place to speculate whether the assemblage format by nature lends itself to holding political content, although it is an appropriate question here. Schwitters was of course apolitical, and his kind of juxtaposition was not entirely heterogeneous (collisionary—perhaps closer to Pudovkin's idea of montage as *linkage* ("bricks arranged in a series to expound an idea"). Again: does Eisenstein's "I get away from realism by going to reality" and "I believe that material things, that matter gives us the basis of all our sensations" hold any relevance for Schwitters (though it seems to for Tatlin)?.

[27] It could even be suggested, therefore, that for the viewer the weighting of formal and iconographical responses is directly proportional to that of saccadic and fixation time in his viewing. But the "reading" of pages and pictures is different, and the analogy cannot be exact. Relevant to the idea of confrontation being in terms either of individual elements or of the whole are some notes to Michael Fried's "Manet's Sources. Aspects of his Art 1859-1865" (*Artforum*, VII, 7, March, 1969), where he discusses the relationship of picture and viewer in total confrontation (note 27) and the problems of portraiture when the subject matter rather than the whole painting effects "facing" (note 91). For Schwitters, the comparison with *group* portraiture, as well as with still life, is instructive.

[28] For a defense of art as making: Robert Morris, "Some notes on the phenomenology of making: The search for the motivated," *Artforum*, VIII, 8, April, 1970. Cf. also the relevant sections of Richard Wollheim's *Art and its Objects* (London, 1968), including: " . . . if it is true that artistic creativity can occur only in so far as certain processes or stuffs are already accredited as the vehicles of art, then it becomes important to know how and why these accreditations are made" (section 47).

[29] Claude Lévi-Strauss, "The Science of the Concrete," *The Savage Mind*, Chicago, 1966, p. 21. Although Lévi-Strauss does not mention Schwitters, he seems a far more appropriate personification of the "bricoleur" of this famous passage than the *facteur* Cheval and the others. Finite tools for diverse tasks, reordering the remains of events, a "significant treasury," and so on: these all bring Schwitters to mind. Lévi-Strauss's later discussion of scale factors is also important here.

[30] Meyer Schapiro, "The Apples of Cézanne: An essay on the meaning of still life," *Art News Annual*, XXXIV, 1968, pp. 34-53 (quoting from George H. Mead, *The Philosophy of the Act*, Chicago, 1938).

Philip Thomson (essay date 1972)

SOURCE: "A Case of Dadaistic Ambivalence: Kurt Schwitters's Stramm-Imitations and 'An Anna Blume,'" in *The German Quarterly*, Vol. XLV, No. 1, January, 1972, pp. 47-56.

[*In the following essay, Thomson evaluates the ambiguous nature of Schwitters's "An Anna Blume" as art and anti-art, sense and nonsense, serious poetry and parody.*]

The recent revival of interest in Dada, accompanying such essentially neo-Dadaist phenomena as pop art, "happenings," and the like, has raised anew the question—properly, for it is a central one—of the Dadaists' attitude to their activities. The question is usually put in the form of contraries: Art or anti-art? Sense or nonsense? Purposeful experimentation or purposeless play? The antithetical formulation reflects a fundamental characteristic of Dadaism, an ambiguity and ambivalence which is quite basic, affecting the very roots of the Dadaistic product. (To say "work of art" would prejudice the issue.)

Not surprisingly in a movement as dedicated to the hoaxing of the public as Dada was, this ambiguity is often translated for the reader, fearful both of being left out and of being drawn in, into the question: Is this meant seriously, or is it wholly a send-up? Will I reveal myself as a Philistine if I reject it as a ridiculous hoax? Will I be made to look a fool if I take it as serious art? Such questions lead on eventually of course to one which is at once more and less fruitful: Where does "art" begin and end? Some discussions of Dada poems have tended to answer these questions by emphasizing their meaningful and in this sense "serious" nature, plumping for art, sense, and purpose against anti-art, nonsense, and arbitrariness. This tendency, while perhaps preferable to the view that sees Dada purely as non-sense and hoax, is nevertheless equally one-sided and can lead not only to over-interpretation but to a blindness to the essentially ambivalent character of Dadaism. In an article entitled "In Defence of Meaning" R. W. Last[1] attempts to decipher Hans Arp's "Kaspar ist tot" as a serious, controlled, and rationally devised if obscure lament, after he has already admitted at the outset that

> One is obliged to accept the coexistence, indeed identity, of apparently irreconcilable forces: "Spiel" and "Ernst"; automatic writing and a guiding, controlling intellect; the destruction of art and the recreation of art.

That Last's search for meaning (in a rather conventional sense) involves him in some extremely far-fetched interpretation should give no cause for surprise: his undertaking was self-admittedly quixotic from the beginning.

Similarly, though much less open to objection, J. C. Middleton, in an examination of Kurt Schwitters' **"Gedicht 25,"**[2] shows that he is well aware of "Schwitters' genius for fooling," but then makes the mistake of assuming that this genius exhausts itself in mere satirizing and thwarting of the mathematical mind, and that outside this the poem is to be taken completely seriously. Far more likely, one is inclined to say that this "poem" (consisting wholly of a series of numbers) falls into the same category as most of Schwitters' work: that of a total ambivalence which prevents any certainty of understanding or interpretation. In the case of "Gedicht 25," for example, while it is quite possible to see the text as "a deflation notably of the declamatory mode in so-called Expressionist poetry," as "a model of patterning and unpredictability in poetic art," and as an attack on the increasing sterilization of life by mathematics and technology, it is equally possible that it is what it looks like at first sight, as Middleton himself says, a prank, designed to trap the enquiring reader or critic, who cannot resist a challenge, into wasting his skill and time in devising "explanations" of what is simply a piece of foolery. This is not meant derisively in the least. My point is merely that such irreconcilable yet undeniably coexistent possibilities, no one of which is more or less likely than the other, are a feature of Dadaistic art and of the art of Kurt Schwitters in particular.

Many of Schwitters' early poems are in the style of August Stramm, imitating the radical reduction of diction to nouns and verbs, the confusion of grammatical function and the frequently breathless and staccato effects achieved by the *Sturm* poet. But these imitations are problematical, raising the kind of question referred to above: serious poetry or nonsense, genuine following of a radically new and, at its best, exciting style, or the parody of this style? Thus the following short poem:

> Ich taumeltürme
> Welkes windes Blatt
> Häuser augen Menschen Klippen
> Schmiege Taumel Wind
> Menschen steinen Häuser Klippen
> Taumeltürme blutes Blatt

would probably pass as a "sincere" imitation of Stramm were it not for its title: **"Ich werde gegangen."** Stramm of course, like all highly mannered writers, lends himself particularly well to parody. It is interesting that, reading the above poem without the title, one can well accept it as "serious." Seeing the comic heading, however, one immediately perceives the text as obvious parody. The dividing line between a radical style and its parody is very thin indeed.

Similarly, the longer poem **"Nächte"** seems "genuine" until the eighth line, which explodes all seriousness:

> Innige Nächte
> Gluten Qual
> Zittert Glut Wonne
> Schmerzhaft umeint
> Siedend nächtigt Brunst
> Peitscht Feuer Blitz
> Zuckend Schwüle
> O wenn ich das Fischlein baden könnte!

Similar ludicrous lines occur in a number of poems Schwitters wrote in the Stramm manner. And yet these poems cannot be simply summed up as parodies or send-ups. One does not have the certainty of a definite deflating aim carried through to the conclusion. In every case Schwitters, having inserted an inverting, ridiculing, or otherwise drastically qualifying line, returns to the "serious" style thus undercut. Thus **"Nächte"** continues in an apparently genuine Stramm-style, as if nothing had happened, as if that eighth line were not there:

> Zagt ein Innen
> Zittert enteint
> Giert schwül
> Herb
> Du—
> Duft der Braut
> Rosen gleiâen im Garten.
> etc.

Similarly, there is nothing in the text of **"Ich werde gegangen"** which takes up the comedy of the title. This strange state of affairs is not confined to poems after the manner of Stramm. A similar ambivalence presents itself in **"Die Welt,"** which is written rather in a style which one might describe as "apocalyptic surrealism":

> Häuser fallen, Himmel stürzen ein.
> Bäume ragen über Bäume.
> Himmel grünt rot.
> Silberne Fische schwimmen in der Luft.
> Sie verbrennen sich nicht.
> Sie sind ja so innig.
> Im ewigen Silber glänzt ihre Frühe.
> Und der Wahn schwillt heran und brüstet sich
>   über die Himmel.
> Millionen silberne Fische zittern über die Weite.
> Doch sengen sie nicht ihre silbernen Flügel.
> Sanft weht die Luft vom silbernen Flügelschlag
> Brüsten sich Menschen—
> Knien Seelen—
> Riesengroâ wächst der Wahn über die Weite.

Here it is of course the sixth line which shatters the apparently serious picture of a crumbling, insane world. Yet once again Schwitters returns to his original, seemingly quite unironic mode, and the poem concludes entirely in the manner of the familiar Expressionist apocalyptic vision.

It may be objected that the merit of much of this poetry is so slight that questions of parody or genuine imitation, nonsense or experimentation are of marginal interest. But it is worth emphasizing that what is demonstrated in the few examples offered is, in a marked and clear form, the most basic characteristic of Dadaism: the willful confusion of art and anti-art, the refusal to make distinctions between "serious" and purely playful or nonsensical creative activity. Even so, Schwitters' imitations (or parodies) of Stramm would be of only slight interest if they did not provide an insight into the poem on which his literary reputation still mainly rests and which has endured as perhaps the most famous creation of Dada: **"An Anna Blume."**

> O du, Geliebte meiner siebenundzwanzig Sinne,
>   ich liebe dir!—Du deiner dich dir, ich dir, du mir.
> —Wir?
> Das gehört (beiläufig) nicht hierher.
> Wer bist du, ungezähltes Frauenzimmer? Du bist
> ——bist du?—Die leute sagen, du wärest,—laâ
> sie sagen, sie wissen nicht, wie der Kirchturm steht.
> Du trägst den Hut auf deinen Füâen und wanderst
>   auf die Hände, auf den Händen wanderst du.
> Hallo, deine roten Kleider, in weiâe Falten zersägt.
> Rot liebe ich Anna Blume, rot liebe ich dir!—Du
> deiner dich dir, ich dir, du mir.—Wir?
> Das gehört (beiläufig) in die Kalte Glut.
> Rote Blume, rote Anna Blume, wie sagen die Leute?
> Preisfrage: 1. Anna Blume hat ein Vogel.
>   2. Anna Blume ist rot.
>   3. Welche Farbe hat der Vogel?
> Blau ist die Farbe deines gelben Haares.
> Rot ist das Girren deines grünen Vogels.
> Du schlichtes Mädchen im Alltagskleid, du
>   liebes grüne
> Tier, ich liebe dir!—Du deiner dich dir, ich dir, du
> mir,—Wir?
> Das gehört (beiläufig) in die Glutenkiste.
> Anna Blume! Anna, a-n-n-a, ich träufle deinen

> Namen. Dein Name tropft wie weiches Rindertalg.
> Weiât du es, Anna, weiât du es schon?
> Man kann dich auch von hinten lesen, und du, du
> Herlichste von allen, du bist von hinten wie von
>   vorne:
> "a - n - n - a."
> Rindertalg träufelt streicheln über meinen Rücken.
> Anna Blume, du tropfes Tier, ich liebe dir!

Schwitters, love poem—or nonsensical send-up of a love poem, for it is a case of antithetical possibilities—elicits as does perhaps no other Dadaistic product the familiar range of questions described above: sense or nonsense, seriousness or facetiousness, organization or willfulness? Not only does the poem chop and change bewilderingly from eulogistic address to Anna to grammatical declension, seemingly destructive intrusions, puns, and back to eulogy, but an antithetical balance is maintained, through all this, between these incompatibles, which we can best subsume under the single antithesis of art/anti-art. But maintenance of balance implies organization and structuring, an order in the apparent chaos or, more accurately in this case, the conscious contriving of the effect of total ambiguity. And that there is some patterning in the poem is obvious enough at a fairly superficial level. Taking the first four lines,[3] down to "Das gehört (beiläufig) nicht hierher," as the introduction, a pattern then emerges of seven lines addressed to and in praise of Anna, followed by the declension of "du" and the line "Das gehört (beiläufig). . . ." The pattern is present twice in full, the last seven lines representing a curtailment. The first four lines can then be seen also as a curtailed version of the pattern, the two curtailed versions combining to complete a full pattern, with one overlapping line, the first.

This says little, however, about the function of such regularity, or about what inner tensions in the poem underlie it. These tensions and conflicts are present from the first line: the ecstatic exaggeration of the lover is laughable yet at the same time peculiarly moving, above all through the beauty of sound and rhythm up to "Sinne." Disconcerting however, and destructive of any "poetry"—i.e. lyrical beauty or emotion—the reader might have felt, is "ich liebe dir." The false grammar seems wholly inexplicable and intrusive. It brings the reader up short, and any amusement he may feel here is probably countered by annoyance at what appears to be a gratuitous piece of foolery. The declension following on this increases the negative response: the ludicrously anti-poetic grammatical exercise (is the poet taking time out to brush up on his grammar after the mistake he has just made?) destroys the hardly begun wooing of Anna.

This is probably the point at which the reader begins to see that he is faced with a decision: he can either dismiss the text as a nonsensical hoax, an anti-poem, or he can think of it—though with some reservations—as a unique blend of the nonsensically comic and the poetic. Searching around for clues, he will possibly reflect that the declension could be an expression of the poet's obsession with the "Du," which leads him to recite in his ecstasy all its forms. "Ich dir, du mir," is then perhaps an expression of the reciprocity of this love, and "Wir?" a wooing question. But the reader will conclude finally that the line is grotesque whichever way one takes it. If it is simply a grammatical exercise its presence in what started out as a love poem is ludicrous and destructive. If it is a reflection of the poet's ecstasy its stammering, barely articulate nature is likewise ludicrously incongruous after the wild expansiveness of the first line.

But Schwitters is a jump ahead: the fourth line admits the reader's strictures on the declension as absolutely correct. (Alternatively, if the reader has decided that the declension is poetically justified, he now discovers that he is wrong, and feels duped.) This fourth line represents a complete withdrawal of the author from his poem. The preceding series of pronouns is declared (apologetically or indifferently?) null and void, an irrelevancy, and the poet hastens back to his interrupted praise of Anna. The alienating effect of this line is so great that even the well-disposed reader is ready to dismiss the whole poem as a kind of self-destructive joke, when the next line draws him back into the lyrical perspective, strange though it may be, of the address to the beloved: "Wer bist du, ungezähltes Frauenzimmer?" There seems to be no rational or contextual justification for "ungezählt," and "Frauenzimmer" is hardly an endearment, but the line is attractive again because of its unusualness and a certain felicity of sound and rhythm—or can it be that, thinking this, one is once again setting oneself up to be duped?

It is significant that one finds oneself analyzing this poem in terms of a contest between author and reader. It is a one-sided contest, for Schwitters invents the rules of the game and calls the play. The game is a kind of "Follow-me-if-you-can," with the reader inevitably a step behind the author. Just when he thinks the poem is one big joke or hoax he is confronted with a line or two which tend to convince him that the praise of Anna is serious: comic and naive perhaps, but convincing in a way *because* of this naivete, because the poet's incoherent, comically ecstatic, and naively excessive language is felt to be proof of a genuinely joyful emotion. Then, however, there inevitably follows a line which is designed to destroy confidence in the genuineness of the praise of Anna and create instead the certainty of frivolous foolery. In this way a balance is produced in the poem as a whole which leaves us at the end unable to take the poem as one thing or the other and obliges us to accept it as both: as both naive but genuine love poem and as the send-up of this, both imaginative expression and frivolity, unique experimentation and hoax, as both art and anti-art. The text "hebt sich selbst auf" and remains standing at the end as an enigma.

The balance between opposites—and it is this which must be seen as the inner pattern of the poem—is so finely calculated that by halfway through the text one is no longer sure which way to take even individual lines. Is "Blau ist die Farbe deines gelben Haares" a successful piece of surrealistic poetry or a debunking of surrealism? Is "Rot ist das Girren deines grünen Vogels" a fine piece of sensually evocative synesthesia, or must one dismiss it, warned by the reference to "Vogel" (in two senses) in the absurd "Preisfrage," as a similarly absurd frivolity?

Such dilemmas are not helped by the realization that Schwitters' problematical imitations (or parodies) of Stramm have left their mark on this poem. It seems a safe guess that the recurring "Du deiner dich dir, ich dir, du mir.—Wir?" is parodistic, in the light of the number of Stramm's love poems which include similar cryptic—or inarticulate—use of personal pronouns. His **"Blüte,"** for example (is it too much to see a connection with Anna *Blume?*), ends thus:

> Blüten! Blüten!
> Küsse! Wein!
> Roter
> Goldner
> Rauscher
> Wein!
> Du
> Du und Ich!
> Ich und Du!
> Du?!

Even more illuminating, and proof that the parodist does not have to exaggerate much (and sometimes not at all) to achieve his purpose, is the following Stramm gem:

> *Wankelmut*
> Mein Suchen sucht!
> Viel tausend wandeln Ich!
> Ich taste Ich
> Und fasse Du
> Und halte Dich!
> Versehne Ich!
> Und Du und Du und Du
> Viel tausend Du
> Und immer Du
> Allwege Du
> Wirr
> Wirren
> Wirrer
> Immer Wirrer
> Durch
> Die Wirrnis
> Du
> Dich
> Ich!

But while it seems we must take Schwitters' "Du deiner dich dir, ich dir, du mir.—Wir?" as a parody of Stramm, this does not necessarily mean that the line is only parody, designed to elicit a knowing laugh. The possibility mentioned earlier, that it can be an expression of the obsession with the "Du," comic in its ecstatic near-incoherence but genuine, still holds good, I suggest. This view—that even such an apparently clear-cut case of parodistic nonsense need not be purely negative—is strengthened not only by the several instances of Schwitters' essentially ambivalent attitude to Stramm occurring in other poems, but also by a further example in **"An Anna Blume."** In the latter part of the poem Schwitters, quite in the manner of Stramm, takes a word—the name "Anna"—and makes it a concrete thing of substance which takes on its own properties: it is glutinous, it drips like beef-tallow. At first this occurs only at the level of simile:

> Anna, a - n - n - a, ich träufle deinen
> Namen. Dein Name tropft wie weiches Rindertalg.

But three lines later (after the revelation of the other remarkable feature of "a-n-n-a," namely that it is the same when spelt backwards) the name has *become* beef-dripping:

> Rindertalg träufelt streicheln über meinen Rücken.

The style of this line, with one of its key words of indeterminate grammatical function (streicheln) is vintage Stramm. But once again it is difficult to decide whether it is a case of imitation or of parody. The line is, if one disregards "Rindertalg," erotically lyrical. But "Rindertalg": anything less lovable or less lyrical is difficult to imagine, suggesting that Schwitters is here employing the favorite parodistic device of comic alienation. Comic too is the last line of the poem, which brings to a conclusion the progression "träufeln, tropfen, Rindertalg" with "du tropfes Tier." The use of "tropf" adjectivally is also typical Stramm style (the confusion of grammatical function being one of the most constant features of his poetry). Yet I would argue with Clemens Heselhaus' assertion that "du tropfes Tier" with its play on the slang "Du Tropf!" is "rein komisch verwendet,"[4] in the belief that nothing in this poem is "purely" anything. Just as the preceding line is erotically lyrical *as well as* comic (through the inappropriateness of "Rindertalg"), so the comic nature of this last line is opposed by the manifest joyfulness, even tenderness, of the poet (he has said "du liebes grünes Tier" earlier). The sense of wonder and triumph in

> Weiât du es Anna, weiât du es schon?
> Man kann dich auch von hinten lesen, und du, du
> Herrlichste von allen, du bist von hinten wie von
>   vorne: "a-n-n-a."

is present again here at the end of the poem: the corny and banal have become wondrous.

This is of course putting a rather "poetic" interpretation on a text which, as this essay has attempted to show, is essentially a balanced mixture of the poetic and the antipoetic. It is a common experience when dealing with Dadaist art that one is compelled to emphasize the "positive" artistic qualities more than one would wish, in order to prevent outright dismissal of it as merely engaging nonsense. **"An Anna Blume"** is both artistic and antiartistic, both love poem and its own send-up, both serious and frivolous at the same time. The reader is obliged to accept the coexistence, indeed inextricability of these irreconcilable opposites: it is the final joke in the game that there is to be no resolution.

There can be no resolution either of the problem of Schwitters' imitations of Stramm. The question "genuine imitation or parody" can only have the answer: "both at once." In this sense the parts of the poem which imitate Stramm are a key to the nature of the whole. For if Schwitters is debunking Stramm he is also in a way debunking himself, who showed a more than slight attraction to Stramm's style. In any case is it not often true that parodists have a "love-hate" relationship to the objects of their parody, that the desire to deflate is not simply directed outward but also inward against a wish or tendency in themselves to write in the style parodied? It is this kind of ambivalence which dictates the whole inner pattern of **"An Anna Blume."** It is an ambivalence involving diametrically opposed possibilities, an ambivalence which the poet raises to the level of a game which he plays with himself and his readers, walking a tightrope between poetry and nonsense, and inviting them to walk it—only is it an invitation to a game for the initiated or for fools?—or for both perhaps?

NOTES

[1] *German Life and Letters,* XXII (New Series), 1969, 333-40.

[2] Ibid., 346-49.

[3] I have adhered to the typography used in *Anna Blume. Dichtungen,* (Hannover: Steegemann, 1919).

[4] C. Heselhaus: *Deutsche Lyrik der Moderne,* (Düsseldorf: 1961), p. 319.

Ulrich Finke (essay date 1973)

SOURCE: "Kurt Schwitters' Contribution to Concrete Art and Poetry," in *Forum For Modern Language Studies,* Vol. IX, No. 1, January, 1973, pp. 75-85.

[*In the following essay, Finke considers Schwitters as an early proponent of concrete poetry and discusses his contribution to the visualization of language in writing and art.*]

"Kurt Schwitters was called the master of collage. He *was* the master of collage. The heresy of giving a new value to odd and overlooked, downtrodden bits of reality—be they bits of wire or bits of words—by putting them together into some specific kind of relationship and creating thus a new entity, was the essence of Schwitters' art."[1] "Although he always emphasized that form alone was important for him, the mounted and pasted objects produced that suggestive spirit of reality in his 'abstract' art that he was so passionately attached to. Above all, the fragments of words that Schwitters took from the daily press, with their terribly distorted letters, flash out the mood of that time between colour and form. In this way they signalize reality with great expressive force, as one can see particularly in the great 'Merz-pictures' of 1919-21 and in several early collages . . . Later on, the writing in his pictures took on an objective character, corresponding to his development towards greater formal strength. Those expressive signal-like letters changed into typographic emblems. . . ."[2]

Kurt Schwitters was concerned with images and words not only in his pictures, but in his writing too. For him they are no longer exclusively "means of communication", they are not an "instrument of thinking", but they are *"behaviour"*.[3] We are accustomed to the fact that printed words, letters and numbers appear in modern pictures, ranging from clearly legible words, such as *Journal* on many still lifes by Braque and Picasso, to purely typographic emblems.

In his book *Les Mots dans la peinture* (1969) Michel Butor has given some very interesting and stimulating comments on the relationship between word and image in painting, dealing with works from the period of Jan van Eyck to modern times. But from the point of view of method the whole question requires investigation.

The Romantics played a decisive part in the break-away of the word from its exclusively representative function. Novalis thought that language had the same concreteness as reality, that it had a quasi real disposition of its material. For him, poetic language is "bloâ wohlklingend, aber auch ohne allen Sinn und Zusammenhang, höchstens einzelne Strophen verständlich, wie lauter Bruchstücke aus den verschiedensten Dingen."[4] Baudelaire and Mallarmé made yet wider the divorce between language and reality, whose final result was an ontological disharmony between language and reality.[5]

It was recognized that the word creates or constitutes its own plasticity or reality and this process found its parallel in modern non-objective painting. Just as words can be a material in their own right, concrete painting refers to itself. Its pictorial intention aims at an expression of the mind indifferent to nature. As the pictorial means no longer have a representative function, it was a decisive step for the Futurists and Cubists to introduce "real details", among them printed letters and words, into their pictures. Umberto Boccioni, in his book *Manifesto tecnico della scultura futurista* (1912), and Apollinaire, in his book *Les Peintres cubistes* (1913) had recommended the painters any material they chose: "c'est légitimement que des chiffres, des lettres moulées apparaissent comme des éléments pittoresques, nouveaux dans l'art, et depuis longtemps déjà imprégnés d'humanité."[6] In his book *Der Weg zum Kubismus,* Kahnweiler also refers to those "real details", which carry with them memory images. Combining the "real" stimulus and the scheme of forms, these images construct the finished object in the *mind.*[7] To facilitate that assimilation the cubist painter should choose descriptive titles, such as "Bottle and Glass", "Playing Cards and Dice". It is evident that these concrete namings of objects should appear in the pictures themselves. The picture plane which is covered with words, letters and numbers thus becomes the constitutive element of such texts. The position of the word-material on the plane, the distance of texts from each other and the compactness of the texture—in the linguistic and optical sense—transform the text into an optical appearance, an additional dimension to the phonetic and semantic articulation of the text.[8] Kandinsky, in his article "Über die Formfrage", refers to this peculiarity of the letter itself.[9] Thus the "innere Klang" of a single letter is the expression of an "inner necessity", which cannot be reduced beyond itself. The conceptual, rather than the merely visual intellectuality of the eye experiences it.

The typographic lay-out of Mallarmé's *Un Coup de dés* (1898) brought back the role of the plane as a constitutive element of the text. We take the text at one and the same time temporally (through memory) and spatially (as a visual entity). The text is given in the shape of a sinking boat or of thrown dice. Apollinaire continued that deliberate optical presentation of the language in many of his poems in *Calligrammes* (1915), where the display of the text offers a shape corresponding to the content of the relevant poem. Word-composition and picture-composition are superimposed. Paul Klee in his picture *Einst dem Grau der Nacht enttaucht . . .* (1918) or Juan Gris in his picture *Nature morte avec poème*[10] superimpose the text as a legible foil to the pictorial composition. Language manifests itself in time and in space. Schwitters had something similar in mind when he wrote:

> Mein Ziel ist das Gesamtkunstwerk, das alle Kunstarten zusammenfaât zur künstlerischen Einheit. Ich habe Gedichte aus Worten und Sätzen so zusammengeklebt, daâ die Anordung rhythmisch eine Zeichnung ergibt. Ich habe Bilder und Zeichnungen geklebt, auf denen Sätze gelesen werden sollen . . . Dies geschah, um die Grenzen der Kunstarten zu verwischen . . . Das Merzgesamtkunstwerk aber ist die Merzbühne . . . Die Merzbühne kennt nur die Verschmelzung aller Faktoren zum Gesamtkunstwerk.[11]

The idea of the *Gesamtkunstwerk,* which is an essential part of German Romanticism and which found in Richard Wagner and in the *Blaue Reiter* group its immediate application, is an important element in Schwitters' artistic conception. The superimposition of text and image, as quoted in Schwitters' own words, is another preoccupation in his work. He called his pictures *Merz-pictures.* "'Do you know what *Merz* means?' he asked me once. 'Isn't it a German word for something you throw away, like rubbish?' I said. 'Well, not really', he said. 'But I'll tell you. There was an advertisement in a newspaper, headed *Kommerz und Privatbank.* I cut the first syllable of the first word off, and *Merz* remained',—and he smiled his innocent and mischievous smile, as if saying: Isn't it all wonderfully simple?"[12] "Das Wort entstand organisch beim Merzen des Bildes, nicht zufällig, denn beim künstlerischen Werten ist nichts zufällig, was konsequent ist. Ich nannte seinerzeit das Bild nach dem lesbaren Teile 'das Merzbild'".[13]

The writing in his pictures of 1919-21 not only forms an integral part of the composition, but was intended to be read and understood. Schwitters frequently chose the visually most dominant word from his pictures as the title of it. When he says about his writing: "Elemente der Dichtkunst sind Buchstabe, Silben, Worte, Sätze. Durch *Werten* der Elemente gegeneinander entsteht die Poesie. Der Sinn ist nur wesentlich, wenn er auch als Faktor gewertet wird. Ich werte Sinn gegen Unsinn",[14] and "In der Dichtung werden die Worte aus ihrem alten Zusammenhang gerissen, entformelt und in einen neuen, künstlerischen Zusammenhang gebracht, sie werden Form-Teile der Dichtung, weiter nichts"[15], that definition could be applied to his pictures, especially to the relationship between word and image. The word, though part of the formal arrangement of the picture plane, has not become illegible; in reading the word *Merz* we understand its "meaning", in regarding its shape we perceive its formal structure. Functionally the word presents reality (mimesis), formally it constitutes reality (poiesis). In his pictures of 1919-21 Schwitters deals mainly with the superimposition of the functional and formal structure of the writing; later he reduced its functional structure in favour of its formal structure. "Sense-less" word fragments, meant to be typographic signs, are perceived entirely by conceptual, rather than the merely visual intellectuality of the eye. A similar tendency can be seen in his writing, where he dissolves the descriptive and representative function of the word, which enables him to arrive at picture-poems, or pure number- or letter-poems, or at his Sonata in primitive sounds, *Sonata in Urlauten.*

Schwitters' early pictures are in a sense exercises in German Expressionism. They find their parallel in his poetry of the same period (1917-19). Like his pictures, which are entitled *Church-yard in the mountains* (1919), *The sun in the high mountain-chain* (1919), *The forest* (1917—Expression No. 1)[16] and which are in the specifically German expressive and romantic tradition, his poems which he wrote under the influence of the Expressionist August Stramm,[17] are reflections of that same, pronouncedly expressionist vital energy. Meaningful words, similar to those which appear as the titles of his paintings, are part of his poetic experiments. "Abstrakte Dichtung wertet Werte gegen Werte. Man kann auch 'Worte gegen Worte' sagen. Das ergibt keinen Sinn, aber es erzeugt Weltgefühl."[18]

Linguistic material produces manifold associations in the poem **"An Johannes Molzahn";**[19] a-logical relations between the words break open the logical structure of the sentence and suspend the familiar continuity of the narrative process. The highly expressive words give way to an independent movement of their own. The leitmotif "Kreisen Welten Du" in the poem **"An Johannes Molzahn"** re-appears as a theme and title in the Merz-picture *Weltenkreise.* Hugo Ball, one of the founders of the Dada movement in Zurich in 1916, spoke of the "Plastizität des Wortes. Auf Kosten des logisch gebauten, verstandesmäßgen Satzes. Wir haben das Wort mit Kräften und Energien geladen, die uns den evangelischen Begriff des 'Wortes' (logos) als eines magischen Komplexgebildes wieder entdecken lieâen."[20]

Max Ernst, who met Schwitters in 1920, defines his technique of collage as the "Systemạtische Ausbeutung des zufälligen oder künstlich provozierten Zusammentreffens von zwei oder mehr wesensfremden Realitäten auf einer augenscheinlich dazu ungeeigneten Ebene—und der Funke Poesie, welcher bei der Annäherung dieser Realitäten überspringt."[21] Ernst's definition refers to his collages and to his poetic writing as well. Hans Arp, Schwitters's friend, applies a similar artistic principle to his poems "Wolkenpumpen" of 1917: "Dialektbildung, altertümelnde Klänge, Jahrmarktslatein, verwirrende Onomatopoesien und Wortspasmen sind in diesen Gedichten besonders auffallend. Die 'Wolkenpumpen' aber sind nicht nur automatische Gedichte, sondern schon Vorläufer meiner 'papiers déchirés'."[22]

In Schwitters' poems and pictures of the years 1917-19 word and pictorial elements have a quality which transcends the expressive values, though they are still controlled by the observation of the visible reality. The a-logical composition of the elements is important, his method of "weighing words against words". In his drawings, such as *Das Herz geht vom Zucker zum Kaffee,* or *Das ist das Biest, das manchmal niest,* Schwitters transfers his former expressionist experiments into Dada art (1919). Here pictorial elements and written words subsist together. Though this technique is not altogether new, Schwitters is the first who applies it consistently to his Merz-pictures. The pictorial space still bears the Futurist qualities of paintings by Delaunay, Chagall, Marc or Feininger.

In his "Stempelzeichnungen", Schwitters uses the imprints of ordinary rubber stamps, which are displayed in a highly decorative and rhythmic composition, as in his drawing *Bahnhof,* which corresponds to his poem of the same title.[23] The rhythmic sequence of imprints, among them "Der Sturm", "Herwarth Walden", "Belegexemplar", "Bezahlt", produces the witty drawing of *Der Kritiker.* The result of such a technique is the apparent de-composition of language and image as a traditional portrayal or representation of visible reality. Expressionist words still embellish those text-collages. In comparison with the poem **"An Johannes Molzahn"** the linguistic structure in his "Stempelzeichnung" and poem **"Bahnhof"** is filled with expressionist word material (sun, heart, etc.) and common words which indicate concrete objects (mill, ladder, etc.). It is this juxtaposition of words that creates a sense of absurdity.

The title and the arrangement of the Merz-picture *Sternenbild* of 1920 still refers to Schwitters' earlier "cosmic" compositions. But the "real details", such as pieces of wood, wire, string or wooden disks, are covered with words and sentences, as for example "eichsk" (for "Reichskanzler"), "Offener Brief E. Mathias Die Korrupt", "erhohung hungersge gegen die Stillegung", "Generalleutnant", etc. It is obvious that these fragments of text have here both an optical and an intellectual function. They point to the political and economic situation of postwar Germany. The Gothic letter type adds a further dimension to the handbill character of these quoted inscriptions. Schwitters continues the Futurist compositional arrangement: the dominating circles and circular segments, further heightened by the varying intensity of painted colours, are joined together with splinter-like elements, which produce a rotating effect to which the inserted texts belong as an integral part. The legible texts are related to the general spatial movement. Indeed, the *Sternenbild* portrays a sky with stars; but it is no longer a metaphor for romantic nostalgia, it is a parody of itself. On these pictures, which are collages and montages, the visually dominant text often re-appears as the title of the relevant picture: *Undbild* (1919), *Arbeiterbild* (1919) (where the words "worker" and "strike" are fused with the rotted material), *Oscar* (1920).[24] The fragments of text are of great importance for the content, the message of the picture itself. Even in the collage *Ohne Titel* of about 1921, the fragments of text are of considerable relevance. They can be deciphered as "Straâenbahn A [ge] lehnt haben, in den Streik abge . . . Die Elektrizitätsarb[eiter] . . . [G]esamthei[t]" and finally the big writing of "Mai 191"; the sequence of the colours black, red, gold are those of the German Republic—and a bit of blue at the right hand corner might suggest hope amidst the social-critical collage. Never does the collage appear to be illustrative, it always works as a very subtle and suggestive signal. Schwitters' merit is that he entirely concentrated on the refuse, leaving the texts mingled with it to illuminate the particular *Zeitgeist.* Though these works may today have lost their historical, critical and even meaningful relevance, they nevertheless are works of art because they fulfil the artistic maxim of "weighing forms against forms".

As text and pictorial forms participate in the overall artistic effect, the texts keep their genuine meaning.[25] The text itself becomes the subject of the collage *Ohne Titel (fec.)* of 1920. The trials of the Supreme Court of Justice, especially their proclamation text, inspired Schwitters to cut up the relevant text and to transfunction it into an apparent linguistic and visual non-sense. The textual collage gains its meaning from that particular transfunctioning of a compromised and corrupted language, displayed optically and linguistically.

The traditional term "text" acquires a totally new meaning: the sequence of movement has been enriched by associations and movable scenery; the linguistic material produces its own autonomous movement; the discrepancy between word and description suggests a new reality. "Merz is form. To form means to de-formalize", proclaimed Schwitters. Because language has become a lifeless formula, Schwitters tries to deformalize (*entformeln*) it and to make its new dimension visible.

In his famous poem **"An Anna Blume"** (**"Eve Blossom"**) (1919) Schwitters had already demonstrated the particular means of the deformalization, when he parodied the narrow-minded views of his beloved Eve Blossom.[26] He even takes language in its logical sense and arrives at absurd results, when he says:

> *Prize question:*
> 1. eve Blossom is red.
> 2. eve Blossom has wheels.
> 3. what colour are the wheels?
> Blue is the colour of your yellow hair,
> Red is the whirl of your green wheels,
> Thou simple maiden in everyday dress,
> Thou small green animal,
> I love thine!
> (Schwitters' own English version).

Schwitters also used his technique of collage in his text **"Auguste Bolte"** (1925), where "die Sprache [. . .] wird zum bloâen Vehikel von Realitätsscherben, Versatzstücken, auch Funktionsmaterialien, die die Geschichte weiter transportieren".[27] The rhythmic sequence of the word material refers back to its own system; it is therefore structurally self-sufficient. Schwitters does it in his i-drawings of around 1920. "Die einzige Tat des Künstlers bei i ist die Entformelung durch Abgrenzung eines in sich rhythmischen Teiles."[28] (Schwitters). For example his i-poem consists of only the small letter i in the German Sütterlin style and the caption: "Lies: rauf, runter, rauf, Pünktchen drauf." Here the tendency is clear, namely to unmask the actual process of writing, whereby the sign becomes more important than the meaning it signifies.[29]

The "de-formalization through separation of a specific rhythmic part" becomes an important artistic principle in Schwitters' writing and collages from 1920 onwards. There is no doubt that his experiments, as early as 1920, gave rise to the works of modern concrete poetry. At the same time the legible texts in Schwitters' collages become less frequent, as the typographic interest gains more attention in the artist's activity.[30] In his collage *Mz Lustig* (1921) the letters "s", "u", and "g", which appear vertically on the right side, seem to be the abbreviation of "Lustig", because one is trying to read the title into the collage. At a second glance one realizes one's own optical mis-reading. Here Schwitters plays with perception. The destruction of the syntactic, orthographic and typographic structure—already evident in his poem **"An Anna Blume"**—results in the use of the typographic material as an autonomous figuration.[31]

As far as the collage *Mz Lustig* is concerned, the typographic "reality" as such refers back to itself and is no longer to be interpreted.[32] The deformalization appears as a transformation of certain materially given elements into signs. This process does not even stop short at the deformalization of letters and numbers, as the following example will show. This leads to the concretisation or materialisation of letters and numbers. Between 1920 and 1933 Schwitters created a large number of works which are very close to concrete art. As Schwitters was in fact involved in these works, it seems rather difficult to accept Werner Schmalenbach's view that "der 'ganze' Schwitters nicht in diesen Kompositionen lebt . . . dass die Gesetze, nach denen sich sein lebenssprühender Geist bewegte, nicht die der 'konkreten Kunst' waren."[33] In contrast to Schmalenbach, Reinhard Döhl has pointed out that the literary works of, for example, Helmut

Heissenbüttel or Franz Mon, cannot be understood without knowing of these relations and scarcely be thought of without the influence of Schwitters.[34] Schwitters used the stylistic means of montage, alienation, parody, permutation, etc., which only function against the background of the conventional forms of language and poetry, from which they distance themselves.

Concrete poetry is poetry insofar as it consists of words, letters or numbers. As his i-poems were a consistent demonstration of the sign and not its meaning, his number-poems, such as **"Zwölf"**, show the extreme consequence of his tendency towards de-formalization:

ZWÖLF
EINS ZWEI DREI VIER FÜNF
FÜNF VIER DREI ZWEI EINS
ZWEI DREI VIER FÜNF SECHS
SECHS FÜNF VIER DREI ZWEI
SIEBEN SIEBEN SIEBEN SIEBEN SIEBEN
ACHT EINS
NEUN EINS
ZEHN EINS
ELF EINS
ZEHN NEUN ACHT SIEBEN SECHS
FÜNF VIER DREI ZWEI EINS.

Here the visual arrangement of the numbers follows a very specific rhythm. The numerical values from one to eleven—the numerical value of twelve is only suggested in the 9th line as the sum of eleven and one—are the elements which constitute the poem. In the abstract rise and decline of the numerical values in the first four lines, in the repetition of the number seven in the fifth line (five times!), in the regular addition of one to the rising numerical value from eight to eleven, and finally in the decline of the numerical values from ten to one, a regular principle in the structure of the poem is evident. The means consist of elementary progressions and regressions, repetitions, inversions, variations, reductions, etc. This "text-reality" means only itself. The decoding of the pattern witnesses to the aesthetic reality of the poem, whose emblems are numerical values.

The visually composed *Gesetztes Bildgedicht* (1922) consists of letters, the smallest units of the language. Here the visual arrangement is of particular importance. The language has been reduced to letters which act as signs establishing a visually perceptible figuration. The picture plane—so to speak—is subdivided into 25 squares. Geometry becomes an integral part of this letter poem. Schwitters visualizes to the extreme what Novalis had defined as poetry, namely magic in connection with "construction" and "algebra". Poetic language is similar to mathematical formulae, "sie machen eine Welt für sich aus, spielen nur mit sich selbst."[35] E. A. Poe saw a relationship between the poetic function and the "strict logic of a mathematical problem"; Baudelaire claimed that

la phrase poétique peut imiter (et par là elle touche à l'art musical et à la science mathématique) la ligne horizontale, la ligne droite ascendante, la ligne droite descendante; qu'elle peut monter à pic

vers le ciel, sans essoufflement, ou descendre perpendiculairement vers l'enfer avec la vélocité de toute pesanteur; qu'elle peut suivre la spirale, décrire la parabole, ou le zigzag figurant une série d'angles superposés.[36]

Mallarmé sought for the "geometry of sentences"—the typographical display of his poem *Un Coup de dés* is a first attempt in that direction. Apollinaire finally required poetry to do everything, in order to rival the boldness of mathematics.

Schwitters has chosen the letters A, B, J, O and Z to point to the entirety of the alphabet, to concentrate on specific geometrical forms, such as the circle (O), the horizontal, vertical and diagonal directions, to take into consideration the phonetic quality of vowels (A, O) and consonants (B, J, Z). (This is in connection with his experiments in phonetic transcriptions, which were to lead to onomatopoeia.) The display of these elements follow obvious structural principles. The letter poem proposes a visual and phonetic identification of the letter material. On the formal (optical) and on the linguistic (phonetic) levels the elements constitute a world of their own, not related to a semantic external world, i.e. it has no meaning that refers beyond itself. Thus the language, reduced to its elements, has been made visible in a spatial and temporal structure. The arrangement or composition of the linguistic material follows a mathematical purpose, linguistic content and optical reference correspond to each other.

We have analysed as "texts" Schwitters' poems consisting of numbers and letters, but an extended meaning has been given to the term *text,* which Max Bense defines in this sense as consisting of

linear, flächig oder auch räumlich angeordnete Mengen von *Material* und *diskret* gegebener *Elementen,* die als *Zeichen* fungieren können, auf Grund gewisser Regeln zu Teilen oder zu einer Ganzheit zusammengefaßt. In dieser Weise konstituierte Texte heißen *materiale Texte* oder *Texturen,* sofern sie nur durch die Materialität oder Realität ihrer Elemente gegeben werden, aber nicht durch Zuordnungen von Bedeutungen, die außerhalb der Konstituierung liegen. Materiale Texte haben also nur eine (semiotische oder linguistische) *Eigenwelt,* jedoch keine (semantische oder metasemiotische) *Außenwelt.*[37]

Schwitters' merit lies in the fact that he has successfully reduced language to its structural and semiotic elements.

Konkrete Texte benutzen im idealen Falle die Sprache nicht nur als *Bedeutungsträger,* sondern darüber hinaus und vielleicht noch betonter als lautlichen und visuellen Akt. Das Wort erscheint also gleichzeitig auf der *Morphem-Ebene* (der Bedeutung), der *Graphem-Ebene* (der figürlichen Wahrnehmung) und der *Phonem-Ebene* (des Klangverlaufs) als poetisches Gestaltungsmittel. Der *Kontext* eines *konkreten Textes* ist gleichzeitig semantischer, visueller und phonetischer Zusammenhang.[38]

Here mention should be made of Schwitters' phonetic poems, for which he discussed the possibilities of a special phonetic script, called "Systemschrift". It had to realize the identity of the phonetic and visual linguistic elements. In 1927 Schwitters had published a long article on **"Anregungen zur Erlangung einer Systemschrift"** in the Dutch periodical *i 10:* "Wie auch immer die zu vermittelnde, zu übersetzende Sprache ist, die Schrift muß optophonetisch sein, wenn sie systematisch gestaltet sein will. Systemschrift verlangt, daß das ganze Bild der Schrift dem ganzen Klang der Sprache entspricht."[39] But the project had proved utopian; Schwitters had transcribed his *Sonata in Urlauten* into the conventional Futura in 1932, though by nature it should have required an optophonetic writing. In his "Explanation of my Sonata in primitive sounds" (1932) Schwitters characterised his work thus: "Sie bewegt sich in einem Zwischenbereich . . . kühn in der konsequenten Anwendung reiner phonetischer Mittel, traditionell in der Durchgliederung als 'Sonate'".[40]

Just as Schwitters' Sonata in primitive sounds needed a conventional structure, so it is "bezeichnend, daß die Konkrete Poesie immer der Ergänzung, Erläuterung durch konventionelle Sprache bedarf, obwohl (und weil) sie selbst sich dem logischen Zugriff entzieht."[41] Eugen Gomringer used the term *concrete poetry* for the first time in 1955, when he spoke of "das aufzeigen der sprachstruktur, ihrer magie, aber auch der transparenz in gehalt und bild." (sic!)[42] The main characteristic of concrete poetry is the visualisation of the language. Schwitters made an impressive contribution to this problem as early as 1920; modern poets owe him a considerable debt.

NOTES

[1] Stefan Themerson, *Kurt Schwitters in England,* London, 1958, p. 15.

[2] Kurt Schwitters, *Retrospective,* UCLA Art Galleries, Los Angeles, 1965, p. 8 (Introduction by Werner Schmalenbach).

[3] Themerson, op. cit., p. 19.

[4] Hugo Friedrich, *Die Struktur der modernen Lyrik. Von Baudelaire bis zur Gegenwart,* rde, Hamburg, 1956, pp. 20-21.

[5] Cf. Friedrich, op. cit., p. 93.

[6] Apollinaire, *Les Peintres cubistes,* ed. P. Cailler, Geneva, 1950, pp. 35-36. Similar tendencies are expressed in Marinetti's "Parole in Libertà" (1913).

[7] Kahnweiler, *Der Weg zum Kubismus,* Munich, 1920. Cf. Jürgen Wismann, "Collagen oder die Integration von Realität im Kunstwerk", in: *Poetik und Hermeneutik II, Immanente Ästhetik, Ästhetische Reflexion,* Munich, 1966.

[8] Franz Mon, *Texte über Texte,* Neuwied/Berlin, 1970, pp. 45-46.

[9] W. Kandinsky, "Über die Formfrage", in: *Der Blaue Reiter* (1912). Dokumentarische Neuausgabe von Klaus Lankheit, Munich 1965, p. 157: "Wenn der Leser irgendeinen Buchstaben dieser Zeilen mit ungewohnten Augen anschaut, d.h. nicht als ein gewohntes Zeichen eines Teiles eines Wortes, sondern als *Ding,* so sieht er in diesem Buchstaben auâer der praktisch-zweckmääigen vom Menschen geschaffenen abstrakten Form, die eine ständige Bezeichnung eines bestimmten Lautes ist, noch eine körperliche Form, die ganz selbständig einen bestimmten äuâeren und inneren Eindruck macht, d.h. unabhängig von der eben erwähnten abstrakten Form. . . . Wir sehen nur, daâ der Buchstabe aus zwei Elementen besteht, die doch schlieâlich *einen* Klang ausdrücken. . . . Und, wie gesagt, ist diese Wirkung doppelt: 1. der Buchstabe wirkt als ein zweckmääiges Zeichen; 2. er wirkt erst als Form und später als innerer Klang dieser Form selbständig und vollkommen unabhängig."

[10] Michel Butor, *Les Mots dans la peinture,* Geneva, 1969, pp. 31-32 (Paul Klee) and p. 173 (Juan Gris), with reproductions.

[11] Werner Schmalenbach, *Kurt Schwitters,* Cologne, 1967, pp. 107-108.

[12] Themerson, op. cit., p. 20.

[13] Schmalenbach, op. cit., p. 96.

[14] Ibid., p. 211.

[15] Ibid., p. 211.

[16] Cf. the works by Franz Marc or Ernst Ludwig Kirchner.

[17] August Stramm, *Das Werk,* herausgegeben von René Radrizzani, Wiesbaden, 1963.

[18] Schmalenbach, op. cit., p. 203.

[19] Ibid., p. 205.

[20] "Die Flucht aus der Zeit", in: R. Döhl, *Das literarische Werk Hans Arps,* Stuttgart, 1967, p. 58.

[21] *Jenseits von Malerei.* Max Ernst exhibition, Cologne-Zurich, 1963, p. 25.

[22] "Wegweiser", in: R. Döhl, op. cit., p. 61.

[23] Schmalenbach, op. cit., pp. 206-207 (text and drawing).

[24] Cf. Schwitters' "cosmic compositions", such as *Das Kreisen, Bild mit heller Mitte,* etc.

[25] Schmalenbach's view is therefore dubious: "Es braucht also nicht zu schaden, obschon es nur selten nützt—, wenn

man sich in die 'Lektüre' einer Merzzeichnung vertieft." And: "Die vielen lesbaren Stellen aber verführen nicht zur Lektüre; derartig plakativ herausgehobene Wortfetzen werden unmittelbar optisch aufgenommen, dringen ins Unterbewuâtsein schneller als ins Bewuâtsein ein. Sie erzeugen das Gefühl einer bedrängenden Realität—der Realität jenes hektischen, politisch überhitzten, von Revolte beunruhigten, auf Inflation und Arbeitslosigkeit zusteuernden Klimas in Deutschland der ersten Nachkriegsjahre." Op. cit., pp. 129, 120.

26 Themerson, op. cit., p. 25.

27 Mon, op. cit., p. 78.

28 Schmalenbach, op. cit., p. 133.

29 Mon, op. cit., p. 60.

30 Kandinsky. Cf. note 9.

31 Schmalenbach, op. cit., pp. 180-193. In this connection we can only make brief mention of Schwitters' great contribution to the new typography in the 1920s—of his collaboration with Jan Tschichold, Lissitzky, Max Burchartz, van Doesburg.

32 Max Bense. Cf. note 37.

33 Schmalenbach, op. cit., p. 150.

34 Döhl, op. cit., p. 75, note 188.

35 Friedrich, op. cit., p. 20.

36 Baudelaire, "Projet de Préface des *Fleurs*", in: *Les Fleurs du Mal,* ed. A. Adam, Paris, Garnier, 1959, p. 249.

37 Max Bense, *Einführung in die informationstheoretische Ästhetik, Grundlegung und Anwendung in der Texttheorie,* rde, Hamburg, 1969, p. 76. This difficult text may be translated as follows: "*discrete* given *elements* and *material,* arranged as linear, plane or also spatial quantities, which can function as *signs* and which are drawn together according to certain rules to form parts or an entirety. Texts constituted in this way are called *material texts* or *textures* insofar as they only exist by virtue of the materiality or reality of their elements, not by virtue of their relation to meanings which exist outside the structure. Material texts have therefore only an *autonomous world* (semiotic or linguistic), but no *external world* (semantic or metasemiotic)."

38 Bense, op. cit., p. 95. Translation: "Ideally, *concrete texts* use language not only as something that *carries a meaning,* but in addition and perhaps more emphatically as a phonetic and a visual act. The word therefore appears as a poetic structural element simultaneously on the *morpheme-level* (meaning), the *grapheme-level* (figurative perception) and the *phoneme-level* (sound-process). The *context* of a *concrete text* is simultaneously that of a semantic, visual and phonetic correlation".

39 Schmalenbach, op. cit., p. 193.

40 Ibid., p. 224.

41 E. Juergens, "Zur Situation der konkreten Poesie", in: *Text + Kritik,* 30, (konkrete Poesie II), April 1971, pp. 48-49.

42 *Vom gedicht zum gedichtbuch,* 1966, p. 291. E. Gomringer was Max Bill's Secretary at the Hochschule für Gestaltung at Ulm. Max Bill applied the term *concrete art,* as Theo van Doesburg defined it in his "Manifesto of concrete art" (1930), and gave a more precise meaning to it in his theoretical writings. Cf. Friedhelm Lach, *Der Merz Künstler Kurt Schwitters,* Cologne, 1971. (On concrete poetry, pp. 112-120): "Die heutige Schule der konkreten Poesie von Gomringer bis Ji í Kolár hat Schwitters wegen dieser Gedichte mit Recht als einen ihrer grossen Anreger genannt" (p. 114).

John Elderfield (essay date 1973)

SOURCE: "Private Objects: The Sculpture of Kurt Schwitters," in *Artforum,* Vol. XII, No. 1, September, 1973, pp. 45-54.

[*In the following essay, Elderfield studies Schwitters's sculptural pieces, characterizing these as the artist's most personal works.*]

Schwitters' output as an artist was prodigious, but of all the arts he worked in, the one most objectlike in character—sculpture—seems somewhat peripheral to his main achievement. The eccentric Dadaist sculptures of the early years appear to be mere offshoots from the far more seriously motivated assemblages that spawned them. The small organic-looking works of wood or plaster and wire dating from the mid-'20s are largely monolithic in effect, and further from the principle of assemblage than any other aspect of his oeuvre. He did, we know, refer to the Hanover Merzbau—the labyrinthlike environmental construction that eventually came to occupy a large proportion of his own home—as being a sculpture; and its importance to his entire oeuvre is not in question. But sculpture as such—as freestanding objects—is not for what Schwitters is remembered.

Given his obsession with objects, and remembering also that "the object" was a central preoccupation for advanced sculpture when Schwitters developed his own art, this fact seems at first surprising. However, objects *as such* were for Schwitters but the raw material of his art. Time and again in his writings, he insisted that the physical components of an assemblage, collage, or whatever, were unimportant on their own behalf. "Essential is only the forming."[1] Committed to the autonomy of art, he sought to minimize the real power of the materials and objects he used, and said hardly anything about what this evocative detritus meant to him. It is hard to believe he chose it only on formal grounds, given his preference for things used, worn, and "already steeped in humanity." While one can agree with Schwitters that it is not what these objects *were* that is important (they are not just objects on display), equally they are also far from being mere functional components "filling out" a given style. The expressive pull of each object *against* its pictorial containment, and the collective mood they create are essential to the character and quality of the art. It was Schwitters' special complicity with objects that brought new feeling to the collection of secondhand styles in which they were used. On several occasions Schwitters almost admitted that it was the unfamiliarity and charged nature of the objects that gave to the known styles he employed their new power. "In the relationship of a known and unknown quality, the unknown varies and modifies the known," he wrote in 1923.[2] Three years later, when reviewing his artistic development, he wrote that his feelings had been "poured into the form," and it was this that kept "forming" from mere decoration.[3]

By and large, when discussing the role of objects in his art he played down anything other than their formal role. Throughout his writings on this subject there run two related images. One is the inherent evocativeness of materials, pulling them out of art's orbit, that must be held in check by forming (that is, by a rigorous abstractness of composition) lest it overwhelm any individual work, thus "loosening its ties to art." The other, and far more guarded image is that the inclusion of objects into art shields their inherent and personal meaningfulness from public view. In sculpture, however (for reasons I will consider in a moment), objects cannot be included and concealed to the extent they can in a two-dimensional art. The objects that comprise Schwitters' Dadaist sculptures seem more simply presented or displayed than in the low relief assemblages, their expressiveness hardly clouded. Given Schwitters' formalist ambitions, this was undoubtedly a handicap; and he never developed an assemblage style for freestanding sculpture which used the same kind of evocative materials that appear elsewhere in his art. The later sculptures do sometimes employ weathered timbers, pieces of furniture, stones, and so on, but they are more regularized and finished—and their components more neutral in expressiveness—than the Dadaist sculptures. Most of them were made of plaster built up on an armature of found objects; objects are physically concealed beneath an artistic front.

The formal necessity of including objects in his art—basic to all Schwitters did—is highlighted by the problems he found in making freestanding sculpture. The sculpture brings to our attention, to a greater degree than any other aspect of his work, the sensitive and difficult topic of what these objects—included only with difficulty in sculpture—actually meant to him. Perhaps the most important question the sculpture poses is the nature of its expressiveness. Other features of the sculpture reinforce this aspect: the quite separate identity of the Dadaist assembled pieces and the monolithic plaster ones asserts the polarity in Schwitters' work of urban and organic themes. The victory of the organic in his sculpture

informs the rest of his activities. Moreover, sculpture in a special sense connected the visual arts Schwitters practiced, as the avenue along which objects had to pass to leave the confines of a painting-based activity and reach the spectacular *Gesamtkunstwerk* of his life's ambition.

II

Excepting some early academic portrait busts,[4] Schwitters' first sculptural venture followed shortly after he established assemblage as the generative principle of his art. In 1919, he invented the word "Merz" to separate his art from previously existing categories. Once so established "Merz" was expanded from its original painting context into a variety of different directions: into drawings and poems that were comprised of distinct material units, and—if only in unrealized theories—into theater and architecture as well. "The reason for this," Schwitters wrote, explaining his moves,

> was not any urge to broaden the scope of my activity, it was my desire not to be a specialist in one branch of art, but an artist. My aim is the Merz composite art work, that embraces all branches of art in an artistic unit.[5]

It is far from surprising, therefore, that sculpture was included in this endeavor. And that Schwitters made sculpture not for its own sake—not to be a "specialist" in sculpture—but because it served to mediate between the modified paintings with which Merz began and the hoped-for "Merz composite art work" explains, in part, why the early Merz sculptures seem ill at ease in any conventional category of sculpture. They have the appearance, rather, of tableaux, or of models for as yet unrealized and larger constructions. Indeed, some were quite specifically created as plans for architecture.

It is impossible to know how many of these sculptures were made. None now exist, though six are known through photographs. Of these the best known are *Der Lustgalgen (Pleasure Gallows)* and *Die Kultpumpe (Cult Pump)*, made presumably in 1919[6] and reproduced as postcards by the Hanover publisher Paul Steegemann in 1920. Schwitters referred to these when first writing about his theory of Merz: "Now I am doing Merz sculptures: *Pleasure Gallows* and *Cult Pump*. Like Merz pictures, the Merz sculptures are composed of various materials. They are conceived as sculptures in the round and present any desired number of views."[7] They are certainly close to the contemporary assembled pictures in the materials they use—wheels and disks, narrow planks and boards, burlap, printed matter, and so on—but whereas in the pictures these materials work as analogues of conventional formal elements, the greater literal presence of sculpture prevents this happening to the same degree.

Within his pictures, objects underwent what Schwitters called *Entformung* (a neologism which has the implication of metamorphosis) as they were absorbed into the context of two-dimensional art. Just as in any art a physical pencil stroke becomes a line, a length of string or wire does so equally for Schwitters. A rectangle of newsprint becomes a plane; wire mesh or burlap becomes overpainting; and transparent papers become varnish. The existing pictorial context of painting—its limited space—separates objects from the outside world and renders them the stuff of art: "The work of art is distinguished from nature by being composed within a limited space, for only within a limited space is it possible to assign compositional values to every part in relation to other parts. . . . "[8] In sculpture, therefore, the *Entformung* is far more difficult to accomplish. The materials and objects keep their "personality poison." Their "ties to art" are looser.

In this respect, Schwitters' early sculptures are among the most overtly Dadaist of all his works, giving a definite "nonart" impression similar to that of Marcel Janco's *Construction 3* of 1917, which Schwitters is almost certain to have seen in reproduction and which perhaps motivated his own pieces.[9] Yet, the actual configurations Schwitters used are far from those of the Zürich construction, closer to forms appearing in the Dadaist drawings and watercolors he made in 1919. These, like the sculptures, were part of Schwitters' expansion of the Merz concept from the formal context of painting, and their more private nature allows far more literary allusions than do the Merz pictures. In both drawings and sculpture, metaphor triumphs over forming; and the connection between these two fringe activities seems confirmed by their occasional sharing of a related imagery. The sculpture *Haus Merz*, 1920, is remarkably close to the small, naively drawn churches that appear in the drawings. Schwitters is also recorded as having made a windmill sculpture,[10] another familiar motif of the drawings. They share also the impression of a mechanical world gone askew—into a Chagall-like fantasy world in the drawings and, in the sculptures, into rubble. *Der Lustgalgen* and *Die Kultpumpe* both look like derelict industrial buildings.

Merz, Schwitters once wrote, "was a prayer about the victorious end of the war, victorious as once again peace had won in the end; everything had broken down in any case and new things had to be made out of fragments: and this is Merz."[11] Like Schwitters' large-scale Merz pictures of 1919, his Dadaist sculptures epitomize that feeling of a new beginning out of a past decimated by war and internal revolution, a feeling common to the German avant-garde at this period. This was perhaps most evident in advanced architectural circles—for obvious reasons, given the condition of cities like Berlin, ravaged by street fighting—and it fostered the creation of organizations like the *Novembergruppe* and the *Arbeitsrat für Kunst,* its architectural inner cell. Although Schwitters never joined any of these organizations (having his own one-man movement to promote), and though his work seems at first sight diametrically opposed to their ideas, there are some significant parallels and connections that deserve investigation.

Schwitters studied architecture for two semesters in 1918, immediately preceding his invention of Merz. The sculpture *Haus Merz*, 1920, is very evidently of architectural inspiration. A model church with a spinning top for a spire, a trouser button for the clock face, and its nave filled with cog wheels (probably the mechanism of a watch), Schwitters called it "my first piece of Merz architecture" and quoted, obviously with approval, what his friend Christof Spengemann had to say about it:

> In *Haus Merz* I see the cathedral: *the* cathedral. Not as a church, no, this is art as a truly spiritual expression of the force that raises us up to the unthinkable: absolute art. This cathedral cannot be used. Its interior is so filled with wheels that there is no room for people . . . that is absolute architecture, it has artistic meaning and no other.[12]

In one way, this reads as a tongue-in-cheek parody of contemporary architectural writing, such as produced by the *Arbeitsrat für Kunst;* and the mock seriousness of tone is far more pronounced if we turn to Spengemann's longer original text.[13] Yet Schwitters does quote it as a serious explanation of this sculpture. If this only raises the further question (and one only too familiar when considering Schwitters' work) of how seriously should one take his more fanciful writings, it should be remembered that despite his predilection for nonsense he was unswervingly committed to pure art. While his Dadaist sculpture is unconvincing as sculpture, it becomes more feasible when thought of as constituting models for an environmental *Gesamtkunstwerk.* The tableaulike *Lustgalgen* and *Kultpumpe* presage the intimate grottoes of Schwitters' Merzbau, into which they were eventually built. Spengemann's reference to "*the* cathedral" becomes explicable when we remember that the Merzbau was to be called *Kathedrale des erotischen Elends* (*Cathedral of Erotic Misery*), and that Schwitters did compare its forms to those of Gothic architecture.[14]

To advanced architectural thought in the Germany of this period, the cathedral was certainly the dominant symbol, for its Expressionist ideals, and for the unity of the arts, recalling as it did a spiritual monument in an imagined Gothic utopia when preindustrial man existed in close harmony with nature, and in social equilibrium. A visionary Expressionist architect, such as Walter Gropius in 1919, wrote that "art's ultimate goal . . . [was] the creative idea of the Cathedral of the Future (*Zukunftskathedrale*) which will once more encompass everything in *one* form, architecture *and* sculpture *and* painting."[15] Gropius' message to practitioners of the fine arts was loud and clear, and almost Dadaist in its iconoclasm:

> You should smash the frames of "Salon Art" that are around your paintings; go into the buildings, endow them with fairy tales of color, engrave your ideas onto their naked walls—and *build in fantasy* without regard for technical difficulties.

Although Gropius and his colleagues at the *Arbeitsrat* were thinking of public and collaboratively created monuments, and Schwitters of private individualistic ones, their sentiments are not so very different. The "protest" of Expressionist architecture was for a return to the *Urbegriff*—to the primeval origins of forms—which, though a reaction to contemporary society, existed autonomously with respect to its real social conditions. This same disinterested, and therefore apolitical rebellion was shared by Schwitters whose art was grounded in Expressionism and who remained a member of the Sturm group though it alienated him from Dadaists in Berlin.

The confrontation of Dada and Expressionism in postwar Berlin was not as clear cut as it sometimes appears. All the Dadaists emerged out of an Expressionist past, and when Club Dada showed signs of collapse some of its members renewed their Expressionist affiliations. Hausmann, Richter, and Eggeling joined the *Novembergruppe* and Golysheff was an active member of the *Arbeitsrat* itself. Conversely, there were certain Dadaist elements within Expressionist architecture. Carl Krayl's *Haus eines Dada* was illustrated in Bruno Taut's first *Frühlicht* publication in 1920; and the Dada character of his work was commented on within his circle—Hans Luckhardt associating it with "the primordial and the primitive" side of their activity.[16] A further work by Krayl was illustrated in *Frühlicht* when it reappeared in Magdeburg in 1921/22; beside it a sculpture by Schwitters, an assembly of weather-beaten timber identified in an accompanying text as *Schloss und Kathedrale mit Hofbrunnen (Castle and Cathedral with Courtyard Well)*. This is the single sure connection between Schwitters and the architectural utopians.

Interestingly, this sculpture (or model) is the only one of Schwitters' early constructions which approximates to a unity of materials; perhaps for this reason it met with Taut's editorial approval. Although almost inconceivable as architecture, it is no less so than most of the other designs Taut published. Indeed, in its organic interpretation of the cathedral theme it has a resemblance to some of the "form-fantasies" by the Luckhardt brothers; just as the Hanover Merzbau looks back to the alliance of the organic and the crystalline that characterized much work produced within Taut's circle. Although the cathedral concept and that of an organic architecture were not peculiar to the *Arbeitsrat* architects (they merely codified themes already current at that time), to look at Schwitters in this context is to be reminded that the Merzbau, and the models that preceded it, are not only eccentricities comparable to the works of Ferdinand Cheval and Simone Rodilla, but bizarre offshoots from the Gaudi-*Zukunftskathedrale* tradition.

What the Expressionist connection reinforces is that Schwitters' insistence on "forming" conceals an essentially spiritual and primitivist understanding of the nature of art as a "primordial concept,"[17] "a spiritual function of man, which aims at freeing him from life's chaos."[18] And despite the "urban" nature of Schwitters' materials (and the assertive geometry of his pictorial style), he saw the autonomy of art as analogous to that of a natural organism, like nature, "a flower of a special kind."[19] This primitivist and organicist understanding of art explains, in part, why—despite all the concern for forming—the confessional and mythical poetry of the bricoleur speaks through the materials Schwitters used. Primitive feelings had been "poured into the form," the art contained their "inner drive," and it became as one with nature. However, this "fossilized evidence of the history of the individual," when displayed outside the limited space of pictorial art, often appeared with an embarrassing clarity. *Der Lustgalgen* is a mechanical scaffold, and *Haus Merz* a mechanical cathedral, irrational, fantastic toys, but ones with private and somehow very specific meanings.

III

To ask—as I believe we are bound to do—what did these objects mean to Schwitters is not to imply that they were *inherently* meaningful to him in their raw state. Rarely are they only presented objects; to interpret them as evidence on display is simplistic. Schwitters' talk of the origins of Merz as a building from past fragments may admit some social connotations to the early work, but the social situation of postwar Germany can hardly explain his unswerving commitment to the use of ephemera over some 30 years of subsequent activity. Obviously, Schwitters' objects do have some external relationship to the world—despite all his denials. It is far more fruitful, however—and more consistent with Schwitters' explanations—to think of them as possessing an internal and personal significance largely irrespective of their original functions.

In most of Schwitters' work, the meaningfulness of individual fragments hardly arises. Objects and materials contribute to a whole variety of complex and evocative moods, far broader than those painting alone could create. Sometimes, in the collages, a whimsical iconographical play takes place, with materials of a similar source or character built up around a specific theme, as with the early Anna Blume imagery.[20] Mostly, however, textures and colors create moods to which individual materials—and their "personalities"—are sublimated. To create these moods, Schwitters depended on the inclusion of objects within a rigorously abstract process of forming. In the sculpture, where, as we have seen, the difficulties of "inclusion" are extreme, abstraction turns out to be a disadvantage. Objects seem placed merely as curiosities lacking the coherence and interdependence which, say, Picasso's fashioning of diverse objects into still-life configurations assured. But even in these sculptures, it is not the outward reference of the objects that is most striking. It is, rather, that they have become Schwitters' objects, uniquely his, and possessed, therefore, by his identity.

It is no mere figure of speech to say that Schwitters identified with these objects. They (and not the styles he borrowed) are what personalize his work. (The styles subordinated the objects to art, and with them Schwitters' own personality, for expression as such was for him "injurious to art.")[21] Objects, for Schwitters, were far more than containers for association; they became extensions of the self, objects which guaranteed him identity. "I myself am now called Merz," he once wrote;[22] and dressed a fictional alter-ego (the artist-hero of his story, *"Revolution in Revon"*) in a costume of planks and wire, to become "a perambulating *Merzplastik.*"[23] In Schwitters' art, as in the Expressionist I-drama, the personality of the artist-hero is expressed through the "characters" with whom he is in contact. They have no personality of their own, being merely what was called *die Ausstrahlungen seiner Innerlichkeit* ("the radiations of the hero's inner nature"). Hence Schwitters' Expressionist background is of crucial importance to an understanding of his uses of objects: their "personality poison" is effaced not only for art's sake, but because they are no less than existentials of the self within the context of art.

How much Schwitters identified with his objects may be gauged by his need to keep them constantly around him. He transformed nearly his whole house in Hanover to accommodate them; while his most grandiose scheme for a *Merzgesamtkunstwerk,* the "Merz-Stage," comprised not actors, but objects given life and performing with each other. The Merz-Stage and the Hanover Merzbau raise issues that can hardly be explored here; yet the beginnings of the Merzbau deserve notice in showing how Schwitters' Dadaist sculpture metamorphosed into an environmental art form. Moreover, the subsequent development of this eccentric architectural fantasy into a geometricized labyrinth, behind which were hidden "grottoes" containing found objects, epitomizes far more than any other aspect of Schwitters' work, that paralleling of formal "inclusion" and masking of personality at the core of his art.

Photographs of Schwitters' studio around 1920 show a room literally overflowing with the collected objects, its walls "merzed" over with collages and pictures. One photograph, printed in the Berlin *Börsenkurier* on October 31, 1924, reveals Schwitters standing beside a construction very different in character to the Dada models previously described: a dressmaker's dummy carrying a collaged box with a crank-handle on one side and a lighted candle on top. Entitled, apparently, *Die heilige Bekümmernis* (*The Holy Affliction*), it was described by the *Börsenkurier* as a "psychoanalytical composition" though Hans Richter has referred to it more simply as Schwitters' Christmas tree.[24] It does in fact bear the inscription, "Wahnsinn! Fröhliche Weihnachten!" ("Insanity! A Merry Christmas!"), which seems to support both interpretations. Clearly, this is far more ephemeral a work than even the architectural models. The humanoid format parallels the topicality of pseudo-personages, especially with machinist connotations, in contemporary Dada art, while the dummy itself comfortably relates to the fashion imagery in a significant group of Schwitters' early collages. This weird construction has disappeared, like all the other Dada objects. Schwitters wrote that the Merzbau had "little Christmas candles in the dark corners . . . (which) when lit make the whole

thing one big unreal Christmas tree."[25] This is perhaps where *Die heilige Bekümmernis* went.

The fate of another columnlike construction (of which at least two separate photographs exist)[26] is clearer. It consisted of a tall rectangular and collaged base surmounted by a wood and plaster column, decorated with tiny figurines and other such ephemera, capped by a doll's head. Later photographs of the Merzbau show what appears to be the same piece protruding above a geometric arrangement of wooden planes.[27] The doll's head is there, though now moved slightly behind the column, which shorn of its decoration reveals itself to be vaguely human in shape, headless, and with a penis prominently attached. We cannot tell what lies behind and beneath the geometric scaffolding. However, this configuration may be a fragment of what Schwitters called "the big Grotto of Love" in his most comprehensive account of the Merzbau's symbolism:

> Shiny broken objects set the mood. In the middle a couple embracing: he has no head, she has no arms; he is holding a huge blank cartridge between his legs. The child with syphilitic eyes in its big twisted-around head is telling the embracing couple to be careful. This is disturbing but there is reassurance in the little round bottle of my own urine in which immortelles are suspended. This is just a tiny part of the column's literary content.[28]

Schwitters' description of the Merzbau (of which this is only a fragment) is a curious and somewhat baffling narrative, not for its illogicalities and fantasies (these we expect), but for its fixation with human object-parts and with the theme of sexual violence and desecration. Grottoes and incidents with names like "the brothel," "the disabled war veteran," "the sex-crime cave" (with "one abominably mutilated corpse of an unfortunate young girl"), and the eccentric sexual encounter described above, populate Schwitters' *Cathedral of Erotic Misery.* Stories tell of his collecting from friends items such as fingernail parings, a broken denture, a necktie, a bottle of urine, and so on. Many of the grottoes were also frankly whimsical ("an exhibition of paintings and sculptures by Michelangelo and myself being viewed by one dog on a leash") or were simply dedicated to friends, present or past ("the Goethe grotto has one of his legs and a lot of pencils worn down to stubs"). Even so, the mood of the grottoes seems to have been that of a rather black humor, far from the exuberant and clownish side of Schwitters' character most often reported. These claustrophobic fetish-lined caves point in a different direction. Kate Steinitz recognized this when she asked Schwitters: "You call the Expressionists painters of their own sour souls, but aren't you emptying your own sour soul into the caves?"[29]

Unfortunately we have to rely on published and verbal reports to judge the effect of the Merzbau, especially since Schwitters only showed the grottoes to his intimate friends. By and large, the sliding doors, movable compartments, and secret panels were opened only for those already sympathetic to his character. It is useful, therefore, to remind ourselves of the impact of the secret grottoes on someone less prepared. They astounded Alexander Dorner, whose encouragement for advanced art through the '20s needs no defense, and who personally did much to advance Schwitters' career.[30] He admired the Merz pictures as "positive pioneering experiments." Confronted with the Merzbau, however, he felt that the "free expression of the socially uncontrolled self had here bridged the gap between sanity and madness." It was "a kind of fecal smearing—a sick and sickening relapse into the social irresponsibility of the infant who plays with trash and filth." Of course, Dorner's sympathies lay primarily with Constructivist-type art (puritan in its looks, and assumed to possess a social justification). Nevertheless, the strong revulsion he evidently felt should serve to temper more publicized responses to the Merzbau, such as Carola Giedion-Welcker's, who wrote of it as being "a little world of branching and building where the imagination is free to climb at will."[31] It hardly seems possible they were talking about the same work.

More than likely the Merzbau was a puzzling experience, even for Schwitters' supporters, as is testified by the widely differing and often erroneous reports as to what it actually comprised. These cannot be corrected here. It suffices for the present purpose to emphasize two basic properties the Merzbau possessed. First, its imagery was essentially erotic and autobiographical, tempered sometimes by humor but often of a disturbingly sadistic character. Second, this imagery was increasingly hidden behind the geometric surfaces that Schwitters applied throughout the '20s.

A strong element of the grotesque runs through much of Schwitters' prose writing, which becomes at times nearly macabre despite its persistently absurd humor. This, however, may be seen as belonging to interests in a specifically German tradition of the introspectively uncanny which affected very many members of the Expressionist generation—and Schwitters' special brand of sadism-tinged fantasy, in the Merzbau imagery and elsewhere, does look back in some interesting respects to that 19th-century Hanoverian, the illustrator Wilhelm Busch. This does not explain just why Schwitters used so erotic an imagery for the most private area of all his work. Kate Steinitz has called each grotto "a time capsule," containing a "sediment of impressions and emotions, with significant literary and symbolistic allusions" to the nature and events of Schwitters' personal life.[32] Elucidation of Schwitters' work, however, (as distinct from his personality) gains more from considering the place and function of the imagery than from delving into his private character to discover motivation. What makes the Merzbau so important is that it was, as Schwitters recognized, "the development into pure form" of all the confessional elements of his autobiography.[33]

In 1923, when Schwitters began to consciously form the Merzbau from the already assembled detritus in his studio, his art was moving toward the geometric. But to see the development of the Merzbau as symbolizing the victory of the geometric over Schwitters' personalized Dadaism is misleading. The geometric pictures are disappointing. Whether Schwitters knew this or not, it is reasonable to assume that he missed the opportunity to personalize his work through objects. There was certainly a crisis in Schwitters' art of the '20s, especially in his large-scale work. The Merzbau became important as a way of keeping contact with the classes of objects withheld from his pictures. The significance he attached to it seems to testify that it was the single work which completely satisfied his ambitions, and which carried his full stamp of identity. Through its development we see Schwitters working out the problems of his new geometricist alignment.

The relative severity of forms which the Merzbau eventually contained are not entirely those of the *neue Sachlichkeit:* they grew, quite literally, from the "darkest erotic caves" of the project's beginning. If, as is so often claimed (and rightly so), the "struggle for pure form . . . finally conquered the chaos" of these caves,[34] equally the new geometry is in no sense a second start effacing the original conception. The new surfaces not merely concealed the images beneath (they are not an applied geometry separate to what they contain), but were the means by which images underwent "dissolution" within the context of "pure form." Although the images (those "injurious" expressions) were "downgraded" by being covered over, their covering grew—"like some jungle vegetation," as Hans Richter put it[35]—from the first-planted seeds of Schwitters' Dada-Expressionist years, and developed its character from this source as well. Hence, although the Merzbau has been described as resembling early sculptures by Domela and Vantongerloo, it looks back to Expressionist architecture, to the crystalline projects of the *Arbeitsrat* group mentioned earlier, and to the zigzag splintery settings that Schwitters' fellow Sturm members devised for *The Cabinet of Dr. Caligari.* In one important sense it is a primitivist or organicist architecture of mood. Seen under Schwitters' controlled illumination it must have appeared more mysterious—sinister even—than photographs reveal. In this sense although an environment—a place of atmospheres—it was not merely a setting. Like Schwitters' Dadaist models "its interior is so filled . . . that there is no room for people." And like the scenery of Expressionist films, these "facades and rooms were not merely backgrounds, but hieroglyphs. . . ."[36] With the ribs and columns that swallowed up the original grottoes Schwitters seems to have been trying to create an amalgam of fabricated objects, each with the same force and potency as the found objects with which he identified. This, of course, was the general problem of Schwitters' geometricist work: to personalize the austerity of his new style. With the Merzbau he let the configuration of the entire work take its form from his collection of found objects. The exuberant growths that remained visible were quite literally the stylized radiations of an inner core.

Much of Schwitters' sculpture from the mid-'20s onward was specifically designed to occupy a place in the Merzbau, and its derivation from this most personal of his works does seem important. As the Merzbau grew it became far more curvilinear in appearance, more organic in its feeling—as if growing itself was manifested in the nature of the forms created. The sculptures that survive often have this character. Searching for a vocabulary of forms with the same charge that found objects possessed, Schwitters turned to analogizing the life-imbued appearance of natural organisms. This development in Schwitters' art culminated in the decidedly "rural" emphasis of his late style. It began, however, within the context of geometric formalism.

IV

Schwitters' early understanding of art as something organic and spiritual in character readily transferred to his new geometric style, because the machine esthetic of the '20s posited a crucial correspondence between the functional efficiency of nature and that of the machine.[37] Nature, the machine—and art—all partook of organic principles: their construction was "economical," their intentions "formative," and they all involved a functional processing of materials. Schwitters wrote in favor of a machine esthetic, and yet seemed far more attracted to the organicist theory attached to the machine than to the machine itself. It is appropriate, therefore, that his allegiance to geometricism was declared in a 1924 issue of the *Merz* magazine called "Nasci" ("Nature"). Here, he compared the structure of modern architecture to that of natural forms, and spoke of Merz as a "new naturalistic work of art [which] grows as nature itself . . . more internally related to nature than an imitation possibly could be." To look at Schwitters' sculpture through the '20s, however, is to see that he espoused not merely an *internal* or functional organicism but the very look of natural organisms as well. Here there is a direct *formal* analogy between a work of art and a work of nature—whereas a true machinist would analogize only the principles of natural growth, and never its appearance. Although nominally working within the machinist ethos of international geometricism, Schwitters' art in fact represents a reaction against it. His empathy with nature favored the primitive over the technological, and this fusion of organicist conception and what is best called soft geometricism places Schwitters' sculpture within that cross-stylistic category known as "vitalist."

Since much of Schwitters' sculpture of the '20s and '30s perished with the Merzbau, it is difficult to trace with any precision his development through geometricism, into the curvilinear, and the "rural" forms of his later style. An orthodox (De Stijl-like) geometric work of 1923 survives; and the angular *gedrehte kleine Plastik* (*Small twisted sculpture*) of 1937/38, as well as photographs of the Merzbau interior, suggest that he practiced a fairly tightly contoured style through the Merzbau period. But with the 1923 sculpture the angles and contours soften and swell away from the geometric to produce a feeling of internal growth. Significantly, both sculptures are columnlike in form, and Schwitters tended to preserve a relatively more angular structure and clean-cut precision of look in the taller pieces—which relates them to the columnar formations in the Merzbau. A tall white pillar, made in Switzerland in 1936, is likewise very close to forms visible in photographs of the Merzbau. Given the private and sexual meanings of Schwitters' *Cathedral of Erotic Misery,* it is tempting to see his various sculptural columns as constituting phallic images.

Only in a pair of related sculptures from the early '40s does this phallic association become explicit and unmistakable.[38] An untitled assemblage of painted wood fragments from 1941/42, now known usually (and appropriately) as *Cathedral,* and an even more blatant phallus from 1944, inscribed with the word *Fant* (Norwegian for "Devil"), consist of strong verticals attended by blockier forms at the base. Seen together they cannot but appear as an organic and an angularist interpretation of the same theme: the aspirative form of the cathedral image given sexual connotations. If the angular piece, without its added title, is not quite supportive of this interpretation, that Schwitters did see the cathedral in phallic terms is confirmed by his writings on the Merzbau and by a unique and curious drawing made on the notepaper of a Yri's Hotel at Olden in Norway in 1939. Here, Schwitters revives the cave and cathedral theme central to the Merzbau, while his obsessively realistic rendering of the impaled eye leaves little to the imagination.

These are anomalous works: the majority of Schwitters' sculptures quite clearly relate to structures in nature, sometimes in a general sense and often specifically to plant forms, stones, and occasionally animals. This became more pronounced when Schwitters left Germany for Norway and later England—when his collages and constructions too took on a "rural" look—although this was also evident through the period of his geometric alignment. *Die Herbstzeitlose* (*Autumn Crocus*) of 1926/28 is close to representing a specific natural form, while a group of relief constructions of around this same date used weathered timbers in their raw state. These constructions, however, belong more to the picture-making side of Schwitters' activity than to the sculptural, in which he made only limited use of the assemblage principle. This concern was with creating fabricated equivalents for natural forms and not generally with using natural forms themselves. When timbers, branches, or pebbles are used (instead of the customary plaster), they are disguised by paint. Their natural surfaces are covered up in a way analogous to putting plaster on an armature of found objects.

To paint a pile of three small pebbles (untitled work of 1946/47) fused them as objects and personalized them in mood. Schwitters added touches and areas of color to his simple plaster pieces probably for the same reason: it keeps them from belonging solely to the natural world. The work of 1943/44 known as *Opening Blossom* is very evidently plantlike in character (a soft version of *Die*

Herbstzeitlose). Its colored-in upper surface and roughened texture is not, however, that of an organic thing but of something man-made. In some respects, Schwitters' vitalist esthetic relates to his friend Arp. Both artists conceived of their forms as primordial, talked of art as growth, and sought to express this in their sculpture. Whereas Arp's meticulous finish gives the impression that the forms have grown (and only just grown) somehow independently of an external forming agent, with Schwitters surface looks handled. He never fully embraced any kind of purist esthetic. In consequence, if Arp's surfaces appear to have been generated from inside, the plaster of Schwitters' sculpture never quite escapes from seeming to be a skin containing an armature of objects beneath.

The use of plaster is at first surprising, given the assemblage structure of most other of Schwitters' activities, and it is not entirely explained either by the cheapness of the method or its traditional obviousness. Yet, its ability to contain objects links it with Schwitters' other techniques.[39] The method of the late sculptures was that of the Merzbau, which stands between them and the early Dada pieces, mediating their transition. The curious small pyramid surmounted by a loop of wire, made between 1942 and 1945, is an organic version of the *Lustgalgen* of over 20 years earlier, just as the late assemblages *Fant* and *Cathedral* relate back to the *Kultpumpe* and the *Haus Merz.* The Expressionist *Urbegriff* of Schwitters' beginnings finds its resolution in the truly primitive ethos of his last sculptures when the forms of nature itself were possessed by Schwitters' art.

But plaster also means modeling, and in many of the late sculptures the armature of found objects becomes only a beginning for independent and invented growths. The plaster and bamboo pieces of 1945-48 are like this—the armature is neutral and purely utilitarian—while the small unitary objects made through the '40s do not appear to use an armature at all. Perhaps the cumulative act of modeling in a single material felt closer to organic creation than construction—as if Schwitters saw in this method a way of literally identifying art and growth. (His last Merzbau, built in Elterwater in the English Lake District, depends on modeling for its structure, certainly in imitation of natural growth.)[40] If this is true, then one cannot but feel that Schwitters misread his talent, which was in formalizing the already created. The further from construction, the weaker his art becomes. Though little of his sculpture is openly constructional, the best of it (*Die Herbstzeitlose,* the Swiss column, a few of the small plaster and wire or wood pieces, and some others) take their form from an evidently fabricated core: the armature appears close to the surface, and comprises the surface itself, or it breaks through and shows itself. When continually modeled—when form is created on and by the surface—his art tends to lose contact with its sources. The invented forms are somehow naive. The modeling is usually as anomalous as the painting Schwitters added to his last pictures. And especially when the forms themselves are unitary, small and completely self-contained, they seem to be closed off to the viewer: a private soliloquy with nature from which we are barred access.

None of Schwitters' sculpture is of major quality. Excepting the Merzbau, it is rarely ambitious enough to be so, appearing but the by-product of a talent whose real fruits were elsewhere. These personal objects of Schwitters' affection shelter in their own private world away from the world of art—away from the context of esthetic forming. In Schwitters' pictures, objects enlarge the art; as sculpture they are raw, unformalized, and not readily separated from the literal world of objects at large—lacking that "limited space" by which "the work of art is distinguished from nature." As keys to Schwitters' personality, and to his feelings for his material environment, they are strangely evocative, and occasionally poignant in their naivete and primitivism. Finally, however, a turn to the primitive was for Schwitters a turn against the tradition that nurtured him. The collages and constructions have all the charge of these sculptures, but far more besides because they hold their place in the modernist tradition, pass on that tradition through Schwitters' personality, and gain in their quality by acknowledging it. The sculptures escape from it almost entirely, as if their utterly personal character has pulled them out of art's orbit.

To call an art personal, and to say that it claims understanding in personal terms, is not necessarily to seek its justification in biography. Often, the more deeply personal an art, the more irrelevant becomes the artist's background—or, better, personal details are less needed to understand the art. Schwitters has so frequently suffered under those emphasizing the personal nature of the materials and objects he used that to even begin to discuss such matters risks grave misinterpretation. Yet the character of his art forces such a discussion. These objects can never be neutral, no matter how much they are formed. One senses in Schwitters' artistic character a basic ambivalence in his attitude to objects: a pull between his attachment to them for their own sake and his constant recognition that they must be formed and made abstract—made impersonal, devalued, included in the art— and this tension is absolutely central to his art's structure. To suggest—as I am doing here—that Schwitters felt a division between what held personal meaning and what was artistic, might seem belied by the closeness of his art to his daily life. The objects of daily life were his artistic materials. The immensity of his output speaks of a continuing and constant absorption of his art in the day-to-day patterns of his life. His unremitting insistence on "forming"—that "injurious" expressions be, if not censured, at least contained—suggests some kind of conflict between his respect for tradition—for the purity of art— and for the objects which carried his identity.

In Schwitters' collages—the works closest to his day-to-day living—the conflict seems resolved: his identity is absorbed; the works personalized without loss in form. But when pure art came to mean the dogmatic geometricism of the '20s, into which Schwitters let himself be drawn, the delicate balance was disturbed; and he seemed to require an escape valve for the feeling cold paint kept out of his pictures. The Merzbau offered such an escape. Begun as a deliberate enterprise in the very year of his geometric alignment, it became a depository for the private and the personal; and from it emerged a way of making sculpture that could not be more in reaction to what geometricism stood for. Escaping the dogmatic and the urban, he retreated to the permissive and the primitive. In the urgency of his flight he left behind the discipline that was not dogmatic, but on which the quality of his art depended. Here are purely private objects, possessed by Schwitters' personality but not by his art as we wish to remember it.

[1] "Merz" (1920), *Der Ararat,* II, 1, January, 1921.

[2] *Merz,* 1, January, 1923.

[3] "Mein Merz und meine Monstre Merz Muster Messe im Sturm," *Der Sturm,* XVII, 7, October, 1926.

[4] None have survived. The photograph of Schwitters' Dada sculpture, *Die Heihge Bekümmernis,* shows one in the background.

[5] "Merz" (1920).

[6] They were shown at Schwitters' April, 1919, exhibition at the Berlin Sturm Gallery.

[7] "Merz" (1920).

[8] "Merz," an unpublished note of April 10, 1938, cited in Werner Schmalenbach, *Kurt Schwitters,* Cologne, 1967.

[9] It was reproduced in the Zürich periodical *Dada,* 1, July, 1917. Schwitters met Arp in Berlin in 1918 and remained in contact with him when he returned to Zürich. Schwitters was also in correspondence with Tzara in 1919 over his contributions to the Zürich magazine *Der Zeltweg,* and it is known that Tzara sent Schwitters publications of the Zürich group.

[10] Bernhard Gröttrup mentions a windmill and a broomstick sculpture in an account of his meeting with Schwitters: *Die Pille,* 7, October 13, 1920.

[11] Heinz and Bodo Rasch, eds., *Gefesselter Blick,* Stuttgart, 1930.

[12] "Merz" (1920).

[13] *Der Zweemann,* I, 4, February, 1920.

[14] *Merz,* 21, "erstes Veilchenheft," 1931.

[15] Pamphlet for the *Ausstellung für Unbekannte Architekten,* Berlin, April, 1919: and for the following quotation.

[16] Letter of July 15, 1920, cited in Ulrich Conrads and Hans G. Sperlich. *Fantastic Architecture,* London, 1963.

[17] "Merz" (1920).

[18] *Merz,* 2, "i," 1923.

[19] "Merz" (1920).

[20] For which (and for further discussion of issues relevant to Schwitters, "meanings" structure), see my "The early work of Kurt Schwitters," *Artforum.* November, 1971.

[21] "Merz" (1920).

[22] *Merz,* 20, "Katalog," 1927.

[23] "Ursachen und Beginn der grossen glorreichen Revolution in Revon," *Der Sturm.* XIII, 11, November, 1922.

[24] Hans Richter, *Dada: Art and anti-art,* New York, 1965.

[25] *Merz,* 21, 1931.

[26] One is a widely reproduced photograph from the Schwitters estate (see Schmalenbach, illus. 160); the other appeared in El Lissitzky and Hans Arp. *Die Kunstismen,* Zürich, 1925.

[27] See Schmalenbach, illus. 163 and 165.

[28] *Merz,* 21, 1931.

[29] Kate Steinitz, *Kurt Schwitters, a portrait from life,* Berkeley and Los Angeles, 1968.

[30] See Samuel Cauman, *The Living Museum. Experiences of an art historian and museum director—Alexander Dorner,* New York, 1958.

[31] Carola Giedion-Welcker, *Contemporary Sculpture,* New York, 1961.

[32] Steinitz.

[33] *Merz,* 21, 1931.

[34] Steinitz.

[35] Hans Richter, *Dada Profile,* Zürich, 1961.

[36] Siegfried Kracauer, *From Caligari to Hitler,* Princeton, 1947.

[37] See, for example, Moholy-Nagy's "biotechnic" principles formulated in *Von Material zu Architektur* (Munich, 1928), and El Lissitzky's attitudes to the natural world as expressed in the "Nasci" issue of Schwitters' *Merz* magazine (8-9, 1924), which he co-edited.

[38] Several of Schwitters' upright sculptures are capped with broadened whorls which may appear to be phallic, but which could equally be said to represent buds, flower heads or the like. Only an untitled work of 1943/45

(*Catalogue of the Marlborough Fine Art Schwitters exhibition,* 1973, no. 77) can readily be seen as a companion (curvilinear) piece to *Fant* and *Cathedral.*

[39] If Schwitters did care about his materials—which I think is self-evident—then the proliferation of estate casts of his sculptures (which, to my knowledge, were first made from works shown at the 1958 Lords Gallery, London, Schwitters exhibition, and which are continuing to be made) does raise some problems at this point. It may seem pedantic to complain that whereas Schwitters' original plasters contain found objects, plaster casts of these sculptures do not; but if Schwitters' principle of containment is important (as I think it is), then these copies must be recognized as essentially different from the originals. However, if the originals remain available for inspection, and plaster casts are made of only plaster sculptures, then little disservice has been done. But when castings in plaster are made from pebble or wood sculptures, or when bronze (itself a material that seems alien to Schwitters sensibility) is used to copy works originally in plaster and wood, serious doubts must be raised as to their value—their esthetic value, that is—regardless of how skillfully they are made.

[40] For discussion of this work (and for further details of Schwitters' "rural" style) see my "The last work of Kurt Schwitters," *Artforum,* October, 1969.

Times Literary Supplement (essay date 1973)

SOURCE: A review of *Das literarische Werk,* in *The Times Literary Supplement,* No. 3735, October 5, 1973, p. 1186.

[*In the following review, the unsigned critic laments the editorial flaws present in the first volume of Schwitters's* Das literarische Werk, *which make Schwitters "seem even more obscure, whimsical, and inaccessible than before."*]

The literary productions of German Dada have long languished under a cloud. They have never been regarded as a respectable object for scholarly investigation, and in any event it has been virtually impossible to study them in depth because the works have for the most part either been out of print for a generation or more, or are published in minute editions under obscure imprints.

Moreover, while immense scholarly effort continues to be lavished on the uttermost minutiae of Goethe's life and works, precious little serious attention has been devoted to this crucial modern movement and to the considerable technical problems facing the critic of the composite poetic forms adopted by the avant-garde, which frequently cross the traditional boundaries between visual, aural and written. As a result, the quality of criticism of the available material is, by and large, pretty deplorable. Nor is the standard of such published primary texts as have been produced excessively high. Hugo Ball's poetry, for example, is collected in an extremely selective volume lacking any proper critical apparatus, and the

Gesammelte Gedichte I of Hans Arp has met with a similar fate. Until now, Schwitters has fared even worse: odd items of his work have appeared piecemeal together with a trickle of secondary material, but there has been little of any substance.

Few publishers have had the courage to market German Dadaists, who owe a particular debt to the enterprise of such houses as the Limes Verlag, and also in Schwitters's case to DuMont, who have so far produced two studies of his life and works, and are now embarking on the publication of his literary work, beginning with the lyric poetry. Volumes two and three promise prose and dramatic works; Volume four will contain manifestos and critical prose.

Outside Germany, Schwitters is best known for his visual works, in particular his Merz collages and constructs; of his other creative activities, virtually nothing is known beyond a narrow specialist circle save for the notorious and much-anthologized and translated **"An Anna Blume".**

Schwitters's poetic career proper began with a series of poems, published in *Der Sturm,* imitative of that journal's first eminent protégé, August Stramm. They are superficially similar but where Stramm compresses every element of his poems (lines, words, length) in his endeavour to concentrate significance in a manner parallel to Futurist linguistic doctrine, Schwitters is content to play with the medium and its technical possibilities, exploiting words as objects in his exploration of a private fantasy-world.

Schwitters progressed from this phase to Merz (a term lifted from "Com*merz*-und Privatbank" which cocks a deliberate snook at the materialism and spiritual emptiness of contemporary society), his own personal form of Dada in which he takes the linguistic and physical leftovers of industrial society, and seeks to translate them into an art of collage poems and pictures. **"An Anna Blume"** is the most celebrated of the Merz poems, and its eponymous heroine became a kind of mascot for Schwitters. The poem itself is a clever parody of bourgeois Romanticism and a huge deflation of the cosmic aesthetic exclusivity of *Der Sturm* (which obligingly published the poem on two separate occasions).

From Merz, Schwitters continued farther along the experimental path, progressing beyond sound poetry to become one of the (little acknowledged) innovators of concrete poetry. He spent his latter years in England, producing some embarrassingly bad verse in English. Poor or not, one of his English poems aptly summarizes his childlike—and not infrequently childish—peregrinations within his own private universe:

> I build my time
> In gathering flowers
> And throwing out the weeds.
> This time will lead me forward
> To death
> And God
> And Paradise.

The edition [*Das literarische Werk,* Volume 1: Lyrik] is rather mystifyingly carved up by Friedhelm Lach into five sections, which not only render the study of chronological development difficult (let alone the task of, say, tracing the order of contributions to *Der Sturm*), but also raise tricky and unnecessary problems of classification. (Should the **"pornographisches i-gedicht"** have been in the concrete poetry section, and should **"What a b what a b what a beauty"** have numbered among the English rather than the concrete poems? And since when has the **"Ursonate"** been a concrete poem?) There is in addition to the main text a welcome selection of illustrations—mainly of Merz pictures—to remind the reader that there are further gradations beyond the concrete, in which printed material is absorbed into a contrastive visual design without totally forfeiting its significance as language.

This volume proclaims itself as the first instalment of a "critical complete edition", and should therefore be judged as such; unfortunately, it falls far short of the minimum requirement, even granted that the Germans are not exactly precipitate in furnishing their men of letters with definitive texts to their *oeuvres.* The inconsistencies, inaccuracies and plain blunders are legion. The poem **"Obervogelsang"** appears to have been quoted from a letter to Raoul Hausmann. Lach's footnote refers to two other published versions, which differ slightly from each other, but which—far more importantly—are substantially at variance with the Hausmann version, lines 6-8 of which run:

> Bekke Dii kee
> P'p'bampédii gaal
> Ii Uü Oo Aa

These lines are rendered in *PIN* (a journal produced by Schwitters and Hausmann) as

> Beckedikee
> Lampedigaal
> P'p'beckedikee

No explanation is offered, and the reader who does not check back with *PIN* will be blissfully ignorant of the fact that these are virtually two different poems. Nor does Lach consider it worth pointing out that the title of the poem as shown in the facsimile of the manuscript, which he reproduces in his own *Der Merzkünstler Kurt Schwitters,* is in fact the more normal form **"Obervogelgesang"**—a red herring for a researcher investigating the suppression of prefixes and the mutations of standard substantive patterns.

The second version of **"Frohe Tage. London Symphony"** is reproduced in the body of the text. A footnote informs us that the first version, dated 1942 (the manuscript of which is lodged in the Kurt Schwitters archive in Oslo) was printed in Stefan Themerson's book *Kurt Schwitters in England* and again in Lach's own monograph. This first version is then reproduced—but in a form which strays considerably from both. One line, indeed, has three distinct renderings (presumably according

to one's skill in reading Schwitters's hand-writing and one's knowledge of English): "Prize Beer", "Price Beer", or "Pike Beer". Again, there is no comment on these variants.

But the most serious blemish of all is the treatment meted out to **"An Anna Blume"**, which is central to an understanding of his Merz period, and indeed to his work as a whole. There are two texts which appear to have established themselves: that which *Der Sturm* published twice (in 1919 and 1926), and a slightly different version employed by anthologizers and which Schwitters himself cites in **Anna Blume und ich.** But there has never been any real certainty about the text of the poem, and Lach does little more than add to the confusion. Instead of accepting one of the "standard" versions, he reproduces Schwitters's "final" version—Lach's editorial policy generally is, to say the least, idiosyncratic—taken from a letter written to Christof Spengemann in 1947 (despite which the poem is labelled "*c.* 1919"). The editor states that the poem appears "with a different typographical arrangement and with variants in *Der Sturm*".

There follows a longish—but not exhaustive—list of locations where the poem has been reproduced, with no information about which version appears where—and then a list of variants which refer back to *Der Sturm* is offered. This list notes two punctuation changes, whereas there are no less than twenty-seven. Lach states that a line 6 variant is "Die Menschen" for "Die Leute". Apart from the fact that he seems to be referring to the wrong line, the words "Die Menschen" do not appear in the *Der Sturm* version.

Lach also passes over in silence a change of spelling and an omitted word and accepts as definitive what is clearly an oversight by Schwitters ("Rot ist die Farbe Deines grünen Vogels"—where every other text has "Girren" for "Farbe"). In one of the French versions cited in the footnotes, the crucial word "rouge" is omitted. The offending line should read: "Le roulement de ta boule rouge est vert." And there is also a silly misprint of "les" for "le" ("Les sais-tu, Eve . . . ?"). The *Urtext* is quoted in the footnotes (with no useful suggestion about chronology; one suspects that it was written in retrospect), in a version which seems to indicate that Lach has copied his own faulty version from *Der Merzkünstler Kurt Schwitters,* except that he has reinserted a line omitted then; particularly unfortunate is the retention of "seines" for "deines" in "die Farbe seines gelben Haares" where the *Der Sturm* text is quite unambiguously in favour of apostrophization.

At one point, Lach makes a passing reference to "the instability of Dadaist texts", and there is no denying that much Dada written material poses considerable technical problems to the would-be editor. But by and large these are no more severe than those which face the editor of a Büchner or a Trakl, let alone of any medieval text. The only German Dadaist whose poetry represents an extreme challenge to editorial skill is Hans Arp. This is because of his organic concept of the work of art; that is, the individual work can undergo several metamorphoses, be divided into separate poems or absorbed into others, rendered from German into French and vice versa, and so on.

None the less, the Dadaist text demands the highest possible level of editorial expertise and accuracy; every comma counts in a situation where language is playing new roles beyond that of carrier of verbal meaning, so that, for example, Lach's lame excuse for normalizing poems written exclusively in lower case (namely, that Schwitters subsequently moved out of this phase) is a travesty of scholarship in a situation where the impact of the physical appearance of the text is at least as significant as its "meaning".

If the Dadaists are to be seriously investigated and properly evaluated (both exercises are long overdue) then genuine critical editions of a high order of reliability and comprehensiveness are essential. Regrettably, this Schwitters volume does not meet these requirements. It is the ultimate Dada joke in the worst possible taste that this attempt to approach Schwitters has succeeded only in making him seem even more obscure, whimsical and inaccessible than before.

Rex W. Last (essay date 1973)

SOURCE: "Kurt Schwitters: The Merz Artist from Revon," in *German Dadaist Literature: Kurt Schwitters, Hugo Ball, Hans Arp,* Twayne Publishers, 1973, pp. 31-61.

[*In the following essay, Last surveys Schwitters's life, prose, and poetry, calling his work "a retreat from reality" into a "private world of shapes and patterns."*]

Each of the Dadaists approached the practical business of creating a work of art—or nonart—in his own unique fashion; although all pursued the same, or at least closely related, objectives, each chose his own unmistakable and distinctive angle of attack. The very lack of uniformity was, in itself, a sign both of their positive strength and richness of ideas and of the fact that they had joined common cause as much in reaction to external circumstances as from the impulse of powerful inner drives.

Kurt Schwitters was perhaps the most carefree and adventurous of all the Dadaists. . . . If Hugo Ball is the Dadaist of cosmic gloom, and if Hans Arp is the childlike admirer of the wonders of the natural world, Schwitters may be designated as the childish figure of the movement, playing with cosmic fire, unaware of the dangerous forces he was meddling with.

A wire sculpture from World War II affords an apt illustration of this point. Schwitters picked up a piece of concrete with wire embedded in it from a bomb-wrecked house. He was on his way to the French Institute in London at the time and took the object with him. Once there, he did not give his full attention to the distinguished speaker—the occasion was the celebration of the tercentenary of the publication of Milton's *Areopagitica*—but

instead concentrated on the object and "was bending it into a space-sculpture while Mr. E. M. Forster was delivering his speech."[1] Schwitters was taking a shattered fragment from a war-torn world and refashioning it, taming it and rendering it harmless, and endowing it with magical qualities remote from the harsh realities of bombing raids and mass destruction. Like Marcel Duchamp, he was taking an object ready made, but instead of simply rendering it useless by depriving it of its context, Schwitters translated it into art and thus belied the object itself. The process would surely have been costigated by his friend Arp, who, in his collection of poetry *Sinnende Flammen,* warned against the insidious attempts on the part of the products of the technological and atomic age to make themselves appear quite harmless and domesticated.[2]

Schwitters was an inveterate picker-up of the leftovers of civilization, some of which were none too savory. In conversation with the present writer, Marguerite Arp-Hagenbach recalled how Schwitters once wrapped a chamber pot, which had clearly seen better days, in brown paper and tied it with string. He then carried this around Paris with him and simply gave it to someone who evinced interest in the package.

The objects which he picked up found their way into collages—Merz pictures—which look shiny and attractive in color reproductions but are essentially drab and untidy. They lack vigor and direction and, above all, conviction. However much the cognoscenti of the art world may seek to obscure the issue in fine phrases, there is no question that Schwitters's pictorial works, with the exception of his typographical experiments, when set alongside parallel experiments by artists of the caliber of Ernst, Picasso, or Arp, lack authority and conclusiveness. There is an air of "take it or leave it" about them which renders it difficult for the critic to approach and judge what appears to be a large number of incomplete visual and written works—incomplete in the sense that Schwitters broke off work at the moment when he himself was personally content with his achievement. Communication and putting a message across do not appear to be primary concerns of his, and he seems not to have made the effort of reaching out to the reader or gallery-visiting public.

For all that, there is equally no doubt that the name of Schwitters is known outside the specialist sphere, much more widely than that of Arp, who is by far the greater artist. Schmalenbach's large-scale study has been rendered into English,[3] and throughout 1971 a lavishly catalogued Schwitters exhibition toured Germany and Switzerland.[4] Schwitters' work is at least superficially more attractive and approachable than that of any other Dadaist, although, in the last analysis, it may lack real depth and significance.

I *A Life of Merz*

Kurt Hermann Eduard Karl Julius Schwitters was born in Hanover on June 20, 1887. He was an only child and was brought up in exemplary middle-class fashion in a city dominated by middle-class sentiment and aspirations.[5] In the lives of many errant Dadaists, one city has come to dominate and mean more than any others: in the case of Ball, Zurich became the peak of his aspirations and the location of their ultimate disappointment; for Arp, Strasbourg and its cathedral left an enduring impact; and for Schwitters, Hanover—which he later rechristened "Revon"—became both a cornerstone of his life and the butt of his satire and antibourgeois mirth. He may have pilloried the city of his birth but was unable to shake himself entirely free from it. Schmalenbach points out that Schwitters's rebellion "had all the colors of the very world it was attacking";[6] and, although Käthe Steinitz says of Schwitters that "he was simply incapable of being conventional,"[7] she nonetheless records, without contradicting the statement, that "someone called Kurt Schwitters the most international petty bourgeois in the world; his daily life lacked any kind of elegance."[8]

Schwitters's father had worked his way up in the world, sold his business, purchased houses, and lived off the proceeds. A more prosperously middle-class example would have been hard for Schwitters to find. Never in the best of health, he seemed to need the security of this background, yet at the same time he was filled with a deep revulsion against what middle-class society had engendered. Perhaps this is why he turned his back on any form of political involvement. At any rate, he was more than typical of his generation of artists (particularly of August Stramm, whose work was to exercise a considerable influence on him) in that he lived a kind of dual existence, part "normal," middle-class, tolerably successful in the practical world, and part *avant-garde,* the crazy artist hurling abuse at bourgeois society and spurning its standards.

Between 1909 and 1914, Schwitters studied at the Academy of Art in Dresden, where he learned his craft as an artist. At the Academy, Georg Grosz—along with Otto Dix the most vicious of the Expressionist satirists—was Schwitters's contemporary. Schwitters seems to have borne up under a regime of representational art and attention to technical detail far better than Arp. The solid background in the theory and practice of art which he gained at the Academy enabled him to earn a living as a commercial artist (a valuable source of income in the many lean years he was to face); but as far as creative work was concerned, Schwitters's time there did not tempt him into a position of complex and esoteric theorizing (despite his subsequent involvement with *Der Sturm*). His point of departure could not be more straightforward: "Liberation became the focal concept of Schwitters's art. At first it was liberation from entanglement in his own emotions, from spiritual depression and melancholy."[9] This starting point was later developed into the notions associated with the term "Merz," but even then the theoretical framework did not assume a substantially more complex structure.

In 1914, with the advent of war, Schwitters returned to Hanover, and in the following year married Helma

Fischer, after an engagement which lasted six years. In 1917, he was called up for military service, but after a couple of months his unsuitability forced him into an office position. Schwitters campaigned for his release, after which he entered industrial service near Hanover as an engineering draftsman. It was during this period that he became fascinated by mechanical shapes and the paraphernalia of technology which can be seen to figure so prominently in his subsequent work.

Schwitters was repelled by war, and he saw the end of World War I as offering the possibility of a new beginning. He sought out other like-minded artists (the conception of Schwitters as a totally isolated figure is erroneous) and began to publish his work. The crucial break came in Berlin, where he was given the opportunity of exhibiting his works in the *Sturm* gallery in January, 1919; and in the same year he began to write for the journal *Der Sturm* itself, becoming one of its most substantial contributors.

In 1919 he also contributed to Christof Spengemann's periodical *Der Zweemann,* and in Spengemann's book series called "Die Silbergäule" he published the collection of prose and verse which was to render him both famous and notorious, not just within the Dadaist movement, but far beyond: ***Anna Blume.*** Schwitters was now also producing abstract visual works. He was extremely active and enthusiastic and soon enjoyed a vast acquaintance and correspondence with other *avant-garde* writers and artists throughout the world.

It was in 1919, too, that he found his own voice and coined the term *"Merzkunst."* Its derivation is well known and frequently referred to: Schwitters took part of the appellation *"Kommerzund Privatbank"* which he found on a scrap of paper, and used it as the title for an art form which based itself on the compulsive collection of all manner of rubbish and the creation of works, both visual and written (there is as close a relationship between the two in the case of Schwitters as there is in the case of Arp), on the basis of collage, an attempt to create a new synthesis from the discarded fragments of things spawned by industrialized society.

Merz (with its subdivisions Merz theater, Merz poem, Merz picture, and so on) tends to be applied as a general descriptive term for the whole of Schwitters's creative output; indeed, Schwitters himself established the precedent for this practice, but it should be recognized both that a substantial part of Schwitters's work (for example, **"Die Zwiebel"**[10]), is not exclusively Merz, and also that two of his most important critics, Lach and Schmalenbach, rightly limit the main period of Merz to the years 1919-1922.[11] However, it should equally be recognized that Schwitters continued to produce Merz works right up to his death nearly a quarter of a century later.

In the immediate postwar years, Schwitters met many fellow Dadaists, notably Tzara and Hausmann, who stimulated him to write sound poems, and—the most important of all—Arp, a similar figure in many ways, a man who also stood on the side-lines of the European *avant-garde,* participating in the artistic revolution, but preferring to go his own way rather than follow the noisome leadership storming the artistic barricades.

Schwitters was something of an entrepreneur as well as an artist, and in 1923 he produced the first issue of his own journal *Merz* (which, according to Käte Steinitz, owes it origin, in part at least, to his need for something to barter with),[12] the last issue of which appeared in 1932. In 1924 he began work on his first *Merzbau* (which was subsequently destroyed in an air raid). The *Merzbau* is a kind of inverted, self-replicating sculpture. Schwitters took over a room and began to disguise its shape and fill out its interior with all manner of strange constructs. The observer finds himself "inside" the sculpture, so to speak, within a context of largely geometrical shapes growing from the floor, the walls, and the ceiling. Schwitters worked on his first *Merzbau* for a decade, and the curiously vulnerable forms ultimately spread over two floors of the house. As Lach points out, the *Merzbau* is the closest realization of Schwitters's ideal of artistic synthesis, the *Gesamtkunstwerk,* "as painting, sculpture and architecture grow together in a totally new manner to form a work of art of considerable impact and bizarre imaginative power."[13] Schwitters produced a second *Merzbau* in Lysaker, Norway, which survived ·his death, only to be destroyed by fire in 1951.

In 1936 Schwitters was represented in the two important exhibitions held at the Museum of Modern Art, New York: Cubism and Abstract Art, on the one hand, and Fantastic Art, Dada, Surrealism on the other. He was also represented in another exhibition, inclusion in which was something of a mixed blessing at the time, namely, *Entartete Kunst,* the 1937 touring exhibition organized by the Nazis to demonstrate the corruption, or even insanity, of "modern art."

At the beginning of the same year, Schwitters had left Germany for Norway, where he took up residence near Oslo and began work on the Lysaker *Merzbau.* When Norway was invaded in 1940, he was forced to move on, this time to England, where he was interned for seventeen months. On his release, he settled in London; after the war, he established what was to prove his last home in Little Langdale, in the Lake District. On Cylinders Farm, Langdale, he was able to start work on his third and final *Merzbau* by a fellowship granted by the trustees of the Museum of Modern Art. The *Merzbau,* which was never completed, occupied the interior of a barn.

In 1946 Schwitters collaborated with Hausmann on a planned journal, *PIN,* which did not come to fruition at the time because of a shortage of funds.[14]

Schwitters died on January 8, 1948, and his remains were buried in Ambleside cemetery.

II *"Die Zwiebel"*

Schwitters's written work falls into three main categories: a relatively brief span under the influence of August Stramm, during which he swiftly abandoned the stern Futurist-inspired discipline of *Sturm* art theory; Merz theory and practice; and concrete poetry. Our survey of his development as an artist begins with an early work, one of his first contributions to *Der Sturm,* called **"Die Zwiebel,"** which exhibits many of the principal characteristics of Schwitters's art and underlines the essential unity of his output. **"Die Zwiebel"** is a short prose piece (about 2,500 words) which begins with a rather startling sentence, whose content would seem, at first glance, to exclude or render extremely unlikely the possibility of first-person narration: "Es war ein sehr begebenwürdiger Tag, an dem ich geschlachtet werden sollte."[15] (It was a most eventful day, on which I was to be butchered.) The narrative continues by explaining that the butcher has been duly booked to appear, that the king is present in person, and that a telephone is at hand in case it should prove necessary to summon medical assistance—not to succor the butchered one, but in case one of those witnessing the proceedings should feel unwell and faint. Four attendants, two male and two female, are standing in readiness. Such is the content of the opening paragraph.

The style of the piece is simple and direct, the tone flat and unemotional. The atmosphere, indeed, is one of cheerful anticipation; the first-person narrator is unruffled and curiously detached. The last sentence of the paragraph underlines this self-depersonalization, the detachment of mind from body: "Es war mir ein angenehmer Gedanke, daâ diese beiden hübschen Mädchen mein Blut quirlen und meine inneren Teile waschen und zubereiten sollten."[16] (It was pleasant for me to think that these two pretty girls were to whisk up my blood and clean and prepare my innards.) The ritual which is about to take place has strong sexual overtones; the scene is being set for some kind of perverted flogging-and-copulation-surrogate sequence for the discriminating voyeur (the chief witness being the victim himself).

As the narrative progresses, the style becomes denser and more intense, staccato and Stramm-like. At the same time, Schwitters tends to introduce short words and phrases in parentheses, which either add another trite perspective and a commentary on the action or seem—like the soap commercial: "auch etwas Seife (Sunlight)"[17]—utterly irrelevant.

The preparations continue: the princess arrives clad in virginal white and in a flurry of non sequiturs. The increasingly compressed style and the violent imagery rub shoulders with banalities reminiscent of Jacob van Hoddis, whose work was an important formative influence on Schwitters.[18] One such example of bathos occurs shortly after the princess's arrival: "Wie schön, daâ sich das Wetter an Ihrem Schlachttage hält, daâ der Schlächter per Rad zu Ihnen fahren kann."[19] (How nice that the weather is holding on this, the day of your butchering, that the butcher can ride over to you on his bicycle.) In a text like this, which is constituted of conflicting styles, and in which the various elements are allowed to stand in contrast without any attempt being made to bring them all together, it is difficult to determine which, if any, is the dominant tone, as ambiguity and interaction are themselves its raison d'être.

The sequence of events portrayed in **"Die Zwiebel"** could be either an ecstasy of cosmic pain, a low-key satire, or a trivialized depiction of suffering, depending on which of the styles ·was dominant; but what in fact dominates here is the conflict between each of these possibilities. The upshot is that the experienced event is, so to speak, rendered harmless and deprived of its potency in any one direction by the strong centrifugal forces at work. The piece is removed from the sphere of reality, a charade in which the reader, like the chief participant, is forced into the role of the outside observer. The moment of execution, for example, is treated by the first-person narrator as an excellent opportunity for a piece of virtuoso acting which is duly greeted by a round of applause.

The sense of play mingled with a fascination for the grotesque and the unequivocally repulsive is typical of Schwitters at this period. The unpleasantness is deliberately canceled out by parenthetical irrelevancies, but it is not easy entirely to obliterate the unsavory sensations engaged by a passage like the following, in which the king, having drunken of the sacrificial victim's blood, expresses an interest in tasting his eyes:

> Runde Kugeln innen glatten Schleim sprangen
> aus die Augen sanfte Hände voll entgegen. Auf
> einem Teller Messer Gabel servierte man die
> Augen. (Schwerhörige und ertaubte Krieger erhalten
> kostenlos Rat und Auskunft.) Austern Augen
> senken Magen schwer.[20]

> (Round balls smooth slime within leapt out the
> eyes toward soft hands. On a plate knife fork
> the eyes were served up. [Soldiers who are hard
> of hearing or deaf can obtain free advice and
> information.] Oysters eyes sink stomach heavily.)

The eyes do not appear to suit the king's palate, for he swoons. While the doctor is fumbling around in the king's vitals, seeking to effect a cure, the whole process of butchering appears to have reached both its climax and its limit, for it now goes into reverse.

First the victim's eyes pop back (gently) into his head and "infolge der mir eigenen inneren magnetischen Ströme"[21] (as a result of my own internal magnetic currents) the whole scene unfolds backward like a film run through the projector in reverse:

> Der Schlächter berührte die Wunde in meiner Seite
> mit dem Messer, stach tief hinein und zog das
> Messer hinaus, und—die Wunde war zu. . . .
> Dann sprang der Schlächter mit einem gewaltigen
> Ruck zurück.[22]

> (The butcher touched the wound in my side with
> the knife, stabbed in deeply and withdrew the knife
> and—the wound closed. . . . Then the butcher
> jumped back with a mighty bound.)

Once more, the application of this technique intensifies the unreality of the whole sequence, at the end of which the victim has more or less recovered, with no scars and no noticeable ill effects. But the situation depicted at the end of the narrative is not the status quo: the victim now becomes the dominant figure. The princess falls at his feet, pleading with him to save her father; but he is adamant that the king will remain dead. The narrative closes with these words:

> Als die Flamme durch die Löcher in den Bauch
> des Königs schlug, explodierte der König. Das Volk
> aber brachte ein Hoch auf mich aus. (Sozialismus
> heiât arbeiten.)[23]

> (When the flames burst through the holes in the
> king's stomach, the king exploded. But the people
> cheered me. [Socialism means work.])

When the onion ("Zwiebel") of the title has been peeled and then reassembled, some changes are inevitably wrought. Chief among these is the downfall of the king, for which the way has been prepared throughout the text by parenthetical references to capitalism and socialism. The political message seems so obvious that it hardly bears repeating; what is significant, however, is the question of the seriousness with which this symbolic overthrow of the monarch is regarded by the poet. Reference has already been made to the fact that Schwitters seeks to remove the pain from the situation, to titillate and amuse rather than repel and horrify (although his predilection for the grotesque often leads him inadvertently in this direction), but this, of itself, does not exclude the possibility that the political message is serious in intent.

However, the content of **"Die Zwiebel"** is as ambiguous in nature as the style, for the death and reconstitution of the victim could also be seen as a commentary on the birth of the Expressionist New Man. The ideas are borrowed from the "classical" Expressionist notions regarding renewal, best exemplified in the dramas of Georg Kaiser, where man is depicted at various stages on the path to the Ideal: the chaos of the old; purification and denial of the self; spiritual rebirth as the New Man; and dedication to the struggle toward the Ideal, which (it is hoped) is the synthesis of the transient and immanent spheres. In Kaiser, the failure to realize this end is essentially tragic (although commitment itself is both noble and ennobling); in **"Die Zwiebel"** the supposed renewal is, in fact, simply a reversal to the status quo with no changes within the individual himself. There is another aspect of renewal and commitment which Schwitters here refers to, and that is the attainment of the Ideal through sexual union. Finally, any political euphoria which may be sensed at the overthrow of the king is swiftly dulled by the last sentence of the text;

the people, now so jubilant, will have to work under socialism at least as hard as before and without the glamor of the monarchy and its attendant splendors.

"Die Zwiebel" is a confusing piece (and deliberately so), in which the meaning or meanings are, in fact, subordinated to fantasy, the delight in play and in sparkling flights of the imagination. It is unfortunate that Schwitters was not equal to his self-imposed task. Instead of creating a rich and varied world, his imagination was evidently limited, his range restricted, and his vision myopic. Thus, the reader rapidly gains the impression of having entered a private, somewhat narcissistic fantasy world of recurring images and a mind preoccupied with sexual perversion.

Schwitters has a penchant for nicknames—Tran, Merz, Erika,[24] Anna Blume, and the like—but the concepts associated with these are both limited and inflexible. In fact, he reiterates the same formulas until they become mere cliché formulations. Typical examples of this are the notions of "whipping" and "fish."

"Die Zwiebel" contains the phrase "oben stachelt Fisch in der Peitscheluft";[25] in the poem **"Nächte"** the same line occurs, only slightly modified: "schlank stachelt Fisch in der Peitscheluft."[26] In **"Mordmaschine 43"** there is a variation: "Schlank stachelt Fisch den Karpfen grün";[27] and in **"Stumm"** there is a modification on the themes of "fish" and "sky": "Der Fisch stirbt in der Luft."[28] As these restricted patterns recur insistently, their repetition becomes more and more monotonous, and the inspiration begins to flag. For Schwitters is merely ringing the changes on the limited set of stock phrases, not opening up new unexplored regions of the imagination.

Nonetheless, Schwitters and his work have exercised a considerable attraction although the intellectual demands made upon the reader or observer are far less rigorous than those imposed by many of the other *Sturm* contributors, notably figures like Blümner and Friedländer (Mynona). Schwitters's work does not present a continuum of theory and practice, of world view and created objects. It is, on the contrary, escapist and insulated against the world outside.

III *Schwitters and Stramm*

The insulation of the created object is most glaring in the case of Schwitters's earliest works (that is, excluding an initial Neo-Romantic phase),[29] the poems written in imitation and admiration of August Stramm for Christof Spengemann's journal *Der Zweemann*[30] and subsequently for *Der Sturm.*[31] It should not be concluded that Schwitters was merely following in the footsteps of Stramm's eccentric staccato verses. The exact nature of the relationship between the two poets can best be demonstrated by comparing and contrasting a poem by Stramm with one in a similar vein written by Schwitters. The most famous and most widely anthologized Stramm poem is the celebrated "Patrouille":

Die Steine feinden.
Fenster grinst Verrat.
Äste würgen
Berge Sträucher blättern raschlig
Gellen
Tod.[32]

(The stones foe.
Window grins betrayal.
Branches throttle
Mountains bushes exfoliate rustling
scream
death.)

This is a typical Stramm product, a poem consciously worked over and compressed on four distinct levels: first, the overall length is severely restricted to six lines (all of Stramm's poetry, with a few exceptions, both special cases, follows a similar pattern); the length of each line is rigorously controlled (frequently being held to a single word); and the individual word is deprived of prefixes, suffixes, and inflexional endings ("feinden" instead of "anfeinden"; "Berge" as a potentially adjectival form; "gellen" instead of "gellenden"). Finally, the poem itself is progressively intensified and compressed (the physical appearance of many of Stramm's poems is clearly that of a pyramidal shape—or a series of such shapes—with the point facing downward), culminating in the single word "Tod," which both concludes and summarizes the action. Everything in the poem is directed toward the single purpose of demonstrating the dehumanizing horrors of war. Stramm, it is true, places image alongside image in a kind of verbal collage, allowing each to comment on the others without losing its separate character or identity. At the same time, the images are balanced in such a way that there is a taut and clearly marked progression. Although there is no reference within the text to specific individuals—in fact, the exclusion of such a reference suggests nature turned against itself in an orgy of self-destruction—the poem conveys both the fear which holds the patrol in its grip, their ambush, and their destruction. The objects presented in successive lines follow the eyes of the patrol, starting down on the ground and then moving higher and higher until the machine-gun fire knocks them to the ground. The poem focuses on stones, then on the flash of sunlight on a window, branches slashing at the soldiers faces, and finally "mountainous" bushes spitting bullets that bring screaming death.

"Patrouille" possesses a rigorous and totally consistent structure and development; a carefully evolved technique is consciously and deliberately applied to a specific and clearly defined end which agrees with Stramm's philosophy.

Stramm's poems are among the most vigorous and dynamic creations of Expressionism, and there is no doubt that Schwitters greatly admired him and recognized his importance: "Stramm was the great poet. We owe *Der Sturm* a great deal for making Stramm known. Poetry itself owes Stramm a great deal."[33] But there is also no doubt that Schwitters's Stramm-like poems are highly selective in their borrowings:

Zagt ein Innen
zittert enteint
giert schwül
herb
Du
Duft der Braut
Rosen gleiâen im Garten
schlank stachelt Fisch in der Peitscheluft[34]

(An inside hesitates
tremblcs un-oned
lusts sultry
bitter
you
scent of the bride
roses glisten in the garden
sleekly fish stabs in the whip air)

Superficially, this extract from **"Nächte,"** the first poem which Schwitters published in *Der Sturm*, bears a strong resemblance to the principal characteristics of Stramm's poetry as outlined above. It is highly compressed, the words are deprived of their articles and endings, and the fifth line represents a culminating point, which seems to be all the more significant when it is noted that, of the sixty times that the word "Du" occurs in Stramm's poetry, it appears as the single word on the line on no less than twenty-two occasions. There are also many other correspondences in vocabulary.[35] Nor is it surprising that there are parallels with Stramm's poems "Zwist"[36] and "Trieb,"[37] which share with **"Nächte"** the theme of sexual intercourse.

But in Schwitters's poem the centrifugal forces are by far the stronger. If the plurality of styles in **"Die Zwiebel"** directed attention away from the act and meaning of the central figure's ritual slaughter, this poem, too, is not concerned with sexual union in its cosmic significance (this is the theme of Stramm's poems on the subject). Schwitters is taking the actions and emotions of love as the basis for artistic experimentation. Stramm marshals alliteration, assonance, and striking imagery to the purpose of heightening and intensifying the impact of the poem, but each of Schwitters's images has a considerable degree of independence from the rest of the poem and also a different frame of reference. The line "Rosen gleiâen im Garten," for instance, owes its existence only partly to the associations sparked off by "Duft" in the previous line. It stands primarily as a separate image conditioned by the initial sounds of "glieâen" and "Garten" (in the same way that the following line is dominated by [ç]) and by the erotic image of roses, which appears elsewhere in his work, for example, in the poem "Senken Schwüle," and more general images associated with flowers, their blossoming and fading, which pervade not only his work but which constitute a significant element in Expressionist imagery at large.

Schwitters's poetry also lacks the forward impetus of Stramm's. "Patrouille" is impelled along by its inner logic to the culminating word "Tod"; but in Schwitters the lack of strong links between one line and the next (indeed the occasional nonsense line bearing no relation to the rest of the text at all) and the absence of a focal or culminating point lead to the suspicion that the relationship between the two poets is neither as strong nor as profound as might at first sight seem to have been the case.

In this respect, it is significant to note that, in his contribution to *Der Sturm*, of which his brief eulogy on Stramm forms part, Schwitters's comments on Stramm are immediately followed by a definition of abstract poetry. The implication is clear. Schwitters is primarily concerned with Stramm's technique: he leans heavily on all his technical devices of compression and his Futuristic breaking of syntactic bonds. But any references there may be to similar themes—the erotic and cosmic union, or war and its dehumanizing effect—are coincidental because, as has been shown in the case of **"Die Zwiebel,"** it is not the subject matter that dominates but the manipulation of the separate constituents of the poem in an endeavor to create an abstract pattern that is removed from the pain of existence into a private fantasy world.

At one time or another, most Dadaists have been accused of writing or creating constructs devoid of meaning in which arbitrary play is the sole detectable consistent feature. In the majority of cases, the accusation is manifestly false, as will be seen with regard to Ball and Arp; but Schwitters comes close to being proven guilty on this score.

IV *Schwitters and Merz*

It seems curious that, despite general critical insistence on the difference between Expressionism and Dada, the two movements rubbed shoulders in many of the leading literary journals of the time. In *Der Zweemann*, edited by Christof Spengemann and predominantly Expressionist in tone and outlook, a declaration by Schwitters on Merz painting appears[38] as does a Dadaist manifesto signed by a galaxy of Dadaists.[39] Schwitters himself did not go through a clearly marked and distinct Expressionist period—his Stramm-like poems were published concurrently with the first Merz works—although he owes his reputation and "discovery" (particularly as a visual artist) almost entirely to *Der Sturm*, the journal which, under Herwarth Walden, promulgated the most exclusive and esoteric brand of Expressionism. Arp, too, appears in the pages of *Der Sturm*, despite the fact that he is highly critical of Expressionism and the concept of the great artist;[40] and in the Dadaist manifesto in *Der Zweemann*, Hausmann, Tzara, Huelsenbeck, Ball, Arp, Otto van Rees, Friedrich Glauser, and others joined forces in a violent attack on Expressionism and its failure to bring about the promised regeneration of art.

The massive weight of scholarship bearing down on Expressionism and Dada tends to crush out of existence the simplest facts, which become lost under a vast superstructure of critical theory; and the simple fact is that the common point of departure meant far more than the specific goals being pursued. Jones underlines this fact in his article on Schwitters's relationship to *Der Sturm*:

The link between Dada anti-idealism and the positive "Sturm"-ideal can be seen as an indirect result of the total negation of all conventions and rules in art by the Dadaists. The destructive impulse left a vacuum; but it also gave the artist the total freedom essential to the creation of the absolute work of art. Schwitters's work is a clear illustration of the successful amalgamation of the art-ideal of *Der Sturm* with the positive "spin-off" from Dada.[41]

And the particular brand of Dada that Schwitters discovered for himself was "Merz."

In his preface to *The Picture of Dorian Grey*, Oscar Wilde asserts that art is useless. Schwitters has stood this declaration on its head: for him, the useless is art. He defines Merz in "Die Merzmalerei" (first published in *Der Zweeman*, subsequently reproduced in *Der Sturm*, shorn of the last paragraph),[42] where he asserts that Merz is abstract, that he gathers the leftovers of society—bits of wood, metal, old tickets, fragments of newspapers for his Merz pictures, and clichés, advertisements, shreds of language for his poems—and creates by withdrawing the materials from their context and treating them as shapes or patterns.[43]

Unlike Arp, Schwitters was not seeking to take an object or word out of its cliché-ridden existence in order to set it in a new, meaningful context, but simply in order to liberate it from all contextual considerations, to remove it from reality into a world of private references and associations. In a dialogue entitled **"Ein solider Artikel,"**[44] which is conducted between "I" and "The Doctor," among all the interpolated parenthetical irrelevancies a fundamental unwillingness to explain Merz, although that is the ostensible object of the exercise, can be detected. Merz is something which exists in Schwitters's imagination and is thence transferred by him to canvas or paper; but overzealous analysis may damage or even destroy Merz. In this awareness, Schwitters takes a malicious pleasure in obscuring the real issues.

This obsessive private world of Schwitters is illustrated by an anecdote (an accretion of such little tales, all sworn not to be apocryphal, has formed about the biographies of most Dadaists), related by Hausmann, who found Schwitters one evening outside groveling on the ground, looking for something amid a pile of pieces of paper. Schwitters explained his presence thus: "It struck me that I just have to slip a piece of blue paper into the left lower corner of my collage 30B1, I won't be a moment."[45] This view of Schwitters as the contented, self-contained artist, utterly wrapped up in his own work, is underlined by Hausmann's statement that "Schwitters was of an harmonious, undivided disposition, and allowed nothing to disturb or deter him."[46] Schwitters peopled this private world with strange figures like Alves Bäsenstiel, Franz Müller, and Auguste Bolte, but the most celebrated of all is a woman, Anna Blume. Schwitters's poem addressed to this lady is his best-known work, **"An Anna Blume"** first appeared in *Der Sturm* in 1919,[47] and subsequently in book form with other, additional texts.[48] The poem has been widely anthologized and has been the object of considerable critical attention.

Heselhaus as an interpreter is typical of the generally tentative and unambitious approach of most critics toward it; he goes little further than giving a straightforward description of Merz. He restricts himself to calling **"An Anna Blume"** grotesque, but he does stress the fact about the Merz poems that "they were by no means as arbitrary as might be thought, but like the Anna Blume poem had their own consistent Merz-unity."[49] This theme of unity is taken up by Thomson, who takes the rather surprising view that the poem is held in a state of balance, in which ambiguity is the key to its significance. "The reader . . . can either dismiss the text as a nonsensical hoax, an anti-poem, or he can think of it—though with some reservations—as a unique blend of the nonsensically comic and the poetic."[50] The major weakness of Thompson's argument derives from his insistence on comparing and contrasting every bit of **"An Anna Blume"** with Stramm (why just Stramm?), which leads him into far wilder realms of speculation than those he accuses Last and Middleton of invading.[51] These two at least make no exclusive claims for their interpretations, recognizing that "meaning" is only one aspect of the poems they are examining. Middleton's close reading of a Schwitters poem (if "close reading" can be applied to a poem consisting entirely of numbers) does at least make the crucial point that Schwitters is taking the banal constituents of the technological society and using them in order to transcend reality: "These deadly designs are answered by Schwitters in this poem with an art of animation which reveals miracle in banality, and which retrieves the breath of human life from the orifices of the robots."[52] Carola Giedion-Welcker also stresses the magical and poetic qualities of **"An Anna Blume"** in particular and Schwitters's poetry in general.[53] And, although Schmalenbach refrains from anything approaching a detailed interpretation of the poem, he does make two important points: first, that Schwitters's poem was not just a *succès d'estime*, but was actually well known and not far short of being a "popular hit"; second, that the poem attacks "petty bourgeois sentimentality."[54] As an advertising copywriter, Schwitters knew how to strike the right note to attract the reader's attention (and **"An Anna Blume"** does read rather like a zany advertisement for this strange product); and, as has been pointed out earlier, he was half a prisoner of his middle-class background, despite the fact that his artistic activities led him to move among the front-line troops of the *avant-garde*.

The observations of Middleton, Giedion-Welcker, and Schmalenbach serve to set **"An Anna Blume"** much more meaningfully in its context than Thomson's simplistic notion of ambiguity, which, like Lach's interpretation, insists too exclusively on the parodistic features of the poem: "The texts are consciously distorted into nonsense as parodies of the language of the *Sturm*-lyrics."[55] The poem is a prose poem; and, like much of Schwitters's Merz Material, it is far less arbitrary and spontaneous than appears at first sight. The apparent spontaneity is more attributable to Schwitters's combinatory skill than to any kind of automatic writing.

It falls into three clearly marked sections, each headed by an apostrophe to Anna Blume, which contains the phrase "ich liebe dir" (I love you—"you" being dative rather than the normal accusative). This has been hailed as an attack on grammar, but it is much more likely to be a deliberately strange (grammatical) case which echoes in the mind until it comes across its rhyming word at the end of the poem, "Tier" (animal).

The three sections, of approximately equal length, each concentrate on a specific attribute or aspect of the beloved. The first section states the poet's (or the lyrical self's) devotion to Anna Blume. The second concerns her appearance, her clothes and color; and the third deals with her animal presence and sexuality. The poem opens thus:

> O du, Geliebte meiner siebenundzwanzig Sinne,
> ich liebe dir!—Du deiner dich dir, ich dir, du
> mir.—Wir?
> Das gehört (beiläufig) nicht hierher.
> Wer bist du, ungezähltes Frauenzimmer? Du bist—
> bist du?—Die Leute sagen, du wärest,—laâ sie
> sagen, sie wissen nicht, wie der Kirchturm steht.
>
> (O thou beloved of my twenty-seven senses, I love
> to thee!—Thou of thee thee to thee, I to thee, thou
> to me.—We?
> That [by the way] does not belong here.
> Who art thou, innumerable lady? Thou art—art
> thou? People say you are—but let them talk, they
> do not know how the churchtower stands.)

The hyperbolic tone is maintained throughout, as are the weird metaphors and other devices with their bathetic effect: they include references to the perfection of the circle, because the name Anna is a palindrome, and the deliberate parallel between Anna Blume (Anna Flower) and the Romantic ideal of the "blue flower," symbol of mystical aspiration toward the infinite. But, typically, Schwitters is not content with straight borrowing: his heroine is green, blue, yellow, and red all at once.

The declension of the second-person singular personal pronoun is, so to speak, a verbal *objet trouvé,* which both reflects the lover's characteristic repetition of "you" and leads to the equally conventional questioning of the durability and strength of the relationship. Typical of Schwitters, this central issue is brushed aside. The repetition of the personal pronoun is, it is true, close to Stramm, and there are a few other traces of Stramm's techniques; but again imitation, if it is that at all, goes no further than that. There is none of Stramm's intensity of meaning and no quest for cosmic union.

Anna Blume herself, a simple homespun maiden, is a parody of the girl of every clean-living young man's dreams. She is described as if she were the miracle ingredient in some grotesque amorous compound. The utter banality of Anna Blume, coupled with the bliss of

definitely noncosmic union which her limp little bourgeois body offers, makes it evident that Schwitters's poem is not sympathetic to the *Sturm* ideal and the esoteric realms inhabited by its high priests. But there is no consistent case being argued: although a highly organized poem, it nonetheless lacks dynamism and a sense of progression. It is essentially a haphazard gathering of independent units, and the lack of focus and consequent abstraction of the poem is closely allied to that noted earlier in the case of **"Die Zwiebel."**

Lach compares **"An Anna Blume"** with Hans Arp's "Kaspar ist tot," which latter in common with many other interpretations of the poem he regards as a parody of a dirge or lament. Even if this funereal interpretation were correct, there would still be essentially very little in common between the two poems, except for the rather superficial correspondence that both concern figures endowed with magical abilities. The differences far outnumber and outweigh any points of comparison: Arp's elegy on a lost harmony is a coherent, developing statement in which parody, if it exists at all, is only a general reference to a conventional form, and one which in no way seeks to devalue or mock the form itself;[57] Schwitters's poem, on the other hand, is not trying to make a political, sociological, cosmic or any other kind of point. There is no message being put across, nor is parody a principal element. In this respect, too, **"An Anna Blume"** follows the example of **"Die Zwiebel"** by withdrawing from reality into a private world; and if the poem is to be subjected to a consistent interpretation, it would be more appropriate to consider it in terms of personal rather than historical issues, that is, with respect to the schizophrenic state of its author, a man torn between *avant-garde* and petit bourgeois, with two most incompatible souls raging within his breast.

V *Revolution in Revon*

Many of the principal features of **"An Anna Blume"** reappear in Schwitters's uncompleted novel ***Franz Müllers Drahtfrühling*** (*Franz Müller's Wire Spring*). It was begun in 1919, but only the first chapter, bearing the title **"Cause and Beginning of the Great and Glorious Revolution, in Revon,"** was actually completed, and published in *Der Sturm.*[58] It was also translated into English for *Transition.*[59]

"Revolution" is a dangerous and tempting word to encounter in a title, particularly of a work composed at a time of revolutionary disturbances; but here again Schwitters removed himself from political and social reality into his own world. And once more he uses a strict and highly developed form. As Elderfield in his stimulating paper on ***Franz Müller's Drahtfrühling*** points out:

> The only political party Schwitters ever supported was one he invented himself: the *KAPD (Kaiserliche Anna Blume Partei Deutschlands).* His lack of interest in politics is well known, and his version of revolution is predictably irreverent. But, as

in much of his work, whether literary or artistic, there exists a duality between what he himself called a "nonsensical" content and a precisely controlled form.[60]

The narrative begins with the simplicity of a fairy tale.[61] A child is asking its mother about a man standing there and doing nothing. The question is repeated with several variations. The man standing there is himself questioned, but he makes no reply. A stranger, Alves Bäsenstiel from **"Die Zwiebel,"** is also present. A couple, Herr Doktor Leopold Feuerhake with his wife, joins the crowd. This pompous pair also questions the reason for the man's presence and apparent lack of mobility. Every time his name is mentioned, Doktor Feuerhake acquires new appellations until his name has grossly inflated itself to "hockwohlgeboren Herr Doktor Friedrich August Leopold Kasimir Amadeus Gneomar Lutetius Obadja Jona Micha Nahum Habakuk Zephanja Hagai Sacharja Maleachi Feuerhake,"[62] editor of the Revon newspaper.

All those present, notably Alves Bäsenstiel and Doktor Feuerhake, condemn the man; for them, his inexplicable presence constitutes a grave affront to public order and the fellow is a criminal and a disgrace. But then, the narrative is suddenly interrupted:

> Hier läât der Autor zunächst ein selbstverfaâtes Gedicht folgen. . . . Und nun folgt zunächst wieder der Anfang dieser Geschichte.[63]

> (At this point the author introduces a poem written by himself. . . . And now there follows once more the beginning of this story.)

Thus, instead of taking up the narrative at the point at which he had left it when he embarked on the poem (which has absolutely no relevance to the rest of the text), Schwitters returns to the beginning of the story, produces a précis of the action described so far, and then proceeds to quote the poem once again, this time with some minor variations.

To borrow a phrase from science fiction jargon, it seems as if Schwitters were caught in a time-loop; but he extricates himself by pointing out that the story has been repeated for the cogent reason that he wishes to make it unambiguously clear to his readers that a man is actually standing there doing nothing.

At this point, Anna Blume appears:

> Anna Blume? Jawohl, geliebter Leser, dieselbe Anna Blume, von hinten wie von vorne A-N-N-A, aber es war noch vor der Zeit, als Steegemann sie verlegt hatte, sie war noch nicht einmal im "Sturm" erschienen, geschweige durch den deutschen Blätterwald mit Anmerkungen der Redaktionen gehetzt. Sie war noch so gut wie unbekannt. (Zur Erhöhung der Betriebssicherheit ist bei der Bergfahrt die vordere Hälfte, bei der Talfahrt die hintere Hälfte stärker zu besetzen. Jeder Miâbrauch wird strafrechtlich verfolgt.)[64]

> (Anna Blume? Yes indeed, dear reader, the selfsame Anna Blume, A-N-N-A read forward and backward, but this was before the time she was published by Steegemann; she had not even appeared in *Der Sturm,* not to mention the thicket of German papers through which she was chased with observations from the publishers. She was still practically unknown. [To increase the safety of operation the front half is to be more fully occupied during the journey up the mountain, the rear half on the journey down. Abuses are punishable by law.])

The parenthetical irrelevancy reminds the reader at once of Anna Blume's function as the mascot of Merz, as does a brief quotation from **"An Anna Blume,"** which pursues her like a leitmotif whenever she is mentioned. She sees the man standing there (now called Franz Müller) with far greater clarity than the others present:

> Der Anzug war auch etwas eigenartig. Anna Blume dachte dabei etwa an die Merzplastiken des Autors. . . . eine wandelnde Merzplastik, d.h. der Mann wandelte ja garnicht, der Mann stand.[65]

> (The suit was also something of an oddity. It reminded Anna Blume of one of the author's Merz sculptures. . . . a walking Merz sculpture, that is, the man wasn't walking at all, he was just standing there.)

The others present fail to see in Franz Müller anything but an obstruction in a public place; they do not recognize that he might be a work of art. Alves Bäsenstiel is particularly wrathful; he denounces the man's presence in a long speech in which a kind of fugue is played on the theme "The man stands." The police are summoned, and since this is a case of an inoffensive and harmless individual causing no violence and posing no danger, an officer of the law agrees to come and apprehend the villain. He addresses the man. For a little while, nothing happens.

> Da geschah das Unerhörte. Der Mann wandte den Kopf zur Seite. Schreck wühlte Augenlichter zischen Eingeweide.[66]

> (Then an amazing thing happened. The man turned his head to one side. Terror raged eyesights hiss bowels.)

The sudden change of style to the Expressionist grotesque seeks to mock the absurdity of the situation rather than parody Expressionist style itself; it is taken a stage further when a child is crushed to death between two fat lady spectators and some of the shorter members of the crowd take possession of the corpse in order to stand on it so that they can the better observe what is happening.

And then the ultimate horror occurs: the man actually walks away. Wild panic breaks out. More people are crushed to death, and the officer of the law stoically notes down the proceedings in legalistic jargon. A crippled youth runs through the streets proclaiming the glad tidings consequent upon the man's moving, namely, the outbreak of the great and glorious revolution in Revon.

Franz Müllers Drahifrühling is Schwitters's most competent and consistent piece of prose writing. The work is supposedly a fragment, but the narrative, as presented in *Der Sturm,* seems to reach the limit of its development and certainly does not break off in mid-action, despite the optimistic note at the end: "Fortsetzung folgt"[67] (to be continued). It has the, by now familiar, strictness of form, here very highly developed. Schwitters operates by a process of repetition with variation, which has the effect of causing the action to move at an uneven pace, even jolting backward in time on occasion. As in **"Die Zwiebel,"** points of crisis are postponed, and when they appear, the reader's attention is split or distracted from the central issue. Elderfield draws the proper conclusion from this situation: "Now, why all this diversion and repetition? It could be argued that it heightens suspense by delaying action. But Schwitters's side-trackings are so assertive that one cannot but conclude that he was as much interested in the form of what he wrote as what he actually said."[68] Schwitters was very preoccupied with technical considerations, and the underlying reason emerges clearly if Elderfield's argument is taken one step further.

The time structure of ***Franz Müllers Drahtfrühling*** is complex, and so is the alternation of different stylistic levels. But Schwitters also operates with an intricate pattern of shifting points of view, ranging from detached omniscient narrator through intrusive first-person narrator to outbursts of·lyricism. The result of this constantly switching standpoint is to generate a state of confusion about levels of reality in the same way that the structure produces an inchoate temporal progression. And the combined effect of this polyvalency of style, time, and viewpoint is to produce within the reader a sensation of alternating involvement and detachment, of being everywhere and nowhere—in effect, of inhabiting and exploring Schwitters's own private world of the imagination.

The more the texture of the narrative is examined, the more complex and consciously worked out it proves to be. Words, phrases, and whole sequences are˙laid out in a linked chain, in which the individual elements appear in this order of progression: a a b a b b c b c c d. Words become structural elements pure and simple. Nowhere else in his work does it emerge more clearly than here that Schwitters's notion of "word play" is radically different from that of other Dadaists like Arp. Arp employs diverse aspects of the meanings of words to produce a punning effect, the object of which is to rejuvenate worn-out concepts and engender new and spontaneous relationships (for example, "habemus papam habemus mamam").[69] In the whole of ***Franz Müllers Drahtfrühling,*** there are only two puns of any significance, neither of them central to the work;[70] it is, rather, the structural role of words and phrases that is crucial. This comes across most forcibly in Schwitters's use of bold type to underscore moments of crisis ("Da geschah das Unerhörte") or for words or phrases with particular importance for the structure of the narrative ("bravo" from the crowd, or the individual expletives directed

against the motionless Franz Müller). Elsewhere, the use of language is extremely conventional with the exception of the Expressionist outbursts. And even here Schwitters is not violently experimental: the Expressionist style is only one of several styles—fairy tale, officialese, the language of advertisements, etc.—which he borrows.

Schwitters creates a magical realm divorced from reality, one with a lesser degree of nastiness than that prevailing in **"Die Zwiebel."** It is peopled with strange characters, like Doktor Feuerhake with his voluble, much-fainting wife. Anna Blume appears to be even more ethereal than elsewhere, for in this narrative she is as yet unknown, not having been "discovered" and made famous.

Schwitters is evidently fascinated by people, their quirks and oddities; and he seems to collect idiosyncrasies just as he collects different styles, pieces of paper, string, and so forth. He even "collects" Hanover, translates it into Revon, and thereby creates a kind of latter-day Seldwyla, Gottfried Keller's immortal hicktown.

The lack of focus generated by this wide range of constituent elements renders an unambiguous interpretation of the meaning of the motionless Müller and his audience somewhat difficult. The central figure is subjected to a variety of approaches, but the only person who is capable of understanding him is Anna Blume, who is placed there by Schwitters in order that the reader might have her insight into Müller's true nature. The other figures are totally uncomprehending and react in a panic-stricken fashion when he moves; but Anna Blume is able to recognize him as a Merz construct, a harmless creation which wishes only to be left alone.

Müller is not a political figure; Schwitters has "collected" the notion of revolution from contemporary events and exploits it here simply as still another weapon in his campaign against the art critics. But even this is not done in deadly earnest. Elsewhere in *Der Sturm* he pokes fun at the scholar and critic of the art world; in one extremely witty article entitled "General-pardon an meine hannoverschen Kritiker in [*sic*] Merzstil" (General pardon to my Hanover critics in Merz style), Schwitters mockingly recommends patent blinkers, which are light, fit easily, and are simple to use.[71] But he is essentially unruffled by critical incomprehension (and one suspects that he would be more than a little bewildered to find himself the object of serious investigation in terms such as the present study offers) and prefers to play happily with his own invented figures in the Revon he has created for himself. As Elderfield observes: "While his methods of working could not help but make reference to his times and their social and political dilemmas . . . Schwitters but used his outer environment to make for himself a personal and absurd abstract world."[72]

VI *Sound Poetry and Concrete Poetry*

Schwitters's creative work continued broadly along the lines of **"Die Zwiebel,"** **"An Anna Blume,"** and *Franz*

Müllers Drahtfrühling, in his novel *Auguste Bolte,*[73] which appeared under the *Sturm* imprint, and in his Merz stage pieces.[74] But there is one important aspect of his work which has yet to be discussed, namely his contribution to the development of sound poetry and concrete poetry.

The dividing line between these two lyric forms (which are partly literary, partly musical, and partly visual in nature) is difficult to determine: perhaps the most straight-forward definition is that, while one appeals principally to the ear and the other to the eye, both employ the word (or part of a word or group of words) as a physical object, not as a conveyor of meanings and associations.

In his statement on Merz painting, Schwitters states that the pictures of Merz painting are "abstract works of art,"[75] and he applies the same epithet to Merz poetry. In his foreword to the book *Anna Blume,* Schwitters defines abstract poetry as a form which "sets values against values. One might also say 'words against words.'"[76] (In the German, Schwitters relates the two concepts by means of the word play between "Worte" and "Werte.") Thus he is concerned with the interplay of forces, the tensions created by verbal and visual structures, whose constituent elements have been deprived of significance because they have been "abstracted" from their context. Schwitters underlines this proclivity by writing poems in which the elements themselves are abstract. The following is an extract from one such poem:

```
        25
    25,  25,  26
    26,  26,  27
    27,  27,  28
    28,  28,  29
31,  33,  35,  37,  39
```
[77]

In a commentary on this poem (for Schwitters gives it this name, incorporating its "first line" into the title: **"Gedicht 25"**), Middleton talks in terms of "patterning and unpredictability,"[78] that is, in relation to a structure whose parts have meaning only by virtue of their relationship to that structure as a whole. Schwitters, he is arguing, is not so much concerned with "25" or any of the other numbers as a cipher, a numerical value, or a quantity with an extrinsic significance (like a magic or lucky number), but as a visual element in a visual pattern, one which hovers between conformity and predictability on the one hand and arbitrariness and chaos on the other. The impact of the poem derives from this conflict between expectation and what actually appears on the printed page.

This manipulation and exploitation of the reader's search for order and pattern is one of the key characteristics of sound poetry and concrete poetry. An absolutely regular pattern would be dull and complete chaos would be bewildering—hence it is possible for the artist to operate between these extremes in order to achieve his desired effect. All too often, Schwitters succeeds only in stimulating without satisfying, asking questions and setting up tensions which he has no intention of resolving. The end product, in such cases, is irritation and alienation on the part of the reader, a frequent response by anyone scanning Schwitters's abstract poetry. Despite the fact that he states in one of his aphorisms, bearing the general title "Banalities from the Chinese," that "Every beginning has its end,"[79] it is evident that here, as elsewhere in his work, the tendency is for Schwitters to lay down his pen (or scissors, or paintbrush, as the case may be) when he has satisfied himself, without reference to the possible response of others. Schwitters may be scathing in his attacks on his critics,[80] but it cannot be said that he goes out of his way to avoid critical censure.

The reduction of the constituents of a poem to the role of building bricks permits Schwitters to approach his central aspiration, namely the uniting of art forms and the destruction of barriers between one form and another. Shapes, words, and sounds all become interchangeable at the point at which they lose their contextual significance. Much of Schwitters's work was written for recitation, notably the *Ursonate,* a long sound poem which has some of the appearance of a musical score and which follows in the tradition of the simultaneous poem.

Schwitters involved himself in the whole range of what might be termed "nonverbal" poetry, but it is in the typographical field that his professional interest created the most substantial impact. All his work in this area was of a high order. In his covers for issues of his journal *Merz* and elsewhere, he exploits the medium with restraint, preferring simplicity of outline, an unornamented typeface, heavy ruled lines, black-edged inserts, and—a favorite device—a block of type at right angles to the main direction of the text. The professionalism of these designs stands in stark contrast to the ineptitude of some of his "straight" poetry, particularly the later material written in England.[81] There is no doubt that Schwitters's technical skills were more visual than literary, particularly the skill of composition and the way in which the eye is guided clockwise round the covers of his *Merz* journal. The long contribution to *Der Sturm,* which bears the title **"Aufruf (ein Epos),"**[82] is a typical mixture of "straight" prose and such typographical experimentation.

Schwitters takes this experimentation a stage further in his stamp pictures, in which an impression of a section of type is employed as part of the design, similar in fashion to certain works by Max Ernst. In "The Critic" (1921),[83] a mixture of type impressions and line drawings presents a visual and verbal picture of a critic: his hair, for example, is composed of repeated impressions of "Der Sturm," and the words "Herwarth Walden" stream in a long line to or from one corner of the critic's mouth. Here Schwitters has arrived at a fusion between pictorial and written statement, a point at which the two are in such a state of balance that it is impossible to categorize the resultant work as either a drawing with typographical elements or a concrete poem with some line drawing.

In a sense, the visual has always tended to dominate with Schwitters: even in the case of the Stramm imitations, the poet was as much concerned with the physical shape of the poems as with their Futuristic rejection of the conventional restraints imposed upon language. The visual pattern generated by the written word often parallels and excites an aural response, as in this poem called **"Fury of Sneezing":**

Tesch, Haisch, Tschiiaa
   Haisch, Tschiiaa

          . . . . .

   Happapeppaisch
   Happapeppaisch
   Happa peppe
TSCHAA![84]

Although hardly a poetic masterpiece, this little poem clearly illustrates Schwitters's overriding concern with shapes and patterns and his avoidance of the inevitable personal and emotional associations generated by traditional lyrical poetry.

The sound poem, which Kreutzer rather tartly, but perhaps not wholly inaccurately, dismisses as a "Pyrrhic victory over language,"[85] has a fairly short pedigree. Although a variety of related forms can be traced back over several centuries,[86] Schwitters, together with Raoul Hausmann, must be regarded as one of the real innovators of this form.[87] A poem by Paul Scheerbart, dating from 1897,[88] and a similar one by Morgenstern, composed a few years later,[89] are frequently cited as standing at the head of the sound poem genealogical tree, but they are only isolated phenomena. The sound poem proper took shape under the influence of the Futurists and their call for the liberation of language from grammatical and syntactical restraints. It should, however, not be forgotten that many other Dadaists tinkered with this type of poetry. . . . Schwitters can also be regarded as a pioneer of concrete poetry, despite the fact that the general impression seems to be that the form did not exist before Eugen Gomringer.[90]

In all of these experimentations on the borderlines between different established art forms, Schwitters constantly pursues his aim of withdrawal from reality into a magical, charmed world in which the cares of the present are a tedious irrelevancy.

VII *Conclusion*

In an essay on Schwitters written shortly after his death, Arp records that he instilled meaning into life by "the metamorphosis of the visible and tangible world into the abstract and absolute."[91]

Schwitters's work is a retreat from reality into this private world of shapes and patterns. He was a true eccentric who lived for himself alone, utterly unorthodox in his conduct, yet constantly looking over his shoulder at the bourgeois world he so despised and sought to escape from. He was never at ease with officialdom and

bureaucracy, the visible exterior of the capitalist industrialized world. Themerson notes that Schwitters's "British passport was granted him on the day before he died."[92] It was certainly a document of little relevance to him; perhaps extracts from it might have found their way into one of his poems, or pieces of it into a picture.

NOTES

[1] S. Themerson, *Kurt Schwitters in England* (London, 1958), p. 10.

[2] Hans Arp, *Sinnende Flammen* (Zurich, 1961), p. 16. The lines referred to are "kleine niedliche Atombomben / für den Hausgebrauch."

[3] London, 1970.

[4] The catalogue is fully illustrated, contains illustrations of, and extracts from, Schwitters's work, and includes brief commentaries on his life and work by important critics in the field.

[5] W. Schmalenbach, *Kurt Schwitters* (Cologne, 1967), p. 11.

[6] Schmalenbach, p. 13.

[7] Käte T. Steinitz, *Kurt Schwitters. Erinnerungen aus den Jahren 1918-1930* (Zurich, 1963), p. 28.

[8] Steinitz, pp. 28-29.

[9] F. Lach, *Der Merz Künstler Kurt Schwitters* (Cologne, 1971), p. 14.

[10] See the discussion of this short story (for want of a better title) in the next section.

[11] See Lach, p. 24.

[12] Steinitz, p. 29.

[13] Lach, p. 26.

[14] For an account of *PIN* see J. Reichardt, "The Story of *PIN*," in R. Hausmann and K. Schwitters, *PIN* (London, 1962), pp. 2-18.

[15] *Der Sturm*, X, 99.

[16] *Der Sturm*, X, 99.

[17] "a little bit of soap too (Sunlight)," *Der Sturm*, X, 99.

[18] See Lach, pp. 88 ff.

[19] *Der Sturm*, X, 99.

[20] *Der Sturm*, X, 100-102.

[21] *Der Sturm*, X, 102.

[22] *Der Sturm,* X, 102-103.

[23] *Der Sturm,* X, 103.

[24] This is the name he gave his typewriter.

[25] *Der Sturm,* X, 99.

[26] *Der Sturm,* X, 35.

[27] *Der Sturm,* XI, 24.

[28] K. Schwitters, *Anna Blume und ich* (Zurich, 1965), p. 193.

[29] See Lach, pp. 85-89. As Lach points out, and as will be seen in the case of Arp, Schwitters is not alone in starting out by writing poems in the neo-Romantic vein. Even more striking is the gulf between the *avant-garde* visual works and the early paintings of a whole range of artists, from Schwitters to Ernst, Duchamp to Arp.

[30] This journal appeared in 1918-19. References subsequently given will be to issue number and page number (the pagination is separate for each issue).

[31] The poems in *Der Sturm* which are written after Stramm are concentrated in volume X, but continue up to volume XII.

[32] *August Stramm. Das Werk,* ed. R. Radrizzani (Wiesbaden, 1963), p. 86.

[33] *Der Sturm,* X, 140.

[34] *Der Sturm,* X, 35.

[35] For example, "Die Schwüle gleiât" ("Mairegen," p. 110); "wenden zagen schauen langen" ("Zwist," p. 22). There are also several references to the poem "Blüte," p. 29. Comparisons are based on *A Computer-Assisted Concordance to the Poetry of August Stramm,* ed. and compiled R. W. Last, Department of German, Hull University, 1972.

[36] P. 22.

[37] P. 34.

[38] *Der Zweemann,* No. 1 (1919), p. 18.

[39] *Der Zweemann,* No. 3 (1920), pp. 15-16.

[40] "Statt einer anonymen Kunst herrscht heute das berühmte Werk, das Meisterwerk." *Unsern täglichen Traum . . .* (Zurich, 1955), p. 80.

[41] M. S. Jones, "Kurt Schwitters, *Der Sturm* and Expressionism," *Modern Languages,* LII (1971), 159.

[42] *Der Zweemann,* No. 1, p. 18; *Der Sturm,* X, 60.

[43] "Der Künstler schafft durch Wahl, Verteilung und Entformung der Materialien."

[44] *Der Sturm,* X, 76.

[45] R. Hausmann, *Am Anfang war Dada,* ed. K. Riha and G. Kämpf (Steinbach, 1972), p. 66.

[46] Hausmann, p. 64. He also states "Er war im Innersten unverletzbar und unangreifbar" (p. 68).

[47] *Der Sturm,* X, 72.

[48] Now reissued, edited by Ernst Schwitters, under the title *Anna Blume und ich* (Zurich, 1965).

[49] C. Heselhaus, *Deutsche Lyrik der Moderne* (Düsseldorf, 1961), p. 319.

[50] P. Thomson, "A Case of Dadaistic Ambivalence: Kurt Schwitters's *Stramm-Imitations* and 'An Anna Blume,'" *German Quarterly,* XLV (1972), 52.

[51] Thomson, p. 47 and p. 48, respectively.

[52] J. C. Middleton, "Pattern without Predictability, or: Pythagoras Saved. A Comment on Kurt Schwitters's 'Gedicht 25,'" *German Life and Letters, NS* XXII (1969-70), 349.

[53] C. Giedion-Welcker, *Anthologie der Abseitigen. Poètes à l'Ecart* (Zurich, 1965), pp. 169-70.

[54] Schmalenbach, pp. 214-15.

[55] Lach, p. 99.

[56] Lach, p. 102.

[57] Compare Ball's poem "Totenklage," which is discussed in the Ball chapter in the section "The secret Alchemy of the Word."

[58] *Der Sturm,* XIII, 158-66.

[59] For this and other versions, see the excellent bibliography in Schmalenbach, pp. 381 ff.

[60] J. Elderfield, "Schwitters's abstract 'Revolution,'" *GLL, NS* XXIV (1970-71), 256. This article concludes with a diagram of the structure of the *Revolution in Revon.*

[61] Schwitters did, in fact, write and illustrate his own *Märchen* for children. See Lach, pp. 140-41.

[62] *Der Sturm,* XIII, 159.

[63] *Der Sturm,* XIII, 160.

[64] *Der Sturm,* XIII, 162.

[65] *Der Sturm,* XIII, 162-63.

[66] *Der Sturm,* XIII, 165.

[67] *Der Sturm,* XIII, 166.

[68] Elderfield, p. 257.

[69] *Jean Arp. Jours effeuillés,* ed. Marcel Jean (Paris, 1966), p. 62.

[70] They are a play on "Summe" and "summen," *Der Sturm,* XIII, 162; and "PRA" (anagram of Arp), *Der Sturm,* XIII, 164 f.

[71] *Der Sturm,* XI, 3.

[72] Elderfield, p. 260.

[73] Published by the Sturm Verlag in 1923.

[74] See Lach, pp. 158-77.

[75] *Der Sturm,* X, 61.

[76] *Der Sturm,* X, 140.

[77] *Kurt Schwitters. Anna Blume und ich,* ed. Ernst Schwitters (Zurich, 1965), p. 182.

[78] J. C. Middleton, 348. See also the commentary on this article: M. McClain, "Kurt Schwitters's 'Gedicht 25': a musicological Addendum," *GLL, NS* XXIII (1969-70), 268-70.

[79] *Anna Blume und ich,* p. 190.

[80] See, for example, *Der Sturm,* XI, 2 ff.

[81] See Themerson, pp. 43 ff.

[82] *Der Sturm,* XII, 201-4.

[83] *Der Sturm,* XIII, 71.

[84] *PIN,* p. 34.

[85] H. Kreuzer, "Exkurs über die Bohème," in *Deutsche Literatur im zwanzigsten Jahrhundert I, loc. cit.,* p. 231.

[86] A. Liede, *Dichtung als Spiel II* (Berlin, 1965), pp. 221-25.

[87] See the chapter "Zur Geschichte des Lautgedichtes" in Hausmann, pp. 35-43.

[88] The poem is entitled "Kikakokú!" and appears in P. Scheerbart, *Ich liebe Dich!* (Berlin, 1897), p. 249.

[89] The poem is entitled "Das groâe Lalul " and was published in C. Morgenstern, *Galgenlieder* (Berlin, 1905), p. 9.

[90] Gomringer is supposedly "the acknowledged father of Concrete poetry" (E. Williams, *An Anthology of Concrete Poetry* [New York, 1967], p. vi); but another anthology does not briefly in the direction of Schwitters and also mentions Arp as a possible ancestor of Gomringer (S. Bann *Concrete Poetry. An International Anthology* [London, 1967], pp. 7-27).

[91] *Jours effeuillés,* p. 334.

[92] Themerson, p. 27.

Rex W. Last (review date 1975)

SOURCE: "One Man's Merz," in *The Times Literary Supplement,* No. 3808, February 28, 1975, p. 231.

[*In the following review, Last describes Schwitters's short prose works "Die Zwiebel" and "Franz Müllers Drahtfrühling."*]

Like many of that generation of the European avant-garde associated with Dada and Surrealism, Kurt Schwitters worked in several artistic media and sought to break down the barriers between the different art forms, and also between what convention deemed to be "art" and "non-art". Although something of a loner, in that he did not join any large group of artists, but preferred to work in relative isolation, cultivating "Merz", his own brand of Dada, Schwitters's work broadly follows a pattern typical of his breed of artistic revolutionary: he painted, sculpted, produced collages, typographical designs, sound and concrete poems—and also prose. This last may come as something of a surprise.

Among the other Dadaists continuous prose is a rare phenomenon, but Schwitters made extensive excursions into the field, and with a fair degree of success. This second volume of ***Das literarische Werk,*** which covers the period 1918-30, does contain items which scarcely fall within the accepted terms of reference of a "prose work", but there are also many tales which seek to convey Schwitters's highly personal world view through the medium of narrative fiction.

It is unfortunate that these short stories should be so little known—the visual extravaganzas create a more immediate impact and cross language barriers with consummate ease, thereby generating a very one-sided view of Schwitters the creative artist—particularly since they reveal him much more clearly than in the visual work as far more than a childlike (and at times, childish) creator of idle fantasies. In his prose tales he comes across as a thoughtful, capable writer with the ability to combine the Dadaist pun with his own Merz techniques, sustaining them through a developing action in order to make a much more complex and powerful "point" than can be achieved by a collage or a few lines of verse.

Some of his verbal vandalism is trifling and tedious, and the narrative situations can be repetitive and trivial, but at the same time he cannot be dismissed as a mere dabbler in words, toying with the Novelle and fairytale conventions to his own arbitrary and private ends, as his two most important prose works, both short stories, demonstrate. **"Die Zwiebel"** and **"Franz Müllers Drahtfrühling"** first appeared in the pages of the Expressionist periodical *Der Sturm*. In both, Schwitters makes lavish use of a wide range of styles, from Stramm-like compressed Expressionistic language to the simplicity of the children's fairytale, and of his Merz technique of incorporating into the artistic construct various discarded items from the world about him: in his visual work, he would include in his collages used bus tickets, pieces of newspaper, wrappings, scraps of wood, along with other less savoury items, and in his prose he employs fragments of advertisements, notices, clichés and proverbial utterances. These are embedded in the text in an apparently random fashion in order to disrupt and deflate the suspension of disbelief and the narrative flow. In the visual works, the result is often confused and lacking in specific direction but in the prose works these linguistic *objets trouvés* are subordinated to the main thread of the action in a way which concentrates, rather than dissipates, the impact of the text.

"Die Zwiebel" takes a rather nasty delight in describing in a first-person narrative an execution—the narrator being the victim—which reaches its climax at the moment when the prisoner has been killed and his body is being carved up for a variety of purposes. Then, suddenly, the action goes into reverse, like a film running backwards through the gate:

> They began to put me together again. First my eyes were popped gently back into their sockets. (Be not afraid, Faith, Love, Hope are the stars.) Then my entrails were fetched. Fortunately, nothing had been cooked yet nor cut up for sausages. (Vaincu, mais non dompté.) Still, people are happy when the harvest is good.

In the end, the *status quo ante* is more or less restored, except that the narrator has lost some blood and the odd shred of flesh, and the king, who is one of the witnesses, dies. In a somewhat tongue-in-cheek fashion, the socialist revolution is proclaimed.

"Franz Müllers Drahtfrühling" is also concerned with revolution, but in this case the central figure, who represents the creative artist or anyone who refuses to become caught up in the aimless bustle of contemporary life, causes first unease, then sensation, and finally uproar by actually standing still and not wishing to move. This affront against public decency stings those who gather round into an increasingly frenzied response, until the man suddenly walks away:

> Then the most shocking thing of all happened. Slowly, and with the composure of a perfect machine, the man started to walk off, greeting all

those about him in a friendly manner, not with the policeman, but in the opposite direction. The women scream, the men are astonished beyond bounds, the children run yelling.

At the end, a hunchback youth runs through the streets proclaiming the outbreak of the glorious revolution.

Like all the Dadaists, Schwitters was repelled by the arrogant self-assertiveness of contemporary man and sought to pillory the narrow materialist aspirations of the society of his day. In these prose works, he employs satire both to point the finger of scorn and also to suggest the direction in which an alternative world might lie. Fantastical and self-indulgent Schwitters's work may be; the tone is none the less fundamentally serious in intent and sincere in its moral objective.

The preceding volume of Schwitters's verse was chastised for falling short of the highest standards of editorial accuracy (*TLS,* October 5, 1973), and this second volume is regrettably not without blemish. The very first item, **"Die Zwiebel"**, six pages in length, contains in its footnotes sixteen omissions with regard to variants, and two misprints. This cannot help but cast further doubt on the quality of the editing.

Annegreth Nill (essay date 1984)

SOURCE: "Weimar Politics and the Theme of Love in Kurt Schwitters' *Das Baumerbild*," in *Dada/Surrealism,* No. 13, 1984, pp. 17-36.

[In the following essay, Nill interprets Schwitters's assemblage Das Bäumerbild *in the context of post-World War I German politics, finding in the work symbols of love and war.]*

While the Hanover Dadaist Kurt Schwitters vociferously rejected using art as political propaganda, he did not reject the use of political propaganda in art, as countless political phrases which function as "material" in his literary works attest.[1] For example, in his prose poem **"Aufruf (ein Epos)"** (1921), Schwitters spliced together newspaper fragments, often overfly political, and lines from his sensational love poem **"An Anna Blume"** (1919):

> O du, Geliebte meiner siebenundzwanzig Sinne,
>   ich liebe dir!
> Du deiner dich dir, ich dir du mir.—Wir?
> (Die letzte Kraftanspannung der Bolschewisten.)
> Sechs Zugbeamte wurden verletzt, darunter drei
> erheblich, und immer wieder erscholl der Ruf:
> "Hoch Hindenburg!" und "Hoch Ludendorff" und
> "Nieder mit der Reaktion"! (Das gehört beiläufig
> nicht hierher.)[2]

> O thou beloved of my twenty-seven senses, I love thine!
> Thou thee thee thine, I thine, thou mine.—We?
> (The last effort of the Bolsheviks.)
> Six train officials were injured, three of them
> seriously, and again and again the cry rang out:

"Hail Hindenburg!" and "Hail Ludendorff" and
    "Down with reaction"! (That by the way does
    not belong here.)

Juxtaposing right-wing ("Hoch Hindenburg!") and left-wing ("Nieder mit der Reaktion") parlance succeeds in both raising the emotional pitch of the epic poem and in establishing its antithetical method.

During the turbulent early phase of the Weimar Republic, political rhetoric also found its way into Schwitters' visual works. One of these is the small but intriguing assemblage entitled *Das Bäumerbild* (1920), which, like *"Aufruf,"* places the theme of love into a political context.[3] Although *Das Bäumerbild* has escaped the attention of Schwitters scholars until now, it yields valuable new information on Schwitters' attitudes toward his subject matter, the artistic process and politics generally.

As will become evident presently, Schwitters was quite aware of the political situation in post-World-War-I Germany. However, it will also become clear that he was first and foremost an artist who was intent on creating works of art with lasting values, no matter how fleeting or topical his materials. Thus, a discussion of Schwitters' political stance at the time falls outside the scope of this essay.[4]

Schwitters' "Bilder" or "pictures" usually received their titles from some key word or image within the work—in a kind of synecdochic or part-for-whole relationship. The ambitious *Das Arbeiterbild* ("Worker Picture") (1919), for instance, derives its name from the word "Arbeiter" printed in red letters and prominently incorporated into the work. Similarly, *Das Bäumerbild* was named after the man in the photograph, the writer Ludwig Bäumer (1888-1928).[5] This makes the work in one sense a "Merz-portrait," Schwitters' term for a portrait created by the artistic manipulation of nonartistic materials. A comparison of the assemblage to Christian Schad's Neue Sachlichkeit portrait of Ludwig Bäumer (1927) reveals how radically Schwitters departs, on the formal level, from the conventional oil portrait. Schad's representation alludes to Bäumer's erotic nature through the orchid and to his refractory, fragmented state of mind by means of the faceted background. These two characterizations of the writer will also be found in Schwitters' work.

The word "Bäumer" itself has a general connotation, which derives from the expressionist-poetic concentration ("Ballung") of the phrase "einer der sich aufbäumt" ("someone who rebels"). Bäumer himself attributed this meaning to the word in the last line of his poem *The Last Judgment:*

Wir sind gegeben, dass wir Erde beben
    Machen Gott Garten Eden, dem wir Bäumer sind.[6]
    We are charged to shake the earth
    to create God's garden, Eden, being rebels.

Thus the ambiguity of the title *Das Bäumerbild* sets the scene both for a general reading of the work, which can be accomplished without knowing the identity of the man in the photograph, and for a more specific reading, which emerges by identifying the two figures and exploring their relationships to each other and to their context.

To create a work of art with multiple levels of meaning, Schwitters combined verbal and visual elements into a complementary whole, as he had done in 1918 in his earliest extant collage, *Zeichnung A2: Hansi,*[7] where a chocolate wrapper provides both a compositional and verbal basis for the work. In *Das Bäumerbild,* the drama unfolds on top of a political broadside realistically tacked onto a board. The image or symbolic object that functions as the visual key to this work, as the cross had done in *Hansi,* is the centrally located table, schematically drawn with heavy black lines on top of the broadside. A black-rimmed red circle and a somewhat faded photograph of flowers create a Cubist-type still life in the plane of the table. Directly beneath it Schwitters has written in cursive script the articles "das" and "der."

The cropped photograph of a man in uniform who gazes intensely out of the picture partially overlaps the table on the left; the man's stick-figure body recalls Schwitters' watercolor drawings of the period. He appears to be holding a red triangle at waist height, and he has a black button-like object attached to his chest. On the right, the table is flanked by a woman whose head and hand holding a flower are also rendered photographically. Her skirt, somewhat displaced to the right, is made up of a red hoodlike shape and newspaper fragments. A tax stamp, pieces of stamp selvage, and a black square add a constructivist quality to a work that appears almost painterly in its richness, an effect partially created by the Gothic script and the green stains in the area around the female figure.

The verbal key to the work, which is insistently pointed out by another red triangle, is the phrase "Vereinigung für ("union for") printed in large, boldface black letters at the bottom of the broadside. Like the word "ade" in *Hansi,* "Vereinigung für" has a double meaning.[8] Its public connotation derives from the partially obscured name of the association that published the broadside "Vereinigung für den Rechtsfrieden" ("Association for a Just Peace"). Its other connotation involves Schwitters' manipulation of the above phrase to read "Vereinigung für . . . eden": thus, the word "eden" is created by truncation from "Frieden," as "ade" was created from "Schokolade."

Weimar Politics in the Context of the Treaty of Versailles

In *Das Bäumerbild* only the man in uniform alludes directly to World War I. But the message of the "Vereinigung für Rechtsfrieden" must be read in relation to the consequences of that war.[9] The broadside's polemic can be reconstructed from a few salient words and phrases that Schwitters left uncovered. Its major subject is peace, as the word "Frieden" appears three times in the text: in the upper righthand corner, directly under the revealing word "Frankreich"; between the man's legs on the left, above which the words "entschiedenen" and "[u]ns weig[ern]"; and underneath the table, partially obscured by the words in cursive and prefaced by the word "[uner]träglichen." This seems to add up to a rejection of an unacceptable peace treaty. But by the same token an appeal is made for "unser Volk" to be patient ("Stunde heisst Geduld"), and not to allow insurrections ("Putsche dürfen uns nicht . . . den wahren") to ruin the chances for a true peace.[10]

These urgent issues, and that of "Rechtsfrieden," had been considered in the debate surrounding the Paris Peace Conference, which began on January 18, 1919. World War I had ended in 1918 with the unexpected and disastrous defeat of Germany, which had transformed it from an empire into an uncertain republic under the tentative leadership of the Majority Socialist party. This new government found itself in the awkward position of having to negotiate the peace terms of a war for which it had been only indirectly responsible.[11] On June 28 at the conclusion of the Paris Peace Conference, under considerable duress, the Germans signed the treaty at Versailles, the very place where Wilhelm I had arranged his coronation as emperor of Germany in 1871 in the wake of the Franco-Prussian War.

In 1920, the year of *Das Bäumerbild* and in response to the Versailles Treaty, Schwitters produced a collage, *Merzzeichnung 170,* which indicts the Majority Socialists of Berlin by cleverly insinuating that "Versaille[s]" belongs to them. The newspaper clipping of May 13, 1919, reports a mass gathering on the "Königsplatz" in support of the already lost "Rechtsfrieden."[12] The work's title, *Leere im Raum* ("Void in Space"), expresses the total despair of the situation. The Majority Socialists and the political right most vociferously invoked the concept of "Rechtsfrieden" against Article 231, the "Kriegsschuldthese" ("war-guilt clause"), which placed the responsibility for the war solely on Germany. This clause was perceived as a violation of the Wilsonian armistice agreement, which would have allowed Germany to pay reparations without a guilt clause.

In *Das Bäumerbild* Schwitters addresses the Versailles issue with less pathos and more irony. Visually, he symbolizes the Paris Peace Negotiations, which produced the unacceptable document, by the centrally placed conference table. Directly beneath the table the phrase "[uner]träglichen Frieden" creates a visual-verbal pun on an insupportable peace, induced by the (super)imposed "articles."

In the context of the Paris Peace Negotiations, however, the concept of a conference table at which opposing parties sit down to negotiate their differences was highly ironic, since the Allies, especially the "big four," France, England, the United States, and Italy (referred to as "Allierten" and "vierm[ächte]" in the newspaper fragment on the bottom right and perhaps symbolized by the black square), indeed sat around the conference table to discuss their ever-increasing demands ("Die Forderung immer mehr") for reparations ("Die Wiedergut[machungen]"), but

they never invited the German delegation to join them. Instead, the "negotiations" consisted of a series of notes or memoranda (mentioned in the newspaper fragment on the right). The cover-notes of the final written exchange achieved notoriety under the term "Mantelnoten." The German "mantle note" of May 28 was a reply to the May 7th draft of the Allied treaty that had caused the original uproar. On June 16th the Allies replied with a "mantle note" of their own, which severely reprimanded the Germans for questioning Article 231 and other matters.[13] In keeping with Schwitters' visual-verbal manipulations, the "skirt" or "mantle" of the female figure doubles as a "mantle note," because it is composed of a series of newspaper notices or notes that refer to the negotiations.

Schwitters also casts doubt more directly on the validity of the conference table by giving it a prominent green leg. This is a pointed reference to the German saying "etwas vom grünen Tisch aus entscheiden" ("to rule something from a green table"), which is a figurative way of alluding to decision-making based on theoretical considerations rather than on the reality of a situation.

Even the meaning of the female figure is perverted. As a veritable personification of peace, she holds and smells a flower, and is surrounded by the fresh green of hope and associated with the word "Frieden." But upon closer examination, Schwitters may be seen to have manipulated a word directly above her flower, which reads as "rüchig" followed by the word "Frankreich." This pungent commentary refers to the peace, negotiated with and in France, land of perfumes, as "stinking."

As noted earlier, a warning against allowing insurrections ("Putsche") to interfere with obtaining genuine peace is the other message of the broadsheet. Even as the Allies negotiated in Paris, many German cities were in a state of civil war. The Social Democrats supported the concept of parliamentary democracy and called for elections for a national assembly on January 19, 1919. For taking this pro-parliamentary position the party was regarded as having betrayed the ideals of the November Revolution by the protocommunist Spartacists and the Independent Socialists, who sought to radicalize the worker and soldier councils that had formed spontaneously during November, 1918, and to establish soviet republics ("Räterepubliken").[14] They were successful in creating temporary but true soviet republics in Bremen and Munich, but most attempts remained on the level of putsches. All leftist revolutionary activity was quickly put down by the government's defense minister, Noske, with the help of the infamous "Freikorps" ("free corps"). These threats of "Bolshevism" did not go unnoticed by the Allies, who were further alarmed by the developments in central Europe. Although the German government attempted to use the Allies' fear of communism to obtain a more favorable treaty, it also felt obligated to put down any insurrection from the left.[15]

The warning expressed in the broadside includes all these developments. To complement the female personification of "Frieden" in *Das Bäumerbild,* Schwitters gave visual expression to the violent overthrow of the government by a male personification of "Putsch." Instead of a flower, his attribute is a bomb, frequently a sign of anarchy. The bomb's smoky effluvium is directed toward the state, represented by the tax stamp in the upper left corner and by the postage stamp selvage just below it.[16] The black and red colors associated with the figure bespeak death and violence.

In 1919 the Russian artist El Lissitzky used a red wedge and a white circle to represent the conflict between the Bolsheviks and the counterrevolutionaries in his famous poster *Beat the Whites with the Red Wedge*.[17] Similarly, by using red triangles Schwitters is commenting on the causes and consequences of the military-controlled counterrevolution known as the "Kapp-Putsch."[18] The small red wedge near "Putsch's" waist is aimed across the table at the red and black hoodlike object, or "Kappe," on the "right." A larger red wedge, emanating from the direction of the "hood," hovers threateningly over the "Vereinigung" ("union").

The military leadership had tried to exonerate itself for its vast defeat in 1918 by blaming the revolution at home. This tactic sought to make the revolutionaries directly responsible for the Treaty of Versailles, which had punished the military particularly severely by demanding drastic reductions in the armed forces. In March, 1920, a small group of military leaders attempted a coup d'etat, which became known as the "Kapp-Putsch" after the name of one of its leaders. The defenseless government fled the capital and called for a general strike by the workers, which effectively ended the takeover. The successful workers, however, recalling their earlier revolutionary activities, began a new revolt centered primarily in the industrial Ruhr district. Again the government stepped in, and at its behest the uprising was crushed by the military, the very forces from whom the workers had earlier saved the government.[19] Small wonder that "Treu[e]" ("loyalty") is in a tenuous position, caught as it is between the table and the "Kappe," symbolizing respectively the Treaty of Versailles and the counterrevolution. Schwitters sums up the transitory nature of political power by invoking the German proverb "ein Keil treibt den andern" which, substituting "wedge" ["Keil"] for the nail in the analogous English proverb, translates idiomatically as "one nail drives out another."

Schwitters has thus created a political portrait of the Weimar Republic in the context of the Paris Peace Negotiations through a sophisticated interplay of verbal and visual elements. The table with the still life of the "green" flowers of peace and the black-rimmed red circle, echoing the bomb of "Putsch," succinctly summarizes the content of peace and violence in a part-for-whole relationship. One is tempted to call *Das Bäumerbild* on this level a "history painting" entitled, according to Schwitters' sense for reversals, *The Consequences of Peace*.

Love and Strife in Worpswede and Bremen

The key to the other level of content of *Das Bäumerbild* is the identity of the two figures and their relationship to each other. But another important element in its meaning is Bäumer's political involvement with the Bremen Soviet Republic, which serves as a case history for the themes of revolution and peace, and therefore links the public and private levels of the work's meaning.

Although the Schwitters literature is silent concerning the name Ludwig Bäumer, one has not far to look in the circles of the Hanover avant-garde to identify him as the author of *Das Wesen des Kommunismus* ("The Nature of Communism"), published in 1919 as Nos. 25-26 in the "radikale Bücherreihe" (radical book series) Die Silbergäule of Paul Steegemann Verlag. Steegemann, who had fought on the barricades in Hanover during the November Revolution of 1918, had also published works by and about his friend Kurt Schwitters, including the famous *Anna Blume Dichtungen* (Die Silbergäule, 39-40). Perhaps one can assume that Paul Steegemann played a role in the Bäumer-Schwitters association.[20]

Schwitters depicts his friend in *Das Bäumerbild* with a bomb and places him in a context of political strife. Such a portrayal has a certain basis in fact. When, on January 10, 1919, the Socialist Republic of Bremen was proclaimed with music and red flags, Ludwig Bäumer, a member of the communist party, had been one of nine men voted into the "Rat der Volksbeauftragten" ("Council of the Peoples' Representatives").[21] His position of responsibility, however, was short-lived: by February 4th, the strong right arm of the socialist government, Noske, had crushed the "Räterepublik."[22] Thirty workers and soldiers lost their lives and Bäumer landed in jail.

A proclamation ("Aufruf!") by the majority Socialists describes the Bremen Soviet Republic from their ruling perspective:

> Dieser Miss- und Gewaltherrschaft war es vorbehalten, das erste Blutvergiessen in Bremen heraufzubeschwören. Damit nicht genug, haben sich die Gewalthaber offen gegen die Reichsregierung aufgelehnt, unbekümmert um die Gefärdung der deutschen Einheit, *unbekümmert darum, dass unsere Feinde einem bolschewistischen Deutschland weder Frieden noch Brot gewähren werden*, unbekümmert auch um die Zukunft Bremens, das vom In-und-Ausland als Hochburg des Terrors, als Feind der Freiheit geächtet, dem wirtschaftlichen Untergang entgegen ging. . . . [23]

> This false and totalitarian rule was left to precipitate the first bloodshed in Bremen. Not satisfied with that, the ruling power openly rebelled against the Federal Government, *indifferent to the fact that our enemies will grant neither peace nor bread to a Bolshevik Germany,* unconcerned also for the future of Bremen, which, proscribed at home and abroad as a stronghold of terror and enemy of freedom, was headed for economic ruin. . . .

This sensitivity to the opinions of the "Feinde" ("enemies"), i.e., the Allies meeting in Paris, helped defeat the revolution. The Bremen Soviet Republic had the added liability that Bremen was a port city; after the war, when the entire German population depended absolutely on food imports for survival, the Berlin government exerted itself to keep Bremen and other key ports out of the hands of the "reds."

Although in *Das Bäumerbild* Schwitters gave Bäumer the attribute of a bomb, it was obviously only symbolic of his involvement in the Bremen revolution and of his syndicalist and left communist leanings.[24] Bäumer's real weapon was the word, written or spoken. He had won notoriety for preserving the unity of the communist party in a crisis by making a fiery speech, and he anticipated great results from his Marxist polemic *Das Wesen des Kommunismus.*[25] In his introduction to the work written in jail, Bäumer thanks the postrevolutionary Socialist government of Bremen for providing him with the leisure to formulate his ideas and for thus helping to bring about its own demise.

> Ein kurzer aber darum nicht weniger ehrlicher Dank sei hier ausgesprochen der Bremischen Regierung und dem Walten ihres herkulischen Armes der Stadtkommandantur. Meine unter Beugung allen bestehenden Rechts erfolgte Verhaftung und Verhängung einer wochenlangen Schutzhaft hat mir die Musse, Ruhe und Geschlossenheit nicht gefunden in der aufreibenden Arbeit meiner auswärten Propaganda. Hilft also dies unter "gütiger, selbstloser" Mitwirkung Allerhöchster Bremischer Stellen entstandene Werk die Klärung revolutionärer proletarischer Bestrebungen bringen, so hilft as auch an der Beseitigung "Allerhöchstderselben" Stellen und ihrer brutalen Vergewaltigungen. So verhelfen sich diese Allerhöchstdieselben Regierungsstellen letzten Endes selbst zu ihrem Schicksal eines gerechten Zusammenbruchs. Grund genug zu danken.
>
> Bremen, Schutzhaft—Worpswede
>
> Ludwig Bäumer[26]

> Brief, but not for that any less sincere gratitude is here expressed to the government of Bremen and the sway of its herculean arm of the garrison headquarters. My arrest and condemnation to weeks of preventive detention, which resulted from the bending of all existing laws, provided me with the leisure, peace, and unity of thought I needed to compose the present text. I would not have found this leisure, peace, and unity while engaged in the demanding work of my outward-bound propaganda. If this work, created with the "charitable, self-sacrificing" cooperation of the supreme authorities of Bremen, helps to bring about a clarification of revolutionary proletarian aspirations, it will also help to bring about the elimination of the "most high" authorities and their brutal oppression. These most high ruling authorities thus finally procure their own fate of a justified collapse. Reason enough for thanks.
>
> Bremen, Preventive Detention—Worpswede
>
> Ludwig Bäumer

Although in fact he languished in preventive detention in Bremen, Bäumer gives his address as "Worpswede," known to the art world as an idyllic artists' colony that had flourished around the turn of the century in the moors outside Bremen. Artists who sought the simplicity of country life, such as Fritz Mackensen, Otto Modersohn, Fritz Overbeck, Hans am Ende, and Heinrich Vogeler were associated with it, as well as the now well-known Paula Modersohn-Becker and, as poet in residence, Rainer Maria Rilke. The Barkenhoff, the beautiful Biedermeier home of the Jugendstil master Heinrich Vogeler, provided an appropriate setting for the group. Vogeler captured the somewhat elegiac mood of those days in his painting of 1905 entitled *Sommerabend (Konzert auf dem Barkenhoff),* which depicts his wife, Martha, standing alone in the center framed by friends listening to and playing music.

It is less well known that after the war Worpswede became the experimental communist community of a group of "Edelkommunisten."[27] Again, the Barkenhoff provided the locus and Heinrich Vogeler the soul of the movement. Many came to hear what Heinrich Vogeler had to say, although the message, brotherly love and mutual aid, sounded more like the Sermon on the Mount than a communist manifesto.[28] Kurt Schwitters was among the visitors to Worpswede at this time.[29]

Heinrich Vogeler later recorded his feelings about the old Barkenhoff with a certain amount of nostalgia:

> Zwanzig Jahre hatte ich wohl an einer Heimat gebaut. Und sie bekam Gestalt als innigste Umwelt einer Frau und ihrer Kinder. Haus, Zimmer und Garten waren aus der Wildernis zu einem kleinen fruchttragenden Paradies erwachsen. Mein Pflug hatte den unberührten Heideboden umgeworfen, meine Hände hatten die Saat zum Keimen versenkt, mit den Kindern hatte ich Bäume und schattige Plätze gepflanzt; Fremde kamen und nahmen teil an unserem Legen. Feste bereitete ich ihnen, konnte sid aber selber nicht feiern. . . . [30]

> I had worked at the creation of a home for perhaps twenty years. It took the shape of the intimate surroundings of a woman and her children. House, chamber, and garden had grown from wilderness into a small, fertile paradise. My plow had turned over the untouched soil, my hands had sunk the seed for sprouting, with the children I had planted trees and shady places; strangers came and shared in our life. I organized festivals for them, but could not celebrate them myself. . . .

Vogeler turned the Barkenhoff into a "paradise," giving every detail his careful attention. This "Gesamtkunstwerk" ("total work of art") even included a girl from the village, Martha Schröder, whom Vogeler carefully groomed to be his wife and muse. The idyll lasted until 1909, when the young, somewhat unstable, aimless law student Ludwig Bäumer arrived and stayed. He and Martha fell in love. And, rather than lose his inspiration and his three daughters completely, Vogeler tacitly allowed Bäumer to live on the Barkenhoff estate.[31]

Without question, Martha Vogeler and Ludwig Bäumer were deeply attracted to one another. Although through Heinrich Vogeler's encouragement Martha had learned to appreciate the finer things in life, she always remained close to the earth, natural and uncomplicated. Bäumer's directness appears to have been better suited to her temperament than was Vogeler's tentative nature. Through Bäumer she experienced love for the first time and abandoned herself to it. Older than he, she could provide him with a refuge for his restless, searching soul. On his part, Bäumer needed to feel that Martha belonged to him. The feeling of possession gave him strength, as he wrote her in a letter: "Das Gefühl, dass Du zu mir gehörst, dass Du an mich gekettet bist, wie mit tausend Fäden, das macht mich immer von neuem stark, froh und glücklich. . . ."[32] ("The feeling that you belong to me, that you are chained to me as with a thousand bonds, makes me again and again strong, glad, and happy.")

There is little doubt that the woman whose photograph appears in *Das Bäumerbild* is Martha Vogeler. The resemblance between the photograph of Martha Schröder taken years earlier at an amateur performance and the woman in *Das Bäumerbild* is convincing, when one allows for the age difference of about twenty years. Furthermore, the setting into which the figure has been placed, the flowers and the green, suggests the Barkenhoff, although Schwitters surely also used them symbolically. Martha's attribute in this context is a symbol of love: "Flower," after all, is the last name of the protagonist of Schwitters' famous love poem *"An Anna Blume.* And green, not red, is the color of love in German folksongs, as Schwitters also seems to know. Anna Blume's admirer loves her both "red" and "green."

Das Bäumerbild thus becomes an homage to Ludwig and Martha's love. United as they are in the picture, Schwitters makes the point verbally as well, by directing attention to the word "Vereinigung." The "union" is for "eden" Schwitters decrees, and underlines the word created from "Frieden" in orange-red. "Eden" on one level clearly refers to the Barkenhoff, the lovers' home until 1921/22. But on another level, Schwitters is probably referring to the "natural state" of their relationships, a condition opposed to the state-sanctioned matrimonial bond, as perhaps indicated by the stamp selvage running above their heads, which unites the lovers visually.

In 1914, inspired by his love for Martha and possibly piqued by a certain amount of guilt for not being able to make her his legal wife, Bäumer wrote what amounts to a diatribe against marriage. In "Das imaginäre Porträt eines 25 jährigen" ("The Imaginary Portrait of a 25-Year-Old"), he calls marriage an erotic relationship and concludes, therefore, that every erotic relationship is a marriage.

> Die Ehe ist ein erotisches Verhältnis, und da der Egoismus die Moral der Erotik ist, so hat die staatliche Ehe mit der wirklichen Ehe nur dann mehr als den Namen gemeinsam, wenn sie ausschliesslich auf erotischen Egoismus aufgebaut ist. Erlischt der sexuelle Wille zweier Ehegatten einseitig oder gleichzeitig zu einander, so hört die Ehe auf zu existieren, und dies Aufhören macht die Staatliche Institution sofort unmoralisch . . .

> Die Ehe ist ein erotisches Verhältnis. Die Schlussfolgerun, dass jedes erotische Verhältnis eine Ehe ist, liegt also nahe und ist eine Tatsache, die nicht zu wiederlegen ist. Und somit erledigt sich der Ehebruch als eine haltlose Fiktion.[33]

> Marriage is an erotic relationship, and as egotism governs the morals of eroticism, marriage sanctioned by the state shares with true marriage more than the name only, when it is exclusively based on erotic egotism. If the sexual pleasure of the two spouses extinguishes on one side or simultaneously on both, the marriage ceases to exist, and this cessation immediately causes the civil institution to become immoral . . .

> Marriage is an erotic relationship. The conclusion that every erotic relationship is a marriage is obvious and a fact which cannot be denied. And thus the concept of adultery discharges itself as an untenable fiction.

Six years later, under similar circumstances, Heinrich Vogeler too was inspired to advocate free love publicly. His pamphlet *Die Freiheit der Liebe in der kommunistischen Gesellschaft* (1920) is dedicated to his lover Marie Griesbach, "die rote Marie" from Dresden, who taught Vogeler that to be pure, love must be free of possessive feelings with regard to the loved one.[34]

Exactly those feelings of possessiveness had caused Vogeler so much suffering when Ludwig Bäumer drove a wedge between him and Martha, as suggested by the threatening aspect of the large red wedge over the "Vereinigung" in *Das Bäumerbild.* But Schwitters' use of the proverb "ein Keil treibt den anderen" also gains new currency in this context, since Bäumer displaced Vogeler as Martha's lover. The small red wedge immediately below Bäumer's photograph has unmistakable sexual connotations here. The analogy to the succession of political takeovers discussed earlier is clear and helps to form a link between the public and the private content of the work. The fact that the small wedge is pointing across the table at the word "Treu[e]" ("fidelity"), left showing on the broadside in the area of Martha's waist, adds a certain instability to the virtue of constancy. Fidelity is relativized, if not made the object of irony.

The table, which in the general, political context of the work represented a questionable conference table, also figures in the more private meaning of the assemblage. The table at once physically separates the lovers and symbolizes their union, according to the general expression "Tisch und Bett miteinander teilen" ("to share bed and board").[35] And one could say that the original table setting emblematic of peace and violence has been overlaid with love and passion.

But Schwitters also puts his formal cards on the table by causing this *Tafel,* a word which in German means both "table" and "picture," to stand, by synecdoche, for the work in which it appears. By unifying the geometric circle and the organic flowers on the "Tafel," he is uniting abstract and representational forms, the two elements with which he composed his work. Finally, in its celebration of the union of opposites, *Das Bäumerbild* becomes a metaphor for the union of form and content.[36]

Schwitters' portrait of Ludwig Bäumer is one of passion and rebellion. So when he places Bäumer in the company of Martha Vogeler personified as Love, and clearly states that their union is for Eden, is he alluding to the classical myth so popular during the Renaissance of strife and love begetting harmony? If so, the creator of Anna Blume and Franz Müller has succeeded in creating a fresh icon of Mars and Venus, timeless symbols of war and love.

NOTES

[1] Schwitters clarifies his position vis-à-vis art as politics through his distinction between the Kern- and the Huelsen-dadaists in "Merz," *Der Ararat* 2 (1921), 3-9. The discussion was prompted by Huelsenbeck's *En Avant Dada: Eine Geschichte des Dadaismus,* published in 1920 by Schwit-ters' friend Paul Steegemann in Die Silbergäule 50/51.

The author thanks Drs. Linda Dalrymple Henderson and T. D. Kelly of the University of Texas at Austin for their helpful suggestions and criticism of this essay.

[2] Kurt Schwitters, *Lyrik,* Vol. I of *Das literarische Werk,* ed. Friedhelm Lach (Köln: M. DuMont Schauberg, 1973), pp. 60-63.

[3] The work measures 6 x 8¼ in. or 17.6 x 21.1 cm. It is signed and dated and belongs to an unidentified collector in Europe. It was most recently exhibited in October 1982, at the Fundación Juan March of Madrid. The catalog of the exhibition includes a color reproduction.

[4] The issue of Schwitters' politics will be considered at length in my forthcoming dissertation on Schwitters' iconography (University of Texas at Austin).

[5] During an interview in Hanover with the author in the summer of 1982, Hilde Bäumer verified the identity of her brother Ludwig in the photograph in *Das Bäumerbild* and attested to a Schwitters-Bäumer friendship. From the available evidence this appears to be the first instance in which Schwitters used real photographs in his work, although he was familiar with the photomontage technique as early as 1918. The use of photographic portraits in art works was quite popular in self-conscious Dada circles in Berlin, and was very much in evidence at the First International Dada Fair (1920), which Schwitters attended.

[6] Ludwig Bäumer, *Das jüngste Gericht,* Vol. 16 of *Der rote Hahn* (Berlin-Wilmersdorf: Die Aktion, 1918), p. 40.

[7] See Annegreth Nill, "Rethinking Kurt Schwitters, Part One: An Interpretation of 'Hansi,'" *Arts* (January 1981), 112-17.

[8] In Schwitters' *Hansi* the word "ade" is used to make two sentences that establish the two readings of the collage. The literal meaning is conveyed by the sentence "Ade Hansi Schokolade" ("goodbye, Hansi chocolate"). The more personal meaning is conveyed by the sentence "Ade Witzgrund, Dresden," in which Schwitters is saying farewell to the academic formation he received in Dresden. See Nill, p. 114.

[9] All attempts so far to identify the organization have failed. Agnes F. Peterson of the Hoover Institution on War, Revolution and Peace, Stanford, Calif., suggests that the organization may have been very small and located near the seat of government (letter dated May 2, 1984). I would like to thank Mrs. Peterson for her considerable effort in this endeavor. I would also like to thank Mrs. E. Möpps at the Deutsche Presseforschung, Universität Bremen, and Mr. Werner Heine at the Stadtarchiv, Landeshauptstadt Hanover, for their attempts to identify the organization in question.

[10] The German words in this paragraph in the order in which they appear mean "peace," "France," "determined," "we refuse," "unbearable," "our people," "hour means patience," and "insurrections may not . . . the true," and "just peace."

[11] Although basically a peace party, the Social Democrats had, under the concept of the "Burgfrieden," voted *en masse* for war credits on August 4, 1914. They had done so out of a sense of patriotism based on their belief that the war was one of defense rather than aggression. See Karl Friedrich Erdmann, *Der Erst Weltkrieg,* Vol. 18 of *Gebhardt, Handbuch der deutschen Geschichte* (München: Deutscher Taschenbuch Verlag, 1980), pp. 165-75.

[12] The Allies had presented the German delegation with the finished treaty on May 7, 1919. On May 12, addressing the national assembly, prime minister Scheidemann proclaimed: "Der Vertrag ist unerträglich und unerfüllbar. Welche Hand müsste nicht verdorren die sich und uns in solche Fesseln legte!". Quoted in Hagen Schulze, *Weimar Deutschland 1917-1933,* Vol. 4 of *Die Deutschen und ihre Nation: Neuere deutsche Geschichte* (Berlin: Severin und Siedler, 1982), p. 196.

[13] For the text of these notes see *Materialien, betr. die Friedensverhandlungen,* ed. Auswertiges Amt (Charlottenburg: Deutsche Verlagsgesellschaft für Politik und Geschichte, 1919).

[14] See "Rätestaat oder parlamentarische Demokratie," in Karl Dietrich Erdmann, *Die Weimarer Republik,* Vol. 19 of *Gebhardt, Handbuch der deutschen Geschichte* (München: Deutsche Taschenbuch Verlag, 1980), pp. 28-52.

[15] For a detailed discussion of this issue, see Arno J. Mayer, *Politics and Diplomacy of Peacemaking* (New York: Alfred A. Knopf, 1967), pp. 753 ff.

[16] Raoul Hausmann expressed antigovernment sentiments in his photomontage *The Art Critic* of 1919 by having a shoe step on a 10-Pfennig "Deutsches Reich" postage stamp.

[17] The forms of the El Lissitzky poster recalled military maps and the terminology "Reds" and "Whites" was in common usage. See Alan C. Birnholz, "Forms, Angles, and Corners: On Meaning in Russian Avant-Garde Art," *Arts* (February 1977), p. 101. One can only speculate as to whether Schwitters knew of the Lissitzky poster in 1920. The Russian artist Iwan Puni, who moved from Vitebsk to Berlin late in 1920, could provide a link. Puni was familiar with El Lissitzky's work because in 1919 both men taught at the academy in Vitebsk, which was headed by marc Chagall. Perhaps at the suggestion of longtime "Sturm-artist" Chagall, Puni established contact with Herwarth Walden's Sturm Gallery upon his arrival in Berlin. Schwitters had close ties to Der Sturm at this time; he would undoubtedly have heard about the newcomers from Russia.

[18] See Erdmann, *Weimarer Republik*, pp. 136 ff. for the "Kapp-Putsch" and its consequences. I am assuming that Schwitters meant the "hood" to be read as a "Kappe," a mantle with hood.

[19] For another point of view, see Schulze, pp. 213-21.

[20] Jochen Meyer, *Der Paul Steegemann Verlag* (Stuttgart: Fritz Eggert, 1975), p. 14.

[21] Peter Kuckuk, *Revolution und Räterepublik in Bremen* (Frankfurt am Main: Suhrkamp, 1969), pp 103-6.

[22] Kuckuk, p. 30.

[23] David Erlay, *Worpswede-Bremen-Moskau: Der Weg des Heinrich Vogeler* (Bremen: Schünemann, 1972), p. 103 (emphasis added).

[24] In the conclusion of *Das Wesen des Kommunismus* (Die Silbergäule, Vols. 25-26 [Hanover: Paul Steegemann Verlag, 1919), p. 26), Ludwig Bäumer calls conventional weapons outmoded bourgeois-capitalist war material: "Es liefert den Nachweis, dass die rückständigen Methoden der bürgerlich-kapitalistischen Kampfmittel, hinterlistiger Mord, Maschinengewehre, Hand- und Gasgranaten, Kanonen, Flammen- und Minenwerfer untaugliche Mittel sind im Kampf um die politische Macht der Zukunft. . . . " ("It furnishes the proof that the antiquated methods of the bourgeois-capitalist means of combat, perfidious murder, machine guns, hand and gas grenades, cannons, flamethrowers, and trench mortars, are unsuitable means in the contest for the political power of the future"). For a detailed discussion of Bäumer's political beliefs, see Lothar Peter, *Literarische Intelligenz und Klassenkampf* (Köln: Prahl-Rungenstein, 1972), pp. 109-15.

[25] Erlay, *Worpswede-Bremen-Moskau,* p. 136.

[26] Bäumer, *Kommunismus,* p. 3.

[27] The Worpswede communists, especially Heinrich Vogeler, were called "Edelkommunisten" (noble communists) on account of their great, almost otherworldly idealism. See David Erlay, *Vogeler, Ein Maler und seine Zeit* (Fischerhude: Atelier im Bauernhaus, 1981), p. 160.

[28] Heinrich Wiegand Petzet, *Heinrich Vogeler: Von Worpswede nach Moskau. Ein Künstler zwischen den Zeiten* (Köln: M. DuMont Schauberg, 1973), p. 126.

[29] Personal interview with Erika Vogt, Worpswede, in the summer of 1982. I would like to thank Professor Ernst Nündel for drawing my attention to the connection between Worpswede and Schwitters. My gratitude also extends to the Fulbright Commission, which not only supported this research financially, but also organized an excursion to Worpswede.

[30] Heinrich Vogeler, *Erinnerungen* (1952), as quoted in Sigrid Weltge-Wortmann, *Worpswede* (Worpswede, 1979), p. 109.

[31] Erlay, *Worpswede,* p. 54 and Petzet, p. 97. In 1914 both Ludwig Bäumer and Heinrich Vogeler went off to war. Both spent some time during the war in mental institutions, and both were committed communists when they returned to the Barkenhoff after the war.

[32] Petzet, p. 97.

[33] *Die Aktion,* 4 (June 1914), 518-23.

[34] Reprinted in Heinrich Vogeler, *Das Neue Leben*, ed. Dieter Pforte (Darmstadt und Neuwied: Hermann Luchterhand, 1972), pp. 92-100. "Die rote Marie" was the name given to Marie Griesbach-Hundt of Dresden on account of the color of her hair and her political views. She was for a time Vogeler's mistress. Schwitters dedicated a poem published in *Der Sturm,* 10 (January 1920), 141 to "Die rote Marie." It provides the only concrete evidence besides *Das Bäumerbild* of Schwitters' Barkenhoff connections.

[35] The converse proverb, "Trennung von Tisch und Bett" ("separation of table and bed"), meaning a judicial separation, also achieves a certain validity when viewed in the context of the Vogeler-Bäumer-Martha triangle.

[36] Schwitters first concerned himself with abstract art in 1910 while attending the Dresden Academy. He recorded his thoughts and readings for a theoretical treatise he planned to write on the problem of abstraction. One of the quotations he copied from Alfred Köppen's *Die moderne Malerei in Deutschland* (Bielefeld, 1902), p. 25, states: "Es ist die Harmonie der Form und des Inhalts, die die Grösse des Kunstwerks ausmacht, das ist das wiederentdeckte Schönheitsgesetz Menzels." ("It is the harmony of form and content that constitutes the significance

of a work of art; that is the principle of beauty rediscovered by Menzel.") Kurt Schwitters, *Werk,* Vol. 5, p. 398. Schwitters surely subscribed to the idea that the harmony of form and content determines the value of a work of art, and he strove to achieve that harmony in *Das Bäumerbild*.

Friedhelm Lach (essay date 1985)

SOURCE: "Schwitters: Performance Notes," in *Dada/Dimensions,* Edited by Stephen C. Foster, UMI Research Press, 1985, pp. 39-45.

[*In the following essay, Lach characterizes Schwitters's* Merz *works as avant-garde performances of creativity.*]

The rediscovery of Kurt Schwitters coincided with the discovery of the "event" character of art—with Pop, neo-Dada, happenings, and performance art. It is this event character of art that allows me to present Kurt Schwitters, who died in 1948, as the father of contemporary art currents and events and to celebrate him as the ingenious inventor who did in the 1920s what became, in the long run, the representative art of the twentieth century.

Even if this critical acclaim is often repeated in general terms by artists and critics alike, art historians and critics are right to smile and to feel uneasiness towards these Merz events. Schwitters' art events and artifacts are a flush of ideas; they are open art forms and outspokenly antisystematic. There are enormous difficulties in gaining a thorough analysis or understanding of his art. But even if one talks about the ambiguous image, one experiences the refreshment of his art as soon as contact is made with it. He is named the bourgeois Dadaist, the hidden provocateur, the abstract painter of naturalistic portraits, the concrete poet who wrote Schlagertexts, fairy tales, and travel reports, a performance artist of the living room, a preacher of consequence who liked fragmentation. You rightly name him a romantic classic of the avant-garde.

Nevertheless, one feels his magnetic attraction for the artists of our time—to musicians inspired by his **"Urlautsonate,"** to art performers, theater groups, directors of museums, and teachers—all trying to transform Schwitters exhibitions and evenings into art events for the public. In a sense, it is proof of the event character of Merz art. Every sensible interpreter feels that the general idea of Merz is the constant happening of creativity. It is essential for this proclaimed creative practice to stimulate, awaken, and deautomatize the public and to incite its activity. To be Merz art is to be a catalytic agent. Therefore, the performance is written into the concept and character of all of Schwitters' articulations. In this sense, and with the help of my analysis of performance, I will share a new, essential perspective for the understanding of Merz and, in general, of Dada.

Everyone will agree that the most obvious documentation of this concept can be cited from the manifesto for and explanations of the Merz stage (*Merzbühne*). Schwitters

formulated: "[The *Merzbühne*] can't be written, or read or heard, it can only be experienced in the theater. Everything is perceived as a complex sensual happening, full of gestures, movements and sounds."[1] But the principle of creative events that leads to a whole new life practice is visible in all actions and creations of Schwitters—in his art, literature, theory, and critiques, even in his life. At the end of his life he wrote about it humorously:

> One needs a medium. The best is, one is his own medium. But don't be serious because seriousness belongs to a past time. This medium called you yourself will tell you to take absolutely the wrong material. That is very good because only the wrong material used in the wrong way will give you the right picture, when you look at it from the right angle, or the wrong angle.[2]

If we take the event character of art seriously and ask about the right and wrong angles of Schwitters research, we have to make a complete turnaround of our research techniques. The event is open-ended, a process in time and context. The structure is replaced by serial technique; attention is paid to the psyche, to behavior, to pretentions and intentions (which are touchy, or forbidden in so-called "scientific research"). In the following, I will use the analysis of a poem performance to demonstrate the value of this perspective for the interpretation of Schwitters' art, and I will further try to clarify the concept of Merz performance.

Interpretation of the Poem "Wall" ("Wand")

In 1922, Schwitters composed a poem with 37 repetitions of the word "wall," in singular and plural forms, with an introductory verse where he counted from one to five. To compose something with walls is different from composing something with brick or stone constructions. Brick is a basic building element, while a wall is an archetypal phenomenon, a functional appearance, a mythic object, and a very personal experience for everyone: for the prisoner, the climber, the architect, the ghetto inhabitant. Walls are built, in a certain sense, by everyone for the purpose of hiding and protecting, a result of ignorance and wisdom. But mainly, we detect walls when we stand in front of them, when they hinder us in our development. They then become signs of authority. We feel the pressure building inside to overrun them, to undo authority. The performer standing in front of his audience feels this wall as well, and he reacts against it. Schwitters' poem is significant because it is a model that shows how to build, how to break, and how to live with walls. He erects, in his poem, the authority of walls and then he overcomes them; he puts the *power of creativity* against them. The poem has to be performed and acquires its meaning only by the performance. This becomes obvious in observing the performer's step by step preparation.

Schwitters makes clear to his public that the main element of construction is not the brick, a basic element, but the wall, a complexity which has, in various cultures, different meanings and connotations. A wall is a means of control for the organizer, of construction for the engineer, of imprisonment for the prisoner, of challenge for the climber, of business for the painter, of information for the informer, of work for the carpenter. At the beginning of the poem, every one of us may have a different understanding and picture of the wall. The performer has to take this into account and must overcome this complex multisignificance by gesturing or by declamation. He has to create his own stage, his own environment; he has to actualize this complexity, the wall, for himself and for the public; he must emotionalize and personalize the "experience" of the wall. Instead of a quick intellectual grasp of the word, he has to aim at a deeper existential understanding, at the archetypal, prenatal comprehension.

This begins with the first occurrence of the word, and it should be reinforced by further occurrences. By repeating the word 27 times in the singular and ten times in the plural, he establishes the serial technique employed in the poem. The repetitions should not be robotlike and mechanical (they do not serve the logical explanation). The series produces a process of variations—a process that makes the word more meaningful and that leads to and builds up to a different and deeper meaning. At the same time, one realizes the inner processes that lead to deeper understanding. The series, "wall wall wall wall," projects the images and experiences, "walls." The multitude of walls is verified by the plural "walls." The identification with the multitude of walls becomes a frightening perception. The inner world realizes the impact of such images and the effect of this emotionalization.

The technique of serial repetition offers a rhythmical stabilization, refers to the breathing rhythm, and establishes the ego as a balancing instance, to the exuberance of the emotionalizations. The affirmative naming of the wall as dialogue partner to the ego reestablishes the inner forces of creativity. The artistic recovery progresses with inventive and playful use of the sound. The poem produces, in this interpretation, a creative practice that is established at the end. The need for it is shown with the beginning of the poem, which includes a countdown from five to one. The wall series starts immediately thereafter. The pressure that is provoked by the counting is released at the end. Countdowns normally lead to explosions or important new events. This new process, heralded by the counting, is obviously the practice of creativity. In a time of severe restraints after the First World War, when everything was destroyed, the constructive energy of creativity was essential for new building.

In the performance of a work, the space in which it happens changes to a stage. The stage makes all actions and messages formalistic. For instance, a demonstration in the street projected to a stage becomes a play with stage character. The intimate admiration of the lover becomes a theater gag. All actions on the stage become plays of actions. The performance of the poem **"Wand"** creates, in this sense, a model that shows how to live with one's wall and how to overcome it with creativity. The performance as a catalytic event is integrated into all of Schwitters' creations, literary and visual. Everything he did was part of a life practice based on creativity and, as a result, everything he could touch became performance art material. The concept of Merz performance states that everything can become material for a performance. It is very important, then, to analyze the conceptualization of this performance.

The Concept of Merz Performance

In **"'Aus der Welt Merz,' a dialogue with interventions of the public,"** (1923) Schwitters describes an example of his performance art. Performing are artists (poets, painters, sculptors, musicians, actors), the public, and the stage. Each of these elements is described as "material" of the performance and produces by itself forces and tensions that all become destructive if they are not controlled by a leader—the so-called "Merzer," who takes all these forces and reactions into account and creates an art performance. He produces the stimulus that leads to feelings of provocation and tension, so that the public wants to change the situation (in this example, he puts the lights out; the public wants light and demands it back). The Merzer has a preconceived concept of the perceptions and reactions of the public. He knows the catalytic effects of darkness and of closed rooms; he knows the dramatic emotional developments from uneasiness to laughter, to unpleasantness, to anger, to shock (terrified state), to horror, to panic. Each situation has this possibility of a latent rise to chaos. Essential is the engagement, the reality and the totality of action.

What is important for the definition of Schwitters' performance art is the non-thought, the non-information in his analysis, which gives us a possibility to systematize his concept. Although stating continuously the availability of all materials (including human beings, emotions, nonsense, and banalities) and the intuitive and improvisational action and reaction of the performer vis-à-vis his public, one does not find any precise thought about control, discipline, and their means (that is, the limiting effects and political and social implications of this artistification). This is the more astonishing considering that he foresees and provokes the very active behavior of the public and hopes to change this public into a Dadaistic society.

The ideal public that Schwitters dreamt of was an unconditioned public, without any conception of what was to follow and without pretentions, preoccupations, prejudgments, codifications, norms, clichés, automatizations—a public that did not know the great restraints of redundancy, of repetition, of predetermined expectations. This proclaimed openness and self-connectedness are integral to the performer and the public. Yet, how can one determine the non-thought of Schwitters and his control mechanisms in order to get a more systematized view of his performance concept?

Since ancient times, the control of time is pursued by three elements: (1) the control of rhythm, (2) the order of certain limited actions, and (3) the regulation of repetitive cycles. Control in ancient times started with purification (with washing hands or with exercises of faith). The Dadaistic cleaning of the human psyche is done by laughter, which is often provoked at the beginning of actions by unexpected happenings.

The discipline of the rhythm is established by the great technician of rhythm, the Merzer. He structures, manages, and modifies all visible, acoustical, and sensual happenings. It is not important for him what performance material is used; anything has equal value. Important is his rhythmic control. The Merzer can use the alphabet and determine, with the rhythmical use of consonants and vowels, the time sequences. Important for him is the uninterrupted control of time. In order to achieve the continuous use of his public's time, certain limitations are necessarily introduced. He, the controller, works with repetitive cycles and serial techniques, and he limits his responses and messages to a limited set of information and orders. The public's reaction, or a limited variety of reactions, is counted on as an evaluation of the event—by applause (positive reaction), by contra or boo calls (negative reaction), or by silence (tension reaction). These reactions, used for time control as well as psychological data, show how deautomatization by new ideas, or by their unusual combination, provoke contradiction and tension. Unpleasant reactions become, in this sense, highlights of art performances. Applause is not considered as a judgment of the performance but as part of the performance. Schwitters pretends that the Merzer can control everything, but he avoids mentioning forbidden reactions by the public in this performance concept (for instance, to converse with each other, to play musical chairs, to watch television, to sleep, to drink alcohol, to tell fairy tales, to pass gas). All activities that hinder control are non-thoughts.

There are other specifics not mentioned; for instance, the specificity of the rhythms. We find countdown rhythms—4, 3, 2, 1—that provoke attention at the beginning and establish control, or we find marching rhythms—1-2, 1-2, 1-2, 1-2—that especially help to control action, by proposing a rhythm program. The public will constantly be tested by the Merzer as to whether it is attentive and responsive to determine the nature of the control. Schwitters states that actions, behavior, and rhythms should be an integral part of the psyche.

As the action of a mother caring for her child can only proceed from her feelings for her child, so can the performer act only out of his feelings for his audience. Each movement, each rhythm is controlled by his psyche. The time control is identical to a body control. The movements and gestures respond to the total behavior. The disciplined body and the artistic use of all articulating body parts are the operational context for the smallest reaction and gesture. The Merzer must inform his public of the right posture and behavior for achieving successful, meaningful, and energized gestures. This explains the combination, during Schwitters' Merz evenings, of performances, dances, and sport exercises. The disciplined body and mind are essential parts of these high-powered performances. In this rhythm

control, one also finds a negative principle—the principle of non-laziness, non-contemplation. It is forbidden to have a negative approach to activity and creativity. What is wanted is the optimum of sensuality within the moment—the total use of forces, the intensification and the exploitation of the psyche, the elementarization and serialization of the life process. High speed is considered the highest effect (probably a Prussian heritage). It is easier to control time if it is segmented into tiny elements and if the speed is regulated. The identification with this control process is not possible by means of rationalization, but by emotionalization and spontaneous identification. Schwitters refused to use drill techniques, and all mechanical or technical time controls, but instead worked with psychological controls to evoke a natural and organic experience of rhythms.

The control of the Merzer is based on optical and mechanical laws. Schwitters describes his *Merzabende* as very spontaneous events composed of individuals with various backgrounds. In the beginning, he asks them to assemble before him or around him. Immediate eye contact is important. He does not talk to the mass, but to the individual. He differentiates between the individual responses and addresses each single participant, coercing him with words, gestures, and eye contact. His position in the center, from where he can best control and observe, is significant. The best place of control is there, where he oversees everything with one glance and to which place everyone's eyes are directed (Schwitters' compositional concepts in his pictures reflect these control stands as well as his performance arrangements).

Direct effect, closeness, and direct communication are essential for the total participation of the public. Schwitters' proclaimed aim for his art—complete liberation and personal inventive creativity—is based on these highly visible control concepts. It became necessary for Schwitters to propose and to create organizations that could promote the new creativity. With the help of his friends, he organized his *Merzabende* and wrote a manifesto and articles in which he proposed a *Merzbühne* (Merz stage) as a permanent institution for Merz performances. This whole artistic articulation and production, his work and life, were considered by him as catalytic agents and examples of the Merz world he promoted. The montages, collages, assemblages, texts, poems, and critiques were all self-imposed tests of his own potential as creator. The vigor and spontaneity of his creations were expressed in ever new explorations of numerous disciplines. He expected to project his creative drive to his public. Creativity is power. It changes the world, not by political means, but by provocation, deautomatization, identification, obsessionalization, and invention. Creativity is perceived as such a power that it transforms the whole world.

Merz Creativity Projects the Merz World

Today we find the recipes, the scores, of Merz events by looking to the visual and poetic heritage of Schwitters. It represents a test of our own ability to invent and to become creative. Merz signals a challenge in a double sense—to become sensitive to the Merz approach and to constitute ourselves as an object of analysis. The art event provokes us to compare and mirror personal data with global and cosmic phenomena, and with collective, archetypal experiences of the mythic world. Merz is based on the experience of the totality and the connectedness of ourselves with this totality. Schwitters emphasizes the counterbalancing effects of art. Whenever the individual or society is unbalanced, for instance by too much emphasis on politics or consumption, the art event becomes treatment for the disease. Only the connection with total knowledge of world functions allows this therapeutical viewpoint.

The participants in a Merz performance were never forced into a participation that they were unable to perform. What was essential was their natural capacity for the action and gesture performance. The influence of the Merzer is not directed to distract, to push away, to mask, to give a role, to veil, to exclude individuality. On the contrary, he wants to produce, through his leadership, a life practice of truth, real experience, and rituals and operations of truth. The creative human being is the projected result of these interventions. Merz stresses the technique to produce creators of disciplines.

NOTES

[1] Kurt Schwitters, *Das literarische Werk,* 5 vols., ed. Friedhelm Lach (Cologne, 1973), vol. 5, p. 42.

[2] Ibid., p. 387.

E. S. Shaffer (essay date 1990)

SOURCE: "Kurt Schwitters, Merzkunstler: Art and Word-Art," in *Word and Image,* Vol. 6, No. 1, January, 1990, pp. 100-18.

[*In the following essay, Shaffer investigates the multiple genres of Schwitters's oeuvre—including visual and literary works: collages, poems, essays, performances, and plays. Shaffer concludes, "We need a new reading of the full verbal and visual core of his work, which is more extensive and more significant for all his work than has been understood hitherto."*]

Kurt Schwitters was born in Hanover in 1887, trained in Dresden (1909-13) and Berlin and, on being condemned by National Socialism as a 'cultural bolshevik' whose works were displayed in the *Entartete Kunst* ('Degenerate Art') exhibition of 1937, fled from Hanover in that year, first to Norway and then in 1940 to England, where he died in Ambleside in 1948. Since the series of retrospectives, beginning in 1956, he has been widely recognised as one of the important German artists of the inter-war period, and a highly talented and original representative of the *avant-garde* movement in the arts which came into being in early 1916 and is identified with international Dada. His own work came into contact with a wide range of other movements in the formative years 1910-20, notably Expressionism (especially the group around Herwarth Walden and *Der Sturm*), Constructivism and Bauhaus, and *De Stijl*.[1] His closest affinities and most productive friendships were, however, with members of Zurich Dada, especially Hans Arp, and of Dutch *De Stijl*, especially Theo van Doesburg. Disagreeing with Berlin Dada, in particular Richard Huelsenbeck, on the political role of art—although affected by the Berlin revolutionary movement in 1919—Schwitters was never prepared to subordinate artistic aims to political ends. He took an independent line and founded his own style, which he labelled *Merz*. Schwitters took this name from one of his own collages, *Merzbild* (1920), no longer extant, which incorporated 'found' materials including the words KOMMERZ UND PRIVATBANK, of which only the letters MERZ were visible. The letters can be related to the German word 'ausmerzen', to eliminate, so that a noun formed from it would mean 'what has been eliminated', or rubbish (in the U.S., *Merz* is rendered as 'trash' or 'junk'). Schwitters turned 'commercial rubbish' into a form of high modern art, in which the rubble of war and the civilization of the past were given new formal coherence and even harmony. He applied the notion *merz,* which he explicated in a number of essays, to a variety of visual and literary works in the course of the 1920s: collages, poems, especially the immediately popular **Anna Blume** (1919), constructions, sometimes on a large scale (*Merzbau*), performances (such as his sound poetry readings and *Dada-Abende*), plays and multi-media events written for a theatre of his own devising (Merzbühne). Despite exile and adversity, Schwitters retained his characteristic style and humour to the end, as his superb letters show, collected under the title **Wir spielen, bis uns der Tod abholt** (*We shall play till Death fetches us*) and by now a minor classic on the Continent. Despite the need to turn his talents to more conventional landscapes and portraits in order to survive in England, he was, in part, able to pursue his own work. For the purposes of this essay, however, we shall discuss primarily works executed in the period 1918-1930.

Far more has been written about Schwitters's visual art than about his literary works. The relative neglect of his literary works, especially his drama, calls for a special effort to focus attention on it. Werner Schmalenbach, in the standard work on Schwitters, relegates drama to the end of a chapter entitled 'Marginal artistic activities', and does not discuss it at all under 'Literary Work'.[2] Yet for both his visual and his literary work, considering the two aspects together offers the most illuminating insight into them both. Unlike artists such as Victor Hugo, whose literary and visual productions were only loosely linked, Schwitters produced a core of work which can be read in both ways and whose distinctive note is the demand for a mode of reading which combines the two. This is the source of much of his innovative power in both spheres. Moreover, consideration of the visual and the literary together will bring us again to his drama, as the locus of the *Gesamtkunstwerk* (Total Work of Art) which he proclaimed as his ultimate aim.

We can, in this limited space, attempt only a very schematic treatment of this central core, while indicating the directions further consideration would have to take. We shall give five readings/viewings (*Sehtexte*) within this core, each of which demands this double reading in a different way: first, poems which explicate art works or seek to convey a pictorial impression or style; second, shaped poems, ranging from purely typographical works through combinations of work and shape to fully sculptural forms (for the sake of clarity we shall follow a major motif in his work, the cathedral, through these transformations); third, the illustrated narrative (*Märchen*, fairy-tale); fourth, sound poems with graphic scores; and fifth, the *Gesamtkunstwerk* as theatrical event. The fourth and fifth types of *Sehtext*, with their strong admixture of sound, also incorporate the musical with the verbal and visual arts.

Schwitters sometimes makes relatively familiar poetic uses of art as a subject or theme, as in **'To a Drawing by Marc Chagall'** (1919), a poem to a drawing by Chagall entitled *The Drinker*, or the 'Portraits' in poetry such as the **'Portrait of Rudolf Blümner'** and **'Portrait of Herwarth Walden',** the latter called by Richard Sheppard 'one of the several convoluted but essentially descriptive poems about various members of the *Sturm-Kreis'*,[3] which derive their titles by analogy with art and attempt to paint the picture in words. These are worth explication in their own right, especially as they may be regarded as a literary interpretation of new styles in art, especially Cubism and Expressionism. The poem on Chagall's drawing, an example of ekphrasis, recreates the drawing while the 'portraits' paint the sitters in their own styles, capturing their inner countenances (*Gesichter*) as visions (*Gesichte*). Both approaches, however, require a highly experimental approach to what the *Sturm* circle called *Wortkunst,* or word-art.

The poem on Chagall's *The Drinker,* by describing the objects in the painting (the playing cards, fish, head in the window, the headless drinker, bottle, hand, knife, drawer of table, etc.) recreates in its own order the unexpected decompositions and juxtapositions of the painting. Nevertheless, it also creates new links between the objects; attempts by poetic means (for example, repetition—especially of the rhyme 'Fisch/Tisch' ('fish/table') and the self-rhyme 'Flasche' ('bottle') to approach the simultaneity of perception that was one of the aims of Dada; and suggests a feeling-tone that interprets their significance, as in the line 'And inwardly rounds knob on the table' ('Und innigrundet Knopf am Tisch').[4] Most strikingly, it creates a climax and a closure through synaesthesia in a way that suggests an interpretation of the drawing while altering the effect for the purposes of verbal form. The whole poem reads as follows:

> Playing-card replays fish, the head in the window.
> The animal head craves the bottle.
> On the babblemouth.
> Man without head.
> Hand waggles sour knife.

Playing-card fish squander dumpling bottle.
And a table-drawer.
Stupid.
And inwardly rounds knob on the table.
Fish presses the table, the stomach takes
    swordstroke ill.
A drinker's stem dumbly eyes the plaintive beast,
The eyes lust after the smell of the bottle.[5]

(Spielkarte leiert Fisch, der Kopf im Fenster.
Der Tierkopf giert die Flasche.
Am Hüpfemund.
Mann ohne Kopf.
Hand wedelt saure Messer.
Spielkarte Fisch verschwenden Knödel Flasche.
Und eine Tischschublade.
Blöde.
Und innig rundet Knopf am Tisch.
Fisch drückt den Tisch, der Magen übelt
    Schwerterstrich.
Ein Säuferstiel augt dumm das klage Tier.
Die Augen lechzen sehr den Duft der Flasche).

The poem recaptures the effect of the drawing by verbal means. The stark catalogue of objects, some 'real' ('Spielkarte', 'Messer') and some imaginary ('Tierkopf', 'Mann ohne Kopf'), suggests the fragmentation of the drawing and its literal intermingling of levels. Through its linearity, as Lessing pointed out, the poem necessarily lays down a sequential ordering of the objects in it; but because the relations set up between them are unexpected, an effect of simultaneity is obtained, though quite different from that of the drawing. Schwitters obtains the isolation of the objects and the institution of new relations between them in four ways. Units that would normally occur only within a sentence ('Am Hüpfemund') are separated out and thus freed; normal grammatical connections are broken down (most simply, by the omission of declined definite articles); the items are arranged in a pseudo-syntactical but semantically meaningless pattern of nouns and verbs ('Spielkarte leiert Fisch', 'Spielkarte Fisch verschwenden Knödel Flasche'); and an intricate sound system is created which draws attention to the essential ('Flasche' ('bottle') is three times strategically placed at the end of a line, including the last line, and reinforced by the assonances of 'Fische' and 'Tisch' and even 'Schwerterstrich') and sets up, by means of its half-rhyming babble, a kind of internal, inconsequential song of unexpected relations ('Tischschublade,/Blöde') like that often experienced in states of intoxication. The ordering in both works is thus that of the drinker whose perceptions are at once disoriented and concentrated on his craving. The last line of the poem goes beyond the recapturing by verbal means of the effects of the drawing: thus, the dots in the background of the drawing are made to represent fragrance escaping from the bottle, which the eyes—all the eyes in the drawing, both those of the disembodied head and those of the animal head looking in at the window, and, by implication, the non-existent eyes of the headless man—lust after. In the poem, this becomes a comment on the pictorial medium itself, which can only indirectly convey the drinker's state through disorientation, yet itself depends on a craving of the eye.

Rudolf Blümner is of particular interest as the main exponent in the *Sturm* circle—itself occupying 'the most extreme position in German poetics in its advocacy of "abstract poetry" '[6]—of sound poetry as performance art, a form that Schwitters learnt from him in private lessons and pursued to great effect in public. Schwitters's **'Portrait'** attempts to give in miniature the principles of Blümner's *Wortkunst* by portraying him in the act of performing a difficult sound exercise: 'Unstrahlend ezen Kreische quäke dreiz'.[7] Blümner is of further interest, inasmuch as a collage of Schwitters, entitled *Der Sturm* (1919), made up largely of the names of the members of the *Sturm* circle, suggests that the name of his best-known poem and collection—***Anna Blume***—is related to 'Blümner' and his word-art: the only names not printed but signed are his own and the name 'Anna Blümner' (and one other).[8] Both names in German suggest flowers/blossoming/blooming, and the translations of 'Anna Blume' into English ('Eve Blossom') and French ('Anna Lafleur') stress this. The usual explanation of the source of 'Anna Blume' is that Schwitters 'found' the phrase 'Anna Blume has a bird' ('Anna Blume hat ein Vogel') scrawled on a board, but as 'to have a bird' can, in German, mean 'to be mad', even this apparently simple (though suspiciously programmatic) explanation plunges us into Schwitters's word-play.[9] Wherever he first found the name, he may well have used the similarity as a compliment to Blümner, since he often paid tribute to those who influenced him by using their names in whole or in part as titles or integral parts of his works, sometimes in rebuses or other verbal puzzles and language games (like *Prapoganda/Arp*). In some cases, these allusions become full-scale 'portraits' in and of the subjects' own styles, such as the constructivist pieces entitled *Moholy* (1922) and *I.K. Bonset* (the pseudonym of Theo van Doesburg, which in this case is inset vertically into the collage) (1925).[10] Sometimes the portraits are mutual, as in the case of Lissitzky's portrait of Schwitters, a photomontage using Schwitters's image, and Schwitters's portrait of Lissitzky, an 'unusually spare Merz collage'.[11] Later, after the War, he incorporated the title of the periodical *De Stijl* and its translation into French and German (*Le Style* and *Der Stil*), together with the publication's slogan, 'le seul organe d'une nouvelle conscience plastique et poétique fondé en', into a largely constructivist collage. This is an example of the use of the stencilled or printed masthead both as title and as an element in the work, as practised in the early *papiers collés* by Braque and Picasso. This is a straightforward example, yet it suggests the way, as in much of Schwitters's work, in which the 'legisign' of the title and the 'sinsign' of the inscription are partial or oblique reminiscences of one another rather than reproductions.[12] In this case, Schwitters created a portrait, a memorial, of the movement.

Shaped poetry is one of the major categories of this central area in which the verbal and the visual reinforce each other. The prominence of shaped poetry in Schwitters's *oeuvre* is striking—indeed, not only many of his stamp-drawings (*Stempelzeichnungen*), but also a large number of his collages may be read as shaped or concrete poetry.

Straightforward examples are a stamp-drawing such as *The Critic* (1921)[13] in which the cartoon-like figure is made up primarily of name-stamps, and the collage *Opened by Customs* (*Vom Zoll Geöffnet*) in which the verbal elements incorporated in the collage are directly relevant to the title. A more complex example is *Milk Flower* (*Milchblume*), where the round milk bottle top is set in the centre of the collage. The bottle top reads at its own centre 'Pure Rich Milk' (seen upside down in the picture), and on this label is inscribed—in the upper semi-circle, 'Nature's finest food', and, in the lower semi-circle, 'Good for Young & Old' (a typographical placing that undoubtedly caught Schwitters's attention). Through the definition of the whole as 'Milk Flower' (which is inset into the picture on the lower left with the artist's signature on a white slip marked in larger letters 'Prize Crop'), the bottle top as the flower's disk organizes the other items of the collage which surround it as rays organically related to it. The inset title together with the organically oriented 'found' elements take on symbolic coherence. This work reaches back to van Doesburg's demonstration of the nature of the aesthetic experience in modern art through four successive representations of the cow, from naturalistic photograph, through a geometrized but still recognizable cow, to the abolition of form by the abandonment of the distinction between ground and figure, and finally, to a completely abstract, geometrical, constructivist design. The annihilation of the natural appearance leads to a new 'organic whole': 'The natural phenomenon is reconstructed in aesthetic accents which re-embody the essence of the object in a new way.'[14] Schwitters carries the process of non-representation of the cow one step further, while lending it a lyricism more reminiscent of Klee than of van Doesburg, thus continuing in his late work the dialogue between abstract art and abstract poetry.

The prominence of shaped poetry in Schwitters's work is in turn not simply an individual achievement, but is representative of the increase in importance of visual or optical poetry in the twentieth century: no longer merely a special sub-genre, it became a central form.[15] That the collages have not been read in this way is due to the complete acceptance (for visual art only) of the hard-won principle of modern art that the elements, whatever their provenance or familiarity, do not signify, and the recognition of Schwitters in the '50s owed much to the acceptance of the orthodoxy of non-objective art. But to take this principle as a premise is to ignore Schwitters's own development towards it in his own work—to ignore the point of departure for the use of *Merz*. It also ignores the complex relation between Dada and Constructivism in Schwitters's development, which makes it essential to read his works in detail as well as to grasp an abstract whole. This was grasped by one of the best American artists of the post-war period, Robert Rauschenberg, who adapted Schwitters's *Merz*-collage/construction techniques in the '50s, in a series of what he dubbed 'combine paintings', of which he said: 'I had to make a surface which invited a constant change of focus and an examination of detail.'[16] Moreover, to fail to read the collages is to acquiesce in the negative valuation by some literary critics of the programme of 'abstract poetry' that was so influential in Schwitters's milieu, which, from the start, used visual art as a model and was practised by visual as well as verbal artists.[17] The art of Schwitters, which uses the tension between signification and non-signification in both the visual and the verbal spheres, deliberately creates an only associatively understandable intentionality. This should be of particular interest in the current critical attempt to reformulate the nature of artistic intentionality. The programme of abstract poetry needs radical reconsideration now that Structuralism and Post-structuralism have taught us to read 'signs', and a counter-movement is rendering up an increasingly sophisticated account of residual 'mimesis'.[18]

Interesting as Schwitters's cubo-expressionist poems and constructivist portraits are, his architectural training led him at a crucial time in his development, the *annus mirabilis* of the 1919, towards one of his major achievements, the monumental shaped poem (or group of poems) entitled *The Cathedral,* which combines a traditional motif with an embodiment both in the immaterial of words and in the material of *Merz*-words: the scrap-cathedral. This is a clear case of the use of a symbol retaining strong reverential overtones in order to produce a Dada shock. *The Cathedral* takes several forms which explore the possibilities in a variety of ways.

Mies van der Rohe relates an anecdote that suggests how, in Schwitters's imagination, materials themselves held the finished form:

> Once Schwitters was on a train, carrying great roots from trees with him. Someone asked him what the roots were, and he replied that they constituted a cathedral. 'But that is no cathedral, that is only wood' the stranger exclaimed. 'But don't you know that cathedrals are made out of wood?' he replied.[19]

Schwitters identified the prototype of *The Cathedral* as the *Merz*-House, 'my first piece of *Merz* architecture', of which Christof Spengemann wrote:

> In *Haus Merz* [*Merz*-House] I see the cathedral. Not as a church, no, this is art as a truly spiritual expression of the force that raises us up to the unthinkable: absolute art. This cathedral cannot be used. Its interior is so filled with wheels that there is no room for people . . . that is absolute architecture, it has an artistic meaning and no other.[20]

Schwitters executed *The Cathedral, 8 Merz Lithographs* in 1920, and of the eight lithographs packed together in an envelope, only two have no verbal element. The cathedral was not only a traditional organic form (from Goethe's famous essay on the Gothic as exemplified by Strasbourg cathedral) it was also a key expressionist symbol taken up with special intensity by Walter Gropius and his circle as the architectural equivalent of the *Gesamt-kunstwerk* of opera: just as Wagner wrote *Zukunftsmusik,* 'the Music of the Future', so now architects would build the *Zukunftskathedrale,* 'the Cathedral of the Future', 'breaking the frames of Salon art' and inscribing a new world within their cathedral as the medieval period had within theirs.[21] This architectural impulse towards large-scale realization is a continuous presence in Schwitters's work even when it is executed on a small scale and in two dimensions; he breaks the mould of 'shaped poetry' almost from the beginning. As usual with Schwitters, there is also an explanation for his procedures at a less rapt and visionary level. The technical medium itself is taken by some critics to be the key to the series: a lithograph is in stone as a cathedral is in stone. Such a reading is, however, still in the realm of the rapt: 'the traditional analogy between book and architecture, between Bible and Church, is validated in astonishingly new ways.'[22] But there is a sense in which this 'technology' is simply a piece of Schwitters's word-play, and one which displays how verbal his technique really is: the lithographed cathedral is 'in stone' primarily at the level of philological joke. Moreover, he alludes to this analogy specifically in order to parody it, as in a poem contained in a letter of the same year to Spengemann, where, in friendly reproof of the exalted note in Spengemann's praise, he redrew the analogy to apply to the book of *Anna Blume* and the cathedral of Spengemann's inner self (note the further pun on 'Christian soul'), and underlined the point with the mock-religious refrain, 'Halleluja tit solei':

> Close by an Anna and a Cathedral—
> Go into thyself, Christian, go into the Dral—
> Let Anna Blume be adored, Crishan!
> Go into the portals of the beloved book
>
> . . . . .
>
> Hallelujah tit solay.
>
> (Anbei eine Anna und eine Kathedrale—
> Geh in Dich, Christian, geh in die Drale—
> Geliebt sei Anna Blume, Crithian!
> Geh ein die Pforten des geliebten Buches
>
> . . . . .
>
> Halleluja tit solei.)[23]

Moreover, Schwitters often mocked the grandiose element in the cathedral motif. *Dom* (*Cathedral*), for example (a poem, drawing or sculpture shaped like a tower or a cathedral façade), is echoed by a purely typographical, tower-shaped poem entitled **'Doof'** (**'Dumb'**) of 1922.[24] Or he combined the two elements so that the word 'DOM' becomes simply a constructive unit in the 'building' of the concrete poem as does the word 'DOF' (along with 'DEN', 'DIE' etc. which yield another version of the misdeclined grammatical building blocks 'der', 'die', 'das' with which the *avant-garde* made so much play—as in Arp's poem beginning 'Ich bin der grosse Derdiedas').[25] Even the typographical mockery is, however, symmetrical and firm, and reminds us that Schwitters often compared typography with architecture.

Opening the portfolio of lithographs, we find a range of items which include linear dadaist works, a group of collage prints made with shoe leather and patterned paper, and two without any verbal elements. This range is typical: as soon as we identify a work as belonging to the core of Schwitters's work where visual and literary overlap, we find that the work itself multiplies into a variety of forms spanning the whole range from the purely visual to the purely verbal. The sense of a gap—and the need to span or fill it—is one of the motors of Schwitters's art and creates an impression of energy, variety and density. In this case, the portfolio cover can be construed as balancing the two extremes.[26]

An inspection of the area of overlap between the visual and the literary uncovers another aspect of Schwitters's work which has been veiled or largely ignored: its multi-directionality. Schwitters often uses *versus retrogradi*: lines which read both backwards and forwards, either being palindromic, like the ANNA of 'Anna Blume', or making sense read either way. Sometimes spelling backwards yields or leads into a joke or a satire, as when in the **'Funeral Oration for Leo Reins' ('Rede am Grabe Leo Reins')**, the name of the critic Leo Reins is spelt backwards—'snieroel'—and Schwitters wishes it were 'Schmieröl' ('grease').[27] A more elaborate example occurs in his reversal of the name of his native city (spelt in German with two n's):

> . . . if one reads Hannover backward, one gets the combination *re von nah*. The word *re* one can translate indifferently as 'backward' or 'back'. I suggest the translation 'backward'. Thus the translation of the word Hannover read backward would be 'backward from near'. [near = *nah*] And that is correct, for then the translation of the word Hannover read forward would be 'forward to far'. This means Hannover strives forward, even to infinity. Note, however that Anna still remains the same whether read backward or forward.[28]

A particularly well-developed example is the novella **Auguste Bolte,** in which 'found rhymes' provide the turning-points in the action and the climax is reached when *â* (German double-s) is found to rhyme with *s*.[29] The pure linguistic artifice as a driving force of the action is familiar from experimental prose of the first decade of the century, like that of Raymond Roussel, but Schwitters uses this device with an almost Kafkaesque sense of the illogic and self-defeating quality of human behaviour pursued with a relentless appearance of logic, and invests it with a personal exuberance and zaniness almost entirely absent from Kafka. Here, pure sound and pure graphic symbol again coalesce. But if reading forwards and backwards is an important experimental technique in some of his literary works, it is essential for the reading of his paintings, where no left-right linear reading is adequate. Schwitters deliberately plays on and frustrates any automatic attempts to read incorporated words in the normal manner. Indeed, the technique of reading both forwards and backwards is given an ideological significance by Schwitters, in the context of an attack on Huelsenbeck and an explication of his own brand of Dada:

> It might be thought that I call myself a Dadaist, especially as the word 'dada' is written on the jacket of my collection of poems, Anna Blume. . . . On the same jacket is a windmill, a head, a locomotive running backwards and a man hanging in the air. This only means that in the world in which Anna Blume lives, in which people walk on their heads, windmills turn and locomotives run backwards, Dada also exists. In order to avoid misunderstandings, I have inscribed 'antidada' on the outside of my Cathedral. This does not mean that I am against Dada, but that there also exists in this world a current opposed to Dadaism. Locomotives run in both directions. Why shouldn't a locomotive run backwards now and then?[30]

Schwitters takes the political mode of antithesis or confrontation and turns it into a constructive and fluid mode of tolerance and Rousselian harmony. Instead of colliding, the opposites are readable in both directions and many even rhyme or become identical. Not infrequently, they are readable up-and-down too, and form a wheel or circle or move in a clockwise-and-counterclockwise manner.

The cathedral was carried out on a still larger, three-dimensional and architectural scale in *Merzbau,* which, like Duchamps' *Large Glass,* developed into a life-work. This occurred in part through unhappy historical circumstances: in exile, Schwitters rebuilt the *Merzbau* twice over, first in Norway, then in England, the original having been destroyed by bombing. But quite apart from the accident of destruction, the *Merzbau* represented one of his most striking and obsessional visions which he continually reworked. The modulation from primarily two-dimensional *Merz*-collages into the large-scale, three-dimensional *Merzbau* parallels the development of Lissitzky over the same period from the PROUN (an abbreviation of the Russian for 'Project for the Affirmation of the New') of 1919 into the PROUN-room created in 1923 for the Berlin Exhibition, and *The Abstract Gallery (Das Abstrakte Kabinett)* built for the Landesmuseum in Hanover in 1927, and destroyed by the Nazis in the late Thirties.[31] Schwitters began the *Merzbau* in his home in Hanover in 1923, building an elaborate interior of Merz items into an imposing cathedral structure which included elements such as the *Merz Column (Merzsäule)* and the Madonna. Later, it was retitled *The Cathedral of Erotic Misery (Die Kathedrale des erotischen Elends)* and took on a dramatic dimension, appearing to be at once a set for an expressionist play and the play itself in sculptural form. Thus, in Schwitters's hands, the 'shaped poem' in its largest and most extended form not only becomes sculptural and architectural but verges on theatre.

Another genre at the verbal-visual core of Schwitters's work is the fairy-tale (*Märchen*), again a traditional German Romantic literary form, but realized by means of pictures as well as text, as for example in *The Cock (Der Hahnepeter)* from *The Fairytales of Paradise* (1924).[32] The stories (or 'Parodies of Paradise') were the inventions of Schwitters, for which he cut up drawings by his friend Kate Steinitz and which he then published in 50 hand-coloured copies in his own *Merz* Press. Another fairytale, *The Scarecrow* (*Der Vogelscheuche*), based on a poem by Schwitters, was created as a collaborative enterprise with Steinitz and van Doesburg (with whom, in 1923, he went on a 'Dada Campaign' in Holland, during which Schwitters staged performance evenings or *Dada-Soirées*).[33] In the new fairytale, if there is a clear link with Morgenstern's *Gallows Songs* (*Galgenlieder*) and books for children, the immediate inspiration was Lissitzky's settings of Mayakovsky's fairytales, where fantasy was constrained by the stipulation that nothing should be used but what was in the normal printer's font. Schwitters and his friends were less strict than Lissitzky, and produced a more whimsical and colourful typographical concoction to which the printer Paul Vogt also willingly lent himself, setting small b's on their backs to make the farmer's feet, and creating extra-large letters not already in the font. The transformation of the fairytale genre is a large topic which requires separate consideration.

Finally, the core of Schwitters's *œuvre* includes the performance genres—ranging from the individual item in an evening programme of readings, through the *Dada-Soirée* as a whole, to the large-scale dramatic spectacle or performed *Gesamtkunstwerk*. Although much of Schwitters's work was small-scale, sometimes by necessity, even his smallest works involve a drive towards the large-scale, all-encompassing embodiment, such as the *Merzbau* itself, or towards the fully theatrical realization, such as the play **Collision** (**Zusammenstoâ**) (1927). Even the small-scale works often convey the impression of being an epitome or miniaturization of something of larger scale. indeed of grandeur, as in the various forms of **The Cathedral**. Behind their modesty and humour is an intense will towards unity and totalization.

In such works, even the notion of the opposite ends of the spectrum—pure words versus pure image—is overcome, as these come full circle and join up as 'analysis of elements', as, for example, Schwitters's performance of the sound poem **"W."** Moholy-Nagy described the scene:

> . . . he showed to the audience a poem containing only one letter on a sheet (1924):
>
> **W**
>
> Then he started to 'recite' it with slowly rising voice. The consonant varied from a whisper to the sound of a wailing siren till at the end he barked with a shockingly loud tone.[34]

This demonstration shows the powerful link that Schwitters was able to forge between the two 'extremes'. To him, sounds, like letters, were materials, and in this 'analysis of elements', the programme of abstract poetry (*Wortkunst*) propounded by the *Sturm* group is still visible, carried out with the uncompromising rigour of the *De Stijl* manifestos rather than the melancholy and doom-laden feeling-tone of August Stramm, usually cited as the most important *Sturm* poet and a model for a few of Schwitters's early poems.[35] But as Scheffer pointed

out, Schwitters's practice was distinctive from the start, and much theoretical significance has been read back into Stramm that his poems scarcely bear out.[36] Both groups agreed that 'Art is production, not reproduction' ('Kunst ist Gabe nicht Wiedergabe'), and banned all imitation of Nature. As van Doesburg put it, using the architectural idiom in which Schwitters was at home: 'The new architecture is elementary. . . . Its elements, such as function, mass, plane, time, space, light, colour, material, etc., are at the same time elements of plasticism.'[37]

Despite this stress on abstract analysis, Moholy-Nagy nevertheless experienced Schwitters's performance as an outcry expressive of the wretched state of post-war Germany:

> The scene is Germany. Inflation after the war; corruption, waste, damage to material and man. An abortive social revolution makes the situation even more hopeless. Schwitters' writings of that time end with a desperate and at the same time challenging cry.[38]

Yet if word and image are analyzed and the elements unforgettably linked in Schwitters's *W,* it remains true that the association between them is arbitrary. That arbitrariness—its total unexpectedness and unpredictability—is a form of wit. Schwitters insisted to such an extent on the meaninglessness of the sounds he used, their lack of denotation, that he objected strongly when, for example, Mies van der Rohe identified one of the sound-clusters of his **Primal Sonata** (**Ursonate**) with the Rumanian word for *Schnaps.*[39] In Schwitters's view, his sounds did not signify by any existing convention—nor, whatever Moholy-Nagy thought, were they to be considered directly expressive of primal emotional conditions such as anguish, despair, or grief. The two major linguistic theories of language—the view that language is expressive and natural, based on primitive onomatopeia and the view that language is a matter of conventional signs in which the link between sound and sign is arbitrary—were both powerful presences in Schwitters's milieu. The theory of primitive poetry, emotional onomatopeia, was rooted deep in German Romanticism, and early experiments in sound poetry by Christian Morgenstern and Paul Scheerbart (which antedated Hugo Ball's often-cited attempts by twenty years and were certainly known to Schwitters) still relied on it for some of their effect. Yet the balance was tipping towards de Saussure's restatement of the view of the conventionality of language, and the notion of the analysis and free combination of elements is associated with it. Schwitters resolved this duality by suggesting a highly individual solution: a combination of the two, a passionately arbitrary 'onomatopeia'. Just as the syntax of his poetic sentences is grammatical only by association, so his pure sounds are expressive only by analogy. There is a further witty dimension, for it is not sound and sense that are conjoined, but sound and senselessness—and that not by an existing link in convention or in Nature, but by arbitrary fiat (*Willkür*): sudden, arresting, and astonishing. This may or may not be the model of ordinary language, but it *is* a language of art.

This short exercise in *W* was at the root of his large-scale, 35-minute-long composition, the **Primal Sonata** (**Ursonate**), or *Sonata in Primal Sounds* (*Sonate in Urlauten*), one of the major works in the genre. Here, sound and sign are linked by phonetics, but phonetics cannot account for the notes or tones produced. As with *W,* there is also a text—in this case, an elaborate 'score' of invented words so that the images simply *are* the words. However meaningful the letters may be at the level of phonetics, when combined into non-signifying words, they become graphic art.

As we move towards Schwitters's most fully elaborated performance art, his theatre, we find that he formulated two models: the '*Merz* Stage' (*Merzbühne*) and the 'Normal *Merz* Stage' (*Normalbühne Merz*). The first came into being in the context of experiments stretching back to the end of the nineteenth-century and was first published in the periodical *Sturm-Bühne* (*Sturm-Theatre*). Schwitters's writings on it convey a visionary enthusiasm and his description of the projected *Merz-Theater* reads like directions for a spectacular production:

> In contrast to the drama or the opera, all parts of the *Merz* stage-work are inseparably bound up together; it cannot be written, read or listened to, it can only be produced in the theatre. . . . The *Merz* stage knows only the fusing of all factors into a composite work. Materials for the stage-set are all solid, liquid and gaseous bodies, such as white wall, man, barbed wire entanglement, blue distance, light cone. Use is made of compressible surfaces, or surfaces capable of dissolving into meshes; surfaces that fold like curtains, expand or shrink. Objects will be allowed to move and revolve, and lines will be allowed to broaden into surfaces.[40]

The second, constructivist model he formulated from 1923 on; it is more functional, stripped down, 'everyday', small-scale and inexpensive, and designed to be adaptable to a variety of uses. This pairing of two opposed kinds of theatre, best known from Max Reinhardt's practice, was common to the whole period: the theatre of grand spectacle on the one hand, and the little theatre of the chamber play and cabaret on the other. Both represented innovation. Schwitters actually built two models, photographs of which survive, one of the 'Normal *Merz* Theatre' for the Exhibition of Theater Technology in Vienna in 1924, and another of an arena stage for the *Merz*-Theatre which was shown with the first in a similar exhibition in New York two years later. But neither type of theatre is confined to one kind of stage: a drawing of 1925 shows an arena stage intended for use by the Normal *Merz* Theatre,[41] and Schwitters also left a number of unpublished writings on the 'Normal *Merz* Theatre'.

On his theatre as on his painting there were, again, many mutually reinforcing influences, emanating from the same set of *avant-garde* sources: the theatrical writings of the Italian Futurists, the idea of the 'total work of art' (*Gesamtkunstwerk*) of Kandinsky and Ball, the Total Theatre (*Theater der Totalität*) of Moholy-Nagy, and the electro-mechanical experiments of Lissitsky and other East European Constructivists. Others, known primarily as writers rather than visual artists, such as Morgenstern and Scheerbart, are also of importance for Schwitters's theatrical writings, for he belonged to a line of experiment in theatre closely related to the practice of Morgenstern, the nonsense poet who prefigured Dada and worked with Reinhardt in the cabaret,[42] and Scheerbart, the visionary exponent of glass architecture and cosmic ballet, who was for a time associated with *Der Sturm* and wrote a number of theatre pieces for a 'little theatre' of fantasy. The writings for the theatre of these men are still little known, even in Germany, and even less performed, like Schwitters's own, despite his recognition as an early theorist of the 'Happening' of the 1960s and the successful mounting of one of his major plays, **Collision** (**Zusammenstoâ**) (1927), in Tübingen in 1976.[43]

Schwitters's plays range from fragments or 'scenes' to the large-scale work—that is, they show the same pattern of analysis into elements and rebuilding into large-scale new forms as does his other work. Schwitters was, of course, himself a performer in those circles where cabaret carried a freight of experimental theatre, and Blümner's writings show that his performance art had its roots in an explicit critique of the theatre.[44] Although in his edition of Schwitters's dramatic work Friedhelm Lach presents Schwitters as a representative of the dramatic movements of Futurism, anti-psychological 'machine' theatre, and *Sturm*-theatre, elsewhere he perceives that Schwitters is actually a parodist of these movements.[45] The affirmation of the *avant-garde* theatre through the parodying of its styles is characteristic of the cabaret tradition from the turn of the century.

The best example of Schwitters's large-scale dramatic work composed of 'scenes' is **Collision.** This resembles an example of Dada 'epic theatre', involving the theme of world collision and apocalypse reminiscent of Schwitters's own expressionist paintings such as *The Circling* (*Das Kreisen*) (1919). The scenes themselves often contain elements of sound poetry, parodies of hit tunes and commercial jingles, café dialogue, familiar quotations from Goethe and snatches of excerpts from film scenarios and radio broadcasts, and they call for organized mass expressive movements and sound effects. For our purposes, the 'multi-media' effects (an extension of Schwitters's 'multi-materiality') are of central importance, and although these would depend in part on the director of the stage productions, Schwitters's action and detailed stage directions give ample indications of what might be done, and are prophetic of technical innovations that have taken place since the time of writing. To give one single example from the riches of **Collision:** scene 10 (the culmination of the play) depicts the crowds of Berlin turning out for the expected disaster of the collision of another planet with the Earth precisely at Berlin Tempelhof. Although a number of settings for the impending disaster have been invoked in the course of the play, it is symptomatic that the scene of the final action is displaced from 'the cathedral' or church (in which traditional prayers/Dada invocations accompanied by organ music, are intoned), via a scene set on Mars, to the airport. The stage direction reads: *'Infinitely open square, countless masses of people' ('Unendlicher freier Platz, unübersehbare Menschenmenge').*[46] The vast crowd and the riot police grapple with one another, shifting each other back and forth by only half a metre at a time, suggesting a ballet of immense power. The other planet, the 'Green Globe', comes into view, and its great shadow darkens the stage. Throughout this scene, sound poetry ('*All run to the left:* Hihiiiiiiiiiiiiiiiiiiiiiiiiiiiiiiiii i i i i i i i i i') is interspersed with *Merz*-chants—the jingles and catch-phrases which have been employed throughout to characterize the various groups and individuals, as well as, at the moment of crisis, half-remembered quotations from Goethe. As the light returns, the crisis barely averted, the scene turns into an immense festival or carnival, again suggesting choreographed movement.

Our understanding of Schwitters's work depends on recognizing that an appeal to all the senses is being made and that their combined forces are being called up. At the same time, the appeal to the senses is always guided by the restraint (sometimes the lash) of wit. **Collision,** for example, the scientist and his assistant, who have predicted the collision and thus caused the panic, now take credit for its aversion, and are awarded the Nobel Prize. The mustering of the senses in the 'total work of art' can also be seen as a satire on the destructive power of self-appointed scientific reason assuming the robes of Nostradamus. Moreover, although the process of transformation of individuals into a mass is conveyed through the mass media and can be related to Brecht's techniques in the political cabaret and epic theatre, **Collision** is best seen as a more elaborate version of Schwitters's short Dada prose work, 'Causes and Outbreak of the Great and Glorious Revolution in Revon' (1919), which analyzes and sums up the irrational moment in which 'a man standing' is converted willy-nilly into 'the revolution'.[47] By extension, the 'Green Globe' may be read as a projected image of our own planet (visible, we now know, from space as the only blue-green planet in our solar system) which is threatened with self-destruction. It is of the essence of Schwitters's art that we must read his logic as well as his illogic, his sense as well as his non-sense, and that we must read him both in fine detail and as a whole. We need a new reading of the full verbal and visual core of his work, which is more extensive and more significant for all his work than has been understood hitherto.

NOTES

[1]—A good account of Schwitters's relations with other movements and tendencies of the years 1910-20 is given by John Elderfield, *Kurt Schwitters* (London: Thames and Hudson, 1985).

[2]—Werner Schmalenbach, *Kurt Schwitters* (Cologne: Du Mont Schauberg, 1967), pp. 198-202.

[3]—Richard Sheppard, 'Kurt Schwitters and Dada: Some Preliminary Remarks on a Complex Topic', in *Dada-Constructivism: The Janus Face of the Twenties* (catalogue) (London: Annely Juda Fine Art, 1984), p. 47.

[4]—Kurt Schwitters, *Das literarische Werk*, ed. Friedhelm Lach, 5 vols (Cologne: Du Mont Schauberg, 1973-81), I, p. 70.

[5]—Translations are my own unless otherwise stated. *Three Painter-Poets: Arp, Schwitters, Klee, Selected Poems*, ed. and transl. Harriet Watts (Harmondsworth: Penguin, 1974), p. 106 offers a more literal reading of line 3 which has the advantage of 'defamiliarization': 'On hop-skip mouth' [hüpfen' = to hop], but thus, perhaps, misses the thematic sense of the coinage in context.

[6]—Richard Brinkmann, 'Zur Wortkunst des *Sturm*-Kreises', in *Unterscheidung und Bewahrung: Festschrift für Hermann Kunisch*, eds. Klaus Lazarowicz and Wolfgang Kron (Berlin: Walter de Gruyter, 1961), pp. 63-78.

[7]—Schwitters, *Das literarische Werk*, I, p. 68.

[8]—*Der Sturn* (1919) is reproduced in Elderfield (Illustration 73) in such a way as to cut off part of the name at the bottom.

[9]—Armin Arnold, 'Kurt Schwitters' Gedicht "An Anna Blume": Sinn oder Unsinn?', *Text + Kritik*, No. 35/36 (October 1972), pp. 16-17. This essay is often regarded as a spoof.

[10]—For reproductions of these, see *Kurt Schwitters* (catalogue) (Dusseldorf: Städtische Kunsthalle, 1971).

[11]—*Berlin/Hanover: the 1920s* (catalogue) (Dallas Museum of Fine Arts, 1977). The introduction by John E. Bowlt gives a useful, brief account of the relations between Russian and German art in this period, and throws light in particular onthe relations between Lissitzky and Schwitters.

[12]—On this Cubist practice, see Stephen Bann, 'The mythical conception is the name: Titles and names in modern and post-modern painting', *Word and Image*, 1/2 (April-June 1985, p. 182 and n. 28.

[13]—*The Critic* is reproduced as Illustration 24 in Elderfield.

[14]—Theo van Doesburg, *Principles of Neo-Plastic Art* (London: Lund Humphries, 1929), p. 18 and figures 5-8. This is a translation of *Grundbegriffe der neuen gestaltenden Kunst* (1925).

[15]—*Text als Figur: Visuelle Poesie von der Antike bis zur Moderne* (exhibition catalogue No. 56 of the Herzog August Bibliothek, Wolfenbüttel), eds. Jeremy Adler and Ulrich Ernst (Wolfenbüttel: Herzog-August-Bibliothek, 1987), p. 254.

[16]—For a dozen of Rauschenberg's 'combine paintings', see *MOCA: The Panza Collection* (catalogue) (Los Angeles; Museum of Contemporary Art, 1988). Unfortunately, the colour reproduction blurs the detail visible in the exhibition.

[17]—Bernd Scheffer, *Anfange experimenteller Literatur* (Bonn: Bouvier, 1978) is the best study of Schwitters's strictly literary output, but does not treat any work that is not exclusively verbal.

[18]—See, for example, Jean-Pierre Dupuy's 'Self-reference in Literature', forthcoming in *Poetics,* ed. Siegfried J. Schmidt.

[19]—Quoted in *The Dada Painters and Poets,* ed. Robert Motherwell (New York: Wittenborn and Schultz, 1951), p. xxi.

[20]—Christof Spengemann, *Der Zweemann,* No. 4, in Motherwell, pp. 61-62.

[21]—Elderfield, pp. 114-115.

[22]—Adler and Ernst, p. 270.

[23]—For the complete poem, see Schwitters's letter of 18 November 1920 to Christof Spengemann, in *Wir spielen, bis uns der Tod abholt,* ed. Ernst Nündel (Berlin: Ullstein, 1975), p. 34.

[24]—Kurt Schwitters, *Anna Blume und Ich,* ed. Ernst Schwitters (Zurich: Die Arche, 1965), p. 199.

[25]—Hans Arp, 'Opus Null', from *Das Pyramidenrock* (1924), in *Gesammelte Gedichte,* 3 vols. (Wiesbaden and Zurich: Limes and Die Arche, 1963-84), I, p. 80.

[26]—Adler and Ernst, p. 271. The portfolio cover appears as figure 184.

[27]—Kurt Schwitters, 'Rede am Grabe Leo Reins', in *Anna Blume und Ich,* p. 29.

[28]—Quoted in Robert Bartlett Haas's translation in Kate T. Steinitz, *Kurt Schwitters: A Portrait from Life* (Berkeley and Los Angeles: California University Press, 1968), p. 5.

[29]—Kurt Schwitters, *Auguste Bolte* (1923) (Zurich: Die Arche, 1966), p. 43.

[30]—Kurt Schwitters, 'Merz', in Motherwell, p. 60.

[31]—For the parallel development of *Merz* and *PROUN,* see *Berlin/Hanover: the 1920s* (footnote 11).

[32]—Steinitz (pp. 30-39) gives an account of the circumstances in which *The Cock* (or, in American translation, *The Rooster*) was created. A translation of *The Scarecrow* appears on pp. 127-129.

[33]—For a chronology and an account of these *Soirées,* see 'Dada: A Chronology' in *New Studies in Dada: Essays and Documents,* ed. Richard Sheppard (Hutton: Hutton Press, 1981), p. 187 and Jane Beckett, 'Dada, Theo van Doesburg and *De Stijl,* in *Dada: Studies of a Movement,*

ed. Richard Sheppard (Chalfont St Giles: Alpha Academic, 1979, pp. 1-25.

[34]—Motherwell, p. xxii.

[35]—Cf. M. S. Jones, 'Kurt Schwitters, *Der Sturm* and Expressionism', *Modern Languages, 52* (1972), pp. 157-160 and Philip Thomson, *'A Case of Dadaistic Ambivalence: Kurt Schwitters' Stramm-Imitations and "An Anna Blume" ',* The German Quarterly, 45 (1972), pp. 47-56.

[36]—Scheffer, pp. 29-30.

[37]—Theo van Doesburg, 'Towards a Plastic Architecture', in *De Stijl,* ed. Hans L. C. Jaffé (London: Thames and Hudson, 1970), p. 185. For the original see *De Stijl,* 6, No. 6/7 (Paris, 1924), p. 78.

[38]—Motherwell, p. xxii.

[39]—*Ibid.*

[40]—Schwitters, 'Merz', transl. Ralph Manheim, in Motherwell, pp. 62-3. Schwitters published the section on *Merz*-theatre half a dozen times between 1919 and 1923. This translation is based on the text as published in *Der Ararat* (Munich, 1921).

[41]—Schmalenbach, p. 36.

[42]—See E. S. Shaffer, 'Christian Morgenstern and the Emergence of Modernism in the Berlin Theatre', in *Facets of Modernism: Essays in Honour of James Walter McFarlane,* ed. Janet Garton (Norwich: University of East Anglia, 1985), pp. 31-75.

[43]—Cf. footnotes 39 and 53 of Richard Sheppard's essay on Kandinsky in this issue of *Word and Image.*

[44]—Rudolf Blümner, *Der Geist des Kubismus und die Künste* (Berlin: Verlag Der Sturm, 1921), pp. 47-54.

[45]—Friedhelm Lach, 'Die Merzbühne von Kurt Schwitters oder Kurt Schwitters als Dramatiker', *Text + Kritik,* No. 35/36 (October 1972), p. 70.

[46]—Schwitters, *Das literarische Werk,* IV, p. 74.

[47]—This was published first in English, in a translation by Eugene Jolas, in *transition,* no. 8 (November, 1926).

Marjorie Perloff (review date 1994)

SOURCE: A review of *pppppp: Poems Performance Pieces Proses Plays Poetics,* in *Sulfur,* Vol. XIV, No. 1, Spring, 1994, pp. 201-08.

[*In the following review of* pppppp: Poems Performance Pieces Proses Plays Poetics, *Perloff discusses the pitfalls of translating Schwitters's "abstract poetry."*]

In a 1924 manifesto called "Consistent Poetry," which appears in Jerome Rothenberg and Pierre Joris's beautifully produced and edited selection of Schwitters's literary works, we read:

> Classical poetry counted on the similarities between people. It considered the association of ideas as unambiguous. It was mistaken. At any rate it built its foci on associations of ideas: "Uber allen Gipfeln ist Ruh" ("O'er every mountain peace does reign"). Here Goethe does not only want to indicate that there is quiet on mountain tops; the reader is supposed to enjoy this peacefulness in the same way the poet, tired from his official duties and usually functioning in an urban environment, does himself. That such associations of ideas are not all that commonly shared can be shown if one were to read such a line to someone from Heidjer (a region of two inhabitants per square kilometer). That person would certainly be much more impressed by a line like "lightning hairy zigzags the subway crushes the skyscraper." At any rate, the realization that all is quiet does not bring forth poetic feelings in him because, for him, quietness is the normal state of affairs. I cite this passage because its combination of common-sense. . . .
>
> Abstract poetry separated—and therein lies its great merit—the word from its associations, and played off word against word; more particularly concept against concept, while taking sound into account. That is more consistent than the evaluation of poetic feelings. . . . (pp. 223-24)

Absurd as it is to contemplate the impact of Goethe's nature lyric on the hypothetical inhabitant of Heidjer, Schwitters is not being merely playful here. What he sees is that, with the breakdown of the traditional class structures—structures that Goethe could take for granted—the transparency of language as carrier of "poetic feeling," directed toward an audience conditioned to "understand,". sharing as it does the poet's own basic feelings, is called into question. No wonder Schwitters longed, as did so many poets of the post-World War I era, to create an "abstract poetry"—a poetry that might remove itself from "concepts" altogether. But how to achieve such a poetry? "Not the word but the letter is the original material of poetry," Schwitters declares in the same manifesto. "Consistent poetry is constructed from letters. Letters have no concepts. Letters in themselves have no sound, they only offer the possibility to be given sound values by the performer. The consistent poem plays off letters and groups of letters against each other" (p. 225).

Shades of Khlebnikov's *zaum* poetry and, in our own day, the chance generated work of Jackson Mac Low (who recently wrote his own *Merzgedichte in memoriam Kurt Schwitters*") and John Cage, who neatly echoes, in his preface to Mureau, Schwitters's assertion that "The elements of poetry are letters, syllables, words, sentences" (p. 215). Indeed as Rothenberg and Joris point out, the sound text and concrete poetry of the past few decades can be traced directly back to such works as Schwitters's famous **"Ur Sonate,"** whose entire text

(some 28 pages) is reproduced in this book, waiting for a set of readers to actualize its score. (A recording of Schwitters reading this amazing tour de force is available from *Gelbe Music* in Hamburg). And certainly Schwitters's alogical and non-grammatical poetry looks ahead to the "language poetry" of the current generation.

But from the translator's perspective, Schwitters's practice is nothing if not a mine field. For if "Not the word but the letter is the original material of poetry," how can translation, usually unable to duplicate the phonemes and morphemes of the original, be adequate? How, for example, to translate a line like "Duumdu" ("Er sie Es"), whose middle syllable "um" ("around") gives us not only the idea of "YOu on you" but also the paragram "Duum" which is a homonym for "dumm" or "stupid," hence "You stupid you." Pierre Joris translates the word as "Thouroundthou" (p. 13), which nicely duplicates the diphthong but loses Schwitters's double entendre.

Like Khlebnikov's often untranslatable (despite the recent valiant efforts of Paul Schmidt) poetry, Schwitters's poems depend so fully on their linguistic base—on pun and paragram, anaphora and rhyme, onomatopoeia and echolalia, that they seem to defy translation, with the result that this great artist, who is also considered a major poet in the German-speaking world (the scholarly Friedhelm Lach edition, published between 1973-76, runs to five large volumes), is almost unknown outside Germany. Indeed, such essays as have been written on his poetic composition are primarily the work of art historians—Werner Schmalenbach and John Elderfield, for example—who understand that Schwitters's writings—his early expressionist poems in the vein of August Schramm, the subsequent Dada poems like **"An Anna Blume"** (the much-anthologized poem which originally made Schwitters famous), the short prose pieces or "proses" as the editors ingeniously call them, the playlets, the visual and sound poems—are not only an integral part of Schwitters's *Merz* (for *Kommerz*) collage art but important in their own right.

The difficulty of translating Schwitters is compounded by the fact that in the last decade of his life when he was living in England, Schwitters translated some of his own early poetry and tried writing new poems in English (see pp. 100-118 of *pppppp*). Poets are not always their own best translators and as Werner Schmalenbach reports, Schwitters's English was always shaky. In 1942, with the help of Stefan Themerson, he translated his 1919 **"An Anna Blume,"** the one poem of his that has made its way into every Dada textbook and anthology. It is the translation unfortunately included by Rothenberg and Joris in *pppppp* as well. I say unfortunately, because I think Schwitters's English version is a travesty of his subtle, witty, playful, and charming 1919 original.

Take the opening line, "O du, Geliebte, meiner 27 Sinne, ich liebe Dir!," which Schwitters translates as "O Thou, beloved of my twenty seven senses, I love thine!" The second-person singular pronoun "Du" is the familiar form of address (vis-à-vis the formal "Sie"), and in German, the pronouns have different endings for every case, singular and plural, whereas our own "you" has no variation, singular or plural, except for the genitive "your." Accordingly, no literal English translation can ever capture the sort of pronoun-play in which the German Schwitters regularly indulges. Still, I find the use of "Thou" ("thou, thee thine") questionable, for Schwitters's German is above all distinguished, as are his collages, by its respect for the ordinary, the everyday, the common, the banal. In this instance, the joke is that Anna, addressed quite naturally and colloquially as "O Du, Geliebte" is immediately deflated by the absurd hyperbole of "my twenty seven senses." And this, in turn, is followed by the absurd "Ich liebe dir"—absurd because "dir" is in the dative case whereas "liebe" takes the accusative "dich." "Ich liebe dir" thus turns Anna, who is after all addressed as "Du, ungezähltes Frauenzimmer" (a much less respectful address than "Thou, uncounted woman"!), into no more than the indirect object of the poet's "love." Grammar, let's remember, produces meanings.

By comparison, "I love thine" strikes me as no more than arch, a sort of pseudo-ee cummings locution. If one were to retranslate **"An Anna Blume,"** perhaps the solution would be to take the literal option: since English designates the indirect object by means of a preposition, we might render the German as "I love to you" or "for you" and let the ambiguities develop. But Schwitters does other things to weaken his original: Anna's "green bird" becomes "wheels" (which eliminates the double entendre of "bird"), her red dress, literally sawed up ("zersägt") into white pleats becomes "thy red dress, clashed in white folds," and so on. Worst of all, the ambiguity of the name Anna Blume—is she an opening bud or a deflowered "schlichtes Mädchen"?—is lost in the coy "Anna Blossom." Schwitters mock-Petrarchan homage to the palindromic Anna of the streets with whom he is sleeping is thus largely deflected.

I mention this particular self-translation because Jerome Rothenberg and Pierre Joris have evidently taken it and related Schwitters's translations at face value. "It's Schwitters," they say in their Introduction, "who gives the green light for our extensive use of second-person thou's, sometimes correctly grammatical, sometimes linked to first-person verbs" (p. xxx). And indeed, "thee" and "thou" are the pronouns of choice in these translations as are certain other archaisms not quite warranted in the supple and racy language of the original. "Ein Säuferstiel augt dumm das klage Tier," for example, has a comic, sardonic edge that is missing from the line "Drunkard's stem dumbly does eye the doleful beast" (p. 24). "Augt dumm" means "gapes" or "gapes stupidly"; "dumbly does eye" seems unnecessarily contrived. Again, "klage" is a coinage from "klagen" ("complain"): it can be read as the "whining" or "pathetic" animal, but "doleful beast"?

But these are minor flaws in what is often a brilliantly inventive rendering of Schwitters's all-but-untranslatable idiom. Take, for example, Rothenberg's "Subway Poem" ("Untergrundgedicht")

Houses eyeball millions cudgel lamps
Windows crunch on eyes
Bellow light the subway-shuttle teeth
German Daily News sleds past and music (super shoeshines)
Adding machines spew numbers, Garden City
Songs tender cannons' gold (physician tested)
Windows live sans light grow numb
Sans coal glass woodens
Flames glass up
Bellow crunch on light the window
Flames glass flames
Houses eyeball millions sparkle lamps
And fire woodens coal light bellows forth
(In case of crowds step to the centre aisle) (p. 35)

Häuser augen Millionen peitschen Lampen
Fenster beissen Augen
Brüllen Licht die Untergrundbahn Zähne
Deutsche Tageszeitung rodelt und Musik (bester Schuhputz)
Additionmaschinen wirren Zahlen, Gartenstadt
Lieder zarten die Kanonen Gold (ärztlich empfohlen)
Fenster leben ohne Licht erstarren
Ohne Kohle holzt das Glas
Flamme glast
Brüllen beissen Licht die Fenster
Flamme glast die Flamme
Häuser augen Millionen funken Lampen
find die Flamme holzen Kohle brüllt das Licht.
(Bei Andrang in den Mittelgang treten.)[1]

This 1920 poem is the counterpart of Schwitters's *Merzbilder*: a catalogue of graphic images aligned with a minimum of punctuation in the tradition of the Futurist *parole in libertà,* which Schwitters surely knew, is "cut" by signboards, advertising slogans, and newspaper bits: "super shoeshines," "physician tested," and so on. The cacophony of the original is caught by onomatopoeic words like "cudgel" and "crunch" and compounds like "subway-shuttle teeth." Throughout, Rothenberg's poem replicates the heavy alliteration and assonance, and the strong-stress rhythm of Schwitters's poem, his use of idiom (e.g., "Flames glass up") captures the sardonic urbanism of this *Merzbau*, the city where everything has turned into commodity ("German Daily News sleds past"). **"Subway poem"** is followed by **"High Fashion Furs" ("Feine Pelzmoden")**, which takes the cataloguing technique of the former lyric even further, juxtaposing a set of images of street scenes (again *parole in libertà* like "Telephones broadcast baskets") with surreal references to the "Boil Intestines Pharmacy," "A-1 intestines" now populating what seems to be the entire city.

The catalogue poems, sentence series, and visual and sound poems bring to the fore all of the ingenuity of the poet-translators. In **"Chinese Banalities"** (p. 32), couplets like "Spice is the variety of life. / Every apron has a wife" has precisely the nursery-rhyme effect of "Würze is des Witzes Kürze. / Jede Frau hat eine Schürze." And Rothenberg's rendition of the title poem provides a masterful verbal-visual equivalent of the erotic play of the original:

p p p p p p p p p
pornographic i-poem
The go
Its bleating is
Sweet & peaceful
And it will not
With its horns |

The black line shows where I cut lengthwise into a harmless poem in a children's picture book. From the goat I got the go.

And it will not | be provoked
With its hams | to shove & poke. (p. 81)

p p p p p p p p p
pornographisches i-Gedicht
Die Zie
Diese Meck ist
Liebe und friedlich
und sie wird sich
Mit den Hörnern |

Der Strich zeigt, wo ich das harmlose Gedichten aus einem Kindergilderbuch durgeschnitten habe, der Länge nach. Aus der Ziege ist so die Zie geworden.

Und sie wird sich | nicht erbossen
Mit den Hörnern | Each zo stossen. (FL 95)

"The go" is even more surprising than the original "Die Zie" (cut-up for "Ziege") because "go" is not a syllable in "goat." The "go" that "bleats" is very suggestive, especially when we learn that "Its bleating is / Sweet & peaceful." What is it that the "go[at]" "will not" . . . "with its horns"? Fill in your own story, a story which is then "explained" by reference to the complete page in the children's book:

And it will not | be provoked
With its horns | to shove & poke.

Here the translation almost betters the original, "shove" and "poke" being paragrammatically inside "provoked" whereas Schwitters's nursery rhyme has the simpler pattern of the rhyme "erbossen" / "stossen."

But perhaps the most important items in the Rothenberg-Joris book, aside from the great **"Ur Sonata,"** which is reproduced in its entirety, are the "proses" like **"The Onion"** and **"Auguste Bolte,"** both important precursors for works like Lyn Hejinian's *My Life* or Gilbert Sorrentino's procedural fictions. These works, almost unknown to the English-speaking reader, have Gertrude Stein-like phrasal permutations, intercut by commercial cliches as is the **"Subway poem"** but on a larger scale. The 28-page **"Auguste Bolte,"** written in 1923 and published in *Der Sturm,* is the fictional equivalent of Schwitters's *Merzbilder.* The title alludes to the cranky Widow Bolte, whom every German schoolchild of the period would have recognized from Wilhelm Busch's famous Max und Moritz. In Schwitters's version, Auguste Bolte becomes a young girl, in search of a PhD in "Lif";

indeed the text is subtitled "a doctoral dissertation." Rather than actually collaging cliches and advertising jingles into the text as he did in **"Subway poem,"** Schwitters here interweaves the language of ordinary people in all its absurdity, comedy, and pathos. Beginning with a "wise saying" pronounced by his five-year old son Ernst ("What one chews turns mush"), Schwitters declares that his "allegory for good old Aart-ccriticism is "a natural and faithful reproduction of the critiques in daily papers. The daily press on art, the so-called daily-artpress, wears a little girl's dress. Chaste and modest, it has tied a tiny apron over it, with embroidery trimmings" (p. 139). Like Joyce's Dublin, where Gerty MacDowell is similarly "chaste and modest," the petit-bourgeois "polite society" of Schwitters's Hannover masks a vicious savagery just underneath its placid surface.

As the story opens, "Augusta Bolte saw about 10 people on the street, who all advanced in one and the same direction. This seemed suspicious to Augusta Bolte, very suspicious indeed. 10 people were walking in one and the same direction. 1, 2, 3, 4, 5, 6, 7, 8, 9, 10. Something was going on there" (p. 140). It becomes Augusta's mission to find out where these ten people are going, a mission complicated when the 10 break into 2 5s, the 5s into 2 + 3 and finally into five 1s. Along the way, Augusta, "who had been such a brilliant girl, so gifted even back in school" (the phrase is repeated again and again), gets "stuck into a metric pattern," and draws conclusions that "went against her grain. For a moment she wondered what that grain was, against which, in a way, it went" (p. 141). When the 10 split into 2 5s, she considers it "a scandalous impertinence of the mass to split up or, better, to divide" (p. 142). "Why indeed," Augusta Bolte wonders, "did 10 people have to split up into groups of 5. That kind of thing was a shrewd tactic of the, in a way, hostile mass." And so on.

The nasty logic and paranoia exhibited in such passages eerily anticipate the Nazi mentality already nascent in Schwitters's Germany. Cliché piles on cliché: Augusta's path now crosses that of one Richard Eckermester, a young ne-er do well who never made it through school: "Neither the carrot nor the stick had had any effect" (159); Eckermester is seen by Augusta descending from a hackney cab and "abscond[ing] into a house":

The die was cast, and the man had absconded into a house. Miss Professor Augusta had her car stop. It was clear that something was going on here. Why else should a man abscond into a house? You can't fit that into a hollow tooth! Why else should a man jump into a hackney cab to abscond into a house? Why? Something was certain: if nothing was happening here, then nothing was happening anywhere. Although the reverse could be true too. And while Augusta realized the equivalence of all values, as she now realized that, depending on one's taste, everything could prove everything or nothing, a new unheard of realization came to her, namely that it did not matter if one attended it or not.

Nobody could attend to everything. Man had to make a choice. And he had to make a choice. And he had to make a choice, not because he had to make a choice, but because in itself it didn't matter if he made a choice or if he didn't make a choice. (p. 162)

The permutations here are less Steinian than reminiscent of Beckett's *Watt*. And indeed, Schwitters' prose, subtly rendered by Rothenberg and Joris here (although the recurrent rhyme "Auguste wusste . . . das sie . . . musste" is not quite conveyed by "Augusta musta"), anticipates the nervousness, anxiety, illogicality, and comic/horrific irresolution of Beckett's fiction as well as his clown plays.

It is a scandal that this edition of Schwitters's work, produced as it is by two of the finest poet-translators writing today, has not (at least so far) gotten the recognition it deserves. The *New York Times Book Review,* the *New York Review of Books,* the *New Republic* and comparable periodicals have not reviewed it. But this silence would hardly have surprised Schwitters. For the bourgeois mindset that he so mercilessly parodizes in works like **"Auguste Bolte"** is the mindset that continues to treat him with "suspicion." He would have shrugged that suspicion off good humoredly with something like the "cadenza" from **Ur Sonata:**

Priimiititti too
Priimiititti taa
Priimiititti too
Priimiititti taa
Priimiititti tootaa

NOTES

[1] Kurt Schwitters, *Das Literarische Werk: Band I, Lyrik,* ed. Friedhelm Lach (Köln: DuMont Shauberg, 1973), p. 81. Subsequently cited as FL.

FURTHER READING

Biography

Steinitz, Kate Trauman. *Kurt Schwitters: A Portrait From Life.* Berkeley: University of California Press, 1968, 221 p.
    Biographical sketch of Schwitters with commentary on some of his better-known literary works.

Criticism

Bacon, Thomas I. "Two From Germany." *Furman Studies* XXI, No. 4 (June 1974): 7-12.
    Mentions Schwitters's poem "In a World of Disappointments" as an example of his "reflective and sentimental" work.

Dietrich, Dorothea. *The Collages of Kurt Schwitters: Tradition and Innovation.* Cambridge: Cambridge University Press, 1993, 240 p.
    Sees Schwitters as an example of avant-garde innovation within a surviving artistic tradition. Dietrich examines Schwitters's relation to Expressionistic theory, postwar politics, the representation of women, and the development of the collage form.

Elderfield, John. "Schwitters's Abstract 'Revolution.'" *German Life & Letters* XXIV, No. 3 (April 1971): 256-61.
    Analyzes the first chapter of Schwitters's unfinished novel *Franz Müllers Drahtfrühling* as an absurd fable concerning the artist's role in society.

———. *Kurt Schwitters.* London: Thames and Hudson, 1985, 424 p.
    Studies Schwitters as a modernist artist, and aims at "providing a clear picture of Schwitters's art as a unified whole and of the ambitions and influences that informed it."

Jones, M. S. "Kurt Schwitters, *Der Sturm* and Expressionism." In *Modern Languages* LII, No. 4 (December 1971): 157-60.
    Considers Schwitters's relationship to the German periodical *Der Sturm*, as it relates to his Expressionist desire for a "total work of art" and his Dadaist negation of all art.

Last, Rex. Review of *Das literarische Prosa 1931-1948,* by Kurt Schwitters. *Times Literary Supplement*, No. 3942 (14 October 1977): 1206.
    Views Schwitters's short prose pieces as arbitrary, uncomposed, and half-
thought out, claiming that they demonstrate "the strange, hermetic, private world that Schwitters inhabited."

Lavin, Maud. "Advertising Utopia: Schwitters as Commercial Designer." *Art in America* 73 (October 1985): 134-39, 69.
    Discusses the years Schwitters spent as an advertising designer, seeing his commercial graphics as both radically utopian and politically conservative.

Middleton, Christopher. "Pattern Without Predictability, or Pythagoras Saved: A Comment on Kurt Schwitters' 'Gedicht 25.'" In *Bolshevism in Art, and Other Expository Writings,* pp. 209-13. Manchester: Carcanet New Press, 1978.
    Explores the Dada spirit of anti-art, chaos, and subversion represented in Schwitters's poem "Gedicht 25."

Paley, Nicholas. "Experiments in Picture Book Design: Modern Artists Who Made Books for Children 1900-1985." *Children's Literature Association Quarterly* 16, No. 4 (Winter 1991-92): 264-69.
    Notes Schwitters's collaboration with Kate Steinitz and Theo Van Doesburg to produce the experimental children's picture book *Die Scheuche (The Scarecrow).*

Retiz, Leonard. "Schwitters and the Literary Tradition." *German Life & Letters* XXVII, No. 4 (July 1974): 303-15.

Claims that Schwitters's poetry, although unique, is not as anti-traditional as its abstruse form and appearance might suggest.

Zeller, Dennis E. "Kurt Schwitters: Unity, Reconstruction and the Missing 'J.'" *German Life & Letters* XXVI, No. 4 (July 1973): 297-306.
   Examines several poems by Schwitters in order to perceive "the ways in which he attempted to upset our normal expectations and forms of artistic thought," including such conceptions as unity and completeness.

Frank Lloyd Wright

1867-1959

American architect.

INTRODUCTION

Wright is considered one of the most important and influential American architects of the twentieth century. Rejecting both the rationalist ideology and rigid machine aesthetic propounded by the leaders of the Modern Movement in Europe, Wright sought to accommodate social, environmental, and technological considerations through the creation of what he called "organic architecture." Wright's architectural philosophy found expression in both his public and private buildings. Of the former, his early office buildings, in particular, are considered advanced for their bold integration of functional and social considerations. However, Wright's numerous designs for private houses are generally thought to constitute his greatest and most enduring work. Acclaimed for their innovations in planning, expressive use of materials, and subtle integration with their natural setting, both the early Prairie houses and the later "Usonian" designs were extremely influential in the formation of postwar attitudes towards the American house.

Biographical Information

Wright was born in Richland Center, Wisconsin. His childhood years were spent traveling with his parents, as his father, a Unitarian minister, sought to improve the family's precarious financial position. In 1877, the Wrights finally settled in Madison, Wisconsin. There Wright attended high school, although he never graduated. Nevertheless, in 1885 he was admitted to the University of Wisconsin, where he studied engineering for two years. His introduction to the architectural profession also came in 1885 when he met J. Lyman Silsbee, a successful architect. Beginning in 1887, Wright assisted Silsbee as a junior draftsman. However, he soon became dissatisfied with Silsbee's conservative approach to design and in 1888 he joined the firm run by Dankmar Adler and the noted commercial architect Louis Sullivan. Wright stayed with Adler and Sullivan until 1893, by which time he was already accepting independent commissions to design houses. By 1909, Wright's reputation as a leading avant-garde architect was solidly established in America. Yet he felt that he had nearly exhausted his creative powers, and frustrated as well by his domestic situation, he left his wife and family in 1909 and went to Europe, accompanied by the wife of a client. Upon his return to America in 1910, Wright found himself alienated from the professional classes that had previously supported him. He relocated to Spring Green, Wisconsin, and there built a home he named Taliesin. The structure

was set ablaze in 1914; several individuals, including Wright's mistress, were killed. He would later build a second and third incarnation of Taliesin after this and another fire. In the mid-thirties, Wright received a number of important commissions. The first of these was a weekend house for the Edgar Kaufmann family known as Falling Water, completed in 1936. That year, Wright also received a commission for the S. C. Johnson and Son Company's administration building, and witnessed the completion of his first Usonian (a term Wright derived from "U. S. A.") house, the Jacobs house, designed as an efficient, low cost dwelling for the lower-middle class. The climax of Wright's postwar career was the construction of the Solomon R. Guggenheim Museum, intended to display Guggenheim's renowned collection of non-representational art. The museum was completed shortly after Wright's death in 1959.

Major Works

Wright's career as an architect may be divided into three phases. Between 1889 and 1899 he designed several houses, most of which were derivative in style. The period from 1900 to 1914 marked the high point of Wright's early career. He designed a great number of houses in and around Chicago that defined what would become known as the Prairie style, which was characterized by an open, asymmetrical plan, interpenetrating spaces, long horizontal planes, and an unprecedented use of glass that brought the house into an intimate relationship with its surroundings. Wright also designed a number of public buildings before the First World War, most importantly the Larkin building and Unity Temple in Oak Park, Illinois. The Larkin Building was distinguished by its open plan and monumental exterior, while Unity Temple was the first example of monolithic reinforced concrete construction in the United States.

The third period of Wright's career, which followed his return from Europe in 1910, features both the first design for his home in Wisconsin, Taliesin, and the Imperial Hotel in Tokyo—a synthesis of Western and Japanese traditions. In the 1920s Wright also designed a series of innovative houses in California. Unlike the Prairie houses, these were formal and monolithic in appearance, typified by the Barnsdall house, a lavish villa, and the Millard house, considered his finest essay in concrete-block construction. Following the 1929 stock market crash and the ensuing depression, Wright increasingly concentrated on writing, publishing *An Autobiography* and a book on urbanism, *The Disappearing City,* in which he advocated a radical decentralization of the traditional city and the creation of a quasi-rural utopia he called Broadacre City. Wright's work of the 1930s includes the well-known Falling Water. A dramatically cantilevered dwelling constructed over a wooded stream in Bear Run, Pennsylvania, Falling Water demonstrates Wright's mastery of reinforced concrete design and great subtlety in the integration of natural and man-made elements. Like that of Falling Water, Wright's design for the Guggenheim Museum exploited the dramatic possibilities of reinforced concrete, and was deliberately envisioned as a free-standing monument in order to set it apart from the surrounding urban landscape of New York City. In the final portion of his career, Wright also offered a number of statements concerning his architectural principles of organic unity and integration, most of which were originally delivered as lectures, notably in *An Organic Architecture.* Late in his career he also published several revisions of *The Disappearing City,* which present minor reassessments of the Broadacre City plan, culminating in *The Living City.*

Critical Reception

Particularly in his early career, Wright is thought to have been principally influenced by the expressive functionalism of Louis Sullivan. Sullivan's *The Autobiography of an Idea* is likewise considered the model for Wright's own *An Autobiography.* Concerning his other literary works, critics have stressed that Wright offered only a small number of architectural ideas—simplicity, decentralization, and an organic integration of nature, art, and living—which he frequently restated in his writings and lectures. His social vision has been typically characterized

as utopian, and perhaps somewhat naïve, relying as it does on the simple extrapolation of his basic design ideals to society as a whole. And, while Frank Lloyd Wright's structures are no longer held in universal regard, such particular monuments as the Guggenheim Museum and the early Prairie houses are still considered important, innovative contributions to twentieth-century American architecture. Moreover, his influence on architectural theory in America persists, given the general acceptance of the open plan as well as the widespread use of natural building materials, both hallmarks of his architectural credo.

PRINCIPAL WORKS

Studies and Executed Buildings by Frank Lloyd Wright. 2 vols. [also published as *Buildings, Plans and Designs* and *Drawings and Plans . . . The Early Period (1893-1909)*] (nonfiction) 1910
The Japanese Print: An Interpretation (nonfiction) 1912
Modern Architecture: Being the Kahn Lectures for 1930 (lectures) 1931
An Autobiography (autobiography) 1932
The Disappearing City [revised and expanded as *When Democracy Builds, The Industrial Revolution Runs Away,* and *The Living City*] (nonfiction) 1932
"Broadacre City: A New Community Plan" (essay) 1935
Architecture and Modern Life [with Baker Brownell] (nonfiction) 1937
An Organic Architecture (lectures) 1939
Genius and the Mobocracy (nonfiction) 1949
An American Architecture [edited by Edgar Kaufmann, Jr.] (nonfiction) 1955
In the Cause of Architecture: Essays by Frank Lloyd Wright for Architectural Record, *1908-1952* [with others] (essays) 1975

CRITICISM

Frank Lloyd Wright (essay date 1908)

SOURCE: "1908: In the Cause of Architecture, I," in *Frank Lloyd Wright on Architecture,* Duell, Sloan and Pearce, 1941, pp. 31-45.

[*In the following essay, originally published in 1908, Wright discusses the principles of his architectural style, which emphasize simplicity, unity, and organic integrity.*]

Radical though it be, the work here illustrated is dedicated to a cause conservative in the best sense of the word. At no point does it involve denial of the elemental law and order inherent in all great architecture; rather, is it a declaration of love for the spirit of that law and order, and a reverential recognition of the elements that made its ancient letter in its time vital and beautiful.

Primarily, nature furnished the materials for architectural motifs out of which the architectural forms as we know them today have been developed, and, although our practice for centuries has been for the most part to turn from her, seeking inspiration in books and adhering slavishly to dead formulae, her wealth of suggestion is inexhaustible; her riches greater than any man's desire. I know with what suspicion the man is regarded who refers matters of fine art back to nature. I know that it is usually an ill-advised return that is attempted, for nature in external, obvious aspect is the usually accepted sense of the term and the nature that is reached. But given inherent vision there is no source so fertile, so suggestive, so helpful aesthetically for the architect as a comprehension of natural law. As nature is never right for a picture so is she never right for the architect; that is, not ready-made. Nevertheless, she has a practical school beneath her more obvious forms in which a sense of proportion may be cultivated, when Vignola and Vitruvius fail as they must always fail. It is there that he may develop that sense of reality that translated to his own field in terms of his own work will lift him far above the realistic in his art; there he will be inspired by sentiment that will never degenerate to sentimentality and he will learn to draw with a surer hand the ever-perplexing and difficult line between the curious and the beautiful.

A sense of the organic is indispensable to an architect; where can he develop it so surely as in this school? A knowledge of the relations of form and function lies at the root of his practice; where else can he find the pertinent object lessons nature so readily furnishes?

Where can he study the differentiations of form that go to determine character as he can study them in the trees? Where can that sense of inevitableness characteristic of a work of art be quickened as it may be by intercourse with nature in this sense?

Japanese art knows this school more intimately than that of any people. In common use in their language there are many words like the word "edaburi," which, translated as near as may be, means the formative arrangement of the branches of a tree. We have no such word in English, we are not yet sufficiently civilized to think in such terms; but the architect must not only learn to think in such terms but he must learn in this school to fashion his vocabulary for himself and furnish it in a comprehensive way with useful words as significant as this one.

For 7 years it was my good fortune to be the understudy of a great teacher and a great architect, to my mind the greatest of his time: Mr. Louis H. Sullivan.

Principles are not invented, they are not evolved by one man or one age; but Mr. Sullivan's perception and practice of them amounted to a revelation at a time when they were commercially inexpedient and all but lost to sight in current practice. The fine art sense of the profession was at that time practically dead; only glimmerings were perceptible in the work of Richardson and of Root.

Adler and Sullivan had little time to design residences. The few that were unavoidable fell to my lot outside of office hours. So, largely, it remained for me to carry into the field of domestic architecture the battle they had begun in commercial building. During the early years of my own practice I found this lonesome work. Sympathizers of any kind were then few and they were not found among the architects. I well remember how "the message" burned within me, how I longed for comradeship until I began to know the younger men and how welcome was Robert Spencer, and then Myron Hunt, and Dwight Perkins, Arthur Heun, George Dean, and Hugh Garden. Inspiring days they were, I am sure, for us all. Of late we have been too busy to see one another often, but the "new school of the Middle West" is beginning to be talked about and perhaps some day it is to be. For why not the same "life" and blood in architecture that is the essence of all true art?

In 1894, with this text from Carlyle at the top of the page, "The ideal is within thyself, thy condition is but the stuff thou art to shape that same ideal out of," I formulated the following "propositions." I set them down here much as they were written then, although in the light of experience they might be stated more completely and succinctly.

I. Simplicity and repose are qualities that measure the true value of any work of art.

But simplicity is not in itself an end nor is it a matter of the side of a barn but rather an entity with a graceful beauty in its integrity from which discord, and all that is meaningless, has been eliminated. A wild flower is truly simple. Therefore:

1. A building should contain as few rooms as will meet the conditions which give it rise and under which we live, and which the architect should strive continually to simplify; then the ensemble of the rooms should be carefully considered that comfort and utility may go hand in hand with beauty. Beside the entry and necessary workrooms there need be but three rooms on the ground floor of any house, living room, dining room, and kitchen, with the possible addition of a "social office"; really there need be but one room, the living room with requirements otherwise sequestered from it or screened within it by means of architectural contrivances.

2. Openings should occur as integral features of the structure and form, if possible, its natural ornamentation.

3. An excessive love of detail has ruined more fine things from the standpoint of fine art or fine living than any one human shortcoming; it is hopelessly vulgar. Too many houses, when they are not little stage settings or scene paintings, are mere notion stores, bazaars or junk shops.

Decoration is dangerous unless you understand it thoroughly and are satisfied that it means something good in the scheme as a whole, for the present you are usually better off without it. Merely that it "looks rich" is no justification for the use of ornament.

4. Appliances or fixtures as such are undesirable. Assimilate them together with all appurtenances into the design of the structure.

5. Pictures deface walls oftener than they decorate them. Pictures should be decorative and incorporated in the general scheme as decoration.

6. The most truly satisfactory apartments are those in which most or all of the furniture is built in as a part of the original scheme. The whole must always be considered as an integral unit.

II. There should be as many kinds (styles) of houses as there are kinds (styles) of people and as many differentiations as there are different individuals. A man who has individuality (and what man lacks it?) has a right to its expression in his own environment.

III. A building should appear to grow easily from its site and be shaped to harmonize with its surroundings if nature is manifest there, and if not try to make it as quiet, substantial, and organic as she would have been were the opportunity hers.

We of the Middle West are living on the prairie. The prairie has a beauty of its own and we should recognize and accentuate this natural beauty, its quiet level. Hence, gently sloping roofs, low proportions, quiet sky lines, suppressed heavy-set chimneys, and sheltering overhangs, low terraces and out-reaching walls sequestering private gardens.

IV. Colors require the same conventionalizing process to make them fit to live with that natural forms do; so go to the woods and fields for color schemes. Use the soft, warm, optimistic tones of earths and autumn leaves in preference to the pessimistic blues, purples or cold greens and grays of the ribbon counter; they are more wholesome and better adapted in most cases to good decoration.

V. Bring out the nature of the materials, let their nature intimately into your scheme. Strip the wood of varnish and let it alone; stain it. Develop the natural texture of the plastering and stain it. Reveal the nature of the wood, plaster, brick or stone in your designs; they are all by nature friendly and beautiful. No architectural treatment can be really a matter of fine art when these truly natural characteristics are, or their essential nature is, outraged or neglected.

VI. A house that has character stands a good chance of growing more valuable as it grows older while a house in the prevailing mode, whatever that mode may be, is soon out of fashion, stale, and unprofitable.

Buildings like people must first be sincere, must be true and then withal as gracious and lovable as may be.

Above all, integrity. The machine is the normal tool of our civilization; give it work that it can do well; nothing is of greater importance. To do this will be to formulate new industrial ideals, sadly needed.

These propositions are chiefly interesting because for some strange reason they were novel when formulated in the face of conditions hostile to them and because the ideas they phrase have been practically embodied in the buildings that were built to live up to them. The buildings of recent years have not only been true to them, but are in many cases a further development of the simple propositions so positively stated then.

Happily, these ideals are more commonplace now. Then the sky lines of our domestic architecture were fantastic abortions, tortured by features that disrupted the distorted roof surfaces from which attenuated chimneys like lean fingers threatened the sky; the invariably tall interiors were cut up into box-like compartments, the more boxes the finer the house; and "architecture" chiefly consisted in healing over the edges of the curious collection of holes that had to be cut in the walls for light and air and to permit the occupant to get in or out. These interiors were always slaughtered with the butt and slash of the old plinth and corner block trim, of dubious origin, and finally smothered with horrible millinery by way of "decoration."

That individuality in a building was possible for each homemaker, or desirable, seemed at that time to rise to the dignity of an idea. Even cultured men and women care so little for the spiritual integrity of their environment; except in rare cases they are not touched, they simply do not care for the matter so long as their dwellings are fashionable or as good as those of their neighbors and keep them dry and warm. A structure has no more meaning to them aesthetically than has the stable to the horse. And this came to me in the early years as a definite discouragement. There are exceptions, and I found them chiefly among American men of business with unspoiled instincts and untainted ideals. A man of this type usually has the faculty of judging for himself. He has rather liked the "idea" and much of the encouragement this work receives comes straight from him because the "common sense" of the thing appeals to him. While the "cultured" are still content with their small châteaux, Colonial wedding cakes, English affectations or French millinery, he prefers a poor thing but his own. He errs on the side of character, at least, and when the lest of time has tried his country's development architecturally, he will have contributed his quota, small enough in the final outcome though it be; he will be regarded as a true conservator.

In the hope that some day America may live her own life in her own buildings in her own way, that is, that we may make the best of what we have for what it honestly is or may become, I have endeavored in this work to establish a harmonious relationship between ground plan and elevation of these buildings, considering the one as a solution and the other an expression of the conditions of a problem of which the whole is a project. I have tried to establish an organic integrity to begin with, forming the basis for the subsequent working out of a significant grammatical expression and making the whole, as nearly as I could, consistent.

What quality of style the buildings may possess is due to the artistry with which the conventionalization as a solution and an artistic expression of a specific problem within these limitations has been handled. The types are largely a matter of personal taste and may have much or little to do with the American architecture for which we hope.

From the beginning of my practice the question uppermost in my mind has been not "what style," but "What is style?" and it is my belief that the chief value of the work illustrated here will be found in the fact that if in the face of our present day conditions any given type may be treated independently and imbued with the quality of style, then a truly noble architecture is a definite possibility, so soon as Americans really demand it of the architects of the rising generation.

I do not believe we will ever again have the uniformity of type which has characterized the so-called great "styles." Conditions have changed; our ideal is democracy, the highest possible expression of the individual as a unit not inconsistent with a harmonious whole. The average of human intelligence rises steadily, and as the individual unit grows more and more to be trusted we will have an architecture with richer variety in unity than has ever arisen before; but the forms must be born out of our changed conditions, they must be *true* forms, otherwise the best that tradition has to offer is only an inglorious masquerade, devoid of vital significance or true spiritual value.

The trials of the early days were many and at this distance picturesque. Workmen seldom like to think, especially if there is financial risk entailed; at your peril do you disturb their established processes mental or technical. To do anything in an unusual, even if in a better and simpler way, is to complicate the situation at once. Simple things at that time in any industrial field were nowhere at hand. A piece of wood without a molding was an anomaly; a plain wooden slat instead of a turned baluster a joke; the omission of the merchantable "grille" a crime; plain fabrics for hangings or floor covering were nowhere to be found in stock.

To become the recognized enemy of the established industrial order was no light matter, for soon whenever a set of my drawings was presented to a Chicago millman for figures he would willingly enough unroll it, read the architect's name, shake his head and return it with the remark that he was "not hunting for trouble"; sagacious owners and general contractors tried cutting out the name, but in vain, his perspicacity was ratlike, he had come to know "the look of the thing." So, in addition to the special preparation in any case necessary for every little matter of construction and finishing, special detail drawings were necessary merely to show the things to be left off or not done, and not only studied designs for every part had to be made but quantity surveys and schedules of millwork furnished the contractors beside. This, in a year or two, brought the architect face to face with the fact that the fee for his service "established" by the American Institute of Architects was intended for something stock and shop, for it would not even pay for the bare drawings necessary for conscientious work.

The relation of the architect to the economic and industrial movement of his time, in any fine art sense, is still an affair so sadly out of joint that no one may easily reconcile it. All agree that something has gone wrong and except the architect be a plan-factory magnate, who has reduced his art to a philosophy of old clothes and sells misfit or made-over, ready-to-wear garments with commercial aplomb and social distinction, he cannot succeed on the present basis established by common practice. So, in addition to a situation already complicated for them, a necessarily increased fee stared in the face the clients who dared. But some did dare, as the illustrations prove.

The struggle then was and still is to make "good architecture," "good business." It is perhaps significant that in the beginning it was very difficult to secure a building loan on any terms upon one of these houses, now it is easy to secure a better loan than ordinary; but how far success has attended this ambition the owners of these buildings alone can testify. Their trials have been many, but each, I think, feels that he has as much house for his money as any of his neighbors with something in the home intrinsically valuable besides, which will not be out of fashion in one lifetime, and which contributes steadily to his dignity and his pleasure as an individual. . . .

Photographs do not adequately present these subjects. A building has a presence as has a person that defies the photographer, and the color so necessary to the complete expression of the form is necessarily lacking, but it will be noticed that all the structures stand upon their foundations to the eye as well as physically. There is good, substantial preparation at the ground for all the buildings and it is the first grammatical expression of all the types. This preparation, or water table, is to these buildings what the stylobate was to the ancient Greek temple. To gain it, it was necessary to reverse the established practice of setting the supports of the building to the outside of the wall and to set them to the inside, so as to leave the necessary support for the outer base. This was natural enough and good enough construction but many an owner was disturbed by private information from the practical contractor to the effect that he would have his whole house in the cellar if he submitted to it. This was at the time a marked innovation, though the most natural thing in the world, and to me, to this day, indispensable.

With this innovation established, one horizontal stripe of raw material, the foundation wall above ground, was eliminated and the complete grammar of type one made possible. A simple, unbroken wall surface from foot to level of second story sill was thus secured, a change of material occurring at that point to form the simple frieze that characterizes the earlier buildings. Even this was frequently omitted as in the Francis Apartments and many other buildings and the wall was let alone from base to cornice or eaves.

"Dress reform houses" they were called, I remember, by the charitably disposed. What others called them will hardly bear repetition.

As the wall surfaces were thus simplified and emphasized the matter of fenestration became exceedingly difficult and more than ever important, and often I used to gloat over the beautiful buildings I could build if only it were unnecessary to cut holes in them; but the holes were managed at first frankly as in the Winslow house and later as elementary constituents of the structure grouped in rhythmical fashion, so that all the light and air and prospect the most rabid client could wish would not be too much from an artistic standpoint; and of this achievement I am proud. The groups are managed, too, whenever required, so that overhanging eaves do not shade them, although the walls are still protected from the weather. Soon the poetry-crushing characteristics of the guillotine window, which was then firmly rooted, became apparent, and single-handed I waged a determined battle for casements swinging out, although it was necessary to have special hardware made for them as there was none to be had this side of England. Clients would come ready to accept any innovation but "those swinging windows," and when told that they were in the nature of the proposition and that they must take them or leave the rest, they frequently employed "the other fellow" to give them something "near," with the "practical" windows dear to their hearts.

With the grammar so far established came an expression pure and simple, even classic in atmosphere, using that much-abused word in its best sense; implying, that is, a certain sweet reasonableness of form and outline naturally dignified.

I have observed that nature usually perfects her forms; the individuality of the attribute is seldom sacrificed; that is, deformed or mutilated by cooperative parts. She rarely says a thing and tries to take it back at the same time. She would not sanction the "classic" proceeding of, say, establishing an "order," a colonnade, then building walls between the columns of the order reducing them to pilasters, thereafter cutting holes in the wall and pasting on cornices with more pilasters around them, with the result that every form is outraged, the whole an abominable mutilation, as is most of the architecture of the Renaissance wherein style corrodes style and all the forms are stultified.

In laying out the ground plans for even the more insignificant of these buildings a simple axial law and order and the ordered spacing upon a system of certain structural units definitely established for each structure in accord with its scheme of practical construction and

aesthetic proportion, is practiced as an expedient to simplify the technical difficulties of execution, and although the symmetry may not be obvious always the balance is usually maintained. The plans are as a rule much more articulate than is the school product of the Beaux-Arts. The individuality of the various functions of the various features is more highly developed; all the forms are complete in themselves and frequently do duty at the same time from within and without as decorative attributes of the whole. This tendency to greater individuality of the parts emphasized by more and more complete articulation will be seen in the plans for Unity Church, the cottage for Elizabeth Stone at Glencoe and the Avery Coonley house in process of construction at Riverside, Ill. Moreover, these ground plans are merely the actual projection of a carefully considered whole. The "architecture" is not "thrown up" as an artistic exercise, a matter of elevation from a preconceived ground plan. The schemes are conceived in three dimensions as organic entities, let the picturesque perspective fall how it will. While a sense of the incidental perspectives the design will develop is always present, I have great faith that if the thing is rightly put together in true organic sense with proportions actually right the picturesque will take care of itself. No man ever built a building worthy the name of architecture who fashioned it in perspective sketch to his taste and then fudged the plan to suit. Such methods produce mere scene painting. A perspective may be a proof but it is no nurture.

As to the mass values of the buildings the aesthetic principles outlined in proposition III will account in a measure for their character.

In the matter of decoration the tendency has been to indulge it less and less, in many cases merely providing certain architectural preparation for natural foliage or flowers, as it is managed in, say, the entrance to the Lawrence house at Springfield. This use of natural foliage and flowers for decoration is carried to quite an extent in all the designs and, although the buildings are complete without this efflorescence, they may be said to blossom with the season. What architectural decoration the buildings carry is not only conventionalized to the point where it is quiet and stays as a sure foil for the nature forms from which it is derived and with which it must intimately associate, but it is always *of* the surface, never *on* it.

The windows usually are provided with characteristic straight line patterns absolutely in the flat and usually severe. The nature of the glass is taken into account in these designs as is also the metal bar used in their construction, and most of them are treated as metal "grilles" with glass inserted forming a simple rhythmic arrangement of straight lines and squares made as cunning as possible so long as the result is quiet. The aim is that the designs shall make the best of the technical contrivances that produce them.

In the main the ornamentation is wrought in the warp and woof of the structure. It is constitutional in the best sense and is felt in the conception of the ground plan. To elucidate this element in composition would mean a long story and perhaps a tedious one, though to me it is the most fascinating phase of the work, involving the true poetry of conception.

The differentiation of a single, certain simple form characterizes the expression of one building. Quite a different form may serve for another, but from one basic idea all the formal elements of design are in each case derived and held well together in scale and character. The form chosen may flare outward, opening flowerlike to the sky as in the Thomas house; another, droop to accentuate artistically the weight of the masses; another be noncommittal or abruptly emphatic, or its grammar may be deduced from some plant form that has appealed to me, as certain properties in line and form of the sumac were used in the Lawrence house at Springfield; but in every case the motif is adhered to throughout so that it is not too much to say that each building aesthetically is cut from one piece of goods and consistently hangs together with an integrity impossible otherwise.

In a fine art sense these designs have grown as natural plants grow, the individuality of each is integral and as complete as skill, time, strength, and circumstances would permit.

The method in itself does not of necessity produce a beautiful building, but it does provide a framework as a basis which has an organic integrity, susceptible to the architects' imagination and at once opening to him nature's wealth of artistic suggestion, ensuring him a guiding principle within which he can never be wholly false, out of tune, or lacking in rational motif. The subtleties, the shifting blending harmonies, the cadences, the nuances are a matter of his own nature, his own susceptibilities and faculties.

But self-denial is imposed upon the architect to a far greater extent than upon any other member of the fine art family. The temptation to sweeten work, to make each detail in itself lovable and expressive, is always great; but that the whole may be truly eloquent of its ultimate function restraint is imperative. To let individual elements arise and shine at the expense of final repose is for the architect a betrayal of trust, for buildings are the background or framework for the human life within their walls and a foil for the nature efflorescence without. So architecture is the most complete of conventionalizations and of all the arts the most subjective except music.

Music may be for the architect ever and always a sympathetic friend whose counsels, precepts, and patterns ever are available to him and from which he need not fear to draw. But the arts are today all cursed by literature; artists attempt to make literature even of music, usually of painting and sculpture and doubtless would of architecture also, were the art not moribund; but whenever it is done the soul of the thing dies and we have not art but something far less for which the true artist can have neither affection nor respect.

Contrary to the usual supposition this manner of working out a theme is more flexible than any working out in a fixed, historic style can ever be, and the individuality of those concerned may receive more adequate treatment within legitimate limitations. This matter of individuality puzzles many; they suspect that the individuality of the owner and occupant of a building is sacrificed to that of the architect who imposes his own upon Jones, Brown, and Smith alike. An architect worthy of the name has an individuality, it is true; his work will and should reflect it, and his buildings will all bear a family resemblance one to another. The individuality of an owner is first manifest in his choice of his architect, the individual to whom he entrusts his characterization. He sympathizes with his work; its expression suits him and this furnishes the common ground upon which client and architect may come together. Then, if the architect is what he ought to be, with his ready technique he conscientiously works for the client, idealizes his client's character and his client's tastes and makes him feel that the building is his, as it really is to such an extent that he can truly say that he would rather have his own house than any other he has ever seen. Is a portrait, say, by Sargent any less a revelation of the character of the subject because it bears his stamp and is easily recognized by anyone as a Sargent. Does one lose his individuality when it is interpreted sympathetically by one of his own race and time who can know him and his needs intimately and idealize them; or does he gain it only by having adopted or adapted to his condition a ready-made historic style which is the fruit of a seedtime other than his, whatever that style may be.

The present industrial condition is constantly studied in the practical application of these architectural ideals and the treatment simplified and arranged to fit modern processes and to utilize to the best advantage the work of the machine. The furniture takes the clean cut, straight-line forms that the machine can render far better than would be possible by hand. Certain facilities, too, of the machine, which it would be interesting to enlarge upon, are taken advantage of; and the nature of the materials is usually revealed in the process.

Nor is the atmosphere of the result in its completeness new and hard. In most of the interiors there will be found a quiet, a simple dignity that we imagine is only to be found in the "old" and it is due to the underlying organic harmony, to the each in all and the all in each throughout. This is the modern opportunity, to make of a building, together with its equipment, appurtenances, and environment, an entity which shall constitute a complete work of art; and a work of art more valuable to society as a whole than has before existed because discordant conditions, endured for centuries, are smoothed away; everyday life here finds an expression germane to its daily existence; an idealization of the common need sure to be uplifting and helpful in the same sense that pure air to breathe is better than air poisoned with noxious gases.

An artist's limitations are his best friends. The machine is here to stay. It is the forerunner of the democracy that is our dearest hope. There is no more important work before the architect now than to use this normal tool of civilization to the best advantage instead of prostituting it as he has hitherto done in reproducing with murderous ubiquity forms born of other times and other conditions and which it can only serve to destroy.

The exteriors of these structures will receive less ready recognition perhaps than the interiors and because they are the result of a radically different conception as to what should constitute a building. We have formed a habit of mind concerning architecture to which the expression of most of these exteriors must be a shock, at first more or less disagreeable, and the more so as the habit of mind is more narrowly fixed by so-called classic training. Simplicity is not in itself an end; it is a means to an end. Our aesthetics are dyspeptic from incontinent indulgence in "Frenchite" pastry. We crave ornament for the sake of ornament; cover up our faults of design with ornamental sensualities that were a long time ago sensuous ornament. We will do well to distrust this unwholesome and unholy craving and look to the simple line, to the clean though living form and quiet color for a time until the true significance of these things has dawned for us once more.

The old structural forms, which up to the present time have spelled "architecture," are decayed. Their life went from them long ago and new conditions industrially, steel and concrete and terra cotta in particular, are prophesying a more plastic art wherein as the flesh is to our bones so will the covering be to the structure; but more truly and beautifully expressive than ever. But that is a long story. This reticence in the matter of ornamentation is characteristic of these structures and for at least two reasons: first, they are the expression of an idea that the ornamentation of a building should be constitutional, a matter of the nature of the structure beginning with the ground plan. In the buildings themselves, in the sense of the whole, there is lacking neither richness nor incident but their qualities are secured not by applied decoration, they are found in the fashioning of the whole, in which color, too, plays as significant a part as it does in an old Japanese wood block print. Second, because as before stated, buildings perform their highest function in relation to human life within and the natural efflorescence without; and to develop and maintain the harmony of a true chord between them making of the building in this sense a sure foil for life, broad simple surfaces and highly conventionalized forms are inevitable. These ideals take the buildings out of school and marry them to the ground; make them intimate expressions or revelations of the exteriors; individualize them regardless of preconceived notions of style. I have tried to make their grammar perfect in its way and to give their forms and proportions an integrity that will bear study, although few of them can be intelligently studied apart from their environment. So, what might be termed the democratic character of the exteriors is their first undefined offense: the lack, wholly, of what the professional critic would deem architecture; in fact, most of the critic's architecture has been left out.

There is always a synthetic basis for the features of the various structures, and consequently a constantly accumulating residue of formula, which becomes more and more useful; but I do not pretend to say that the perception or conception of them was not at first intuitive, or that those that lie yet beyond will not be grasped in the same intuitive way; but, after all, architecture is a scientific art, and the thinking basis will ever be for the architect his surety, the final court in which his imagination sifts his feelings.

The few draftsmen so far associated with this work have been taken into the drafting room, in every case almost wholly unformed, many of them with no particular previous training, and patiently nursed for years in the atmosphere of the work itself, until, saturated by intimate association, at an impressionable age, with its motifs and phases, they have become helpful.

To develop the sympathetic grasp of detail that is necessary before this point is reached has proved usually a matter of years, with little advantage on the side of the college-trained understudy. These young people have found their way to me through natural sympathy with the work, and have become loyal assistants. The members, so far, all told here and elsewhere, of our little university of 14 years' standing are: Marion Mahony, a capable assistant for 11 years; William Drummond, for 7 years; Francis Byrne, 5 years; Isabel Roberts, 5 years; George Willis, 4 years; Walter Griffin, 4 years; Andrew Willatzen, 3 years; Harry Robinson, 2 years; Charles E. White, Jr., 1 year; Erwin Barglebaugh and Robert Hardin, each 1 year; Albert McArthur, entering.

Others have been attracted by what seemed to them to be the novelty of the work, staying only long enough to acquire a smattering of form, then departing to sell a superficial proficiency elsewhere. Still others shortly develop a mastery of the subject, discovering that it is all just as they would have done it, anyway, and, chafing at the unkind fate that forestalled them in its practice, resolve to blaze a trail for themselves without further loss of time. It is urged against the more loyal that they are sacrificing their individuality to that which has dominated this work; but it is too soon to impeach a single understudy on this basis, for, although they will inevitably repeat for years the methods, forms, and habit of thought, even the mannerisms of the present work, if there is virtue in the principles behind it that virtue will stay with them through the preliminary stages of their own practice until their own individualities truly develop independently. I have noticed that those who have made the most fuss about their "individuality" in early stages, those who took themselves most seriously in that regard, were inevitably those who had least.

Many elements of Mr. Sullivan's personality in his art (what might be called his mannerisms) naturally enough clung to my work in the early years, and may be readily traced by the casual observer; but for me one real proof of the virtue inherent in this work will lie in the fact that some of the young men and women who have given themselves up to me so faithfully these past years will some day contribute rounded individualities of their own, and forms of their own devising to the new school.

This year I assign to each a project that has been carefully conceived in my own mind, which he accepts as a specific work. He follows its subsequent development through all its phases in drawing room and field, meeting with the client himself on occasion, gaining an all-round development impossible otherwise, and insuring an enthusiasm and a grasp of detail decidedly to the best interest of the client. These privileges in the hands of selfishly ambitious or overconfident assistants would soon wreck such a system; but I can say that among my own boys it has already proved a moderate success, with every prospect of being continued as a settled policy in future.

Nevertheless, I believe that only when one individual forms the concept of the various projects and also determines the character of every detail in the sum total, even to the size and shape of the pieces of glass in the windows, the arrangement and profile of the most insignificant of the architectural members, will that unity be secured which is the soul of the individual work of art. This means that fewer buildings should be entrusted to one architect. His output will of necessity be relatively small; small, that is, as compared to the volume of work turned out in any one of fifty "successful offices" in America. I believe there is no middle course worth considering in the light of the best future of American architecture. With no more propriety can an architect leave the details touching the form of his concept to assistants, no matter how sympathetic and capable they may be, than can a painter entrust the painting in of the details of his picture to a pupil; for an architect who would do individual work must have a technique well developed and peculiar to himself, which, if he is fertile, is still growing with his growth. To keep everything "in place" requires constant care and study in matters that the old-school practitioner would scorn to touch.

As for the future, the work shall grow more truly simple; more expressive with fewer lines; fewer forms; more articulate with less labor; more plastic; more fluent, although more coherent; more organic. It shall grow not only to fit more perfectly the methods and processes that are called upon to produce it, but shall further find whatever is lovely or of good repute in method or process, and idealize it with the cleanest, most virile stroke I can imagine. As understanding and appreciation of life matures and deepens, this work shall prophesy and idealize the character of the individual it is fashioned to serve more intimately, no matter how inexpensive the result must finally be. It shall become in its atmosphere as pure and elevating in its humble way as the trees and flowers are in their perfectly appointed way, for only so can architecture be worthy of its high rank as a fine art, or the architect discharge the obligation he assumes to the public, imposed upon him by the nature of his own profession.

Frank Lloyd Wright (essay date 1914)

SOURCE: "1914: In the Cause of Architecture," in *Frank Lloyd Wright on Architecture*, Duell, Sloan and Pearce, 1941, pp. 46-58.

[*In the following essay, originally published in 1914, Wright responds to detractors of the "Prairie School" of architecture—a movement formed of his disciples and imitators—by dissociating himself from this school.*]

"Nature has made creatures only; art has made men." Nevertheless, or perhaps for that very reason, every struggle for truth in the arts and for the freedom that should go with the truth has always had its own peculiar load of disciples, neophytes, and quacks. The young work in architecture here in the Middle West, owing to a measure of premature success, has for some time past been daily rediscovered, heralded and drowned in noise by this new characteristic feature of its struggle. The so-called "movement" threatens to explode soon in foolish exploitation of unripe performances or topple over in pretentious attempts to "speak the language." The broker, too, has made his appearance to deal in its slender stock in trade, not a wholly new form of artistic activity certainly, but one serving to indicate how profitable this intensive rush for a place in the "new school" has become.

Just at this time it may be well to remember that "every form of artistic activity is not art."

Obviously this stage of development was to be expected and has its humorous side. It has also unexpected and dangerous effects, astonishingly in line with certain prophetic letters written by honest "conservatives" upon the publication of the former paper of 1908.

Although an utterance from me of a critical nature is painful, because it must be a personal matter, perhaps a seeming retraction on my part, still all that ever really happens is "personal matter" and the time has come when forbearance ceases to be either virtue or convenience. A promising garden seems to be rapidly overgrown with weeds, notwithstanding the fact that "all may raise the flowers now, for all have got the seed." But the seed has not been planted; transplanting is preferred, but no amount of transplanting can raise the needed flowers.

To stultify or corrupt our architectural possibilities is to corrupt our aesthetic life at the fountain head. Her architecture is the most precious of the susceptibilities of a young, constructive country in this constructive stage of development; and maintaining its integrity in this respect, therefore, distinctly a cause.

When, 21 years ago, I took my stand, alone in my field, the cause was unprofitable, seemingly impossible, almost unknown, or, if known, was, as a rule, unhonored and ridiculed; Montgomery Schuyler was the one notable exception to the rule. So swiftly do things "come on" in this vigorous and invigorating age that although the cause itself has had little or no recognition, the work has more than its share of attention and has attracted to itself abuses seldom described (never openly attacked) but which a perspective of the past 6 years will enable me to describe, as I feel they must render the finer values in this work abortive for the time being, if they do not wholly defeat its aim. Many a similar work in the past has gone prematurely to ruin owing to similar abuses; to rise again, it is true; but retarded generations in time.

I still believe that the ideal of an organic architecture forms the origin and source, the strength and, fundamentally, the significance of everything ever worthy the name of architecture.

And I know that the sense of an organic architecture, once grasped, carries with it in its very nature the discipline of an ideal at whatever cost to self-interest or the established order.

It is itself a standard and an ideal and I maintain that only earnest artist integrity, both of instinct and of intelligence, can make any forward movement of this nature in architecture of lasting value.

The ideal of an organic architecture for America is no mere license for doing the thing that you please to do as you please to do it in order to hold up the strange thing when done with the "see what I have made" of childish pride. Nor is it achieved by speaking the fancied language of "form and function"; cant terms learned by rote; or prating foolishly of "progress before precedent"; that unthinking, unthinkable thing! In fact, it is precisely the total absence of any conception of this ideal standard that is made conspicuous by this folly and the practices that go with it. To reiterate the statement made in 1908: this ideal of an organic architecture for America was touched by Richardson and Root, and perhaps other men; but was developing consciously 28 years ago in the practice of Adler and Sullivan when I went to work in their office. This ideal combination of Adler and Sullivan was then working to produce what no other combination of architects nor any individual architect at that time dared even preach: a sentient, rational building that would owe its "style" to the integrity with which it was individually fashioned to serve its particular purpose; a "thinking" as well as "feeling" process, requiring the independent work of true artist imagination; an ideal that is dynamite, cap and fuse, in selfish, insensible hands; personal ambition, the lighted match.

At the expiration of a 6-year apprenticeship, during which time Louis Sullivan was my master and inspiration, 21 years ago I entered a field he had not, in any new spirit, touched, the field of domestic architecture, and began to break ground and make the forms I needed, alone, absolutely alone.

These forms were the result of a conscientious study of materials and of the machine which is the real tool, whether we like it or not, that we must use to give shape

to our ideals; a tool which at that time had received no such artistic consideration from artist or architect. And that my work now has individuality, the strength to stand by itself, honors Mr. Sullivan the more. The principles, however, underlying the fundamental ideal of an organic architecture, common to his work and to mine, are common to all work that ever rang true in the architecture of the world, and free as air to any pair of honest young lungs that will breathe deeply enough. But I have occasion to refer only to that element in this so-called "new movement" which I have characterized by my own work and which should and, in a more advanced stage of culture, would be responsible to me for use or abuse of the forms and privileges of that work. Specifically, I speak only to that element within this element, now beyond private reach or control, ruthlessly characterizing and publicly exploiting the cause it does not comprehend or else that it cannot serve.

Someone for the sake of that cause must have some conscience in the matter and tell the truth. Since disciples, neophytes, and brokers will not, critics do not, and the public cannot, I will. I will be suspected of the unbecoming motives usually ascribed to any man who comes to the front in behalf of an ideal, or his own; nevertheless, somehow, this incipient movement, which it has been my life work to help outfit and launch, must be protected or directed in its course. An enlightened public opinion would take care of this, but there is no such opinion. In time there will be; meantime good work is being wasted, opportunities destroyed or, worse, architectural mortgages on future generations forged wholesale; and in architecture they must be paid with usurious interest.

The sins of the architect are permanent sins.

To promote good work it is necessary to characterize bad work as bad.

Half-baked, imitative designs (fictitious semblances) pretentiously put forward in the name of a movement or a cause, particularly while novelty is the chief popular standard, endanger the cause, weaken the efficiency of genuine work, for the time being at least; lower the standard of artistic integrity permanently; demoralize all values artistically; until utter prostitution results. This prostitution has resulted in the new work partly, I have now to confess, as a byproduct of an intimate, personal touch with the work, hitherto untried in the office of an American architect; and partly, too, perhaps, as one result of an ideal of individuality in architecture, administered in does too strong, too soon, for architectural babes and sucklings; but chiefly, I believe, owing to almost total lack of any standard of artist integrity among architects, as a class, in this region at least. Of ethics we hear something occasionally; but only in regard to the relation of architects to each other when a client is in question; never in relation to sources of inspiration, the finer material the architect uses in shaping the thing he gives to his client. Ethics that promote integrity in this respect are as yet unformed and the young man in architecture is adrift in the most vitally important of his experiences; he cannot know where he stands in the absence of any well-defined principles on the part of his confreres or his elders. Such principles must now be established.

If I had a right to project myself in the direction of an organic architecture 21 years ago, it entailed the right to my work and, so far as I am able, a right to defend my aim. Also, yet not so clearly, I am bound to do what I can to save the public from untoward effects that follow in the wake of my own break with traditions. I deliberately chose to break with traditions in order to be more true to tradition than current conventions and ideals in architecture would permit. The more vital course is usually the rougher one and lies through conventions oftentimes settled into laws that must be broken, with consequent liberation of other forces that cannot stand freedom. So a break of this nature is a thing dangerous, nevertheless indispensable, to society. Society recognizes the danger and makes the break usually fatal to the man who makes it. It should not be made without reckoning the danger and sacrifice, without ability to stand severe punishment, nor without sincere faith that the end will justify the means; nor do I believe it can be effectively made without all these. But who can reckon with the folly bred by temporal success in a country that has as yet no artistic standards, no other god so potent as that same success? For every thousand men nature enables to stand adversity, she, perhaps, makes one man capable of surviving success. An unenlightened public is at its mercy always; the "success" of the one thousand as well as of the one in a thousand; were it not for the resistance of honest enmity, society, nature herself even would soon cycle madly to disaster. So reaction is essential to progress, and enemies as valuable an asset in any forward movement as friends, provided only they be honest; if intelligent as well as honest, they are invaluable. Some time ago this work reached the stage where it sorely needed honest enemies if it were to survive. It has had some honest enemies whose honest fears were expressed in the prophetic letters I have mentioned.

But the enemies of this work, with an exception or two, have not served it well. They have been either unintelligent or careless of the gist of the whole matter. In fact, its avowed enemies have generally been of the same superficial, time-serving spirit as many of its present load of disciples and neophytes. Nowhere even now; save in Europe, with some few notable exceptions in this country; has the organic character of the work been fairly recognized and valued; the character that is perhaps the only feature of lasting vital consequence.

As for its peculiarities; if my own share in this work has a distinguished trait, it has individuality undefiled. It has gone forward unswerving from the beginning, unchanging, yet developing, in this quality of individuality, and stands, as it has stood for 19 years at least, an individual entity, clearly defined. Such as it is, its "individuality" is as irrevocably mine as the work of any painter, sculptor, or poet who ever lived was irrevocably his. The form of a work that has this quality of individuality is never the product of a composite. An artist knows this; but the general public, near artist and perhaps "critic," too, may have to be reminded or informed. To grant a work this quality is to absolve it without further argument from anything like composite origin, and to fix its limitations.

There are enough types and forms in my work to characterize the work of an architect, but certainly not enough to characterize an architecture. Nothing to my mind could be worse imposition than to have some individual, even temporarily, deliberately fix the outward forms of his concept of beauty upon the future of a free people or even of a growing city. A tentative, advantageous forecast of probable future utilitarian development goes far enough in this direction. Any individual willing to undertake more would thereby only prove his unfitness for the task, assuming the task possible or desirable. A socialist might shut out the sunlight from a free and developing people with his own shadow, in this way. An artist is too true an individualist to suffer such an imposition, much less perpetrate it; his problems are quite other. The manner of any work (and all work of any quality has its manner) may be for the time being a strength, but finally it is a weakness; and as the returns come in, it seems as though not only the manner of this work or its "clothes," but also its strength in this very quality of individuality, which is a matter of its soul as well as of its forms, would soon prove its undoing, to be worn to shreds and tatters by foolish, conscienceless imitation. As for the vital principle of the work (the quality of an organic architecture) that has been lost to sight, even by pupils. But I still believe as firmly as ever that without artist integrity and this consequent individuality manifesting itself in multifarious forms, there can be no great architecture, no great artists, no great civilization, no worthy life. Is, then, the very strength of such a work as this is its weakness? Is it so because of a false democratic system naturally inimical to art? Or is it so because the commercialism of art leaves no noble standards? Is it because architects have less personal honor than sculptors, painters, or poets? Or is it because fine buildings are less important now than fine pictures and good books?

In any case, judging from what is exploited as such, most of what is beginning to be called the "New School of the Middle West" is not only far from the ideal of an organic architecture, but getting farther away from it everyday.

A study of similar situations in the past will show that any departure from beaten paths must stand and grow in organic character or soon fall, leaving permanent waste and desolation in final ruin; it dare not trade long on mere forms, no matter how inevitable they seem. Trading in the letter has cursed art for centuries past, but in architecture it has usually been rather an impersonal letter of those decently cold in their graves for sometime.

One may submit to the flattery of imitation or to caricature personally; everyone who marches or strays from beaten paths must submit to one or to both, but never will one submit tamely to caricature of that which one loves. Personally, I too am heartily sick of being commercialized and traded in and upon; but most of all I dread to see the types I have worked with so long and patiently drifting toward speculative builders, cheapened or befooled by senseless changes, robbed of quality and distinction, dead forms or grinning originalities for the sake of originality, an endless string of hacked carcasses, to encumber democratic front yards for five decades or more. This, however, is only the personal side of the matter and to be endured in silence were there any profit in it to come to the future architecture of the "melting pot."

The more serious side and the occasion for this second paper is the fact that emboldened or befooled by its measure of "success," the new work has been showing weaknesses instead of the character it might have shown some years hence were it more enlightened and discreet, more sincere and modest, prepared to wait, to wait to prepare.

The average American man or women who wants to build a house wants something different, "something different" is what they say they want, and most of them want it in a hurry. That this is the fertile soil upon which an undisciplined "language-speaking" neophyte may grow his crop to the top of his ambition is deplorable in one sense but none the less hopeful in another and more vital sense. The average man of business in America has truer intuition, and so a more nearly just estimate of artistic values, when he has a chance to judge between good and bad, than a man of similar class in any other country. But he is prone to take that "something different" anyhow; if not good then bad. He is rapidly outgrowing the provincialism that needs a foreign-made label upon "art," and so, at the present moment, not only is he in danger of being swindled, but likely to find something peculiarly his own, in time, and valuable to him, if he can last. I hope and believe he can last. At any rate, there is no way of preventing him from getting either swindled or something merely "different"; nor do I believe it would be desirable if he could be, until the inorganic thing he usually gets in the form of this "something different" is put forward and publicly advertised as of that character of the young work for which I must feel myself responsible.

I do not admit that my disciples or pupils, be they artists, neophytes, or brokers, are responsible for worse buildings than nine-tenths of the work done by average architects who are "good school"; in fact, I think the worst of them do better; although they sometimes justify themselves in equivocal positions by reference to this fact. Were no more to come of my work than is evident at present, the architecture of the country would have received an impetus that will finally resolve itself into good. But to me the exasperating fact is that it might aid vitally the great things we all desire, if it were treated on its merits, used and not abused. Selling even good versions of an original at second hand is in the circumstances not good enough. It is cheap and bad, demoralizing in every sense. But, unhappily, I have to confess that the situation seems worse where originality, as such, has

thus far been attempted, because it seems to have been attempted chiefly *for its own sake,* and the results bear about the same resemblance to an organic architecture as might be shown were one to take a classic column and, breaking it, let the upper half lie carelessly at the foot of the lower, then setting the capital picturesquely askew against the half thus prostrate, one were to settle the whole arrangement as some structural feature of street or garden.

For worker or broker to exhibit such "designs" as efforts of creative architects, before the ink is yet dry on either work or worker, is easily done under present standards with "success," but the exploit finally reflects a poor sort of credit upon the exploited architect and the cause. As for the cause, any growth that comes to it in a "spread" of this kind is unwholesome. I insist that this sort of thing is not "new school," nor this the way to develop one. This is piracy, lunacy, plunder, imitation, adulation, or what you will; it is not a developing architecture when worked in this fashion, nor will it ever become one until purged of this spirit; least of all is it an organic architecture. Its practices belie any such character.

"Disciples" aside, some 15 young people, all entirely inexperienced and unformed—but few had even college educations—attracted by the character of my work, sought me as their employer. I am no teacher; I am a worker; but I gave to all, impartially, the freedom of my workroom, my work, and myself, to imbue them with the spirit of the performances for their own sakes; and with the letter for my sake; so that they might become useful to me; because the nature of my endeavor was such that I had to train my own help and pay current wages while I trained them.

The nature of the profession these young people were to make when they assumed to practice architecture entails much more careful preparation than that of the "good school" architect; theirs is a far more difficult thing to do technically and artistically, if they would do something of their own. To my chagrin, too many are content to take it "ready-made," and with no further preparation hasten to compete for clients of their own. Now 15 good, bad, and indifferent are practicing architecture in the Middle West, South, and Far West and with considerable "success." In common with the work of numerous disciples (judging from such work as has been put forward publicly), there is a restless jockeying with members, one left off here, another added there, with varying intent; in some a vain endeavor to reindividualize the old types; in others an attempt to conceal their origin, but always—ad nauseam—the inevitable reiteration of the features that gave the original work its style and individuality. To find fault with this were unfair. It is not unexpected nor unpromising except in those unbearable cases where badly modified *inorganic* results seem to satisfy their authors' conception of originality; and banalities of form and proportion are accordingly advertised in haste as work of creative architects of a "new school." That some uniformity in performance should have obtained for some years is natural; it could not be otherwise, unless unaware I had harbored marked geniuses. But when the genius arrives nobody will take his work for mine; least of all will he mistake my work for his own creation.

"The letter killeth." In this young work at this time, still it is the letter that killeth, and emulation of the "letter" that gives the illusion or delusion of "movement." There is no doubt, however, but that the sentiment is awakened which will mean progressive movement in time. And there are many working quietly who, I am sure, will give a good account of themselves.

Meanwhile, the spirit in which this use of the letter has its rise is important to any noble future still left to the cause. If the practices that disgrace and demoralize the soul of the young man in architecture could be made plain to him; if he could be shown that inevitably equivocation dwarfs and eventually destroys what creative faculty he may possess; that designing lies, in design to deceive himself or others, shuts him out absolutely from realizing upon his own gifts; no matter how flattering his opportunities may be; if he could realize that the artist heart is one uncompromising core of truth in seeking, in giving, or in taking; a precious service could be rendered him. The young architect who is artist enough to know where he stands and man enough to use honestly his parent forms as such, conservatively, until he feels his own strength within him, is only exercising an artistic birthright in the interest of a good cause; he has the character at least from which great things may come. But the boy who steals his forms; "steals" them because he sells them as his own for the moment of superficial distinction he gains by trading on the results; is no artist, has not the sense of the first principles of the ideal that he poses and the forms that he abuses. He denies his birthright, an act characteristic and unimportant; but for a mess of pottage, he endangers the chances of a genuine forward movement, insults both cause and precedent with an astounding insolence quite peculiar to these matters in the United States, ruthlessly sucks what blood may be left in the tortured and abused forms he caricatures and exploits, like the parasite he is.

Another condition as far removed from creative work is the state of mind of those who, having in the course of their day's labor put some stitches into the "clothes" of the work, assume, therefore, that style and pattern are rightfully theirs and wear them defiantly unregenerate. The gist of the whole matter artistically has entirely eluded them. This may be the so-called "democratic" point of view; at any rate it is the immemorial error of the rabble. No great artist nor work of art ever proceeded from that conception, nor ever will.

Then there is the soiled and soiling fringe of all creative effort, a type common to all work everywhere that meets with any degree of success, although it may be more virulent here because of low standards; those who benefit by the use of another's work and to justify themselves depreciate both the work and worker they took it from; the type that will declare, "In the first place, I never had your shovel; in the second place, I never broke your shovel; and in the third place, it was broken when I got it, anyway;" the type that with more crafty intelligence develops into the "coffin worm." One of Whistler's "coffin worms" has just wriggled in and out.

But underneath all, I am constrained to believe, lies the feverish ambition to get fame or fortune "quick," characteristic of the rush of commercial standards that rule in place of artist standards, and consequent unwillingness to wait to prepare thoroughly.

"Art to one is high as a heavenly goddess; to another only the thrifty cow that gives him his butter," said Schiller; and who will deny that our profession is prostitute to the cow, meager in ideals, cheap in performance, commercial in spirit: demoralized by ignoble ambition? A foolish optimism regarding this only serves to perpetuate it. Foolish optimism and the vanity of fear of ridicule or "failure" are both friends of ignorance.

In no country in the world do disciples, neophytes, or brokers pass artist counterfeit so easily as in these United States. Art is commercialized here rather more than anything else, although the arts should be as free from this taint as religion. But has religion escaped?

So the standard of criticism is not only low; it is often dishonest or faked somewhere between the two, largely manufactured to order for profit or bias. Criticism is worked as an advertising game, traders' instincts subject to the prevailing commercial taint. Therein lies a radically evil imposition that harms the public; that also further distorts, confuses and injures values and promotes bad work; that tends to render the integrity of artist and commerce alike a stale and unprofitable joke, and to make honest enemies even harder to find than honest friends. The spirit of fair play, the endeavor to preserve the integrity of values, intelligently, on a high plane in order to help in raising the level of the standard of achievement in the country, and to refrain from throwing the senseless weight of the mediocre and bad upon it; all this is unhappily too rare among editors. The average editor has a "constituency," not a standard. This constituency is largely the average architect who has bought the "artistic" in his architecture as one of its dubious and minor aspects, or the sophisticated neophyte, the broker, and the quack, to whom printers' ink is ego-balm and fortune.

So until the standard is raised any plea for artist integrity is like a cry for water in the Painted Desert. As for competent criticism, the honest work of illuminating insight, where is it? Nothing is more precious or essential to progress. Where is the editor or critic not narrow or provincial? Or loose and ignorant? Or cleverly or superficially or cowardly commercial? Let him raise this standard! Friend or foe, there is still a demand for him even here; but if he did, he would fail, gloriously fail, of "success."

Is architecture, then, no longer to be practiced as an art? Has its practice permanently descended to a form of mere "artistic activity"?

The art of architecture has fallen from a high estate, lower steadily since the men of Florence patched together fragments of the art of Greece and Rome and in vain endeavor to reestablish its eminence manufactured the Renaissance. It has fallen from the heavenly "Goddess of Antiquity" and the Middle Ages to the thrifty cow of the present day. To touch upon these matters in this country is doubly unkind, for it is to touch upon the question of "bread and butter" chiefly. Aside from the conscienceless ambition of the near artist (more sordid than any greed of gold) and beneath this thin pretense of the ideal that veneers the curious compound of broker and neophyte there lurks, I know, for any young architect an ever present dread of the kind of "failure" that is the obverse of the kind of "success" that commercialized standards demand of him if he is to survive. Whosoever would worship his heavenly goddess has small choice; he must keep his eye on the thrifty cow or give up his dream of "success"; and the power of discrimination possessed by the cow promises ill for the future integrity of an organic architecture. The net result of present standards is likely to be a poor wretch, a coward who aspires pretentiously or theoretically, advertises cleverly and milks surreptitiously. There is no real connection between aspiration and practice except a tissue of lies and deceit; there never can be. The young architect before he ventures to practice architecture with an ideal, today, should first be sure of his goddess and then, somehow, be connected with a base of supplies from which he cannot be cut off, or else fall in with the rank and file of the "good school" of the hour. Anyone who has tried it knows this; that is, if he is honest and is going to use his own material as soon as he is able. So the ever present economic question underlies this question of artist integrity, at this stage of our development, like quicksand beneath the footing of a needed foundation, and the structure itself seems doomed to shreds and cracks and shores and patches, the deadening compromises and pitiful makeshifts of the struggle to "succeed"! Even the cry for this integrity will bind the legion together, as one man, against the crier and the cry.

This is art, then, in a sentimental democracy, which seems to be only another form of self-same hypocrisy? Show me a man who prates of such "democracy" as a basis for artist endeavor, and I will show you an inordinately foolish egotist or a quack. The "democracy" of the man in the American street is no more than the gospel of mediocrity. When it is understood that a great democracy is the highest form of aristocracy conceivable, not of birth or place or wealth, but of those qualities that give distinction to the man as a man, and that as a social state it must be characterized by the honesty and responsibility of the absolute individualist as the unit of its structure, then only can we have an art worthy the name. The rule of mankind by mankind is one thing; but false "democracy," the hypocritical sentimentality politically practiced and preached here, usually the sheep's clothing of the proverbial wolf, or the egotistic dream of self-constituted patron saints is quite another thing. "The letter killeth," yes; but more deadly still is the undertow of false democracy that poses the man as a creative artist and starves him to death unless he fakes his goddess or persuades himself, with "language," that the cow is really she. Is the lack of an artist conscience, then, simply the helpless surrender of the would-be artist to this wherewith democracy with which a nation soothes itself into subjection? Is the integrity for which I plead here no part of this time and place? And is no young aspirant or hardened sinner to blame for lacking it? It may be so. If it is, we can at least be honest about that, too. But what aspiring artist could knowingly face such a condition? He would choose to dig in the ditch and trace his dreams by lamplight, on scrap paper, for the good of his own soul; a sweet and honorable, if commercially futile, occupation.

It has been my hope to have inspired among my pupils a personality or two to contribute to this work, some day, forms of their own devising, with an artistic integrity that will help to establish upon a firmer basis the efforts that have gone before them and enable them in more propitious times to carry on their practice with a personal gentleness, wisdom, and reverence denied to the pioneers who broke rough ground for them, with a wistful eye to better conditions for their future.

And I believe that, cleared of the superficial pose and push that is the inevitable abuse of its opportunity and its nature, and against which I ungraciously urge myself here, there will be found good work in a cause that deserves honest friends and honest enemies among the better architects of the country. Let us have done with "language" and unfair use of borrowed forms; understand that such practices or products are not of the character of this young work. This work is a sincere endeavor to establish the ideal of an organic architecture in a new country; a type of endeavor that alone can give lasting value to any architecture and that is in line with the spirit of every great and noble precedent in the world of forms that has come to us as the heritage of the great life that has been lived, and in the spirit of which all great life to be will still be lived.

And this thing that eludes the disciple, remains in hiding from the neophyte, and in the name of which the broker seduces his client, What is it? This mystery requiring the catch phrases of a new language to abate the agonies of the convert and in the name of which ubiquitous atrocities have been and will continue to be committed, with the deadly enthusiasm of the ego-mania that is its plague. First, a study of the nature of materials you elect to use and the tools you must use with them, searching to find the characteristic qualities in both that are suited to your purpose. Second, with an ideal of organic nature as a guide, so to unite these qualities to serve that purpose, that the fashion of what you do has integrity or is *natively fit*, regardless of preconceived notions of style. *Style* is a byproduct of the process and comes of the man or the mind in the process. The style of the thing, therefore, will be the man; it is his. *Let his forms alone.*

To adopt a "style" as a motive is to put the cart before the horse and get nowhere beyond the "styles"; never to reach *style*.

It is obvious that this is neither ideal nor work for fakers or tyros; for unless this process is finally so imbued, informed, with a feeling for the beautiful that grace and proportion are inevitable, the result cannot get beyond good engineering.

A light matter this, altogether? And yet an organic architecture must take this course and belie nothing, shirk nothing. Discipline! The architect who undertakes his work seriously on these lines is emancipated and imprisoned at the same time. His work may be severe; it cannot be foolish. It may lack grace; it cannot lack fitness altogether. It may seem ugly; it will not be false. No wonder, however, that the practice of architecture in this sense is the height of ambition and the depth of poverty!

Nothing is more difficult to achieve than the integral simplicity of organic nature, amid the tangled confusions of the innumerable relics of form that encumber life for us. To achieve it in any degree means a serious devotion to the "underneath" in an attempt to grasp the *nature* of building a beautiful building beautifully, as organically true in itself, to itself and to its purpose, as any tree or flower.

That is the need, and the need is demoralized, not served, by the same superficial emulation of the letter in the new work that has heretofore characterized the performances of those who start out to practice architecture by selecting and electing to work in a ready-made "style."

Meyer Schapiro (review date 1938)

SOURCE: "Architect's Utopia," in *Partisan Review*, Vol. IV, No. 4, March, 1938, pp. 42-47.

[*In the following review, Schapiro critiques Wright's social vision as it is represented in* Architecture and Modern Life, *observing numerous "contradictions and naivetés" in the work.*]

Frank Lloyd Wright believes that only "organic architecture" or primitive Christianity—"Jesus, the gentle anarchist"—can solve the crisis. This was also the theme of his earlier book, ***The Disappearing City,*** written in the depths of the depression. If we forget the undergraduate poetizing of the great architect, now seventy years old ("the earth is prostrate, prostitute to the sun"), and his no less profound philosophizing ("what, then, is life?"), and if we strip his argument of the grand, neo-Biblical and neo-Whitmanesque theogonic jargon of "integral," "organic" and the man "individual," we come at last to a familiar doctrine of innocence and original sin and a plan of redemption ·by rural housing. According to Wright (and this is developed in detail by [Baker] Brownell) a primitive state of democratic individualism in the Eden of the small towns and the farms was perverted by the cities. A privileged class arose which did not know how to administer its wealth in the common interest; and what remained of the native culture was corrupted by the immigrants. But by an internal law that regulates the fortunes of mankind, swinging life back to its healthy starting-point when it has gone too far toward decay, salvation comes through the evil itself. As the city grows, it is choked by its own traffic and reawakens the nomadic instincts of man. Its own requirements of efficiency gradually bring about decentralization. And the insecurity of life in the city forces people back to the soil where their living depends on themselves alone and a healthy individualism can thrive. In the Broadacre City, already designed by Wright in his earlier book, the urban refugee will have his acre of ground on which to grow some vegetables; he will work several days a week in a factory some miles away, accessible in his second-hand Ford; the cash income will supplement the garden; and through these combined labors he will enjoy a balanced life in nature. The new integrity of the individual will bring about the end of speculation and commercial standards.

The deurbanizing of life, the fusion of city and country on a high productive level, is an ideal shared by socialists and anarchists. But when presented as in Wright's books as an immediate solution of the crisis, it takes on another sense. It is the plan of Ford and Swope, a scheme of permanent subsistence farming with a corvée of work sharing in the distant mill, of scattered national company villages under a reduced living standard. The homes of Broadacre City may be of the most recent and efficient materials; they may be designed by the ablest architects—"integrated" and "organic" as Wright assures us they will be; but all these are perfectly consistent with physical and spiritual decay. Social well-being is not. simply an architectural problem. A prison may be a work of art and a triumph of ingenuity. The economic conditions that determine freedom and a decent living are largely ignored by Wright. He foresees, in fact, the poverty of these new feudal settlements when he provides that the worker set up his own factory-made house, part by part, according to his means, beginning with a toilet and kitchen, and adding other rooms as he earns the means by his labor in the factory. His indifference to property relations and the state, his admission of private industry and second-hand Fords in this idyllic world of amphibian labor, betray its reactionary character. Already under the dictatorship of Napoleon III, the state farms, partly inspired by the old Utopias, were the official solution of unemployment. The democratic Wright may attack rent and profit and interest, but apart from some passing reference to the single-tax he avoids the question of class and power.

The outlines of Wright's new society are left unclear; they are like the content of his godless religion for which he specifies a church in Broadacre City. After all, he is an architect telling you what a fine home he can build you in the country; it is not his business to discuss economics and class relations. But in the chapters by his collaborator, Brownell, who has more to say about technology, economics and culture (although the consequences are not faced in any field), the reactionary side of this shabby, streamlined Utopia becomes more evident.

The core of his argument is the critique of bourgeois society made over a hundred years ago by both the right and the left and repeated since, that it destroys idyllic values, dehumanizes man, disperses his interests and activity and subjects him to the machine. But following the right, he opposes to it the ideal of a self-sufficient agrarian culture on the Borsodi plan, with its elaborate household industry. By converting the middle class—the real subject of his anxiety—into a conservative peasantry, he hopes to restore their "human integrity." There is little direct reference to exploitation and war and the everyday brutalities of class power; where he has to deal with the clash of interests, his thought becomes blurred or allegorical. The historical movements of our time are transposed into conflicts between shadowy principles. The great and primary struggle is between "relativism" and "absolutism": an inherent tendency toward freedom and creativeness (relativity) meets an opposite inherent tendency toward "absolutism." Beside this "primarily intellectual conflict" there are three lesser ones: Urbanism vs. Agrarianism, Security vs. Opportunity, Specialization vs. Integrity, the latter two being individual, not social, problems. Ignorant of socialist theory, of which he has acquired some elements of the vocabulary, he caricatures socialist ideas in a half-baked manner. He is against socialism because it is necessarily centralized and urban, surrendering freedom for security, but also because it is "essentially insecure, unstable, destructive of human values of life." He can speak in the same work of the economic causes of crises, but also of the decay of western Europe and the economic disasters of the United States as "natural functions of the overgrown urbanism and cosmopolitanism of these times." He cannot explain why security should decline as productive power increases; "the disorganization of personal life" is not the cause, as he thinks, but only an effect.

His own agrarian solution involves a similar indifference to economic facts. The interdependence of agriculture and industry, of production and the market, is nowhere analyzed and the obvious practical objections remain unanswered. He does not ask: what will be the effect of such a return to the soil and the self-sufficiency he advocates on the millions of farmers (with their tenants and laborers) who depend on cash crops and already find their market dwindling? or the effect of the lower income of the semi-industrial workers on the same agricultural market? He recommends a revival of household industry with modern machines as an essential part of the new agrarianism. But how can the farmer who grows crops only for himself afford this elaborate plant for producing his own household goods?

Characteristically enough, Brownell approves the trend toward industrial decentralization, not seeing that it coincides with an even greater concentration of ownership and a greater poverty of the masses. He innocently looks forward to a broader distribution of productive property as one of the results of this trend; but in the name of a mysterious concept of balance he would preserve centralized private control of some industries and a decentralized private ownership of others. Although the self-sufficiency of the farms in his ideal America is to rest upon the use of machines, he deplores the drift of the farm youth to the cities, which is due precisely to the mechanizing of agriculture.

His whole approach is based on the pathetic polarities of stability and movement, order and restlessness, the land and the city, formulated by the folk-loving, but anti-democratic, romantic reaction at the beginning of the nineteenth century. He has inherited its stock antitheses of security and insecurity, the whole and the fragment, the organic and the inorganic; and added like his predecessors other categories appropriate to the politics and science of the moment. There are indeed personal nuances, but in the muddled form of the whole, with its eclectic hyphenation of doctrines, they are as insignificant as the lyrical delicacies of the more learned Nazis. Like the religious and feudal reactionaries of the last century and their fascist successors, Brownell wants a "balanced" and an "integral" society. But balance, he admits, is not good in all fields. In population, for example, a homogeneous racial and national stock is preferable to a "balance of stocks." Nevertheless, he finds "an integrated life" only in the South. And as he goes on to specify the ideals of his "natural" agrarian culture, he begins to resemble the fascists to a hair. He attacks the declining birth-rate and the increasing longevity. The old are uncreative and useless; big families, especially big rural families, with plenty of young men, are needed to effect the balance and the integration. And these big families must produce in their domestic factories an American "folk art and a folk religion and even a folk education" to end the cultural crisis. Brownell shares the Nazi enthusiasm and vagueness about the folk as a classless primordial "natural" mass which he opposes to the landless immigrants with their "unnatural" and un-American urban interests. "Surely one of the main influences toward a more integrated life and culture is the nature of the American people. They are not suited to urban lives and extreme specialization. The agrarian tradition is deeply in them." But strangely enough jazz music in its dynamic character becomes for him an American folk product, although in his yearning for repose he has criticized this dynamism as a foreign and urban perversion.

The contradictions and naivetés of this book are so numerous that the informed reader can have little confidence in the authors. He is struck again and again by the contrast between their reverence for technique and science and their complete failure to analyze the social mechanism they have in mind and the means for realizing their goals. They are obsessed by modern life as an expression of something peculiar to the moment, but are wholly unable to make an historical explanation. The idea that society is known through its reflections permits a crude analogical thinking and the flattest impressionist substitutes for a rounded historical study. The pages devoted by Wright to architectural style are no better; he says little that is precise about the forms of contemporary building, and his survey of past architecture is a grotesque parody of the views of the 1880s, a home-made affair based on old readings and the artistic propaganda of the pioneers of the modern movement. All architecture after the fourteenth century is regarded as decadent, and post-mediaeval painting as merely photographic.

The social imagination of Wright should not be classed with that of the great Utopians whom he seems to resemble. Their energy, their passion for justice and their constructive fantasy were of another and higher order and embodied the most advanced insights of their time. The thought of Wright, on the other hand, is improvised, vagrant and personal at a moment when the social values and relations he expounds have already long been the subject of critical analysis and scientific formulation. He is not in the direct line of the Utopians, but his social criticism as an architect is in many ways characteristic of modern architectural prophecy and has its European parallels, though addressed to an American middle class. During the last fifty years the literature of building has acquired a distinctive reformist and prophetic tone. The architects demand a new style to fit a new civilization, or if the civilization has become problematic, they propose a new architecture to reform it. In either case, the architect, unlike the poet or the painter, is a practical critic of affairs. Even his aesthetic programs are permeated with the language of efficiency, and underneath his ideals of simplicity and a flexible order we can detect the emulation of the engineer. As a technician who must design for a widening market, he can foresee endless material possibilities of his art, and by the existing standards he can judge the wretchedness of the average home. The whole land cries out to be rebuilt, while he himself, inventive and energetic, remains unemployed. But his social insight is limited by his professional sphere; in general, the architect knows the people whom he serves mainly in terms of their resources and their tastes. Their economic role, their active relation to other classes, escape him. His certainty that architecture is a mirror of society does not permit him to grasp the social structure. The correspondences of architecture and "life" by which he hopes to confirm the historic necessity of his new style, these are largely on the surface, reflections of reflections: architecture, for Wright, is "a spirit of the spirit of man." Hence Le Corbusier could wonder how such pillars of efficiency and honor as the bankers tolerated the sham façades of their banks; he offered to protect them from revolution by designing hygienically superior workers' homes. Today, Wright returning from Russia finds it hard "to be reconciled to the delays Russia is experiencing no matter how cheerfully in getting the architecture characteristic of her new life and freedom." But he explains the "falsity" of the current bureaucratic classicism of the public buildings by Stalin's eagerness to please the people who want the luxuries once enjoyed by their masters. "If Stalin is betraying the revolution, then I say he is betraying it into the hands of the Russian people" (*Architectural Record,* Oct. 1937).

This blindness to the facts of social and economic power makes possible the visionary confidence with which architects like Wright correct society on the drawing-board.

Accustomed to designing plans, which others will carry out and for which the means of realization already exist, they assume for themselves the same role or division of labor in the work of social change. The conditions which inspired their architectural inventiveness are more like those which preside over reforms than over revolution. Through their designs they have effected the almost daily transformation of the cities, and when society has to be rebuilt, their self-assurance as prophetic forces is strengthened by the current demands for housing and public works as the only measures against ruin. Their reformist sentiments are echoed by the architectural metaphors of planning, construction, foundations, bases and frameworks in the language of economic and social reform. Advanced architects who have only contempt for the grandiose, unrealistic projects of academic architectural competitions, relapse into social planning of the same vastness and practical insignificance. They are subject especially to the illusion that because they are designing for a larger and larger mass of people they are directly furthering democracy through their work; Mumford, for example, supposed that the use of the same kind of electric bulb by the rich and the poor was a sign of the inherent democratic effects of modern technology. The existence of fascism is the brutal answer to such fantasies.

To the degree that the crisis is judged psychologically as the result of "restlessness" and is neurotically laid to a "faulty environment" or to mistakes of the past, the architectural utopia of Wright, the specialist in new environments, must seem really convincing to those from whom the economic reality is hidden. Around the private middle-class dwelling cluster such strong and deep memories of security that the restoration of the home appears in itself a radical social cure. Throughout his books Wright insists that architecture is the art which gives man a sense of stability in an unstable world, and that of all styles of building the modern is the most "organic." "The old is chaos, restlessness"; the new, "integral, organic, is order, repose," he writes,—like the modern mystics of the state and church. In his survey of modern architecture—otherwise so meagre—Wright tells in detail how he built the Imperial Hotel of Tokyo on marshy ground, and how this building alone withstood the earthquake of 1923. But social earthquakes are not circumvented by cantilevers and light partitions.

In spite of the exaggerations and errors of Wright in giving architecture an independent role in shaping social life, the experience of his profession has a vital bearing on socialism. But it is just this bearing that Wright and Brownell, as spokesmen for the middle class, ignore. They have failed to recognize—what must be apparent on a little reflection—that the progress of architecture today depends not only on large-scale planning and production, but also on the continuity of this production and on a rising living standard of the whole mass of the people—conditions irreconcilable with private control of industry. It is only when all three conditions are present that the architect can experiment freely and control the multiplicity of factors which now enter invariably into his art. Monopoly capitalism and its political regimes also plan on a large scale, within certain limits, but they are fatally tied to crises and war and declining standards of life (not to mention political and cultural repression) which limit the architect at every point. The masses cannot afford good homes and the intervention of the capitalist state in housing is tentative and even reactionary, since it helps to perpetuate lower standards and supports the familiar speculative swindles. Moreover, even under more prosperous conditions, the great mass of architects have no chance for original artistic creation; they are salaried workers submerged in a capitalist office, with little possibility of self-development. The architect cannot be indifferent to these as merely economic and material factors inferior to creative problems. The latter are not posed unless the architect can really build, and the quality of the solutions depends in part on the freedom of the architect in realizing his designs. In our day the best architects have built very little during the last eight years, at a time when the need of new construction was universally admitted. Even the slight upswing just experienced has already subsided and architects face a desperate future. A return to the soil, far from stimulating architecture, can only depress it further.

Nikolaus Pevsner (essay date 1939)

SOURCE: "Frank Lloyd Wright's Peaceful Penetration of Europe," in *The Rationalists,* The Architectural Press Ltd, 1978, pp. 34-41.

[*In the following essay, originally published in 1939, Pevsner assesses Wright's influence on European architecture.*]

There lived near London an architect known to many for his adventurous early buildings and designs, his brilliant writings on the social movement of the arts and crafts, his Campden experiment in craftsmanship, husbandry and community life, and his charming personality, Mr C. R. Ashbee. He was about seventy-five, [C. R. Ashbee died in 1942.] and could claim amongst his other titles to fame that of having discovered Frank Lloyd Wright for Europe. They got to know each other when Mr Ashbee was staying in Chicago in 1900. Correspondence ensued, and when Wright came over to Europe in 1910 he visited Mr Ashbee at Campden. Some time before this journey, Professor Kuno Francke, a German professor in aesthetics at Harvard, had visited Wright and strongly suggested to him to go to Germany, where his work would be hailed by the progressive architects. Soon after this visit, a proposal came from E. Wasmuth, the best-known German architectural publishers, to bring out a complete monograph of Wright's work. While in Florence, Wright signed the introduction to this first portfolio, a copy of which is now at the Architectural Association. Immediately afterwards he suggested to Mr Ashbee to write the text to a second smaller and more popular volume also to be brought out by Wasmuth's. This appeared in 1911, and can now be studied in the library of the Victoria and Albert Museum.

The two books, including all that was most important of Wright's early style from Winslow to the Robie and Martin Houses, must have had an almost instantaneous effect on young German architects. This is most clearly reflected in certain details of Gropius's model factory at the Cologne Exhibition of 1914. The brick technique, above all, in the odd long slots of the upper floor windows, the heavy entrance with the two bands of windows on the left and the right, the projecting string courses above and the flat slab roofs, all these motifs prove beyond doubt the impression of Wright's (besides Peter Behrens's) work on Gropius. In the meantime, however, Berlage, the great old man of Dutch architecture, had gone to the United States in 1911, unacquainted in all probability with the Wasmuth volumes. Travelling in America he discovered Wright again independently. In articles published in the *Schweizerische Bauzeitung* of September 14, 21 and 28, 1912, and in a Dutch book of 1913 dealing with his American impressions, Berlage praised Wright as 'a master without an equal in Europe'. In discussing the Martin House, he stressed its bare ground floor walls, the long bands of windows on the upper floor, the living-rooms leading into each other without separating doors, the lovely vistas across caused by this spatial arrangement, the intimate connection between house and garden, and the widely projecting roofs. It can be assumed that those young Dutch architects who learned their craft or set up in practice just before the war became familiar with a man so sincerely admired by their great example, Berlage, and with the two German publications of 1910 and 1911. One of the first palpable proofs of Wright's influence on building in Holland is a house designed by Van't Hoff in 1915. Similar features can easily be detected in the early work of Jan Wils and H. Th. Wijdeveld (who, incidentally, saw illustrations of some houses by Wright in an American book as early as 1900, when he was only fifteen years old. He says: 'I could not sleep the first night I possessed the book; I was so thrilled'). During the first postwar decade Wright's idiom became one of the chief ingredients of Dutch architectural expression. There was, eg, the Kijkduin Estate near the Hague, by Bijvoet and Duiker, there were private houses by Wouda, La Croix (ill. *Nieuw Nederl. Bouwkunst,* 1924, Figs. 21-23), and even by Berlage himself. The centre of Wright enthusiasm, however, was Wijdeveld, not by imitating Wright's style, but by spreading knowledge of it. In 1921 and again in 1925 he published in a magazine, *Wendingen,* then edited by him, illustrated articles on Wright, and collected these in 1925 into a lavishly produced book with English text and contributions by Oud, Mendelsohn, Mallet-Stevens, and others. This book, it seems, opened at last the eyes of young English architects to Wright's genius, although nothing comparable to the Dutch vogue followed. When Wijdeveld splendidly finished his propaganda for Wright by staging an exhibition of his work at the Municipal Museum in Amsterdam, which was then sent round to Berlin, Cologne, Munich, and Antwerp, no arrangements could be made for the exhibition to be shown in London. Paris does not appear to have been interested either, and this came probably from the strangely isolated development of the Modern Movement in France until after the war. To those eager for innovation and a true contemporaneity, Garnier's Cité Industrielle of 1904, and Perret's achievements in ferro-concrete had played the part assumed in Germany to a certain extent by Wright's forms and experiments. However, despite this, it seems unlikely that Mallet-Stevens or Le Corbusier can have been in complete ignorance of Wright when they formed and evolved their styles. Mallet-Stevens, in fact, paid a debt of gratitude to Wright in his article for Heer Wijdeveld's volume. But Le Corbusier, although he had lived in Berlin for about six months just in 1910-11, answered, when asked to contribute to the Wijdeveld book: 'I do not know this architect'.

Here is a first instance of the difficulties which one meets in trying to follow the course of one man's style in the intricate tissue of European postwar architecture. Wright's influence on early Gropius—a transitory one—or on Dutch buildings of about 1920-24, is comparatively easy to grasp, but the historian of style finds himself in a much more precarious position directly he tries to analyse certain deeper and wider effects of Wright on Europe. A few examples may illustrate this.

There are, eg, the so-called Phantasts in Holland, the school of architects recognizable by their odd, deliberately crude, chaotic details, originally, one may surmise, instigated by Indian native temple art. De Klerk is perhaps the best known of them (Eigen Haard 1914 and 1917, Spaarndamerplantoen 1913 and 1917, Amstellaan 1920); Kromhout and, for a time, Piet Kramer were other representatives of this mood which leads back to Van der Mey's mad Scheepvaarthuis of 1912-13, and even to certain details in Berlage interiors. When the large estates of tenement houses around Amsterdam were erected immediately after the war and began to impress German town planners and architects, it was in this fantastic attire that they became known. And as at exactly the same time riotous post-war feelings prevailed in Germany, sometimes of a constructive revolutionary, sometimes of a post-defeat desperado, and sometimes of a jazzy *Après-nous-le-Déluge* character, the Dutch Phantasts found response in more than one school in Germany. Poelzig's and Bruno Taut's most soaring architectural dreams belong to these years, but Mendelsohn also succumbed to such feelings for a short time, and even Gropius's now destroyed War Memorial of 1920 at Weimar re-echoed the strident outbreaks of Expressionism.

Now, Expressionism was originally a pictorial movement, and the effects on architects of new forms in painting should not be underestimated. Cubism, the French counterpart of German Expressionism, has certainly deeply impressed architects, and helped them to develop compositions of bare cubes and façades without any mouldings mediating between different planes. But Cubism again could be interpreted decoratively and functionally, and both interpretations can be found in buildings of the first ten years after the war. The Rue Mallet-Stevens of 1927 can serve to illustrate the decorative, J. J. P. Oud's splendid Rotterdam estates the functional exegesis of Cubist tenets. Dudok, one may say, stands between the two.

Functionalism, however, is in itself a complex phenomenon. Even without Cubist pictures—and pre-war Cubism of Picasso and Braque or pre-war abstract art of Kandinsky were far from precise and geometrically rigid—Functional architecture would probably have found its own immediate expression, simply by evolving Loos's and Peter Behrens's forms of about 1910. This is what Gropius did. He certainly understood Cubist painters or else he would not have appointed them to professorships in the Bauhaus, but while teaching there they probably adopted more from his direct and courageous architectural style than he from their configurations in the flat.

The Dutch and German Phantasts, Expressionism, Cubism, Functionalism—an intricate pattern of tendencies in European art between 1920 and 1925, and yet, in fact, not intricate enough, for once more Frank Lloyd Wright's influence must be introduced into it. There was not one of these conflicting schools of thought which has not at one time or other experienced some stimulus from Wright. And as if this were not enough of confusion yet, one has to add that by then—as is known—Wright had changed his own style considerably. Midway Gardens, Chicago (1913), and the Imperial Hotel, Tokio (1916-20), represent a new Wright, gone all romantic, fantastic, Eastern—far more personal and inimitable now than he had been when Europe first got to hear of him. To copy this new style or even to accept influence from it was bound to be fatal to any but the strongest decorative genius. How far now did the Dutch Phantasts find themselves confirmed in Wright's *seconda maniera?* Van der Mey comes before Midway Gardens, but Berlage may have felt the first symptoms of a change, the result of which was naturally just as palatable to him as Wright's earlier style. Wijdeveld's volume of 1925 is certainly an instance of Wrightian Phantasm interpreted by a Dutch architect who had gone through a phase of native Dutch Phantasm.

It is the same with Cubism. An architect grown up in admiration of Wright's genius would find access to Cubist painting easy; an architect ready to translate Cubist revelations into building would see his theories corroborated in Wright's practice. Who would be prepared to define what comes from Wright in Dudok's work at Hilversum, and what from Cubism, or what in Mendelsohn's uncouth brick houses of 1922 and 1923 is the outcome of Wright's idiom and what of Dudok's?

However, these questions seem simple when held against any arising from a consideration of Wright's most profoundly architectural qualities. So far, only forms have been discussed. But what effects of Wright's research into modern building materials can be traced, what effects of his brilliant spatial flexibility, or his revolutionary theories on the social future of art and architecture? It will, in all probability, never be possible to assess correctly the share, in the use of composite walling materials in German post-war experiments (Gropius, Luckhardt, etc), which belonged to Wright's Unity Temple of 1908, a monolith with walls all of concrete slabs. And how far would Gropius himself be able to remember whether the lovely unity of house and garden in his Bauhaus staff dwellings at Dessau owed something to early impressions gathered from the perusal of the Wasmuth volumes? Or take Mies van der Rohe's ravishing ballets of space, his Barcelona Exhibition Pavilion of 1929 and the famous Tugendhat House at Brünn with rooms rhythmically flowing into each other and no inner divisions. Had Le Corbusier spurred him, or at a much earlier stage Wright, who was the first so boldly to unite room with room? And—to mention one last instance— what of Wright's ideas on art education? Taliesin, his Wisconsin community, is only a few years old. But it was preceded by his plan for what was to be called the Hillside Home School of the Allied Arts. The prospectus of this went out about the end of 1931, and Heer Wijdeveld was mentioned as future principal, Heer Wijdeveld who only a few months before had published his own plan for an international guild of architectural and general artistic training and community life to be built in Holland. Did Wijdeveld know about the Bauhaus? Is the name of guild derived in some roundabout way from Mr Ashbee's Guild and School of Handicraft at Chipping Campden, which Wright on his part knew? If there is a connection here, it would be a welcome proof of an ultimate derivation of Taliesin as well as Heer Wijdeveld's Elckerlic school from the Arts and Crafts Movement and William Morris. But these relations are, of course, not meant to be in any way direct or conscious. They are subtler, more concealed, and therefore perhaps all the more important. For the deeper the impression an architect of original genius receives from another of equal calibre, the less apparent will the links be . . .

Paul Goodman and Percival Goodman (essay date 1942)

SOURCE: "Frank Lloyd Wright on Architecture," in *Kenyon Review*, Vol. 4, No. 1, Winter, 1942, pp. 7-28.

[*In the following essay, Goodman and Goodman summarize Wright's architectural thought and compare his concept of Organic Architecture with the International Style of Le Corbusier.*]

As is natural to a teacher and polemicist, a propagandist when he cannot build and a critic of what he has built,— and all this for forty-seven years!—the publications of Wright are voluminous, the more so since his larger conception of architecture as "organically" related to society and the cosmos leads him to talk of nearly everything. For the same reasons, however, these writings are so repetitive that it is possible in a brief essay to reduce them to a few headings and even to do justice to the main details: the polemicist hammers at the same points and this particular organic-philosopher soon comes home to his simple lesson.

What is lost in such a reduction is the character of Wright's remarkably continuing activity, the unfailing energy and bold essays, loose connections and plenty of ignorance, and the faith in good principles.[1]

I. ORGANIC ARCHITECTURE

"Architecture," as used by Wright with a capital A, is a universal term. By this I mean that it signifies every object and subject-matter so far as it is excellent. Sometimes he distinguishes Organic Architecture from mere architecture, where Organic means "a structure wherein features or parts are so organized in form and substance as to be, applied to purpose, *integral*." But all organisms are architectural, and all purposes are spoken of as integral to the architecture of the Universe: "Architecture is whatever is organic. It is the organic pattern of all things. This remains the hidden mystery of creation until the architect has grasped and revealed it." Thus Organic Architecture is architectural architecture. Again, Architecture is something taken as the abstract structure of living, reality, etc.; but in the end nothing has significance except this structure, so that Architecture is the significance of everything: "Architecture is abstract. Abstract form is the pattern of the essential. It is spirit in objectified forms." It is the Good and, in fact, the Real. Thus, poetry is Architecture; Bach and Beethoven were the greatest architects, "the architecture of the future is the only hope for the painter and sculptor"; it is the keystone of Art, Science, and Religion; it is the Creative Spirit itself; "The Man of Galilee himself was an humble architect, in those days called carpenter"; the Universe itself is nothing but a grand Machine; Taliesin is a "research station toward—Reality."

Again, with respect to action: Statesmanship is Architecture; Economics is Architecture. And Architecture is the cure for War and conscription, as he told the British public in the summer of 1939. He therefore refutes the charge that the school at Taliesin is "escapist" by insisting that only there, through an organic architectural education, will young men come to grips with social problems.

The use of such universal terms is unobjectionable; they were used by Plato. And it is certain that Wright's way of conceiving Architecture has fortified him in his most valuable attitudes: for instance, in limiting himself to simply machined surfaces that do not do formal violence to the other surfaces of 20th Century life; in analyzing the *living* in the house, as when he opened the interior space; in combating the teaching of architecture as a speciality apart from social considerations; in relating form to site; in building-in the furniture and fixtures; in freeing the architectural imagination from axes and the other Beaux-Arts conventions. No doubt any of these might be arrived at by reasoning other than Organic Architecture; but Organic Architecture has certainly been Wright's way of explaining them to himself and his audiences.

Nevertheless, to handle language so freely demands in the end a mind infinitely flexible and astonishingly well-informed, for it is necessary to reach out into every field and do justice to the problems *of that field,* as well as merely to say "this also is Architecture." Otherwise, he will surely offend the experts who know their separate business; and he will come out, as always happens when the context of statements is not analyzed, with contradictions and loose talk. I don't mean to dwell on this master's weak points, but the mere mention of some of his "architectural" visions will show how vulnerable he is.

The architect-economist finds that Major Douglas has solved the problems of distribution. He imagines that rent can be abolished without political change. His ignorance of the financial structure is such that he imagines that gasoline, for instance, can be given gratis to the public without upsetting the ownership of "industry."

The architect-statesman finds that in Broadacre City there will be no police, but "it follows naturally from all this genuinely constructive way of life that in the administration of Broadacre City the county architect . . . has a certain disciplinary as well as cultural relationship to the whole; and since he maintains the harmony of the whole his must be one of the best minds the city has; and it will inevitably be the best trained." He finds that Organic Architecture will prevent war; but on the other hand, one reason why cities are *in*organic is that they are vulnerable to air-attack!

The architect-theologian favors us with the observation: "Of course there will be religion. Protestants, Catholics, Darkies, and the Synagogue will be with us"!!

The architect-educator has only contempt for classical education; but he avows that the students of his academy will work in close cooperation with private industrialists, so that they may at once be employed in private industry—as if the dangers of trade-schools had never been thought of. Is this the Research Station toward Reality?

The architect-painter most often writes as if all painting were mural-painting in a Wright house, as if easel-painting did not speak mind to mind precisely in a certain isolation in a frame.

These offensive observations could be multiplied a hundred-fold, and I assure the reader that they are not isolated slips, but seem to Wright to be as peculiar to his thought as the sentence "Form and Function are One."

(It is worth while to compare such loose talk of Wright's with the *Kindergarten Chats* of his Lieber Meister, Louis Sullivan. The *Kindergarten Chats* deal almost entirely with the themes of free imagination and cultural integrity, both dear to Wright. But Sullivan everywhere has an intimate sense of cultural atmosphere, whereas Wright's is more distant and schematic; Sullivan is a psychologist and an erotic, able to portray the genesis of imagination; and his flair for pedagogy is simply exquisite, as contrasted with Wright's authoritarianism. Then Sullivan's style, though often odd, is always graceful and witty;

whereas when he is not energetic, Wright is affected, and blunders from violence to coyness. Yet it is Wright who says: "Language is comparatively easy to use; it will always be easier to phrase an ideal than to build it." But Louis Sullivan says: "If you are to use words, be careful that you understand their values, their form, texture, color, their literal, their figurative meanings, their inborn tendency to shift and transform themselves, and their inclination to gravitate toward other words. Words are alive. Drive them carefully . . . otherwise they will slip away." Lieber Meister found plenty of truth in that wine he used to drink. In fact the only thing that prevents the *Kindergarten Chats* from being a major classic is—that there is no concrete discussion of architecture in them.)

Let me mention one shift of Wright's words extremely important for his later career. The climax of the Hull House Lecture of 1903 proclaiming the architecture of the Machine Age is a vivid vision of Chicago at night, its power and color, its pulsating life of almost physiological interrelations, "a magnificent truth with no guise of beauty," capable of unimaginable compositions. But when he comes to speak in England in 1939, every city in his eyes is a poor moribund thing; "all that is possible now in the buildings you build in your city is a kind of merciful mitigation"; "in any good organic structure it is difficult to say where the garden ends and the house begins"; this is the ideal of Broadacres, "an acre per person." Now either of these visions, or both, may be true; and it is easy to understand how—war, depression, and technological advance intervening—one might come from one to the other; but it is just this variation of contexts that Wright never seems to make clear to himself. Values that once seemed great are suddenly no values, yet without reconsideration or new proof. By this method it is always possible to say something different, but quite impossible to say anything wiser.

Through these changes, however, persists a developing architectural theme, continually absorbing more and more of Wright's theorizing; it is *the creation of domestic architecture for independent and increasingly self-subsistent people permanently attached to their own ground.* Wright says that it was by accident that in the firm of Sullivan and Adler the small houses were assigned to him; but as the years pass it is astonishing how few large buildings or even projects come from his board,—the Imperial Hotel, the Johnson Wax Building, Saint Mark's Towers, a few others. I am not referring merely to his success and skill in domestic architecture, but to the cause of this success, an inward sympathy for a certain attitude and way of life, where the house is the castle. This sympathy is expressed in his Wisconsin progressivism, "capitalism broad-based on the ground"; Barsodianism and neo-agrarianism. He speaks everywhere of the new mobility, but architecture, as opposed to engineering, consists in repose; all values are at home. Broadacre City pretends to be a synthesis of all modern functions; but the fact is that on the subject of *community planning* he has absolutely nothing original to say (he does not even try), whereas in 1938 he is still able to prepare to plan 40 completely different small dwellings. Therefore, if I may advance an hypothesis, is it not permissible to say that what so fascinates him in Broadacre City is just the fact that the formula "an acre per person" seems at last *both to confirm his real interest as a domestic architect and to put to rest his dreams of a universal architecture?* As a community-plan it touches on all values, but it imposes on them the uncriticized standard of a domestic architect.

II. DOMESTIC ARCHITECTURE

In innumerable places Wright has listed and explained the characteristic excellences of his small houses.[2] These excellences are not merely the criticism of existent works, but are advanced as prescriptions for all building, for domestic houses and for buildings like the Imperial Hotel. It is reasonable to say that such a typical list is for Wright the general *poetics* of architecture, and the particulars are the *parts* of architecture.

These parts are the site, both geographical and historical; the living functions; what might be called the idea of the living functions; the surfaces; the structure; the "basic design idea"; the plan; the nature of materials; the technology; the personalities of both architect and client. The order of these parts—I have roughly followed *Two Lectures*—is not crucial, because as Wright repeatedly and truly says, the art consists in the mutual expression of them all. You can tell the true artist by the way in which he brings his own formal parts, such as the plan and design, to the interpretation of the material parts, to constitute one whole.

(The excellent categories of Plasticity, Organic Simplicity, Individuality, Naturalness which Wright often introduces to describe this wholeness, belong rather to general aesthetics than to architecture especially.)

Now the glory of Frank Lloyd Wright is that *throughout this fundamental list*—fundamental because it is inconceivable that a great architect should omit expressing a single one of the points—*he has everywhere made strong and original contributions.* Contributions, moreover, in the teeth of almost universal architectural malpractice by his contemporaries, one of whom (like White) would be excellent in the façade, another (like Sullivan and Adler) in the structure, but none in the whole.

(There is one significant omission from all of Wright's lists up to the latest years; it is the Community Plan.)

1. *Site.* An example of appropriateness to the Site is the famous invention of the Prairie Style, the long horizontals of eaves, window-strips, balconies, and projecting base-course, adapted to the plain. The base-course projects so that the building is seen to rest on the ground rather than to spring from under it. (A tall city building, like St. Mark's Towers, is made smaller below than above.) The basement itself is above soil. The colors are prairie neutrals. (b) But this adaptation is not only to the formal appearance of the site, but also to its physical

nature. The prairie-basement is dry, etc. The Imperial Hotel floats in mud which is the real basis of Tokyo rather than stands on the few feet of superimposed clay. (c) Now in Wright's later houses he comes more and more to *rely* on peculiarities of the site for formal inspiration both in the plan and design (the Kaufmann house over the brook, the Oboler house on the peak). (d) But such reliance on the *peculiar* site is likely to lead, is it not, to domestic architecture for wealthy clients, for reasons of both real estate and construction. Here is an ironic contradiction between Wright's theory and practice: his sincere ambition is to build cheaply for every one; his most striking successes involve luxury expenditure. (e) The other buildings in the environment, Wright said in the early days, will take care of themselves without a general imposed plan, because the place, the individual needs and spirits, will have enough in common to insure community of style, *if* the buildings are built with integrity. In fact, of course, we find such a typical Wright house as that on Woodlawn and 58th in Chicago squatting alone in the midst of the Rockefeller-College-Gothic of the University.

2. Historical appropriateness means fitness to the mores and traditions: "I design a Negro schoolhouse in the South; make it theirs in point of life and color, form, etc. . . . I build a home for myself in southern Wisconsin, a stone, wood, and plaster building; make it as much a part of my grandfather's ground as the rocks and trees and hills." Thus in designing the Imperial Hotel, Wright was unwilling to import a purely occidental style, as had been done elsewhere in Tokyo; his idea was to design for the *transition* of Japan from "its knees to its feet" (surely he means from kneeling to sitting). Later he says, "All great architecture is transitional architecture." (b) The principle here is irrefutable, but Wright does not seem to realize the difficulties in the application. Let me point to a somewhat ridiculous contrast of paragraphs in *Organic Architecture.* Describing Taliesin West in Arizona he says: "Instead of sculpture we have used native rocks written on centuries ago by the American Indians and which we found on our own piece of ground. The camp has grown out of that ground, according to the spirit of environment and climate." In describing Taliesin in Wisconsin he says: "Most of our ornaments at Taliesin are ancient Chinese. . . . They seem to have the modern spirit which characterizes modern buildings and the more ancient they are the more of that spirit they seem to have." (c) The fact is that the spirit of an environment is in large part given by the prejudice of the critic; the Internationalists too see their spirit everywhere. Wright is on much surer ground, when he relies for the Zeitgeist on the client's needs and his own feelings: "The building will be characteristic of those it was built to serve because it necessarily is a solution of conditions they make, and is made to serve their ends in their way. . . . The architect is their technician and interpreter . . . he is too keenly sensible of the nature of his client as a fundamental condition in his problem to cast him off, although he may give him something to *grow to*. . . . An architect is bound to educate his client to the extent of his true skill

and capacity in what he as a professional believes to be fundamentally right." Wright has lived up to this program too. (d)In his early doctrine following directly after Sullivan, just what Wright saw as the spirit of the environment was the Machine Age. He was among the first to use the word streamline-design; his houses were called "Dress-Reform Houses," as later he called the International Style "Cardboard Houses." It was mainly in opposition to the Internationalists that he later laid such verbal stress on parochial peculiarities. His present position seem to be: "The house must not seem incompatible with the motor car that drives up to the door," yet "the house itself is not a machine."

3. *Function.* We come next to the architectural abstraction of the Functions of Living, or at least of a kind of living of a kind of individual. It was Wright who broke down the interior partitions of multiple rooms and restored freedom of living-movement; and he has tried to destroy the box-room built on a major and minor axis. He talks in terms of the Zones of living: activity and repose. His intention in these changes was partly to give himself freedom for handling the enclosed space; but this free handling in itself results in variety of perspective and the possibility of furniture and activity grouping according to more individual requirements. (b) He has opened up the inside to the outside by combining the windows and by extensive use of balconies; although, apparently temperamentally averse to flat roofs, he does not use terraces and roof-gardens with the lavishness of the Internationalists. (c) Again, he says "Always in the human scale in all proportions," so that he lowered the ceilings—leading to the criticism that if he himself had been 3 inches taller the proportion of all his buildings would have been different! But though the atmosphere is intimate, it is free and light, because of the extensive use of glass. A Wright house looks dark and is light, whereas a Le Corbusier house looks light and is light.

4. Nevertheless, Wright is not a functionalist; for along with the calculation of objective functions, he lays enormous stress on what we must call the *basic idea of the function,* as when he says: "I liked the sense of *shelter* in the 'look of the building'" and offers this as an explanation for the characteristic jutting eaves. This point is of capital importance. Wright's is the logical interpretation of Sullivan's formula "Form follows Function," for it is clear in the *Kindergarten Chats* that Sullivan conceived of a number of architectural genres, "to be a store," "to be a bank," etc., and it was these types of which the form was to be expressive. A simon-pure functionalist might, e.g., leave the lighting and plumbing exposed, but to Wright this would violate the proper repose of Shelter. (b) Similar is Wright's formula, "The horizontal is the line of domesticity." He himself sometimes dispenses with these horizontals in the interest of considerations of site or construction. Or again when he says of the Hanna or Honeycomb House: "The hexagonal is better suited to human movement than the rectangle"—he seems to be borrowing from Buckminster Fuller's Dymaxion House—if he really believes this, he must abjure every rectangular

room he ever designed; but instead he has gone on to the curious *Circle* House in California. (c) The fact is that such formulae of horizontals, hexangles, or circles constitute the *basic plan and design idea* by means of which Wright feels that he is able to impose a unity on the manifold parts. The process is first to abstract from the functions some simple formal conception, and then to exfoliate this into the ground plan and ornament of the house. This is certainly architecture, but it is certainly not functionalism. (d) The bother is that even now Wright keeps disclaiming any intention of imposing a pattern on living; he speaks of the "Declaration of Independence from any imposition on life . . . the interpretation of life is the true function of the Architect." Must we then conclude that to him these few patterns exhaust whatever is possible in living? The *architectural* conception of "an acre per person" is nothing but the most grandiose, though least productive, of such imposed patterns. This is indeed the architect exercising a "certain disciplinary as well as cultural authority." What he means or at least should mean is that *any* creation is an imposition and the architect has a proper right to his own; but that architecture is *only* architecture and may impose itself only after taking due account of other things, never forgetting the warning of the poet,

"as I build, you move."

5. The same doubleness—of affirming the demands of the parts as absolute yet imposing an ideal upon them—runs through what Wright has to say of surfaces, plan, materials, construction, and technology. This doubleness is of course nothing but the tension of art itself, the medium and the imaginative solution fertilizing each other; but it is inaccurate to pass off as nature what is precisely art.

Surfaces. Wright was one of the first to fight for simpler machined-surfaces: he omitted the imitation hand-carving on the mouldings and sometimes the mouldings themselves. He reduced the number of materials and, following Sullivan, insisted that the surfaces should indicate and not conceal the underlying structure, as the flesh of the hand, to use his favorite simile, does not conceal the skeleton. He sought to achieve *plasticity,* "the quality and nature of materials seen as 'flowing' or 'growing' into form instead of as built up out of cut and joined pieces"; to "eliminate the insignificant"—e.g. he was in at the Passing of the Cornice—where by significance is meant just this property of one surface expressing another in appearance (quality) and structure (nature). The "perfect style" or ultimate success would be to use a single material; thus he often boasts of the Unity Temple as the first example of monolithic concrete. (b) A major invention to achieve plasticity was to build in the furniture and fixtures; and in general to design the furniture as part of the house. (He complains that the style of his early houses disappeared as soon as the client moved in his old junk.) Unfortunately the T-square dominates the furniture; Wright's furniture is square and bulky, not especially functional—"all my life I have been black and blue from contact with my own furniture." Certain shapes, elegant in themselves and graceful to the anatomy, are suppressed; Wright asks, for instance, that the piano-shape be concealed except for the keyboard. (c) When the furniture is architecturally designed the inhabitant is organically inseparable from his house: he must remain a long time. The alternative possibility for plastic furniture, that chosen by Le Corbusier for example, is to make both house and furniture so *un*-individual that it makes no difference in which house one lives. (d) Again, imposed on the whole is the one Idea: "The differentiation of a single simple form characterizes the expression of one building . . . from one basic idea all the formal elements of design are in each case derived. . . . The form chosen may flare outward, opening flowerlike to the sky, as in the Thomas house; another droop, to accentuate artistically the weight of the masses . . . or its grammer may be deduced from some plant form that has appealed to me, as certain properties in line and form of the sumac were used in the Lawrence house at Springfield. But in every case the motif is adhered to throughout."

6. *Plan.* The analysis of functions into a few large zones gives clarity and simplicity to the Plan. In theory, not especially in Wright's practice, this is marked by the absence of connecting corridors, and therefore still more living space; and wardrobes in place of closets, relieving the plan from what is properly part of the furniture. (b) The zones of the plan may then become the chief elements of the exterior design, as in the house Wing Spread; and further, they may be marked by changes in material and construction, as from stone to wood, where the change in material not only satisfies a change in function, e.g. in the kind of lighting required, but may itself appear as part of the interior decoration. None of this would be possible if the plan were cut up into small parts. (Of course nowhere here, it must be said, does Wright achieve the interior openness and exterior clarity of the Internationalists who use screens instead of walls and often zone by furniture alone.) (c) Again, the logical expansion of small plan elements, such as windows or balconies, into large plan elements, such as window-strips and balconies that run the length of the wall, makes them automatically the chief elements of the exterior design. "The forms are complete in themselves and frequently do duty at the same time from within and without as decorative attributes of the whole." We thus, *from within,* escape the dilemma of "a wall punctured with holes." (d) It is in the Plan, finally, that the architectural imagination works under most tension, *for the Plan, the immediate expression of the functions, is in the best cases also the relation between the construction and the design.* That Wright grasps this is beautifully shown by his insistence on keeping the plan as far as possible in the fluid imagination: "If the original concept is lost as the drawing proceeds throw away all and begin afresh. To throw away a concept *entirely* to make way for a fresh one, that is a faculty of the mind . . . few architects have. . . . What I am trying to express is the fact that the plan is the gist of all truly creative matter and must gradually mature as such." Would that Wright showed the same flexibility everywhere!

7. Lastly, let us lump together a few remarks about *materials, construction,* and *technology.* What he has added most, says Wright, to Sullivan's conception of function and form and function and construction, is the analysis of the nature of materials. Each material is to be finished and constructed according to its primary physical characteristics, as grain, crystal, or sheet; terra cotta must not imitate stone nor one wood be painted to look like another. Surface and ornament will then express material and construction. Thus, "the stick is the natural post. It is also the natural beam. Post and beam construction was, by nature, first wood"; the Greeks were in error to imitate this construction in stone. In separate discussions he takes up the "proper uses" of wood, brick, glass, metal. (b) An important consequence of the "honest" handling of materials is that Wright's buildings wear and weather well; he does not have to fear the moment when the veneer cracks and discloses the material beneath. (c) But in another sense, the nature of material is like the spirit of the environment in that the potentialities are very numerous and it is possible to see quite different properties as primary. Further, Wright is not always a careful observer. Thus, though indeed the Greeks imitated wood in ornamental details—and this perhaps largely for the sake of religious tradition—the total effect is always a graceful massiveness, perfectly appropriate to marble. Again, in what sense is wood "the natural beam"? The engineering of a tree seems to be more usually a system of cantilevers with members more and more in tension, rather than in units of compression and tension. (d) Further, he seems to have an aversion for certain materials. There is not much to say about Wright on Steel, though this was so dear to Sullivan and Adler. (But even here he has the profound intuition that steel must be built "as a spiderweb," that is triangulated.) When the Internationalists expose the steel skeleton, he calls it "rattling the bones" and building "as a machine"; but why is such a structure less formal than exposing the wood beams of a ceiling in Taliesin West? Likewise, on the one hand when he analyzes the steel and concrete construction of St. Mark's Towers, he says "the outer enclosing shell of glass and copper is pendent from the cantilever slabs," and in a similar context, "the walls are mere screens"; but then he complains that the walls of the Le Corbusier houses are "artificially thin, like cardboard, bent, folded, and glued." It seems clear that he is here substituting temperament for analysis. (e) The same in his attitude toward machine-technology. On the one hand he was certainly among the first to celebrate simple machine-finish: "If I wanted to realize new forms, I should have to make them not only appropriate to old and new materials, but so design them that the machines that would have to make them could and would make them well." But this is a negative concept of technology; the affirmative concept would be to say, not "here are materials designed for machinery," but "here are machine-products to employ." This diffidence is fundamental in Wright because he is interested really in the integration and differentiation of rather small wholes, and to this enterprise mass-production is obviously a menace. The key to technology in architecture is pre-fabrication; but on this subject Wright

says contemptuously, "Assembly-line houses." (How revealing that the moment he thinks in terms of a larger whole, the St. Mark's Towers, he says, "The building is a complete standardization for prefabrication." But pre-fabrication would be economical only if there were a number of St. Mark's Towers; then what becomes of Broadcres?) The issue is not, as Wright thinks, whether to make a house look like a machine, but how to use the machine as a tool according to its own potentialities. These considerations cast a blinding light on Broadacres and "an acre per person"; he is thinking (rightly!) of every single acre; but he is not thinking of all the persons in the City.

But passing by all objections, let us ask: What is architecture as learned from the practice of a master builder?

Architecture consists first in the analysis of the conditions: "the terrain, the native industrial conditions, the nature of materials, and the purpose of the building"; to these we must certainly add the community-life and the general economy. Next, from these we abstract "simple basic ideas," adequate to the conditions but also capable of combination and mutual expression. Lastly, these basic ideas are unified by the plan, the construction, the design, which add nothing material of their own (such as Axes or Orders), but are just the formal principles which combine the parts into a whole. For the first step knowledge is required; for the second, insight into the essential; and for the final step, imagination.

III. Organic Architecture and the International Style

Since the late twenties Wright has been obsessed by the polemic with Le Corbusier and his Esprit Nouveau; he returns everywhere to the attack on the Cardboard House, the Imitation Machine, and Modern: Latest of the Styles. The cause of the attacks is certainly partly pique at the enthusiastic reception that the younger men gave to ideas imported from Paris to which Wright had a claim not only of 20 years priority but of direct influence. But there are also the deepest differences both in social thought and in aesthetics between Le Corbusier and Wright, so that their contrast shows up the merits and demerits of each.

The pity is that these *complementary* positions do not exhaust the analysis of modern architecture, so that even adding Wright and Le Corbusier together we do not get an adequate philosophy; yet apart from these two there is no modern articulate successful builder (so that my story here has no conclusion). This failure to exhaust the field springs perhaps from certain attitudes that both men *share:* they are both political messiahs (Le Corbusier's *Voisin Plan for Paris,* e.g., was to be a cure for war); at the same time the explicit purpose of both men is to preserve the political status quo and prevent revolution ("Architecture or Revolution" is the conclusion of *Towards a New Architecture*); for both, Architecture can solve all problems and pervades every subject (*The City of Tomorrow* sets out to insure that "the people of our city must never become bored"). These common faiths make it extremely difficult for either

man to see building for just what it is in relation to society. At the same time certain other attitudes that they share have helped both men to become great planners: as, their forthright break with the Beaux Arts; the sense of architecture as involved in living problems in a social matrix; the understanding of part and whole, plasticity, and the elimination of the insignificant; functionalism; and the insistence on both reason and passion.

Wright's attack proceeds all along the line: The International Style neglects "the Nature of Materials, the Third Dimension, Integral Ornament . . . Surface and Mass are subordinate to this Trinity . . . they are a by-product." Then we are told that a house should not "outrage the Machine by trying to make a dwelling-place too complementary to Machinery." "The simplicity of these houses is too easily read, visibly an attitude, strained or forced." We need "heartfelt instead of head-made simplicity." The International Style, the Left Wing of Organic Architecture, is the "mere countenance"; it is not built from inside out. "Proportion is nothing in itself. . . . Le Corbusier, hard as nails and sane as a hammer up to this point, here goes superstitious." "There is this essential difference between a machine and a building. A building is not an appliance nor a mobilization. The building as architecture is born out of the heart of man, permanent consort to the ground, comrade to the trees, true reflection of man in the realm of his spirit. . . . Architecture expresses human life . . . appliances only serve life." Lastly, to Organic Architecture the City is dead, whereas Le Corbusier thinks it is the center of architecture.

My aim is not of course to answer these charges for Le Corbusier; I am writing about Wright. But the positive content of such answers show clearly the limitations of Wright's perspective; it is in this sense that Wright and Le Corbusier are complimentary.

Some of the argument is a matter of dialectical formulation. Thus, Wright does not believe cities will disappear, but he relegates them to Engineering; they cannot be architecture because they do not express the individual spirit in repose. To Le Corbusier, however, Engineering and Architecture, though not identical, are continuous; whatever can be put together can be beautifully put together. Again (to contrast their higher flights): for Wright, Architecture is nature, but not external nature; it is an abstraction of the organic principles of external nature. To Le Corbusier, "A city is a human operation directed against nature. It is a creation. All the poetry we find in nature is but the creation of our own spirit. . . . Nature presents itself to us as a chaos." Yet—"the spirit which animates Nature is a spirit of order; this we come to know." So that their metaphysics are compatible after all!

At the same time, such verbal and dialectical differences, even when they do not result in contradictions, never fail to correspond to profound differences in interest.

1. To Wright, the essential of architectural aesthetics is "space enclosed." Space is enclosed by gripping the site

and by the substance of materials. This is three-dimensionality. From this point of view the "abstractions" of Le Corbusier are not 3-dimensional at all, they "ignore depth of matter to get effects characteristic of painting." To Le Corbusier, on the other hand, Space is the universal which is abstracted from matter in geometry; to him we have 3-dimensionality when we have cubes, spheres, and cones. Mass, then, is the first principle of architecture; and surface is that which by its lines can reinforce the impression of the mass. To Wright, a house of Le Corbusier has no inside, therefore no real outside; but dealing in the universal space, Le Corbusier would say just that we must not enclose it, but let the eye pass freely from inside to outside. Therefore, instead of emphasizing the materials, he tries deliberately to negate them, by giving them all a uniform surface, surface color, etc.

Thus, speaking of the Parthenon, Wright at once points out that this is stone imitating wood; and being too heavy for the imitation it destroys the interior space. But the first thing that strikes Le Corbusier is the disposition of the Parthenon among the buildings of the Acropolis and the axial relation of the whole Acropolis to the sea and Mt. Pentelicon.

Again, for Le Corbusier proportion is the fundamental part of beauty: proportion is nothing but the animation and repose of the universal space. To Wright, Integral Ornament is "the heart of architecture so far as art is concerned," where again the integrity of the ornament is that it expresses the Plan or enclosed space, the structure, the materials, and the site. But to Le Corbusier, just what must be avoided is the expression of the site: we must "build on a clear site to replace the accidental layout by the formal layout." To Wright the final grace of a building is that it belongs to its soil; to Le Corbusier it is the silhouette ("profile") against the sky. And still again, the great tool of the designer for Le Corbusier is the "Regulating Line"—the length or angle whose simple products or repetitions measure out the whole space; but for Wright we have seen that it is the basic design idea, the upward flare, the wing-spread, etc.

Proceeding, we find that Le Corbusier's settled habit is to begin with the largest visible space, that is the whole environment. Then, in order to achieve form in this wide view, it is necessary to count it off in identical parts: therefore he comes to Standardization *as a principle of design;* we must have variety in the whole, but standardization in all the parts. To Wright, standardization in this sense is the negation of organism.

2. Now if we turn from such purely formal considerations to the moral and the social, it is not surprising to see Le Corbusier interested in environment-plans, country-wide circulation, and mass-production, whereas Wright is interested in domestic architecture, reposeful life, and making every one of his 40 new small houses individually different. (In dealing with great artists there is obviously no sense in asking whether the aesthetics or the appropriate subject-matter came first, since they are artists because of their habits of thinking plastically and selectively about their subject-matter.) Viewed as a whole, the scheme for Broadacre City has no plastic interest whatsoever; but we know that every one of the 40 houses will contain a plastic discovery. But Le Corbusier's *Plan for Paris* or *Contemporary City* or *Plan for Algiers* are plastically remarkable in the view of the foreground against the horizon.

Both men are much concerned with the new mobility; but to Wright freedom of motion is the way to get home; it is there that life and architecture begin. Le Corbusier, on the other hand, is simply fascinated by traffic-problems, 3 and 4 level autostrades, grade-crossings, the place for straight and the place for curving roads; his architecture is essentially a matter of circulation. And where Wright, as we have seen, plans for his people to move in for a "long long time," Le Corbusier announces: "We must arrive at the house-machine . . . designed for a succession of tenants. The idea of the 'old home' disappears, and with it local architecture, etc., for labor will shift about as needed, and must be ready to move *bag and baggage.* The words 'bag and baggage' . . . express the kind of furniture needed. Standardized houses with standardized furniture."

The moral interest of Wright, there is no doubt, is in individual ways-of-life. For the most part, to be sure, he is thinking of his own way of life and willing to impose this at large; but it is a good enough way, as is proved by the fact that for him no "problem of leisure" arises. We have touched on some of his inventions for living and might have multiplied them many times. But Le Corbusier's insights into personal habits are simply calamitous, from the exposed privies on; this is not the place to discuss them, but let me merely cite the passage where he declares that the differing desires within the "private cells" are precisely the "menace" to the architect. (To Wright they are theoretically precisely the opportunity.) Rather reticent about himself he leans heavily on social statistics. His great fear is that the people of his city may become bored with their leisure-time! To prevent this he provides sports and gardening. To provide a mean between the human-beings and the houses, it is necessary to plant trees: this is called "keeping to the Human Scale."

Though both are authoritarian, Wright is so in a more negative way, because what he wants ultimately to defend is the liberty of each inhabitant or at least *of each acre;* the meaning of living for him is what spontaneously occurs there; and the authoritarianism, when it crops up, takes the form of his individual caprice dominating every other life. Le Corbusier is affirmative; he realizes that vast enterprises require strong measures; and the meaningful enterprises for him are especially the vast ones, the steamships and skyscrapers. Therefore, though Broadacre is more capricious, unstatistical, and reactionary, it is much less conservative; whereas the Contemporary City attempts to rationalize just what we have at its most intense: this gives us, "The real Revolution lies in the solution of existing problems."

Wright is temperamentally opposed to class-stratification—though, if he is willing to preserve capitalism and the differences of wealth (the 1-car house, the 5 car house), he ought to make clear how the corresponding class-attitudes are to be avoided. But Le Corbusier in a curious passage points out that just the differences of classes give the variety of standards that the community-planner requires for plastic manipulation. In general, Le Corbusier is, within very narrow limits, acutely aware of group attitudes, emotions, and peculiarities; in this sphere Wright is quite blank. It is reasonable to say that Wright everywhere expresses a group-attitude in his buildings and writings, the attitude of a relatively static fraction of the middle-class, professionals, etc., which still has real personal satisfactions but is increasingly suspicious; but no one would say that he is conscious of what he is expressing,—in fact this very unconsciousness is a property of his group. But Le Corbusier is a remarkable panegyrist of finance-capital—"the morality of industry," he says, "has been transformed; big business is today [1923] a healthy and moral organism"; and he allows himself the phrase "Captains of Industry." He imagines he has arguments to prove that private capitalists will make money by tearing down the center of Paris and rebuilding it according to the spirit of their other vast enterprises; he calls especially on international capital (this is the Paris internationalism of the devaluation of the franc.) But Wright does not think as a great entrepreneur; he merely rather hopes that Broadacres is inevitable. (In fact it must be said of him that throughout his long career he has never mixed in the schemes nor compromised with the tastes of his wealthy clients. It is mysterious in these circumstances how he has managed to get along—except that God takes care of his saints.)

NOTES

[1] The numerous writings of Wright include: *Modern Architecture,* Princeton University Press, 1931; *Two Lectures on Architecture,* Art Institute of Chicago, 1931; *Autobiography,* Longmans Green, 1932; *Architecture and Modern Life,* Harper, 1937; *An Organic Architecture* (London), 1939; *On Architecture,* Duell Sloan and Pearce, 1941.

[2] Relatively complete lists are given, e.g., in the paper *In the Cause of Architecture,* 1908; in the preface to *Ausgefuehrte Bauten und Entwuerfe,* 1910; in the first of the *Two Lectures,* 1930; in the second chapter of *Modern Architecture.*

Paul Buitenhuis (essay date 1957) .

SOURCE: "Aesthetics of the Skyscraper: The Views of Sullivan, James and Wright," in *American Quarterly,* Vol. 9, No. 3, Fall, 1957, pp. 316-24.

[*In the following essay, Buitenhuis examines the development of the skyscraper in relation to the views of American life held by Louis Sullivan, Henry James, and Wright.*]

When a new form is invented, whether it be in art, literature or architecture, a new aesthetic has to be created so that the form, in its various manifestations, can be evaluated and criticized. Some of the worst and most misguided criticism is always written during the infancy of a new form, but also some of the most original and incisive. The views of Louis Sullivan, Henry James and Frank Lloyd Wright on the typically American innovation of the skyscraper are not only constructive but also show how far men of different generations, backgrounds and temperaments can agree on aesthetic judgments.

Before the evolution of the steel skeleton frame, the weight and relatively low tensile strength of masonry limited the height of the office building to about twelve floors. The demand for taller buildings became stronger and stronger, however, as American cities rapidly grew in the closing years of the nineteenth century and commercial land values soared. The steel frame was a direct response to this demand. The first office building to utilize the technique was constructed in 1885. It soon became obvious that a steel-framed building could rise at least four times as high as a masonry building. In little over ten years the technique had revolutionized tall office-building design.

The center of development of this new architectural form was Chicago. It was a place peculiarly well-suited to the idea of the skyscraper. The bustling, booming city, with a tremendous sense of its destiny as the future metropolis of the Midwest, was the city in America most individualistic in its enterprise. In the tall building the American tycoon found a fitting symbol for his restless drive and buoyant hopes. In the 1880's and 1890's large numbers of skyscrapers were built in Chicago. The impetus rapidly spread to other cities, especially New York. Many of the architects called upon to design skyscrapers worked within established forms, merely elongating these forms to fit the needs of the tall building. The wealth of their clients stimulated them also to decorate their designs with lavish copies of classical and Gothic models. Some Chicago architects were, however, dissatisfied with this approach to a new form. One of the most visionary of these was Louis Sullivan.

Frank Lloyd Wright, who worked in Sullivan's office between 1887 and 1894, recounts how one day Sullivan entered his cubicle, placed a piece of manila paper on Wright's desk, and left without a word. On the paper was an elevation of the Wainwright Building, "the very first human expression," Wright called it, "of a tall steel office-building as Architecture."[1] Wright pointed out that Sullivan had hit upon the fundamental principle of skyscraper design in his replacement of the broken, opaque walls of previous tall buildings with sheer, transparent screens. The only part of the building that Wright disliked was the elaborate cornice. In such designs as that for the Reliance Building (1895), Sullivan corrected his tendency toward ornamentation and produced soaring, well-proportioned, curtain-walled skyscrapers.[2]

Sullivan himself first raised the aesthetic problem of the skyscraper in an article that appeared in March, 1896, called "The Tall Office Building Artistically Considered."

> How shall we impart to this sterile pile, this crude, harsh, brutal agglomeration, this stark, staring exclamation of eternal strife, the graciousness of those higher forms of sensibility and culture that rest on the lower and fiercer passions? How shall we proclaim from the dizzy heights of this strange, weird, modern housetop the peaceful evangel of sentiment, of beauty, the cult of a higher life?[3]

The answer to this question lay in his own famous apothegm: "form follows function."

The function of the office-building, as Sullivan saw it, was to supply a large number of identical, well-lit offices. He therefore proposed a modular unit on which the design of the skyscraper should be based.

> The practical horizontal and vertical division or office unit is naturally based on a room of comfortable area and height, and the size of this standard office room as naturally predetermines the standard structural unit, and, approximately, the size of window openings. In turn, these purely arbitrary units of structure form in an equally natural way the true basis of the artistic development of the exterior.[4]

The building was to be, simply, a tier of identical floors, except for a main entrance floor and an attic for tanks, pipes and machinery. Sullivan denied the need for cornice or frieze or any other embellishment of the building. He pointed out that although nine out of ten skyscrapers then being built were used as a display for "architectural knowledge in the encyclopaedic sense," it was obvious that such decoration was mere folly. The architect was in this way only speaking "a foreign language with a noticeable American accent," instead of expressing with "native instinct and sensibility" that which was in him to say in "the simplest, most modest, most natural way. . . . "[5]

In a style that savors of Walt Whitman, Sullivan justified the form of the skyscraper.

> What is the chief characteristic of the tall office building? And at once we answer, it is lofty. This loftiness is to the artist nature its thrilling aspect. It is the very organ-tone in its appeal. It must be in turn the dominant chord in his expression of it, the true excitant of his imagination. It must be tall, every inch of it tall. The force and power of altitude must be in it, the glory and pride of exaltation must be in it. It must be every inch a proud and soaring thing, rising in sheer exultation that from bottom to top it is a unit without a single dissenting line—that it is the new, the unexpected, the eloquent peroration of most bald, most sinister, most forbidding conditions.[6]

From the start, Sullivan was well aware of these "forbidding conditions" in which skyscrapers were built. He saw that they were a response to a selfish commercial need, and a direct result of the rapidly rising value of city lots in good business locations. In his skyscrapers he sought to transmute these drives into a soaring form which signified the endeavor but made no concessions to the "lower passions" which provided the original impetus for the form. The steel frame was boldly outlined on the exterior of the building. It provided both the frame for the huge windows and the unit of construction. In the Carson Pirie Scott Department Store (1899) and the McClurg Building (1900), the form is seen at its best. The soaring vertical piers of steel are regularly and cleanly intersected by the horizontal girders which mark the level of floors and ceilings.[7]

While the Chicago skyline soon revealed the results of the work of Sullivan and like-minded architects, that of New York showed no such change. Although New York architects lost no time in adopting the steel frame principle, they retained the thick masonry construction of the old tall buildings on the exterior, to give the illusion that the stone was securely bearing the weight. There was no grace in the heavy vertical stone pillars nor in the horizontal bands of masonry and cast iron of these new skyscrapers. They struggled up into the sky encumbered by layers of brick, stone, iron and marble. For them, "rising in sheer exultation" was out of the question.

These were the skyscrapers that Henry James saw when he sailed into the harbor in 1904, after an absence of more than twenty years, and looked across at what he called in *The American Scene* the "serried, bristling city" of New York. Nearly thirty years earlier, in 1878, James had written a story, *An International Episode,* in which an English nobleman, visiting New York, is to his surprise shot up in an elevator to the seventh floor of a "fresh, light, ornamental structure, ten stories high." He looks out of the window of the office in which he finds himself to see the weather vane of a church steeple on a line with his eyes.[8] It is probable that this is a fictional account of a visit that James himself paid to an office on Wall Street. The weather vane surely belonged to the spire of Trinity Church. He returned to the scene on his visit of 1904-5 and gazed in astonishment at "the special sky-scraper that overhangs poor old Trinity to the north—a south face as high and wide as the mountainwall that drops the alpine avalanche, from time to time, upon the village, and the village spire, at its foot. . . . "[9] The difference between the "ornamental structure, ten stories high" and this "mountain-wall" must have been a measure to James of the difference made by the intervening years to his "old" New York.

James found many reasons to dislike these new skyscrapers. To him the "flash of innumerable windows and flicker of subordinate gilt attributions" seemed like "the flare, up and down their long, narrow faces, of the lamps of some general permanent 'celebration.'"[10] The windows of most New York skyscrapers at this time were set deeply into the thick masonry, as if the buildings had been thought of as substantial houses extended almost indefinitely upwards. As a result, the skyline was dense with the flashing, broken facades that James found so distasteful.

It was natural that he should seek to compare the sky-scraper with some analogous structure in European architecture, deeply versed as he was in this aspect of the older civilization. He found his analogy in the Renaissance bell-towers of Italy. Yet how different they were from these "towers of glass"! "Such a structure," he wrote, "as the comparatively windowless bell-tower of Giotto, in Florence, looks supremely serene in its beauty. You don't feel it to have risen by the breath of an interested [money] passion that, restless beyond all passions, is for ever seeking more pliable forms." In the Giotto tower James found a successful solution to the eternal quest for form. "Beauty," he continued, "has been the object of its creator's idea, and, having found beauty, it has found the form in which it splendidly rests."[11] We have seen that Sullivan started his quest from another quarter—a quarter typically American in its pragmatism. Function had been his first objective; form was to follow it, and beauty was to be the result. Paradoxically, Sullivan's finest curtain-walled skyscrapers have in them much of the sheer elegance of the Italian windowless towers.

Implicit in Sullivan's justification for the form of the skyscraper is the premise that the building should stand in isolation. A lofty building has little "force and power of altitude" if it is crowded by other tall buildings. The New York skyscrapers seemed to James to be "extravagant pins in a cushion already overplanted, and stuck in as in the dark, anywhere and anyhow . . ."[12] Land values had soared so rapidly in Manhattan at the end of the nineteenth century that landowners had competed among themselves to put up tall buildings. Already, in 1904, they huddled together and hemmed in the streets. "Quiet interspaces." James wrote, "always half the architectural battle, exist no more in such a structural scheme."[13] However, on a few occasions, Henry James saw skyscrapers as Louis Sullivan intended them to be seen, when tricks of light softened their broken outlines. In the later afternoons of some summer and winter days, a "refinement of modelling," James observed, "descends from the skies and lends the white towers, all new and crude and commercial and over-windowed as they are, a fleeting distinction."[14] Even when, one foggy morning, he had been gazing up at the skyscraper that had "extinguished" Trinity, he had been aware that "the vast money-making structure quite horribly, quite romantically justified itself, looming through the weather with an insolent cliff-like sublimity."[15]

James's most radical criticism of the New York skyscrapers was that the commercial motive which had caused them to be built, the motive which Sullivan had successfully sublimated, dominated the form. *"They,"* James ironically and balefully observed, "ranged in this terrible recent erection, were going to bring in money—and was not money the only thing a self-respecting structure could be thought of as bringing in?"[16] Convinced as he was that the mercenary spirit was, of all, the most restless, he saw little chance that the form should remain as it was.

Crowned not only with no history, but with no credible possibility of time for history, and consecrated by no uses save the commercial at any cost, they are simply the most piercing notes in that concert of the most expensively provisional into which your supreme sense of New York resolves itself. They never begin to speak to you, in the manner of the builded majesties of the world as we have heretofore known such—towers or temples or fortresses or palaces—with the authority of things of permanence or even of things of long duration. One story is good only till another is told, and sky-scrapers are the last word of economic ingenuity only till another word be written. This shall be possibly a word of still uglier meaning, but the vocabulary of thrift at any price shows boundless resources, and the consciousness of that truth, the consciousness of the finite, the menaced, the essentially *invented* state, twinkles ever, to my perception, in the thousand glassy eyes of these giants of the mere market.[17]

Even the windows themselves seemed to James to have a sinister purpose. "Doesn't it," he asked, "take in fact acres of window-glass to help even an expert New Yorker to get the better of another expert one, or to see that the other expert one doesn't get the better of *him*?" The answer was apparently self-evident. "It is easy to conceive," he went on, "that, after all, with this origin and nature stamped upon their foreheads, the last word of the mercenary monsters should not be their address to our sense of formal beauty."[18]

Frank Lloyd Wright's observations on the New York skyscrapers, written twenty-five years later, are remarkably similar in ideas, if not in language, to those of Henry James. As a basis for his criticism, however, were the principles of skyscraper construction that he had learned from Sullivan. Looking back in 1930 to those visionary designs by his old master, he could see how little they had affected the designs of the contemporary skyscrapers. In his lecture **"The Tyranny of the Skyscraper,"** given at Princeton, he said: "The light that shone in the Wainwright Building as a promise, flickered feebly and is fading away."[19]

By this time, skyscrapers had clustered so thickly that the city had been forced to pass some "set-back" laws, so that some light should filter down into the street canyons and into the lower offices. Set-back skyscrapers lose of course that single soaring line that Sullivan postulated as the basis for design. Wright pointed out:

> The Skyscraper of today is only the prostitute semblance of the architecture it professes to be. The heavy brick and stone that falsely represents walls is, by the very set-back laws, unnaturally forced onto the interior steel stilts to be carried down by them through twenty, fifty or more stories to the ground. The picture is improved, but the picturesque element in it all is false work built over a hollow box. These new tops are shams, too—box-balloons.[20]

James had used the same image as Wright, characteristically muted, to call all the gilding on the skyscrapers the efforts of a "compromised charmer" to cover up the temporary nature and insincerity of the building.[21] Also in the same vein as James, Wright observed: "The skyscraper envelope is not ethical, beautiful or permanent. It is a commercial exploit or a mere expedient. It has no higher ideal of unity than commercial success." Wright also recognized that the congestion of the skyscrapers had robbed them of what distinction they might have gained from their height. "Utterly barbaric," he wrote, "they rise regardless of special consideration for environment or for each other, except to win the race or get the tenant. Space as a becoming psychic element of the American city is gone."[22] As Sullivan had before him, Wright scorned those native architects who had tried to bring Beaux-Arts ideas to bear on the design of the skyscraper and to see it as a column, with base, shaft and capital. He derided those architects who saw it as "Gothic—commercial competitor to the Cathedral."[23] He demanded integrity and sanity in the design and erection of skyscrapers in American cities.

Sullivan had treated the skyscraper as a form without taking into consideration the rest of the city scene. Both Wright and James, however, realized that it was impossible to deal with the skyscraper apart from the aesthetic and utilitarian aspects of the whole city. Both saw in what James called "the original sin of longitudinal avenues perpetually, yet meanly intersected" and Wright "the original village grid-iron" the root of New York's trouble. James wrote darkly:

> There is violence outside, mitigating sadly the frontal majesty of the monument, leaving it exposed to the vulgar assault of the street by the operation of those dire facts of absence of margin, of meagreness of site, of the brevity of the block, of the inveteracy of the near thoroughfare, which leave 'style,' in construction, at the mercy of the impertinent cross-streets, make a detachment and independence, save in the rarest cases, an insoluble problem, preclude without pity any element of court or garden, and open to the builder in quest of distinction the one alternative, and the great adventure, of seeking his reward in the sky.[24]

Wright observed:

> Barely tolerable for a village, the grid becomes a dangerous criss-cross check to all forward movements even in a large town where horses are motive power. But with the automobile and skyscraper that opposes and kills the automobile's contribution to the city, stop-and-go attempts to get across to somewhere or to anywhere, for that matter, in the great Metropolis, are inevitable waste—dangerous and maddening to a degree where sacrificial loss, in every sense but one, is for everyone.
>
> Erstwhile village streets become grinding pits of metropolitan misery. Frustration of all life, in the village-that-became-a-city, is imminent in this, the great unforeseen Metropolis. . . . "[25]

Unlike James, however, Frank Lloyd Wright believed that the skyscraper as form had great possibilities. He was strongly of the opinion that the commercial motive behind the building of skyscrapers was a force for good. "Business ethics," he wrote, "make a good platform for true Aesthetics in this Machine Age or in any other." In Wright's eyes, the trouble was that the dominating force in the construction of the New York skyscrapers was not business ethics alone but "a conscious yearn, a generosity, a prodigality in the name of taste and refinement" that led only to pretension and artificiality. Were this mummery only dropped, Wright believed (as had Sullivan) that "space-manufacturing-for-rent," as he called it, "might become genuine architecture and be beautiful as standardization in steel, metals and glass."[26] Perhaps to prove this point, Wright built his superb skyscraper for the Johnson Wax Company at Racine, Wisconsin. The building is suspended from a central core of steel and concrete, and the sheer glass walls, accented with vertical metal strips, are banded by the parapets of the alternate floors which are cantilevered out from the core. The intermediate floors, which are circular, do not reach the exterior walls, so that the horizontal planes are not overemphasized. Equally important, this skyscraper stands apart from other tall buildings, so that its "force and power of altitude" can be seen and appreciated.[27]

To bring order out of the chaos of New York, Wright recommended that immediate action be taken to control the erection of further skyscrapers. He also urged the broadening of roadbeds and the removal of pedestrians to a higher level. James made no such specific recommendation. He only reflected wryly on the endless abuse of natural beauty and constant scorn of opportunity in New York. As he looked at the tall buildings that marched relentlessly northwards up Manhattan and along the Hudson, he came to what was for him, a life-long conservative and individualist, a remarkable conclusion.

> The whole thing is the vividest of lectures on the subject of individualism, and on the strange truth, no doubt, that this principle may in the field of art—at least if the art be architecture—often conjure away just that mystery of distinction which it sometimes so markedly promotes in the field of life. . . . And yet why *should* the charm ever fall out of the 'personal,' which is so often the very condition of the exquisite? Why should conformity and subordination, that acceptance of control and assent to collectivism in the name of which our age has seen such dreary things done, become on a given occasion the one *not* vulgar way of meeting a problem?[28]

Henry James expressed in this question the whole dilemma of the city-planner. The irony of the situation is that the skyscraper, symbol of American individual enterprise, should be that form of construction most necessary to control in order to bring back not only some measure of convenience to the American city, but also to restore to it the aesthetic appeal of its own loftiness.

In the views of Sullivan, James and Wright, we can see then a spectrum of architectural criticism. Firstly, there is the definition and the justification of the form, secondly the criticism of the misuses of the form, and lastly an attempt to relate the special problems that the skyscraper raises to the planning of the city. Although James was, basically, opposed to the idea of the skyscraper, he yet gave it the benefit of the consideration due any significant new form, as few had done before him. In criticizing the form, however, he sought always to find in it the expression of the "money-passion" which he came to believe was corrupting so much of twentieth-century American life. Sullivan and Wright were both aware of this commercial motive in the form, but they turned their critical and creative talents to separating what they considered to be the gold of American enterprise and endeavor from the dross of prodigality, ostentation and historicism. All three recognized in the skyscraper a peculiarly American form and strove to evaluate it in terms of their vision of American life.

NOTES

[1] Frank Lloyd Wright, "The Tyranny of the Skyscraper," *Modern Architecture* (Princeton: Princeton University Press, 1931), p. 85.

[2] William Alex, "The Skyscraper: USA," *Perspectives 8,* Summer 1954, Plate 10.

[3] Louis Sullivan, "The Tall Office Building Artistically Considered," *Kindergarten Chats* (rev. ed.), ed., Isabella Athey (New York: Wittenborn, Schultz, 1947), p. 202.

[4] Sullivan, *Kindergarten Chats,* p. 203.

[5] *Ibid.,* pp. 208, 213.

[6] *Ibid.,* p. 206.

[7] Alex, "The Skyscraper: USA," plates 12 & 13.

[8] Henry James, "An International Episode," *The Great Short Novels of Henry James,* ed. Philip Rahv (New York: Dial Press, 1944), p. 157.

[9] Henry James, *The American Scene* (London: Chapman & Hall, 1907), p. 83.

[10] *Ibid.,* p. 76.

[11] James, *The American Scene,* pp. 77-78.

[12] *Ibid.,* p. 76.

[13] *Ibid.,* p. 95.

[14] *Ibid.,* p. 81.

[15] *Ibid.,* p. 83.

[16] James, *The American Scene,* p. 94.

[17] *Ibid.,* p. 77.

[18] *Ibid.,* p. 96.

[19] Wright, *Modern Architecture,* p. 98.

[20] Wright, *Modern Architecture,* pp. 94-95.

[21] James, *The American Scene,* pp. 110-11.

[22] Wright, *Modern Architecture,* p. 98.

[23] *Ibid.,* p. 94.

[24] James, *The American Scene,* p. 100.

[25] Wright, *Modern Architecture,* pp. 90-91.

[26] *Ibid.,* p. 96.

[27] Alex, "The Skyscraper: USA," plates 31-33.

[28] James, *The American Scene,* pp. 141-42.

Edgar Kaufmann, Jr. (essay date 1963)

SOURCE: "The Fine Arts and Frank Lloyd Wright," in *Four Great Makers of Modern Architecture,* 1963, pp. 27-37.

[*In the following essay, Kaufmann explores Wright's relationship to modern art, highlighting the architect's desire that art be integrated with life.*]

Frank Lloyd Wright spent the last decade of his life blasting away at (among other things) modern art; at the same time, he was engaged in a long and eventually successful campaign to build the Solomon Guggenheim Museum for modern art. On these grounds he is accused of designing the museum to show the superiority of his own art—architecture—over the arts of painting and sculpture. Now Wright dearly loved a fight and even more a paradox, but it would never have occurred to him to betray a professional trust. When he accepted any commission, it was not as a self-monumentalizer; else he would have aimed his whole career differently. His original museum clients, Solomon Guggenheim and Hilla Rebay, had a specialized, didactic, and developmental program which offered him a chance to build for what Wright thought were the hopeful aspects of modern art. With a change of clients after Solomon Guggenheim's death, came the clash of purposes which transformed the Guggenheim museum into a half-thing. Even as a half-thing, it has proved astonishingly vital.

Did Wright really hate the fine arts generally, as competitors with architecture? A simple survey of his long practice, in contrast to his many words, shows that Frank Lloyd Wright was in love with fine arts, that life without them was inconceivable to him. His was an astonishingly old-fashioned love, however, with manifestations that require some effort before they can be comprehended today. In fact, to understand them at all, some thought must needs be given to the ideas of art that were current when Wright was young, particularly among people like his pious, well-read, and progressive family.

Wright's heritage in the arts was centered on ideas and ideals common to liberal British intellectuals of the mid-nineteenth century, when many able men and women, like Wright's forebears, found it necessary to leave the over-populated homeland of the Industrial Revolution. This specific heritage has been encapsuled by one of Wright's favorite authors, Emerson, in his essay, "Art," published in 1841. Emerson thought that rather than being imitative, "the painter should give . . . only . . . the spirit . . . the gloom of gloom and the sunshine of sunshine"; he should "convey a larger sense by simpler symbols." Yet the writer continued, "The office of painting and sculpture seems to be merely initial. The best pictures can easily tell us their last secret. . . . Painting and sculpture are gymnastics of the eye, its training. . . . Away with your nonsense of oils and easels, of marble and chisels; except to open your eyes. . . . Under an oak-tree loaded with leaves and nuts, under a sky full of eternal eyes, I stand in a thoroughfare, but in the works of our plastic arts and especially of sculpture, creation is driven into a corner. And the individual in whom simple tastes and susceptibility to all the great human influences overpower the accidents of a local and special culture, is the best critic of art. . . . Art has not yet come into its maturity if it does not put itself abreast with the most potent influences in the world, if it is not practical and moral. . . . But the artist and the connoisseur now seek in art the exhibition of their talent, or an asylum from the evils of life. . . . Art makes the same effort which a sensual prosperity makes: namely to detach the beautiful from the useful, to do up the work as unavoidable, and hating it, pass on to enjoyment. These solaces and compensations, this division of beauty from use, the laws of nature do not permit. . . . Now men do not see Nature to be beautiful. . . . They reject life as prosaic, and create a death which they call poetic. . . . Beauty must come back to the useful arts, and the distinction between the fine and the useful arts be forgotten. . . ." He concludes the essay, "Find holiness and beauty in new and necessary facts, in the field and roadside, in the shop and mill. . . . When science is learned in love, and its powers are wielded by love, they will appear the supplements and continuations of the material creation." His last point was polemically elaborated years later by William Morris, who said, "It is allowing the machines to be our masters and not our servants that so injures life nowadays."

Wright followed these thoughts and developed them; all his reactions to modern art are inherent in Emerson's formulation. To understand Wright's hopes and fears for art, one should keep in mind the Emersonian text. Emerson represented a synthesis of attitudes that had been built up by men like Cobbett and Coleridge, Southey and Owen. They were followed by Carlyle, John Stuart Mill, Pugin, Ruskin, and Morris. Many of these men's works were actually read by Wright as a youngster,

along with those of Victor Hugo, penny dreadfuls, the poetry of Blake, and the essays of Viollet-le-duc.

It will suffice merely to mention Wright's early fascination with Froebel's educational toys and the music of Beethoven and Bach, for these are well-investigated aspects of his education. Less notice has been taken of his childhood recreations: painting, drawing, piano playing, singing, and reading aloud. To these add decorating crockery and confecting trifles to be sold before Christmas for pocket money, and you have the very image of a progressive, provincial upbringing in the era of the esthetic movement. After all, it was just as Frank Lloyd Wright was being trained in physical and moral fortitude on his uncle's farm that Oscar Wilde lectured in America on the beauty of the machine, and *Patience* opened in London. A few years later, when Wright determined to seek his fortune in Chicago, his cultural equipment was pretty much that sketched here; he had acquired a knowledge of engineering, to be sure, and an enduring enthusiasm for Maya, Aztec, and Inca ruins.

When he arrived in Chicago, Wright, still in his teens, found his place at Louis Sullivan's elbow in the Adler and Sullivan office. The great Auditorium Building was the center of activity. It was designed to be the most superb home for grand occasions—opera, concerts, and political rallies—in the New World. It was abundantly ornamented within; numerous oil paintings were commissioned as murals. The concept of architecture and fine arts working together was never questioned, despite the results!

About this time, too, the Art Institute of Chicago began to form its collections. The heroic El Greco, the lovely set of Hubert Roberts, and many Dutch seventeenth-century paintings were on view, along with the contemporary Salon art of France. (Chicago's great impressionist paintings were just entering private collections.) The Art Institute held numerous passing shows of contemporary American painting, sculpture, and artistic crafts in those years, and a large collection of casts, some architectural, were also seen.

All this was grist to Wright's mill, but perhaps even more important to him were the opportunities Chicago provided to enjoy full-scale professional performing arts. Sullivan and his friends were alert to these influences. Wright eagerly went along. Hard after the successful opening of the Auditorium, came preparations for the World's Columbian Exposition; Chicago filled with aspiring artist-decorators. In 1892, while this was going on, Sullivan's firm opened the Schiller theater building, where, not for the first time, they employed a sculptor to complete the decorations. Then, if not earlier, Wright met this sculptor, Richard Bock, who later worked closely with him over many years.

Probably in the same year, Wright and his friends learned to admire another young sculptor, fresh from the Indian Southwest and, earlier, a student in the Paris academies, Hermon Atkins MacNeil. In 1895 or 1896, MacNeil left his brief but successful Chicago career for the American

Academy at Rome. His works may be seen in photographs of Wright's own home, in the company of oriental painting and assorted bric-a-brac, and deliberately featured in the entrance hall of Wright's first independent house of great quality, the Winslow. Wright's statuette, a Hopi runner, was reputedly modeled at the Villa Aurelia, where it must have looked extra exotic; it probably should be dated 1895 or later. In that same year, the sculptor Bock helped Wright complete the entrance to a studio annexed to the architect's home. Flanking the entry, two cowering muscle men on plinths seem pure Bock; the four pilaster caps, however, were sketched and programmed by Wright. Some similar collaboration, with Wright guiding a painter, would account for a mural in a new children's playroom added to the residence about then; the correctly drawn figures seem outside Wright's skills. Within the studio annex, other photos show a landscape in oils and numerous, rather lively, naturalistic statuettes.

There can be no question that at this point Wright was absorbed in an attempt to mix architecture, painting, and sculpture, as he had learned to do with Sullivan. To compare Wright's use of painting and sculpture with examples from Sullivan's works in the years around 1890, is to see progress on the side of the younger man. Not all of it was due to cumulative experience; Wright had a more acute sense than his erstwhile master of scale, composition, and rhythm. In 1897, when Sullivan's only New York building was going up with vaguely classical winged figures modeled in the topmost spandrels, Bock executed very similar but freer figures for a roof loggia on Wright's Heller house. Such ladies, no doubt inspired by figure 4 of Viollet's essay on Roman architecture, appeared in flat paint only on the Transportation Building, Sullivan's masterpiece at the Fair; but fortunately for American art, after 1897 they never winged their way to the top of another Sullivan or Wright building. Russell Lynes has reminded us that in 1898 Wright gave one of his popular talks at the annual meeting of the Central Art Association on "Art in the Home." He lived with what he talked about; Bock even modeled Wright's young son life-size in bronze, adding wings. Seemingly, it was a volatile period in American sculpture.

At the turn of the century, C. R. Ashbee, a leading light of the English Arts and Crafts movement, spent some time in Chicago; we know he and Wright became friendly. Wright agreed to head a committee for the preservation of historic buildings which Ashbee wanted set up in connection with the English equivalent. Ten years later, when Wright's executed buildings were published in a German volume, Ashbee wrote an enthusiastic introduction. Likely enough it was Ashbee who provoked Wright's famous Hull House lecture on "The Art and Craft of the Machine" in 1901. This aired views contrary to Ashbee's, but by 1911, the year of his introduction to Wright's book, Ashbee announced himself ready to work with, rather than against, the current of the times, as Wright had done at Hull House.

The original contact with Ashbee around 1900 may have spurred Wright to consider how far he had drifted from the ideals of his youth, from the concepts of Emerson's essay. Over the next ten years, Wright made extraordinary and remarkably successful efforts to integrate the fine arts and the applied with his architecture. Three great houses testify to this: the Dana, 1902-04; the Martin, 1904; and the Coonley, 1908; to these should be added the famous and unique Larkin office building, 1904; Browne's Bookstore, 1908; and the Thurber Art Gallery, 1909; commissions offering special but smaller opportunities. Even a mid-decade vacation in Japan, the first visit to a land Wright admired and learned to love, exerted no perceptible effect on his work (though his ten- or twelve-year-old passion for Japanese prints increased). One great building of the period, Unity Temple, 1906, was barren of fine arts no doubt because funds and interest were equally absent among the clients. When one considers how St. Bartholomew's in New York had just been artistically enriched, it is clear how much Wright was able to achieve in the Midwest in the 1900's, with artists considerably inferior to those that architects in the East or in Europe could call on.

Wright's extra-legal nuptial flight to Europe in 1910 was spent largely in Florence working on drawings for a luxurious publication of his works which was issued in Berlin just prior to the more modest volume of photographs that Ashbee introduced. Projects for himself, a studio in Florence and a city house in Chicago, show Wright more ready than ever to make a feature of exterior sculpture. The first country home that Wright built for himself, called, like its sequels, Taliesin, after the Welsh bard, was also fully, but less formally, embellished. Few records of it survived the fire that destroyed it in 1914.

This disaster occurred just as Midway Gardens, a complex of restaurants and clubs complete with large garden and music shell, opened in Chicago. Wright had designed it with wonderful boldness. Sculpture and painting played important roles, upholding a festive, exhilarating mood. Here, significantly enough, Wright seized the initiative, designing murals (and, in part, the sculptures) in an abstract idiom all his own, one as fully abstract and asymmetric as any avant-garde European art of the moment. Midway Gardens was executed in a rush, and this may well have forced Wright to impose, rather than to elicit, the artistic qualities needed to complete the architecture and furnishings. Whatever the cause, Midway Gardens marked an epoch in Wright's reactions to fine arts. He was forced to see that the painters and sculptors around him felt an intrinsic affinity to his work. The teamwork of the arts that Ruskin and Morris predicated, that Wright had witnessed in Japan and in Europe's monuments, was broken; art was intent on making "the effort . . . to detach the beautiful from the useful" that Emerson had observed three quarters of a century earlier.

Wright's new-found skill to design his own fine arts for his buildings can be traced back to humble beginnings in colored window compositions, abstract and derived from his Froebel training, that he used in his own house as early as 1895. The earliest of Wright's fully elaborated, asymmetric abstractions for glass seems to have been made in 1911 or 1912 for the Coonley playhouse. These are exactly contemporary with the first documented European abstractions, by Kupka, Larionov, and Delaunay. Wright designed a timidly asymmetric and very nearly abstract relief for a house in Milwaukee, 1916. Nothing prior in modern art is recalled, but a similar spirit is seen in an entirely abstract ornamental relief of 1902 by Josef Hoffmann. Wright was well aware of the Sezession and its works, thanks to his admiration for Hoffmann's teacher, Otto Wagner.

After Midway Gardens, Japan called Wright, and the next years were largely devoted to the complicated commission of the Imperial Hotel. Its rich ornamentation reached a peak in the ballroom. Neither Japanese influence nor the taste of the White Russian refugees with whom Wright then associated can be traced in this work. It is tempting to attribute its rather overcharged air to psychological pressures exerted on Wright by his extremely erratic, bohemian mistress. However that may be, Wright's next expansive client belonged to a similar, if less hectic, world and over the fireplace in the livingroom of Olive Hill in Hollywood, 1920, the architect presented himself more effectively as a sculptor than, perhaps, anywhere else in his career. Here, his stone abstraction is as free of symmetry as his murals and glass had been long since.

Here also, oriental art is used—in the form of Japanese screens built into the room. Here Wright found an art that had the quality of repose that he sought and that—more than his own and more than any modern art he could commission—seemed to have been created according to the Emersonian recipe "only the spirit . . ."; able to "convey a larger sense by simpler symbols." The more Wright understood Far Eastern art, the less tempted he was by the introspective trend of some Western art or by its unsophisticated abstractions, laboring under the weight of inappropriate techniques and caught in the tangle of European ideology. The characteristics he could admire in Western art were better deployed in Eastern.

Wright then designed in California several houses for owners devoted to visual arts. I remember visiting Mrs. Millard and her Renaissance antiques: they looked charmingly at home. Taliesin in Wisconsin was again rebuilt after a second fire in 1925, again replete with oriental art of every kind and of various qualities. A Gustav Klimt, donated by the decorator Paul Frankl, represented modern art in a notably insufficient way; later, a handsome O'Keeffe, a gift of the artist, was in evidence.

About this time Wright began publicly to sing the praise of the Japanese *tokonoma* niche. The reserved place, a chance to group painting, sculpture, and flowers (or other fragments of nature) appropriately to a season or an event, seemed an ideal way to acclimatize the very personal quality of much modern art. Painting and sculpture, thus temporarily exposed and treated preciously, were closer to the performing arts of music, theatre, dance, and recitation, which Wright had always loved. In these arts,

he had never shied away from strongly personal effects, since they could be displayed or set aside as seemed fitting. What seemed wrong to the architect was a permanent display of such effects in a home or public building (other than an art gallery). The *tokonoma* was a cogent solution to these problems, but, even in Wright's own surroundings, it had limited application. The major works of art in both Taliesins tended to remain in place for long periods of time.

With the resurgence of interest in Frank Lloyd Wright in the 1930's (due to his remarkably winning autobiography and to better times), opportunities returned for the association of the arts in his work. Abstract pattern, like that he formerly used in ornamental glass, now was allocated graphic duties: as part-titles in *An Autobiography* and on the cover of the January, 1938 *Architectural Forum*.

But in his seventh decade the architect increasingly looked toward broader horizons: he developed ideas of area planning and of type-homes for modest living. He surrounded himself with young people, forming a community to evolve a way of life that he believed the necessary pre-condition to learning any of the arts: performing arts and *tokonoma*-like arrangements were both features of this life. In 1938, the community built Taliesin West, designed by Wright, as its winter home, and art, mostly oriental, was introduced as part of the ensemble.

One of Wright's last architecturally sculptured walls was designed for my father's office. In plywood, it was more delicate than the stone abstractions of fifteen years earlier. Fallingwater, the country house for the same client, was conspicuously free of Wrightian ornament. As the years went on, Wright used to come to visit at Fallingwater, and he was always very aware of the modern sculpture that accrued around it. He was, of course, as outspoken in our house as everywhere else, but curiously he never made a sarcastic remark about these works to us, nor attempted to persuade us to other tastes. However, he would invariably ask to have new statues relocated, often only a few feet from where they were. Then he would settle back to enjoy the new piece, directing the sculpture into a telling position where it accentuated a feature of the architecture, and in turn gained the support of its setting. From this experience, I feel sure that Frank Lloyd Wright retained his early enthusiasm for and sensitivity to the fine arts.

He found the artists near him during his life working on problems of their own rather than on mutual ones. When he built a museum for them, it was with equal amounts of questioning and hope, but not with disrespect. It wouldn't occur to him to demean his own architecture by assigning to it the task of demeaning another's work. He was too proud and strong an artist himself for that.

In looking back over Wright's long career, then, we see a series of episodes in his relations to the fine arts. First, there are the home-taught attitudes, typical of the Arts and Crafts era and admirably summarized forty years before in Emerson's essay, "Art." These attitudes remained influential, though not decisive, throughout Wright's development. Then came a period of experimentation with the works of artists around him, modeled on Sullivan's usage, which was no more than a measured application of Beaux-Arts conventions. About 1900 (perhaps stimulated by discussions with the Arts-and-Craftser Ashbee), Wright assayed an integration of the arts, using mediocre sculptors and painters to extraordinary effect. Then came the adventure of Midway Gardens, 1914, and the start of Wright's experiments with his own painted and carved architectural embellishments. The years in Japan confirmed his ready affinity with certain aspects of oriental arts, though, encouraged by artistic and bohemian associates in Japan and in California, Wright continued to develop his own expressions for some time. Eventually, oriental arts proved more apt to his sense of architecture as space for living than either his own works or any Western painting and sculpture available to him. By the 1930's, Wright's attitudes towards the arts had jelled, and the full flowering of his architecture at the end of his life had little or no effect on this aspect of his practice. Assuming the role of senior prophet, which in some degree he had earned, Wright castigated modern art for its failure to conform to the image of arts integrated with life, found in the Emerson essay. Yet, faced with particular instances of the power of modern art and its exploratory courage, Wright responded to its value. He willingly worked with modern art despite instinctive reservations expressed in verbal denunciations; he hoped to see it round the corner into a fertile relationship with architecture, which to him remained the key art in human cultural expression.

G. Thomas Couser (essay date 1979)

SOURCE: "Two Prophetic Architects: Louis Sullivan and Frank Lloyd Wright," in *American Autobiography*, University of Massachusetts Press, 1979, pp. 120-47.

[*In the following essay, Couser evaluates and compares the autobiographies of Wright and his mentor Louis Sullivan, emphasizing the prophetic scheme of both works.*]

The contributions of Louis Sullivan and Frank Lloyd Wright to the growth of modern architecture in America are familiar; their achievements as autobiographers are less well known. The similarities between their autobiographies should not be surprising, for the two men had closely linked careers and closely parallel lives. Both cherished their rural childhoods, yet both achieved professional maturity in the raw urban environment of Chicago. Both attributed their success as architects not to their academic education but to the influence of nature and talented contemporaries. Adapting Transcendental theories of art to architecture, they cooperated in the creation of an indigenous, modern, "democratic" architecture. Both disseminated their ideas by lecturing and writing, but as architectural innovators, both suffered, at times, from public neglect or hostility. Thus, in periods

of professional inactivity, both wrote autobiographies in which they portrayed themselves as benevolent yet persecuted geniuses dedicated to revitalizing American architecture and society.

The prophetic tendencies of their autobiographies derived from their conception of the architect's role in society, which clearly reflects the new maturity of American architecture and the self-confidence of the American artist in the High Victorian age. Toward the end of the nineteenth century, American visual artists came to think of themselves not merely as independent creative personalities but as cultural leaders and even as interpreters of reality and arbiters of value—as seers whose visions of truth would lead society to greater accomplishments in a progressive evolutionary scheme.[1] This change in the self-concept of the artist was evident when, as their arts matured, painters and architects adopted Transcendental ideas about the artist. Just as the emergence of Sullivan and Wright as architects marks the period during which American architecture began to receive international recognition, their emergence as prophets clearly marks the point at which Transcendental principles were carried over into architecture and into the mainstream of our intellectual life. Sullivan and Wright, like the earlier Transcendentalists, believed man to be innately creative, potentially inspired, and fundamentally in harmony with a unified nature representing divine order. Furthermore, both believed that the development of American society as an ideal democracy was dependent on the establishment of an indigenous, organic architecture.

For our purposes, the most significant similarity between the autobiographies is that both reflect and dramatize the predicament of the architect who is also a Transcendental prophet. More than any other kind of artist, perhaps, the architect needs clients and commissions in order to realize his ideas. To function as an architect, he needs to persuade other people to enable him to give his ideas physical embodiment. As innovative architects, both Sullivan and Wright suffered—personally and professionally—from being ahead of their times. Lacking the academic architect's ability to appeal to hallowed precedent and cultural snobbery, the progressive architect, as Wright put it, "can talk only principle and sense";[2] he has to depend on the integrity of his ideas and the ability of his clients to recognize it. To some extent, then, the prophetic architect is at the mercy of his society; he has to lead while seeming to follow. As latter-day Transcendentalists, Sullivan and Wright endorsed idealistic metaphysics, but as architects they depended on materials to express their ideas. As Wright put it, "a poetic idea . . . had to conquer this stubborn, suspicious, mean, possessive old world—all its refractory materials in between—in order to appear at all . . ." (p. 231). In his autobiography, Louis Sullivan resolved this dilemma in favor of the idea, stressing theory rather than practice. This is appropriate in view of the fact that his theory was more radical than his buildings. Wright—a daring engineer as well as an architect, and a prophet whose social interests were more highly developed than Sullivan's—faced a more difficult predicament, and he resolved it differently. Whereas Sullivan devoted his autobiography to tracing the development of his philosophy of man, of architecture, and of society, Wright concentrated on the difficulties of enacting such a philosophy both in his career and in his personal life.

Louis Sullivan

Louis Sullivan's refusal to accommodate himself to the shift in American taste toward academic eclecticism after the Columbian Exposition of 1893, combined with certain personal problems, led to a precipitous and tragic decline in his professional career after 1900. Written after two decades of increasing poverty and inactivity, *The Autobiography of an Idea* (1924) might have been a bitter and defensive book. To some extent, Sullivan did portray himself as a neglected genius, a victim of the betrayal of American ideals by a group of reactionary architects. But the mood of the narrative is self-celebratory, not self-pitying; its major motives were self-restoration and prophecy, not self-defense and apology. In writing it, he managed to recapture both a sense of his own youthful energy and an optimistic vision of America's destiny. On his deathbed, he regarded this—the last, most consistent, and most readable of his prophetic works—and a companion volume, *A System of Ornament,* as the consummating achievements of his career.

Sullivan's two most important predecessors were, for different reasons, Whitman and Adams. Probably he regarded Whitman less as an autobiographer than as a poet and prophet; "There Was a Child Went Forth" and *Democratic Vistas* were more important for Sullivan than "Song of Myself" and *Specimen Days.* Whitman's influence, then, is less evident in the form than in the content of Sullivan's autobiography. In addition to Transcendental philosophy, Sullivan's strong emphasis on childhood probably derives from Whitman. Sullivan's idealistic metaphysics may help to account for his unique conception of writing the "autobiography of an idea," but, as we have noted, neither Thoreau nor Whitman wrote a chronological narrative of the development of his own thought. Thus, it is likely that Sullivan's conception of his autobiography owes more to English examples of developmental autobiography. However, Sullivan adapts the developmental form to his own purposes and to his own philosophy, which is explicitly opposed to the utilitarianism and Darwinism of most British developmental autobiographers.[3]

Sullivan was similarly aware of the formal model and philosophy of Adams's *Education* and seems to have attempted implicitly to answer his prophecy with a modern Transcendentalism which took into account some of the realities Adams claimed the "Concord church" ignored. Sullivan's consciousness of Adams's example is suggested by the fact that Sullivan desired to assign the royalties from his autobiography to the educational fund of the American Institute of Architects, just as Adams had given the Institute the rights to his *Chartres.*[4] While Sullivan imitated Adams's magnanimous gesture, he must have hoped that his own contributions, financial and intellectual, would counteract Adams's pernicious "feudal" influence. Similarly, as Sherman Paul has noted, although Sullivan's formal gesture of adopting the third-person point of view recalled Adams's method, it served significantly different ends.[5] Perhaps out of deference to Adams, Sullivan acknowledged the shocks of his education and the ominous nature of modern realities; nevertheless, he boldly asserted his ability to absorb, organize, and express in plastic forms contemporary social, economic, and technological forces.[6] Thus, Sullivan acknowledged Adams's example while refuting his vision of man and history.

Ultimately, *The Autobiography of an Idea* is the spiritual autobiography of a latter-day Transcendentalist, for it narrates the growth of a religious idea and the nurture of the creative powers man shares with God rather than the development of an intellectual system or the course of a professional career. Unlike Thoreau or Whitman, Sullivan offers a chronological narrative of a long portion of his life, but, in contrast to Franklin and Adams, he tends to suppress historical fact in order to create an aura of myth or legend around his experience. Structurally, the narrative seems to have three main sections. The first and significantly the longest section (chapters 1-8) is devoted to childhood and primary education; the second part (chapters 9-12), to Sullivan's secondary and architectural education; the third (chapters 13-15), to his career and mature thought.

The first section is novelistic in its richly detailed re-creation of sensation and incident, and nostalgic in mood. For the most part, the narrative avoids sentimentality because the nostalgia, evoked by a rural America, establishes a reference point against which to measure subsequent change. Indeed, part of Sullivan's prophetic message, which, like Wright's, is essentially conservative, is that although both the boy and the nation must change, certain qualities of their early stages should be nurtured rather than eclipsed: "To disdain our fertile childhood is precisely equivalent to disdain of our maturity. Hence the illusion that we are no longer the child; the delusion that we are other than grown children."[7] The narrative is to measure not growth from naive childhood into wise maturity but the development of the vision and the latent powers of the child. Growth is not, as it was for Adams, a matter of response to dislocation but of continuous expansion from a stable center.

Childhood for Sullivan, as for Adams, involved a rhythmic alternation between town and country. But Adams used this polarity mainly to establish the theme of the duality of all experience. For Sullivan, the specific content of the polarity became a theme; it was one of the contradictions of nineteenth-century American life he hoped to resolve. Indeed, one manifestation of his growth is his changing attitude toward the city. At first, he perceives it as a prison cutting him off from nature; later, he learns to view it as an environment capable of enlarging his powers; finally, he endeavors to make Chicago truly a "Garden City."

Adams, too, had begun with a description of childhood sensations, but he had quickly moved from a world of the senses and instinct to one of intellect, abstraction, and analysis. He used the third-person narration to suggest the gulf between the narrator and his youthful self, to express his sense of the fragmentation of the psyche, and to exert the pressure of irony on his earlier impressions. Sullivan's use of the third person shares only one motive with Adams's—to thrust his ideas rather than himself into prominence. Otherwise, Sullivan manages to use the same device for very different purposes—to suggest the continuity of experience, the wholeness of the self, and the validity of the child's viewpoint. The third-person narration allows Sullivan to re-create the child's consciousness impersonally, with a minimum of sentimentality. At times, the narrator recalls the child's vision in order to affirm its wisdom, as when he records his perception of a Baptist minister's preaching as a perversion of religion. At other times, Sullivan uses the third-person technique to illustrate the process by which raw sensory data is converted into ideas which can then be tested. One such sequence, in which young Louis learns to appreciate, then to worship, a bridge he had naively mistaken for a monster, serves as a paradigm of American society's adjustment to its new technology.

As was the case with Adams, Sullivan's childhood illusions were often abruptly shattered. The crucial difference is that for Sullivan reality often proved less frightening than illusion. One such beneficial shock occurred when Louis's father revealed to him the nature of visual perspective. This archetypal crisis profoundly disturbed the boy, "for had not that son built up a cherished world all of his own, a world made up of dreams, of practicalities, of deep faith, of unalloyed acceptance of externalities, only now to find that world trembling and tottering on its foundations threatening to collapse upon him, or to vanish before this new and awful revelation from the unseen" (p. 104). The architectural metaphor here is significant, for this experience was crucial to the education of the architect. He not only made a discovery necessary to a draftsman; he also learned to see that reality or truth does not always lie in the apparent or obvious. What seemed an experience destructive of the world of the child eventually enabled him to found his buildings upon a true vision—to realize his creative powers in designs which expressed the latent or "suppressed" functions of a building.

Such shocks were not typical of Sullivan's childhood, which he portrays as characterized by reverie and enjoyment of nature. Much time was spent observing and being absorbed in nature. Sullivan's gardening, his delight in spring, and his excursions to explore and establish—to "possess"—his own domain in the rural countryside are all reminiscent of Thoreau. Building a dam represents not a change in his attitude toward nature but a further development of a natural creative power. His allusion in the following passage suggests that he saw no necessary contradiction between contemplating nature and manipulating it: "Then he loafed and invited his soul as was written by a big man about the time this proud hydraulic engineer

was born" (p. 56). Even more characteristic of his invocation of Whitman is his description of his solitary experience of his first sunrise: "Surely the child that went forth every day became part of the sunrise even as this sunrise became forevermore part of him" (p. 61).

Rivalling his experience of nature as he grew older was his schooling, which he found oppressive, and his intuitive response to buildings, which he found liberating: "His history books told him that certain buildings were to be revered, but the buildings themselves did not tell him so, for he saw them with a fresh eye, an ignorant eye, an eye unprepared for sophistries and a mind empty of dishonesty" (p. 117). The climax of this section occurs with Sullivan's decision to become an architect. This event resembles Franklin's adoption of the role of printer because it engages Sullivan in a profession that allowed him to concentrate his powers and employ them in a publicly useful way. It does not resolve the dualities of his childhood, but it suggests a means of their eventual resolution. Furthermore, it gives him a medium for the expression of his prophetic vision.

If the first section focused on Sullivan's unplanned and unconscious experience of nature, the middle section concentrates on his education in institutions, for the boy was in need of having his intuitions translated into ideas and his innate powers disciplined. At Boston English, Moses Woolson taught Sullivan not only the Franklinian lesson that true freedom comes only through discipline of power but also the symbolic language of algebra, which enabled Sullivan to probe the unknown. Sullivan's critical and analytical faculties began to develop alongside his creative ones. Schooling no longer distracted him from nature, but began to make nature's lessons conscious and systematic. Sullivan summarized this crucial phase of his education in a way that contrasts sharply with Adams's comments on his academic education; according to Sullivan, Woolson "had brought order out of disorder, definition out of what was vague . . . [and] made of Louis a compacted personality, ready to act on his own initiative, in an intelligent and purposeful way" (p. 168).

At M.I.T., however, Sullivan became restless with the Beaux Arts method and decided to go "to headquarters to learn if what was preached *there* as gospel really signified glad tidings" (p. 188-89). The main benefits of his time in Europe came not from his education at the École but from his intensive preparation for the exams and from his vacation travel. A mathematics tutor, M. Clopet, who valued only rules so broad as to admit of no exceptions, stimulated Sullivan's quest for an equivalent approach to architecture. Similarly, his study of history and his immersion in European culture led to his discovery of his vocation as a prophet. He came to see history as "a processional of the races and nations, whose separate deeds seemed to flow from their separate thoughts, and whose thoughts and deeds seemed, as he himself progressed, toward them, to coalesce into a mass movement of mankind, carrying the burden of a single thought" (p. 237). His subsequent devotion to the pursuit and expression of that idea reveals that his aspiration was to become a prophet as well as an architect—one who would further the progress of mankind by revealing and realizing the ideals of his society. This new endeavor marks, also, the beginnings of self-education. Armed with his new vision of history, Sullivan quickly became impatient with the architectural training at the École, which he felt offered technique without inspiration.

In the last three chapters, Sullivan sets forth his philosophy and discusses his attempts to realize it in his architecture. At the beginning of "The Garden City," he establishes the nature of the environment in which the idea was finally discovered. He reverts to the fairy-tale tone of the book's opening in order to remove the city from the realm of history into that of myth: "There was a time a city some three hundred thousand strong stood beside the shore of a great and very wonderful lake with a wonderful horizon and wonderful daily moods" (p. 241). According to Sullivan, the city, which had been devastated by a fire, was preparing for recovery and for transformation into a totally new and wholesome environment.

For a time, Sullivan's personal growth, his architectural education, and the growth of the city proceed in parallel fashion. But the narrative focuses not, like a memoir, on the career but, like a spiritual autobiography, on the vision and values of the author. Sullivan's concern is to establish his prophetic stature rather than his professional standing. Only in this chapter does he make explicit what he means by "an idea" and specify what the idea is: "This steadfast belief in the power of man was an unalloyed childhood instinct, an intuition and a childhood faith which never for a day forsook him, but grew stronger, like an indwelling daemon. . . . as he grew on through his boyhood, and through passage to manhood and to manhood itself, he began to see the powers of nature and the powers of man coalesce in his vision into an IDEA *of power.* Then and only then he became aware that this idea was a *new idea,*—a complete reversal and inversion of the commonly accepted intellectual and theological concept of the Nature of man" (p. 248).

It becomes clear, finally, that by "idea" Sullivan means philosophy or even vision, and that the "new idea" consists essentially of the principles of Transcendentalism. The next chapter, "Face to Face," summarizes Sullivan's personal philosophy and uses it as the basis for a prophetic interpretation of human history. Thus, this penultimate chapter corresponds closely in function, though not in content, to Adams's "Dynamic Theory of History." Whereas Adams's vision focused on impersonal forces and made room for man's salvation only by admitting that he too was a force, Sullivan concentrates on making man's latent powers visible to him. In Sullivan's scheme, nature is a beneficent servant of man, who wields impressive powers: "He changes his own situations, he creates an environment of his own" (p. 264).

According to Sullivan, all previous civilizations had been based on delusions and misconceptions—on a tragic underestimation of man's abilities. Sullivan presents his own idea as the successor to two previous "inversions"— the Christian and the Copernican—which had begun to dispel man's self-delusion: "The world of heart and head is becoming dimly sentient that man in his power is Free Spirit—Creator. The long dream of inverted self is nearing its end" (p. 266). In announcing this new and presumably final inversion, Sullivan, of course, assumes the role of a new messiah; the chapter title, which echoes I Corinthians 13, implies that Sullivan's gospel enables man to see himself clearly and hence to realize his divine potential.

Although Sullivan goes on in Whitmanic fashion to enumerate the powers of man and to prophesy the overthrow of "feudalism" in America, his performance is not very convincing. For one thing, his view of history is oversimplified to a point that suggests willful distortion rather than inspired vision. Thus, his optimistic version of the future appears to be without foundation; with regard to history, at least, he seems to have lost his traumatically acquired sense of perspective. Or perhaps his vision was properly graphic and autobiographical rather than prophetic, for, ironically, it is when his idea is presented in bald expository form, divorced from the intuition and experience from which it evolved, that it is least impressive. As his commercial buildings attest, Sullivan's architectural vision was capable of spiritualizing the material, but his autobiographical vision led him to extract an idea from its experiential context and project it upon a vague future. The result seems not, like Adams's synthesis, arduously derived from the minutely detailed history that preceded it but artificially distilled from Sullivan's mythic childhood. The soft focus and latent sentimentality of the earlier chapters are exposed here as liabilities. Instead of revealing man to himself, Sullivan seems to project his own wishes upon nature and to see himself reflected in it—face to face.

If Charles Whitaker, the editor of the *Journal* of the A.I.A. who solicited the autobiography, had not urged Sullivan to add another chapter, the book would have ended on this positive, but false note.[8] Having set forth his idea, or his prophecy, Sullivan had done what he had set out to do, but he had said little about either his architectural theory or his buildings. In a final and somewhat uneven chapter, he dealt with his attempts to enact the idea whose evolution he had traced in the earlier chapters. In doing so, he had to account for the decline of his career and his failure to convert the American public to his viewpoint, either through his writings or his buildings. His solution to this autobiographical problem was to portray himself as a victim of the struggle between "democratic" and "feudal" principles in American civilization.

Sullivan characterizes himself as ignorant of the politics of architectural practice, armed only with the revolutionary concept that form should follow function in architecture—an architectural corollary of the idea of power elaborated in the previous chapter. Thus buildings, like men, were to realize their greatest beauty by making manifest their latent functions or powers. Theoretically, this architectural concept was the seed of an organic architecture which would symbolize the achievement of the final inversion and the arrival of a kind of democratic millennium.

But the new formula for organic architecture, like Sullivan's prophetic writings, failed to transform the contemporary scene. Sullivan quickly sketched in the forces assembling for a showdown between opposing principles within the culture. On the one hand, there were many personalities and technological factors making for vital developments in Chicago architecture in the 1880s, as the city began to recover from the fire of 1871 and the panic of 1873. The rise of the tall office building, with its true skeletal frame, and Sullivan's solution to the problem of expressing it esthetically are prime examples of these creative developments: "The true steel frame structure stands unique in the flowing of man's works; a brilliant expression of man's capacity to satisfy his needs through the expression of his natural powers" (p. 313). On the other hand were the values and activities of men like Daniel Burnham, whose architectural practice embodied for Sullivan the "tendency toward bigness, organization, delegation, and intense commercialism" of the "feudal" trusts (p. 314). Burnham was cast as a traitor and villain because of his deference to the academic eastern architects in the design of the Columbian Exposition of 1893.

The Exposition became the focus of Sullivan's final chapter, as it had been for Henry Adams's "Chicago"; for both, it was an event revealing the destiny of the community. But whereas Adams viewed the attempt "to impose classical taste on plastic Chicago"[9] as a sign of possible improvement in American taste, Sullivan saw signs of cultural regression in the plaster classicism of the fair, which he denounced as "a naked exhibitionism of charlatanry in the higher feudal and domineering culture, conjoined with expert salesmanship of the materials of decay" (p. 322). Similarly, while the bemused Adams found more questions than answers among the fair's exhibits, Sullivan portrayed it as a decisive betrayal of American ideals: "Here was to be the test of American culture, and here it failed" (p. 318).

Sullivan makes his account of the Exposition the occasion for some bitterly satiric writing on eclecticism and commercialism and also for an ironic epitaph for American architecture: "Thus Architecture died in the land of the free and the home of the brave,—in a land declaring its fervid democracy, its inventiveness, its resourcefulness, its unique daring, enterprise, and progress" (p. 325). This interpretation of the significance of the Exposition is, of course, highly personal. As an autobiographer who substitutes an account of the defeat of his revolutionary idea for an account of his personal and professional decline, Sullivan may be accused of shifting the blame from himself to society—of portraying himself, for egotistical reasons, as a genius ignored by an unappreciative public. Still, there is a certain amount of truth to Sullivan's version of events. His career and the development of progressive architecture did suffer from the triumph of academic classicism in the design of the Exposition—

a triumph symptomatic of an important shift in taste in the 1890s. Furthermore, the pose of the persecuted genius, in both Sullivan and Wright, is consistent with their portrayal of themselves as prophets. Their exaggeration of public indifference or hostility may derive, not from self-pity or self-delusion, but from their desire to function as prophets in writing autobiography; as prophets, they would inevitably judge society by high ideals. Certainly, Sullivan's indignation and anger seem more authentic than his blandly optimistic prophecy in the previous chapter. His editor's coaxing another chapter out of him seems to have unleashed a power of vituperation latent in the rest of the narrative; Sullivan's performance as a prophet is thus strengthened by his continuation of the narrative.

Still, one remains unsure of Sullivan's motives. While the episode of the Exposition serves as a valuable reminder of the vulnerability of American ideals, it also excuses, without confronting, the subsequent decline of Sullivan's career. Moreover, Sullivan goes on to reassert his faith in America's future, arguing that the masses are withdrawing their consent from the architectural travesty of eclecticism: "Dogma and the rule of the dead are passing. The Great *Modern* Inversion, for which the world of mankind has been preparing purblindly through the ages, is now underway in its world-wide awakening" (p. 328). Sullivan's major motive in his treatment of the Exposition may have been to make the contemporary plight of progressive architecture seem more urgent by citing a recent defeat for its ideals. His own suffering as a result of that failure may make his faith in the final triumph of his ideals more moving to some readers, less convincing to others. Thus, this second reversal may be, to some, evidence of Sullivan's resilience, self-composure, and magnanimity; to others, of his ambivalence toward the American public. One wonders whether he willfully revived his earlier optimism for the sake of consistency, in the hope of pleasing his audience, or out of genuine prophetic conviction.

To unsympathetic readers, Sullivan's subordination of personal experience to the development of his philosophy or vision will seem a ploy for avoiding the unpleasant facts of his later life; to sympathetic readers, it may seem a way of transcending self-concern in order to serve the needs of the community in the manner of the prophetic autobiographer. Another perspective is to view the autobiography as an attempt to resurrect and preserve the self. Unlike some of his predecessors, Sullivan never prophesied his own immortality. Rather, he expressed a sense of self-transcendence which made it superfluous. Thus, he informs the reader that in a moment of spiritual illumination, he had experienced a sense of "peace which is life's sublimation, timeless and spaceless. Yet he never lost his footing on the earth; never came the sense of immortality: One life surely is enough if lived and fulfilled" (p. 298). Still, Sullivan's autobiographical strategy seems calculated to guarantee his immortality in more ways than the obvious and inevitable one. In treating his autobiography as the record of the growth of an idea, rather than as an account of his career, he focused on a contribution—a life-product—which would outlast even his buildings. And, like Whitman, he identified his life with the process of evolution; according to Sullivan, the history of his life simply recapitulated the history of civilization, which is also the autobiography of an idea.

Frank Lloyd Wright

Since Sullivan was the man who most strongly influenced Wright's thought and expression, as well as his design, the connection between their autobiographies is a firm one. Wright discusses their relationship in *An Autobiography* (1932), but its importance to him is even more apparent in a later book, *Genius and the Mobocracy* (1949). In it, he sets out to "right" the art historians' account of their relationship and, in doing so, to write the personal history of that relationship as well. Wright follows the relationship from the beginning, during the crucial period when Sullivan was designing the Auditorium Building, through Wright's dismissal from the firm for violating his contract, to their reunion in Sullivan's declining years. Thus, the book becomes a declaration of allegiance to Sullivan and even a work of confession and atonement. However, Wright portrays himself not as a disciple or imitator but as a co-worker carrying on the master's work. He insists on the mutuality of their relationship, pointing out that at one time Sullivan could not distinguish between their drawings, and claiming that the master owed him as much as he owed the master. Indeed, the relationship between them is so close that the book becomes autobiographical; in concluding, Wright describes it as "neither biograph nor autobiograph but a combination of both."[10] Elsewhere he asserts, "This book is not about him—it is about our work-life and struggle while we were together" (p. 155). More than a biography of Sullivan, the book is finally a meditation on the predicament of the inspired artist in a democracy that has failed to honor individual freedom. Louis Sullivan is the prime example of the tragic fate of a genius in such a society. But, seeing himself in Sullivan, Wright tends to portray his own predicament indirectly.

Yet here, as in the autobiography, Wright is careful to distinguish himself from his master in several respects. Wright argues that he is more aware than Sullivan of the significance of the machine for modern architecture and more sensitive to the nature of materials. Restating Sullivan's dictum more positively as "Form and Function are one," he claims to have refined the master's architectural theory and to have extended its application beyond the treatment of facades. And although his characterization of Sullivan as "untroubled by a social conscience" seems unfair (pp. 53-54), it reflects Wright's sense that he was more concerned than his master with social problems and the function of the institutions for which he designed buildings.

The similarities and differences between them are reflected in their autobiographies. Much of the early part of Wright's reads like a recapitulation of Sullivan's, while the later part reads like its sequel. However, whereas Sullivan fulfilled the role of the prophet explicitly in his writing and implicitly in his architecture, Wright tended to function as a prophet both in his personal life and in his architecture and writing. Sullivan, like Emerson, announced the principles of a radical philosophy; Wright, like Thoreau and Whitman, attempted to explore the implications of these principles by enacting them in his life, which became part of his design. Instead of subordinating his experience to his ideas, Wright chose to treat his experience as a test and demonstration of them; indeed, he calls his book "an autobiographical study of Life-as-Idea and Idea-as-Life."[11] Wright's autobiography is more personal, more concrete, and more inclusive of failure than Sullivan's because, as a self-conscious prophet, he tried to extend his organic principles into a design for his entire society.

Book One of the autobiography is preceded by a "Prelude" which graphically illustrates Wright's sense of his own life. As the nine-year-old Wright and his Uncle John walk across a snow-covered field, the difference between their personalities is revealed by the paths they trace in the snow: "There was the wavering, searching, heedful line embroidering the straight one like some free, engaging vine as it ran back and forth across it" (p. 1). Wright clearly intends to indicate here that although the pattern of his life departs from the purposeful straightness of his uncle's, it does so only because he was seeking for and heedful to a *natural* principle.

The first part of Book One, "Family," is largely devoted to an impressionistic rendering of a rural boyhood. The content and tone of this section are Sullivanesque; minimizing the financial insecurity of his family and the nomadic pattern of his boyhood years, Wright stresses the wholesome influence of nature and the healthy rhythm of farm work. Like Sullivan, he portrays himself as a dreamy, mystical youth susceptible to the influence of music and educated primarily by the "Book of Creation" rather than by school or society: "Something in the nature of an inner experience had come to him that was to make a sense of the supremacy of interior order like a religion to him" (p. 47).

In treating his boyhood, then, Wright portrays not so much its reality as the ideals to which he became devoted. He finds their intellectual sources in his family's Unitarianism and their enthusiasm for what he calls "the transcendentalism of the sentimental group at Concord: Whittier, Lowell, Longfellow, yes, and Emerson, too" (p. 15). But a harsher heritage is implicit in his family's motto, "Truth against the world." Thus, in addition to an appreciation for the beneficence of nature, of rural life, and of the sheltering clan of Welsh relatives within which he lived, Wright, like Thoreau and Adams, acquired a testiness and intolerance for institutions or individuals that threatened his ideals. Even as a youth, he questioned society in the manner of Thoreau: " . . . the boy already wondered why 'culture' . . . shouldn't consist in getting rid of the inappropriate in everything" (p. 57).

Like Sullivan, Wright can record only impatience with his schooling, which he evaluates as an educational blank. His most important architectural lesson came not from his courses in civil engineering at the University of Wisconsin but from witnessing the collapse of a shoddily built section of the state Capitol. This event impressed him with the urgency of structural as well as professional integrity, and provided him with an image of avoidable catastrophe which shaped his professional and prophetic conscience: "The horror of the scene has never entirely left his consciousness and remains to prompt him to this day" (p. 55).

The first real turning point in the narrative comes when, at the end of Part One, Wright runs away from college and family in Madison to seek a practical architectural education in Chicago, "the Eternal City of the West." The significance of this break with the restrictive influence of his family and school is suggested by the change from a third-person point of view to a first-person narration: "Here say goodby to 'the boy.' Henceforward, on my own, I am I" (p. 60). Wright's use of the third person in this section may be, in part, a gesture of deference to Sullivan's example, but he uses it largely to distinguish a period of vague memory of dependent childhood from a period of conscious selfhood. At the point in the narrative at which the character first assumes responsibility for his destiny, the narrator recognizes his identity with him by means of a simple formal gesture.

If the entire narrative is intended to record an attempt to live a life according to natural principles, the "Family" section of Book One establishes Wright's intuitive harmony with nature, while the "Fellowship" section records the articulation of personal ideals. Thus, this section of the autobiography, like the middle section of *The Autobiography of an Idea,* is concerned with the activities and education of the budding architect—his reading, acquaintances, employers, and the development of his personal taste and style as a designer. But as his individuality develops, Wright becomes increasingly aware of conventional obstacles to the enactment of his ideas, both in his personal life and his architectural practice: "I began to see that in spite of all the talk about Nature 'natural' was the last thing they would let you be if they could prevent it" (p. 88). His relationship with Sullivan became especially important because " . . . the very sense of things I had been feeling as rebellion was—in him—at work" (p. 101). From the beginning of his architectural career, Wright's sense of himself as an antinomian and heretic in opposition to the prevailing culture developed rapidly. Thus, like Thoreau and unlike Whitman, Wright tended to take a prophetic stance which opposed him to the public. This tendency helped him to define his prophetic message, but it also sometimes frustrated his attempts at reform. He simultaneously thrived on and was thwarted by his antagonistic attitude toward social conventions.

Book Two, "Work," begins where Louis Sullivan chose to conclude his autobiography—with the year 1893. Unlike Sullivan, Wright did not suffer a personal and professional decline after the Exposition, and he does not focus on it as a personal and communal catastrophe, as Sullivan had done. However, he does imply that it represented a betrayal of organic principles when he treats "Uncle Dan" Burnham's offer to send him to the École des Beaux Arts as a kind of temptation scene. He portrays himself here as facing a crisis similar to the test Sullivan claimed confronted the nation in the Exposition. But instead of reenacting the communal failure in his personal life, Wright remains true to his and Sullivan's ideals and turns down the offer: "Suddenly the whole thing cleared up before my eyes as only keeping faith with what we call 'America'" (p. 125). Like Sullivan before him, Wright chooses the more difficult route, asserting his faith in the future of America and his own role in bringing about progress.

Unlike Sullivan, Wright includes a detailed account of his career; thus his autobiography seems to display some of the characteristics of the memoir. Yet he resists the impersonality of that form, pointing out that his career cannot be considered separately from his self: "These creations of ours! I see as we look back upon them how we ourselves belong to them" (p. 129). On the other hand, he succeeds, to some extent, in avoiding narrow egocentricity by treating his commissions not as personal achievements but as embodiments of ideals which are, or should be, communal ones: "All true building in our land of the brave and the home of the free is a soul-trying crusade . . ." (p. 24).

During the late 1890s, Wright's dual concern for the family as an institution and for the architectural expression of organic principles came together in his first creative breakthrough—the development of the prairie house.[12] In the autobiography, Wright explains this achievement in terms of the expression of two distinctively American "commodities"—unity and space. In these houses, Wright sought to create an architectural environment which would maximize both a communal sense of shelter and a personal sense of freedom. Like Thoreau, he saw his dwellings not only as embodiments of his spiritual ideals but as environments with regenerative capabilities: "As these ideals worked away from house to house, finally freedom of floor space and elimination of useless heights worked a miracle in the new dwelling place. A sense of appropriate freedom had changed its whole aspect. The whole became different, but more fit for human habitation, and natural for its site" (p. 145). Thus, while Sullivan had tried to translate Whitman's poetic ideals into architectural equivalents, Wright came much closer to fulfilling Thoreau's prophetic architectural program.[13]

Wright was less successful in his attempt to realize in his life the ideal he expressed in the prairie house—an optimum combination of stability and freedom. In 1909, he settled a domestic crisis by choosing individual freedom at the expense of his family's stability, leaving home to go off to Europe with the wife of a neighbor and client. His inclusion of domestic problems introduces a confessional element wholly lacking in Sullivan's autobiography and generally uncharacteristic of American autobiography. There is also an element of the apology in the "sociological tract" concerning marriage, fatherhood, and divorce which serves as the defense of his action. Yet both elements—confession and apology—are still subsumed under his prophetic purpose, for Wright explains his actions as part of an attempt to live a life as true to organic principles as his architecture: " . . . I went out into the unknown to test faith in freedom, test faith in life as I had already proved faith in work" (p. 167).

Hostile publicity about Wright's actions aroused his sense of righteousness and moved him toward the role of an antagonistic prophet. Unable to accept social conventions and reluctant to suffer the consequences of ignoring them, Wright resorted to elitism in his own defense, portraying himself as a genius mistreated by the mob. There is certainly an element of paranoia in Wright's consistent exaggeration of the public's hostility to his architecture and his conduct of his personal life.[14] Yet to some extent, Wright earned his role as a persecuted genius, for he spent more than one night in jail as a result of his unconventional behavior. Furthermore, Wright's predicament stemmed in part from his interpretation of the prophet's role. He was sincere and passionate in his rejection of certain conventions; his devotion to his ideas and his very self-concept demanded a certain amount of public resistance.[15] Yet the dilemma was one he, unlike Woolman, never satisfactorily resolved. Throughout his life he continued to offend the public and to complain of their hostility to his actions and ideas.

The period following this turning point, from 1910 to 1914, was one of little architectural activity.[16] But Wright's retreat from suburban Oak Park to the rural isolation of Taliesin accomplished some of the benefits for Wright that Thoreau's removal to Walden Pond gained for him. It gave him a self-constructed retreat from which to reexamine and reestablish his personal relationship to society, and it supplied him with an environment suitable to his needs, expressive of his ideals, and conducive to harmony with nature. Moreover, at Taliesin, Wright was able to create an exemplary social unit consisting of "a garden and a farm behind a workshop and a home" (p. 172). He sought both to reenter the world of his youth and to make that world the site of his mature creative development. Like Thoreau, he invoked as an analogue for his change of residence the discovery and settlement of the New World by immigrant pioneers: "I turned to the hill in the Valley as my Grandfather before me had turned to America—as a hope and a haven . . ." (p. 172). There he proceeded to build, at last, a natural house for himself as the site of his future perfect home.

However, once again, Wright's work was opposed by "something not in the reckoning"—this time not a mere temptation but a devastating tragedy: one of his employees at Taliesin went berserk, killing Wright's mistress and six other people and burning down much of Taliesin. Coming two weeks after the outbreak of World War I, this episode marks the nadir of the narrative. In marked contrast to Henry Adams, Wright includes a personal tragedy which might have broken his life in order to show that he had overcome it and kept his life and personality intact. His recovery, which was slow and arduous, began with temporary self-isolation and agonizing self-doubt: "Was this trial for heresy too? Was this trial at some judgment seat . . . to quell a spirit that would not be quelled?" (p. 192). Finally, however, with the activity of rebuilding Taliesin, he felt a sense of self-redemption and triumph.

Nearly as important for his recovery was the time Wright spent in Japan. Japanese culture embodied many of Wright's ideals, both esthetic and religious, and the Japanese print, an indigenous art form based on simplification, was as comforting and inspiring to him as the Gothic cathedral was for Henry Adams. In his autobiography, Wright uses Japan as Adams uses medieval France and Thoreau uses Cape Cod—as cultural ideals with which to reproach and inspire American civilization. Impressed by the physical and spiritual cleanliness favored by the Shinto religion, he declares, "We of the West couldn't live in Japanese houses and shouldn't. But we could live in houses disciplined by an ideal at least as high and true as this one of theirs, if we went about it—for a century or two" (p. 199).

But like Thoreau's Cape Cod, Wright's Japan harbored a threat to his Transcendental philosophy; the earthquake, like the unbridled Atlantic, furnished evidence of potential chaos in nature. Like Thoreau, Wright responded by adapting his organic principles to native conditions, but Wright's trial was more severe since it required not only intellectual accommodation but the creation of a physical construct—a hotel—able to withstand an earthquake. The construction of the Imperial Hotel looms larger in the autobiography than it would in an "objective" biography or an account of his architectural career, because Wright saw this achievement as a supreme and dramatic example of the ability of organic principles of design to transcend natural disasters and of his personal capacity to rise above tragic catastrophe. When the hotel survived an earthquake which flattened much of Tokyo in 1923, Wright's triumph was not only professional but personal, not only real but symbolic.

Wright took advantage of the disappointment in his career and the turmoil in his personal life between 1914 and 1932 to emphasize the difficulty of his struggle to realize his ideals. The stories of certain commissions come to epitomize the lifelong process of conceiving and nurturing an idea. Wright comments with irony but without bitterness on the architect's peculiar predicament, which involves overcoming human as well as material resistance to the force of his idea: "Seeking simplicity in the spirit in which it was sought in La Miniatura, you shall never fail to find beauty—though contractors do betray, workmen botch, all friends backslide, bankers balk, the jaws of heaven open wide to hitherto unsuspected deluge, and all the Gods—but one—be jealous" (p. 250).

Wright did not stint in recording his personal trials during this period. Another fire nearly destroyed Taliesin, but there was no loss of life and a storm quenched the fire before devastation was complete. Wright's recovery was aided by the support of Olgivanna Milanoff, but his joy in his family was dampened by the harassment of his estranged and unbalanced wife, Miriam Noel. Interestingly, the interpretive framework of this part of the narrative has to do with two opposing prophetic principles. One, instilled in him by his grandfather, is a principle of judgment which Wright associates with Isaiah, the prophet of a severe, masculine deity. The other represents a principle of acceptance which he associates with the Welsh prophet Taliesin, the prophet of a deity with the gentle nature of Adams's Virgin: "Isaiah is the vengeful prophet of an antique wrath. Taliesin is a nobler prophet and he is not afraid of him. . . . Taliesin loves and trusts—man" (p. 273). Thus, Wright often interprets favorable events, such as the reconstruction of Taliesin, as evidence of the strength of the gentler prophet. While not providential, his framework is teleological, and the struggle between these opposing principles is reminiscent of the Puritan's vacillation between forgiving and condemning texts.

Book Three, the final book of the 1932 version of the autobiography, is entitled "Freedom" because the death of Miriam Noel removed a large obstacle to a free personal life and the resumption of creative activity. However, the coming of the Depression meant a lack of construction and hence of commissions. Faced with a period of professional inactivity, Wright's creative energy, like that of Sullivan in similar circumstances, expressed itself in a flood of articles and speeches. Thus, Book Three also records the liberation of Wright's ideas from the necessity of realization in material form for paying clients. In a time of national crisis, Wright fully assumed the role of prophet, and his ideas are increasingly presented in pure expository form. Book Three corresponds, then, to Sullivan's "Face to Face" chapter, for here Wright explicitly states the essence of his prophetic message.

Freedom is the theme of this somewhat anticlimactic section in another sense, for the theme of Wright's prophecy is that the challenge facing America is the reestablishment of freedom in a designed society. In the 1930s, his thought turned increasingly to the city, which he thought had been outmoded by modern communications and transportation. His hope was that decentralization would ruralize Usonia, as he liked to call the United States, and reestablish the family home as the primary social unit. But in the meantime, he recognized the need "to mitigate . . . the horror of life held helpless or caught unaware in the machinery that is the city . . ." (p. 324). Thus, he offered his own project for St. Mark's Tower as a humane and organic design for a skyscraper. Although he was generally optimistic about the future, he also felt, like Adams, that American civilization was facing a crisis, and that its salvation might lie in education: "Publicizing organic educational influences, by way of information, may avert the organic disaster that overtook earlier civilizations. It may also precipitate disaster, be it said" (p. 318).

One section of this book, entitled "Journeyman Preacher," describes Wright's travels as an itinerant prophet. One of his goals is to prevent the Chicago World's Fair of 1933, in which he had not been invited to participate, from becoming another setback for organic architecture like the Columbian Exposition. As the title of this section indicates, however, the format for the presentation of his ideas tends to be expository rather than narrative, and the effect is rather flat. In introducing a complete lecture into the text, he admits that the procedure may not seem autobiographical and that the lecture may be skipped, but implies that it ought to be read since it contains "compact, the essence of work and life as philosophy of form, line, material and symbol" (p. 344). Like any prophet, he endeavors to involve the reader by suggesting his inevitable implication in the future of his community: "Let us see what illusions we are cherishing in these prisons for life that we have built, and then see what freedom is possible for us if we will take it" (p. 313). Wright remains optimistic, believing that in his work and his writing he leaves a legacy sufficient to inspire the creation of an organic society. As illustration, one of the final scenes offers an image of Wright's instruction of posterity in the means of their salvation. Describing a game in which he and his five-year-old daughter take turns adding colored blocks to a cooperative construction, he comments: "Always the little form and color exercises would make a good thesis in 'Modern Art.' In fact, that is what I intend them to be" (p. 368).

As Wright brought his narrative to a close, he appeared ready to accept death as part of natural change: "The inevitable is friend to natural order in any true culture founded on this reality. Age, then, becomes a desirable qualification, . . . death a crisis of growth" (p. 371). However, although Wright was in his mid-sixties when *An Autobiography* was first published, he did not die until 1959. Moreover, in the late 1930s, he entered into a new creative phase which surpassed even his "first golden age" in the first decade of the century. During this time, he continued to write, and one of his many projects was a continuation of the autobiography. In the enlarged 1943 edition, he divided Book One into two separate books, "Family" and "Fellowship"; revised "Freedom," which now became Book Four; added a fifth book, "Form"; and suggested in his closing lines that "Broadacres City" be considered the sixth and final book. This new version of *An Autobiography* was composed during the early years of World War II, but this event seems to have had little impact on its content. For Wright, who was a pacifist and an isolationist, the war would not have been cause for any cessation of his criticism of the nation. Nor did he see it as a communal crisis worthy of treatment in his added book, "Form." It afforded the occasion for this writing project not because it posed a threat to the community but because it brought about a dearth of commissions. The decisive historical context for the new version of the autobiography, as for the old, seems to have been the Depression, with its national introspection and its experimentation with new approaches to social problems. In the enlarged autobiography, Wright's concern for the community is very apparent, for Book Five concentrates on the Taliesin Fellowship and Book Six explicitly suggests a design for the nation as a whole.

The establishment of the Taliesin Fellowship was, in part, a way of responding to the professional inactivity caused by the Depression: "No buildings to build at the harrowing moment but, capitalizing thirty five years of past experience, why not build the builders of buildings against the time when buildings might again be built?"[17] But it was also a way of making an institution of Wright's creative and prophetic self, and once the Fellowship was established, Taliesin became even more of an "anti-city" on a hill than it had been when only Wright's immediate family lived there. With this act, Wright extended his nuclear family into a creative fellowship which amalgamated elements of Christian pietism, early monasticism, and Arthurian romance.[18] Thus, the fellowship was a nearly self-sufficient community intended both to inspire the large community by its example and to assume leadership in the process of designing an ideal democratic society. It differed from Thoreau's experiment at Walden in being a group enterprise. Yet a similar effort was made to reconstruct life from the essentials, beginning with the acquisition of materials through activities like logging and lime-burning. The same attempt was made to live a totally designed life. Moreover, like Thoreau, Wright suggests that his experiment is an effort to complete the American Revolution: " . . . this search of ours for democratic FORM is revolutionary. Necessarily. But a Revolution utterly essential to the life of this our country" (p. 416).

In the Taliesin Fellowship, Wright again confronted the dilemma of the genius or prophet in a democracy—how much to anticipate the needs and desires of his people. While the impulse behind the community may have been democratic, the actual arrangements were anything but egalitarian: policy was made rather autocratically by Wright and his wife, and eccentricity seems to have been exclusively Wright's privilege.[19] Certainly, the hierarchical arrangement of the community suggests that Wright developed a community which demanded little self-sacrifice from him and permitted much self-assertion. The fellowship represented an extension, not an annihilation, of Wright's self. The dichotomy between individual freedom and social order was one he was never able to resolve comfortably or consistently; as Robert Twombly has observed, "His own life-style extolled the one, his intellectual constructs the other."[20]

The relationship between the fellowship and the commissions executed by Wright in this period is complex. Detractors have argued that Wright exploited his apprentices in order to rebuild his practice; in the sense that the fellowship supplied cheap assistance which multiplied Wright's efforts, it *was* a means toward an architectural end-product. But the commissions also provided both a creative and a financial stimulus to the fellowship; thus, they were a means toward the end of sustaining and developing the community. Ultimately, of course, both were means of releasing Wright's creative and reform energies.

Among other commissions Wright chose for inclusion in this section is the Administration Building for the Johnson Wax Company in Racine, Wisconsin (1936). This building, which he describes as "a socio-economic interpretation of modern business at its top and best" (p. 472), was a kind of counterpart of Taliesin for a commercial community. As with Taliesin, the ideal embodied was conservative in that the building gave clear architectural expression to the administrative hierarchy of this small, paternalistic firm. In a period when unemployment was high and the value of work was being undermined by programs like National Relief, Wright deliberately sought to create a visual symbol of the therapeutic power of work. Like its predecessor, the Larkin Building, this building was intended to reaffirm the quasireligious gospel of work: "Organic architecture designed this great building to be as inspiring a place to work in as any cathedral was in which to worship" (p. 472).

The story of the construction of this building, which required some novel engineering devices, brings Wright back to the theme of testing his ideas. In the manner of a Transcendentalist, he develops a mundane fact into a comprehensive autobiographical symbol: "Nearly every structure I have built, large or small, required some test. Or many. . . . Frequently one test would require others. One experience would lead to the next until the building process extending back over a period of forty-five years resembles the continuous test to which life itself subjects the architect himself" (p. 478). The tests demanded by bureaucratic building commissions reflect their distrust or incomprehension of the genius's designs. But Wright learns to welcome them for two reasons. First, they are a good experimental way of discovering nature's inherent tolerances and equilibriums—which building codes merely attempt to estimate on the basis of conventional building methods. As natural methods of learning natural laws, they are a means of self-education. Second, the tests offer Wright a way of proving himself to skeptics. Thus, they are a means of educating the public about organic design; as a means of communication, they can help to close the gaps between the designer, the contractor, the client, and the commissions.

Book Five might have properly concluded the autobiography, since it portrayed Wright's life as combining the values of the previous four books—family, fellowship, work, and freedom—in a happier form than ever before. But as if to answer questions raised by his critics, Wright chose to add another book, which he introduces in this fashion: "I wish to build a city for Democracy: the Usonian city that is nowhere yet everywhere. Since this search for FORM ends there, the Usonian City, Broadacres, will be the sixth book of 'An Autobiography.' The natural Conclusion" (p. 560). Thus, Wright decided to end this enlarged version of the narrative as he had the earlier one, with speculative prophecy rather than retrospective autobiography.

As its interpreters have been quick to point out, Broadacres City is not a city at all. Rather, it is a section of a national scheme that attempts to resolve the urban-rural polarity with a mix of residential, industrial, agricultural, and service areas in a uniformly populated county. It is not relevant to discuss the plan in detail here, but it is worthwhile to point out that it belongs not in the tradition of Franklin's projects for urban improvement, but in the tradition of the cooperative communities which proliferated in the United States beginning in the mid-nineteenth century. As its name suggests, it was a bit of a conundrum—a paradoxical resolution of some of the polarities of American civilization that had concerned Wright. He was vague about the nature of its economic and political systems, and he failed to specify how the scheme could be realized. But it was not really intended to be practicable; Wright was not interested in the specific economic and social arrangements but in the values and the pattern of life they encouraged.[21] Historically, the plan represents a conservative ideal, for it perpetuates many of the qualities of the rural America he and Sullivan had known as youths. Mythically, it represents a kind of timeless ideal beyond history and yet worth striving for, a combination of two Christian images of Paradise—heaven as a garden and heaven as a strong city.[22]

As a conclusion for the autobiography, it is appropriate in several respects. First, it is self-revelatory. Its comprehensiveness and its prophetic nature reveal Wright's desire to design a total society rather than unrelated buildings. Also, its installation of the architect as the highest authority exposes his personal and professional self-esteem. But it is also a statement about the possibilities of the self in general; it is a scheme designed to ensure that the individual would remain in wholesome contact with his essential powers and in control of his destiny. In Norris Kelly Smith's words, it is "an assertion . .. about Wright's own self and, in general, about a kind of sacred and central selfhood which he believed is being obliterated in the present-day world."[23] Finally, it is a statement about responsibility and self-reliance; like Thoreau, Wright communicates the individual's responsibility to account for himself by the exemplary act of creating his own ideal world.

NOTES

[1] Alan Gowans, *Images of American Living* (New York: J. B. Lippincott, 1964), pp. 356, 416-17.

[2] Frank Lloyd Wright, *An Autobiography* (New York: Longmans, Green, 1932), p. 162.

[3] For a discussion of developmental autobiography, see Wayne Shumaker, *English Autobiography* (Berkeley: University of California Press, 1954), pp. 85-88.

[4] Willard Connely, *Louis Sullivan As He Lived* (New York: Horizon Press, 1960), p. 304.

[5] Sherman Paul, *Louis Sullivan* (Englewood Cliffs, N. J.: Prentice-Hall, 1962), p. 133.

[6] Albert Bush-Brown, *Louis Sullivan* (New York: George Braziller, 1960), p. 7.

[7] Louis Sullivan, *The Autobiography of an Idea* (1924; rpt., New York: Dover, 1956), p. 175. Hereafter page numbers will be cited in the text.

[8] Paul, *Louis Sullivan*, p. 135.

[9] Henry Adams, *The Education of Henry Adams,* ed. Ernest Samuels (1918; rpt., Boston: Houghton Mifflin, 1974), p. 340.

[10] Frank Lloyd Wright, *Genius and the Mobocracy* (1949; rpt., New York: Horizon, 1971), p. 166. Hereafter page numbers will be cited in the text.

[11] Wright, *Autobiography,* p. 314. Hereafter page numbers will be cited in the text.

[12] Robert C. Twombly, *Frank Lloyd Wright* (New York: Harper and Row, 1973), pp. 26, 32-33.

[13] Theodore M. Brown, "Thoreau's Prophetic Architectural Program," *New England Quarterly* 38, no. 1 (1965): 20.

[14] Twombly, *Frank Lloyd Wright,* pp. 132-33.

[15] Ibid., pp. 132, 216.

[16] Ibid., p. 112.

[17] Frank Lloyd Wright, *An Autobiography* (New York: Duell, Sloan, and Pearce, 1943), p. 389. Hereafter page numbers will be cited in the text.

[18] Norris Kelly Smith, *Frank Lloyd Wright* (Englewood Cliffs, N. J.: Prentice-Hall, 1966), p. 124.

[19] Twombly, *Frank Lloyd Wright,* p. 173.

[20] Ibid., p. 177.

[21] Smith, *Frank Lloyd Wright,* pp. 148-52.

[22] Ibid., p. 162.

[23] Ibid., p. 170.

James Dougherty (essay date 1981)

SOURCE: "Broadacre City: Frank Lloyd Wright's Utopia," in *The Centennial Review*, Vol. 25, No. 3, Summer, 1981, pp. 239-56.

[*In the following essay, Dougherty describes Wright's utopian vision of a reintegrated America—"Broadacre City."*]

I

For the last thirty years of his long life, Frank Lloyd Wright's work was directed by his vision of an ideal city, called Broadacre City. Though primarily a domestic architect, and a resident of rural Wisconsin and the Arizona desert, he wanted to plan a city. In *The Disappearing City* (1932) he proclaimed that the megalopolis soon would begin to disappear, absorbed into a new city invisible because it would extend over the entire nation. In 1935 he and the apprentices of his Taliesin Fellowship assembled a twelve-foot-square model of a representative section of Broadacre City, a model displayed first in Rockefeller Center and then in other exhibitions in America and Europe. In the 1940's he revised and expanded his book on the city, now called *When Democracy Builds.* His last book, *The Living City* (1958), amplified once more his vision of a new form of urban life.[1]

Because of the idealism of his plan, and because he held aloof from political programs, Wright's visionary city has been dismissed as utopian; but part of his dream has come true, and "utopian" will not serve to dismiss the rest of it.

Decentralization is the first principle of Broadacres. Wright's plan would redistribute the population of America widely across the continent, affording every citizen at least an acre of ground—more if warranted by climate or personal need. Although Wright endowed owning and tilling land with that moral mystique once invoked by Jefferson and Crèvecoeur, he did not yearn for a nation of simple cultivators, uniform in their enjoyment of a decent but minimum competence. He proposed to retain all the diversity of urban life, scattering factories and skyscrapers across the landscape, providing regional markets and local centers of culture, entertainment, and education. His plan further provides for diversity in mode of life: minimum housing on single-acre plots, small farms with more complex buildings, luxury housing near country clubs; single dwellings, quadriplexes, small and large apartment buildings. Broadacres *is* a city, he insists; telecommunications and convenient motor transport have altered the scale according to which we must measure propinquity. A man's neighborhood may measure twenty miles across, but within it he will find all the benefactions of urban life. And yet within it are none of the evils of that life—the overcrowding, the traffic, the alienation from nature and creative work, the social and economic oppression, all of which Wright associated with the present concentrated form of the city and with the economic and political interests—rentiers and autocrats—that thrive upon a concentrated population. In the great city, machines use men, and devour them. In Broadacres, men use machines to enhance their own freedom. Wright called his new America "Usonia."

This vision of a garden city, where work does not enslave man to machine, certainly seems indebted to late-nineteenth-century utopian novels by Edward Bellamy (*Looking Backward*), Samuel Butler (*Erewhon*), and William Morris (*News from Nowhere*), all of whom Wright mentions in his essays. And a manifest lack of specifics about how politically to accomplish this redistribution of land, population and industry has led unfriendly critics to label his city as a utopia. Morton and Lucia White so called it, as they dismissed Wright as yet another of those American

intellectuals unable to come to terms with the city.[2] Robert Fishman more sympathetically associated Broadacres with Karl Mannheim's definition of utopia as "a coherent program for action arising out of thought that 'transcends the immediate situation'"; however, Fishman noted that Wright proposed no scheme to mediate between his transcendent vision and political reality.[3]

A recent review of forty years' reaction to Broadacres by architects and planners noted that Wright's design has been more severely criticized by those whose views of the city matured before 1969, while younger planners have begun to recognize that the diffused city, however unworkable as a unified architectural design, is nevertheless a socio-economic fact plainly evident in such western cities as Phoenix and Los Angeles and in the periphery of every other American city.[4] The centerless congeries of low-density housing, industrial parks, and regional markets (now known as shopping malls) is not a vision, but reality; while Jane Jacobs' and Lewis Mumford's dense, various and urbane city neighborhoods are rapidly becoming visionary and nostalgic—perhaps utopian. Wright himself understood this, in *The Living City* claiming that his city was not a utopia because "my interest lies in sincerely appraising . . . elemental changes I see existing or surely coming." "The free city," he says, "is already here all around us in the haphazard making . . . all about us and no plan." "America needs no help to Broadacre City. It will haphazard build itself. Why not plan it?"[5]

Decentralization indeed we have; in that regard Wright has proved to be not a utopian, but a prophet. Plan, however, we do not have. The diffusion of the American city has brought us only the spoliation of farmland and village, engulfed in dunes of housing whose pretensions as architecture and as habitation are false beyond any horror that Wright at his most saturnine could have foreseen. And while Wright had hoped that his "regional markets" would foster an indigenous regional culture, instead today's shopping malls thrive on a homogeneous formula of chains and franchises, circumscribing and trivializing human needs. Further, the recent diffusion of metropolitan life has been largely residential, imposing on suburban wage-earners a burden of vacuous commutation from which the thrill of the Open Road has altogether vanished. To look at the Broadacre model today in Taliesin in Wisconsin is to see a familiar suburban landscape, a dream of decentralization come true. But to read the explanatory notices accompanying the model, and to read Wright's books, is to discover that the physical structures are only the bodying-forth of an inner, spiritual revolution, with a consequent socio-economic revolution, that has certainly not been accomplished.

Such a revolution, Wright acknowledged, might be long in coming. But, he said, "We can have a good architecture meantime by way of good architects working for good individuals. We may have valuable exemplars without waiting for the entire mass to come along."[6] From the 1930's onward, Wright thought of his commissioned buildings, especially the residences, as such exemplars.[7]

Oneida and New Harmony, in nineteenth-century America, had been conceived also as the yeast by which a whole society might be leavened; that Wright should see single-family dwellings, not small communities, as his exemplars reflects both his own practice as a domestic architect and also the importance of the home in his ideal city: "The true center (the only centralization allowable) in Usonian democracy, is the individual in his true Usonian family home."[8] But more, it reveals Wright's sense of a correspondence between the individual, his home, and his city, an identity in form which it is the architect's business to discover and to enhance. In that identity of form, and in the role of the architect, we find the true nature of Wright's utopianism.

II

The earliest versions of the Broadacre City proposal speak of a "county architect," an officer wielding extraordinary powers to redistribute land and to regulate its use. "The agent of the state in all matters of land allotment or improvement, or in matters affecting the harmony of the whole, is the architect."[9] Wright subsequently effaced this commissar-like figure from the accounts of his city, saying more blandly that "Architecture would, necessarily, again become the natural backbone (and architects the broad essential leaders) of such cultural endeavor."[10] Nevertheless, Wright's critics have focussed much attention on the county architect, one calling him a "Philosopher-King of the County Seat" and questioning how his authority could be reconciled with the freedom of the Usonian citizen, another connecting this "odd mixture of radical equalitarianism and autocracy" with the comparable figures of John Humphrey Noyes at Oneida and Robert Owen at New Lanark.[11]

When one asks political questions about this architectural vision, it is natural to conclude that the county architect must be the local agent of a political force powerful enough to uproot railroads, relocate industries, annual corporate landholding, and redistribute populations, all to provide greater personal liberty for its citizens. In Broadacres, it might seem, one is compelled to be free. Yet such questions appear to miss Wright's point, for his books do not even address them. This suggests that his city is utopian not in the political sense invented by Engels to dismiss Wright's nineteenth-century predecessors, but in an imaginative sense linking him with the tradition of Plato and Thomas More. It is not Wright's model, but Wright's words, that specify the utopianism of Broadacres. The "plan" he called for is not a political program, but a regeneration of the human spirit.

One of Wright's critics has said, "Frank Lloyd Wright would probably not have been happy in Broadacre City."[12] Nor would Plato in his Republic, nor More in Utopia, if we were to take as literal proposals the political institutions and processes they describe. Discussing the implicit tyranny that permeates not only the classical utopias but also more recent works like *Looking Backward* and *Walden Two,* Northrop Frye warns us "A utopia should not be read simply as a description of a most perfect state, even if the author believes it to be one. Utopian thought is imaginative, with its roots in literature, and the literary imagination is less concerned with achieving ends than with visualizing possibilities. . . . [The utopian writer] is communicating a vision to his readers, not sharing a power or fantasy dream with them."[13]

The key to that vision is to be found not in the word "decentralize," the process which architectural plans and models can represent, but in the term which Wright always twinned with it, "reintegrate," an ideal which the model can only indirectly symbolize, and only to those who know the values that Wright attributes to the city in his essays. Reintegration is not merely a physical matter of uniting workplace with residence or field with factory. Rather it is a vision of spiritual integrity, of moral and psychological harmony, set against the fragmentation of technopolitan consciousness. To convey this ideal, Wright turns to the utopia, a dialectical mode in which ethical alternatives can be clearly distinguished and made to comment on each other. In utopian writing, the here and now is limned in gray or black, while the there and then shines forth in rose and gold. More's *Utopia* begins with a vivid account of the evils and injustices of Tudor England; and then we hear Hythloday's tale of an island that lies opposite to England both geographically and morally. The space- and time-travellers of nineteenth-century utopian romances are always harking back upon the evils of the place they left behind. So Wright's books on his ideal city devote their first third to a prophetic denunciation of the evils of present society. Conditions of modern work and dwelling have alienated man from his work and have betrayed the promise of American Democracy: he attacks "rent" (on land, on money, on ideas in the form of patents); he denounces the city for its demoralizing crowd, its acceleration of production and consumption, and its substitution of false, "vicarious" pleasures for true satisfactions; he condemns mechanization under conditions which dehumanize the worker while multiplying benefits for the rentier. These themes bespeak Wright's acknowledged affiliation with Morris, Bellamy, Thorstein Veblen and Henry George, reflecting the nineteenth-century view of the city as a dark satanic mill, a paleotechnic engine which reduced its human attendants to grotesque fragments—"hands," or feet or eyes—and eventually consumed them. "City" meant the atrophy of all human qualities not useful in economic survival, including those senses of freedom, moral integrity, and esthetic consciousness which Wright held most dear. He propounds Broadacres as More did Utopia, as a standard against which to measure the wickedness of his place and time. It is a counter-city, the symbol of reintegration.

Unlike Bellamy and Butler, the Fourierists and the Shakers, Wright does not propose to reintegrate man by reformulating institutions. On that point his utopia tends toward an arcadian anarchy. The integrity of Broadacres is the integrity of its single citizens (and of the family, in Wright's view the only natural institution). Nevertheless, Wright's utopia is not completely atomistic: the individual does find his place in larger social forms. As Frye has observed, many ideal commonwealths depend on an assumed analogy between the individual and the social order.[14] The proper way to read this analogy is "inward," understanding the utopian society as a macrocosmic symbol of the single human being—as in the *Republic,* where Socrates undertakes his depiction of a commonwealth specifically so that the qualities of the just man may be more easily comprehended because "written large" in the hierarchies and operations of the city. In the *Timaeus* Plato expounds his theory of the cosmos as a series of nested, corresponding spheres, world within Idea, earth within heavens, man within earth, so that his analogy of state with man appears not fanciful but necessary. In Wright's neoplatonic world too, the integrated human being is contained within its two isomorphs, the Usonian house and the Usonian state. It is in this correspondential sense that the Usonian house, sensitively designed to complement the family it houses, can be seen as the "exemplar" of the Usonian state. And likewise the city is the figure of both organic man and natural house. What might seem political compulsion directed through the county architect, or a behaviorist faith in architecture's power to determine attitude and conduct, can be better understood—if the analogy is read "inward"—as the spiritual process of setting one's house in order. In *The Living City* Wright says:

> [Man's] own nature may be so attuned to the nature of the cosmos that he in himself would be a new, more vital, kind of success. Only through such interior organic process is he (or are we) going to be able to build the city of democracy.[15]

III

The specific form of Wright's neoplatonism is that of the American transcendentalists, who are so often cited in his prose as influences or sources of mottos and epigraphs. *When Democracy Builds* begins by quoting Whitman's "Song of the Universal"; *The Living City* ends with an excerpt from Emerson's "Farming," which calls the countryman the noblest and most creative of men. And it has become a commonplace to observe that Wright's architectural style, that "sense of space in spaciousness," was anticipated by Thoreau's description of his ideal house:

> I sometimes dream of a larger and more populous house, standing in a golden age, of enduring materials, and without gingerbread work, which shall still consist of only one room. . . . A house whose inside is as open and manifest as a bird's nest, and you cannot go in at the front door and out at the back without seeing some of its inhabitants; where to be a guest is to be presented with the freedom of the house, and not to be carefully excluded from seven eighths of it, shut up in a particular cell, and told to make yourself at home there,—in solitary confinement.[16]

However, it should be understood that Thoreau too inhabited a concentrically linked symbolic world, and that earlier in his book he had written of the house as the image of the soul:

> It would be worth the while to build still more deliberately than I did, considering, for instance, what foundation a door, a window, a cellar, a garret, have in the nature of man. . . . What of architectural beauty I now see, I know has gradually grown from within outward, out of the necessities and character of the indweller, who is the only builder,— out of some unconscious truthfulness, and nobleness, without ever a thought for the appearance.[17]

In the organic cosmology of Emerson, Whitman, Thoreau and Wright, the world and the soul correspond point for point; whatever intermediary structures man creates— poem or house or state—should tally with that natural correspondence. To affirm this linking of inner and outer worlds, Wright's essays repeatedly conjoin Lao-tze ("The reality of the building does not consist in the four walls and roof but in the space within to be lived in") with Jesus Christ ("The Kingdom of God is within you"). The kingdom within is to be spacious, harmonious, organically unified; the space of the house, and the style of the city, are larger images of that inner kingdom. In that spiritual house there are no impervious partitions, no walling-in or walling-out; in that city there is no overdevelopment of one area at the expense of others, no preference of one function over another. In that kingdom all the powers of the whole are available to each of its parts. Wright's epithet for Broadacres—"the city that is nowhere or everywhere"—can be seen to refer not only to a process of decentralization, but also to the spiritual inclusiveness—nowhere yet everywhere—which is at the heart of his city metaphor.[18]

Now Wright's "county architect" can be understood as the presiding genius of that inner kingdom, the equivalent of Whitman's prototypical "Self," Thoreau's or Emerson's Poet. Wright sometimes called this figure the artifex, the one "who by manual toil or by concentration of superior ability upon actual production, physical, aesthetic, intellectual or moral—render[s] 'value received' to human life."[19] Elsewhere he calls him the poet: "We speak of genius as though it were the extrusion of some specialty or other. No, the quality is not there. Find genius, and you will find a poet."[20] In the divided state of man, the artifex is a specialist, a professional—an architect, a writer, a philosopher. In Usonia, the artifex is a power common to all human beings and freely exercised by all. This poetic power, he explains in his *Autobiography,* is the capacity to discover "the nature-pattern in the expression of actual construction."[21] This is the Emersonian hero, that universal man who discerns the form latent in the heart of nature, and utters it as a creation with an architecture of its own. Civilization owes its existence to the artifex, for it is he who has created its true capital wealth—not tangible goods, but those usable patterns which the imagination half discovers in nature, and half creates: epics and symphonies, the principles of aerodynamics and the design of the transistor, the logarithmic spiral and the spiral of the Guggenheim Museum. In his dystopian description of the old centralized megalopolis, Wright portrays the artifex as the victim of a materialist economic system which rewards not the creation of forms but only the production of commodities derived from those forms.—While in Broadacres, the artifex is the ordinary citizen, or, as Wright would have put it, the extraordinary citizen.

"Man lives in a fragmented world," said Berdyaev, "and dreams of a world reintegrated. The hallmark of utopia is wholeness. Utopia is destined to surmount fragmentation and restore wholeness."[22] If fragmentation is a perennial motive for Utopian imagining, it was an evil historically acute to Emerson and to Wright. Industrial civilization, based on specialization of function and division of process, had shaped the city in its own false image. In its clutch, human personality disintegrated. Man in the factory, Emerson wrote, is reduced to a hand; the mechanic becomes a machine himself. "Out of the Machine that his city has become," says Wright, "no citizen can create more than more machinery. . . . He has traded the Book of Creation for emasculation by way of the Substitute."[23] The hero whom both writers propose is Man undivided, Man redeemed from the machine.

Emerson never gave full treatment to a utopian enlargement of his reintegrated man,[24] but Wright spent almost thirty years sketching, modeling, and describing Broadacre City. It is the macrocosm of that integrated, unspecialized man which he, like Emerson, believed we all might become. In Broadacres the citizen is at once farmer, factory worker, builder, artisan, and patron of arts and education. Broadacres is where man and machine strike a balance, machinery used not to accelerate production or to enslave and disintegrate man, but to lighten and simplify work and to enhance the craftsman-like use of materials. Broadacres is where work and leisure are so re-defined as not to seem antithetical, since in Wright's Gesellian economy it is consumption, not production, that dictates the conditions of labor, and in his Ruskinian culture the public demand is not for quantity but for quality. Broadacres is where the farmstead nurtures the integrity of the family, man's natural social setting; where the self-reliant citizen is accommodated within an undemanding democratic society. Where not only the physical but also the cultural distinctions between city and country are effaced, Broadacres providing both the country's intimacy with nature and—thanks partly to telecommunications, partly to regional decentralization—the city's opportunities for entertainment, education and service. Broadacres is man in full possession of all his faculties.

> If you can see the varied, multiple parts all thus contributing to a great dramatic whole in which you sense the repose of individual human contentment and the exuberance of plenty—the life of the imagination truly aesthetic, in the over-all view from wherever you may happen to stand—then you will get a glimpse of the country-loving life in agronomy of the new Usonian city.[25]

Northrop Frye distinguishes the *utopia* proper, with its emphasis on hierarchy, industry, and urbanized man's ascendancy over nature, from the *arcadia,* which stresses simplicity and equality, leisure and art, and the integration

of man with nature.[26] One further integrative function of Wright's symbolic city is to overcome even this disjunction, providing a mechanized arcadia, where the Cougar lies down with the lamb.

In a utopia that unites man and machine, art and labor, nature and society, the representative citizen is indeed the architect. As Robert Fishman has pointed out, the architect is both artist and engineer:[27] he works with the stuff of dreams and with the tolerances of steel and plywood. He reconciles his personal vision with social purposes.[28] Discerning the patterns integral in his materials and in the site, he fabricates a space that is natural to man, an interior space both physical and metaphysical. "This new sense of Architecture as integral-pattern . . . may awaken the United States to fresh beauty," Wright declared in his *Autobiography;* "Integral-pattern becomes 'the sound of the Usonian heart.'"[29] This architect plans not for a county, but for a state of mind. He might indeed be called the Philosopher King, who in Plato's allegory symbolizes the human power to comprehend Form and to translate it into personal spiritual harmony. This is the architecture, says Wright, of man's soul.[30]

IV

When utopian planners turn to actual physical design, their instinct has been to produce radiocentric, symmetrical cities: Plato's semi-utopian Atlantis, More's Amaurote, Campanella's City of the Sun, Considerant's Phalanx, Ebenezer Howard's Garden City. It is easy to postulate, in their resemblance to the Jungian mandala, some link between the utopian imagination and a search for symbols of personal integrity. Wright's model of course eschews such centripetal physical designs. Nevertheless, some details of the model do use physical form to express spiritual aspirations. Of course there are the linear highway and the broad regional field, which were to Wright the "integral-pattern" of freedom. A "Temple of Universal Worship," three concentric hexagons encompassing a circle, reflects Wright's belief that "religion is necessary to good life and work," serving "the depths and the breadths of the universal soul," to restore "complete human harmony."[31] And the one-acre allotments are so platted that each takes the form of the Golden Section, that ancient Pythagorean symbol of personal and cosmic harmony.[32] The true center of Broadacre City, once again, is the Kingdom Within.

Broadacres may have no center save in each citizen's heart and hearth; but a delimited model representing four square miles must have a physical center also. The model was built in four sections, each six feet square. What did Wright place at the intersection of these quadrants, as the focus of his display? If automotive decentralization were the paramount theme of Broadacre City, the linear highway would pass through the model's center, to dramatize its role as connector, axis of design, and symbol of liberation. But rather it is set at the extreme edge; and at the model's heart stand the three main schools of this district. Education is an essential theme in Wright's books on his city, as it is in most utopian writing. Condemning present schools and universities as too big and too specialized, he proposes small, unspecialized, practical schools, and "design centers" where apprentices study with a master. The revolution that will bring about Broadacres, he writes, is not a violent political stroke but "earnest educational revolution."[33] An education in natural patterning, in the meaning of work, in the esthetic use of industrial techniques: an education in the architecture of man's world.

Education not only goes on *in* Broadacres; it goes on *through* Broadacres, through Wright's description of his city. Northrop Frye has observed that "the literary convention of an ideal state is really a by-product of a systematic view of education."[34] In Plato's *Republic,* the ideal city is introduced frankly as a heuristic device; Campanella's City of the Sun and Skinner's Walden II are preoccupied with the instruction of the young. (And how many utopian communities, their millennial fever spent, have like Owen's New Harmony settled at last for some reform in education!) Broadacre City was conceived about the time when Wright founded his own educational enterprise, the Taliesin Fellowship. The model was built by his apprentices, and was for a time a prescribed part of their course of study. Today it is displayed on the wall of a studio adjacent to the drafting room at Taliesin North in Wisconsin. Wright once said that with some money for food and materials, he and the Fellowship "might have started Broadacre City right then and there, ourselves."[35]

Like the pylon that stands in its civic center as "Beacon to the Lost Tribes of a Continent," Broadacres was articulated by Wright to counterpoint his diatribe against the evils of a dystopian over-urbanized society, to symbolize his faith in the harmonious development of all of an individual's human faculties, and to actualize his vision of moral integrity, his "truth against the world." Like any teacher, he redeems his materials—in this case fields, factories, shops, roads and dwellings—from the random disorder of experience, and ranges them into an intelligible, unified structure. He asks, Socratically, what foundation a city has in the nature of man. When Judith Shklar identified the significance of More's utopia, she described Wright's city as well:

> Utopia was a model, an ideal pattern that invited contemplation and judgment but did not entail any other activity. It is a perfection that the mind's eye recognizes as true and which is described as such, and so serves as a standard of moral judgment. . . . As such it is an expression of the craftsman's desire for perfection and permanence. That is why utopia, the moralist's artifact, is of necessity a changeless harmonious whole, in which a shared recognition of truth unites all the citizens.[36]

Shklar's last two sentences here suggest another characteristic of utopian imagining that Broadacres may embody. Utopias occur in clusters, one germinating another, as *Looking Backward* did *News from Nowhere* and a score of ephemeral responses. Epochs of acute political discord, like the Renaissance and the later nineteenth century, may generate utopias not only to focus political debate but to symbolize a lost and much-desired social stability. The 1930's, when Wright designed Broadacres, was likewise rife with utopias and model cities, each offering at once a solution to, and an escape from, the confusions of that era. Le Corbusier's are perhaps the most memorable, tracing between two wars his search for a principle of social authority. Further, utopias as macrocosmic symbols of perfection and permanence often seem to spring from times of dissolution in the lives of their creators. *Looking Backward* unites its reforming zeal with a valetudinarian's desire to rise from his bed transformed by a long mesmeric sleep. *News from Nowhere,* written six years before Morris's death and five months before the final collapse of his health, presents a hero who longs to regain his youth in that childlike land where years are not a burden. The ideal city may become for its creator the symbol of an escape from confusion, a deliverance from time.[37]

With its avowed correspondence between the nation and the single soul, Broadacre City had an evident personal significance for Wright. Conceived literally in the desert, at the end of a decade and a half of great personal turmoil and professional neglect, Broadacres symbolized both a still-tentative grasp at personal reintegration and a bid for recognition as not merely a domestic architect but a planner who could engineer for all America, a nation gripped by a depression he attributed to forces inherent in the industrial megalopolis. Undertaken when he was past sixty, Broadacres became the lodestar of Wright's long old age, his image of life's culmination, a millennial city. "In the organic city," he wrote, "we might live indefinitely! . . . Both buildings and city should be more truly [a] defense against time."[38] And so they are, for Wright's housing plans imply a timeless, static relationship of citizen, house and land. First, acreage allotments are not the disposable property of those who dwell there. They are inalienable and indivisible (though evidently they can be reassigned by the county architect). They seem not subject to the temporal rhythms of inhabitation—to changes in employment or family size, or in capacity for work; to wanderlust, or migration, or the desire to cluster near water, friends or scenery. Also, each house is built by its residents, to reflect their particular needs and temperaments. Such a dwelling might grow, but it is not foreseen that it should later shrink, or that others might someday live there who had no share in planning or building it. To account for this inflexibility, one might invoke Wright's frequently authoritarian relationship with his personal clients, or reflect on whether the absolute ownership of land has proven an unmixed blessing to America; but also one might recognize that Broadacres was for Wright a symbol of completion and immortality, a city where time would be no more.

Broadacres also stood as a symbol of fulfillment in some of the architect's other books. In 1932 he completed the first version of his autobiography, a casting-back over his life which organized its narrative around a series of images of harmony and integration, some of them persons (his mother, his first family, Olgivanna and his second family) and some of them places (the Wisconsin valley of his boyhood, Chicago, Japan, Taliesin); its last section, "Freedom," a distillation of sixty years' learning, is an indictment of urban and industrial slavery, dominated by the counter-image of Broadacre City. In the same year, 1932, he published the first account of that city, *The Disappearing City.* In 1943 he extended the memoir with a chapter of incidents from the preceding decade, and published privately a sixth "book" of the autobiography, titled *Broadacre City,* not a description of his city at all, but a political and economic essay, for which the city evidently stood as a symbol of culminated wisdom, like the Celestial City at the end of *The Pilgrim's Progress.* In 1945 he incorporated *Broadacre City* into a third edition of the *Autobiography,* and published *When Democracy Builds,* an amplification of *The Disappearing City* and the most readable of his essays on Broadacres. In 1958, as his final testament, he issued *The Living City,* a work enhanced by the inclusion of many plans, sketches and photographs of the city model and its Usonian dwellings, though at the same time marred by a line-for-line revision of the text in which Wright, now striving to say everything in one last book, overloaded or redistributed the members of every sentence without regard for the relative importance of their content. In those same years, Broadacres became for him the very landscape of his mind, like Eliot's London or Faulkner's Yoknapatawpha.[39] The 1935 model had included some of his then-unrealized plans for both high-rise and two-story apartments and for a luxurious private home. New sketches for the 1958 book incorporated into Broadacres a full score of his projects, both realized and unrealized, from barges for Lake Tahoe to the Price Tower in Bartlesville, to a "Steel Cathedral" for Manhattan. The style of the sketching became futurist, almost surreal. "The drawings," his biographer Robert Twombly has said, "represent Wright's last attempt at synthesis, his ultimate depiction of America as he would have planned it."[40] Wright had given his life the archetypal image of a journey from a paradisal valley, through the cities of the plain and through the desert, to a celestial city, harmonious as music, where all that had seemed lost would be gathered together.

"This commonwealth we have been founding in the realm of discourse," says Glaucon near the end of the *Republic,* "—I think it nowhere exists on earth." No, replies Socrates, it does not; "but perhaps there is a pattern set up in the heavens for one who desires to see it and, seeing it, to found one in himself."[41] Broadacre City, Wright insisted, would be everywhere and nowhere. In the late 1920's he appraised the impact of the machine on the city's fabric—the auto, the truck, the telephone, electrification. He saw that the energy of the city was almost exhausted, that soon it would collapse inward upon itself and disappear. Today we can see the lineaments of Broadacres around every city, beginning just where the old city's taxation area ends. Decentralization is indeed everywhere. Reintegration, however, is not everywhere. It is, as the word utopia itself reminds us, nowhere. But,

as Plato told Glaucon, this is not to say that it does not exist. It exists in a twelve-foot-square model in a quiet studio in Wisconsin. It exists in the forty or fifty "exemplars" of Wright's Usonian buildings—for we must remember that in his concentric imagination the house is the microcosm of the city, exhibiting the city's qualities on a scale that is easy to comprehend. Primarily, though, it exists as utopia always does, as an articulated vision of truth and integrity, set against the sometimes false and always chaotic world of our everyday experience. Broadacres is the communal form that Wright created to mediate between the patterns of Nature and the architecture of the Soul.

NOTES

[1] *The Disappearing City* (New York: William Farquhar Payson, 1932); "Broadacre City: A New Community Plan," *The Architectural Record,* 77.4 (April 1935), 243-254; "Broadacre City," *The American Architect,* 146 (May 1935), 55-63; When *Democracy Builds* (Chicago: University of Chicago Press, 1945); *The Living City* (1958; rpt. New York: The New American Library, 1970). I am grateful to the officers of the Frank Lloyd Wright Fellowship for letting me examine the Broadacre model at Taliesin, Spring Green, Wisconsin, and to Charles Montooth of the Fellowship for discussing it with me.

[2] *The Intellectual vs. the City* (1962; rpt. New York: The New American Library, 1964), p. 199.

[3] *Urban Utopias of the Twentieth Century* (New York: Basic Books, 1977), pp. x, 146. John Sergeant disagrees, arguing in *Frank Lloyd Wright's Usonian Houses* (New York: Whitney Library of Design, 1976), that Wright was firmly in touch with the progressive thinking of the 1930's.

[4] Stephen Grabow, "Frank Lloyd Wright and the American City: The Broadacres Debate," *The Journal of the American Institute of Planners,* 43.2 (April 1977), 122; see also Sergeant, pp. 129-134.

[5] pp. 230, 120, 159.

[6] Baker Brownell and Frank Lloyd Wright, *Architecture and Modern Life* (New York: Harper & Brothers, 1937), p. 331.

[7] Sergeant, p. 138.

[8] *The Living City,* p. 231.

[9] "Broadacre City: A New Community Plan," *The Architectural Record,* 246-247.

[10] *The Living City,* p. 215.

[11] Fishman, p. 143; Norris Kelly Smith, *Frank Lloyd Wright: A Study in Architectural Content* (Englewood Cliffs, N.J.: Prentice-Hall Inc., 1966), p. 152.

[12] Grabow, p. 119.

[13] "Varieties of Literary Utopias," *Daedalus,* 94.2 (Spring 1965), 329-330.

[14] pp. 331-332. In Plato's view, he writes, "the disciplined individual is the only free individual. . . . He is free because a powerful will is ready to spring into action to help reason do whatever it sees fit. . . . [But] it is true that what frees the individual seems to enslave society, and that something goes all wrong with human freedom when we take an analogy between individual and social order literally."

[15] p. 244.

[16] *Walden,* ed. Sherman Paul (Boston: Houghton Mifflin Co., 1960), pp. 166-167 ("House-Warming").

[17] pp. 31-32 ("Economy").

[18] A similarly correspondential world is propounded in the poetry of William Blake, whose name appears twice on the signboards accompanying the Broadacres model, once as "required reading" for those who would understand his city, once among those social and economic reformers—Tolstoi, Kropotkin, Gesell—whom Broadacres "commemorates." Though it is hard to imagine Wright reading patiently through *Jerusalem* or *Milton,* he might have found there a vision of correspondences, an urgency of rhetoric, and a sense of psycho-political mission similar to those offered by the more accessible (and quotable) Americans.

[19] *The Disappearing City,* p. 10.

[20] "Foreword Concluded," *Architectural Forum,* 68.1 (January 1938), 101. Then he quotes Whitman's description of the poet as the "equable man," from the 1855 Preface to *Leaves of Grass.* See also *A Testament* (New York: Horizon Press, 1957), p. 192: "We must recognize the creative architect as poet and interpreter of life."

[21] *An Autobiography* (New York: Horizon Press, 1977), pp. 371-372.

[22] Nicolas Berdyaev, *Royaume de l'Esprit et Royaume de César,* trans. Philippe Sabant (Neuchâtel: Delachaux & Niestlé, 1951), p. 166; cited in Robert C. Elliott, *The Shape of Utopia* (Chicago: The University of Chicago Press, 1970), p. 90.

[23] *When Democracy Builds,* p. 1.

[24] Michael Cowan has traced the outlines of Emerson's Utopia in *City of the West: Emerson, America, and Urban Metaphor* (New Haven: Yale University Press, 1967). The first part of chapter 5, "The Organic City," seems closely to describe Broadacres.

[25] *The Living City,* p. 98.

[26] pp. 338-339.

[27] pp. 106-109.

[28] Norris Kelly Smith, pp. 58-59, questions how successful Wright was in doing so.

[29] p. 374.

[30] *The Living City,* p. 240.

[31] *When Democracy Builds,* p. 107.

[32] Each acre, according to Wright's annotations of the model, measures 165 x 264 feet: see "Broadacre City: A New Community Plan," *The Architectural Record,* 251. "Pythagoras" is the first of the spiritual influences which Wright acknowledges in a postscript to his autobiography (p. 617), though it seems to have been the philosopher's disciples who attributed spiritual significance to the .618 ratio. Wright's *Autobiography* everywhere displays a Pythagorean faith in cosmic harmony: "The pattern of reality *is* supergeometrical, casting a spell or a charm over any geometry" (p. 181).

[33] *When Democracy Builds,* p. 44; *The Living City,* p. 85. See Fishman, pp. 136-138, for an interpretive summary.

[34] pp. 335-336.

[35] *Autobiography,* p. 439.

[36] "The Political Theory of Utopia: From Melancholy to Nostalgia," *Daedalus,* 94.2 (Spring, 1965), 371. See also Robert C. Twombly, *Frank Lloyd Wright: An Interpretive Biography* (New York: Harper & Row, 1973): "Broadacres City was a platform for criticism and a standard against which to measure prevailing conditions" (p. 183). And Norris Kelly Smith: "Broadacre City . . . should not be looked upon as a practicable plan for social action but as a declaration of ultimate principle" (p. 165).

[37] In financial ruin and artistic obscurity, Le Corbusier designed his Contemporary City; Louis Napoleon solaced himself in exile with plans for a new Paris; even Adolf Hitler in prison in 1924 planned a grandiose center for Berlin.

[38] *The Living City,* pp. 82, 111; Wright italicized the first four words of this quotation.

[39] Twombly, p. 305, suggests this analogy. He and Smith, p. 153, both catalog the buildings which Wright incorporated into Broadacre City.

[40] p. 305.

[41] *The Republic,* trans. Francis MacDonald Cornford (1945; rpt., New York: Oxford University Press, 1969), pp. 319-320 (ix. 592).

John Roche (essay date 1988)

SOURCE: "Democratic Space: The Ecstatic Geography of Walt Whitman and Frank Lloyd Wright," in *Walt Whitman Quarterly Review,* Vol. 6, No. 1, Summer, 1988, pp. 16-32.

[*In the following essay, Roche considers the shared conception of America's limitless space held by Walt Whitman and Wright, and discusses other affinities in their geographical outlook.*]

> The map speaks across the barriers of language; . . .
> A map invites attention alike synoptically and
>   analytically.
> —Carl Sauer, "The Education of a
>   Geographer"

Walt Whitman is our great poet of geography—a fact readily apparent to any of his countrymen as soon as they read him. Whitman was an augur, but of a discrete, American type, absorbed ecstatically in considerations of spatial form even as contemporary Europe was either attuned to the approach of the temporal shock waves of intellectual and political revolution, or hearing, with Arnold, the "long, withdrawing roar" of a secure past.

Whitman could also look back. He was among the first historians of the city of Brooklyn, author of *Brooklyniana.* And he certainly spoke of the future in his familiar prophetic mode. But Walt, as an American, was comfortable with space, which represented to him, as to Jefferson or Boone, Greeley or Benton, both a divine gift and a "safety valve"[1] for alleviating poverty and political instability.

Though Whitman usually remained ensconced in the insular space of Manhattan, or at other points along the continent's easternmost edge, he yet provided the American people with their first articulate mental map. In *Leaves of Grass,* the vectors all point westwards, as though the continent were a tilted billiards table. Yet, paradoxically, the image of Mannahatta is superimposed over the whole of this non-Euclidean and defiantly subjective map. By "Mannahatta," an Algonquin term, Whitman refers to a united and transfigured Manhattan-Brooklyn. Mannahatta is the idiosyncratic city of Whitman's experience, the ex-reporter's record of an increasingly energetic and cosmopolitan Eastern city. But it is, simultaneously, the type for the democratic cities, the New Mannahattas, which would emerge in the Western, "dominion-heart of America."[2] These would grow more easily from their aboriginal ground, he believed, than had their predecessor; more easily admitting that direct interaction between man and nature, as between man and man, which Whitman longed for in spite of his enjoyment of the "Broadway Pageant."

Frank Lloyd Wright, too, "was born an American / child of the ground and space, welcoming spaciousness as a modern human need,"[3] as he himself said in 1936. Wright as a native Midwesterner was especially situated to perceive and welcome that spaciousness. Despite childhood stays in Massachusetts and Rhode Island, he returned frequently, and by his eleventh birthday, permanently, to his Wisconsin birthplace. Speaking of this move, Wright said that, "fate took me out to the prairies of the United States of America—Usonia let us say—and there in the tall grass I grew up . . ."[4]

This idyllic scene is not so different from Whitman's descriptions of his own boyhood—Paumanok even had "the spreading Hempstead plains, then (1830-40) quite prairie-like"[5]—yet Wright's experience is of an even vaster space. Both men shared a Westward tropism, but Wright lacked the antipodal attraction which Whitman felt for the East, especially for the New York islands.[6]

Wright's imagined city, Broadacre City, was grounded therefore in the physical and cultural terrain of the Midwest. Though attempting, like Whitman, to set a pattern for a new and more democratic city for all America, Wright rejected the Eastern model whose elements Whitman had, in large part, incorporated as he looked towards the West and the future. Where Whitman sensed exuberance and egalitarian fraternity, Wright saw (a half-century later) congestion and stratification. Wright was unapologetic in claiming that "America begins west of Buffalo. The greatest and most nearly beautiful city of our young nation is probably Chicago."[7]

If any discrete city contributed to the continuous city which Broadacres represents it is Chicago, which at the turn of the century taught the nation about modern office building, effective occupation of lakeside sites, and gracious suburban living. But it is the prairie itself which is the greatest contributor.

Broadacre City stretches out like that great shelf which extends westward from the Mississippi as far as the Rockies of the U.S. and Canada, and southward across Texas to the Sonora desert. A twelve square-foot scale model is all that was "built," and that represented only four square miles of this vast city. To locate Broadacres one needs a continental map, for it is intended to occupy at least all of the contiguous U.S.; and one needs maps that indicate the existing topography, rainfall, agricultural patterns, and ethnocultural concentrations, for Broadacre City is meant to be built with all of these conditions in mind. The population density, for instance, although always much closer to that of a small town or village than a typical city, would vary according to the terrain and its agricultural suitability. The unbroken line to the horizon that one sees from the prairie is the prime image representing Broadacres. It connects with the "Earth line" or "Horizontal" principle that Wright spoke of in connection to his building, a factor immediately recognizable in his early "Prairie-style" homes, and more subtly in later works like Taliesin West or the Marin County Center. Broadacres is to be, no less than the nation, connected architecturally and politically to the land.

Wright attempted an interweaving here of contrasting American ideals. He introduced extreme privacy by granting to each family a house of their own on a mini-mum of two "broad acres" of good land, yet made use of the most up-to-date innovations in transportation and communications—from the automobile and radio in the thirties, to the helicopter in his fifties revision—to en-courage community. He, in fact, was anticipating the "hub-less" cities made possible for the eighties and nine-ties by the computer revolution, although he would have strongly disagreed with the economic stratification and cultural poverty prevailing in our day, as he did of the ugly, sprawling suburbs of the post-war period which parodied his planning vision even as their "ranch houses" debased his prairie-and-Usonian styles in home design.

For Broadacres is not merely an exercise in massive ur-ban planning, it is fundamentally a radical vision for America. Wright proposes the expropriation and free redistribution of land on a continental scale.[8] He pro-poses returning government and culture to the people by making the individual county the seat for most po-litical and economic decisions, as well as the center for education and the arts.[9] He proposes, finally, to combine urban and rural living in an esthetic manner that does the least possible harm to the people or to the land; for example, by streamlining factories, regulating pollu-tion, emphasizing landscaping, allowing wilderness pres-ervation, and so on.

"Maps Yet Unmade"

Any attempt to compare and contrast Mannahatta with Broadacre City must acknowledge the inherent difficul-ties of such a proposition. Both are unbuilt, but each differs in its degree of explicitness. Mannahatta is, above all, an ideal, but one upon whose pristine sur-face has been etched the topical and social features of New York City. As such it resembles the panoramic paintings and photographs of Whitman's contemporaries, as Peter Conrad relates:

> The panoramas popular at the time are models of Whitman's all-embracing urban pantheism, his capacity to comprehend the city in a single omni-scient survey. Burckhardt's panorama wrapped New York into a sectional circle and placed the viewer at its midpoint, while in E. Porter Belden's you looked down on it, seeing it all at once like Whitman in "Mannahatta."[10]

The Western cities incorporate the same ideal, but are more sketchily drawn.

Broadacre City, on the other hand, as represented in its 1935 scale model, is deceptively detailed considering that Wright claimed, "Broadacre City does not represent in any way a proposed plan, a fixed formal arrangement..."[11] But this scale model was itself an outgrowth of twenty years of considerations and sketches, and the concept of Broadacres as presented in *The Disappearing City* of 1932 would undergo continuous revisions until its best known and most specific embodiment, *The Living City,* was pub-lished in 1958, near the end of Wright's life.

To varying degrees, nevertheless, in the cases of Manna-hatta and Broadacres, an ideal is proposed, and yet that ideal is confused, in seemingly deliberate fashion, with a set of particulars—each is given a geography, not merely a geometry. The dangers of such an approach are evident, for no explicit model could possibly fit the diverse ter-rains, climates, and cultures of this capacious nation. In Whitman's case, one expects, correctly, that this quintessen-tial poet of the particular (the cataloger of each "kelson of the creation,")[12] will rapturously devote himself to the incidences of his own city, whose streets he celebrates.

To Whitman, in 1860, the extension of present marvels like paved streets and the innovative iron work and other technologies he had seen at New York's Crystal Palace exhibition into the heartland of the nation must have seemed prophecy indeed. New York and New England were inescapably the centers and the symbols of this technological revolution in America, and so it was not surprising that he would see the future in the East as well as in the frontier West, complementary contributors to a prosperous new nation egalitarian in art, manners, gov-ernment, and economy.[13]

Yet, especially after the Civil War, when populating the new lands became a national priority and when the fail-ures of the existing cities and their society became appar-ent, he focused more often on those "mighty inland cities yet unsurvey'd and unsuspected."[14] He saw in the West "Our Real Culmination"[15] as a nation, and wrote that, "In a few years the dominion-heart of America will be far inland, toward the West."[16] One wishes that he had been more de-tailed about these prophecies, but in his later prose pieces he drew some appealing portraits of the new communities where the citizens would reside, "millions of comfortable city homestead and moderate-sized farms, healthy and independent"[17] in neo-Jeffersonian sufficiency.

Whitman, however, acknowledged the limitations of all his projections, as he acknowledged those of his poetry: "Then . . . we have to say there can be no complete or epical presentation of democracy in the aggregate, or any-thing like it, at this day, . . . Thus we presume to write, as it were, upon things that exist not, and travel by maps yet unmade and a blank."[18] Though Whitman was relatively comfortable with this pregnant uncertainty, he was a poet of life-as-lived, and so he included on his maps the makings and wanderings of the ordinary people he encountered.

Wright, too, was aware of the incomplete and essentially incompletable order of his Broadacres task, though as an architect it was his duty to delineate and not just cel-ebrate the new city. The new sketches that he included a year before his death, while not significantly altering the Midwest-like landscape of the 1930s model, did intro-duce several buildings from his later repertoire, including those meant for California or Southwestern sites.[19]

It is interesting that one of the Whitman passages which Wright chose for his 1938 *Architectural Forum* issue also illustrated the theme of the ever-constructive imagination:

"Say on—sayers! Dig, model, pile up the words of the earth. Work on age after age—nothing is to be lost; it may have to wait long, but it will certainly come in use; when the materials are all prepared, the architects shall appear."[20] The idea that artistic and social creations, of which Mannahatta and Broadacres are two, must be on-going constructs is an evolutionary one, in the wider sense. Whitman and Wright were familiar with compatible concepts, such as, for example, Jefferson's belief in a revolution repeated each generation, Fichte's ever-unfinished temple of philosophy, and Emerson's dictum: "neither can any artist entirely exclude the conventional, the local, the perishable from his book . . . Each age, it is found, must write its own books; or rather, each generation for the next succeeding."[21]

In the geographical analogue, based on a narrower sense of "local" than Emerson fully intended,[22] it is the *topos* or site which provides the counterbalance to the general space which, for these artists, is usually America. The necessity of localizing their ideal cities, of subtracting *ous* from "utopia," was as clear to each man as the necessity of rooting a poem in topical occurrences was to Whitman ("Crossing Brooklyn Ferry"), or orienting a house to its ground ("Fallingwater") was to Wright.

Geography is important to Whitman and Wright, then, both as continental focus and as local study. Geography, of course, has many definitions, and as a discipline many specializations. Foremost, for our concerns, is the phenomenology of space, the area of Perceptual Geography. A second is Cultural Geography, or what Carl Sauer called "Human Geography," especially as it relates to the "localization of ways of living,"[23] and including Urban Geography insofar as that deals with the city's relationship to its land. Finally, Geography is of interest in its concern with mapping, as Whitman and Wright were both engaged in a search for analogues to their and their nation's experience. The present concern will be, primarily, with Perceptual Geography.

Ecstatic Geography

For geographers, architects, and psychologists, the study of the ways in which we perceive space has become, in recent years, an enormously important undertaking, spurred on by the failure of the housing projects of the 1960s, the emergence of a strong Environmental movement in the 1970s, and the complexities surrounding attempts at urban revitalization in this decade. For geographers, especially, the notion of a "mental map," or subjective apprehension of space, first introduced by Charles Trowbridge early in the century, is quite useful. It has since been used not only by geographers like Peter Gould and Yi Fu Tuan, but by figures from various disciplines, like architect and urban planner Kevin Lynch and psychologist James Hillman.

It was remarked earlier how Whitman and Wright both conceived of American space as an immense vastness, yet neither reacted to vastness with the inescapable dread one finds, say, in *Moby Dick*.[24] Instead, both men are agoraphiles, reveling in the experience of inexhaustible space as a renewable source of personal and artistic energy, impervious to time's ephemerality. (In this, they stay close to the ancient sense of space as a verb: "to increase," "to hope," or "to prosper.")[25] References to this revivifying experience of space permeate *Leaves of Grass;* a particularly intricate example occurs in "To the Sun-Set Breeze," where that breeze entering his sickroom has a recuperative effect and is envisioned by the poet as first, a "messenger-magical strange bringer to body and spirit of me," and second, as North American space: "I feel the sky, the prairies vast—I feel the mighty northern lakes, / I feel the ocean and the forest—somehow I feel the globe itself swift-swimming in space. . . . "[26] Like the coolness that comes in through his window, space here is the very thing denied the sick man—which is of course why it is a fitting representation of freedom and, moreover, a fitting analogue to that other lake, the breath of life.

Space is, in the poem, directly related to a "dialectic of outside and inside"; the phrase is from Gaston Bachelard's brilliant phenomenological romp, *The Poetics of Space*.[27] Inside, Bachelard observes, is usually associated in the imagination with the concrete, as outside with the vast, but these are not absolute opposites,[28] as they are not in "To the Sun-Set Breeze." Rather, the space within the room becomes continuous with that beyond it, as in Whitman's perception where it becomes equally filled by the "universal concrete's distillation,"[29] or filled (in Bachelard's psychological, not metaphysical, view) by a common "immensity."[30] As Bachelard writes: " . . . it is through their 'immensity' that these two kinds of space— the space of intimacy and world space—blend. When human solitude deepens, then the two immensities touch and become identical."[31] This moment of deepening solitude, this "inner state that is so unlike any other,"[32] is identified by Bachelard with the creative "reverie," an associational condition which proceeds by a "dialectic of superposition."[33] Reverie does not seek to resolve or synthesize the generated images, but lets these apparitions "reverberate" with multiple meanings.[34] This experience, which Bachelard also depicts oxymoronically as one of "intimate immensity,"[35] is similar to what Whitman referred to as "ecstasy," a state of happiness[36] giving vent to poetry or song which is linked, as in the following short poem, to a contemplation of particulars:

> Beginning my studies the first step pleas'd me so
> much,
> The mere fact of consciousness, these forms, the
> power of motion,
> The least insect or animal, the sense, eyesight, love,
> The first step I say awed me and pleas'd me so
> much,
> I have hardly gone and hardly wish'd to go any
> further,
> But stop and loiter all the time to sing it in ecstatic
> songs.[37]

As in reverie, there is no urge to go beyond the first step of apprehension to the following analytic stage; the narrator is content to take in natural forms and to utter, in its original sense, corresponding words.[38]

Recognizable in the previous sentence is a description of Whitman's poetic method, which is based on naming as a holy act: "*Names* are magic—One word can pour such a flood through the soul."[39] Place names are the most common of such utterances in Whitman's poetry.

The parallels between the creative act and religious or mystical ecstasy have often been remarked on, as in works by Otto Rank and Rudolf Otto.[40] Whitman makes this connection frequently, recognizing the interrelation of poetic, spiritual and even erotic stimuli (or "excitations" in Otto's term), within the shared space of his own mind, as well as the "essential correspondence"[41] of that inner space[42] to the extended landscape. An example occurs as he discusses his ideal society:

> I say the question of Nature, largely consider'd, involves the questions of the esthetic, the emotional, and the religious—and involves happiness. A fitly born and bred race, growing up in right conditions of out-door as much as in-door harmony, activity and development, would probably, from and in those conditions, find it enough merely *to live*— and would, in their relations to the sky, air, water, trees, &c., and to the countless common shows, and in the fact of life itself, discover and achieve happiness—with Being suffused night and day by wholesome extasy, surpassing all . . . [43]

This correspondence between Whitman's images of landscape and his psychic states Gay Wilson Allen called "panpsychism,"[44] and he found in it "ideas of transmission and identification resembling the imitative magic of animistic religions."[45] Allen himself is most interested in topographical images as symbols of Whitman's interior processes, as they certainly can be read. But it is equally important to dwell on the power, for Whitman, of geographic space to initiate or catalyze events in consciousness, and also to define a national political and esthetic identity.

In the case of those central events or ecstasies—no longer the special province of mad monks or artists, but as common as daydreams in Whitman's democratic citizenry—the landscape provides both a coherent matrix for metaphorical representations and a major type of excitation or trigger for the experiences themselves. The first instance, the geographical image as metaphor, is quite prominent in *Leaves of Grass*—even in the title—and has received sufficient critical attention so as to hardly necessitate illustration, but a passage from the opening section of "Salut Au Monde!" renders Whitman's method particularly transparent:

> What widens within you Walt Whitman?
> What waves and soils exuding?
> What climes? what persons and cities are here?[46]

Moving on to Whitman's proclivity for spatial metaphors of psychological states, guideposts may be found in Bachelard's *Poetics of Space* and Yi Fu Tuan's *Topophilia*,[47] which separately explain how spatial apprehension, with its close relationship to our awareness of the structure of our bodies, is central to most ways of representing the fact of ourselves in the world. It is, for example, nearly impossible in English to speak of mental states without using spatial metaphors. We speak of "inner" states and "areas" of behavior. Our words for the soul are derived from the breath, with its inward-and-outward pattern. Greek- or Latin-based words like "proclivity," "derangement," and even "emotion" have spatial reference. The term "ecstasy," which is central to Whitman's imaginal and geographical concerns, means literally "to put out of place" or "to stand outside."[48] Ecstasy, or "extasy," as Whitman also spelled it, is used by him to indicate anything from simple exuberance to an overwhelming experience not unlike that reported by mystics, although Whitman's democratic vantage would see both as degrees of an identical experience.

A report of a spiritual "transformation" by the English writer Edward Carpenter,[49] a friend and admirer of Whitman, emphasizes the spatial nature—the feeling of extending outwards into space or of "standing outside" one's body—often accompanying mystical states:

> Or again a strange sense of Extension comes on me—and of presence in distant space and time. Mine is an endless Life, unconquerable, limitless in subtlety and expanse; and strange intimations that it is so come to me even in my tiny earth-cell— intimations of power inexhaustible, of knowledge mysterious and unbounded, and of far presence through all forms and ranges of being.[50]

Whitman's philosophy of "Personalism" demands that he maintain and expand his ego: his wisdom comes from "dilation," not from denial of self; from an equation of self with Self, not from self-sacrifice. As a poet Whitman seeks not to transcend the self, but to transcend such categories as self/not-self, inner/outer, etc. He continually subverts expected dichotomies, affirming both body and psyche, granting the poet a political role, and adhering to cultural pluralism; these are not the ecstasies of a narcissist, but a possible transversing of the solipsistic minefield that, we are told by Freudian or Marxist analyses,[51] underlies most poetics of the sublime.

It is not surprising, therefore, that he prefers those representations of ecstasy which emphasize space even as they transcend it. Neither is it surprising that he gives us many examples of ecstasy that are either directly triggered by awe of panoramic vistas and similar topophilic experiences, or indirectly aided by the sublimity of some landscape upon which love, battle, patriotic celebrations, or the excitement of the ferry ride induce a heightened state.

If questions remain as to why and how geographical images figure so prominently and seemingly easily as representations of Whitman's interior life, particularly in regard to such intensely felt and possibility-filled experiences, one might iterate the obvious yet impenetrable fact of American space as utterly new, discrete, and numinous:

A boundless field to fill! A new creation, with needed orbic works launch'd forth, to revolve in free and lawful circuits—to move, self-poised, through the ether, and shine like heaven's own suns! With such, and nothing less, we suggest that New World literature, fit to rise upon, cohere, and signalize in time, these States.[52]

Such is the promise of America's "momentous spaces."[53] They provide both the inspiration and the resources necessary for an unprecedented literature and government—the former represented by Whitman through a metaphor of galactic space, which indicates both the strangeness and the spiritualness that America derives from her setting.

Beyond the inescapability of American geography as perception, the above passage makes clear the uses to which Whitman puts spatial imagery on behalf of his program for a national esthetic which would, in turn, consolidate the democratic society and political union of the U.S.[54] If the goal was to celebrate America's space, it was also necessary to celebrate its places and place-names.

Lacking the accrued significances of an ancient history, American sites must be discovered for the imagination. Although Irving, Cooper, and Longfellow had done the preliminary work of poetic founding for the Northeast by the time Whitman entered the scene, and Thoreau and Hawthorne were completing theirs, little but Paul Bunyan tales were available to imaginatively locate the West (Beadle Dime-Novels had not even begun[55]). Whitman's emphasis on place-names and topography is partially to this end, although as an Easterner it is not surprising that his specific focusings on the West are few relative to his references to New York and Long Island geography and, until his 1879 trip to Denver, less detailed.

What he lacks in number of specific references to Western sites, however, Whitman compensates for in his frequent references to American space as a unified, continental presence, and to that vastness as a unifying force in the nation's life. Whitman sought always to correct the amorphic vision that fragments the continental field into competing regions, each with an opposed perspective—in this he resembles his hero, Lincoln. An American must not be defined by space as a boundary, but by the common experience of inhabiting an infinity. They wanted us to stretch.

Space Unbound

Among the Whitman passages which Frank Lloyd Wright chose for his special issue of the *Architectural Forum* in January 1938 can be found the following lines: "I inhale great draughts of space. / The East and the West are mine, and the North and the South are mine . . ."[56] Wright's *Autobiography* opens with the following scene:

Light blanket of snow fresh-fallen over sloping fields, gleaming in the morning sun. Clusters of pod-topped weeds woven of bronze here and there sprinkling the spotless expanse of white. Dark

sprays of slender metallic straight lines, tipped with quivering dots. Pattern to the eye of the sun, as the sun spread delicate network of more pattern in blue shadows on the white beneath.[57]

Between the continental expanse and epic tone of the first passage and the undulating, broken expanse of the lyrical second, there is little in common besides an attention to space. The first is sublime, while the second is beautiful. The first communicates power—the power of untamed spaces, the power of men who become giants by absorbing some of the vastness they live within, and the power of the first poem elastic enough to swallow those nearly infinite spaces that only chaos, it was previously thought, could hold. Yet the second passage is an eclogue of early winter, telling of a localized and humanized landscape— a "place" or "piece of the whole environment that has been claimed by feelings," as Alan Gussow defines it.[58]

One cannot ascribe any contrasting characteristics to Whitman and to Wright based on these two isolated passages, of course. Wright clearly admired the titan in Whitman, which is one reason he selected the above quote. There are many selections from Whitman which consider space as discrete and tame places—"Sounds of the Winter,"[59] for instance, could be placed alongside Wright's descriptive narrative. And even though Whitman as an epic poet is obliged to present the American continent in panorama whereas Wright as an architect must necessarily attend to the individual site, it is also the case that Whitman includes the lyrical and the individual, as Wright frequently shifts to an apprehension of expansive space in his architectural theorizings and conceptions of Broadacres.

Yet, the two passages do reintroduce a "dialectic of outside and inside" in respect to continuous, usually continental space versus discrete, localized space—a polarity which Wright incorporated, as would become evident in his concept of the "Earth Line."[60] The passages, moreover, are evidences of Wright's preoccupation with geography—that he is a "child of space," or as Mumford referred to him, a "poet of space,"[61] and that he is, like Whitman, receptive to its ecstasies.

The first book of Wright's *Autobiography* is interspersed with boyhood memories of the Taliesin valley, with its "sloping fields," "wooded hills," and "wild Wisconsin pastures" in whose "marvelous book-of-books, Nature-Experience" the young Wright was discovering a corresponding "inner experience for what he heard or saw."[62]

The opening passage, in fact, presents Midwestern nature as seen through an inner, geometrically cognizant eye more sophisticated than the nine-year-old Frank can be expected to possess. Pattern is quite visible in the bronze-"woven" weeds and the "delicate network" of shadows, as the author envisions a landscape composed of "metallic straight lines," "clusters," and "dots" (one might almost have the elements of a Louis Sullivan façade instead of a landscape!).

A later passage also has a split focus, but is more attendant to the boy's awareness, with its ecstatic fusion of place, eros, and the infinite:

> Sometimes . . . he would get out of bed, sweaty jeans pulled on, rolled above his knees, and barefoot and bareheaded slowly climb the path up the hill behind the house. Climb to the long, quiet ride that ran to the north high in the moonlight, ornamented here and there with scattered hazel-brush and trees. Climbing to wander, look forward and imagine, enjoy waking dreams in a high place. . . .
>
> On either side of the ridge lay fertile valleys luminously bathed and gentled by the moon. The different trees all made their special kinds of pattern when the moon shone on them and their favorite deep-dark silhouettes when it shone against them. . . . Broad, shallow mists, distilled from heavy dews, . . . were lying free over the treetops in long, thin, flat ribands. . . . The ancient element of moisture seemed to prevail there as a kind of light flooding over all. The deep shadows held mysteries alluring and friendly to the boy. No haste now.[63]

Wright is known as the leading architect of the "Prairie Style," and the majority of those early houses were set in the Oak Park outskirts of Chicago. Today a suburban village, in the 1890s Oak Park fronted the prairie. Wright's own Home-and-Studio, a precursor of that style, is situated so that the design studio faced the edge of town where, a couple of hundred yards off, cattle grazed; the home more sociably flanked an existing house, and faced several houses Wright had recently built. There is a third direction apparent here, as in, to varying degrees, all of Wright's houses: an interior, hearth-centered space whose reflective windows allow in light but not strangers' gazes, and whose domestic comforts provide shelter from that same prairie which Wright's imagination found indispensable. Taliesin, Wright's next home, looks over a river valley adjacent to Wisconsin's prairies, so it is also a place shielded from the awful sameness of the prairie—that "scene of desolate stillness . . . with unbroken horizon, under a cloudless sky,"[64] as Schopenhauer envisions the sublime. Wright, in abandoning his practice and family in the suburb of Oak Park almost as impetuously as his fellow Midwesterner, Sherwood Anderson, left his family and conventional job to become a writer, did not head for the interior of some metropolis. But neither did he search out the forbidding wilds, or even the cultivated-yet-uninterrupted prairies. Instead, he settled, after a tour of Europe, in the Wisconsin vale that was scene to his childhood idylls.

Inhabiting Taliesin, Wright, the advocate of a prairie architecture, might resemble Whitman, the poet of the open road, whose peripatetics were limited, aside from one trip to New Orleans, one to Canada, and one to the West, to an ellipse whose points include Boston, New York, Camden, Washington, D.C., and Long Island. Taliesin was a garden in the original sense of enclosed, sacralized space. It was a place he could work with few

distractions, and also a refuge for himself and his lover, Mamah Borthwick Cheney, against the unrelenting voices of the scandal sheets. Mannahatta, as an island, is symbolically a garden in this sense for Whitman, too. Whitman found his safety within the anonymity of the crowds that strolled down Fifth Avenue, or rode the trolleys.

The dialectics of outside and inside, however, are often beyond our ken as they relate to the creative choices of a particular artist, as are the needs which go into those choices. Whitman seems to have needed Mannahatta as a place in his poem more than he needed it as a place to remain in. Wright used Taliesin as a workshop and occasional retreat, but his place as an architect was out supervising construction wherever and whenever there was a project. It is possible that the tragic fire of 1914, in which a madman murdered Mamah and her children, and two subsequent fires at Taliesin, deprived it of some of its talismanic power and womb-like serenity for Wright. That *memento mori* which appeared on seventeenth-century landscape paintings would be appropriate in regard to Taliesin: *"Et in Arcadia Ego,"* or, "I (Death) also am in Arcadia."[65]

Perhaps a reduction in the symbolic safety of Taliesin's discrete space was a factor in Wright's construction of Taliesin West in Arizona, where he would live for decades with his last wife, Olgivanna, although other factors such as his growing enchantment with the Southwest and a health problem which demanded a warm climate were primary.[66] In any case it is interesting to consider this move—occurring shortly after his Broadacre model—as part of a significant transformation in his artistic career. The journey from the discrete and humanized spaces of Wisconsin to the floor of a vast desert was a step in the larger journey Wright took in his "second" career towards an architecture evolving into radically innovative forms which were, nevertheless, more and more finely attuned to the nature of materials and topographies.

Robert Twombly discusses the Taliesin West site as an expression of emotional reorientation, and, one could add, an affirmation of unlimited space as the American reality:

> This close interrelationship (between building and site) had contributed to a fortresslike atmosphere at Spring Green, but in the desert worked in completely different ways. Alone with his mistress in 1911, Wright had valued privacy, protection from hostile outsiders, and a sense of shelter above all. Happily married for a decade by 1938 with commissions coming and new ideas developing rapidly, he now faced the world confidently, without fear. Taliesin East achieved its security and its architectural success from its commanding hilltop position, overlooking the valley and controlling its own access routes like the castle of a feudal baron. Taliesin West, on the other hand, sits alone and unprotected on the desert floor, dominated by the mountains to which it pays tribute, exposed on all sides like the lonely home of a pioneer. . . . But the sand and the canvas and the water suggested a certain impermanence, as if Wright had learned

that the strongest fortress guaranteed nothing. Only the looming mountain was certain of immortality.[67]

Wright had, in several senses, come to his bedrock, and found it was sand. Heraclitean as he had always, at heart, been,[68] Wright was becoming more resolvedly aware of "The Inexorable Law of Change."[69] And he was realizing, in an architecture newly based on the shifting of elemental materials and forms,[70] the temporal and spatial freedom he had always sought: "In the realm of his own imagination come forms found only in freedom of spirit. Space outflowing instead of static containment. Liberation a fulfillment. Architecture no longer any kind of fortification but generously spacious and plastic."[71]

This statement was written by Wright in the 1950s, but as early as the thirties Wright had promulgated a socio-esthetic based on "THE NEW STANDARD OF SPACE MEASUREMENT,"[72] stressing mobility, centrigual directionality, and horizontality in emulation of the "democratic" nomad versus the fearful cavedweller. In this parable Wright distinguished the imaginative, adventurous, and innovative in man from the obedient, laboring, and bourgeois; the latter qualities he associated with repressive government and repressed society, and with the city, an overcrowded "WHIRLING VORTEX"[73] constricting individuality.

Wright was forced to admit at the time that the two aspects of humanity have blended and fought throughout history, and that each aspect is found in any individual. Even so, the urge to fortify seems to have been stronger in himself than Wright might then have realized. Luckily, he and his architecture were able to subsume this need into the improvisatory and less restrictive forms of shelter required by new climates and ways of life, gaining in the process that mobility which was second nature to Whitman and his poetry.

Wright was, thus, akin to Whitman in his sensitivity to the presence and importance of American spaciousness, and was equally agoraphilic. Both men valued centrifugality; for Whitman it was indicative of the emergence of words from the mouth of the poet, of the unfolding of the "kosmos" in evolution, of the soul's voyage, and of sympathy as the principle of extension of self.

Wright embraced, for the most part, these insights of Whitman, but with two differences. First, Wright applied this centrifugal necessity to his solution for the congested city in a far more drastic way than the crowd-energized Whitman would have approved. And, second, Wright was less apt to view the spread of democracy as equivalent to the spread of America's boundaries, though growing older Whitman had himself grown less chauvinistic.

The American continent is not the only space which Whitman's imagination gauges, of course, but this great envelope is the "stubborn fact," in Whitehead's terminology, "which at once limits and provides opportunity for the actual occasion"[74] of *Leaves of Grass.* In the same way, as Wright's European commentators unanimously point out, the Broadacres model could never be applied on the older Continent, which simply lacks the *Lebensraum* such an experiment requires. Yet such an inexhaustible space, in our time, when even the solar system is becoming man's junkyard, seems all too finite. But North American space was also, for Whitman and Wright, a symbolic work space where necessary creations on whatever level—esthetic, political, spiritual—could occur, and for this there's still room:

> Others take finish, but the Republic is ever
>   constructive and ever keeps vista, . . .
> O America because you build for mankind I build
>   for you,
> O well-beloved stone-cutters, I lead them who
>   plan with decision and science,
> Lead the present with friendly hand toward the
>   future.[75]

NOTES

[1] As Henry Nash Smith has observed in *Virgin Land* (New York: Vintage, 1970); see ch. 20, also chs. 11 and 15.

[2] Walt Whitman, "Democratic Vistas," *Prose Works 1892,* ed. Floyd Stovall (New York: New York University Press, 1968), 2:384.

[3] Frank Lloyd Wright, from *Architect's Journal,* London: July 16-August 6, 1936, included in Wright, *An American Architecture,* ed. Edgar Kaufmann, Jr. (New York: Bramhall House, 1955), 61.

[4] Wright, *The Master Architect: Conversations with Frank Lloyd Wright,* ed. Justin Meehan (New York: Wiley, 1984), 241.

[5] Whitman, "Specimen Days," *PW,* 1:11.

[6] It is worth keeping in mind that Whitman is foremost an islander and his earliest experience of expansive space must have come, as for Melville's Nantucketers, from the sea. See Joan Berbrich, *Three Voices from Paumanok* (Port Washington: Friedman, 1969), 170-195. As illustration, see "From Montauk Point," *Leaves of Grass: Comprehensive Reader's Edition,* ed. Harold W. Blodgett and Sculley Bradley (New York: Norton, 1965), 508. (References are to this edition unless otherwise specified.)

[7] Wright, London Lecture no. 3 (1939), *The Future of Architecture* (New York: Horizon, 1953), 282. On p. 289, Wright answers a questioner as to why Chicago is the most beautiful city:

> First of all because it has a generous park system, the greatest on earth . . . Chicago seems to be the only great city in our States to have discovered its own waterfront . . . Chicago takes pride in building things in a big substantial broad way . . . even gangsters.

The first two points here are remarkably parallel to planning trends in the 1880s, even though the final comment betrays the passage's date.

[8] Wright cites Henry George as his model here, yet opposes George's Single Tax, favoring instead some system of just compensation for the expropriated; Wright appears to be following Silvio Gesell on this point.

[9] County Seat: Surrounds small lake near eastern edge of model; County Architect's building & Crafts center on one side of lake, government & corporate office buildings on other side; Arena with festival pole just north. Adjacent to Arena is a north-south strip of museums, zoo, aquarium, etc. East of Arena, secluded, are country club and sanitarium; County Building: Consolidates all governmental functions (public safety, legislative, judicial, administrative); Community Center; " . . . salient feature of every countryside development of the county, wherever the county seat might be . . . Golf courses, race tracks, the zoo, aquarium, planetarium—all would be found at this general center. Good buildings grouped in architectural ensemble with botanical gardens, art museums, libraries, galleries, opera, etc." (Wright, *The Living City* [New York: Horizon, 1958], 174-176).

[10] *The Art of The City: Views and Versions of New York* (New York: Oxford University Press, 1984), 18.

[11] Wright, cited by Lionel March, "An Architect in Search of Democracy: Broadacre City," *Writings on Wright,* ed. H. Allen Brooks (Cambridge: MIT Press, 1981), 204.

[12] "Song of Myself" 5:95, *Leaves,* 33.

[13] Despite the fact that many inventions in what John Kouwenhoven called the American "vernacular" occurred in the West as improvisations due to the lack of standard materials or procedures—see *The Arts in Modern American Civilization* (New York: Norton, 1948), also published as *Made in America.* For Whitman's reaction to the Crystal Palace, see Justin Kaplan, *Walt Whitman: A Life* (New York: Simon and Schuster, 1980), 179-183.

[14] Whitman, "Thoughts" 2:26, *Leaves,* 494.

[15] Whitman, *PW,* 2:539-540.

[16] "Vistas," *PW,* 1:384.

[17] "Our Real Culmination," *PW,* 2:539.

[18] "Vistas," *PW,* 2:389, 391.

[19] See Robert C. Twombly, *Frank Lloyd Wright: An Interpretive Biography* (New York: Harper, 1973), 304-305. The drawings appear in many of Wright's books and anthologies, including *The Living City, Writings and Buildings,* and *The Master Architect.*

[20] Whitman, "A Song of the Rolling Earth," 4: 121-126, 127-130, cited in Wright, "Broadacre City" insert to *The Architectural Forum,* January 1938.

[21] "The American Scholar," *Selections from Ralph Waldo Emerson,* ed. Stephen E. Whicher (Boston: Houghton Mifflin, 1957), 67.

[22] The term "local" in Emerson's passage implies the philosophical sense of "accidental" or "particular."

[23] Carl Sauer, *Land and Life* (Berkeley: University of California Press, 1963), 358.

[24] Melville frequently alludes to the treacherous sublimity of the vast oceans, as in the following passage: "Already we are boldly launched upon the deep; but soon we shall be lost in its unshored, harborless immensities." (*Moby Dick* [1851: Baltimore: Penguin, 1972], 227.) Olson, in *Call Me Ishmael* (San Francisco: City Lights, 1947), 11-13, observed that space in America "comes large here. Large and without mercy." And that Melville "had all space concentrated into the form of a whale called Moby Dick."

[25] From Indo-European root *spe,* related to Sanskrit *sphayati,* "he increases," and Latin *spes,* "hope."—*American Heritage Dictionary of Indo-European Roots,* ed. Calvert Watkins (Boston: Houghton-Mifflin, 1985), and *Origins,* ed. Eric Partridge (New York: Greenwich, 1983).

[26] Whitman, "To the Sun-Set Breeze" 8, 10-11, *Leaves,* 546.

[27] Gaston Bachelard, *The Poetics of Space,* trans. Maria Jolas (1958; Boston: Beacon, 1964) title of ch. 9. Bachelard shares with Whitman and Wright an affinity to Coleridge and his German post-Kantian predecessors; see Neil Forsyth, "Gaston Bachelard's Theory of the Poetic Imagination: Psychoanalysis to Phenomenology," *The Quest for Imagination: Essays in Twentieth-Century Aesthetic Criticism,* ed. O. B. Hardison, Jr. (Cleveland: Case Western Reserve University Press, 1971), 225-253.

[28] See Bachelard, 215.

[29] Whitman, "To the Sun-Set Breeze" 15, *Leaves,* 546.

[30] Bachelard, 203.

[31] Bachelard, 203.

[32] Bachelard, 183.

[33] Bachelard, *On Poetic Imagination and Reverie: Selections,* trans. Colette Gaudin (New York: Merrill, 1971), 8.

[34] Bachelard, *Imagination,* 82-83.

[35] Bachelard, *Space,* 183; see 202-203.

[36] Whitman's "ecstasy" was always a condition associated with health and happiness—not at all the "derangement" (*existant*) which it sometimes implies.

[37] Whitman, "Beginning My Studies," *Leaves,* 9.

[38] The word "utter," as "to direct outward."

[39] Whitman, *An American Primer* (Boston: Small, 1904), 18; see 17, 19, 31-32. Wright is also fond of the magic of names: e.g., "Taliesin" (Welsh: "Shining Brow"), "Hollyhock," "Fallingwater."

[40] See Otto Rank, *Art and Artist* (1932; New York: Agathon, 1968), 85-87, on the similarities and differences among the "aesthetic," "religious," and "erotic" experiences. Also see Rank, 291-293, and ch. 14; see Rudolph Otto, *The Idea of the Holy* (New York: Oxford University Press, 1958), 42-49.

[41] Otto, 45.

[42] See Gay Wilson Allen, "Walt Whitman's Inner Space," *Papers on Language and Literature* 5 (Supplement, Summer 1969), 7. Bachelard, in *Imagination,* 36, says of this connection: "In a general way, I believe that the psychology of aesthetic emotion would profit from studying the kinds of material reveries which precede contemplation. We dream before contemplating. Any landscape is an oneiric experience before becoming a conscious spectacle."

[43] Whitman, "Vistas" *PW,* 2:416.

[44] Allen, "Inner Space," 10.

[45] Allen, "Inner Space," 10.

[46] Whitman, "Salut Au Monde!" 5-8, 11-16, 20-21, *Leaves,* 137-138.

[47] Yi Fu Tuan, *Topophilia* (Englewood Cliffs: Prentice-Hall, 1974).

[48] From Greek *ex,* "out" and *histanai,* "to cause to stand" (Webster's); Greek *histanai,* "to set, place" (*American Heritage Dictionary*).

[49] Bucke included both Whitman and Carpenter in his examples of men who had attained to visionary states, in his book *Cosmic Consciousness.* Carpenter, by the way, was involved in Chicago Arts and Crafts Society activities at the same time Wright was, according to Peter I. Abernathy, in "Frank Lloyd Wright/Walt Whitman: The Expatriate's Dream of Home," *American Studies* 18 (Fall 1982), 47. He also notes the presence in that circle of Whitman biographer Oscar Lovell Triggs and also C. R. Ashbee, an early critic of both Whitman and Wright. Triggs was a friend of Sullivan and Wright.

[50] Edward Carpenter, *The Art of Creation,* 3rd ed. (London: Allen, 1912), 231. See *Religious Ecstasy,* ed. Nils G. Holm (Stockholm: Almqvist, 1982), for some recent neurological and psychological findings on the subject.

[51] I am thinking especially of Thomas Weiskel's *The Romantic Sublime: Studies in the Structure and Psychology of Transcendence* (Baltimore: Johns Hopkins University Press, 1976).

[52] "Vistas," *PW,* 2:404-405.

[53] "Vistas," *PW,* 2:404.

[54] See Lee Schlesinger, "Toward Infinite Expanse: The Use of Spatial Imagery in Nineteenth and Twentieth Century Poetry: A Phenomenological Study," Ph.D. Dissertation, Yale University, 1973, 13.

[55] See Henry Nash Smith, *Virgin Land,* ch. 9. Erastus Beadle was a Buffalo publisher who moved to New York City in 1860 to begin a weekly series of mass-market Westerns.

[56] Whitman, "Song of the Open Road" 5:53-59, as cited by Wright, *The Architectural Forum,* January 1938.

[57] Wright, *An Autobiography,* 3rd (expanded) ed. (New York: Horizon, 1977), 23.

[58] Alan Gussow, *A Sense of Place: The Artist and the American Land* (San Francisco: Friends of the Earth, 1971), 27.

[59] Whitman, *Leaves,* 548.

[60] Wright, *A Testament* (New York: Horizon, 1957), 219.

[61] Lewis Mumford, "The Social Background of Frank Lloyd Wright," *The Work of Frank Lloyd Wright,* ed. Olgivanna Lloyd Wright (New York: Horizon, 1965), 74.

[62] Wright, *Autobiography,* 45.

[63] Wright, *Autobiography,* 67-68.

[64] Arthur Schopenhauer, *The World as Will and Idea* (London: 1886), 1:454.

[65] Leo Marx, *The Machine in the Garden* (New York: Oxford University Press, 1964), 26.

[66] See Twombly, 185.

[67] Twombly, 186, 188.

[68] Wright, *An Autobiography,* 617; see also Wright, *The Living City,* 49, and Twombly, 228.

[69] Wright, *The Living City,* 49 (and elsewhere).

[70] One of the main themes of current investigations into Wright, as apparent in the Columbia University Symposium on Fallingwater of November 1986.

[71] Wright, *Testament,* 130.

[72] Wright, *The Disappearing City* (New York: Payson, 1932), 25.

[73] Wright, *The Disappearing City,* 21.

[74] Alfred North Whitehead, *Process and Reality: An Essay in Cosmology* (New York: Macmillan, 1929), 129.

[75] Whitman, "Blue Ontario's Shore" 8:119, 122-124, 9:128-129; *Leaves,* 346.

Larzer Ziff (essay date 1988)

SOURCE: "The Prairie in Literary Culture and The Prairie Style of Frank Lloyd Wright," in *The Nature of Frank Lloyd Wright,* edited by Carol R. Bolon, Robert S. Nelson, and Linda Seidel, The University of Chicago Press, 1988, pp. 173-85.

[*In the following essay, Ziff investigates the effect of the Midwestern prairie landscape on American literature and architecture.*]

"My dear and honored Walt Whitman," Louis Sullivan began the letter of February 3, 1887, in which he introduced himself to the poet. When he read *Leaves of Grass,* he told him, "you then and there entered my soul, have not departed, and will never depart."[1] The democratic faith of Whitman, it seemed, would be justified by the art of the Midwest where it could be embodied, free of the older patterns of the colonial past from which popular democracy was never quite separate on the Atlantic seaboard. So great was Whitman's influence on Sullivan's ideas that in his study of Sullivan Sherman Paul felt it appropriate to head his chapters with titles taken from Whitman: "Starting from Paumanok"; "Democratic Vistas"; "A Backward Glance."

But although Frank Lloyd Wright also admired the Whitman of democratic optimism and organic style directly as well as, it may be assumed, reflexively during his fruitful association with Sullivan, it would not be good judgment to parallel his career with epigraphs from *Leaves of Grass.* Despite his genealogical credentials from New England and some childhood years spent there, Wright springs undeniably from Wisconsin. When the poetic mood is on his prose, as it frequently is, it is the mood of the Welsh bards rather than of Whitman. Like those of the Celtic chanters, the exhortations in Wright's prose are also dappled with obscurities. The play of light and shade is not confined to his buildings.

Yet Whitman does supply the most striking similarity that American literature affords to Wright's work. Although it is not my intention to center on parallels between literature and architecture—a subject beyond my knowledge and also, I suspect, one that is vulnerable to all sorts of well-meant misrepresentations—before I come to my central concern, that of the literary perception of the prairies against which Wright's Prairie style asserted itself, some sense of Whitman will not be amiss. Whatever his specific influence may have been in the latter decades of nineteenth-century America, Whitman's was the only literary voice that insisted that the opportunity which the American West once symbolized—the establishment of the community of democratic brotherhood—was still possible to realize despite the setbacks of the Civil War, the rise of caste if not classes in an industrializing society, and the corruption of political processes by the pirates of finance. Henry James chose to focus on Americans only after they had emerged from native ground onto a finer soil, and Mark Twain saw them, increasingly saw all mankind, as different in kind from the truths they proclaimed. But Whitman took them for the promise they represented.

If Whitman alone sounded the optimistic note convincingly, it was because of the way he said what he said, not because of the message itself. The truth he proclaimed was validated not by the facts—he spoke a good deal about promises rather than fulfillment—but by his demonstration. If America represented the arrival of new values—the death of hierarchy and the establishment of the dignity of the common man—then it represented also the death of the old art forms and the arrival of new forms generated by the new values.

> I harbor for good or bad, I permit to speak at
>   every hazard,
> Nature without check with original energy,

Whitman announced in his first masterpiece,[2] signifying that he wished to bring into consciousness the great primal resource which underlay all life and art but which traditional art had formalized out of existence. He did not, therefore, offer poems, but promised his reader that if he stopped with the poet he would "possess the origin of all poems" (l. 33). To read the words of *Leaves of Grass* was to be enabled rather than informed, to become a poet rather than to remain an audience.

Whitman thus attempted to move Americans out from the delusions which had arisen from cultures that denied the democratic principle and to locate them in a radical awareness of the reality they inhabited. In the process, his imagery characteristically associated buildings with dead forms and the out-of-doors with American reality:

> Houses and rooms are full of perfumes, the
>   shelves are crowded with perfumes,
> I breathe the fragrance myself and know it and
>   like it,
> The distillation would intoxicate me also, but I
>   shall not let it.
>
> The atmosphere is not a perfume, it has no taste of
>   the distillation, it is odorless,
>
> It is for my mouth forever, I am in love with it,
> I will go to the bank by the wood and become
>   undisguised and naked,
> I am mad for it to be in contact with me.
>
>   (ll. 14-20)

It is tempting, treacherously so, to label this manner organic. Certainly in the presence of Whitman's poems we feel that the spill of words, which visually defy margins and refuse to arrange themselves in the black-and-white architecture of the sonnet or the heroic couplet, represents the striving of meaning to find signifiers and of signifiers to extend themselves to whatever shape is necessary for them to arrive at full signification. But beyond this, questions arise which trouble the simple notion of organic. Is the written word not different in kind from the spoken? Are the seemingly artificial forms in which poetry is arranged inorganic if they assist the signifier to signify? In the light of such questions, it is prudent to suggest that what Whitman liked to call his swimming shapes also have their form, a form which in its seeming formlessness may be called the convention of the organic, just as Mark Twain's colloquial style may be called the convention of the colloquial, actual talk being far more repetitious and inconsequential than the literary similitude he constructs to stand for it.[3]

Still, the impulse that propels Whitman is a pulse that throbbed in the American Romantic period, but which he alone maintained toward century's end. In 1852, for example, three years before the first edition of *Leaves of Grass,* the Yankee sculptor Horatio Greenough published his manifesto:

> By beauty I mean the promise of function.
> By action I mean the presence of function.
> By character I mean the record of function.[4]

Yet in response to whatever constraints, Greenough himself sculpted Washington in a toga, engaged, that is, in what a disappointed Emerson called a futile endeavor to revive dead forms.[5] Whitman, however, frankly and fully acknowledged a social function for his poetry and throughout the century continued to be a symbol—an increasingly lone one as decades passed—of the coherence of nature, democracy, the United States, and a new art.

The idea of the American West was central to this faith. There was, all agreed, something more American about the West. "The damned shadow of Europe," as Hawthorne called it,[6] had not fallen over the plains, and from that region, it was to be expected, democracy's true voice would speak through an art which took its clues from limitless space and the voice of nature speaking from its midst, unfiltered by human conventions. Yet while writers spoke often of the westerners who were destined to fulfill the promise of the nation, the great works of the 1850s were neither by westerners nor about the West, except as it stood on the margin as a place in the imagination. Emerson, Thoreau, Hawthorne, and Melville were centered elsewhere even when they departed from the literal settings of their native regions. Whitman's celebration of the outdoors insofar as it invoked the plains was just that, an invocation of a rising region of the mind rather than a rendering of the life that was taking shape on it.

This is hardly surprising since the plains were not yet settled and so furnished scant material for arts dependent upon lived life and the social values that emerged from it. And yet it is remarkable because in the period immediately prior to the great outburst of literary creativity in the 1850s, when Cooper, Bryant, and Irving occupied the stage as America's three most distinguished men of letters, the prairies were such a powerful presence in the culture that each of them not only wrote about them but even titled a major work after them. In 1827 Cooper published his novel *The Prairie;* in 1833 Bryant published his poem "The Prairies"; and in 1835 Irving published his narrative *A Tour on the Prairies.* The absence of similar attention among the next generation of writers, therefore, is not so much an indication of the prematurity of the subject as it is of a collapse of interest in it.

The word "prairie" first entered literary English when Sir Thomas Browne used it to describe the grassy savanna of Provence. The term crossed the Atlantic in 1778 when its first printed appearance was in application to the grasslands of Virginia. In 1787 it appeared in an English work concerned with the region we now call the prairies, doubtless prompted by the early penetration of that territory by the French from whom the word was taken. The word became increasingly common in English as the landscape it denoted came under the control of English-speaking America after the Louisiana Purchase of 1803. Political and economic curiosity ran high, and explorers' accounts soon sprang up to feed it. Not too long after, writers began the literary exploration of its cultural potential.

Bryant's 124-line poem, "The Prairies," is a model of the conventions that were adapted to encompass the new subject matter. It begins:

> These are the gardens of the Desert, these
> The unshorn fields, boundless and beautiful,
> For which the speech of England has no name—
> The Prairies.[7]

The originality of the challenge they present to the imagination is most immediately signaled by the observation that England—not English—has no name for them; the very term in English is uniquely American. The more precise nature of their uniqueness as well as the way in which that uniqueness is to be comprehended imaginatively is captured in a phrase which was to reecho through the century, "gardens of the Desert," an oxymoron of controlled growth and emptiness, human endeavor and divine creation, which is rephrased throughout the poem, as in the term "verdant Waste" (l. 35) in the following stanza.

The thrust of Bryant's contemplation of this awesome phenomenon is to reduce it to human scale without trivializing its wondrous features. Although the prairies possess characteristics conventionally associated in aesthetics with the sublime—they are like the ocean; man has no part in the glorious work but they come directly from God's hand—Bryant resists the upward movement toward the sublime and works to comprehend his subject within the less rarefied category of the beautiful. So, for example, after seeing the prairie as a fitting floor for the magnificent temple of the sky, with flowers "whose glory and whose multitude / Rival the constellations!" (ll. 29-30), he checks the rise toward pure awe and curves it downward to a human scale:

> The great heavens
> Seem to stoop down upon the scene in love,—
> A nearer vault, and of a tenderer blue,
> Than that which bends above our Eastern hills.
>
> (ll. 31-34)

That downward curve initiates the next movement of the poem, which is a consideration of the prairies as the scene of a social life that is now extinct. Taking up the popular notion that the Mound Builders whose barrows yet stood were a people separate from the North American Indians of his day racially as well as chronologically, he paints a picture of the prairies' past when an agricultural people harvested their crops, tamed the bison to the yoke, and

> Heaped with long toil, the earth, while yet the Greek
> Was hewing the Pentelicus to forms
> Of symmetry, and rearing on the rock
> The glittering Parthenon.
>
> (ll. 47-50)

A "forgotten language" (l. 56) had once domesticated the desert, and the verdant waste the poet now beholds is not, after all, primal, but a second growth, the mighty grave of a cultured people overwhelmed and annihilated by the "warlike and fierce" (l. 59) red man. The prairie wolf and the gopher, like the Indian, are not original occupants of the scene, and the waste is humanized by its dead and fertilized to yield another social harvest. The poem's closing, then, can see the prairies which are now quick with the life of insects, flowers, and "gentle quadrupeds, / And birds," (ll. 105-6) as the inevitable site of another agricultural people, and the poet dreams of this:

> Comes up the laugh of children, the soft voice
> Of maidens, and the sweet and solemn hymns
> Of Sabbath worshippers. The low of herds
> Blends with the rustling of the heavy grain
> Over the dark brown furrows.
>
> (ll. 117-22)

Different as his *Prairie* is from Bryant's "Prairies," Cooper nevertheless shares with Bryant a concern with the literary strategy that will comprehend this unique phenomenon and a belief that that strategy is best developed in terms of the society that will live on the prairies, even though the period in which his fiction is set precedes such settlement. While Cooper is more given to stressing the sublimity of the vacant wastes than Bryant, at the same time as a novelist he is in need of social life. So he cannot merely dream of the future but must, at the risk of losing all probability, introduce onto his prairies a cast of characters who represent civilized society, in addition to the trapper and the Indians, even though fully half of the members of this assemblage have no real business being where he puts them. As a result, to the extent that he is open to the sublime he is also vulnerable to bathos.

Two remarkable death scenes close the novel, and while one may make the general observation that no literary convention is a trustier supplier of closure than death, still, in *The Prairie* the deaths assume a function peculiar to the problem of the setting itself. Bryant needed to feel the presence of the dead before he could comprehend the prairies as an appropriate site for the living. Cooper, eschewing the Mound Builders myth, leaves his scene as vacant of social life at the close as he had found it at the opening, save that it is marked by two graves. In one lies a man of mythic stature, the first white man to traverse the region, whose gifts blend the natural rhythms of the land to the sensibilities of civilization. In the other lies the first white man to commit willful murder on the prairie and that against a member of his family. Symbolic Adam and symbolic Cain provide the landmarks for the society to follow; without death there is no life.

As Henry Nash Smith has shown, Cooper's view of the West does advance significantly beyond that of his peers in one important respect.[8] He introduces Ishmael Bush as representative of the class of rude husbandmen scarcely emerged from the hunter state who will first plow the prairies, and he employs him to symbolize the necessarily coarse life preliminary to culture. However, he uncovers in him a moral sublimity that is not to be attributed to the kind of refined sensibility his novels, including *The Prairie,* consistently assert to be the property of civilization and thus the justification for the conquest of the wild. Bush's power is primal. He embodies the notion that the prairies shape human culture to their own standard of unlicensed truth rather than exist in order to be shaped by socialized versions of truth. The notion is isolated in the character of Bush and is at war with the thematic values Cooper more explicitly maintains, but it remains as a buried message, available to those who will exhume it.[9] In the context of the 1830s, however, Ishmael Bush was an exception, a character who momentarily escaped from the restraints of the conscious mind. As his name indicated, he was to be read more conventionally as another formulation of the oxymoron governing the conceptualization of the prairies: Ishmael, a wanderer; Bush, a rooted plant.

"We send our youth abroad to grow luxurious and effeminate in Europe," Washington Irving wrote in his *Tour on the Prairies,* "it appears to me that a previous tour on the prairies would be more likely to produce that manliness, simplicity, and self-dependence most in unison with our political institutions."[10] His prairies are a finishing school which the civilized should attend, a reenforcer of a democratic culture but not its generator. Those who actually reside on the prairies are not as a result manly, simple, and self-dependent, but are characterized, rather, as a "rabble rout of nondescript beings that keep about the frontier between civilised and savage life; as those equivocal birds, the bats, hover about the confines of light and darkness" (p. 19). If we smile at the concluding pages of Irving's *Tour,* in which his party after a month's hunting sport on the prairies straggles back to the despised frontier in a condition so far from manly self-dependence that their survival depends upon their reaching a friendly farm before starvation overtakes them, the irony is lost on the author.

The prairies thus settled into the literary, which is to say the essentially eastern, imagination as a wild space awaiting a social life and a culture which would replicate the civilization of the Atlantic seaboard. Their appeal was greater in the promise than in the early realization, since the latter would for some while be marked by the nondescript beings of whom Irving wrote. Until the replication of the eastern town was accomplished, there was little to add to the tale told by Bryant, Cooper, and Irving. The writers of the remarkable generation which succeeded theirs focused on other matters. Left to the popular imagination, the prairies were pictured as the opposite of home, the negation of the enclosed and the snug. A microcosmic view of popular beliefs is afforded by the metamorphosis undergone by the poetic offering the Reverend E. H. Chapin published in *The Southern Literary Messenger* of September 1839. It was called "The Ocean-Buried," and began:

> "Bury me not in the deep deep sea!"
> The words came faint and mournfully,
> From the pallid lips of a youth, who lay
> On the cabin couch, where day by day
> He had wasted and pined.[11]

The lad asks rather to be laid in the churchyard on the green hillside by his father's grave, near the home, cot, and bower where he was raised so that his mother's prayers and his sister's tears can attend his rest. In the event, however, the unfortunate youth is lowered over the ship's side, "Where the billows bound and the wind sports free."

Within ten years the poem had acquired a printed musical score. Twenty years on it was not much heard in the parlors of America, but something called a "traditional cowboy song" was. It began:

> "Oh, bury me not on the lone prairie,"
> These words came low and mournfully
> From the pallid lips of a youth, who lay
> On his dying bed at the close of day.[12]

Unsurprisingly, this youth wants precisely the same green hillside grave as the luckless sailor and for exactly the same reasons. Alas, he had no better luck, and

> In a narrow grave just six by three
> We buried him there on the lone prairie

The graves depicted by Bryant and Cooper continued to dot the prairies of the imagination, a landscape so devoid of human meaning that words about the ocean could be applied to it also.

And then came the flood of indignation. At the time of the Midwest's great announcement of its self-discovery in the World's Columbian Exposition in 1893, a literary generation born on the prairies came into maturity and its theme was a double betrayal: the promise of the land betrayed by men—farmers, that is, betrayed by speculators; and the promise of men betrayed by the land—upright men coerced by labor to the stoop of beasts, and passionate women gone mad in shacks at the crossroad of the winds. Hamlin Garland, son of a westering Civil War veteran who homesteaded in Wisconsin, then Iowa, then South Dakota, only to go bust and backtrail to Wisconsin, sounded the keynote in *Main-Travelled Roads* (1891). The rudest stage of yeomanry had indeed succeeded the period of exploration, as earlier writers had predicted, but this was not followed by the New Englandy village of town green, trim houses, and bookish culture. Rather the home of toil was at one end of a road "hot and dusty in summer, and desolate and drear with mud in fall and spring," while in winter it was impassable, and at the other end was a town of shacks and tin.[13] The poor and weary predominated. Such culture as there was preached profit and the sinfulness of art.

The fantasized replication of Americanized European civilization had not occurred because between the emergence of the farmer and the growth of the market town, finance capital had intervened. Whatever their geographical proximity, the road from farm to town led through the metropolitan offices of banks, railroads, and land companies. Their lives were not in the control of the prairies' inhabitants. Their culture could neither grow coherently from their relationship to the land nor could the values of traditional culture—the best that man has thought and done—find a home in their midst. The latter culture was to be sought in the metropolis where social stratification and patronage American-style made it possible. In the amused dissection of Columbian Chicago found in the fiction of Henry Blake Fuller, artists and reformers go after Chicago with a will, but regardless of their projects—a painting or a settlement house—the paths they follow to accomplishment lead through the drawing rooms of Mrs. Eudoxia Pence.

The resulting prairie culture appeared mean, drab, and blighted to its native sons and daughters, and they sought the conscious life in Boston, New York, and Chicago, the mizzen, main, and fore masts of the American ship of culture. There, like Garland, they soon became deracinated and grafted themselves to a culture alien to their upbringing even as they bewailed the degradation of their home soil which made this necessary.

Some ten years after the Prairie style in architecture had been fully articulated, Carol Milford of Minneapolis married a doctor from Gopher Prairie, Minnesota, and made her home there. Anticipating her new life, Carol planned to bring beauty to a town which, however drab it then appeared, was bordered by lakes and flowed into a boundless prairie. But she seems never to have heard of the Prairie style, and the beautiful Gopher Prairie of her fantasy is Georgian. Her failure is a defeat at the hands of the powerfully corrosive culture of Gopher Prairie. But the narrative in which she lives is not called *Carol Kennicott* nor *Gopher Prairie,* but *Main Street.* The title is both a tip of Sinclair Lewis's hat to Hamlin Garland, who led the literary revolt from the prairie, and a reminder that a Gopher Prairie may be found wherever there is an American town big enough to have a Main Street.

The Prairie style has sometimes been regarded as a mis-nomer, a label that helps to distinguish a unique and consequential architectural achievement, but only a label, not an accurate description. The houses were, after all, designed in Chicago and not built on the real prairie. Such reservations have been countered by the contention that the coming-of-age of the Midwest, although drama-tized by the rise of Chicago, was nevertheless regional and so should be identified in terms of the region's char-acteristic topography. Wright himself said, "We of the Middle West are living on the prairie. The prairie has a beauty of its own and we should recognize and accentu-ate this natural beauty, its quiet level."[14] Moreover, the effect of architectural space-in-motion not only blended inside and outside space but also captured a singularly po-tent feature of the prairies. Bryant in his poem, for example, had noted how still the prairies stood, only to add:

> Motionless?
> No—they are all unchained again. The clouds
> Sweep over with their shadows, and, beneath
> The surface rolls and fluctuates to the eye.
>
> (ll. 10-13)

The matter of greater significance is not whether the term Prairie style validly grows from other meanings of prai-rie, but whether that style once so named validly attached itself to the locale, made, as it were, the prairie its own. Of this there can be no doubt. Wright's Prairie style marked not only a major event in architectural history, it led to a major revision of cultural attitudes.

When we consider this revision in the context of the lit-erary history of the prairie, we recognize that it is in good part a return to the outlook of the Romantic visionaries who had either little or no first-hand knowledge of the landscape. By Wright's day the real children of the prairie had lost the vision in pained reaction to the actuality. Also a native son, Wright transcended the actuality to embody what had only been vision for Bryant and Whitman.

Several years ago I took part in a symposium on the American Renaissance in art in connection with a show of paintings and artifacts from the period of 1878 to 1917. As now, my assignment then was to consider the literary context of the fine arts that formed the occasion. Then I was struck by how far in advance the writers were. The literary renaissance had preceded that in the fine arts by a quarter of a century; the painters were working in close cooperation with a patronage system which the writers of their day were exposing as the outgrowth of a social structure that denied the values that American lit-erary artists had fought so hard to establish—denied what Whitman would have called American identity.

Now I am struck by quite the reverse. At a time when writers stood baffled and dismayed at the edge of the abyss which had opened between the promise of the prai-ries and the actuality of its culture and concluded that their literary task could only be a dismantling, a fellow artist, Frank Lloyd Wright, showed them the way to re-turn to the dreamed-of ground and there to build.

NOTES

[1] Sherman Paul, *Louis Sullivan: An Artist in American Thought* (New York: Prentice-Hall, 1962), 1.

[2] Walt Whitman, "Song of Myself," *Leaves of Grass,* ed. Sculley Bradley and Harold W. Blodgett (New York: Norton, 1973), lines 12-13.

[3] See, for example, Richard Bridgman, *The Colloquial Style in America* (New York: Oxford University Press, 1966).

[4] Horatio Greenough, *The Travels, Observations, and Experiences of a Yankee Stonecutter* (Gainesville, Fla.: Scholars Facsimiles and Reprints, 1958), 33.

[5] Ralph Waldo Emerson, *The Journals and Miscella-neous Notebooks,* 16 vols. (Cambridge, Mass.: Harvard University Press, 1961-82), 5:150.

[6] William Dean Howells, *Literary Friends and Acquaintan-ces* (Bloomington: Indiana University Press, 1968), 49.

[7] William Cullen Bryant, "The Prairies," *The Literature of America,* 3 vols., ed. Irving Howe, Mark Schorer, and Larzer Ziff (New York: McGraw-Hill, 1971), 1:505, lines 1-4.

[8] Henry Nash Smith, *Virgin Land* (Cambridge, Mass.: Harvard University Press, 1950), 220-24.

[9] See, for example, two notable works of the 1920s: D. H. Lawrence, *Studies in Classic American Literature* (New York: Doubleday, 1951), and William Carlos Williams, *In the American Grain* (New York: New Di-rections, 1956).

[10] Washington Irving, *A Tour on the Prairies* (London, 1835), 69.

[11] Reverend E. H. Chapin, "The Ocean-Buried," *Southern Literary Messenger* 5, no. 9. (September 1839): 615-16.

[12] "Bury Me Not on the Lone Prairie," *Songs of the Great American West,* ed. Irwin Silber (New York: Macmillan, 1967), 202.

[13] Hamlin Garland, *Main-Travelled Roads* (New York: Signet, 1962), 12.

[14] Quoted in Marcus Whiffen, *American Architecture Since 1780: A Guide to the Styles* (Cambridge, Mass.: MIT Press, 1969), 202.

FURTHER READING

Biography

Secrest, Meryle. *Frank Lloyd Wright*. New York: Alfred A. Knopf, 1992, 634 p.

  Biography of Wright that makes use of previously unavailable photographs, letters, books, and other materials from the Frank Lloyd Wright Memorial Foundation.

Twombly, Robert C. *Frank Lloyd Wright: An Interpretive Biography*. New York: Harper & Row, 1973, 373 p.

  Biographical and critical study emphasizing the impact of Wright's complex personality on his architectural designs. This work features an extensive bibliography.

Wright, John Lloyd. *My Father Who Is On Earth*. New Edition. Carbondale: Southern Illinois University Press, 1994, 231 p.

  Noncritical biography by Wright's second son.

Wright, Olgivanna Lloyd. *The Shining Brow: Frank Lloyd Wright*. New York: Horizon Press, 1960, 300 p.

  A laudatory account of the latter portion of Wright's architectural career.

Criticism

Alofsin, Anthony. *Frank Lloyd Wright, The Lost Years, 1910-1922: A Study of Influence*. Chicago: University of Chicago Press, 1993, 397 p.

  Asserts that Wright's contact with European architecture from 1909 to 1911 "had a greater impact on Wright than he had on European architecture."

Brooks, H. Allen, ed. *Writings on Wright: Selected Comment on Frank Lloyd Wright*. Cambridge, Mass.: The MIT Press, 1981, 229 p.

  Extensive collection of thematically-organized statements on Wright by the "people with whom he actually lived, worked, and argued, not just the views of critics and historians."

————. *Frank Lloyd Wright and the Prairie School* New York: George Braziller, Inc., 1984, 120 p.

  A brief synopsis of the Prairie school of architecture (c. 1890-1914), stressing the importance of Wright's position as a leader of the movement. Includes annotated illustrations of buildings and decorative designs by Wright and other members of the movement.

Ellis, Russell. "Wright's Written People." In *Architects' People*, edited by Russell Ellis and Dana Cuff, pp. 44-54. New York: Oxford University Press, 1989.

  Considers some of Wright's statements on human nature, social order, and his view of the *living* building.

Levine, Neil. "Abstraction and Representation in Modern Architecture: The International Style of Frank Lloyd Wright." *A A Files* II (Spring 1986): 3-21.

  Analyzes the relationship between abstraction and representation in Wright's buildings, arguing that Wright must be classed as a modernist along with the European leaders of the International Style.

————. *The Architecture of Frank Lloyd Wright*. Princeton, N.J.: Princeton University Press, 1996, 524 p.

  Study that considers "Wright's career and work as a continuous field, embedded in a larger cultural and historical context" while acknowledging the major shift in focus that occurred in 1909-10 with his exposure to European modernism.

McCarter, Robert, ed. *Frank Lloyd Wright: A Primer on Architectural Principles*. New York: Princeton Architectural Press, 1991, 308 p.

  Collection of essays by various contributors on the central ideals of Wright's architectural vision.

Riley, Terence, ed. *Frank Lloyd Wright: Architect*. New York: The Museum of Modern Art, 1994, 344 p.

  Five essays on such subjects as Wright's relationship to modernism, technology, and landscape.

Smith, Norris Kelly. *Frank Lloyd Wright: A Study in Architectural Content*. Englewood Cliffs, N. J.: Prentice-Hall, 1966, 332 p.

  A survey of Wright's career, focusing on the theoretical aspects of his designs.

Storrer, William Allin. *The Frank Lloyd Wright Companion*. Chicago: University of Chicago Press, 1993, 492 p.

  Includes textual commentary, plans, and photographs related to Wright's more than five hundred known architectural works.

Weisberg, Gabriel. "Frank Lloyd Wright and Pre-Columbian Art—The Background for His Architecture." *Art Quarterly* XXX, No. 1 (Spring 1967): 40-51.

  Traces the influence of pre-Columbian architecture on Wright's early work.

Twentieth-Century Literary Criticism

Cumulative Indexes
Volumes 1-95

How to Use This Index

The main references

```
┌─────────────────────────────────────┐
│  Calvino, Italo                      │
│     1923–1985 ....... CLC 5, 8, 11, 22, 33, 39,  │
│                          73; SSC 3   │
└─────────────────────────────────────┘
```

list all author entries in the following Gale Literary Criticism series:

BLC = *Black Literature Criticism*
CLC = *Contemporary Literary Criticism*
CLR = *Children's Literature Review*
CMLC = *Classical and Medieval Literature Criticism*
DA = *DISCovering Authors*
DAB = *DISCovering Authors: British*
DAC = *DISCovering Authors: Canadian*
DAM = *DISCovering Authors: Modules*
    DRAM: *Dramatists Module*; *MST*: *Most-Studied Authors Module*;
    MULT: *Multicultural Authors Module*; *NOV*: *Novelists Module*;
    POET: *Poets Module*; *POP*: *Popular Fiction and Genre Authors Module*
DC = *Drama Criticism*
HLC = *Hispanic Literature Criticism*
LC = *Literature Criticism from 1400 to 1800*
NCLC = *Nineteenth-Century Literature Criticism*
PC = *Poetry Criticism*
SSC = *Short Story Criticism*
TCLC = *Twentieth-Century Literary Criticism*
WLC = *World Literature Criticism, 1500 to the Present*

The cross-references

```
┌─────────────────────────────────────┐
│                                      │
│    See also CANR 23; CA 85-88;       │
│       obituary CA116                 │
│                                      │
└─────────────────────────────────────┘
```

list all author entries in the following Gale biographical and literary sources:

AAYA = *Authors & Artists for Young Adults*
AITN = *Authors in the News*
BEST = *Bestsellers*
BW = *Black Writers*
CA = *Contemporary Authors*
CAAS = *Contemporary Authors Autobiography Series*
CABS = *Contemporary Authors Bibliographical Series*
CANR = *Contemporary Authors New Revision Series*
CAP = *Contemporary Authors Permanent Series*
CDALB = *Concise Dictionary of American Literary Biography*
CDBLB = *Concise Dictionary of British Literary Biography*
DLB = *Dictionary of Literary Biography*
DLBD = *Dictionary of Literary Biography Documentary Series*
DLBY = *Dictionary of Literary Biography Yearbook*
HW = *Hispanic Writers*
JRDA = *Junior DISCovering Authors*
MAICYA = *Major Authors and Illustrators for Children and Young Adults*
MTCW = *Major 20th-Century Writers*
NNAL = *Native North American Literature*
SAAS = *Something about the Author Autobiography Series*
SATA = *Something about the Author*
YABC = *Yesterday's Authors of Books for Children*

See also CA 89-92; 134

Antoine, Marc
 See Proust, (Valentin-Louis-George-Eugene-) Marcel

Antoninus, Brother
 See Everson, William (Oliver)

Antonioni, Michelangelo 1912- .... **CLC 20**
 See also CA 73-76; CANR 45, 77

Antschel, Paul 1920-1970
 See Celan, Paul
 See also CA 85-88; CANR 33, 61; MTCW 1

Anwar, Chairil 1922-1949 .... **TCLC 22**
 See also CA 121

Apess, William 1798-1839(?) ... **NCLC 73; DAM MULT**
 See also DLB 175; NNAL

Apollinaire, Guillaume 1880-1918**TCLC 3, 8, 51; DAM POET; PC 7**
 See also Kostrowitzki, Wilhelm Apollinaris de
 See also CA 152; MTCW 1

Appelfeld, Aharon 1932- .... **CLC 23, 47**
 See also CA 112; 133

Apple, Max (Isaac) 1941- .... **CLC 9, 33**
 See also CA 81-84; CANR 19, 54; DLB 130

Appleman, Philip (Dean) 1926- .... **CLC 51**
 See also CA 13-16R; CAAS 18; CANR 6, 29, 56

Appleton, Lawrence
 See Lovecraft, H(oward) P(hillips)

Apteryx
 See Eliot, T(homas) S(tearns)

Apuleius, (Lucius Madaurensis) 125(?)-175(?) **CMLC 1**
 See also DLB 211

Aquin, Hubert 1929-1977 .... **CLC 15**
 See also CA 105; DLB 53

Aquinas, Thomas 1224(?)-1274 .... **CMLC 33**
 See also DLB 115

Aragon, Louis 1897-1982**CLC 3, 22; DAM NOV, POET**
 See also CA 69-72; 108; CANR 28, 71; DLB 72; MTCW 1, 2

Arany, Janos 1817-1882 .... **NCLC 34**

Aranyos, Kakay
 See Mikszath, Kalman

Arbuthnot, John 1667-1735 .... **LC 1**
 See also DLB 101

Archer, Herbert Winslow
 See Mencken, H(enry) L(ouis)

Archer, Jeffrey (Howard) 1940- .. **CLC 28; DAM POP**
 See also AAYA 16; BEST 89:3; CA 77-80; CANR 22, 52; INT CANR-22

Archer, Jules 1915- .... **CLC 12**
 See also CA 9-12R; CANR 6, 69; SAAS 5; SATA 4, 85

Archer, Lee
 See Ellison, Harlan (Jay)

Arden, John 1930- **CLC 6, 13, 15; DAM DRAM**
 See also CA 13-16R; CAAS 4; CANR 31, 65, 67; DLB 13; MTCW 1

Arenas, Reinaldo 1943-1990**CLC 41; DAM MULT; HLC**
 See also CA 124; 128; 133; CANR 73; DLB 145; HW 1; MTCW 1

Arendt, Hannah 1906-1975 .... **CLC 66, 98**
 See also CA 17-20R; 61-64; CANR 26, 60; MTCW 1, 2

Aretino, Pietro 1492-1556 .... **LC 12**

Arghezi, Tudor 1880-1967 .... **CLC 80**
 See also Theodorescu, Ion N.
 See also CA 167

Arguedas, Jose Maria 1911-1969 .. **CLC 10, 18; HLCS 1**
 See also CA 89-92; CANR 73; DLB 113; HW 1

Argueta, Manlio 1936- .... **CLC 31**
 See also CA 131; CANR 73; DLB 145; HW 1

Ariosto, Ludovico 1474-1533 .... **LC 6**

Aristides
 See Epstein, Joseph

Aristophanes 450B.C.-385B.C. .... **CMLC 4; DA; DAB; DAC; DAM DRAM, MST; DC 2; WLCS**
 See also DLB 176

Aristotle 384B.C.-322B.C. **CMLC 31; DA; DAB; DAC; DAM MST; WLCS**
 See also DLB 176

Arlt, Roberto (Godofredo Christophersen) 1900-1942 .... **TCLC 29; DAM MULT; HLC**
 See also CA 123; 131; CANR 67; HW 1, 2

Armah, Ayi Kwei 1939-**CLC 5, 33; BLC 1; DAM MULT, POET**
 See also BW 1; CA 61-64; CANR 21, 64; DLB 117; MTCW 1

Armatrading, Joan 1950- .... **CLC 17**
 See also CA 114

Arnette, Robert
 See Silverberg, Robert

Arnim, Achim von (Ludwig Joachim von Arnim) 1781-1831 .... **NCLC 5; SSC 29**
 See also DLB 90

Arnim, Bettina von 1785-1859 .... **NCLC 38**
 See also DLB 90

Arnold, Matthew 1822-1888 .... **NCLC 6, 29; DA; DAB; DAC; DAM MST, POET; PC 5; WLC**
 See also CDBLB 1832-1890; DLB 32, 57

Arnold, Thomas 1795-1842 .... **NCLC 18**
 See also DLB 55

Arnow, Harriette (Louisa) Simpson 1908-1986 **CLC 2, 7, 18**
 See also CA 9-12R; 118; CANR 14; DLB 6; MTCW 1, 2; SATA 42; SATA-Obit 47

Arouet, Francois-Marie
 See Voltaire

Arp, Hans
 See Arp, Jean

Arp, Jean 1887-1966 .... **CLC 5**
 See also CA 81-84; 25-28R; CANR 42, 77

Arrabal
 See Arrabal, Fernando

Arrabal, Fernando 1932- .... **CLC 2, 9, 18, 58**
 See also CA 9-12R; CANR 15

Arrick, Fran .... **CLC 30**
 See also Gaberman, Judie Angell

Artaud, Antonin (Marie Joseph) 1896-1948**TCLC 3, 36; DAM DRAM**
 See also CA 104; 149; MTCW 1

Arthur, Ruth M(abel) 1905-1979 .... **CLC 12**
 See also CA 9-12R; 85-88; CANR 4; SATA 7, 26

Artsybashev, Mikhail (Petrovich) 1878-1927 **TCLC 31**
 See also CA 170

Arundel, Honor (Morfydd) 1919-1973 ... **CLC 17**
 See also CA 21-22; 41-44R; CAP 2; CLR 35; SATA 4; SATA-Obit 24

Arzner, Dorothy 1897-1979 .... **CLC 98**

Asch, Sholem 1880-1957 .... **TCLC 3**
 See also CA 105

Ash, Shalom
 See Asch, Sholem

Ashbery, John (Lawrence) 1927-**CLC 2, 3, 4, 6, 9, 13, 15, 25, 41, 77; DAM POET; PC 26**
 See also CA 5-8R; CANR 9, 37, 66; DLB 5, 165; DLBY 81; INT CANR-9; MTCW 1, 2

Ashdown, Clifford
 See Freeman, R(ichard) Austin

Ashe, Gordon
 See Creasey, John

Ashton-Warner, Sylvia (Constance) 1908-1984 **CLC 19**
 See also CA 69-72; 112; CANR 29; MTCW 1, 2

Asimov, Isaac 1920-1992 **CLC 1, 3, 9, 19, 26, 76, 92; DAM POP**
 See also AAYA 13; BEST 90:2; CA 1-4R; 137; CANR 2, 19, 36, 60; CLR 12; DLB 8; DLBY 92; INT CANR-19; JRDA; MAICYA; MTCW 1,

2; SATA 1, 26, 74

Assis, Joaquim Maria Machado de
 See Machado de Assis, Joaquim Maria

Astley, Thea (Beatrice May) 1925- .... **CLC 41**
 See also CA 65-68; CANR 11, 43, 78

Aston, James
 See White, T(erence) H(anbury)

Asturias, Miguel Angel 1899-1974**CLC 3, 8, 13; DAM MULT, NOV; HLC**
 See also CA 25-28; 49-52; CANR 32; CAP 2; DLB 113; HW 1; MTCW 1, 2

Atares, Carlos Saura
 See Saura (Atares), Carlos

Atheling, William
 See Pound, Ezra (Weston Loomis)

Atheling, William, Jr.
 See Blish, James (Benjamin)

Atherton, Gertrude (Franklin Horn) 1857-1948 **TCLC 2**
 See also CA 104; 155; DLB 9, 78, 186

Atherton, Lucius
 See Masters, Edgar Lee

Atkins, Jack
 See Harris, Mark

Atkinson, Kate .... **CLC 99**
 See also CA 166

Attaway, William (Alexander) 1911-1986**CLC 92; BLC 1; DAM MULT**
 See also BW 2, 3; CA 143; DLB 76

Atticus
 See Fleming, Ian (Lancaster); Wilson, (Thomas) Woodrow

Atwood, Margaret (Eleanor) 1939-**CLC 2, 3, 4, 8, 13, 15, 25, 44, 84; DA; DAB; DAC; DAM MST, NOV, POET; PC 8; SSC 2; WLC**
 See also AAYA 12; BEST 89:2; CA 49-52; CANR 3, 24, 33, 59; DLB 53; INT CANR-24; MTCW 1, 2; SATA 50

Aubigny, Pierre d'
 See Mencken, H(enry) L(ouis)

Aubin, Penelope 1685-1731(?) .... **LC 9**
 See also DLB 39

Auchincloss, Louis (Stanton) 1917-**CLC 4, 6, 9, 18, 45; DAM NOV; SSC 22**
 See also CA 1-4R; CANR 6, 29, 55; DLB 2; DLBY 80; INT CANR-29; MTCW 1

Auden, W(ystan) H(ugh) 1907-1973**CLC 1, 2, 3, 4, 6, 9, 11, 14, 43; DA; DAB; DAC; DAM DRAM, MST, POET; PC 1; WLC**
 See also AAYA 18; CA 9-12R; 45-48; CANR 5, 61; CDBLB 1914-1945; DLB 10, 20; MTCW 1, 2

Audiberti, Jacques 1900-1965 ..... **CLC 38; DAM DRAM**
 See also CA 25-28R

Audubon, John James 1785-1851 .... **NCLC 47**

Auel, Jean M(arie) 1936-**CLC 31, 107; DAM POP**
 See also AAYA 7; BEST 90:4; CA 103; CANR 21, 64; INT CANR-21; SATA 91

Auerbach, Erich 1892-1957 .... **TCLC 43**
 See also CA 118; 155

Augier, Emile 1820-1889 .... **NCLC 31**
 See also DLB 192

August, John
 See De Voto, Bernard (Augustine)

Augustine 354-430 . **CMLC 6; DA; DAB; DAC; DAM MST; WLCS**
 See also DLB 115

Aurelius
 See Bourne, Randolph S(illiman)

Aurobindo, Sri
 See Ghose, Aurabinda

Austen, Jane 1775-1817**NCLC 1, 13, 19, 33, 51; DA; DAB; DAC; DAM MST, NOV; WLC**
 See also AAYA 19; CDBLB 1789-1832; DLB 116

Auster, Paul 1947- .... **CLC 47**
 See also CA 69-72; CANR 23, 52, 75; MTCW 1

See also CA 1-4R; CANR 5, 20; DLB 88;
MTCW 1

Biruni, al 973-1048(?) .... **CMLC 28**

Bishop, Elizabeth 1911-1979 **CLC 1, 4, 9, 13, 15,
32; DA; DAC; DAM MST, POET; PC 3**
See also CA 5-8R; 89-92; CABS 2; CANR 26, 61;
CDALB 1968-1988; DLB 5, 169; MTCW 1, 2;
SATA-Obit 24

Bishop, John 1935- .... **CLC 10**
See also CA 105

Bissett, Bill 1939- .... **CLC 18; PC 14**
See also CA 69-72; CAAS 19; CANR 15; DLB
53; MTCW 1

Bissoondath, Neil (Devindra) 1955- .. **CLC 120;
DAC**
See also CA 136

Bitov, Andrei (Georgievich) 1937- .... **CLC 57**
See also CA 142

Biyidi, Alexandre 1932-
See Beti, Mongo
See also BW 1, 3; CA 114; 124; CANR 81; MTCW
1, 2

Bjarme, Brynjolf
See Ibsen, Henrik (Johan)

Bjoernson, Bjoernstjerne (Martinius) 1832-1910
TCLC 7, 37
See also CA 104

Black, Robert
See Holdstock, Robert P.

Blackburn, Paul 1926-1971 .... **CLC 9, 43**
See also CA 81-84; 33-36R; CANR 34; DLB 16;
DLBY 81

Black Elk 1863-1950 ..... **TCLC 33; DAM MULT**
See also CA 144; MTCW 1; NNAL

Black Hobart
See Sanders, (James) Ed(ward)

Blacklin, Malcolm
See Chambers, Aidan

Blackmore, R(ichard) D(oddridge) 1825-1900
TCLC 27
See also CA 120; DLB 18

Blackmur, R(ichard) P(almer) 1904-1965 **CLC 2,
24**
See also CA 11-12; 25-28R; CANR 71; CAP 1;
DLB 63

Black Tarantula
See Acker, Kathy

Blackwood, Algernon (Henry) 1869-1951 **TCLC 5**
See also CA 105; 150; DLB 153, 156, 178

Blackwood, Caroline 1931-1996 .. **CLC 6, 9, 100**
See also CA 85-88; 151; CANR 32, 61, 65; DLB
14, 207; MTCW 1

Blade, Alexander
See Hamilton, Edmond; Silverberg, Robert

Blaga, Lucian 1895-1961 .... **CLC 75**
See also CA 157

Blair, Eric (Arthur) 1903-1950
See Orwell, George
See also CA 104; 132; DA; DAB; DAC; DAM
MST, NOV; MTCW 1, 2; SATA 29

Blair, Hugh 1718-1800 .... **NCLC 75**

Blais, Marie-Claire 1939- .. **CLC 2, 4, 6, 13, 22;
DAC; DAM MST**
See also CA 21-24R; CAAS 4; CANR 38, 75; DLB
53; MTCW 1, 2

Blaise, Clark 1940- .... **CLC 29**
See also AITN 2; CA 53-56; CAAS 3; CANR 5,
66; DLB 53

Blake, Fairley
See De Voto, Bernard (Augustine)

Blake, Nicholas
See Day Lewis, C(ecil)
See also DLB 77

Blake, William 1757-1827 **NCLC 13, 37, 57; DA;
DAB; DAC; DAM MST, POET; PC 12; WLC**
See also CDBLB 1789-1832; CLR 52; DLB 93, 163;
MAICYA; SATA 30

Blasco Ibanez, Vicente 1867-1928 **TCLC 12;
DAM NOV**
See also CA 110; 131; CANR 81; HW 1, 2;
MTCW 1

Blatty, William Peter 1928- . **CLC 2; DAM POP**
See also CA 5-8R; CANR 9

Bleeck, Oliver
See Thomas, Ross (Elmore)

Blessing, Lee 1949- .... **CLC 54**

Blish, James (Benjamin) 1921-1975 ..... **CLC 14**
See also CA 1-4R; 57-60; CANR 3; DLB 8;
MTCW 1; SATA 66

Bliss, Reginald
See Wells, H(erbert) G(eorge)

Blixen, Karen (Christentze Dinesen) 1885-1962
See Dinesen, Isak
See also CA 25-28; CANR 22, 50; CAP 2; MTCW
1, 2; SATA 44

Bloch, Robert (Albert) 1917-1994 .... **CLC 33**
See also AAYA 29; CA 5-8R; 146; CAAS 20;
CANR 5, 78; DLB 44; INT CANR-5; MTCW
1; SATA 12; SATA-Obit 82

Blok, Alexander (Alexandrovich) 1880-1921
TCLC 5; PC 21
See also CA 104

Blom, Jan
See Breytenbach, Breyten

Bloom, Harold 1930- .... **CLC 24, 103**
See also CA 13-16R; CANR 39, 75; DLB 67;
MTCW 1

Bloomfield, Aurelius
See Bourne, Randolph S(illiman)

Blount, Roy (Alton), Jr. 1941- .... **CLC 38**
See also CA 53-56; CANR 10, 28, 61; INT CANR-
28; MTCW 1, 2

Bloy, Leon 1846-1917 .... **TCLC 22**
See also CA 121; DLB 123

Blume, Judy (Sussman) 1938- **CLC 12, 30; DAM
NOV, POP**
See also AAYA 3, 26; CA 29-32R; CANR 13, 37,
66; CLR 2, 15; DLB 52; JRDA; MAICYA;
MTCW 1, 2; SATA 2, 31, 79

Blunden, Edmund (Charles) 1896-1974 **CLC 2, 56**
See also CA 17-18; 45-48; CANR 54; CAP 2; DLB
20, 100, 155; MTCW 1

Bly, Robert (Elwood) 1926- **CLC 1, 2, 5, 10, 15, 38;
DAM POET**
See also CA 5-8R; CANR 41, 73; DLB 5; MTCW
1, 2

Boas, Franz 1858-1942 .... **TCLC 56**
See also CA 115

Bobette
See Simenon, Georges (Jacques Christian)

Boccaccio, Giovanni 1313-1375 **CMLC 13; SSC 10**

Bochco, Steven 1943- .... **CLC 35**
See also AAYA 11; CA 124; 138

Bodel, Jean 1167(?)-1210 .... **CMLC 28**

Bodenheim, Maxwell 1892-1954 .... **TCLC 44**
See also CA 110; DLB 9, 45

Bodker, Cecil 1927- .... **CLC 21**
See also CA 73-76; CANR 13, 44; CLR 23;
MAICYA; SATA 14

Boell, Heinrich (Theodor) 1917-1985 **CLC 2, 3, 6,
9, 11, 15, 27, 32, 72; DA; DAB; DAC; DAM
MST, NOV; SSC 23; WLC**
' See also CA 21-24R; 116; CANR 24; DLB 69;
DLBY 85; MTCW 1, 2

Boerne, Alfred
See Doeblin, Alfred

Boethius 480(?)-524(?) .... **CMLC 15**
See also DLB 115

Bogan, Louise 1897-1970 **CLC 4, 39, 46, 93; DAM
POET; PC 12**
See also CA 73-76; 25-28R; CANR 33; DLB 45,
169; MTCW 1, 2

Bogarde, Dirk .... **CLC 19**
See also Van Den Bogarde, Derek Jules Gaspard

Ulric Niven
See also DLB 14

Bogosian, Eric 1953- .... **CLC 45**
See also CA 138

Bograd, Larry 1953- .... **CLC 35**
See also CA 93-96; CANR 57; SAAS 21; SATA
33, 89

Boiardo, Matteo Maria 1441-1494 .... **LC 6**

Boileau-Despreaux, Nicolas 1636-1711 ..... **LC 3**

Bojer, Johan 1872-1959 .... **TCLC 64**

Boland, Eavan (Aisling) 1944- **CLC 40, 67, 113;
DAM POET**
See also CA 143; CANR 61; DLB 40; MTCW 2

Boll, Heinrich
See Boell, Heinrich (Theodor)

Bolt, Lee
See Faust, Frederick (Schiller)

Bolt, Robert (Oxton) 1924-1995 .. **CLC 14; DAM
DRAM**
See also CA 17-20R; 147; CANR 35, 67; DLB 13;
MTCW 1

Bombet, Louis-Alexandre-Cesar
See Stendhal

Bomkauf
See Kaufman, Bob (Garnell)

Bonaventura .... **NCLC 35**
See also DLB 90

Bond, Edward 1934- **CLC 4, 6, 13, 23; DAM DRAM**
See also CA 25-28R; CANR 38, 67; DLB 13;
MTCW 1

Bonham, Frank 1914-1989 .... **CLC 12**
See also AAYA 1; CA 9-12R; CANR 4, 36; JRDA;
MAICYA; SAAS 3; SATA 1, 49; SATA-Obit
62

Bonnefoy, Yves 1923- **CLC 9, 15, 58; DAM MST,
POET**
See also CA 85-88; CANR 33, 75; MTCW 1, 2

Bontemps, Arna(ud Wendell) 1902-1973 **CLC 1,
18; BLC 1; DAM MULT, NOV; POET**
See also BW 1; CA 1-4R; 41-44R; CANR 4, 35;
CLR 6; DLB 48, 51; JRDA; MAICYA; MTCW
1, 2; SATA 2, 44; SATA-Obit 24

Booth, Martin 1944- .... **CLC 13**
See also CA 93-96; CAAS 2

Booth, Philip 1925- .... **CLC 23**
See also CA 5-8R; CANR 5; DLBY 82

Booth, Wayne C(layson) 1921- .... **CLC 24**
See also CA 1-4R; CAAS 5; CANR 3, 43; DLB 67

Borchert, Wolfgang 1921-1947 .... **TCLC 5**
See also CA 104; DLB 69, 124

Borel, Petrus 1809-1859 .... **NCLC 41**

Borges, Jorge Luis 1899-1986 **CLC 1, 2, 3, 4, 6, 8,
9, 10, 13, 19, 44, 48, 83; DA; DAB; DAC;
DAM MST, MULT; HLC; PC 22; SSC 4; WLC**
See also AAYA 26; CA 21-24R; CANR 19, 33, 75;
DLB 113; DLBY 86; HW 1, 2; MTCW 1, 2

Borowski, Tadeusz 1922-1951 .... **TCLC 9**
See also CA 106; 154

Borrow, George (Henry) 1803-1881 ...... **NCLC 9**
See also DLB 21, 55, 166

Bosman, Herman Charles 1905-1951 . **TCLC 49**
See also Malan, Herman
See also CA 160

Bosschere, Jean de 1878(?)-1953 .... **TCLC 19**
See also CA 115

Boswell, James 1740-1795 **LC 4, 50; DA; DAB;
DAC; DAM MST; WLC**
See also CDBLB 1660-1789; DLB 104, 142

Bottoms, David 1949- .... **CLC 53**
See also CA 105; CANR 22; DLB 120; DLBY 83

Boucicault, Dion 1820-1890 .... **NCLC 41**

Boucolon, Maryse 1937(?)-
See Conde, Maryse
See also BW 3; CA 110; CANR 30, 53, 76

Bourget, Paul (Charles Joseph) 1852-1935 **TCLC
12**
See also CA 107; DLB 123

See also CA 13-16R; CANR 15
Carlsen, Chris
See Holdstock, Robert P.
Carlson, Ron(ald F.) 1947- .... CLC 54
See also CA 105; CANR 27
Carlyle, Thomas 1795-1881NCLC 70; DA; DAB;
    DAC; DAM MST
See also CDBLB 1789-1832; DLB 55; 144
Carman, (William) Bliss 1861-1929TCLC7; DAC
See also CA 104; 152; DLB 92
Carnegie, Dale 1888-1955 .... TCLC 53
Carossa, Hans 1878-1956 .... TCLC 48
See also CA 170; DLB 66
Carpenter, Don(ald Richard) 1931-1995 CLC 41
See also CA 45-48; 149; CANR 1, 71
Carpenter, Edward 1844-1929 .... TCLC 88
See also CA 163
Carpentier (y Valmont), Alejo 1904-1980CLC 8,
    11, 38, 110; DAM MULT; HLC; SSC 35
See also CA 65-68; 97-100; CANR 11, 70; DLB
    113; HW 1, 2
Carr, Caleb 1955(?)- .... CLC 86
See also CA 147; CANR 73
Carr, Emily 1871-1945 .... TCLC 32
See also CA 159; DLB 68
Carr, John Dickson 1906-1977 .... CLC 3
See also Fairbairn, Roger
See also CA 49-52; 69-72; CANR 3, 33, 60; MTCW
    1, 2
Carr, Philippa
See Hibbert, Eleanor Alice Burford
Carr, Virginia Spencer 1929- .... CLC 34
See also CA 61-64; DLB 111
Carrere, Emmanuel 1957- .... CLC 89
Carrier, Roch 1937- ... CLC 13, 78; DAC; DAM
    MST
See also CA 130; CANR 61; DLB 53; SATA 105
Carroll, James P. 1943(?)- .... CLC 38
See also CA 81-84; CANR 73; MTCW 1
Carroll, Jim 1951- .... CLC 35
See also AAYA 17; CA 45-48; CANR 42
Carroll, Lewis .... NCLC 2, 53; PC 18; WLC
See also Dodgson, Charles Lutwidge
See also CDBLB 1832-1890; CLR 2, 18; DLB 18,
    163, 178; DLBY 98; JRDA
Carroll, Paul Vincent 1900-1968 .... CLC 10
See also CA 9-12R; 25-28R; DLB 10
Carruth, Hayden 1921-CLC 4, 7, 10, 18, 84; PC
    10
See also CA 9-12R; CANR 4, 38, 59; DLB 5, 165;
    INT CANR-4; MTCW 1, 2; SATA 47
Carson, Rachel Louise 1907-1964CLC 71; DAM
    POP
See also CA 77-80; CANR 35; MTCW 1, 2; SATA
    23
Carter, Angela (Olive) 1940-1992CLC 5, 41, 76;
    SSC 13
See also CA 53-56; 136; CANR 12, 36, 61; DLB
    14, 207; MTCW 1, 2; SATA 66; SATA-Obit 70
Carter, Nick
See Smith, Martin Cruz
Carver, Raymond 1938-1988 CLC 22, 36, 53, 55;
    DAM NOV; SSC 8
See also CA 33-36R; 126; CANR 17, 34, 61; DLB
    130; DLBY 84, 88; MTCW 1, 2
Cary, Elizabeth, Lady Falkland 1585-1639 LC 30
Cary, (Arthur) Joyce (Lunel) 1888-1957TCLC 1,
    29
See also CA 104;.164; CDBLB 1914-1945; DLB
    15, 100; MTCW 2
Casanova de Seingalt, Giovanni Jacopo 1725-1798
    LC 13
Casares, Adolfo Bioy
See Bioy Casares, Adolfo
Casely-Hayford, J(oseph) E(phraim) 1866-1930
    TCLC 24; BLC 1; DAM MULT
See also BW 2; CA 123; 152

Casey, John (Dudley) 1939- .... CLC 59
See also BEST 90:2; CA 69-72; CANR 23
Casey, Michael 1947- .... CLC 2
See also CA 65-68; DLB 5
Casey, Patrick
See Thurman, Wallace (Henry)
Casey, Warren (Peter) 1935-1988 .... CLC 12
See also CA 101; 127; INT 101
Casona, Alejandro .... CLC 49
See also Alvarez, Alejandro Rodriguez
Cassavetes, John 1929-1989 .... CLC 20
See also CA 85-88; 127
Cassian, Nina 1924- .... PC 17
Cassill, R(onald) V(erlin) 1919- .... CLC 4, 23
See also CA 9-12R; CAAS 1; CANR 7, 45; DLB 6
Cassirer, Ernst 1874-1945 .... TCLC 61
See also CA 157
Cassity, (Allen) Turner 1929- .... CLC 6, 42
See also CA 17-20R; CAAS 8; CANR 11; DLB
    105
Castaneda, Carlos (Cesar Aranha) 1931(?)-1998
    CLC 12, 119
See also CA 25-28R; CANR 32, 66; HW 1; MTCW
    1
Castedo, Elena 1937- .... CLC 65
See also CA 132
Castedo-Ellerman, Elena
See Castedo, Elena
Castellanos, Rosario 1925-1974 . CLC 66; DAM
    MULT; HLC
See also CA 131; 53-56; CANR 58; DLB 113; HW
    1; MTCW 1
Castelvetro, Lodovico 1505-1571 .... LC 12
Castiglione, Baldassare 1478-1529 .... LC 12
Castle, Robert
See Hamilton, Edmond
Castro, Guillen de 1569-1631 .... LC 19
Castro, Rosalia de 1837-1885NCLC 3, 78; DAM
    MULT
Cather, Willa
See Cather, Willa Sibert
Cather, Willa Sibert 1873-1947 TCLC 1, 11, 31;
    DA; DAB; DAC; DAM MST, NOV; SSC 2;
    WLC
See also AAYA 24; CA 104; 128; CDALB 1865-
    1917; DLB 9, 54, 78; DLBD 1; MTCW 1, 2;
    SATA 30
Catherine, Saint 1347-1380 .... CMLC 27
Cato, Marcus Porcius 234B.C.-149B.C.CMLC 21
See also DLB 211
Catton, (Charles) Bruce 1899-1978 ...... CLC 35
See also AITN 1; CA 5-8R; 81-84; CANR 7, 74;
    DLB 17; SATA 2; SATA-Obit 24
Catullus c. 84B.C.-c. 54B.C. .... CMLC 18
See also DLB 211
Cauldwell, Frank
See King, Francis (Henry)
Caunitz, William J. 1933-1996 .... CLC 34
See also BEST 89:3; CA 125; 130; 152; CANR 73;·
    INT 130
Causley, Charles (Stanley) 1917- .... CLC 7
See also CA 9-12R; CANR 5, 35; CLR 30; DLB
    27; MTCW 1; SATA 3, 66
Caute, (John) David 1936- . CLC 29; DAM NOV
See also CA 1-4R; CAAS 4; CANR 1, 33, 64;
    DLB 14
Cavafy, C(onstantine) P(eter) 1863-1933TCLC 2,
    7; DAM POET
See also Kavafis, Konstantinos Petrou
See also CA 148; MTCW 1
Cavallo, Evelyn
See Spark, Muriel (Sarah)
Cavanna, Betty .... CLC 12
See also Harrison, Elizabeth Cavanna
See also JRDA; MAICYA; SAAS 4; SATA 1, 30
Cavendish, Margaret Lucas 1623-1673 ... LC 30
See also DLB 131

Caxton, William 1421(?)-1491(?) .... LC 17
See also DLB 170
Cayer, D. M.
See Duffy, Maureen
Cayrol, Jean 1911- .... CLC 11
See also CA 89-92; DLB 83
Cela, Camilo Jose 1916- .. CLC 4, 13, 59; DAM
    MULT; HLC
See also BEST 90:2; CA 21-24R; CAAS 10; CANR
    21, 32, 76; DLBY 89; HW 1; MTCW 1, 2
Celan, Paul .... CLC 10, 19, 53, 82; PC 10
See also Antschel, Paul
See also DLB 69
Celine, Louis-FerdinandCLC 1, 3, 4, 7, 9, 15, 47
See also Destouches, Louis-Ferdinand
See also DLB 72
Cellini, Benvenuto 1500-1571 .... LC 7
Cendrars, Blaise 1887-1961 .... CLC 18, 106
See also Sauser-Hall, Frederic
Cernuda (y Bidon), Luis 1902-1963CLC 54; DAM
    POET
See also CA 131; 89-92; DLB 134; HW 1
Cervantes (Saavedra), Miguel de 1547-1616LC 6,
    23; DA; DAB; DAC; DAM MST, NOV; SSC
    12; WLC
Cesaire, Aime (Fernand) 1913-CLC 19, 32, 112;
    BLC 1; DAM MULT, POET; PC 25
See also BW 2, 3; CA 65-68; CANR 24, 43, 81;
    MTCW 1, 2
Chabon, Michael 1963- .... CLC 55
See also CA 139; CANR 57
Chabrol, Claude 1930- .... CLC 16
See also CA 110
Challans, Mary 1905-1983
See Renault, Mary
See also CA 81-84; 111; CANR 74; MTCW 2;
    SATA 23; SATA-Obit 36
Challis, George
See Faust, Frederick (Schiller)
Chambers, Aidan 1934- .... CLC 35
See also AAYA 27; CA 25-28R; CANR 12, 31, 58;
    JRDA; MAICYA; SAAS 12; SATA 1, 69, 108
Chambers, James 1948-
See Cliff, Jimmy
See also CA 124
Chambers, Jessie
See Lawrence, D(avid) H(erbert Richards)
Chambers, Robert W(illiam) 1865-1933TCLC 41
See also CA 165; DLB 202; SATA 107
Chandler, Raymond (Thornton) 1888-1959TCLC
    1, 7; SSC 23
See also AAYA 25; CA 104; 129; CANR 60;
    CDALB 1929-1941; DLBD 6; MTCW 1, 2
Chang, Eileen 1920-1995 .... SSC 28
See also CA 166
Chang, Jung 1952- .... CLC 71
See also CA 142
Chang Ai-Ling
See Chang, Eileen
Channing, William Ellery 1780-1842 . NCLC 17
See also DLB 1, 59
Chao, Patricia 1955- .... CLC 119
See also CA 163
Chaplin, Charles Spencer 1889-1977 ... CLC 16
See also Chaplin, Charlie
See also CA 81-84; 73-76
Chaplin, Charlie
See Chaplin, Charles Spencer
See also DLB 44
Chapman, George 1559(?)-1634 .... LC 22; DAM
    DRAM
See also DLB 62, 121
Chapman, Graham 1941-1989 .... CLC 21
See also Monty Python
See also CA 116; 129; CANR 35
Chapman, John Jay 1862-1933 .... TCLC 7
See also CA 104

CDALB 1968-1988; DLB 2, 173, 185; DLBY 81, 86; MTCW 1, 2

Dietrich, Robert
See Hunt, E(verette) Howard, (Jr.)

Difusa, Pati
See Almodovar, Pedro

Dillard, Annie 1945-**CLC 9, 60, 115; DAM NOV**
See also AAYA 6; CA 49-52; CANR 3, 43, 62; DLBY 80; MTCW 1, 2; SATA 10

Dillard, R(ichard) H(enry) W(ilde) 1937- **CLC 5**
See also CA 21-24R; CAAS 7; CANR 10; DLB 5

Dillon, Eilis 1920-1994 .... **CLC 17**
See also CA 9-12R; 147; CAAS 3; CANR 4, 38, 78; CLR 26; MAICYA; SATA 2, 74; SATA-Essay 105; SATA-Obit 83

Dimont, Penelope
See Mortimer, Penelope (Ruth)

Dinesen, Isak .... **CLC 10, 29, 95; SSC 7**
See also Blixen, Karen (Christentze Dinesen)
See also MTCW 1

Ding Ling .... **CLC 68**
See also Chiang, Pin-chin

Diphusa, Patty
See Almodovar, Pedro

Disch, Thomas M(ichael) 1940- .... **CLC 7, 36**
See also AAYA 17; CA 21-24R; CAAS 4; CANR 17, 36, 54; CLR 18; DLB 8; MAICYA; MTCW 1, 2; SAAS 15; SATA 92

Disch, Tom
See Disch, Thomas M(ichael)

d'Isly, Georges
See Simenon, Georges (Jacques Christian)

Disraeli, Benjamin 1804-1881 . **NCLC 2, 39, 79**
See also DLB 21, 55

Ditcum, Steve
See Crumb, R(obert)

Dixon, Paige
See Corcoran, Barbara

Dixon, Stephen 1936- .... **CLC 52; SSC 16**
See also CA 89-92; CANR 17, 40, 54; DLB 130

Doak, Annie
See Dillard, Annie

Dobell, Sydney Thompson 1824-1874 .. **NCLC 43**
See also DLB 32

Doblin, Alfred .... **TCLC 13**
See also Doeblin, Alfred

Dobrolyubov, Nikolai Alexandrovich 1836-1861
NCLC 5

Dobson, Austin 1840-1921 .... **TCLC 79**
See also DLB 35; 144

Dobyns, Stephen 1941- .... **CLC 37**
See also CA 45-48; CANR 2, 18

Doctorow, E(dgar) L(aurence) 1931-. **CLC 6, 11, 15, 18, 37, 44, 65, 113; DAM NOV, POP**
See also AAYA 22; AITN 2; BEST 89:3; CA 45-48; CANR 2, 33, 51, 76; CDALB 1968-1988; DLB 2, 28, 173; DLBY 80; MTCW 1, 2

Dodgson, Charles Lutwidge 1832-1898
See Carroll, Lewis
See also CLR 2; DA; DAB; DAC; DAM MST, NOV, POET; MAICYA; SATA 100; YABC 2

Dodson, Owen (Vincent) 1914-1983**CLC 79; BLC 1; DAM MULT**
See also BW 1; CA 65-68; 110; CANR 24; DLB 76

Doeblin, Alfred 1878-1957 .... **TCLC 13**
See also Doblin, Alfred
See also CA 110; 141; DLB 66

Doerr, Harriet 1910- .... **CLC 34**
See also CA 117; 122; CANR 47; INT 122

Domecq, H(onorio Bustos)
See Bioy Casares, Adolfo

Domecq, H(onorio) Bustos
See Bioy Casares, Adolfo; Borges, Jorge Luis

Domini, Rey
See Lorde, Audre (Geraldine)

Dominique

See Proust, (Valentin-Louis-George-Eugene-) Marcel

Don, A
See Stephen, Sir Leslie

Donaldson, Stephen R. 1947-**CLC 46; DAM POP**
See also CA 89-92; CANR 13, 55; INT CANR-13

Donleavy, J(ames) P(atrick) 1926- . **CLC 1, 4, 6, 10, 45**
See also AITN 2; CA 9-12R; CANR 24, 49, 62, 80; DLB 6, 173; INT CANR-24; MTCW 1, 2

Donne, John 1572-1631 .... **LC 10, 24; DA; DAB; DAC; DAM MST, POET; PC 1; WLC**
See also CDBLB Before 1660; DLB 121, 151

Donnell, David 1939(?)- .... **CLC 34**

Donoghue, P. S.
See Hunt, E(verette) Howard, (Jr.)

Donoso (Yanez), Jose 1924-1996**CLC 4, 8, 11, 32, 99; DAM MULT; HLC; SSC 34**
See also CA 81-84; 155; CANR 32, 73; DLB 113; HW 1, 2; MTCW 1, 2

Donovan, John 1928-1992 .... **CLC 35**
See also AAYA 20; CA 97-100; 137; CLR 3; MAICYA; SATA 72; SATA-Brief 29

Don Roberto
See Cunninghame Graham, R(obert) B(ontine)

Doolittle, Hilda 1886-1961**CLC 3, 8, 14, 31, 34, 73; DA; DAC; DAM MST, POET; PC 5; WLC**
See also H. D.
See also CA 97-100; CANR 35; DLB 4, 45; MTCW 1, 2

Dorfman, Ariel 1942- **CLC 48, 77; DAM MULT; HLC**
See also CA 124; 130; CANR 67, 70; HW 1, 2; INT 130

Dorn, Edward (Merton) 1929- .... **CLC 10, 18**
See also CA 93-96; CANR 42, 79; DLB 5; INT 93-96

Dorris, Michael (Anthony) 1945-1997 **CLC 109; DAM MULT, NOV**
See also AAYA 20; BEST 90:1; CA 102; 157; CANR 19, 46, 75; CLR 58; DLB 175; MTCW 2; NNAL; SATA 75; SATA-Obit 94

Dorris, Michael A.
See Dorris, Michael (Anthony)

Dorsan, Luc
See Simenon, Georges (Jacques Christian)

Dorsange, Jean
See Simenon, Georges (Jacques Christian)

Dos Passos, John (Roderigo) 1896-1970**CLC 1, 4, 8, 11, 15, 25, 34, 82; DA; DAB; DAC; DAM MST, NOV; WLC**
See also CA 1-4R; 29-32R; CANR 3; CDALB 1929-1941; DLB 4, 9; DLBD 1, 15; DLBY 96; MTCW 1, 2

Dossage, Jean
See Simenon, Georges (Jacques Christian)

Dostoevsky, Fedor Mikhailovich 1821-1881**NCLC 2, 7, 21, 33, 43; DA; DAB; DAC; DAM MST, NOV; SSC 2, 33; WLC**

Doughty, Charles M(ontagu) 1843-1926**TCLC 27**
See also CA 115; DLB 19, 57, 174

Douglas, Ellen .... **CLC 73**
See also Haxton, Josephine Ayres; Williamson, Ellen Douglas

Douglas, Gavin 1475(?)-1522 .... **LC 20**
See also DLB 132

Douglas, George
See Brown, George Douglas

Douglas, Keith (Castellain) 1920-1944 **TCLC 40**
See also CA 160; DLB 27

Douglas, Leonard
See Bradbury, Ray (Douglas)

Douglas, Michael
See Crichton, (John) Michael

Douglas, (George) Norman 1868-1952 **TCLC 68**
See also CA 119; 157; DLB 34, 195

Douglas, William

See Brown, George Douglas

Douglass, Frederick 1817(?)-1895 . **NCLC 7, 55; BLC 1; DA; DAC; DAM MST, MULT; WLC**
See also CDALB 1640-1865; DLB 1, 43, 50, 79; SATA 29

Dourado, (Waldomiro Freitas) Autran 1926-**CLC 23, 60**
See also CA 25-28R; CANR 34, 81; DLB 145; HW 2

Dourado, Waldomiro Autran
See Dourado, (Waldomiro Freitas) Autran

Dove, Rita (Frances) 1952- . **CLC 50, 81; BLCS; DAM MULT, POET; PC 6**
See also BW 2; CA 109; CAAS 19; CANR 27, 42, 68, 76; CDALBS; DLB 120; MTCW 1

Doveglion
See Villa, Jose Garcia

Dowell, Coleman 1925-1985 .... **CLC 60**
See also CA 25-28R; 117; CANR 10; DLB 130

Dowson, Ernest (Christopher) 1867-1900**TCLC 4**
See also CA 105; 150; DLB 19, 135

Doyle, A. Conan
See Doyle, Arthur Conan

Doyle, Arthur Conan 1859-1930 .. **TCLC 7; DA; DAB; DAC; DAM MST, NOV; SSC 12; WLC**
See also AAYA 14; CA 104; 122; CDBLB 1890-1914; DLB 18, 70, 156, 178; MTCW 1, 2; SATA 24

Doyle, Conan
See Doyle, Arthur Conan

Doyle, John
See Graves, Robert (von Ranke)

Doyle, Roddy 1958(?)- .... **CLC 81**
See also AAYA 14; CA 143; CANR 73; DLB 194

Doyle, Sir A. Conan
See Doyle, Arthur Conan

Doyle, Sir Arthur Conan
See Doyle, Arthur Conan

Dr. A
See Asimov, Isaac; Silverstein, Alvin

Drabble, Margaret 1939- **CLC 2, 3, 5, 8, 10, 22, 53; DAB; DAC; DAM MST, NOV, POP**
See also CA 13-16R; CANR 18, 35, 63; CDBLB 1960 to Present; DLB 14, 155; MTCW 1, 2; SATA 48

Drapier, M. B.
See Swift, Jonathan

Drayham, James
See Mencken, H(enry) L(ouis)

Drayton, Michael 1563-1631 **LC 8; DAM POET**
See also DLB 121

Dreadstone, Carl
See Campbell, (John) Ramsey

Dreiser, Theodore (Herman Albert) 1871-1945 **TCLC 10, 18, 35, 83; DA; DAC; DAM MST, NOV; SSC 30; WLC**
See also CA 106; 132; CDALB 1865-1917; DLB 9, 12, 102, 137; DLBD 1; MTCW 1, 2

Drexler, Rosalyn 1926- .... **CLC 2, 6**
See also CA 81-84; CANR 68

Dreyer, Carl Theodor 1889-1968 .... **CLC 16**
See also CA 116

Drieu la Rochelle, Pierre(-Eugene) 1893-1945 **TCLC 21**
See also CA 117; DLB 72

Drinkwater, John 1882-1937 .... **TCLC 57**
See also CA 109; 149; DLB 10, 19, 149

Drop Shot
See Cable, George Washington

Droste-Hulshoff, Annette Freiin von 1797-1848 **NCLC 3**
See also DLB 133

Drummond, Walter
See Silverberg, Robert

Drummond, William Henry 1854-1907 **TCLC 25**
See also CA 160; DLB 92

See also DLB 95

Finch, Robert (Duer Claydon) 1900- .... **CLC 18**
See also CA 57-60; CANR 9, 24, 49; DLB 88

Findley, Timothy 1930-**CLC 27, 102; DAC; DAM MST**
See also CA 25-28R; CANR 12, 42, 69; DLB 53

Fink, William
See Mencken, H(enry) L(ouis)

Firbank, Louis 1942-
See Reed, Lou
See also CA 117

Firbank, (Arthur Annesley) Ronald 1886-1926
TCLC 1
See also CA 104; 177; DLB 36

Fisher, Dorothy (Frances) Canfield 1879-1958
TCLC 87
See also CA 114; 136; CANR 80; DLB 9, 102; MAICYA; YABC 1

Fisher, M(ary) F(rances) K(ennedy) 1908-1992
CLC 76, 87
See also CA 77-80; 138; CANR 44; MTCW 1

Fisher, Roy 1930- .... **CLC 25**
See also CA 81-84; CAAS 10; CANR 16; DLB 40

Fisher, Rudolph 1897-1934**TCLC 11; BLC 2; DAM MULT; SSC 25**
See also BW 1, 3; CA 107; 124; CANR 80; DLB 51, 102

Fisher, Vardis (Alvero) 1895-1968 .... **CLC 7**
See also CA 5-8R; 25-28R; CANR 68; DLB 9, 206

Fiske, Tarleton
See Bloch, Robert (Albert)

Fitch, Clarke
See Sinclair, Upton (Beall)

Fitch, John IV
See Cormier, Robert (Edmund)

Fitzgerald, Captain Hugh
See Baum, L(yman) Frank

FitzGerald, Edward 1809-1883 .... **NCLC 9**
See also DLB 32

Fitzgerald, F(rancis) Scott (Key) 1896-1940
TCLC 1, 6, 14, 28, 55; DA; DAB; DAC; DAM MST, NOV; SSC 6, 31; WLC
See also AAYA 24; AITN 1; CA 110; 123; CDALB 1917-1929; DLB 4, 9, 86; DLBD 1, 15, 16; DLBY 81, 96; MTCW 1, 2

Fitzgerald, Penelope 1916- .... **CLC 19, 51, 61**
See also CA 85-88; CAAS 10; CANR 56; DLB 14, 194; MTCW 2

Fitzgerald, Robert (Stuart) 1910-1985 .. **CLC 39**
See also CA 1-4R; 114; CANR 1; DLBY 80

FitzGerald, Robert D(avid) 1902-1987 ... **CLC 19**
See also CA 17-20R

Fitzgerald, Zelda (Sayre) 1900-1948 ... **TCLC 52**
See also CA 117; 126; DLBY 84

Flanagan, Thomas (James Bonner) 1923- .. **C L C 25, 52**
See also CA 108; CANR 55; DLBY 80; INT 108; MTCW 1

Flaubert, Gustave 1821-1880**NCLC 2, 10, 19, 62, 66; DA; DAB; DAC; DAM MST, NOV; SSC 11; WLC**
See also DLB 119

Flecker, Herman Elroy
See Flecker, (Herman) James Elroy

Flecker, (Herman) James Elroy 1884-1915**TCLC 43**
See also CA 109; 150; DLB 10, 19

Fleming, Ian (Lancaster) 1908-1964 **CLC 3, 30; DAM POP**
See also AAYA 26; CA 5-8R; CANR 59; CDBLB 1945-1960; DLB 87, 201; MTCW 1, 2; SATA 9

Fleming, Thomas (James) 1927- .... **CLC 37**
See also CA 5-8R; CANR 10; INT CANR-10; SATA 8

Fletcher, John 1579-1625 .... **LC 33; DC 6**
See also CDBLB Before 1660; DLB 58

Fletcher, John Gould 1886-1950 .... **TCLC 35**
See also CA 107; 167; DLB 4, 45

Fleur, Paul
See Pohl, Frederik

Flooglebuckle, Al
See Spiegelman, Art

Flying Officer X
See Bates, H(erbert) E(rnest)

Fo, Dario 1926-**CLC 32, 109; DAM DRAM; DC 10**
See also CA 116; 128; CANR 68; DLBY 97; MTCW 1, 2

Fogarty, Jonathan Titulescu Esq.
See Farrell, James T(homas)

Folke, Will
See Bloch, Robert (Albert)

Follett, Ken(neth Martin) 1949- .. **CLC 18; DAM NOV, POP**
See also AAYA 6; BEST 89:4; CA 81-84; CANR 13, 33, 54; DLB 87; DLBY 81; INT CANR-33; MTCW 1

Fontane, Theodor 1819-1898 .... **NCLC 26**
See also DLB 129

Foote, Horton 1916- .. **CLC 51, 91; DAM DRAM**
See also CA 73-76; CANR 34, 51; DLB 26; INT CANR-34

Foote, Shelby 1916- .. **CLC 75; DAM NOV, POP**
See also CA 5-8R; CANR 3, 45, 74; DLB 2, 17; MTCW 2

Forbes, Esther 1891-1967 .... **CLC 12**
See also AAYA 17; CA 13-14; 25-28R; CAP 1; CLR 27; DLB 22; JRDA; MAICYA; SATA 2, 100

Forche, Carolyn (Louise) 1950-**CLC 25, 83, 86; DAM POET; PC 10**
See also CA 109; 117; CANR 50, 74; DLB 5, 193; INT 117; MTCW 1

Ford, Elbur
See Hibbert, Eleanor Alice Burford

Ford, Ford Madox 1873-1939**TCLC 1, 15, 39, 57; DAM NOV**
See also CA 104; 132; CANR 74; CDBLB 1914-1945; DLB 162; MTCW 1, 2

Ford, Henry 1863-1947 .... **TCLC 73**
See also CA 115; 148

Ford, John 1586-(?) .... **DC 8**
See also CDBLB Before 1660; DAM DRAM; DLB 58

Ford, John 1895-1973 .... **CLC 16**
See also CA 45-48

Ford, Richard 1944- .... **CLC 46, 99**
See also CA 69-72; CANR 11, 47; MTCW 1

Ford, Webster
See Masters, Edgar Lee

Foreman, Richard 1937- .... **CLC 50**
See also CA 65-68; CANR 32, 63

Forester, C(ecil) S(cott) 1899-1966 .... **CLC 35**
See also CA 73-76; 25-28R; DLB 191; SATA 13

Forez
See Mauriac, Francois (Charles)

Forman, James Douglas 1932- .... **CLC 21**
See also AAYA 17; CA 9-12R; CANR 4, 19, 42; JRDA; MAICYA; SATA 8, 70

Fornes, Maria Irene 1930- **CLC 39, 61; DC 10; HLCS 1**
See also CA 25-28R; CANR 28, 81; DLB 7; HW 1, 2; INT CANR-28; MTCW 1

Forrest, Leon (Richard) 1937-1997**CLC 4; BLCS**
See also BW 2; CA 89-92; 162; CAAS 7; CANR 25, 52; DLB 33

Forster, E(dward) M(organ) 1879-1970 **CLC 1, 2, 3, 4, 9, 10, 13, 15, 22, 45, 77; DA; DAB; DAC; DAM MST, NOV; SSC 27; WLC**
See also AAYA 2; CA 13-14; 25-28R; CANR 45; CAP 1; CDBLB 1914-1945; DLB 34, 98, 162, 178, 195; DLBD 10; MTCW 1, 2; SATA 57

Forster, John 1812-1876 .... **NCLC 11**
See also DLB 144, 184

Forsyth, Frederick 1938-**CLC 2, 5, 36; DAM NOV, POP**
See also BEST 89:4; CA 85-88; CANR 38, 62; DLB 87; MTCW 1, 2

Forten, Charlotte L. .... **TCLC 16; BLC 2**
See also Grimke, Charlotte L(ottie) Forten
See also DLB 50

Foscolo, Ugo 1778-1827 .... **NCLC 8**

Fosse, Bob .... **CLC 20**
See also Fosse, Robert Louis

Fosse, Robert Louis 1927-1987
See Fosse, Bob
See also CA 110; 123

Foster, Stephen Collins 1826-1864 ..... **NCLC 26**

Foucault, Michel 1926-1984 ...... **CLC 31, 34, 69**
See also CA 105; 113; CANR 34; MTCW 1, 2

Fouque, Friedrich (Heinrich Karl) de la Motte 1777-1843 .... **NCLC 2**
See also DLB 90

Fourier, Charles 1772-1837 .... **NCLC 51**

Fournier, Henri Alban 1886-1914
See Alain-Fournier
See also CA 104

Fournier, Pierre 1916- .... **CLC 11**
See also Gascar, Pierre
See also CA 89-92; CANR 16, 40

Fowles, John (Philip) 1926-**CLC 1, 2, 3, 4, 6, 9, 10, 15, 33, 87; DAB; DAC; DAM MST; SSC 33**
See also CA 5-8R; CANR 25, 71; CDBLB 1960 to Present; DLB 14, 139, 207; MTCW 1, 2; SATA 22

Fox, Paula 1923- .... **CLC 2, 8, 121**
See also AAYA 3; CA 73-76; CANR 20, 36, 62; CLR 1, 44; DLB 52; JRDA; MAICYA; MTCW 1; SATA 17, 60

Fox, William Price (Jr.) 1926- .... **CLC 22**
See also CA 17-20R; CAAS 19; CANR 11; DLB 2; DLBY 81

Foxe, John 1516(?)-1587 .... **LC 14**
See also DLB 132

Frame, Janet 1924-**CLC 2, 3, 6, 22, 66, 96; SSC 29**
See also Clutha, Janet Paterson Frame

France, Anatole .... **TCLC 9**
See also Thibault, Jacques Anatole Francois
See also DLB 123; MTCW 1

Francis, Claude 19(?)- .... **CLC 50**

Francis, Dick 1920- . **CLC 2, 22, 42, 102; DAM POP**
See also AAYA 5, 21; BEST 89:3; CA 5-8R; CANR 9, 42, 68; CDBLB 1960 to Present; DLB 87; INT CANR-9; MTCW 1, 2

Francis, Robert (Churchill) 1901-1987 **CLC 15**
See also CA 1-4R; 123; CANR 1

Frank, Anne(lies Marie) 1929-1945**TCLC 17; DA; DAB; DAC; DAM MST; WLC**
See also AAYA 12; CA 113; 133; CANR 68; MTCW 1, 2; SATA 87; SATA-Brief 42

Frank, Bruno 1887-1945 .... **TCLC 81**
See also DLB 118

Frank, Elizabeth 1945- .... **CLC 39**
See also CA 121; 126; CANR 78; INT 126

Frankl, Viktor E(mil) 1905-1997 .... **CLC 93**
See also CA 65-68; 161

Franklin, Benjamin
See Hasek, Jaroslav (Matej Frantisek)

Franklin, Benjamin 1706-1790**LC 25; DA; DAB; DAC; DAM MST; WLC**
See also CDALB 1640-1865; DLB 24, 43, 73

Franklin, (Stella Maria Sarah) Miles (Lampe) 1879-1954 .... **TCLC 7**
See also CA 104; 164

Fraser, (Lady) Antonia (Pakenham) 1932- . **C L C 32, 107**
See also CA 85-88; CANR 44, 65; MTCW 1, 2; SATA-Brief 32

Fraser, George MacDonald 1925- .... **CLC 7**

See Kuttner, Henry

Gardons, S. S.
See Snodgrass, W(illiam) D(e Witt)

Garfield, Leon 1921-1996 .... **CLC 12**
See also AAYA 8; CA 17-20R; 152; CANR 38, 41, 78; CLR 21; DLB 161; JRDA; MAICYA; SATA 1, 32, 76; SATA-Obit 90

Garland, (Hannibal) Hamlin 1860-1940
TCLC 3; SSC 18
See also CA 104; DLB 12, 71, 78, 186

Garneau, (Hector de) Saint-Denys 1912-1943
TCLC 13
See also CA 111; DLB 88

Garner, Alan 1934-.. **CLC 17; DAB; DAM POP**
See also AAYA 18; CA 73-76; CANR 15, 64; CLR 20; DLB 161; MAICYA; MTCW 1, 2; SATA 18, 69; SATA-Essay 108

Garner, Hugh 1913-1979 .... **CLC 13**
See also CA 69-72; CANR 31; DLB 68

Garnett, David 1892-1981 .... **CLC 3**
See also CA 5-8R; 103; CANR 17, 79; DLB 34; MTCW 2

Garos, Stephanie
See Katz, Steve

Garrett, George (Palmer) 1929- **CLC 3, 11, 51; SSC 30**
See also CA 1-4R; CAAS 5; CANR 1, 42, 67; DLB 2, 5, 130, 152; DLBY 83

Garrick, David 1717-1779 . **LC 15; DAM DRAM**
See also DLB 84

Garrigue, Jean 1914-1972 .... **CLC 2, 8**
See also CA 5-8R; 37-40R; CANR 20

Garrison, Frederick
See Sinclair, Upton (Beall)

Garth, Will
See Hamilton, Edmond; Kuttner, Henry

Garvey, Marcus (Moziah, Jr.) 1887-1940 . **TCLC 41; BLC 2; DAM MULT**
See also BW 1; CA 120; 124; CANR 79

Gary, Romain .... **CLC 25**
See also Kacew, Romain
See also DLB 83

Gascar, Pierre .... **CLC 11**
See also Fournier, Pierre

Gascoyne, David (Emery) 1916- .... **CLC 45**
See also CA 65-68; CANR 10, 28, 54; DLB 20; MTCW 1

Gaskell, Elizabeth Cleghorn 1810-1865 **NCLC 70; DAB; DAM MST; SSC 25**
See also CDBLB 1832-1890; DLB 21, 144, 159

Gass, William H(oward) 1924-**CLC 1, 2, 8, 11, 15, 39; SSC 12**
See also CA 17-20R; CANR 30, 71; DLB 2; MTCW 1, 2

Gasset, Jose Ortega y
See Ortega y Gasset, Jose

Gates, Henry Louis, Jr. 1950-.. **CLC 65; BLCS; DAM MULT**
See also BW 2, 3; CA 109; CANR 25, 53, 75; DLB 67; MTCW 1

Gautier, Theophile 1811-1872**NCLC 1, 59; DAM POET; PC 18; SSC 20**
See also DLB 119

Gawsworth, John
See Bates, H(erbert) E(rnest)

Gay, John 1685-1732 .... **LC 49; DAM DRAM**
See also DLB 84, 95

Gay, Oliver
See Gogarty, Oliver St. John

Gaye, Marvin (Penze) 1939-1984 .... **CLC 26**
See also CA 112

Gebler, Carlo (Ernest) 1954- .... **CLC 39**
See also CA 119; 133

Gee, Maggie (Mary) 1948- .... **CLC 57**
See also CA 130; DLB 207

Gee, Maurice (Gough) 1931- .... **CLC 29**
See also CA 97-100; CANR 67; CLR 56; SATA

46, 101

Gelbart, Larry (Simon) 1923- .... **CLC 21, 61**
See also CA 73-76; CANR 45

Gelber, Jack 1932- .... **CLC 1, 6, 14, 79**
See also CA 1-4R; CANR 2; DLB 7

Gellhorn, Martha (Ellis) 1908-1998 **CLC 14, 60**
See also CA 77-80; 164; CANR 44; DLBY 82, 98

Genet, Jean 1910-1986**CLC 1, 2, 5, 10, 14, 44, 46; DAM DRAM**
See also CA 13-16R; CANR 18; DLB 72; DLBY 86; MTCW 1, 2

Gent, Peter 1942-................................... **CLC 29**
See also AITN 1; CA 89-92; DLBY 82

Gentlewoman in New England, A
See Bradstreet, Anne

Gentlewoman in Those Parts, A
See Bradstreet, Anne

George, Jean Craighead 1919- .... **CLC 35**
See also AAYA 8; CA 5-8R; CANR 25; CLR 1; DLB 52; JRDA; MAICYA; SATA 2, 68

George, Stefan (Anton) 1868-1933 .. **TCLC 2, 14**
See also CA 104

Georges, Georges Martin
See Simenon, Georges (Jacques Christian)

Gerhardi, William Alexander
See Gerhardie, William Alexander

Gerhardie, William Alexander 1895-1977**CLC 5**
See also CA 25-28R; 73-76; CANR 18; DLB 36

Gerstler, Amy 1956- .... **CLC 70**
See also CA 146

Gertler, T. .... **CLC 34**
See also CA 116; 121; INT 121

Ghalib .... **NCLC 39, 78**
See also Ghalib, Hsadullah Khan

Ghalib, Hsadullah Khan 1797-1869
See Ghalib
See also DAM POET

Ghelderode, Michel de 1898-1962**CLC 6, 11; DAM DRAM**
See also CA 85-88; CANR 40, 77

Ghiselin, Brewster 1903- .... **CLC 23**
See also CA 13-16R; CAAS 10; CANR 13

Ghose, Aurabinda 1872-1950 .... **TCLC 63**
See also CA 163

Ghose, Zulfikar 1935- .... **CLC 42**
See also CA 65-68; CANR 67

Ghosh, Amitav 1956- .... **CLC 44**
See also CA 147; CANR 80

Giacosa, Giuseppe 1847-1906 .... **TCLC 7**
See also CA 104

Gibb, Lee
See Waterhouse, Keith (Spencer)

Gibbon, Lewis Grassic .... **TCLC 4**
See also Mitchell, James Leslie

Gibbons, Kaye 1960- ..... **CLC 50, 88; DAM POP**
See also CA 151; CANR 75; MTCW 1

Gibran, Kahlil 1883-1931**TCLC 1, 9; DAM POET, POP; PC 9**
See also CA 104; 150; MTCW 2

Gibran, Khalil
See Gibran, Kahlil

Gibson, William 1914-**CLC 23; DA; DAB; DAC; DAM DRAM, MST**
See also CA 9-12R; CANR 9, 42, 75; DLB 7; MTCW 1; SATA 66

Gibson, William (Ford) 1948-**CLC 39, 63; DAM POP**
See also AAYA 12; CA 126; 133; CANR 52; MTCW 1

Gide, Andre (Paul Guillaume) 1869-1951**TCLC 5, 12, 36; DA; DAB; DAC; DAM MST, NOV; SSC 13; WLC**
See also CA 104; 124; DLB 65; MTCW 1, 2

Gifford, Barry (Colby) 1946- .... **CLC 34**
See also CA 65-68; CANR 9, 30, 40

Gilbert, Frank

See De Voto, Bernard (Augustine)

Gilbert, W(illiam) S(chwenck) 1836-1911 **TCLC 3; DAM DRAM, POET**
See also CA 104; 173; SATA 36

Gilbreth, Frank B., Jr. 1911- .... **CLC 17**
See also CA 9-12R; SATA 2

Gilchrist, Ellen 1935-. **CLC 34, 48; DAM POP; SSC 14**
See also CA 113; 116; CANR 41, 61; DLB 130; MTCW 1, 2

Giles, Molly 1942- .... **CLC 39**
See also CA 126

Gill, Eric 1882-1940 .... **TCLC 85**

Gill, Patrick
See Creasey, John

Gilliam, Terry (Vance) 1940- .... **CLC 21**
See also Monty Python
See also AAYA 19; CA 108; 113; CANR 35; INT 113

Gillian, Jerry
See Gilliam, Terry (Vance)

Gilliatt, Penelope (Ann Douglass) 1932-1993**CLC 2, 10, 13, 53**
See also AITN 2; CA 13-16R; 141; CANR 49; DLB 14

Gilman, Charlotte (Anna) Perkins (Stetson) 1860-1935 .... **TCLC 9, 37; SSC 13**
See also CA 106; 150; MTCW 1

Gilmour, David 1949-............................ **CLC 35**
See also CA 138, 147

Gilpin, William 1724-1804 .... **NCLC 30**

Gilray, J. D.
See Mencken, H(enry) L(ouis)

Gilroy, Frank D(aniel) 1925- .... **CLC 2**
See also CA 81-84; CANR 32, 64; DLB 7

Gilstrap, John 1957(?)- .... **CLC 99**
See also CA 160

Ginsberg, Allen 1926-1997 **CLC 1, 2, 3, 4, 6, 13, 36, 69, 109; DA; DAB; DAC; DAM MST, POET; PC 4; WLC**
See also AITN 1; CA 1-4R; 157; CANR 2, 41, 63; CDALB 1941-1968; DLB 5, 16, 169; MTCW 1, 2

Ginzburg, Natalia 1916-1991 . **CLC 5, 11, 54, 70**
See also CA 85-88; 135; CANR 33; DLB 177; MTCW 1, 2

Giono, Jean 1895-1970 .... **CLC 4, 11**
See also CA 45-48; 29-32R; CANR 2, 35; DLB 72; MTCW 1

Giovanni, Nikki 1943-**CLC 2, 4, 19, 64, 117; BLC 2; DA; DAB; DAC; DAM MST, MULT, POET; PC 19; WLCS**
See also AAYA 22; AITN 1; BW 2, 3; CA 29-32R; CAAS 6; CANR 18, 41, 60; CDALBS; CLR 6; DLB 5, 41; INT CANR-18; MAICYA; MTCW 1, 2; SATA 24, 107

Giovene, Andrea 1904- .... **CLC 7**
See also CA 85-88

Gippius, Zinaida (Nikolayevna) 1869-1945
See Hippius, Zinaida
See also CA 106

Giraudoux, (Hippolyte) Jean 1882-1944**TCLC 2, 7; DAM DRAM**
See also CA 104; DLB 65

Gironella, Jose Maria 1917- .... **CLC 11**
See also CA 101

Gissing, George (Robert) 1857-1903**TCLC 3, 24, 47**
See also CA 105; 167; DLB 18, 135, 184

Giurlani, Aldo
See Palazzeschi, Aldo

Gladkov, Fyodor (Vasilyevich) 1883-1958**TCLC 27**
See also CA 170

Glanville, Brian (Lester) 1931- .... **CLC 6**
See also CA 5-8R; CAAS 9; CANR 3, 70; DLB 15, 139; SATA 42

Glasgow, Ellen (Anderson Gholson) 1873-1945

See also CA 5-8R; CANR 6; CLR 47; DLB 88; JRDA; MAICYA; SAAS 10; SATA 6, 74
Harris, Frank 1856-1931 .... **TCLC 24**
See also CA 109; 150; CANR 80; DLB 156, 197
Harris, George Washington 1814-1869**NCLC 23**
See also DLB 3, 11
Harris, Joel Chandler 1848-1908**TCLC 2; SSC 19**
See also CA 104; 137; CANR 80; CLR 49; DLB 11, 23, 42, 78, 91; MAICYA; SATA 100; YABC 1
Harris, John (Wyndham Parkes Lucas) Beynon 1903-1969
See Wyndham, John
See also CA 102; 89-92
Harris, MacDonald .... **CLC 9**
See also Heiney, Donald (William)
Harris, Mark 1922- .... **CLC 19**
See also CA 5-8R; CAAS 3; CANR 2, 55; DLB 2; DLBY 80
Harris, (Theodore) Wilson 1921- .... **CLC 25**
See also BW 2, 3; CA 65-68; CAAS 16; CANR 11, 27, 69; DLB 117; MTCW 1
Harrison, Elizabeth Cavanna 1909-
See Cavanna, Betty
See also CA 9-12R; CANR 6, 27
Harrison, Harry (Max) 1925- .... **CLC 42**
See also CA 1-4R; CANR 5, 21; DLB 8; SATA 4
Harrison, James (Thomas) 1937-**CLC 6, 14, 33, 66; SSC 19**
See also CA 13-16R; CANR 8, 51, 79; DLBY 82; INT CANR-8
Harrison, Jim
See Harrison, James (Thomas)
Harrison, Kathryn 1961- .... **CLC 70**
See also CA 144; CANR 68
Harrison, Tony 1937- .... **CLC 43**
See also CA 65-68; CANR 44; DLB 40; MTCW 1
Harriss, Will(ard Irvin) 1922- .... **CLC 34**
See also CA 111
Harson, Sley
See Ellison, Harlan (Jay)
Hart, Ellis
See Ellison, Harlan (Jay)
Hart, Josephine 1942(?)- .... **CLC 70; DAM POP**
See also CA 138; CANR 70
Hart, Moss 1904-1961 ..... **CLC 66; DAM DRAM**
See also CA 109; 89-92; DLB 7
Harte, (Francis) Bret(t) 1836(?)-1902**TCLC 1, 25; DA; DAC; DAM MST; SSC 8; WLC**
See also CA 104; 140; CANR 80; CDALB 1865-1917; DLB 12, 64, 74, 79, 186; SATA 26
Hartley, L(eslie) P(oles) 1895-1972 ... **CLC 2, 22**
See also CA 45-48; 37-40R; CANR 33; DLB 15, 139; MTCW 1, 2
Hartman, Geoffrey H. 1929- .... **CLC 27**
See also CA 117; 125; CANR 79; DLB 67
Hartmann, Sadakichi 1867-1944 .... **TCLC 73**
See also CA 157; DLB 54
Hartmann von Aue c. 1160-c. 1205 ..... **CMLC 15**
See also DLB 138
Hartmann von Aue 1170-1210 .... **CMLC 15**
Haruf, Kent 1943- .... **CLC 34**
See also CA 149
Harwood, Ronald 1934- .. **CLC 32; DAM DRAM, MST**
See also CA 1-4R; CANR 4, 55; DLB 13
Hasegawa Tatsunosuke
See Futabatei, Shimei
Hasek, Jaroslav (Matej Frantisek) 1883-1923 **TCLC 4**
See also CA 104; 129; MTCW 1, 2
Hass, Robert 1941- .... **CLC 18, 39, 99; PC 16**
See also CA 111; CANR 30, 50, 71; DLB 105, 206; SATA 94
Hastings, Hudson
See Kuttner, Henry
Hastings, Selina .... **CLC 44**

Hathorne, John 1641-1717 .... **LC 38**
Hatteras, Amelia
See Mencken, H(enry) L(ouis)
Hatteras, Owen .... **TCLC 18**
See also Mencken, H(enry) L(ouis); Nathan, George Jean
Hauptmann, Gerhart (Johann Robert) 1862-1946 **TCLC 4; DAM DRAM**
See also CA 104; 153; DLB 66, 118
Havel, Vaclav 1936-**CLC 25, 58, 65; DAM DRAM; DC 6**
See also CA 104; CANR 36, 63; MTCW 1, 2
Haviaras, Stratis .... **CLC 33**
See also Chaviaras, Strates
Hawes, Stephen 1475(?)-1523(?) .... **LC 17**
See also DLB 132
Hawkes, John (Clendennin Burne, Jr.) 1925-1998 **CLC 1, 2, 3, 4, 7, 9, 14, 15, 27, 49**
See also CA 1-4R; 167; CANR 2, 47, 64; DLB 2, 7; DLBY 80, 98; MTCW 1, 2
Hawking, S. W.
See Hawking, Stephen W(illiam)
Hawking, Stephen W(illiam) 1942-**CLC 63, 105**
See also AAYA 13; BEST 89:1; CA 126; 129; CANR 48; MTCW 2
Hawkins, Anthony Hope
See Hope, Anthony
Hawthorne, Julian 1846-1934 .... **TCLC 25**
See also CA 165
Hawthorne, Nathaniel 1804-1864 **NCLC 39; DA; DAB; DAC; DAM MST, NOV; SSC 3, 29; WLC**
See also AAYA 18; CDALB 1640-1865; DLB 1, 74; YABC 2
Haxton, Josephine Ayres 1921-
See Douglas, Ellen
See also CA 115; CANR 41
Hayaseca y Eizaguirre, Jorge
See Echegaray (y Eizaguirre), Jose (Maria Waldo)
Hayashi, Fumiko 1904-1951 .... **TCLC 27**
See also CA 161; DLB 180
Haycraft, Anna
See Ellis, Alice Thomas
See also CA 122; MTCW 2
Hayden, Robert E(arl) 1913-1980**CLC 5, 9, 14, 37; BLC 2; DA; DAC; DAM MST, MULT, POET; PC 6**
See also BW 1, 3; CA 69-72; 97-100; CABS 2; CANR 24, 75; CDALB 1941-1968; DLB 5, 76; MTCW 1, 2; SATA 19; SATA-Obit 26
Hayford, J(oseph) E(phraim) Casely
See Casely-Hayford, J(oseph) E(phraim)
Hayman, Ronald 1932- .... **CLC 44**
See also CA 25-28R; CANR 18, 50; DLB 155
Haywood, Eliza (Fowler) 1693(?)-1756 . **LC 1, 44**
See also DLB 39
Hazlitt, William 1778-1830 .... **NCLC 29**
See also DLB 110, 158
Hazzard, Shirley 1931- .... **CLC 18**
See also CA 9-12R; CANR 4, 70; DLBY 82; MTCW 1
Head, Bessie 1937-1986**CLC 25, 67; BLC 2; DAM MULT**
See also BW 2, 3; CA 29-32R; 119; CANR 25; DLB 117; MTCW 1
Headon, (Nicky) Topper 1956(?)- .... **CLC 30**
Heaney, Seamus (Justin) 1939-**CLC 5, 7, 14, 25, 37, 74, 91; DAB; DAM POET; PC 18; WLCS**
See also CA 85-88; CANR 25, 48, 75; CDBLB 1960 to Present; DLB 40; DLBY 95; MTCW 1, 2
Hearn, (Patricio) Lafcadio (Tessima Carlos) 1850-1904 .... **TCLC 9**
See also CA 105; 166; DLB 12, 78, 189
Hearne, Vicki 1946- .... **CLC 56**
See also CA 139

Hearon, Shelby 1931- .... **CLC 63**
See also AITN 2; CA 25-28R; CANR 18, 48
Heat-Moon, William Least .... **CLC 29**
See also Trogdon, William (Lewis)
See also AAYA 9
Hebbel, Friedrich 1813-1863 .... **NCLC 43; DAM DRAM**
See also DLB 129
Hebert, Anne 1916-**CLC 4, 13, 29; DAC; DAM MST, POET**
See also CA 85-88; CANR 69; DLB 68; MTCW 1, 2
Hecht, Anthony (Evan) 1923-**CLC 8, 13, 19; DAM POET**
See also CA 9-12R; CANR 6; DLB 5, 169
Hecht, Ben 1894-1964 .... **CLC 8**
See also CA 85-88; DLB 7, 9, 25, 26, 28, 86
Hedayat, Sadeq 1903-1951 .... **TCLC 21**
See also CA 120
Hegel, Georg Wilhelm Friedrich 1770-1831 **NCLC 46**
See also DLB 90
Heidegger, Martin 1889-1976 .... **CLC 24**
See also CA 81-84; 65-68; CANR 34; MTCW 1, 2
Heidenstam, (Carl Gustaf) Verner von 1859-1940 **TCLC 5**
See also CA 104
Heifner, Jack 1946- .... **CLC 11**
See also CA 105; CANR 47
Heijermans, Herman 1864-1924 .... **TCLC 24**
See also CA 123
Heilbrun, Carolyn G(old) 1926- .... **CLC 25**
See also CA 45-48; CANR 1, 28, 58
Heine, Heinrich 1797-1856 . **NCLC 4, 54; PC 25**
See also DLB 90
Heinemann, Larry (Curtiss) 1944- .... **CLC 50**
See also CA 110; CAAS 21; CANR 31, 81; DLBD 9; INT CANR-31
Heiney, Donald (William) 1921-1993
See Harris, MacDonald
See also CA 1-4R; 142; CANR 3, 58
Heinlein, Robert A(nson) 1907-1988**CLC 1, 3, 8, 14, 26, 55; DAM POP**
See also AAYA 17; CA 1-4R; 125; CANR 1, 20, 53; DLB 8; JRDA; MAICYA; MTCW 1, 2; SATA 9, 69; SATA-Obit 56
Helforth, John
See Doolittle, Hilda
Hellenhofferu, Vojtech Kapristian z
See Hasek, Jaroslav (Matej Frantisek)
Heller, Joseph 1923- **CLC 1, 3, 5, 8, 11, 36, 63; DA; DAB; DAC; DAM MST, NOV, POP; WLC**
See also AAYA 24; AITN 1; CA 5-8R; CABS 1; CANR 8, 42, 66; DLB 2, 28; DLBY 80; INT CANR-8; MTCW 1, 2
Hellman, Lillian (Florence) 1906-1984**CLC 2, 4, 8, 14, 18, 34, 44, 52; DAM DRAM; DC 1**
See also AITN 1, 2; CA 13-16R; 112; CANR 33; DLB 7; DLBY 84; MTCW 1, 2
Helprin, Mark 1947- .. **CLC 7, 10, 22, 32; DAM NOV, POP**
See also CA 81-84; CANR 47, 64; CDALBS; DLBY 85; MTCW 1, 2
Helvetius, Claude-Adrien 1715-1771 .... **LC 26**
Helyar, Jane Penelope Josephine 1933-
See Poole, Josephine
See also CA 21-24R; CANR 10, 26; SATA 82
Hemans, Felicia 1793-1835 .... **NCLC 71**
See also DLB 96
Hemingway, Ernest (Miller) 1899-1961**CLC 1, 3, 6, 8, 10, 13, 19, 30, 34, 39, 41, 44, 50, 61, 80; DA; DAB; DAC; DAM MST, NOV; SSC 1, 25; WLC**
See also AAYA 19; CA 77-80; CANR 34; CDALB 1917-1929; DLB 4, 9, 102, 210; DLBD 1, 15, 16; DLBY 81, 87, 96, 98; MTCW 1, 2

See also CA 97-100; CAAS 22; CANR 19, 43
Kelman, James 1946- .... **CLC 58, 86**
See also CA 148; DLB 194
Kemal, Yashar 1923- .... **CLC 14, 29**
See also CA 89-92; CANR 44
Kemble, Fanny 1809-1893 .... **NCLC 18**
See also DLB 32
Kemelman, Harry 1908-1996 .... **CLC 2**
See also AITN 1; CA 9-12R; 155; CANR 6, 71;
DLB 28
Kempe, Margery 1373(?)-1440(?) .... **LC 6**
See also DLB 146
Kempis, Thomas a 1380-1471 .... **LC 11**
Kendall, Henry 1839-1882 .... **NCLC 12**
Keneally, Thomas (Michael) 1935- **CLC 5, 8, 10,
14, 19, 27, 43, 117; DAM NOV**
See also CA 85-88; CANR 10, 50, 74; MTCW 1, 2
Kennedy, Adrienne (Lita) 1931-**CLC 66; BLC 2;
DAM MULT; DC 5**
See also BW 2, 3; CA 103; CAAS 20; CABS 3;
CANR 26, 53; DLB 38
Kennedy, John Pendleton 1795-1870 ..... **NCLC 2**
See also DLB 3
Kennedy, Joseph Charles 1929-
See Kennedy, X. J.
See also CA 1-4R; CANR 4, 30, 40; SATA 14, 86
Kennedy, William 1928-**CLC 6, 28, 34, 53; DAM
NOV**
See also AAYA 1; CA 85-88; CANR 14, 31, 76;
DLB 143; DLBY 85; INT CANR-31; MTCW 1,
2; SATA 57
Kennedy, X. J. .... **CLC 8, 42**
See also Kennedy, Joseph Charles
See also CAAS 9; CLR 27; DLB 5; SAAS 22
Kenny, Maurice (Francis) 1929- . **CLC 87; DAM
MULT**
See also CA 144; CAAS 22; DLB 175; NNAL
Kent, Kelvin
See Kuttner, Henry
Kenton, Maxwell
See Southern, Terry
Kenyon, Robert O.
See Kuttner, Henry
Kepler, Johannes 1571-1630 .... **LC 45**
Kerouac, Jack .... **CLC 1, 2, 3, 5, 14, 29, 61**
See also Kerouac, Jean-Louis Lebris de
See also CA 25; CDALB 1941-1968; DLB 2,
16; DLBD 3; DLBY 95; MTCW 2
Kerouac, Jean-Louis Lebris de 1922-1969
See Kerouac, Jack
See also AITN 1; CA 5-8R; 25-28R; CANR 26,
54; DA; DAB; DAC; DAM MST, NOV, POET,
POP; MTCW 1, 2; WLC
Kerr, Jean 1923- .... **CLC 22**
See also CA 5-8R; CANR 7; INT CANR-7
Kerr, M. E. .... **CLC 12, 35**
See also Meaker, Marijane (Agnes)
See also AAYA 2, 23; CLR 29; SAAS 1
Kerr, Robert .... **CLC 55**
Kerrigan, (Thomas) Anthony 1918- .... **CLC 4, 6**
See also CA 49-52; CAAS 11; CANR 4
Kerry, Lois
See Duncan, Lois
Kesey, Ken (Elton) 1935-**CLC 1, 3, 6, 11, 46, 64;
DA; DAB; DAC; DAM MST, NOV, POP;
WLC**
See also AAYA 25; CA 1-4R; CANR 22, 38, 66;
CDALB 1968-1988; DLB 2, 16, 206; MTCW 1,
2; SATA 66
Kesselring, Joseph (Otto) 1902-1967 .. **CLC 45;
DAM DRAM, MST**
See also CA 150
Kessler, Jascha (Frederick) 1929- .... **CLC 4**
See also CA 17-20R; CANR 8, 48
Kettelkamp, Larry (Dale) 1933- .... **CLC 12**
See also CA 29-32R; CANR 16; SAAS 3; SATA 2
Key, Ellen 1849-1926 .... **TCLC 65**

Keyber, Conny
See Fielding, Henry
Keyes, Daniel 1927- .. **CLC 80; DA; DAC; DAM
MST, NOV**
See also AAYA 23; CA 17-20R; CANR 10, 26, 54,
74; MTCW 2; SATA 37
Keynes, John Maynard 1883-1946 ...... **TCLC 64**
See also CA 114; 162, 163; DLBD 10; MTCW 2
Khanshendel, Chiron
See Rose, Wendy
Khayyam, Omar 1048-1131**CMLC 11; DAM
POET; PC 8**
Kherdian, David 1931- ....**CLC 6, 9**
See also CA 21-24R; CAAS 2; CANR 39, 78; CLR
24; JRDA; MAICYA; SATA 16, 74
Khlebnikov, Velimir .... **TCLC 20**
See also Khlebnikov, Viktor Vladimirovich
Khlebnikov, Viktor Vladimirovich 1885-1922
See Khlebnikov, Velimir
See also CA 117
Khodasevich, Vladislav (Felitsianovich) 1886-1939
TCLC 15
See also CA 115
Kielland, Alexander Lange 1849-1906 .. **TCLC 5**
See also CA 104
Kiely, Benedict 1919- .... **CLC 23, 43**
See also CA 1-4R; CANR 2; DLB 15
Kienzle, William X(avier) 1928- . **CLC 25; DAM
POP**
See also CA 93-96; CAAS 1; CANR 9, 31, 59;
INT CANR-31; MTCW 1, 2
Kierkegaard, Soren 1813-1855 ..... **NCLC 34, 78**
Kieslowski, Krzysztof 1941-1996 .... **CLC 120**
See also CA 147; 151
Killens, John Oliver 1916-1987 .... **CLC 10**
See also BW 2; CA 77-80; 123; CAAS 2; CANR
26; DLB 33
Killigrew, Anne 1660-1685 .... **LC 4**
See also DLB 131
Kim
See Simenon, Georges (Jacques Christian)
Kincaid, Jamaica 1949-**CLC 43, 68; BLC 2; DAM
MULT, NOV**
See also AAYA 13; BW 2, 3; CA 125; CANR 47,
59; CDALBS; DLB 157; MTCW 2
King, Francis (Henry) 1923- .. **CLC 8, 53; DAM
NOV**
See also CA 1-4R; CANR 1, 33; DLB 15, 139;
MTCW 1
King, Kennedy
See Brown, George Douglas
King, Martin Luther, Jr. 1929-1968**CLC 83; BLC
2; DA; DAB; DAC; DAM MST, MULT;
WLCS**
See also BW 2, 3; CA 25-28; CANR 27, 44; CAP
2; MTCW 1, 2; SATA 14
King, Stephen (Edwin) 1947-**CLC 12, 26, 37, 61,
113; DAM NOV, POP; SSC 17**
See also AAYA 1, 17; BEST 90:1; CA 61-64;
CANR 1, 30, 52, 76; DLB 143; DLBY 80; JRDA;
MTCW 1, 2; SATA 9, 55
King, Steve
See King, Stephen (Edwin)
King, Thomas 1943-**CLC 89; DAC; DAM MULT**
See also CA 144; DLB 175; NNAL; SATA 96
Kingman, Lee .... **CLC 17**
See also Natti, (Mary) Lee
See also SAAS 3; SATA 1, 67
Kingsley, Charles 1819-1875 .... **NCLC 35**
See also DLB 21, 32, 163, 190; YABC 2
Kingsley, Sidney 1906-1995 .... **CLC 44**
See also CA 85-88; 147; DLB 7
Kingsolver, Barbara 1955-**CLC 55, 81; DAM POP**
See also AAYA 15; CA 129; 134; CANR 60;
CDALBS; DLB 206; INT 134; MTCW 2
Kingston, Maxine (Ting Ting) Hong 1940- **C L C
12, 19, 58, 121; DAM MULT, NOV; WLCS**

See also AAYA 8; CA 69-72; CANR 13, 38,
74; CDALBS; DLB 173, 212; DLBY 80; INT
CANR-13; MTCW 1, 2; SATA 53
Kinnell, Galway 1927-**CLC 1, 2, 3, 5, 13, 29; PC
26**
See also CA 9-12R; CANR 10, 34, 66; DLB 5;
DLBY 87; INT CANR-34; MTCW 1, 2
Kinsella, Thomas 1928- .... **CLC 4, 19**
See also CA 17-20R; CANR 15; DLB 27; MTCW
1, 2
Kinsella, W(illiam) P(atrick) 1935- . **CLC 27,
43; DAC; DAM NOV, POP**
See also AAYA 7; CA 97-100; CAAS 7; CANR
21, 35, 66, 75; INT CANR-21; MTCW 1, 2
Kinsey, Alfred C(harles) 1894-1956 ... **TCLC 91**
See also CA 115; 170; MTCW 2
Kipling, (Joseph) Rudyard 1865-1936**TCLC 8, 17;
DA; DAB; DAC; DAM MST, POET; PC 3;
SSC 5; WLC**
See also CA 105; 120; CANR 33; CDBLB 1890-
1914; CLR 39; DLB 19, 34, 141, 156; MAICYA;
MTCW 1, 2; SATA 100; YABC 2
Kirkup, James 1918- .... **CLC 1**
See also CA 1-4R; CAAS 4; CANR 2; DLB 27;
SATA 12
Kirkwood, James 1930(?)-1989 .... **CLC 9**
See also AITN 2; CA 1-4R; 128; CANR 6, 40
Kirshner, Sidney
See Kingsley, Sidney
Kis, Danilo 1935-1989 .... **CLC 57**
See also CA 109; 118; 129; CANR 61; DLB 181;
MTCW 1
Kivi, Aleksis 1834-1872 .... **NCLC 30**
Kizer, Carolyn (Ashley) 1925- . **CLC 15, 39, 80;
DAM POET**
See also CA 65-68; CAAS 5; CANR 24, 70; DLB
5, 169; MTCW 2
Klabund 1890-1928 .... **TCLC 44**
See also CA 162; DLB 66
Klappert, Peter 1942- .... **CLC 57**
See also CA 33-36R; DLB 5
Klein, A(braham) M(oses) 1909-1972 .. **CLC 19;
DAB; DAC; DAM MST**
See also CA 101; 37-40R; DLB 68
Klein, Norma 1938-1989 .... **CLC 30**
See also AAYA 2; CA 41-44R; 128; CANR 15,
37; CLR 2, 19; INT CANR-15; JRDA;
MAICYA; SAAS 1; SATA 7, 57
Klein, T(heodore) E(ibon) D(onald) 1947-**CLC 34**
See also CA 119; CANR 44, 75
Kleist, Heinrich von 1777-1811**NCLC 2, 37; DAM
DRAM; SSC 22**
See also DLB 90
Klima, Ivan 1931- .... **CLC 56; DAM NOV**
See also CA 25-28R; CANR 17, 50
Klimentov, Andrei Platonovich 1899-1951
See Platonov, Andrei
See also CA 108
Klinger, Friedrich Maximilian von 1752-1831
NCLC 1
See also DLB 94
Klingsor the Magician
See Hartmann, Sadakichi
Klopstock, Friedrich Gottlieb 1724-1803**NCLC 11**
See also DLB 97
Knapp, Caroline 1959- .... **CLC 99**
See also CA 154
Knebel, Fletcher 1911-1993 .... **CLC 14**
See also AITN 1; CA 1-4R; 140; CAAS 3; CANR
1, 36; SATA 36; SATA-Obit 75
Knickerbocker, Diedrich
See Irving, Washington
Knight, Etheridge 1931-1991 ... **CLC 40; BLC 2;
DAM POET; PC 14**
See also BW 1, 3; CA 21-24R; 133; CANR 23;
DLB 41; MTCW 2
Knight, Sarah Kemble 1666-1727 .... **LC 7**

Lamartine, Alphonse (Marie Louis Prat) de
1790-1869 **NCLC 11; DAM POET; PC 16**

Lamb, Charles 1775-1834 ..... **NCLC 10; DA;**
DAB; DAC; DAM MST; WLC
See also CDBLB 1789-1832; DLB 93, 107, 163;
SATA 17

Lamb, Lady Caroline 1785-1828 .... **NCLC 38**
See also DLB 116

Lamming, George (William) 1927-**CLC 2, 4, 66;**
BLC 2; DAM MULT
See also BW 2, 3; CA 85-88; CANR 26, 76;
DLB 125; MTCW 1, 2

L'Amour, Louis (Dearborn) 1908-1988 **C L C**
25, 55; DAM NOV, POP
See also AAYA 16; AITN 2; BEST 89:2; CA 1-
4R; 125; CANR 3, 25, 40; DLB 206; DLBY 80;
MTCW 1, 2

Lampedusa, Giuseppe (Tomasi) di 1896-1957
TCLC 13
See also Tomasi di Lampedusa, Giuseppe
See also CA 164; DLB 177; MTCW 2

Lampman, Archibald 1861-1899 .... **NCLC 25**
See also DLB 92

Lancaster, Bruce 1896-1963 .... **CLC 36**
See also CA 9-10; CANR 70; CAP 1; SATA 9

Lanchester, John .... **CLC 99**

Landau, Mark Alexandrovich
See Aldanov, Mark (Alexandrovich)

Landau-Aldanov, Mark Alexandrovich
See Aldanov, Mark (Alexandrovich)

Landis, Jerry
See Simon, Paul (Frederick)

Landis, John 1950- .... **CLC 26**
See also CA 112; 122

Landolfi, Tommaso 1908-1979 .... **CLC 11, 49**
See also CA 127; 117; DLB 177

Landon, Letitia Elizabeth 1802-1838 ... **NCLC 15**
See also DLB 96

Landor, Walter Savage 1775-1864 ...... **NCLC 14**
See also DLB 93, 107

Landwirth, Heinz 1927-
See Lind, Jakov
See also CA 9-12R; CANR 7

Lane, Patrick 1939- .... **CLC 25; DAM POET**
See also CA 97-100; CANR 54; DLB 53; INT 97-
100

Lang, Andrew 1844-1912 .... **TCLC 16**
See also CA 114; 137; DLB 98, 141, 184;
MAICYA; SATA 16

Lang, Fritz 1890-1976 .... **CLC 20, 103**
See also CA 77-80; 69-72; CANR 30

Lange, John
See Crichton, (John) Michael

Langer, Elinor 1939- .... **CLC 34**
See also CA 121

Langland, William 1330(?)-1400(?) **LC 19; DA;**
DAB; DAC; DAM MST, POET
See also DLB 146

Langstaff, Launcelot
See Irving, Washington

Lanier, Sidney 1842-1881 **NCLC 6; DAM POET**
See also DLB 64; DLBD 13; MAICYA; SATA 18

Lanyer, Aemilia 1569-1645 .... **LC 10, 30**
See also DLB 121

Lao-Tzu
See Lao Tzu

Lao Tzu fl. 6th cent. B.C.- .... **CMLC 7**

Lapine, James (Elliot) 1949- .... **CLC 39**
See also CA 123; 130; CANR 54; INT 130

Larbaud, Valery (Nicolas) 1881-1957 .... **TCLC 9**
See also CA 106; 152

Lardner, Ring
See Lardner, Ring(gold) W(ilmer)

Lardner, Ring W., Jr.
See Lardner, Ring(gold) W(ilmer)

Lardner, Ring(gold) W(ilmer) 1885-1933**TCLC 2,**
14; SSC 32

See also CA 104; 131; CDALB 1917-1929;
DLB 11, 25, 86; DLBD 16; MTCW 1, 2

Laredo, Betty
See Codrescu, Andrei

Larkin, Maia
See Wojciechowska, Maia (Teresa)

Larkin, Philip (Arthur) 1922-1985**CLC 3, 5, 8, 9,**
13, 18, 33, 39, 64; DAB; DAM MST, POET;
PC 21
See also CA 5-8R; 117; CANR 24, 62; CDBLB
1960 to Present; DLB 27; MTCW 1, 2

Larra (y Sanchez de Castro), Mariano Jose de
1809-1837 .... **NCLC 17**

Larsen, Eric 1941- .... **CLC 55**
See also CA 132

Larsen, Nella 1891-1964 **CLC 37; BLC 2; DAM**
MULT
See also BW 1; CA 125; DLB 51

Larson, Charles R(aymond) 1938- .... **CLC 31**
See also CA 53-56; CANR 4

Larson, Jonathan 1961-1996 .... **CLC 99**
See also AAYA 28; CA 156

Las Casas, Bartolome de 1474-1566 .... **LC 31**

Lasch, Christopher 1932-1994 .... **CLC 102**
See also CA 73-76; 144; CANR 25; MTCW 1, 2

Lasker-Schueler, Else 1869-1945 .... **TCLC 57**
See also DLB 66, 124

Laski, Harold 1893-1950 .... **TCLC 79**

Latham, Jean Lee 1902-1995 .... **CLC 12**
See also AITN 1; CA 5-8R; CANR 7; CLR 50;
MAICYA; SATA 2, 68

Latham, Mavis
See Clark, Mavis Thorpe

Lathen, Emma .... **CLC 2**
See also Hennissart, Martha; Latsis, Mary J(ane)

Lathrop, Francis
See Leiber, Fritz (Reuter, Jr.)

Latsis, Mary J(ane) 1927(?)-1997
See Lathen, Emma
See also CA 85-88; 162

Lattimore, Richmond (Alexander) 1906-1984**CLC**
3
See also CA 1-4R; 112; CANR 1

Laughlin, James 1914-1997 .... **CLC 49**
See also CA 21-24R; 162; CAAS 22; CANR 9, 47;
DLB 48; DLBY 96, 97

Laurence, (Jean) Margaret (Wemyss) 1926-1987
CLC 3, 6, 13, 50, 62; DAC; DAM MST; SSC
7
See also CA 5-8R; 121; CANR 33; DLB 53;
MTCW 1, 2; SATA-Obit 50

Laurent, Antoine 1952- .... **CLC 50**

Lauscher, Hermann
See Hesse, Hermann

Lautreamont, Comte de 1846-1870**NCLC 12; SSC**
14

Laverty, Donald
See Blish, James (Benjamin)

Lavin, Mary 1912-1996 .... **CLC 4, 18, 99; SSC 4**
See also CA 9-12R; 151; CANR 33; DLB 15;
MTCW 1

Lavond, Paul Dennis
See Kornbluth, C(yril) M.; Pohl, Frederik

Lawler, Raymond Evenor 1922- .... **CLC 58**
See also CA 103

Lawrence, D(avid) H(erbert Richards) 1885-1930
TCLC 2, 9, 16, 33, 48, 61, 93; DA; DAB;
DAC; DAM MST, NOV, POET; SSC 4, 19;
WLC
See also CA 104; 121; CDBLB 1914-1945; DLB
10, 19, 36, 98, 162, 195; MTCW 1, 2

Lawrence, T(homas) E(dward) 1888-1935 **TCLC**
18
See also Dale, Colin
See also CA 115; 167; DLB 195

Lawrence of Arabia
See Lawrence, T(homas) E(dward)

Lawson, Henry (Archibald Hertzberg) 1867-
1922 .... **TCLC 27; SSC 18**
See also CA 120

Lawton, Dennis
See Faust, Frederick (Schiller)

Laxness, Halldor .... **CLC 25**
See also Gudjonsson, Halldor Kiljan

Layamon fl. c. 1200- .... **CMLC 10**
See also DLB 146

Laye, Camara 1928-1980**CLC 4, 38; BLC 2; DAM**
MULT
See also BW 1; CA 85-88; 97-100; CANR 25;
MTCW 1, 2

Layton, Irving (Peter) 1912- .. **CLC 2, 15; DAC;**
DAM MST, POET
See also CA 1-4R; CANR 2, 33, 43, 66; DLB 88;
MTCW 1, 2

Lazarus, Emma 1849-1887 .... **NCLC 8**

Lazarus, Felix
See Cable, George Washington

Lazarus, Henry
See Slavitt, David R(ytman)

Lea, Joan
See Neufeld, John (Arthur)

Leacock, Stephen (Butler) 1869-1944 . **TCLC 2;**
DAC; DAM MST
See also CA 104; 141; CANR 80; DLB 92; MTCW
2

Lear, Edward 1812-1888 .... **NCLC 3**
See also CLR 1; DLB 32, 163, 166; MAICYA;
SATA 18, 100

Lear, Norman (Milton) 1922- .... **CLC 12**
See also CA 73-76

Leautaud, Paul 1872-1956 .... **TCLC 83**
See also DLB 65

Leavis, F(rank) R(aymond) 1895-1978 .. **CLC 24**
See also CA 21-24R; 77-80; CANR 44; MTCW 1,
2

Leavitt, David 1961- .... **CLC 34; DAM POP**
See also CA 116; 122; CANR 50, 62; DLB 130;
INT 122; MTCW 2

Leblanc, Maurice (Marie Emile) 1864-1941**TCLC**
49
See also CA 110

Lebowitz, Fran(ces Ann) 1951(?)- .... **CLC 11, 36**
See also CA 81-84; CANR 14, 60, 70; INT CANR-
14; MTCW 1

Lebrecht, Peter
See Tieck, (Johann) Ludwig

le Carre, John .... **CLC 3, 5, 9, 15, 28**
See also Cornwell, David (John Moore)
See also BEST 89:4; CDBLB 1960 to Present; DLB
87; MTCW 2

Le Clezio, J(ean) M(arie) G(ustave) 1940- . **C L C**
31
See also CA 116; 128; DLB 83

Leconte de Lisle, Charles-Marie-Rene 1818-1894
NCLC 29

Le Coq, Monsieur
See Simenon, Georges (Jacques Christian)

Leduc, Violette 1907-1972 .... **CLC 22**
See also CA 13-14; 33-36R; CANR 69; CAP 1

Ledwidge, Francis 1887(?)-1917 .... **TCLC 23**
See also CA 123; DLB 20

Lee, Andrea 1953-**CLC 36; BLC 2; DAM MULT**
See also BW 1, 3; CA 125

Lee, Andrew
See Auchincloss, Louis (Stanton)

Lee, Chang-rae 1965- .... **CLC 91**
See also CA 148

Lee, Don L. .... **CLC 2**
See also Madhubuti, Haki R.

Lee, George W(ashington) 1894-1976 . **CLC 52;**
BLC 2; DAM MULT
See also BW 1; CA 125; DLB 51

Lee, (Nelle) Harper 1926-**CLC 12, 60; DA; DAB;**
DAC; DAM MST, NOV; WLC

74, 77; CDALB 1968-1988; DLB 2, 16, 28, 185; DLBD 3; DLBY 80, 83; MTCW 1, 2

Maillet, Antonine 1929- ...... **CLC 54, 118; DAC**
See also CA 115; 120; CANR 46, 74, 77; DLB 60; INT 120; MTCW 2

Mais, Roger 1905-1955 .... **TCLC 8**
See also BW 1, 3; CA 105; 124; DLB 125; MTCW 1

Maistre, Joseph de 1753-1821 .... **NCLC 37**

Maitland, Frederic 1850-1906 .... **TCLC 65**

Maitland, Sara (Louise) 1950- .... **CLC 49**
See also CA 69-72; CANR 13, 59

Major, Clarence 1936- .. **CLC 3, 19, 48; BLC 2; DAM MULT**
See also BW 2, 3; CA 21-24R; CAAS 6; CANR 13, 25, 53; DLB 33

Major, Kevin (Gerald) 1949- .... **CLC 26; DAC**
See also AAYA 16; CA 97-100; CANR 21, 38; CLR 11; DLB 60; INT CANR-21; JRDA; MAICYA; SATA 32, 82

Maki, James
See Ozu, Yasujiro

Malabaila, Damiano
See Levi, Primo

Malamud, Bernard 1914-1986**CLC 1, 2, 3, 5, 8, 9, 11, 18, 27, 44, 78, 85; DA; DAB; DAC; DAM MST, NOV, POP; SSC 15; WLC**
See also AAYA 16; CA 5-8R; 118; CABS 1; CANR 28, 62; CDALB 1941-1968; DLB 2, 28, 152; DLBY 80, 86; MTCW 1, 2

Malan, Herman
See Bosman, Herman Charles; Bosman, Herman Charles

Malaparte, Curzio 1898-1957 .... **TCLC 52**

Malcolm, Dan
See Silverberg, Robert

Malcolm X .... **CLC 82, 117; BLC 2; WLCS**
See also Little, Malcolm

Malherbe, Francois de 1555-1628 .... **LC 5**

Mallarme, Stephane 1842-1898**NCLC 4, 41; DAM POET; PC 4**

Mallet-Joris, Francoise 1930- .... **CLC 11**
See also CA 65-68; CANR 17; DLB 83

Malley, Ern
See McAuley, James Phillip

Mallowan, Agatha Christie
See Christie, Agatha (Mary Clarissa)

Maloff, Saul 1922- .... **CLC 5**
See also CA 33-36R

Malone, Louis
See MacNeice, (Frederick) Louis

Malone, Michael (Christopher) 1942- .. **CLC 43**
See also CA 77-80; CANR 14, 32, 57

Malory, (Sir) Thomas 1410(?)-1471(?)**LC 11; DA; DAB; DAC; DAM MST; WLCS**
See also CDBLB Before 1660; DLB 146; SATA 59; SATA-Brief 33

Malouf, (George Joseph) David 1934-**CLC 28, 86**
See also CA 124; CANR 50, 76; MTCW 2

Malraux, (Georges-)Andre 1901-1976**CLC 1, 4, 9, 13, 15, 57; DAM NOV**
See also CA 21-22; 69-72; CANR 34, 58; CAP 2; DLB 72; MTCW 1, 2

Malzberg, Barry N(athaniel) 1939- .... **CLC 7**
See also CA 61-64; CAAS 4; CANR 16; DLB 8

Mamet, David (Alan) 1947-**CLC 9, 15, 34, 46, 91; DAM DRAM; DC 4**
See also AAYA 3; CA 81-84; CABS 3; CANR 15, 41, 67, 72; DLB 7; MTCW 1, 2

Mamoulian, Rouben (Zachary) 1897-1987**CLC 16**
See also CA 25-28R; 124

Mandelstam, Osip (Emilievich) 1891(?)-1938(?)
TCLC 2, 6; PC 14
See also CA 104; 150; MTCW 2

Mander, (Mary) Jane 1877-1949 .... **TCLC 31**
See also CA 162

Mandeville, John fl. 1350- .... **CMLC 19**

See also DLB 146

Mandiargues, Andre Pieyre de .... **CLC 41**
See also Pieyre de Mandiargues, Andre
See also DLB 83

Mandrake, Ethel Belle
See Thurman, Wallace (Henry)

Mangan, James Clarence 1803-1849 .. **NCLC 27**

Maniere, J.-E.
See Giraudoux, (Hippolyte) Jean

Mankiewicz, Herman (Jacob) 1897-1953**TCLC 85**
See also CA 120; 169; DLB 26

Manley, (Mary) Delariviere 1672(?)-1724**LC 1, 42**
See also DLB 39, 80

Mann, Abel
See Creasey, John

Mann, Emily 1952- ....**DC 7**
See also CA 130; CANR 55

Mann, (Luiz) Heinrich 1871-1950 .... **TCLC 9**
See also CA 106; 164; DLB 66, 118

Mann, (Paul) Thomas 1875-1955**TCLC 2, 8, 14, 21, 35, 44, 60; DA; DAB; DAC; DAM MST, NOV; SSC 5; WLC**
See also CA 104; 128; DLB 66; MTCW 1, 2

Mannheim, Karl 1893-1947 .... **TCLC 65**

Manning, David
See Faust, Frederick (Schiller)

Manning, Frederic 1887(?)-1935 .... **TCLC 25**
See also CA 124

Manning, Olivia 1915-1980 .... **CLC 5, 19**
See also CA 5-8R; 101; CANR 29; MTCW 1

Mano, D. Keith 1942- .... **CLC 2, 10**
See also CA 25-28R; CAAS 6; CANR 26, 57; DLB 6

Mansfield, KatherineTCLC 2, 8, 39; DAB; SSC 9, 23; WLC
See also Beauchamp, Kathleen Mansfield
See also DLB 162

Manso, Peter 1940- .... **CLC 39**
See also CA 29-32R; CANR 44

Mantecon, Juan Jimenez
See Jimenez (Mantecon), Juan Ramon

Manton, Peter
See Creasey, John

Man Without a Spleen, A
See Chekhov, Anton (Pavlovich)

Manzoni, Alessandro 1785-1873 .... **NCLC 29**

Map, Walter 1140-1209 .... **CMLC 32**

Mapu, Abraham (ben Jekutiel) 1808-1867**NCLC 18**

Mara, Sally
See Queneau, Raymond

Marat, Jean Paul 1743-1793 .... **LC 10**

Marcel, Gabriel Honore 1889-1973 .... **CLC 15**
See also CA 102; 45-48; MTCW 1, 2

Marchbanks, Samuel
See Davies, (William) Robertson

Marchi, Giacomo
See Bassani, Giorgio

Margulies, Donald .... **CLC 76**

Marie de France c. 12th cent. - **CMLC 8; PC 22**
See also DLB 208

Marie de l'Incarnation 1599-1672 .... **LC 10**

Marier, Captain Victor
See Griffith, D(avid Lewelyn) W(ark)

Mariner, Scott
' See Pohl, Frederik

Marinetti, Filippo Tommaso 1876-1944 **TCLC 10**
See also CA 107; DLB 114

Marivaux, Pierre Carlet de Chamblain de 1688-1763 ....**LC 4; DC 7**

Markandaya, Kamala .... **CLC 8, 38**
See also Taylor, Kamala (Purnaiya)

Markfield, Wallace 1926- .... **CLC 8**
See also CA 69-72; CAAS 3; DLB 2, 28

Markham, Edwin 1852-1940 .... **TCLC 47**
See also CA 160; DLB 54, 186

Markham, Robert

See Amis, Kingsley (William)

Marks, J
See Highwater, Jamake (Mamake)

Marks-Highwater, J
See Highwater, Jamake (Mamake)

Markson, David M(errill) 1927- .... **CLC 67**
See also CA 49-52; CANR 1

Marley, Bob .... **CLC 17**
See also Marley, Robert Nesta

Marley, Robert Nesta 1945-1981
See Marley, Bob
See also CA 107; 103

Marlowe, Christopher 1564-1593**LC 22, 47; DA; DAB; DAC; DAM DRAM, MST; DC 1; WLC**
See also CDBLB Before 1660; DLB 62

Marlowe, Stephen 1928-
See Queen, Ellery
See also CA 13-16R; CANR 6, 55

Marmontel, Jean-Francois 1723-1799 .... **LC 2**

Marquand, John P(hillips) 1893-1960 **CLC 2, 10**
See also CA 85-88; CANR 73; DLB 9, 102; MTCW 2

Marques, Rene 1919-1979**CLC 96; DAM MULT; HLC**
See also CA 97-100; 85-88; CANR 78; DLB 113; HW 1, 2

Marquez, Gabriel (Jose) Garcia
See Garcia Marquez, Gabriel (Jose)

Marquis, Don(ald Robert Perry) 1878-1937**TCLC 7**
See also CA 104; 166; DLB 11, 25

Marric, J. J.
See Creasey, John

Marryat, Frederick 1792-1848 .... **NCLC 3**
See also DLB 21, 163

Marsden, James
See Creasey, John

Marsh, (Edith) Ngaio 1899-1982**CLC 7, 53; DAM POP**
See also CA 9-12R; CANR 6, 58; DLB 77; MTCW 1, 2

Marshall, Garry 1934- .... **CLC 17**
See also AAYA 3; CA 111; SATA 60

Marshall, Paule 1929-**CLC 27, 72; BLC 3; DAM MULT; SSC 3**
See also BW 2, 3; CA 77-80; CANR 25, 73; DLB 157; MTCW 1, 2

Marshallik
See Zangwill, Israel

Marsten, Richard
See Hunter, Evan

Marston, John 1576-1634 .. **LC 33; DAM DRAM**
See also DLB 58, 172

Martha, Henry
See Harris, Mark

Marti (y Perez), Jose (Julian) 1853-1895 **NCLC 63; DAM MULT; HLC**
See also HW 2

Martial c. 40-c. 104 .... **PC 10**
See also DLB 211

Martin, Ken
See Hubbard, L(afayette) Ron(ald)

Martin, Richard
See Creasey, John

Martin, Steve 1945- .... **CLC 30**
See also CA 97-100; CANR 30; MTCW 1

Martin, Valerie 1948- .... **CLC 89**
See also BEST 90:2; CA 85-88; CANR 49

Martin, Violet Florence 1862-1915 ..... **TCLC 51**

Martin, Webber
See Silverberg, Robert

Martindale, Patrick Victor
See White, Patrick (Victor Martindale)

Martin du Gard, Roger 1881-1958 ...... **TCLC 24**
See also CA 118; DLB 65

Martineau, Harriet 1802-1876 .... **NCLC 26**
See also DLB 21, 55, 159, 163, 166, 190; YABC 2

See also AITN 2; BEST 89:2; CA 25-28R;
CANR 26, 70; DLB 185; INT CANR-26

McGivern, Maureen Daly
See Daly, Maureen

McGrath, Patrick 1950- .... **CLC 55**
See also CA 136; CANR 65

McGrath, Thomas (Matthew) 1916-1990 **CLC 28, 59; DAM POET**
See also CA 9-12R; 132; CANR 6, 33; MTCW 1;
SATA 41; SATA-Obit 66

McGuane, Thomas (Francis III) 1939- **CLC 3, 7, 18, 45**
See also AITN 2; CA 49-52; CANR 5, 24, 49;
DLB 2, 212; DLBY 80; INT CANR-24; MTCW 1

McGuckian, Medbh 1950- ..... **CLC 48; DAM POET**
See also CA 143; DLB 40

McHale, Tom 1942(?)-1982 .... **CLC 3, 5**
See also AITN 1; CA 77-80; 106

McIlvanney, William 1936- .... **CLC 42**
See also CA 25-28R; CANR 61; DLB 14, 207

McIlwraith, Maureen Mollie Hunter
See Hunter, Mollie
See also SATA 2

McInerney, Jay 1955- . **CLC 34, 112; DAM POP**
See also AAYA 18; CA 116; 123; CANR 45, 68;
INT 123; MTCW 2

McIntyre, Vonda N(eel) 1948- .... **CLC 18**
See also CA 81-84; CANR 17, 34, 69; MTCW 1

McKay, Claude **TCLC 7, 41; BLC 3; DAB; PC 2**
See also McKay, Festus Claudius
See also DLB 4, 45, 51, 117

McKay, Festus Claudius 1889-1948
See McKay, Claude
See also BW 1, 3; CA 104; 124; CANR 73; DA;
DAC; DAM MST, MULT, NOV, POET; MTCW
1, 2; WLC

McKuen, Rod 1933- .... **CLC 1, 3**
See also AITN 1; CA 41-44R; CANR 40

McLoughlin, R. B.
See Mencken, H(enry) L(ouis)

McLuhan, (Herbert) Marshall 1911-1980 **CLC 37, 83**
See also CA 9-12R; 102; CANR 12, 34, 61; DLB
88; INT CANR-12; MTCW 1, 2

McMillan, Terry (L.) 1951- .... **CLC 50, 61, 112; BLCS; DAM MULT, NOV, POP**
See also AAYA 21; BW 2, 3; CA 140; CANR 60;
MTCW 2

McMurtry, Larry (Jeff) 1936- **CLC 2, 3, 7, 11, 27, 44; DAM NOV, POP**
See also AAYA 15; AITN 2; BEST 89:2; CA 5-
8R; CANR 19, 43, 64; CDALB 1968-1988; DLB
2, 143; DLBY 80, 87; MTCW 1, 2

McNally, T. M. 1961- .... **CLC 82**

McNally, Terrence 1939- **CLC 4, 7, 41, 91; DAM DRAM**
See also CA 45-48; CANR 2, 56; DLB 7; MTCW 2

McNamer, Deirdre 1950- .... **CLC 70**

McNeal, Tom .... **CLC 119**

McNeile, Herman Cyril 1888-1937
See Sapper
See also DLB 77

McNickle, (William) D'Arcy 1904-1977 **CLC 89; DAM MULT**
See also CA 9-12R; 85-88; CANR 5, 45; DLB 175,
212; NNAL; SATA-Obit 22

McPhee, John (Angus) 1931- .... **CLC 36**
See also BEST 90:1; CA 65-68; CANR 20, 46, 64,
69; DLB 185; MTCW 1, 2

McPherson, James Alan 1943- ...... **CLC 19, 77; BLCS**
See also BW 1, 3; CA 25-28R; CAAS 17; CANR
24, 74; DLB 38; MTCW 1, 2

McPherson, William (Alexander) 1933- **CLC 34**

See also CA 69-72; CANR 28; INT CANR-28

Mead, George Herbert 1873-1958 .... **TCLC 89**

Mead, Margaret 1901-1978 .... **CLC 37**
See also AITN 1; CA 1-4R; 81-84; CANR 4;
MTCW 1, 2; SATA-Obit 20

Meaker, Marijane (Agnes) 1927-
See Kerr, M. E.
See also CA 107; CANR 37, 63; INT 107; JRDA;
MAICYA; MTCW 1; SATA 20, 61, 99

Medoff, Mark (Howard) 1940- **CLC 6, 23; DAM DRAM**
See also AITN 1; CA 53-56; CANR 5; DLB 7;
INT CANR-5

Medvedev, P. N.
See Bakhtin, Mikhail Mikhailovich

Meged, Aharon
See Megged, Aharon

Meged, Aron
See Megged, Aharon

Megged, Aharon 1920- .... **CLC 9**
See also CA 49-52; CAAS 13; CANR 1

Mehta, Ved (Parkash) 1934- .... **CLC 37**
See also CA 1-4R; CANR 2, 23, 69; MTCW 1

Melanter
See Blackmore, R(ichard) D(oddridge)

Melies, Georges 1861-1938 .... **TCLC 81**

Melikow, Loris
See Hofmannsthal, Hugo von

Melmoth, Sebastian
See Wilde, Oscar

Meltzer, Milton 1915- .... **CLC 26**
See also AAYA 8; CA 13-16R; CANR 38; CLR
13; DLB 61; JRDA; MAICYA; SAAS 1; SATA
1, 50, 80

Melville, Herman 1819-1891 **NCLC 3, 12, 29, 45, 49; DA; DAB; DAC; DAM MST, NOV; SSC 1, 17; WLC**
See also AAYA 25; CDALB 1640-1865; DLB 3,
74; SATA 59

Menander c. 342B.C.-c. 292B.C. **CMLC 9; DAM DRAM; DC 3**
See also DLB 176

Mencken, H(enry) L(ouis) 1880-1956 . **TCLC 13**
See also CA 105; 125; CDALB 1917-1929; DLB
11, 29, 63, 137; MTCW 1, 2

Mendelsohn, Jane 1965(?)- .... **CLC 99**
See also CA 154

Mercer, David 1928-1980 .. **CLC 5; DAM DRAM**
See also CA 9-12R; 102; CANR 23; DLB 13;
MTCW 1

Merchant, Paul
See Ellison, Harlan (Jay)

Meredith, George 1828-1909 **TCLC 17, 43; DAM POET**
See also CA 117; 153; CANR 80; CDBLB 1832-
1890; DLB 18, 35, 57, 159

Meredith, William (Morris) 1919- **CLC 4, 13, 22, 55; DAM POET**
See also CA 9-12R; CAAS 14; CANR 6, 40; DLB 5

Merezhkovsky, Dmitry Sergeyevich 1865-1941
TCLC 29
See also CA 169

Merimee, Prosper 1803-1870 **NCLC 6, 65; SSC 7**
See also DLB 119, 192

Merkin, Daphne 1954- .... **CLC 44**
See also CA 123

Merlin, Arthur
See Blish, James (Benjamin)

Merrill, James (Ingram) 1926-1995 **CLC 2, 3, 6, 8, 13, 18, 34, 91; DAM POET**
See also CA 13-16R; 147; CANR 10, 49, 63; DLB
5, 165; DLBY 85; INT CANR-10; MTCW 1, 2

Merriman, Alex
See Silverberg, Robert

Merriman, Brian 1747-1805 .... **NCLC 70**

Merritt, E. B.

See Waddington, Miriam

Merton, Thomas 1915-1968 **CLC 1, 3, 11, 34, 83; PC 10**
See also CA 5-8R; 25-28R; CANR 22, 53; DLB
48; DLBY 81; MTCW 1, 2

Merwin, W(illiam) S(tanley) 1927- **CLC 1, 2, 3, 5, 8, 13, 18, 45, 88; DAM POET**
See also CA 13-16R; CANR 15, 51; DLB 5, 169;
INT CANR-15; MTCW 1, 2

Metcalf, John 1938- .... **CLC 37**
See also CA 113; DLB 60

Metcalf, Suzanne
See Baum, L(yman) Frank

Mew, Charlotte (Mary) 1870-1928 .... **TCLC 8**
See also CA 105; DLB 19, 135

Mewshaw, Michael 1943- .... **CLC 9**
See also CA 53-56; CANR 7, 47; DLBY 80

Meyer, June
See Jordan, June

Meyer, Lynn
See Slavitt, David R(ytman)

Meyer-Meyrink, Gustav 1868-1932
See Meyrink, Gustav
See also CA 117

Meyers, Jeffrey 1939- .... **CLC 39**
See also CA 73-76; CANR 54; DLB 111

Meynell, Alice (Christina Gertrude Thompson)
1847-1922 .... **TCLC 6**
See also CA 104; 177; DLB 19, 98

Meyrink, Gustav .... **TCLC 21**
See also Meyer-Meyrink, Gustav
See also DLB 81

Michaels, Leonard 1933- .... **CLC 6, 25; SSC 16**
See also CA 61-64; CANR 21, 62; DLB 130;
MTCW 1

Michaux, Henri 1899-1984 .... **CLC 8, 19**
See also CA 85-88; 114

Micheaux, Oscar (Devereaux) 1884-1951 **TCLC 76**
See also BW 3; CA 174; DLB 50

Michelangelo 1475-1564 .... **LC 12**

Michelet, Jules 1798-1874 .... **NCLC 31**

Michels, Robert 1876-1936 .... **TCLC 88**

Michener, James A(lbert) 1907(?)-1997 **CLC 1, 5, 11, 29, 60, 109; DAM NOV, POP**
See also AAYA 27; AITN 1; BEST 90:1; CA 5-
8R; 161; CANR 21, 45, 68; DLB 6; MTCW 1, 2

Mickiewicz, Adam 1798-1855 .... **NCLC 3**

Middleton, Christopher 1926- .... **CLC 13**
See also CA 13-16R; CANR 29, 54; DLB 40

Middleton, Richard (Barham) 1882-1911 **TCLC 56**
See also DLB 156

Middleton, Stanley 1919- .... **CLC 7, 38**
See also CA 25-28R; CAAS 23; CANR 21, 46, 81;
DLB 14

Middleton, Thomas 1580-1627 .... **LC 33; DAM DRAM, MST; DC 5**
See also DLB 58

Migueis, Jose Rodrigues 1901- .... **CLC 10**

Mikszath, Kalman 1847-1910 .... **TCLC 31**
See also CA 170

Miles, Jack .... **CLC 100**

Miles, Josephine (Louise) 1911-1985 . **CLC 1, 2, 14, 34, 39; DAM POET**
See also CA 1-4R; 116; CANR 2, 55; DLB 48

Militant
See Sandburg, Carl (August)

Mill, John Stuart 1806-1873 .... **NCLC 11, 58**
See also CDBLB 1832-1890; DLB 55, 190

Millar, Kenneth 1915-1983 . **CLC 14; DAM POP**
See also Macdonald, Ross
See also CA 9-12R; 110; CANR 16, 63; DLB 2;
DLBD 6; DLBY 83; MTCW 1, 2

Millay, E. Vincent
See Millay, Edna St. Vincent

Millay, Edna St. Vincent 1892-1950 **TCLC 4, 49; DA; DAB; DAC; DAM MST, POET; PC 6;**

Peck, Richard (Wayne) 1934- .... **CLC 21**
    See also AAYA 1, 24; CA 85-88; CANR 19,
        38; CLR 15; INT CANR-19; JRDA;
        MAICYA; SAAS 2; SATA 18, 55, 97
Peck, Robert Newton 1928- **CLC 17; DA; DAC;**
        DAM MST
    See also AAYA 3; CA 81-84; CANR 31, 63; CLR
        45; JRDA; MAICYA; SAAS 1; SATA 21, 62;
        SATA-Essay 108
Peckinpah, (David) Sam(uel) 1925-1984 **CLC 20**
    See also CA 109; 114
Pedersen, Knut 1859-1952
    See Hamsun, Knut
    See also CA 104; 119; CANR 63; MTCW 1, 2
Peeslake, Gaffer
    See Durrell, Lawrence (George)
Peguy, Charles Pierre 1873-1914 .... **TCLC 10**
    See also CA 107
Peirce, Charles Sanders 1839-1914 **TCLC 81**
Pena, Ramon del Valle y
    See Valle-Inclan, Ramon (Maria) del
Pendennis, Arthur Esquir
    See Thackeray, William Makepeace
Penn, William 1644-1718 .... **LC 25**
    See also DLB 24
Pepece
    See Prado (Calvo), Pedro
Pepys, Samuel 1633-1703 **LC 11; DA; DAB; DAC;**
        DAM MST; WLC
    See also CDBLB 1660-1789; DLB 101
Percy, Walker 1916-1990 **CLC 2, 3, 6, 8, 14, 18,**
        47, 65; DAM NOV, POP
    See also CA 1-4R; 131; CANR 1, 23, 64; DLB 2;
        DLBY 80, 90; MTCW 1, 2
Percy, William Alexander 1885-1942 . **TCLC 84**
    See also CA 163; MTCW 2
Perec, Georges 1936-1982 .... **CLC 56, 116**
    See also CA 141; DLB 83
Pereda (y Sanchez de Porrua), Jose Maria de 1833-
        1906 .... **TCLC 16**
    See also CA 117
Pereda y Porrua, Jose Maria de
    See Pereda (y Sanchez de Porrua), Jose Maria de
Peregoy, George Weems
    See Mencken, H(enry) L(ouis)
Perelman, S(idney) J(oseph) 1904-1979 **CLC 3, 5,**
        9, 15, 23, 44, 49; DAM DRAM; SSC 32
    See also AITN 1, 2; CA 73-76; 89-92; CANR 18;
        DLB 11, 44; MTCW 1, 2
Peret, Benjamin 1899-1959 .... **TCLC 20**
    See also CA 117
Peretz, Isaac Loeb 1851(?)-1915 **TCLC 16; SSC 26**
    See also CA 109
Peretz, Yitzhok Leibush
    See Peretz, Isaac Loeb
Perez Galdos, Benito 1843-1920 **TCLC 27; HLCS**
        2
    See also CA 125; 153; HW 1
Perrault, Charles 1628-1703 .... **LC 2**
    See also MAICYA; SATA 25
Perry, Brighton
    See Sherwood, Robert E(mmet)
Perse, St.-John
    See Leger, (Marie-Rene Auguste) Alexis Saint-
        Leger
Perutz, Leo(pold) 1882-1957 .... **TCLC 60**
    See also CA 147; DLB 81
Peseenz, Tulio F.
    See Lopez y Fuentes, Gregorio
Pesetsky, Bette 1932- .... **CLC 28**
    See also CA 133; DLB 130
Peshkov, Alexei Maximovich 1868-1936
    See Gorky, Maxim
    See also CA 105; 141; DA; DAC; DAM DRAM,
        MST, NOV; MTCW 2
Pessoa, Fernando (Antonio Nogueira) 1888-1935
        TCLC 27; DAM MULT; HLC; PC 20

See also CA 125
Peterkin, Julia Mood 1880-1961 .... **CLC 31**
    See also CA 102; DLB 9
Peters, Joan K(aren) 1945- .... **CLC 39**
    See also CA 158
Peters, Robert L(ouis) 1924- .... **CLC 7**
    See also CA 13-16R; CAAS 8; DLB 105
Petofi, Sandor 1823-1849 .... **NCLC 21**
Petrakis, Harry Mark 1923- .... **CLC 3**
    See also CA 9-12R; CANR 4, 30
Petrarch 1304-1374 **CMLC 20; DAM POET; PC 8**
Petrov, Evgeny .... **TCLC 21**
    See also Kataev, Evgeny Petrovich
Petry, Ann (Lane) 1908-1997 .... **CLC 1, 7, 18**
    See also BW 1, 3; CA 5-8R; 157; CAAS 6; CANR
        4, 46; CLR 12; DLB 76; JRDA; MAICYA;
        MTCW 1; SATA 5; SATA-Obit 94
Petursson, Halligrimur 1614-1674 .... **LC 8**
Peychinovich
    See Vazov, Ivan (Minchov)
Phaedrus c. 18B.C.-c. 50 .... **CMLC 25**
    See also DLB 211
Philips, Katherine 1632-1664 .... **LC 30**
    See also DLB 131
Philipson, Morris H. 1926- .... **CLC 53**
    See also CA 1-4R; CANR 4
Phillips, Caryl 1958- **CLC 96; BLCS; DAM MULT**
    See also BW 2; CA 141; CANR 63; DLB 157;
        MTCW 2
Phillips, David Graham 1867-1911 ...... **TCLC 44**
    See also CA 108; 176; DLB 9, 12
Phillips, Jack
    See Sandburg, Carl (August)
Phillips, Jayne Anne 1952- **CLC 15, 33; SSC 16**
    See also CA 101; CANR 24, 50; DLBY 80; INT
        CANR-24; MTCW 1, 2
Phillips, Richard
    See Dick, Philip K(indred)
Phillips, Robert (Schaeffer) 1938- .... **CLC 28**
    See also CA 17-20R; CAAS 13; CANR 8; DLB
        105
Phillips, Ward
    See Lovecraft, H(oward) F(hillips)
Piccolo, Lucio 1901-1969 .... **CLC 13**
    See also CA 97-100; DLB 114
Pickthall, Marjorie L(owry) C(hristie) 1883-1922
        TCLC 21
    See also CA 107; DLB 92
Pico della Mirandola, Giovanni 1463-1494 **LC 15**
Piercy, Marge 1936- .... **CLC 3, 6, 14, 18, 27, 62**
    See also CA 21-24R; CAAS 1; CANR 13, 43, 66;
        DLB 120; MTCW 1, 2
Piers, Robert
    See Anthony, Piers
Pieyre de Mandiargues, Andre 1909-1991
    See Mandiargues, Andre Pieyre de
    See also CA 103; 136; CANR 22
Pilnyak, Boris .... **TCLC 23**
    See also Vogau, Boris Andreyevich
Pincherle, Alberto 1907-1990 **CLC 11, 18; DAM**
        NOV
    See also Moravia, Alberto
    See also CA 25-28R; 132; CANR 33, 63; MTCW
        1
Pinckney, Darryl 1953- .... **CLC 76**
    See also BW 2, 3; CA 143; CANR 79
Pindar 518B.C.-446B.C. .... **CMLC 12; PC 19**
    See also DLB 176
Pineda, Cecile 1942- .... **CLC 39**
    See also CA 118
Pinero, Arthur Wing 1855-1934 **TCLC 32; DAM**
        DRAM
    See also CA 110; 153; DLB 10
Pinero, Miguel (Antonio Gomez) 1946-1988 **C L C**
        4, 55
    See also CA 61-64; 125; CANR 29; HW 1
Pinget, Robert 1919-1997 .... **CLC 7, 13, 37**

See also CA 85-88; 160; DLB 83
Pink Floyd
    See Barrett, (Roger) Syd; Gilmour, David; Ma-
        son, Nick; Waters, Roger; Wright, Rick
Pinkney, Edward 1802-1828 .... **NCLC 31**
Pinkwater, Daniel Manus 1941- .... **CLC 35**
    See also Pinkwater, Manus
    See also AAYA 1; CA 29-32R; CANR 12, 38; CLR
        4; JRDA; MAICYA; SAAS 3; SATA 46, 76
Pinkwater, Manus
    See Pinkwater, Daniel Manus
    See also SATA 8
Pinsky, Robert 1940- **CLC 9, 19, 38, 94, 121; DAM**
        POET
    See also CA 29-32R; CAAS 4; CANR 58; DLBY
        82, 98; MTCW 2
Pinta, Harold
    See Pinter, Harold
Pinter, Harold 1930- **CLC 1, 3, 6, 9, 11, 15, 27,**
        58, 73; DA; DAB; DAC; DAM DRAM,
        MST; WLC
    See also CA 5-8R; CANR 33, 65; CDBLB 1960 to
        Present; DLB 13; MTCW 1, 2
Piozzi, Hester Lynch (Thrale) 1741-1821 **N C L C**
        57
    See also DLB 104, 142
Pirandello, Luigi 1867-1936 ... **TCLC 4, 29; DA;**
        DAB; DAC; DAM DRAM, MST; DC 5; SSC
        22; WLC
    See also CA 104; 153; MTCW 2
Pirsig, Robert M(aynard) 1928- .. **CLC 4, 6, 73;**
        DAM POP
    See also CA 53-56; CANR 42, 74; MTCW 1, 2;
        SATA 39
Pisarev, Dmitry Ivanovich 1840-1868 .. **NCLC 25**
Pix, Mary (Griffith) 1666-1709 .... **LC 8**
    See also DLB 80
Pixerecourt, (Rene Charles) Guilbert de 1773-1844
        NCLC 39
    See also DLB 192
Plaatje, Sol(omon) T(shekisho) 1876-1932 **T C L C**
        73; BLCS
    See also BW 2, 3; CA 141; CANR 79
Plaidy, Jean
    See Hibbert, Eleanor Alice Burford
Planche, James Robinson 1796-1880 .. **NCLC 42**
Plant, Robert 1948- .... **CLC 12**
Plante, David (Robert) 1940- **CLC 7, 23, 38; DAM**
        NOV
    See also CA 37-40R; CANR 12, 36, 58; DLBY 83;
        INT CANR-12; MTCW 1
Plath, Sylvia 1932-1963 **CLC 1, 2, 3, 5, 9, 11, 14,**
        17, 50, 51, 62, 111; DA; DAB; DAC; DAM
        MST, POET; PC 1; WLC
    See also AAYA 13; CA 19-20; CANR 34; CAP 2;
        CDALB 1941-1968; DLB 5, 6, 152; MTCW 1,
        2; SATA 96
Plato 428(?)B.C.-348(?)B.C. **CMLC 8; DA; DAB;**
        DAC; DAM MST; WLCS
    See also DLB 176
Platonov, Andrei .... **TCLC 14**
    See also Klimentov, Andrei Platonovich
Platt, Kin 1911- .... **CLC 26**
    See also AAYA 11; CA 17-20R; CANR 11; JRDA;
        SAAS 17; SATA 21, 86
Plautus c. 251B.C.-184B.C. ...... **CMLC 24; DC 6**
    See also DLB 211
Plick et Plock
    See Simenon, Georges (Jacques Christian)
Plimpton, George (Ames) 1927- .... **CLC 36**
    See also AITN 1; CA 21-24R; CANR 32, 70; DLB
        185; MTCW 1, 2; SATA 10
Pliny the Elder c. 23-79 .... **CMLC 23**
    See also DLB 211
Plomer, William Charles Franklin 1903-1973
        CLC 4, 8
    See also CA 21-22; CANR 34; CAP 2; DLB 20,

Reiner, Max
See Caldwell, (Janet Miriam) Taylor (Holland)
Reis, Ricardo
See Pessoa, Fernando (Antonio Nogueira)
Remarque, Erich Maria 1898-1970 **CLC 21; DA; DAB; DAC; DAM MST, NOV**
See also AAYA 27; CA 77-80; 29-32R; DLB 56; MTCW 1, 2
Remington, Frederic 1861-1909 .... **TCLC 89**
See also CA 108; 169; DLB 12, 186, 188; SATA 41
Remizov, A.
See Remizov, Aleksei (Mikhailovich)
Remizov, A. M.
See Remizov, Aleksei (Mikhailovich)
Remizov, Aleksei (Mikhailovich) 1877-1957
TCLC 27
See also CA 125; 133
Renan, Joseph Ernest 1823-1892 .... **NCLC 26**
Renard, Jules 1864-1910 .... **TCLC 17**
See also CA 117
Renault, Mary .... **CLC 3, 11, 17**
See also Challans, Mary
See also DLBY 83; MTCW 2
Rendell, Ruth (Barbara) 1930-**CLC 28, 48; DAM POP**
See also Vine, Barbara
See also CA 109; CANR 32, 52, 74; DLB 87; INT CANR-32; MTCW 1, 2
Renoir, Jean 1894-1979 .... **CLC 20**
See also CA 129; 85-88
Resnais, Alain 1922- .... **CLC 16**
Reverdy, Pierre 1889-1960 .... **CLC 53**
See also CA 97-100; 89-92
Rexroth, Kenneth 1905-1982 **CLC 1, 2, 6, 11, 22, 49, 112; DAM POET; PC 20**
See also CA 5-8R; 107; CANR 14, 34, 63; CDALB 1941-1968; DLB 16, 48, 165, 212; DLBY 82; INT CANR-14; MTCW 1, 2
Reyes, Alfonso 1889-1959 ... **TCLC 33; HLCS 2**
See also CA 131; HW 1
Reyes y Basoalto, Ricardo Eliecer Neftali
See Neruda, Pablo
Reymont, Wladyslaw (Stanislaw) 1868(?)-1925
TCLC 5
See also CA 104
Reynolds, Jonathan 1942- .... **CLC 6, 38**
See also CA 65-68; CANR 28
Reynolds, Joshua 1723-1792 .... **LC 15**
See also DLB 104
Reynolds, Michael Shane 1937- .... **CLC 44**
See also CA 65-68; CANR 9
Reznikoff, Charles 1894-1976 .... **CLC 9**
See also CA 33-36; 61-64; CAP 2; DLB 28, 45
Rezzori (d'Arezzo), Gregor von 1914-1998 **CLC 25**
See also CA 122; 136; 167
Rhine, Richard
See Silverstein, Alvin
Rhodes, Eugene Manlove 1869-1934 ... **TCLC 53**
Rhodius, Apollonius c. 3rd cent. B.C.- **CMLC 28**
See also DLB 176
R'hoone
See Balzac, Honore de
Rhys, Jean 1890(?)-1979**CLC 2, 4, 6, 14, 19, 51; DAM NOV; SSC 21**
See also CA 25-28R; 85-88; CANR 35, 62; CDBLB 1945-1960; DLB 36, 117, 162; MTCW 1, 2
Ribeiro, Darcy 1922-1997 .... **CLC 34**
See also CA 33-36R; 156
Ribeiro, Joao Ubaldo (Osorio Pimentel) 1941-
CLC 10, 67
See also CA 81-84
Ribman, Ronald (Burt) 1932- .... **CLC 7**
See also CA 21-24R; CANR 46, 80
Ricci, Nino 1959- .... **CLC 70**
See also CA 137
Rice, Anne 1941- .... **CLC 41; DAM POP**

See also AAYA 9; BEST 89:2; CA 65-68; CANR 12, 36, 53, 74; MTCW 2
Rice, Elmer (Leopold) 1892-1967**CLC 7, 49; DAM DRAM**
See also CA 21-22; 25-28R; CAP 2; DLB 4, 7; MTCW 1, 2
Rice, Tim(othy Miles Bindon) 1944- .... **CLC 21**
See also CA 103; CANR 46
Rich, Adrienne (Cecile) 1929-**CLC 3, 6, 7, 11, 18, 36, 73, 76; DAM POET; PC 5**
See also CA 9-12R; CANR 20, 53, 74; CDALBS; DLB 5, 67; MTCW 1, 2
Rich, Barbara
See Graves, Robert (von Ranke)
Rich, Robert
See Trumbo, Dalton
Richard, Keith .... **CLC 17**
See also Richards, Keith
Richards, David Adams 1950- ..... **CLC 59; DAC**
See also CA 93-96; CANR 60; DLB 53
Richards, I(vor) A(rmstrong) 1893-1979**C L C 14, 24**
See also CA 41-44R; 89-92; CANR 34, 74; DLB 27; MTCW 2
Richards, Keith 1943-
See Richard, Keith
See also CA 107; CANR 77
Richardson, Anne
See Roiphe, Anne (Richardson)
Richardson, Dorothy Miller 1873-1957 **TCLC 3**
See also CA 104; DLB 36
Richardson, Ethel Florence (Lindesay) 1870-1946
See Richardson, Henry Handel
See also CA 105
Richardson, Henry Handel .... **TCLC 4**
See also Richardson, Ethel Florence (Lindesay)
See also DLB 197
Richardson, John 1796-1852 .... **NCLC 55; DAC**
See also DLB 99
Richardson, Samuel 1689-1761 ... **LC 1, 44; DA; DAB; DAC; DAM MST, NOV; WLC**
See also CDBLB 1660-1789; DLB 39
Richler, Mordecai 1931- **CLC 3, 5, 9, 13, 18, 46, 70; DAC; DAM MST, NOV**
See also AITN 1; CA 65-68; CANR 31, 62; CLR 17; DLB 53; MAICYA; MTCW 1, 2; SATA 44, 98; SATA-Brief 27
Richter, Conrad (Michael) 1890-1968 ... **CLC 30**
See also AAYA 21; CA 5-8R; 25-28R; CANR 23; DLB 9, 212; MTCW 1, 2; SATA 3
Ricostranza, Tom
See Ellis, Trey
Riddell, Charlotte 1832-1906 .... **TCLC 40**
See also CA 165; DLB 156
Ridgway, Keith 1965- .... **CLC 119**
See also CA 172
Riding, Laura .... **CLC 3, 7**
See also Jackson, Laura (Riding)
Riefenstahl, Berta Helene Amalia 1902-
See Riefenstahl, Leni
See also CA 108
Riefenstahl, Leni .... **CLC 16**
See also Riefenstahl, Berta Helene Amalia
Riffe, Ernest
See Bergman, (Ernst) Ingmar
Riggs, (Rolla) Lynn 1899-1954 . **TCLC 56; DAM MULT**
See also CA 144; DLB 175; NNAL
Riis, Jacob A(ugust) 1849-1914 .... **TCLC 80**
See also CA 113; 168; DLB 23
Riley, James Whitcomb 1849-1916 .... **TCLC 51; DAM POET**
See also CA 118; 137; MAICYA; SATA 17
Riley, Tex
See Creasey, John
Rilke, Rainer Maria 1875-1926 . **TCLC 1, 6, 19; DAM POET; PC 2**

See also CA 104; 132; CANR 62; DLB 81; MTCW 1, 2
Rimbaud, (Jean Nicolas) Arthur 1854-1891
NCLC 4, 35; DA; DAB; DAC; DAM MST, POET; PC 3; WLC
Rinehart, Mary Roberts 1876-1958 .... **TCLC 52**
See also CA 108; 166
Ringmaster, The
See Mencken, H(enry) L(ouis)
Ringwood, Gwen(dolyn Margaret) Pharis 1910-1984
CLC 48
See also CA 148; 112; DLB 88
Rio, Michel 19(?)- .... **CLC 43**
Ritsos, Giannes
See Ritsos, Yannis
Ritsos, Yannis 1909-1990 .... **CLC 6, 13, 31**
See also CA 77-80; 133; CANR 39, 61; MTCW 1
Ritter, Erika 1948(?)- .... **CLC 52**
Rivera, Jose Eustasio 1889-1928 .... **TCLC 35**
See also CA 162; HW 1, 2
Rivers, Conrad Kent 1933-1968 .... **CLC 1**
See also BW 1; CA 85-88; DLB 41
Rivers, Elfrida
See Bradley, Marion Zimmer
Riverside, John
See Heinlein, Robert A(nson)
Rizal, Jose 1861-1896 .... **NCLC 27**
Roa Bastos, Augusto (Antonio) 1917- . **CLC 45; DAM MULT; HLC**
See also CA 131; DLB 113; HW 1
Robbe-Grillet, Alain 1922- **CLC 1, 2, 4, 6, 8, 10, 14, 43**
See also CA 9-12R; CANR 33, 65; DLB 83; MTCW 1, 2
Robbins, Harold 1916-1997... **CLC 5; DAM NOV**
See also CA 73-76; 162; CANR 26, 54; MTCW 1, 2
Robbins, Thomas Eugene 1936-
See Robbins, Tom
See also CA 81-84; CANR 29, 59; DAM NOV, POP; MTCW 1, 2
Robbins, Tom .... **CLC 9, 32, 64**
See also Robbins, Thomas Eugene
See also BEST 90:3; DLBY 80; MTCW 2
Robbins, Trina 1938- .... **CLC 21**
See also CA 128
Roberts, Charles G(eorge) D(ouglas) 1860-1943
TCLC 8
See also CA 105; CLR 33; DLB 92; SATA 88; SATA-Brief 29
Roberts, Elizabeth Madox 1886-1941 .. **TCLC 68**
See also CA 111; 166; DLB 9, 54, 102; SATA 33; SATA-Brief 27
Roberts, Kate 1891-1985 .... **CLC 15**
See also CA 107; 116
Roberts, Keith (John Kingston) 1935- . **CLC 14**
See also CA 25-28R; CANR 46
Roberts, Kenneth (Lewis) 1885-1957 .. **TCLC 23**
See also CA 109; DLB 9
Roberts, Michele (B.) 1949- .... **CLC 48**
See also CA 115; CANR 58
Robertson, Ellis
See Ellison, Harlan (Jay); Silverberg, Robert
Robertson, Thomas William 1829-1871**NCLC 35; DAM DRAM**
Robeson, Kenneth
See Dent, Lester
Robinson, Edwin Arlington 1869-1935 . **TCLC 5; DA; DAC; DAM MST, POET; PC 1**
See also CA 104; 133; CDALB 1865-1917; DLB 54; MTCW 1, 2
Robinson, Henry Crabb 1775-1867 ..... **NCLC 15**
See also DLB 107
Robinson, Jill 1936- .... **CLC 10**
See also CA 102; INT 102
Robinson, Kim Stanley 1952- .... **CLC 34**
See also AAYA 26; CA 126; SATA 109

Silkin, Jon 1930- .... **CLC 2, 6, 43**
See also CA 5-8R; CAAS 5; DLB 27

Silko, Leslie (Marmon) 1948- **CLC 23, 74, 114;
DA; DAC; DAM MST, MULT, POP; WLCS**
See also AAYA 14; CA 115; 122; CANR 45, 65;
DLB 143, 175; MTCW 2; NNAL

Sillanpaa, Frans Eemil 1888-1964 .... **CLC 19**
See also CA 129; 93-96; MTCW 1

Sillitoe, Alan 1928- .... **CLC 1, 3, 6, 10, 19, 57**
See also AITN 1; CA 9-12R; CAAS 2; CANR 8,
26, 55; CDBLB 1960 to Present; DLB 14, 139;
MTCW 1, 2; SATA 61

Silone, Ignazio 1900-1978 .... **CLC 4**
See also CA 25-28; 81-84; CANR 34; CAP 2;
MTCW 1

Silver, Joan Micklin 1935- .... **CLC 20**
See also CA 114; 121; INT 121

Silver, Nicholas
See Faust, Frederick (Schiller)

Silverberg, Robert 1935- ...... **CLC 7; DAM POP**
See also AAYA 24; CA 1-4R; CAAS 3; CANR 1,
20, 36; CLR 59; DLB 8; INT CANR-20;
MAICYA; MTCW 1, 2; SATA 13, 91; SATA-
Essay 104

Silverstein, Alvin 1933- .... **CLC 17**
See also CA 49-52; CANR 2; CLR 25; JRDA;
MAICYA; SATA 8, 69

Silverstein, Virginia B(arbara Opshelor) 1937-
CLC 17
See also CA 49-52; CANR 2; CLR 25; JRDA;
MAICYA; SATA 8, 69

Sim, Georges
See Simenon, Georges (Jacques Christian)

Simak, Clifford D(onald) 1904-1988 . **CLC 1, 55**
See also CA 1-4R; 125; CANR 1, 35; DLB 8;
MTCW 1; SATA-Obit 56

Simenon, Georges (Jacques Christian) 1903-1989
CLC 1, 2, 3, 8, 18, 47; DAM POP
See also CA 85-88; 129; CANR 35; DLB 72; DLBY
89; MTCW 1, 2

Simic, Charles 1938- **CLC 6, 9, 22, 49, 68; DAM
POET**
See also CA 29-32R; CAAS 4; CANR 12, 33, 52,
61; DLB 105; MTCW 2

Simmel, Georg 1858-1918 .... **TCLC 64**
See also CA 157

Simmons, Charles (Paul) 1924- .... **CLC 57**
See also CA 89-92; INT 89-92

Simmons, Dan 1948- .... **CLC 44; DAM POP**
See also AAYA 16; CA 138; CANR 53, 81

Simmons, James (Stewart Alexander) 1933-**CLC
43**
See also CA 105; CAAS 21; DLB 40

Simms, William Gilmore 1806-1870 .... **NCLC 3**
See also DLB 3, 30, 59, 73

Simon, Carly 1945- .... **CLC 26**
See also CA 105

Simon, Claude 1913-1984**CLC 4, 9, 15, 39; DAM
NOV**
See also CA 89-92; CANR 33; DLB 83; MTCW 1

Simon, (Marvin) Neil 1927-**CLC 6, 11, 31, 39, 70;
DAM DRAM**
See also AITN 1; CA 21-24R; CANR 26, 54; DLB
7; MTCW 1, 2

Simon, Paul (Frederick) 1941(?)- .... **CLC 17**
See also CA 116; 153

Simonon, Paul 1956(?)- .... **CLC 30**

Simpson, Harriette
See Arnow, Harriette (Louisa) Simpson

Simpson, Louis (Aston Marantz) 1923-**CLC 4, 7,
9, 32; DAM POET**
See also CA 1-4R; CAAS 4; CANR 1, 61; DLB 5;
MTCW 1, 2

Simpson, Mona (Elizabeth) 1957- .... **CLC 44**
See also CA 122; 135; CANR 68

Simpson, N(orman) F(rederick) 1919- . **CLC 29**
See also CA 13-16R; DLB 13

Sinclair, Andrew (Annandale) 1935- . **CLC 2,
14**
See also CA 9-12R; CAAS 5; CANR 14, 38;
DLB 14; MTCW 1

Sinclair, Emil
See Hesse, Hermann

Sinclair, Iain 1943- .... **CLC 76**
See also CA 132; CANR 81

Sinclair, Iain MacGregor
See Sinclair, Iain

Sinclair, Irene
See Griffith, D(avid Lewelyn) W(ark)

Sinclair, Mary Amelia St. Clair 1865(?)-1946
See Sinclair, May
See also CA 104

Sinclair, May 1863-1946 .... **TCLC 3, 11**
See also Sinclair, Mary Amelia St. Clair
See also CA 166; DLB 36, 135

Sinclair, Roy
See Griffith, D(avid Lewelyn) W(ark)

Sinclair, Upton (Beall) 1878-1968**CLC 1, 11, 15,
63; DA; DAB; DAC; DAM MST, NOV; WLC**
See also CA 5-8R; 25-28R; CANR 7; CDALB 1929-
1941; DLB 9; INT CANR-7; MTCW 1, 2;
SATA 9

Singer, Isaac
See Singer, Isaac Bashevis

Singer, Isaac Bashevis 1904-1991**CLC 1, 3, 6, 9,
11, 15, 23, 38, 69, 111; DA; DAB; DAC; DAM
MST, NOV; SSC 3; WLC**
See also AITN 1, 2; CA 1-4R; 134; CANR 1, 39;
CDALB 1941-1968; CLR 1; DLB 6, 28, 52;
DLBY 91; JRDA; MAICYA; MTCW 1, 2;
SATA 3, 27; SATA-Obit 68

Singer, Israel Joshua 1893-1944 .... **TCLC 33**
See also CA 169

Singh, Khushwant 1915- .... **CLC 11**
See also CA 9-12R; CAAS 9; CANR 6

Singleton, Ann
See Benedict, Ruth (Fulton)

Sinjohn, John
See Galsworthy, John

Sinyavsky, Andrei (Donatevich) 1925-1997**CLC 8**
See also CA 85-88; 159

Sirin, V.
See Nabokov, Vladimir (Vladimirovich)

Sissman, L(ouis) E(dward) 1928-1976 **CLC 9, 18**
See also CA 21-24R; 65-68; CANR 13; DLB 5

Sisson, C(harles) H(ubert) 1914- .... **CLC 8**
See also CA 1-4R; CAAS 3; CANR 3, 48; DLB 27

Sitwell, Dame Edith 1887-1964**CLC 2, 9, 67; DAM
POET; PC 3**
See also CA 9-12R; CANR 35; CDBLB 1945-1960;
DLB 20; MTCW 1, 2

Siwaarmill, H. P.
See Sharp, William

Sjoewall, Maj 1935- .... **CLC 7**
See also CA 65-68; CANR 73

Sjowall, Maj
See Sjoewall, Maj

Skelton, John 1463-1529 .... **PC 25**

Skelton, Robin 1925-1997 .... **CLC 13**
See also AITN 2; CA 5-8R; 160; CAAS 5; CANR
28; DLB 27, 53

Skolimowski, Jerzy 1938- .... **CLC 20**
See also CA 128

Skram, Amalie (Bertha) 1847-1905 .... **TCLC 25**
See also CA 165

Skvorecky, Josef (Vaclav) 1924-**CLC 15, 39, 69;
DAC; DAM NOV**
See also CA 61-64; CAAS 1; CANR 10, 34, 63;
MTCW 1, 2

Slade, Bernard .... **CLC 11, 46**
See also Newbound, Bernard Slade
See also CAAS 9; DLB 53

Slaughter, Carolyn 1946- .... **CLC 56**
See also CA 85-88

Slaughter, Frank G(ill) 1908- .... **CLC 29**
See also AITN 2; CA 5-8R; CANR 5; INT
CANR-5

Slavitt, David R(ytman) 1935- .... **CLC 5, 14**
See also CA 21-24R; CAAS 3; CANR 41; DLB 5,
6

Slesinger, Tess 1905-1945 .... **TCLC 10**
See also CA 107; DLB 102

Slessor, Kenneth 1901-1971 .... **CLC 14**
See also CA 102; 89-92

Slowacki, Juliusz 1809-1849 .... **NCLC 15**

Smart, Christopher 1722-1771**LC 3; DAM POET;
PC 13**
See also DLB 109

Smart, Elizabeth 1913-1986 .... **CLC 54**
See also CA 81-84; 118; DLB 88

Smiley, Jane (Graves) 1949- **CLC 53, 76; DAM
POP**
See also CA 104; CANR 30, 50, 74; INT CANR-
30

Smith, A(rthur) J(ames) M(arshall) 1902-1980
CLC 15; DAC
See also CA 1-4R; 102; CANR 4; DLB 88

Smith, Adam 1723-1790 .... **LC 36**
See also DLB 104

Smith, Alexander 1829-1867 .... **NCLC 59**
See also DLB 32, 55

Smith, Anna Deavere 1950- .... **CLC 86**
See also CA 133

Smith, Betty (Wehner) 1896-1972 .... **CLC 19**
See also CA 5-8R; 33-36R; DLBY 82; SATA 6

Smith, Charlotte (Turner) 1749-1806 . **NCLC 23**
See also DLB 39, 109

Smith, Clark Ashton 1893-1961 .... **CLC 43**
See also CA 143; CANR 81; MTCW 2

Smith, Dave .... **CLC 22, 42**
See also Smith, David (Jeddie)
See also CAAS 7; DLB 5

Smith, David (Jeddie) 1942-
See Smith, Dave
See also CA 49-52; CANR 1, 59; DAM POET

Smith, Florence Margaret 1902-1971
See Smith, Stevie
See also CA 17-18; 29-32R; CANR 35; CAP 2;
DAM POET; MTCW 1, 2

Smith, Iain Crichton 1928-1998 .... **CLC 64**
See also CA 21-24R; 171; DLB 40, 139

Smith, John 1580(?)-1631 .... **LC 9**
See also DLB 24, 30

Smith, Johnston
See Crane, Stephen (Townley)

Smith, Joseph, Jr. 1805-1844 .... **NCLC 53**

Smith, Lee 1944- .... **CLC 25, 73**
See also CA 114; 119; CANR 46; DLB 143; DLBY
83; INT 119

Smith, Martin
See Smith, Martin Cruz

Smith, Martin Cruz 1942-**CLC 25; DAM MULT,
POP**
See also BEST 89:4; CA 85-88; CANR 6, 23, 43,
65; INT CANR-23; MTCW 2; NNAL

Smith, Mary-Ann Tirone 1944- .... **CLC 39**
See also CA 118; 136

Smith, Patti 1946- .... **CLC 12**
See also CA 93-96; CANR 63

Smith, Pauline (Urmson) 1882-1959 ... **TCLC 25**

Smith, Rosamond
See Oates, Joyce Carol

Smith, Sheila Kaye
See Kaye-Smith, Sheila

Smith, Stevie .... **CLC 3, 8, 25, 44; PC 12**
See also Smith, Florence Margaret
See also DLB 20; MTCW 2

Smith, Wilbur (Addison) 1933- .... **CLC 33**
See also CA 13-16R; CANR 7, 46, 66; MTCW 1, 2

Smith, William Jay 1918- .... **CLC 6**
See also CA 5-8R; CANR 44; DLB 5; MAICYA;

173; DLBY 81

Suknaski, Andrew 1942- .... **CLC 19**
See also CA 101; DLB 53

Sullivan, Vernon
See Vian, Boris

Sully Prudhomme 1839-1907 .... **TCLC 31**

Su Man-shu .... **TCLC 24**
See also Su, Chien

Summerforest, Ivy B.
See Kirkup, James

Summers, Andrew James 1942- .... **CLC 26**

Summers, Andy
See Summers, Andrew James

Summers, Hollis (Spurgeon, Jr.) 1916- **CLC 10**
See also CA 5-8R; CANR 3; DLB 6

Summers, (Alphonsus Joseph-Mary Augustus)
Montague 1880-1948 .... **TCLC 16**
See also CA 118; 163

Sumner, Gordon Matthew .... **CLC 26**
See also Sting

Surtees, Robert Smith 1803-1864 .... **NCLC 14**
See also DLB 21

Susann, Jacqueline 1921-1974 .... **CLC 3**
See also AITN 1; CA 65-68; 53-56; MTCW 1, 2

Su Shih 1036-1101 .... **CMLC 15**

Suskind, Patrick
See Sueskind, Patrick
See also CA 145

Sutcliff, Rosemary 1920-1992 .... **CLC 26; DAB;**
DAC; DAM MST, POP
See also AAYA 10; CA 5-8R; 139; CANR 37;
CLR 1, 37; JRDA; MAICYA; SATA 6, 44, 78;
SATA-Obit 73

Sutro, Alfred 1863-1933 .... **TCLC 6**
See also CA 105; DLB 10

Sutton, Henry
See Slavitt, David R(ytman)

Svevo, Italo 1861-1928 .... **TCLC 2, 35; SSC 25**
See also Schmitz, Aron Hector

Swados, Elizabeth (A.) 1951- .... **CLC 12**
See also CA 97-100; CANR 49; INT 97-100

Swados, Harvey 1920-1972 .... **CLC 5**
See also CA 5-8R; 37-40R; CANR 6; DLB 2

Swan, Gladys 1934- .... **CLC 69**
See also CA 101; CANR 17, 39

Swarthout, Glendon (Fred) 1918-1992 .. **CLC 35**
See also CA 1-4R; 139; CANR 1, 47; SATA 26

Sweet, Sarah C.
See Jewett, (Theodora) Sarah Orne

Swenson, May 1919-1989 **CLC 4, 14, 61, 106; DA;**
DAB; DAC; DAM MST, POET; PC 14
See also CA 5-8R; 130; CANR 36, 61; DLB 5;
MTCW 1, 2; SATA 15

Swift, Augustus
See Lovecraft, H(oward) P(hillips)

Swift, Graham (Colin) 1949- .... **CLC 41, 88**
See also CA 117; 122; CANR 46, 71; DLB 194;
MTCW 2

Swift, Jonathan 1667-1745 **LC 1, 42; DA; DAB;**
DAC; DAM MST, NOV, POET; PC 9; WLC
See also CDBLB 1660-1789; CLR 53; DLB 39, 95,
101; SATA 19

Swinburne, Algernon Charles 1837-1909 **TCLC**
8, 36; DA; DAB; DAC; DAM MST, POET;
PC 24; WLC
See also CA 105; 140; CDBLB 1832-1890; DLB
35, 57

Swinfen, Ann .... **CLC 34**

Swinnerton, Frank Arthur 1884-1982 .. **CLC 31**
See also CA 108; DLB 34

Swithen, John
See King, Stephen (Edwin)

Sylvia
See Ashton-Warner, Sylvia (Constance)

Symmes, Robert Edward
See Duncan, Robert (Edward)

Symonds, John Addington 1840-1893 . **NCLC 34**

See also DLB 57, 144

Symons, Arthur 1865-1945 .... **TCLC 11**
See also CA 107; DLB 19, 57, 149

Symons, Julian (Gustave) 1912-1994 **CLC 2, 14,**
32
See also CA 49-52; 147; CAAS 3; CANR 3, 33,
59; DLB 87, 155; DLBY 92; MTCW 1

Synge, (Edmund) J(ohn) M(illington) 1871-1909
TCLC 6, 37; DAM DRAM; DC 2
See also CA 104; 141; CDBLB 1890-1914; DLB
10, 19

Syruc, J.
See Milosz, Czeslaw

Szirtes, George 1948- .... **CLC 46**
See also CA 109; CANR 27, 61

Szymborska, Wislawa 1923- .... **CLC 99**
See also CA 154; DLBY 96; MTCW 2

T. O., Nik
See Annensky, Innokenty (Fyodorovich)

Tabori, George 1914- .... **CLC 19**
See also CA 49-52; CANR 4, 69

Tagore, Rabindranath 1861-1941 ... **TCLC 3, 53;**
DAM DRAM, POET; PC 8
See also CA 104; 120; MTCW 1, 2

Taine, Hippolyte Adolphe 1828-1893 ... **NCLC 15**

Talese, Gay 1932- .... **CLC 37**
See also AITN 1; CA 1-4R; CANR 9, 58; DLB
185; INT CANR-9; MTCW 1, 2

Tallent, Elizabeth (Ann) 1954- .... **CLC 45**
See also CA 117; CANR 72; DLB 130

Tally, Ted 1952- .... **CLC 42**
See also CA 120; 124; INT 124

Talvik, Heiti 1904-1947 .... **TCLC 87**

Tamayo y Baus, Manuel 1829-1898 .... **NCLC 1**

Tammsaare, A(nton) H(ansen) 1878-1940 **TCLC**
27
See also CA 164

Tam'si, Tchicaya U
See Tchicaya, Gerald Felix

Tan, Amy (Ruth) 1952-**CLC 59, 120; DAM MULT,**
NOV, POP
See also AAYA 9; BEST 89:3; CA 136; CANR
54; CDALBS; DLB 173; MTCW 2; SATA 75

Tandem, Felix
See Spitteler, Carl (Friedrich Georg)

Tanizaki, Jun'ichiro 1886-1965 . **CLC 8, 14, 28;**
SSC 21
See also CA 93-96; 25-28R; DLB 180; MTCW 2

Tanner, William
See Amis, Kingsley (William)

Tao Lao
See Storni, Alfonsina

Tarassoff, Lev
See Troyat, Henri

Tarbell, Ida M(inerva) 1857-1944 .... **TCLC 40**
See also CA 122; DLB 47

Tarkington, (Newton) Booth 1869-1946 **TCLC 9**
See also CA 110; 143; DLB 9, 102; MTCW 2;
SATA 17

Tarkovsky, Andrei (Arsenyevich) 1932-1986**CLC**
75
See also CA 127

Tartt, Donna 1964(?)- .... **CLC 76**
See also CA 142

Tasso, Torquato 1544-1595 .... **LC 5**

Tate, (John Orley) Allen 1899-1979**CLC 2, 4, 6, 9,**
11, 14, 24
See also CA 5-8R; 85-88; CANR 32; DLB 4, 45,
63; DLBD 17; MTCW 1, 2

Tate, Ellalice
See Hibbert, Eleanor Alice Burford

Tate, James (Vincent) 1943- .... **CLC 2, 6, 25**
See also CA 21-24R; CANR 29, 57; DLB 5, 169

Tavel, Ronald 1940- .... **CLC 6**
See also CA 21-24R; CANR 33

Taylor, C(ecil) P(hilip) 1929-1981 .... **CLC 27**
See also CA 25-28R; 105; CANR 47

Taylor, Edward 1642(?)-1729 ..... **LC 11; DA;**
DAB; DAC; DAM MST, POET
See also DLB 24

Taylor, Eleanor Ross 1920- .... **CLC 5**
See also CA 81-84; CANR 70

Taylor, Elizabeth 1912-1975 .... **CLC 2, 4, 29**
See also CA 13-16R; CANR 9, 70; DLB 139;
MTCW 1; SATA 13

Taylor, Frederick Winslow 1856-1915 **TCLC 76**

Taylor, Henry (Splawn) 1942- .... **CLC 44**
See also CA 33-36R; CAAS 7; CANR 31; DLB 5

Taylor, Kamala (Purnaiya) 1924-
See Markandaya, Kamala
See also CA 77-80

Taylor, Mildred D. .... **CLC 21**
See also AAYA 10; BW 1; CA 85-88; CANR 25;
CLR 9, 59; DLB 52; JRDA; MAICYA; SAAS
5; SATA 15, 70

Taylor, Peter (Hillsman) 1917-1994**CLC 1, 4, 18,**
37, 44, 50, 71; SSC 10
See also CA 13-16R; 147; CANR 9, 50; DLBY 81,
94; INT CANR-9; MTCW 1, 2

Taylor, Robert Lewis 1912-1998 .... **CLC 14**
See also CA 1-4R; 170; CANR 3, 64; SATA 10

Tchekhov, Anton
See Chekhov, Anton (Pavlovich)

Tchicaya, Gerald Felix 1931-1988 .. **CLC 101**
See also CA 129; 125; CANR 81

Tchicaya U Tam'si
See Tchicaya, Gerald Felix

Teasdale, Sara 1884-1933 .... **TCLC 4**
See also CA 104; 163; DLB 45; SATA 32

Tegner, Esaias 1782-1846 .... **NCLC 2**

Teilhard de Chardin, (Marie Joseph) Pierre 1881-
1955 .... **TCLC 9**
See also CA 105

Temple, Ann
See Mortimer, Penelope (Ruth)

Tennant, Emma (Christina) 1937- .. **CLC 13, 52**
See also CA 65-68; CAAS 9; CANR 10, 38, 59;
DLB 14

Tenneshaw, S. M.
See Silverberg, Robert

Tennyson, Alfred 1809-1892 . **NCLC 30, 65; DA;**
DAB; DAC; DAM MST, POET; PC 6; WLC
See also CDBLB 1832-1890; DLB 32

Teran, Lisa St. Aubin de .... **CLC 36**
See also St. Aubin de Teran, Lisa

Terence c. 184B.C.-c. 159B.C. . **CMLC 14; DC 7**
See also DLB 211

Teresa de Jesus, St. 1515-1582 .... **LC 18**

Terkel, Louis 1912-
See Terkel, Studs
See also CA 57-60; CANR 18, 45, 67; MTCW 1, 2

Terkel, Studs .... **CLC 38**
See also Terkel, Louis
See also AITN 1; MTCW 2

Terry, C. V.
See Slaughter, Frank G(ill)

Terry, Megan 1932- .... **CLC 19**
See also CA 77-80; CABS 3; CANR 43; DLB 7

Tertullian c. 155-c. 245 .... **CMLC 29**

Tertz, Abram
See Sinyavsky, Andrei (Donatevich)

Tesich, Steve 1943(?)-1996 .... **CLC 40, 69**
See also CA 105; 152; DLBY 83

Tesla, Nikola 1856-1943 .... **TCLC 88**

Teternikov, Fyodor Kuzmich 1863-1927
See Sologub, Fyodor
See also CA 104

Tevis, Walter 1928-1984 .... **CLC 42**
See also CA 113

Tey, Josephine .... **TCLC 14**
See also Mackintosh, Elizabeth
See also DLB 77

Thackeray, William Makepeace 1811-1863**NCLC**
5, 14, 22, 43; DA; DAB; DAC; DAM MST,

NOV; WLC
See also CDBLB 1832-1890; DLB 21, 55, 159, 163; SATA 23

Thakura, Ravindranatha
See Tagore, Rabindranath

Tharoor, Shashi 1956- .... **CLC 70**
See also CA 141

Thelwell, Michael Miles 1939- .... **CLC 22**
See also BW 2; CA 101

Theobald, Lewis, Jr.
See Lovecraft, H(oward) P(hillips)

Theodorescu, Ion N. 1880-1967
See Arghezi, Tudor
See also CA 116

Theriault, Yves 1915-1983 **CLC 79; DAC; DAM MST**
See also CA 102; DLB 88

Theroux, Alexander (Louis) 1939- .... **CLC 2, 25**
See also CA 85-88; CANR 20, 63

Theroux, Paul (Edward) 1941- **CLC 5, 8, 11, 15, 28, 46; DAM POP**
See also AAYA 28; BEST 89:4; CA 33-36R; CANR 20, 45, 74; CDALBS; DLB 2; MTCW 1, 2; SATA 44, 109

Thesen, Sharon 1946- .... **CLC 56**
See also CA 163

Thevenin, Denis
See Duhamel, Georges

Thibault, Jacques Anatole Francois 1844-1924
See France, Anatole
See also CA 106; 127; DAM NOV; MTCW 1, 2

Thiele, Colin (Milton) 1920- .... **CLC 17**
See also CA 29-32R; CANR 12, 28, 53; CLR 27; MAICYA; SAAS 2; SATA 14, 72

Thomas, Audrey (Callahan) 1935-**CLC 7, 13, 37, 107; SSC 20**
See also AITN 2; CA 21-24R; CAAS 19; CANR 36, 58; DLB 60; MTCW 1

Thomas, D(onald) M(ichael) 1935-**CLC 13, 22, 31**
See also CA 61-64; CAAS 11; CANR 17, 45, 75; CDBLB 1960 to Present; DLB 40, 207; INT CANR-17; MTCW 1, 2

Thomas, Dylan (Marlais) 1914-1953 **TCLC 1, 8, 45; DA; DAB; DAC; DAM DRAM, MST, POET; PC 2; SSC 3; WLC**
See also CA 104; 120; CANR 65; CDBLB 1945-1960; DLB 13, 20, 139; MTCW 1, 2; SATA 60

Thomas, (Philip) Edward 1878-1917 ... **TCLC 10; DAM POET**
See also CA 106; 153; DLB 98

Thomas, Joyce Carol 1938- .... **CLC 35**
See also AAYA 12; BW 2, 3; CA 113; 116; CANR 48; CLR 19; DLB 33; INT 116; JRDA; MAICYA; MTCW 1, 2; SAAS 7; SATA 40, 78

Thomas, Lewis 1913-1993 .... **CLC 35**
See also CA 85-88; 143; CANR 38, 60; MTCW 1, 2

Thomas, M. Carey 1857-1935 .... **TCLC 89**

Thomas, Paul
See Mann, (Paul) Thomas

Thomas, Piri 1928- .... **CLC 17; HLCS 2**
See also CA 73-76; HW 1

Thomas, R(onald) S(tuart) 1913- **CLC 6, 13, 48; DAB; DAM POET**
See also CA 89-92; CAAS 4; CANR 30; CDBLB 1960 to Present; DLB 27; MTCW 1

Thomas, Ross (Elmore) 1926-1995 .... **CLC 39**
See also CA 33-36R; 150; CANR 22, 63

Thompson, Francis Clegg
See Mencken, H(enry) L(ouis)

Thompson, Francis Joseph 1859-1907 .. **TCLC 4**
See also CA 104; CDBLB 1890-1914; DLB 19

Thompson, Hunter S(tockton) 1939- **CLC 9, 17, 40, 104; DAM POP**
See also BEST 89:1; CA 17-20R; CANR 23, 46, 74, 77; DLB 185; MTCW 1, 2

Thompson, James Myers

See Thompson, Jim (Myers)

Thompson, Jim (Myers) 1906-1977(?) .. **CLC 69**
See also CA 140

Thompson, Judith .... **CLC 39**

Thomson, James 1700-1748**LC 16, 29, 40; DAM POET**
See also DLB 95

Thomson, James 1834-1882**NCLC 18; DAM POET**
See also DLB 35

Thoreau, Henry David 1817-1862**NCLC 7, 21, 61; DA; DAB; DAC; DAM MST; WLC**
See also CDALB 1640-1865; DLB 1

Thornton, Hall
See Silverberg, Robert

Thucydides c. 455B.C.-399B.C. .... **CMLC 17**
See also DLB 176

Thurber, James (Grover) 1894-1961 . **CLC 5, 11, 25; DA; DAB; DAC; DAM DRAM, MST, NOV; SSC 1**
See also CA 73-76; CANR 17, 39; CDALB 1929-1941; DLB 4, 11, 22, 102; MAICYA; MTCW 1, 2; SATA 13

Thurman, Wallace (Henry) 1902-1934 . **TCLC 6; BLC 3; DAM MULT**
See also BW 1, 3; CA 104; 124; CANR 81; DLB 51

Ticheburn, Cheviot
See Ainsworth, William Harrison

Tieck, (Johann) Ludwig 1773-1853 **NCLC 5, 46; SSC 31**
See also DLB 90

Tiger, Derry
See Ellison, Harlan (Jay)

Tilghman, Christopher 1948(?)- .... **CLC 65**
See also CA 159

Tillinghast, Richard (Williford) 1940- **CLC 29**
See also CA 29-32R; CAAS 23; CANR 26, 51

Timrod, Henry 1828-1867 .... **NCLC 25**
See also DLB 3

Tindall, Gillian (Elizabeth) 1938- .... **CLC 7**
See also CA 21-24R; CANR 11, 65

Tiptree, James, Jr. .... **CLC 48, 50**
See also Sheldon, Alice Hastings Bradley
See also DLB 8

Titmarsh, Michael Angelo
See Thackeray, William Makepeace

Tocqueville, Alexis (Charles Henri Maurice Clerel, Comte) de 1805-1859 .... **NCLC 7, 63**

Tolkien, J(ohn) R(onald) R(euel) 1892-1973**CLC 1, 2, 3, 8, 12, 38; DA; DAB; DAC; DAM MST, NOV, POP; WLC**
See also AAYA 10; AITN 1; CA 17-18; 45-48; CANR 36; CAP2; CDBLB 1914-1945; CLR 56; DLB 15, 160; JRDA; MAICYA; MTCW 1, 2; SATA 2, 32, 100; SATA-Obit 24

Toller, Ernst 1893-1939 .... **TCLC 10**
See also CA 107; DLB 124

Tolson, M. B.
See Tolson, Melvin B(eaunorus)

Tolson, Melvin B(eaunorus) 1898(?)-1966 .. **C L C 36, 105; BLC 3; DAM MULT, POET**
See also BW 1, 3; CA 124; 89-92; CANR 80; DLB 48, 76

Tolstoi, Aleksei Nikolaevich
See Tolstoy, Alexey Nikolaevich

Tolstoy, Alexey Nikolaevich 1882-1945**TCLC 18**
See also CA 107; 158

Tolstoy, Count Leo
See Tolstoy, Leo (Nikolaevich)

Tolstoy, Leo (Nikolaevich) 1828-1910**TCLC 4, 11, 17, 28, 44, 79; DA; DAB; DAC; DAM MST, NOV; SSC 9, 30; WLC**
See also CA 104; 123; SATA 26

Tomasi di Lampedusa, Giuseppe 1896-1957
See Lampedusa, Giuseppe (Tomasi) di
See also CA 111

Tomlin, Lily .... **CLC 17**

See also Tomlin, Mary Jean

Tomlin, Mary Jean 1939(?)-
See Tomlin, Lily
See also CA 117

Tomlinson, (Alfred) Charles 1927- **CLC 2, 4, 6, 13, 45; DAM POET; PC 17**
See also CA 5-8R; CANR 33; DLB 40

Tomlinson, H(enry) M(ajor) 1873-1958 **TCLC 71**
See also CA 118; 161; DLB 36, 100, 195

Tonson, Jacob
See Bennett, (Enoch) Arnold

Toole, John Kennedy 1937-1969 ...... **CLC 19, 64**
See also CA 104; DLBY 81; MTCW 2

Toomer, Jean 1894-1967**CLC 1, 4, 13, 22; BLC 3; DAM MULT; PC 7; SSC 1; WLCS**
See also BW 1; CA 85-88; CDALB 1917-1929; DLB 45, 51; MTCW 1, 2

Torley, Luke
See Blish, James (Benjamin)

Tornimparte, Alessandra
See Ginzburg, Natalia

Torre, Raoul della
See Mencken, H(enry) L(ouis)

Torrey, E(dwin) Fuller 1937- .... **CLC 34**
See also CA 119; CANR 71

Torsvan, Ben Traven
See Traven, B.

Torsvan, Benno Traven
See Traven, B.

Torsvan, Berick Traven
See Traven, B.

Torsvan, Berwick Traven
See Traven, B.

Torsvan, Bruno Traven
See Traven, B.

Torsvan, Traven
See Traven, B.

Tournier, Michel (Edouard) 1924-**CLC 6, 23, 36, 95**
See also CA 49-52; CANR 3, 36, 74; DLB 83; MTCW 1, 2; SATA 23

Tournimparte, Alessandra
See Ginzburg, Natalia

Towers, Ivar
See Kornbluth, C(yril) M.

Towne, Robert (Burton) 1936(?)- .... **CLC 87**
See also CA 108; DLB 44

Townsend, Sue .... **CLC 61**
See also Townsend, Susan Elaine
See also AAYA 28; SATA 55, 93; SATA-Brief 48

Townsend, Susan Elaine 1946-
See Townsend, Sue
See also CA 119; 127; CANR 65; DAB; DAC; DAM MST

Townshend, Peter (Dennis Blandford) 1945-**CLC 17, 42**
See also CA 107

Tozzi, Federigo 1883-1920 .... **TCLC 31**
See also CA 160

Traill, Catharine Parr 1802-1899 .... **NCLC 31**
See also DLB 99

Trakl, Georg 1887-1914 .... **TCLC 5; PC 20**
See also CA 104; 165; MTCW 2

Transtroemer, Tomas (Goesta) 1931-**CLC 52, 65; DAM POET**
See also CA 117; 129; CAAS 17

Transtromer, Tomas Gosta
See Transtroemer, Tomas (Goesta)

Traven, B. (?)-1969 .... **CLC 8, 11**
See also CA 19-20; 25-28R; CAP 2; DLB 9, 56; MTCW 1

Treitel, Jonathan 1959- .... **CLC 70**

Tremain, Rose 1943- .... **CLC 42**
See also CA 97-100; CANR 44; DLB 14

Tremblay, Michel 1942-**CLC 29, 102; DAC; DAM MST**
See also CA 116; 128; DLB 60; MTCW 1, 2

Waldo, Edward Hamilton
See Sturgeon, Theodore (Hamilton)
Walker, Alice (Malsenior) 1944-**CLC 5, 6, 9, 19,**
27, 46, 58, 103; BLC 3; DA; DAB; DAC;
DAM MST, MULT, NOV, POET, POP; SSC
5; WLCS
See also AAYA 3; BEST 89:4; BW 2, 3; CA 37-
40R; CANR 9, 27, 49, 66; CDALB 1968-1988;
DLB 6, 33, 143; INT CANR-27; MTCW 1, 2;
SATA 31
Walker, David Harry 1911-1992 .... **CLC 14**
See also CA 1-4R; 137; CANR 1; SATA 8; SATA-
Obit 71
Walker, Edward Joseph 1934-
See Walker, Ted
See also CA 21-24R; CANR 12, 28, 53
Walker, George F. 1947-**CLC 44, 61; DAB; DAC;**
DAM MST
See also CA 103; CANR 21, 43, 59; DLB 60
Walker, Joseph A. 1935- **CLC 19; DAM DRAM,**
MST
See also BW 1, 3; CA 89-92; CANR 26; DLB 38
Walker, Margaret (Abigail) 1915-1998**CLC 1, 6;**
BLC; DAM MULT; PC 20
See also BW 2, 3; CA 73-76; 172; CANR 26, 54,
76; DLB 76, 152; MTCW 1, 2
Walker, Ted .... **CLC 13**
See also Walker, Edward Joseph
See also DLB 40
Wallace, David Foster 1962- .... **CLC 50, 114**
See also CA 132; CANR 59; MTCW 2
Wallace, Dexter
See Masters, Edgar Lee
Wallace, (Richard Horatio) Edgar 1875-1932
TCLC 57
See also CA 115; DLB 70
Wallace, Irving 1916-1990**CLC 7, 13; DAM NOV,**
POP
See also AITN 1; CA 1-4R; 132; CAAS 1; CANR
1, 27; INT CANR-27; MTCW 1, 2
Wallant, Edward Lewis 1926-1962 .... **CLC 5, 10**
See also CA 1-4R; CANR 22; DLB 2, 28, 143;
MTCW 1, 2
Wallas, Graham 1858-1932 . ... **TCLC 91**
Walley, Byron
See Card, Orson Scott
Walpole, Horace 1717-1797 .... **LC 49**
See also DLB 39, 104
Walpole, Hugh (Seymour) 1884-1941 ... **TCLC 5**
See also CA 104; 165; DLB 34; MTCW 2
Walser, Martin 1927- .... **CLC 27**
See also CA 57-60; CANR 8, 46; DLB 75, 124
Walser, Robert 1878-1956 .... **TCLC 18; SSC 20**
See also CA 118; 165; DLB 66
Walsh, Jill Paton .... **CLC 35**
See also Paton Walsh, Gillian
See also AAYA 11; CLR 2; DLB 161; SAAS 3
Walter, Villiam Christian
See Andersen, Hans Christian
Wambaugh, Joseph (Aloysius, Jr.) 1937-**CLC 3,**
18; DAM NOV, POP
See also AITN 1; BEST 89:3; CA 33-36R; CANR
42, 65; DLB 6; DLBY 83; MTCW 1, 2
Wang Wei 699(?)-761(?) .... **PC 18**
Ward, Arthur Henry Sarsfield 1883-1959
See Rohmer, Sax
See also CA 108; 173
Ward, Douglas Turner 1930- .... **CLC 19**
See also BW 1; CA 81-84; CANR 27; DLB 7, 38
Ward, E. D.
See Lucas, E(dward) V(errall)
Ward, Mary Augusta
See Ward, Mrs. Humphry
Ward, Mrs. Humphry 1851-1920 .... **TCLC 55**
See also DLB 18
Ward, Peter
See Faust, Frederick (Schiller)

Warhol, Andy 1928(?)-1987 .... **CLC 20**
See also AAYA 12; BEST 89:4; CA 89-92; 121;
CANR 34
Warner, Francis (Robert le Plastrier) 1937-**CLC**
14
See also CA 53-56; CANR 11
Warner, Marina 1946- .... **CLC 59**
See also CA 65-68; CANR 21, 55; DLB 194
Warner, Rex (Ernest) 1905-1986 .... **CLC 45**
See also CA 89-92; 119; DLB 15
Warner, Susan (Bogert) 1819-1885 .... **NCLC 31**
See also DLB 3, 42
Warner, Sylvia (Constance) Ashton
See Ashton-Warner, Sylvia (Constance)
Warner, Sylvia Townsend 1893-1978 **CLC 7, 19;**
SSC 23
See also CA 61-64; 77-80; CANR 16, 60; DLB 34,
139; MTCW 1, 2
Warren, Mercy Otis 1728-1814 .... **NCLC 13**
See also DLB 31, 200
Warren, Robert Penn 1905-1989 . **CLC 1, 4, 6, 8,**
10, 13, 18, 39, 53, 59; DA; DAB; DAC; DAM
MST, NOV, POET; SSC 4; WLC
See also AITN 1; CA 13-16R; 129; CANR 10, 47;
CDALB 1968-1988; DLB 2, 48, 152; DLBY 80,
89; INT CANR-10; MTCW 1, 2; SATA 46;
SATA-Obit 63
Warshofsky, Isaac
See Singer, Isaac Bashevis
Warton, Thomas 1728-1790 **LC 15; DAM POET**
See also DLB 104, 109
Waruk, Kona
See Harris, (Theodore) Wilson
Warung, Price 1855-1911 .... **TCLC 45**
Warwick, Jarvis
See Garner, Hugh
Washington, Alex
See Harris, Mark
Washington, Booker T(aliaferro) 1856-1915
TCLC 10; BLC 3; DAM MULT
See also BW 1; CA 114; 125; SATA 28
Washington, George 1732-1799 .... **LC 25**
See also DLB 31
Wassermann, (Karl) Jakob 1873-1934 . **TCLC 6**
See also CA 104; 163; DLB 66
Wasserstein, Wendy 1950-**CLC 32, 59, 90; DAM**
DRAM; DC 4
See also CA 121; 129; CABS 3; CANR 53, 75;
INT 129; MTCW 2; SATA 94
Waterhouse, Keith (Spencer) 1929- ..... **CLC 47**
See also CA 5-8R; CANR 38, 67; DLB 13, 15;
MTCW 1, 2
Waters, Frank (Joseph) 1902-1995 .... **CLC 88**
See also CA 5-8R; 149; CAAS 13; CANR 3, 18,
63; DLB 212; DLBY 86
Waters, Roger 1944- .... **CLC 35**
Watkins, Frances Ellen
See Harper, Frances Ellen Watkins
Watkins, Gerrold
See Malzberg, Barry N(athaniel)
Watkins, Gloria 1955(?)-
See hooks, bell
See also BW 2; CA 143; MTCW 2
Watkins, Paul 1964- .... **CLC 55**
See also CA 132; CANR 62
Watkins, Vernon Phillips 1906-1967 .... **CLC 43**
See also CA 9-10; 25-28R; CAP 1; DLB 20
Watson, Irving S.
See Mencken, H(enry) L(ouis)
Watson, John H.
See Farmer, Philip Jose
Watson, Richard F.
See Silverberg, Robert
Waugh, Auberon (Alexander) 1939- .... **CLC 7**
See also CA 45-48; CANR 6, 22; DLB 14, 194
Waugh, Evelyn (Arthur St. John) 1903-1966**CLC**
1, 3, 8, 13, 19, 27, 44, 107; DA; DAB; DAC;

DAM MST, NOV, POP; WLC
See also CA 85-88; 25-28R; CANR 22; CDBLB
1914-1945; DLB 15, 162, 195; MTCW 1, 2
Waugh, Harriet 1944- .... **CLC 6**
See also CA 85-88; CANR 22
Ways, C. R.
See Blount, Roy (Alton), Jr.
Waystaff, Simon
See Swift, Jonathan
Webb, (Martha) Beatrice (Potter) 1858-1943
TCLC 22
See also Potter, (Helen) Beatrix
See also CA 117; DLB 190
Webb, Charles (Richard) 1939- .... **CLC 7**
See also CA 25-28R
Webb, James H(enry), Jr. 1946- .... **CLC 22**
See also CA 81-84
Webb, Mary (Gladys Meredith) 1881-1927 **TCLC**
24
See also CA 123; DLB 34
Webb, Mrs. Sidney
See Webb, (Martha) Beatrice (Potter)
Webb, Phyllis 1927- .... **CLC 18**
See also CA 104; CANR 23; DLB 53
Webb, Sidney (James) 1859-1947 .... **TCLC 22**
See also CA 117; 163; DLB 190
Webber, Andrew Lloyd .... **CLC 21**
See also Lloyd Webber, Andrew
Weber, Lenora Mattingly 1895-1971 ..... **CLC 12**
See also CA 19-20; 29-32R; CAP 1; SATA 2;
SATA-Obit 26
Weber, Max 1864-1920 .... **TCLC 69**
See also CA 109
Webster, John 1579(?)-1634(?)**LC 33; DA; DAB;**
DAC; DAM DRAM, MST; DC 2; WLC
See also CDBLB Before 1660; DLB 58
Webster, Noah 1758-1843 .... **NCLC 30**
See also DLB 1, 37, 42, 43, 73
Wedekind, (Benjamin) Frank(lin) 1864-1918
TCLC 7; DAM DRAM
See also CA 104; 153; DLB 118
Weidman, Jerome 1913-1998 .... **CLC 7**
See also AITN 2; CA 1-4R; 171; CANR 1; DLB
28
Weil, Simone (Adolphine) 1909-1943 .. **TCLC 23**
See also CA 117; 159; MTCW 2
Weininger, Otto 1880-1903 .... **TCLC 84**
Weinstein, Nathan
See West, Nathanael
Weinstein, Nathan von Wallenstein
See West, Nathanael
Weir, Peter (Lindsay) 1944- .... **CLC 20**
See also CA 113; 123
Weiss, Peter (Ulrich) 1916-1982 **CLC 3, 15, 51;**
DAM DRAM
See also CA 45-48; 106; CANR 3; DLB 69, 124
Weiss, Theodore (Russell) 1916- .. **CLC 3, 8, 14**
See also CA 9-12R; CAAS 2; CANR 46; DLB 5
Welch, (Maurice) Denton 1915-1948 .. **TCLC 22**
See also CA 121; 148
Welch, James 1940-**CLC 6, 14, 52; DAM MULT,**
POP
See also CA 85-88; CANR 42, 66; DLB 175;
NNAL
Weldon, Fay 1931-**CLC 6, 9, 11, 19, 36, 59; DAM**
POP
See also CA 21-24R; CANR 16, 46, 63; CDBLB
1960 to Present; DLB 14, 194; INT CANR-16;
MTCW 1, 2
Wellek, Rene 1903-1995 .... **CLC 28**
See also CA 5-8R; 150; CAAS 7; CANR 8; DLB
63; INT CANR-8
Weller, Michael 1942- .... **CLC 10, 53**
See also CA 85-88
Weller, Paul 1958- .... **CLC 26**
Wellershoff, Dieter 1925- .... **CLC 46**
See also CA 89-92; CANR 16, 37

Literary Criticism Series
Cumulative Topic Index

This index lists all topic entries in Gale's *Classical and Medieval Literature Criticism, Contemporary Literary Criticism, Literature Criticism from 1400 to 1800, Nineteenth-Century Literature Criticism,* and *Twentieth-Century Literary Criticism.*

Topic Index

Topic Index

Twentieth-Century Literary Criticism
Cumulative Nationality Index

Nationality Index

Chekhov, Anton (Pavlovich) **3, 10, 31, 55**
Der Nister **56**
Eisenstein, Sergei (Mikhailovich) **57**
Esenin, Sergei (Alexandrovich) **4**
Fadeyev, Alexander **53**
Gladkov, Fyodor (Vasilyevich) **27**
Gorky, Maxim **8**
Gumilev, Nikolai (Stepanovich) **60**
Gurdjieff, G(eorgei) I(vanovich) **71**
Guro, Elena **56**
Hippius, Zinaida **9**
Ilf, Ilya **21**
Ivanov, Vyacheslav Ivanovich **33**
Kandinsky, Wassily **92**
Khlebnikov, Velimir **20**
Khodasevich, Vladislav (Felitsianovich) **15**
Korolenko, Vladimir Galaktionovich **22**
Kropotkin, Peter (Aleksieevich) **36**
Kuprin, Aleksandr Ivanovich **5**
Kuzmin, Mikhail **40**
Lenin, V. I. **67**
Mandelstam, Osip (Emilievich) **2, 6**
Mayakovski, Vladimir (Vladimirovich) **4, 18**
Merezhkovsky, Dmitry Sergeyevich **29**
Pavlov, Ivan Petrovich **91**
Petrov, Evgeny **21**
Pilnyak, Boris **23**
Platonov, Andrei **14**
Prishvin, Mikhail **75**
Remizov, Aleksei (Mikhailovich) **27**
Shestov, Lev **56**
Sologub, Fyodor **9**
Stalin, Joseph **92**
Tolstoy, Alexey Nikolaevich **18**
Tolstoy, Leo (Nikolaevich) **4, 11, 17, 28, 44, 79**
Trotsky, Leon **22**
Tsvetaeva (Efron), Marina (Ivanovna) **7, 35**
Zabolotsky, Nikolai Alekseevich **52**
Zamyatin, Evgeny Ivanovich **8, 37**
Zhdanov, Andrei Alexandrovich **18**
Zoshchenko, Mikhail (Mikhailovich) **15**

SCOTTISH
Barrie, J(ames) M(atthew) **2**
Bridie, James **3**
Brown, George Douglas **28**
Buchan, John **41**
Cunninghame Graham, R(obert) B(ontine) **19**
Davidson, John **24**
Frazer, J(ames) G(eorge) **32**
Gibbon, Lewis Grassic **4**
Lang, Andrew **16**
MacDonald, George **9**
Muir, Edwin **2, 87**
Sharp, William **39**
Tey, Josephine **14**

SOUTH AFRICAN
Bosman, Herman Charles **49**
Campbell, (Ignatius) Roy (Dunnachie) **5**
Mqhayi, S(amuel) E(dward) K(rune Loliwe) **25**
Plaatje, Sol(omon) T(shekisho) **73**
Schreiner, Olive (Emilie Albertina) **9**
Smith, Pauline (Urmson) **25**
Vilakazi, Benedict Wallet **37**

SPANISH
Alas (y Urena), Leopoldo (Enrique Garcia) **29**
Barea, Arturo **14**
Baroja (y Nessi), Pio **8**
Benavente (y Martinez), Jacinto **3**
Blasco Ibanez, Vicente **12**

Echegaray (y Eizaguirre), Jose (Maria Waldo) **4**
Garcia Lorca, Federico **1, 7, 49**
Jimenez (Mantecon), Juan Ramon **4**
Machado (y Ruiz), Antonio **3**
Martinez Sierra, Gregorio **6**
Martinez Sierra, Maria (de la O'LeJarraga) **6**
Miro (Ferrer), Gabriel (Francisco Victor) **5**
Ortega y Gasset, Jose **9**
Pereda (y Sanchez de Porrua), Jose Maria de **16**
Perez Galdos, Benito **27**
Ramoacn y Cajal, Santiago **93**
Salinas (y Serrano), Pedro **17**
Unamuno (y Jugo), Miguel de **2, 9**
Valera y Alcala-Galiano, Juan **10**
Valle-Inclan, Ramon (Maria) del **5**

SWEDISH
Bengtsson, Frans (Gunnar) **48**
Dagerman, Stig (Halvard) **17**
Ekelund, Vilhelm **75**
Heidenstam, (Carl Gustaf) Verner von **5**
Key, Ellen **65**
Lagerloef, Selma (Ottiliana Lovisa) **4, 36**
Soderberg, Hjalmar **39**
Strindberg, (Johan) August **1, 8, 21, 47**

SWISS
Ramuz, Charles-Ferdinand **33**
Rod, Edouard **52**
Saussure, Ferdinand de **49**
Spitteler, Carl (Friedrich Georg) **12**
Walser, Robert **18**

SYRIAN
Gibran, Kahlil **1, 9**

TURKISH
Sait Faik **23**

UKRAINIAN
Aleichem, Sholom **1, 35**
Bialik, Chaim Nachman **25**

URUGUAYAN
Quiroga, Horacio (Sylvestre) **20**
Sanchez, Florencio **37**

WELSH
Davies, W(illiam) H(enry) **5**
Evans, Caradoc **85**
Lewis, Alun **3**
Machen, Arthur **4**
Thomas, Dylan (Marlais) **1, 8, 45**

TCLC-95 Title Index

ISBN 0-7876-3208-2

90000